FROMMER'S

COMPREHENSIVE TRAVEL GUIDE

California '95

by Dan Levine

MACMILLAN • USA

ABOUT THE AUTHOR

Dan Levine, who has a degree in history from New York University, is an incessant traveler. In addition to *California '95,* he has written Frommer guides to Los Angeles and San Francisco, as well as Miami. He is also the coauthor of *Frommer's Walking Tours: London* and has contributed to *Europe on $50 a Day.* When he is not on the road, Dan lives in Santa Barbara.

MACMILLAN TRAVEL
A Prentice Hall Macmillan Company
15 Columbus Circle
New York, NY 10023

ISBN 0-02-860057-6
ISSN 1044-2146

Design by Michele Laseau
Maps by Ortelius Design

SPECIAL SALES

Bulk purchases (10+ copies) of Frommer's Travel Guides are available to corporations at special discounts. The Special Sales Department can produce custom editions to be used as premiums and/or for sales promotion to suit individual needs. Existing editions can be produced with custom cover imprints such as corporate logos. For more information write to: Special Sales, Prentice Hall, 15 Columbus Circle, New York, NY 10023.

Manufactured in the United States of America

Contents

4 San Francisco 54

SPECIAL FEATURES

5 The Wine Country 228

SPECIAL FEATURES

6 Northern California 256

SPECIAL FEATURES

List of Maps

What the Symbols Mean

Frommer's Favorites Hotels, restaurants, attractions, and entertainments you should not miss.

$ Super-Special Values Really exceptional values.

Abbreviations in Hotel and Other Listings

The following symbols refer to the standard amenities available in all rooms:

- A/C air conditioning
- MINIBAR refrigerator stocked with beverages and snacks
- TEL telephone
- TV television

The following abbreviations are used for credit cards:

- AE American Express
- CB Carte Blanche
- DC Diners Club
- DISC Discover
- EC Eurocard
- ER enRoute
- JCB (Japan)
- MC MasterCard
- V Visa

Trip Planning with this Guide

USE THE FOLLOWING FEATURES:

What Things Cost To help you plan your daily budget

Calendar of Events To plan for or avoid

What's Special About Checklist A summary of each region's highlights

Suggested Itineraries For seeing the regions or cities

Easy-to-Read Maps Walking tours, city sights, hotel and restaurant locations—all referring to or keyed to the text

Fast Facts All the essentials at a glance: currency, embassies, emergencies, safety, taxes, tipping, and more

Frommer's Smart Traveler Tips Hints on how to secure the best value for your money

OTHER SPECIAL FROMMER FEATURES

Did You Know? Offbeat, fun facts

Famous People The state's greats

Invitation to the Readers

In researching this book, I have come across many wonderful establishments, the best of which I have included here. I am sure that many of you will also come across appealing hotels, inns, restaurants, guesthouses, shops, and attractions. Please don't keep them to yourself. Share your experiences, especially if you want to comment on places that have been included in this edition that have changed for the worse. You can address your letters to:

Dan Levine
Frommer's California '95
c/o Macmillan Travel
15 Columbus Circle
New York, NY 10023

Disclaimer

Readers are advised that prices fluctuate in the course of time, and travel information changes under the impact of the varied and volatile factors that influence the travel industry. Neither the author nor the publisher can be held responsible for the experiences of readers while traveling. Readers are invited to write to the publisher with ideas, comments, and suggestions for future editions.

Safety Advisory

Whenever you're traveling in an unfamiliar city or country, stay alert. Be aware of your immediate surroundings. Wear a moneybelt and keep a close eye on your possessions. Be particularly careful with cameras, purses, and wallets, all favorite targets of thieves and pickpockets.

Getting to Know California

1

OFTEN IDEALIZED AS A CAREFREE LAND OF ALMOST EXCESSIVE BEAUTY, CALIFORNIA is known for its glitzy cities, sunny seashores, dramatic coastlines, and upscale, trend-setting citizens. Visitors often discover that all their preconceptions of paradise are true: This is the golden land, and the people who live here are the lucky ones.

Think of California as a country; it is larger, richer, and more diverse than any other U.S. state. California's fantastic growth and seemingly endless wealth are embodiments of the American Dream. In California, snowcapped mountain majesties really *do* tower above densely fruited plains. California is a land of superlatives: It's the most populous American state and boasts one of the world's largest economies. It is home to the world's tallest forest (Redwood National Park), the continent's highest waterfall (Yosemite Falls), the western hemisphere's lowest point (Death Valley), and the tallest peak in the 48 contiguous states (Mount Whitney). More than 1,200 miles of calendar-art coastline fronts bountifully productive farms and some of nature's most awe-inspiring wonders, including Yosemite Valley, the Sierra Nevada mountain range, and the Big Sur coast. In a state equally devoted to outdoor recreation and cosmopolitan living, you can fish, windsurf, cycle, ski, hike, swim, beachcomb, or run river rapids by day; and dine, dance, and attend the theater or a concert by night.

Of course, California has its share of social, environmental, and geological problems. But, somehow, when you're cruising down the coast in an open-top car, it seems as though nothing can tarnish the reputation of America's Golden State.

1 Geography, History & Politics

GEOGRAPHY

More than 1,200 miles long and 350 miles wide, America's westernmost contiguous state occupies much of this country's Pacific seaboard. California is best known for spectacular seashores, but it's the geology of the state's interior that best defines California's multiplicity of regions. A succession of coastal mountain ranges runs from the Oregon border to Oxnard, about 45 miles north of Los Angeles. Most of the state's population lives on the relatively narrow strip of land between these mountains and the ocean. Closer to California's eastern border, a second set of mountain ranges—the most notable of which is the Sierra Nevada—also runs from Oregon to Los Angeles. Between these two ranges is the 400-mile-long Central Valley, one of the most fertile and productive farming regions in the world. The Mojave Desert, which sprawls over much of the southeastern part of the state, is separated from Los Angeles and the rest of California by the Sierra Nevada and other north-south mountain ranges.

HISTORY

EUROPEAN DISCOVERY & COLONIZATION Although very little remains to mark the existence of West Coast Native Americans, anthropologists estimate that as many as half a million aboriginals flourished on this naturally abundant land for thousands of years before the arrival of Europeans in the mid-16th century. Sailing from a small colony, established 10 years before, on the southern tip of Baja (Lower) California, Portuguese explorer Juan Rodrígues Cabrillo (in the service of Spain) is credited

Dateline

- 1542 Juan Cabrillo enters San Diego Bay and sails up California's coast, in first documented European visit.
- 1579 Sir Francis Drake drops anchor in the San Francisco Bay area and claims the land for England's Queen Elizabeth I.

➤

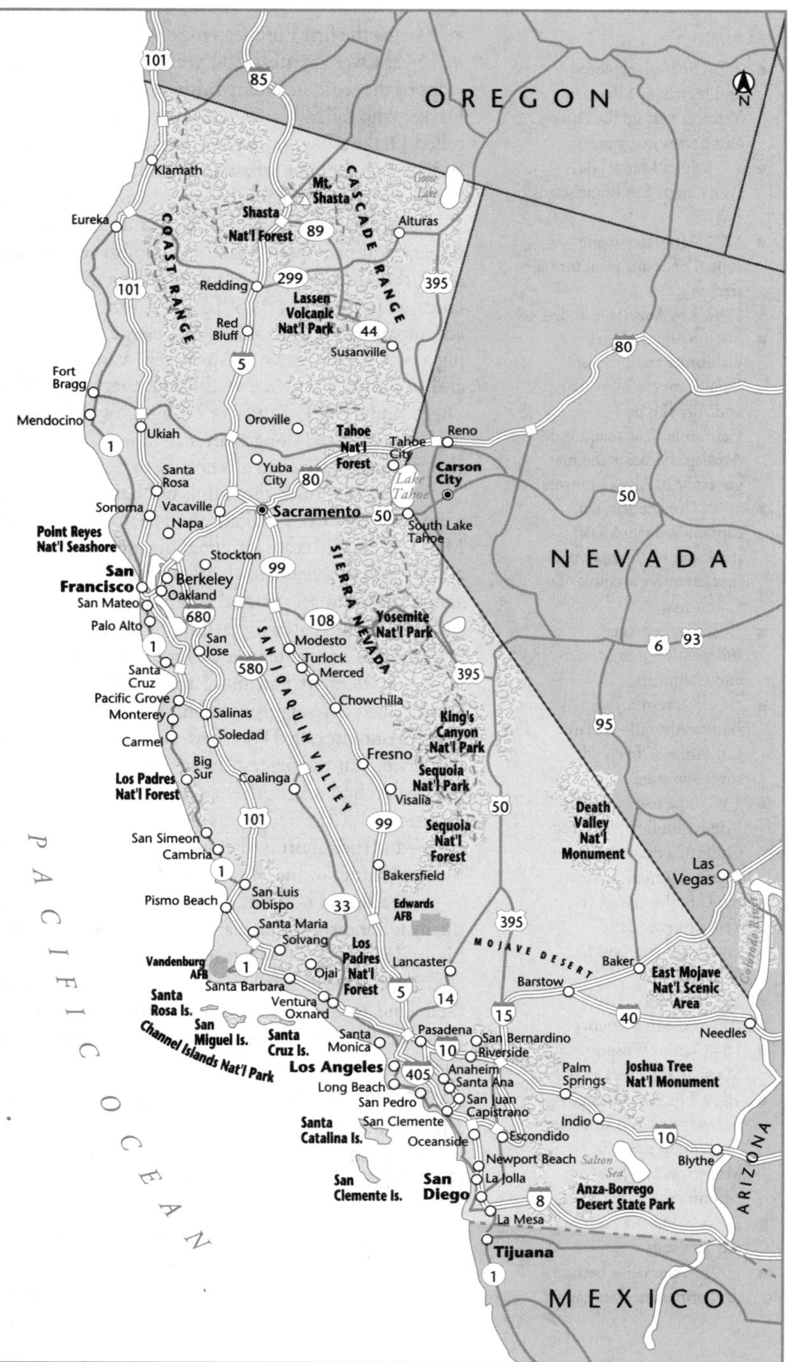
OREGON
101
85
N
Klamath
Mt. Shasta
CASCADE RANGE
Goose Lake
Eureka
Shasta Nat'l Forest
89
Alturas
COAST RANGE
Redding
299
101
Lassen Volcanic Nat'l Park
395
Red Bluff
44
Susanville
5
80
Fort Bragg
Mendocino
Oroville
Ukiah
Tahoe Nat'l Forest
Reno
Tahoe City
1
Carson City
Yuba City
Santa Rosa
80
Lake Tahoe
Sonoma
Vacaville
Sacramento
50
50
Napa
South Lake Tahoe
Point Reyes Nat'l Seashore
Stockton
SIERRA NEVADA
NEVADA
San Francisco
Berkeley
99
Oakland
San Mateo
680
108
Yosemite Nat'l Park
Palo Alto
San Jose
SAN JOAQUIN VALLEY
Modesto
1
6
93
Turlock
Santa Cruz
580
Merced
395
Pacific Grove
Chowchilla
Monterey
Salinas
King's Canyon Nat'l Park
95
Carmel
Soledad
Fresno
Big Sur
Sequoia Nat'l Park
Los Padres Nat'l Forest
Coalinga
Visalia
50
Death Valley Nat'l Monument
101
99
Sequoia Nat'l Forest
San Simeon
Cambria
PACIFIC OCEAN
1
Bakersfield
Las Vegas
San Luis Obispo
Pismo Beach
Edwards AFB
33
395
Santa Maria
Solvang
MOJAVE DESERT
Colorado River
Los Padres Nat'l Forest
Vandenburg AFB
1
Ojai
Lancaster
Baker
East Mojave Nat'l Scenic Area
Santa Barbara
Barstow
5
Santa Rosa Is.
Ventura
14
Oxnard
15
40
San Miguel Is.
Needles
Santa Cruz Is.
Santa Monica
Pasadena
San Bernardino
Channel Islands Nat'l Park
10
Riverside
Los Angeles
405
Anaheim
Palm Springs
Joshua Tree Nat'l Monument
Long Beach
Santa Ana
San Pedro
San Juan Capistrano
Santa Catalina Is.
San Clemente
Indio
Oceanside
Escondido
10
ARIZONA
Newport Beach
Salton Sea
Blythe
San Clemente Is.
San Diego
La Jolla
Anza-Borrego Desert State Park
8
La Mesa
Tijuana
1
MEXICO

Dateline

- 1602 Spanish explorer and merchant Sebastian Vizcano sails up the coast and names many areas.
- 1775 Juan Manuel de Ayala maps San Francisco Bay.
- 1777 Monterey made capital of Spain's California territory.
- 1791 Los Angeles founded.
- 1804 Spain divides its California territory into Baja (Lower) California and Alta (Upper) California; Jose Joaquin de Arrillaga becomes the first governor of Alta California.
- 1808 Connecticut sea captain William Shaler publishes his *Journal,* the first extensive account of California.
- 1821 Spain grants independence to Mexico and California.
- 1836 Governor Juan Batista Alvarado declares California a "free and sovereign state."
- 1846 The so-called Bear Flag Republic proclaimed; California drawn into the Mexican-American War; the U.S. flag raised in Yerba Buena (San Francisco) and Los Angeles.
- 1847 Yerba Buena renamed San Francisco.
- 1848 James Wilson Marshall discovers gold.
- 1849 The Gold Rush in full swing. A constitutional convention meets in Monterey; San Jose becomes the state capital.
- 1850 California becomes the 31st state.
- 1854 Sacramento becomes the permanent state capital.

➤

with being the first European to "discover" California, in 1542. Over the next 200 years, dozens of sailors mapped the coast, including British explorer Sir Francis Drake, who sailed his *Golden Hind* into what is now called Drake's Bay, north of San Francisco, in 1579; and Spanish explorer Sebastian Vizcano, who, in 1602, bestowed most of the place-names that survive today.

European colonial competition and Catholic missionary zeal prompted Spain to establish settlements along the Alta (Upper) California coast and claim the lands as its own. In 1769, Father Junípero Serra, accompanied by 300 soldiers and clergy, began forging a path from Mexico to Monterey. A small mission and presidio (fort) were established that year at San Diego, and by 1804 a chain of 21 missions, each a day's walk from the next along a dirt road called *Camino Real* (Royal Road), stretched all the way to Sonoma.

During that time, thousands of Native Americans were converted to Christianity and coerced into labor. Many others died from imported diseases. Because not all the natives welcomed their conquerors with open arms, many missions and pueblos (small towns) suffered repeated attacks, leading to the construction of California's now ubiquitous, fireproof red-tile roofs.

No settlement had more than 100 inhabitants when Spain's sovereignty was compromised by an 1812 Russian outpost called Fort Ross, 60 miles north of San Francisco. But the biggest threat came from the British—who had strengthened their own claims to America with the Hudson's Bay Company trading firm—and their shortlived, last-ditch effort to win back their territories in the War of 1812.

Embattled at home as well as abroad, the Spanish finally relinquished their claim to Mexico and California in 1821. Under Mexican rule, Alta California's Spanish missionaries fell out of favor and lost much of their land to the increasingly wealthy *Californios*—Mexican immigrants who'd been granted vast tracts of land.

AMERICAN EXPANSION Beginning in the late 1820s, Americans from the east began to make their way to California, via a three-month sail around Cape Horn. Most of them settled in the territorial capital of Monterey and in northern California.

From the 1830s on, inspired by the doctrine of Manifest Destiny—an almost religious belief that the United States was destined to cover the continent from coast to coast—more and more settlers headed west.

Along with them came daring explorers. In 1843, Marcus Whitman, a missionary, seeking to prove that settlers could travel overland through the Oregon Territory's Blue Mountains, helped blaze the Oregon Trail; the first covered-wagon train made the four-month crossing in 1844. Over the next few years, several hundred Americans made the trek to California over the Sierra Nevada range via Truckee Pass, just north of Lake Tahoe.

As the drive to the west increased, the U.S. government sought to extend its control over Mexican territory north of the Rio Grande, the river that now divides the United States and Mexico. In 1846, President James Polk offered Mexico $40 million for California and New Mexico. The offer might have been accepted, but America's simultaneous annexation of Texas, to which Mexico still laid claim, resulted in a war between the two countries. Within months, the United States overcame Mexico and took possession of the entire west coast.

GOLD & STATEHOOD In 1848, California's non–Native American population was around 7,000. That same year, flakes of gold were discovered by workers building a sawmill along the American River. Word of the find spread quickly. By 1850 the state's population exceeded 92,000, although very few settlers unearthed a gold mine. Within 15 years the gold had dissipated, but the new residents remained.

In 1850, California was admitted to the Union as the 31st state. The state constitution on which California applied for admission included several noteworthy features. In order to protect the miners, slavery was prohibited. To attract women from the east coast, legal recognition was given to the separate property of a married woman. (California was the first state to offer such recognition.) By 1870, almost 90% of the state's Native American population had been wiped out, and the bulk of the rest were removed to undesirable inland reservations.

Mexican and Chinese laborers were brought in to help local farmers and to work on the transcontinental railroad, which was completed in 1869. The new rail line transported easterners to California in just five days, marking a turning point in the settlement of the west. In 1875, when the Santa Fe railroad reached Los Angeles, southern California's population of just 10,000 was divided equally between Los Angeles and San Diego.

Dateline

- 1862 The first telegraph line established between San Francisco and New York.
- 1867 Anti-Chinese demonstrations in San Francisco in the wake of rising immigration.
- 1869 The transcontinental railroad completed.
- 1873 The University of California opens its campus at Berkeley. The first cable car appears in San Francisco.
- 1879 The University of Southern California founded.
- 1881 The *Los Angeles Times* begins publication.
- 1906 San Francisco decimated by an earthquake and fire.
- 1911 Hollywood's first film studio established.
- 1915 The first transcontinental telephone call made from San Francisco to New York.
- 1922 The Hollywood Bowl and amphitheater opens.
- 1924 The first transcontinental airmail flight made from San Francisco to New York.
- 1936 The San Francisco–Oakland Bay Bridge opens.
- 1937 The Golden Gate Bridge opens.
- 1945 The United Nations founded in San Francisco.
- 1955 Disneyland opens.
- 1960 San Francisco's Candlestick Park opens.
- 1972 The BART system opens in San Francisco.
- 1984 Los Angeles hosts the Summer Olympic Games.

➤

Dateline

- 1991 Fire rages through the Berkeley/Oakland hills, destroying 2,800 homes.
- 1992 Los Angeles experiences the worst race riots in modern American history; 50 dead, hundreds injured.
- 1993 Firestorms sweep through Los Angeles area; an earthquake registering 6.2 on the Richter scale strikes.

GROWTH & INDUSTRY Los Angeles began to grow in 1911, when the film industry moved there from the east coast to take advantage of cheap land and a warm climate that enabled movies to be shot outdoors year round. The movies' glamorous, idyllic portrayal of California boosted the region's popularity and population, especially during the Great Depression of the 1930s, when thousands of families (like the Joads in John Steinbeck's novel *The Grapes of Wrath*) packed up their belongings and headed west in search of a better life.

World War II brought heavy industry to California, in the form of munitions factories, shipyards, and airplane manufacturing. Freeways were built, military bases were opened, and suburbs were developed. In the 1950s, California in general, and San Francisco in particular, became popular with artists and intellectuals. The so-called beat generation appeared, later to inspire alternative-culture groups, most notably the "flower children" of the 1960s, in San Francisco's Haight-Ashbury district. During the "Summer of Love" in 1967, as the war in Vietnam escalated, student protests increased at Berkeley and elsewhere in California, as they did across the country. A year later, amid rising racial tensions, Martin Luther King, Jr., was killed, setting off riots in the Watts section of Los Angeles and in other cities. Soon thereafter, Robert F. Kennedy was fatally shot in Los Angeles after winning the California Democratic Party presidential primary. Antiwar protests continued into the 1970s.

Perhaps in response to an increasingly violent society, the 1970s also gave rise to several exotic religions and cults, which found eager adherents in California. The spiritual "New Age" continued into the 1980s, along with a growing population, environmental pollution, and escalating social ills, especially in Los Angeles. California also became very rich. Real-estate values soared, the computer industry, centered in "Silicon Valley," south of San Francisco, boomed, and banks and businesses prospered. The late 80s and early 90s, however, have brought a devastating recession to the state.

In the early 1990s, Californians, like many other Americans, have become more conservative. Though they remain keenly concerned about the nation's problems—economic competition from abroad, the environment, drugs, the blight of homelessness afflicting cities large and small—their fascination with alternative lifestyles may have ebbed and the former campus rebels among them may have settled into comfortable positions in industry and politics. But Californians still like to think of themselves as being on the cutting edge of American society. Whatever happens in the country, they say proudly, takes place here first.

POLITICS

After Democrat Jerry Brown, an avowed liberal, succeeded conservative Republican Governor Ronald Reagan in the 1970s, California gained a reputation for progressive leadership. The state enacted some of the most stringent antipollution measures in the world, actively encouraged the development of renewable forms of energy, and protected the coastline from development and despoliation. At the same time, San Francisco emerged at the forefront of the gay rights movement, and there was a general resurgence of interest among Californians in alternative lifestyles and the exploration of foreign cultures.

California's reputation as a liberal mecca, however, is largely mistaken, for the state, as a whole, has leaned traditionally to the right. Governor Brown's tenure seems almost an aberration. In 1990, Republican Pete Wilson won election as governor, succeeding Republican George Deukmejian, whose conservative fiscal and social policies, he promised to continue. Wilson won re-election in 1994 after a closely contested race with Kathleen Brown, sister of Jerry Brown.

Wealthy Orange County and to a lesser extent Los Angeles (surprisingly) have always been more conservative than the rest of the state. Residents of Orange County, who have consistently voted for right-wing candidates since their firm support of Barry Goldwater in 1964, are mocked by other Californians as living in splendid isolation behind the "Orange Curtain." San Diego, with a large military presence, is also predominantly Republican, supporting the kind of administration in Washington that it thinks will best serve its economic interests.

In 1992, California became the first state in the union to send two female senators to Washington when it elected Barbara Boxer and Dianne Feinstein.

2 Famous Californians

Francis Ford Coppola (b. 1939) One of America's most successful contemporary filmmakers, Coppola is best known for *Apocalypse Now* and *The Godfather.* His movie *The Conversation* was filmed in San Francisco, where Coppola lives and works.

Joe DiMaggio (b. 1914) DiMaggio was one of the greatest baseball players of all time. He began his career with the San Francisco Seals before becoming the New York Yankees' star center fielder. His marriage to Marilyn Monroe in the 1950s drew world headlines.

Lawrence Ferlinghetti (b. 1920) A prominent figure in the beat movement of the 1950s, Ferlinghetti is a poet extraordinaire with close links to major cultural figures. In 1953, he founded San Francisco's City Lights bookstore.

Jerry Garcia (b. 1942) Lead guitarist and vocalist of the Grateful Dead, Jerry still lives in the San Francisco Bay Area, as does the rest of the band.

Dashiell Hammett (1894–1961) Drawing on his experience with the Pinkerton Detective Agency, Hammett penned hard-boiled detective novels, including *The Maltese Falcon* and *The Thin Man.* He was imprisoned for refusing to testify during the House Un-American Activities Committee "witch-hunts" of the 1950s.

William Randolph Hearst (1863–1951) Famous for his opulent lifestyle and grand castle at San Simeon, Hearst was a publishing magnate, who, as a young man, worked on the *San Francisco Examiner.*

Janis Joplin (1943–70) One of the most charismatic rock-and-roll voices, Joplin began her career in San Francisco with Big Brother and the Holding Company.

Jack Kerouac (1922–69) The Massachusetts-born leader of the beat generation moved to San Francisco in the 1950s and there wrote the beat's bible, *On the Road.*

Orville Redenbacher (b. 1907) A resident of San Diego, Redenbacher developed a hybrid yellow popping corn in 1952 that won nationwide popularity.

Carl Rogers (1902–87) Founder of the Center for Studies of the Person, in La Jolla in 1963, Rogers is known as the father of humanistic psychology. He wrote a seminal study, *On Becoming a Person,* in 1961.

Jonas Salk (b. 1914) Best known as the developer of the polio vaccine (1953), Salk founded the Institute for Biological Studies in La Jolla in 1963.

H. W. Scripps (1854–1926) A San Diegan, Scripps was a prominent newspaper publisher. He helped develop the United Press International news wire service and founded the Scripps-McRae League of Newspapers, which later became Scripps-Howard Newspapers.

"Dr. Seuss" (1904–81) Theodore Seuss Geisel wrote and illustrated many beloved children's books, including *The Cat in the Hat* and *How the Grinch Stole Christmas,* both published in 1957.

3 Architecture & Literature

ARCHITECTURE California's buildings reflect several historical styles of architecture. The first, dating from the late 18th century, during the era of Mexican rule, consists of Spanish-style adobe structures, often topped with red-tile roofs. Dozens of homes on the Monterey Peninsula and in Santa Barbara, as well as many of the state's missions, exemplify the style of this period. The missions usually employed distinctive Native American construction methods.

The second major style, popularized about a century later, reflects a Victorian tendency in design and ornateness. Both homes and office buildings were constructed in this style. The most stunning examples are in San Francisco, where many of the more than 14,000 colorfully painted "gingerbread" structures, dating from the second half of the 19th century, have beautifully restored painted exteriors. The Alamo Square district has one of the city's largest concentrations of these "Painted Ladies," in which the local residents take particular pride. Many Victorian-style structures, such as the Haas-Lillienthal House and the Sheraton Palace Hotel's Garden Court, are open to the public (see Chapter 4 for more information).

Later architectural styles include 1930s art-deco buildings, largely in Los Angeles, and 1950s kitsch diners, near main roads and highways throughout the state. Concrete was the preferred building material in the late 1960s and in the 1970s; consequently, a plethora of almost uniformly ugly concrete structures mar almost every urban

Did You Know ?

- The official state animal, the grizzly bear, is extinct in California.
- California's ubiquitous Spanish missions are among the oldest buildings in the state.
- California boasts more than 1,200 miles of coastline.
- San Diego was the first of California's original 27 counties.
- San Francisco is the fourth-largest city in California, after Los Angeles, San Diego, and San Jose.
- One in every seven Americans lives in California.

area. Glass-and-steel office buildings—a trend that took hold in the 1980s—dominate much of downtown San Francisco, Los Angeles, and San Diego and give Silicon Valley its sleek, urban look.

LITERATURE Almost from the beginning, novelists and poets were an essential part of the cultural mosaic that makes up California. Although their personal stays were often in the nature of passing through, their works have left lasting records of the history of America's fastest-changing region. From Mark Twain, who created vivid tales of the Comstock Lode silver mines and the 1860s frontier, to Joan Didion and Amy Tan, contemporary novelists who write about the California of their childhoods, there has been no lack of talent here. Writing in between we find Dashiell Hammett, whose seminal detective novels were often set in San Francisco; Aldous Huxley, who lived in and wrote about California and Hollywood; and Jack Kerouac, who was the most influential of the beat writers.

Jack London, author of *Call of the Wild* and other stories, grew up on the docks of Oakland and spent most of his life in California. John Steinbeck, one of the state's best-known authors, would have achieved his reputation with just one of the many books he wrote about life in the center of the state. His *Grapes of Wrath* remains the classic account of Midwestern migrants coming to California in the midst of the Great Depression. *Cannery Row* has forever made the Monterey waterfront famous, and *East of Eden* brings a deep insight into the way of life in the Salinas Valley. (See "Recommended Books, Films, and Recordings," below, for more information on California literature.)

4 Cultural & Social Life

The first time I drove down the California coast, I was awed not only by the beauty of the country but also by the seemingly staggering wealth of its residents. To this day I have not seen anywhere else such a consistently rich stretch of real estate as the sliver of land that hugs the coast from San Francisco to San Diego. What you can't see from your car is that California's cultural, social, and economic mix is as diverse as its geography. Oceanfront land is the highest-priced of the state's parcels, often topped with spectacular houses. But for every wealthy landlord there are several struggling tenants, whose work-a-day lifestyles are California's real bread and butter. Mexicans make up the largest share of the state's immigrant population, and large communities of Mexican-Americans can be found in almost every town in California. And in recent years, Asian immigrants have also flocked to California in record numbers.

Settlers, dreamers, speculators, spirituality seekers, political idealists, economic immigrants—all are lured by California's sunshine and laid-back lifestyle, and by the state's magical ability to assume the shape of any dream. Anything still seems possible in this new land that is relatively unburdened by the past. Few of California's many aspirants have ever discovered gold, struck oil, or achieved stardom. But that reality has not stifled the state's incredible growth (from more than 10.5 million in 1950 to more than 25 million in 1990) or withered the region's mystique as the Promised Land.

5 Food & Drink

California cuisine is one of the newest and most important genres in regional American cooking. The style stresses local ingredients and light preparations that are both calorie- and health-conscious. "Designer" vegetables are often used, as are fresh local spices and locally produced wines.

A strong Mexican influence is apparent; avocados are everywhere, and salsa is served with almost every meal. Mexican restaurants are the most popular ethnic eateries, so you're never very far from a taco or a burrito. Yet nearly every other ethnic cuisine is also represented here, especially in San Francisco and Los Angeles. Sushi is fresh and popular; Chinese food, especially in San Francisco, is excellent; and superior French cuisine can be found in the state's major cities.

The growing emphasis on health food has inspired a debate about whether California's water is safe to drink. Opinions vary, as borne out by studies. The state consumes more bottled water per capita than any other region in America, but many more locals drink water straight from the tap. Suffice it to say that if you do decide to order bottled water at a restaurant, there are usually plenty of brands, both domestic and foreign, from which to choose.

Few will argue, however, with the assertion that California is wine country. You will find that what supremely enhances a good California meal is a bottle of local wine. Many restaurants offer excellent selections, which usually include several good buys. Try some new wines from a vineyard you've never heard of, and enjoy further exploration of a region you may have thought you knew well.

6 Recommended Books, Films & Recordings

Books

GENERAL Mark Twain and Bret Harte were in the center of the action during the height of the Gold Rush, writing it all down. Harte's collection of stories *The Luck of Roaring Camp and Other Sketches* reveals the tough lives of Gold Rush miners. Mark Twain's *San Francisco* is a collection of articles that Twain wrote about what he called "the liveliest, heartiest community on our continent." His book *Roughing It* includes a moment-by-moment description of the 1906 San Francisco earthquake.

Joan Didion, in her novel *Slouching Toward Bethlehem,* and Hunter S. Thompson, in his columns for the *San Francisco Examiner,* both used a "new journalistic" approach in their studies of San Francisco in the 1960s. Thompson's essays have recently been brought together in the collection *Generation of Swine.* Tom Wolfe's early work *The Electric Kool-Aid Acid Test* follows the Hell's Angels, the Grateful Dead, and Ken Kesey's Merry Pranksters as they ride through the hallucinogenic 1960s.

FICTION & BIOGRAPHY Frank Norris's *McTeague: A Story of San Francisco* is a violent tale of love and revenge set in that city at the turn of the century. Dashiell Hammett's classic, *The Maltese Falcon,* is a steamy detective novel that captures the seedier side of San Francisco in the 1920s. *Martin Eden* is Jack London's semiautobiographical account of his boyhood on the Oakland shores.

IMPRESSIONS

Californians are a race of people; they are not merely inhabitants of a state.
—O. Henry, *A Municipal Report*

California—a state so blessed . . . none had ever died there a natural death.
—Robert Frost, *New Hampshire*

In the 1950s, Jack Kerouac came to California to write *On the Road*, the bible of the beat generation. Its bopping prose chronicles a series of cross-country adventures, including high-jinks in San Francisco. Thomas Pynchon, in *The Crying of Lot 49,* chronicles the adventures of 1960s potheads.

More recently, Amy Tan's gentle, engrossing novels *The Joy Luck Club* and *The Kitchen God's Wife* evoke the lives of several generations of women in San Francisco's Chinatown.

Films

California's varied venues and beautiful sites, and their proximity to Hollywood, make the state a natural for directors searching for captivating, yet relatively inexpensive, film locations. Tens of thousands of movies have been shot here, the lion's share in and around Los Angeles. Below is a small selection.

Here Comes the Navy (1934), with James Cagney and Pat O'Brien, was filmed at the U.S. Naval Training Station in San Diego.

Citizen Kane (1941), based loosely on the life of newspaper publisher William Randolph Hearst, is widely regarded as the best film ever made.

The Maltese Falcon (1941), John Huston's film about San Francisco private eye Sam Spade (Humphrey Bogart), may be one of the best detective films ever made.

Hellcats of the Navy (1956), starring Ronald Reagan and Nancy Davis, was shot in San Diego.

Some Like It Hot (1959), one of Marilyn Monroe's best pictures, with Jack Lemmon and Tony Curtis, was filmed in San Diego's Hotel del Coronado.

Bird Man of Alcatraz (1962) is about real-life convicted killer Robert Stroud (Burt Lancaster), who studies birds while doing time in the high-security prison.

Alfred Hitchcock's classic thriller *The Birds* (1963) is set on the rugged coast just north of San Francisco.

The Graduate (1967) features Dustin Hoffman as a college graduate who expresses no interest in the prospect of a career in "plastics." UCLA doubles for the Berkeley campus.

Bullit (1968) is a cop thriller starring Steve McQueen. It contains what is still the quintessential San Francisco car chase.

Harold and Maude (1971) is a black comedy about a death-obsessed teenager and his octogenarian friend. Filmed in San Francisco, it's a cult classic.

Dirty Harry, Magnum Force, and *The Enforcer* (1971, 1973, and 1976), three thrillers about a fascist-minded San Francisco cop, affirmed Clint Eastwood's place in the American psyche.

What's Up Doc? (1972), a screwball comedy starring Barbra Streisand and Ryan O'Neal, offers plenty of shots of San Francisco.

American Graffiti (1973), a remarkably popular teen rite-of-passage film, is based on director George Lucas's hometown of Modesto.

The Sting (1973) featured Santa Monica Pier's Carousel, among other Los Angeles locations.

The Conversation (1974), by director Francis Ford Coppola and starring Gene Hackman, is set in and around San Francisco's Union Square.

Freaky Friday (1976), with Jodie Foster, was shot in San Diego.

Attack of the Killer Tomatoes (1978), the cult classic thriller, was made in San Diego.

California Suite (1978), Neal Simon's sentimental comedy, is set in the Beverly Hills Hotel.

Foul Play (1978), filmed in San Francisco, was one of Goldie Hawn's biggest movies. Dudley Moore and Chevy Chase costar.

Blade Runner (1982) featured downtown L.A.'s art deco–style Union Station as a 21st-century police station.

Chan Is Missing (1982) was director Wayne Wang's low-budget sleeper about the Chinese-American experience in San Francisco's Chinatown.

48 Hours (1982) offers great shots of San Francisco as Eddie Murphy prances around with Nick Nolte trying to wrap up a homicide case.

Beverly Hills Cop (1984), a runaway hit, stars Eddie Murphy in the role of a Detroit police officer in Los Angeles.

Top Gun (1986), Tom Cruise's top-grossing film, was shot in San Diego, at the Naval Air Station and in the city's Kansas City Barbecue restaurant.

Little Nikita (1988), starring Sydney Poitier and River Phoenix, was also filmed in San Diego, which has come to rival California's two other major cities as a favorite movie location.

Bagdad Café (1988) is German director Percy Adlon's view of life in an oasis in the Mojave Desert.

Pretty Woman (1989), starring Richard Gere and Julia Roberts, was filmed in L.A.'s Beverly Wilshire Hotel.

City Slickers (1990), one of Billy Crystal's successful comedies, was shot, in part, at Los Angeles International Airport.

The Player (1991), Robert Altman's award-winning film about behind-the-scenes Hollywood, proves that everything we think about "The Industry" is true.

In the Line of Fire (1994), which starred Clint Eastwood and John Malkovich, featured the glass elevators and renovated ballroom of L.A.'s Westin Bonaventure during the climactic conclusion.

Recordings

California has made such a major contribution to the American music scene, from the classical to the popular, that this section can only be a brief overview. Composer Arnold Schoenberg, violinist Jascha Heifitz, and conductor Zubin Mehta are just a few of the figures who attracted world attention to Los Angeles and gave the city a fittingly prominent place in classical music. And in the 1950s Los Angeles mounted the only serious challenge New York has faced as the world's jazz capital; players such as Dave Brubeck, Dexter Gordon, Chet Baker, Ornette Coleman, Gerry Mulligan, and Art Pepper developed a fresh sound known as "west coast cool," and bebop legend Charlie Parker made some of his greatest recordings in L.A.'s Dial Recording Studios. Popular composers from George Gershwin and Jerome Kern to Henry Mancini have enriched America's musical heritage with the songs and scores they wrote for the silver screen, a medium that helped to spread American culture abroad and made it as likely that you would hear their tunes hummed in Paris or Buenos Aires as in New York and St. Louis.

In recent decades, California has been a major force in rock and pop, beginning with the various groups that emerged in San Francisco in the mid-1960s and changed American popular culture. Of those groups, the Grateful Dead, formed in 1965, are the only surviving psychedelic band. Santana, a group known for its innovative blending of Latin rhythms and virtuosic rock guitar, made its debut at San Francisco's Fillmore

West; before long, they'd become one of the stars of the famous Woodstock music festival. Other groups with California roots from this era included Jefferson Airplane, Big Brother and the Holding Company (with Janis Joplin), the political country band Country Joe and the Fish, Frank Zappa and his supremely creative Mothers of Invention, and the Doors.

While all these groups were part of the stridently rebellious counterculture of the 1960s, another strand of California pop rock, epitomized by the Beach Boys and a slew of "surf" bands that featured the ripping guitar solos of Dick Dale, was built around sweet harmonies or lyrics that centered on fun, sun, and sand. As the 1970s rolled on, this goodtime sensibility grew into the classic "California sound" purveyed by laid-back artists such as the Eagles, the Steve Miller Band, Steely Dan, and the Doobie Brothers, or rowdier rockers such as Van Halen.

Chris Isaak and San Francisco's Counting Crows prove that the California sound lingers on, but in the last 10 years most California bands that have hit it big have features an aggressive, in-your-face sound and attitude. In the mid-1980s Los Angeles was the U.S. birthplace of hardcore punk, spawning bands like X, the Minutemen, and Black Flag. The latter's Henry Rollins remains in the forefront of the new music scene with the Rollins Band, along with California contemporaries the Red Hot Chili Peppers, Bad Religion, and the Offspring. And there's no mistaking the dominant musical export from California today: rap and hip-hop, including the controversial "gangster" variety performed by a slew of artists, most notably N.W.A., Ice Cube, Dr. Dre, Ice-T, and Snoop Doggy-Dog.

2 Planning a Trip to California

How you get to the Golden State and how you get around it obviously depend on where you're coming from, how much you want to spend, and how much time you have. It is possible to arrive in California without an itinerary or reservations, but your trip will be much more rewarding with a little bit of advance planning. This chapter will help you discover your options and plan the trip that's best suited to your needs and interests.

1 Information & Money

Information

Tourism is big in California, and the state is rich with information about what to see and do. For information on the state as a whole, contact the **California Office of Tourism,** 801 K St., Suite 1600, Sacramento, CA 95814 (☎ toll free **800/862-2543**). They mail out a free information packet. In addition, almost every city and town in the state has a dedicated tourist bureau or chamber of commerce that will be happy to send you information on its particular parcel. These visitor information addresses and telephone numbers are listed under the appropriate headings in the geographically organized chapters that follow. Foreign travelers should also see Chapter 3, "For Foreign Visitors," for entry requirements and other pertinent information.

Money

Soaring real-estate values have made California one of America's most expensive states. U.S. dollar traveler's checks are the safest, most negotiable way to carry currency. They are accepted by most restaurants, hotels, and shops and can be exchanged for cash at banks and check-issuing offices. **American Express** offices are usually open weekdays from 9am to 5pm and Saturdays from 9am until noon. See "Fast Facts" in the chapters on San Francisco, Los Angeles, and San Diego for office locations in those cities.

Most banks offer **Automated Teller Machines** (ATMs), which accept cards connected to a particular network. The ubiquitous Bank of America accepts Plus, Star, and Interlink cards, while First Interstate Bank is on-line with the Cirrus system. Each bank has dozens of branches all around the state. For additional locations, dial toll free **800/424-7787** for the Cirrus network and **800/843-7587** for the Plus system.

Credit cards are widely accepted in California. MasterCard and Visa are most commonly accepted, followed by American Express, Carte Blanche, Diner's Club, and Discover. ATMs at the above-listed banks will make cash advances against MasterCard and Visa cards. American Express cardholders can write a personal check, guaranteed against the card, for up to $1,000 in cash at an American Express office. Foreign travelers should also see Chapter 3, "For Foreign Visitors," for monetary descriptions and currency exchange information.

2 When to Go

Summer is California's primary tourist season, but moderate temperatures and year-round visitor services make it a pleasure to travel during less busy seasons as well. The cities are particularly delightful from early autumn to late spring, when skies are bluest, when theater, opera, and ballet seasons are in full swing, and when restaurants and stores are less crowded. But California's climate is so varied that it is impossible to generalize about the state as a whole.

What Things Cost in San Francisco	U.S. $
Taxi from the airport to the city center	30.00
Bus fare to any destination within the city	1.00
Double at the Four Seasons Clift Hotel (very expensive)	205.00
Double at Villa Florence (moderate)	139.00
Double at Edward II Inn & Carriage House (budget)	67.00
Lunch for one at Little City (moderate)	15.00
Lunch for one at Amerasian Café (budget)	7.00
Dinner for one, without wine, at Fleur de Lys (expensive)	75.00
Dinner for one, without wine, at Cha Cha Cha (moderate)	17.00
Dinner for one, without wine, at Hamburger Mary's (inexpensive)	10.00
Glass of beer	2.75
Coca-Cola	1.25
Cup of coffee	.80
Admission to the top of Coit Tower	3.00
Movie ticket	7.50
Theater ticket	10.00–40.00

What Things Cost in Los Angeles	U.S. $
Taxi from the airport to downtown	25.00
Bus fare to any destination within the city	1.10
Double at the Beverly Hills Ritz (very expensive)	250.00
Double at the Radisson-Huntley Hotel (moderate)	145.00
Double at the Royal Palace Westwood Hotel (budget)	66.00
Lunch for one at Tom Bergin's Tavern (moderate)	12.00
Lunch for one at Roscoe's House of Chicken (budget)	6.00
Dinner for one, without wine, at Spago (expensive)	60.00
Dinner for one, without wine, at Antonio's (moderate)	25.00
Dinner for one, without wine, at the Source (budget)	12.00
Glass of beer	2.75
Coca-Cola	1.25
Cup of coffee	1.00
Admission to the J. Paul Getty Museum	Free
Movie ticket	7.50
Theater ticket	20.00

San Francisco's temperate marine climate means relatively mild weather year round. In summer, temperatures rarely top 70°F, and the city's famous fog rolls in most mornings and evenings. In winter, the mercury seldom falls below freezing, and snow is almost unheard of. Because of San Francisco's fog, summer seldom sees more than a few hot days in a row.

Los Angeles is usually much warmer than the Bay Area, and it gets significantly more sun. L.A.'s beaches are the golden sands that have given the entire state a worldwide reputation for tropical temperatures and the laid-back lifestyle they conduce. Even in winter, daytime thermometer readings regularly reach into the 60s and warmer. Summers can be stifling inland, but this city's beach communities are always comfortable. Don't pack an umbrella. When it rains, southern Californians go outside to look at the novelty.

San Francisco's Average Temperatures

	Jan	Feb	Mar	Apr	May	June	July	Aug	Sept	Oct	Nov	Dec
Avg. High (°F)	56	59	60	61	63	64	64	65	69	68	63	57
Avg. Low (°F)	46	48	49	49	51	53	53	54	56	55	52	47

Los Angeles's Average Temperatures

	Jan	Feb	Mar	Apr	May	June	July	Aug	Sept	Oct	Nov	Dec
Avg. High (°F)	65	66	67	69	72	75	81	81	81	77	73	69
Avg. Low °F)	46	48	49	52	54	57	60	60	59	55	51	49

Natives argue about the location of the border that separates southern and northern California; it is more psychological than physical. But as far as weather is concerned, seasonal changes have less effect south of San Luis Obispo, where temperatures remain relatively stable year round. Above this weather line, seasons are very much in evidence, and you should prepare accordingly. Also, once you turn inland, where the ocean has less of a stabilizing effect, winters bring ice and snow, and summers mean unending 100-plus degree days. Sightseeing in these parts is best during spring and autumn.

San Francisco Calendar of Events

January

- **San Francisco International Boat Show,** Moscone Center. Draws thousands of boat enthusiasts over a nine-day period. Call **415/469-6065** for details. Early January.

February

☆ Chinese New Year

In 1995, the Year of the Boar, public celebrations will again spill onto every street in Chinatown. Festivities climax during the "Miss Chinatown U.S.A." pageant parade, an incredible mixture of marching bands, rolling floats, barrages of fireworks, and a wonderful block-long dragon writhing in and out of the crowds. Not to be missed.

Where: Chinatown. **When:** Late January or early February, depending on the lunar calendar. **How:** Arrive early for a good viewing spot on Grant Avenue. For information, call **415/982-3000.**

March

- **St. Patrick's Day Parade.** Starts at 12:30pm at Market Street and Second Street, and continues past City Hall. The city's large Irish community is in evidence. Call **415/391-2000** for details. The Sunday before March 17.

★ San Francisco International Film Festival

This is one of America's oldest film festivals. Tickets are relatively inexpensive, and screenings are very accessible to the general public. Entries include new films by beginning and established directors.

Where: The AMC Kabuki 8 Cinemas, at Fillmore Street and Post Street. **When:** During two weeks early in the month. **How:** You can charge tickets by phone through BASS Ticketmaster at **415/835-3849.** For a schedule or information, call **415/931-FILM.**

April

- **Cherry Blossom Festival,** Japantown and at Golden Gate Park's Japanese Tea Garden. Traditional drumming, flower arranging, origami, and Kabuki theater celebrate the blooming of the cherry trees' pretty pink petals. Around the middle of April.
- **Yachting Season Opening Day.** Fills the bay with boats—it seems as though every craft in the Bay Area takes part in this aquatic salute to sailing. Good views can be had from the Golden Gate Bridge, Fisherman's Wharf, and the Marin Headlands. On a Saturday or Sunday at the end of April.

May

- **Bay to Breakers Foot Race,** Golden Gate Park. One of the city's most popular annual events, it's really more fun than run. Thousands of entrants show up dressed in their best Halloween-style costumes for the approximately seven-mile run across the park. The event is sponsored by the *San Francisco Examiner* (☎ **415/777-7770**). Third Sunday of May.
- **Black and White Ball,** Civic Center. A biennial fund-raiser for the San Francisco Symphony. At $150 each, tickets aren't cheap, but this is no ordinary black-tie event. Festivities take place in several Civic Center buildings, and the streets between them are cordoned off for the party. Food and drink are donated by local restaurants and wineries, and the thousands of revelers dress—appropriately enough—in black and white. For information, call **415/431-5400.** Usually held late in May, and scheduled in 1995.

★ Carnaval

San Francisco's Mission District's largest annual event, Carnaval is a week-long series of festivities that culminates with a parade on Mission Street over Memorial Day Weekend. Over a half-million spectators line the route and the samba musicians and dancers continue to play on 14th Street, near Harrison at the end of the march.

Where: Mission Street, between 14th and 24th streets. **When:** Memorial Day Weekend, late May. **How:** Just show up. Phone the Mission Economic Cultural Association (☎ **415/826-1401**) for more information.

June

- **Union Street Spring Festival,** along Union Street. This is the first of a series of city street fairs. From Fillmore Street to Gough Street, stalls sell arts and crafts, as well as food and drink. Music and entertainment are usually provided on a number of stages. Call **415/346-4446** for more information. First weekend of June.
- **Haight Street Fair.** Features alternative crafts, ethnic foods, rock bands, and a healthy number of hippies. For details, call **415/661-8025.** A Saturday in the middle of June.
- **Lesbian and Gay Freedom Day Parade,** Market Street. A prideful event drawing up to half a million participants. The parade ends at Civic Center Plaza, where hundreds of food, art, and information booths are set up around several sound stages. Call **415/864-3733** for information. Last weekend of June.
- **Stern Grove Midsummer Music Festival,** in the natural amphitheater at 19th Avenue and Sloat Boulevard. Free jazz, classical, and pop concerts are held every Sunday at 2pm. Call **415/252-6252** for listings. Mid-June through August.

July

- **Independence Day,** July 4th is celebrated all over town, but the largest festivities are on the waterfront, at Crissy Field. In addition to a 50-cannon salute, there are music concerts, comedy acts, food stands, and fireworks in front of the Golden Gate Bridge at 9pm.
- **San Francisco Marathon.** One of the largest marathons in the world. For entry information, contact the Pamakid Runners Club at **415/391-2123.** Mid-July.
- **Comedy Celebration Day,** at the Polo Field in Golden Gate Park. A free comedy marathon featuring dozens of famous and not-so-famous funny people. For information, call **415/777-7120.**

September

★ San Francisco Fair

There are no tractor pulls or monster trucks at San Francisco's rendition of an annual county fair. This sophisticated urban party is attended by thousands and includes restaurant and winery booths, street artists, fine artists, and high-quality local entertainment.
Where: Fort Mason Center. **When:** Early September. **How:** For information call **415/391-2000.**

★ Sausalito Art Festival

A juried exhibit of over 160 artists is accompanied by music by Bay Area jazz, rock, and blues performers while international cuisine is washed down by wines from some 50 different Napa and Sonoma producers.
Where: Sausalito. **When:** Labor Day Weekend, early September. **How:** For more information, call **415/332-3555.** Parking is impossible; take the Red & White Fleet (☎ **415/546-2628**) ferry from Fisherman's Wharf to the festival site.

- **San Francisco Blues Festival,** on the grounds of Fort Mason. The largest outdoor blues music event on the West Coast. Local and national musicians perform back-to-back during two marathon days. You can charge tickets by phone through BASS Ticketmaster (☎ **415/835-3849**). For schedule information, call **415/826-6837.** Usually in mid-September.
- **Castro Street Fair.** Celebrates life in the city's most famous gay neighborhood. Late September.

October

- **Columbus Day Festivities.** The 1995 party will celebrate the 503rd anniversary of Christopher Columbus's landing in America. The city's Italian community leads the festivities, around Fisherman's Wharf, which include street food fairs, fireworks, the usual curbside entertainment, and a reenactment of the explorer's landing, at Aquatic Park. On Columbus Day itself, a parade marches up Columbus Avenue. Phone **415/434-1492** for information.

December

- **The Nutcracker,** War Memorial Opera House. Performed annually by the San Francisco Ballet (☎ **415/776-1999**). Tickets to this Tchaikovsky tradition should be purchased well in advance.

Los Angeles Calendar of Events

January

★ Tournament Of Roses

An annual celebration of the first day of the new year. Festivities include the spectacular parade down Colorado Boulevard, famous for its lavish floats, music, and extraordinary equestrian entries; followed by the Rose Bowl Game.

Where: Pasadena. **When:** January 1. **How:** Contact the Pasadena Tournament Of Roses office at 391 S. Orange Grove Blvd., Pasadena, CA 91105 **(818/449-4100)** for more details.

- **Oshogatsu.** The Japanese New Year is celebrated annually at the Japanese American Cultural and Community center in Little Tokyo. Participate in traditional Japanese ceremonies and enjoy ethnic foods and crafts. It takes place during the first weekend in January. For more information, call **213/628-2725.**
- **Martin Luther King Parade.** Long Beach's annual parade down Alameda and Seventh Streets, ending with a festival in Martin Luther King Park. For more information, contact the Council of Special Events at **310/570-6816**.

February

- **Chinese New Year.** Colorful dragon dancers parade through the streets of downtown's New Chinatown. An event not to be missed. Contact the Chinese Chamber of Commerce, 977 N. Broadway, Room E, Los Angeles, CA 90012 (☎ **213/617-0396**) for this year's schedule.

March

★ Los Angeles Marathon

It might seem counterproductive healthwise, but this 26.2-mile run through the streets of Los Angeles attracts thousands of participants.
Where: Downtown Los Angeles. **When:** Early March. **How:** Call **310/444-5544** for registration or spectator information.

★ American Indian Festival And Market

Showcase and Festival of Native American arts and culture. The fun includes traditional dances, storytelling, and a display of arts and crafts as well as a chance to sample ethnic foods.
Where: Los Angeles Natural History Museum. **When:** Late March. **How:** Admission to museum includes festival tickets. Call **213/774-3414.**

April

★ Renaissance Pleasure Fair

One of America's largest Renaissance festivals, this annual happening, set in L.A.'s relatively remote countryside, looks very much like an authentic, albeit somewhat touristy, old English village. The fair provides an entire day's activities, shows and festivities, food and crafts. Participants are encouraged to come in costume.
Where: Glen Ellen Regional Park, San Bernardino. **When:** Weekends from April through June. **How:** For ticket information phone toll free **800/523-2473.**

★ Toyota Grand Prix

An exciting weekend of Indy car auto racing and entertainment in and around the streets of downtown Long Beach.
Where: Long Beach. **When:** Mid-April. **How:** Contact Grand Prix Association, 300 Pacific Ave., Long Beach, CA 90806 **(310/436-9953).**

May

★ Cinco De Mayo

A week-long celebration of one of Mexico's most jubilant holidays takes place throughout the city of Los Angeles. The fiesta's carnival-like atmosphere is created by large crowds, live music, dances, and food.
Where: Main festivities held in El Pueblo De Los Angeles State Historic Park, downtown. Other events around the city. **When:** One week surrounding May 5th. **How:** Phone **213/625-5045** for information.

- **Redondo Beach Wine Festival.** The largest outdoor wine-tasting event in Southern California is held in early May in Redondo Beach. For exact dates and this year's locations, contact the Redondo Chamber of Commerce, 200 N. Pacific Coast Highway, Redondo Beach, CA 90277 (**310/376-6912**).
- **National Orange Show.** This 11-day county fair includes various stadium events, celebrity entertainment, livestock shows, and carnival rides. It's held in San Bernardino in mid-May. Phone **909/888-6788** for information.

June

- **Playboy Jazz Festival.** Usually held in the Hollywood Bowl, this mid-June event is widely recognized for the great artists it attracts. Phone **310/246-4000** for details.

★ **Annual Grand National Irish Fair And Music Festival**

Bagpipes, Gaelic music, song, and dance ring in this traditional event. You may even see a leprechaun, if you're lucky.
Where: Griffith Park. **When:** June. **How:** Phone **310/395-8322** for dates and more information.

July

★ **Fourth Of July Celebration**

Southern California's most spectacular display of fireworks follows an evening of live entertainment.
Where: The Rose Bowl, 1001 Rose Bowl Dr., Pasadena. **When:** July 4th. **How:** Phone **818/577-3106** for further information.

- **Fireworks Display at the Marina.** Burton Chase Park in Marina Del Rey is a favorite place to view traditional Fourth of July fireworks. Arrive in the afternoon for best parking and viewing sites.

★ **Hollywood Bowl Summer Festival**

Summer season at the Hollywood Bowl brings the world's best sounds of jazz, pop, and classical music to an open-air setting. The season includes an annual Fourth of July concert.
Where: 2301 N. Highland Blvd., Hollywood. **When:** July through mid-September. **How:** Phone the Bowl's box office at **213/850-2000** for information.

★ **International Surf Festival**

Four beachside cities collaborate in the oldest international surf festival in California. Competitions include surfing, boogie boarding, sand-castle building, and other beach-related categories.
Where: Hermosa Beach/Manhattan Beach/Redondo Beach/Torrance. **When:** The end of July or the beginning of August. **How:** Contact the International Surf Festival Committee at **310/376-6911** for information.

August

- **Nisei Week Japanese Festival.** A week-long celebration of Japanese culture and heritage is held in mid-August in the Japanese-American Cultural and Community Center Plaza, in Little Tokyo. Festivities include parades, food, music, arts, and crafts. Phone **213/687-7193** for details.
- **African Marketplace and Cultural Fair.** African arts, crafts, food, and music are featured during this mid-August cultural awareness event held in Rancho Cienega Park. Phone **213/734-1164** for more information.
- **Long Beach Sea Festival.** The last two weeks of August are dedicated to a variety of water-related events, including a sailboat regatta and jet ski and swimming competitions. Contact the Long Beach Department of Parks, and Marine Recreation, 2760 Studebaker Rd., Long Beach, CA 90815 (☎ **310/421-9431,** ext. 3370) for specific scheduling information.

September

Los Angeles County Fair

Horse racing, arts, agricultural displays, celebrity entertainment, and carnival rides are among the attractions of the largest county fair in the world. **Where:** Los Angeles County Fair and Exposition Center in Pomona. **When:** September. **How:** Call **909/623-3111** for information.

- **Long Beach Blues Festival.** An annual outdoor festival featuring top names in blues music, usually held toward the end of September. Call **310/985-5566** for information.

October

- **Annual Bob Hope Celebrity Golf Tournament.** Bob Hope is the honorary chairman of this annual golf tournament in Riverside. For ticket and other information, contact the Riverside Visitors and Convention Bureau, 3443 Orange St., Riverside, CA 92507 (**909/787-7950**).

November

- **Bandfest.** Bands participating in the Hollywood Christmas Parade compete in various categories in a battle of the marching bands. Call **213/469-8311** for details.

Hollywood Christmas Parade

This spectacular star-studded parade marches through the heart of Hollywood just after Thanksgiving. **Where:** Hollywood Boulevard. **When:** End of November. **How:** For information, phone **213/469-2337.**

3 Health, Insurance & Other Concerns

Health and safety are serious issues. Take a little time before your trip to make sure these concerns don't ruin it. Foreign travelers should see Chapter 3, "For Foreign Visitors," for entry information and other related matters.

INSURANCE Most travel agents sell low-cost health, loss, and trip-cancellation insurance to their vacationing clients. Compare these rates and services with those offered by local banks, as well as with those from your personal insurance carrier.

Most American travelers are covered by their hometown health insurance policies in the event of an accident or sudden illness while away on vacation. Make sure your Health Maintenance Organization (HMO) or insurance carrier can provide services for you in California. If there is any doubt, a health insurance policy that specifically covers your trip is advisable. Foreign travelers should check if they are covered by their home insurance companies and see Chapter 3, "For Foreign Visitors," for more information.

You can also protect your travel investment with travel-related insurance that covers lost or damaged baggage and trip-cancellation or interruption costs. These coverages are often combined into a single comprehensive plan, sold through travel agents, credit-card companies, and automobile and other clubs.

SAFETY Innocent tourists are rarely the victims of violent crime. Still, there are precautions you can take to protect yourself and your possessions.

When sightseeing, it's best to plan your route in advance; consult maps indoors before leaving your hotel room. Ask directions from service providers—hotel desk staff, telephone or power company employees, or police officers. Avoid asking strangers for directions, and don't discuss your plans with them. If you get lost, find an open business and ask for directions there. Always be aware of your surroundings and leave an area if it appears unsafe. Remember, alcohol consumption diminishes awareness.

Use traveler's checks or credit cards whenever possible. Carry only as much cash as you will need and never display it openly. Carry your wallet in the front pocket of your pants or inside your jacket. Carry pocketbooks and other bags under your arm, not by the handle. While sitting, keep your handbag in your lap. In a restaurant, never sling your purse over the back of a chair. Keep your bag next to you in a public restroom instead of using door hooks. Consider using a "fanny-pack" or a concealable money-belt to carry cash and credit cards. Carry some of your cash and credit cards separately, in a second pocket or wallet, and carry new purchases in old bags. Stay especially alert in crowded situations, such as in department stores, at bus stops, and on public transportation.

Don't let your car advertise that you are a visitor. Place maps, travel brochures, this guidebook, and valuables out of sight—in the glove compartment or trunk. Never leave wallets, credit cards, checkbooks, or purses anywhere in the vehicle. Always lock your vehicle and take the keys. Park in well-lighted, busy areas. Check the interior of your vehicle before getting in, and when parking for the night, ask yourself if you've left anything in your car that could be of any value whatsoever—then remove it.

Keep an eye on your luggage when checking in and out of your hotel. Make sure no one hears your name and room number while at the front desk. Phone the front desk to verify the identity of room service and other hotel employees—especially if you did not call for them. Know what the hotel identification badge looks like. Deposit your valuables in the hotel safe and keep an inventory of what was deposited; never leave cash or other valuables in your room. Lock your luggage when it is left in the room, know how to double lock your room door, and use the door viewer to identify anyone trying to gain entry to your room. Never leave your room key at an unattended front desk.

California's homeless problem is immense—panhandlers are especially prevalent in San Francisco and Los Angeles. Most homeless people are harmless; however, some street people are chronic law violators who may infringe upon the rights of others. We suggest a combination of respect and caution around panhandlers and other strangers.

See "Fast Facts" in the San Francisco, Los Angeles, and San Diego chapters for city-specific safety tips.

Driving Safety while driving is particularly important. Question your rental agency about personal safety or ask for a brochure on traveler safety tips when you pick up your car. Obtain written directions, or a map with the route marked in red, from the agency showing how to get to your destination. And, if possible, arrive and depart during daylight hours.

Recently more and more crime has involved cars and drivers. If you drive off a highway into a doubtful neighborhood, leave the area as quickly as possible. If you have an accident, even on the highway, stay in your car with the doors locked until you assess the situation, or until the police arrive. If you are bumped from behind on the street or are involved in a minor accident with no injuries and the situation appears to be suspicious, motion to the other driver to follow you. *Never* get out of your car in such situations. You can also keep a pre-made sign in your car that reads: "PLEASE

FOLLOW THIS VEHICLE TO REPORT THE ACCIDENT." Show the sign to the other driver and go directly to the nearest police precinct, well-lighted service station, or all night store.

If you see someone on the road who indicates a need for help, do not stop. Take note of the location, drive on to a well-lighted area, and telephone the police by dialing **911.**

Park in well-lighted, well-traveled areas, if possible. Always keep the doors of your vehicle locked, whether it is attended or unattended. Look around you before you get out of your car, and never leave any packages or valuables in sight. If someone attempts to rob you or steal your car, *do not try to resist.* Report the theft or carjacking to the police department immediately.

See also the "Fast Facts" entry on safety below and in the chapters on San Francisco, Los Angeles, and San Diego for safety tips relating specifically to those cities.

SUNBURN The sun is healthful only in moderation. Too much exposure to the sun's rays over a long period of time can be detrimental, and even cause cancer. Sunning should be fun, but you should also take it seriously, and take precautions.

Protect yourself with a high Sun Protection Factor (SPF) lotion or screen and don't expose yourself to too much sun in one day—*especially* if you've been out of the sun for months. If you burn easily, a product with an SPF of at least eight is recommended. Also, wear sunglasses—the kind that block out ultraviolet rays—and bring a hat with a wide bill or rim. You may laugh now, but when you're walking on the beach in the middle of the afternoon, or driving west while the sun is setting, you'll want your hat.

4 What to Pack

It's unwise to bring more than you can carry. There is no need to overpack and be a slave to your luggage; many smaller hotels do not have porters. Don't worry if you forget something or need an emergency item. Everything you could possibly want can be purchased in California.

California's weather ranges from freezing cold to blistering hot. If you're driving down the coast, you'll be crossing several climate zones, so you should pack for all eventualities. Any time of year, an all-weather coat is a good idea, and it is best to dress in layers. Good walking shoes are also a must if you want to explore the state's many wonderful towns and neighborhoods.

San Francisco's weather can be freezing cold in summer and pleasantly balmy in winter. It can also be both on any given day, summer or winter, thus making packing for your trip particularly difficult. In general, San Francisco's weather is usually cooler than you might expect, especially during summer, when you should pack at least one warm sweater and a light jacket.

Down south, warm weather translates into informal dress. Few places require jackets and ties, and if you're on vacation, you'll rarely feel out of place without these business staples. During winter, plan for cold snaps and cool nights with clothes appropriate to more northerly climes. Of course, you should bring shorts, a bathing suit, and sunglasses. Keep your rain gear at home; the chances that you'll need it are few.

Other items of necessity include prescriptions if you are currently taking medication, just in case your pills are lost. Eyeglass wearers should also carry their prescriptions.

5 Tips for Special Travelers

FOR THE DISABLED Most of California's major museums and tourist attractions are fitted with wheelchair ramps to accommodate physically challenged visitors. In addition, many hotels offer special accommodations and services for wheelchairbound and other visitors with disabilities. These include large bathrooms, ramps, and telecommunication devices for the deaf. The **California Travel Association,** 2500 Wilshire Blvd., Suite 603, Los Angeles, CA 90057 (☎ **310/645-1500**), provides information and referrals to specially equipped sights and hotels around the state. California issues special license plates to physically disabled drivers and honors plates issued by other states. Special "handicapped" parking spots are located near entrances to most buildings.

Local tourist bureaus have specialized information on their area for disabled visitors. See listings in individual cities and towns for information.

FOR SENIORS "Senior citizens" usually means those who are 65 and older. Seniors regularly receive discounts at museums and attractions; when available, these discounts have been listed in the following chapters. Ask for discounts everywhere—at hotels, movie theaters, museums, restaurants, and attractions. You may be surprised how often you will be offered reduced rates. When making airline reservations, ask about a senior discount, but find out if there is a cheaper promotional fare before committing yourself.

Older travelers are particularly encouraged to purchase travel insurance (see "Insurance" above) and would be well advised to exercise frugality when packing.

FOR FAMILIES Children add joys and a different level of experience to travel. They help you see things in a different way and will draw sometimes reticent local people like a magnet. Taking kids to California also obviously means additional, more thorough planning. On airplanes, order children's meals as far in advance as possible. Most airlines don't carry baby food, but they will be glad to heat up any you've brought with you. Pack essential first-aid supplies, such as Band-Aids, a thermometer, children's Tylenol, and cough drops; and always carry with you some snacks, such as raisins, crackers, and fruit, as well as water or juice.

Frommer's California with Kids (Macmillan) is an excellent, specialized guide to the state for parents with kids in tow. California is full of sightseeing opportunities and special activities geared toward children. If you're headed specifically for Los Angeles or San Francisco, you'll find *Frommer's Los Angeles with Kids* and *Frommer's San Francisco with Kids* (also Macmillan) equally invaluable as family guides to all the fun places in those cities. In this guide, see the "Cool for Kids" listings for restaurant and hotel suggestions in the chapters on Los Angeles, San Diego, and San Francisco.

FOR STUDENTS Students will find that their valid high school or college I.D. will often mean discounts to museums and attractions. When student prices are available, they are noted in this book.

6 Alternative/Adventure Travel

Ever increasingly, the world of travel is being segmented into small, specialized packages geared toward like-minded travelers. These special-interest vacations encompass everything from adventure and wilderness tours to self-improvement workshops, political retreats, and educational packages. California's diversity and size ensure plenty of opportunities for alternative travel; some of the best are listed below.

Educational/Study Travel

Elderhostel, 75 Federal St., Boston, MA 02110 (☎ **617/426-7788**), is one of the most successful and inexpensive vacation plans for persons 60 and older. The organization offers short-term study tours at colleges and universities in California and elsewhere in the United States, as well as around the world. Classes last usually from one to three weeks, and a single fee covers tuition, room, and board. Accommodations are often university residence halls. Programs can cost as little as $250 per week, plus airfare, and usually include daily classroom instruction. Single travelers usually constitute about one-third of the Elderhostel's participants, of whom at least 60% are women. Write or call for a free catalog of upcoming events.

Idyllwild School of Music and the Arts (ISOMATA), P.O. Box 38, Idyllwild, CA 92549 (☎ **714/659-2171** or **213/622-0355**), is a school for the applied arts like no other. Tucked away among the rustic San Jacinto Mountains on 205 pine-topped acres, the school takes a spiritually oriented approach to the study of music, dance, theater, and the visual and applied arts. It offers one- and two-week classes, from June through September, on a variety of subjects, including wilderness photography, painting, drawing, collage, visual-language development, study of mystical symbols, papermaking, science-fiction writing, poetry, and sculpture. The school is best known for its Mother Earth, Father Sky workshops in Native American arts. These special classes include weaving, pottery, basketry, sculpture, jewelry making, and mask carving using the same methods and materials as the Navajo, Hopi, Acoma, Papago, and other native peoples.

The children's center at Idyllwild offers special arts programs for kids ages 5 to 12. Classes include arts, crafts, movement, and music, which are then integrated into a single performance of an original play based on the children's own ideas.

Classes cost from $195 per week, plus room and board. There are a limited number of residence hall–style accommodations, each of which is fitted with twin beds and private bath. Units can accommodate one or two adults and cost $275 to $375 per person per week, including three meals, based on double occupancy. Tent and trailer sites are also available and cost $40 and $80 per week, respectively. Finally, the school can recommend private motels and bed-and-breakfast establishments located in the nearby town of Idyllwild. A charming mountain hamlet, Idyllwild has several B&Bs and eateries, as well as a village market, bookstores, and gift shops.

The school is located about 2½ hours by car inland from both Los Angeles and San Diego. It will arrange to have you picked up from either Palm Springs or Ontario Airport for an additional $50 charge in each direction. Call or write for a free catalog detailing the school's workshops and environs.

Adventure Travel

BACKPACKING To receive an excellent guide to California's state parks, contact the **California Department of Parks and Recreation,** Publications Unit, P.O. Box 942896, Sacramento, CA 94296 (☎ **916/653-6995**). Enclose $2 for the guide and postage and handling.

Cal Adventures, University of California, 2301 Bancroft Way, Berkeley, CA 94720 (☎ **510/642-4000**), is the outdoor recreation program of the University of California at Berkeley. For 10 years, this excellent program has offered a wide variety of top-notch outdoor trips throughout the year. Dozens of adventures are offered each season; most last three to four days. Rock climbing and extended backpacking trips are also offered to Yosemite, Death Valley, Big Sur, and beyond. Hikes are rated for difficulty and cost from $99 to $208. Write or call for a comprehensive brochure outlining upcoming programs.

Minarets Pack Station, 23620 Robertson Blvd., Chowchilla, CA 93610 (☎ **209/868-3405**), in the southeastern part of Yosemite National Park, high on the Sierra Nevada's west side, serves visitors to the Ansel Adams Wilderness Area in the Sierra National Forest. Whether you want to explore the awe-inspiring heights of Banner Peak and Mount Ritter or the roaring San Joaquin River, Minarets Pack Station can outfit you for an extraordinary vacation. The company will supply you with anything from trail information to donkeys, a guide, and a cook. For an intimate adventure with yourself, the pack station will bring you and your gear to a secluded campsite and return to pick you up on a specified date. A five-day, hands-on, professionally taught packing course is also offered. Minarets Pack Station is located in Miller Meadow, 95 miles northeast of Fresno. It's open from June through October only. Prices vary considerably, depending on your specifications. Write or call before June 1 and you'll receive a very informative folder with rates, dates, and an area map.

BICYCLING Excellent, inexpensive bicycle tours around California are offered by **American Youth Hostels (AYH),** Central California Council, P.O. Box 28148, San Jose, CA 95159 (☎ **408/298-0670**). Some trips are specially designed for specific age groups; despite the organization's title, however, you don't have to be a youth to join, just high-spirited and in good shape. A host of camping, hostel, and country-inn tours are offered throughout the summer. One of the most popular is a 22-day California coast cycling trip that journeys from San Francisco to San Diego and costs about $700. Hiking, motor, and other adventure journeys are also offered. Write or call for a current catalog.

Backroads, 1516 Fifth St., Suite Q427, Berkeley, CA 94710-1740 (☎ **510/527-1555,** or toll free **800/245-3874**), offers several weekend and week-long luxury bike excursions through some of the state's most spectacular countryside. Tours vary in difficulty and comfort; some are camping trips, while others accommodate in B&Bs. Two or three professional leaders accompany each group, while a support van trails with gear, baggage, and provisions. Most tours cost from $100 to $200 per day (the camping tour costs about $100 per day). Write or call for further information and a free copy of the firm's award-winning 104-page catalog.

CAMPING TOURS One organization, **Green Tortoise,** P.O. Box 24459, San Francisco, CA 94124 (☎ **415/821-0803,** or toll free **800/227-4766** outside California), offers one of America's unique approaches to touring. The 1960s are still celebrated aboard this "hostel on wheels," where up to 35 passengers stretch out on a seatless bus while rolling around the countryside. Participants explore, camp out, hike, and swim; each trip is a new adventure, with a flexible schedule. Most California trips start in San Francisco and head north through the Napa Valley and on to Lassen Volcanic National Park, Shasta National Forest, Redwoods National Park, or Fern

Canyon, before returning to the Bay Area. The price of a typical six-day loop is about $200. Write or call for detailed itineraries and prices.

TrekAmerica, P.O. Box 470, Blairstown, NJ 07825 (☎ **908/362-9198,** or toll free **800/221-0596**), one of the largest and most successful cooperative camping-tour operators in America, has been offering regular packages to California destinations since 1972. Cruising by day and camping at night, up to 14 people share a van complete with camping equipment and a professional tour escort. Participants range in age from 18 to 38 and quickly become a tight-knit group. Members take turns shopping for food along the way, and everyone helps prepare meals and set up camp. West coast camping tours often depart from Los Angeles and travel east to Nevada and the Grand Canyon or north toward San Francisco and Seattle. Tours are two to four weeks in length and cost from $550 to $1,200. Write or call for a free detailed color brochure.

HORSEBACK TREKKING **Rock Creek Pack Station,** P.O. Box 248, Bishop, CA 93514 (☎ **619/935-4493** in summer, **619/872-8331** in winter), schedules four-day mustang-tracking trips in the rarely visited Pizona area of the Inyo National Forest—the natural habitat of wild mustangs. Participants ride horseback, camp out, and eat chuck-wagon style. The trek is led by experienced trackers, who share their knowledge of the horses' social behavior and environment, and costs about $425 per person.

Other excursions include fly-fishing angler rides, fall-foliage wilderness trail rides, and a horse drive between the winter range in the Owens Valley and the summer corrals in Rock Creek. There are so many variations that it is impossible to list them all here. Write or call for a brochure outlining all the tours.

HOUSEBOATING One of America's largest houseboat rental companies is **Seven Crown Resorts,** P.O. Box 1409, Boulder City, NV 89005 (☎ toll free **800/752-9669**). It rents fully equipped cruisers on Lake Shasta, 3 1/2 hours north of San Francisco; and near Stockton, at the Sacramento River Delta, about one hour east of San Francisco. Standard amenities usually include fully equipped kitchen, bathroom, shower, hot water, air conditioning, heating, built-in beds, deck chairs, ice chests, and barbecue. All you need to bring is food, a bathing suit, hiking boots, a picnic basket, and fishing tackle. The boats are easy to operate, even if you've never been at the helm before. They can also be relatively economical, depending on how many of your friends you're sharing the boat with. Houseboats that sleep six adults range in cost from $970 to $1,290 per week, depending on season and location. Larger boats, accommodating as many as 10, are also available.

RIVER RAFTING A non-profit river-rafting organization, **American River Touring Association (ARTA),** Star Rte. 73, Groveland, CA 95321 (☎ **209/962-7873,** or toll free **800/323-2782**), offers one-, two-, and three-day raft adventures down California's Tuolumne and Merced rivers. On the Tuolumne, when miners once panned for gold, three-day excursions depart during July and August and cost $380. The river pours out of the Yosemite National Park and rushes down a thrilling and relentless series of rapids through a breathtakingly beautiful canyon. On the untamed Merced, one- and two-day trips run from late April to early July and cost $85 to $190. This river booms out of the Sierras and winds its way down through Yosemite Valley. Other excursions are also available. Write or call for ARTA's comprehensive booklet on this year's offerings.

Mariah Wilderness Expeditions, P.O. Box 248, Point Richmond, CA 94807 (☎ **510/233-2303,** or toll free **800/462-7424**), is another top operator that can take you white-water rafting on the state's rivers. The majority of its California packages are one- and two-day excursions offered daily from April through September. One particularly excellent family-oriented river trip is accompanied by a professional storyteller, who spins tales during lunches and around the evening campfire. A second package combines hot-air ballooning with white-water rafting and offers accommodations in a country-style B&B. Prices average about $100 per day. Write or call for a detailed brochure.

Sierra Mac River Trips, P.O. Box 366, Sonora, CA 95370 (☎ **209/532-1327,** or toll free **800/457-2580**), offers white-water rafting trips down the Tuolumne and Stanislaus rivers, as well as more challenging rides along the American River and Cherry Creek. The easiest runs are family affairs, open to paddlers ages 5 to 75. More difficult trips include class V rapids, which require participants to pass a test at the conclusion of a training seminar. Prices range from $75 for a one-day excursion to $395 for a high-end three-day package. The cost includes rafts, guides, meals, equipment, and wet suits; sleeping gear can be rented for an additional $20. Write or call for complete information.

ROCK CLIMBING Introductory climbing packages to various sites around the state are offered by **Cal Adventures** (see "Backpacking," above). Trips to some of the most magnificent landscapes in the west typically last from one to three days, with camping and climbing equipment provided. Prices range from $80 to $150. Whether you're a beginning climber or into advanced multipitched ascensions, California Adventures can coach you with private, customized rock-climbing instruction for individuals and small groups.

Yosemite Mountaineering School, Yosemite, CA 95389 (☎ **209/372-1244**), has a worldwide reputation for excellence in rock-climbing instruction. Classes of varying length and skill are offered from June to September to climbers of all levels of expertise. Write or call for a brochure outlining specific dates and costs.

WHALE WATCHING Few events attract as much attention and interest in California as the annual migration of whales between Mexico and Alaska.

Biological Journeys, 1696 Ocean Dr., McKinleyville, CA 95521 (☎ **707/839-0178,** or toll free **800/548-7555**), is one of the largest whale-watching organizations in the state. From January to mid-April, small cruise ships depart from San Diego and travel along the Baja coast to Mexico's San Ignacio Lagoon and Magdalena Bay, the primary breeding grounds for California gray whales. March cruises to the Sea of Cortez offer a close look at the calving of blue and fin whales. Travel farther south to observe humpback whales in the waters of Cabo San Lucas. Excursions take 8 to 12 days, accommodate 14 to 28 passengers, and cost $2,295 to $2,995 per person.

Pacific Sea Fari Tours, 2803 Emerson St., San Diego, CA 92106 (☎ **619/222-1144**), also makes journeys down to Baja's San Ignacio Lagoon and other well-known Mexican whale-watching spots. Conducting naturalist-led seagoing expeditions for over 20 years, Pacific Sea Fari is a first-class tour, operating small boats that accommodate 12 to 30 passengers. Each vessel has air conditioning, large galleys, and comfortable lounge facilities, including color TVs, VCRs, and natural-history libraries. Tours last from 8 to 11 days and cost $1,400 to $2,000. Write or call for complete information.

Meditation & Yoga Retreats

The **Esalen Institute,** Big Sur, CA 93920 (☎ **408/667-3000**), was established in 1962 as a center for experiential learning. Esalen has since evolved into one of California's most dynamic residential retreats for personal growth. Its setting is spectacular, wedged in a lush valley, overlooking the surf, just south of the Monterey Peninsula. Natural stone hot springs and a casual, friendly atmosphere are the perfect surroundings for personal exploration.

A full schedule of classes includes such workshops as "Focusing," "Dream Work and the Helping Relationship," "Letting Go—Moving On," and "Non-adversarial Child Care," to name but a few. No matter what your interests, don't miss the center's famous massage—$60 for an hour of sheer bliss. During winter, it is possible to stay at Esalen without enrolling in any seminar or workshop; you may simply want to meditate, write, or quietly relax. The cost of a shared room and three meals is from $70 to $125 per night. Including workshops and seminars, a weekend will cost from $200 to $380; a week from $375 to $740. Some accommodations have patios and ocean views, but you can hear the sound of the surf from any room. Meals are served buffet style, and the food is both wholesome and delicious. Many of the vegetables served come from Esalen's own gardens.

The Expanding Light, c/o Ananda World Brotherhood Village, 14618 Tyler Foote, Nevada City, CA 95959 (☎ toll free **800/346-5350**), is a meditation and yoga retreat located 17 miles from Nevada City and about 70 miles northeast of Sacramento. It can accommodate up to 125 visitors. Classic yoga routines are emphasized and include special morning and afternoon asanas (yogic poses) for beginning and advanced students. Meditation training and classes on both Christian and Eastern themes are also offered. Rates vary, but expect to pay about $400 per person per week for a shared room, activities, and meals.

Macrobiotic Center, 1511 Robinson St., Oroville, CA 95965 (☎ **916/533-7702**), about 70 miles due north of Sacramento, offers wonderful week-long retreats on healthful living. The center is located in a charming town full of old Victorian homes and shops. Directors Cornellia and Herman Aihara are hands-on managers, involved with every aspect of the center. They are both authors and macrobiotic teachers and offer morning tea talks and afternoon cooking classes daily. Guests share rooms and sleep on pine beds with futon mattresses. Rates, including full board, average about $595 per week.

Mount Madonna Center, 445 Summit Rd., Watsonville, CA 95076 (☎ **408/722-7175** or **847-0406**), is a popular yoga-oriented conference and personal retreat facility. Weekend and week-long seminars have both broad and directed themes, such as "Healing the Child Within" and "Living Your Yoga." The center is located in the Santa Cruz mountains, equidistant from Monterey and Santa Cruz, and enjoys sweeping views of Monterey Bay. Room rates, which include two vegetarian meals daily, range from $35 for dormitory accommodations to $60 for a private room with bath. Seminars cost an additional $100 or so. Write or call for complete details on upcoming events.

Sivananda Ashram Vrindavan Yoga Farm, 14651 Ballantree Lane, Grass Valley, CA 95949 (☎ **916/272-9322**), is a small center located off a dirt road about 60 miles northeast of Sacramento. Life here is rustic, simple, and quiet, consisting of a changeless routine of meditation, meals, and exercise. Participation in classes and twice-daily meditation is required. During free time, guests can hike among the hills and view the timeless beauty of the magnificent Sierras. Sivananda is among the smallest of California's residential ashrams and one of the cheapest, too. With space for only 30 guests, it charges just $25, $35, and $50 per person per night for, respectively, camping, dormitory, and private accommodations, including breakfast and dinner. Rates are even lower for those who wish to work for their room and board.

7 Getting There

California is easy to reach, but not all transportation options are created equal. Shopping around will ensure that you get there the right way at the best price.

By Plane

Almost every major scheduled airline flies into the international airports in Los Angeles, San Jose, San Diego, and San Francisco. Many carriers also service the dozens of smaller gateways located in between these points. Almost every city in the state is accessible by air, though sometimes it requires a short commuter hop on a smaller propeller-driven plane. If you are not planning to visit a major city, it might be wise to avoid it entirely and fly into a smaller regional airport. Airlines often offer special deals that can make it as cheap to fly into Santa Barbara, for instance, as it is to fly into Los Angeles. Explore this option before buying your ticket.

British and Canadian travelers should also see "Getting To and Around the U.S." in Chapter 3.

THE MAJOR AIRLINES Several major U.S. carriers offer regular flights to California. They are (along with their toll-free telephone numbers): **Alaska Airlines (800/426-0333)**, **American Airlines (800/433-7300)**, **Delta Airlines (800/221-1212)**, **Northwest Airlines (800/225-2525)**, **Southwest Airlines (800/531-5601)**, **Tower Airlines (800/221-2500)**, **TWA (800/221-2000)**, **United Airlines (800/241-6522)**, and **USAir (800/428-4322)**.

REGULAR FARES Depending on your point of origin, an inexpensive ticket to California might not be worthwhile enough to travel agents to make them really dig. To get the lowest price, I usually do the legwork and make the reservation myself, and then visit my travel agent for ticketing. Check the newspapers for advertisements and call a few of the major carriers before committing yourself.

The cheapest standard economy-class fare usually comes with serious restrictions and steep penalties for altering dates and itineraries. When purchasing these tickets, don't use terms like "APEX" (Advance Purchase Excursion) and "excursion" or other airline jargon; just ask for the lowest fare. If you are flexible with dates and times, say so. Ask if you can get a cheaper fare by staying an extra day or by flying during the middle of the week; many airlines won't volunteer this kind of information. At the time of this writing, the lowest round-trip fare to San Francisco or Los Angeles from New York was $498 and from Chicago $398; the lowest round-trip fare to San Francisco from Los Angeles was $198. You may even get it cheaper.

BUSINESS CLASS & FIRST CLASS Business-class seats can easily cost twice what coach seats go for. When buying a full-fare ticket to either San Francisco or Los Angeles, expect to pay about $1,600 from New York and about $1,100 from Chicago. Note, however, that competition is stiff for luxury-class passengers, and prices are sometimes more elastic in this category than they are in economy class. Call several airlines and compare prices before committing yourself.

Many short hops to California don't carry a first-class section. When they do, they're predictably expensive. Expect to pay about $2,500 from New York and about $2,000 from Chicago to San Francisco or Los Angeles.

DISCOUNTED AIRFARES Alternatives to the traditional travel agent ticket have their advantages (usually price) and their drawbacks (usually lack of flexibility).

By negotiating directly with airlines, consolidators, or "bucket shops," can sell tickets on major scheduled carriers at deeply discounted rates—often 20% to 30% lower. Such fares are often the least-expensive means of traveling to California, lower in most instances than charter-flight fares. For example, in winter from New York, you can buy bucket-shop tickets to San Francisco or Los Angeles on well-known international airlines for as little as $150 each way; prices rise to about $225 in summer. There are drawbacks, however. The tickets are restrictive, valid only for a particular date or flight, usually nontransferable, and nonrefundable except directly from the bucket shop. Also, consolidators usually don't offer travel counseling, and don't book hotels or rental cars. On the plus side, bucket shop tickets are rarely restricted by advance purchase requirements; if space is available, you can buy your ticket just days before departure.

The lowest-priced bucket shops are usually local operations with low profiles and overheads. Look for their advertisements in the travel or classified section of your local newspaper. Ads for consolidators are typically small, usually a single column in width and a few lines deep. They contain a list of cities and, opposite it, a list of corresponding prices. Short and to the point.

While prices for flights available through bucket shops are low, at times they may be eclipsed by special offers by the airlines. As usual, compare prices before you buy.

Nationally advertised consolidators are usually not as competitive as the smaller boiler-room operations, but they have toll-free telephone numbers, and are easily accessible. Such consolidators include Travac, 989 Sixth Ave., New York, NY 10018 (☎ **212/563-3303,** or toll free **800/TRAV-800**), and Unitravel, 1177 N. Warson Rd., (P.O. Box 12485), St. Louis, MO 63132 (☎ **314/569-0900**, or toll free **800/325-2222**).

Competition from the bucket shops, not to mention fiercely competitive commercial airlines, has pared the number of charters somewhat, but there are still plenty from which to choose. Most charter operators advertise and sell their seats through travel agents, making these local professionals your best source of information for available flights. Before deciding to take a charter flight, check the restrictions on the ticket. You may be asked to purchase a tour package, pay far in advance of the flight, be amenable if the day of departure or the destination is changed, pay a service charge, fly on an airline with which you are not familiar, and pay harsh penalties if you cancel, but be understanding if the charter does not fill up and is cancelled up to 10 days before departure. Summer charters fill up more quickly than others and are almost sure to fly, but if you decide on a charter flight, seriously consider cancellation and baggage insurance.

GOING AS A COURIER Courier flights are primarily long-haul jobs and are not usually available for short, domestic hops. But if you are crossing the country, or an ocean, becoming a mule might be the bargain for you. Companies who hire couriers use your luggage allowance for their business baggage; in return, you get a heavily discounted ticket. Flights are often offered at the last minute, and you may have to arrange a pretrip interview to make sure you're right for the job. Now Voyager, Inc. (☎ **212/431-1616** Monday through Friday from 10am to 5pm, and Saturday from 10am to 4:30pm), flies from New York and sometimes has flights to San Francisco and Los Angeles for as little as $199 round-trip.

By Train

Traveling by train takes longer than by plane. But if you want to save money, if you're afraid of airplanes, or want to take a leisurely ride through America's countryside, rail may be a good option. **Amtrak** (☎ toll free **800/USA-RAIL**), the nation's most complete long-distance passenger railroad network, connects about 500 American cities with points all over California.

Trains bound for Los Angeles and San Francisco leave daily from New York and cross the country through Chicago and Denver. The journey takes about 3½ days, and seats fill up quickly. As of this writing, the lowest round-trip fare was $359 from New York and $280 from Chicago. These heavily restricted tickets are good for 45 days and allow up to three stops along the way.

Amtrak offers family plans, tours, and many other money-saving fares. Call for an excellent brochure outlining routes and prices for the entire system.

By Bus

Bus travel is an inexpensive and often flexible, least time-efficient, option. **Greyhound/ Trailways** (☎ toll free **800/231-2222**) can get you here from anywhere, and offers several money-saving multiday bus passes. Round-trip fares vary, depending on your point of origin, but few, if any, ever exceed $200.

By Car

California is well connected to the rest of the United States by several major highways. Among them are **Interstate 5,** which comes into the state from the north; **Interstate 10,** which originates in Jacksonville, Florida, and terminates in Los Angeles; and **U.S. 101,** which follows the western seaboard from Los Angeles north to the Oregon state line. Traveling by car is a great way to go if you want to become acquainted with the countryside, but after figuring in food, lodging, and automobile expenses, it may not be your cheapest option. Still, driving down the California coast is one of the world's ultimate journeys. Always drive within the speed limit, and keep an eye out for "speed traps," where the limit suddenly drops. For tips on getting around the major cities by car, see the chapters on San Francisco, Los Angeles, and

Frommer's Smart Traveler: Airfares

1. Shop all the airlines that fly to your destination.
2. Always ask for the lowest fare, not "discount," "APEX," or "excursion."
3. Keep calling the airline—the availability of cheap seats changes daily.
4. Seek out budget alternatives. Phone bucket shops, charter companies, and discount travel agents.
5. Plan to travel midweek, when rates are usually lower.

San Diego. For automobile association information, see "Breakdowns and Assistance" in Section 8, "Getting Around," below.

Package Tours

Tours and packages are put together by airlines, charter companies, hotels, and tour operators and are sold to travelers either directly or through travel agents. A **tour** usually refers to an escorted group and often includes transportation, sightseeing, meals, and accommodations. The entire group travels together and shares the same preplanned activities. A **package,** on the other hand, can include any or all of the above components, but travelers are usually unescorted and free to make their own itinerary. Many travelers purchase airfare, hotel, and airport transfers from a travel agent, without even knowing that they are buying a tour operator's package. This is perfectly fine; packages can be a very good value. Since packagers buy in bulk, they can sometimes sell their services at a discount.

To find out what tours and packages are available to you, check the ads in the travel section of your newspaper or visit your travel agent. Before signing up, however, read the fine print carefully and do some homework:

- **How reputable is the tour operator?** Ask for references of people who have participated in tours run by the same company. Call travel agents and the local Better Business Bureau, and check with the consumer department of the U.S. Tour Operators Association, 211 East 51st St., Suite 12B, New York, NY 10022 (☎ **212/750-7371**). Be leery of any outfit that doesn't give you details of the itinerary.
- **What is the size of the tour?** Decide whether you can handle an experience shared by 40 other people, or if your limit is 20. A smaller tour is generally a better-quality tour.
- **What kinds of hotels will be used and where are they located?** Get the names of the hotels and then look them up in guidebooks or in your travel agent's hotel guide. If you sense that the hotels provide only minimal essentials, so might the entire tour. If the hotel is not conveniently located, it will be less expensive, but you may feel isolated or unsafe, and you'll spend extra money and time getting to and from attractions and nightspots.
- **If meals are included, how elaborate are they?** Is breakfast continental, English, or buffet? Is the menu for the group limited to a few items?
- **How extensive is the sightseeing?** You may have the chance to get on and off the bus many times to explore several attractions, or you may see them only from the bus window. If you like to explore, pick an attraction you're interested in and ask the operator precisely how much time you can expect to spend there. Find out whether all admissions are included in the price of the tour.
- **Are the optional activities offered at an additional price?** This is usually the case, so make sure the activities that particularly interest you are included in the tour price.
- **What is the refund policy should you cancel?** Check this carefully; some tour operators are more lenient than others regarding trip cancellations.
- **How is the package price paid?** If a charter flight is involved, make sure that you can pay into an escrow account (ask for the name of the bank) to ensure proper use of the funds or their return in case the operator cancels the trip.

Most of the airlines listed above offer both escorted tours and on-your-own packages. Dozens of other companies also compete for this lucrative business. Discuss your options with a travel agent and compare tour prices with those in this guide.

8 Getting Around

BY PLANE In addition to the major carriers listed above, several smaller airlines are known for the excellent and comprehensive service they provide up and down the California coast. **America West** (toll free **800/247-5692**), **American Eagle** (toll free **800/433-7300**), **Skywest** (toll free **800/453-9417**), and **United Express** (toll free **800/241-6522**) are some of the biggest carriers offering regular service between California cities.

BY TRAIN Amtrak (☎ toll free **800/USA-RAIL**) runs trains up and down the California coast, connecting San Francisco with San Diego and all points in between. A one-way ticket can often be had for as little as $50. San Francisco–bound trains actually arrive in Oakland and connect with regularly scheduled buses to San Francisco's Transbay Terminal (☎ **415/982-8512**). From San Francisco north, trains run inland to the Oregon border through Sacramento, Chico, and Redding.

Southern Pacific (☎ **415/541-1000**) operates commuter train services between San Francisco and the towns of the peninsula. The San Francisco depot is at 700 Fourth Street, at Townsend Street.

BY BUS You can get almost anywhere in California on **Greyhound.** The main San Francisco bus station is Transbay Terminal, at First and Mission Streets (☎ **415/558-6789**). In Los Angeles, the main Greyhound terminal is located downtown at 1716 E. Seventh St. (☎ **213/620-1200**). In San Diego, the main terminal is at 120 West Broadway (☎ **619/239-9171**). Greyhound no longer operates a single nationwide telephone number, so consult your local directory for the office nearest you.

BY CAR In every chapter of this book, easy-to-follow driving directions are regularly provided. Buy a good road map of the state before you start your trip and keep it handy in the glove compartment for easy reference. Before setting out for a long drive, call **415/557-3755** for a recorded announcement on California road conditions. See individual city chapters for specific information on renting and driving in San Francisco, Los Angeles, and San Diego.

Rentals California is one of the cheapest places in America in which to rent a car. Major national car-rental companies usually offer their cheapest economy vehicles for about $35 per day and $125 per week with unlimited mileage. The best-known firms, with locations up and down the California coast, include **Alamo** (toll free **800/327-9633**), **Avis** (toll free **800/331-1212**), **Budget** (toll free **800/527-0700**), **Dollar** (toll free **800/421-6868**), **General** (toll free **800/327-7607**), **Hertz** (toll free **800/654-3131**), **National** (toll free **800/328-4567**), and **Thrifty** (toll free **800/367-2277**).

Local rental companies have lower overhead costs than the big chains and are often cheaper than their larger competitors. Names and telephone numbers of regional rental firms are listed by city in the chapters on San Francisco, Los Angeles, and San Diego.

Most rental firms pad their profits by selling a Loss/Damage Waiver (LDW), which usually costs an extra $9 per day. Before agreeing to this, however, check with your insurance carrier and credit-card companies. Many people don't realize that they are already covered by either one or both. If you're not already protected, the LDW is a wise investment.

A minimum age (ranging from 19 to 25) is usually required of renters. Some agencies also have set maximum ages. If you are concerned that these limits may affect you, ask about rental requirements at the time of booking to avoid problems later.

Finally, think about splurging for a convertible. Few things in life can match the feeling of flying along warm California freeways with the sun on your shoulders and the wind whipping through your hair.

Gasoline Prices vary, but expect to pay anywhere between $1.20 and $1.60 for one U.S. gallon of "regular" unleaded gasoline. Gas is cheapest in Los Angeles, San Diego, and the Central Valley. Prices rise slightly in coastal resort towns, in downtown San Francisco, in state and national parks, and in places at higher elevations. Higher-octane fuels are almost always available at slightly higher prices. Taxes are already included in the price.

Driving Rules California law requires both drivers and passengers to wear seat belts. The car's registration and proof of insurance must always be on hand, whether you're driving your own vehicle or a rented one. Pay attention to signs and arrows on the streets and roadways or you may find yourself in a lane that requires exiting or turning when you want to go straight on. You can turn right at a red light, unless otherwise indicated—but be sure to come to a stop first. Even in major cities, pedestrians *always* have the right-of-way; stop if a pedestrian steps into a crosswalk in front of you. See individual city chapters for specific information on driving in San Francisco, Los Angeles, and San Diego.

Road Maps California's freeway signs frequently indicate direction by naming a town rather than a point on the compass. If you have never heard of Canoga Park you might be in trouble, unless you have a map. The best state road guide is the comprehensive *Thomas Bros. California Road Atlas,* a 300-plus-page book of maps with schematics of towns and cities statewide. It costs $19 but is a good investment if you plan on doing any amount of exploring. Smaller accordion-style maps are handy for the state as a whole or for individual cities and regions. These foldout maps usually cost $2 to $3 and are available at gas stations, pharmacies, supermarkets, and tourist-oriented shops everywhere.

Breakdowns and Assistance Before taking a long car trip you should seriously consider joining a major automobile association. Not only do automobile associations offer travel insurance and helpful information, but they can also perform vacation-saving roadside services, including towing. The **American Automobile Association (AAA),** 1000 AAA Dr., Heathrow, FL 32746-5063 (☎ **407/444-7000,** or toll free **800/763-6600**), is the nation's largest auto club, with more than 850 offices. Membership fees range from about $20 to $60, depending on where you join.

Other recommendable auto clubs include the **Allstate Motor Club,** 1500 Shure Dr., Arlington Heights, IL 60004 (☎ **708/253-4800**) and the **Amoco Motor Club,** 200 E. Randolph Dr., mail code 0607, Chicago, IL 60601 (☎ toll free **800/334-3300**).

HITCHHIKING Thumbing a ride is the cheapest and most unpredictable way of traveling. Unfortunately, it can also be dangerous. Small country roads are best, and cities are worst. Use common sense: Sit next to an unlocked door, keep your bags within reach, and refuse a ride if you feel uneasy. The best way to become a rider is to strike up a conversation at a gas station or truck stop. Better still, find a driver through a ride board, located at most colleges, and in some local cafes.

Suggested Itineraries

Most of California's top tourist attractions are located near the coast. The best way to see the state is to drive north or south along the coast, and head inland at desired locations.

California is car country, and **Highway 1,** which hugs the shores of the Pacific, is the most famous road in the state. Also known as Calif. 1 and the Pacific Coast Highway, it comes in from Oregon and parallels the water, over the Golden Gate Bridge, through San Francisco, down to the Mexican border. At various points the road takes on different names, merges with larger freeways, and becomes a main commercial street through cities and towns. There is a significant stretch, between San Luis Obispo and Gaviota, north of Santa Barbara, where the highway parts with the shore to avoid the militarily sensitive Vandenberg Air Force Base. Apart from this significant exception, however, the Pacific Coast Highway remains true to its name.

If you haven't yet figured it out, Hwy. 1 is the number-one recommended route to travel in California. Take it slowly—the wild, crashing beauty of the ocean and the rugged cliffs along this spectacular road are meant to be savored. Most bicyclists who travel the Pacific coast route travel from north to south, the direction of the prevailing winds. If you have your choice when driving, however, I recommend you travel from the south to the north; since the coast keeps edging west, you will be treated to continually unfolding coastline vistas.

Several freeways complement the coastal road, offering fast routes to the major sights (there are times, especially north of San Francisco, when you may tire of the endless winding of smaller roads). And when you are pressed for time, the freeway is the fastest way to go. **U.S. 101** is the most important artery in the state. It runs from Los Angeles north to Eureka, where it meets with Hwy. 1, and continues along the coast into Oregon. Most of the way it is close enough to the coast and the state's major population centers that you can easily exit near your destination. U.S. 101 is big, but it's not all bad. The freeway has its own sort of beauty and travels through a lot of unspoiled countryside. The area between Goleta and Santa Maria, on the central coast, is largely undeveloped and looks as the old west must have looked—if you ignore the utility poles. Between San Luis Obispo and San Jose are gentle rolling hills and grazing cattle.

Interstate 5 is an inland freeway, located on the east side of the Coast Mountain range. It is also the fastest link between San Francisco, Los Angeles, and San Diego. It is prettiest between L.A. and San Diego, when it skirts the Pacific Ocean.

CITY HIGHLIGHTS California's three major urban centers are particularly special for the way in which they are so different from one another.

Mist-enshrouded San Francisco, draped delicately over steep hillsides, has the cosmopolitan feel of a much larger city. Small, enchanting, elegant, independent, and somewhat outrageous, this beautiful city by the bay enjoys an east coast sophistication at a more comfortable west coast pace.

Los Angeles is just 400 miles down the coast, but it's a world away in atmosphere and attitude. The unofficial capital of southern California sprawls across endless miles of flat, uneventful terrain, marked by monotonous housing developments and unending strip malls. In both quality and quantity, the city has some of the best restaurants in the world, yet for most of the diners food often takes a backseat to seeing and being seen. Home to the world's most important film industry, it's sometimes hard to separate art from reality on the streets of Santa Monica or Hollywood. And yet this smoggy suburbia, crisscrossed by an astonishing number of freeways, is somehow intensely magnetic. A colossal Technicolor ode to modernity, Los Angeles is a scene like no other. Whether you love it or hate it, no trip to California is complete without some time in L.A.

San Diego, the second-most-populous city in California, boasts an ideal climate, the best beaches in the state, a world-renowned zoo, and some of the most laid-back people you'll ever meet. It's also one of America's largest military towns and is heavily populated with Mexicans, surfers, and political conservatives. With more retirees and golf courses than either Los Angeles or San Francisco, San Diego is a city for enjoying life, and a beautiful place to visit.

9 Notes on Accommodations, Dining & Shopping

WHERE TO STAY Every kind of accommodation is available in California, from sophisticated city hotels to small B&Bs, coastal resorts, and wooded RV parks and campgrounds. Cities offer the broadest range of choices, but smaller towns up and down the coast compete favorably when it comes to quality and service. In fact, some of the state's best accommodations are smaller hotels and inns located in romantic seaside resort towns.

There are so many hotels in California—in every price range—that few regularly fill to capacity. Even during the height of the tourist season, you can usually drive right into a city or town and find decent accommodations fairly quickly. But be careful. If you have your sights set on a specific hotel, if you have to have a water view, or if you want to locate in an area where accommodations are not particularly plentiful, you should book your room in advance.

WHERE TO DINE Top chefs, innovative cuisines, creative surroundings, and a startling number of restaurants make San Francisco and Los Angeles two of America's best cities for dining out. Ethnic restaurants are particularly plentiful, as are cafes, diners, burger joints, and fast-food restaurants. See "Food & Drink," in Chapter 1, for a rundown of what to expect gastronomically, and see individual chapters for specific information on area restaurants.

WHAT TO BUY Go ahead and purchase postcards, T-shirts, and sun visors, but California's best buys are handmade arts and crafts sold in boutiques, at fairs, and on quaint little shopping streets in almost every touristy town in the state. Both San Francisco and Los Angeles are major fashion centers, with international and local retailers selling urban outfits that aren't available elsewhere. Sports lovers might want to pick up some quintessentially Californian goods, such as surfboards, in-line roller skates, and skateboards. Distinctively styled beachwear and sportswear are also indigenous to these parts.

Fast Facts: California

American Express To report lost or stolen traveler's checks, call toll free **800/221-7282.** Local office locations are listed in the appropriate chapters below.

Business Hours Most businesses in the state are open Monday through Friday from 9am to 5pm. Banking hours vary, but most banks are open Monday through Friday from 9am to 3pm. Several stay open until 5pm or so at least one day during the week, and many banks feature Automated Teller Machines (ATMs) for 24-hour banking (see "Information & Money" in this chapter). Most stores are usually open Monday through Saturday from 10am to 6pm and are closed Sunday. Malls are the most notable exceptions; they keep longer hours and are usually open Sundays. See individual chapters for specific city listings. Restaurant hours vary, but most serve lunch from about 11:30am to 3pm and dinner from 5:30 to 11pm. You can sometimes get served later on weekends. Nightclubs and bars are usually open daily until 2am, when they are legally required to stop serving alcohol.

Climate See "When to Go," earlier in this chapter.

Crime See "Safety," below.

Customs See "Preparing for Your Trip" in Chapter 3.

Documents Required Foreign travelers should consult "Preparing for Your Trip" in Chapter 3.

Driving Rules See "Getting Around," earlier in this chapter.

Drug Laws California lawmakers are becoming increasingly strict about use and possession of illegal drugs. Whatever you do, don't carry any drugs or related paraphernalia when leaving the state by air.

Drugstores Walgreens is the state's largest drugstore chain. In addition to prescription and over-the-counter remedies, pharmacies usually sell everything from food to cosmetics, hair supplies, tobacco, and small electronic equipment.

Earthquakes There will always be earthquakes in California—most of which you won't even notice. Nevertheless, in case of a significant shaker, there are a few basic precautionary measures you should know. When you are inside a building, seek cover; do not run outside. Move away from windows toward what would be the center of the building. Duck under a large, sturdy piece of furniture or stand against a wall or under a doorway. When you do exit the building, use stairwells, not elevators. If you are in your car, pull over to the side of the road and stop—but not until you are safely away from bridges, overpasses, telephone poles, and power lines. Stay in your car. If you are out walking, stay outside and away from trees, power lines, and the sides of buildings. If you are in an area with tall buildings, find a doorway in which to stand.

Embassies and Consulates See "Fast Facts: For the Foreign Traveler" in Chapter 3.

Emergencies To reach the police, ambulance service, or fire department, dial **911** from any telephone. No coins are needed.

Gasoline See "Getting Around," earlier in this chapter.

Hitchhiking See "Getting Around," earlier in this chapter.

Information See "Information & Money" in this chapter and specific city listings for local information offices.

Liquor Laws Liquor and grocery stores, as well as some drugstores, can legally sell packaged alcoholic beverages between 6am and 2am. Most restaurants, nightclubs, and bars are licensed to serve alcoholic beverages during the same hours. The legal age for the purchase and consumption of alcoholic beverages is 21; proof of age is required.

Mail Domestic first-class letters cost 29¢ for the first ounce and 23¢ for each additional ounce. Postcards cost 19¢ to send to any U.S. destination. Letters to Canada cost 40¢ for up to one ounce, and Mexico-bound mail costs 45¢ for up to one ounce. All other international airmail letters cost 50¢ for up to 1/2 ounce.

Maps Local maps can usually be obtained free from area tourist offices. See specific city listings for information. State and regional maps are sold at gas stations, in drugstores, and in tourist-oriented shops all around the state.

Newspapers and Magazines The state's largest and best daily newspapers are *The Los Angeles Times, The San Diego Union, The Sacramento Bee, The San Francisco Chronicle,* and *The San Francisco Examiner.* Almost every sizable town also has its own regional daily, and many offer supplemental weekly listings magazines. Look for local publications in sidewalk vending machines and in cafes, hotels, and restaurants. California's major cities also have namesake magazines; most are monthlies. Look for local periodicals in bookstores and at larger newsstands.

Pets Not all hotels allow pets in their rooms. If you're traveling with the family dog, tell the reservationist prior to check-in to avoid problems later.

Photographic Needs Camera shops and film-processing labs are located in almost every California town, usually in a mall. Check the local telephone directory for locations. Drugstores and supermarkets are probably the cheapest places at which to purchase film. You'll pay much more for the same product at specialized kiosks near major tourist attractions.

Police In an emergency, dial **911.** For other matters, dial **555-1212** and ask for the nonemergency telephone number for the local police.

Radio and Television About four dozen radio stations can be heard from any point along the California coast. See "Fast Facts" in the chapters on San Francisco, Los Angeles, and San Diego for specific information on stations in those cities. In addition to the cable television stations, available in most hotels, all the major networks and several independent stations can usually be received. Check with your hotel for specific channel information.

Restrooms Stores rarely let customers use the restrooms, and many restaurants offer their facilities for customers only. But most malls have bathrooms, as do the ubiquitous fast-food restaurants. Many public beaches and large parks provide toilets, though in some places you have to pay, or tip, an attendant. If you have the time, look for one of the large hotels; most have well-stocked, clean restrooms in their lobbies.

Safety Heavily touristed areas are always prime targets for petty thieves. Whenever you're traveling in an unfamiliar city or country, stay alert. Be aware of your immediate surroundings. To avoid an unpleasant incident or an end to a pleasurable trip, use common sense. One practical option is to leave valuables in the hotel safe. Wear a moneybelt and don't sling your camera or purse over your shoulder. This will minimize the possibility of your becoming a victim of crime. It's your responsibility to be aware and alert, especially in the most heavily touristed areas.

Taxes California's state sales tax is 7.75%. Some municipalities include an additional percentage, so tax varies throughout the state. Hotel taxes are almost always higher than tariffs levied on goods and services. In restaurants, stores, and hotels, tax is not included in the printed price; it's tacked on at the register.

Time California and the entire west coast are in the Pacific standard time zone, eight hours behind Greenwich mean time and three hours behind eastern standard time.

Tipping In restaurants, waiters and waitresses, as well as bartenders, expect a 15% tip; so do taxi drivers and hairdressers. Porters should be tipped 50¢ to $1 per bag, and parking valets should be given $1. Lavatory attendants will appreciate whatever change you have.

Tourist Offices See "Information & Money," earlier in this chapter, as well as specific city chapters later in this guide.

3

For Foreign Visitors

Many first time visitors to the United States arrive with a sense of familiarity; through their acquaintance with American culture—which is popular the world over—they feel that they already know the country, its people, and its customs. And in a way they do. The impressions they have culled from American films, music, books, and the whirl of ever-changing fads and fashions do present, if taken together, a general portrait of the United States. What this chapter does is fill in the essential details as they concern the traveler.

It offers information on entry requirements and Customs duties, transportation and telephone services, currency exchange and tipping. It advises you on drinking laws and legal aid, on safety and emergencies. Together with the previous chapter, it seeks to help you plan your trip properly, so that your visit to California will be as smooth and enjoyable as possible.

1 Preparing for Your Trip

ENTRY REQUIREMENTS

DOCUMENT REGULATIONS Canadian citizens may enter the United States without visas; they need only proof of residence.

Citizens of the United Kingdom, New Zealand, Japan, and most western European countries traveling on valid passports may not need a visa for fewer than 90 days of holiday or business travel to the United States, providing that they hold a round-trip or return ticket and enter the United States on an airline or cruise line participating in the visa waiver program.

(Note that citizens of these visa-exempt countries who first enter the United States may then visit Mexico, Canada, Bermuda, and/or the Caribbean islands and then reenter the United States by any mode of transportation, without needing a visa. Further information is available from any United States embassy or consulate.)

Citizens of countries other than those stipulated above, including citizens of Australia, must have two documents: a valid passport, with an expiration date at least six months later than the scheduled end of the visit to the United States, and a tourist visa, available without charge from the nearest United States Consulate.

To obtain a visa, the traveler must submit a completed application form (either in person or by mail) with a 1½-inch square photo and demonstrate binding ties to a residence abroad. Usually you can obtain a visa at once or within 24 hours, but it may take longer during the summer rush from June to August. If you cannot go in person, contact the nearest U.S. embassy or consulate for directions on applying by mail. Your travel agent or airline office may also be able to provide you with visa applications and instructions. The U.S. consulate or embassy that issues your visa will determine whether you will be issued a multiple- or single-entry visa and any restrictions regarding the length of your stay.

MEDICAL REQUIREMENTS No inoculations are needed to enter the United States unless you are coming from, or have stopped over in, areas known to be suffering from epidemics, particularly cholera or yellow fever.

If you have a disease requiring treatment with medications containing narcotics or drugs requiring a syringe, carry a valid signed prescription from your physician to allay any suspicions that you are smuggling drugs.

CUSTOMS REQUIREMENTS Every adult visitor may bring in free of duty: one liter of wine or hard liquor; 200 cigarettes or 100 cigars (but no cigars from Cuba) or three pounds of smoking tobacco; $100 worth of gifts. These exemptions are offered to travelers who spend at least 72 hours in the United States and who have not claimed them within the preceding six months. It is altogether forbidden to bring into the country foodstuffs (particularly cheese, fruit, cooked meats, and canned goods) and plants (vegetables, seeds, tropical plants, and so on). Foreign tourists may bring in or take out up to $10,000 in U.S. or foreign currency with no formalities; larger sums must be declared to Customs on entering or leaving.

INSURANCE

There is no national health system in the United States. Because the cost of medical care is extremely high, we strongly advise every traveler to secure health coverage before setting out.

You may want to take out a comprehensive travel policy that covers (for a relatively low premium) sickness or injury costs (medical, surgical, and hospital); loss or theft of your baggage; trip-cancellation costs; guarantee of bail in case you are arrested; costs of accident, repatriation, or death. Such packages (for example, "Europe Assistance" in Europe) are sold by automobile clubs at attractive rates, as well as by insurance companies and travel agencies.

MONEY

CURRENCY & EXCHANGE The U.S. monetary system has a decimal base: one American **dollar ($1)**= 100 **cents** (100¢).

Dollar bills commonly come in $1 ("a buck"), $5, $10, $20, $50, and $100 denominations (the last two are not welcome when paying for small purchases and are not accepted in taxis or at subway ticket booths). There are also $2 bills (seldom encountered).

There are six denominations of coins: 1¢(one cent or "a penny"), 5¢(five cents or "a nickel"), 10¢(ten cents or "a dime"), 25¢(twenty-five cents or "a quarter"), 50¢(fifty cents or "a half dollar"), and the rare $1 piece.

The "foreign-exchange bureaus" so common in Europe are rare even at airports in the United States, and nonexistent outside major cities. Try to avoid having to change foreign money, or traveler's checks denominated other than in U.S. dollars, at a small-town bank, or even a branch in a big city; in fact, leave any currency other than U.S. dollars at home—it may prove more nuisance to you than it's worth.

TRAVELER'S CHECKS Traveler's checks denominated in U.S. dollars are readily accepted at most hotels, motels, restaurants, and large stores. But the best place to change traveler's checks is at a bank. Do not bring traveler's checks denominated in other currencies.

CREDIT CARDS The method of payment most widely used is the credit card: Visa (BarclayCard in Britain), MasterCard (EuroCard in Europe, Access in Britain, Chargex in Canada), American Express, Diners Club, Discover, and Carte Blanche. You can save yourself trouble by using "plastic money" rather than cash or traveler's checks in most hotels, motels, restaurants, and retail stores (a growing number of food and liquor stores now accept credit cards). You must have a credit card to rent a car. It can also be used as proof of identity (often carrying more weight than a passport), or as a "cash card," enabling you to draw money from banks that accept them.

SAFETY

GENERAL While tourist areas are generally safe, crime is on the increase everywhere, and U.S. urban areas tend to be less safe than those in Europe or Japan. Visitors should always stay alert. This is particularly true of large U.S. cities. It is wise to ask the city's or area's tourist office if you're in doubt about which neighborhoods are safe. Avoid deserted areas, especially at night. Don't go into any city park at night unless there is an event that attracts crowds. Generally speaking, you can feel safe in areas where there are many people, and many open establishments.

Avoid carrying valuables with you on the street, and don't display expensive cameras or electronic equipment. Hold on to your pocketbook, and place your billfold in an inside pocket. In theaters, restaurants, and other public places, keep your possessions in sight.

Remember also that hotels are open to the public, and in a large hotel, security may not be able to screen everyone entering. Always lock your room door—don't assume that once inside your hotel you are automatically safe and no longer need be aware of your surroundings.

DRIVING Safety while driving is particularly important. Question your rental agency about personal safety, or ask for a brochure of traveler safety tips when you pick up your car. Obtain written directions, or a map with the route marked in red, from the agency showing how to get to your destination. And, if possible, arrive and depart during daylight hours.

Recently more and more crime has involved cars and drivers. If you drive off a highway into a doubtful neighborhood, leave the area as quickly as possible. If you have an accident, even on the highway, stay in your car with the doors locked until you assess the situation or until the police arrive. If you are bumped from behind on the street or are involved in a minor accident with no injuries and the situation appears to be suspicious, motion to the other driver to follow you. *Never* get out of your car in such situations. You can also keep a pre-made sign in your car which reads: PLEASE FOLLOW THIS VEHICLE TO REPORT THE ACCIDENT. Show the sign to the other driver and go directly to the nearest police precinct, well-lighted service station, or all-night store.

If you see someone on the road who indicates a need for help, do *not* stop. Take note of the location, drive on to a well-lighted area, and telephone the police by dialing 911.

Park in well-lighted, well-traveled areas if possible. Always keep your car doors locked, whether attended or unattended. Look around you before you get out of your car, and never leave any packages or valuables in sight. If someone attempts to rob you or steal your car, do *not* try to resist the thief/carjacker—report the incident to the police department immediately.

See also the "Fast Facts" entry on safety in the chapters on San Francisco, Los Angeles, and San Diego for safety tips relating specifically to those cities.

2 Getting To & Around the U.S.

GETTING TO THE U.S. In addition to the domestic American airlines listed in Chapter 2, several international carriers also serve San Francisco and Los Angeles international airports. Among them are **Air Canada** (toll free **800/422-6232**), **British Airways** (toll free **800/247-9297**), **Japan Airlines** (toll free **800/525-3663**), and **SAS** (toll free **800/221-2350**).

Some large American airlines (for example, TWA, American Airlines, Northwest, United, and Delta) offer travelers—on their transatlantic or transpacific flights—special discount tickets under the name **Visit USA,** allowing travel between any U.S. destinations at minimum rates. They are not for sale in the United States, and must, therefore, be purchased before you leave your foreign point of departure. This system is the best, easiest, and fastest way to see the United States at low cost. You should obtain information well in advance either from your travel agent or from the office of the airline concerned, since the conditions attached to these discount tickets can be changed without advance notice.

The visitor arriving by air, no matter what the port of entry, should cultivate patience and resignation before setting foot on U.S. soil. Getting through Immigration control may take as long as two hours on some days, especially summer weekends. Add the time it takes to clear Customs and you'll see that you should make very generous allowance for delay in planning connections between international and domestic flights—an average of two to three hours at least.

In contrast, travelers arriving by car or by rail from Canada will find border-crossing formalities streamlined to the vanishing point. And air travelers from Canada, Bermuda, and some places in the Caribbean can sometimes go through Customs and Immigration at the point of departure, which is much quicker and less painful.

For further information about travel to California, see "Getting There" in Chapter 2.

GETTING AROUND THE U.S. Visitors should be aware of the limitations of long-distance rail travel in the United States. With a few notable exceptions (for instance, the Northeast Corridor line between Boston and Washington, D.C.), service is rarely up to European standards: Delays are common, routes are limited and often infrequently served, and fares are rarely significantly lower than discount airfares. Thus, cross-country train travel should be approached with caution.

International visitors can also buy a **USA Railpass,** good for 15 or 30 days of unlimited travel on Amtrak. The pass is available through many foreign travel agents. Prices in 1994 for a 15-day pass were $208 off-peak, $308 peak; a 30-day pass cost $309 off-peak, $389 peak. (With a foreign passport, you can also buy passes at some Amtrak offices in the United States, including locations in San Francisco, Los Angeles, Chicago, New York, Miami, Boston, and Washington, D.C.) Reservations are generally required and should be made for each part of your trip as early as possible.

The cheapest way to travel the United States is by **bus.** Greyhound, the nation's nationwide bus line, offers an **Ameripass** for unlimited travel for 7 days (for $250), 15 days (for $350), and 30 days (for $450). Bus travel in the United States can be both slow and uncomfortable, so this option is not for everyone.

Fast Facts: For the Foreign Traveler

Accommodations Most of the major hotels listed in this book maintain overseas reservation networks and can be booked either directly or through travel agents. Some hotels are also included in tour operators' package tours. Since tour companies buy rooms in bulk, they can often offer them at a discount. Discuss this option with your travel agent and compare tour prices with those in this guide.

Automobile Organizations Auto clubs will supply maps, suggest routes, guidebooks, accident and bail-bond insurance, and emergency road service. The major auto club in the United States, with 955 offices nationwide, is the **American**

Automobile Association (AAA). Members of some foreign auto clubs have reciprocal arrangements with the AAA and enjoy its services at no charge. If you belong to an auto club, inquire about AAA reciprocity before you leave. The AAA can provide you with an **International Driving Permit** validating your foreign license. You may be able to join the AAA even if you are not a member of a reciprocal club. To inquire call toll free 800/336-4357. In addition, some automobile rental agencies now provide these services, so you should inquire about their availability when you rent your car.

Automobile Rentals To rent a car you need a major credit card. A valid driver's license is required, and you usually need to be at least 25. Some companies do rent to younger people but add a daily surcharge. Be sure to return your car with the same amount of gas you started out with; rental companies charge excessive prices for gasoline.

Business Hours Banks are open weekdays from 9am to 3 or 4pm, although there's 24-hour access to the automatic tellers (ATMs) at most banks and other outlets. Generally, offices are open weekdays from 9am to 5pm. Stores are open six days a week, with many open on Sunday, too; department stores usually stay open until 9pm at least one day a week.

Climate See "When to Go" in Chapter 2.

Currency See "Money" in "Preparing for Your Trip," above.

Currency Exchange You will find currency-exchange services in major airports with international service. Elsewhere, they may be quite difficult to come by.

Money-changing offices in San Francisco include Bank of America, 345 Montgomery St. (☎ **415/622-2451**), open Monday through Thursday from 9am to 4pm, on Friday from 9am to 6pm, and on Saturday from 9am to 1pm; and Thomas Cook Travel, 75 Geary Ave. (☎ **415/362-3452**), open Monday through Friday from 9am to 5pm. In Los Angeles, try Thomas Cook Travel, 900 Wilshire Blvd. (☎ **213/624-4221**). Thomas Cook Currency Services (formerly Deak International) offers a wide variety of services: more than 100 currencies, commission-free traveler's checks, drafts and wire transfers, check collections, and precious-metal bars and coins. Rates are competitive and service excellent. Some hotels will also exchange currency if you are a registered guest.

Drinking Laws The legal age for purchase and consumption of alcoholic beverages is 21; proof of age is required. Liquor is sold in supermarkets and grocery stores, daily from 6am to 2am. Licensed restaurants are permitted to sell alcohol during the same hours. Note that many eateries are licensed only for beer and wine.

Electric Current The United States uses 110–120 volts, 60 cycles, unlike the 220–240 volts, 50 cycles used in Europe. Besides a 100-volt converter, small appliances of non-American manufacture, such as hairdryers or shavers, will require a plug adapter with two flat parallel pins.

Embassies and Consulates All embassies are located in the national capital, Washington, D.C.; some consulates are located in major cities, and most nations have a mission to the United Nations in New York City.

Listed here are the embassies and east and west coast consulates of the major English-speaking countries. Travelers from other countries can get telephone numbers for their embassies and consulates by calling "Information" in Washington, D.C. (☎ **202/555-1212**).

The *Australian Embassy* is at 1601 Massachusetts Ave. NW, Washington, D.C. 20036 (**202/797-3000**). Consulates and trade offices are maintained in New York, at the International Building, 630 Fifth Ave., Suite 420, NY, NY 10111 (**212/245-4000**); in Los Angeles, at 611 N. Larchmont Blvd., Los Angeles, CA 90004 (**213/469-4300**); and in San Francisco, at 1 Bush St., San Francisco, CA 94104 (**415/362-6160**).

The *Canadian Embassy* is at 501 Pennsylvania Ave. NW, Washington, D.C. 20001 (**202/682-1740**). Consulates are maintained in New York at 1251 Avenue of the Americas, NY, NY 10020 (**212/596-1600**); and in Los Angeles, at 300 Grand Ave., 10th Floor, Los Angeles, CA 90071 (**213/687-7432**).

The *Irish Embassy* is at 2234 Massachusetts Ave. NW, Washington, D.C. 20008 (**202/462-3939**). Consulates are maintained in New York, at 515 Madison Ave., NY, NY 10022 (**212/319-2555**); and in San Francisco, at 655 Montgomery St., Suite 930, San Francisco, CA 94111 (**415/392-4214**).

The *New Zealand Embassy* is at 37 Observatory Circle NW, Washington, D.C. 20008 (**202/328-4800**). The consulate is located in Los Angeles, at 12400 Wilshire Blvd., 11th Floor, Los Angeles, CA 90025 (**310/477-8241**).

The *British Embassy* is at 3100 Massachusetts Ave. NW, Washington, D.C. 20008 (**202/462-1340**). Consulates are maintained in New York, at 845 Third Ave., NY, NY 10022 (**212/745-0200**); and in Los Angeles, at 11766 Wilshire Blvd., Suite 400, Los Angeles, CA 90025 (**310/477-3322**).

Emergencies Call 911 for fire, police, and ambulance. If you encounter traveler's problems, check the local directory to find an office of the Traveler's Aid Society, a nationwide, nonprofit, social-service organization geared to helping travelers in difficult straits. Their services might include reuniting families separated while traveling, providing food and/or shelter to people stranded without cash, or even emotional counseling. If you're in trouble, seek them out.

Fax See telephones.

Gasoline [Petrol] One U.S. gallon equals 3.8 liters, while 1.2 U.S. gallons equals one Imperial gallon. You'll notice there are several grades (and price levels) of gasoline available at most gas stations. And you'll also notice that their names change from company to company. The unleaded ones with the highest octane are the most expensive (most rental cars take the least expensive "regular" unleaded) and leaded gas is the least expensive, but only older cars can take this any more, so check if you're not sure.

Holidays On the following legal national holidays, banks, government offices, post offices, and many stores, restaurants, and museums are closed: January 1 (New Year's Day); Third Monday in January (Martin Luther King Day); Third Monday in February (Presidents Day, Washington's Birthday); Last Monday in May (Memorial Day); July 4 (Independence Day); First Monday in September (Labor Day); Second Monday in October (Columbus Day); November 11 (Veteran's Day/Armistice Day); Last Thursday in November (Thanksgiving Day); December 25 (Christmas).

Finally, the Tuesday following the first Monday in November is Election Day, and is a legal holiday in presidential-election years.

Languages Major hotels may have multilingual employees. Unless your language is very obscure, they can usually supply a translator on request.

Legal Aid The ordinary tourist will probably never become involved with the American legal system. If you are pulled up for a minor infraction (for example, of the highway code, such as speeding), never attempt to pay the fine directly to a police officer; you may wind up arrested on the much more serious charge of attempted bribery. Pay fines by mail, or directly into the hands of the clerk of the court. If accused of a more serious offense, it's wise to say and do nothing before consulting a lawyer. Under U.S. law, an arrested person is allowed one telephone call to a party of his or her choice. Call your embassy or consulate.

Mail If you want your mail to follow you on your vacation and you aren't sure of your address, your mail can be sent to you, in your name, c/o General Delivery at the main post office of the city or region where you expect to be. The addressee must pick it up in person and produce proof of identity (driver's license, credit card, passport, etc.).

Generally to be found at intersections, mailboxes are blue with a red-and-white stripe and carry the inscription U.S. MAIL. If your mail is addressed to a U.S. destination, don't forget to add the five-figure postal code, or ZIP (Zone Improvement Plan) Code, after the two-letter abbreviation of the state to which the mail is addressed (CA for California, FL for Florida, NY for New York, and so on).

Newspapers/Magazines National newspapers include the *New York Times, USA Today,* and the *Wall Street Journal.* National news weeklies include *Newsweek, Time,* and *U.S. News & World Report.*

Radio and Television Audiovisual media, with four coast-to-coast networks—ABC, CBS, NBC, and Fox—joined in recent years by the Public Broadcasting System (PBS) and the Cable News Network (CNN), play a major part in American life. In big cities, televiewers have a choice of about a dozen channels (including the UHF channels), most of them transmitting 24 hours a day, without counting the pay-TV channels showing recent movies or sports events. All options are usually indicated on your hotel TV set. You'll also find a wide choice of local radio stations, each broadcasting particular kinds of talk shows and/or music—classical, country, jazz, pop, gospel—punctuated by news broadcasts and frequent commercials.

Safety See "Safety" in "Preparing for Your Trip," above.

Taxes In the United States there is no VAT (Value-Added Tax) or other indirect tax at a national level. Every state, and each city in it, has the right to levy its own local tax on all purchases, including hotel and restaurant checks, airline tickets, and so on. In California, sales tax is 7.75%.

Telephone, Fax, Telegraph, and Telex The telephone system in the United States is run by private corporations, so rates, particularly for long distance service and operator-assisted calls, can vary widely—especially on calls made from public telephones. Local calls in the United States usually cost 25¢.

Generally, hotel surcharges on long-distance and local calls are astronomical. You are usually better off using a **public pay telephone,** which you will find clearly marked in most public buildings and private establishments as well as on the street. Outside metropolitan areas, public telephones are more difficult to find. Stores and gas stations are your best bet.

Most **long-distance and international calls** can be dialed directly from any phone. For calls to Canada and other parts of the United States, dial 1 followed by the area code and the seven-digit number. For international calls, dial 011 followed by the country code, city code, and the telephone number of the person you wish to call.

For **reversed-charge or collect calls,** and for **person-to-person calls,** dial 0 (zero, *not* the letter "O") followed by the area code and number you want; an operator will then come on the line, and you should specify that you are calling collect, or person-to-person, or both. If your operator-assisted call is international, ask for the overseas operator.

Note that all phone numbers with the area code 800 are toll free.

For local **directory assistance** ("information"), dial **411**; for **long-distance information,** dial 1, then the appropriate area code and **555-1212**.

Facilities for sending and receiving **faxes** are widely available, and can be found in most hotels and many other establishments. Try Mailboxes Etc. or any photocopying shop.

Like the telephone system, **telegraph** and **telex** services are provided by private corporations like ITT, MCI, and above all, Western Union, the most important. You can bring your telegram in to the nearest Western Union office (there are hundreds across the country), or dictate it over the phone (a toll-free call, **800/325-6000**). You can also telegraph money, or have it telegraphed to you, very quickly over the Western Union system.

Telephone Directory There are two kinds of telephone directories available to you. The general directory is the so-called **White Pages,** in which private and business subscribers are listed in alphabetical order. The inside front cover lists the emergency number for police, fire, and ambulance, and other vital numbers (like the Coast Guard, poison-control center, crime-victims hotline, and so on). The first few pages are devoted to community-service numbers, including a guide to long-distance and international calling, complete with country codes and area codes.

The second directory, printed on yellow paper (hence its name, *Yellow Pages*), lists all local services, businesses, and industries by type of activity, with an index at the back. The listings cover not only such obvious items as automobile repairs by make of car, or drugstores (pharmacies), often by geographical location, but also restaurants by type of cuisine and geographical location, bookstores by special subject and/or language, places of worship by religious denomination, and other information that the tourist might otherwise not readily find. The *Yellow Pages* also include city plans or detailed area maps, often showing postal ZIP Codes and public transportation routes.

Time The United States is divided into four **time zones** (six, if Alaska and Hawaii are included). From east to west, these are eastern standard time (EST), central standard time (CST), mountain standard time (MST), Pacific standard time (PST), Alaska standard time (AST), and Hawaii standard time (HST). Always keep changing time zones in mind if you are traveling (or even telephoning) long distances in the United States. For example, noon in New York City (EST) is 11am in Chicago (CST), 10am in Denver (MST), 9am in Los Angeles (PST), 8am in Anchorage (AST), and 7am in Honolulu (HST).

California observes Pacific standard time. **Daylight saving time** is in effect from the last Sunday in April through the last Saturday in October (actually, the change is made at 2am on Sunday) except in Arizona, Hawaii, part of Indiana, and Puerto Rico. Daylight saving time moves the clock one hour ahead of standard time.

Tipping This is part of the American way of life, on the principle that you must expect to pay for any service you get (many service personnel receive little direct salary and must depend on tips for their income). Here are some rules of thumb:

In **hotels,** tip bellhops at least $1 per piece ($2 to $3 if you have a lot of luggage) and tip the chamber staff $1 per day. Tip the doorman or concierge only if he or she has provided you with some specific service (for example, calling a cab for you or obtaining difficult-to-get theater tickets).

In **restaurants, bars, and nightclubs,** tip service staff 15% to 20% of the check, tip bartenders 10% to 15%, tip checkroom attendants $1 per garment, and tip valet-parking attendants $1 per vehicle. Tip the doorman only if he has provided you with some specific service (such as calling a cab for you). Tipping is not expected in cafeterias and fast-food restaurants.

Tip **cab drivers** 15% of the fare.

As for **other service personnel,** tip redcaps at airports or railroad stations at least 50¢ per piece ($2 to $3 if you have a lot of luggage) and tip hairdressers and barbers 15% to 20%.

Tipping ushers in cinemas, movies, and theaters and gas-station attendants is not expected.

Toilets Foreign visitors often complain that public toilets are hard to find in most U.S. cities. True, there are none on the streets, but the visitor can usually find one in a bar, restaurant, hotel, museum, department store, or service station—and it will probably be clean (although the last-mentioned sometimes leaves much to be desired). Note, however, a growing practice in some restaurants and bars of displaying a notice that "toilets are for the use of patrons only." You can ignore this sign, or better yet, avoid arguments by paying for a cup of coffee or soft drink, which will qualify you as a patron. The cleanliness of toilets at railroad stations and bus depots may be more open to question, and some public places are equipped with pay toilets, which require you to insert one or more coins into a slot on the door before it will open.

The American System of Measurements

Length

1 inch (in.)	=	2.54cm				
1 foot (ft.)	=	12 in.	=	30.48cm	=	.305m
1 yard	=	3 ft.	=	.915m		
1 mile (mi.)	=	5,280 ft.	=	1.609km		

To convert miles to kilometers, multiply the number of miles by 1.61 (for example, 50 mi. × 1.61 = 80.5km). Note that this conversion can be used to convert speeds from miles per hour (m.p.h.) to kilometers per hour (km/h).

To convert kilometers to miles, multiply the number of kilometers by .62 (for example, 25km × .62 = 15.5 mi.). Note that this same conversion can be used to convert speeds from kilometers per hour to miles per hour.

Capacity

1 fluid ounce (fl. oz.)	=	.03 liter				
1 pint	=	16 fl. oz. =	.47 liter			
1 quart	=	2 pints =	.94 liter			
1 gallon (gal.)	=	4 quarts =	3.79 liter	=	.83 Imperial gal.	

To convert U.S. gallons to liters, multiply the number of gallons by 3.79 (example, 12 gal. × 3.79 = 45.58 liters)

To convert U.S. gallons to Imperial gallons, multiply the number of U.S. gallons by .83 (example, 12 U.S. gal. × .83 = 9.96 Imperial gal.).

To convert liters to U.S. gallons, multiply the number of liters by .26 (example, 50 liters × .26 = 13 U.S. gal.).

To convert Imperial gallons to U.S. gallons, multiply the number of Imperial gallons by 1.2 (example, 8 Imperial gal. × 1.2 = 9.6 U.S. gal.).

Weight

1 ounce (oz.)	=	28.35 grams				
1 pound (lb.)	=	16 oz.	=	453.6 grams	=	.45 kilograms
1 ton	=	2,000 lb.	=	907 kilograms	=	.91 metric ton

To convert pounds to kilograms, multiply the number of pounds by .45 (example, 90 lb. × .45 = 40.5kg).

To convert kilograms to pounds, multiply the number of kilos by 2.2 (example, 75kg × 2.2 = 165 lb.).

Area

1 acre	=	.41 hectare				
1 square mile (sq. mi.)	=	640 acres	=	2.59 hectar	=	2.6km

To convert acres to hectares, multiply the number of acres by .41 (example, 40 acres × .41 = 16.4ha).

To convert square miles to square kilometers, multiply the number of square miles by 2.6 (example, 80 sq. mi. × 2.6 = 208km.)

To convert hectares to acres, multiply the number of hectares by 2.47 (example, 20ha × 2.47 = 49.4 acres).

To convert square kilometers to square miles, multiply the number of square kilometers by .39 (example, 150km2 × .39 = 58.5 sq. mi.).

Temperature

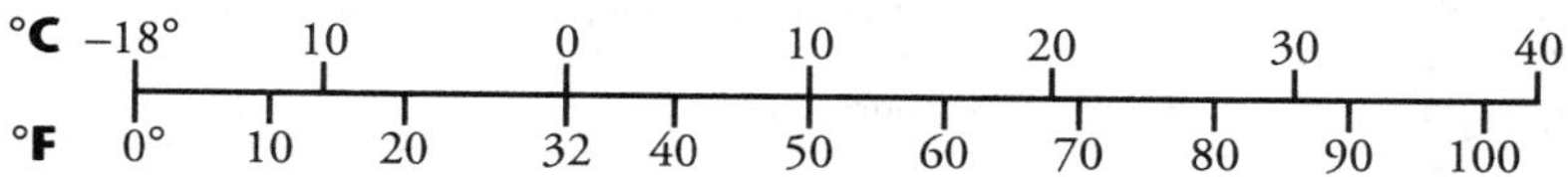

To convert degrees Fahrenheit to degrees Celsius, subtract 32 from °F, multiply by 5, then divide by 9 (example, 85°F – 32 × 5 ÷ 9 = 29.4°C).

To convert degrees Celsius to degrees Fahrenheit, multiply °C by 9, divide by 5, and add 32 (example, 20°C × 9 ÷ 5 + 32 = 62.6°F).

4 San Francisco

SAN FRANCISCO'S ENCHANTING BEAUTY IS ITS PRIMARY CHARM. BUILT ACROSS dozens of hills, the city is shaped like a compressed accordion, its gingerbread houses clinging to steep hillsides like displaced alpine cottages. Both first-time visitors and longtime locals are stirred by the sights and sounds of San Francisco: the glitter of sunshine on the golden pagoda roofs of Chinatown, the unexpected glimpses of ocean when you stop climbing and look back over your shoulder, and the bell-clanking onrush of toy-like cable cars that seem to have escaped from an amusement park.

At the turn of the 20th century, just less than half of California's population lived in San Francisco. Today, the city is home to about 724,000 people, fewer than 5% of the state total. The nine Bay Area counties that surround the city hold an additional 6 million inhabitants. Despite its small size, San Francisco is highly diversified culturally. One out of every three San Franciscans comes from a home where a language other than English is spoken. The city is about 13% Chinese, 9% Irish, 8% German, and 6% Italian. Filipinos, Mexicans, Russians, French, and Japanese are also significantly represented.

In addition to its unusually broad ethnicity, San Francisco is known as a spawning ground and haven for alternative lifestyles. This was the town that sheltered the hippie counterculture and, prior to that, the beat generation. Most of all, however, the Bay Area is internationally known as a liberal oasis for gays and lesbians. The Castro district remains the center of the city's gay community, while the lesbian stronghold is in Oakland, across the bay.

1 Orientation

San Francisco occupies the tip of a 32-mile-long peninsula between San Francisco Bay and the Pacific Ocean. Its land area measures about 46 square miles, comparable to that of Manhattan but minute by the standards of, say, Chicago or Los Angeles. Don't be misled by this. The city's downtown section is wonderfully compact, and North Beach and Chinatown more compact still, but the rest of the city meanders over some 40 hills, many of which become positively mountainous when you're in the process of climbing them. Twin Peaks, in the geographic center of the city, is over 900 feet high. San Francisco's hills count among the city's chief charms. They offer sudden, breathless views of moving ships and creeping fog banks on the harbor below or rolling stretches of open countryside at what seems arm's length. It has been said that when you get tired of walking around San Francisco, you can always lean against it.

ARRIVING

BY PLANE Two major airports serve the Bay Area, San Francisco International and Oakland International.

San Francisco International Airport Served by almost four dozen major scheduled carriers, San Francisco International Airport (☎ **415/761-0800**)—currently undergoing a $2.4 billion improvement—is one of the busiest in the world. The airport is located 14 miles south of downtown San Francisco, directly on U.S. 101. Travel time to the downtown area during commuter rush hours is about 40 minutes, 25 minutes at other times. There are several ways of making your way from the airport to your hotel.

What's Special About San Francisco

The Arts

- ACT and other city theater companies, well known for their excellent, innovative staging.
- The world-renowned San Francisco Opera and Ballet.
- The city's many galleries, some exhibiting works by local artists.

Neighborhoods

- North Beach, the city's Italian and bohemian quarter, known for its restaurants and nightlife.
- Haight-Ashbury, the famed hippie district, still a great place to shop for the latest street fashions.
- The Castro, a unique neighborhood synonymous with gay life.
- Chinatown, one of the occidental world's largest Asian immigrant communities, excellent for strolling, shopping, and eating.

Public Transportation

- The city's trademark cable cars—cute, fun, historic, and utilitarian.
- BART, fast and futuristic, one of the world's best high-speed commuter railways.

Bridges

- The Golden Gate Bridge, one of the world's most elegant spans, connecting the city with the countryside.
- The San Francisco–Oakland Bay Bridge, a spectacular engineering feat.

Geographical Features

- Golden Gate Park, where it's easy to get lost amid the ponds, trees, and museums.
- The Presidio of San Francisco, which is in an exciting stage of transformation.
- The city's hills, each with a unique perspective of San Francisco.
- The bay, San Francisco's most important asset.

Taxis are plentiful and line up in front of a dispatcher's desk outside the airport's arrival terminals. Cabs are metered and cost $25 to $30, plus tip, to a downtown location.

The **SFO Airporter bus** (☎ **415/495-8404**) departs from the lower-level luggage claim area and travels nonstop to downtown San Francisco. Buses leave every 10 minutes from 6am to 11pm daily and stop at several Union Square–area hotels, including the San Francisco Hilton, San Francisco Marriott, Westin St. Francis, and Parc Fifty Five. Additional hotels are served every 20 minutes. No reservations are needed. The cost is $8 one way, $14 round trip, $4 each way for children ages 2 to 12 (with an accompanying adult), and free for infants under 2.

Several private shuttle companies offer door-to-door airport service, in which you share a van with other passengers. **SuperShuttle** (☎ **415/558-8500**) and **Yellow Airport Shuttle** (☎ **415/282-7433**) both charge about $11 per person. Each stops every 20 minutes or so and picks up passengers from marked areas outside the terminals' upper level. Reservations are required for the return trip to the airport only and should be made one day prior to departure.

The **San Mateo County Transit system (Sam Trans; ☎ 415/508-6200**, or toll free **800/660-4287** in Northern California) runs two buses between the airport and the Transbay Terminal at First and Mission Streets. The 7B bus costs 85¢ and makes the trip in about 55 minutes. The 7F bus costs $1.50 and takes only 35 minutes, but permits only one carry-on bag. Both buses run daily, every half-hour from about 6am to 7pm, then hourly until about midnight.

Oakland International Airport Located about five miles south of downtown Oakland, at the Hegenberger Road Exit of Calif. 17 (U.S. 880), Oakland International Airport (☎ **510/577-4000**) is used primarily by passengers with East Bay destinations. Some San Franciscans, however, prefer this uncrowded, accessible airport when flying during busy periods.

Again, taxis from Oakland Airport to downtown San Francisco are expensive, costing approximately $55, plus tip.

If you make advance reservations, the **AM/PM Airporter,** P.O. Box 2902, Oakland, CA 94609 (☎ **510/547-2155**), will take you from Oakland Airport to your hotel any time of the day or night. The price of the ride varies, depending on the number of passengers sharing the van, but usually it's $35 or less; get a quote when you call.

The **AirBART shuttle bus** (☎ **510/832-1464**) connects Oakland International Airport with Bay Area Rapid Transit (BART) trains. Buses run every 15 minutes or so and stop in front of Terminals 1 and 2, near the "Ground Transportation" signs. The shuttle ride to BART's Coliseum Station costs $2. BART fares vary, depending on your destination; the trip to downtown San Francisco costs $1.90 and takes 45 minutes. AirBART operates Monday through Saturday from 6am to midnight, Sunday from 8am to midnight.

BY TRAIN Passengers traveling to San Francisco by train (see "Getting There," in Chapter 2) actually disembark at the **Amtrak** 16th Street depot in Oakland (☎ toll free **800/872-7245**). Free transport shuttles connect the Oakland depot with San Francisco's Transbay Terminal at First and Mission Streets. The ride takes about 40 minutes. Unfortunately, none of the major car-rental companies has an office at the train station; you'll have to pick up your car from a downtown Oakland or San Francisco location. Hertz (☎ toll free **800/654-3131**) will reimburse your cab fare from the train station to its Oakland office at 1001 Broadway, two miles away.

BY BUS Buses from **Greyhound/Trailways** (☎ **415/558-6789**) arrive and depart from the Transbay Terminal at First and Mission Streets. See "Getting There," in Chapter 2, for complete information on traveling by bus.

BY CAR There are several approaches into San Francisco:

From the north: U.S. 101 crosses the Golden Gate Bridge at the northernmost tip of the peninsula and feeds into the city.

From the east: Interstate 80 crosses the San Francisco–Oakland Bay Bridge and terminates in the city's South of Market (SoMa) district.

From the south: Both Interstate 280 and U.S. 101 come up the peninsula and drop into the city via several downtown off-ramps.

From all three directions, off-ramps are well marked, pointing to Union Square, Financial District, and Waterfront destinations. Once you're on city streets, you'll see directional signs pointing the way to Chinatown, Fisherman's Wharf, and North Beach.

TOURIST INFORMATION

If you have any questions about what to do and where to go in San Francisco, the people with answers are the cheerful experts at the **San Francisco Visitor Information Center,** 900 Market St., on the lower level of Hallidie Plaza, at Powell and Market Streets (☎ **415/391-2000**). They can render answers in German, French, Spanish, Italian, Portuguese, Chinese, Hungarian, and Japanese, as well as in English. They're open Monday through Friday from 9am to 5:30pm, on Saturday from 9am to 3pm, and on Sunday from 10am to 2pm. To find the office, descend the escalator at the cable car turnaround.

When in town, you can get **information by telephone** by dialing **391-2001** any time of day or night for a recorded message about current cultural, theater, music, sports, and special events. This information is also available in German (☎ **391-2004**), French (☎ **391-2003**), Spanish (☎ **391-2122**), and Japanese (☎ **391-2101**).

The **Visitors Information Center of the Redwood Empire Association,** 785 Market St., 15th floor (☎ **415/543-8334**), offers informative brochures and a very knowledgeable desk staff who are able to plan tours both in San Francisco and north of the city. Their annual *Redwood Empire Visitors' Guide* ($3 by mail, free in person) is crammed with detailed information on everything from San Francisco walking tours and museums to visits to Marin County and the timetable of the *Super Skunk* train through Mendocino County. The office is open Monday through Friday from 9am to 5pm.

CITY LAYOUT

San Francisco may seem confusing at first, but it quickly becomes easy to negotiate. The city's downtown streets are arranged in a simple grid pattern, with the exception of Market Street and Columbus Avenue, which cut across the grid at right angles to each other. Hills appear to distort this pattern, however, and can seem disorienting. But as you learn your way around, these same hills will become your landmarks and reference points.

MAIN ARTERIES & STREETS San Francisco's main thoroughfare is **Market Street.** Most of the city's buses ply this strip on their way to the Financial District from the bedroom communities to the west and south. The tall office buildings that punctuate the city's skyline are clustered at the northeast end of Market; one block beyond lie the Embarcadero and the bay.

The Embarcadero curves north along San Francisco Bay, around the perimeter of the city. It terminates at Fisherman's Wharf, the famous tourist-oriented pier, which is full of restaurants and T-shirt stands. Aquatic Park and the Fort Mason complex are just ahead, occupying the northernmost point of the peninsula.

From here, **Van Ness Avenue** runs due south, back to Market Street. The area I have just described forms a rough triangle, with Market Street as its eastern, the waterfront as its northern, and Van Ness Avenue as its western boundary. Within this triangle lie most of the city's main tourist sights.

FINDING AN ADDRESS Since most of the city's streets are laid out in a grid pattern, finding an address is easy when you know the nearest cross street. All the listings in this chapter include cross-street information. In addition, the city of San Francisco encompasses over a dozen distinct neighborhoods. To help you stay oriented, I have listed hotels and restaurants under area headings. When asking for directions, find out the nearest cross street and the neighborhood in which your destination is located.

STREET MAPS Because San Francisco is relatively compact, and the streets generally follow a rigid grid pattern, the maps included in this guide may be all you need in order to find your way around. The maps printed in the free tourist weeklies *Bay City Guide* and *Key* are also very good for visitors who don't plan on leaving the main tourist areas. These small magazines can be found at most large hotels, around major tourist sites, and in the San Francisco Visitor Information Center (see "Tourist Information" above). More serious explorers should buy one of the accordion-style foldout maps of the city that are sold in hotels, bookshops, and tourist-oriented stores all over town.

Neighborhoods in Brief

Distinct neighborhoods like North Beach, Haight-Ashbury, and the Castro have made San Francisco a city of villages. Each is unique and fun to explore.

Union Square Although it's not in the geographic center of the city, Union Square is the true heart of San Francisco. Surrounded by both the city's swankiest and seediest shops, the square is also home to large department stores, busy hotels, and tourist-oriented restaurants. It's likely that your hotel will be near here. But even if you're not bedding down within walking distance of Union Square, you'll probably pass by on your way to the theater or as you go to shop or to ride the famous cable cars, which terminate just three blocks south, on the corner of Powell Street and Market Street. The grassy square itself was named for a series of violent pro-Union mass demonstrations staged there on the eve of the Civil War. Today the well-manicured little park, which sits atop a huge underground garage, is planted with palms, yews, boxwood, and flowers—centered around a towering memorial to Admiral George Dewey's 1898 victory at Manila Bay. Lunching office workers and assorted homeless people occupy the park's benches, while traffic perpetually jams the surrounding streets.

Financial District Northeast of Union Square, toward San Francisco Bay, is the city's suit-and-tie district. This conservative quarter, centered around Kearny and Sansome Streets, swarms with smartly dressed workers on weekdays, and is almost deserted on weekends and at night. The Transamerica Pyramid, at Montgomery and Clay Streets, is one of the district's most conspicuous architectural features. To its east stands the sprawling Embarcadero Center, an 8½-acre complex housing offices, shops, and restaurants. Farther east is the World Trade Center, standing adjacent to the old Ferry Building, the city's pre-bridge transportation hub. Ferries to Sausalito and Larkspur still leave from this point.

Chinatown A short distance north of Union Square and the Financial District, this 24-block labyrinth of restaurants, markets, temples, and shops is one of the largest in North America. For tourists, it is one of the most marvelous walking, shopping, and eating areas in San Francisco.

IMPRESSIONS

The extreme geniality of San Francisco's economic, intellectual and political climate makes it the most varied and challenging city in the United States.
—James Michener

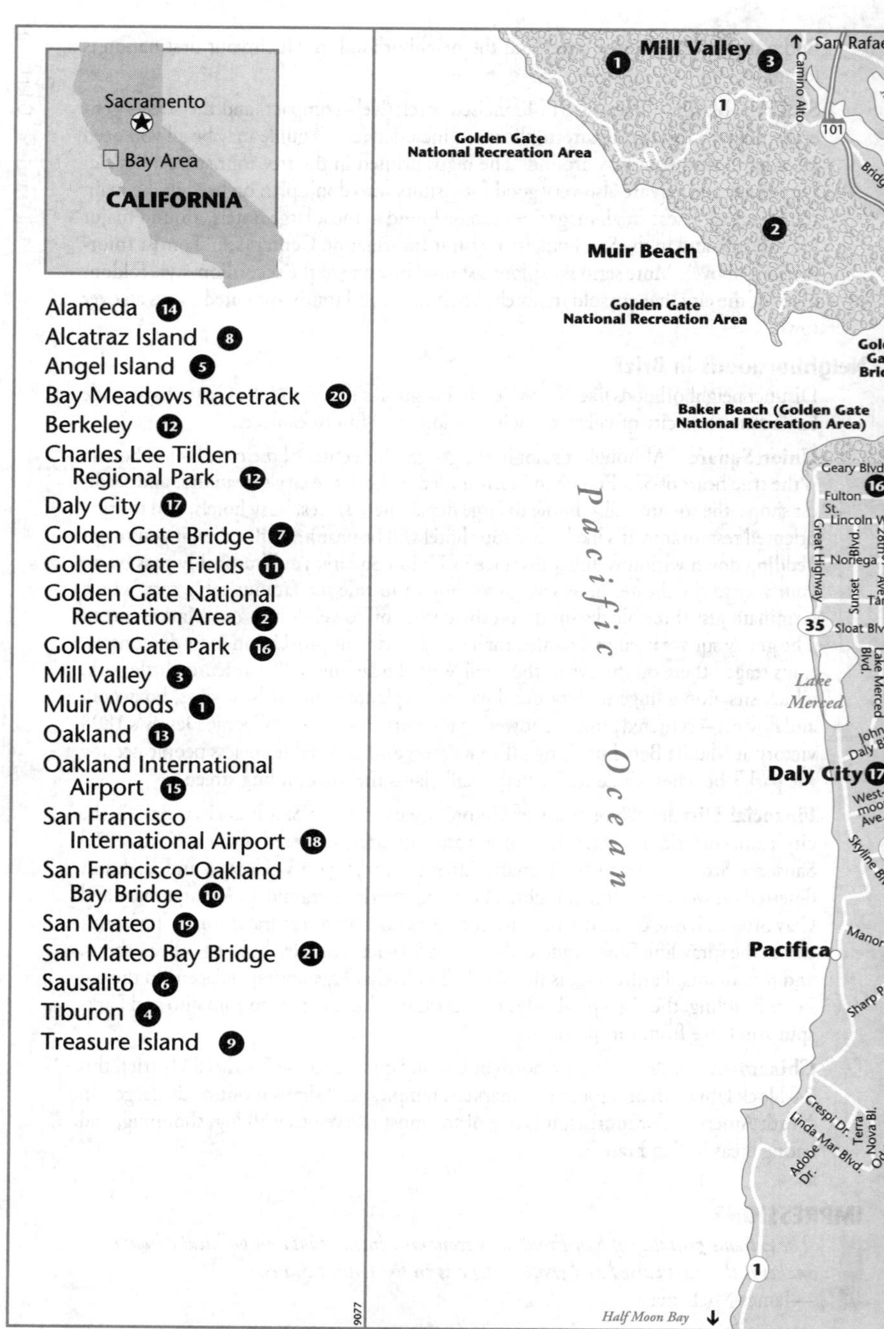
Sacramento
Bay Area
CALIFORNIA
Alameda 14
Alcatraz Island 8
Angel Island 5
Bay Meadows Racetrack 20
Berkeley 12
Charles Lee Tilden Regional Park 12
Daly City 17
Golden Gate Bridge 7
Golden Gate Fields 11
Golden Gate National Recreation Area 2
Golden Gate Park 16
Mill Valley 3
Muir Woods 1
Oakland 13
Oakland International Airport 15
San Francisco International Airport 18
San Francisco-Oakland Bay Bridge 10
San Mateo 19
San Mateo Bay Bridge 21
Sausalito 6
Tiburon 4
Treasure Island 9
Mill Valley
San Rafael
Camino Alto
101
Golden Gate National Recreation Area
Muir Beach
Golden Gate National Recreation Area
Baker Beach (Golden Gate National Recreation Area)
Geary Blvd.
Fulton St.
Great Highway
Sunset Blvd.
Noriega St.
35
Sloat Blvd.
Lake Merced
Lake Merced Blvd.
Pacific Ocean
Daly City
West-moor Ave.
Skyline Blvd.
Pacifica
Manor
Crespi Dr.
Linda Mar Blvd.
Adobe Dr.
Terra Nova Bl.
1
Half Moon Bay
9077

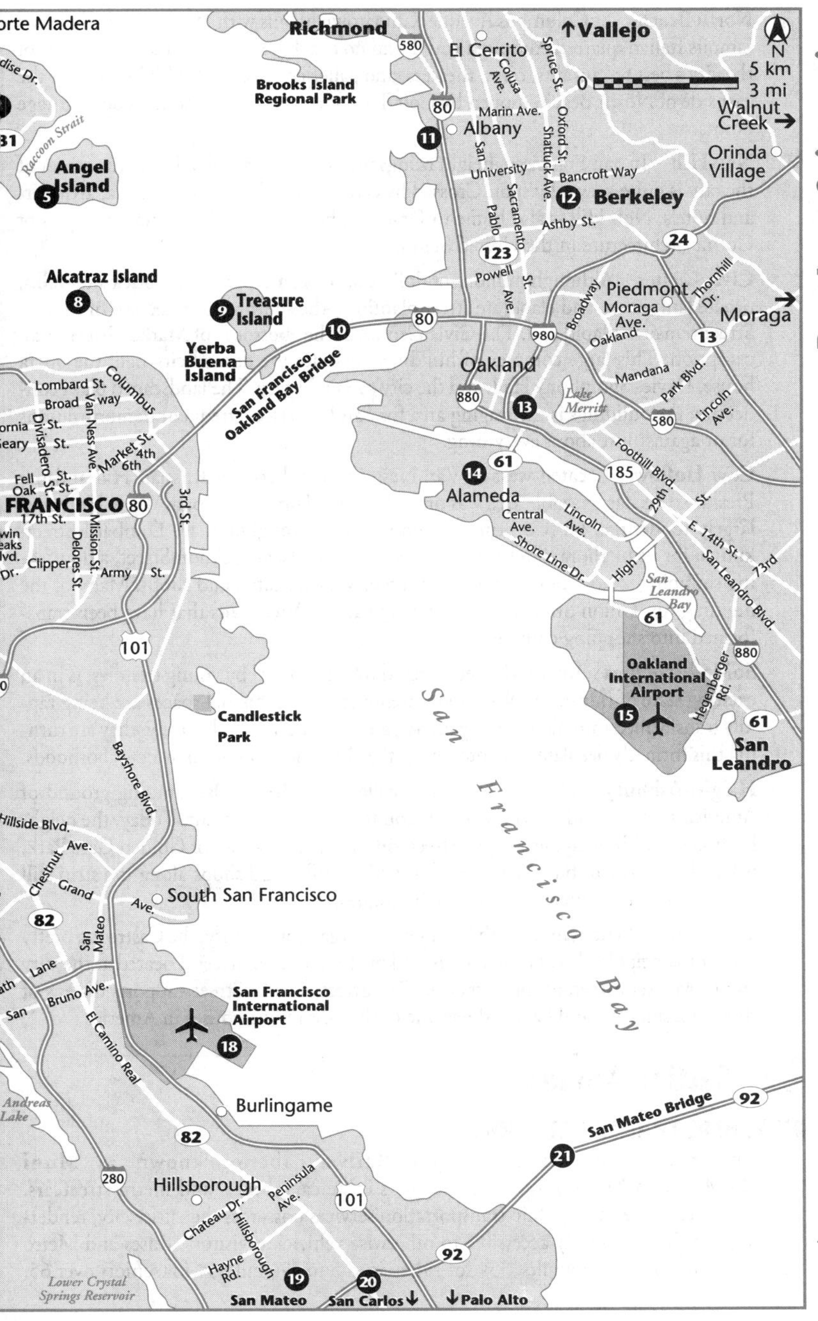

Bay Area Orientation

North Beach At Columbus Avenue, Chinatown blends with North Beach, the city's famous Italian quarter. Although you'll find no beach here, you will discover some of the city's best restaurants, cafes, theaters, and galleries. Telegraph Hill looms over the east side of North Beach, topped by Coit Tower, one of San Francisco's best vantage points.

Nob Hill In San Francisco, height brings prestige, and this high hill in the center of the city is quite a swanky spot. Crossed by cable cars and topped by ritzy apartments and hotels, Nob Hill is also home to Grace Cathedral, one of the finest examples of Gothic architecture in the United States.

Civic Center Although millions of dollars have been expended on brick sidewalks, ornate lampposts, and elaborate street plantings, the southwestern section of Market Street remains dilapidated. The Civic Center, at the "bottom" of Market Street, is an exception. This large complex of buildings includes the domed city hall, the opera house, Davies Symphony Hall, and the city's main library. The landscaped plaza connecting the buildings is the staging area for San Francisco's frequent demonstrations for or against just about everything.

Cow Hollow Located west of Van Ness Avenue, between Russian Hill and the Presidio, this flat, grazable area was once the city's dairy land. Today, Cow Hollow is largely residential. Its two primary commercial thoroughfares are Lombard Street, known for its plethora of relatively inexpensive motels, and Union Street, a flourishing shopping sector crammed with restaurants, pubs, cafes, and shops. Many of the buildings on Union Street are handsomely painted Victorians that have been transformed into shopping complexes.

SoMa The area south of Market Street, dubbed "SoMa" by young trendies, is in an exciting state of transition. Working warehouses and industrial spaces are being rapidly transformed into nightclubs, galleries, and restaurants. Collectively, they are turning this formerly desolate area into one of the city's most vibrant new neighborhoods.

Haight-Ashbury The Haight, as it is called, was the 1960s stamping ground of America's hippies and the center of the counterculture movement. Today, the neighborhood straddling upper Haight Street, on the eastern border of Golden Gate Park, is largely gentrified, but the street life is still colorful, and shops along the strip still include a good number of alternative boutiques.

The Castro Synonymous with San Francisco's gay community, the Castro is a pretty residential neighborhood centered around bustling Castro Street. Located at the very end of Market Street, at the corner of 17th Street, Castro Street supports dozens of shops, restaurants, and bars and has one of the best movie houses in America.

2 Getting Around

BY PUBLIC TRANSPORTATION

The **San Francisco Municipal Railway,** better known as **Muni** (☎ **415/673-MUNI**), operates the city's cable cars, buses, and metro streetcars. Together, these three public-transportation services crisscross the entire city, rendering San Francisco fully accessible to otherwise vehicleless visitors. Buses and Metro streetcars cost $1 for adults, 35¢ for riders aged 5 to 17, and 35¢ for seniors over 65.

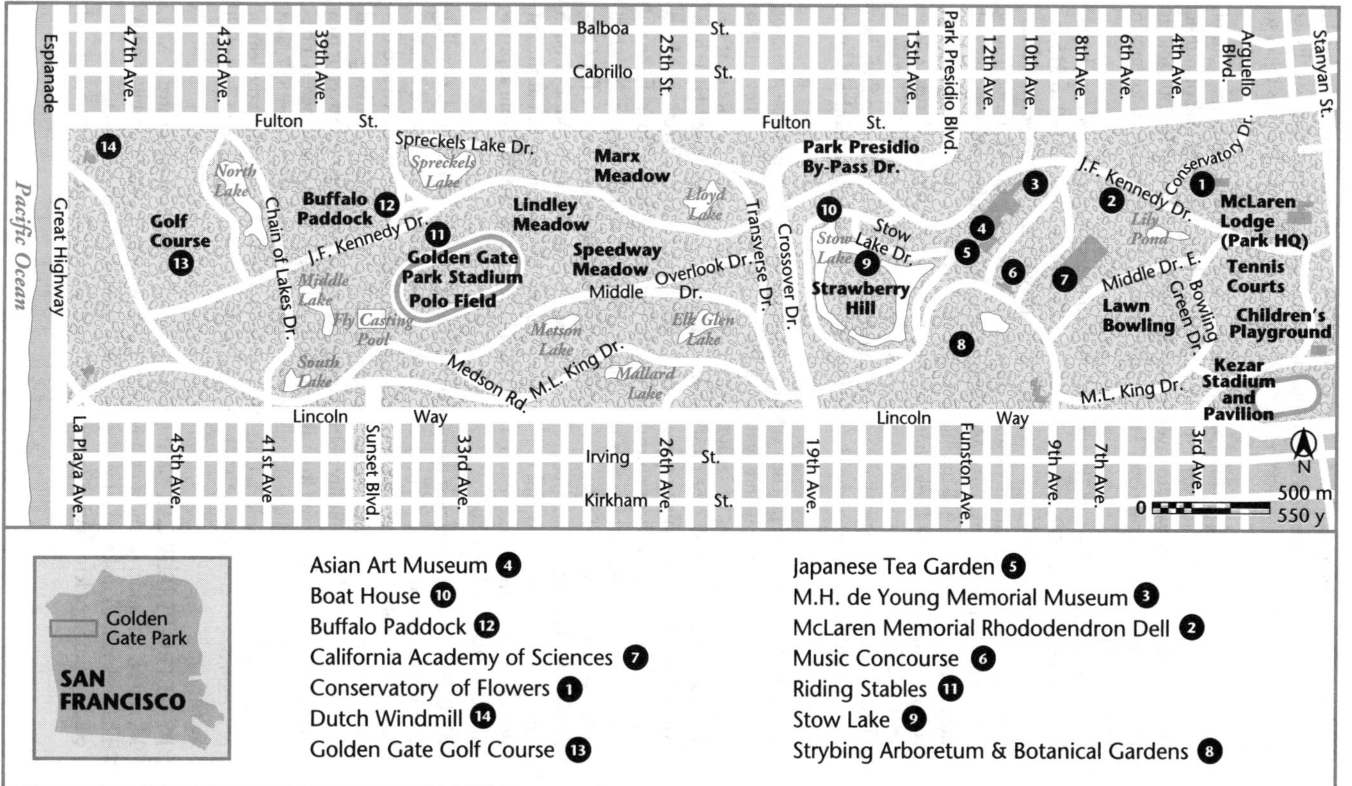
Golden Gate Park
Balboa St.
Cabrillo St.
Fulton St.
Stanyan St.
Arguello Blvd.
4th Ave.
6th Ave.
8th Ave.
10th Ave.
12th Ave.
Park Presidio Blvd.
15th Ave.
25th St.
39th Ave.
43rd Ave.
47th Ave.
Esplanade
Great Highway
Pacific Ocean
Spreckels Lake Dr.
Spreckels Lake
North Lake
Golf Course 13
Buffalo Paddock 12
J.F. Kennedy Dr.
Chain of Lakes Dr.
Middle Lake
Fly Casting Pool
South Lake
Golden Gate Park Stadium
Polo Field
Lindley Meadow
Marx Meadow
Speedway Meadow
Lloyd Lake
Overlook Dr.
Middle Dr.
Transverse Dr.
Crossover Dr.
Elk Glen Lake
Metson Lake
Mallard Lake
Medson Rd.
M.L. King Dr.
Park Presidio By-Pass Dr.
Stow Lake Dr.
Stow Lake
Strawberry Hill
Conservatory Dr.
McLaren Lodge (Park HQ)
Lily Pond
Middle Dr. E.
Bowling Green Dr.
Tennis Courts
Lawn Bowling
Children's Playground
Kezar Stadium and Pavilion
Lincoln Way
La Playa Ave.
45th Ave.
41st Ave
Sunset Blvd.
33rd Ave.
Irving St.
Kirkham St.
26th Ave.
19th Ave.
Funston Ave.
9th Ave.
7th Ave.
3rd Ave.
N
0
500 m
550 y
Golden Gate Park
SAN FRANCISCO
Asian Art Museum 4
Boat House 10
Buffalo Paddock 12
California Academy of Sciences 7
Conservatory of Flowers 1
Dutch Windmill 14
Golden Gate Golf Course 13
Japanese Tea Garden 5
M.H. de Young Memorial Museum 3
McLaren Memorial Rhododendron Dell 2
Music Concourse 6
Riding Stables 11
Stow Lake 9
Strybing Arboretum & Botanical Gardens 8

Cable cars cost a whopping $2 for adults and $1 for seniors from 9pm to midnight and from 6 to 7pm. Needless to say, they're packed primarily with tourists. Exact change is required on all vehicles except cable cars. Fares quoted here are subject to change.

For detailed route information, call Muni or consult the bus map at the front of the San Francisco *Yellow Pages.* If you plan on making extensive use of public transportation, you may want to invest in a comprehensive route map ($1.50), sold at the visitor information center (see "Tourist Information" above) and many downtown retail outlets.

Muni discount passes, or **"Passports,"** entitle holders to unlimited rides on buses, metro streetcars, and cable cars. A passport costs $6 for one day, and $10 to $15 for three or seven consecutive days. As a bonus, your passport also entitles you to admission discounts at 24 of the city's major attractions, including the M. H. de Young Memorial Museum, the Asian Art Museum, the California Academy of Sciences, and the Japanese Tea Garden—all in Golden Gate Park—as well as the Museum of Modern Art, Coit Tower, the Exploratorium, the zoo, and the National Maritime Museum and Historic Ships (where you may visit the USS *Pampanito* and the S.S. *Jeremiah O'Brien*). Among the places where you can purchase a passport are the San Francisco Visitor Information Center, the Holiday Inns, and the Tix Bay Area booth at Union Square.

BY CABLE CAR San Francisco's cable cars may not be the most practical means of transportation, but these rolling symbols of the city are the best loved. They are also official historic landmarks, designated as such by the National Parks Service in 1964. There are three lines in all. The most scenic—and exciting—is the Powell-Hyde line, which follows a zigzag route from the corner of Powell and Market Streets, over both Nob Hill and Russian Hill, to a turntable at gaslit Victorian Square in front of Aquatic Park. The Powell-Mason line starts at the same intersection and climbs over Nob Hill before descending to Bay Street, just three blocks from Fisherman's Wharf. The California Street line begins at the foot of Market Street and runs a straight course through Chinatown and over Nob Hill to Van Ness Avenue. All riders must exit at the last stop and wait in line for the return trip. The cable-car system operates from approximately 6:30am to 12:30am.

BY BUS Buses reach almost every corner of San Francisco and beyond, traveling over the bridges to Marin County and Oakland. Some buses are powered by overhead electric cables; others use conventional gas engines. All are numbered and display their destinations on the front. Stops are designated by signs, curb markings, and yellow bands on adjacent utility poles. Most buses travel along Market Street or pass near Union Square. They run from about 6am to midnight, after which there is infrequent all-night "owl" service. Popular tourist routes are traveled by buses 5, 7, and 71, all of which run to Golden Gate Park; by buses 41 and 45, which ply the length of Union Street; and by bus 30, which runs between Union Square and Ghirardelli Square.

BY METRO STREET CAR Muni's five metro street car lines, designated J, K, L, M, and N, run underground downtown and on the street in the outer neighborhoods. The sleek railcars make the same stops as BART (see below) along Market Street, including Embarcadero Station (in the Financial District), Montgomery Street and

Powell Street (both near Union Square), and the Civic Center (near city hall). Past the Civic Center, the routes branch off in different directions: The J line will take you to Mission Dolores; the K, L, and M lines to Castro Street; and the N line parallels Golden Gate Park. Metro streetcars run about every 15 minutes—more frequently during rush hours. Service is offered Monday through Friday from 5am to 12:30am, on Saturday from 6am to 12:20am, and on Sunday from 8am to 12:20am.

BY BART BART, an acronym for Bay Area Rapid Transit (☎ **788-BART**), is a futuristic-looking, high-speed rail network that connects San Francisco with the East Bay—Oakland, Richmond, Concord, and Fremont. Four stations are located along Market Street (see "By Metro Street Car" above). Fares range from 80¢ to $3, depending on how far you go. Tickets are dispensed from machines in the stations and are magnetically encoded with a dollar amount. Computerized exits automatically deduct the correct fare. Children 4 and under ride free. Trains run every 15 to 20 minutes, Monday through Friday from 4am to midnight, on Saturday from 6am to midnight, and on Sunday from 8am to midnight.

BY TAXI

Taxis ply major thoroughfares and can be hailed on the street. When a cab is available for hire, the sign on its roof will be lighted. Like police when you need them, taxis can become suddenly scarce during rain or rush hour. If you can, it's best to call in advance and request a cab to pick you up at a designated location. The following licensed private companies compete for customers: **Veteran's Cab (552-1300)**, **Desoto Cab Co. (673-1414)**, **Luxor Cabs (282-4141)**, **Yellow Cab (626-2345)**, **City (468-7200)**, and **Pacific (986-7220)**. Rates are approximately $2 for each mile.

BY CAR

You certainly don't need a car to explore San Francisco proper. In fact, in some areas, such as Chinatown and the Financial District, a car is a positive handicap. If, however, you plan on extensive exploration of outlying neighborhoods or want to tour the Bay Area in general, a car will prove extremely handy. See Section 8, "Getting Around," in Chapter 2, for general information on driving around California.

RENTALS Most of the large, national car-rental firms have outlets in San Francisco. See "Getting Around" in Chapter 2 for information and toll-free telephone numbers. In addition to the big chains, there are dozens of regional rental places in San Francisco; many offer lower rates. These include **A-One Rent-A-Car,** 434 O'Farrell St. (**415/771-3977**); and **Bay Area Rentals,** 440 O'Farrell St. (**415/441-4779**).

PARKING Street parking in San Francisco is extremely limited—and the local cops are the quickest tow I've ever seen. Parking is particularly tough in Chinatown, around Nob Hill, by Fisherman's Wharf, in North Beach, and on Telegraph Hill. Where street parking is not metered, signs will tell you when you can park and for how long. **Curb colors** also indicate parking regulations—and mean it! Red means no stopping or parking; blue is reserved for disabled drivers with a California-issued disabled plate or a placard; white means there's a five-minute limit; green indicates a 10-minute limit; and yellow and yellow-black curbs are reserved for commercial vehicles only. Also, don't park at a bus stop or in front of a fire hydrant; watch out, too, for street-cleaning signs. If you violate the law, you may be "booted" (immobilized) or towed away,

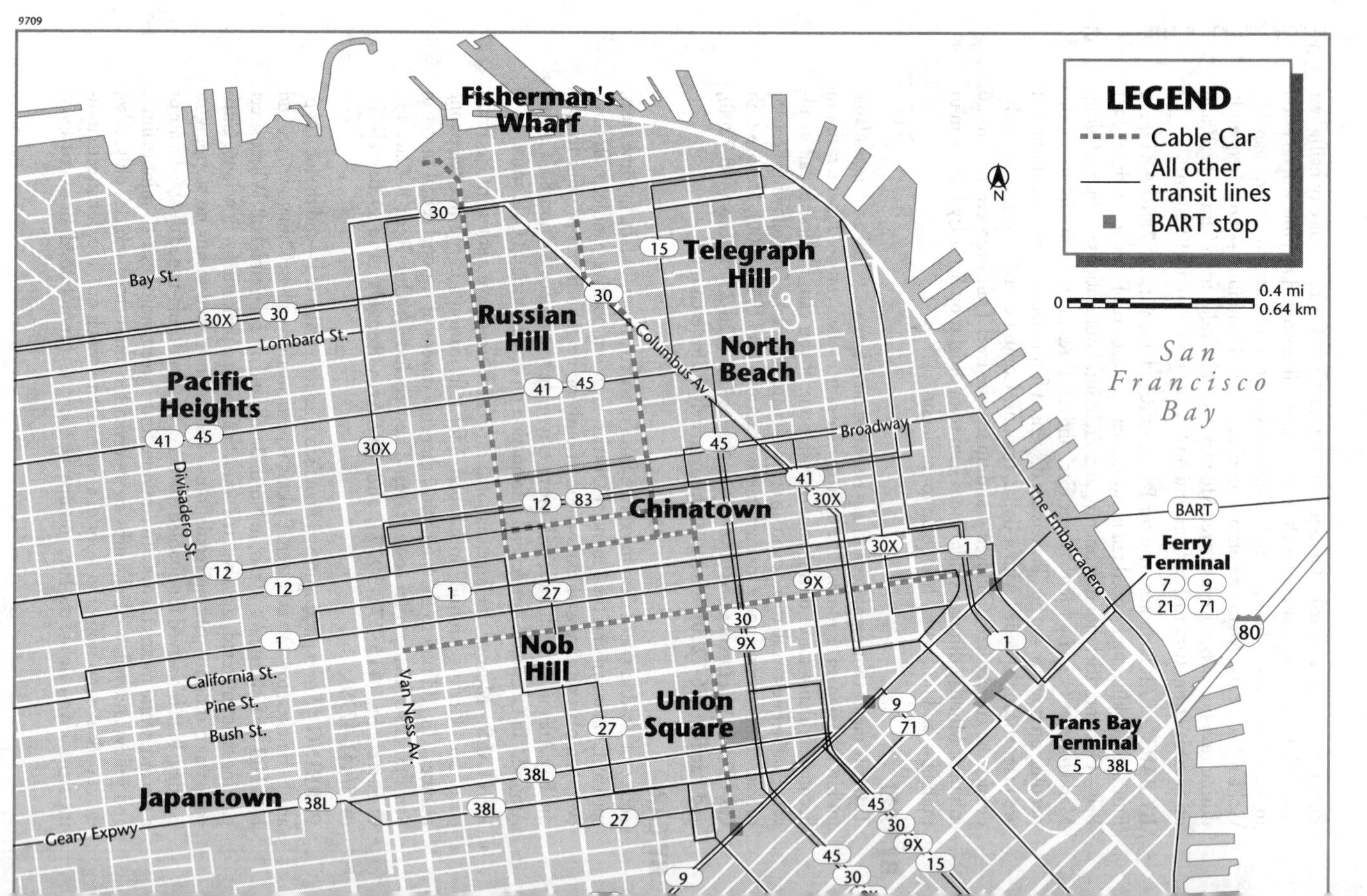
9709
LEGEND
Cable Car
All other transit lines
BART stop
N
0
0.4 mi
0.64 km
San Francisco Bay
Fisherman's Wharf
Telegraph Hill
Russian Hill
North Beach
Pacific Heights
Chinatown
Nob Hill
Union Square
Japantown
Ferry Terminal
Trans Bay Terminal
Bay St.
Lombard St.
Columbus Av.
Broadway
Divisadero St.
Van Ness Av.
California St.
Pine St.
Bush St.
Geary Expwy
The Embarcadero
BART
80

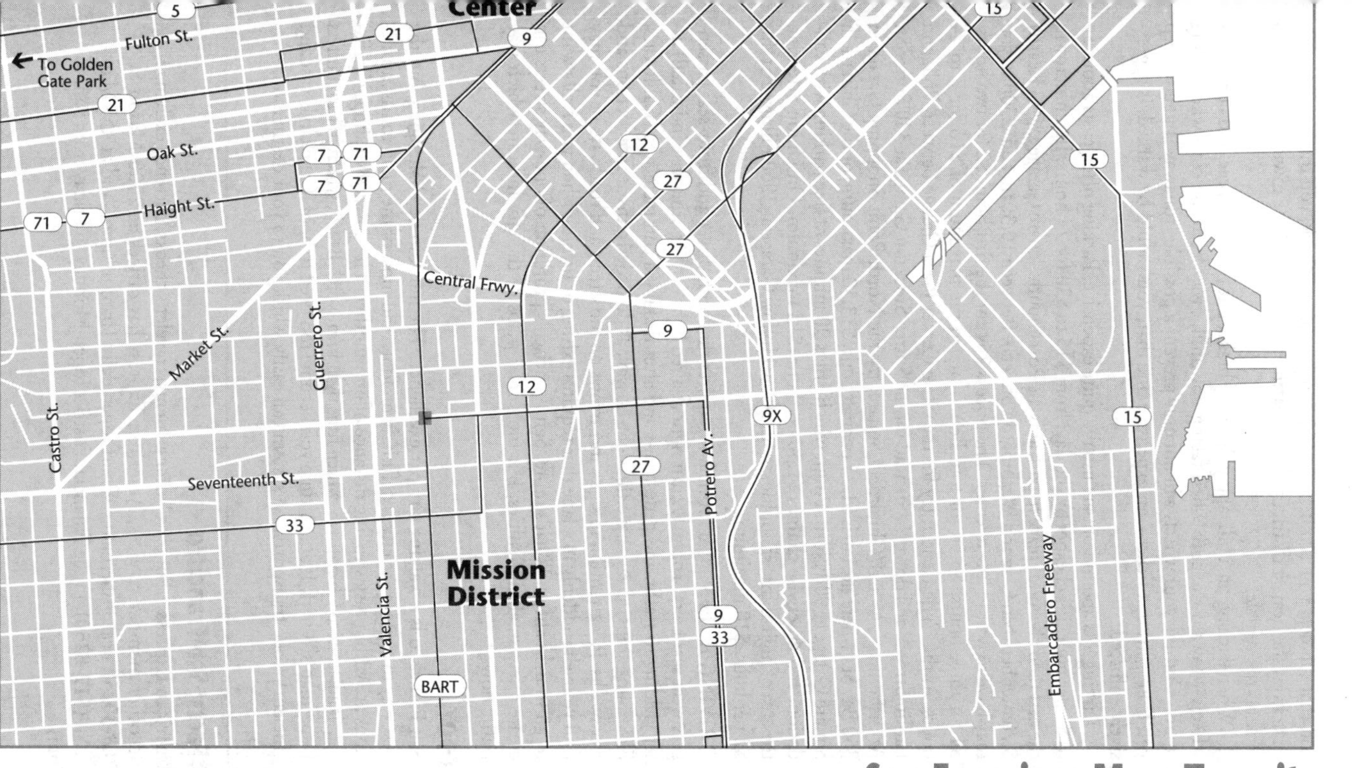
Center
Fulton St.
To Golden Gate Park
Oak St.
Haight St.
Castro St.
Market St.
Guerrero St.
Seventeenth St.
Valencia St.
Central Frwy.
Mission District
Potrero Av.
Embarcadero Freeway
BART
5
21
9
7
71
12
27
33
9X
15

and that can cost you as much as $100. To get your car back, you must obtain a release from the nearest district police department, then go to the towing company to pick up the vehicle.

When parking on a hill, apply the hand brake, put the car in gear, and **curb your wheels**—toward the curb when facing downhill, away from the curb when facing uphill. Curbing your wheels will not only prevent a possible "runaway" but also keep you from getting a ticket—an expensive fine that, you should be warned, is aggressively enforced.

Parking lots abound but are usually quite expensive. Parking often costs about $4 to $5 per hour. It's cheaper by the day: from $15 to $20 for 24 hours. In Chinatown, the best (and cheapest) place to park at is the Portsmouth Square Garage at 733 Kearny St. (enter between Clay and Washington Streets). Between 10:30am and 2:30pm, you may have to wait in line to enter. The price is 75¢ for the first hour, $2 for two hours, $4 for three hours, $6.50 for four hours—up to the maximum of $16 for 7 to 24 hours. At the Civic Center, try for the Civic Center Plaza Garage between Polk and Larkin Streets, and downtown, head for the Sutter-Stockton Garage at 330 Sutter St. At Fisherman's Wharf/Ghirardelli Square, try the North Point Shopping Garage at 350 Bay St., where the tab is $1.25 per half hour, $13.50 maximum; or the Ghirardelli Square Garage at 900 North Point, which offers 90 minutes of free parking with validation, and otherwise charges $1.50 per hour, $15 maximum. On Union Street, in the area of high-traffic shopping, try the Cow Hollow Garage at 3060 Fillmore St. for $2 per hour, $10 maximum.

DRIVING RULES California law requires that both driver and front-seat passengers wear seat belts. You may turn right at a red light (unless otherwise indicated) after yielding to traffic and pedestrians and after making a complete stop. Cable cars, like sailing ships, always have the right-of-way, as do pedestrians at intersections and crosswalks. Pay attention to signs and arrows on the streets and roadways or you may find yourself suddenly in a lane that requires exiting or turning when you really want to go straight ahead. What's more, San Francisco's profusion of one-way streets can create a few small difficulties, but most road maps of the city indicate which way traffic flows.

ON FOOT

San Francisco is a walking city par excellence. The hills can be challenging, but the best way to explore the city is definitely on foot. And most of the main tourist attractions are within easy strolling distance of one another. The downtown shopping district is adjacent to Chinatown, which runs right into North Beach, which in turn buffets Fisherman's Wharf. If at any time you become too tired to hoof it, the city's vast and efficient public transportation system can easily whisk you to your destination.

Fast Facts: San Francisco

American Express For travel arrangements, traveler's checks, currency exchange, and other member services, American Express has offices at 2500 Mason St. (**788-3025**), near Fisherman's Wharf (open daily 10am to 6pm), and at 455 Market St. (**512-8250**), in the Financial District (open Monday to Friday from 9am to 5pm).

Area Code There are two area codes in the San Francisco Bay Area. The city of San Francisco and the entire peninsula is identified by the 415 area code. Oakland, Berkeley, and much of the East Bay uses the 510 area code. All phone numbers in this book assume San Francisco's 415 area code, unless otherwise noted.

Babysitters Hotels can often recommended a babysitter or child-care service. If yours can't, try *Temporary Tot Tending* (**355-7377,** or **871-5790** after 6pm), which offers child care by licensed teachers, by the hour or day, for children from 3 weeks to 12 years of age. It's open Monday through Friday from 6am to 7pm (weekend service is available only during convention times).

Barbers See "Hairdressers/Barbers," below.

Bookstores Chain bookstores can be found in almost every shopping center in the city, including B. Dalton at 2 Embarcadero Center (**982-4278**) and Brentano's at Ghirardelli Square (**474-8328**) and the San Francisco Shopping Center on Market and Fifth Streets (**543-0933**). See "San Francisco Savvy Shopping" for a complete list of the city's excellent specialty booksellers.

Business Hours Most banks are open Monday through Friday from 9am to 3pm, several staying open until 5pm or later at least one day a week. Most stores are open Monday through Saturday from 10am to 6pm and are closed on Sunday. But there are exceptions: Stores in Chinatown are generally open daily from 10am to 10pm; Ghirardelli Square and Pier 39 shops are open Monday through Thursday from 10am to 6pm and on Friday and Saturday from 10am to 9pm (later during the summer).

Hours in restaurants vary, but most serve lunch from about 11:30am to 3pm and dinner from 5:30 to 11pm. You can sometimes get served later on weekends. Nightclubs and bars are usually open daily until 2am, when they are legally bound to stop serving alcohol.

Cameras See "Photographic Needs," below.

Car Rentals See "Getting Around," earlier in this chapter.

Cleaners See "Laundry/Dry Cleaning," below.

Climate See "When to Go," in Chapter 2.

Currency and Exchange See "Fast Facts: For the Foreign Traveler" in Chapter 3.

Dentist In the event of an emergency, see your hotel concierge or contact the San Francisco Dental Society (**421-1435**) for 24-hour referral to a specialist. The San Francisco Dental Office, 132 The Embarcadero (**777-5115**), between Mission and Howard Streets, offers emergency service and comprehensive dental care on Monday and Friday from 8am to 4:30pm, and Tuesday through Thursday from 8:30am to 7pm.

Doctor In an emergency, call an ambulance by dialing **911** from any telephone; no coins are required. Saint Francis Memorial Hospital, 900 Hyde St., on Nob Hill (**353-6000**), provides urgent-care service 24 hours daily; no appointment is necessary. The hospital also operates a physician-referral service (**353-6566**).

Drugstores There are Walgreens Pharmacies all over town, including one at 135 Powell St. (**391-4433**) that's open Monday through Saturday from 8am to midnight and on Sunday from 9am to 9pm. The branch on Divisadero Street at Lombard (**931-6415**) is open 24 hours. Merrill's Drug Center, 805 Market St. (**781-1669**), is open Monday through Friday from 7am to 10pm and on Saturday and Sunday from 7:30am to 10pm. Both chains accept MasterCard and Visa.

Embassies and Consulates See "Fast Facts: For the Foreign Traveler," in Chapter 3.

Emergencies To reach the police, an ambulance, or the fire department, dial **911** from any telephone; no coins are needed. Emergency hotlines include the Poison Control Center (**476-6600**), Suicide Prevention (**221-1424**), and Rape Crisis (**647-7273**).

Eyeglasses For emergency replacement of lost or broken glasses, Lens Crafters, 685 Market St., at Third Street (**896-0680**), offers one-hour service. They're open Monday through Friday from 8am to 7pm, Saturday from 9am to 6pm, and Sunday from 9am to 5pm. Pearle Express, 720 Market St. (**677-9701**), offers similar services, selections, and prices. It's open Monday through Friday from 10am to 9pm, Saturday and Sunday 11am to 6pm. For top name-brand frames, visit Spectacles of Union Square, 177 Maiden Lane at Kearny Street (**781-8556**). It features one-hour service, in-stock contact lenses, and a full-time staff technician. It's open Monday through Saturday from 10am to 6pm.

Film See "Photographic Needs," below.

Hairdressers/Barbers In addition to haircutters in the top hotels, respected salons include the avant-garde Architects & Heroes, 207 Powell St., at O'Farrell Street (**391-8833**); the English coiffeur David Oliver, 3356 Sacramento St., at Presidio Avenue (**563-2044**); and the classic Vidal Sassoon, 130 Post St., at Grant Street (**397-5105**).

Holidays See "Fast Facts: For the Foreign Traveler," in Chapter 3.

Hospitals See "Doctor" above.

Information See "Tourist Information" under "Orientation," earlier in this chapter.

Laundry/Dry Cleaning Laundries abound; inquire at your hotel for the closest one. If you want to have some fun while you wash your clothes, visit Brain Wash, 1122 Folsom St., South of Market (**431-WASH**). It features dozens of washers and dryers, along with a cafe and bar and live music Tuesday through Thursday. It's open daily from 7:30am to 11pm. Dry cleaning is also available.

Libraries The main branch of the San Francisco Public Library (**557-4400**) is located in Civic Center Plaza, just north of Market Street, and houses some 1.2 million volumes. Call for hours and the location and hours of other branches.

Lost Property If you lose any personal property on the street, it's probably gone for good, but call the local police anyway (**553-0123**). If you lose something on a Muni cable car, bus, or Metro street car, call the lost-and-found office (**923-6168**).

Newspapers and Magazines The city's two main dailies are the *San Francisco Chronicle* and the *San Francisco Examiner;* both are widely distributed throughout the city. The two papers combine for a massive Sunday edition that includes a pink "Datebook" section, an excellent preview of the week's upcoming events. The free weeklies *San Francisco Bay Guardian* and *San Francisco Weekly*, competing news and listings tabloids, are indispensable for nightlife information; they are widely distributed through street corner dispensers and city cafes and restaurants.

Of the many free tourist-oriented publications, the most widely read are *Key* and *San Francisco Guide*. Both of these handbook-size weeklies include basic information and current events. They can be found in most hotels and in shops and restaurants in the major tourist areas.

Photographic Needs Brooks Cameras, 45 Kearny St., at Maiden Lane (**392-1900**), has a complete inventory of cameras and accessories. It also offers an authorized repair service and one-hour photo-finishing. It's open Monday through Friday from 8:30am to 6pm and on Saturday from 9:30am to 5:30pm.

Phone For emergencies, dial **911** from any phone; no coins are needed. For other matters, call **553-0123.**

Post Office There are dozens of post offices located all around the city. The closest office to Union Square is inside Macy's department store, 121 Stockton St. (**956-3570**). You can pick up mail addressed to you, and marked "General Delivery," (Poste Restante) at the Civic Center Post Office Box Unit, P.O. Box 429991, San Francisco, CA 94142-9991.

Radio About four dozen radio stations can be heard in San Francisco. On the AM dial, 740 (KCBS) and 810 (KGO) are the top picks for news, sports, talk, and information. The best music stations on the FM dial include KQED (88.5) for classical, KSAN (94.9) for country, and KRQR (97.3) and KFOG (104.5) for album-oriented rock; KBLX (102.9) and KUSF (90.3) play dance and alternative rock, respectively.

Religious Services San Francisco has houses of worship for all major faiths, including the following: First Friendship Institutional Baptist Church, 501 Steiner St. (**431-4775**); Buddha's Universal Church, 720 Washington St. (**982-6116**); Congregation Emanu-El (Jewish), 21 Lake St. (**751-2535**); Mission Dolores Basilica (Roman Catholic), 3321 16th St. (**621-8203**); Grace Cathedral (Episcopal), 1051 Taylor St. (**776-6611**); and New Liberation Presbyterian Church, 1100 Divisadero St. (**929-8881**).

Restrooms Stores rarely let customers use the restrooms, and many restaurants offer their facilities for customers only. But most malls have bathrooms, as do the ubiquitous fast-food restaurants. Many public beaches and large parks provide toilets, though in some places you have to pay, or tip, an attendant. If you have the time, look for one of the large hotels; most have well-stocked, clean restrooms in their lobbies.

Safety Innocent tourists are rarely the victims of violent crime. Still, few locals would recommend that you walk alone late at night. The Tenderloin, between Union Square and the Civic Center, is one of San Francisco's most infamous areas. Compared with similar areas in other cities, however, even this section of San Francisco is relatively tranquil. Other areas where you should be particularly alert are the Mission District, around 16th and Mission Streets; the Fillmore area, around lower Haight Street; and the SoMa area, south of Market Street. See "Earthquakes," in "Fast Facts: California," in Chapter 2, and "Health, Insurance & Other Concerns," in Chapter 2, for additional safety tips.

Shoe Repairs There are dozens of shoe- and leather-repair shops around the city. Check the San Francisco *Yellow Pages* for the location nearest you, or visit Jack's Shoe Service, 53 Sutter St., between Montgomery and Sansome Streets (**392-7336**). It's open Monday through Friday from 7:30am to 5:30pm.

Taxes An 8¼% sales tax is added on at the register for all goods and services purchased in San Francisco. In restaurants, a 7¼% tax will be tacked onto your bill. The city hotel tax is a whopping 11¼%. No additional airport tax is charged to international travelers.

Taxis See "Getting Around," earlier in this chapter.

Television In addition to the cable stations, available in most hotels, all the major networks and several independent stations are represented. They include Channel 2, KTVU (Fox network); Channel 4, KRON (NBC); Channel 5, KPIX (CBS); Channel 7, KGO (ABC); and Channel 9, KQED (PBS).

Transit Information The San Francisco Municipal Railway, better known as Muni, operates the city's cable cars, buses, and metro streetcars. Information is available 24 hours by calling **415/673-6864.**

Useful Telephone Numbers Tourist information (**391-2001**); highway conditions (**557-3755**); time (**767-8900**); KFOG Entertainment Line (**777-1045**); KJAZ Jazz Entertainment Line (**510/769-4818**); KKSF Bay Line, which covers movies, theaters, and lectures (**392-1037**); KMEL's Movie Phone Line (**777-FILM**); Grateful Dead Hotline (**457-6388**); Morrison Planetarium Sky Line (**750-7141**).

Weather Call **936-1212** to find out when the next fog bank is rolling in.

3 Accommodations

San Francisco is well known for its excellent accommodations—from deluxe hotels to modest family establishments. In terms of facilities, services, cleanliness, and courtesy, hotels here represent some of the best values in the world. In addition, the many hostelries appeal to a multiplicity of personalities and pocketbooks. There are over a dozen international luxury-class hotels—remarkable for a city with fewer than one million inhabitants. And a large number of historic buildings, both large and small, have been reconstituted, reworked, and refurbished (most of them successfully) into handsome new hotels. Many are very posh, exuding a sophisticated European elegance, beauty, and charm. Most of the hotels listed below are within easy walking distance of Union Square. This central area is close to both the city's major shops and the Financial District, so it's understandably popular with tourists and businesspeople alike.

Prices listed below do not include state and city taxes, which total a whopping 11¼%. Be aware that most hotels impose additional charges for parking (with in-and-out privileges, except where noted) and levy heavy surcharges for telephone use. Many have their own on-site health facilities. When they don't, an arrangement has often been made with a nearby club, allowing you to use the club's facilities on a per day basis. Charges usually run $8 to $15. Inquire about these extras before committing yourself.

Finally, even in the budget categories, all the following listings meet my pretty exacting standards of comfort and cleanliness.

There are so many hotels in San Francisco—in every price range—that few regularly fill to capacity. Even during the height of the tourist season, you can usually drive right into the city and find decent accommodations fairly quickly. But be careful. If you have your sights set on a particular hotel, if you have to have a Nob Hill view, or if you want to locate in an area where accommodations are not particularly plentiful, you should book your room in advance.

Bed and Breakfast International, P.O. Box 282910, San Francisco, CA 94128 (☎ **415/696-1690,** or toll free **800/872-4500;** fax 415/696-1699), specializes in unique accommodation arrangements in San Francisco and the entire Bay Area. The cost of these private B&Bs range from $60 to $150 per night, and there's a two-night minimum. Accommodations vary depending on price, and range from simple rooms in private homes to luxurious, full-service carriage houses, houseboats, and Victorian homes. I've been very impressed with the quality and consistency offered by this established company, which can help you with arrangements throughout California.

Hotel-operated toll-free telephone numbers can also help you with your search. These "800" numbers will save you time and money when you're inquiring about rates and availability. When available, toll-free numbers are listed below, under the heading of each hotel. Some of the larger hotel chains with properties in the San Francisco area, as well as toll-free numbers, include **Best Western** (**800/528-1234**), **Days Inn** (**800/325-2525**), **Holiday Inn** (**800/465-4329**), **Quality Inns** (**800/228-5151**), **Ramada Inns** (**800/272-6232**), and **TraveLodge** (**800/255-3050**).

To help you decide on the accommodations option that's best for you, I've classified the hotels below first by area and then by price, using the following guide:

Very Expensive—more than $160 per night
Expensive—between $120 and $159 per night
Moderate—between $80 and $119 per night
Budget—less than $80 per night

These categories reflect the price of an average double room during the tourist season. Read each of the entries carefully: Many hotels also offer rooms at rates above and below the price category that they have been assigned here.

The city's tourist season is loosely defined; it runs from about April through September. In general, hotel rates are rather inelastic; they don't vary much throughout the year. But recent economic sluggishness has seen a small rate reduction throughout the city, and bargains and special packages can be had. Ask about weekend discounts, corporate rates, and family plans.

Union Square

VERY EXPENSIVE

Campton Place Hotel, 340 Stockton St., San Francisco, CA 94108.

☎ **418/781-5555,** or toll free **800/428-3135.** Fax 415/955-5536. 117 rms, 10 suites. No-smoking rooms available. A/C MINIBAR TV TEL **Cable Car:** Powell-Hyde and Powell-Mason, one block away. **Bus:** 2, 3, 4, 30, or 45.

Rates: $185–$320 single or double; from $395 suite. AE, CB, DC, MC, V. **Parking:** $19.

This intimate hotel between Post and Sutter Streets offers all the luxury of its larger competitors. It occupies the early 20th-century buildings of the former Drake-Wiltshire

Abigail Hotel 55
Albion House Inn 12
Alexander Inn 49
ANA Hotel San Francisco 58
AYH Hostel at Union Square 43
Bed & Breakfast Inn 6
Bedford Hotel 32
Beresford Arms 33
Brady Acres 40
Campton Place Hotel 29
Cartwright Hotel 28
Chelsea Motor Inn 4
Cow Hollow Motor Inn 3
Donatello 37
Edward II Inn & Carriage House 2
Fairmont Hotel and Tower 15
The Fitzgerald 34
Four Seasons Clift 42
Galleria Park Hotel 31
Golden Gate Hotel 22
Grand Hyatt San Francisco on Union Square 30
Grant Plaza Hotel 25
Handlery Union Square Hotel 45
Hotel Beresford 27
Hotel Nikko 51
Hotel Savoy 41
Hotel Triton 24
Hotel Union Square 53
Hotel Vintage Court 23
Huntington Hotel 16
Hyatt Regency San Francisco 20
Inn at the Opera 11
Kensington Park Hotel 35
King George Hotel 38
Lombard Hotel 39
The Mansions 8
Mark Hopkins Inter-Continental 14
Miyako Hotel 10
Monticello Inn 52
Nob Hill Lambourne Spa 19
Pacific Bay Inn 47
Pensione International 33
Phoenix Inn 54
Pied a Terre 7
Prescott Hotel 36
Queen Anne Hotel 9
Raphael 43
Ritz-Carlton 18
San Francisco Hilton and Towers 50
San Francisco International Hostel 1
San Francisco Marriott 56
Shannon Court 48
Sheehan 26
Sheraton at Fisherman's Wharf 13
Sheraton Palace Hotel 57
Stouffer Stanford Court Hotel 17
Union Street Inn 5
Villa Florence 46
Westin St. Francis 44
White Swan Inn 21

MARINA
Chestnut St.
2 3 4
5
6
PACIFIC HEIGHTS
Divisadero St.
Scott St.
Pierce St.
Steiner St.
Fillmore St.
Webster St.
Buchanan St.
Laguna St.
Alta Plaza
7
Lafayette Park
8
Sacramento St.
California St.
Pine St.
Bush St.
9
10
Post St.
JAPANTOWN
Geary Expwy.
O'Farrell St.
WESTERN ADDITION
Octavia St.
McAllister St.
Grove St.
Hayes St.
Fell St.
Oak St.
Page St.
Haight St.
14th St.
15th St.
16th St.
9080

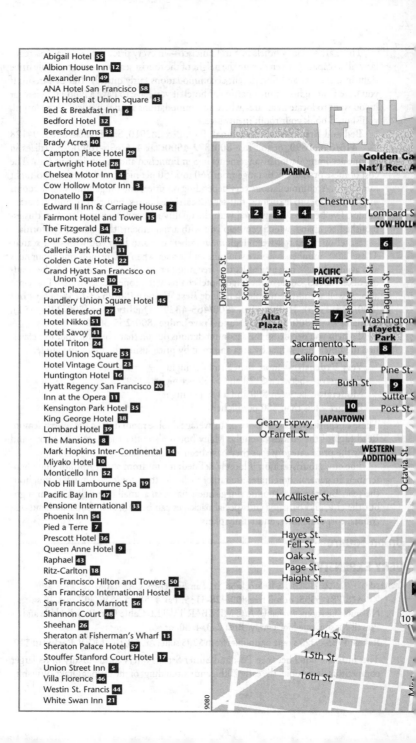

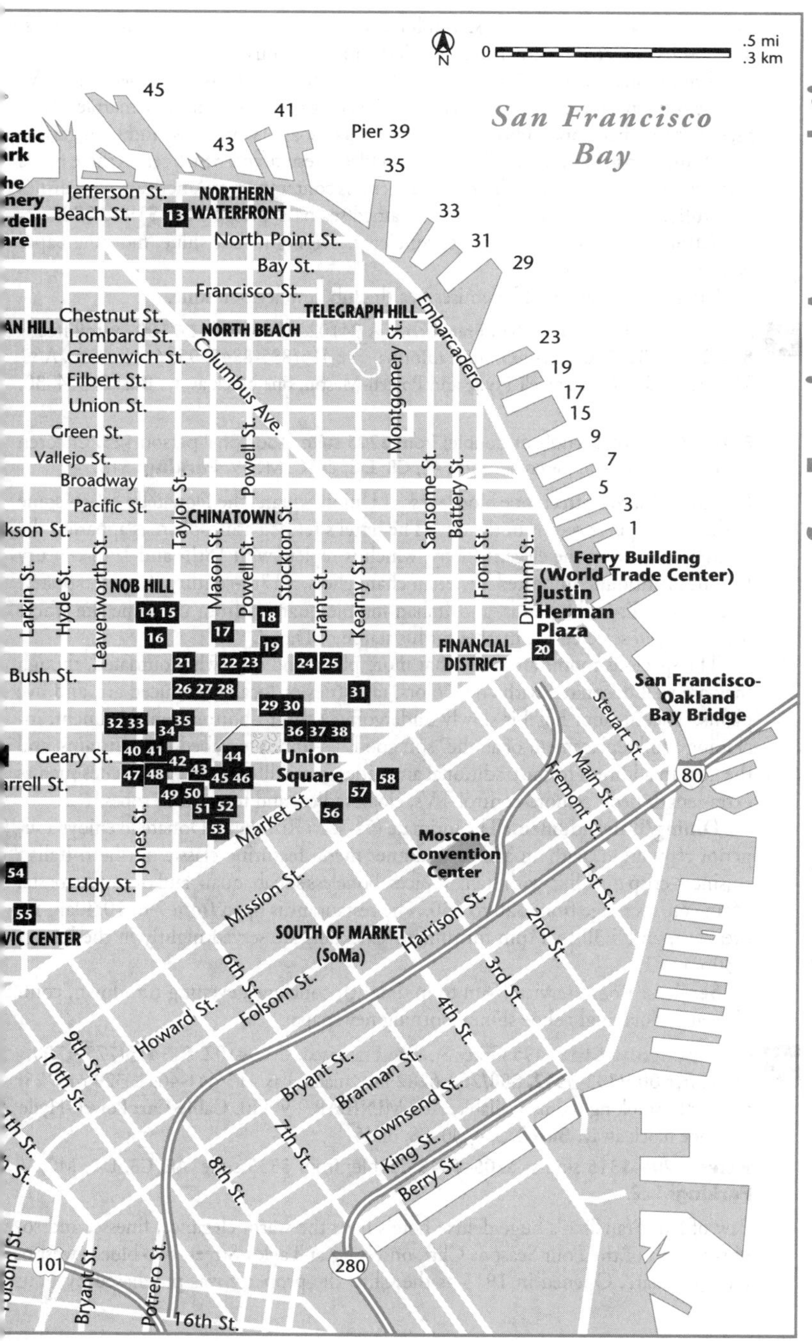
N
0
.5 mi
.3 km
San Francisco Bay
45
41
43
Pier 39
35
33
31
29
23
19
17
15
9
7
5
3
1
Jefferson St.
Beach St.
13
NORTHERN WATERFRONT
North Point St.
Bay St.
Francisco St.
TELEGRAPH HILL
NORTH BEACH
Embarcadero
Chestnut St.
Lombard St.
Greenwich St.
Filbert St.
Union St.
Green St.
Vallejo St.
Broadway
Pacific St.
Columbus Ave.
Powell St.
Montgomery St.
Sansome St.
Battery St.
Taylor St.
CHINATOWN
Stockton St.
Mason St.
Front St.
Drumm St.
Ferry Building (World Trade Center)
Justin Herman Plaza
Larkin St.
Hyde St.
Leavenworth St.
NOB HILL
Grant St.
Kearny St.
14 15
16
17
18
19
20
FINANCIAL DISTRICT
21
22 23
24 25
Bush St.
26 27 28
31
San Francisco-Oakland Bay Bridge
29 30
32 33
34 35
36 37 38
Steuart St.
Geary St.
40 41
42
44
Union Square
Main St.
Fremont St.
80
47 48
43
45 46
58
57
49 50
51 52
56
53
Market St.
Jones St.
Moscone Convention Center
54
Eddy St.
Mission St.
1st St.
55
Harrison St.
SOUTH OF MARKET (SoMa)
2nd St.
6th St.
Folsom St.
3rd St.
Howard St.
4th St.
9th St.
10th St.
Bryant St.
Brannan St.
Townsend St.
7th St.
King St.
8th St.
Berry St.
101
280
Bryant St.
Potrero St.
16th St.

Hotel, and was reopened after $25 million worth of renovations and improvements. The results are terrific—luxurious, modern, and gorgeous.

Guest rooms are beautifully appointed, with extra-large beds, concealed color TVs with remote control, and AM/FM clock radios. Elegant bathrooms have marble floors, brass fixtures, bathrobes, phone, and goodies like soaps, shampoos, and bath gels.

Dining/Entertainment: The Campton Place Restaurant, which serves three meals a day, is especially popular at lunch. The menu is contemporary American, with dishes like stuffed braised oxtail and saffron-steamed sea bass, priced from $19 to $30.

Services: 24-hour room service, concierge, overnight shoe shine, morning paper delivered to your door.

Facilities: Access to off-premises health club, jewelry boutique.

★ **Donatello,** 501 Post St., San Francisco, CA 94102. ☎ **415/441-7100,** or toll free **800/227-3184**, **800/792-9837** in California. Fax 415/885-8842. 95 rms, 7 suites. A/C TV TEL **Cable Car:** Powell-Hyde and Powell-Mason, one block away. **Bus:** 2, 3, 4, 30, or 45.

Rates: $175–$225 single or double; from $295 suite. Additional person $25. Children under 12 stay free in parents' room. AE, CB, DC, DISC, MC, V. **Parking:** $15.

Located at Mason Street, one block west of Union Square, the Donatello boasts some of the largest guest rooms in the city. The hotel's refined atmosphere is apparent the moment you enter the elegant lobby, which is replete with 18th- and 19th-century European antiques, imported Venetian chandeliers, a 17th-century Belgian tapestry, museum-quality lithographs, and Italian marble quarried from the same site where Michelangelo selected the marble for his statue of David.

The spacious rooms are somewhat more plain, and somewhat outdated, though they are well decorated with cool colors, tapestries or locally produced art, and live plants. The 14-floor hotel is slowly undergoing a top-to-bottom refurbishment, including a full replacement of all the "soft goods"—upholstery, bedding, curtains, and the like. In addition to the traditional amenities, you will find special touches such as extra-length beds, remote-control TVs, clock radios, and terry-cloth robes.

Dining/Entertainment: The intimate (54-seat) Ristorante Donatello enjoys a superior reputation, with an à la carte dinner menu featuring classic northern Italian cuisine—crisp duckling with Italian spices, boneless squab, quail, and of course, pasta. Main courses range from $20 to $30. The restaurant is open from 7 to 10:30am for breakfast, and 5:30 to 11pm for dinner. Cocktails are served nightly in the lounge 5:30pm to 1am.

Services: Room service (6am to midnight), concierge, evening turndown, complimentary overnight shoe shine, morning newspaper.

★ **Four Seasons Clift,** 495 Geary St., San Francisco, CA 94102. ☎ **415/775-4700,** or toll free **800/332-3442, 800/268-6282** in Canada. Fax 415/441-4621. 329 rms, 25 suites. No-smoking rooms available. A/C MINIBAR TV TEL **Cable Car:** Powell-Hyde line, one block away. **Bus:** 2, 3, 4, 30, 38, or 45.

Rates: $205–$315 single; $205–$345 double; from $355 suite. AE, CB, DC, MC, V. **Parking:** $22.

Few of San Francisco's huge deluxe hotels have the warm elegance, finesse, and sophistication of the Four Seasons Clift, on Geary at Taylor Street, two blocks west of Union Square. Opened in 1915 as the Clift, the property was purchased by Four

Seasons in 1974 and was completely restored. Subsequent renovations have left the rooms tastefully and individually decorated with cool color schemes and plush furnishings. Today the hotel sets the city's standard for luxury accommodations, and claims an aristocratic clientele.

Guest rooms are spacious, with high ceilings, restored moldings and woodwork, fine Georgian reproductions, and marble bathrooms with everything from hairdryers to plush terry-cloth robes. Thoughtful extras include padded hangers, individual climate control, two-line telephone, shampoos and bath gels, and a scale in your dressing room.

The Very Important Kids program provides traveling families with baby blankets, teddy bears, Nintendo video games, children's-size robes, and other amenities to help children and their parents feel at home. The hotel also accepts pets.

Dining/Entertainment: The French Room offers breakfast, lunch, and dinner and specializes in seasonally appropriate California-French cuisine. Dinner might spotlight potato risotto with proscuitto, asparagus, and shaved parmesan, or medallion of venison with roasted pears and bacon. Main courses cost from $25 to $32. More health-conscious "spa-style" meals (like Pinot noir poached salmon) are also always available. The hotel's Redwood Room, a true art-deco beauty, is one of San Francisco's poshest piano bars. Its gorgeous redwood interior was built from a single 2,000-year-old tree. The Lobby Lounge serves cocktails daily and a traditional English tea Monday through Saturday.

Services: 24-hour room service, concierge, twice-daily maid service, overnight laundry and shoe shine, evening turndown, complimentary in-room fax and computers.

Facilities: Business center, gift shop; small exercise room with free weights, stair machines, and stationary bicycles.

Hotel Nikko, 222 Mason St., San Francisco, CA 94102. ☎ **415/394-1111,** or toll free **800/645-5687.** Fax 415/421-0455. 500 rms, 22 suites. A/C MINIBAR TV TEL

Rates: $185–$275 single; $215–$305 double; from $375 suite. AE, CB, DC, MC, V. **Parking:** $23.

Top-of-the-line business standards make the Hotel Nikko a reliable choice in the Union Square area. Most rooms have king-size beds and fantastic floor-to-ceiling windows that overshadow the rooms' nondescript wall art. Cotton upholstery on room furnishings is upgraded to silk on the Concierge Level, where guests also get continental breakfast and evening cocktails. Every room features voice-mail telephones, computer modem lines, and pay-for-view movies. Particularly large marble bathrooms feature

Frommer's Smart Traveler: Hotels

1. A hotel room is a perishable commodity; if it's not sold, the revenue is lost forever. Always ask if the hotel has a lower rate, and make it clear that you're shopping around.
2. For the best rates, seek out business-oriented hotels on weekends and in the summer, and tourist-oriented B&Bs during the off-season.
3. Ask about summer discounts, corporate rates, and special packages. Most hotel reservation offices don't tell you about promotional rates unless you ask.
4. Always inquire about telephone and parking charges. In San Francisco it could add $25 per night for your car and $1 per local call.

separate showers and baths, and are outfitted with hairdryers and (sometimes) duel sinks.

At $975 per night, the Nikko's Tokyo-priced Japanese-style suites are not cheap. But they offer a unique indulgence that's not easily replicated in this country. In addition to a Western style sitting room, Japanese suites include a traditional tatami room, complete with a well for performing the tea ceremony, and a small rock garden overlooking all of San Francisco. Silk-covered futons are unrolled each night.

The Nikko is one of the few hotels in San Francisco to have its own swimming pool, and the entire property is accessible to wheelchair-bound guests.

Dining/Entertainment: The bistro-style Cafe 222 serves California cuisine enlivened with Japanese spices. A new lobby-level sushi bar has all the favorites, but is open for lunch only.

Services: 24-hour room service, twice-daily maid service, massage, weight training, business center, concierge.

Facilities: Swimming pool, fitness center, sauna, hot tub, tanning booth, Japanese soaking tubs, gift shop.

San Francisco Hilton and Towers, 333 O'Farrell St., San Francisco, CA 94142. ☎ **415/771-1400,** or toll free **800/445-8667.** Fax 415/771-6807. 1,900 rms, 180 suites. No-smoking rooms available. A/C MINIBAR TV TEL **Cable Car:** Powell-Hyde line, one block away. **Bus:** 2, 3, 4, 30, 38, or 45.

Rates: $175–$240 single; $200–$265 double; from $300 suite. Children of any age stay free in parents' room. AE, CB, DC, DISC, MC, V. **Parking:** $22.

One of the largest hotels on the West Coast is this conveniently situated, first-class hotel on O'Farrell at Mason Street. The San Francisco Hilton is a city within a city, composed of three connecting buildings: the original 19-story main building, a 46-story tower topped by a panoramic restaurant, and a new, 23-story landmark with an additional 386 luxurious rooms and suites. This is a grand-scale group hotel, with plenty of bus and business traffic.

After you get past the sweeping grand lobby entrance, you'll find well-proportioned guest rooms competently furnished in typical Hilton style. If you can tear yourself away from the memorable floor-to-ceiling view, you'll find a color TV with first-run movies, minibar, radio, and a marble bathroom. There are 40 rooms located poolside.

Dining/Entertainment: Cityscape, on the 46th floor, serves classic Californian cuisine in a breathtaking setting. The magnificent 360-degree view encompasses both the Golden Gate Bridge and the Bay Bridge, as well as Sausalito, Telegraph Hill, and the East Bay; the retractable skylight exposes the night sky in all its grandeur. Kiku of Tokyo presents authentic Japanese cuisine. The Mason Street Deli serves breakfast and lunch, and Intermezzo, serves Italian-style food to go.

An elegant sidewalk Café on the Square, provides a lovely spot for spectators to eye the passing parade and the promenade of hotel shops.

Services: Room service (available from 6am to midnight), concierge, car rental, tour desk, laundry, shoe shine.

Facilities: Swimming pool, health club, rooms equipped for the handicapped, shopping arcade.

Westin St. Francis, 335 Powell St., San Francisco, CA 94102. ☎ **415/397-7000,** or toll free **800/228-3000.** Fax 415/774-0124. 1,200 rms, 83 suites. No-smoking rooms available. A/C MINIBAR TV TEL **Cable Car:** Powell-Hyde and Powell-Mason, direct stop. **Bus:** 2, 3, 4, 30, 45, or 76.

Rates: Main building $150–$195 single; $180–$225 double; from $300 suite. Tower $205–$230 single; $235–$260 double; from $425 suite. Extra person $30. AE, CB, DC, MC, V. **Parking:** $20.

Located in the heart of the city—on verdant Union Square between Geary and Post Streets—is the elegant grande dame of San Francisco hotels. The splendid rosewood-marble-columned lobby extends back to the carpeted foyer of the 32-story tower building, and it's here that the main desk and an open cocktail area are located.

Resembling exotic space capsules, the five outside elevators whisk guests to their rooms. The rooms are attractively furnished and supplied with many amenities, such as color TVs with in-room movies and direct-dial phones. The older rooms of the main building vary in size and have more charm than the newer and more expensive tower rooms. But the tower is remarkable for its great views of the city, once you rise above the 18th floor.

Dining/Entertainment: High above the city, on the tower's top floor, are the award-winning Victor's, featuring excellent Californian-cuisine dinners, and the adjoining Oz, one of the city's hottest dance clubs. Additional dining facilities include the Dutch Kitchen breakfast and lunch restaurant, open from 6am to 11:30am. Fresh seafood, steaks, and other grilled items are offered at the handsome, oak-paneled St. Francis Grill, open daily for dinner. Soup-and-sandwich fare is served daily at the hotel's Dewey's Bar. The Compass Rose is open daily for lunch and high tea, and is the perfect spot for an afternoon drink in a plush, nostalgic setting.

Services: 24-hour room service, babysitting referral, laundry, car rental, tour desk.

Facilities: Health club with life cycles and rowing machines, business center, accommodations for the handicapped, barber/beauty salon, gift shop.

EXPENSIVE

Grand Hyatt San Francisco on Union Square, 345 Stockton St., San Francisco, CA 94108. ☎ **415/398-1234,** or toll free **800/233-1234.** Fax 415/391-1780. 693 rms, 30 suites. No-smoking rooms available. A/C MINIBAR TV TEL **Cable Car:** Powell-Hyde line, one block away. **Bus:** 2, 3, 4, 30, 38, or 45.

Rates: $149–$220 basic single or double; $185–$245 Regency rooms; from $350 suite. AE, CB, DC, MC, V. **Parking:** $22.

One of the most enjoyable hotels in town is the conveniently located Grand Hyatt, between Post and Sutter Streets. Although not as startlingly innovative as the Hyatt Regency San Francisco (see below), this is a handsome, modern hotel with an elegant old-world courtyard graced by Ruth Asawa's bronze fountain sculpture.

The rooms, renovated in 1990 at a cost of $20 million, are ultramodern, with mirrored walls, beige rugs, and gold, brown, or royal-blue drapes and spreads. Accommodations include such amenities as TV in both the bedroom and the bath, first-run movies, and a phone with computer-connection capability. Regency rooms are larger and come with continental breakfast and evening hors d'oeuvres.

Dining/Entertainment: The hotel's signature Plaza Restaurant has floor-to-ceiling windows overlooking Union Square. Breakfast, lunch, and dinner are served in a garden setting, created by bamboo furnishings, a fountain, potted palms, and a stained-glass skylight dome. Napper's Deli, an indoor/outdoor bistro, serves custom-cut sandwiches, seasonal salads, soups, and desserts. Continental breakfasts are served here on weekends beginning at 8:30am. Club 36, located on the 36th floor, serves cocktails with live jazz nightly.

Services: 24-hour room service, concierge, free weekday morning towncar service to the Financial District, car-rental desk, tour desk.

Facilities: Fitness center, fully equipped business center.

Hotel Triton, 342 Grant Ave., San Francisco, CA 94108. ☎ **415/394-0500,** or toll free **800/433-6611.** Fax 415/394-0555. 140 rms, 7 suites. No-smoking rooms available. A/C MINIBAR TV TEL **Cable Car:** Powell-Hyde and Powell-Mason, three blocks away.

Rates: $169 single or double; $259 suite. AE, DC, DISC, MC, V. **Parking:** $20.

One of San Francisco's most stylish hotels is located directly across from Chinatown's ornate dragon-gate entrance, at Bush Street. The hotel's plain-brick exterior belies a whimsical interior that's designed to make you smile. Playful murals, original art, and Daliesque custom-made furniture make the lobby look more like a contemporary museum. Sapphire theater curtains, colorful original art, and mahogany furniture, designed with geometric shapes, turn guest rooms into veritable artist showcases. It's all done with excellent crafting and terrific style. Complimentary wine is served each evening in the hotel lobby.

Dining/Entertainment: Café Aioli, an Italian restaurant and bar, serves breakfast, lunch, and dinner. Home-cured prosciutto and veal carpaccio top the appetizers, while wild-boar ravioli, snapper ratatouille, and braised rabbit are some of the more unusual entree selections. None tops $16.

Services: Room service, same-day laundry, complimentary morning limousine to the South of Market Design District.

Prescott Hotel, 545 Post St., San Francisco, CA 94102. ☎ **415/563-0303,** or toll free **800/283-7322.** Fax 415/563-6831. 167 rms, 36 suites. No-smoking rooms available. A/C MINIBAR TV TEL **Cable Car:** Powell-Hyde line, one block away. **Bus:** 2, 3, 4, 30, 38, or 45.

Rates: $165 standard single or double; $185 concierge-level single or double; from $235 suite. AE, CB, DC, MC, V. **Parking:** $15.

The Prescott, between Mason and Taylor Streets, is just one block from Union Square and the Powell Street cable car. It opened in 1989 following a complete renovation of the old Hotel Cecil, built in 1917. This prestigious medium-size, first-class hotel offers elegance and gracious personal service. Each room has a simple neoclassical design and custom-made cherry furnishings—beds with columned headboards, bow-front armoires, and faux-marble bedside lamps. Bedspreads and draperies are beautifully done in hunter green, cerise, purple, and saffron. Amenities include a phone with call waiting and an extra-long cord, a color TV with remote control and complimentary HBO, and a digital clock radio, all in a thoroughly soundproofed environment. Bathrooms are black and taupe in color scheme and are supplied with terry-cloth robes and hairdryers.

Concierge-level rooms include plusher furnishings, free continental breakfast, evening cocktails, and exercise bicycles or rowing machines brought to your room on request. Suites have an adjoining parlor with a comfortable overstuffed sofa, upholstered chairs, a coffee table, and an oval dining/desk table; other pleasant touches include a VCR and a whirlpool bathtub.

Dining/Entertainment: Chef Wolfgang Puck's popular Postrio restaurant adjoins the Prescott. Make reservations when you book your room. The restaurant serves contemporary San Franciscan cuisine. (See "San Francisco Dining," later in this chapter, for complete information.)

Services: Complimentary coffee and tea each morning, wine and hors d'oeuvres every evening in the library, limousine service weekday mornings to the Financial District, concierge, evening turndown, same-day valet/laundry service, overnight shoe shine, room service from the Postrio.

Facilities: Access to off-premises health club, including swimming pool, free weights, and sauna.

San Francisco Marriott, 55 Fourth St., San Francisco, CA 94103. ☎ **415/896-1600,** or toll free **800/228-9290.** Fax 415/442-0141. 1,500 rms, 134 suites. No-smoking rooms available. A/C MINIBAR TV TEL **Cable Car:** Powell-Hyde and Powell-Mason, one block away. **Bus:** 7, 8, or 71.

Rates: $169–$245 standard single or double; $195–$265 concierge-level single or double; from $325 suite. AE, CB, DC, MC, V. **Parking:** $24.

The Marriott has variously been referred to as a giant jukebox, a 40-story robot, and the world's biggest parking meter. Architectural criticisms aside, it is the only hotel that can lay claim to opening its doors during the week of the October 1989 quake. The Marriott is one block from the Moscone Convention Center and the Powell Street cable-car turnaround and a short stroll to Nordstrom department store. It's also one of the largest buildings in San Francisco; enter from Fourth Street, between Market and Mission Streets, to avoid a long, long trek to the registration area.

Amenities include remote-control color TVs and plush baths. Rooms on the concierge level are more spacious and provide a lengthy list of complimentary services, including continental breakfast, afternoon snacks and beverages, evening hors d'oeuvres and canapes, and an open honor bar.

Dining/Entertainment: The Kinoko is a Japanese teppanyaki restaurant and sushi bar. The Garden Terrace, facing the hotel's central fountain, has a breakfast bar and two buffets that prepare made-to-order omelets, and it serves a varied lunch and dinner menu. As for lounge areas, the Atrium Lounge is on the atrium level, the View Lounge is on the 39th floor and has a truly spectacular view of the bay and Golden Gate Bridge (assuming there's no fog) as well as live entertainment, and Treats serves refreshments in the Golden Gate Foyer.

Services: Room service, concierge, car-rental and airline desk, tour desk.

Facilities: Indoor pool and health club, business center, gift shop.

White Swan Inn, 845 Bush St., San Francisco, CA 94108. ☎ **415/775-1755.** Fax 415/775-5717. 26 rms, 1 suite. MINIBAR TV TEL **Cable Car:** Powell-Hyde and Powell-Mason, one block away. **Bus:** 1, 2, 3, 4, 27, or 45.

Rates (including breakfast): $145–$160 double; $260 suite. Extra person $15. AE, MC, V. **Parking:** $15.

Just 2 1/2 blocks from Union Square, 2 blocks from Nob Hill, and 1 1/2 blocks from the Powell Street cable cars, the White Swan Inn enjoys an excellent location between Taylor and Mason Streets. This tasteful hotel was constructed in the early 1900s and renovated by Four Sisters Inns. The handsome reception area features a cheery fireplace, a carousel horse, and an antique oak breakfront cabinet. With the charm and serenity of an English garden inn, the White Swan still offers service and style to fit the needs of the most discriminating traveler. It's a delightful, romantic discovery.

Each spacious room comes with its own teddy-bear companion. Soft English wallpaper and floral-print bedspreads add to the feeling of warmth and comfort, as do the working fireplaces, fluffy oversize towels, color TVs, and bedside phones.

Dining/Entertainment: Each morning a generous breakfast is served in a lovely common room just off a tiny garden. Afternoon tea is also served, with hors d'oeuvres, sherry, wine, and home-baked pastries. You can have your sherry in front of the fireplace while you browse through the books in the library.

Services: Concierge, laundry, evening turndown, morning newspaper, overnight shoe shine.

Facilities: Off-premises health club.

MODERATE

Bedford Hotel, 761 Post St., San Francisco, CA 94109. ☎ **415/673-6040,** or toll free **800/227-5642.** Fax 415/563-6739. 144 rms, 7 suites. No-smoking rooms available. MINIBAR TV TEL **Bus:** 2, 3, 4, or 27.

Rates: $109–$119 single or double, from $175 suite. AE, CB, DC, MC, V. **Parking:** $15.

A charming European-style hotel in a quiet but convenient location three blocks from Union Square, the Bedford is on the southwest slope of Nob Hill between Leavenworth and Jones Streets. Each room is well furnished with king-size, queen-size, or two double beds, VCR, AM/FM clock radio, writing desk, and armchair. Color schemes are a cheerful pale blue, peach, or yellow, and many rooms have remarkable views of the city. The Bedford's staff is enthusiastic, attentive, and very professional.

The hotel's Wedgwood Lounge is a small bar opposite the registration desk. Café Bedford, an elegant, award-winning gourmet eatery located behind the lobby, is under separate management. Services include room service, valet parking, and complimentary wine in the lobby each evening from 5 to 6pm. There's a video library, and free morning limousine service to the Financial District.

Beresford Arms, 701 Post St., San Francisco, CA 94109. ☎ **415/673-2600,** or toll free **800/533-6533.** Fax 415/474-0449. 92 rms, 52 suites. MINIBAR TEL TV **Cable Car:** Powell-Hyde line three blocks away. **Bus:** 2, 3, 4, 27, or 38.

Rates: $75 single, $85 double, $105 Jacuzzi suite, $135 parlor suite. Extra person $10. Children under 12 stay free in parents' room. Senior citizen discount available. AE, CB, DC, DISC, MC, V. **Parking:** $15 valet.

Under the same management as the Hotel Beresford (see below), this hostelry at Jones Street has a friendly, helpful staff. All units are equipped with color TV, direct-dial phone, and complete bath. A recent renovation reduced the number of guest rooms and added Jacuzzis to some of the suites, which also have kitchen units or wet bars. Complimentary coffee, tea, and pastries are served in the lobby each morning, and a complimentary tea and wine social is held each afternoon in the lobby.

Cartwright Hotel, 524 Sutter St., San Francisco, CA 94102. ☎ **415/421-2865,** or toll free **800/227-3844.** Fax 415/421-2865. 170 rms, 5 suites. No-smoking rooms available. TV TEL **Cable Car:** Powell-Hyde and Powell-Mason, direct stop. **Bus:** 2, 3, 4, 30, or 45.

Rates: $119 single; $129 double or twin; $160–$170, family suite sleeping four. AE, CB, DC, DISC, MC, V. **Parking:** $12.

A charming and distinctly cozy establishment on Sutter at Powell Street, the recently renovated Cartwright is remarkably quiet despite its convenient location near one of the busiest downtown corners. The hotel takes great pride in its reputation for comfort, cleanliness, and efficiency. And it's well earned—reflected in every nook and cranny, from the small, well-groomed lobby to the rooms furnished with antiques and brightened with fresh flowers. Each unit is decorated in a unique, charming style and has direct-dial phone and color TV. Although water pressure could be better, baths feature shower massages, thick fluffy towels, and terry-cloth robes. Accommodations with air conditioning or refrigerator are available on request at no additional charge. Special attention is paid to the guests' comfort. In addition to turndown service, there are such extras as irons, hairdryers, and large reading pillows.

Guests have access to a nearby health club. Complimentary tea and cakes are served in a wonderful library adjacent to the lobby from 4 to 6pm. Teddy's restaurant, located behind the lobby, serves good country breakfasts, including waffles, pancakes, and omelets.

The Fitzgerald, 620 Post St., San Francisco, CA 94109. ☎ **415/775-8100,** or toll free **800/334-6835.** Fax 415/775-1278. 42 rms, 5 suites. TEL TV **Bus:** 2, 3, 4, or 27.

Rates (including continental breakfast): $59–$69 single; $69–$99 double; from $95 suite. Extra person $10. Lower rates in the off-season. AE, DISC, MC, V. **Parking:** $15.

One of Union Square's newest moderately priced hotels, The Fitzgerald is also one the best. The building has been miraculously transformed from a dilapidated welfare hotel into one that's both stylish and modern. A clean, plush little lobby gives way to immaculately maintained guest rooms outfitted with new plumbing and decorations that include bright bedspreads and carpets with overly busy designs. Smallish rooms and positively tiny closets are a drawback, but they are fully functional and well-maintained. For space, the rooms with queen-size beds are particularly recommendable. Suites, some of which are located on no-smoking floors, include an additional sitting room furnished with a fold-out couch. The hotel's telephones feature private voice mail service.

Breakfasts include home-baked breads, scones, muffins, juice, tea, and coffee. An off-premises swimming pool, located about two blocks away, is available free for guests' use. All and all a good value.

Frommer's Cool for Kids: Hotels

Donatello (see p. 76) Having some of the biggest rooms in the city means there's plenty of space for romping. The Donatello is not cheap, but children under 12 stay free in their parents' room.

Four Seasons Clift (see p. 76) The hotel's Very Important Kids (VIK) program provides traveling families with baby blankets, teddy bear, Nintendo video games, children-size robes, and other amenities to help kids feel as pampered as their parents.

The Mansions (see p. 97) Furnished with theatrical originality, this hotel will appeal to childrens' creative fantasies. On-site entertainment includes nightly performances by virtuoso pianist Claudia the Ghost, who is sometimes accompanied by owner Bob Pritikin on the saw.

Handlery Union Square Hotel, 351 Geary St., San Francisco, CA 94102. ☎ **415/781-7800,** or toll free **800/843-4343.** Fax 415/781-0269. 375 rms, 20 suites. TV TEL **Cable Car:** Powell-Hyde and Powell-Mason line, one block away. **Bus:** 2, 3, 4, 30, 38, or 45.

Rates: $120–$130 basic single or double; club section, $145 single, $155 double; from $220 suites. Extra person $10. AE, CB, DC, MC, V. **Parking:** $12.50.

This establishment, between Mason and Powell Streets, is the attractive offspring of the Handlery Motor Inn and the Hotel Stewart, following a $10-million renovation and merger completed in 1989. The shopping, theater, and financial districts are easily accessible from this location, which is half a block from Union Square.

Every room contains a handy safe; 100 rooms have minibars. The club section offers services that one usually expects only from a larger hotel. The rooms are truly large and luxurious, with such frills as electric shoe polishers, coffeemakers, two phones, dressing rooms with makeup mirrors, custom bathroom amenities, scales, robes, and hairdryers. The club section also provides a complimentary morning newspaper and turndown service. Hotel services include a multilingual concierge staff, tour desk, same-day laundry, and babysitting. Complimentary coffee and tea are served each morning. The hotel also has a heated outdoor swimming pool and sauna, barbershop, gift shop, candy store, and art gallery.

Hotel Beresford, 635 Sutter St., San Francisco, CA 94102. ☎ **415/673-9900,** or toll free **800/533-6533.** Fax 415/474-0449. 114 rms. MINIBAR TV TEL **Cable Car:** Powell-Hyde line, one block away. **Bus:** 2, 3, 4, 30, 38, or 45.

Rates (including continental breakfast): $75 single; $85–$94 double. Extra person $5. Children under 12 stay free in parents' room. Senior citizen discounts available. AE, CB, DC, MC, V. **Parking:** $15.

A small, lively, and friendly hostelry, the Hotel Beresford, near Mason Street, is a good, moderately priced choice near Union Square.

There is a writing parlor off the lobby, with wicker furniture, desks, a color TV, and a portrait of Lord Beresford. The rooms, which are priced according to occupancy rates, have color-coordinated bedspreads, sparkling white drapes, wall-to-wall carpeting, a refrigerator, a direct-dial telephone, and color TV. There's an Olympic-sized swimming pool and health facilities just across the street.

The White Horse restaurant, an attractive replica of an old English pub, serves a complimentary continental breakfast, as well as lunch and dinner.

Hotel Savoy, 580 Geary St., San Francisco, CA 94102. ☎ **415/441-2700,** or toll free **800/227-4223.** Fax 415/441-2700. 83 rms, 13 suites. No-smoking rooms available. MINIBAR TV TEL **Bus:** 2, 3, 4, 27, or 38.

Rates (including continental breakfast): $119–$129 single or double; from $169 suite. AE, CB, DC, DISC, MC, V. **Parking:** $16.

Located between Taylor and Jones Streets, the Savoy likes to think of itself as a bit of provincial France in the middle of San Francisco. Completely renovated in 1990, the medium-size rooms are decorated with 18th-century, period-style furnishings and feature feather pillows, remote-control color TVs, and hairdryers. The little extras are here too: triple sheets, turndown service, full-length mirrors, and two-line telephones. Guests also enjoy concierge service and overnight shoe-shine services. Rates include complimentary late-afternoon sherry and tea, and continental breakfast, served in the Brasserie Savoy, a seafood restaurant complete with a raw bar.

Hotel Union Square, 114 Powell St., San Francisco, CA 94102. ☎ **415/397-3000,** or toll free **800/553-1900.** Fax 415/399-1874. 131 rms, 7 suites. No-smoking rooms available. MINIBAR TV TEL **Cable Car:** Powell-Hyde or Powell-Mason lines. **Muni Metro:** J, K, L, M, or N. **Bus:** 7, 8, or 71.

Rates: $99 single or double; from $129 suite. AE, CB, DC, DISC, MC, V. **Parking:** $16.

At the foot of Powell Street, fronting the cable-car turnaround, the Hotel Union Square is pleasant, friendly, and very well located. It also proudly claims its place in American literary history: In the 1920s, as the Golden West Hotel, it was an occasional stop for then–Pinkerton detective Dashiell Hammett, creator of Sam Spade.

The hotel has been renamed and considerably modernized since those days, but it retains its early charm. Its refurbished guest rooms feature art deco decor and soft floral-print bedspreads and curtains. Shampoos, conditioners, and soaps are supplied in the bathrooms. Complimentary coffee, tea, and croissants are served each morning. Weekday newspapers are available. The hotel's penthouse suites come complete with redwood decks and garden patios, and are especially nice during sunny weather.

The hotel has no restaurant, but there are dozens of eating establishments within a block or two of the front door.

Hotel Vintage Court, 650 Bush St., San Francisco, CA 94108. ☎ **415/392-4666,** or toll free **800/654-1100.** Fax 415/433-4065, ext. 137. 106 rms, 1 suite. No-smoking rooms available. A/C MINIBAR TV TEL **Cable Car:** Powell-Hyde or Powell-Mason lines, direct stop. **Bus:** 2, 3, 4, 30, 45, or 76.

Rates: $109–$149 single or double; $250 penthouse suite. AE, CB, DC, DISC, MC, V. **Parking:** $15.

This handsome European-style hotel, between Powell and Stockton Streets, is two blocks from Union Square and half a block from the cable car. Its relatively small size allows for excellent personal service, and it's so popular that you should make reservations at least two or three weeks in advance. Supremely comfortable sofas, a lobby fireplace, soft classical music, and the warm tones of the furnishings create an intimate, cozy feeling.

Grape clusters embossed on custom-made bedspreads and drapes are complemented by impressionistic prints of the wine country. Each room has a private refrigerator and minibar stocked daily, as well as the usual color TV and phone, and a well-lit writing desk. The deluxe two-room penthouse suite includes an original 1912 stained-glass skylight, wood-burning fireplace, whirlpool tub, a complete entertainment center, and magnificent views of the city.

The hotel's eatery, Masa's, serving traditional French fare, is one of the top restaurants in San Francisco (see "San Francisco Dining," below, for complete information). Complimentary continental breakfast is served daily, and a variety of California wines are poured free in the evening. Services include complimentary morning limousine service to the Financial District, tour desk, and car-rental service. There is also access to an off-premises health club.

Kensington Park Hotel, 450 Post St., San Francisco, CA 94102. ☎ **415/788-6400,** or toll free **800/553-1900.** Fax 415/399-9484. 86 rms, 1 suite. No-smoking rooms available. TV TEL **Cable Car:** Powell-Hyde or Powell-Mason lines, one block away.

Rates: $115 single or double; $350 suite. 50% discount for post-midnight check-in. Extra person $10. AE, CB, DC, MC, V. **Parking:** $16.

Very well maintained, this cozy choice two blocks from Union Square impresses with its cathedral-like lobby, complete with a hand-painted Gothic ceiling, crystal chandelier, and baby grand piano. Rooms do not disappoint either. Mahogany furnishings, highlighted with warm blue and rose accents, and brass-and-marble bathrooms, are comforts usually known only to more expensive hotels. Complimentary coffee and croissants are available on each floor every morning from 7 to 10am. Tea and sherry are served in the lobby each afternoon.

The hotel offers 50% off rack rates to guests who arrive after midnight. No advance reservations are accepted in connection with this late-night offer, and a one-night maximum applies. Check-out is noon.

Among the hotel's amenities are room service, concierge, same-day laundry service, and morning newspaper, complimentary morning limousine to the Financial District. Fax and secretarial services are available. In addition, there's access to an off-premises health club.

★ **King George Hotel,** 334 Mason St., San Francisco, CA 94102. ☎ **415/781-5050,** or toll free **800/288-6005.** Fax 415/391-6976. 139 rms, 2 suites. TV TEL **Cable Car:** Powell-Hyde or Powell-Mason lines, one block away. **Bus:** 2, 3, 4, 30, 38, or 45.

Rates: $107 single; $117 double; $185 suite. Special value season packages available. AE, CB, DC, DISC, MC, V. **Parking:** $15.50.

Full of charm and personality, this particularly beautiful European-style restoration is located just one block from Union Square. The hotel is entered through an elegant lobby with an air of quiet sophistication and a fine collection of European period prints. The rooms have been completely renovated in subtle pastel tones and are equipped with color TVs, direct-dial phones, and private baths. Laundry, valet, and 24-hour room service are available.

On the mezzanine above the lobby, the Bread & Honey Tearoom offers continental breakfast daily from 7 to 10am. Monday through Saturday from 3 to 6:30pm the hotel offers a proper high tea, complete with scones, trifle, tea sandwiches, and assorted pastries. The hotel also has a comfortable cocktail lounge and piano bar. Services include laundry, concierge, and a business center. Guests have access to an off-premises health club, which includes free weights, bikes, and a swimming pool.

Monticello Inn, 127 Ellis St., San Francisco, CA 94102. ☎ **415/392-8800,** or toll free **800/669-7777.** Fax 415/398-2650. 91 rms, 36 suites. No-smoking rooms available. A/C MINIBAR TV TEL **Cable Car:** Powell-Hyde or Powell-Mason, direct stop. **Muni Metro:** J, K, L, M, or N lines. **Bus:** 7, 8, and 71.

Rates (including continental breakfast): $120 single, $135 double, $145–$180 suite. AE, CB, DC, DISC, MC, V. **Parking:** $15 weekdays, $25 weekends.

Opened in 1987, between Cyril Magnin and Powell Streets, the Monticello is a first-rate addition to the neighborhood. Colonial American charm is the theme, and Thomas Jefferson, whose bust is displayed in the lobby, would have been pleased with the inn's simplicity and elegance. The spacious lobby features early American reproductions, a Federal-period desk, a stately grandfather clock, fresh floral displays, and a cozy library where you can enjoy a complimentary evening glass of wine by the fireplace. Should you need information, directions, or reservations, the friendly staff is very helpful.

Each soundproof room is decorated in country-colonial style, and features elegant canopied beds, digital clock radios, cable TV, and computer hookups. The hotel's restaurant, the Corona Bar & Grill, features southwestern cuisine; it's located next door. The hotel offers complimentary limousine service to the Financial District, same-day laundry and valet service, a business center, and a tour desk.

The Raphael, 386 Geary St., San Francisco, CA 94102. ☎ **415/986-2000,** or toll free **800/821-5343.** Fax 415/397-2447. 152 rms, 2 suites. No-smoking rooms available. A/C TV TEL **Cable Car:** Powell-Hyde or Powell-Mason lines, one block away. **Bus:** 2, 3, 4, 30, 38, or 45.

Rates: $99–$134 single; $109–$134 double; $145–$195 suite. Weekend discounts available. AE, CB, DC, DISC, MC, V. **Parking:** $15.75.

Billing itself as San Francisco's "little elegant hotel," the Raphael, at Mason Street, one block from Union Square, provides quite luxurious accommodations at moderate prices. Its rooms occupy 12 stories, and the door to each is individually hand painted, making for very cheerful hallways. Each interior is uniquely attractive. All rooms have two phones, color TVs with pay-for-view movies, AM/FM radios, individually controlled air and heat, clocks, hairdryers, and makeup mirrors. Room service is available from 7am to 11pm.

The Shannon Court, 550 Geary St., San Francisco, CA 94102. ☎ **415/775-5000,** or toll free **800/228-8830.** Fax 415/928-6813. 173 rms, 5 suites. No-smoking rooms available. TV TEL **Cable Car:** Powell-Hyde or Powell-Mason lines, two blocks away. **Bus:** 2, 3, 4, 30, 38, or 45.

Rates: $110–$115 single; $100–$135 double or twin; from $200 suite. Extra person $13. AE, CB, DC, MC, V. **Parking:** $13.

Originally constructed in 1929, this historic landmark building between Jones and Taylor Streets has a distinctly Spanish flavor, with graceful curved arches, white stucco walls, and highly polished brass fixtures. While still retaining the ambience of the original building, the Shannon Court offers spacious guest rooms and suites in delicate pastels with a comfortable contemporary look. All rooms have outside exposures and are equipped with color TVs and phones. The hotel's five luxury suites are on the 16th floor; two have rooftop terraces. Complimentary morning coffee and donuts and afternoon tea are available in the lobby. Accommodations for the handicapped are available.

The City of Paris restaurant and bar is the hotel's latest addition. It's open every day, serving three meals from 7am to midnight, while the bar remains open until 2am. Well-priced lunch and dinner entrees include a half herb-roasted chicken for $9, and seared yellowfin tuna for $15; there's also an oyster bar and a great wine list.

Villa Florence, 225 Powell St., San Francisco, CA 94102. ☎ **415/397-7700,** or toll free **800/553-4411.** Fax 415/397-1006. 177 rms, 36 suites. No-smoking rooms available. A/C MINIBAR TV TEL **Cable Car:** Powell-Hyde or Powell-Mason lines, direct stop. **Bus:** 2, 3, 4, 30, 38, or 45.

Rates: $139–$149 single or double; $159–$169 junior suite; $249 deluxe suite. AE, CB, DC, DISC, MC, V. **Parking:** $16.

If there were nothing more to be said about the Villa Florence, its price and location would make it an exceptional buy. Near Union Square and Geary Street, it's ideal for anyone who wants to be downtown. The hotel is two blocks from the heart of the

Financial District, the Moscone Convention Center, and the BART and Muni stations. It's adjacent to Saks Fifth Avenue, Macy's, Neiman-Marcus, and enough specialty shops to satisfy even the most dedicated shopper.

The Villa Florence is the superb result of a $6.5 million renovation of what was the turn-of-the-century Manx Hotel. As soon as you enter, you'll have an idea of the magnificent refurbishing job done throughout: The arched entryway, graceful palms, marble columns, murals of Florence, huge marble fireplace, rich maroon upholstered chairs, Etruscan-style table lamps, giant urns, and fresh flowers all reflect an aura of Italian grandeur.

The beautiful, elegant bedrooms feature pink-and-blue floral chintz drapes and matching spreads, as well as white furnishings. The rooms are a bit small, but the light decor and the high ceilings contribute a feeling of airiness. Modern amenities include color TVs, pullout writing tables, direct-dial phones, and well-stocked refrigerators. The bath has make-up mirror lighting, overhead heat lamps, and hand-milled soap. Kuleto's, to the left of the hotel's main lobby, is a gem of a northern Italian restaurant with specialties from Tuscany (see "San Francisco Dining," below, for complete information).

BUDGET

Alexander Inn, 415 O'Farrell St., San Francisco, CA 94102. ☎ **415/928-6800,** or toll free **800/843-8709.** Fax 415/928-3354. 48 rms, 50 suites (all with bath). No-smoking rooms available. TV TEL **Cable Car:** Powell-Hyde or Powell-Mason lines, two blocks away.

Rates: $48–$72 single or double; $58–$78 triple; $64–$84 family suite. **Parking:** Garage nearby.

Far from fancy, but both clean and comfortable, the Alexander gets marks for affordable accommodations in a notoriously high-rent district. Most rooms in this six-floor hotel are twins, and all have extra touches like a direct-dial telephone, a color TV, and even a coffee- and teamaker. Located at Taylor Street, the hotel is just three blocks from Union Square.

AYH Hostel at Union Square, 312 Mason St., San Francisco, CA 94102 ☎ **415/788-5604.** 200 beds. **Bus:** 7B, 38. **Cable Car:** Powell-Mason line.

Rates: $14 per person for AYH members, $17 for nonmembers, half price for persons under 18 when accompanied by a parent. Maximum stay six nights, MC, V.

The city's newest hostel is located smack-dab in the middle of the city, at Union Square. Occupying five sparsely decorated floors, rooms here are simple and clean; each room has two or three beds, its own sink, and a closet. Although most rooms share hallway baths, a few en-suite rooms are reserved for families. Freshly painted hallways are adorned with laminated posters, and there are several common rooms, including a reading room, a smoking room, and a large kitchen with lots of tables, chairs, and refrigerator space. There are laundry facilities nearby, and a helpful information desk

IMPRESSIONS

Cities are like gentlemen. They are born, not made. Site has nothing to do with it. I bet San Francisco was a city from the very first time it had a dozen settlers.
—Will Rogers

offering tour reservations and sightseeing tips. The hostel is open 24 hours; reservations are necessary.

$ **Brady Acres,** 649 Jones St., San Francisco, CA 94102. ☎ **415/929-8033,** or toll free **800/627-2396.** Fax 415/441-8033. 25 rms (all with bath). MINIBAR TV TEL **Bus:** 2, 3, 4, 27, or 38.

Rates: $50–$55 single, $60–$75 double. Weekly rates available. MC, V. **Parking:** Garage nearby.

Inside this small, four-story brick building is one of the best budget hotels in the city. Enter through a black-and-gold door, with lamp sconces on either side. Inside, you'll find very clean rooms accessorized with microwave ovens, small refrigerators, direct-dial phones (with free local calls), answering machines, toasters, and coffeemakers. Baths are newly remodeled, with tiled tubs. A coin-operated washer and dryer are located in the basement, along with free laundry soap. Resident proprietor Deborah Liane Brady is usually on hand to offer friendly, personal service.

Golden Gate Hotel, 775 Bush St., San Francisco, CA 94108. ☎ **415/392-3702,** or toll free **800/835-1118.** Fax 415/392-6202. 23 rms (14 with bath). TV **Cable Car:** Powell-Hyde or Powell-Mason lines, one block away. **Bus:** 2, 3, 4, 30, 38, or 45.

Rates (including continental breakfast): $55–$65 single or double without bath, $89 single or double with bath. AE, CB, DC, MC, V. **Parking:** $14.

Among San Francisco's small, charming hotels born near the turn of the century are some real gems—the Golden Gate Hotel, between Powell and Mason Streets, is one. It's two blocks north of Union Square and two blocks down (literally) from the crest of Nob Hill. The cable car stops at the corner for easy access to Fisherman's Wharf and Chinatown. The city's theaters and best restaurants are also within walking distance.

Part of the charm of the Golden Gate is that it is family run by John and Renate Kenaston, delightful, hospitable innkeepers who take obvious pleasure in making their guests comfortable. They offer lovely rooms that have been individually redecorated with handsome antique furnishings from the early 1900s. Draperies and spreads with floral prints add to the quaintness and warmth, as do fresh flowers in each room. The antique claw-foot tubs are great for long hot soaks. Most, but not all, rooms have phones, so request one when you make your reservation.

Complimentary afternoon tea is served daily from 4 to 7pm. Concierge services are available and sightseeing tours can be arranged with a pickup at the hotel.

Grant Plaza Hotel, 465 Grant Ave., San Francisco, CA 94108. ☎ **415/434-3883,** or toll free **800/472-6899.** Fax. 415/434-3886. 72 rms. TV TEL **Cable Car:** Powell-Hyde and Powell-Mason lines (2 blocks west).

Rates: $39–$42 single; $42–$65 double. MC, V. **Parking:** $8.50.

Offering basic, clean rooms overlooking Chinatown's main street, the Grant Plaza, at the corner of Pine Street, represents one of the best accommodations deals in San Francisco. The six-story hotel's simple, clean lobby and equally modest rooms are conscientiously cared for by a particularly hospitable Chinese management. Guest rooms, which contain little more than a bed, desk, and chair, are on the small side. Corner rooms on higher floors are both larger and brighter. There are ice and soda machines in the lobby, and no visitors are permitted in the rooms after 11pm.

Grant Plaza is not for everybody; its motel-quality rooms occupy one of the city's busiest urban corners. But if you're happy with basic accommodations, and relish being right in the heart of the hustle, this hotel is thoroughly recommendable. Rooms in back are quieter.

$ **Pacific Bay Inn,** 520 Jones St., San Francisco, CA 94102. ☎ **415/673-0234,** or toll free **800/445-2631.** Fax 415/673-4781. 84 rms (all with bath). No-smoking rooms available. TV TEL **Cable Car:** Powell-Hyde or Powell-Mason lines, three blocks away. **Bus:** 2, 3, 4, 27, or 38.

Rates: $45–$65 single or double. AE, CB, DC, DISC, MC, V. **Parking:** $12.

This pleasant, recently renovated little hotel between Geary and O'Farrell Streets, three blocks west of the Powell Street cable car and Union Square, offers no frills to budget-conscious visitors. The inn is easily identified by the international flags flying outside. The lobby has recently been given a comfortable high-tech look, and there's 24-hour desk service.

Cozy and light, accommodations are done in airy peach tones with maroon floral-print spreads and maroon-and-gray carpeting throughout. The rooms have showers only, no tubs.

Pensione International, 875 Post St., San Francisco, CA 94109 ☎ **415/775-3344.** 46 rms (15 with bath).

Rates (including continental breakfast): $30–$40 single without bath, $40–$55 single with bath; $40–$50 double without bath, $50–$75 double with bath. AE, DISC, MC, V.

Popular with budget-minded Europeans, this small Union Square–area hotel, complete with molded doors, gilded mirrors, and framed art, could easily fit into Rome or Paris. While it's not a fancy place, the Pensione International offers basic, stylish rooms, located on two floors atop narrow staircases. Accommodations tend to be small, and are outfitted with mismatched furniture and decor. All rooms have sinks and mirrors; the more expensive ones have a TV and a private bath.

★ **The Sheehan,** 620 Sutter St., San Francisco, CA 94102. ☎ **415/775-6500,** or toll free **800/654-6835.** Fax 415/775-3271. 68 rms (51 with bath), 2 suites. No-smoking rooms available. TV **Cable Car:** Powell-Hyde or Powell-Mason lines, one block away. **Bus:** 2, 3, 4, 30, 38, or 78.

Rates (including continental breakfast): $40–$47 single without bath, $60–$75 single with bath; $50–$57 double without bath, $75–$98 double with bath; $85–$90 suite. AE, CB, DC, MC, V. **Parking:** $12.

Formally a YWCA hotel, the Sheehan, near Mason Street, is well located just two blocks from Union Square. You can easily walk from here to most places in the downtown area. Mostly remodeled in 1990, the rooms are carpeted, comfortable, clean, and well furnished. In addition to beds, each has a table, chairs, and cableless color TV. The hotel has a clean and pleasant lobby, a comfortable tea room, open for light lunches and afternoon tea, and an indoor, heated swimming pool, and a work-out area—a very good value.

Nob Hill

VERY EXPENSIVE

Fairmont Hotel and Tower, 950 Mason St., San Francisco, CA 94108. ☎ **415/772-5000,** or toll free **800/527-4727.** Fax 415/772-5013. 600 rms, 62 suites.

No-smoking rooms available. A/C MINIBAR TV TEL **Cable Car:** Powell-Hyde, Powell-Mason, or California lines, one block away.

Rates: Main building, $179–$209 single or double, from $450 suite; tower, $239–$300 single or double, from $500 suite. Extra person $30. AE, CB, DC, DISC, MC, V. **Parking:** $25.

Perhaps the most famous hotel in San Francisco, the luxurious Fairmont, atop Nob Hill, is an ornate marble palace sheltering hundreds of opulent rooms, six good restaurants, several cocktail lounges, and conveniences ranging from a pharmacy to a full-service bank. The huge lobby, with its marbleized columns, high silver-and-white ceilings, and red-velvet-covered furnishings, is more kitsch than classic and is often full with doctors, lawyers, conventioneers, and red-jacketed bellhops.

In addition to the usual luxuries, guests will appreciate such details as goose-down pillows, electric shoe buffers, hair dryers, bath scales, huge walk-in closets, and multiline phones with private voice-mail message capability. All suites are equipped with personal fax machines.

Dining/Entertainment: The Bella Voce Restaurant, open for three meals daily, features Italian cuisine served by a singing staff. The Crown offers lavish buffet meals and a spectacular view of the Bay Area. The exotic Tonga Restaurant and Hurricane Bar has an extensive selection of Chinese and Polynesian specialties in a lavish South Seas ambience. There is dancing on a boat deck, and simulated indoor "thundershowers." Masons serves contemporary Californian cuisine in a sophisticated atmosphere, with a good view of the cable cars. Afternoon tea is served daily in the hotel's magnificent lobby.

Services: 24-hour room service, evening turndown, concierge, babysitting services, doctor on call, overnight laundry, complimentary morning limousine to the Financial District.

Facilities: Health club, business center, barbershop, beauty salon, pharmacy, travel agency, bank, shopping arcade.

★ **Huntington Hotel,** 1075 California St., San Francisco, CA 94108.
☎ **415/474-5400,** or toll free **800/227-4683, 800/652-1539** in California.
Fax 415/474-6227. 140 rms, 40 suites. MINIBAR TV TEL **Cable Car:** Powell-Hyde, Powell-Mason, or California lines, direct stop. **Bus:** 1.

Rates: $165–$215 single; $185–$250 double; from $315 suite. Special packages available. AE, CB, DC, MC, V. **Parking:** $16.50.

Discreet Nob Hill elegance and old-world charm are the hallmarks of the Huntington, between Mason and Taylor Streets. It's not for attention-loving glitterati. The stately hotel's low-key elegance is attractive to guests who appreciate strict privacy and unobtrusive service.

Extra-large rooms offer a view of the city or the bay and overlook Huntington Park and Grace Cathedral. From Irish linens, and imported silks to Ming Dynasty treasures and signature artwork, each room and suite is individually decorated with custom-made and antique furnishings, as well as modern amenities, such as color TVs and hair dryers.

Dining/Entertainment: The Big Four restaurant is one of the city's most handsome cocktail lounges and dining rooms. Named for the Central Pacific Railroad's "big four" tycoons—Huntington, Stanford, Crocker, and Hopkins—the restaurant serves excellent contemporary continental cuisine, with seasonally-inspired dinner selections ranging from $13 to $29. Its walnut-paneled interior showcases an impressive collection of 19th-century photos and memorabilia. There is live piano music in the lounge nightly from 5 to 11:30pm.

Services: Room service, concierge, complimentary limousine to the Financial District and Union Square (available 8am to 4pm daily), overnight shoe shine, laundry, evening turndown, complimentary morning newspaper, complimentary formal tea or sherry service upon arrival.

Facilities: Access to off-premises health club.

Mark Hopkins Inter-Continental, 1 Nob Hill, San Francisco, CA 94108. ☎ **415/392-3434,** or toll free **800/327-0200.** Fax 415/421-3302. 390 rms. 271 suites. No-smoking rooms available. A/C MINIBAR TV TEL **Cable Car:** Powell-Hyde, Powell-Mason, or California lines, direct stop. **Bus:** 1.

Rates: $180–$275 single; $200–$305 double or twin; from $400 suite. AE, CB, DC, MC, V. **Parking:** $20.

The elegant Mark Hopkins, at the crest of Nob Hill, stands 19 stories tall and offers a marvelous view from every one of its gracious rooms. It opened in 1926 on the spot where railroad millionaire Mark Hopkins's turreted monster of a mansion once stood. The hotel gained global fame during World War II, when Pacific-bound servicepeople toasted their good-bye to the States in the Top of the Mark cocktail lounge.

The Mark Hopkins is now a member of the Inter-Continental Hotel Group. Guests are still treated to classic decor and excellent service. All the rooms have sumptuous baths, color TVs, alarm clocks, and radios. Suites offer more of the same, and the Jacuzzi Suite has a view of the Golden Gate Bridge from its private terrace. One problem with the hotel is that it has only three guest elevators, making a quick trip up to your room difficult during busy periods.

Dining/Entertainment: In addition to the famous Top of the Mark lounge, the Legends at the Mark serves breakfast, lunch, and dinner daily. Its menu is best described as international with a Californian flair. The Lower Bar, under a skylight roof, is a delightful setting for cocktails and piano bar entertainment Tuesday through Saturday nights.

Services: 24-hour room service, concierge, evening turndown, overnight shoe shine, car-rental desk.

Facilities: Business center, health club.

Ritz-Carlton, 600 Stockton St., San Francisco, CA 94108. ☎ **415/296-7465,** or toll free **800/241-3333.** Fax 415/296-0288. 336 rms, 44 suites. No-smoking rooms available. A/C MINIBAR TV TEL **Cable Car:** Powell-Hyde, Powell-Mason, or California lines, one block away.

Rates: $205–$305 standard single, double, or triple; $345 club-level single, double, or triple; from $460 suite. Weekend discounts and packages available. AE, CB, DC, DISC, MC, V. **Parking:** $25.

In April 1991, after a massive 3½-year, multimillion-dollar restoration, the Ritz-Carlton opened in an 83-year-old Nob Hill landmark. The building's majestic facade, with its 17 Ionic columns, rich filigree, winged hourglasses, carvings, and lions' heads is indeed exquisite. The lobby is less opulent and is sometimes crowded with conventioneers and tour groups.

The new rooms, however, are up to par and, like the rest of the hotel, offer every amenity and service known to the hotel industry: Italian-marble bathrooms with double sinks and name-brand toiletries, phone, remote-control TV, a stocked bar and refrigerator, and plush terry-cloth bathrobes. The more expensive rooms take advantage of the hotel's location, on the south slope of Nob Hill, and have a good view over the city. There is twice-daily maid service, including nightly turndown. Club rooms, located on the eighth and ninth floors, have a dedicated concierge, separate elevator-key access, and continuous complimentary meal presentations, including continental breakfast, afternoon tea, cocktails and hors d'oeuvres, and late-evening cordials and chocolates.

Of the many services and facilities mentioned below, the most outstanding is the fitness center, which is free to guests. A large indoor swimming pool and an adjacent whirlpool are complemented by saunas, free weights, and Nautilus machines.

Dining/Entertainment: The Dining Room, the hotel's flagship restaurant, seats 96 people for intimate, elegant dining. Critically-acclaimed chef Gary Danko presents his American version of classic French cuisine using strictly seasonal ingredients. The Dining Room is open Tuesday through Saturday for dinner only. The hotel's second eatery, named simply The Terrace, is the city's only hotel restaurant offering courtyard seating (weather permitting). Menus offer light or hearty international meals. It's open daily for breakfast, lunch, dinner, and Sunday Jazz Brunch. The relatively plain Lobby Lounge offers afternoon tea and cocktails daily, with low-key live entertainment from 3pm to 1am.

Services: Same-day valet, 24-hour room service, concierge, child care, morning newspapers delivered to guest rooms, car-rental desk.

Facilities: Business center, fitness center, gift boutique, VCR and video library.

★ **Stouffer Stanford Court Hotel,** 905 California St., San Francisco, CA 94108. ☎ **415/989-3500,** or toll free **800/227-4736, 800/622-0957** in California. Fax 415/391-0513. 402 rms, 18 suites. No-smoking rooms available. A/C TV TEL **Cable Car:** Powell-Hyde, Powell-Mason, or California lines, direct stop. **Bus:** 1.

Rates: $195–$295 single; $225–$325 double; from $450 suite. Extra person 18 or over $30. AE, CB, DC, DISC, MC, V. **Parking:** $22.

The Stouffer Stanford Court stands at the top of Nob Hill (at the corner of Powell Street), and all three cable-car lines pass by its doors. Once the site of the Leland Stanford mansion and the luxurious Stanford Court Apartments, the building was constructed in 1912 and is considered a historic landmark. A lofty stained-glass dome highlights the entrance of the hotel, and its furnishings consist of antiques and period pieces.

Many of the guest rooms have partially canopied beds, and all have a writing desk with dictionary, marble bedside tables, etchings of old San Francisco on the walls, and oak armoires that cleverly conceal the TV. Bathrooms include remote-control TV, phone, heated towel racks, overhead heat lamps, hand-milled soap, and pre-threaded sewing kits.

Dining/Entertainment: Fournou's Ovens, the hotel's award-winning restaurant, features a massive, tile-faced European roasting oven and contemporary American cuisine. Dinners here might begin with marinated lobster, scallops, and oysters with buckwheat noodles and proceed to the likes of roast rack of lamb and grilled salmon. Main courses cost $19 to $28, and the menu is often augmented with seasonal specialties. The Stanford Court wine cellar is truly extensive, featuring a choice of some 20,000 bottles. The adjacent International Bar offers limited skyline views and terrific martinis. It's worth a visit just for their antique travel-poster collection.

Services: 24-hour room service, complimentary limo service to downtown destinations in a Mercedes stretch limousine, complimentary morning newspaper and coffee or tea, evening turndown service, complimentary overnight shoeshine, on-call babysitters.

Facilities: Concierge; business services, including no surcharges for collect and credit-card phone calls; access to off-premises health club.

EXPENSIVE

Nob Hill Lambourne Spa, 725 Pine St., San Francisco, CA 94108 ☎ **415/433-2287.** 12 rms, 8 suites. A/C TV TEL MINIBAR **Cable Car:** California Street line (1 block north).

Rates (including continental breakfast): $119–$145 single or double; from $199 suite. AE, CB, DC, DISC, MC, V. **Parking:** $13 self, $18 valet.

A small "boutique" hotel, the Lambourne bills itself as an urban spa, offering on-site massages, clay-wraps, body oilings, and yoga lessons. Even without this "hook," the Lambourne deserves a top-of-the-class rating. Sporting one of San Francisco's most stylish interiors, the hotel flaunts every penny's worth of its recent multi-million-dollar renovation that, happily, has not favored form over function. Top-quality, hand-sewn mattresses and goose down comforters are complemented by a host of in-room accoutrements that include desktop computers, fax machines, stereos, coffee makers, and smartly designed contemporary furnishings. Bathrooms contain oversized tubs and hair dryers, as well as an "honor bar" of Neal's Yard brand pamperings like geranium and orange bath oil, herbal lip balm, and Jasmine moisturizer, sold for $6 to $10 each.

Guest rooms are priced according to size, but even those at the top end are relatively small. Suites include an additional sitting room, and all guests are treated to a complimentary ten-minute neck and shoulder massage, offered each afternoon.

Services: Evening turndown, business services, spa treatments.

Facilities: Spa treatment room.

Financial District

VERY EXPENSIVE

ANA Hotel San Francisco, 50 Third St., San Francisco, CA 94103. ☎ **415/974 6400,** or toll free **800/262-4683.** Fax 415/543-8268. 641 rms, 26 suites. No smoking rooms available. A/C MINIBAR TV TEL **Bus:** All Market Street buses. **Muni Metro:** All Market Street trams.

Rates: $170–$190 single or double; from $300 suite. AE, MC, V. **Parking:** $22.

Originally known as Le Meridian, this skyscraper hotel received a $28-million face-lift along with its name change in 1992, when it was purchased by the company that owns Japan's second-largest airline. The hotel's large number of uniformly decorated rooms and its fine location—just one block south of Market Street, and one block from the Moscone Convention Center—make the ANA attractive to both groups and business travelers. Intelligently designed separate check-in facilities for conventioneers keeps the main lobby clear and welcoming for independent guests.

From the outside, the ANA Hotel is an unspectacular glass-and-steel monolith. Inside, the design makes itself understood with dramatic floor-to-ceiling windows that dominate most every guest room. Packed with accessories, rooms are well outfitted with three telephones (with voice mail), a minibar, and interesting original art work. Corner suites look across the Bay Bridge to Candlestick Park, and Executive Level rooms include continental breakfast and evening hors d'oeuvres.

Specially outfitted "Green Rooms," located on the hotel's third floor, contain special air and water filtration systems, and environmentally friendly products like facial and bathroom tissues made from recycled paper; pens made from recycled plastics; and all-natural, biodegradable, "cruelty-free" soaps, shampoos, conditioners, and body lotions. Part of the rooms' $10 surcharge is donated to a non-profit environmental organization.

Dining/Entertainment: Cafe Fifty-Three serves three meals daily, and a special Sunday brunch. The adjacent loungy Lobby Bar serves cocktails, wine, beer, and appetizers.

Services: Room service, concierge, twice-daily maid service, overnight laundry and dry cleaning.

Facilities: Fitness center, business center, complimentary use of nearby tennis club, gift shop.

Hyatt Regency San Francisco, 5 Embarcadero Center, San Francisco, CA 94111. ☎ **415/788-1234,** or toll free **800/233-1234.** Fax 415/398-2567. 803 rms, 44 suites. No-smoking rooms available. TV TEL **Muni Metro:** J, K, L, M, or N. **Bus:** 7, 8, or 71.

Rates: $175–$260 single or double; from $350 suite. AE, CB, DC, MC, V. **Parking:** $20.

The architecturally impressive Hyatt Regency rises from the edge of the Embarcadero Center at the foot of Market Street. The structure is shaped like a vertical triangle, with two sides forming a right angle and the stunning third side sweeping inward from ground level like an Egyptian pyramid, serrated with long rows of jutting balconies.

Closed for three months in 1993, the hotel reopened after a $27 million renovation that completely redesigned the public areas and updated all the hotel's technology. The stunning lobby, illuminated by museum-quality theater lighting, features flowing water and a natural environment of California grasslands and wildflowers.

Rooms are comfortably furnished; their rich browns and earth tones are set off by bold splashes of color. Each room has a color TV, clock radio, voice-mail telephone, and computer ports for modems. Some rooms have coffee- and tea-making facilities; private fax machines are available free on request. Rooms with two double beds also include a sofa, easy chair, and cocktail table. The hotel's 16th and 17th floors house the Regency Club, with 102 larger guest rooms, private bar-lounges and games rooms, complimentary continental breakfast, after-dinner cordials, and private concierge.

Dining/Entertainment: The Eclipse Café is an open-air lobby restaurant serving three meals daily; the new Thirteen-Views Bar seats about 200 and is open for morning coffee and evening cocktails; the rooftop Equinox is a revolving lunch, dinner, and cocktail spot that gives you a complete panorama of San Francisco every 45 minutes. But perhaps the most charming place for lunch is the Street Café, where on sunny days you can watch the passing brokers, bankers, secretaries, and artists while listening to street musicians in the Embarcadero Center.

Services: 24-hour room service, concierge, laundry, overnight shoe shine.

Facilities: Business center; access to off-premises health club, swimming pool, and tennis courts.

 **Sheraton Palace Hotel,** 2 New Montgomery St., San Francisco, CA 94105. ☎ **415/392-8600,** or toll free **800/325-3535.** Fax 415/543-0671. 550 rms, 32 suites. No-smoking rooms available. A/C TV TEL **Muni Metro:** J, K, L, M, or N lines. **Bus:** 7, 8, or 71.

Rates: $225–$295 single; $255–$315 double; from $500 suite. Additional person $20. Children under 18 sharing existing bedding stay free in parents' room. Weekend rates and packages available. AE, CB, DC, DISC, MC, V. **Parking:** $20.

Completed in 1875, the original Palace Hotel was one of the world's largest and most luxurious hostelries. After a two-year, $150-million renovation, the hotel reopened in April 1991. Today, behind a relatively unassuming facade, this Sheraton hides what is without question the most spectacular lobby in San Francisco. It's the Garden Court, a San Francisco landmark that has been restored to its original 1909 elegance. It is graced by a $7 million dome ceiling of iridescent glass, through which the sun filters, creating an amber glow. The Court is flanked by a double row of massive Italian-marble Ionic columns and is further enhanced by 10 huge chandeliers valued at $50,000 each. The on-site, fourth-floor health club features a pretty, skylight-covered lap pool, whirlpool, sauna, and exercise room.

The nostalgic elegance of every room has been lovingly restored; new coverings bless the original antiques with new life. Each room has a refrigerator, safe, color TV, and radio. In the bathrooms, high ceilings contrast with sparkling fittings, built-in hairdryers, and other contemporary accoutrements.

Dining/Entertainment: The Garden Court serves breakfast daily from 6:30 to 11am, lunch Monday through Saturday from 11:30am to 2pm, and dinner daily from 5:30 to 10pm. Its menu offers American cuisine. Afternoon tea is served Monday through Saturday from 2:30 to 5pm, and brunch is served on Sunday from 10:30am to 2pm. The Court is open for drinks Monday through Saturday until 1am.

In Maxfield's Restaurant, a traditional San Francisco grill, guests can enjoy a more intimate meal with turn-of-the-century charm, enhanced by a stained-glass ceiling and mosaic tile floor. Open daily for lunch and dinner. The Pied Piper Bar, one of the best watering holes in San Francisco, is named for the Maxfield Parrish mural that hangs inside. Valued at approximately $2.5 million, the mural hung in the M. H. de Young Memorial Museum while the hotel underwent restoration.

Services: 24-hour room service, concierge, evening turndown, overnight dry cleaning.

Facilities: Business service center, health club, lobby-level shops.

EXPENSIVE

Galleria Park Hotel, 101 Sutter St., San Francisco, CA 94104. ☎ **415/781-3060,** or toll free **800/792-9639.** Fax 415/433-4409. 177 rms, 15 suites. No-smoking rooms available. A/C MINIBAR TV TEL **Muni Metro:** J, K, L, M, or N. **Bus:** 7, 8, or 71.

Rates: $149 single or double; from $185 suite. AE, CB, DC, DISC, MC, V. **Parking:** $14.

From its impressive black-marble facade and stylized lobby—complete with fireplace and crystal skylight—to its beautifully appointed rooms and suites, the Galleria Park, at Kearny Street, has been totally restored in the art nouveau style of its original 1911 construction. A good, upscale, business-class hotel, the Galleria Park offers all the expected necessities and some unusual extras, like a rooftop jogging track.

Dining/Entertainment: Bentley's seafood restaurant, on the lobby level, serves fresh seafood specialties, a variety of oysters and grand-scale raw bar, and a good selection of non-fish dishes. There's also a bar. The adjacent piano lounge features a pianist nightly. Brasserie Chambord is the house French restaurant, serving an inspired country cuisine. Both restaurants are open daily for breakfast, lunch, and dinner.

Services: Room service, concierge.

Facilities: Rooftop running track and park, fitness room.

Japan Center & Environs

EXPENSIVE

The Mansions, 2220 Sacramento St., San Francisco, CA 94115. ☎ **415/929-9444.** 21 rms, 5 suites. TV TEL **Bus:** 1, 3, or 83.

Rates (including breakfast): $129–$190 single or double; from $250 suite. AE, DC, DISC, MC, V. **Parking:** $10.

Bob Pritikin's unique inn, between Laguna and Buchanan Streets, is one of San Francisco's most unusual and eclectic hideaways, attracting the likes of Robin Williams and Barbra Streisand. Set in a terraced garden adorned with sculptures, the Mansions are actually two historic buildings connected by an interior corridor. Their total and often theatrical originality is reflected in Pritikin's philosophy that "The Mansions is only as good as its last performance."

Guests are greeted by a host in Victorian attire and offered a glass of wine or sherry upon check-in. Each room is different, but most rooms look out on a rose or sculpture garden, and all are furnished with well-chosen antiques, brass beds, and Victorian memorabilia. All have fresh flowers, direct-dial phones, and TVs (delivered on request). Each unit is named for a famous San Franciscan—Bufano, Coit, Huntington, or Pritikin—and includes a wall mural depicting that person's story. The ultimate indulgence is the opulent Empress Josephine Room, furnished with priceless antiques. There's even an all-glass Garden Room, partly done in spectacular stained glass.

Dining/Entertainment: Breakfast includes English crumpets, English-style banger sausages, fruit, fresh-squeezed orange juice, coffee, and more. The Victorian Cabaret Theater stages nightly performances by virtuoso pianist Claudia the Ghost, playing requests with invisible fingers. Some nights, she performs extraordinary feats of magic, and Pritikin, "America's foremost saw player," also entertains. There's also a games room with billiard tables.

Miyako Hotel, 1625 Poet St., San Francisco, CA 94115. ☎ **415/922-3200,** or toll free **800/533-4567.** Fax 415/921-0417. 218 rms, 11 suites. No-smoking rooms available. A/C TV TEL **Bus:** 38 to Geary.

Rates: $99–$159 single; $129–$189 double or twin; from $279 suite. Children 18 and under stay free in parents room. AE, CB, DC, MC, V. **Parking:** $20.

Just a mile from the heart of downtown, the Miyako is located in the Japan Center at Laguna Street, which borders Nihonmachi, the city's Japanese quarter. The center was opened in 1968 and the hotel's 15-story tower and five-story garden wing overlook

IMPRESSIONS

In all my travels I have never seen the hospitality of San Francisco equaled anywhere in the world.

—Conrad Hilton, Hotelier

its fascinating complex of shops and restaurants. From the moment you enter the peaceful lobby, with its beautiful flock of origami birds at the bell desk, you know this is a successful merger of East and West. Bay area residents often come for the weekend, hire a Japanese suite, settle into the bathtub, and leave it only for forays to Nihonmachi.

Most of the rooms are equipped with American-style beds and chairs, carpets, color TVs, and Japanese baths. Shoji screens slide away to frame views of the city. Two of the luxury suites have their own private redwood saunas and deep-tub Japanese baths. Six of the Miyako's accommodations are done in all-Japanese decor, which means you sleep on a floor laid with tatami mats and spread with huge down futons. A bamboo and rock garden runs the length of the wall and can be contemplated in peace from your sunken bathtub. Four rooms combine Eastern- and Western-style accommodations and are ideal for families.

Dining/Entertainment: The Asuka Brasserie offers continental-Japanese cuisine prepared and presented in a contemporary Californian garden setting. The restaurant serves breakfast, lunch, and dinner, as well as Sunday brunch, with dinner dishes at $15 to $30. The mezzanine cocktail lounge is open from 10am to 1am daily.

Services: Room service, concierge, evening turndown, overnight shoe shine, car-rental desk.

Facilities: Business center, access to an off-premises health club.

MODERATE

Queen Anne Hotel, 1590 Sutter St., San Francisco, CA 94109. ☎ **415/441-2828,** or toll free **800/227-3970.** Fax 415/775-5212. 49 rms, 4 suites. No-smoking rooms available. TV TEL **Bus:** 2, 3, 4, or 38.

Rates (including continental breakfast): $99–$150 single or double; from $175 suite. Extra person $10. AE, DC, MC, V. **Parking:** $12.

This handsomely restored Victorian mansion, one mile west of Union Square, at Octavia Street, was Miss Mary Lake's School for Girls at the turn of the century. Later it became a private gentlemen's club, then returned to its original gender as the Girl's Friendly Society Lodge. After a complete restoration it opened as the Queen Anne in 1981.

The pretty English oak-paneled lobby is furnished with antiques. The unique guest rooms preserve a turn-of-the-century atmosphere while providing all-modern conveniences. The rooms have been individually decorated: Some have corner turret bay windows that look out on tree-lined streets, as well as separate parlor areas and wet bars; others have cozy reading nooks and fireplaces. All rooms have a telephone with extensions in the bathroom and remote-control color TV. The Queen Anne serves complimentary continental breakfast. Services include room service, concierge, morning newspaper, and complimentary afternoon tea and sherry. There's access to an off-premises health club, with lap pool and Nautilus machines. Accommodations for the handicapped are available.

Civic Center

EXPENSIVE

★ **The Inn at the Opera,** 333 Fulton St., San Francisco, CA 94102. ☎ **415/863-8400,** or toll free **800/325-2708, 800/423-9610** in California.

Fax 415/861-0821. 30 rms, 18 suites. No-smoking rooms available. MINIBAR TV TEL **Bus:** 5, 21, 47, or 49.

Rates (including continental breakfast): $130–$180 single or double; from $185 suite. Extra person $10. AE, MC, V. **Parking:** $16.

The Inn at the Opera is a small, elegant hotel specializing in luxurious accommodations and attentive, personalized service. This is the city's premier "boutique hotel." Tucked away in the heart of the performing-arts center, the inn has become a hideaway for both performers and patrons of the arts.

The hotel's plain facade belies its handsome interior. The reception area is light and airy, with European furnishings, fresh flowers, and old brass inkwells on the front desk. Rooms, which underwent a complete renovation in January 1992, reflect the same warmth, with subtle pastel shades, opulent furnishings, and huge stuffed pillows. Each features queen-size beds draped with half canopies, fully stocked minibars, fresh flowers, and a microwave oven. Baths include hair dryers, scales, terry-cloth robes and French milled soaps. The beautifully appointed suites are especially recommended.

Dining/Entertainment: Act IV Restaurant, the hotel's fine dining room, provides an intimate setting with fireside seating, plush furnishings, original art, and soft piano accompaniment. Executive chef Kenneth Fredsted oversees the preparation of daily special menus of Mediterranean cuisine with Californian influences. It's open for breakfast, lunch, and dinner, as well as Sunday brunch.

Services: 24-hour room service, concierge, evening turndown, complimentary light pressing and overnight shoe shine, morning newspaper, staff physician, complimentary limousine service to the Financial District.

Facilities: Access to off-premises health club.

MODERATE

Phoenix Inn, 601 Eddy St., San Francisco, CA 94109. ☎ **415/776-1380,** or toll free **800/248-9466.** Fax 415/885-3109. 44 rms, 3 suites. TV TEL **Bus:** 19, 31, or 38.

Rates (including continental breakfast): $89 single or double; $129–$139 suite. AE, DC, MC, V. **Parking:** Free.

A stylish, offbeat spot on Eddy Street at Larkin Street, the Phoenix is an unusual motel that wouldn't look out of place in the heart of Miami Beach. The fun owners like to think of this gathering place for visiting rock musicians, writers, and filmmakers as a little bit of Los Angeles transplanted to San Francisco. Indeed, the Phoenix is an island of creativity in the middle of a less-than-prosperous area. And if you'd like to say that you've stayed at the same inn as Linda Ronstadt, Arlo Guthrie, and the Dance Theater of Harlem, this is the place. At the center of this oasis is a small, heated outdoor pool set in a spacious courtyard and modern-sculpture garden.

Rooms are spacious, bright, comfortable, and attractively decorated in pastels. Oversize furnishings and chairs are handmade of Philippine bamboo. Potted plants and original local art add attractive touches. The high ceilings and overhead lighting, in addition to the usual standing lamps, give an airy outdoor feeling to the rooms. In addition to the usual amenities, the inn's own closed-circuit channel exclusively shows films made in or about San Francisco, among them *The Maltese Falcon, Vertigo,* and *Foul Play.*

Miss Pearl's Jam House is the hotel's lobby restaurant (see "San Francisco Dining," below, for complete information).

BUDGET

Abigail Hotel, 246 McAllister St., San Francisco, CA 94102. ☎ **415/861-9728,** or toll free **800/243-6510.** Fax 415/861-5848. 62 rms, 1 suite. TV TEL **Muni Metro:** J, K, L, M, or N lines. **Bus:** 7, 8, or 71.

Rates: $79 single or double; $140 suite. Extra person $10. AE, DC, MC, V. **Parking:** $5.

What the Abigail lacks in luxury it more than makes up for in charm. The handsome white exterior, with its canopy and polished brass, might have been picked up in London and set down two blocks from the San Francisco Opera. In the lobby you'll find a small desk, contemporary furnishings, and a popular cafe.

Guest rooms contain blue floral drapes, white curtains, old prints, down comforters, and an occasional antique table or lamp. Most rooms are bright and quiet.

Man's Justice, the Abigail's new restaurant/cafe is open for breakfast, lunch, and dinner.

Albion House Inn, 135 Gough St., San Francisco, CA 94102. ☎ **415/621-0896.** 9 rms. TEL **Muni Metro:** J, K, L, M, or N lines. **Bus:** 7, 8, or 71.

Rates (including breakfast): $75–$150 single or double. AE, MC, V. **Parking:** $3.50.

Albion House Inn, at Lily Street, is a delightful example of a successful San Francisco B&B. Built as a small hotel in 1907, it has since been remodeled to reflect the contemporary charm of a moderately priced Northern European bed-and-breakfast. Each room is decorated differently. Sonoma, for example, evokes images of the Wine Country with a double-size brass bed and floral prints; and Cypress, inspired by the Lone Cypress in Monterey, is decorated in tans and furnished with a queen-size bed. All rooms have phones and private baths; some rooms have color TVs.

The heart of the Albion House is the common room, a large living room decorated in cool pinks, with exposed redwood beams and a fireplace. A full breakfast is served here each morning, set on china and silver service. Coffee and tea are available throughout the day and complimentary brandy is served each evening. There is evening turndown service.

Cow Hollow

EXPENSIVE

Union Street Inn, 2229 Union St., San Francisco, CA 94123. ☎ **415/346-0424.** 5 rms (all with bath). All no-smoking rooms. TV TEL **Bus:** 22, 41, 45, or 47.

Rates (including continental breakfast): $125–$175 standard single or double; $225 cottage. AE, MC, V. **Parking:** $10.

Helen Stewart's Union Street Inn is a renovated Victorian-era beauty, located between Fillmore and Steiner Streets. Its five rooms are well furnished with carefully selected antiques. Downstairs is a beautiful, homey parlor with apricot velvet walls, a velvet sofa, and a fireplace.

Rooms are fancifully named (Wildrose, Holly, Golden Gate, English Garden, New Yorker) and charmingly decorated. They have canopied or brass beds with polished cotton spreads, well-chosen art on the walls, a table and chairs, live plants and beautifully arranged flowers, and magazines to read. All have private baths, multipaned bay windows, and garden views. TVs are available on request. The Cottage is similarly decorated, nuzzles up against the garden, and has a Jacuzzi in its own huge bathroom. You can have breakfast (fresh-baked croissants, with Helen's homemade kiwi or plum jam, fresh-squeezed orange juice, fruit, and coffee) in the parlor, in your room, or on an outdoor terrace overlooking a lovely garden with its own lemon tree.

MODERATE

Chelsea Motor Inn, 2095 Lombard St., San Francisco, CA 94123. ☎ **415/563-5600.** Fax 415/346-9127. 60 rms. A/C TV TEL **Bus:** 22, 28, 30, or 76.

Rates: $73–$85 single; $78–$95 double. AE, CB, DC, MC, V. **Parking:** Free.

An attractive establishment on the "motel strip" that stretches from the Golden Gate Bridge to Van Ness Avenue, the Chelsea Inn, at Fillmore Street, is perfectly located for a stroll along Union Street. Rooms are very comfortable and pleasantly decorated in shades of rose, blue, or brown.

Cow Hollow Motor Inn & Suites, 2190 Lombard St., San Francisco, CA 94123. ☎ **415/921-5800.** Fax 415/922-8515. 117 rms, 12 suites (all with bath). A/C TV TEL **Bus:** 28, 43, or 76.

Rates: $73 single; $78–$86 double; from $175 suite. Extra person $10. AE, DC, MC, V. **Parking:** Free.

Located at Steiner Street, this modest brick hotel comes loaded with such amenities as cable TV, free local phone calls, free covered parking lot, and in-room coffeemaker. The inn is well run by hospitable co-managers Warren and Catherine Murphy.

BUDGET

Bed & Breakfast Inn, 4 Charlton Court, San Francisco, CA 94123. ☎ **415/921-9784.** 11 rms, 2 suites (7 with bath). TV TEL **Bus:** 41 or 45.

Rates (including continental breakfast): $70–$90 single or double without bath; $115–$140 single or double with bath; $190–$215 suite. No credit cards. **Parking:** $7.50 a day at nearby garage.

Located in a charming courtyard just off Union Street between Buchanan and Laguna Streets, this B&B is Bob and Marily Kavanaugh's noteworthy addition to the Bay Area's hostelries. The Bed & Breakfast Inn offers exquisite accommodations, with a good level of luxury and personal service. Guests are greeted by name and introduced to each other. There's a library for guests, furnished with a writing desk, TV, and pay phone.

Rooms are located in three Victorian houses that predate the 1906 earthquake by several decades. Each room is uniquely and charmingly decorated—perhaps in a Casablanca motif with a peacock chair and a ceiling fan, perhaps with a Victorian or brass bed. All are wonderfully cozy and contain cherished family antiques, original art, plants and fresh flowers, fruit, a Thermos of ice water, clocks, down pillows, and a selection of quality books and magazines. All the rooms with private baths also have color TVs and direct-dial phones. Those rooms without baths have doors leading to the lovely enclosed garden out back. The Mayfair Suite, formerly the Kavanaughs' flat, has a latticed terrace and a private garden. The largest room is the Garden Suite, with a full kitchen, two fireplaces, a Jacuzzi, two bedrooms, a study, and French doors leading out into the garden. Breakfast (freshly-baked croissants, orange juice, coffee, fancy teas, or cocoa) is either brought to your room on a tray with flowers and a morning newspaper or served in a sunny Victorian breakfast room with antique china. Sherry is available at all times.

Edward II Inn & Carriage House, 3155 Scott St., San Francisco, CA 94123. ☎ **415/922-3000,** or toll-free **800/473-2846.** Fax 415/931-5784. 31 rms (20 with bath), 6 suites. TV TEL **Bus:** 28, 30, 43, or 76.

Rates (including continental breakfast): $67 single or double without bath; $85 single or double with bath; $150–$200 suite. Rates reduced Jan–Feb Sun–Thurs. AE, MC, V. **Parking:** $9.

Located at Lombard Street, the well-appointed and well-priced Edward II was originally built in 1914 for the Pan-Pacific Exposition. It has since been transformed into a smoothly run European-style bed-and-breakfast. Guest rooms are simple and charming, with quilted bedspreads, antique and English-country rattan dressers, and white plantation shutters. All rooms have color TVs with cable hookups. Each of the suites is different, but all are beautifully furnished and represent some of the best values in San Francisco. Four have a whirlpool bath and wet bar, while others have full kitchens and living rooms. They're highly recommended.

Haight-Ashbury

Stanyan Park Hotel, 750 Stanyan St., San Francisco, CA 94117. ☎ **415/751-1000.** Fax 415/668-5454. 36 rms, 6 suites. No-smoking rooms available. TV TEL **Muni Metro:** N. **Bus:** 7, 33, 71, or 73.

Rates (including continental breakfast): $78–$96 single or double; from $130 suite. Extra person $20. AE, CB, DC, DISC, MC, V. **Parking:** $5.

Another inn-style hostelry is the Stanyan Park, at Waller Street, across from Golden Gate Park. It has operated as a hotel under a variety of names since 1904. In its current incarnation, it's a charming, three-story establishment decorated with antique-style furnishings, Victorian wallpaper, and pastel quilts, curtains, and carpets. Modern amenities include color TVs, direct-dial phones, and tub/shower baths, complete with massaging shower head, shampoos, and fancy soaps.

There are one-bedroom and two-bedroom suites. Each has a full kitchen, formal dining and living rooms, and can sleep up to six comfortably; they're ideal for families. Complimentary tea and cookies are served each afternoon.

Around Town

EXPENSIVE

Pied a Terre, 2424 Washington St., San Francisco, CA 94115. ☎ **415/922-8033,** or toll free **800/627-2396.** 2 apts. A/C TV TEL

Rates: $150–$200 double. Weekly rates available. **Parking:** On street only.

If you want to live like the locals—the rich locals—then I can make no better suggestion than the Pied a Terre apartments. The fully-equipped rentals are superbly located in Pacific Heights, between Alta Plaza Park and Lafayette Park, just a block from the upper Fillmore shopping area. Each apartment has two bedrooms, a living room, two fireplaces, and a gourmet kitchen complete with stylish dishwashers, gas ranges, large refrigerators, and microwave ovens. Adjacent dining areas have room for up to eight guests, and laundry facilities are available.

The Sheraton at Fisherman's Wharf, 2500 Mason St., San Francisco, CA 94133. ☎ **415/362-5500,** or toll free **800/325-3535.** Fax 415/956-5275. 525 rms, 6 suites.

No-smoking rooms available. A/C TV TEL **Cable Car:** Powell-Mason, three blocks away. **Bus:** 15, 32, or 42.

Rates: $139–$190 single or double; from $275 suite. Extra person $20. AE, CB, DC, DISC, MC, V. **Parking:** $12.

Built in the mid-1970s, this modernistic, three-story hotel is not architecturally outstanding, but it offers some of the most reliably comfortable rooms in the Fisherman's Wharf area. The no-bones business hotel features attractive, though nondescript, guest rooms decorated in soft pastels. The hotel is well situated, on Beech Street, near the water, and its relatively high tariff is a reflection of its fine location.

Dining/Entertainment: The Mason Beach Grill serves breakfast, lunch, and dinner daily. The menu is heavy on seafood. Chanen's Lounge is a Victorian-style piano bar offering live jazz several nights a week, along with cocktails and assorted appetizers.

Services: 24-hour room service, concierge, evening turndown, car-rental desk, travel desk.

Facilities: Outdoor heated swimming pool, access to nearby health club, business center, hair salon.

MODERATE

The Archbishop's Mansion, 1000 Fulton St., San Francisco, CA 94117. ☎ **415/563-7872,** or toll free **800/543-5820.** 10 rms, 5 suites. A/C TV TEL **Bus:** 19, 31, or 38.

Rates (including continental breakfast): $115–$207 single or double; from $289 suite. AE, MC, V. **Parking:** Free.

Built in 1904 for the Archbishop of San Francisco, this authentic turn-of-the-century parkfront mansion is one of the city's most unusual and upscale bed-and-breakfasts. A historical landmark, the mansion offers elegant rooms that are each unique in character, color, shape, and size. Furnishings include oversized four-poster and canopied beds, copious antiques, and embroidered linens; suites offer the extra bonus of private sitting areas. Most rooms have working fireplaces, as well as large old-fashioned bathtubs or Jacuzzis. The home's interior is decorated with polished redwood paneling, beamed ceilings, and a magnificent palatial staircase.

The mansion's considerable size and sturdy wall construction provide guests with more privacy than they'd experience at most B&Bs. The trade-off is lost intimacy, as well as a lack of services and facilities that can be expected at most similarly priced hotels.

Services: Complimentary morning newspaper and afternoon wine. Breakfast is served each morning in guests' rooms.

Lombard Hotel, 1015 Geary St., San Francisco, CA 94109. ☎ **415/673-5232,** or toll free **800/777-3210.** 100 rms. TV TEL **Bus:** 2, 3, 4, 19, or 38.

Rates: $83–$89 single or double. Extra person $10. Children under 12 stay free in parents' room. AE, CB, DC, DISC, MC, V. **Parking:** $10.

The Lombard Hotel, at Polk Street, is the kind of hostelry you might expect to find on a fashionable London street. It's about six blocks west of Union Square and half a dozen blocks north of the Civic Center. Most rooms feature queen-size beds; all have private baths with tubs and/or showers. There is a billiards room and sun deck, and complimentary morning limousine service to the Financial District.

The marble-floored lobby boasts a grand piano and fireplace and is perfect for an afternoon tea or sherry. Also in the lobby is the small Gray Derby restaurant, where breakfast is served.

BUDGET

San Francisco International Hostel, Building 240, Fort Mason. ☎ **415/771-7277.** 156 beds. **Bus:** 19, 30, 42, 47, or 49.

Rates: $13 per person. Maximum stay five nights. MC. V (to hold reservation only).

Some of the cheapest accommodations in San Francisco are these well-located dormitory rooms, inside a park between the Golden Gate Bridge and Fisherman's Wharf. Anyone can use the dormitory, regardless of age, and the facility is handicapped accessible. For families or compatible couples, there are three rooms with four bunks, obviously in great demand. Kitchen facilities are available, as are lockers, laundry facilities, snack-vending machines, and several community rooms with fireplaces, stereo, piano, and a wide selection of books. You'll also find several bulletin boards with information on tours and places to go during your stay. Rooms are closed to guests from 11am to 1pm. Call to find out if there's space, from 7am until midnight.

4 Dining

According to San Francisco columnist laureate Herb Caen, "A city has to be a place where you can get blinis and caviar, fisherman's spaghetti, white figs and prosciutto, a '45 Mouton Rothschild, or a movie in any one of six languages." San Francisco is such a city—and more. You can also get Moroccan couscous, Szechuan shrimp, Indonesian rijstaffel, and a decent pastrami on rye—all within walking distance of one another.

Ethnic flavors have a solid history here. Spanish and Mexican cuisines were established in the Bay Area long before the Anglos arrived. Scores of Chinese, French, and Germans who came for the Gold Rush remained in the city to cook. They were followed by Russians, Italians, Basques, Filipinos, Japanese, Greeks, and Scandinavians, most of whom started by catering to their own compatriots. Vietnamese and Thai immigrants have added the newest culinary options.

With the exception of New York and Los Angeles, San Francisco is quite possibly the most cuisine-conscious city in the United States. Its citizens take food seriously. One reason may be the local wine—San Francisco is within minutes of some of the world's finest vineyards. The vast majority of city restaurants offer a good selection of California wines, including house table wines that are often served from unlabeled bottles—French rural style.

To help you choose where to eat, restaurants below are divided first by area, then by price, using the following guide:

Expensive: more than $40 per person
Moderate: $20 to $40 per person
Inexpensive: $10 to $20 per person
Budget: less than $10 per person

These categories reflect the price of the majority of dinner menu items and include an appetizer, main course, coffee, dessert, tax, and tip.

Union Square

EXPENSIVE

Fleur de Lys, 777 Sutter St., at Jones St. ☎ **673-7779.**

Cuisine: FRENCH. **Reservations:** Recommended. **Bus:** 2, 3, 4, 27, or 38.
Prices: Appetizers $7.50–$15; main courses $22–$35; five-course tasting menu $62.50; four-course vegetarian menu $50. AE, CB, DC, MC, V.
Open: Dinner only, Mon–Thurs 6–10pm, Fri–Sat 5:30–10:30pm.

Visually and gastronomically delightful, Fleur de Lys is one of the city's most celebrated and romantic dining spots. The lovely interior, designed by the late Michael Taylor, elegantly captures a feeling of the French countryside. Tables are set under an immense, burgundy color garden tent, made of locally hand-printed fabric, that evokes an autumnal, rustic mood.

Host Maurice Rouas and executive chef Hubert Keller are also the restaurant's co-owners, ensuring perfect preparations and top service to each patron. Chef Keller has distinguished himself by serving under such great French masters as Roger Verge, Paul Haeberlin, and Paul Bocuse. The Provençal fare includes such appetizers as foie gras salad, venison with black chanterelle sauce, and crispy sweetbreads with rock shrimp mousse and citrus peppercorn vinaigrette. Main courses include grilled swordfish with whole-grain mustard and spinach-wrapped lamb with garlic and truffle oil. In addition to the impressive à la carte menu, a five-course tasting menu is offered, featuring daily market selections. An appropriately extensive wine list features both French and Californian vintages.

Masa's, 648 Bush St., at Stockton St. ☎ **989-7154.**

Cuisine: FRENCH. **Reservations:** Required; accepted up to 21 days in advance. **Cable Car:** Powell-Hyde, Powell-Mason, or California lines. **Bus:** 2, 3, 4, 30, or 45.
Prices: Appetizers $11.50–$19; main courses $30–$38.50; fixed-price dinner $68–$75. AE, CB, DC, DISC, MC, V.
Open: Dinner only, Tues–Sat 6–9:30pm. **Closed:** First week in Jan; July 4th week.

After the death of founder Masataha Kobayashi in 1984, local gourmets questioned the future of Masa's, but no more. Chef Julian Serrano's brilliant cuisine and the elegant but simple decor have solidified the restaurant's reputation as one of the country's great French outposts.

Either fixed price or à la carte, dinner is a memorable experience from start to finish. You might begin with fresh foie gras smothered in pan juices, cognac, and black truffles. The sautéed medallions of venison, served with a rich brown sauce, is also recommended, as are any of the game-bird dishes. The wine list includes some excellent older French wines as well as an impressive cache of California bottles.

The restaurant is located in the Hotel Vintage Court, and no smoking is allowed.

Postrio, 545 Post St. ☎ **776-7825.**

Cuisine: AMERICAN. **Reservations:** Required. **Cable Car:** Mason and Hyde. **Bus:** 2, 3, 4, or 38.
Prices: Breakfast $6–$15; appetizers and pastas $8–15; main courses $18–$25. AE, CB, DC, DISC, MC, V.
Open: Breakfast Mon–Fri 7–10am; lunch daily 11:30am–2pm; dinner daily 5:30–10:30pm; brunch Sat–Sun 9am–2pm; bar daily 11:30am–2am.

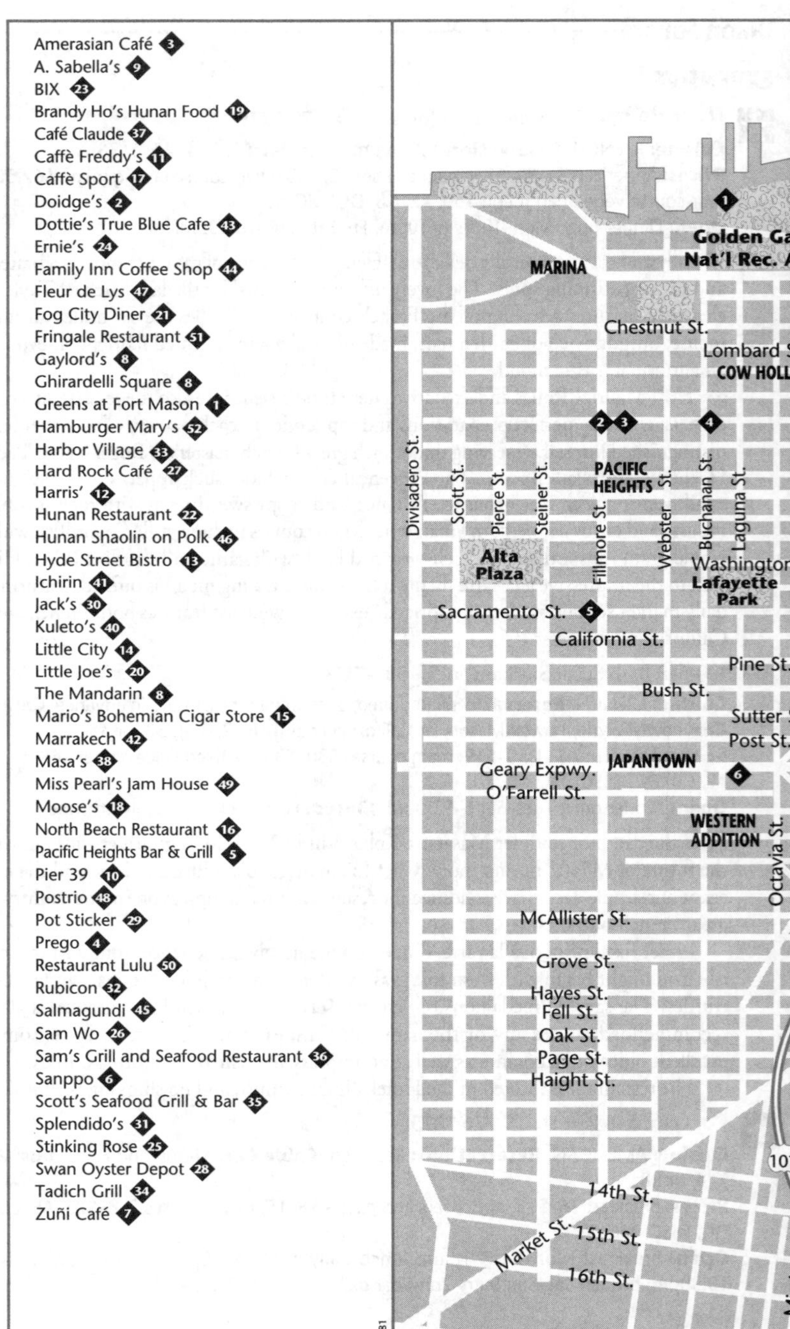

Amerasian Café 3
A. Sabella's 9
BIX 23
Brandy Ho's Hunan Food 19
Café Claude 37
Caffè Freddy's 11
Caffè Sport 17
Doidge's 2
Dottie's True Blue Cafe 43
Ernie's 24
Family Inn Coffee Shop 44
Fleur de Lys 47
Fog City Diner 21
Fringale Restaurant 51
Gaylord's 8
Ghirardelli Square 8
Greens at Fort Mason 1
Hamburger Mary's 52
Harbor Village 33
Hard Rock Café 27
Harris' 12
Hunan Restaurant 22
Hunan Shaolin on Polk 46
Hyde Street Bistro 13
Ichirin 41
Jack's 30
Kuleto's 40
Little City 14
Little Joe's 20
The Mandarin 8
Mario's Bohemian Cigar Store 15
Marrakech 42
Masa's 38
Miss Pearl's Jam House 49
Moose's 18
North Beach Restaurant 16
Pacific Heights Bar & Grill 5
Pier 39 10
Postrio 48
Pot Sticker 29
Prego 4
Restaurant Lulu 50
Rubicon 32
Salmagundi 45
Sam Wo 26
Sam's Grill and Seafood Restaurant 36
Sanppo 6
Scott's Seafood Grill & Bar 35
Splendido's 31
Stinking Rose 25
Swan Oyster Depot 28
Tadich Grill 34
Zuñi Café 7

9081

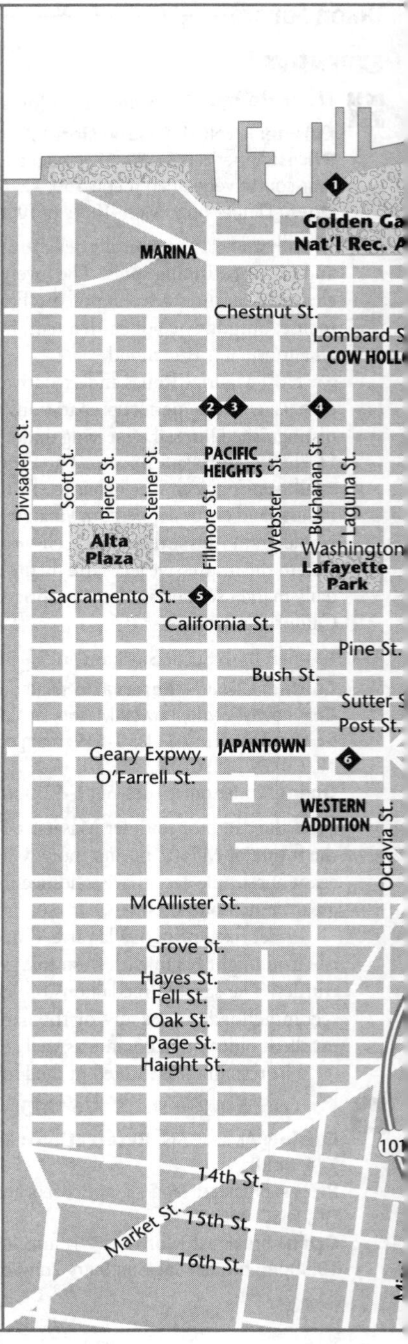
Golden Ga
Nat'l Rec. A
MARINA
Chestnut St.
Lombard S
COW HOLL
PACIFIC HEIGHTS
Divisadero St.
Scott St.
Pierce St.
Steiner St.
Fillmore St.
Webster St.
Buchanan St.
Laguna St.
Alta Plaza
Washington
Lafayette Park
Sacramento St.
California St.
Pine St.
Bush St.
Sutter S
Post St.
JAPANTOWN
Geary Expwy.
O'Farrell St.
WESTERN ADDITION
Octavia St.
McAllister St.
Grove St.
Hayes St.
Fell St.
Oak St.
Page St.
Haight St.
101
14th St.
15th St.
16th St.
Market St.

N
0
.5 mi
.3 km
San Francisco Bay
45
41
Pier 39
43
35
33
31
29
23
19
17
15
9
7
5
3
1
uatic
ark
The
nnery
rardelli
quare
SIAN HILL
Jefferson St.
Beach St.
NORTHERN WATERFRONT
North Point St.
Bay St.
Francisco St.
Columbus Ave.
TELEGRAPH HILL
Embarcadero
Chestnut St.
Lombard St.
NORTH BEACH
Greenwich St.
Filbert St.
Union St.
Green St.
Vallejo St.
Broadway
Pacific St.
kson St.
Montgomery St.
Powell St.
Taylor St.
CHINATOWN
Sansome St.
Battery St.
Stockton St.
Mason St.
Kearny St.
Front St.
Drumm St.
Polk St.
Larkin St.
Hyde St.
Leavenworth St.
NOB HILL
Jones St.
Grant St.
Ferry Building
(World Trade Center)
Justin
Herman
Plaza
FINANCIAL
DISTRICT
Bush St.
San Francisco-
Oakland
Bay Bridge
Steuart St.
Main St.
Fremont St.
Geary St.
Union
Square
Farrell St.
Market St.
80
Moscone
Convention
Center
1st St.
Eddy St.
Mission St.
SOUTH OF MARKET
(SoMa)
2nd St.
CIVIC CENTER
Harrison St.
3rd St.
6th St.
Folsom St.
arket St.
Howard St.
4th St.
9th St.
10th St.
Bryant St.
Brannan St.
11th St.
Townsend St.
7th St.
King St.
th St.
8th St.
Berry St.
Folsom St.
101
Bryant St.
Potrero St.
280
16th St.
1
8
9
10
11
13
14
15
16
17
18
19
20
21
22
23
24
25
26
29
30
31
32
33
34
35
36
37
38
39
40
41
42
43
44
45
47
48
49
50
51
52

Celebrity chef Wolfgang Puck, who is best known for his Los Angeles restaurant Spago, has brought his fame and formula to San Francisco in the form of this trendy eatery on Post Street, at Mason Street, adjacent to the Prescott Hotel. Postrio is named for the combined talents of its three executive chefs—Wolfgang and Anne and David Gingrass, all of whom hail from L.A.

The dramatic art-gallery interior is as creative as the cuisine. Breakfast here means cinnamon-raisin French toast with strawberry jam and maple syrup, or a trio of salmon, sturgeon, and white fish served on homemade bagels.

Lunchtime pastas can be ordered as appetizer or main-course portions. Whimsical concoctions include clam-filled dumplings with angel hair pasta, and crispy grilled sweetbreads with pumpkin ravioli. Spago won fame for its designer pizzas, many of which have been imported here. Toppings like smoked salmon, crème fraîche, and golden caviar have never even been imagined in Naples.

The gloves come off at dinner, when elegant first courses include home-smoked sturgeon with potato pancakes, and crab cakes served with smoked red-pepper sauce. Selecting just one main course is equally frustrating. Possibilities may include roast Dungeness crab with spicy curry risotto, crispy Wolf Ranch quail with spicy pineapple sauce, or grilled squab with noodle cakes and blackberry sauce. An exceptionally diverse wine selection spans the globe and deserves special attention. Gourmet pizzas are served at the bar well into the night, pleasing a see-and-be-seen crowd. Reservations are essential, as this is one of the hottest restaurants in the city.

MODERATE

Café Claude, 7 Claude Ln. ☎ **392-3505.**

Cuisine: FRENCH. **Reservations:** Accepted. **Cable Car:** Powell-Hyde and Powell-Mason lines.
Prices: Appetizers $3–$7; main courses $5–$9.50. AE, MC, V.
Open: Mon–Thurs 8:30am–9:30pm, Fri–Sat 8:30am–10pm.

Cramped and crazy, Café Claude, situated on a quaint little lane near Union Square, is San Francisco's most authentic Parisian bistro. Seemingly everything—every table, every spoon, every salt shaker, and every waiter—is imported from France. A tin "Buvez Pepsi" sign attracts young trendies who create a fun, lively atmosphere. There is usually live jazz on weekends, and with prices topping out at about $9 for entrees like pan-fried sturgeon, Café Claude is a terrific value.

Ichirin, 330 Mason St., at O'Farrell St. ☎ **956-6085.**

Cuisine: JAPANESE. **Reservations:** Accepted. **Cable Car:** Mason and Hyde lines. **Bus:** 7, 8, 27, 38, or 71. **Muni Metro:** J, K, L, M, or N lines.
Prices: Appetizers $3–$8; main courses $15–$20. AE, DC, MC, V.
Open: Dinner daily 5–10:30pm.

First-rate food and service sets Ichirin apart from other local Japanese eateries. In addition to a full sushi bar, the restaurant specializes in shabu shabu—thinly sliced beef, vegetables, and tofu cooked tableside by kimono-clad waitresses. Some 28 appetizers include gyoza, deep-fried chicken wings, and marinated broiled beef wrapped with green onion. Fixed-price dinners are a chef's choice of appetizer, main course, and dessert, in traditional Japanese fashion. Private tatami rooms are available.

★ **Kuleto's,** 221 Powell St., at Geary St. ☎ **397-7720.**

Cuisine: NORTHERN ITALIAN. **Reservations:** Recommended. **Cable Car:** Mason and Hyde lines. **Bus:** 2, 3, 4, or 38.
Prices: Appetizers $4–$9; main courses $8–$17. AE, CB, DC, DISC, MC, V.
Open: Breakfast daily 8–10:30am; lunch/dinner daily 11:30am–11pm.

There are hundreds of Italian restaurants in the city, but few rival Kuleto's for exceptionally good food, unusual preparations, a comfortable setting, and moderate prices. For the full effect, enter through the Powell Street bar. Between yesteryear's high ceilings and the black-and-white-marble tile floors hang strings of dried peppers and garlic, over a magnificently long mahogany bar. Kuleto's is the familiar, friendly restaurant you've known for years—even if you've never been here before.

The same extensive northern Italian menu filled with Tuscan specialties is offered at both lunch and dinner. Antipasti include calamari fritti and roasted garlic, which is meant to be squeezed and spread over the crusty Italian bread. For a main dish the management suggests sausage and peppers with Parmesan polenta or roast duck with grappa-soaked cherries. But go with what you like; I favor the fresh fish, which is grilled over hardwoods. The well-selected wine list includes some fine champagnes.

Marrakech, 419 O'Farrell St., at Taylor St. ☎ **776-6717.**

Cuisine: MOROCCAN. **Reservations:** Recommended. **Cable Car:** Mason and Hyde lines. **Bus:** 38 or any Market Street bus. **Muni Metro:** J, K, L, M, or N lines.
Prices: Fixed-price dinner $20–$24. AE, MC, V.
Open: Dinner only, daily 6–10pm.

Both a belly- and an eye-full, a meal at Marrakech is a ritual feast. The restaurant itself is a sumptuous regal palace. Enter past a marble pool and take your place on a goatskin ottoman atop high-quality Oriental rugs. At once you are served by waiters in kaftans, who wash and dry your hands while a belly dancer weaves her way between the tables.

Choose from four award-winning, multiple-course, fixed-price menus, each of which includes a piquant Moroccan salad, meant to be scooped up with chunks of homemade bread, and b'stila, a mixture of chicken, egg, and almonds encased in filo dough. Next, choose between chicken with lemons, lamb with honey, lamb with onions, and hare with paprika, all eaten by hand. Couscous is served as well, followed by fruit and mint tea.

Frommer's Smart Traveler: Restaurants

1. Go ethnic. The city has some great, inexpensive ethnic dining.
2. Eat your main meal at lunch, when prices are lower; you can sample gourmet hot spots for a fraction of the price charged at dinner.
3. Watch the liquor; it can add greatly to the cost of any meal.
4. Look for fixed-price menus, two-for-one specials, and coupons in local newspapers and magazines.

BUDGET

The Family Inn Coffee Shop, 505 Jones St., at Geary St. ☎ **771-5995.**

Cuisine: AMERICAN. **Cable Car:** Mason and Taylor lines. **Bus:** 2, 3, 4, or 38.
Prices: Appetizers $1–$3; main courses $4–$6. No credit cards.
Open: Tues–Sat 7am–6pm.

For a really hearty yet inexpensive meal, it's hard to top the Family Inn. The menu varies daily, but homemade soups are featured at lunch, along with a special so cheap that it's practically being given away—a main course served with mashed potatoes, a vegetable, bread, and dessert costs less than $5. The restaurant is not the least bit fancy—just counter seats in front of a hard-working kitchen—but the food is good and wholesome, and the price is right.

 **Salmagundi,** 442 Geary St., at Taylor St. ☎ **441-0894.**

Cuisine: SOUP/SALADS. **Reservations:** Not accepted. **Cable Car:** Mason and Taylor lines. **Bus:** 2, 3, 4, or 38.
Prices: Soups and salads $3–8. AE, MC, V.
Open: Tues–Sat 11am–11pm, Sun–Mon 11am–9pm.

Modern, bright, and pleasant, Salmagundi is a casual spot, offering three unusual varieties of soup daily. Among the possibilities are English country Cheddar, Hungarian goulash, North Beach minestrone, Barbary Coast bouillabaisse, and Ukrainian beef borscht. Sandwiches and salads are also available. The atmosphere is pleasant, clean, and casual. Highly polished wood floors are topped with Formica tables and bentwood chairs. Seats in the rear look out onto a tiny garden.

Financial District

EXPENSIVE

Ernie's, 847 Montgomery St. ☎ **397-5969.**

Cuisine: CONTEMPORARY FRENCH. **Reservations:** Recommended. **Bus:** 15 or 41.
Prices: Appetizers $10–$17; main courses $24–$30, fixed-price dinner $66. AE, CB, DC, MC, V.
Open: Dinner only, Mon–Sat 6–10:30pm. **Closed:** First 2 weeks of Jan; major holidays.

Two blocks from Broadway, on Montgomery Street at Pacific Avenue, Ernie's is a study in elegance, offering exquisite French cuisine and polished service. The champagne-colored silk walls, richly tapestried upholstery, and fragrant floral arrangements make you feel as if you're dining in a fine home. In fact, much of the handsome furniture was salvaged from San Francisco's splendid turn-of-the-century mansions. The massive mahogany and stained-glass bar in the cocktail lounge is an authentic relic of the Barbary Coast.

Chef Alain Rondelli turns out a playful mix of classic French cuisine prepared in a contemporary style. Soy sauce, balsamic vinegar, lime juice, ginger, Indian spices, and champagne replace butter and cream, creating lighter, more health-conscious dishes. The menu, which changes with the seasons four times annually, might feature onion and niçoise olive tart with rosemary-scented veal juice or sage-scented Maine lobster sautéed with artichokes in a thyme flower juice with fresh herbs. Fixed-price dinners are available Monday through Thursday only. A stellar selection of over 350 fine wines includes excellent buys on some older vintages. Expect to spend at least $60 per person—a worthy splurge. Jackets are required for men.

Harbor Village, 4 Embarcadero Center, Lobby Level, at Sacramento St. ☎ **781-8833.**

Cuisine: CHINESE. **Reservations:** Recommended. **Bus:** 15, 45, or 76.
Prices: Appetizers $8–$14; main courses $15–$30. AE, DC, MC, V.
Open: Lunch Mon–Fri 11am–2:30pm, Sat 10:30am–2:30pm, Sun 10am–2:30pm; dinner daily 5:30–9:30pm.

One of the city's most upscale Chinese restaurants, Harbor Village claims to have introduced Imperial cuisine—the classical Cantonese cuisine of Hong Kong—to this country. Five hand-picked, imported specialty chefs work under the direction of executive chef Andy Wai. And though most of the dishes are steadfastly Cantonese, the kitchen seems equally at home with spicy Szechuan dishes and such popular "northern" specialties as crackling Peking duck. Crystal chandeliers, porcelain place settings, and delicate engraved chopsticks aren't chop suey either. Nor are the six opulent private dining rooms, each laid with Chinese antiquities and teak furnishings.

The courteous staff can guide you through the extensive menu, which includes some 30 seafood dishes alone. Unique appetizers include shredded spicy chicken and minced squab in lettuce cups. Stir-fried garlic prawns and sizzling beef in black pepper sauce are excellent main-course choices. Among several wine selections, the house Chardonnay is especially drinkable, at about $14 a bottle.

The restaurant offers free validated parking at all the Embarcadero Center garages (located at the foot of Clay Street) after 5pm Monday through Friday and all day on Saturday, Sunday, and holidays.

Scott's Seafood Grill & Bar, 3 Embarcadero Center (3rd Floor). ☎ **981-0622.**

Cuisine: SEAFOOD. **Reservations:** Recommended.
Prices: Appetizers $3–$11; main courses $11–$28; lunch $9–$19. AE, CB, DC, DISC, MC, V.
Open: Mon–Thurs 11am–10pm, Fri–Sat 11am–11pm, Sun 4:30–9:30pm.

Although there are several Scott's Seafood Grills around California, this is no corporate-style chain eatery. The restaurant's chefs and managers are encouraged to experiment and create an environment that's appropriate to their location. This Scott's, located in the heart of San Francisco's Financial District, has earned an excellent reputation for its seafood dishes, prepared with lots of fresh herbs and spices and served in a modern French country setting. White-clothed tables, each topped with a small hurricane lamp and separated by massive gray stone pillars and brass railings, front floor-to-ceiling windows. During warm weather, diners can choose to eat alfresco, on a terrace under large green umbrellas.

Creamy clam chowder, seafood salads, and pan-fried sole are Scott's signature lunch dishes. Dinners are more exotic and include local sand dabs and Cajun-style fried oyster pasta, as well as a selection of fresh fish that changes daily. There is a good wine list available by the glass, as well as an unusual wheat beer.

MODERATE

Jack's, 615 Sacramento St., at Montgomery St. ☎ **986-9854.**

Cuisine: CONTINENTAL. **Reservations:** Recommended. **Bus:** 15 or 41.
Prices: Appetizers $2.50–$9; main courses $9–$22; fixed-price dinner $19. AE.
Open: Mon–Fri 11:30am–9:30pm, Sat 5–9:30pm.

Founded in 1864, this venerated San Francisco institution claims a fanatically faithful following. The wooden Thonet chairs, worn tile floors, and sure-footed waiters all look as they might have appeared a century ago. Despite all appearances, this is a relatively fancy place, and jackets are suggested for men.

Choices run the gamut from cheese blintzes to Thanksgiving-style roast-turkey dinners, but the real specialty here is the rex sole. Fixed-price dinners are served from 5 to 9pm only and are usually a particularly good buy.

★ **Sam's Grill and Seafood Restaurant,** 374 Bush St., near Kearny St. ☎ **421-0594.**

Cuisine: SEAFOOD. **Reservations:** Accepted for parties of six or more. **Bus:** 15, 45, or 76.
Prices: Appetizers $4–$13; main courses $7–$20. AE, DC, MC, V.
Open: Mon–Fri 11am–8:30pm.

Power-lunching at Sam's is a San Francisco tradition; the restaurant has been doing a brisk business with Financial District types for more than 40 years. The entry, which holds a lovingly polished small mahogany bar, opens onto a main dining room, where most of the setting is in booths with shoulder-high partitions. It's pretty noisy at midday; but if privacy is your primary concern, choose one of the individually curtained booths that line the corridor to the left of the main dining room.

For lunch, consider the clam chowder, charcoal-broiled filet of fish, and a dessert of French pancakes anisette. Luncheon specials might include boned rex sole à la Sam or fresh crab au gratin.

★ **Splendido's,** 4 Embarcadero Center. ☎ **986-3222.**

Cuisine: MEDITERRANEAN/AMERICAN. **Reservations:** Accepted. **Bus:** 15, 45, or 76.
Prices: Appetizers $5–$10; main courses $7–$14 at lunch, $10–$23 at dinner. AE, DC, DISC, MC, V.
Open: Lunch Mon–Fri 11:30am–2:30pm, dinner daily 5:30–10pm.

It's difficult to believe that the feel of a small Mediterranean village could be captured within such an architecturally sophisticated building, but designer Pat Kuleto (who also worked magic on Postrio) has done just that, using 200-year-old olivewood doors, Moorish arches, rustic French stone walls, Italian tiles, Spanish wrought-iron banisters, and a Portuguese pewter-top bar. Stone pillars, huge hand-hewn beams, wormwood cabinetry, and soft rose lighting are used to create intimate dining areas. When the weather is pleasant, you can eat under a canopy on the outdoor patio or choose the exhibition seating in front of the full-display kitchen, complete with an open grill and wood-burning pizza oven.

And then there's the food. Beautifully presented starters might include curry soup with spiced chicken, or ravioli of prosciutto, mascarpone, and shallots. Main courses may feature pan-roasted quail with lemon and herb dumplings; sautéed sweetbreads with pancetta vinaigrette, wild mushrooms, and chestnuts; or grilled loin of lamb with white-bean and garlic flan. The dessert creations of pastry chef Cameron Ryan are surely procured from somewhere beyond the pearly gates. The list may include polenta cake with fresh strawberry sauce; a frozen terrine of pears, chocolate, Armagnac, and prunes; tiramisu with chocolate pine-nut bark; or my favorite, pistachio crème brûlée. Like the pasta and baked goods, all the desserts are prepared fresh daily in the restaurant's hard-working bakery. The excellent wine list is especially notable for its good selection of wines by the glass. The restaurant is located between Clay and Drum streets.

Tadich Grill, 240 California St. ☎ **391-1849.**

Cuisine: SEAFOOD. **Reservations:** Not accepted. **Bus:** 7, 8, or 71. **Muni Metro:** J, K, L, M, or N lines.
Prices: Appetizers $7–$13; main courses $12–$25. MC, V.
Open: Mon–Fri 11am–9pm, Sat 11:30am–9pm.

This famous, venerated old California institution arrived with the Gold Rush in 1849 and maintains the handsome dignity of the successful survivor that it is. Tradition is honored by an ageless mahogany bar that extends the entire length of the restaurant. No-nonsense white-linen-draped tables are topped with big plates of sourdough bread. Power-lunchers get one of the seven enclosed private booths.

Tadich's claims to be the very first to broil seafood over mesquite-hardwood charcoal, back in the early 1920s. Then it was known simply as charcoal broiling. The restaurant's reputation was immediately solidified, and it continues to be fantastic. For a light meal you might try one of the delicious seafood salads, such as shrimp or prawn Louis, with a glass of wine and fresh sourdough bread with butter. Hot dishes include baked avocado with shrimp diablo, baked casserole of stuffed turbot with crab and shrimp à la Newburg, and mesquite-charcoal-broiled petrale sole with butter sauce—a local favorite. Anyone who's anyone gets a side order of big, tasty french fries. The restaurant is located between Battery and Front streets.

BUDGET

Hunan Restaurant, 924 Sansome St. ☎ **956-7727.**

Cuisine: CHINESE. **Reservations:** Accepted. **Bus:** 15, 45, or 76.
Prices: Appetizers $4–$7; main courses $7–$11. AE, DC, DISC, MC, V.
Open: Daily 11am–9:30pm.

It's not much to look at, but Craig Claiborne, formerly of the *New York Times,* and Tony Hiss, of the *New Yorker* magazine, have both sung the praises of this restaurant near Broadway. Regulars choose either the onion cakes or the dumplings (often called pot stickers) as an appetizer, then move on to hot-and-sour beef, chef Henry Chung's special chicken, or bean curd (tofu) with pickled vegetables. There are several spicy dishes, but the kitchen does its best to accommodate delicate palates.

North Beach

EXPENSIVE

BIX, 56 Gold St. ☎ **433-6300.**

Cuisine: CALIFORNIA. **Reservations:** Recommended. **Bus:** 15, 30, 41, or 45.
Prices: Appetizers $5–$10; main courses $11–$25; lunch $5–$12. AE, CB, DC, DISC, MC, V.
Open: Mon–Thurs 11:30am–11pm, Fri–Sat 11:30am–midnight, Sun 6–10pm.

Located in the middle of a narrow alley near Columbus Avenue, BIX looks very much like an upscale 1930s-era speakeasy. A small, dimly lit dining room that's taller than it is wide is overlooked by a second seating area on a wraparound balcony. Clubby tables are topped with lampshaded candles that cast shadows on the room's dark redwood walls and ornately capitaled columns. Perfectly suited to the see-and-be-seen set, the restaurant offers good sightlines, and a particularly busy bar. A singer usually sits at a grand piano, though it's hard to hear him over the din of the crowd.

BIX is not the place to rush through a meal; diners linger for the night, and table turnover is low. Consequently, food is expensive, but happily, it's worth it. Lobster bisque pasta is especially recommendable, as are the potato-and-leek pancakes wrapped around smoked salmon, caviar, and crème fraîche. Entrées, which are heavy on seafood, include sand dabs with asparagus, and salmon with aioli and fried capers. Grilled meats include pork and lamb chops and thick-cut steaks. At lunch, smaller portions are offered at smaller prices.

Caffè Sport, 574 Green St. ☎ **981-1251.**

Cuisine: ITALIAN. **Reservations:** Accepted only for parties of four or more. **Bus:** 15, 30, 41, or 45.
Prices: Appetizers $5–$9; main courses $14–$29. AE, DC, MC, V.
Open: Lunch Tues–Thurs noon–2pm, Fri–Sat noon–2:30pm, dinner seatings Tues–Thurs at 5, 6:30, 8:30, and 10pm; Fri–Sat at 6:30, 8:30, and 10pm.

You either love or hate this robust Sicilian eatery between Grant and Columbus Avenues. The dining room is a clutter of hanging hams and sausages, fishnets, decorative plates, dolls, and mirrors. Artful tables and chairs are hand painted and colorfully collaged. The restaurant is better known for its surly staff and eclectic ambience than for its fine food. Owner, chef, and artiste Antonio Latona serves up healthy portions of attitude along with garlic-laden pasta dishes; he is happy to report that this is former mayor Dianne Feinstein's favorite eatery.

Lunch is less hectic than the mobbed and lively dinner scene. Disregard the framed menu that sits on each table, and accept the waiter's suggestions. Whatever arrives—whether it be a dish of calamari, mussels, and shrimp in tomato-garlic sauce or pasta in pesto sauce—it will be delicious. Bring a huge appetite—but don't be late if you have a reservation.

Moose's, 1652 Stockton St. ☎ **989-7800.**

Cuisine: CONTINENTAL. **Reservations:** Recommended. **Bus:** 15, 30, 41, or 45.
Prices: Appetizers $5–$11; main courses $8–$25; lunch $7–$14. AE, CB, DC, MC, V.
Open: Sun–Thurs 11:30am–11pm, Fri–Sat 11:30am–midnight. Bar stays open later.

Overlooking Washington Square Park, a big blue stylized neon moose beckons diners into this restaurant's two huge dining rooms, which are enlivened with blown-glass chandeliers and Romanesque archways. Most of the herd that grazes here are well-dressed locals who are very much a part of the young establishment scene. Nicely lit, Moose's is small enough to feel intimate, yet big enough for customers to get a table, even on busy nights.

An open kitchen turns out creative continental meals with a quasi-Mediterranean flair. Menus, which change weekly, might include Dungeness crab cakes with vanilla bean coleslaw; goat cheese, roasted peppers, and garlic-stuffed calzone; pan-roasted fish; or grilled veal marinated in port wine and served with a potato-onion tart. Similar meals, with smaller portions and prices are served at lunch.

The adjacent bar, which is separated from the main dining room by a low frosted glass partition, remains busy long after the kitchen closes.

Rubicon, 558 Sacramento St. ☎ **434-4100.**

Cuisine: CONTINENTAL. **Reservations:** Recommended.
Prices: Appetizers $7–$14; main courses $17–$23. AE, MC, V.
Open: Lunch Mon–Fri 11:30am–2:30pm; dinner Mon–Thurs 5:30–10:30pm, Fri–Sat 5:30–11pm.

Debuting in 1994, Rubicon won instant publicity because its owners happen to be film director Francis Ford Coppola and actor Robert De Niro–both of whom are part of the Myriad investment group, which opened the Tribeca Grill and Montrachet in New York. Named for Coppola's Napa Valley wine, Rubicon, on the corner of Leidesdorff Street, features a contemporarily conservative dining room that feels like the proper place for an expensive dinner.

The menu is short and to the point, offering favorite delicacies like sautéed foie gras with rhubarb, and house-cured salmon with crisp potato cakes. Equally opulent entrées like rabbit and tuna are accompanied by creamy corn, polenta, or chickpea pancakes with tomato confit.

MODERATE

Little City, 673 Union St., at Powell St. ☎ **434-2900.**

Cuisine: ITALIAN/MEDITERRANEAN. **Reservations:** For parties of six or more. **Cable Car:** Mason Street line. **Bus:** 15, 30, 41, or 45.
Prices: Appetizers $5–$9; main courses $10–$16. AE, MC, V.
Open: Daily 11:30am–midnight, bar 11:30am–2am.

Once one of the most fashionable restaurants in San Francisco, Little City attracts upscale young people. Colorful prints and paintings line the exposed brick walls, while brass fans whirl slowly overhead. Burgundy cafe curtains frame the large windows, and white linen napkins sit upon heavy, dark-wood tables, which are spread over two levels.

The excellent food is what originally attracted the trendies, and it still never disappoints. The menu is heavy on antipasti—you'd do well to circumvent the main course entirely and make a meal of the appetizers. Among the best choices are grilled sausage and polenta, baked Brie with roasted garlic (served with plenty of bread), Manila clams, and prawns borracho (marinated in tequila, chiles, garlic, and lime). The best pasta is covered with a sauce of Gorgonzola, walnuts, and sun-dried tomatoes. If you must, other dishes (which change daily) include fresh fish, pot roast, osso buco. The sacripantina is a must—rum-soaked sponge cake, layered with zabaglione ($4 and worth it). The limited wine list is acceptable; the scotch and grappa selections are exceptional.

Little Joe's, 523 Broadway, near Columbus Ave. ☎ **433-4343.**

Cuisine: ITALIAN. **Reservations:** Not accepted. **Bus:** 15, 30, 41, or 45.
Prices: Appetizers $2–$3; main courses $8–$12. MC, V.
Open: Mon–Thurs 11am–10pm, Fri–Sat 11am–11pm, Sun noon-10pm.

Little Joe's is a real San Francisco experience. It's a wide-open grillroom, completely without pretension. Joe's gets so busy that tables often have to be shared with other patrons, and that's part of the fun. Portions are huge and preparations straightforward. The menu is heavy on veal and chicken, prepared in several styles—parmigiana, piccata, saltimbocca, scaloppine. A half dozen pastas, with at least as many sauces, are also available. But the specialty here is Caciucco, a stew of clams, cod, crab, mussels, and prawns, cooked in a tomato-and-garlic sauce. Also recommended are the gamberoni (prawns), which are served over a big plate of spaghetti.

North Beach Restaurant, 1512 Stockton St., between Union St. and Green St. ☎ **392-1587.**

Cuisine: ITALIAN. **Reservations:** Accepted for parties of three or more. **Bus:** 15, 30, 41, or 45.

Prices: Appetizers $5–$8; main courses $12–$30; fixed-price dinner $25–$35. AE, DC, MC, V.
Open: Daily 11:30am–11:45pm.

Highest praise goes to chef Bruno Orsi for the first-rate cucina Toscana at this trattoria. The unpretentious decor includes white table cloths, tabletop candles in red holders, hanging plants, and the requisite braids of garlic suspended overhead. But the atmosphere is flamboyantly Italian, marked by robust conversation, charming waiters, and attentive service. Dining here is something of an occasion.

The top appetizer is easily melon with home-cured prosciutto, along with a side order of homemade pasta; it makes a great light meal. In addition to a choice of cooked-to-order dishes, such as cioppino, eggplant parmigiana, and veal scaloppine marsala, full seven-course, fixed-price dinners include an enormous antipasto, salad, soup, fresh vegetable, and pasta with prosciutto sauce. A la carte choices include a selection of 22 homemade pasta dishes. Desserts range from an excellent zabaglione to a tray of cheese, walnuts, apples, and figs. You'll want to order a bottle of wine from the excellent cellar.

Stinking Rose, 325 Columbus Ave. ☎ **781-7673.**

Cuisine: ITALIAN/INTERNATIONAL. **Reservations:** Accepted. **Bus:** 15, 30, 41, or 45.
Prices: Appetizers $4–$10; main courses $8–$18; lunch about half price. AE, MC, V.
Open: Sun–Thurs 11am–11pm, Fri–Sat 11am–midnight.

Garlic, of course, is the "flower" from which this restaurant gets its name. From soup to ice cream, the supposedly healthful herb is a star ingredient in most every dish. From a strictly gourmet point of view, the Stinking Rose is nothing special—pizzas, pastas, and meats smothered in simple, overpowering garlic sauces are tasty, but memorable only for their singular garlicky intensity. That said, this is a fun place; the restaurant's lively atmosphere and themed menu is good entertainment. Several casually decorated dining areas with black-and-white checkerboard linoleum floors sport gray marble tables. Large windows overlooking an enviable Columbus Avenue corner location put passersby on display. The best dishes here include garlic-steamed clams and mussels, garlic pizza, and 40-clove garlic chicken (served with garlic mashed potatoes).

So what if tourists are the restaurant's "regulars?" It's a gimmick, to be sure, but as a unique theme restaurant, the Stinking Rose works.

Frommer's Cool for Kids: Restaurants

Hard Rock Cafe (see p. 124) Touristy but fun, the famous Hard Rock chain flips one of the best burgers in town.

Little Joe's (see p. 115) Although it's often busy, Joe's is not cramped—it's fun. Children will like the convivial atmosphere, as well as the simple pasta and meat dishes.

Marrakech (see p. 109) What child wouldn't like to eat with his or her hands in a fancy restaurant? Marrakech is dining entertainment, complete with music, dancing, and a totally themed environment—for adventurous children only.

INEXPENSIVE

Caffè Freddy's, 901 Columbus Ave. ☎ **922-0151.**

Cuisine: CONTINENTAL. **Reservations:** Accepted.
Prices: Appetizers $3–$7; main courses $5–$8; lunch $4–$7; brunch $2–$8. MC, V.
Open: Mon lunch only, 11:30am–3pm; Wed–Fri 11:30am–10pm; Sat 9am–10pm; Sun 9am–9pm.

Recognizable by the large, painted palms that frame the doorway, Caffè Freddy's, at the corner of Lombard Street, is an attractive Italian-American diner with large storefront windows overlooking Columbus Avenue. Inside, under an exceptionally high ceiling, are large modern prints, lots of small matte black tables, and a few gray booths.

It would take several pages to mention all the different offerings that are prepared in this restaurant's open kitchen. Those with small appetites might opt for one of the many sandwiches or salads available in full or half orders (a representative salad is warm cabbage with goat cheese, currants, walnuts, rosemary, and spinach). The large assortment of appetizers includes a plate of bruschetta, fresh melon, ham, sun-dried tomatoes, and pesto. One of the restaurant's specialties is polenta (grilled corn meal) topped with one or more ingredients that may include salmon, cheese, and assorted vegetables. Gourmet pizzas and creative pastas are topped with everything from grilled chicken to green beans, red onions, lemon, garlic, bread crumbs, and parmesan cheese.

BUDGET

 **Mario's Bohemian Cigar Store,** 566 Columbus Ave. ☎ **362-0536.**

Cuisine: ITALIAN. **Bus:** 15, 30, 41, or 45.
Prices: Sandwiches $5–$6.
Open: Mon–Sat 10am–midnight, Sun 10am–11pm. **Closed:** Dec 24-Jan 1.

Kitty-corner to Washington Square is North Beach's friendliest neighborhood joint. Mario's is best known for its foccacia sandwiches, such as meatball or eggplant—they're great. Cap your meal with an excellent cappuccino or a Campari as you watch the people stroll by.

Chinatown

A delightful prelude to the pleasure of eating in Chinatown is strolling up and down its streets trying to choose a restaurant. There are hundreds of places, but if you find yourself overwhelmed, it's nice to know that you can always rely on these following suggestions.

MODERATE

 **Brandy Ho's Hunan Food,** 217 Columbus Ave., at Pacific Ave. ☎ **788-7527.**

Cuisine: CHINESE. **Reservations:** Accepted. **Bus:** 15 or 41.
Prices: Appetizers $4–$9; main courses $8–$13. AE, DC, DISC, MC, V.
Open: Sun–Thurs 11:30am–11pm, Fri–Sat 11:30am–midnight.

Because it offers great food in a down-to-earth atmosphere, Brandy Ho's is one of my hippest friends' favorite restaurants. The simple, pleasant interior features black-and-white, faux-granite tabletops and a large open kitchen.

Fried dumplings with sweet-and-sour sauce make a good starter, as do several uncommon soups, including moo shu soup with eggs, pork, vegetables, and tree-ear mushrooms and fish-ball soup with spinach, bamboo shoots, noodles, and other goodies.

The best main course is Three Delicacies, a combination of scallops, shrimp, and chicken with onion, bell pepper, and bamboo shoots, seasoned with ginger, garlic, and wine and served with black-bean sauce. Most dishes here are quite hot and spicy, but the kitchen will adjust the level to meet your specifications. There is a small selection of wines and beers, including plum wine and sake.

BUDGET

Pot Sticker, 150 Waverly Place. ☎ **397-9985.**

Cuisine: CHINESE. **Reservations:** Not accepted. **Bus:** 15, 30, 41, or 45.
Prices: Appetizers $3–$6; main courses $7–$11. AE, MC, V.
Open: Daily 11:30am–9:45pm.

It's nice to know about a simple, quiet, untouristed Chinatown oasis patronized largely by locals in the know. This restaurant's specialty is pot stickers, an appetizer of pan-fried or steamed, thin-skinned dumplings stuffed with seasoned meat or vegetables. These staples of Mandarin cooking do just what their name suggests—stick to the pot they're cooked in. The full menu of authentic standards reads like a survey of Chinese cooking. Moo shu pork, Mongolian beef, General Tsao's chicken, and other specialties are traditionally prepared by extremely experienced hands. The restaurant is located just east of Grant Avenue, between Clay and Washington Streets.

Civic Center

EXPENSIVE

 **Zuñi Cafe**, 1658 Market St. ☎ **552-2522.**

Cuisine: MEDITERRANEAN. **Reservations:** Suggested. **Bus:** 6, 7, 71, or 75. **Muni Metro:** All Market Street lines.
Prices: Appetizers $6–$10; main courses $17–$23.
Open: Tues–Sun 7:30am–midnight, Sun 7am–11pm.

This wedge-shaped restaurant, near the corner of Page Street, attracts one of the most electric crowds in the city. It is perpetually packed. The common denominators between diners in black leather and those in pinstripes are good looks, success, and a taste for a good martini. Regulars come for the scene as much as for the food. The changing menu always includes meat, such as New York steak with Belgian endive gratin, but the fish is best, either grilled or braised in the kitchen's brick oven. Whatever you do, be sure to order the shoestring potatoes—they're the best in the world. A separate, foot-long oyster menu has half a dozen or so varieties on hand at all times. The restaurant is located three blocks south of the Opera House.

MODERATE

Miss Pearl's Jam House, 601 Eddy St., at Larkin St. ☎ **775-5267.**

Cuisine: CARIBBEAN. **Reservations:** Accepted. **Bus:** 31.
Prices: Appetizers $3–$7; small plates $5–$10; main courses $15–$17. DC, MC, V.
Open: Lunch Tues–Fri 11:30am–2:30pm; dinner Tues–Thurs 6–10pm, Fri–Sat 6–11pm, Sun 5:30–9:30pm; brunch Sun 11am–2:30pm (bar open until 2am).

Popular with a young, artistic, gold-card crowd, Miss Pearl's is a wacky, lively restaurant and bar with a ridiculous, Caribbean-inspired, "Gilligan's Island" interior. It adjoins the Phoenix Inn, an equally esoteric motel (see "San Francisco Accommodations" above).

Starters may include black-eyed-pea fritters or catfish fingers with Trinidadian pepper and cilantro pesto. Salads include hearts of palm and jicama and cold calamari with ginger, chiles, lime, and peppers. Blackened fish, "jerked" chicken, and rock shrimp quesadillas often make the list of main courses. The dinner menu also includes a terrific selection of small plates (tapas) that can be combined into a fulfilling meal. Grilled tequila-marinated prawns might complement chicken-mango sausage or eggplant with wild-mushroom risotto. The restaurant has a full bar and a limited selection of Californian wines. On weekends stick around after dinner for drinks and dancing to steel drums and other island sounds. The restaurant is located four blocks north of the Civic Center.

Japan Center & Environs

Pacific Heights Bar & Grill, 2001 Filmore St., at Pine St. ☎ **567-5226.**

Cuisine: SEAFOOD. **Reservations:** Recommended for dinner. **Bus:** 2, 3, or 22.
Prices: Appetizers $5–$8; main courses $6–$17. AE, CB, DC, MC, V.
Open: Lunch Wed–Sat 11:30am–2:30pm; dinner Sun–Thurs 5:30–9:30pm, Fri–Sat 5:30–10:30pm; Sun brunch 10:30am–2:30pm.

Handsome and spacious, this friendly spot enjoys a warm neighborhood patronage. A long oak bar fronts comfortable lounge chairs, arranged around small cocktail tables. The dining room is dominated by a broad front window, which puts every diner on display. Pictureless frames decorate an entire wall, while color is provided by fresh flowers and a lively clientele.

The menu changes nightly but always includes 12 to 16 varieties of oysters—including Belon, jumbo Blue Point, and Portuguese. Clams and mussels are also available on the half shell. Prices average $1.10 to $1.30 each or $6.50 to $7.50 per half dozen. From amberjack to sturgeon, fresh fish is the house specialty, followed by seafood stews, paella, and cioppino. Understandably, the selection changes daily. A good selection of Californian wines is available by the glass.

 **Sanppo,** 1702 Post St., at Laguna St. ☎ **346-3486.**

Cuisine: JAPANESE. **Reservations:** Not accepted. **Bus:** 2, 3, 4, or 38.
Prices: Appetizers $3–$6; main courses $6–$13; combination dishes $10–$17. MC, V.
Open: Tues–Sat 11:45am–10pm, Sun 3–10pm.

Simple and unpretentious though it is, Sanppo, across from the Japan Center, serves excellent down-home Japanese food. You may be asked to share one of the few tables that surround a square counter in the small dining room.

Lunches and dinners include miso soup, rice, and pickled vegetables. At lunch you might have an order of fresh, thick-cut sashimi, teriyaki, tempura, beef donburi, or gyoza (dumplings filled with savory meat and herbs) for $6 to $12. The same items are available at dinner for an additional dollar or so. Combination dishes, such as tempura, sashimi, and gyoza or tempura and teriyaki, are also available. Beer, wine, and sake are served.

Union Street

MODERATE

Prego, 2000 Union St., at Buchanan St. ☎ **563-3305.**

Cuisine: ITALIAN. **Reservations:** Accepted. **Bus:** 41 or 45.

Prices: Appetizers $3–$7, pasta and pizza $6–12, meat and fish courses $10–$18. AE, CB, DC, MC, V.
Open: Daily 11:30am–midnight.

A light and airy trattoria, Prego is pretty and pleasant, with a veritable garden of seasonal flowers blossoming in the windows. Pasta is the house specialty, but competently prepared meat, fowl, and fish dishes are also designed to please. Spit-roasted free-range chickens are prepared from a rotisserie, and served with potatoes and vegetables. Did I mention the crusty pizzas that emerge from the oak-fired brick ovens? A good selection of wines is also available by the glass or bottle.

BUDGET

Amerasian Café, 2165 Union St. ☎ **963-9638.**

Cuisine: CHINESE. **Reservations:** Not accepted. **Bus:** 22, 41, 45, or 47.
Prices: Appetizers $2–$6; main courses $5–$8; sandwiches $4–$6. AE.
Open: Mon–Sat 11am–10pm, Sun 10:30am–7pm.

Occupying a small storefront in the middle of the Union Street shopping district, the Amerasian Café serves upscale cuisine in a decidedly down-home dining room. Order at the counter that separates the kitchen from the 10-table dining area, then take a seat and wait for your hamburger, pot stickers, or kung pao chicken to arrive. The Asian chefs who prepare the wholly à la carte menu are as adept at grilling chicken as they are at stir-frying vegetables.

Haight-Ashbury

MODERATE

Cha Cha Cha, 1805 Haight St., at Schrader St. ☎ **386-5758.**

Cuisine: CARIBBEAN. **Reservations:** Not accepted. **Bus:** 6, 7, 66, 71, or 73. **Muni Metro:** N line.
Prices: Small plates $4–$7; main courses $9–$13. No credit cards.
Open: Lunch Mon–Fri 11:30am–3pm, Sat–Sun 10am–4pm; dinner Mon–Thurs 5–11pm, Fri–Sun 5–11:30pm.

I hesitate to recommend this culinary party because the line is already long enough. But this is the restaurant I dream about when I'm away, and the wait is well worth it. Colorful booths and tables sit under Créole shrines, while small plates (tapas) of out-of-this-world delights are served by an unpretentious, friendly young staff. The chicken paillard is something to die for. Sangria is served by the pitcher and is particularly potent. Squeeze in with the hip Haight Street crowd and have some drinks while you wait an hour or more.

BUDGET

Zona Rosa, 1797 Haight St. ☎ **668-7717.**

Cuisine: MEXICAN. **Reservations:** Not accepted. **Bus:** 6, 7, 66, 71, or 73. **Muni Metro:** N line.
Prices: Burritos $3–$4. No credit cards.
Open: Daily 11am–11pm.

Zona Rosa, at the corner of Haight and Shrader Streets, has absolutely the best burritos in the world. Period. Don't argue—just walk up to the counter, choose your ingredients (beans, rice, cheese, salsa, steak, chicken, and so on) and watch your guacamole dreams be rolled right before your eyes. It's pretty nice for a dive. You can sit on a stool at the window or at one of five colorful interior tables. Zona Rosa is cheap and it's one of the best meals around. It's located in the Haight, two blocks from Golden Gate Park.

Mission District

Val 21, 995 Valencia St. ☎ **821-6622.**

Cuisine: CALIFORNIAN. **Reservations:** Recommended. **Muni Metro:** J line to 16th Street Station.
Prices: Appetizers $4–$10; main courses $8–$18. AE, MC, V.
Open: Sun–Thurs 11am–11pm, Fri–Sat 11am–midnight.

In this dining age, when New San Francisco cuisine also usually means high-tech lighting, Kenneth Cole shoes, and smoked pesto pizzas, Val 21, a Mission District standout, proves refreshingly different. Located at 21st Street, the restaurant's dining room is contemporarily stylish, yet not too opulent or trendy. The food is top quality, though you never know what will be on the menu, a drawback for some. Inspired meals depend on availability, ensuring quality and freshness. Wonderfully spiced chicken and fish dishes arrive with surprise accompaniments like black beans or fried plantains. Preparations are somewhat exotic, but not too far out, and portions are generous.

Around Town

EXPENSIVE

A. Sabella's, Fisherman's Wharf, 2766 Taylor St., 3rd Floor. ☎ **771-6775.**

Cuisine: ITALIAN/SEAFOOD. **Reservations:** Accepted. **Cable Car:** Powell-Hyde, Powell-Mason, or California lines.
Prices: Appetizers $7–$10; main courses $16–$38. AE, DC, MC, V.
Open: Daily 11am–10:30pm.

The Sabella family has been serving seafood in San Francisco since the turn of the century, and has operated A. Sabella's on the Wharf continuously since 1920. Today, the traditionally creative kitchen is under the direction of fourth-generation chef Michael Sabella, a graduate from New York's Culinary Institute of America.

The freshest local and imported fish, crab, shrimp, and other seafoods are served cooked or in cocktails, as well as on top of pastas. The restaurant's dedicated sous chefs also make steak, veal, and other "turf" dishes special. The truly special wine list is particularly strong with selections from Napa and other Californian regions.

Flying Saucer, 1000 Guerrero St. ☎ **641-9955.**

Cuisine: INTERNATIONAL. **Reservations:** Recommended.
Prices: Appetizers $7–$17; main courses 15–$24. No credit cards.
Open: Dinner only, Tues–Sat 5:30–9:30pm.

Never have I seen food so outrageously and artfully presented—not even in Hong Kong, New York, or Japan. Peering into the open kitchen, diners might catch a chef carefully standing a jumbo prawn on its head atop a baked column of potato polenta, which is itself the centerpiece of a commotion of food art. Fish, beef, and fowl dishes are competently grilled, baked, or flamed before being surrounded by a flurry of sauces and accoutrements. While the pricey food is flavorful, the overwhelming emphasis at this restaurant is visual. The party extends from the plate to the decor, where toy plastic flying saucers mingle with colorful murals and creative lighting. The menu changes frequently, and there are almost always specials. If you ask your waiter to bring you the chef's most flamboyant *looking* offering, you won't be disappointed.

One word of warning: The restaurant is located in the Mission District, at 22nd Street. This is not the city's safest neighborhood, and you may wish to take a cab.

Harris', 2100 Van Ness. ☎ **673-1888.**

Cuisine: AMERICAN. **Reservations:** Recommended.
Prices: Appetizers $6–$10; main courses $16–25. AC, CB, DC, DISC, MC, V.
Open: Dinner Mon–Fri 6–11pm, Sat–Sun 5–11pm.

Every great city has a great steak restaurant, and in San Francisco it's Harris'. Proprietor Ann Lee Harris knows steaks. She grew up on a cattle ranch and married the owner of the largest feed lot in California. In 1976 the couple opened the Harris Ranch Restaurant on Interstate 5, in central California, where they built a rock-solid reputation up and down the coast. Harris' well-marbled, corn-fed midwestern steaks tempt diners through a glass-walled aging room. They are cut thick—either New York style or T-bone—and are served with a baked potato and seasonal vegetables.

For those who like to visit steak houses and order something else, Harris' offers roast duckling in a light orange sauce, lamb chops, pork tenderloin with peppercorn sauce, and fresh fish and lobster. My friends who like brains rave about the restaurant's sautéed brains in brown butter.

Harris' light, brick-walled dining room, upholstered in muted florals, is more casual than the restaurant's tie-and-jacket dress code would suggest.

MODERATE

Fog City Diner, 1300 Battery St. ☎ **982-2000.**

Cuisine: AMERICAN. **Reservations:** Accepted.
Prices: Appetizers $2–$9; main courses $11–$14. CB, DC, DISC, MC, V.
Open: Sat–Thurs 11:30am–11pm, Fri 11:30am–midnight.

Looking like a dressed-up diner, but smelling like a bar, Fog City Diner is a good pick South of Market. Made famous by a Visa credit card commercial, the restaurant looks like a genuine American metallic diner—but only from the outside. Inside, dark polished woods, inspired lighting, and a well-stocked raw bar tell you this is no hash slinger.

Dressed-up diner dishes include gourmet chili dogs, salads, pork chops, and pot roast. Fancier fish and meat meals include grilled catches of the day and thick-cut steaks. Lighter eaters can make a meal out of the long list of "small plates" that include sautéed mushrooms with garlic custard and seasoned walnuts, and a quesadilla with chili peppers and almonds.

Fringale Restaurant, 570 Fourth St. ☎ **543-0573.**

Cuisine: FRENCH. **Reservations:** Recommended.
Prices: Appetizers $4–$10; main courses $8–$18; lunch $4–$12. AE, MC, V.
Open: Lunch Mon–Fri 11:30am–2:30pm; dinner Mon–Sat 5:30–10:30pm.

A celebrated newcomer, Fringale, which is French for "urge to eat," is an upscale bistro-style restaurant with an ebullient owner and fine food. The cozy, low-key South of Market dining room can only accommodate about 15 tables, all of which are usually in service.

French-Basque cuisine means starters like onion pie with roquefort, prosciutto, and walnuts; and cucumber salad with smoked salmon and crème fraîche. Main courses like sautéed sea scallops Basquaise with shaved fennel or veal scallops with wild mushrooms are equally adventuresome, and well within the chef's substantial range. Roquefort ravioli with basil and pine nuts, and roasted lamb and eggplant sandwiches are added to the lunch menu. Serious wine drinkers will appreciate the restaurant's long, well-chosen list of domestic and international selections.

Greens Restaurant, Fort Mason, in Building A, Fort Mason Center. ☎ **771-6222.**

Cuisine: VEGETARIAN. **Reservations:** Recommended two weeks in advance. **Bus:** 30.
Prices: Appetizers $5–$7; main courses $10–$12, fixed-price dinner $36; brunch $8–$10. DISC, MC, V.
Open: Lunch Tues–Thurs 11:30am–2pm, Fri–Sat 11:30am–2:30pm; dinner Mon–Thurs 5:30–9:30pm, Fri–Sat 6–9:30pm; brunch Sun 10am–2pm (bakery, Tues–Sat 9:30am–4:30pm, Sun 10am–3pm).

Knowledgeable locals swear by Greens, one of natural food's best ambassadors. Located in an old warehouse, with enormous windows overlooking the marina and the bay, the restaurant is both a pioneer and a legend. Haute vegetarian cuisine includes North African vegetable stew, packed with a garden of greens and served with raisin-almond couscous; pizza with shiitake and porcini mushrooms, Gruyère and fontina cheeses, tomatoes, and thyme; and marinated, mesquite-grilled tofu and vegetables, with wild-rice pilaf. Appetizers and soups are equally adventuresome, as are fresh desserts such as polenta cake with strawberry-rhubarb compote, and cherry-almond biscotti. Dinner is served à la carte Tuesday through Thursday. The place is particularly clubby Friday and Saturday nights, when a single, fixed-price dinner menu is offered exclusively.

Lunch and brunch are somewhat simpler but equally inventive. Lunch offerings include overstuffed pita sandwiches, designer lettuce salads, chili, soup, and such specials as spinach frittata and grilled tofu on potato bread. Brunch encompasses a variety of breads, muffins, omelets, and sandwiches. An extensive wine list is always available.

Like the restaurant, the adjacent bakery is also operated by the Zen Center. It sells homemade breads, sandwiches, and pastries to take home. Enter Fort Mason opposite the Safeway at Buchanan and Marina Streets.

Hyde Street Bistro, 1521 Hyde St. ☎ **441-7778.**

Cuisine: NORTHERN ITALIAN. **Reservations:** Recommended. **Cable Car:** Mason and Hyde line.
Prices: Appetizers $5–$7; main courses $12–$16.
Open: Daily 5:30–10:30pm.

Chef and owner Albert Rainer combines his Austrian background with Californian style to create consistently good dishes, such as strudel filled with a melange of

IMPRESSIONS

San Francisco is the city that knows how.
—President William Howard Taft

San Francisco is the city that knows chow.
—Trader Vic, Restaurateur

vegetables and a roasted Sonomo chicken with a potato pancake and vegetables. Pasta dishes are particularly abundant. Albert recommends ravioli with wild-mushroom sauce or penne with sausage, peppers, tomato, and eggplant. Hyde Street Bistro is exceptionally romantic. Despite the bustle, the small European dining room feels singular and special. Albert greets diners personally at the door and makes you feel pampered and special. The prices are exceptionally reasonable for food of such high caliber. The restaurant is located on the northwestern slope of Nob Hill, between Pacific and Jackson Streets.

Restaurant Lulu, 816 Folsom St. ☎ **495-5775.**

Cuisine: CONTINENTAL. **Reservations:** Recommended. **Bus:** 15, 30, 32, 42, or 45.
Prices: Appetizers $5–$8; main courses $9–$18; lunch $7–$17. AE, MC, V.
Open: Mon–Sat 11:30am–10:30pm, Sun 5:30–10:30pm.

Lulu's excellent food, upscale casual surroundings, and pulsing atmosphere combine to make this South of Market newcomer one of San Francisco's most terrific bargains. Enormous windows and high ceilings represent the current local style. The single large dining room suffers from such high decibel levels that the cooks must wear headsets with microphones in order to communicate with each other.

The restaurant's not-to-be-missed roasted mussels arrive at the table piled high on an iron skillet. While you might skip the rather ordinary pastas and gourmet pizzas, meats from the wood-fired rotisserie are simply delicious, including leg of lamb, rosemary chicken, and pork loin. Sandwiches, like fresh tuna with sweet pepper or roasted chicken, are served at lunchtime. Lulu's wine list is particularly interesting, and includes an excellent selection of rare and oversized bottles ranging from California's Clos Du Val Cabernet Sauvignon, 1983 ($50), to France's Vieux Telegraphe Châteauneuf du Pape, 1990 ($500).

INEXPENSIVE

Hamburger Mary's, 1582 Folsom St., at 12th St. ☎ **626-5767.**

Cuisine: AMERICAN. **Reservations:** Recommended. **Bus:** 9, 12, 42, or 47.
Prices: Breakfast $5–$9; lunch/dinner $5–$11. AE, MC, V.
Open: Tues–Thurs 11am–1am, Fri 11:30am–2am, Sat 10am–2am, Sun 10am–1am.

Easily the hippest burger joint in San Francisco, Hamburger Mary's is packed with an ever-trendy crowd of South of Market dance clubbers. The restaurant's kitsch decor includes thrift-shop floral wallpaper, family photos, garage-sale prints, stained glass, religious drawings, and Asian screens. You'll get to know the bar well—it's where you'll stand with the masses while you wait for a table. Don't despair. They mix a good drink—and anyway hanging out is the reason you're here. Best of all, Hamburger Mary's serves some of the best burgers in town. Top it with grilled mushrooms, avocado spread, salsa, bleu cheese, or a swamp of chili and cheese. Order home fries instead of french fries any day.

You have no reason to be anywhere near here come breakfast, but if you are, it's a good stop for a three-egg omelet, banana bread, or French or Hawaiian toast.

Hard Rock Cafe, 1699 Van Ness Ave., at Sacramento St. ☎ **885-1699.**

Cuisine: AMERICAN. **Reservations:** Not accepted. **Cable Car:** California Street line. **Bus:** 1.
Prices: Appetizers $3–$6; main courses $4.50–$13. AE, MC, V.
Open: Sun–Thurs 11am–11:30pm, Fri–Sat 11am–midnight.

What can I say about one of the most popular tourist-oriented eateries ever to gimmick the public out of hard-earned vacation money? Like its sibling restaurants around the world, this loud, nostalgia-laden place is the home of the guaranteed wait. Don't arrive hungry, especially on weekend nights, when the line can run down the block.

Formerly an auto showroom, the cafe is decorated with gold records, historic front pages, and the usual "Save the Planet" clutter. It's a convention center with ceiling fans. Despite the hype, the menu is decent—the place flips a pretty good burger—and the prices are moderate. Baby back ribs, grilled fish, and chicken are also available, as are salads and sandwiches. The restaurant is located about six blocks west of Nob Hill's summit.

Swan Oyster Depot, 1516 Polk St. ☎ **673-1101.**

Cuisine: OYSTER BAR. **Reservations:** Not accepted. **Bus:** 27.
Prices: Seafood cocktails $5–$8; clams and oysters on the half shell $6–$7.50 per half dozen. No credit cards.
Open: Mon–Sat 8am–5:30pm.

Almost 85 years old and looking even older, the Swan Oyster Depot is classic San Francisco. Opened in 1912, this tiny hole-in-the-wall with the city's friendliest servers, is little more than a narrow fresh fish market that decided to slap down some stools. There are only 20 or so seats here; chairs jammed toe-to-toe at a long marble bar. Most of the patrons come for a quick cup of chowder or a plate of half-shelled oysters that arrive chilling on crushed ice. Indeed, there's little more than that available here. The menu is limited to crab, shrimp, oyster and clam cocktails, Maine lobster, and Boston-style clam chowder. Fish is only available raw and to go.

BUDGET

Hunan Shaolin on Polk, 1150 Polk St. ☎ **771-6888.**

Cuisine: CHINESE. **Reservations:** Not accepted. **Bus:** 2, 3, or 4.
Prices: Appetizers $2–$5; main courses $5–$9; fixed-price lunch about $4. AE, CB, DC, DISC, MC, V.
Open: Daily 11am–10pm.

Some of the city's best Chinese restaurants lie outside Chinatown, and Hunan Shaolin, smack in the middle of "Polk Gulch," between Sutter and Post Streets, proves it. Pink, plastic-covered tablecloths, bentwood chairs, an odd assortment of lighting fixtures, and cheap Asian art surely must mean that the food is good. Indeed, the hot-and-sour soup is the best in the city. Of the main courses, I highly recommend the iron-platter specials (sizzling prawns, for one). Traditional dishes, such as cashew chicken, are also available. Lunch specials, offered weekdays from 11:30am to 2:30pm, are particularly a bargain at about $4. The restaurant is located seven blocks west of Union Square.

Marcello's, 420 Castro. ☎ **863-3900.**

Cuisine: PIZZA. **Muni Metro:** J line to Castro Street Station.
Prices: Pizza slices $1.50–$2.50; pies $10–$15.
Open: Mon–Fri 11am–2pm, Sat–Sun 11am–1pm.

Marcello's is not a fancy place, just a traditional pizza joint with a couple of tables and pizza by the slice. But, hey, this New Yorker thinks it's pretty good.

The Metro, 3600 16th St. ☎ **703-9750.**

Cuisine: CHINESE. **Reservations:** Accepted for parties of four or more. **Bus:** 8. **Muni Metro:** K, L, or M lines.

Prices: Appetizers $3–$7; main courses $5–$10. AE, MC, V.
Open: Dinner only, daily 5:30–11pm; bar daily 3:30pm–2am.

Located at the intersection of Market and Noe Streets, the Metro is an outstanding dinner selection in the Castro district. Touched here and there with slim gold lines, the black lacquer restaurant sports a stylish art-deco Parisian decor.

The lively Hunan menu is varied enough and includes many items not commonly seen in your neighborhood Chinese restaurant (unless, of course, you live in San Francisco). Among the beef and lamb dishes is a first-rate hot braised beef and delicious curried lamb. The list of seafood choices is lengthy, but you can always rely on scallops with black mushrooms. And the bean curd, garlic-braised eggplant, and black mushrooms in oyster sauce are great whether or not you're a vegetable aficionado. The restaurant's cocktail lounge is popular with locals Wednesday through Saturday.

Specialty Dining

DINING COMPLEXES

Ghirardelli Square

This outdoor shopping complex encompasses several good restaurants, most of which have great views of the water. Below are the best.

Gaylord's, 900 North Point St., Ghirardelli Square. ☎ **771-8822.**

Cuisine: INDIAN. **Reservations:** Recommended. **Cable Car:** Hyde Street line. **Bus:** 19, 42, 47, or 49.
Prices: Appetizers $4–$8; main courses $12–$19; fixed-price meals, $14–$18 at lunch, $22–$28 at dinner. AE, CB, DC, DISC, MC, V.
Open: Lunch Mon–Sat 11:45am–1:45pm, Sun noon–2:45pm; dinner daily 5–10:45pm.

With branches in London, New York, Beverly Hills, and New Delhi, this far-flung chain may be the most successful Indian restaurant in the world. Opened in 1976, San Francisco's Gaylord's has earned its reputation by serving an accessible North Indian haute cuisine in stunning surroundings. The warm, candlelit interior is spiced with superb bay views from almost every seat.

A la carte selections are available, but the fixed-price dinners are the most sensible choice. Almost everything on the menu is offered, including soup, tandoori chicken, lamb kebabs, chicken tikka, Indian breads, saffron rice, dessert, and tea and coffee. Lunch is a choice of fixed-price menus only. Dining here is not cheap, but Gaylord's is good and equals some of the finest restaurants in India.

A second Gaylord's is located at One Embarcadero Center (**397-7775**).

The Mandarin, 900 North Point, Ghirardelli Square. ☎ **673-8812.**

Cuisine: CHINESE. **Reservations:** Accepted. **Cable Car:** Hyde Street line. **Bus:** 19, 30, 42, or 49.
Prices: Appetizers $5–$12; main courses $15–$38; fixed-price dinners $22, $25, $28, and $38. AE, CB, DC, MC, V.
Open: Daily 11:30am–11:30pm.

Created by Madame Cecilia Chiang in 1968, the Mandarin is meant to feel like a cultured northern Chinese home and features beamed twig ceilings, fine furnishings, silk-covered walls, and good-quality Asian art. Tables are spaced comfortably apart, and the better of two softly lit dining rooms offers matchless views of the bay.

True to its name, the Mandarin offers exceptional Peking-style cookery. Dinner might start with sizzling rice soup—a chicken broth with shrimp, mushrooms, and fried rice that actually sizzles as it goes into the bowl. Unusual dishes include walnut chicken, minced squab, tangerine beef, Szechuan string beans, and smoked tea duck. Dim sum are served daily from 11:30am to 3pm.

Pier 39

Seafood restaurants are the pier's specialty. While none of the restaurants below rate among the city's best, most are atmospheric and well located and have good bay views. Good choices include the art-nouveau **Chic's Place** (**421-2442**), a seafood bar-and-grill eatery with a particularly fine wine selection.

The two-level **Dante's Italian Seafood Restaurant** (**421-5778**) is also very art nouveau, with a plush living room–style cocktail lounge upstairs, an exquisite food display up front, and incredible bay views. Char-broiled seafood and steaks, pasta, generous drinks, and sumptuous desserts are featured.

A bit of old San Francisco can be found at the **Eagle Café** (**433-3689**). The cafeteria-style service is perfect as you share space at long tables. It's open for breakfast, lunch, and dinner.

Then there's **Vannelli's** (**421-7261**), with its gorgeous mahogany bar and large variety of seafood dishes and wines.

Non-seafood samplings include a branch of **Yet Wah** (**434-4430**), a very popular San Francisco Chinese restaurant with first-rate Mandarin fare and terrific views.

Another Bay Area tradition, **Swiss Louis** (**421-2913**), moved to the pier from Broadway, where it had been located for more than 40 years. It's not Swiss, by the way—it's Italian.

If you *do* want Swiss fare (French Swiss, actually), you can have it in the homey and charming **Old Swiss House** (**434-0432**), complete with alpine-style carved chairs, lace-curtained windows, and a blazing fireplace in the cocktail lounge.

Most pier restaurants open for lunch at 11:30am and serve food until 10:30 or 11pm nightly. Call for specific information.

BREAKFAST/BRUNCH

If I could choose to be in any city in the world come breakfast time, I'd choose San Francisco. This city has no peer when it comes to honest, filling American morning food. Go out for breakfast in San Francisco, even if you have to retire early the night before in order to wake up in time.

Doidge's, 2217 Union St. ☎ **921-2149.**

Cuisine: AMERICAN. **Reservations:** Required Sat–Sun. **Bus:** 41 or 45.
Prices: Breakfast $5–$8; lunch $5–$10. MC, V.
Open: Mon–Fri 8am–1:45pm, Sat–Sun 8am–2:45am.

Started in 1971 with counter service and six tables, Doidge's has quickly become the quintessential breakfast joint. The restaurant has since expanded to include a comfortable dining room that sports a distinctly French look: fresh table flowers, oak sideboards, and the like. But seats at the original mahogany counter are still the most coveted by locals, who like to be close to the coffee pots.

Doidge's fame lies in its eggs Benedict, quite possibly the best you've ever tasted. Its eggs Florentine run a close second, prepared with thinly sliced Motherlode ham. Loggers and other hearty eaters would do well to order breakfast casserole—a medley of ham or Italian sausage, potato, onion, and tomato, baked with cheese and topped with a poached egg. French toast, fresh fruits, and buttermilk pancakes are offered along with an extensive list of omelets for the wide-eyed. Champagne and mimosas are also available.

Dottie's True Blue Cafe, 522 Jones St. ☎ **885-2767.**

Cuisine: BREAKFAST. **Reservations:** Not accepted. **Cable Car:** California Street Line.
Prices: Most items $2–$6. No credit cards.
Open: Daily 7:30am–2pm.

This family-owned breakfast restaurant in the Pacific Bay Inn has only 10 tables and a handful of counter stools. The traditional coffeeshop serves standard American morning fare (French toast, pancakes, bacon and eggs, omelets, and the like) delivered to blue-and-white checkerboard tablecloths on rugged diner-quality plates. Whatever you order, include bread, muffins, or scones, all of which are made on the premises.

★ **Pork Store Cafe,** 1451 Haight St. ☎ **864-6981.**

Cuisine: AMERICAN. **Reservations:** Not accepted. **Bus:** 6, 7, 66, 71, or 73. **Muni Metro:** N line.
Prices: Breakfast $3–$6. No credit cards.
Open: Mon–Fri 7am–3pm, Sat–Sun 8am–4pm.

Despite its unappealing, carnivorous name, the Pork Store serves the Haight's best breakfast, and everybody knows it. The usual omelet and pancake fare is supplemented by good oatmeal, great biscuits, and heaps of crunchy home fries. If possible, avoid weekends, when everyone who couldn't get up early enough during the week is here.

★ **Sears Fine Foods,** 439 Powell St., at Sutter St. ☎ **986-1160.**

Cuisine: AMERICAN. **Reservations:** Not accepted. **Bus:** 7, 8, or 71. **Muni Metro:** J, K, L, M, or N lines.
Prices: Meals $5–$10. No credit cards.
Open: Wed–Sun 6:30am–3:30pm.

Sears would be the perfect place to breakfast on the way to work, but you can't always be sure you'll get in the door before 9am. It's not just a diner, it's an institution, famous locally for its luscious dark-brown waffles, light sourdough French toast, and unbelievably delicious pancakes. Be prepared to wait, especially during rush hour.

LATE-NIGHT/24-HOUR DINING

Sam Wo, 813 Washington St., by Grant Ave. ☎ **982-0596.**

Cuisine: CHINESE. **Reservations:** Not accepted. **Bus:** 15, 30, 41, or 45.
Prices: Appetizers $2–$3; main courses $4–$5. No credit cards.
Open: Mon–Sat 11am–3am, Sun 12:30–9:30pm.

Very handy for late nighters, Sam's is a total dive that's well known and often packed. The restaurant's two pocket-size dining rooms are located on top of each other, on the second and third floors—take the stairs past the first-floor kitchen. You'll have to share a table, but this place is for mingling almost as much as it is for eating.

The house specialty is jook (known as congee in its native Hong Kong)—a disgustingly thick rice gruel flavored with fish, shrimp, chicken, beef, or pork. The best is Sampan, with rice and seafood. Several other dishes you've never seen are just as famous. Try sweet-and-sour pork rice, wonton soup with duck, or a roast-pork/rice-noodle roll. Chinese doughnuts sell for 50¢ each.

AFTERNOON TEAS

Fairmont Hotel, 950 Mason St. ☎ **772-5000.**

Reservations: Accepted. **Cable Car:** California Street line (direct stop). **Prices:** $15 set tea; à la carte available.
Tea Served: Mon–Sat 3–6pm, Sun 1–6pm.

Served in Connoisseur's Corner, away from the hotel's usually busy lobby, this serene lounge offers plush red velvet chairs and plentiful sandwiches and pastries along with hot tea and cider.

Four Seasons Clift Hotel, 495 Geary St. ☎ **775-4700.**

Reservations: Accepted. **Cable Car:** Powell-Hyde and Powell-Mason lines (2 blocks east). **Bus:** 2, 3, 4, 30, 38, or 45.
Prices: $10 light tea; à la carte available.
Tea Served: Mon–Sat 3–5pm.

The Clift's lobby bar is one of the coziest tea rooms in the city. Diners relax on comfortable chairs and love seats while tea is served on small lace-draped tables.

Neiman-Marcus, 150 Stockton St., Union Square. ☎ **362-3900.**

Reservations: Accepted. **Cable Car:** Powell-Hyde and Powell-Mason lines (one block west). **Bus:** 2, 3, 4, 30, 38, or 45.
Prices: $9 set tea; à la carte available.
Tea Served: Mon–Sat 3–5pm.

The Rotunda Restaurant has long offered fine dining under the department store's famous turn-of-the-century glass dome. During tea time, finger sandwiches, scones, and pastries are brought to your table on a silver tiered tray. Sadly, however, tea here is brewed from bags.

Sheraton Palace Hotel, 2 New Montgomery St. ☎ **392-8600.**

Reservations: Accepted. **Muni Metro:** All Market Street trams. **Bus:** All Market Street buses.
Prices: $16 set tea; $20 with champagne.
Tea Served: Daily 2:30–5pm.

It's hard to beat this grand hotel's fantastic glass-roofed Garden Court, especially at tea time, when changing sunlight and moody clouds turn the room into a dramatic light show. A harpist or other lone musician adds a theatrical score.

5 Attractions

San Francisco is an outdoor city; it's meant to be strolled in, gazed at, climbed, and admired. Accordingly, the best sights are outdoors—bridges, monuments, vantage points, and neighborhoods. Of course, San Francisco has terrific museums and galleries, but somehow, when you think about sightseeing in this city, you think about the beauty of the bay, the history of Alcatraz, the whimsy of Lombard Street, the exotic bustle of Chinatown, the toy-like cable cars, and a leisurely stroll along Fisherman's Wharf.

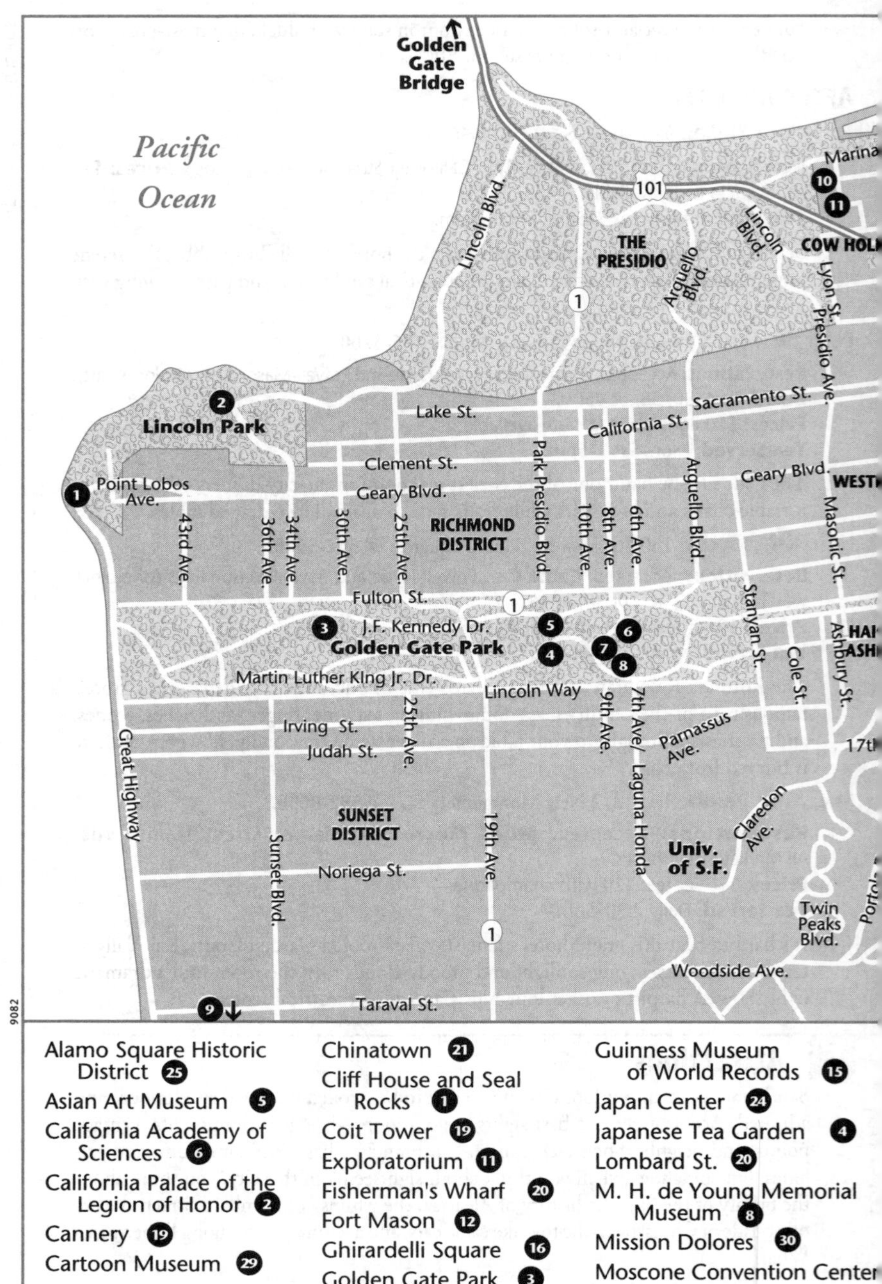

Golden Gate Bridge
Pacific Ocean
101
Marina
10
11
Lincoln Blvd.
THE PRESIDIO
Arguello Blvd.
Lincoln Blvd.
COW HOL
1
Lyon St.
Presidio Ave.
2
Lincoln Park
Lake St.
Sacramento St.
California St.
Clement St.
Geary Blvd.
Geary Blvd.
WEST
1
Point Lobos Ave.
43rd Ave.
36th Ave.
34th Ave.
30th Ave.
25th Ave.
RICHMOND DISTRICT
Park Presidio Blvd.
10th Ave.
8th Ave.
6th Ave.
Arguello Blvd.
Masonic St.
Fulton St.
1
Stanyan St.
3
J.F. Kennedy Dr.
5
6
HAI
ASH
Golden Gate Park
4
7
8
Ashbury St.
Cole St.
Martin Luther King Jr. Dr.
Lincoln Way
9th Ave.
7th Ave/ Laguna Honda
25th Ave.
Irving St.
Judah St.
Parnassus Ave.
17t
Great Highway
SUNSET DISTRICT
19th Ave.
Claredon Ave.
Univ. of S.F.
Sunset Blvd.
Noriega St.
Twin Peaks Blvd.
1
Woodside Ave.
9
Taraval St.
9082
Alamo Square Historic District 25
Asian Art Museum 5
California Academy of Sciences 6
California Palace of the Legion of Honor 2
Cannery 19
Cartoon Museum 29
Chinatown 21
Cliff House and Seal Rocks 1
Coit Tower 19
Exploratorium 11
Fisherman's Wharf 20
Fort Mason 12
Ghirardelli Square 16
Golden Gate Park 3
Guinness Museum of World Records 15
Japan Center 24
Japanese Tea Garden 4
Lombard St. 20
M. H. de Young Memorial Museum 8
Mission Dolores 30
Moscone Convention Center

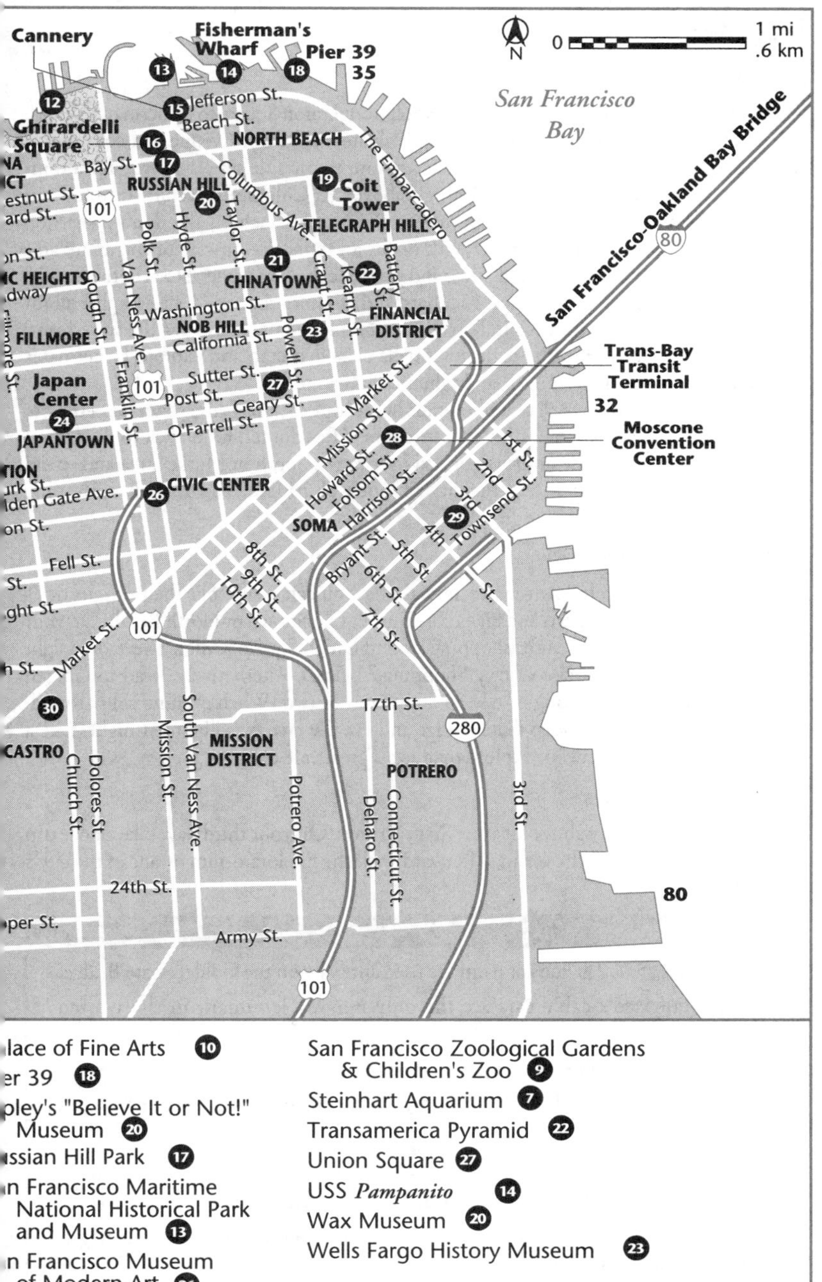

…lace of Fine Arts 10
…er 39 18
…pley's "Believe It or Not!" Museum 20
…ssian Hill Park 17
…n Francisco Maritime National Historical Park and Museum 13
…n Francisco Museum of Modern Art 26
San Francisco Zoological Gardens & Children's Zoo 9
Steinhart Aquarium 7
Transamerica Pyramid 22
Union Square 27
USS *Pampanito* 14
Wax Museum 20
Wells Fargo History Museum 23

Suggested Itineraries

If You Have One Day

Put on your walking shoes for a hearty stroll from Union Square to Fisherman's Wharf. From Union Square, head north along Chinatown's Grant Avenue and continue to Columbus Avenue. Take your time to explore exotic side streets or stop for a dim-sum lunch (see "San Francisco Dining," above). At Columbus Avenue, turn left and you'll be heading straight through the heart of North Beach. Again, don't rush. Stop for a rest in Washington Square Park or for a cappuccino in one of the many area cafes. Look left down Lombard Street and you'll see the "crookedest street in the world." If you feel hearty, turn right on Lombard and climb to the top of Telegraph Hill for a magnificent view from Coit Tower. Columbus Avenue ends near the waterfront, where you can take in the delicious smells of boiled crab and explore Fisherman's Wharf, Pier 39, the Cannery, and Ghirardelli Square.

For dinner, walk back to a restaurant in North Beach or Chinatown, or better yet hop on a cable car to your dinner destination. After dinner, head back to the Union Square area for a show or drinks or taxi over to the South of Market area and spend the night dancing in one of the city's hippest clubs (see "San Francisco Evening Entertainment," below).

If You Have Two Days

On your first day, follow the itinerary above. You can easily split the previous day's sightseeing into two parts and take more time in Chinatown or North Beach. On your second day, spend some time shopping around Union Square, Union Street, or Haight Street (see "San Francisco Savvy Shopping," below). Alternatively, head to Golden Gate Park and go boating or take in a museum or two. When evening rolls around, make your way to Golden Gate Bridge and eye the city at twilight. At night, take a North Beach bar crawl or explore that area's great cafe culture.

If You Have Three Days

Follow the itinerary above for your first two days. On your third day, take a boat trip to Alcatraz and tour the island. Afterward, visit the Exploratorium or one of the city's

Did You Know?

- More than 5,000 gallons of paint are used annually on the Golden Gate Bridge.
- San Francisco's cable cars are the only moving landmark in the United States.
- Twenty-six foghorns blast in San Francisco Bay.
- Most of San Francisco rests on a foundation of sandstone, shale, and volcanic rock.
- There are 43 hills in San Francisco.
- "I Left My Heart in San Francisco" is the city's official ballad.
- San Francisco, which has about 775,000 inhabitants, hosts nearly 3 million hotel guests annually.
- Mission Dolores, dedicated on August 2, 1791, is San Francisco's oldest extant structure.

small specialized museums. If you have kids in tow, you might want to visit the zoo or take a tour of the submarine USS *Pampanito* docked at Fisherman's Wharf. After an early dinner, go to a sports event (depending on the season, a baseball, football, or basketball game), take in a show, or go to the opera, symphony, or ballet.

If You Have Five Days or More

It's unlikely that you've exhausted all the opportunities of interest to you in the city, but if you can, take a boat trip across the bay to Sausalito or Larkspur. Better still, drive to the Wine Country or to Muir Woods. It's amazing how, just across the Golden Gate Bridge, you are suddenly in the country, surrounded by trees and vineyards. Hike through the Marin Headlands or take a day trip to Sonoma or Napa.

The Top Attractions

Golden Gate Park, extending from Stanyan Street to the Pacific Ocean between Fulton Street and Lincoln Way. ☎ **666-7201.**

One of the best and largest urban parks in America, San Francisco's Golden Gate Park is an integral part of the city. Three miles long and half a mile wide, this strip of green offers an outstanding variety of attractions, including a fantastic glass Victorian greenhouse, a Japanese tea garden, bowling greens, tennis courts, polo and football fields, checker pavilions, a botanical garden, a boat house with rentals, a golf course, baseball diamonds, riding stables, a bandstand where free summer concerts are held, and 27 miles of footpaths.

Free guided walking tours are offered every weekend from May through October by Friends of Recreation and Parks (221-1311). Call for information and reservations.

See "More Attractions" later in this section for details on three major museums located in the park: the M.H. de Young Memorial Musem, the Asian Art Museum, and the California Academy of Sciences.

Alcatraz Island, San Francisco Bay. ☎ **546-2700.**

Spanish explorer Juan Manuel de Ayala sighted this oblong chunk of rock in 1775 and christened it "Isla de los Alcatraces," or Island of the Pelicans, after the thousands of birds that made their home here. American settlers drove the birds off and successively transformed the island into a fortress, an army prison, and a maximum-security prison. The last incarnation occurred in 1934, at the peak of America's gangster scare, when tough guys like John Dillinger and "Pretty Boy" Floyd seemed to bust out of ordinary jails with toothpicks. An alarmed public demanded an escape-proof "tiger cage"—and the federal government fingered Alcatraz for the part.

The choice seemed ideal. The Rock, as it became known, is ringed by strongly swirling, bone-chilling water, enough to defeat even the strongest swimmer. At great cost, the old army cages were made into tiers of tiny, tool-proof, one-person cells, guarded by machine-gun turrets, high walls, steel panels, and electronic metal detectors called "snitch boxes." Even more forbidding than the walls were the prison rules: no talking, no newspapers, no canteen, no card playing . . . and no rewards for good behavior—merely punishment for bad.

The Rock resembled a gigantic, absolutely spotless tomb with the hush of death upon it. Into that living cemetery went most of the criminal big shots who let themselves be taken alive—Al Capone, "Machine Gun Kelly," "Doc" Barker, "Creepy" Karpis, and dozens more. All were broken by Alcatraz—except those who died while trying to escape from the island prison.

Although in some respects, Alcatraz seemed a macabre success, it was a huge white elephant from the start. Its cells were designed to hold 300 convicts, but there simply weren't that many top torpedoes in captivity. Consequently, more and more small fry were added just to maintain the population, which eventually included ordinary car thieves, forgers, and burglars—tin-pot crooks who could just as well have been jailed elsewhere. Yet the cost of maintaining the prison was colossal (drinking water, for instance, had to be ferried across in tank boats), and by the 1950s the money required to keep a single inmate on the Rock could have housed him in a luxury hotel suite. When three men seemed to have staged a successful escape from Alcatraz in June 1962, the federal government took the opportunity to order the prison "phased out"—closed. I say "seemed" because it's far from certain whether the trio actually did get away. They may have drowned while swimming for shore (as did several others), but their bodies were never recovered—a good mystery for modern tourists.

In the decade that followed, Alcatraz was abandoned, a rock without a purpose. The only tenants were a caretaker, his wife, and an assistant. In 1969 a group of protesters occupied the island with the intention of establishing a Native American cultural center; they left in 1971.

Once a major colony for thousands of seabirds, the island saw its wildlife population dwindle during federal prison days. The birds were frightened away by guard dogs, and the island's flora was kept trim to reduce the number of hiding places. Since Alcatraz joined the Golden Gate National Recreation Area in 1972, rangers have noticed birds returning—the black-crowned night-heron and western gull both nest here in abundance. You can take a ranger-guided nature tour (schedules are posted at the dock) or buy a self-guided walking trail map (25¢).

Today, great numbers of visitors explore the island's grim cells and fortifications. Tours are conducted by the U.S. National Parks Service and include fascinating accounts by park rangers on the island's history, an award-winning audio tour in the prison cell house, and a slide show.

A trip to Alcatraz is a popular excursion, and space is limited. Try to make reservations as far in advance as possible. Tours and tickets are available through **Red and White Fleet** (☎ **415/546-2700,** or toll free **800/229-2784** in California) and can be charged to your American Express, MasterCard, or Visa card. You can also purchase tickets on the day of sailing from the Red and White Fleet ticket office on Pier 41.

Be sure to wear comfortable shoes and take a heavy sweater or windbreaker. Even if the sun is shining when you embark, the bay can turn bitterly cold in minutes. You should know that hiking around the island is not easy; there's a steep rise, and you have to climb several flights of stairs. The National Parks Service advises those with a heart or respiratory condition to reconsider taking the tour if climbing stairs leaves them short of breath.

For those who want to get a closer look at Alcatraz without all the hiking, two boat-tour operators offer short circumnavigations of the island—Red and White Fleet, above, and Blue and Gold Fleet (☎ **415/781-7890**). (See "Organized Tours," below, for complete information.)

IMPRESSIONS

San Francisco is the most civilized city in America, full of delightful people.
—W. Somerset Maugham

Admission: Tours, $8.75 adults, $7.75 seniors 62 and older, $4.25 children ages 5–11.

Open: Winter, daily 9:30am–2:45pm; summer, daily 9:15am–4:15pm. Ferries depart from Pier 41 by Fisherman's Wharf every half hour at 15 and 45 minutes after the hour. You should arrive at least 20 minutes prior to sailing time.

Cable Cars. ☎ 673-6864.

Although they may not be San Francisco's most practical means of transportation, cable cars are the best loved. Designated official historic landmarks by the National Parks Service in 1964, these rolling symbols continuously cross the city like mobile museum pieces.

Cable cars owe their existence to the soft heart and mechanical genius of London-born engineer Andrew Hallidie. It all started in 1869, when Hallidie was watching a team of overworked horses haul a heavily laden carriage up a steep San Francisco slope. One horse slipped and the car rolled back, dragging the other tired beasts with it. Right then and there the engineer decided to invent a mechanical contraption to replace horses, and just four years later, in 1873, the first cable car made its maiden run from the top of Clay Street. Promptly ridiculed as "Hallidie's folly," the cars were slow to gain acceptance. One early onlooker voiced general opinion by exclaiming, "I don't believe it—the damned thing works!"

Even today a good many visitors have difficulty believing that these vehicles work. The cable cars' basic design hasn't changed in over a century—and still they have no engines! Each weighing about six tons, the cars are hauled along by a steel cable, enclosed under the street in a center rail. You can't see the cable unless you peer straight down into the crack, but you'll hear its characteristic clanking sound whenever you're nearby.

The cars move when the gripper (not the driver) pulls back a lever that closes a pincerlike "grip" on the cable. The speed of the car, therefore, is the speed of the cable—a constant 9½ m.p.h., never more or less. This may strike you as a snail's pace, but it doesn't feel that way when you're cresting an almost perpendicular hill and look down at what seems like a bobsled dive straight into the ocean. And when you're slamming around a horseshoe curve, you'd swear you were on two wheels. But in spite of the nerve tingles they can produce, cable cars are eminently safe. They have four separate braking devices, and most of the crew's time is spent applying them. The gripper operates the wheel brakes and the track brakes. The conductor frequently helps him by turning the hand lever of the rear brakes on the rear platform. And in real emergencies, there's a lever that rams a metal wedge into the cable slot, stopping the car so effectively that it takes a welding crew to dislodge it.

The two types of cable cars in use hold, respectively, a maximum of 90 and 100 passengers—and the limits are rigidly enforced. The best views are had from the outer running boards, where you have to hold on tightly when taking curves. Everyone, it seems, prefers to ride on the running boards. It's quite a sight to see a beehive-like cluster of people inching uphill, with a cable car tucked away somewhere in their midst.

Because some of the cars have only one-way controls, they have to be reversed manually on a turntable by their crews. Cable-car crews may be hardworking, but they're an elite corps—the marines of Muni. They're also an integral part of the show, ringing the famous bell and hollering "Heeeeere we go!" and, at the appropriate moments,

"Hold on tight for the curve!" Conductors and grippers positively bask in the admiration of local kids and tourists alike, and never cease polishing their image as "characters."

By the turn of the century, Hallidie's cable cars were running in most parts of the globe. Since then, they have been scrapped, one by one, in favor of more "modern" forms of transportation—Melbourne, Australia, was among the last cities to give up their trolleys. On several occasions, the San Francisco municipality wanted to follow suit. But each time it encountered so much opposition that, in 1955, the cable car's perpetuation was written into the city charter. This mandate cannot be revoked without the approval of a majority of voters—a prospect that is not soon forthcoming.

San Francisco's three existing lines comprise the world's only surviving system of cable cars. (For complete information on riding them, see "Getting Around," in Section 2.)

Coit Tower, atop Telegraph Hill. ☎ **362-0808.**

In a city known for its great views and vantage points, Coit Tower is tops. Located atop Telegraph Hill, just east of North Beach, the round stone tower offers magnificent 360-degree views of San Francisco.

Completed in 1933, the tower is the legacy of Lillie Hitchcock Coit, a wealthy eccentric who left San Francisco a $125,000 bequest "for the purpose of adding beauty to the city I have always loved." Inside the base are some colorful murals titled *Life in California, 1934.* Commissioned by the Public Works of Art Project, under President Franklin D. Roosevelt's New Deal program, the frescoed paintings, recently restored, are a curious melange of art and politics—a social realist's vision of America and Americans during the Great Depression.

Admission: Base, free; tower $3 adults, $2 students, $1 children ages 6–12.

Open: Daily 10am–7pm. **Bus:** 39 ("Coit").

The Exploratorium, in the Palace of Fine Arts, 3601 Lyon St. ☎ **563-7337,** or **561-0360** for recorded information.

The only museum to make this "Top Attractions" list is the thoroughly mind-boggling Exploratorium, on Lyon Street at Marina Boulevard. This fun, hands-on science fair is a participatory venture in which you use all your senses and stretch them to new dimensions. More than 650 permanent exhibits explore everything from color theory to Einstein's Theory of Relativity. Optics are demonstrated in booths where you can see a bust of a statue in three dimensions—but when you try to touch it, you discover it isn't there! The same surreal experience occurs with an image of yourself: When you stretch your hand forward, a hand comes out to touch you from the opposite direction, and the hands pass—or appear to pass—in midair. Every exhibit is designed to be used. You can whisper into a concave reflector and have a friend hear you 60 feet away, or you can design your own animated abstract art—using sound.

The museum is located on one of the prettiest parcels in the city in the only building left standing from the Panama-Pacific Exposition of 1915, which celebrated the opening of the Panama Canal. The adjoining lagoon is home to ducks, swans, seagulls, and sawgrass.

Admission: $8 adults, $6 senior citizens, $4 children ages 6–17, free for children under 6; free for everyone first Wed of each month.

Open: Memorial Day–Labor Day and holidays, Tues and Thurs–Sun 10am–5pm, Wed 10am–9:30pm; the rest of the year, Tues and Thurs–Sun 10am–5pm, Wed 10am–9:30pm. **Closed:** Mon from Labor Day–Memorial Day (except holidays),

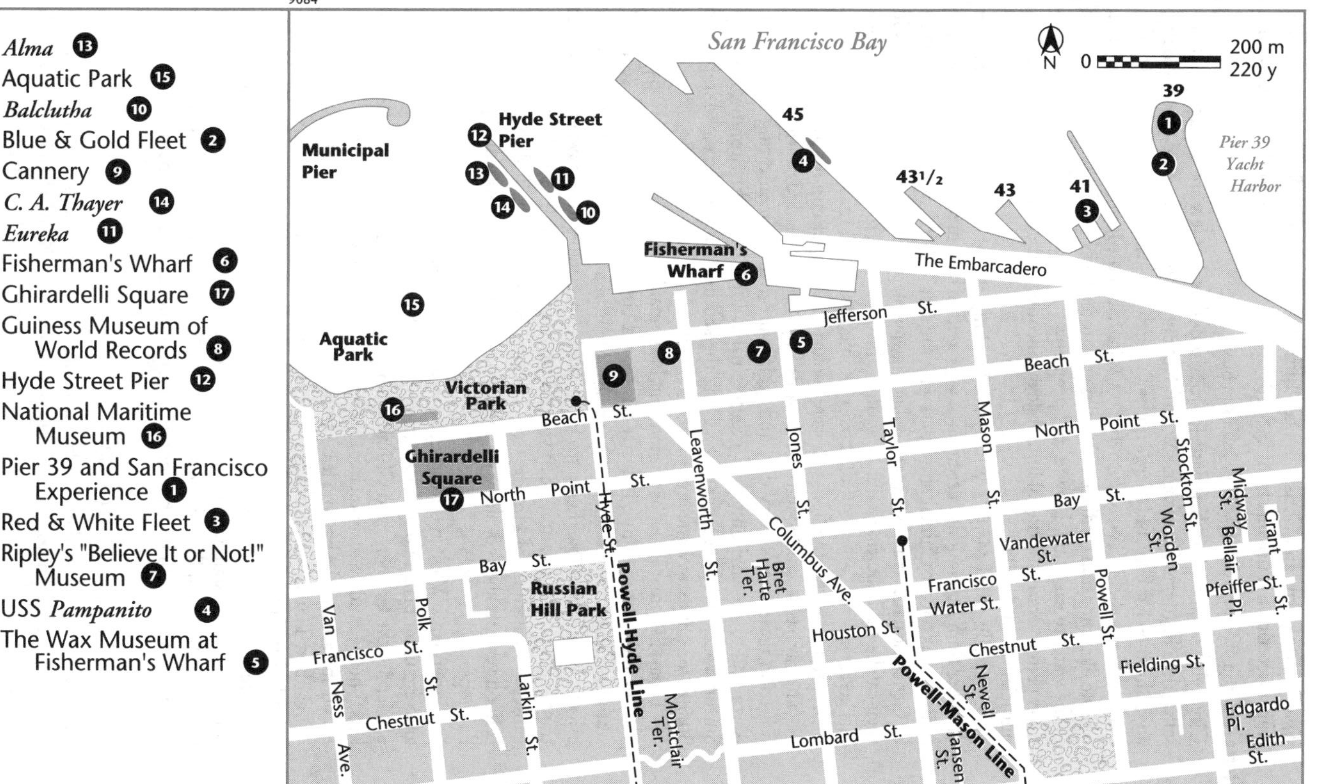

The Northern Waterfront

Thanksgiving Day, and Christmas Day. **Bus:** 30 from Stockton Street to the Marina stop. **Directions:** If driving, from U.S. 101 North, take the last exit before the bridge.

Fisherman's Wharf & Vicinity, Jefferson St.

City sights often exploit their pasts for tourist dollars, but few are as adept at wholesaling their history as Fisherman's Wharf. Not only would you be hard-pressed to find any fishermen left here, but there's not even much around to remind visitors that this dock was once theirs. Today, Fisherman's Wharf, and the festive area surrounding it, pulsate like a nonstop carnival. Sidewalks are jammed with strollers, who come down to the water to eat, shop, browse, and people-watch. Crowds jostle for space around street performers, consisting of immobile mannequins, mimes, puppeteers, magicians, musicians, and the like.

Originally called Meigg's Wharf, this bustling strip of waterfront got its present moniker from generations of fishermen who used to base their boats here. The high-prowed junks of the Chinese shrimpers were the first "fishers" on the wharf, followed by Genovese feluccas and southern Italian trawlers. Upon landing, the fishermen sold their catch—crab, herring, salmon, shrimp, abalone, perch, squid, sand dabs, sea bass, mackerel, and cod—fresh off the boat to homemakers and restaurants. Small stands then sprouted where the fresh fish were cooked to order for curious passersby.

The bay has become polluted with toxins; bright yellow placards warn against eating fish from these waters every day, and against pregnant women eating them at all. According to the environmental group Citizens for a Better Environment, several Silicon Valley–based companies that ring the southern end of the bay dump some 30,000 tons of toxic waste into the bay annually.

Today, fish are still caught offshore, but Fisherman's Wharf has become too popular and the bulk of the fishing industry has moved elsewhere. There are now scores of seafood restaurants and stalls—as well as dozens of stores, selling everything from original art to cans of "San Francisco Fog"—and innumerable street hawkers and tourist traps. You can buy a caricature of yourself (drawn in three minutes) or visit the Wax Museum's Chamber of Horrors (see "Cool for Kids," below). T-shirt hawkers and balloon vendors abound, along with the usual cluster of tourist-oriented paraphernalia shops.

Fisherman's Wharf is only one part of a long, strollable strip of shopping arcades and restaurant plazas along the waterfront on Jefferson Street. The nearby complexes of Pier 39, the Cannery, and Ghirardelli Square are discussed in detail under "Markets," below, and "San Francisco Savvy Shopping, Section 7." Cruises to Alcatraz Island and around the bay also leave from this area. (See "Alcatraz Island," above, and "Organized Tours," below, for information on these aquatic excursions.)

Admission: Free.

Open: The Wharf, 24 hours; most area shops, daily 11am–8pm (later during the summer); most restaurants, Sun–Thurs 10am–midnight, Fri–Sat 10am–2am. **Cable Car:** Powell-Mason line (it climbs to Nob Hill, swings around Chinatown, and descends through North Beach to its terminus near the east end of Fisherman's Wharf—a great ride!).

Golden Gate Bridge. ☎ 921-5858.

The year 1995 marks the 58th birthday of what is possibly the most beautiful—certainly the most photographed—bridge in the world. Often half-veiled by the city's trademark rolling fog, San Francisco's Golden Gate spans tidal currents, ocean waves, and battering winds to connect the "City by the Bay" with the "Redwood Empire" to the north.

With its gracefully swung single span, spidery bracing cables, and sky-zooming twin towers, the bridge looks more like a work of abstract art than the practical engineering feat that it is—among the greatest of this century. Construction began in January 1933 and was completed in May 1937 at the then colossal cost of $35 million. Contrary to pessimistic predictions, the bridge neither collapsed in a gale or an earthquake nor proved to be a white elephant. A symbol of hope when the country was afflicted with widespread joblessness, the Golden Gate single-handedly changed the Bay Area's economic life, encouraging the development of areas north of San Francisco.

The mile-long steel link, which reaches a towering height of 746 feet above the water, is an awesome bridge to cross. Traffic usually moves quickly, so crossing by car won't give you too much time to see the sights. If you drive ($3 toll, payable southbound), park in the lot at the foot of the bridge (on the city side) and make the crossing by foot. Back in your car, continue to Marin's Vista Point by making the first left turn at the bridge's northern end. Look back and you'll be rewarded with one of the greatest views of San Francisco.

Millions of pedestrians walk across the bridge each year, gazing up at the tall red towers, out at the vistas of San Francisco and Marin County, and down into the stacks of oceangoing liners. You can walk out onto the span from either end. But be prepared: It's usually windy and cold, and the bridge vibrates. Still, walking even a short distance is one of the best ways to experience the immense scale of the structure.

You can park your car at the foot of the bridge on the San Francisco side of the span. When approaching the bridge, drive slowly, stay in the right-hand lane, and exit into the parking lot at the base of the bridge.

Transportation: Bridge-bound Golden Gate Transit buses (☎ **332-6600**) depart every half hour during the day for Marin County, starting from the Transbay Terminal at Mission and First Streets and making convenient stops at Market and Seventh Streets, at the Civic Center, and along Van Ness Avenue and Lombard Street. Consult the route map in the *Yellow Pages* of the telephone directory or call for schedule information.

Lombard Street, between Hyde and Leavenworth Sts.

Known as the "crookedest street in the world," the whimsically winding block of Lombard Street between Hyde and Leavenworth Streets puts smiles on the faces of thousands of visitors each year. The elevation is so dramatic that the road has to snake back and forth to make a descent possible. The street zigzags around bright flower gardens that explode with color during warmer months. This short stretch of Lombard Street is one way, downhill, and great fun to drive. Take the curves slowly and in low gear. Save your photographing for the bottom, where you can find a parking space and gaze to your heart's content. You can also walk the block, either up or down, via staircases (without curves) on either side of the street.

The NAMES Project, 2362 Market St. ☎ **863-1966.**

The NAMES Project began in 1987 as a memorial for people who have died from Acquired Immune Deficiency Syndrome (AIDS). The idea was to direct grief into positive action and help the world understand the devastating impact of AIDS. Sewing machines and fabric were acquired, and the public was invited to make coffin-sized panels for a giant memorial quilt. More than 26,000 individual panels now commemorate the lives of individuals who have died of complications related to AIDS. Each has been uniquely designed and sewn by the victims' friends, lovers, and family members.

The quilt, which would cover 10 football fields if laid out end to end, was first displayed on the Capitol Mall in Washington, D.C., during a 1987 national march on Washington for Lesbian and Gay Rights. Although the quilt is often on tour in pieces throughout the world, portions of the heart-wrenching art project are on display here. A sewing machine and fabrics are also available here, free, for your use.

Open: Mon noon–6:30pm, Tues–Wed and Fri noon–7pm, Sat–Sun noon–5pm. **Muni Metro:** J line to Castro Street Station.

More Attractions

ARCHITECTURAL HIGHLIGHTS

Alamo Square Historic District

San Francisco's plethora of beautiful Victorian homes is one of the city's greatest assets. Most of the 14,000 extant structures date from the second half of the 19th century and are private residences. Spread throughout the city, many have been beautifully restored and ornately painted by residents, who are proud of their city's heritage. The small area bordered by Divisadero Street on the west, Golden Gate Avenue on the north, Webster Street on the east, and Fell Street on the south—about 10 blocks west of the Civic Center—has one of the city's greatest concentrations of these "Painted Ladies." One of the most famous views of San Francisco—seen on postcards and posters all around the city—depicts sharp Financial District skyscrapers behind a row of delicate Victorians. This fantastic juxtaposition is the view from Alamo Square, a small, picnic-quality park in the center of this historic district, at Fulton and Steiner Streets.

San Francisco's traditionally designed Victorian homes have little to do with the British queen after whom they're named. They were built en masse, in developments, and were designed to thrive in the Bay Area's climate and topography. Almost uniformly tall and narrow, many of these houses share common walls. They are called "Victorian" only because they were built during the reign of Queen Victoria.

The Garden Court, in the Sheraton Palace Hotel, 2 New Montgomery St. ☎ **392-8600.**

This spectacular enclosed courtyard is topped by a lofty, iridescent glass roof supported by 16 Doric columns. Rebuilt in 1909 after the Great Earthquake, the elegant court has been painstakingly restored, with marble floors, crystal chandeliers, and a leaded-glass ceiling. The hotel, situated between Market and Third Streets, reopened, after restoration, in 1991. Even if you're not staying here (see "San Francisco Accommodations," above), it's definitely worth a look.

Admission: Free.

Open: Daily 24 hrs.

Transamerica Pyramid, 600 Montgomery St.

The tallest structure in San Francisco's skyline is this corporate headquarters between Clay and Washington Streets. The building's unique white wedge is 48 stories tall, capped by a 212-foot spire. It was completed in 1972.

San Francisco–Oakland Bay Bridge. ☎ **510/464-1148.**

Although it's visually less appealing than the nearby Golden Gate, the Bay Bridge is in many ways more spectacular. The silvery giant that links San Francisco with Oakland has a total length of 8 1/4 miles and is one of the world's longest steel bridges. The San Francisco–Oakland Bay Bridge opened in 1936, six months before the Golden Gate. Both of its two decks contains five automobile lanes. The Bay Bridge is not a single bridge at all but a superbly dovetailed series of spans joined in midbay—at Yerba Buena Island—by one of the world's largest (in diameter) tunnels. To the west of Yerba Buena, the bridge is really two separate suspension bridges, joined at a central anchorage. East of the island is a 1,400-foot cantilever span, followed by a succession of truss bridges. And it looks even more complex than it sounds.

Directions: You can reach the bridge by car via Lombard Street (the bridge toll is $1, paid westbound), or you can catch a bus at the Transbay Terminal (Mission at First Street) and ride to downtown Oakland.

CHURCHES

Glide Memorial United Methodist Church, 330 Ellis St. ☎ **771-6300.**

There would be nothing so special about this plain Tenderloin area church if it weren't for its exhilarating pastor, Cecil Williams. Williams's enthusiastic and uplifting preaching and singing with homeless and poor people of the neighborhood has attracted nationwide fame. Last year, during the pastor's 30th anniversary celebrations, singers Angela Bofill and Bobby McFerrin joined with comedian Robin Williams, author Maya Angelou, and talk show queen Oprah Winfrey to honor him publicly. Williams's nondogmatic, fun Sunday services attract a diverse audience that crosses all socioeconomic boundaries.

Services held: Sun 9am and 11am.

Mission Dolores, 16th St. at Dolores St. ☎ **621-8203.**

In 1776, at the behest of Franciscan missionary Junipero Serra, Fr. Francisco Palou came to the Bay Area to found the sixth in a chain of missions that dotted California's howling wilderness. From these humble beginnings grew what was to become the city of San Francisco. Surrounded by a four-foot-thick wall, the adobe Mission Dolores is the oldest structure in the city. The mission's small, simple chapel was built by Native Americans who were converted to Christianity. Its interior is a curious mixture of native construction methods and Spanish-colonial style. A statue of Father Serra stands in the mission garden. Lovingly preserved by the Roman Catholic diocese, the mission is a relatively tranquil oasis in a funky part of town. Even when tour buses are lined up in front, the mission's walls are an interesting, calm counterpoint to the busy neighborhood that surrounds them.

Admission: $1.

Open: May–Oct, daily 9am–4:30pm; Nov–Apr, daily 9am–4pm; Good Fri 10am–noon. **Closed:** Thanksgiving Day and Christmas Day. **Muni Metro:** J line, down Market Street to the corner of Church and 16th Streets.

MARKETS

In addition to Fisherman's Wharf (see above), three market complexes front the bay on or near Jefferson Street.

Ghirardelli Square, 900 North Point St. ☎ **775-5500.**

The Ghirardelli complex, at Polk and Larkin Streets, dates back to 1864, when it served as a factory making Civil War uniforms. But it's best known as the former chocolate-and-spice factory of Domingo Ghirardelli. Saved from demolition in 1962, the 10-level streamlined mall is now a beehive of terraces, shops, theaters, cafés, restaurants, and exhibitions—and one of the city's most popular rendezvous spots. The largely unchanged exterior still retains its historic charm. Inside are some 50 stores, retailing everything from clothing and family coats of arms to hand-cut lead crystal. (Many of these shops are described in "San Francisco Savvy Shopping," below.) Ghirardelli Square also boasts the best restaurants of any of the malls on the waterfront. Close to 20 eateries, in all price categories, can satisfy almost any craving. So if you're exploring the entire wharf area, plan to end up here at mealtime. (See "San Francisco Dining," above, for specific recommendations.) Scheduled street performers—including mimes, magicians, and puppeteers—play regularly in the west plaza.

The whole complex is crowned by a charming clock tower, an exact replica of the one at France's Château Blois. Inside the tower, on the mall's plaza level, is the Ghirardelli soda fountain, where small amounts of chocolate are still made and are available for purchase, along with other candy and ice cream. A free guide to the mall, together with a map, is available from the information booth, located in Ghirardelli's center courtyard. Illustrated with photographs, it contains a history of the square and details all the shops, restaurants, and attractions.

Incidentally, the Ghirardelli Chocolate Manufactory still turns out magnificent chocolate, but in a lower-rent district in the East Bay.

Admission: Free.

Open: Shops, Memorial Day through Labor Day, Mon–Sat 10am–9pm, Sun 10am–6pm; the rest of the year, Mon–Thurs 10am–7pm, Fri–Sat 10am–9pm, Sun 10am–6pm. Restaurants, times vary (see the individual listings in "San Francisco Dining," above, for complete information). **Cable Car:** Powell-Hyde line to Aquatic Park.

The Cannery, 2801 Leavenworth St. ☎ **771-3112.**

Built in 1894 as a fruit-canning plant for the Del Monte company, the structure was abandoned in 1963 and acquired by developer Leonard V. Martin. Inspired by the chocolate factory–cum–shopping mall up the street, Martin left the red-brick exterior intact and transformed the structure into a vaguely Florentine, three-story shopping, eating, and entertainment complex. Divided by a zigzagging alley, the mall is lined with arcades, spanned by bridges, and fitted with elevators and escalators. There are about a dozen eateries here and more than 50 shops, many of which are detailed in "San Francisco Savvy Shopping," below.

The Museum of the City of San Francisco (☎ **928-0289**) also recently opened here. Dedicated solely to the city's history, the museum outlines the city's chronological development with displays of artifacts, including the head of the 22-foot Goddess of Progress statue that topped City Hall until the building was demolished in 1909.

In the courtyard, amid a grove of century-old olive trees, are vendors' stalls and sidewalk cafés. On summer weekends some of the city's best street talents perform here.

Admission: Free.

Open: Winter, Mon–Sat 10am–6pm, Sun 11am–6pm; summer and hols, Mon–Sat 10am–8pm, Sun 11am–8pm. **Cable Car:** Powell-Hyde line to Aquatic Park.

Pier 39, on the Waterfront at Embarcadero and Beach St. ☎ **981-7437.**

This $54-million, 4½-acre waterfront complex, a few blocks east of Fisherman's Wharf, is San Francisco's latest tourist-oriented bayside conversion. Constructed on an abandoned cargo pier, it is, ostensibly, a re-creation of a turn-of-the-century street scene. The walkways are built of aged and weathered wood salvaged from demolished piers. This is the busiest mall of the bunch, drawing visitors with its shops, restaurants, and usual assortment of street entertainers. The complex, which has parking for 1,000 cars, contains more than 100 shops selling games, toys, jewelry, luggage, trinkets, mugs, and kites, among a plethora of other items. To please the palate, there are 10 restaurants of varying quality, cuisine, ambience, and price, some of them with great views of the bay. In addition, more than a dozen nosheries serve everything from clam chowder to Mexican pastries.

Two marinas—which, combined, accommodate over 350 boats—flank the pier and house the Blue and Gold bay-sightseeing fleet. In recent years a large group of California sea lions has taken up residence on the adjacent floating docks. They arrived without warning and may abandon their new resting ground just as fast. But, for now, the silent sunning and playful yelping of these cute, blubbery creatures creates one of the best diversions in the entire city.

Admission: Free.

Open: Shops, daily 10:30am–8:30pm; restaurants, daily 11:30am–11:30pm; bars, daily 11:30am–2am. **Cable Car:** Powell-Mason line to Bay Street.

Japan Center, Post and Buchanan Sts. ☎ **922-6776.**

The immense Japan Center is an Asian-oriented shopping mall located in San Francisco's revitalized Japantown, about a mile west of Union Square. At its center is a serenely noble, five-tiered Peace Pagoda, designed by world-famous Japanese architect Yoshiro Taniguchi "to convey the friendship and goodwill of the Japanese to the people of the United States." Surrounding the pagoda, in a network of arcades, squares, and bridges, are dozens of shops and showrooms featuring everything from cameras and transistor radios to pearls, bonsai (dwarf trees), and kimonos. When it opened, with fanfare, in 1968, the complex seemed as modern as a jumbo jet. Today, the aging concrete structure seems less impressive, but it still holds some interesting surprises.

The renowned **Kabuki Hot Spring,** 1750 Geary Blvd. (☎ **922-6000**), is the center's most famous tenant. The Kabuki is an authentic traditional Japanese bathhouse with deep ceramic communal tubs as well as private baths. In addition to steaming water and restful rooms, the Kabuki features Japanese-style shiatsu finger-pressure massages. Facilities include a *furo* (hot bath) and *mizoburo* (cold bath), dry-heat saunas, a steam room, steam cabinets, and Japanese-style sit-down showers. Appointments are required. The Japan Center also houses several restaurants (including sushi bars) and teahouses, the AMC Kabuki 8 cinema, and the luxurious, 14-story Miyako Hotel (see "San Francisco Accommodations," above, for complete information).

There is often live entertainment on summer weekends, including Japanese music and dance performances, tea ceremonies, flower-arranging demonstrations, martial-arts presentations, and other cultural events. Japanese festivals are celebrated here four times a year: the Northern California **Cherry Blossom Festival** (Sakura Matsuri) in April, the **Buddhist Bon Festival** in July, the **Nihonmachi Street Fair** in August, and an **Autumn Festival** (Aki Matsuri) in September or October.

Japantown, or Nihonmachi, San Francisco's Japanese quarter, stretches for seven square blocks directly north of the Japan Center. Though less exotic and colorful than Chinatown, this area is notable for some interesting gift stores and several good Japanese restaurants. In the Buchanan Street Mall, between Post and Sutter Streets, there is a cobblestone walkway, designed to resemble a meandering stream. It is lined on either side with flowering cherry and plum trees and contains two origami-inspired fountains by Ruth Asawa.

Admission: Free.

Open: Mon–Fri 10am–10pm, Sat–Sun 9am–10pm. **Bus:** 2, 3, or 4 (exit on Buchanan Street and Sutter Street), 22 or 38 (exit on the northeast corner of Geary Boulevard and Fillmore Street).

A MULTIMEDIA SHOW

The San Francisco Experience, at Pier 39, on the waterfront, at Embarcadero and Beach St. ☎ **982-7394,** or **982-7550** for recorded information.

Two centuries of San Francisco history are condensed into about 30 minutes in this slightly dated multimedia show that lets you see, hear, and even feel events from the city's past. From the city's founding to the Gold Rush, the Great Earthquake, and the Summer of Love, the life and times of San Francisco are neatly pieced together for a lightly informative and highly entertaining look at the forces that made the Bay City what it is today. Three film and 32 slide projectors coordinate their images in an extraordinarily fast-paced presentation on a 70- by 35-foot screen. In addition, famous historical events and conditions unique to the city are simulated by many three-dimensional surprises, including a San Francisco "fog" that really rolls in.

Admission: $7 adults, $6 seniors over 55, $4 children ages 5–16.

Open: Jan–Mar, shows daily (every half hour) 10am–8:30pm; the rest of the year, shows daily (every half hour) 10am–9:30pm.

MUSEUMS

San Francisco Museum of Modern Art, 151 Third St. ☎ **357-4000.**

Scheduled to move into a new home in early 1995, the Museum of Modern Art originally opened in 1935 as the first collection on the West Coast devoted solely to 20th-century art.

International in scope, the permanent collection consists of more than 4,000 paintings, sculptures, and works on paper, as well as a selection of objects relating to architecture, design, and the media arts. The museum is strong on American abstract expressionism and other major schools of the 20th century. Rotating displays regularly include works by Clyfford Still, Jackson Pollock, Mark Rothko, and Willem de Kooning. It also has a significant representation of German expressionism, fauvism, Mexican paintings, and local art. It stands out as one of the first major galleries to recognize photography as a serious art form. The collection of approximately 8,000 photographs includes works by Alfred Stieglitz, Ansel Adams, and Edward Weston, as well as good examples of 1920s German avant-garde and 1930s European surrealist photographers.

Temporary exhibits cover a broad spectrum of styles and media. Past shows included a major Alberto Giacometti retrospective, the paintings of New York artist Julian Schnabel, a survey of turn-of-the-century Chicago architecture, and the drawings of the celebrated Californian artist Richard Diebenkorn.

The new red-colored museum building, designed by Mario Botto, is a funky, futuristic construction combining simple primary shapes. It's located two blocks south of Market Street in a revitalized neighborhood newly named Yerba Buena Gardens.

Guided tours are offered daily at 1:15pm and on Thursday at 7:15 and 7:45pm. In addition, the museum regularly organizes special artistic events, lectures, concerts, dance performances, poetry readings, conceptual-art events, and special activities for children. Phone for current details.

Admission: $7 adults, $3.50 students 14–18 and seniors, free for children 13 and under; half price for everyone Thurs 5–9pm, and free for everyone the first Tues of each month.

Open: Tues–Wed and Fri–Sun 11am–6pm, Thurs 11am–9pm. **Closed:** Holidays. **Muni Metro:** J, K, L, M to Montgomery Station. **Bus:** 15, 30, or 45.

M. H. de Young Memorial Museum, in Golden Gate Park near 10th Ave. and Fulton St. ☎ **750-3600,** or **863-3330** for recorded information.

One of the city's oldest museums, the de Young is also the most diversified, housing a hodgepodge of art that spans continents and centuries. Located on the Music Concourse of Golden Gate Park, the museum is best known for its American art, from colonial times to the 20th century, and includes paintings, sculptures, furniture, and decorative arts by Paul Revere, Winslow Homer, John Singer Sargent, and Georgia

Frommer's Favorite San Francisco Experiences

Riding the Cable Cars Roller-coasting over the city's hills, and hanging on tightly on curves, is understandably one of San Francisco's top tourist draws.

Walking Across the Golden Gate Bridge It might be windy and cold, but nothing matches the thrill of viewing San Francisco's spectacular stalactites from the world's most famous suspension bridge.

Eating in North Beach or Chinatown If you had only one meal in the city, it would be tough to choose where to eat it. These two colorful neighborhoods are adjacent to one another, making restaurant window-shopping a breeze.

Shopping Along Haight Street The chain stores are moving in, but there are still plenty of outrageous boutiques in America's most famous psychedelic neighborhood.

Dancing in a South Market Club Even if you've forgotten your black clothes, you're guaranteed a good time hanging out with the trendies in up-and-coming SoMa.

Cruising to Alcatraz Beautiful, scary, fun, and fascinating, Alcatraz is one of the best sightseeing attractions to be found anywhere.

Day-Tripping to the Wine Country Just a short drive from the city are some of the world's greatest vineyards. Have fun discovering new vintages on a wine-tasting tour of the Napa Valley.

O'Keeffe. Special note should be taken of the American landscapes, as well as the fun trompe-l'oeil and still-life works from the turn of the century.

Named for the late 19th-century publisher of the *San Francisco Chronicle*, the museum also possesses an important textile collection, with primary emphasis on rugs from central Asia and the Near East. Other collections on view include ancient art from Egypt, Greece, and Rome; decorative art from Africa, Oceania, and the Americas; and British art by Gainsborough, Reynolds, Lawrence, Raeburn, and others. Major traveling exhibitions are equally eclectic, including everything from ancient rugs to great Dutch paintings. Call the museum to find out what's on. Guided tours are offered daily; call for times.

The museum's eatery, the Café de Young, is an exceptional cafeteria serving rotating specials that include Peruvian stew, Chinese chicken salad, and Italian vegetables in tomato-basil sauce. In summer, dining is in the garden, among bronze statuary. The cafe is open Wednesday through Sunday from 10am to 4pm.

Admission (including the Asian Art Museum and California Palace of the Legion of Honor): $5 adults, $3 seniors over 65, $2 youths ages 12–17, free for young visitors 11 and under (fees may be higher for special exhibitions); reduced admission for everyone the first Wed and first Sat of each month.

Open: Wed 10am–8:45pm, Thurs–Sun 10am–5pm. **Bus:** 44.

Asian Art Museum, in Golden Gate Park near 10th Ave. and Fulton St. ☎ **668-8921,** or **752-2635** for the hearing impaired.

Adjacent to the M. H. de Young Museum and the Japanese Tea Garden, this exhibition space, opened in 1966, contains an academically oriented array of art and artifacts from the entire Asian continent. Only about 1,800 pieces from the museum's vast collection of 12,000 are shown at any one time. About half of the works on display are in the ground-floor Chinese and Korean galleries and include sculptures, paintings, bronzes, ceramics, jades, and decorative objects. There is also a wide range of exhibits from Pakistan, India, Tibet, Japan, and Southeast Asia, including the world's oldest-known, dated Chinese Buddha. The museum's daily guided tours are highly informative and sincerely recommended. Call for times.

Admission (including the M. H. de Young Memorial Museum): $5 adults, $3 seniors 65 and over, $2 youths 12–16, free for young visitors 11 and under (fees may be higher for special exhibitions); reduced admission for everyone the first Wed and first Sat of each month.

Open: Wed–Sun 10am–5pm. **Bus:** 44.

California Palace of the Legion of Honor, Lincoln Park. ☎ **750-3600,** or **863-3330** for recorded information.

The white architectural sculpture that rises unexpectedly from a green hilltop above the bay is San Francisco's most beautiful museum. Designed as a memorial to California's World War I casualties, the neoclassical structure is an exact replica of the Legion of Honor Palace in Paris, right down to the inscription HONNEUR ET PATRIE above the portal.

Scheduled to reopen in late 1995 after a two-year, $29 million renovation and seismic upgrading project that was stalled by the discovery of almost 300 turn-of-the-century coffins, the museum houses a collection of paintings, sculpture, and decorative arts from Europe, as well as international tapestries, prints, and drawings. The chronological display of over 800 years of European art includes one of the world's finest collections of Rodin sculpture.

Admission (including the Asian Art Museum and M. H. de Young Memorial Museum): $5 adults, $3 seniors 65 and over, $2 youths 12–17, free for children 11 and under. Fees may be higher for special exhibitions; reduced admission for everyone the first Wed and first Sat of each month.

Open: Hours were not set at press time; phone for details. **Bus:** 38 or 18.

PARKS & GARDENS

In addition to Golden Gate Park, San Francisco boasts more than 2,000 acres of city park, most of which are perfect for picnicking.

Aquatic Park, at the foot of Hyde St. ☎ **556-2904.**

Adjacent to Ghirardelli Square, three blocks west of Fisherman's Wharf, this green lawn and protected marina was built in 1937 as a project of the federal Works Progress Administration. It's popular with sunbathers as well as strollers who walk out on the long pier. The large white building fronting the water is the National Maritime Museum (see "Cool for Kids," below).

Fort Mason, Bay and Franklin Sts. ☎ **441-5706.**

Aquatic Park quickly gives way to the expansive waterfront grounds of Fort Mason. A former military installation and headquarters for the Pacific Fleet in World War II, the park now contains the Fort Mason Center, a complex of buildings housing theaters, galleries, and various arts programs. More than 1,000 activities are held here monthly, including concerts and fairs on the adjacent piers.

Marin Headlands, across the Golden Gate Bridge. ☎ **331-1540.**

Administered by the Golden Gate National Recreation Area, the headlands' 70,000 acres encompass ocean beaches, wildlife sanctuaries, and more than 100 miles of trails. Protected by a 1972 act of Congress, the rolling hills of this expansive park start just across the Golden Gate Bridge, where an excellent view can be had of the entire city.

Justin Herman Plaza, at the foot of Market St.

More of a landscaped concrete plaza than a park, this square in the Financial District is popular with office workers at lunchtime. At its center is Vaillancourt Fountain, a free-form water sculpture that was designed to be walked through. The surrounding sidewalks are dotted with cafes and stalls selling leather goods, jewelry, pottery, paintings, and sculpture. The plaza is particularly packed on sunny weekday afternoons.

Lincoln Park, Clement St. and 34th Ave.

One of my personal favorites is this 270-acre green on the northeastern side of the city. The California Palace of the Legion of Honor is here (see "Museums," above), as is a scenic 18-hole municipal golf course (see "Sports & Recreation," below). But the best thing about this park are the 200-foot cliffs that overlook the Golden Gate Bridge and San Francisco Bay.

Presidio of San Francisco, at the foot of Golden Gate Bridge. ☎ **556-3111.**

After more than 200 years as a military stronghold guarding the entrance to the Golden Gate and San Francisco Bay, the Presidio Army base is being decommissioned and transferred to the National Park Service's Golden Gate National Recreation Area. The 1,400-acre waterfront park has its own golf course, water system, and more than 800 buildings, over half of which are of historical significance. One of America's most wonderful products of the "peace dividend," the Presidio is resplendent with natural treasures that include a forest of windblown cypress trees and the only free-flowing stream left in the city. Among the park's habitats are coastal scrub, sand dunes, and prairie grasslands that contain many rare plants. In addition, there are about 170 species of birds, some 50 of which nest here.

Planning for the new Presidio is still underway and debate rages about the park's future. An environmental learning center is in the works, at least some of the historic homes will be opened to the public, and park officials are projecting annual visitor rates in excess of 20 million. The Presidio will have a visitor center, food service, trails, public transportation within the park, historical programs, and traditional military ceremonies. For a free 16-page summary of the proposed Presidio plan, write to Presidio Information Center, Fort Mason Building 201, San Francisco 94123, or phone the number above.

Cool for Kids

With few exceptions, most of the major sights in San Francisco are just as cool for kids as they are for adults. Windy **Lombard Street,** the majestic **Golden Gate Bridge,** Golden Gate Park's **Japanese Tea Garden, Alcatraz Island** . . . they're all fun destinations, which is why San Francisco is one of America's favorite cities. For all its vaunted sophistication, the Bay City is a kid's paradise. Children usually take one look at the **cable cars** and decide they want to take them home. The whole of the **Fisherman's Wharf** area is like one gigantic playground, and children are just as enthralled as adults by the view from **Coit Tower** and the excitement of **Chinatown.**

In addition to those sights listed above, the following attractions are of particular interest to kids. A few of them, at least, are bound to capture yours as well.

Wells Fargo History Museum, 420 Montgomery St., at California St. ☎ **396-2619.**

Wells Fargo, one of California's largest banks, got its start in the Wild West. Its history museum, at the bank's head office, houses hundreds of genuine relics—pistols, photographs, early banking articles, posters, and mining equipment—from the company's whip and six-shooter days.

In the center of the main room stands a genuine Concord stagecoach, probably the most celebrated vehicle in American history. This was the 2,500-pound buggy that opened the west as surely as the Winchester and the iron horse. The interior seems cramped even when empty; it's hard to believe that it could hold nine passengers "passing comfortably"—with six more perched on the roof. That's not counting the "knight of the whip," who drove the six-horse team, and the essential "shotgun rider" beside him.

On the mezzanine, you can take an imaginary ride in a replica stagecoach or send a telegraph message in code using a telegraph key and the codebooks, just the way the Wells Fargo agents did more than a century ago. The Wiltsee Collection of western stamps and postal franks will interest collectors. In addition, there are samples of the treasure that Wells Fargo carried—gold nuggets and coins from the fabulous Mother Lode mines—and mementos of the men who were after it. Chief among them was "Black Bart," a verse-writing humorist who robbed 27 stages single-handedly. Identified by a laundry mark on his handkerchief, he was captured in 1883 by Wells Fargo's top detective, James B. Hume.

Admission: Free.

Open: Mon–Fri 9am–5pm. **Closed:** Bank holidays. **Muni Metro:** J, K, L, M, or N lines to Montgomery Street. **Bus:** 7, 8, 27, 38, or 71.

San Francisco Maritime National Historical Park and Museum, at the foot of Polk St. ☎ **929-0202.**

Shaped like an art-deco ship and located near Fisherman's Wharf, the National Maritime Museum is a treasure trove of sailing, whaling, and fishing lore. Remarkably good exhibits include intricate model craft, scrimshaw, and a terrific collection of shipwreck photographs and historic marine scenes, including an 1851 snapshot of hundreds of abandoned ships, deserted en masse by crews rushing off to participate in the latest gold strike. The museum's walls are lined with beautifully carved, high-busted, brightly painted wooden figureheads from old windjammers.

Two blocks east, on Aquatic Park's Hyde Street Pier, are several museum-operated historic ships, now moored and open to the public.

The ***Balclutha*** (☎ **929-0202**), one of the last surviving square-riggers and the handsomest vessel in San Francisco Bay, was built in Glasgow, Scotland, in 1886 and used to carry grain from California at a near-record speed of 300 miles a day. The *Balclutha* was one of the legendary "Cape Horners" of the windjammer age; it rounded the treacherous cape 17 times in its career. It survived a near wreck off the coast of Alaska and was refitted in 1906. The ship is now completely restored. Visitors are invited to spin the wheel, squint at the compass, and imagine they're weathering a mighty blow. Kids can climb into the bunking quarters, visit the "slop chest" (galley to you, matey), and read the sea chanties (clean ones only) that decorate the walls.

The 1890 ***Eureka*** still carries a cargo of nostalgia for San Franciscans. The last of 50 paddle-wheeled ferries that regularly plied the bay, it made its final trip in 1957. Restored to its original splendor at the height of the ferryboat era, the side-wheeler is loaded with deck cargo, including antique cars and trucks.

The "steam schooner" ***Wapama,*** built in 1915, is a good example of ships of the Industrial Revolution. Originally built as a sailing ship, it was later fitted with a steam engine, after the technology became available.

The black-hulled, three-masted ***C. A. Thayer,*** built in 1895, was crafted for the lumber trade and carried logs felled in the Pacific Northwest to the carpentry shops of California.

Other historic ships docked here include the tiny two-masted ***Alms,*** one of the last scow schooners to bring hay to the horses of San Francisco; and the ***Hercules,*** a huge 1907 oceangoing steam tug; and the ***Eppleton Hall*** a side-wheeled tugboat built in England in 1914 to operate on London's River Thames.

At the pier's small-boat shop, visitors can follow the restoration progress of historic boats from the museum's collection. It's located behind the maritime bookstore on your right as you approach the ships.

Admission: Museum, free; ships, $3 adults, $1 children ages 11–17, free for youngsters under 11 and for seniors over 62.

Open: Museum, daily 10am–5pm. Hyde Street Pier, Apr–Oct, daily 10am–6pm, the rest of the year, daily 9:30am–5pm. **Closed:** Thanksgiving Day, Christmas Day, and New Year's Day. **Cable Car:** Hyde Street line to the last stop. **Bus:** 19, 30, 32, 42, or 47.

California Academy of Sciences, on the Music Concourse of Golden Gate Park. ☎ **221-5100,** or **750-7145** for recorded information.

This group of related museums and exhibitions is clustered around the Music Concourse in Golden Gate Park.

The **Steinhart Aquarium** houses one of the largest and most diverse collections of aquatic life in the nation. Some 14,000 specimens call Steinhart home, including amphibians, reptiles, marine mammals, and penguins. The aquarium contains a California tidepool and a hands-on area where children can touch starfish and sea urchins. Their living coral reef is the largest display of its kind in the country and the only one in the west. In the Fish Roundabout—a unique, 100,000-gallon tank—visitors are surrounded by fast-swimming schools of open-ocean fish. Seals and dolphins are fed every two hours, beginning at 10:30am; the penguins are fed at 11:30am and 4pm.

The **Morrison Planetarium** is northern California's largest indoor theater of the outdoors. Its awesome sky shows are projected onto a 65-foot domed ceiling. Approximately four major exhibits, with titles such as "Star Death: The Birth of Black Holes" and "The Universe Unveiled," are presented each year. Related cosmos exhibits are located in the adjacent Earth and Space Hall. Call for show schedules and information.

In the Earth and Space Hall you can weigh yourself on other planets, see a real moon rock, experience one of San Francisco's infamous earthquakes on the "Safe Quake," and learn about the rotation of the planet at the Foucault Pendulum.

In **Meyer Hall,** the "Wild California" exhibition includes a 14,000-gallon aquarium and seabird rookery, life-size battling elephant seals, and two larger-than-life views of microscopic life forms. There's also a poisonous twin-headed snake.

In **McBean-Peterson Hall,** visitors are encouraged to "walk through time" as they are presented with evidence of human evolution. This massive exhibit walks you through 3.5 billion years of history, from the earliest life forms to the present day.

Admission: Aquarium and science exhibits, $7 adults, $4 students ages 12–17 and seniors 65 and over, $1.50 children ages 6–11, free for children under 6; free for everyone the first Wed of every month. Planetarium Shows, $2.50 adults, $1.25 youngsters under 18 and seniors 65 and over. Show a valid Muni transfer for $2 off the admission price.

Open: July 4–Labor Day, daily 10am–7pm; rest of the year, daily 10am–5pm; first Wed of every month 10am–9pm. **Muni Metro:** N line to Golden Gate Park. **Bus:** 5, 71, or 44.

San Francisco Zoological Gardens and Children's Zoo, Sloat Blvd. and 45th Ave. ☎ **753-7080,** or **753-7083** for recorded information.

Located between the Pacific Ocean and Lake Merced, in the southwest corner of the city, the San Francisco Zoo is among America's highest-rated animal parks. Begun in 1889 with a grizzly bear named Monarch, donated by the *San Francisco Examiner,* the zoo now sprawls over 65 acres and is growing. It attracts more than a million visitors each year. Most of the 1,000-plus inhabitants are contained in realistically landscaped enclosures guarded by cunningly concealed moats. The innovative Primate Discovery Center is particularly noteworthy, known for its many rare and endangered species. Soaring outdoor atriums, sprawling meadows, and a midnight world for exotic nocturnal primates house a speedy Patas monkey that can run up to 35 miles per hour and the Senegal bush baby, a pint-size primate that can jump up four feet.

Other highlights include Koala Crossing, patterned after an Australian outback station; Gorilla World, one of the world's largest exhibits of these gentle giants; and Penguin Island, home to the largest breeding colony of Magellanic penguins. Musk

Ox Meadow is a $2^{1}/_{2}$-acre habitat for a herd of rare, white-fronted musk oxen brought from Alaska. And the Lion House is home to four species of cats and includes Prince Charles, a rare white tiger (you can watch them being fed at 2pm daily except Monday).

The Children's Zoo, adjacent to the main park, allows both kids and adults to get close to animals, including zoo babies being tended in the nursery. The barnyard is alive with strokable, cuddly baby animals. And then there's my personal favorite, the fascinating Insect Zoo—the only one in the western United States and one of only three such exhibits in the country. More than 6,000 specimens include a colony of velvet ants, honey bees, scorpions, and several hissing cockroaches. On weekends, at 2:30pm, you can see the popular "Amazing Insects in Action," which gives an intimate look at live insects through a "macro" video system.

A free, informal walking tour of the zoo leaves from Koala Crossing at 12:30 and 2:30pm on weekends. The *Zebra Zephyr* tour train takes visitors on a 20-minute "safari" daily (in winter, only on weekends). The tour is $2.50 for adults, $1.50 for youngsters ages 15 and under, and seniors.

Admission: Main zoo, $6.50 adults, $3 seniors and youths 12–15, $1 for children 6–11, and free for children under 5 if accompanied by an adult. Children's zoo, $1, free for children under 3.

Open: Main zoo, daily 10am–5pm; children's zoo, daily 11am–4pm. **Muni Metro:** L line from downtown Market Street to the end of the line.

KIDS' FAVORITES AT FISHERMAN'S WHARF

The following sights are all clustered on or near Fisherman's Wharf, along Jefferson Street. To reach this area by cable car, take the Mason line to the last stop and walk toward the water to the wharf; by bus, take 30, 32, or 42. If you're arriving by car, park on adjacent streets or on the Wharf between Taylor and Jones Streets.

USS *Pampanito*, Pier 45, Fisherman's Wharf. ☎ **441-5819.**

This popular, battle-scarred World War II fleet submarine saw plenty of action in the Pacific. It has been completely restored, and visitors are free to crawl around inside. An audio tour is available.

Admission: $4 adults, $3 students ages 12–17, $2 children ages 6–12 and seniors 65 and over, free for children under 6.

Open: May–Oct, daily 9am–8pm; Nov–Apr, daily 9am-6pm.

Ripley's "Believe It Or Not!" Museum, 175 Jefferson St. ☎ **771-6188.**

Believe it or not, this amazing and silly "museum" is still open. A bizarre collection of 2,000 wax figures, photos, and models depict natural oddities from Robert LeRoy Ripley's infamous arsenal. There's a one-third-scale wooden-matchstick-made replica of a cable car, a dinosaur made of old car bumpers, and the usual "freak-show" assortment of midgets, sword swallowers, and the like. Some examples from the collection of "humorous" gravestone epitaphs can be seen at the door, including such gems as "HERE LIES JONATHAN BLAKE, STEPPED ON THE GAS, INSTEAD OF THE BRAKE."

Admission: $7.75 adults, $6.25 teens ages 13–17 and seniors over 60, $4.75 children ages 5–12, free for children under 5.

Open: June 15–Labor Day, daily 9am–11pm; the rest of the year, Sun–Thurs 10am–10pm, Fri–Sat 10am–midnight.

Wax Museum, 145 Jefferson St. ☎ **202-0400.**

Conceived in the Madame Tussaud mold, San Francisco's wax museum features over 250 eerily lifelike figures of the rich and famous. The "museum" donates the lion's share of its space to images of modern superstars like singer Michael Jackson and political figures like former President George Bush. Tableaux include "Royalty," "Great Humanitarians," "Wickedest Ladies," "World Religions," and "Feared Leaders," the last including Adolf Hitler, Benito Mussolini, Nikita Khrushchev, and Fidel Castro. The Chamber of Horrors—which features Dracula, Frankenstein's monster, and a werewolf, along with bloody victims hanging from meathooks—is the stuff tourist traps are made of. It may also scare younger children.

Admission: $8.95 adults, $6.95 seniors over 60, $4.95 children ages 6–12, free for children under 6.

Open: Summer, Sun–Thurs 9am–11:30pm, Fri–Sat 9am–midnight; winter, Sun–Thurs 9am–10pm, Fri–Sat 9am–11pm.

Haunted Gold Mine, 113 Jefferson St. ☎ **202-0400.**

Under the same ownership as the Wax Museum, the Haunted Gold Mine is a fun house complete with mazes, a hall of mirrors, spatial-disorientation tricks, wind tunnels, and animated ghouls. Even very young children will probably not find it too scary, but it's fun.

Admission: $4.95 adults, $3.95 seniors, $2.95 children ages 6–12, free for children under 6.

Open: Summer, Sun–Thurs 9am–11pm, Fri–Sat 9am–midnight; winter, Sun–Thurs 9am–10pm, Fri–Sat 9am–11pm.

The Guinness Museum of World Records, 235 Jefferson St. ☎ **771-9890.**

You've read the book, now see the displays. Kids, and kids only, will enjoy this large collection of superlatives. Your arms won't reach around a plastic replica of the world's fattest man; he tipped the scales at 1,069 pounds! You can march over to the participation area and try to break records of your own. There are also movies and videotapes of record-breaking events—like the world's longest domino tumble. And artifacts such as the world's smallest camera, or the most expensive shoes.

Admission: $6.50 adults, $5.25 students, $5.50 seniors 60 and over, $3.50 children ages 5–12, free for children under 5.

Open: Summer, Sun–Thurs 10am–11pm, Fri–Sat 10am–midnight; the rest of the year, Sun–Thurs 10am–10pm, Fri–Sat 10am–midnight.

CHILDREN'S PLAYGROUNDS

Cow Hollow Playground, Baker St., between Greenwich and Filbert Sts.

Surrounded by apartment buildings on three of four sides, this lushly gardened ground features a bi-level play area fitted with well-conceived colorful play structures, including a tunnel, slides, swings and a miniature cable car.

Huntington Park, Taylor St., between Sacramento and California Sts.

Located atop Nob Hill, this tony play area contains several small play structures that are particularly well suited to children under 5.

Julius Kahn Playground, West Pacific Ave., at Spruce St.

A popular playground, Julius Kahn is situated inside San Francisco's great Presidio park. Larger play structures and pretty, forested surroundings make this ground attractive to children and adults alike.

Special-Interest Sightseeing

SPECIALIZED MUSEUMS

Octagon House, 2645 Gough St. ☎ **441-7512.**

Located at Union Street, this unusual, eight-sided, cupola-topped house dates from 1861 and is maintained by the National Society of Colonial Dames of America. Inside, you'll find furniture, silverware, and American pewter from the Colonial and Federal periods. There are also some historic documents, including signatures of 54 of the 56 signers of the Declaration of Independence. Even if you're not able to visit during opening hours, this strange structure is worth a look.

Admission: Free (donation requested).

Open: Second Sun and second and fourth Thurs of each month noon–3pm. **Closed:** Jan and holidays.

FOR RAPID-TRANSIT LOVERS

Bay Area Rapid Transit [BART], 800 Madison St., Oakland. ☎ **788-BART.**

One of the world's best commuter systems, BART's 71 miles of rail links eight San Francisco stations with Daly City to the south and 25 stations in the East Bay. Under the bay, BART runs through one of the longest underwater transit tubes in the world. This link opened in September 1974, two years behind schedule and six months after the then-general manager resigned under fire. The train cars are 70 feet long and were designed to represent the last word in public transport luxury. Almost 20 years later they no longer seem futuristic, but they're still attractively modern, with carpeted floors, tinted picture windows, automatic air conditioning, and recessed lighting. The trains can hit a top speed of 80 miles per hour, a computerized control system monitors and adjusts their speed.

The people who run BART think so highly of their trains and stations that they sell a $2.60 "Excursion Ticket," which allows you, in effect, to "sightsee" the BART system. Tour as much as you like, then exit from the same station you entered. If this is your idea of fun, you can buck the system and save some money by buying an 80¢ ticket at any station, then riding as much as you like before exiting three blocks away at an adjacent station.

Walking & Driving Tours

The City by the Bay is a stroller's paradise, just as Los Angeles is a motorist's metropolis. The most popular walking tour is surely the one through Chinatown detailed below. Here, in this famous quarter of San Francisco, while exploring the architectural sights, the museums and other cultural points of interest, the Buddhist temples and churches, the bazaars and shops, the stroller experiences the ethnic vitality of this coastal city, which does much of its trade with the Far East.

If you want a **self-guided driving tour** of the scenic and historic spots of San Francisco and have access to a car, there is no better way to see the city than to follow the blue-and-white seagull signs of the beautiful 49-mile scenic drive, originally designed for the benefit of visitors to San Francisco's 1930–40 Golden Gate International Exposition. Virtually all the best-known sights are on this tour, which follows a rough circle around the city, as well as some great views of the bay and ocean.

In theory, this mini-excursion can be done in half a day, but if you stop to walk across the Golden Gate Bridge or have tea in the Japanese Tea Garden in Golden Gate Park, or enjoy many of the panoramic views, you'll spend the better part of a day.

The San Francisco Visitors Information Center at Powell and Market Streets can supply you with a free map of the route. The blue-and-white seagull signs along the way will direct you counterclockwise, but since a few are missing, the map will be especially useful. Try to avoid the downtown area during the weekday rush hours from 7 to 9am and 4 to 6pm.

For alternative walking tours, consult *Frommer's San Francisco* and *Frommer's Walking Tours: San Francisco* (both Macmillan). While Chinatown is a popular district for strolling, there are, as you'll discover, many other areas of the city worth exploring.

Walking Tour

Chinatown

Start Grant Avenue and Bush Street.
Finish Grant and Columbus Avenues.
Time 1½ hours, not counting refueling stops.
Best Times Daily from 11am to 9pm, when the streets are in full swing.
Worst Times Very early or very late, when shops are closed and the quarter is not at its most cluttered.

The first Chinese immigrants reached San Francisco during the Gold Rush of 1849. They called the collection of huts around the bay, somewhat optimistically, Gum San Dai Foo—"Great City of the Golden Hill." The Chinese were not concentrated here entirely by choice—they were segregated by anti-Asian prejudice. Chinatown was a cramped, hideously overcrowded ghetto. The opium trade and child prostitution flourished here, as did disease, poverty, and hunger.

Conditions worsened until the Great Earthquake and subsequent fire wiped out the area in 1906. Since it was rebuilt, Chinatown has become the renowned commercial and culinary quarter that it is today. The seven-block-long, three-block-wide district is now one of the largest Chinese settlements outside Asia—and growing, as immigrants from Hong Kong and even from mainland China arrive on the coast.

Start at the corner of Grant Avenue and Bush Street. You'll know you're at the right place when you spot the:

1. **Chinatown Arch,** a two-story, green-tiled, dragon-topped gate. This pretty Chinese portal is the main entrance to San Francisco's Chinatown. Erected in 1970, it was a gift from the Republic of China (Taiwan).

   Walk uphill, under the arch, and you are strolling on:

2. **Grant Avenue,** the eight-block-long mainstem of Chinatown. This primary thoroughfare is a multi-ethnic parade every day of the year. The shops are crammed with goods, ranging from ordinary utility wares to exotic treasures and—of course—mountains of "souvenirs." Some of it is pure junk, not even of Chinese origin.

   Walk two blocks up Grant Avenue, just past the corner of California Street. On your right you'll see:

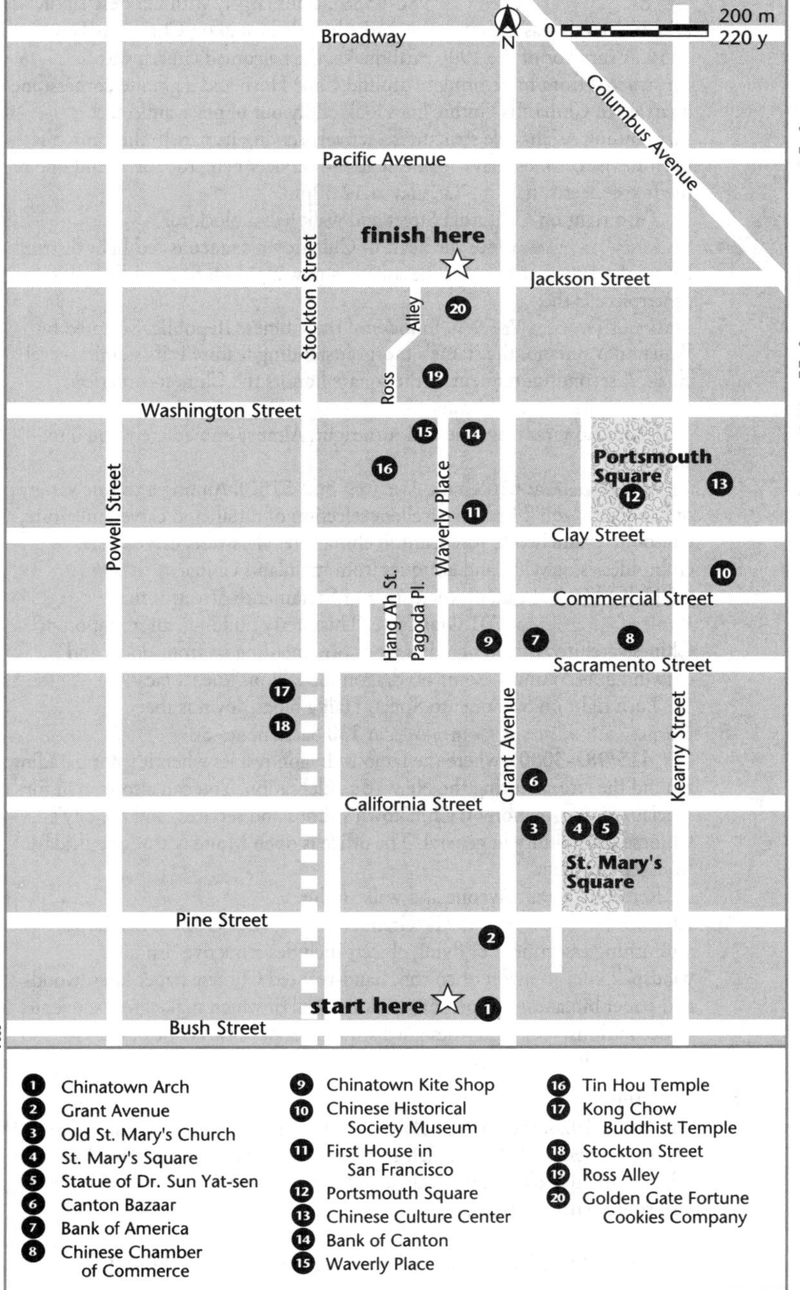

Broadway
N
0
200 m
220 y
Columbus Avenue
Pacific Avenue
finish here
Jackson Street
Stockton Street
Ross Alley
Washington Street
Powell Street
Waverly Place
Portsmouth Square
Clay Street
Commercial Street
Hang Ah St.
Pagoda Pl.
Sacramento Street
Grant Avenue
Kearny Street
California Street
St. Mary's Square
Pine Street
start here
Bush Street
1 Chinatown Arch
2 Grant Avenue
3 Old St. Mary's Church
4 St. Mary's Square
5 Statue of Dr. Sun Yat-sen
6 Canton Bazaar
7 Bank of America
8 Chinese Chamber of Commerce
9 Chinatown Kite Shop
10 Chinese Historical Society Museum
11 First House in San Francisco
12 Portsmouth Square
13 Chinese Culture Center
14 Bank of Canton
15 Waverly Place
16 Tin Hou Temple
17 Kong Chow Buddhist Temple
18 Stockton Street
19 Ross Alley
20 Golden Gate Fortune Cookies Company

Walking Tour—Chinatown

3. **Old St. Mary's Church** (☎ **986-4388**). Built largely with Chinese labor, Old St. Mary's was the city's first cathedral, dedicated on Christmas Day 1854. A survivor of the 1906 earthquake, the balconied church was constructed from brick brought around Cape Horn and a granite cornerstone quarried in China. Its Gothic lines look oddly out of place amid the surrounding Asian-style structures. Actively serving its parish, the church is open to visitors most days. You can attend services here, too, or attend one of the free concerts, held on Tuesday at 12:30pm.

   Turn right on California Street and walk half a block to:
4. **St. Mary's Square.** Once the heart of Chinatown's raucous red-light district before the 1906 earthquake, the square is now a placid, flower-filled park. Its centerpiece is the:
5. **Statue of Dr. Sun Yat-Sen,** founder of the Chinese Republic. Sculpted by Beniamino Bufano, the statue's most outstanding feature is its stainless-steel cloak. A second monument in the square honors the Chinese-American victims of the two world wars.

   Return to Grant Avenue and turn right. Almost immediately you'll see the:
6. **Canton Bazaar,** at 616 Grant Ave. (☎ **362-5750**). Among a terrific variety of handcrafts you'll find an excellent selection of rattan and carved furniture, cloisonne enamelwork, rose Canton chinaware, glassware, carved jade, embroideries, jewelry, and antiques from mainland China.

   Half a block ahead, on the corner of Sacramento Street, is the:
7. **Bank of America,** at 701 Grant Ave. This pretty building, an imitation of Chinese architecture, has gold dragons ornamenting its front doors and entwining its columns. Some 60 dragon medallions line its facade.

   Turn right on Sacramento Street. Half a block down is the:
8. **Chinese Chamber of Commerce,** at 730 Sacramento St. (☎ **415/982-3000**), where the famous dragon resides when it's not parading around the streets during the New Year celebration. You can also stop in for specialized information on Chinatown's shops and services, and the city's Chinese community in general. The office is open Monday through Friday from 9am to 5pm.

   Return to Grant Avenue and walk to the:
9. **Chinatown Kite Shop,** at 717 Grant Ave. (☎ **989-5182**). This shop's astonishing assortment of flying objects includes attractive fish kites, windsock kites in nylon or cotton, hand-painted Chinese paper kites, wood-and-paper biplanes, and pentagonal kites—all of which make great souvenirs or decorations. Computer-designed stunt kites have two control lines to manipulate loops and dives.

Refueling Stop

Opened in 1924, the **Eastern Bakery,** at Commercial Street, is the oldest Chinese-American bakery in San Francisco. Stop for some fermented soybean cakes, almond cookies, mooncakes, and other Asian sweets that will probably take some getting used to.

Turn right down Commercial Street, and walk two blocks to the:

10. **Chinese Historical Society Museum,** at 650 Commercial St. (☎ **391-1188**). This pocket-size museum traces the history of Chinese immigrants in California through Gold Rush relics, photos, and artifacts.

Return to Grant Avenue, turn right, and walk half a block to the corner of Clay Street. At this corner once stood:

11. **The First House in San Francisco.** Constructed in 1836 when the fledgling town was called Yerba Buena, the house was built by a merchant named Jacob Leese, next to the tent then occupied by Captain Richardson, the settlement's first harbormaster.

Turn right down Clay Street. A few steps down on your left is:

12. **Portsmouth Square,** a quiet little park atop a parking garage. This was the birthplace of Yerba Buena—the central plaza around which grew the city of San Francisco. It was also a favorite contemplation spot for Jack London, Rudyard Kipling, and Robert Louis Stevenson. Today this grassy slope is not the most restful park in the city, but is interesting as the gathering place for Chinatown's older men, who perform tai chi, gamble over games of mahjong and Chinese cards, and chat with each other. The wooden pagoda-style structures were only placed here in 1990.

Cross the hideously ugly footbridge over Kearny Street into the:

13. **Chinese Culture Center,** at 750 Kearny St., inside the Financial District Holiday Inn. Pass display cases of antique puppets into a gallery presenting changing exhibits on Chinese history and culture. Depending on what's on, it can be very interesting. It's open Tuesday through Saturday from 10am to 4pm; admission is free.

Return to Portsmouth Square, walk to the far end, and turn right on the path, toward Washington Street. Before you exit the green, notice the statue of Robert Louis Stevenson that stands on your left in the park's northwest corner. Turn left onto Washington Street, back toward Grant Avenue. Here you'll see the:

14. **Bank of Canton,** at 743 Washington St., which boasts the oldest (1909) Asian-style edifice in Chinatown. This three-tiered temple-style building once housed the China Telephone Exchange, known as "China-5" until 1945; operators spoke five dialects, and were famous for their phenomenal memories. Operators reputedly knew every subscriber by name and would often correct a caller—"No, that's not Mrs. Wu's number; you're calling Mr. Chang."

Cross Grant Avenue, walk half a block and turn left onto:

15. **Waverly Place,** the best known of Chinatown's side streets. This small street is popular because of its especially colorful architecture. Most of the balconied buildings that line this thoroughfare are private family associations and temples, few of which are open to the public. An exception is the:

16. **Tin Hou Temple,** at 125 Waverly Place. Accessed by a narrow stairway, this incense-laden sanctuary is decorated in traditional black, red, and gold lacquered woods. Chinese Buddhists don't attend scheduled services—they enter temples to pray, meditate, and send offerings to their ancestors. You are welcome to visit, but do so unobtrusively. It's customary to drop a dollar in the offering box, or to buy a bundle of stick incense.

Refueling Stop

If you're ready for a snack, try **Pot Sticker,** 150 Waverly Place (☎ **397-9985**), a simple, quiet oasis, patronized largely by locals in the know. The name comes from its specialty: pot stickers—pan-fried, thin-skinned dumplings stuffed with seasoned meat or vegetables, a staple of Mandarin cooking.

Back on the street, continue for just a few steps and turn right on Clay Street. Walk one block, and turn left onto Stockton Street. On the right-hand side, above the post office you'll find the:

17. Kong Chow Buddhist Temple, at 855 Stockton St., fourth floor. This is the oldest and prettiest of Chinatown's many temples. Feel free to take a look, but have respect for those who have come to pray. Exit the temple and backtrack up:

18. Stockton Street. This stretch of Stockton is the center of the Chinese food market district, an unusual conglomeration of glazed ducks, bamboo shoots, sharks fins, ginger roots, fish, and chickens.

Walk one block and turn right onto Washington Street. After half a block, turn left into the small:

19. Ross Alley, a passage connecting Washington and Jackson Streets. Along the left-hand side of this alley are a number of Chinese sweat shops, hiding behind boarded-up screen doors—an eery reminder of the bad old days.

Toward the end of the block is the:

20. Golden Gate Fortune Cookies Company, at 56 Ross St. (☎ **781-3956**). It's a tiny place, where a single woman sits at the end of a conveyer belt and folds messages into the warm cookies. The manager will try to sell you a big bag of cookies. X-rated fortunes are their specialty.

Turn right at the end of Ross Alley, walk half a block, then turn left and you're back on Grant Avenue. Chinatown terminates at Columbus Avenue, where it fades into strip joints and the beginning of North Beach. Turn around and explore Chinatown on your own, or turn left, up Columbus Avenue, and take a tour of North Beach, San Francisco's Italian quarter.

A Final Refueling Stop

Turn right on Columbus and walk half a block to **Brandy Ho's Hunan Food,** 217 Columbus Ave. (☎ **788-7527**). This down-to-earth place with great food is one of my favorite restaurants in Chinatown. (See Section 4, "Dining," above, for complete information.)

Organized Tours

WALKING TOURS

You should know about the free walking tours of historic areas sponsored by the **Friends of the San Francisco Public Library** (☎ **558-3857**). Volunteers conduct these informative tours from May through October. A recorded schedule of the day's tours can be obtained by calling **558-3981.** The walks usually last about 1½ hours, and reservations are not required. Tour destinations include City Hall, Coit Tower, North Beach, Victorian Houses of Pacific Heights, and Japantown.

Wok Wiz Chinatown Walking Tours, 750 Kearny St., Suite 800, San Francisco, CA 94108. ☎ **415/355-9657.**

San Francisco's Chinatown is always fascinating, but for many visitors with limited time it's hard to know where to search out the "nontouristy" shops, restaurants, and historical spots in this magnificent microcosm of Chinese culture. Founded by author, TV personality, cooking instructor, and restaurant critic Shirley Fong-Torres, Wok Wiz tours take you into nooks and crannies not usually seen by tourists. Each of her guides is Chinese, speaks fluent Cantonese or Mandarin, and is intimately acquainted with all of Chinatown's backways, alleys, and small enterprises, which are generally known only to those who live here. You'll learn about dim sum (a "delight of the heart") and the Chinese tea ceremony, meet a Chinese herbalist, stop at a pastry shop to watch rice noodles being made (noodles and other pasta forms originated in China, not Italy), watch the famous Chinese artist Y. K. Lau do his delicate brush painting, learn about jook (a traditional Chinese breakfast), stop in at a fortune-cookie factory, and visit a Chinese produce market and learn about the very unusual vegetables you may never identify at lunch or dinner.

All in all, you'll learn more about Chinatown than you'll ever remember. And you'll also learn enough to return on your own because you'll know that there's more to Chinatown than just the Grant Avenue gift shops.

Wok Wiz Chinatown Walking Tours are conducted daily from 10am to 1:30pm, and include a complete Chinese lunch. The tour begins in the lobby of the Chinatown Holiday Inn, at 750 Kearny St. (between Washington and Clay Streets). It's an easy walk, fun and fascinating, and you're bound to make new friends. Groups are generally held to a maximum of 12, and reservations are essential.

Prices (including lunch): $35 adults, $33 seniors ages 60 and older, $25 children under 12.

Cruisin' The Castro, 375 Lexington St., San Francisco, CA 94110. ☎ **415/550-8110.**

This fascinating, fun, and informative historical tour of San Francisco's most famous gay quarter will give you a totally new insight into the contribution of the gay community to the political maturity, growth, and beauty of San Francisco.

Tours are personally conducted by Ms. Trevor Hailey, who was part of the development of the Castro in the 1970s and knew Harvey Milk—the first openly gay politician elected to office in the United States. You'll learn about Milk's rise from shopkeeper to city supervisor and visit Harvey Milk Plaza, where most marches, rallies, and protests begin. Then there are the beautifully restored Victorian homes on the Castro's side streets. The area is also rich in community pride. It is filled with unusual gift shops, bookstores, restaurants, and businesses—and there's not a single hill to climb.

Ms. Hailey, a resident of the gay community since 1972, knows most of the local business owners personally. She therefore offers a view of the Castro that tourists seldom see. She's the originator of the Palace Guides (docents for the city's Palace of Fine Arts) and a fervent historical researcher, so her acquaintance with tours is not happenstance.

Tours are conducted Tuesday through Saturday, from 10am to 1:30pm, and begin at Harvey Milk Plaza, atop the Castro Street Muni station. The cost includes brunch at the historic Elephant Walk Restaurant. Reservations are required.

Prices (including brunch): $30 adults, $25 seniors ages 62 and older and children ages 16 and under.

BUS TOURS

Gray Line, Transbay Terminal, First and Mission Streets. ☎ **558-9400,** or toll free **800/826-0202.**

San Francisco's largest bus-tour operator offers several itineraries on a daily basis. There is a free pickup and return service between centrally located hotels and departure locations. Reservations are required for most tours.

The one-hour **Motorized Cable Car Tour** continuously loops around the city's downtown, passing Union Square, Nob Hill, Chinatown, North Beach, and Fisherman's Wharf. Passengers ride aboard an authentic cable car–cum-bus. You can get off the bus at either Union Square or Pier 39 and board again later. Tickets cost $12 for adults, $6 for children ages 5 to 11. Buses depart from Union Square, at the corner of Powell and Geary Streets, or from Pier 39. No reservations are required.

The company's 3½-hour **Deluxe City Tour** is a panoramic ride past the city's major sights. You pass by the Opera House, visit Golden Gate Park, and cross the Golden Gate Bridge for the magnificent view from Vista Point (see "The Top Attractions," above). Stops include Mission Dolores, the Japanese Tea Garden, and Cliff House. All tours are led by a driver/guide. Tours cost $25 for adults, $12.50 for children aged 5 to 11. Buses depart from the Transbay Terminal, at First and Mission Streets, daily at 9, 10, and 11am and at 1:30 and 2:30pm. From May 4 to September 30, there's an additional departure at 3:30pm.

The three-hour **San Francisco by Night Tour** starts with a bus ride to the glittering lights of Ghirardelli Square, the Cannery, and Fisherman's Wharf. Then it's on to a walking tour of Chinatown with an Asian guide to point out the Painted Balconies, the Dragon Lanterns, and the Tongs. Tours cost $25 for adults, $12.50 for children ages 5 to 11. Buses depart nightly at 7pm from Union Square, at Powell and Geary Streets.

Three Babes and a Bus. ☎ **552-2582.**

Perhaps the world's hippest scheduled-tour operator, this unique company runs regular nightclub trips for out-of-towners and locals who want to brush up on San Francisco's loudest sights. Although the 3½-hour roller-coaster ride through trendy SoMa and adjacent regions begins a little early for the most hardened clubbers, there is no lack of black clothes on the bus. The Babes' ever-changing itinerary waltzes into four different clubs per night, cutting in front of every line with priority entry. The party continues en route, when the Babes entertain. The bus departs on weekends only, at locations throughout the city. Call for complete information and reservations.

Cost: $30, including club entrances.

Tours: Fri and Sat nights only, from 9:30pm to 1:30am.

BOAT TOURS

One of the best ways to look at San Francisco is from a boat bobbing on the bay. There are several cruises to choose from, many of which start from Fisherman's Wharf.

Red and White Fleet, Pier 41, Fisherman's Wharf. ☎ **546-2700,** or toll free **800/229-2784** in California.

The city's largest boat-tour operator offers more than half a dozen itineraries on the bay. The fleet's primary ships are two-toned double- and triple-deckers, capable of holding 150 to 500 passengers. You can't miss the observation-tower ticket booth, at Pier 43½, located next to the Franciscan Restaurant.

The **Golden Gate Bay Cruise** is a 45-minute cruise by the Golden Gate Bridge, Angel Island, and Alcatraz Island. Tours cost $15 for adults, $12 for juniors 12 to 18 and seniors 55 and older, $8 for children 5 to 11. Tour price includes audio narration in one of six languages: English, French, Spanish, German, Japanese, or Mandarin. Tours depart from Pier 41 and Pier 43½ daily, every hour and a half, from 10:45am to 3:45pm.

Blue and Gold Fleet, Pier 39, Fisherman's Wharf. ☎ **705-5444.**

Blue and Gold's Bay Cruise tours the bay year round in a sleek 400-passenger sightseeing boat, complete with food-and-beverage facilities. The fully narrated 1¼-hour cruise passes beneath the Golden Gate Bridge and the Bay Bridge, and comes within yards of Alcatraz Island. Frequent daily departures from Pier 39's West Marina begin at 10am during summer and 11am in winter. Tickets cost $15 for adults, $7 for juniors ages 5 to 18 and seniors over 62; children under 5 sail free.

6 Sports & Recreation

SPECTATOR SPORTS

The Bay Area's sports scene includes several major professional franchises, including football, baseball, and basketball. Check the local newspapers' sports sections for daily listings of local events.

Baseball

San Francisco Giants, Candlestick Park, Giants Dr. and Gilman Ave. ☎ **467-8000.**

From April through October the National League Giants play their home games at Candlestick Park, off U.S. 101, about eight miles south of downtown. Tickets are usually available up until game time, but they can be dreadfully far from the action. Tickets may be obtained at Candlestick Park; from Giants Dugout, 170 Grant Ave. (☎ **982-9400**); or by phone through BASS TicketMaster (☎ **510/762-2277**). Special $4 express bus service is available from Market Street on game days, call Muni (☎ **673-6864**) for pickup points and schedule information. Bring a coat, as this 60,000-seat stadium is known for chilly winds.

Oakland Athletics, Oakland Coliseum Complex, at the Hegenberger Rd. Exit from 1-880, in Oakland. ☎ **510/430-8020.**

The A's play across the bay in the Oakland Coliseum Stadium. Part of the Oakland Coliseum Complex, the stadium holds close to 50,000 spectators and is serviced by BART's Coliseum station. Tickets are available from the Coliseum Box Office or by phone through BASS TicketMaster (☎ **510/762-2277**).

Basketball

Golden State Warriors, Oakland Coliseum Complex, at the Hegenberger Rd. Exit from 1-880, in Oakland. ☎ **510/638-6300.**

The NBA Warriors play basketball in the 15,025-seat Oakland Coliseum Arena. The season runs from November through April, and most games are played at 7:30pm. Tickets are available at the arena, and by phone, through BASS TicketMaster (☎ **510/762-2277**).

Football

San Francisco 49ers, Candlestick Park, Giants Dr. and Gilman Ave. ☎ **468-2249.**

The football 49ers call Candlestick Park home. The stadium is off U.S. 101, about eight miles south of downtown. Games are played on Sunday from August through December; kickoff is usually at 1pm. Tickets sell out early in the season, but are available at higher prices through ticket agents beforehand and from scalpers at the gate. Ask your hotel concierge, or visit City Box Office, 141 Kearny St. (☎ **392-4400**). Special $4 express bus service is available from Market Street on game days; call Muni (☎ **673-6864**) for pickup points and schedule information.

University of California Golden Bears, 61 Harmon Gym, University of California, Berkeley. ☎ **642-5150,** or toll free **800/GO-BEARS.**

The Berkeley Bears play their home games in Memorial Stadium, on the university campus across the bay. Tickets are usually available at game time. Call for schedules and information.

Horse Racing

Golden Gate Fields, Gilman St., off 1-80, in Albany. ☎ **510/559-7300.**

Scenic Thoroughbred races are held here from January to June. The park is located on the seashore, 10 miles northeast of San Francisco. Call for admission prices and post times.

Bay Meadows, 2600 S. Delaware St., off U.S. 101, in San Mateo. ☎ **574-7223.**

The nearest autumn racing is at this Thoroughbred and quarter-horse track on the peninsula. Located about 20 miles south of downtown San Francisco, the course hosts races four or five days each week from September through January. Call for admission and post times.

RECREATION

Although San Francisco's climate is not perfectly suited to outdoor recreation, the city does offer a good deal of terrific activities when the sun does shine.

Ballooning

Over a dozen hot-air-ballooning companies will take you up for a silent flight over the nearby Wine Country.

Adventures Aloft, P.O. Box 2500, Vintage 1870, Yountville, CA 94599. ☎ **707/944-4408,** or toll free **800/367-6272.**

The Napa Valley's oldest hot-air-balloon company is staffed with full-time professional pilots. Groups are small, and the flight will last about an hour. The cost of $165 per person includes a preflight continental breakfast, postadventure champagne brunch, and a framed "first-flight" certificate. Flights are daily between 6 and 8am.

Once in a Lifetime Balloon Co., P.O. Box 795, Calistoga, CA 94515. ☎ **707/942-6541,** or toll free **800/659-9915** in California.

Daily launches are made between 6 and 8am. The one-hour balloon flight is followed by a gourmet champagne brunch. The cost of $175 per person includes a photo and flight certificate.

Beaches

Ocean Beach, at the end of Golden Gate Park, on the westernmost side of the city, is San Francisco's prettiest beach. Just offshore, in front of Cliff House, are the jagged

Seal Rocks. These dangerous-looking formations are usually inhabited by various shore birds and a large colony of barking sea lions. Bring binoculars if you have any. Ocean Beach is great for strolling or sunning, but don't swim here—tides are tricky, and each year bathers drown in the rough surf.

Hike up the hill to explore the ruins of Sutro Baths. These magnificent baths were once the largest indoor pools in the world.

Bicycling

Two city-designated bike routes are maintained by the Recreation and Parks Department. One tours 7½ miles through Golden Gate Park to Lake Merced; the other traverses the city, starting in the south, and follows a route over the Golden Gate Bridge. These routes are not dedicated to bicyclists, and care must be taken to avoid cars. Helmets are recommended. A bike map is available from the San Francisco Visitor Information Center at Powell and Market Streets (see Section 1, "Orientation," above) and from bicycle shops all around town.

A massive new seawall, constructed to buffer Ocean Beach from storm-driven waves, doubles as an attractive public walk and bike way along five waterfront blocks of the Great Highway between Noriega and Santiago Streets. It's an easy ride from Cliff House or Golden Gate Park.

Park Cyclery, 1865 Haight St. ☎ **221-3777.**

This is one of two shops in the Haight Street/Stanyan Street area that rents bikes to day trippers. Located next to Golden Gate Park, the Cyclery rents mountain bikes exclusively, along with helmets, locks, and accessories. The charge is $5 per hour, and it's open daily from 9:30am to 5:30pm.

Boating

Cass's Marina, 1702 Bridgeway, Sausalito. ☎ **332-6789** or toll free **800/472-4595.**

Sailboats measuring 22 to 101 feet are available for rent on San Francisco Bay. Sail under the Golden Gate Bridge on your own or with a licensed skipper. In addition, large sailing yachts leave from Sausalito on a regularly scheduled basis. Call for schedules, prices, and availability of sailboats.

Open: Daily 9am–sunset.

Golden Gate Park Boat House, at Stow Lake. ☎ **752-0347.**

At Stow Lake, the park's largest body of water, you can rent a rowboat or pedalboat by the hour, and steer over to Strawberry Hill, a large round island in the middle of the lake, for lunch. There's usually a line on weekends.

Open: June–Sept, daily 9am–4pm; the rest of the year, Tues–Sun 9am–4pm.

City Stair Climbing

Many health clubs now have stair-climbing machines and step classes, but in San Francisco, you need only go outside. The following city stair climbs will not only provide you with a good workout, but offer great sightseeing, too.

Filbert Street Steps, between Sansome St. and Telegraph Hill.

Scaling the sheer eastern face of Telegraph Hill, this 377-step climb from Sansome and Filbert Streets wends its way through verdant flower gardens and charming 19th-century cottages. Napier Lane, a narrow wooden plank walkway, leads to Montgomery Street. Turn right, and follow the path to the end of the cul-de-sac where another stairway continues to Telegraph's panoramic summit.

Lyon Street Steps, between Green St. and Broadway.

Built in 1916, this historic stairway street contains four steep sets of stairs totaling 288 steps in all. Begin at Green Street and climb all the way up, past manicured hedges and flower gardens to an iron gate that opens into the Presidio. A block east, on Baker Street, another set of 369 steps descends to Green Street.

Croquet

The San Francisco Croquet Club (☎ **776-4104**) offers public lessons from 11am to 2pm on the first Saturday of each month (or anytime by reservation for parties of four or more). The game is taught according to international six wicket rules at the croquet lawns, in Stern Grove, at 19th Avenue and Wawona Street. Members over 60 years of age can play free from 1 to 4pm on the first and third Wednesdays of each month.

Fishing

New Easy Rider Sport Fishing, 561 Prentiss St. ☎ **285-2000.**

From June to October, Easy Rider makes daily salmon runs from Fisherman's Wharf. Fishing equipment is available; the cost of $47 per person includes bait. Reservations are required. Departures are daily at 6am, returning at 2pm; from June through October there's a second daily departure at 3pm, returning at dusk.

Sea Breeze Sportfishing at Fisherman's Wharf, P.O. Box 713, Mill Valley, CA 94942. ☎ **415/381-FISH** or **474-7748.**

Salmon-fishing trips depart from Fisherman's Wharf daily at 6am, returning at 2pm. Equipment is available, and reservations are required. The cost is $45 per person.

Golf

Golden Gate Park Course, 47th Ave. and Fulton St. ☎ **751-8987.**

This small nine-hole course covers 1,357 yards and is par 27. All holes are par 3, tightly set, and well trapped with small greens. Greens fees are very reasonable: $8 per person per day Monday through Friday and $11 on Saturday and Sunday. The course is open daily from 9am to dusk.

Lincoln Park Golf Course, 34th Ave. and Clement St. ☎ **221-9911.**

San Francisco's prettiest municipal course has terrific views and fairways lined with Monterey cypress trees. Its 18 holes encompass 5,081 yards, for a par 68. This is the oldest course in the city and one of the oldest in the west. Greens fees are $13 per person Monday through Friday and $17 on Saturday and Sunday. The course is open daily from 9am to dusk.

Handball

The city's best handball courts are in Golden Gate Park, opposite Seventh Avenue, south of Middle Drive East. Courts are available free on a first-come, first-served basis.

Roller Skating

Although people skate in Golden Gate Park all week long, Sunday is best, when John F. Kennedy Drive, between Kezar Drive and Transverse Road, is closed to automobiles. A smooth "skate pad" is located on your right, just past the Conservatory.

Skates on Haight, 1818 Haight St. ☎ **752-8376.**

The best place to rent either in-line or conventional skates is at this well-stocked shop one block from the park. Although protective wrist guards and knee pads are included free, inexperienced skaters should walk past the cars to the park before lacing up their skates. The cost is $7 per hour for in-line Rollerblades, $6 per hour for "conventionals." Major credit card and I.D. deposit are required. The shop is open Monday to Friday from 11:30am to 6:30pm, and Saturday and Sunday from 10am to 6pm.

Running

The **San Francisco Marathon,** held annually in the middle of July, is one of the largest in the world. For entry information, contact Pamakid Runners Club (☎ **415/681-2322**). At other times of the year, call **543-RACE** for up-to-date running-event information.

Tennis

More than 100 courts throughout the city are maintained by the **San Francisco Recreation and Parks Department** (☎ **753-7001**). All are available free, on a first-come, first-served basis. The exception are the 21 courts in Golden Gate Park; a nominal fee is charged for their use, and courts must be reserved in advance for weekend play. Call the number above on Wednesday from 7 to 9pm, or on Thursday and Friday from 9am to 5pm.

7 Savvy Shopping

If New York and Chicago are department store cities, then San Francisco is a boutique town. Sure, there are plenty of large emporiums here, but this city's main shopping attractions are small, smart specialty shops, selling distinctive and unusual clothes, crafts, books, antiques, jewelry, and gifts. It is relevant that San Francisco is a great walking city, making it both fun and easy to stroll and shop along the many fashionable streets.

The Shopping Scene

GREAT SHOPPING AREAS • Union Square and Environs San Francisco's downtown, centered around Union Square and enclosed by Bush, Taylor, Market, and Montgomery Streets, contains several fashionable department stores, many of the city's high-end specialty shops, and some of the most respected names in international retailing. Maiden Lane, a tree-lined walk that runs east from Union Square, is lined with some of the most elegant showcases in town. From Market Street, running north, the first four blocks of Grant Avenue are lined with several top-name shops, including Tiffany & Co., Shreve & Co., and Brooks Brothers. Post Street, which marks Union Square's northern perimeter, is another chic shopping strip, most densely packed with prestigious shops between Kearny and Taylor Streets.

• Chinatown In many ways, Chinatown is the antithesis of Union Square, selling an exceptional variety of cheap goods, T-shirts, knockoffs, and innumerable tourist-oriented trinkets. The best shops in this crowded area are the colorful bazaars, crammed with an eclectic assortment of unrelated objects, from postcards and water pipes to Chinese tableware and plastic toys. Grant Avenue is the area's main thoroughfare, and side streets between Bush Street and Columbus Avenue are full of restaurants, markets, and interesting shops. Walking is best, since traffic through this area is slow and parking is next to impossible. Most of the stores in Chinatown are open daily from 10am to 10pm.

• **Union Street** Real San Franciscans are those who know the difference between Union Square and Union Street. Though similarly named, these two shopping areas are located far away from each other. The Cow Hollow section of this trendy street, between Van Ness Avenue and Steiner Street, is an "in" stretch for antiques, handcrafts, hip fashions, and deluxe glassware. A stroll along Union Street, poking through the many boutiques and highly original stores, makes for a very pleasant afternoon. Several excellent eateries are also worth the trip (see "Dining," above, for complete information). The area is serviced by bus lines 41 and 45.

• **Haight Street** The neighborhood known as Haight-Ashbury is most famous as a spawning ground for hippies in the 1960s. Although there are no longer so many flower children here, the Haight still has an active street scene and is home to a good number of writers and musicians as well as younger, upwardly mobile types. The six blocks of upper Haight Street, between Central Avenue and Stanyan Street, is the best place in the city to shop for trendy street styles from Europe and America. Along this thoroughfare is a healthy mix of boutiques, secondhand shops, and inexpensive restaurants. Bus lines 7, 66, 71, and 73 run the length of Haight Street. Muni metro line N stops at Waller and Cole Streets.

• **Fisherman's Wharf and Environs** The nonstop strip of waterfront malls that runs along Jefferson Street includes hundreds of shops, restaurants, and attractions. Ghirardelli Square, the Cannery, and the Anchorage are all outlined under "Shopping Centers & Complexes," below.

HOURS, TAXES & SHIPPING Store hours are generally Monday through Saturday from 10am to 6pm, and Sunday from noon to 5pm. Most department stores stay open later, as do shops around Fisherman's Wharf—the most heavily touristed area.

The **sales tax** in San Francisco is 8¼%, added on at the register for all goods and services purchased.

For **shipping,** most of the city's shops can wrap your purchase and ship it anywhere in the world via United Parcel Service (UPS). If they can't, you can send it yourself, either through UPS (☎ **952-5200**) or through the U.S. mail (see "Fast Facts: San Francisco" above).

Shopping A to Z

ANTIQUES

Jackson Square, a historic district just north of the Financial District's Embarcadero Center, is the place to go for the top names in high-end furniture and fine art. There are also many Asian-art dealers here. Over a dozen dealers on the two blocks between Columbus and Sansome Streets specialize in European furnishings from the 17th to the 19th centuries. Most shops here are open Monday through Friday from 9am to 5pm, and Saturday from 11am to 4pm.

Fumiki Fine Asian Arts, 2001 Union St. ☎ **922-0573.**

Specializing in fine Asian art and antiques, including Japanese baskets and Chinese artifacts and embroidery, the shop has one of the largest collections of antique Japanese Imari and Korean and Japanese tansus in the country. Open Monday through Saturday from 10am to 6pm and Sun noon to 5pm.

ART

The ***San Francisco Gallery Guide,*** a comprehensive, bimonthly publication listing the city's current shows, is available free of charge from the William Sawyer Gallery, 3045 Clay St., San Francisco, CA 94115 (☎ **921-1600**). Most of the city's major art galleries are clustered downtown, in the Union Square area. Below is a select list of the city's most interesting offerings. All the shops host changing exhibitions. Call for current information.

Atelier Dore, 771 Bush St. ☎ **391-2423.**

American and European painting from the 19th and 20th centuries is featured, including some WPA art. Open Tuesday through Saturday from 11am to 5pm.

Erika Meyerovich, 231 Grant Ave. ☎ **421-9997.**

Contemporary exhibitions by Warhol, Haring, Lichtenstein, Hockney, and others are sold alongside works by Picasso, Matisse, Chagall, Miró, and others. Open Monday through Friday from 10am to 5pm and Saturday from 11am to 5pm.

Fraenkel Gallery, 49 Geary St. ☎ **981-2661.**

This photography gallery features works by contemporary American and European artists. The excellent shows change frequently. Open Tuesday through Friday from 10:30am to 5:30pm and Saturday from 11am to 5pm.

Harcourts Modern and Contemporary Art, 460 Bush St. ☎ **421-3428.**

This is an international contemporary gallery featuring works on paper as well as a variety of other media. Open Tuesday through Saturday from 10am to 5:30pm.

Images of the North, 1782 Union St. ☎ **673-1273.**

This gallery features one of the most extensive collections of Inuit art—Canadian and Alaskan—in the United States. There's also a fine collection of Native American masks and jewelry. Open Monday through Saturday from 11am to 5:30pm and Sunday from noon to 4pm.

BOOKS

The Booksmith, 1644 Haight St. ☎ **863-8688.**

Haight Street's best selection of new books is housed in this large, well-maintained shop. It carries all the top titles, along with works from smaller presses, and over 1,000 different magazines. Open Monday through Saturday from 10am to 9pm and Sunday from 10am to 6pm.

Charlotte's Web, 2278 Union St. ☎ **441-4700.**

A terrific children's bookstore, Charlotte's Web is notable for its particularly knowledgeable owner, who sells everything from cloth books for babies, to histories and poetry for young adults. Non-literary items include music cassettes, videos, posters, and cards. Open Monday through Saturday from 10am to 6pm, and Sunday from 10am to 5pm.

City Lights Book Store, 261 Columbus Ave. ☎ **362-8193.**

Owned by Lawrence Ferlinghetti, the renowned beat-generation poet, this excellent two-level bookshop prides itself on a comprehensive collection of art, poetry, and political paperbacks, as well as more mainstream books. Open daily from 10am to midnight.

Clean Well-Lighted Place, 601 Van Ness Ave. ☎ **441-6670.**

A really good general bookstore, this independently owned shop sells a wide variety of titles, and has an educated staff that's quite knowledgeable about them. Open Monday through Saturday from 10am to 7pm, and Sunday from noon to 5pm.

Eastwind Books and Arts, 1435A Stockton St. ☎ **772-5877.**

The emphasis here is on Asian-American and Chinese books, including fiction, medicine, history, and language. Open Monday through Saturday from 10am to 6pm and Sunday noon to 5pm.

Markus Books, 1721 Fillmore St. ☎ **346-4222.**

Markus has the Bay Area's best selection of books relating to African-American and African culture. In addition to a good collection of children's books, there are titles on fiction, history, politics, art, and biography. Open Monday through Saturday from 10am to 7pm, and Sunday from noon to 5pm.

McDonald's Bookshop, 48 Turk St. ☎ **673-2235.**

San Francisco's biggest used-book shop claims to stock over a million volumes, including out-of-print, esoteric, and hard-to-find books in all categories and languages. As a birthday novelty, they'll find a copy of *Life* magazine from the month and year in which you were born. It's quite a shop. Open Monday, Tuesday, and Thursday from 10am to 6pm; Wednesday, Friday and Saturday from 10:30am to 6:30pm.

Rand-McNally Map and Travel, 595 Market St. ☎ **777-3131.**

Hands down, the best travel-book store in the city, this corner shop features maps, atlases, and travel guides to all destinations. Open Monday through Friday from 9am to 6:30pm and Saturday from 10am to 6pm.

Staceys, 581 Market St. ☎ **421-4687.**

Although it's widely known for its technical, computer, and business sections, Staceys is equally well stocked with fiction and trade books. Open Monday through Friday from 9am to 6:30pm and on Saturday from 10am to 6pm.

CHINA, SILVER & GLASS

The Enchanted Crystal, 1895 Union St. ☎ **885-1335.**

This shop has an extensive collection of fine crystal, art glass, jewelry, and one-of-a-kind decorative art, including one of the largest crystal balls in the world (from Madagascar). Open Monday through Saturday from 10am to 6pm and Sunday from noon to 5pm.

Gump's, 250 Post St. ☎ **982-1616.**

San Francisco's most impressive museum/store is located between Grant Avenue and Stockton Street. Founded more than a century ago, this supremely elegant establishment offers beautiful objects ranging from Asian antiques and porcelain to Steuben glass and Baccarat and Lalique crystal. It also claims to have the largest collection of freshwater pearls in the United States, and designs and manufactures much of its own jewelry. If you're in the market for a family of hand-carved Chilean lapis-lazuli penguins or for a Venetian opaline glass vase, then Gump's is the place. The store also encompasses an art gallery, a scent shop, and an interior-design salon. Open Monday through Saturday from 10am to 5:30pm.

CRAFTS

The Canton Bazaar, 616 Grant Ave. ☎ **362-5750.**

Amid a terrific variety of handcrafts you'll find an excellent selection of rattan and carved furniture, cloisonné enamelwork, rose Canton chinaware, glassware, carved jade, embroideries, jewelry, and antiques from mainland China. Open daily from 10am to 10pm.

Yankee Doodle Dandy, 1974 Union St. ☎ **346-0346,** or **346-3337.**

This shop features America's largest collection of pre-1935 quilts, many more than 100 years old. In addition, there are folk-art carvings, contemporary primitive paintings, and handmade collector teddy bears. Everything in this country-style store is unique and intriguing, beautiful, or cuddly. Open Monday through Saturday from 10:30am to 5:30pm and Sunday from noon to 5pm.

DEPARTMENT STORES

Emporium, 835 Market St. ☎ **764-2222.**

Located between Fourth Street and Fifth Street, adjacent to the San Francisco Shopping Centre (see "Shopping Centers & Complexes," below), Emporium is one of northern California's major chains. This is a full-line department store, including fashions, kitchenware, home furnishings, and electronics. Open Monday through Friday from 9:30am to 8pm, Saturday from 9:30am to 6pm, and Sunday from 11am to 6pm.

I. Magnin, Union Square. ☎ **362-2100.**

Founded in 1876, this is one of the city's oldest businesses, and the flagship shop in the Magnin chain. Ten upscale floors merchandise the finest fashions for women, men, and children. The store's Estée Lauder skin-care spa is almost as famous as its opulent ladies' powder room. Open Monday, Tuesday and Wednesday from 10am to 6pm, Saturday from 10am to 7pm, and on Sunday from 11am to 6pm.

Macy's, Stockton St. and O'Farrell St., Union Sq. ☎ **397-3333.**

One of the largest stores in San Francisco, Macy's is divided into two distinct buildings. The seven-story Macy's West features contemporary fashions for women and juniors, including jewelry, fragrances, cosmetics, and accessories. The top floors contain home furnishings, while the Cellar sells kitchenware and gourmet foods. Across the street, Macy's East has five floors of men's and children's fashions, as well as one of the best electronics departments in the city. Open Monday through Saturday from 10am to 8pm, Sunday from 11am to 7pm.

Neiman-Marcus, 150 Stockton St., Union Sq. ☎ **362-3900.**

Famous for its classic rotunda, this unit of the Texas-based chain features upscale men's and women's clothes, precious gems, and conservative formal wear. Other departments sell gourmet foods, gifts, and cosmetics. The Rotunda Restaurant, on the top floor, is a beautiful, relaxing place for lunch. Open Monday, Thursday, and Friday from 10am to 8pm; Tuesday, Wednesday, and Saturday from 10am to 6pm; and Sunday from noon to 6pm.

Nordstrom, in the San Francisco Shopping Centre, 865 Market St. ☎ **243-8500.**

Well known for its personalized service, this is the largest member of the Seattle-based fashion department-store chain. Nordstrom occupies the top five floors of the San Francisco Shopping Centre (see "Shopping Centers & Complexes," below), and is that mall's primary anchor. Equally devoted to women's and men's fashions, the store has one of the best shoe selections in the city, and thousands of suits in stock. The Nordstrom Café, on the top floor, has a terrific view and is a great place for an inexpensive lunch or light snack. Open Monday through Saturday from 9:30am to 9pm, and Sunday from 11am to 7pm.

Saks Fifth Avenue, 384 Post St. ☎ **986-4300.**

San Francisco's branch of this famous New York–based shop is as opulent as any. Saks sells fashions and gifts for men, women, and children, and has a well-regarded restaurant on the top floor. Open Monday, Thursday, and Friday from 10am to 8pm; Tuesday, Wednesday, and Saturday from 10am to 6:30pm; and Sunday from noon to 5pm.

FASHIONS

Burberrys, 225 Post St. ☎ **392-2200.**

One of the biggest names in traditional fashions is most famous for its plaid-lined trenchcoat. Luggage, accessories, and other clothes items can also be found in Burberrys plaid. Open Monday through Saturday from 9:30am to 6pm and Sunday from noon to 5pm.

Cable Car Clothiers, 246 Sutter St. ☎ **397-4740.**

Inside a beautiful landmark building at the corner of Market Street, this fine clothier features Aquascutum coats, English Church's shoes, McGeorge sweaters, Countess Mara neckwear, and other top fashions. Open Monday through Saturday from 9:30am to 5:30pm.

Polo/Ralph Lauren, 90 Post St. ☎ **567-7656.**

This beautifully assembled, multilevel store at Kearny Street is a tribute to the elegance and taste of its namesake designer. It features the entire collection of Polo apparel, from casual and roughwear to couture clothing, footwear, and accessories. Open Monday through Saturday from 10am to 6pm.

Men's Fashions

All American Boy, 463 Castro St. ☎ **861-0444.**

Long known for setting the mainstream style for gays, All American Boy is the quintessential Castro clothing shop. Open Monday to Saturday from 10am to 8pm, and Sunday 11am to 7pm.

Citizen Clothing, 536 Castro St. ☎ **558-9429.**

The Castro has some of America's best casual mens' clothing stores, and this is one of them. Stylish, but not faddish, pants, tops and accessories are sold. Open daily from 10am to 8pm.

Culot of San Francisco, 1969B Union St. ☎ **931-2413.**

Specializing in mens' undergarments and accessories, Culot sells high-quality underwear in a variety of styles, as well as cufflinks, suspenders, and tie clips. Open daily from 10:30am to 6:30pm.

Bolla, 1764 Haight St. ☎ **386-3290.**

The beautiful wooden floors of this Haight Street shop are topped with metal racks displaying trendy English-style clothes. Women's fashions are available, but the best offerings here are men's dress shirts, ties, belts, socks, watches, and accessories. Open Monday through Saturday from 11am to 7pm and Sunday from noon to 6:30pm.

Brooks Brothers, 201 Post St. ☎ **397-4500.**

In San Francisco, this bastion of tradition is located near Grant Avenue, one block east of Union Square. Brooks Brothers introduced the button-down collar and single-handedly changed the standard of the well-dressed businessman. The multilevel shop also sells traditional casual wear, including sportswear, sweaters, and shirts. Open Monday through Saturday from 9:30am to 6pm and Sunday from noon to 5pm.

Women's Fashions

The Chanel Boutique, 151 Maiden Lane. ☎ **981-1550.**

The entire elegant Chanel line is under one roof, and includes clothing, accessories, scents, cosmetics, and jewelry. Open Monday through Friday 10am to 6:30pm, Saturday from 10am to 6pm, and Sunday from 10am to 5pm.

The Dinostore, 1553 Haight St. ☎ **861-3933.**

A great Haight Street boutique for women's shoes and hip, contemporary fashions. Cute summer dresses, skirts, and tops are complemented by bustiers, scarves, and accessories. Look for the small green dinosaur out front. Open Monday through Saturday from 11am to 7pm and Sunday from noon to 6pm.

Imperial Fashion, 838 Grant Ave. ☎ **362-0981.**

Near Washington Street you'll find some of the most attractive merchandise in Chinatown, most of it from mainland China—silk blouses, jackets, and kimonos, and also silk fabrics that can be custom-tailored especially for you. Beautiful embroideries, handkerchiefs, and linens are also available. Open daily from 10am to 9:30pm.

Solo Fashion, 1599 Haight St. ☎ **621-0342.**

One of my favorite shops in the Haight for original women's fashions. There is a good selection of upbeat, contemporary English-style street wear, along with a collection of dresses designed exclusively for this shop.

Jaeger International, 272 Post St. ☎ **421-3714.**

Jaeger, near Stockton Street, has an international reputation for conservative designs and superb fabrics, especially lightweight wools. No one has ever accused this place of being on the cutting edge; it specializes in classic cuts in women's jackets, sweaters, pants, and skirts. Open Monday through Saturday from 10am to 6pm.

Children's Fashions

Kids Only, 1608 Haight St. ☎ **552-5445.**

Among the more conservative children's clothes here can be found a small selection of funky outfits that sport the Haight Street look. Tie-dyed fabrics are sold along with Nature's Wear brands that are made from all-natural, dye-free fabrics. Open Monday through Saturday from 10am to 6pm, and Sunday from 11am to 5pm.

Minis by Profili, 2042 Union St. ☎ **567-9537.**

Christina Profili, a San Franciscan clothing maker who used to design for The Gap, opened this children's clothing store in 1994 to sell her wonderful line of pint-sized pants, shirts, and dresses. Everything Profili designs matches with everything else—the colors and fabrics in every outfit in the store perfectly complement one another. A small toy corner includes storybooks that are sold with matching dolls. Open Monday through Thursday from 11:30am to 5:30pm, Saturday from 10am to 5:30pm, and Sunday from noon to 5:30pm.

Secondhand Clothing

Aardvark's, 1501 Haight St. ☎ **621-3141.**

One of San Francisco's largest secondhand clothing dealers, Aardvarks has seemingly endless racks of shirts, pants, dresses, skirts, and hats from the last 30 years. Open daily from 11am to 7pm.

Buffalo Exchange, 1555 Haight St. ☎ **431-7733.**

This large storefront on upper Haight Street is crammed with racks of antique and new fashions from the 1960s, '70s, and '90s. It stocks everything from suits and dresses to neckties, hats, handbags, and jewelry. Buffalo Exchange anticipates some of the hottest new street fashions. Open Monday through Saturday 11am to 7pm and Sunday noon to 6pm. A second shop is located at 1800 Polk St. (☎ **346-5741**).

La Rosa, 1711 Haight St. ☎ **668-3744.**

On a street packed with vintage clothing shops, this is the most upscale, featuring a very good selection of high-quality secondhand goods. Formal suits and dresses are its specialty, but you'll also find sport coats, slacks, and shoes.

Wasteland, 1660 Haight St. ☎ **863-3150.**

The enormous art-filled exterior fronts a large collection of vintage and contemporary clothes for men and women. Leathers, natural fibers, and dark colors predominate. Grandma's furniture is also for sale. Open daily from 11am to 7pm.

Factory Outlets

There are many factory-outlet stores in San Francisco, selling overstocked and discontinued fashions at very good prices. All the following shops are located south of Market Street, in the city's warehouse district.

Esprit Outlet Store, 499 Illinois St. ☎ **957-2550.**

All the Esprit collections and Susie Tompkins merchandise are available here at 30% or more off regular prices. In addition to clothes, the store sells accessories, shoes, and assorted other items. The bargain bins at the back of the store are especially appealing. Open Monday through Friday 10am to 8pm, Saturday 10am to 7pm, Sunday 11am to 5pm.

Glasser Designs, 32 Otis St. ☎ **552-3188.**

The beautiful soft-leather handbags, totes, and business bags sold here are all handmade in San Francisco. The outlet is located a half block west of Mission Street and South Van Ness Avenue. Open Monday through Friday from 9am to 5:30pm, Saturday from noon to 5pm.

The North Face, 1325 Howard St., at Ninth Street. ☎ **626-6444.**

Well known for its sporting, camping, and hiking equipment, this off-price outlet carries a good selection of high-quality skiwear, boots, sweaters, and goods like tents, packs, and sleeping bags. The North Face makes heavy use of Gore-Tex, down, and other durable light-weight materials. Open Monday through Saturday from 10am to 6pm.

FOOD

Bepples Pie Shop and Restaurant, 1934 Union St. ☎ **931-6225.**

One of the most celebrated shops on Union Street is this mouth-watering noshery selling soups, muffins, breads, and pies. Open Monday through Wednesday from 7am to 11:30pm, Thursday from 7am to midnight, Friday from 7 to 2am, Saturday from 9 to 2am, and Sunday from 9am to 10:30pm.

The Golden Gate Fortune Cookies Co., 56 Ross Alley. ☎ **781-3956.**

This tiny, touristy factory sells fortune cookies hot off the press. You can purchase them in small bags or in bulk, and if your order is large enough, you may even be able to negotiate your own message. Even if you're not buying, stop in to see how these sugary treats are made. Open Monday through Friday from 10am to 7pm.

Ten Ren Tea Company, 949 Grant Ave. ☎ **362-0656.**

At the Ten Ren Tea Company, between Jackson and Washington Streets, you will be offered a steaming cup of roselle tea, made of black tea and hibiscus. In addition to a selection of almost 50 traditional and herbal teas, the company stocks related paraphernalia, such as pots, cups, and infusers. If you can't make up your mind, take home a mail-order form. Open daily from 9:30am to 9pm.

GIFTS

Art Of China, 829-843 Grant Ave. ☎ **981-1602.**

Amid a wide variety of collectibles, this shop features exquisite hand-carved Chinese figurines. You'll also find a lovely assortment of ivory beads, bracelets, necklaces, and earrings. Pink-quartz dogs, jade figurines, porcelain vases, cachepots, and blue-and-white barrels suitable for use as table bases are just some of the many collectibles on offer. Open daily from 10am to 6pm.

Aud's, 1960 Union St. ☎ **931-7765.**

Located inside one of the street's most beautiful Victorians, the shop sells one-of-a-kind "fun things," including toys and wearable art. The jewelry is priced from $10 to $60; the shop's proceeds benefit Bay Area artists. Open daily from 10:30am to 6:30pm.

Babushka, 333 Jefferson. ☎ **673-6740.**

Located near Fisherman's Wharf, adjacent to the Anchorage Shopping Center, Babushka sells exclusively Russian products, most of which are wooden or papier-mâché nesting dolls. Open daily from 10am to 10pm.

Body Time, 2072 Union St. ☎ **922-4076.**

All the oils, lotions, soaps, and pamperings sold here are natural, biodegradable, and not tested on animals. Soaps come in over 30 scents, including China Lily, Rain, Pikaki, and Black Rose. And if you don't find the fragrance you want, the shop will create it to your specifications. Other items include aloe vera fresheners, clay masks, and cleansing grains. Body Time also has related application utensils, such as sponges and bath brushes. Open Monday through Saturday from 10am to 6:30pm and Sunday from 11am to 6pm.

Distractions, 552 Haight St. ☎ **252-8751.**

This is the best of the Haight Street shops selling pseudo-sixties psychedelia. Retro hippie clothes, pipes, toys, and stickers are liberally intermixed with tie-dyed Grateful Dead paraphernalia and lots of cool stuff to look at. Open Monday through Saturday from 11am to 6:45pm, and Sunday from 11am to 6pm.

The Dolls and Bears of Charlton Court, 1957 Union St. ☎ **775-3740.**

A pint-sized shop cluttered with bears and dolls in all sizes, Charlton Court is not a toy shop, but a collector's emporium, crammed with antique Raggedy Anns and teddys of all sizes. The store is located in a tiny alleyway off Union Street. Open Monday through Saturday from 10:30am to 3pm.

Exploratorium Store, in the Palace of Fine Arts, 3601 Lyon St. ☎ **561-0390.**

The best museum gift shop in the city is this fanciful store inside a terrific hands-on science museum (see "San Francisco Attractions," above). Gifts include Space Age Super Balls, high-bouncing rubber balls that never seem to slow down; chime earrings and magnets; and other gizmos and gadgets. Open Wednesday from 10am to 9pm and Tuesday and Thursday through Sunday from 10am to 5:30pm.

Forma, 1715 Haight St. ☎ **751-0545.**

Perhaps the most unusual store in San Francisco is this celebration of urban kitsch between Cole and Shrader Streets. In addition to colorful handmade dioramas, you'll find voodoo dolls, ant farms, sea monkeys, Rocky and Bullwinkle toys, Elvis toilet seats, and games like Lite-Brite and Twister. Open Monday through Saturday from noon to 7pm, and Sunday from noon to 6pm.

Oggetti, Inc., 1846 Union St. ☎ **346-0631.**

This fascinating Florentine shop specializes in objects decorated with marbleized paper. The decorative marbleizing technique was invented in the 17th century by Mace Ruette, the royal bookbinder to Louis XIII. Oggetti continues this elegant tradition, featuring covered frames, jewelry boxes, pencils, pencil boxes, and blank books, among other lovely objects. About 95% of their items are imported from Italy and are exclusive to the store. Open Monday through Saturday from 10am to 6pm, and Sunday from 11am to 6pm.

Planetweavers Treasures Store, 1573 Haight St. ☎ **864-4415.**

There truly are real "treasures" here; a huge selection of unusual arts and collectibles including drums, dolls, incense, cards, and clothing from around the world. Proceeds from the shop go directly to the United Nations UNICEF fund, which helps save children worldwide from disease and malnutrition. Open daily 11am to 7pm.

Revival of the Fittest, 1701 Haight St. ☎ **751-8857.**

On the corner of Cole Street, this window-wrapped shop sells retro and contemporary clocks, candleholders, picture frames, stemware, dinnerware, telephones, and collectibles. It also carries a good selection of silver and surgical steel jewelry, as well as art postcards. Open Monday through Saturday from 11am to 7pm and Sunday from noon to 6pm.

Smile, 500 Sutter St. ☎ **362-3436.**

The shop is a treasure trove of unique, contemporary sculpture and gifts, all made by craftspeople with a sense of humor. A must-see. Open Monday through Saturday from 9:30am to 5:30pm.

Union Street Music Box Co., 2201 Union St. ☎ **563-5181.**

Although these dust collectors aren't for everybody, memento collectors will love this shop full of wind-up and electric-run music boxes. If your experience with these novelties is limited to twirling ballerinas, come check out the miniature cable car that climbs a hill, then turns around and descends it. Open daily from 10am to 7pm.

HOUSEWARES

The Wok Shop, 718 Grant Ave. ☎ **989-3797.**

This shop, at Clay Street, has every conceivable implement for Chinese cooking, including woks, brushes, cleavers, circular chopping blocks, dishes, oyster knives, bamboo steamers, strainers—you name it. The shop also sells a wide range of kitchen utensils, baskets, hand-made linens from China, and aprons. Open Sunday through Friday from 10am to 6pm, Saturday from 10am to 10pm.

Z Gallerie, 2071 Union St. ☎ **346-9000.**

A California-based chain, selling a good selection of poster art, along with unusual gifts, and matte black furnishings and kitchenware. Other stores are located in the San Francisco Shopping Centre (see "Shopping Centers & Complexes," below) and at 1465 Haight St. (☎ **863-5331**). Open Monday through Thursday, and Sunday from 10am to 7pm, Friday and Saturday from 10am to 11pm.

IMPORTS

Cost Plus Imports, 2552 Taylor St. ☎ **928-6200.**

Between Bay Street and North Point, at the Fisherman's Wharf cable-car turntable, Cost Plus is a vast warehouse crammed to the rafters with Chinese baskets, Indian camel bells, Malaysian batik scarves, and innumerable other items from Algeria to Zanzibar. More than 20,000 well-priced items from 40 nations are purchased directly from their country of origin and packed into this warehouse. Open Monday through Saturday from 9am to 9pm and Sunday from 10am to 8pm.

JEWELRY

Cartier, Inc., 231 Post St. ☎ **397-3180.**

One of the most respected names in jewelry and luxury goods operates its San Francisco shop between Grant Avenue and Stockton Street. The boutique's setting is as elegant as the beautifully designed jewelry, watches, crystal, and accessories it sells. Open Monday through Saturday from 10am to 5:30pm.

Jerusalem Shoppe, 531 Castro St. ☎ **626-7906.**

Known for its fine collection of funky silver jewelry, this small shop in the middle of Castro Street also sells unusual amber pieces. Open Monday through Thursday from 10am to 8pm, Friday and Saturday from 10am to 8:30pm, and Sunday from 10am to 6pm.

Old & New Estates, 2181 A Union St. ☎ **346-7525.**

Top-of-the-line antiques including pendants, diamond rings, necklaces, bracelets, watches, and natural pearls make this San Francisco's best jewelry museum. Bring your checkbook. Open Monday through Saturday from 11:30am to 6pm, Sunday noon to 5pm.

Pearl Empire, 127 Geary St. ☎ **362-0606.**

Located between Stockton Street and Grant Avenue, the Pearl Empire has been importing jewelry directly from Asia since 1957. They are specialists in unusual pearls and jade, and offer restringing on the premises. Open Monday through Saturday from 9:30am to 5:30pm.

Union Street Goldsmith, 1909 Union St. ☎ **776-8048.**

A showcase for Bay Area goldsmiths, this exquisite shop sells custom-designed jewelry in all karats. Many pieces emphasize colored stones in their settings. Open Monday through Saturday from 11am to 5:45pm and Sunday from noon to 4:45pm.

LEATHER

Mark Cross, 170 Post St. ☎ **391-7770.**

For more than 100 years this store has been known for the quality and beauty of its fine crafting. All leather goods are hand constructed and classically styled of calfskin, pigskin, ostrich, and lizard. The store will emboss your purchase with gold initials, free of charge. Open Monday through Saturday from 10am to 6pm, Sunday from noon to 5pm.

North Beach Leather, 1365 Columbus Ave. ☎ **441-3208.**

Primarily selling leather jackets and dresses, this shop has up-to-the-minute fashions at high prices. Other leather items from casual to elegant are sold. A second shop is located at 190 Geary St. (☎ **362-8300**). Open Monday through Thursday from 10am to 7pm, Friday and Saturday from 10am to 8pm, and Sunday from noon to 6pm.

Overland Sheepskin Co., 21 Grant Ave. ☎ **296-9180.**

Inside this pretty wooden southwestern-style shop just off Market Street are beautiful sheepskin hats, jackets, booties, and bears. They stock some of the nicest sheep styles I've ever seen. Open daily from 8am to 8pm.

LINGERIE

Backseat Betty, 1584 Haight St. ☎ **431-8393.**

This is San Francisco's best intimate-apparel shop. Their eclectic collection of synthetic cotton and rubber goods makes Victoria's Secret seem tame. Sexy dresses, skirts, and assorted outerwear are also sold, beneath a shrine to Cher. Open daily from 11am to 7pm.

Carol Doda's Champagne & Lace Lingerie Boutique, 1850 Union St., ☎ **776-6900.**

Carol Doda, one of the country's most famous strippers, won fame at the Condor in North Beach, when she danced on the opening night of the 1964 Republican National Convention. Today she runs a shop at Union Street courtyard. Lingerie and bodywear for men and women include bras, bustieres, and teddies. Open daily from 11am to 7pm.

Under Cover, 535 Castro St. ☎ **864-0505.**

This Castro shop sells men's underwear, exercise wear, robes, Lycra shorts, and minitops. Dozens of Porn-star Polaroids line the wall behind the cash register. Open Monday through Friday from 11am to 8pm, Saturday from 10am to 8pm, and Sunday from 11am to 7pm.

MUSIC

Recycled Records, 1377 Haight St. ☎ **626-4075.**

Easily one of the best used-record stores in the city, this loud shop in the Haight has a good selection of promotional CDs, and cases of used "classic" rock LPs. Sheet music, tour programs, and old *TV Guides* are also sold. Open daily from 10am to 10pm.

Rough Trade Records, 1529 Haight St. ☎ **621-4395.**

Both mainstream and alternative new and used CDs, tapes, and vinyl are sold in this well-stocked, preowned-music shop. Some local bands and hard-to-find international titles are available. Open Monday through Saturday from 10am to 11pm and Sunday 10am to 8pm.

Streetlight Records, 3979 24th St. ☎ **282-3550.**

Overstuffed with used music in all three formats, this place is best known for its records and excellent CD collection. Rock music is cheap here, and a money-back guarantee guards against defects. Open Monday through Saturday from 10am to 10pm and Sunday from 11am to 8pm.

SHOES

Birkenstock Natural Footwear, 1815 Polk St. ☎ **776-5225.**

Located at Washington Street, this relaxed store is known for its California-style form-fitting sandals. Other orthopedically correct brands are also available, including Finn Comforts, ECCO, and Reikers. Open daily from 10:30am to 6pm.

Kenneth Cole, in the San Francisco Shopping Center, 865 Market St. ☎ **227-4536.**

High-fashion footwear for men, women, and children is sold at this trendy shop. In addition to shoes, there is an innovative collection of handbags and small leather goods and accessories. A second shop is located at 2078 Union St. (☎ **346-2161**). Open Monday through Saturday from 9:30am to 8pm and Sunday from 11am to 6pm.

Taming of the Shoe, 1736 Haight St. ☎ **221-4453.**

For both men and women, this contemporary shoe and boot shop is filled with the hippest names from America and Europe. It also sells many original styles under their own name, and vintage footwear from the '50s, '60s, and '70s. Open Monday through Saturday from 11am to 7pm, and Sunday from 11am to 5pm.

SHOPPING CENTERS & COMPLEXES

Like any city, San Francisco's malls are filled with carbon-copy chain stores, but they are also dotted with a good selection of local specialty shops and a taste of the avant garde.

The Anchorage, 2800 Leavenworth St., at Beach St. and Jefferson St., Fisherman's Wharf. ☎ **775-6000.**

The newest of the waterfront complexes, the Anchorage offers still more shopping and dining near Fisherman's Wharf. The mall is fronted by an impressive, two-story anchor sculpture and continues the nautical theme throughout its outdoor promenades and decks. Close to 50 units offer everything from music boxes to home furnishings. The **Incredible Christmas Store (928-5700)** sells holiday items year round. There is also a fair assortment of restaurants and specialty food shops. In the courtyard, musicians, mimes, jugglers, and other street performers entertain. Open summer, daily from 10am to 9pm; the rest of the year, daily from 10am to 6pm.

The Cannery, 2801 Leavenworth St., at Jefferson St. ☎ **771-3112.**

Once a Del Monte fruit-canning plant, this complex is now occupied by a score or two of shops, restaurants, and nightspots. Mercifully, there are few chain stores here. Top shops include the **Gourmet Market (673-0400)**, selling international foods, coffees, and teas; the **Print Store (771-3576)** offering a well-chosen selection of fine art prints and local original art; and the **Basic Brown Bear Factory (931-6670)**, where you can stuff your own teddy bear.

Cobb's Comedy Club (see "San Francisco Evening Entertainment" below) is also here, along with several restaurants that offer a variety of cuisines in all price ranges. Open daily 10am to 6pm, extended hours during summer and on holidays.

Crocker Galleria, 50 Post St. ☎ **393-1505.**

Modeled after Milan's Galleria Vitorio Emmanuelle, this glass-domed, three-level pavilion, about three blocks east of Union Square, features about 40 high-end shops. Fashions include Stephane Kelian designs, Nicole Miller, Gianni Versace, and Polo. Restaurants and gift and specialty shops round out the offerings. Open Monday through Friday from 9:30am to 6pm and Saturday from 10am to 5pm.

Ghirardelli Square, 900 North Point. ☎ **775-5500.**

This former chocolate factory is one of the city's largest malls and most popular landmarks. Many chain stores are located here, including the women's clothier **Ann Taylor, Benetton,** for Italian knitwear, **Crabtree & Evelyn** for English soaps and scents, the **Nature Company** for earth-related gifts, and the **Sharper Image** for unique, upscale electronics and designs.

The complex is open daily from 10am to 6pm. Main plaza shops are open Monday through Thursday from 10am to 6pm, Friday and Saturday from 10am to 9pm, and Sunday from 11am to 6pm (extended hours during summer).

San Francisco Shopping Centre, 865 Market St. ☎ **495-5656.**

Opened in 1988, this $140-million complex is one of the few vertical malls in the United States. Its most stunning features are the four-story spiral escalators that circle their way up to **Nordstrom,** the center's primary anchor and the largest unit in the Seattle-based fashion specialty chain (see "Department Stores," above). More than 90 specialty shops and restaurants include designer clothiers **Adrienne Vittadini, Ann Taylor, Bebe,** and **Mondi.** Lower-fashion outlets include **Benetton, Foot Locker, J. Crew,** and **Victoria's Secret.** The mall's nine-story atrium is covered by a retractable skylight. Open Monday through Saturday from 9:30am to 8pm and Sunday from 11am to 6pm; holiday hours may vary.

TOBACCO

Alfred Dunhill of London, 290 Post St. ☎ **761-3368.**

This tobacconist near Stockton Street has been specializing in custom-blended tobacco since the turn of the century. Accessories have been added more recently—Dunhill lighters are among the most elegantly designed and consistently functional. Today the mark also covers an exquisite line of men's clothing, including sweaters, jackets, and shirts. Leather goods and luggage are also of Dunhill quality. Open Monday through Saturday from 9:30am to 6pm and Sunday from noon to 5pm.

TOYS

The Chinatown Kite Shop, 717 Grant Ave. ☎ **989-5182.**

This shop's astonishing assortment of flying objects includes attractive fish kites, windsocks in nylon or cotton, hand-painted Chinese paper kites, wood-and-paper biplanes, and pentagonal kites—all of which make great souvenirs or decorations. Computer-designed stunt kites have two control lines to manipulate loops and dives. Open daily from 10am to 9pm.

F.A.O. Schwarz, 48 Stockton St. ☎ **394-8700.**

The world's greatest toy store for both children and adults is filled with every imaginable plaything, from hand-carved, custom-painted carousel rocking horses, dolls, and stuffed animals to gas-powered cars, train sets, and hobby supplies. At the entrance is a singing 22-foot clock tower with 1,000 different moving parts. If you're with kids and don't want to buy, tell them it's a museum. Open Monday through Wednesday and Friday and Saturday from 10am to 6:30pm; Thursday from 10am to 8pm; and on Sunday from 11am to 6pm.

TRAVEL GOODS

On the Road Again, Pier 39. ☎ **434-0106.**

In addition to lightweight luggage, this smart shop sells toiletry kits, travel bottles, travel-size items, and a good selection of other related goods. Open daily from 10am to 8:30pm.

Thomas Brothers Maps, 550 Jackson St. ☎ **981-7520,** or toll free **800/969-3072.**

The best map shop in the city, Thomas Brothers sells street, topographic, and hiking maps depicting San Francisco, California, and the world. A selection of travel-related books is also sold. Open Monday through Friday from 9:30am to 5:30pm.

WINES

The Napa Valley Winery Exchange, 415 Taylor St. ☎ **771-2887** or toll free **800/653-9463.**

Situated in the heart of downtown, between Geary Street and O'Farrell Street, this is a convenient place to shop for Californian wines and champagnes. The selection is excellent, encompassing varieties from every region in the state. Major wineries as well as smaller, limited-release vintners are represented (about 250 different brands in all). The staff is expert at packing wines for travel or shipping. They take phone orders and credit cards are accepted. Open Monday through Saturday from 10am to 7pm.

8 Evening Entertainment

As the west coast's cultural capital, San Francisco does not disappoint. The city's opera is justifiably world-renowned, the ballet is respected, and the theater is high in both quantity and quality. Dozens of piano bars and top-notch drinking rooms are augmented by one of the best dance-club cultures this side of New York. For a city with fewer than a million inhabitants, San Francisco's overall artistic enterprise is nothing short of phenomenal. In fact, the only U.S. city to better it is New York—which is more than 10 times its size.

For up-to-date nightlife information, turn to the *San Francisco Weekly* and the *San Francisco Bay Guardian,* both excellent guides to current activities around the city, with comprehensive listings. They are available free at bars and restaurants, and from street-corner boxes all around the city. *Key,* a free touristy monthly, also has information on programs and performance times; it's available in hotels and around the major tourist sights. The local daily newspapers also have good previews of upcoming events. The Sunday edition of the *San Francisco Examiner and Chronicle,* for example, features a "Datebook" section, printed on pink paper, with information and listings on the week's upcoming events.

American Conservatory Theatre (ACT) 9
Climate Theatre 16
Curran Theatre 19
Eureka Theatre 18
Golden Gate Theatre 14
Great American Music Hall (GAMH) 8
Herbst Theatre 10
Life on the Water 2
Lorraine Hansberry Theatre 7
Louis M. Davies Symphony Hall 12
Magic Theatre 1
Orpheum 13
San Francisco Ballet (War Memorial Opera House) 11
San Francisco Opera (War Memorial Opera House) 11
San Francisco Symphony (Davies Hall) 12
Theatre Artaud 17
Theatre on the Square 6
Theatre Rhinoceros 15
Tix Bay Area 4 5
War Memorial Opera House 11
Zephyr Theatre 3

N
0
.5 mi
.3 km
San Francisco
Bay
45
41
43
Pier 39
35
33
31
29
23
19
17
15
9
7
5
3
1
Jefferson St.
Beach St.
NORTHERN
WATERFRONT
North Point St.
Bay St.
NORTH BEACH
TELEGRAPH HILL
Embarcadero
Chestnut St.
Lombard St.
Columbus Ave.
Union St.
Green St.
Vallejo St.
Broadway
Pacific St.
Montgomery St.
Sansome St.
Battery St.
CHINATOWN
Larkin St.
Hyde St.
Leavenworth St.
Jones St.
Taylor St.
Mason St.
Powell St.
Stockton St.
Grant St.
Kearny St.
Front St.
Drumm St.
Ferry Building
(World Trade Center)
Justin
Herman
Plaza
NOB HILL
FINANCIAL
DISTRICT
Bush St.
Union
Square
San Francisco-
Oakland
Bay Bridge
Steuart St.
Main St.
Fremont St.
80
O'Farrell St.
Market St.
Moscone
Convention
Center
Eddy St.
Mission St.
1st St.
Harrison St.
SOUTH OF MARKET
(SoMa)
2nd St.
6th St.
Folsom St.
3rd St.
4th St.
Howard St.
9th St.
10th St.
Bryant St.
Brannan St.
Townsend St.
7th St.
King St.
8th St.
Berry St.
101
280
Bryant St.
Potrero St.
16th St.
4
7
9
6
5
8
14
13
16
17
18

The Performing Arts

Tix Bay Area (☎ **433-7827**), sells half-price tickets to theater, dance, and music performances on the day of the show only; tickets for Sunday and Monday events, if available, are sold on Saturday. They also sell advance, full-price tickets for most performance halls, sporting events, concerts, and clubs. A service charge, ranging from $1 to $3, is levied on each ticket. Only cash or traveler's checks are accepted for half-price tickets, Visa and MasterCard are accepted for full-price tickets. Tix is located on Stockton Street, on the east side of Union Square (opposite Maiden Lane). It's open Tuesday through Saturday from noon to 7:30pm.

Tickets to most theater and dance events can also be obtained through **City Box Office,** Sherman Clay & Co., 141 Kearny St. (☎ **392-4400**).

BASS Ticketmaster (☎ **510/762-2277**) sells computer-generated tickets to concerts, sporting events, plays, and special events. Downtown BASS Ticketmaster offices include Tix Bay Area (see above) and the Emporium Department Store, 835 Market St.

Special concerts and performances are staged in San Francisco all year long. **San Francisco Performances,** 500 Sutter St., Suite 710 (☎ **398-6449**), has been bringing acclaimed artists to the Bay Area for more than a dozen years. Shows run the gamut from classical to jazz and sometimes include ethnic and other styles of dance. Performances are staged all around town, including the city's Performing Arts Center, Davies Hall, and Herbst Theater, with occasional productions at the Cowell Theater at Fort Mason. The season lasts from October through May. Tickets cost $12 to $47 and are available through City Box Office (☎ **392-4400**). There is also a 6pm Thursday afterwork concert series at the EC Cabaret, 3 Embarcadero Center in the fall and winter; admission price is $6, paid at the door. For more information, call **398-6449.**

Other festivals and events are especially heavy during the summer, when workers are on vacation and the tourist season is in full swing. One of the best and longest-running summer programs is the free Stern Grove Midsummer Music Festival (☎ **398-6551**), held every Sunday at 2pm in Golden Gate Park. The first concert is traditionally offered by the San Francisco Symphony Orchestra; other performances include ballet, jazz, and theater. For more than 50 years the festival has run from mid-June through August. Stern Grove is located near 19th Avenue and Sloat Boulevard; arrive early for a good view, and bring a picnic.

The Major Concert/Performance Halls

Cow Palace, Geneva and Santos Sts., Daly City (☎ **469-6065**).

Louis M. Davies Symphony Hall, 201 Van Ness Ave., at Grove St. (☎ **431-5400**).

The Great American Music Hall (GAMH), 859 O'Farrell St. (☎ **885-0750**).

Herbst Theatre, 401 Van Ness Ave. (☎ **392-4400**).

Theatre Artaud, 450 Florida St. (☎ **621-7797**).

War Memorial Opera House, 301 Van Ness Ave. (☎ **864-3330**).

Zephyr Theatre, 25 Van Ness Ave. (☎ **861-6655**).

MAJOR PERFORMING ARTS COMPANIES

Opera & Classical Music

Philharmonia Baroque Orchestra, 57 Post St., Suite 705. ☎ **391-5252.**

Acclaimed by the *New York Times* as "the country's leading early-music orchestra," the Philharmonia Baroque performs in San Francisco and all around the Bay Area. The season lasts from September to April. In the city, they play at Herbst Theatre.

Prices: Tickets $20–$29.

San Francisco Opera, War Memorial Opera House, 301 Van Ness Ave. ☎ **864-3330.**

The San Francisco Opera was the United States' first municipal opera, and is one of the cultural bastions that has given this city such a good artistic reputation. Brilliantly balanced casts feature celebrated international stars along with promising newcomers for whom this is often the greatest break of their careers. Staging and direction are a wonderful blend of traditional effects and avant-garde innovations. All productions have English supertitles.

The opera season starts in September and lasts just 14 weeks. Performances are considered social as well as artistic events, so that tickets, unfortunately, are not cheap ($20 to $130, or $8 for standing room sold starting at 10:30am on the day of the performance) or easy to acquire. Tickets go on sale as early as August, and the best seats quickly sell out. Unless a performer like Luciano Pavarotti or Plácido Domingo is in town, less-coveted views are usually available until curtain time. Performances are held most evenings, except Monday, with matinees on Saturday and Sunday.

Prices: Tickets $15–$115.

San Francisco Symphony, Louise M. Davies Symphony Hall, 201 Van Ness Ave., at Grove St. ☎ **431-5400.**

Founded in 1911, the internationally respected San Francisco Symphony has long been an important part of this city's cultural life. Led by Music Director Herbert Blomstedt and Music Director Designate Michael Tilson Thomas, the symphony moved to the acoustically superior Davies Hall in 1980. Their long season runs from September to May and is always packed with internationally acclaimed guest artists. Summer symphony activities include a Composers festival, a summer pops series, and a presentation in concert with the Joffrey Ballet.

Prices: Tickets $8–$65.

Theater

American Conservatory Theatre [ACT], Stage Door Theatre, 440 Mason St. ☎ **749-2228.**

The American Conservatory Theatre (ACT) made its debut in 1967 and quickly established itself as the city's premier resident theater group. The troupe is so venerated that ACT has been compared to the superb British National Theatre, the Berliner Ensemble, and the Comédie Française. ACT offers solid, well-staged, and brilliantly acted theater, and performs both classical drama and new and experimental works. It won a Tony Award for excellence in repertory theater and actor training in 1979. Whatever's on, the repertoire is always exciting and upbeat. The ACT season runs from October through May. Performances are held at various venues around the city, including the Stage Door Theatre, Theater on the Square, and the Orpheum Theater. Specific locations and transit information can be obtained from the box office.

Prices: Tickets $12–$38.

Eureka Theatre Company, 2730 16th St. ☎ **243-9899.**

Eureka produces a number of outstanding, award-winning plays in its own 200-seat facility near Harrison Street, south of Market Street. Productions are both contemporary and classical, and usually deal with political or social issues. Eureka's season runs from September to June, and usually presents performances Wednesday through Sunday.

Prices: Tickets $13–$25; half price for students and seniors 10 minutes prior to the performance.

Lorraine Hansberry Theatre, 620 Sutter St. ☎ **474-8800.**

San Francisco's top African American troupe performs in a 300-seat theater off the lobby of the Sheehan Hotel, near Mason Street, Special adaptations from literature are performed along with contemporary dramas, reworked classics, and world premieres.

Prices: Call for dates, programs, and ticket prices.

Magic Theatre, Fort Mason, Bld. D, Marina Blvd. and Buchanan St. ☎ **441-8822.**

The city's fifth-largest non-profit performing arts institution is best known for its premieres of Sam Shepard and Michael McClure as well as frequent nudity. The Magic also has the reputation of being the most socially unconscious of the midsize Bay Area theaters. It was something of a welcome turnaround in 1993 when the theater staged the first play based on the Clarence Thomas–Anita Hill sexual harassment scandal.

The season usually runs from October to July; performances are offered Wednesday through Sunday.

Prices: Tickets cost $17 to $21, and $12 for students, children, and seniors.

Theatre Rhinoceros, 2926 16th St. ☎ **861-5079.**

At the time of its founding in 1977, this was America's first and foremost theater ensemble devoted solely to works addressing gay and lesbian issues. The company presents two dozen fully mounted productions of new and classical works each year. The theater is located one block east of the 16th St./Mission BART station.

Prices: Call for dates, programs, and ticket prices.

Dance

In addition to the local companies, top traveling troupes like the Joffrey Ballet and American Ballet Theatre make regular appearances. Primary modern dance spaces include the Theatre Artaud, 450 Florida St. (☎ **621-7797**); the Cowell Theater, Fort Mason Center (☎ **441-5706**); Dancer's Group/Footwork, 3221 22nd St., at Mission Street (☎ **824-5044**); and the New Performance Gallery, 3153 17th St. (☎ **863-9834**). Check the local papers for schedules or contact the theater box offices directly.

★ **The San Francisco Ballet,** 455 Franklin St. ☎ **861-5600,** or **703-9400.**

The San Francisco Ballet has won the highest possible praise from around the world, even from London critics, who are notoriously spoiled by their own superlative Royal Ballet company and accept only the Russians and the Danes as equals. This city's troupe, founded in 1933, is the oldest permanent ballet company in the United States, and is widely regarded as one of the best. Under the artistic direction of Helgi Tomasson, former choreographer and principal dancer with the New York City Ballet, the San Francisco Ballet performs classics and world premieres in equal parts.

The season usually lasts from January to May, with short gaps in between. Performances are staged at the War Memorial Opera House, Van Ness Avenue and Grove Street, almost nightly (except Mondays). *The Nutcracker,* performed in December of every year, is one annual tradition worth supporting.

Prices: Tickets $10–$75.

MAJOR CONCERT HALLS & ALL-PURPOSE AUDITORIUMS

Cow Palace, Geneva and Santos Sts., Daly City. ☎ **469-6065.**

Located about 10 miles south of downtown, this 14,500-seat multipurpose facility features a plethora of concerts, exhibits, conventions, trade shows, and sporting events. In addition to top-name musicians like Van Halen and Neil Diamond, the palace hosts Disney's World on Ice, the Grand National Rodeo, the San Francisco Sports and Boat Show, and the Ringling Bros. and Barnum & Bailey Circus. Tickets are usually available through BASS Ticketmaster (see above), as well as the Cow Palace box office. Prices vary, depending on the performance.

The Great American Music Hall (GAMH), 859 O'Farrell St., between Polk and Larkin Sts. ☎ **885-0750.**

From the exterior, this 1907 building looks as though it could house anything from a restaurant to an insurance company, and over the years it probably has. The charming interior sports carved plaster cupids on the ceiling, while huge marble pillars support gilded mezzanine boxes. The hall's eclectic and adventurous booking policy intersperses top names like Etta James, Wynton Marsalis, B. B. King, and Carmen McRae, with rising stars, a cappella groups, satirical comedy, rock 'n' roll, and swing dance bands. Light meals, snacks, and drinks are available.

Prices: Tickets $5–$30, depending on the performer.

Herbst Theatre, 401 Van Ness Ave. ☎ **392-4400.**

Opened in 1932 as the Veterans Auditorium and rechristened the Herbst after its 1978 renovation, it has become the city's top hall for local and visiting musicians and artists; the stage is lit almost every night of the year. The 928-seat auditorium was the site of the 1945 signing of the United Nations Charter. Its walls are hung with eight paintings commissioned for the 1915 Panama Pacific International Exposition, created by renowned muralist Frank Brangwyn.

Prices: Tickets $10–$50, depending on the performance.

Louise M. Davies Symphony Hall, 201 Van Ness Ave., at Grove St. ☎ **431-5400.**

This Civic Center hall, having undergone a recent renovation, is the premier concert space for the San Francisco Symphony; classical, pop, and jazz musicians; and top traveling orchestras. The auditorium features an 8,000-pipe Ruffatti organ.

Prices: Symphony tickets $8–$65; ticket prices for other shows depend on the performance.

Theatre Artaud, 450 Florida St. ☎ **621-7797.**

This 300-seat theater, located in the former American Can Company building, is an innovative showplace for dance, music, and drama performances.

Prices: Tickets $5–$25, depending on the performance.

War Memorial Opera House, 301 Van Ness Ave., at Grove St. ☎ **864-3330.**

This magnificent 3,252-seat, European-style opera house opened in 1932. It is a terrific example of Beaux Arts architecture. As the premier city stage for top opera and ballet, the auditorium offers good sightlines, and superior acoustics.

Prices: Ballet tickets, \$5–\$75; opera tickets, \$20–\$130; other shows vary, depending on the performance.

Zephyr Theatre, 25 Van Ness Ave. ☎ **441-6655.**

Three separate theaters are housed in this renovated Masonic Temple, a San Francisco landmark. A busy stage schedule is filled by everything from poetry readings to dance, theater, and music.

Prices: Ticket prices vary, depending on the performance.

THEATERS

Most of San Francisco's stages are clustered together, on the blocks just east of Union Square. This semi-official "theater district" is the closest thing San Francisco has to a Broadway or West End. The city's theater offerings—known for solid staging and acting—are easily the best in the west. The high quality of performances matches the unusual quantity of productions, a result of the large numbers of artists who have made the Bay Area their home.

Climate Theatre, 252 Ninth St. ☎ **626-9196.**

After eight successful years, Climate is still going strong, showcasing avant-garde and experimental works in a casual and intimate atmosphere. It's located at Howard Street.

Curran Theatre, 445 Geary St. ☎ **474-3800.**

Erected in the 1920s, the Curran was one of the last great theaters to be built in San Francisco. Although it once hosted operas, plays, and ballets, the Curran now specializes in big-name Broadway musicals and comedies, usually with major stars, like Judd Hirsch in *I'm Not Rappaport,* James Earl Jones in *Fences,* Lily Tomlin in *The Search for Signs of Intelligent Life in the Universe,* and *Les Misérables.*

Golden Gate Theatre, 1 Taylor St. ☎ **474-3800.**

Lavishly appointed, the theater was built in 1922 and has hosted many famous acts from the Marx Brothers to Carmen Miranda. The original building was so plush that it included a lounge and library solely for orchestra members. Reopened in 1979 after a massive restoration that revealed its original grandeur, the theater once again features marble floors, gilt trimmings, French carpeting, and rococo ceilings. The immense size of the house forces its owners to book popular Broadway-style musicals almost exclusively. Legendary productions in years past have included *The Music Man,* starring Dick Van Dyke; *My Fair Lady,* with Rex Harrison; and *Camelot,* featuring Richard Burton. It's located at Market Street and Golden Gate Avenue.

★ **Life on the Water,** Building B, Fort Mason. ☎ **776-8999.**

Easily the most innovative stage in the city for avant-garde performances of all kinds, Life on the Water is a must-see for anyone interested in alternative theater and performance art.

Marine's Memorial Theatre, 609 Sutter St. ☎ **771-6900.**

Located in the Marines Memorial Association building at Sutter and Mason Streets, this stage features shows running the gamut from one-act, performance-art pieces to full-blown Broadway musicals.

The Orpheum, 1192 Market St. ☎ **474-3800.**

This handsomely refurbished vaudeville palace is architecturally patterned after a cathedral in Spain. Located at Eighth Street, the theater primarily features Broadway revivals starring top names. Productions have included *Man of La Mancha* and *Secret Garden.* Concerts with stars like Shirley MacLaine and Linda Ronstadt are also featured.

Theatre on the Square, 450 Post St. ☎ **433-6461.** Box office **433-9500.**

Comedies, musicals, and dramas are all staged in this 750-seat, Gothic-Mediterranean-style, second-floor theater. Prepackaged productions are booked here almost exclusively, and most take full advantage of the flexible seating and close contact with the audience. It's located near Union Square, inside the Kensington Park Hotel, between Powell and Mason Streets.

The Club & Music Scene

Always a pioneer in arts and entertainment, San Francisco is well known for its liberal policies and alternative culture. The city is credited with popularizing topless entertainment in the early 1960s and made headlines in the 1970s for its particularly promiscuous gay nightlife. Today, most of the city's strip clubs are rather seedy places, and the AIDS crisis has curtailed the gay party scene. Like other major American metropolitan areas, San Francisco offers a good variety of dance clubs and live-music venues. The hippest dance places are located South of Market Street (SoMa) in former warehouses. The city's most popular music and cafe culture is still centered around North Beach; a walk along Columbus Avenue any night of the week will be rewarded with a number of exciting finds. Check the local papers for the latest.

CABARET & COMEDY

Bay Area Theatresports, 450 Geary Blvd. ☎ **824-8220.**

Combining comedic improvisation with competitive spirit, Bay Area Theatresports (BATS) is comprised of several four-player teams who take on challenges formed with audience suggestions. Judges then flash score cards good-naturedly, or honk a horn—Gong Show style—for scenes that just aren't working. Shows are staged on Mondays only. Phone for reservations.

Admission: $10.

Beach Blanket Babylon, at Club Fugazi, 678 Green St. ☎ **421-4222.**

Now a San Francisco tradition, Beach Blanket Babylon evolved from Steve Silver's Rent-a-Freak service—a group of party-givers extraordinaire who hired themselves out as a "cast of characters" to entertain, complete with fabulous costumes and sets, props, and gags. After their act caught on, it was moved into the Savoy-Tivoli, a North Beach bar. By 1974 the audience grew too large for the facility and Beach Blanket has been at the 400-seat Club Fugazi ever since.

Tiny tables now face the medium-size stage, where a delightful, funny, and original production is staged nightly. Beach Blanket is a comedic musical send-up that is best known for its outrageous costumes and oversize head dresses. It's been almost 20 years now and almost every performance still sells out. The show is updated with enough regularity that it still draws a fair number of locals along with the hordes of tourists. Persons under 21 are welcome at Sunday matinees at 3pm when no alcohol is served; photo ID is required for evening performances. It's wise to write for tickets at least three weeks in advance or obtain them through Tix Bay Area (see "The Performing Arts" section, above). **Note:** When you purchase tickets they will be in a specific section depending upon price; seating, however, is still first-come/first-seated in that section. Performances are given on Wednesday and Thursday at 8pm, Friday and Saturday at 7 and 10pm, and Sunday at 3 and 7pm.

Admission: $17–$40.

Cobb's Comedy Club, 2801 Leavenworth St. ☎ **928-4320.**

Located in the Cannery at Fisherman's Wharf, Cobb's attracts an upscale audience with national headliners such as George Wallace, Emo Philips, and Jake Johannsen. There is comedy every night, including a 13-comedian, all-pro Monday showcase (a three-hour marathon). Cobb's is open to those 18 and over, as well as kids ages 16 and 17 if they are accompanied by a parent or legal guardian. Shows are on Tuesday through Thursday and Sunday at 9pm; Friday and Saturday at 9 and 11pm.

Admission: Tues–Sun $8–$15, plus a two-drink minimum nightly.

★ **Finocchio's,** 506 Broadway, ☎ **982-9388.**

For more than 50 years this family-run cabaret club, on Broadway at Kearny Street, has showcased the best female impersonators. This funny, kitschy establishment sets the standard to which all others should strive. There are three different lavish reviews nightly (usually staged Thursday through Saturday at 8:30, 10, and 11:30pm), and a single admission charge is good for the entire evening. Parking is available next door at the Flying Dutchman.

Admission: $12, no drink minimum.

Holy City Zoo, 408 Clement St. ☎ **386-4242.**

Holy City Zoo, on Clement Street between Fifth and Sixth Avenues, is San Francisco's longest-running comedy club. This intimate space is home to many comics, and has helped launch numerous stars, most notably Robin Williams, who used to tend bar here when he wasn't performing. Sunday and Monday are "open-mike" nights, which means that anybody—amateur or pro—can drop in and do a routine. Tuesday nights are the All-Pro Comedy Showcases. Wednesday night is Improvisation, featuring local improv artists. Thursday through Saturday nights headline the best local and national comedic talents. Shows are Sunday through Thursday at 8:30pm and on Friday and Saturday at 8:30 and 10:30pm.

Admission: $5–$10 (depending on the performers), plus a two-drink minimum.

Punch Line, 444 Battery St., plaza level. ☎ **397-4337,** or **397-7573** for recorded information.

This spot between Washington and Clay Streets, adjacent to the Embarcadero One office building, is the largest comedy nightclub in the city. The Punch Line has been San Francisco's premier comedy club since 1978, showcasing top talent plus up-and-coming comedians. Three-person shows with top national and local talent are featured Tuesday through Saturday. Showcase night is on Sunday with 15 to 20 rising stars. There's an all-star showcase or a special event on Monday nights. It's advisable to buy tickets in advance if you don't want to wait in line; advance tickets are available through BASS Ticketmaster outlets (☎ **510/762-2277**). Shows are Sunday through Thursday at 9pm; Friday at 9 and 11pm; and Saturday at 7, 9, and 11pm.

Admission: Sun $5, Mon–Thurs $7–$10, Fri–Sat $12, plus a two-drink minimum.

ROCK & BLUES CLUBS

In addition to the following listings, see "Dance Clubs," below, for live, (usually) danceable rock.

The Fillmore, 1805 Geary St. (at Fillmore). ☎ **346-6000.**

Reopened after years of neglect, The Fillmore, made famous by promoter Bill Graham in the 1960s, is once again attracting big names. Check the local listings magazines, or call the theater for information on upcoming events.

Grant and Green, 1371 Grant Ave. ☎ **956-9605.**

The atmosphere at this North Beach dive rockery is not that special, but the local bands are pretty good. Look for daytime shows on the weekends, and call to see what's on. Open daily from 1pm to 2am.

Admission: Fri–Sat $3.

★ **I-BEAM,** 1748 Haight St. ☎ **668-6023,** or **668-6006** for recorded information.

Except for the line out front, you'd hardly know that above Haight Street's hippest storefronts is one of the largest and loudest clubs in the city. Struggling local and national bands perform almost nightly, while a DJ spins dance discs between sets. There's a lot of new metal here, along with a healthy dose of post-punk and traditional rock. Sunday is gay tea dance night—one of the longest running in the city. Thursday is Club 1970, where bell-bottoms and platform shoes are still in fashion. Open Monday through Saturday from 8pm to 2am and Sunday from 5pm to 2am.

Admission: Mon–Sat free–$20, depending on the night and performer; Sun $5–$7.

Lost & Found Saloon, 1353 Grant Ave. ☎ **397-3751.**

Beer is the main drink at this North Beach blues bar. Leave your tie at home. Open daily from 6pm to 2am.

Admission: Free.

★ **The Saloon,** 1232 Grant Ave. ☎ **989-7686.**

An authentic Gold Rush survivor, this North Beach dive is the oldest extant bar in the city—and smells like it. Popular with both bikers and daytime pin-stripers, there's live blues several nights a week. Drinks run $3 to $5. It's open daily from noon to 2am, and a $3 to $5 admission is charged Friday and Saturday.

Admission: Free.

Slim's, 333 11th St. ☎ **621-3330.**

New Orleans–style Slims is co-owned by musician Boz Scaggs, who sometimes takes the stage under the name "Presidio Slim." Located south of Market Street (SoMa), at Folsom Street, this shiny, slightly overpriced restaurant/bar seats 300, serves Californian cuisine, and specializes in excellent American music—home-grown rock, jazz, and blues—almost nightly. Open Tuesday through Sunday from 8pm to 2am.

Admission: $10–$20, plus a two-drink minimum.

JAZZ & LATIN CLUBS

Bahia Tropical, 1600 Market St. ☎ **861-8657.**

Now four years old, this tropical Brazilian club opened with the lambada craze. But it's not cheesy; this is the real McCoy. Excellent bands are featured nightly, and samba dancers often perform. The music starts at 9pm, and there's a dance floor show every weekend at 11:30pm. Open daily from 8am to 2am.

Admission: $5–$10.

Cesar's Latin Palace, 3140 Mission St. ☎ **648-6611.**

Live Latin bands perform to a very mixed crowd—ethnically, economically, and generationally. There's plenty of dancing and drinking in this ultra-fun club. Open Wednesday through Sunday from 9pm to 2am.

Admission: $4–$8.

Jazz at Pearl's, 256 Columbus Ave. ☎ **291-8255.**

Behind large windows directly on North Beach's busy Columbus Avenue, Pearl's is a large and rather elegant restaurant specializing in ribs, chicken, and jazz. The live jams last until 2am nightly. Open daily from 5pm to 2am.

Admission: Free, but there's a two-drink minimum.

Kimball's, 300 Grove St. ☎ **861-5585,** or **861-5555.**

In addition to being a popular pretheater restaurant, Kimball's has become one of the city's top jazz clubs. It's located right across the street from Davies Symphony Hall and the Opera House, at Franklin Street, inside a particularly handsome old brick building. The cavernous interior encompasses two levels, and attracts top names like Ahmad Jamal, along with superior local talent. Food is served daily from 5pm to midnight or so, but live music is only offered Wednesday through Sunday. Call for prices and information before setting out. Open Wednesday through Sunday from 5pm to 1am.

Admission: $12–$15, depending on the performer.

The Mason Street Wine Bar, 342 Mason St. ☎ **391-3454.**

Formerly a bank, this funky, intimate drinkery, bedecked with contemporary, oversized paintings, attracts a mixed crowd of office workers, locals, and tourists with nightly live jazz. Small cabaret tables with black club chairs face a small stage, while the old bank safe is used as a private room and a wine storage area. Over 150 different wines are served from the half-moon-shaped bar. Open nightly from 4pm to 2am.

Admission: Free, except during occasional special performances.

The New Orleans Room, in the Fairmont Hotel, 950 Mason St., at California St. ☎ **772-5259.**

Solo jazz pianists perform Monday and Tuesday. Local jazz vocalists perform Wednesday. International jazz stars from be-bop to fusion play Thursday through Saturday. Cover charge varies with artists. Open nightly from 3pm to 2am. Drinks run $3 to $5.

Admission: Call for details.

Rasselas, 2801 California St. ☎ **567-5010.**

One of my favorite jazz rooms is this prominently windowed corner near Fillmore Street. An amply sized, casual jazzery, Rasselas is packed with small tables and comfortable couches, and is backed by a Victorian bar. Hot local jazz and R&B combos play nightly from 9pm to 1am. The adjacent restaurant serves Ethiopian cuisine under an elegant Bedouin tent. Open Sunday through Thursday from 5pm to midnight, Friday and Saturday from 5pm to 2am.

Admission: Free–$5.

DANCE CLUBS

The up-and-coming area South of Market Street (SoMa) is the center of San Francisco's nightlife scene. A virtual ghost town during the day, SoMa awakes only once the sun sets.

The very nature of the club scene demands frequent fresh faces, outdating recommendations before ink can dry on a page. Most of the venues below are promoted as different clubs on various nights of the week, each with its own look, sound, and style. The weekly listings magazines *San Francisco Bay Guardian* and *San Francisco Weekly* contain the latest. Discount passes and club announcements are often available at trendy clothing stores; shop along upper Haight Street.

Three Babes and a Bus (☎ **552-2582**) runs regular nightclub trips on Friday and Saturday nights to the city's busiest clubs. See "Organized Tours," in Section 5, "Attractions," above, for complete information.

City Nights, 715 Harrison St. ☎ **546-7938.**

This popular club at Third Street sprawls over three levels and has one of the largest dance floors in the city. The weekend has been divided into two distinctly different programs, each with its own name, personality, and crowd. Wednesday and Friday is **The X** (**561-1432**), a modern music party with caged dancers, and a multimedia show that rivals any in San Francisco. Saturday is **City Nights** (**561-9782**), playing contemporary, Top 40, house, and hip hop music. Call for information on occasional live performances. Drinks run $3.50 to $4. Open Friday and Saturday from 9:30pm to 3am.

Admission: $10.

Club DV8, 540 Howard St. ☎ **777-1419,** or **957-1730** for recorded information.

King of the SoMa club scene, DV8 has been attracting the black-clothes-and-pointy-shoes crowd longer than almost any other establishment. There are two DJs spinning music on separate dance floors, each perpetually packed with a lively 20-something crowd. The decor is an interesting mix of trompe l'oeil, pop art, candelabras, mirrors, and some extraordinary Dalíesque props. Several quieter VIP lounges provide necessary relief from the pounding. Open Thursday through Sunday from 9pm to 4am.

Admission: Thurs $5, Fri $10, Sat $10, Sun $5; usually free before 10pm.

Oasis, 278 11th St. ☎ **621-8119.**

Club O, on 11th at Folsom Street, is one of the trendiest danceterias in the city. Live bands alternate with in-crowd theme nights. In addition to the usual light show and videos, there's a Plexiglas dance floor on top of a swimming pool; it's sometimes uncovered for parties. Open Tuesday through Sunday from 9pm to 2am.

Admission: Free–$10 (call for details).

Oz, in the St. Francis Hotel, 32nd floor, Powell St. ☎ **774-0116.**

Euro-chic DJs mix contemporary American dance music with the latest European sounds. Reached via glass elevator, Oz has a marble dance floor and good lighting, including mirrored columns with Tivoli lights that bounce to the beat. The interior attempts to mimic a forest glade, complete with birch trees, ferns, and rockery. Look out the windows for superb views of the glittering city. Open Sunday through Thursday from 9pm to 1:30am and Friday and Saturday from 9pm to 2:30am.

Admission: Sun–Thurs $8, Fri–Sat $15, Sun $5.

Paradise Lounge, 1501 Folsom St. ☎ **861-6906.**

Labyrinthine Paradise features three dance floors simultaneously vibrating to different beats. Smaller auxiliary spaces include a pool room with half a dozen tables. Open daily from 3pm to 2am.

Admission: $5–$15.

 **Ten 15 Folsom,** 1015 Folsom St., at Sixth St. ☎ **431-0700.**

Three levels, and three dance floors, have long made this a stylish stop on the nightclub circuit. Weekends are best, when the club is a carnival of beautiful people. Currently, Friday is **Club Martini (431-1200)**, one of the city's hottest tickets, and Saturday is **gay night (431-BOYS)**. Open on Thursday from 10pm to 3am, Friday from 10pm to 4am, Saturday from 10pm to 6am, and Sunday from 5pm to 2:30am, plus various other special days. Call the club for information.

Admission: $5–$15.

The Bar Scene

There are so many bars in San Francisco it would be impossible to catalog them all. Below is a good cross section of the best that the city has to offer.

Albion, 3139 16th St. ☎ **552-8558.**

This Mission District club is a gritty, leather, in-crowd place packed with artistic slummers and various SoMa hipsters. Open daily from 2pm to 2am.

Caribbean Zone, 55 Natoma St. ☎ **541-9465.**

Not just another restaurant bar, Caribbean Zone is a visual Disneyland, jam-packed with a cluttered tropical decor that includes a full-size airplane fuselage. They don't have this in Iowa. Open Monday through Thursday from 11:30am to 10pm, Friday 11:30am to 11pm, Saturday 5 to 11pm, Sunday 5 to 11pm.

Edinburgh Castle, 950 Geary St. ☎ **885-4074.**

Opened in 1958, this legendary Scottish pub is still known for unusual British ales on tap and the best selection of single-malt scotches in the city. The huge pub, located near Polk Street, is decorated with Royal Air Force mementos, horse brasses, steel helmets, and an authentic Ballentine caber, used in the annual Scottish games. On Saturday nights, live bagpipers supplement the jukebox. Fish and chips, and other traditional foods are always available. Drinks cost $3 to $5. Open Monday through Thursday from 5pm to midnight, Friday from 5pm to 2am, Saturday from 2pm to 2am, and Sunday from noon to midnight.

Harry Denton's, 161 Stuart St. ☎ **882-1333.**

The dismantling of the Embarcadero Freeway after the 1989 earthquake has had the effect of revitalizing the Rincon Center neighborhood below. Harry Denton's, just a short walk away, in the shadow of the Ferry Building, is a popular restaurant, but even better known as a great bar with lots of energy. Especially happening with an after-work crowd, the bar bustles until late. Harry Denton's is always a safe bet for a drink. The food, unfortunately, is not as memorable. Open Monday through Friday from 7am to 1:30am, Friday and Saturday from 8am until 1:30am.

IMPRESSIONS

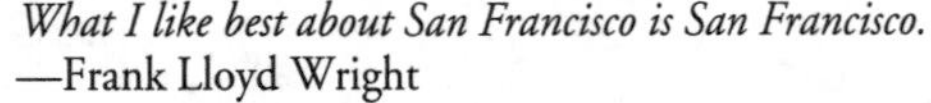

What I like best about San Francisco is San Francisco.

—Frank Lloyd Wright

Johnny Love's, 1500 Broadway. ☎ **931-6053.**

Attracting the same youngish power crowd as Harry Denton's (see above), Johnny Love's is a happy place, perpetually packed with corporate assistant-types and first-tier managers who go directly here from work to buy rounds for their friends. There's a small dance floor and live music several nights a week; when it's jumping, this joint is a real scene. Love's serves decent food too, but your money is best spent here on drinks. Open nightly from 5pm to 1:30am.

Li Po Cocktail Lounge, 916 Grant Ave. ☎ **982-0072.**

A divey Chinese bar, Li Po is made special by a clutter of dusty Asian furnishings and mementos that include an unbelievably huge ricepaper lantern hanging from the ceiling, and a glittery golden shrine to Buddha behind the bar. It would be the perfect place to hold a private party, if it weren't for the video game machines and the bad sound system. Open daily from 2pm to 2am.

Perry's, 1944 Union St. ☎ **922-9022.**

San Francisco's young, thirty-something crowd has long patronized this attractive bar. Decorated with tiled floors, brass rails, a pressed-tin ceiling, and dark mahogany paneling, Perry's is pickuppy and attracts a successful urban clientele, most of whom are dressed as though they're ready to work. A separate, secluded dining room features breakfast, lunch, dinner, and brunch at candlelit tables. It's a good place for hamburgers, easy fish dishes, and pasta. Drinks run $3 to $5. Open daily from 9am to midnight.

★ **Persian Aub Zam Zam,** 1633 Haight St. ☎ **861-2545.**

Step through the forbidding metal doors and you'll feel as if you're in Casablanca. And although it's full of character, regulars come here for the acerbic owner/bartender, Bruno, who kicks almost everyone else out. Order a Finlandia vodka martini and you'll be allowed to stay. Sit at the bar; the tables are "closed." Usually open Monday through Friday from 4pm to midnight, and at the owner's whim.

The Savoy-Tivoli, 1434 Grant Ave. ☎ **362-7023.**

With your back to Chinatown, walk two blocks up Grant from Columbus Avenue to one of the area's most atmospheric neighborhood bars. The large room offers unobstructed sightlines, making it easy to see and be seen. Popular with a wanna-be-artist, cigarette-smoking, Campari-and-soda crowd. Open Tuesday through Sunday from 3:15pm to 2am.

BREWPUBS

Gordon-Biersch Brewery, in the Embarcadero, 2 Harrison St. ☎ **243-8726.**

Gordon-Biersch Brewery is San Francisco's largest brew-restaurant, serving decent food and tasty homemade "barley-pop." There are always several brews to choose from, ranging from light to dark. Most of the brewery's well-dressed clientele look like they are marketers from The Gap, whose headquarters are located across street. Open Sunday through Wednesday 11am to 11pm, Thursday 11am to midnight, Friday and Saturday 11am to 1am.

San Francisco Brewing Company, 155 Columbus Ave. ☎ **434-3344.**

Surprisingly low-key for an ale house, this cozy brewpub serves its barley pop along with burgers, fries, and the like. It's located on North Beach's Columbus Avenue, at

Pacific Avenue. Open Sunday noon to 11:30pm, Monday through Thursday from noon to 12:30am, Friday and Saturday from noon to 1:30am.

★ **20 Tank Brewery,** 316 11th St. ☎ **255-9455.**

Right in the heart of SoMa's most "happening" strip, 11th Street at Folsom Street, this huge, upscale bar is known for enormous windows that look out onto the street, as well as a decent ale. Open daily from 11:30am to 2am.

CAFES/BARS

San Francisco in general, and North Beach in particular, is loaded with Italian-style cafes, many of which also have full bars. These character-laden places encourage patrons to linger and are one of the city's greatest assets.

★ **Cafe Picaro,** 3120 16th St. ☎ **431-4089.**

None of the tables match at this huge, informal literary cafe in the Mission. Picaro is part used-book store, part bohemian hangout, and part restaurant. Few cognoscenti, however, eat here. Wine and beer are served along with the cappuccinos. It's located on 16th Street at Valencia Street. Open Sunday through Thursday from 9am to 10pm, and Friday and Saturday from 9am to midnight.

Caffè Greco, 423 Columbus Ave. ☎ **397-6261.**

Relatively recent for North Beach, Caffè Greco opened about seven years ago and has quickly become one of the best places to linger. Sophisticated and relaxed, they serve beer, wine, a good selection of coffee drinks, and delicious desserts. Open Monday through Thursday from 7am to 11pm and Friday through Sunday from 7am to midnight.

Caffè Trieste, 601 Vallejo St. ☎ **392-6739.**

Opera is always on the jukebox at this classic beatnik North Beach coffeehouse. Its somehow provincial European feel is augmented by live arias sung to the lucky few who get to squeeze in on Saturday afternoons. Open Sunday through Thursday from 6:30am to 11:30pm and Friday and Saturday from 6:30am to 12:30am.

★ **Specs' Adler Museum Cafe,** 12 Saroyan Place. ☎ **421-4112.**

Specs' is located on Saroyan Place, a tiny alley at 250 Columbus Avenue that's named for William Saroyan, a local author and playwright who penned *The Time of Your Life,* which described a 1930s dive somewhat like this bar. Specs' is one of the liveliest—and most likable—pubs in North Beach. Inside this small wooden bar, near the intersection of Columbus Avenue and Broadway, you'll find one of the city's friendliest crowds. Maritime flags hang from the ceiling, while the exposed-brick walls are lined with posters, photos, and various oddities. The "museum," protected beneath a few glass cases, contains memorabilia and items brought back by seamen who drop in between sailings. Beer and wine cost $2.50 to $3.50; mixed drinks, $3 to $5. Open Sunday through Thursday from 4:30pm to 2am and Friday and Saturday from 5pm to 2am.

Vesuvio, 255 Columbus Ave. ☎ **362-3370.**

Situated across Jack Kerouac Alley from the famed City Lights Bookstore, this established cafe/bar at Broadway is one of North Beach's best beatnik-style hangouts. Popular with neighborhood writers, artists, songsters, and wanna-be's, Vesuvio also gets its share of longshoremen, cab drivers, and business types. Did I mention tourists? The walls are hung with a changing exhibition of locally produced art, complemented by an ongoing slide show. In addition to well-priced drinks, Vesuvio features an espresso machine, along with a staff that knows how to use it. No credit cards are accepted. Open daily from 6am to 2am.

COCKTAILS WITH A VIEW

The Carnelian Room, in the Bank of America Building, 555 California St. ☎ **433-7500.**

Located between Kearny and Montgomery Streets, on the 52nd floor of one of the city's tallest and most revered buildings, the Carnelian Room offers dramatic and spectacular uninterrupted views of the entire city. From a window-front table it feels possible to reach out, pluck up the Transamerica Pyramid, and stir your martini with it. In addition to cocktails, sunset dinners are served nightly, for about $32 per person. Jackets and ties are required for men. Drinks are $5 to $7. Open nightly from 5pm to midnight.

Cityscape, atop Hilton Tower I, 46th floor. ☎ **776-0215.**

Topped by a glass roof, Cityscape gives the illusion of drinking under the stars, with superlative views of the bay. There's dancing to a live orchestra Tuesday through Saturday from 8pm. The rich gold-and-blue carpeting, mirrored columns, and floor-to-ceiling draperies are both elegant and romantic. Drinks run $4 to $6. Open nightly from 6pm to 2am.

Sherlock Holmes, Esq. Lounge, in the Union Square Holiday Inn, 30th floor. ☎ **398-8900.**

A theme bar, this 30th-floor lounge pays homage to the world's greatest fictional detective. Collections of related "memorabilia" are hung throughout this replica of Holmes's study at 221B Baker Street, complete with recorded London street sounds. Hats and pipes aside, attractions include plush velvet chairs, two wood-burning fireplaces, a terrific 360-degree view, and live piano music Tuesday through Saturday. Drinks run $5 to $6. Open nightly from 4pm to 1:30am.

★ **Top of the Mark,** in the Mark Hopkins Hotel, atop Nob Hill, California and Mason Sts. ☎ **392-3434.**

One of the most famous cocktail lounges in the world, the Top of the Mark offers traditional drinks in a nostalgia-laden atmosphere. During World War II it was considered de rigueur for Pacific-bound servicemen to toast their good-bye to the States here. The spectacular glass-walled room features an unparalleled view; nobody will mind if you wander around with your drink, sampling each direction. Sunday brunch is served from 10am to 2pm and costs about $28. Drinks cost $6 to $8. Open daily from 4pm to 1:30am.

PIANO BARS

San Francisco is lucky to have several terrific piano bars. As in other cities, these specialized lounges are perfectly suited to the posh hotels in which they are usually located.

The Lower Bar, in the Mark Hopkins Hotel, 1 Nob Hill. ☎ **392-3434.**

Drinks are served nightly in a delightfully intimate, skylighted room with hand-painted murals. The bar is located just off the hotel lobby. Drinks run $5 to $8. Open Sunday through Thursday from 2 to 10pm, Friday and Saturday from 1pm to midnight.

The Redwood Room, in the Four Seasons Clift Hotel, 495 Geary St. ☎ **775-4700.**

A true art-deco beauty, this ground-floor lounge is one of San Francisco's poshest piano bars. Its gorgeous redwood interior was built completely from a single 2,000-year-old tree. The piano player, Ricardo Scales, is easily one of the best in the city, while the staff is terrifically trained and particularly attentive. The Redwood Room is intimate, luxurious, and fun. Drinks go for $6 to $7. Open Sunday through Thursday from 11am to midnight, Friday and Saturday from 11am to 2am.

GAY BARS & CLUBS

As with straight establishments, gay bars and clubs each attract a different clientele, from the leather crowd to three-piece-suit types. Because most of the area's lesbians live in Oakland, across the bay, clubs here are primarily male oriented. The Castro, South of Market (SoMa), and Mission sections of town have especially good bar selections. Check the appropriate sections of the free weeklies, the *San Francisco Bay Guardian* and *San Francisco Weekly,* for listings of events and happenings. The dedicated gay papers *San Francisco Sentinel* and *Bay Area Reporter* have the most comprehensive listings, including a weekly calendar of events, social gatherings, art classes, sports events, meetings, and the like. All the above papers are free and are distributed weekly on Thursday. They can be found stacked at the corner of 18th and Castro Streets, and Ninth and Harrison Streets, as well as in bars, bookshops, and stores around town.

Listed below are some of the city's more established, mainstream gay hangouts.

Kennel Club, 628 Divisadero St. ☎ **931-1914.**

This warehouse bar features both DJ dancing and live bands in equal parts. On Thursday and Saturday nights it's called **The Box,** which is currently one of the best gay men and lesbian clubs around. Call for further details.

Admission: $5–$15.

Rawhide II, 280 Seventh St. ☎ **621-1197.**

Gay or straight, this is one of the city's top country-and-western dance bars. Whether or not you brought your chaps, this is a jeans joint, patronized by both sexes. Free dance lessons are offered Monday through Thursday from 7:30 to 9:30pm. Rawhide II is located by Folsom Street. Drinks cost $2.50 to $5. Open daily from noon to 2am.

Admission: Free.

The Stud, 399 Ninth St. ☎ **863-6623.**

Despite its aggressive name, the Stud, on Ninth at Harrison Street, is a pretty mellow hangout. This classic SoMa place has been around forever, and is so tame that straights will feel comfortable here, too. The interior has an antique-shop look and a miniature train circling over the bar and dance floor. The music is a balanced mix of old and new. Open nightly from 5pm to 2am.

Admission: Sun–Thurs free, Fri–Sat $3.

Twin Peaks Tavern, 401 Castro St. ☎ **864-9470.**

Right at the intersection of Castro, 17th, and Market Streets is one of the Castro's most famous hangouts. This is a drinking bar catering to a thirty-something crowd. Because of its relatively small size and great location, the place gets pretty full by 8pm or so. Drinks run $2 to $5. Open daily from noon to 2am.

Admission: Free.

More Entertainment

FILMS

The **San Francisco International Film Festival,** held in March of each year, is one of America's oldest film festivals. Tickets are relatively inexpensive, and screenings are very accessible to the general public. Entries include new films by beginning and established directors. For a schedule or information, call **415/931-FILM.** Tickets can be charged by phone through BASS Ticketmaster (☎ **510/762-2277**).

Even if you're not here in time for the festival, don't despair. The classic, independent, and mainstream cinemas in San Francisco are every bit as good as the city's other cultural offerings.

Revival Houses

Castro, 429 Castro St. ☎ **621-6120.**

One of the largest and prettiest theaters in the city, the Castro is known for its screenings of classics and for its bold Wurlitzer organ, played before each show. There's a different feature here almost nightly, and more often than not it's a double feature. Bargain matinees are usually offered on Wednesday, Saturday, Sunday, and holidays. Phone for schedules, prices, and show times.

Red Vic, 1727 Haight St. ☎ **668-3994.**

The worker-owned Red Vic movie collective recently moved from the Victorian building that gave it its name. The theater specializes in old Hollywood films, independent releases, and contemporary cultish hits. Call for schedules, prices, and show times.

Roxie, 3117 16th St. ☎ **863-1087.**

Located on 16th at Valencia Street, the Roxie consistently screens the best new alternative films anywhere. The low-budget contemporary features shown here are largely devoid of Hollywood candy-coating; many are west coast premieres. Films change weekly, sometimes sooner. Phone for schedules, prices, and show times.

First-Run Houses

In addition to a small number of classic theaters that have not (yet) been cut up into bite-size cinemas, there are plenty of multiplex theaters featuring postage-stamp-size screens. Check the newspaper advertisements and listings for current showings.

Balboa, 3630 Balboa St. ☎ **221-8184.**

Operated by the Levin family since its opening in 1926, this grand old art-deco theater encompasses twin cinemas showing recent double features, exclusively.

Admission: $5.50 evenings, $3.50 matinees.

Clay, 2261 Fillmore St. ☎ **346-1123.**

Opened in 1910, the Clay, on Fillmore at Clay Street, is the oldest continuously operating movie house in San Francisco. The 400-seat theater, now shows first-run foreign films.

Admission: $7 evenings, $4 first show.

Coronet, 3575 Geary Blvd. ☎ **752-4400.**

Well known for its large screen, the Coronet shows Hollywood blockbusters.

Admission: $7 evenings, $4 matinees.

Northpoint, 2290 Powell St. ☎ **989-6060.**

Located on Powell at Bay Street, near Fisherman's Wharf, this modern film house boasts one of the biggest screens in the city. It's also fitted with a Dolby sound system.

Admission: $7, $4 for shows before 6pm Monday through Friday, and for first show Saturday and Sunday.

9 Easy Excursions from San Francisco

Although you can spend a lifetime exploring San Francisco, save some time to take in the surrounding regions as well. The Bay City is a captivating place, but don't let it ensnare you to the point of ignoring its environs.

San Francisco is set amid the most fascinating and diverse area in northern California—possibly in the United States. And the contrasts of the region are even more spellbinding than its beauties. There are silent forests of 1,200-year-old trees and smartly sophisticated seaside resorts. Humming industrial cities and serene, sun-drenched Spanish missions contrast with rolling wine country, wildly rugged mountain ranges, an island transformed into an oceanarium, and two of America's greatest universities. With San Francisco as either your travel base or your spring board, you can reach any of these points in a few hours or less by car or public transport.

Tower Tours, 77 Jefferson St. (☎ **434-8687**), operates regularly scheduled tours of San Francisco's neighboring towns and countryside. Half- and full-day trips visit Muir Woods, Sausalito, Napa, and Sonoma. Other excursions trek to Yosemite as well as to the Monterey Peninsula. Phone for price and departure information.

Oakland

10 miles E of San Francisco

GETTING THERE • By BART Bay Area Rapid Transit (BART) makes the trip from San Francisco to Oakland through one of the longest underwater transit tubes in the world. Fares range from 80¢ to $3, depending on your station of origin; children ages four and under ride free. BART trains operate Monday through Saturday from 6am to midnight and on Sunday from 9am to midnight. Exit at the 12th Street station for downtown Oakland. (See map on p. 201.)

• By Car From San Francisco, take I-80 across the San Francisco–Oakland Bay Bridge. Exit at Grand Avenue south for the Lake Merritt area.

ESSENTIALS Downtown Oakland is bordered by Grand Avenue on the north, I-980 on the west, Inner Harbor on the south, and Lake Merritt on the east. Between these landmarks are three BART stations (12th Street, 19th Street, and Lake Merritt), city hall, the Oakland Museum, Jack London Square, and several other sights.

For a recorded update on Oakland's arts and entertainment happenings, phone **510/835-2787.**

Few San Francisco locals would suggest that any tourist leave the beautiful peninsula for Oakland, the East Bay's largest city. It's largely true; Oakland is chiefly a sprawling industrial city, and is almost entirely devoid of San Francisco's unique charm. It does, however, boast a number of outstanding attractions.

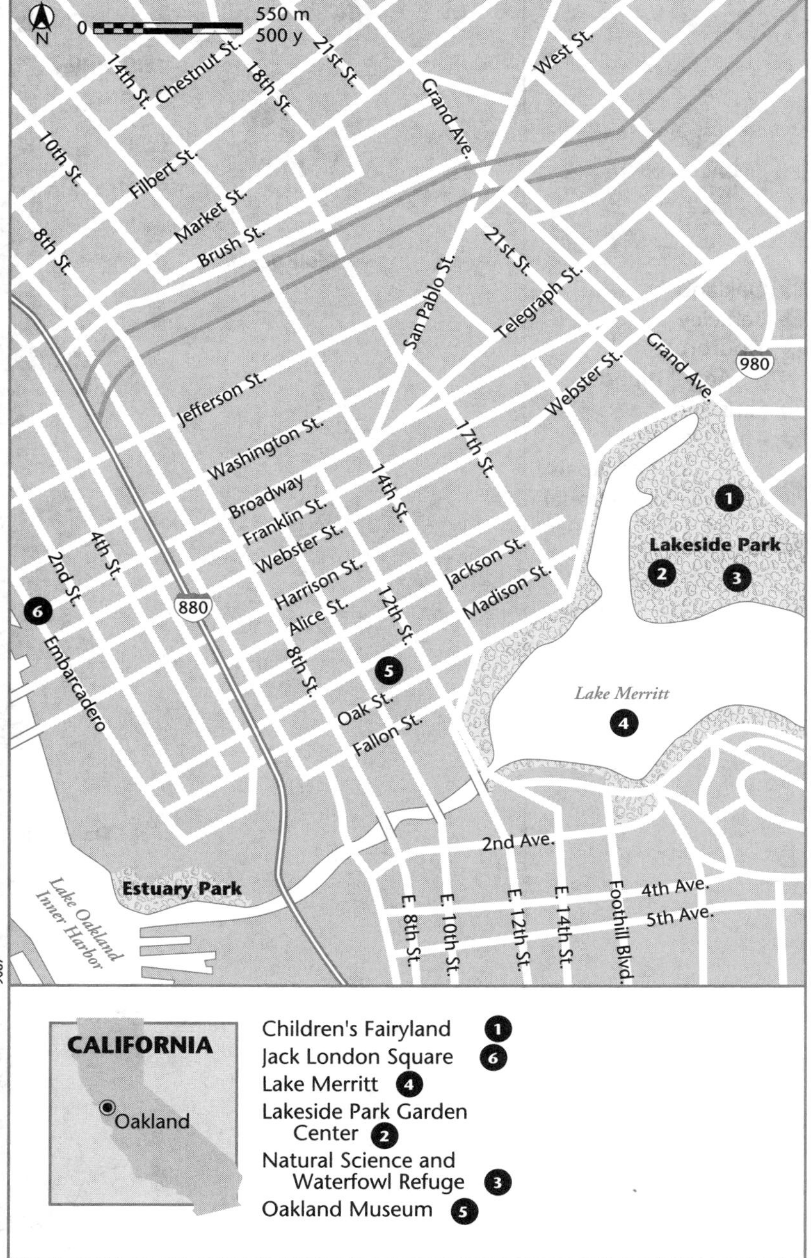
N
0
550 m
500 y
14th St.
Chestnut St.
18th St.
21st St.
West St.
Grand Ave.
10th St.
Filbert St.
Market St.
Brush St.
8th St.
21st St.
San Pablo St.
Telegraph St.
980
Grand Ave.
Webster St.
Jefferson St.
Washington St.
17th St.
Broadway
14th St.
Franklin St.
Webster St.
Lakeside Park
4th St.
2nd St.
Harrison St.
Jackson St.
Madison St.
880
Alice St.
12th St.
Embarcadero
8th St.
Lake Merritt
Oak St.
Fallon St.
2nd Ave.
Estuary Park
Lake Oakland Inner Harbor
E. 8th St.
E. 10th St.
E. 12th St.
E. 14th St.
Foothill Blvd.
4th Ave.
5th Ave.
CALIFORNIA
Oakland
Children's Fairyland 1
Jack London Square 6
Lake Merritt 4
Lakeside Park Garden Center 2
Natural Science and Waterfowl Refuge 3
Oakland Museum 5

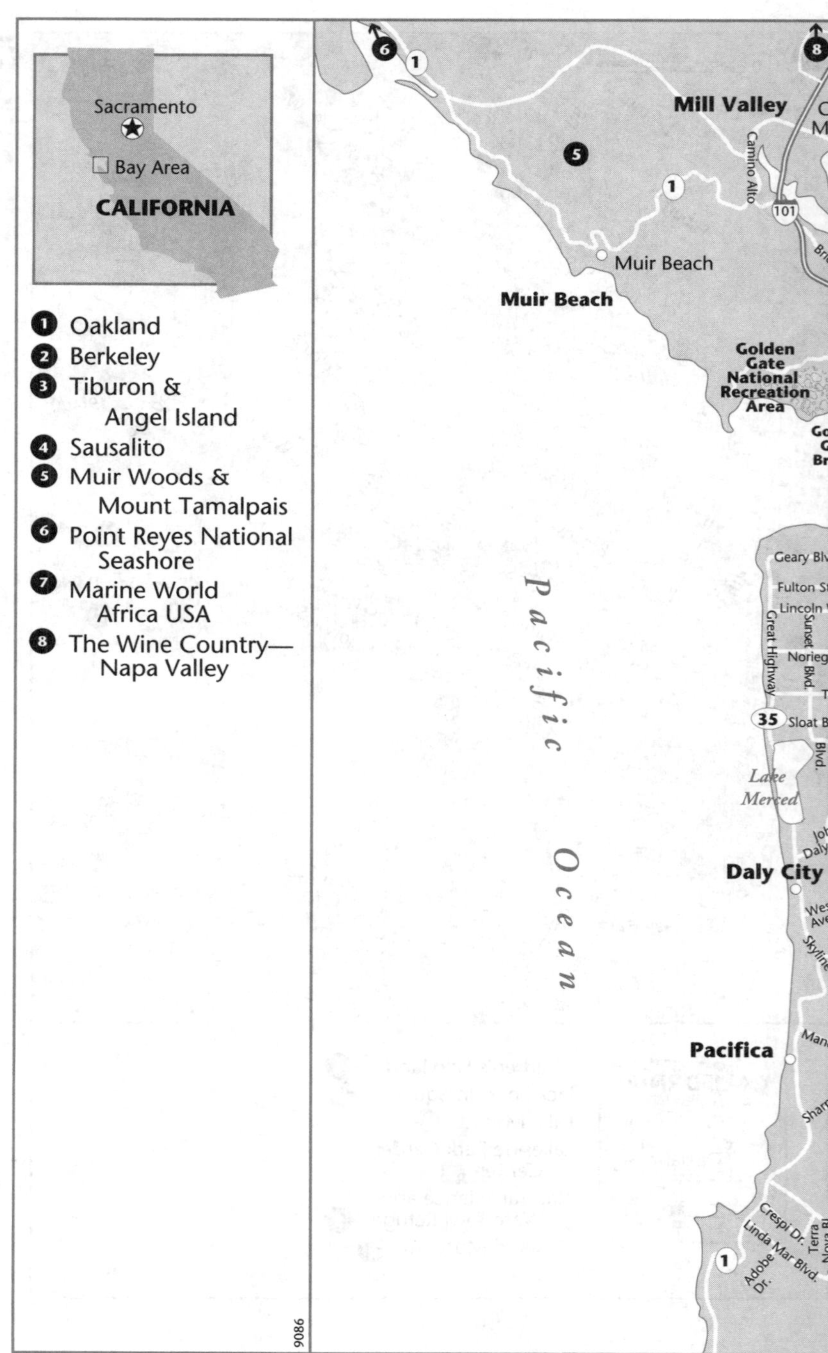
Sacramento
Bay Area
CALIFORNIA
1 Oakland
2 Berkeley
3 Tiburon & Angel Island
4 Sausalito
5 Muir Woods & Mount Tamalpais
6 Point Reyes National Seashore
7 Marine World Africa USA
8 The Wine Country—Napa Valley
9086
Mill Valley
Camino Alto
101
Muir Beach
Muir Beach
Golden Gate National Recreation Area
Pacific Ocean
Geary Blvd.
Fulton St.
Great Highway
Sunset Blvd.
Noriega
35
Sloat Blv
Lake Merced
Lake Merced Blvd.
Daly City
Pacifica
Crespi Dr.
Linda Mar Blvd.
Adobe Dr.
Terra Nova Bl.
1

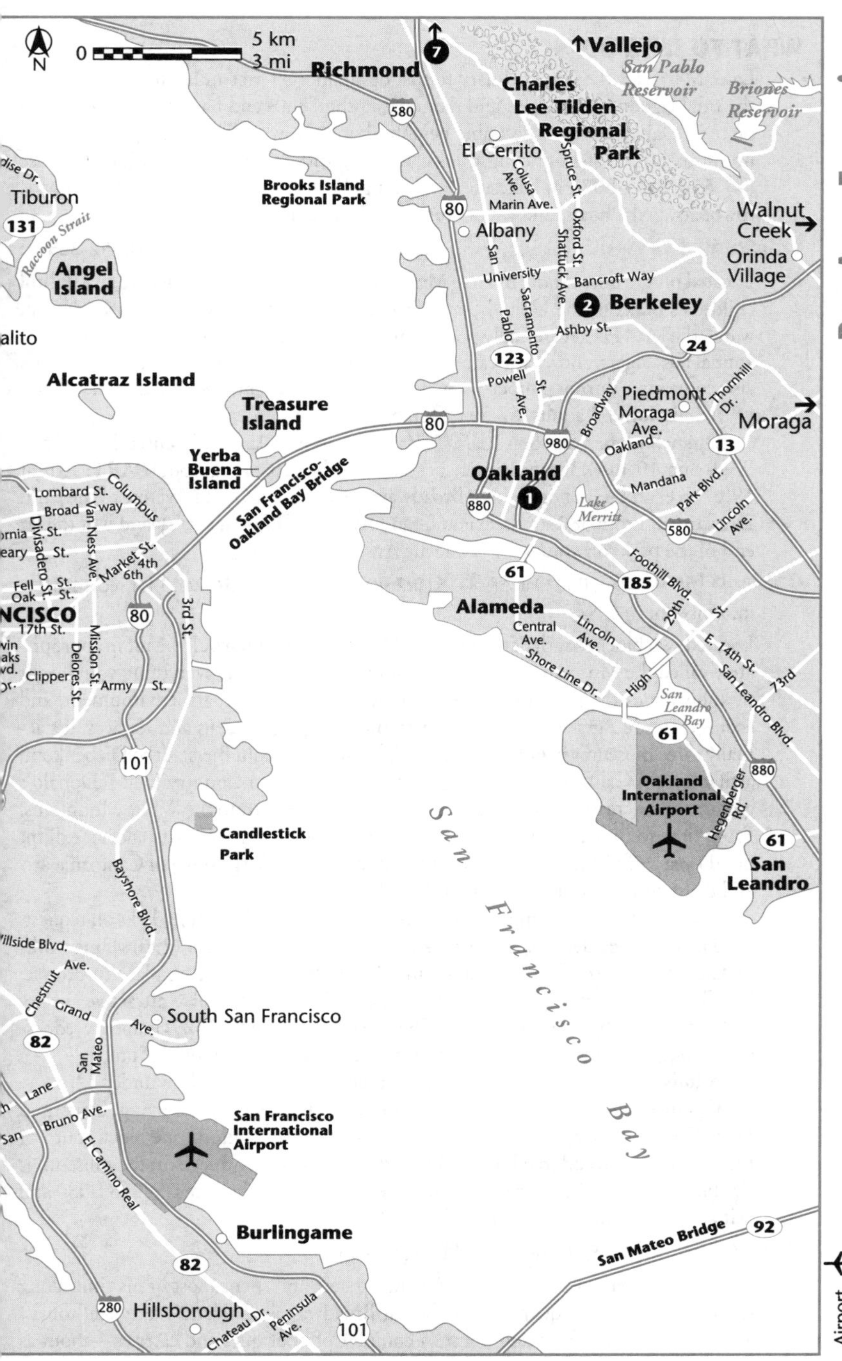
N
0
5 km
3 mi
Richmond
7
580
Vallejo
San Pablo Reservoir
Briones Reservoir
Charles Lee Tilden Regional Park
El Cerrito
Colusa Ave.
Spruce St.
Brooks Island Regional Park
Tiburon
131
Raccoon Strait
Angel Island
80
Marin Ave.
Albany
Oxford St.
Shattuck Ave.
San Pablo
University
Sacramento St.
Bancroft Way
Walnut Creek
Orinda Village
2
Berkeley
Ashby St.
24
123
Powell
Ave.
Alcatraz Island
Treasure Island
Broadway
Piedmont
Moraga Ave.
Thornhill Dr.
Moraga
980
Oakland
13
Yerba Buena Island
San Francisco-Oakland Bay Bridge
Oakland
1
880
Lake Merritt
Mandana
Park Blvd.
580
Lincoln Ave.
Lombard St.
Columbus
Broad way
Van Ness Ave.
Divisadero St.
St.
Market St.
4th
6th
Fell St.
Oak St.
61
185
Foothill Blvd.
80
3rd St.
Alameda
17th St.
Mission St.
Delores St.
Clipper
Army
St.
Central Ave.
Lincoln Ave.
29th
St.
E. 14th St.
Shore Line Dr.
High
San Leandro Bay
73rd
San Leandro Blvd.
61
101
880
Oakland International Airport
Hegenberger Rd.
61
San Leandro
Candlestick Park
San Francisco Bay
Bayshore Blvd.
Hillside Blvd.
Ave.
Chestnut
Grand Ave.
South San Francisco
82
San Mateo
Lane
Bruno Ave.
San
San Francisco International Airport
El Camino Real
Burlingame
San Mateo Bridge
92
82
280
Hillsborough
Chateau Dr.
Peninsula Ave.
101
Airport

WHAT TO SEE & DO

Lake Merritt is the city's primary tourist destination. Three miles in circumference, the tidal lagoon was bridged and dammed in the 1860s and has become the centerpiece of Oakland's most desirable neighborhood. Now a wildlife refuge, the lake is home to flocks of migrating ducks, herons, and geese. At the Sailboat House (☎ **510/444-3807**), in Lakeside Park, along the north shore, you can rent sailboats, rowboats, pedal boats, and canoes for $6 to $20 per hour.

Children's Fairyland, Lakeside Park, Grand Ave. and Bellevue Dr. ☎ **510/452-2259.**

Located on the north shore of Lake Merritt is one of the most imaginative and skillful children's parks in the United States. You can peer into old Geppetto's workshop, watch the Mad Hatter eternally pouring tea for Alice, see Noah's Ark overloaded with animal passengers, and view Beatrix Potter's village of storybook characters. Fairy tales also come alive during puppet-show performances at 11am, and 2 and 4pm.

Admission: $3 adults, $2.50 children ages 12 and under.

Open: Summer, Sat–Sun 10am–5:30pm; Mon–Fri 10am–4:30pm; spring and fall, Wed–Sun 10am–4:30pm; winter, Fri–Sun and hol 10am–4:30pm. **BART:** Exit at 19th Street and walk north along Broadway; turn right on Grand Avenue to the park. **Directions:** From 580 south, exit at Grand Avenue; Children's Fairyland is at the far end of the park, on your left at Bellevue Avenue.

Oakland Museum, 1000 Oak St. ☎ **510/238-3401,** or **510/834-2413** for recorded information.

Located two blocks south of the lake, the Oakland Museum would be more appropriately called the Museum of California—it includes just about everything you'd want to know about the state, its people, history, culture, geology, art, environment, and ecology. Inside a graceful building, set among sweeping gardens and terraces, it's actually three museums in one: works by California artists from Bierstadt to Diebenkorn; artifacts from California's history, from Pomo basketry to Country Joe McDonald's guitar; and re-creations of California habitats from the coast to the White Mountains. From time to time the museum has major shows of California artists, like an exhibit of 200 years of California folk painting and sculpture. A large show of California arts and crafts from 1890 to 1930 opened in 1993.

There are 45-minute guided tours leaving the gallery information desks on request.

There's a fine cafe, inexpensive parking, and a gallery (**510/834-2296**) selling works by California artists. The book and gift shop is also an interesting place to browse. You'll find a wide variety of books, posters, and gift items, as well as attractive jewelry and wearable art by California artists. The snack bar (**510/834-2329**) is open Wednesday through Saturday from 10am to 4pm and Sunday from noon to 5pm.

Admission: $4 adults, $2 students and seniors, free for children under 12.

Open: Wed–Sat 10am–5pm, Sun noon–7pm. **Closed:** Thanksgiving, Christmas Day, New Year's Day, and July 4. **BART:** Lake Merritt station (one block south of the museum). **Directions:** From I-80 north, take the Oak Street exit; the museum is five blocks east of I-80 at Oak and 10th Streets. Alternatively, take I-580 to I-980 and exit at the Jackson Street ramp.

Jack London Square, Broadway and Embarcadero.

Jack London was an Oaklander who grew up here and spent most of his time along the waterfront. This square, at the foot of Broadway, is Oakland's only real tourist area. It fronts the harbor and houses a complex of boutiques and eateries—about as far away from the call of the wild as you can get. In the center of the square is the small, reconstructed, rustic Yukon cabin in which Jack London lived while prospecting in the Klondike during the gold rush of 1897.

At 56 Jack London Square, at the foot of Webster Street, you'll find the oddly named First and Last Chance Saloon, where London did some of his writing and much of his drinking. The corner table he used has remained exactly as it was 75 or so years ago (except for his photos on the wall). Have a schooner in Jack's memory. Also in the square are the mast and nameplate from the USS *Oakland,* a ship that saw extensive action in the Pacific during World War II.

Admission: Free.

Open: Thurs 10am–6pm, Mon–Sat 10am–9pm (some restaurants stay open later). **BART:** 12th Street station; then walk south along Broadway (about half a mile), or take bus 51A to the foot of Broadway. **Directions:** Take I-80 to Broadway, turn south, and go to the end.

Alice Arts Center, 1428 Alice St. ☎ **510/238-7222.**

The $14 million Alice Arts Center, a five-story mixed-use building four blocks from downtown Oakland opened to raves in 1993. The five-story complex, situated on a quiet residential street, houses the Oakland Ballet, Oakland Ensemble Theater, and City Center Dance. The latter is primarily a school of Jazz, Caribbean, and African dance. Dimensions Dance Theatre, the Bay Area's oldest modern dance company performs here, as well as in downtown's spectacular Paramount Theater (**510/465-6400**).

Prices: $5–$20, depending on the program.

Berkeley

10 miles E of San Francisco

GETTING THERE • By BART Berkeley station is two blocks from the university. The fare from San Francisco is $1.80.

• By Car From San Francisco, take I-80 east to the University exit. Drive straight to the university. Count on walking some distance because chances are you won't find a place to park near the university.

ESSENTIALS Telegraph Avenue is the main drag for the student populace. It is most colorful around Bancroft Way and Ashby Avenue. Telegraph Avenue deadends at the university's Sproul Plaza and the Student Union.

Phone the Visitor Hotline (**510/549-8710**) for general information on events and happenings in Berkeley.

Berkeley is actually an East Bay factory town that has achieved fame, glory, and notoriety through harboring an educational institution that has produced 15 Nobel Prize winners—more than any other university—and spawned some of the worst (best?) campus riots in the nation. More than any other city, Berkeley conjures up images of dissent and is closely identified with the radical 1960s. Politically, the student populace has moved somewhat to the right, but come Election Day, this college town still becomes more boisterous than most.

Telegraph Avenue, the main shopping and strolling street, is seemingly lined in equal numbers by coffee bars and bookshops, both overflowing with students. It's also packed with people selling everything from T-shirts and jewelry to I Ching and tarot-card readings. On Telegraph Avenue the 1960s have never left.

Just before Telegraph Avenue runs into the university campus, it crosses **Bancroft Way.** This is the hub of student activities, a great many of which seem to take place right on the corner. Stand here for a few minutes and you're bound to have leaflets thrust at you, hear an impromptu debate, or the jingling and rattling of a Hare Krishna chant. And you can likely purchase anything from a curried-beef pie to falafel from food stands here while you're being converted to the current cause. The university's **Sproul Plaza** is across the street and contains the Student Union, a lively building as spacious and hectic as the rest of the university. Go to the information desk on the second floor to pick up a free map of Berkeley, as well as the local student newspaper.

WHAT TO SEE & DO

University Of California—Berkeley. ☎ **510/642-5215.**

You might call Berkeley a city with a split personality, or at least two faces. The western part is flat, chock-a-block with factories and garages, and decidedly drab. The eastern portion undulates over a series of hills, with little houses clinging all over them and lush green patches smiling right into the main shopping streets. This is the university section, dominated by students and professors, and catering to their particular tastes like no other town in the United States.

You're not likely to see any rioting on campus in the now-tame 1990s, but you will see hordes of students—there are about 30,000 of them. Built in the wide-open California style, the campus is not exceptionally beautiful. Still, it's interesting to see.

The Visitor Information Center at UC—Berkeley offers free, regularly-scheduled campus tours Monday, Wednesday, and Friday at 10am and 1pm. Phone ahead for information and reservations. No tours are offered from mid-December to mid-January.

People's Park, Berkeley.

In late 1967, the University demolished an entire block of buildings north of Telegraph Avenue. The destruction, which forced hippies and other "undesirables" from the slum housing that stood there, was done under the guise of university expansion and urban renewal. But after the lot lay vacant for almost two years, a group of Berkeley radicals that reads like a Who's Who of 1960s leftists—including Jerry Rubin, Bobby Seale, and Tom Hayden—decided to seize the land for "the people." On April 29, 1969, hundreds of activists invaded the vacant lot with gardening tools and transformed the muddy ground into a park. One month later, Berkeley's Republican mayor sent 250 police officers into the park, and 4,000 demonstrators materialized to challenge them. A riot ensued, the police fired buckshot at the crowd, and one rioter was killed and another blinded. Gov. Ronald Reagan sent in the National Guard, and for the next 17 days the Guardsmen repeatedly gassed innocent students, faculty, and passersby. Berkeley was a war zone, and People's Park became the 1960s' most important symbol of "people power."

People's Park once again sparked controversy in 1992, when university officials decided to build volleyball courts there. In August of that year, a park activist broke into the campus home of the university's chancellor. When a police officer arrived, the activist lunged at him with a machete and was shot dead. On the victim's body was a note with the message: "We are willing to die for this land. Are you?" On news of the contemporary radical's death, over 150 of her supporters rioted. Today you can visit the park and watch the volleyballers self-consciously setting, bumping, and spiking.

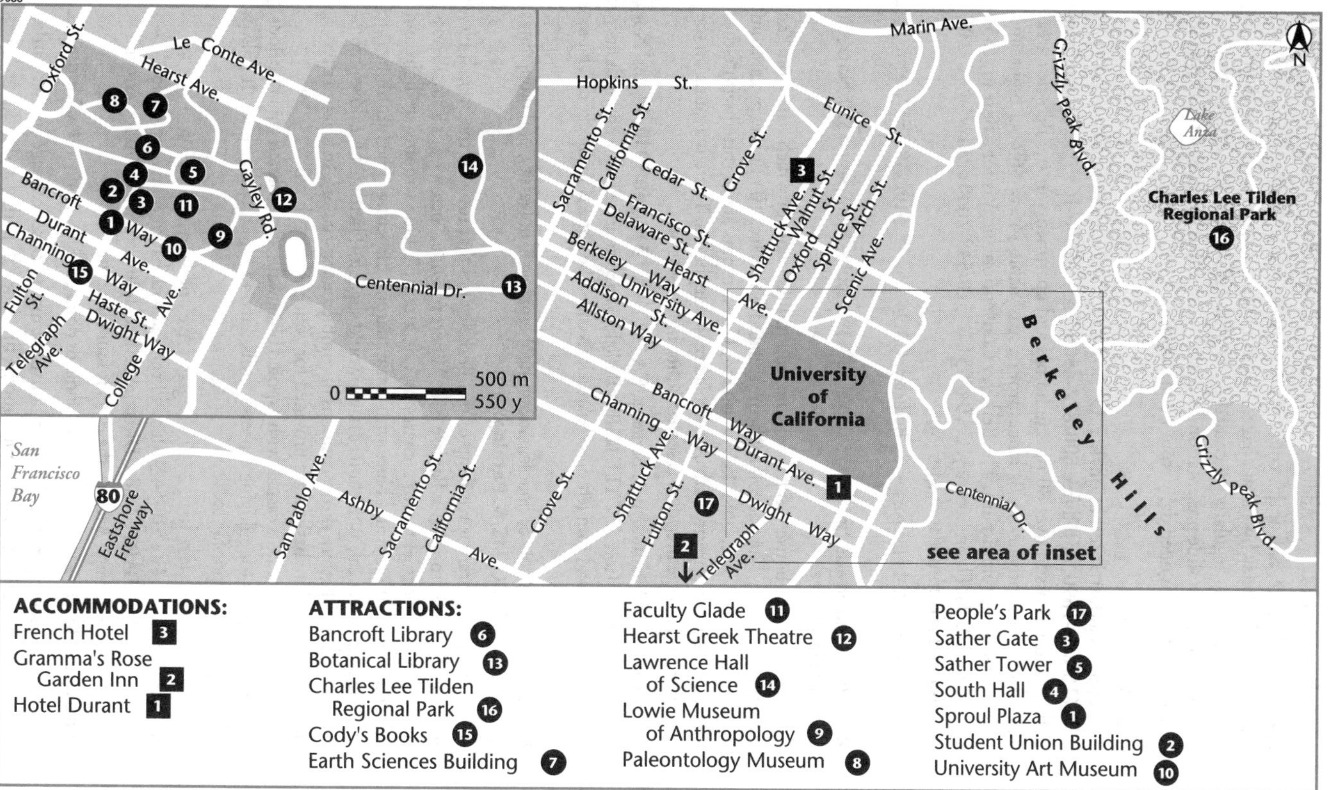
Oxford St.
Le Conte Ave.
Hearst Ave.
Gayley Rd.
Bancroft Way
Durant Ave.
Channing Way
Haste St.
Dwight Way
Fulton St.
Telegraph Ave.
College Ave.
Centennial Dr.
0 500 m 550 y
Marin Ave.
Hopkins St.
Eunice St.
Grizzly Peak Blvd.
Lake Anza
Charles Lee Tilden Regional Park
Sacramento St.
California St.
Cedar St.
Grove St.
Francisco St.
Delaware St.
Hearst
Berkeley Way
University Ave.
Addison St.
Allston Way
Shattuck Ave.
Walnut St.
Oxford St.
Spruce St.
Arch St.
Scenic Ave.
University of California
Berkeley Hills
see area of inset
San Francisco Bay
80
Eastshore Freeway
San Pablo Ave.
Ashby Ave.
ACCOMMODATIONS:
French Hotel 3
Gramma's Rose Garden Inn 2
Hotel Durant 1
ATTRACTIONS:
Bancroft Library 6
Botanical Library 13
Charles Lee Tilden Regional Park 16
Cody's Books 15
Earth Sciences Building 7
Faculty Glade 11
Hearst Greek Theatre 12
Lawrence Hall of Science 14
Lowie Museum of Anthropology 9
Paleontology Museum 8
People's Park 17
Sather Gate 3
Sather Tower 5
South Hall 4
Sproul Plaza 1
Student Union Building 2
University Art Museum 10

Berkeley

Takara Sake USA Inc., 708 Addison St., Berkeley. ☎ **510/540-8250.**

Sho Chiku Bai sake, one of this country's most popular brands, is not Japanese—it's made here in Berkeley by Takara Sake USA, America's largest sake maker. Unfortunately, there are no regularly scheduled tours of the plant, but you can learn about sake making from a slide presentation, and taste three different types of the rice wine. The tasting room is open daily from noon to 6pm.

WHERE TO STAY

Bed and Breakfast International, P.O. Box 282910, San Francisco, CA 94128 (☎ **415/696-1690,** or toll free **800/872-4500,** fax 415/696-1699), accommodates tourists and visitors in over 80 private homes and apartments in the Berkeley area. The cost of these private B&Bs ranges from a reasonable $45 to $69 per night, and there's a two-night minimum. The Berkeley Convention and Visitor's Bureau, 1834 University Ave. 1st Floor, Berkeley, CA 94703 (☎ **510/549-7040** or **510/549-8710**), can also find accommodations for you.

Hillegass House, 2834 Hillegass Ave., Berkeley, CA 94705. ☎ **510/548-5517.** 4 rms. TEL

Rates (including breakfast): $65–$75 single, $80–$90 double. Extra person $20. No credit cards. **Parking:** Free.

Built in 1904, the house is filled with many antiques, most of which date from the turn of the century. The tradeoff for being situated as much as 10 minutes by car from the university, is a nice, quiet neighborhood. Guest rooms are outfitted with either king or queen beds, private baths, and voice-mail telephones. There is a sauna on the property, and a large breakfast is served either indoors or out.

French Hotel, 1538 Shattuck Ave., Berkeley, CA 94709. ☎ **510/548-9930.** 18 rms. No-smoking rooms available. TV TEL **BART:** Berkeley. **Directions:** From I-80 north, take the University exit and turn left onto Shattuck Avenue; the hotel is six blocks down on your left.

Rates: $85–$125 single or double. Government employee, university, and group rates available. AE, CB, DC, MC, V. **Parking:** Free.

If Gallic contemporary is your cup of tea, Berkeley has that too—at the French Hotel, directly across from Chez Panisse (see "Where to Dine," below). It's a small, relatively new establishment with a charming cafe attached. Guest rooms are light and airy, done in quiet grays and blues with warm maroon carpeting. The furnishings are attractive and practical, as the hotel's name would suggest. There are blue downy comforters and floral-pattern throw cushions in complementary colors. In lieu of a dresser, stacked sliding white baskets are provided for your personal things.

The downstairs cafe is casual, with exposed brick walls, rust-colored concrete floor, and outdoor tables for enjoying espresso, croissants, and fresh orange juice. It's also a relaxed gathering spot for locals.

Gramma's Rose Garden Inn, 2740 Telegraph Ave., Berkeley, CA 94705. ☎ **510/549-2145.** Fax 510/549-1085. 40 rms (all with bath). All rooms are no-smoking. TV TEL **BART:** Ashby. **Directions:** Take I-80 north to the Ashby exit and turn left onto Telegraph Avenue; the hotel is four blocks up.

Rates (including breakfast): $85–$150 single or double. AE, DC, MC, V. **Parking:** Free.

Gramma's charming restored Tudor houses (a main house, carriage house, garden house, and the Fay house) offer guest rooms furnished in period style with antiques, floral-print wallpapers, and pretty patchwork quilts on the beds. Accommodations in the restored carriage house overlook a garden and have fireplaces and king beds.

Guests are served a complimentary breakfast in the downstairs dining room or on the deck overlooking the garden. Sunday brunch is served free to guests staying over Saturday night.

Hotel Durant, 2600 Durant Ave., Berkeley, CA 94704. ☎ **510/845-8981,** or toll free **800/238-7268.** Fax 510/486-8336. 140 rms, 10 suites. No-smoking rooms available. TV TEL **BART:** Berkeley. **Directions:** Take I-80 north to the University exit, turn right onto Shattuck Avenue and left onto Durant Avenue; the hotel is five blocks ahead on the right.

Rates (including breakfast): $85–$95 single, $95–$105 double, from $180 suite. AE, DC, DISC, MC, V. **Parking:** $5.

Just one block from the university is the very pleasant Hotel Durant, at Bowditch Street. Built in 1928, it's the only full-service hotel this close to the university. New ownership restored it nicely to keep the best of its earlier days while providing conveniences now expected by vacationers and travelers. The rooms are straight-forwardly furnished, and all have cable TV, in-room movies, and radio. Some of the rooms can be connected for families.

The hotel's restaurant, Henry's Publick House and Grille, serves American cuisine in an English-pub atmosphere.

WHERE TO DINE

You can eat on campus Monday through Friday in the building directly behind the Student Union. The least expensive food is available downstairs in the cafeteria, on Lower Sproul Plaza. Adjacent to it are Bear's Lair Pub and Coffee House, the Deli, and the Ice Creamery. Upstairs, at the Terrace you can get breakfast, snacks, and lunch. Also on this level of the building is the handsome Golden Bear Restaurant. All the university eateries have both indoor and outdoor seating.

Telegraph Avenue has a wonderful array of small restaurants of many nationalities. Walk along, read the posted menus, and take your pick.

★ **Chez Panisse,** 1517 Shattuck Ave. ☎ **510/548-5525.**

Cuisine: CALIFORNIAN. **Reservations:** Restaurant, essential; cafe, accepted for lunch, not accepted for dinner. **BART:** Berkeley. **Directions:** From I-80 north take the University exit and turn left onto Shattuck Avenue.

Prices: Appetizers $6–$8; main courses $13–$18; lunch $14–$18; fixed-price dinner $35–$65. AE, CB, DC, MC, V.

Open: Restaurant, dinner seatings Mon–Sat 6, 6:30, 8:30, and 9:15pm. Cafe, lunch Mon–Thurs 11:30am–3pm, Fri–Sat 11:30am–4pm; dinner Mon–Thurs 5–10:30pm, Fri–Sat 5–11:30pm.

Between Cedar and Vine Streets is Alice Waters's extraordinary Chez Panisse. Californian cuisine is so much a product of Waters's genius that all other restaurants following in her wake should be dated "A.A.W." (After Alice Waters). This delightful redwood-and-stucco cottage is entered via a brick terrace filled with flowering potted plants. There are two separate dining areas—the upstairs cafe and the downstairs restaurant, both offering a Mediterranean-inspired cuisine.

In the upstairs cafe there are displays of pastries and fruit, and large bouquets of fresh flowers adorning an oak bar. The menu is posted daily out front, and luncheon dishes are à la carte. Offerings might include a delicately smoked gravlax or a roasted eggplant soup with pesto, followed by lamb ragout garnished with apricots, onions, and spices served with couscous. Your luncheon tab includes gratuity and tax. A glass of wine will usually add another $4. Brick-oven pizza, salads, homemade pastas, and a fabulous calzone stuffed with mozzarella, goat cheese, and prosciutto, are among the exceptional dinner offerings. Even the ice creams and sherbets are homemade. Since dinner reservations are not taken for the cafe your wait may be lengthy, but it's worth it.

In the cozy downstairs restaurant, only one fixed-price, five-course gourmet dinner is served each night. The menu, which has changed daily since the restaurant opened in 1971, is posted outside the restaurant on Saturday for each day of the week. The dining area is redwood-paneled and has a working fireplace, art deco lamps, and big bouquets of fresh flowers everywhere. A typical meal might include pan-fried oysters with Chino Ranch curly endive, spinach-and-fennel soup, veal saltimbocca, straw potatoes, salad, and orange ice cream in almond-cookie cups. Is this expensive? Of course. Is it worth it? Absolutely. The wine list ($20 to $200) is also excellent.

Bishop's Sweet Potato Pie Company, 1786 Shattuck Ave. ☎ **510/841-1277.**

Cuisine: MEAT AND FRUIT PIES.
Prices: $1.65–$3 per mini pie; $7–$13 per large pie. No credit cards.
Open: Mon–Sat 7:30am–7pm.

This tiny take-out at Delaware Street bakes some of the best meat and fruit pies to be found anywhere. As the name says, sweet potato pie is the house specialty, but pecan, apple, pumpkin, and berry are also recommendable. Hearty entrée-type pies include chicken, beef, and vegetable. Most every flavor comes in single-serving pies and full-pie sizes.

Blondie's Pizza, 2340 Telegraph Ave., Berkeley. ☎ **510/548-1129.**

Cuisine: PIZZA.
Prices: $7–$14 pizza; $1.50 slice of cheese. No credit cards.
Open: Mon–Thurs 5pm–1am, Fri–Sat 5pm–2am, Sun noon–midnight.

Always busy, loud, and somewhat messy, this pizza parlor with the decidedly un-Italian name is a Berkeley institution. Pizza is the only menu item—your choice of thick, thin, or whole wheat crust.

Cafe Intermezzo, 2422 Telegraph Ave. ☎ **510/849-4592.**

Cuisine: SALADS/SANDWICHES.
Prices: $3–$5. No credit cards.
Open: Daily 10am–10pm.

Although Intermezzo's menu is strictly salads and sandwiches, it's easy to understand why this is one of the busiest restaurants in Berkeley: ingredients are of uniformly high standards, portions are huge, and prices are rock-bottom. Roast beef, ham, turkey, salami, tuna, chicken, egg, and vegetables are mounded between slices of homemade oversized thick-sliced bread. Huge natural salads contain lettuce, avocado, egg, beans,

IMPRESSIONS

When I was a child growing up in Salinas we called San Francisco "The City." Of course it was the only city we knew but I still think of it as The City as does everyone else who has ever associated with it.
—John Steinbeck

tomatoes, cabbage, and more. Order cafeteria-style, then take a seat at one of about 15 varnished wooden tables. At lunch time during the school year, there's a line out the door.

Noah's Bagels, 2344 Telegraph Ave., Berkeley. ☎ **510/849-9951.**

Cuisine: JEWISH.
Prices: $1–$7. No credit cards.
Open: Mon–Fri 7am–9pm, Sat–Sun 7:30am–6pm.

I've never had a good bagel in San Francisco. Until now. Noah's corner shop is permeated by a heavenly fresh-baked smell. A large appetizing section contains six different kinds of cream cheese, a dozen kinds of salads, and several smoked fish selections. In deference to their native Berkeley customers, peanut butter and hummus are also available. It's still not New York, but you can get the Sunday *Times* at a newsstand just a block away.

Triple Rock Brewery Company, Inc., 1920 Shattuck Ave., Berkeley. ☎ **510/843-2739.**

Cuisine: AMERICAN. **Reservations:** Not accepted.
Prices: $6–$9. No credit cards.
Open: Sun–Thurs 11:30am–1am, Fri–Sat 11:30am–2am.

Although I don't particularly recommend eating here, this top-notch brewpub/ restaurant is a must for any beer lover worthy of the title. It's not much to look at—very frat-like with wooden floors and a good juke box—but the beer is one of the tastiest around.

Tiburon & Angel Island

8 miles N of San Francisco

GETTING THERE • By Boat Ferries of the Red and White Fleet (☎ **415/546-2700**) leave from Pier 43½ (Fisherman's Wharf) and travel to both Tiburon and Angel Island. Boats run on a seasonal schedule; call for departure information. The round-trip fare is $9 to Tiburon, $8 to Angel Island; half price for kids ages 5 to 11.

Alternatively, you can drive to Tiburon (see below), then board the Angel Island Ferry (☎ **415/435-2131,** or **415/388-6770**) for the short, 15-minute hop to the island. The round-trip costs $5.

• By Car Take U.S. 101 to the Tiburon/Belvedere exit and then follow Tiburon Boulevard all the way into downtown, a 40-minute drive from San Francisco. Catch the ferry from the dock located at Tiburon Boulevard and Main Street.

ESSENTIALS • Orientation Tiburon is tiny. The aptly named Main Street is the town's primary thoroughfare. It fronts the water and is a popular bike path. Main intersects with Tiburon Boulevard (known as Paradise Drive). Opposite is a handsome and posh shopping and eating plaza with wood-shingled buildings and brick walkways overlooking its own small body of water. Just across the Beach Road Bridge is Belvedere Island, a pretty little place full of fancy houses.

Angel Island is only 730 acres big. There are picnic sites with tables, benches, barbecue pits, and rest rooms at Ayala Cove, where you land. Miles of hiking trails lead you around the island and to the peak of Mount Caroline Livermore, 776 feet above the bay.

• **Information** The rangers at Angel Island State Park (☎ **415/435-1915**) will be happy to answer any of your questions.

A federal and state wildlife refuge, Angel Island is the prettiest of the San Francisco Bay's three islets (the others are Alcatraz and Yerba Buena). Most of the people who visit here never leave the large green lawn that fronts the docking area; they bring picnics and enjoy the view of Tiburon across the way. Behind the lawn, inside the ranger station, are displays detailing the history of this largest bay island. Angel Island has been, at various times, a prison, a favorite site for duels, a quarantine station for immigrants, and a Nike missile base. Today, in addition to picnics, it is popular for hiking and biking. Over 12 miles of trails include the Perimeter Road, a partly paved path that circles the island and winds its way past unused troop barracks, former gun emplacements, and other military buildings. Sometimes referred to as the "Ellis Island of the west," Angel Island, from 1910 to 1940, held Chinese immigrants as they waited to have their citizenship papers processed. You can still see some faded Chinese scrawlings on the walls of the barracks where the immigrants were held. During warmer months it's possible to camp on the island. There are a limited number of sites, and reservations are required. Call **415/323-2988** for information.

Tiburon, situated on a peninsula of the same name, looks like a cross between a fishing village and a Hollywood western set—imagine San Francisco reduced to toy dimensions, with just a dash of stagecoach atmosphere thrown in. This decidedly odd seacoast town rambles over a series of green hills and ends up at a spindly, multicolored pier on the waterfront, like a Fisherman's Wharf in miniature. But in reality it's an extremely plush patch of yacht-club suburbia, as you'll see by both the marine craft and the homes of their owners. This, ladies and gentlemen, is the "good life."

Main Street is lined with ramshackle, color-splashed old frame houses that hide chic little boutiques, expensive antique shops, and art galleries. Other roads are narrow, winding, and hilly, and lead up to ultramodern villas that stand in glaring contrast to the old village atmosphere of the shopping center. But this contrast is the town's primary charm. The pace here is sleepy, the bay view bewitching, and the hill setting glorious. The view of San Francisco's skyline and the islands in the bay is almost worth the price of living here.

Whether you reach Tiburon by car or by boat, it'll give you a pang of envy for its lucky inhabitants, who enjoy city sophistication and village air in one breath. Several hundred upper-bracket businesspeople feel exactly the same way; that's why they live here and commute daily to their San Francisco offices.

WHAT TO SEE & DO

The main thing to do here is stroll along the waterfront, pop into the boutiques, and end up at a restaurant in time for lunch or dinner. While you're at it, enjoy a taste of the Wine Country at Windsor Vineyards, 72 Main St. (☎ **415/435-3113,** or toll free **800/214-9463**). Their Victorian tasting room dates from 1888. You may choose from more than 35 fine Windsor Vineyards wines, including many award winners, for complimentary sampling. Windsor has been awarded more than 200 medals at prestigious wine-tasting competitions. They also carry a good selection of wine accessories and gifts—glasses, cork pullers, gourmet sauces, posters, maps, and so on. Carry packs are available (they hold six bottles). Ask about personalized labels for your own selections. The shop is open Sunday through Thursday from 10am to 6pm, and Friday and Saturday from 10am to 7pm.

WHERE TO DINE

Guaymas Restaurante, 5 Main St. ☎ **415/435-6300.**

Cuisine: MEXICAN. **Reservations:** Accepted. **Ferry:** Walk about 10 paces from the landing. **Directions:** From U.S. 101, exit at Tiburon/Belvedere, follow Tiburon Boulevard five miles and turn right onto Main Street. The restaurant is situated directly behind the bakery.

Prices: Appetizers $3–$8; main courses $7–$15. AE, CB, DC, MC, V.

Open: Mon–Fri 11am–9:30pm, Sat–Sun 11am–10:30pm.

Guaymas is quite possibly the only restaurant in the Bay Area offering both authentic Mexican regional dishes and a spectacular panoramic view of San Francisco and the bay. In good weather, dining on either one of the two outdoor patios is particularly pleasing. Bright-pink walls are hung with colorful Mexican masks, illuminated by modern track lighting. To the rear of the dining room is a rounded fireplace reminiscent of those shaped by Native Americans of the Southwest.

Guaymas is named after a fishing village on Mexico's Sea of Cortez. Both the town and its restaurant are famous for their camarones (giant shrimp). In addition, the restaurant features ceviche, handmade tamales, and charcoal-grilled beef, seafood, and fowl. Save room for dessert—among the tempting choices is an outrageously delicious fritter with "drunken" bananas and ice cream, or you might opt for the white-chocolate mousse with fresh strawberry sauce. In addition to a good selection of California wines, the restaurant offers an exceptional variety of tequilas, Mexican beers, and mineral waters flavored with flowers, grains, and fruits.

Sam's Anchor Cafe, 27 Main St. ☎ **415/435-4527.**

Cuisine: SEAFOOD. **Reservations:** Accepted. **Ferry:** Walk from the landing. **Directions:** From U.S. 101, exit at Tiburon/Belvedere, follow Tiburon Boulevard four miles, and turn right onto Main Street.

Prices: Appetizers $4–$9, main courses $8–$16. AE, MC, V.

Open: Mon–Thurs 11am–10pm, Fri 11am–10:30pm, Sat 10am–10:30pm, Sun 9:30am–10pm.

Tiburon is liveliest on summer Sundays, when weekend boaters tie up to the docks of waterside restaurants. For over 70 years now, the traditional place to dock is Sam's, which boasts two 110-foot piers and a large wooden deck that's filled to overflowing with blithe Sunday spirits. Sam's is the kind of place where you can take off your shoes and shirt—everyone's home-away-from-home neighborhood bar. During Prohibition days it was a rendezvous point for bootleggers, who used to pull in under the restaurant and bring liquor in through trap doors.

At lunch you might order a bay shrimp, a tomato and cheddar-cheese sandwich on a toasted English muffin, or the soup du jour and half a sandwich for $4.50 to $9.95. Dinner might be any one of the fresh seafood specials or deep-fried oysters served with fresh vegetables. Delicious sourdough bread and butter comes with all main courses.

Sweden House Bakery-Cafe, 35 Main St. ☎ **415/435-9767.**

Cuisine: SWEDISH/AMERICAN. **Reservations:** Not accepted. **Ferry:** Walk from the landing. **Directions:** From U.S. 101, exit at Tiburon/Belvedere, follow Tiburon Boulevard five miles and turn right onto Main Street.

Prices: Omelets $5–$6, sandwiches $6–$8. MC, V.

Open: Mon–Fri 8am–5pm, Sat–Sun 8am–7pm.

This quaint little eatery with gingham-covered walls adorned with copperware and other kitchen things is one of my favorite places in Tiburon. I love sitting on the terrace, gazing out over the bay with an espresso in one hand and a home-baked Swedish pastry in the other. The raspberry-iced, cream-filled napoleon is especially good.

Full breakfasts are served daily—perhaps scrambled eggs with cheese, mushrooms, shrimp, or slices of smoked salmon? Everything comes with the restaurant's own toasted Swedish limpa bread. At lunch there are traditional open-face sandwiches like avocado and bacon, or delicious asparagus tips rolled in Danish ham; you can also order such American standards as chicken and garden salads. Beer and wine are available.

Sausalito

8 miles N of San Francisco

GETTING THERE • By Boat Ferries of the Red and White Fleet (☎ **415/546-2700**) leave from Pier 43½ (Fisherman's Wharf) and cost $9 round-trip, half price for kids ages 5 to 11. Boats run on a seasonal schedule call for departure information.

• **Golden Gate Ferry Service** (☎ **415/332-6600**) boats dash back and forth between the San Francisco Ferry Building, at the foot of Market Street, and downtown Sausalito. Service is frequent, departing at reasonable intervals, every day of the year except New Year's Day, Thanksgiving, and Christmas Day. Call for exact schedule information. The ride takes half an hour, and costs $3.75 for adults and $2.80 for youths ages 6 to 12. Seniors and physically disabled passengers ride for $1.85, kids 5 and under ride free.

• **By Car** From U.S. 101 north, take the first right after the Golden Gate Bridge (Alexander exit). Alexander becomes Bridgeway in Sausalito.

ESSENTIALS Sausalito's main street is Bridgeway, which runs along the water. Just about everything notable is somewhere on or just off this roadway, which plays the combined role of shopping center and promenade.

Sausalito makes no attempt to hide what it is—a slightly bohemian, nonchalant, and studiedly quaint adjunct to San Francisco, designed for folks who want to have their metropolitan cake and eat it outdoors too. With approximately 7,500 residents, Sausalito feels rather like St. Tropez on the French Riviera—minus the starlets and the social rat race. It has its quota of paper millionaires, but they rub their permanently suntanned shoulders with a good number of hard-up artists, struggling authors, shipyard workers, and fishermen. Next to the swank restaurants, plush bars, and expensive antique shops, you'll see hamburger joints, beer parlors, and secondhand bookstores.

Above all, Sausalito has scenery and sunshine, for once you cross the Golden Gate Bridge you're out of the San Francisco fog patch and under blue California sky. The town's steep hills are covered with white houses that overlook a forest of masts on the water below. The gleaming spires of bustling San Francisco can be seen in the comfortably far-off distance.

WHAT TO SEE & DO

Bay Model Visitors Center, 2100 Bridgeway. ☎ **415/332-3871.**

In this 1.5-acre model of San Francisco's bay and delta, the U.S. Army Corps of Engineers can make water behave as it does in the bay and observe just what changes in water flow will mean. It's a scientific tool used by engineers, scientists, and planners to analyze problems that can't be resolved through textbooks, experience, or mathematical models alone. The model reproduces (in scale) the rise and fall of tides, the flows and currents of water, the mixing of fresh and salt water, and indicates trends in sediment movement.

An introductory film that lasts about 10 minutes orients visitors to the purpose and operation of the bay model. Here you can see the impact of pollution, view the Sacramento and San Joaquin rivers flowing into the bay, and even see the swift flow of water around Alcatraz. In addition to rangers, who are available to answer questions, the center has a 30-minute tour on tape in English, Russian, Japanese, German, French, and Spanish. The model is most interesting when it's actually in operation, and that happens only when a test is being conducted. It pays to call before you go and ask about testing.

Admission: Free.

Open: Winter, Tues–Sat 9am–4pm; summer, Tues–Fri 9am–4pm, Sat–Sun 10am–6pm.

Shopping

A mecca for handmade, original, and offbeat clothes and footwear, Sausalito boasts many charming shops, featuring a wide variety of unusual arts and crafts, antiques, gifts, and souvenirs. The town's best offbeat shops can be discovered by prowling through the alleys, malls, and second-floor boutiques reached by steep, narrow staircases on and off **Bridgeway.** Shops here come and go fairly quickly, as the goods are fairly pricey. But the merchandise is original, and it's always colorful and fun.

If you have energy enough to push on farther, new shops, pubs, and restaurants are mushrooming on **Caledonia Street,** which runs parallel to, and one block inland from, Bridgeway. This street may be as busy as the main drag by the time this book is in your hands, but, as yet, the strollers are mainly natives, and the baseball game in the schoolyard helps remind you that this tourist-thronged town on woody hillsides has real people in residence.

Burlwood Gallery, 721 Bridgeway. ☎ **415/332-6550.**

Visit this gallery for one-of-a-kind redwood furniture plus fine jewelry, metal sculptures, hand-blown glass, Oriental rugs, and other interesting gifts. It's well worth browsing. Open daily from 10am to 6pm.

Pegasus Leather Company, 30 Princess St. ☎ **415/332-5624.**

Turn right off Bridgeway onto Princess Street and look into the Pegasus store, vendors of beautiful leather clothing and extensive accessories collections. Some of the leathers are so soft they seem to be made of flowing fabric and in colors sure to add excitement to a wardrobe. Clothing will be custom made, and altered for a perfect fit at no extra charge. Along with jackets, coats, skirts, and blouses, there are handsome leather belts, boots, gloves, and purses. Open daily from 10am to 5:30pm.

Pegasus Men's Store, 28 Princess St. ☎ **415/332-1718.**

Pegasus Men's Store offers ruggedly good-looking jackets in award-winning designs. The men's shop is where you'll find a fine selection of leather briefcases, belts, hats, boots, and wallets. Open daily from 10am to 5:30pm.

The Sausalito Country Store, 789 Bridgeway. ☎ **415/332-7890.**

This place sells oodles of wonderful handmade country-style goods. Many of these items—ceramic, stuffed, and painted-wood animals, aprons, baskets, embossed quilt prints, and lithographs—are made by local artists and artisans. Open daily from 10am to 6pm.

Stoneflower Gallery, 795 Bridgeway. ☎ **415/332-2995.**

The shop specializes in wood, ceramics, and unusual hand-crafted creations with a somewhat ethnic flair. The Stoneflower carries artwork from major American and international artists. Open daily from 10am to 6pm.

Village Fair, 777 Bridgeway.

This is Sausalito's closest approximation to a mall. It's a fascinating complex of 30 shops, souvenir stores, coffee bars, and gardens. Leaning against the hillside and spilling over in all directions from what used to be an old warehouse, Village Fair is almost a community unto itself, and could occupy an afternoon's exploring. **Quest Gallery** (☎ **415/332-6832**) features fine ceramics, whimsical chess sets, contemporary glass, hand-painted silks, woven clothing, art jewelry, and graphics. The shop specializes in the works of celebrated California artists; many of these artists sell exclusively through this store.

Most shops are open daily from 10am to 6pm; restaurants stay open later.

WHERE TO STAY

Casa Madrona, 801 Bridgeway, Sausalito, CA 94965. ☎ **415/332-0502,** or toll free **800/288-0502.** Fax 415/332-2537. 34 rms, 1 suite. MINIBAR TEL **Ferry:** Walk across the street from the landing. **Directions:** From U.S. 101 north, take the first right after the Golden Gate Bridge (Alexander exit); Alexander becomes Bridgeway in Sausalito.

Rates: $105–$225 single or double, $370 Madrona Villa suite. Extra person $10. Two-night minimum stay on weekends. AE, MC, V. **Parking:** $5.

Sooner or later most visitors to Sausalito look up and wonder at the ornate mansion on the hill. It's part of Casa Madrona, a hideaway-by-the-bay built in 1885 by a wealthy lumber baron. The epitome of luxury in its day, the mansion slipped, with the passage of time, into decay. It was saved by a Frenchman, Henri Deschamps, who converted it into a hotel and restaurant. Successive renovations and additions have included a rambling New England–style building that was added to the hillside below the main house. Now a certified historic landmark, the hotel offers rooms, suites, and cottages. The 16 newest units are each uniquely decorated by different local designers. The "1,000 Cranes" is Asian in theme, with lots of ash and lacquer. "Artist's Loft" is reminiscent of a rustic Parisian artist's studio, complete with easel, brushes, and paint. "Summer House" is decked out in white wicker, and "Chateau Charmant" evokes the genteel French countryside. Up in the mansion, the rooms are also decorated in a variety of styles. Amenities include quilts and baskets of luxury shampoos, soaps, and bath gels in the bathroom; some even have Jacuzzis. Other rooms have a fireplace. The newest rooms are located on the water, with panoramic views of the San Francisco skyline and bay.

The Casa Madrona Restaurant (☎ **415/331-5888**), offering breathtaking views of the bay, serves contemporary American cuisine. It's open for lunch Monday through Friday, for Sunday brunch 10am to 2:30pm, and for dinner nightly. A meal will cost $30 to $40 without wine.

WHERE TO DINE

Feng Hian Chinese Restaurant, 2650 Bridgeway. ☎ **415/331-5300.**

Cuisine: CHINESE. **Reservations:** Accepted. **Directions:** From U.S. 101 north, take the first right after the Golden Gate Bridge (Alexander exit); Alexander becomes Bridgeway in Sausalito. The restaurant is located near the intersection of Bridgeway and Harbor Drive, before downtown Sausalito.

Prices: Appetizers $4–$6.50; main courses $6–$13; lunch specials $4–$5.50. AE, DC, MC, V.

Open: Mon and Wed–Fri 11:30am–9:30pm, Sat 11:30am–10pm, Sun noon–9:30pm.

Some of the best and most interesting Chinese food outside of San Francisco proper is served in this pretty restaurant with an orange awning, at the south end of a small mall.

Feng Nian has such a wide selection of appetizers that a combination of several would make a delicious meal in itself. The crispy roast duck is a personal preference, but if you'd like an assortment, try the flaming combination (enough for two) that includes egg roll, fried prawn, paper-wrapped chicken, barbecued ribs, fried chicken, and teriyaki ($9.50). There are nine soups, including a sizzling rice soup with sliced chicken, prawns, mushrooms, and snow peas on a golden rice crust; or go for broke and order a truly exceptional, rich crabmeat/shark's-fin soup with shredded crab-leg meat.

Choosing one of the chef's suggestions isn't easy. The Peking duck requires about a half hour of patience before it arrives, but it's always superb. If you especially enjoy seafood, try the Twice Sizzling Seafood with prawns, scallops, squid, and fresh vegetables in oyster sauce; it's prepared at your table. Beef dishes are prepared in almost every conceivable manner: Mongolian, Szechuan, Hunan, Mandarin; with ginger, curry, and broccoli—just to name a few of the choices. The restaurant offers over 90 main dishes, including a select number of main courses for vegetarians.

Guernica, 2009 Bridgeway. ☎ **415/332-1512.**

Cuisine: FRENCH/BASQUE. **Reservations:** Recommended. **Directions:** From U.S. 101 north, take the first right after the Golden Gate Bridge (Alexander exit): Alexander becomes Bridgeway in Sausalito.

Prices: Appetizers $2.50–$6.50; main courses $10–$18. AE, MC, V.

French-Basque proprietor Roger Minhondo runs this terrific restaurant with a firm but friendly hand. The atmosphere is homey; Roger greets regulars by name and welcomes first-timers with a smile. In its decade of operation, Guernica has developed quite a large following, both in Sausalito and in San Francisco. The small dining room is tastefully decorated, with walls of stone, brick, wood, and white stucco, large wood-and-leatherette booths, and white-clothed tables with flowers and candles. On one wall there's a large print of Picasso's *Guernica.* Classical music plays softly in the background.

Begin with an appetizer of artichoke hearts or escargots. Some of the main courses from which you can choose are grilled rabbit with devil sauce, the daily fresh fish special, paella, and medallions of veal with mustard sauce. Terrific desserts include such in-season specialties as strawberry tarte and peach Melba.

Horizons, 558 Bridgeway, Sausalito. ☎ **415/331-3232.**

Cuisine: SEAFOOD/AMERICAN. **Reservations:** Accepted weekdays only.
Prices: Appetizers $3–$10; main courses $9–$14; salads and sandwiches $4–$10. AE, MC, V.
Open: Mon–Fri 11am–10pm, Fri–Sat 10am–10pm.

Everybody goes to Horizons for the view. On warm days you can sit out on the wooden waterside terrace and watch dreamy sailboats glide past San Francisco's toylike skyline. The heavily varnished clunky built-in furnishings inside are hardly as inviting. The food here can't touch the view, but it's pretty good. Seafood dishes are the main bills of fare, and include steamed clams and mussels, and fresh shucked oysters. Almond chicken, Dungeness crab, and bay shrimp lead a long list of salads, and lunchtime sandwiches are filled with chicken or turkey breast. Dinners are heartier, and include tiger prawns sautéed in basil-sherry cream sauce, chicken dijon, and a variety of pastas.

In fine Marin tradition, Horizons has an herb tea bar, and is a totally nonsmoking restaurant.

Scoma's, 588 Bridgeway. ☎ **415/332-9551.**

Cuisine: ITALIAN/SEAFOOD. **Reservations:** Not accepted. **Ferry:** Walk 5 minutes south from the landing. **Directions:** From U.S. 101 north, take the first right after the Golden Gate Bridge (Alexander exit); Alexander becomes Bridgeway in Sausalito.
Prices: Appetizers $6–$8, main courses $10–$26. AE, CB, DC, MC, V.
Open: Thurs–Mon 11:30am–10pm, Tues–Wed 5:30–10pm.

Scoma's is yet another one of Sausalito's attractive, right-on-the-bay eateries. Boxes of geraniums line the entranceway, and the interior is beautifully finished with gray wood-paneled walls and select antique furnishings. A scrumptious cioppino and linguine with clam sauce are among the Italian-style seafood dishes at this charming establishment. A la carte main courses usually come with a vegetable and pasta or rice.

The Spinnaker, 100 Spinnaker Dr. ☎ **415/332-1500.**

Cuisine: AMERICAN. **Reservations:** Accepted. **Ferry:** Walk from the landing. **Directions:** From U.S. 101 north, take the first right after the Golden Gate Bridge (Alexander exit); Alexander becomes Bridgeway in Sausalito. The restaurant is located just off Bridgeway, near the ferry landing.
Prices: Appetizers $3–$6, main courses $7–$14, fixed-price dinner $12–$20. AE, CB, DC, MC, V.
Open: Daily 11am–11pm.

The food at the Spinnaker is almost as great as the superb panoramic view of the bay. The restaurant itself actually projects out onto the bay, and diners sit on comfortable tufted banquettes facing 14-foot-high picture windows overlooking the water.

Fir-trunk columns add a warm natural nautical air. Main courses include the likes of rex sole meunière, New York steak, and scallops sauté. A good selection of chicken, pasta, and veal dishes is also available.

Picnic Fare

There are picnic areas and benches all along Bridgeway, offering superb views of the bay. On a nice day, picnicking beats a restaurant meal hands-down.

The Stuffed Croissant Etc., 43 Caledonia St. ☎ **415/332-7103.**

The most notable shop on Caledonia, in my hungry opinion, is the Stuffed Croissant, where you can get anything from a nosh to a meal. There are all sorts of gourmet sandwich croissants filled with almond-chicken salad or a scrumptious roast-beef barbecue with garlic and onions, bagels, plus soups and stews of the day. Hot meals like chicken curry and Italian meatballs are also popular. For your sweet tooth there are croissants stuffed with fruits—strawberries and cream cheese, or apples, raisins, and cinnamon, as well as pain au chocolat—and a fantastic variety of delicious fresh muffins, like honey bran, pumpkin raisin, carrot pineapple, poppy seed, banana nut, and blueberry, as well as cakes, cookies, and gourmet homemade brownies. All these goodies are freshly baked, and cost a mere $1.50 to $4.50 each. There's always a variety of gourmet coffees brewing (including cappuccino and espresso), and juices, tea, and mineral waters are available.

Open: Mon–Wed 6:45am–9pm, Thurs–Sat 6:45am–10pm, Sun 7:30am–8pm.

Venice Gourmet Delicatessen, 625 Bridgeway. ☎ **415/332-3544.**

This place has all the makings for a superb picnic—wines, cheeses, fruits, stuffed vine leaves, mushroom-and-artichoke salad, quiche, delicious sandwiches made to order on sourdough bread, olives, and fresh-baked pastries.

Open: Daily 9am–6pm.

Muir Woods & Mount Tamalpais

20 miles N of San Francisco

GETTING THERE • By Car To get to Mount Tamalpais, drive across the Golden Gate Bridge and take the exit for Calif, 1/Mount Tamalpais. Follow the shoreline highway about 2½ miles and turn onto the Panoramic Highway. After about 5½ miles, turn onto Pantoll Road and continue for about a mile to Ridgecrest Boulevard. Ridgecrest winds to a parking lot below East Peak. From there, it's a 15-minute hike up to the top.

To get to Muir Woods, follow the Mount Tamalpais directions to the Panoramic Highway. After about a mile, take the signed turnoff and follow successive signs.

Also in Marin county, but in silent, majestic contrast to the bustle of Marin County's seacoast towns, lies one of America's most enchanting nature preserves. Mount Tamalpais is the great landmark of the country, its outline towering over the entire scenery. At its foot nestle the Muir Woods.

WHAT TO SEE & DO

Amid the quiet grandeur of the forest are the world-famous **California redwoods.** Although these magnificent trees have been successfully transplanted to five continents, their homeland is a 500-mile strip along the mountainous coast of southwestern Oregon and northern California, where they grow inland "as far as the fog flows"—about 30 miles.

The coast redwood, or *Sequoia sempervirens,* is the tallest tree in that section of the earth—the largest-known specimen towers 167.8 feet. It has an even-larger relative, the *Sequoiadendron giganteum* of California's Sierra Nevada, but the coastal variety is stunning enough. There is no other forest like it anywhere in the world—soaring like a wooden cathedral up to the sky while spreading over a lush green carpet of ferns underfoot.

You can drive the 2,600 feet to the top of Mount Tam, as the locals call it, or hike along one of two clearly marked trails (one gentle, the other fairly rough) to the summit. The mountain offers a special picnic camp and some wonderful forest trails undulating for miles beneath the spreading green canopy above. The redwoods range from months-old seedlings to 1,200-year-old elders that were fully grown when Charlemagne ruled France. And from the peak you get a 100-mile sweep in all directions, from the foothills of the Sierras to the western horizon.

What is known as Marin today, incidentally, was actually the first "New England." In June 1579, Sir Frances Drake sailed his sturdy *Golden Hind* into the bay named after him. One of his first acts was to order a "plate of brasse, fast nailed to a great and firm post," claiming his discovery for his tough and level-headed sovereign, Queen Elizabeth I of England. He then named the land "Nova Albion."

However, this turned out to be one of the rare historical instances when the English were unable to follow through on their exploration by occupation—they were too busy elsewhere on the globe. Instead, the Spaniards arrived two centuries later and made Marin part of their empire.

Larkspur

25 miles N of San Francisco

GETTING THERE • By Ferry The fleet of the **Golden Gate Ferry Service** (☎ **415/332-6600**) dashes back and forth between the San Francisco Ferry Building, at the foot of Market Street, and Larkspur. Boats make the trip in about 50 minutes and cost $2.50 each way for adults, $2 for young riders ages 6 to 12. On weekends, prices rise to $4 for adults and $3 for young riders. Seniors and physically disabled passengers ride for $1.85, kids 5 and under ride free.

• **By Car** Take U.S. 101 north to the Larkspur/Corte Madera turnoff, proceed west on Tamalpais Road, which turns into Magnolia Avenue, and you'll soon arrive in Larkspur.

North of the highly developed tourist towns of Tiburon and Sausalito, Marin County opens into vistas of housing developments and rolling hills. In places, the marshes of the upper bay can still be seen within a short distance of U.S. 101.

Does Larkspur look familiar? If so, it's probably because so many period movies have been shot here. A walk through the town reveals drugstores, banks, and other shops, unique only in that they have not changed in style since the 1930s. Just three blocks south of town is a delightful creekside shopping center painted daffodil yellow and grass green.

WHERE TO DINE

Lark Creek Inn, 234 Magnolia Ave. ☎ **415/924-7766.**

Cuisine: CALIFORNIAN. **Reservations:** Recommended. **Directions:** Take U.S. 101 north to the Larkspur/Corte Madera turnoff, proceed west on Tamalpais Road, which turns into Magnolia Avenue.
Prices: Appetizers $4–$8, main courses $13–$24. AE, MC, V.
Open: Lunch Mon–Fri 11:30am–2:30pm; dinner Mon–Thurs 5:30–10pm, Fri–Sat 5–10:30pm; Sun brunch 10am–1:30pm.

Okay, the real reason to visit Larkspur is to dine at the slightly snobbish Lark Creek Inn. On the banks of Lark Creek, just 20 minutes north of San Francisco, this charming American country restaurant was built as a private home in 1888. In 1989 it came into the hands of chef Bradley Ogden, formerly of the Campton Place Hotel restaurant in San Francisco, and his partner, Michael Dellar. Here, chef Ogden has created a menu of old and new classics well suited to this magnificent setting among the redwoods.

The menu varies seasonally, but you'll find great dishes, such as red garlic and potato soup with turnip greens and croutons, or air-dried beef with roasted artichoke salad, to start off your meal, perhaps followed by citrus-basted sand dabs (my very favorite) with sweet-potato chips, homemade ravioli with shredded ham hocks and Swiss chard, or perhaps a spit-roasted free-range chicken from the restaurant's wood-burning brick oven. Desserts are equally delicious—try one of the many homemade ice creams or the old-fashioned banana cake. The restaurant's wine list features more than 100 moderately priced American wines—from Napa Valley to New York State vineyards.

Point Reyes National Seashore

35 miles N of San Francisco

GETTING THERE • By Car From San Francisco, cross the Golden Gate Bridge and stay on U.S. 101 north. Shortly before Corte Madera, turn left onto Sir Francis Drake Boulevard and drive 20 miles to Bear Valley Road. The information center is half a mile down Bear Valley Road. To get to the lighthouse, return to Sir Francis Drake Boulevard and continue to its end at a parking lot. The lighthouse is a half-mile walk down a paved road.

ESSENTIALS This 65,000-acre park encompasses several surf-pounded beaches, beautiful bird estuaries, and open swaths of land with roaming elk. Before you leave for the lighthouse, call the Visitor Center (☎ **415/669-1534**) for a weather and whale-activity report.

This remarkable, beautiful stretch of shoreline is located about an hour's drive from San Francisco. Comprised primarily of sand beach and scrubland, it's home to birds, sea lions, and a variety of tidepool creatures.

WHAT TO SEE & DO

There are three distinct areas of interest that you can visit.

Point Reyes Beach faces the Pacific and withstands the full brunt of ocean tides and winds—so much so that the water is much too rough for swimming, surfing, or even wading. It's a wild, tormented, and moody place to walk, and not one that you'll soon forget.

Drake's Beach, along the south coast, evokes different feelings entirely. The waters here are as tranquil and serene as Point Reyes's waters are turbulent. Drake's Beach was named for the English explorer who landed here. Locals come here to sun and picnic; occasionally a hearty soul ventures into the quiet but cold waters of Drake's Bay.

The main road of the park, Sir Francis Drake Boulevard, which passes by Point Reyes Beach and branches off to reach Drake's Beach, leads right out to Point Reyes itself. The **Point Reyes Lighthouse** juts out almost 15 miles from the mainland and is one of the best places on the West Coast to watch for whales. Gray whales pass by the point as they migrate between Alaska and the lagoons of Baja California. The annual round-trip encompasses 10,000 miles and represents one of the longest mammal migrations known. The whales head south in December and January, and return north in March. The last group of migrators are mothers swimming with their newborn calves.

If you plan to drive out to the lighthouse to whale watch, be sure to arrive early since there's a limited amount of parking space. If possible, come on a weekday. If you come on a weekend or holiday, it's wise to park at the Drake's Beach Visitor Center and take the free shuttle bus to the lighthouse. Be sure to dress warmly—it's often quite cold and windy. Also, bring binoculars if you have any.

But whale watching, as spectacular as it is, is not the only interesting activity the Point Reyes National Seashore offers. There are excellent ranger-conducted tours: You can walk along the **Bear Valley Trail,** where you'll see the wildlife and inhabitants of the ocean's edge; get a good look at the birds and some of the very secretive waterfowl of Fivebrooks Pond; explore tidepools; view some of North America's most beautiful ducks in the wetlands of Limantour; hike to the promontory overlooking Chimney Rock to see the sea lions, harbor seals, and sea birds; or take a guided walk along the San Andreas fault to look at the site of the epicenter of the famous 1906 earthquake and learn about the regional geology. And this is just a sampling. Since available tours and their lengths vary seasonally, you can either call the ranger station (☎ **415/663-1092**), with pencil and paper handy, or ask to be sent a copy of *Park Paper*, which includes a schedule of activities and much other useful information. Many of the tours are suitable for the handicapped. Two important no-no's: pets are not permitted on any trails, and no swimming or wading is permitted at the outer Point Reyes beaches—surf and rip tides are extremely dangerous.

WHERE TO DINE

Station House Cafe, Main St., Point Reyes Station. ☎ **415/663-1515.**

Cuisine: AMERICAN. **Reservations:** Recommended.
Prices: Appetizers $4.50–$7; main courses $8.50–$15; breakfast $4–$6.50. MC, V.
Open: Sun–Thurs 8am–9pm, Fri–Sat 8am–10pm.

I don't know why sea air gives you an appetite, but when it does, treat yourself to the remarkable gastronomic glories of the Station House, located in the tiny town of Point Reyes Station. The cafe has a fireplace, an open kitchen, a full-service bar, live music on weekends, and a lovely garden for dining—in addition to superb food. For breakfast you might be offered bread pudding with stewed fruit compote, or frittata with asparagus, goat cheese, and olives. Regular omelets and Belgian waffles are also on offer. The lunch special might be fettuccine with fresh local mussels steamed in white wine and butter sauce, or two-cheese polenta served with fresh spinach sauté and grilled garlic-buttered tomato. Organically grown beef is always on the menu; it's raised locally and is of an exceptionally superior quality. Rounding out the delicious choices are homemade chili, steamed clams, fresh soup made daily, and fish and chips. The cafe has an extensive list of fine California wines, plus local and imported beers.

Marine World Africa USA

30 miles NE of San Francisco; 10 miles S of Napa

GETTING THERE • By Ferry The **Red and White Fleet** (☎ **415/546-2700** in San Francisco, or toll free **800/229-2784** in California) operates a high-speed catamaran service from Pier 41 at Fisherman's Wharf. The pretty cruise, passing Alcatraz and the Golden Gate Bridge, takes 55 minutes, including a brief bus ride. The round trip, including park admission, is $36 for adults, $30 for seniors 62 and over and students ages 13 to 18, and $20.50 for kids ages 4 to 12. Service is limited; call for departure times.

• **By Car** From San Francisco, take I-80 north to Calif. 37 and follow the signs to the park; it's less than an hour's drive.

WHAT TO SEE & DO

Marine World Africa USA, Marine World Pkwy. in Vallejo (☎ **707/643-ORCA** for a recording), is a kind of Disney-meets–Wild Kingdom theme park, where humans and animals perform for visitors. The park is the interesting conjunction of two distinct outfits: Marine World, which specializes in aquatic attractions, and Africa USA, which features trained animals of land and air in daily shows.

A variety of events are scheduled throughout the day. There's a Killer Whale and Dolphin Show, during which the front seven rows of seats are set aside for guests who don't mind getting a thorough drenching. In the Sea Lion Show you can pet some of the oldest and largest performers in the country. In Shark Experience, a moving walkway takes visitors through a clear acrylic tunnel that cuts through a 300,000-gallon tropical shark-filled tank.

When you cross the bridge over the waterfall, heading through the trees and past the flamingos, you enter **Africa USA.** Here you'll find Elephant Encounter, where guests can interact with the park's 11 Asian and African elephants. In addition to shows, rides are offered, costing $3 per person. At Tiger Island, a habitat for the park's hand-raised Bengal tigers, you can see trainers and tigers playing and swimming together. An informative show about the park's exotic and endangered animals is performed in the **Wildlife Theater.**

The Bird Show is one of the park's best, and proves that the avian performers' peanut-sized brains are capable of more than we think! There's also an enclosed Butterfly World and a Small Animal Petting Kraal (with llamas); both are particularly popular with kids. Even better is Gentle Jungle, a unique playground that combines education, fun, and adventure. It's one of the most innovative play areas of its type. Inside the Prairie Crawl, children can crawl through burrows in the prairie dog village and pop up into Plexiglas domes so they can see the world as these cute little animals view it.

And finally there's a 55-acre lake that is the stage for a waterski and boat show April through October. Daredevil athletes jump, spin, and even perform a human pyramid while wearing waterskis.

A wide variety of fast food is available at Lakeside Plaza—everything from burgers and sandwiches to nachos and chicken. Prices are moderate, averaging about $6 to $7 for a light bite. A sit-down restaurant completes the food choices. Or you can bring your own picnic—there are barbecue facilities on the grounds. The best way to cope with the full schedule of shows is to get there early, make up your own itinerary from the leaflet and map given to you at the entrance—and then stick to it. Otherwise, you'll find yourself missing parts of each presentation and feeling frustrated.

Admission is $24.95 for adults, $16.95 for kids 4 to 12 and $19.95 for seniors over 60, free for children under 4. CB, DC, MC, and V are accepted. The park is open from Memorial Day through Labor Day, daily from 9:30am to 6pm; the rest of the year, Wednesday through Sunday from 9:30am to 5:30pm.

San Jose

48 miles S of San Francisco

GETTING THERE • By Car From San Francisco, follow U.S. 101 south for almost 50 miles and turn left onto Santa Clara Street. This main thoroughfare runs through the heart of downtown.

ESSENTIALS • Orientation San Jose sits in the center of a relatively flat valley, its center surrounded by a triangle of freeways: U.S. 101 to the east, U.S. 880 to the west, and U.S. 280 to the south. The main "downtown" commercial district is laid out in a grid pattern and is centered at First Street and Santa Clara Street.

• Information The San Jose Convention and Visitors Bureau, 333 W. San Carlos St., Suite 1000, San Jose, CA 95110 (☎ **408/283-8833**), offers general and specialized information on the city. Their free **Visitors Guide** spotlights local shops, sights, dining, lodging, and entertainment.

• Transportation Restored turn-of-the-century streetcars run a circular route on downtown tracks, drawing electrical power from overhead lines. They offer a fun, inexpensive way to familiarize yourself with the city. Streetcars run Monday through Friday from 9am to 3:30pm, and Saturday and Sunday from 11am to 6pm; they run every 20 minutes up First Street and down Second Street, between Devine and San Carlos Streets. Fares are 25¢ for adults and 10¢ for young ones ages 5 to 17 and seniors 65 and older.

San Jose was California's state capital between 1849 and 1851. Today the city, along with the surrounding Santa Clara Valley—popularly known as Silicon Valley—is home to one of the world's largest concentrations of electronic and microchip technology firms. It is also California's third-largest city, after Los Angeles and San Diego. A lot has changed here since Burt Bacharach immortalized this town with the musical question: "Do you know the way to San Jose?"

Silicon Valley and San Jose's most dramatic growth occurred during the late 1960s and early 1970s when new electronics firms seemed to spring up overnight. The county's population grew fourfold, and low concrete buildings soon overran the valley's orchards. San Jose is now primarily a manufacturing city, but there are several top sightseeing attractions that make a stop in Silicon Valley's capital worthwhile.

WHAT TO SEE & DO

Winchester Mystery House, 525 S. Winchester Blvd. ☎ **408/247-2101.**

Begun in 1884, the Winchester Mystery House is the legacy of Sarah L. Winchester, widow of the son of the famous rifle magnate. After the deaths of her husband and baby daughter, Mrs. Winchester became convinced that continuous building would appease the evil spirits of those killed with Winchester repeaters. The widow used much of her $20-million inheritance to finance the construction, which continued 24 hours a day, 7 days a week, 365 days a year, for 38 years. Now known as the Winchester Mystery House, this structure is a testament to one woman's madness. It is immediately apparent that this is no ordinary home. The red-roofed, stylized Victorian mansion contains 160 rooms and sprawls across a half-dozen acres. But more amazing than its size are the mansion's eccentric peculiarities; staircases lead to nowhere, a chimney rises four floors to stop just before reaching the ceiling, doors open onto blank walls, and a window is built into the floor. Such schemes were designed to confound the spirits that seemed to endlessly haunt the heiress. Mrs. Winchester's occult beliefs are also evident by her obsession with the number 13: There are 13 bathrooms, 13 windows and doors in the old sewing room, 13 palms lining the main driveway, 13 hooks in the seance room, and 13 lights in the chandeliers—just to give a few examples.

The house is filled with the usual treasures contained within an extraordinary mansion, including exquisite gold chandeliers, silver and bronze inlaid doors, Tiffany stained-glass windows, intricate parquet floors, Japanese tiled mantels, and the like. Several rooms have been restored and furnished with period pieces. Admission includes a tour of the manicured gardens and entrance to the Winchester Historic Firearms and Antique Products Museums, which holds, in addition to a large collection of Winchesters and many other rifles, displays featuring other items made by the Winchester company in the early 1900s—knives, roller skates, fishing tackle, tools, flashlights, and the like.

Admission: $12.50 adults, $9.50 seniors 60 and older, $6.50 children ages 6–12, free for children under 6.

Tours: Summer daily 9am–5:30pm; spring–fall daily 9am–4:30pm; winter daily 9am–4pm. **Directions:** From San Francisco, take U.S. 101 south to U.S. 880, exit west onto Stevens Creek Boulevard, and after 1 mile turn left onto Winchester Boulevard. The Mystery House is straight ahead on your left.

Rosicrucian Park, 1342 Naglee Ave. ☎ **406/947-3636.**

California is full of unique and unusual sights, and this is one of them. Owned and operated by the Rosicrucian Order, an ancient order claiming Egyptian roots, this large complex encompasses several entities. The order's imposing **administration building** is an architectural copy of Egypt's Great Temple of Rameses III. The **Egyptian Museum** houses the largest collection of ancient Egyptian, Babylonian, Assyrian, and Sumerian artifacts on exhibit on the west coast. Thousands of original antiquities are on display, including statuary, textiles, jewelry, and paintings, as well as a variety of mummies—both animal and human—and a full-size reproduction of an Egyptian limestone tomb. The adjacent **Contemporary Art Gallery** exhibits an eclectic variety of multimedia works, with emphasis on emerging and local artists. An on-site **planetarium (408/947-3634)** offers regular star shows that emphasize both the scientific and cultural aspects of astronomy. Currently under development, the park's **Science Center** features exhibits on earth and space sciences. The center's "Geological Gems" displays quartz gemstones, and crystals. The "Earth's Geophysical Weather Report," which is on permanent display, includes a seismograph station that reports on earthquakes detected from Loma Prieta, and a National Oceanic and Atmospheric satellite data station, which reports on the earth's geomagnetic field and solar activities that affect our home planet.

Admission: Egyptian Museum and Contemporary Art Gallery: $6 for adults, $4 for students and seniors over 65, $3.50 for children aged 7–15, children under 7 enter free. Planetarium: $4 adults, $3.50 seniors over 65, $3 children aged 7–15, under 7 enter free. Science Center: free.

Open: Museums, daily 9am–5pm; Planetarium, varies (call for exact show times). **Directions:** From San Francisco take U.S. 101 south to I-880, then take the Alameda/ Santa Clara exit and turn south (left) onto The Alameda. After about five blocks, turn right on Naglee Avenue; Rosicrucian Park is four blocks ahead on your left, at the corner of Park Avenue.

San Jose Historical Museum, 1600 Senter Rd. ☎ **408/287-2290.**

Located inside Kelley Park, the city's prettiest green, this 25-acre outdoor museum is a re-creation of the city as it existed near the close of the 19th century. Over 26 buildings and structures include restored homes, stables, a firehouse, a bank, a print shop, and a trolley barn. The imposing 115-foot Electric Light Tower stands in the center of the museum and is surrounded by original and faithfully reproduced Victorian buildings.

Admission: $4 adults, $3 seniors 65 and over, $2 children ages 6–17.

Open: Mon–Fri 10am–4:30pm, Sat–Sun noon–4:30pm. **Directions:** From San Francisco, take U.S. 101 south to Story Road west; after 1 mile, turn left onto Senter Road. The museum entrance is on your left.

The Tech Museum of Innovation, 145 West San Carlos St. ☎ **408/279-7150.**

This "hands-on" museum represents the initial phase of a major science and technology museum and center that's slated for completion by the mid-1990s. The Tech introduces visitors to a world of evolving technology and engages you with high-tech interactive exhibits. In the "clean room," a million transistors are fitted onto a computer chip. Using computers, visitors can design an aerodynamic bicycle, and solve a mystery using DNA "fingerprints." The Materials Bar features fabric that can stop a speeding bullet, a ceramic knife that is sharper than a metal one, and a plastic that conducts electricity.

Admission: $6 adults, $4 children ages 6–18 and seniors 65 and older, under 6 free.

Open: Tues–Sun 10am–5pm. **Directions:** From San Francisco, take U.S. 101 south to Calif. 87 south, exit east (left) onto West San Carlos Street. The Tech is 3 blocks ahead on your left across from the Convention Center.

Children's Discovery Museum, 180 Woz Way, Guadalupe River Park. ☎ **408/298-5437.**

Opened in June 1990, this fanciful facility encourages visitors to touch, smell, talk, listen, and use their imaginations in a dynamic display of scientific humanistic and technological exhibits. And although this is reputedly the largest children's museum in the west, it's not just for kids. Innovative interactive activities are both fun and informative.

Admission: $6 adults, $4 children ages 4–18, $5 seniors 65 and older.

Open: Tues–Sat 10am–5pm, Sun noon–5pm. **Directions:** From U.S. 101 south, exit onto Santa Clara Street. After driving through the downtown district, turn left on Almaden Boulevard, and take the fifth right onto Woz Way.

Santa Cruz

74 miles S of San Francisco

GETTING THERE • By Bus Greyhound buses from San Francisco stop four times daily at Santa Cruz Terminal, 425 Front St. (☎ **408/423-1800**).

• By Car The fastest way from San Francisco is to take U.S. 101 south to Calif. 17, a 90-minute drive. The most scenic route is via Calif. 1, the beautiful coastal highway that hugs the ocean right into the city center. It takes about two hours, depending on traffic.

ESSENTIALS • Orientation Located two blocks west of the sluggish San Lorenzo River, the town's primary commercial center straddles Pacific Avenue, and the streets that surround it. The Pacific Garden Mall, a central, landscaped pedestrian stretch of Pacific Avenue is packed with upscale strollers, ancient homeless hippies, and a good cross-section of assorted others. The Santa Cruz Municipal Wharf, and its attendant boardwalk, are located about a half-mile south of the mall, and together make up the main tourist areas.

INFORMATION The Santa Cruz County Conference and Visitors Council, 701 Front St. (☎ **408/425-1234,** or toll free **800/833-3494**), has general and specialized information on the entire Greater Santa Cruz area. An information booth on Ocean Street, between Water and Soquel Streets, is open during summer months only.

Santa Cruz is a study in contrasts. Known for its 1960s liberalism and immortal hippie culture, the city is appropriately packed with Summer of Love holdouts and dropouts, as well as modern-day children of Flower Children, occultists, and alternative religion followers. But not everyone here wears tie-dyed clothing and eats whole grains out of hand-thrown earthenware bowls. Santa Cruz is also a conservative farming community, and, despite the city's progressive politics, there are plenty of locals who wouldn't be out of place at a rodeo in California's Central Valley or at a monster truck pull in America's heartland.

Although most of the rubble has been cleared, Santa Cruz is still rebuilding from the October 1989 earthquake that was centered nearby. Thankfully, few people were injured, and most of the town's visitor attractions, restaurants, and accommodations were unhurt.

WHAT TO SEE & DO

Santa Cruz Boardwalk, 400 Beach St. ☎ **408/423-5590.**

The city's old-fashioned Boardwalk is the hub of beach activities from May to mid-September and weekends throughout the year. Visitors and locals spend entire days digging their toes into the sand, surfing, sunbathing, and swimming. But the Boardwalk is more than a beach. It's an amusement park with over 25 rides, including a roller coaster, log flume, haunted castle, bumper cars, and a beautiful, hand-carved merry-go-round. There are two big penny arcades, miniature golf, and, of course, food concessions where you can buy hot dogs, corn on the cob, cotton candy, and other health foods.

Santa Cruz Municipal Wharf. ☎ **408/429-3628.**

A short ramble west along the Boardwalk will soon put you at the foot of Municipal Wharf, a fisherman's pier with picturesque shops, fish markets, and seafood restaurants. You can bring your own tackle or rent it here at the bait shop, and then fish off the wharf or in a rented boat. Deep-sea fishing trips depart daily from here from about February 1 to November 15, and on weekends during December and January, weather permitting.

Nearby Attractions

The Mystery Spot, 1953 Branciforte Dr. ☎ **408/423-8897.**

Situated in a redwood forest 2½ miles north of Santa Cruz is a 150-foot section of woodlands where the laws of physics are seemingly not enforced. Wildlife avoids the area and birds will not nest here. Trees grow aslant and instruments on planes flying overhead go dead. Strangely, when climbing uphill you'll find that you're walking as straight-legged as you would on level ground. The cause of such peculiarities puzzles some scientists: perhaps a meteor, minerals, or a magnet is buried deep underground, exerting a magnetic force or distorting the sun's rays. But it's more fun to believe that it's all due to some mysterious, unexplainable "force." Excellent guided tours include a series of demonstrations that exhibit the unusual properties of this spot. A ball set down on a slanted plank apparently rolls uphill (skeptics can place the ball themselves or try another object like a lipstick). And in one of the most amazing demonstrations, the guide places two people on either side of a level block (tested with a carpenter's level) and one appears to shrink while the other seems to grow. Remember, if you do go, wear rubber-soled shoes.

Admission: $3 adults, $1.50 children ages 5–11.

Open: Daily 9:30am–5pm.

Roaring Camp and Big Trees Narrow-Gauge Railroad, Graham Hill Rd., near Felton. ☎ **408/335-4484.**

Nestled in the Santa Cruz Mountains off Calif. 17, the railroad is America's last steam-powered passenger train and a colorful reminder of Gold Rush days. Scheduled runs, using authentic 1880 and 1890 equipment, make a magnificent round-trip journey through towering redwood forests.

The 6½-mile, 75-minute tour chugs past quaint unused stations to the summit of Bear Mountain. Passengers may leave the train to hike or picnic, and return on a later train. On spring, summer, and fall weekends there's lively country music on board. You can take this delightful ride any day during summer, and on weekends and holidays the rest of the year.

Round-trip Fare: $12 adults, $8.75 children ages 3–15, under 3 free.

Departures: Summer, daily every 75 minutes from 11am–4pm; Nov–Dec Mon–Fri at noon, Sat–Sun and hols at noon, 1:30pm, and 3pm; Jan–Mar Wed–Fri at noon, Sat–Sun and hols at noon, 1:30pm, and 3pm. **Directions:** From downtown Santa Cruz, take Calif. 17 to the Mt. Hermon/Glen Canyon exit; after 3½ miles, turn left onto Graham Hill Road. Roaring Camp is a half mile on your right.

Shopping

Pacific Garden Mall, Santa Cruz's primary commercial thoroughfare, is an auto-free shopping plaza right in the heart of town. A free shuttle operates between Santa Cruz beach and the mall, in summer daily every 20 minutes from 10am to 7pm. You can walk it, too—a short hike along Pacific Avenue. In addition to hosting a wide variety of shops and restaurants, the mall provides space for frequent craft fairs and festivities and is well worth exploring.

WHERE TO DINE

Municipal Wharf restaurants run the gamut from snack to banquet. If you're not in the mood for something fancy, you can stop in at any one of numerous shops and snack bars here for a light bite.

Gilbert's, Municipal Wharf. ☎ **408/423-5200.**

Cuisine: SEAFOOD. **Reservations:** Accepted. **Directions:** From Calif. 1 south, turn west (right) on Bay Street, and follow the signs to the pier.

Prices: Appetizers $4–$7; main courses $10–$22. AE, DC, DISC, MC, V.
Open: Sun–Thurs 11:30am–9pm, Fri–Sat 11:30am–10pm.

Gilbert's overlooks the water and serves seasonally fresh seafood in a friendly atmosphere. It's a pretty place, with plank-wood walls and ceilings, but a bit pricey—you pay for the view. The food is good, though, and the service is friendly.

Miramar, Municipal Wharf. ☎ **408/423-4441.**

Cuisine: SEAFOOD. **Reservations:** Accepted. **Directions:** From Calif. 1 south, turn west (right) on Bay Street, and follow the signs to the pier.
Prices: Appetizers $4–$7; lunch main courses $7–$9; dinner main courses $11–$14. AE, CB, DC, DISC, MC, V.
Open: Tues–Fri lunch 11:30am–4pm; dinner Tues–Sat 4:30–9:30pm; Sun 10:30am–9:30pm.

Open since 1945, this wharf restaurant is fancier than most, with green wall-to-wall carpeting and large windows overlooking Monterey Bay. The menu is heavy on seafood, with such appetizers as fried calamari, shrimp cocktail, steamed clams, and oysters on the half shell. Grilled or broiled fish is the house specialty; and whether it's salmon, snapper, or sole, it's topped with lemon butter, dijonnaise, or another good sauce.

5 The Wine Country

CALIFORNIA'S ADJACENT NAPA AND SONOMA VALLEYS ARE TWO OF THE MOST FAMOUS wine-growing regions in the world. Hundreds of wineries nestle amongst the vines, and most are open to visitors. But Napa and Sonoma are more than wine and beautiful countryside. The workaday valleys that are a way of life for thousands of vintners are also a worthy must-see for any wine-lover and a downright good time for any traveler with a curious sense of adventure. Even if you can only visit California's celebrated wine country as a day trip from San Francisco, it's well worth the extended drive.

SEEING THE WINE COUNTRY

Like the rest of California, Wine Country is car country; best toured by automobile. Conveniently, most of the large wineries are located along a single road, California 29, which starts at the mouth of the Napa River, near the north end of San Francisco Bay, and continues north to Calistoga to the top of the growing region. With the exception of Sonoma, located due west of the Napa Valley, every town and winery listed here can be reached from Calif. 29. The Napa Valley wineries and towns listed below are organized geographically, from south to north, along Calif. 29, beginning in Napa village.

1 Napa County

55 miles N of San Francisco

GETTING THERE • **By Car** From San Francisco, cross the Golden Gate Bridge and continue north on U.S. 101. Turn east on Calif. 37, then north on Calif. 29. This road is the main thoroughfare through the Wine Country.

ESSENTIALS • **Orientation** Calif. 29 runs the length of Napa Valley, which is just 35 miles long. You really can't get lost—there's just one north-south road on which most of the wineries, hotels, shops, and restaurants are located. Towns are small and easy to negotiate. Any local can give you directions.

• **Information** For a detailed description of the following and many other wineries, pick up free wine country maps and brochures, from the Wine Institute at 425 Market St., Suite 1000, San Francisco, CA 94105 (☎ **415/512-0151**). Once in the Napa Valley, make your first stop the Napa Chamber of Commerce, 1556 First St., in downtown Napa (☎ **707/226-7455**). They have information on the local vineyards, as well as listings of antiques dealers and walking tours. All over Napa and Sonoma, you can pick up a very informative—and free—weekly publication called *Wine Country Review.* It will give you the most up-to-date information on wineries and related area events.

Most of the delicious California wines you've been enjoying with your meals in San Francisco hail from a warm, narrow valley about a 90-minute drive from San Francisco. Napa Valley's fame began with Cabernet Sauvignon and, except for white Chardonnay, more acreage is devoted to the growth of this grape than any other. The valley is home to about 225 wineries and an exceptional selection of fine restaurants and hostelries at all price levels. If you can, plan on spending more than one day here, if you'd like to tour even a small segment of the valley and its wineries. The valley is just 35 miles long, so whether you stay in Napa, Yountville, Rutherford, or St. Helena, you can dine, wine, shop, and sightsee without traveling very far.

What's Special About the Wine Country

Winery Tours

- Artfully designed and impeccably run, many winery tours are as fine as a good bottle of wine.
- Informative talks on how wine is made and the characteristics of different varieties.

Beautiful Countryside

- Napa, Yountville, Oakville, and the other small towns of the Wine Country—both charming and elegant.
- Driving through the endless miles of verdant, fragrant vineyards.

Invigorating Spas

- Experiencing a restorative mud bath at Calistoga, a popular resort famed for its mineral waters.

Museums

- The Silverado Museum, in St. Helena, devoted to the life and works of Robert Louis Stevenson, who honeymooned here in 1880.

Historical Sights

- Bear Flag Monument, in Sonoma, marking spot where the Bear Flag was raised in 1846 to signal the end of Mexican rule.
- The estate of Mexican Gen. Mariano Guadalupe Vallejo, where settlers declared California's independence.

WHEN TO GO The beauty of the valley is striking any time of the year but is most memorable in September and October. This is when the grapes are being pressed, and the very air in the valley seems intoxicating. It's the time of the year when the rain in Napa has its own quiet, soft-spoken love affair with the hills, where the mists lie softly and lovingly. The colors are breathtaking as the vine leaves change to gold, rust brown, and deep maroon—all in preparation for the next season of grapes.

THE WINERIES

Most wineries offer tours daily from 10am to 5pm. And there's considerably more to them than merely open vineyards. Huge presses feed through an elaborate system of pipes into blending vats. From there, wines are mellowed gracefully in giant oak casks in the deep cellars. As you drive through the Napa Valley, you'll see nonstop welcoming signs put out by rows of wineries, most of which not only take visitors on conducted tours but also offer samples of their product, most of them free. Be careful—just a few visits can affect your driving in no uncertain manner.

Newlan Vineyards, 5225 Solano Ave., Napa, CA 94558. ☎ **707/257-2399.**

This small, family-owned winery produces only about 10,000 cases a year. It all started in 1967 when physicist Brunc Newlan planted 11 acres of Cabernet Sauvignon along Dry Creek. Three years later 16 more acres were planted, and in five years Bruce and his wife, Jonette, had a winery. Cabernet Sauvignon, Pinot Noir, Chardonnay, Zinfandel, and Late Harvest Johannisberg Riesling are estate bottled. Excellent tours are offered by appointment only.

Trefethen Vineyards, 1160 Oak Knoll Ave. (P.O. Box 2460), Napa, CA 94558. ☎ **707/255-7700.**

Tours are offered here by appointment only, and are well worth arranging. Listed on the National Register of Historical Places, Trefethen's main building was built in 1886 and remains Napa's only wooden, gravity-powered winery. The bucolic brick courtyard is surrounded with oak and cork trees. Unlike many of the region's wineries, which try to outdo one another with modernity, Trefethen embraces its history, displaying old farming tools and machines along with plaques explaining their functions. Although it is one of the region's granddaddies, Trefethen did not vinify its first case of Chardonnay until 1973; but since then it's been winning awards year after year. Tastings take place in Trefethen's brick-floored, jazz-filled tasting room, under a wood-beamed ceiling.

To reach Trefethen Vineyards from Calif. 29, take Oak Knoll Avenue east. The winery is ahead, on your left.

Open: Daily 10am–4:30pm.

Stag's Leap Wine Cellars, 5766 Silverado Trail, Napa, CA 94558. ☎ **707/944-2020.**

The man who has guided the destiny of this now-famous winery and attracted the attention of France's noted wine experts is Warren Winiarski. A hill hides the group of buildings at its foot that comprise Stag's Leap Wine Cellars. The first building of the group, which once housed the entire operation, now houses a summary exhibit of wine making from start to finish. Undoubtedly one of the best-known wines is the Cabernet Sauvignon Cask 23. Winiarski also offers good-value wines under the Hawk Crest label. You can taste selected current releases during sales hours for $3 per person.

Open: Sales and tasting daily 10am–4pm, tours by appointment only.

Domaine Chandon, California Drive, Yountville, CA 94599. ☎ **707/944-2280.**

Back on Calif. 29 at its intersection with California Drive, you'll find Domaine Chandon. The firm produces about 450,000 cases annually of method champenoise sparkling wines, Chandon Brut Cuvée, Carneros Blanc de Noirs, Chandon Réserve, and étoile. Founded in 1973, this is a California version of a champagne house. You can take a guided tour here to find out all about the making of sparkling wines. Wines are sold by the bottle or glass, and are accompanied by complimentary hors d'oeuvres. There's also a gift shop and a small gallery housing artifacts from the vineyard's parent company, Moët et Chandon, depicting the history of champagnes. The Domaine Chandon Restaurant is one of the best in the valley (see "Where to Dine" in "Yountville," below for complete information).

Open: Nov–Apr Wed–Sun 11am–6pm, May–Oct daily 11am–6pm.

Robert Mondavi Winery, 7801 St. Helena Hwy. (Calif. 29), Oakville, CA 94562. ☎ **707/963-9611.**

If you continue on Calif. 29 up to Oakville, you'll arrive at the Robert Mondavi Winery. This is the ultimate high-tech Napa Valley winery, housed in a magnificent mission-style facility. Almost every conceivable processing variable in their wine making is computer controlled—fascinating, especially if you've never watched the procedure before.

Reservations are recommended for the guided tour. It's wise to make them one to two weeks in advance, especially if you plan to go on a weekend. After the guided tour, you can taste the results of all this attention to detail with selected current wines. The Vineyard Room usually features an art show, and you'll find some exceptional antiques in the reception hall. During the summer the winery has some great outdoor jazz concerts.

Open: May–Oct, daily 9:30am–5:30pm; Nov–Apr, daily 9:30am–4:30pm.

Inglenook–Napa Valley Winery, 1991 St. Helena Hwy. (Calif. 29), Rutherford, CA 94573. ☎ **707/967-3362.**

Farther north on Calif. 29 (opposite Rutherford Cross Road) you will reach Rutherford and the Inglenook–Napa Valley Winery. Inglenook's history dates back to 1879, when the vineyards were bought by Gustave Niebaum. The original winery, designed and built by Captain McIntyre, the architect of several neighboring wineries, is now the tasting room and starting point for tours. You can taste current releases as well as older vintages during sales hours.

Open: Daily 10am–5pm.

Beaulieu Vineyard, 1960 St. Helena Hwy. (Calif. 29), Rutherford, CA 94573. ☎ **707/963-2411.**

A bit farther on from Inglenook is the Beaulieu Vineyard, founded by a Frenchman named Georges De Latour. The original winery looks as French baronial as a turn-of-the-century transplant can be. The winery is larger than when first built, but you can still see the complete tradition-oriented process of wine making from start to finish-beginning with the crusher, on to bottling, and then the tasting, the last step being yours.

Open: Daily 10am–5pm, tours daily 11am–3:30pm.

Flora Springs Wine Co., 1978 W. Zinfandel Lane, St. Helena, CA 94574. ☎ **707/963-5711.**

Flora Springs Wine Co. is at the end of West Zinfandel Lane, off Calif. 29. While this handsome stone winery dates back to Napa Valley's early days, the Flora Springs label first appeared in 1978. The current owners have vineyards throughout Napa Valley and select choice lots for their own label. They are especially known for their barrel-fermented Chardonnay, a Cabernet Sauvignon, and Trilogy, a Bordeaux-style blend.

Flora Springs offers an excellent two-hour "familiarization seminar," which almost everyone interested in wines would enjoy. And best of all, it's tailored to all levels of wine enthusiasts. Limited to groups of 10, the course is held on Saturdays at 10am. The program begins in the vineyards, where you'll see a good-growing vine and taste the grapes. While the grapes are being crushed, you taste the must (the just-pressed juice) and ultimately see how it becomes a beautiful, clear wine. Then you are taught how to evaluate wines: You'll blind-taste different ones and learn to distinguish between them, trying an older and a younger wine, for example, to see what happens with aging. You'll also learn to pair wines with different foods.

Open: By reservation only; call Fritz Draeger at **707/963-5711** or write to him at the above address.

Beringer Vineyards, 2000 Main St. (Calif. 29), St. Helena, CA 94574. ☎ **707/963-7115.**

Be sure to stop just north of St. Helena's business district at Beringer Vineyards if only to look at this remarkable Rhine House and view the hand-dug tunnels carved out of the mountainside, the site of the original winery.

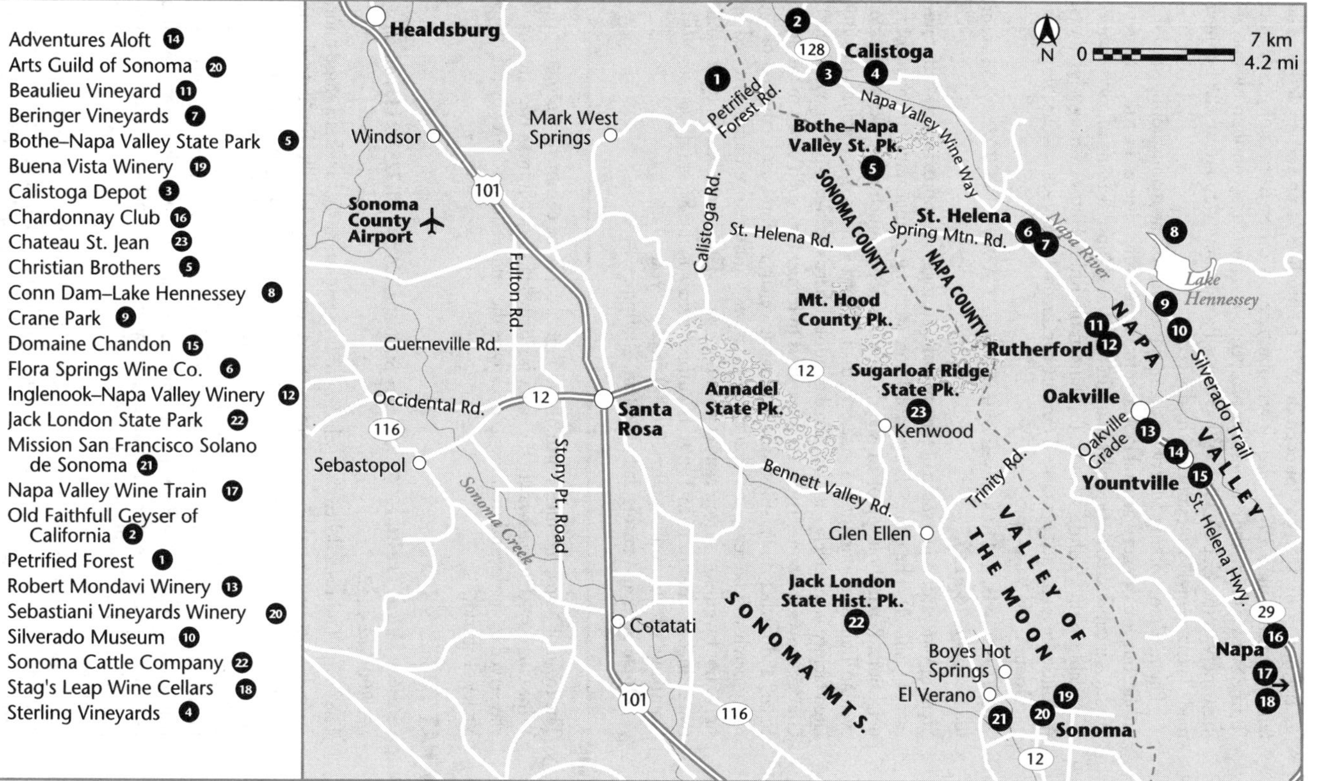
Adventures Aloft 14
Arts Guild of Sonoma 20
Beaulieu Vineyard 11
Beringer Vineyards 7
Bothe–Napa Valley State Park 5
Buena Vista Winery 19
Calistoga Depot 3
Chardonnay Club 16
Chateau St. Jean 23
Christian Brothers 5
Conn Dam–Lake Hennessey 8
Crane Park 9
Domaine Chandon 15
Flora Springs Wine Co. 6
Inglenook–Napa Valley Winery 12
Jack London State Park 22
Mission San Francisco Solano de Sonoma 21
Napa Valley Wine Train 17
Old Faithfull Geyser of California 2
Petrified Forest 1
Robert Mondavi Winery 13
Sebastiani Vineyards Winery 20
Silverado Museum 10
Sonoma Cattle Company 22
Stag's Leap Wine Cellars 18
Sterling Vineyards 4
Healdsburg
Windsor
Mark West Springs
Sonoma County Airport
101
Fulton Rd.
Guerneville Rd.
Occidental Rd.
12
116
Sebastopol
Sonoma Creek
Stony Pt. Road
Santa Rosa
Cotatati
Calistoga Rd.
Petrified Forest Rd.
128
Calistoga
Napa Valley Wine Way
Bothe–Napa Valley St. Pk.
St. Helena Rd.
SONOMA COUNTY
NAPA COUNTY
St. Helena
Spring Mtn. Rd.
Napa River
Lake Hennessey
Mt. Hood County Pk.
Annadel State Pk.
Sugarloaf Ridge State Pk.
Kenwood
Rutherford
NAPA VALLEY
Silverado Trail
Oakville
Oakville Grade
Yountville
St. Helena Hwy.
29
Napa
Bennett Valley Rd.
Trinity Rd.
VALLEY OF THE MOON
Glen Ellen
Jack London State Hist. Pk.
SONOMA MTS.
Boyes Hot Springs
El Verano
Sonoma
7 km
4.2 mi
N

The Wine Country

Beringer Vineyards was founded in 1876 by brothers Jacob and Frederick. The family owned it until 1971, when it was purchased by the Swiss firm of Nestlé, Inc. In true Swiss fashion, the business has prospered. It is the oldest continuously operating winery in the Napa Valley. "What about Prohibition?" you might ask. Beringer made "sacramental" wines during the dry years.

The modern working winery on the opposite side of the road is not open to the public, but you can get a general look at it from the Rhine House. Tasting of current products is conducted during sales hours in the Rhine House. Tasting of reserve wines is available in the Founders' Room (upstairs in the Rhine House) during sales hours. A modest fee is charged per taste. Tours are conducted by very knowledgeable guides.

Open: Daily 9am–5pm.

Sterling Vineyards, 1111 Dunaweal Lane, Calistoga, CA 94515. ☎ **707/942-3344,** or toll free **800/726-6136.**

Sterling Vineyards is just south of the town of Calistoga and approximately half a mile east of Calif. 29. The winery is probably more startling in appearance than any of its neighbors. Perched on top of an island of rock, it looks much more like a Greek or even an Italian mountaintop monastery than a Napa winery. Yet reaching this isolated facility is relatively easy; via aerial gondola (there's a $6-per-person visitor fee). Gravity moves the wine. You'll go downstairs to fermentors, then down to the aging cellar, and farther down still to the final aging cellar. A climb up to the top of the rocky perch will be rewarded by a tasting. The very informative tour is directed by signs, not by guides, so you can set your own pace. The winery has changed hands twice since its founding in 1969; its current owner is the Seagram Classics Wine Company, which produces over 200,000 cases per year.

Open: Sales and tasting daily 10:30am–4:30pm.

Napa

The town of Napa, 57 miles north of San Francisco, is the commercial center of the Wine Country. This gateway to the valley is situated at the juncture of two streams; it was served by ferries and steamboats as early as the mid-1800s and later by the Napa Valley Railroad.

WHAT TO SEE & DO

Napa Valley Wine Train, 1275 McKinstry St., Napa, CA ☎ **707/253-2111,** or toll free **800/522-4142.**

The Wine Train is a deliciously relaxing rolling restaurant that makes a three-hour, 36-mile journey through the vineyards of Napa, Yountville, Oakville, Rutherford, and St. Helena. The cars—finished with polished Honduran mahogany paneling, brass accents, etched glass partitions, and fine fabrics, and colored burgundy, champagne, and grapeleaf green—re-create the opulence and sophistication of the 1920s and 1930s. Gourmet meals are served by an attentive staff, complete with all the accoutrements of gracious living—damask linen, bone china, silver flatware, and etched crystal. Menus are fixed, consisting of three or four courses, which might include poached Norwegian salmon court bouillion or Black Angus filet mignon served with a Cabernet and Roquefort sauce.

In addition to the luxuriously appointed dining rooms, the train pulls a Wine Tasting Car, a Deli Car, and three 50-passenger lounges. Tours depart from, and return to, Napa's McKinstry Street depot, near First Street and Soscol Avenue.

Admission: Train fare only, $29 brunch and lunch trains, $14.50 dinner train; additional cost for fixed-price meals, $22 for brunch trains, $25 for lunch, $45 for dinner.

Open: Departures for brunch trains, Sat–Sun and holidays at 8:30am; lunch trains, Mon–Fri at 11:30am, Sat–Sun and holidays at noon; dinner trains, Tues–Sun and holidays at 6pm. Reduced departure schedule during winter; call for information.

Chardonnay Club, Calif. 12, Napa, CA ☎ **707/257-8950.**

South of downtown Napa, 1 1/3 miles east of Calif. 29, is a classy, stunning, mean, beautiful, and challenging 36-hole land-links golf complex with first-class service. You pay just one fee, which makes you a member for the day. Privileges include the use of a golf cart, the practice range (including a bucket of balls), and services usually found only at a private club. The day I played, a snack cart came by on the course with a full complement of sandwiches and soft drinks. And at the end of the round, my clubs were cleaned. Chardonnay is not surrounded by condominiums, and there are no tennis courts or swimming pools; it's just beautiful championship golf—a test of strength, accuracy, and touch. The course ambles through and around 325 acres of vineyards, hills, creeks, canyons, and rock ridges. There are three nines of similar challenge, all leaving from the clubhouse so that you can play the 18 of your choice. Five sets of tees provide you with a course measuring from 5,300 yards to a healthy 7,100. Starting times can be reserved up to one week in advance. Chardonnay Club services include the golf shop, locker rooms, and a restaurant and grill.

Admission: Greens fees $55 Mon–Thurs, $70 Fri–Sun, including mandatory cart and practice balls.

Open: Year round.

WHERE TO STAY

Expensive

Silverado Country Club & Resort, 1600 Atlas Peak Rd., Napa, CA 94558. ☎ **707/257-0200,** or toll free **800/532-0500.** Fax 707/257-2867. 281 rms, 28 suites. A/C MINIBAR TV TEL **Directions:** Drive north on Calif. 29 to Trancas Street, then turn east to Atlas Peak Road.

Rates: $175 studio, $235 one-bedroom suite, $340–$465 2- or 3-bedroom suite. Seasonal packages available. AE, CB, DC, MC, V. **Parking:** Free.

Silverado is a 1,200-acre resort lavishly spread out in the Wine Country foothills. The main building looks more like an old southern mansion than a California country resort. It features spacious accommodations, ranging from very large studios with a king-size bed, kitchenette, and a roomy, well-appointed bath, to one-, two-, or three-bedroom cottage suites, each with a wood-burning fireplace. Each room is individually decorated. The setting is superb: the cottage suites are in private, low-rise groupings, each sharing tucked-away courtyards and peaceful walkways. This arrangement allows for a feeling of privacy and comfort despite the size of the resort.

Occupying some 360 acres, the hotel's two golf courses are very cleverly designed by Robert Trent Jones, Jr. The south course is 6,500 yards, with a dozen water crossings; the north course is 6,700 yards, somewhat longer but a bit more forgiving. There is a staff of pros on hand. Greens fee is $95 for 18 holes on either course, including a mandatory cart. There are also a tournament's worth of tennis courts, and several swimming pools.

Dining/Entertainment: The Royal Oak is the quintessential steak restaurant, with high-back chairs, carved-wood tables, and exposed beams and brickwork. Vintner's Court offers superb Californian cuisine in a chandeliered salon with a view of the surrounding eucalyptus and beautifully groomed flowerbeds. The Silverado Bar & Grill is a large indoor terrace/bar and outdoor deck that overlooks the north course and serves breakfast, lunch, and cocktails.

Services: Room service, concierge, laundry.

Facilities: Eight swimming pools, 20 tennis courts, two 18-hole golf courses, tour desk.

Moderate

Cedar Gables Inn, 486 Coombs St., Napa, CA 94559 ☎ **707/224-7969.** Fax 707/224-4838. 6 rms. **Directions:** From Calif. 29 north, exit onto First Street and follow signs to "Downtown." The house is at the corner of Oak Street.

Rates (including breakfast): $79–$149 single or double. AE, MC, V.

Easily one of the best buys in tab-happy Napa, Cedar Gables is a darling Victorian mansion made cozy by the personal attention of innkeepers Margaret and Craig Snasdell. The thoroughly romantic bed-and-breakfast, located in Old Town Napa, was built in 1892. Rooms are decorated with tapestries and antiques, and gilded in rich, Old World colors. Some include fireplaces and others have whirlpool tubs. The biggest room, called Churchill Chamber, was the mansion's original master bedroom. The inn's ground-floor sunken family room is cozy, and contains a large-screen TV.

Château Hotel, 4195 Solano Ave., Napa, CA 94558. ☎ **707/253-9300,** or toll free **800/253-6272** in California. Fax 707/253-0906. 115 rms, 6 suites. A/C TV TEL **Directions:** From Calif. 29 north, turn left just past Trower Avenue, at the entrance to the Napa Valley wine region.

Rates (including buffet breakfast): Nov–Mar, $70 single, $80 double; Apr–Oct. $85 single, $95 double. AE, CB, DC, MC, V. **Parking:** Free.

The Château is a contemporary two-story hotel complex with the exterior charm of a country inn and the interior look of a Motel 6. Rooms are spacious and are furnished with individually controlled heating and air conditioning, direct-dial phones, cable TVs, and oversize beds. Most have refrigerators, and 10 rooms are especially designed for handicapped guests. The bath is well sized and comes with a separate vanity-dressing area. In addition to breakfast, rates include a daily newspaper.

If you're used to a daily swim, the Château has a heated pool and spa. If you prefer golf, tennis, bicycling, or even hot-air ballooning, the staff will be happy to arrange it.

Tall Timbers Chalets, 1012 Darms Lane, Napa, CA 94558. ☎ **707/252-7810.** 7 cottages. A/C TV MINIBAR **Directions:** From Calif. 29 north, turn left onto Darms Lane before you reach Yountville.

Rates: Dec–Feb, Sun–Thurs $75 single or double, Fri–Sat and hols $90–$105 single or double; Mar–Nov, Sun–Thurs $80–$95 single or double, Fri–Sat and hols $95–$125 single or double. Extra person $10. Children under 11 stay free in parents' room. AE, MC, V. **Parking:** Free.

Tall Timbers is a group of seven whitewashed, roomy cottages surrounded by pines and eucalyptus. It ranks as one of the best bargains in the Napa Valley: the rates are exceptional, the location convenient. The cottages' proximity to Yountville makes it ideal for sightseeing, shopping, and dining. It's also a good starting point for trips through the surrounding countryside and up to Calistoga. The Newlan Vineyards are located next door and Domaine Chandon is within walking distance.

All the cottages are nicely decorated and well furnished. Amenities include a refrigerator, a toaster-oven, and a coffee maker, all located in a stoveless breakfast nook. And it's really quite pleasant to find, on your arrival, a basket of fresh fruit in the breakfast area of your cottage, as well as breakfast treats in the refrigerator and a complimentary bottle of champagne. There are no phones in the cottages, but there is one in the main office. Each unit can sleep four (there's a bedroom plus a queen-size sofa bed in the living room). Several have decks—ideal for watching the colorful hot-air balloons as they float over in the morning.

While it is not particularly difficult to find the Tall Timbers Chalets, be sure to ask for specific directions. No smoking is allowed in the chalets.

Budget

Napa Valley Budget Inn, 3380 Solano Ave., Napa, CA 94558. ☎ **707/257-6111.**

58 rms. A/C TV TEL **Directions:** From Calif. 29 north, turn left onto the Redwood Road turnoff and go one block to Solano Avenue; then turn left and go a half block to the motel.

Rates: $40–$57 single; $46–$66 double. AE, DC, DISC, MC, V. **Parking:** Free.

The location of this no-frills lodging is excellent—close to Calif. 29 and just across the street from a pleasant mini-mall. Rooms are simple, clean, and comfortable. Local calls are free, and there is a small heated pool on the premises.

WHERE TO DINE

Moderate

The Red Hen Cantina, 5091 St. Helena Hwy., Napa. ☎ **707/255-8125.**

Cuisine: MEXICAN. **Reservations:** For large parties only.
Prices: Appetizers $4–$10; main courses $8–$14; lunches $4–$9. AE, DC, MC, V.
Open: Sun–Thurs 11am–9pm, Fri–Sat 11am–10pm.

Looking very much like a Swiss chalet that got lost somewhere south of the border, The Red Hen is one of the most popular taquerías north of San Francisco. Both moderately priced and decorated the cantina contains several good-sized dining rooms and a large outdoor dining deck.

Gastronomically, Mexican traditionals are dotted with a healthy number of seafood dishes that include burritos, tacos, and Pollo Mexicano (chicken strips sautéed in white wine, onion, mushrooms, and tomatoes).

Yountville

Yountville is both casual and posh, and inarguably the most charming village along Calif. 29. Of less historical interest than St. Helena or Calistoga, it is nonetheless an excellent jumping-off point for a wineries tour or for the simple enjoyment of the beauties of the valley. What's more, it has several lovely places to stay, good shops, and excellent restaurants at various price levels. Best of all, intimate Yountville is walkable—you can easily take a very enjoyable stroll from one end of the town to the other.

WHAT TO SEE & DO

At the center of the village is Vintage 1870 (☎ **707/944-2451**), once a winery (from 1871 to 1955) and now a gallery with specialty shops selling antiques, wine accessories, country collectibles, and more. It is also home to three restaurants. One of the best shops in the complex is **Basket Bazaar**—where, in addition to wickery, you'll also find lamps, vine wreaths, chairs, chests, baskets, and rockers. And then there's **Gami's Scandia Imports** for Scandinavian and European imports—Copenhagen figurines, jewelry, and a troll or two to bring along.

Ballooning silently over the grape vines is a popular Napa pastime. **Adventures Aloft,** Vintage 1870 (P.O. Box 2500, Yountville, CA 94599, ☎ **707/252-7067**), is Napa Valley's oldest hot-air balloon company, with full-time professional pilots. Groups are small and flights last about an hour. Like all ballooneries, Adventures Aloft flies in the early morning, when the winds are gentle and the air is cool. The cost includes a preflight continental breakfast, a postflight champagne brunch, and a framed first-flight certificate. The cost is $165 per person.

WHERE TO STAY

Burgundy House Country Inn, 6711 Washington St., P.O. Box 3156, Yountville, CA 94599. ☎ **707/944-0889.** 5 rms (all with bath). A/C **Directions:** From Calif. 29 north, take the Yountville exit and turn left onto Washington Street.

Rates (including breakfast): $100 single; $115 double. MC, V. **Parking:** Free.

Decidedly charming, this distinctly French country inn was built in the early 1870s of local fieldstone and river rock. Burgundy House is tiny yet impressive, with exposed hand-hewn beams and handsome antique country furniture. Each of the five cozy guest rooms has colorful quilted spreads and comfortable beds. Delightful touches include fresh flowers in each of the rooms and a complimentary decanter of local white wine. The full breakfast can be taken inside, or outdoors in the inn's lovely garden.

Vintage Inn, 6541 Washington St., Yountville, CA 94599. ☎ **707/944-1112,** or toll free **800/351-1133.** Fax 707/944-1617. 72 rms, 8 suites. A/C MINIBAR TV TEL **Directions:** From Calif. 29 north, take the Yountville exit and turn left on Washington Street.

Rates: $134–$174 single; $144–$184 double; $184–$204 minisuites and villas. Extra person $25. AE, CB, DC, MC, V. **Parking:** Free.

The Vintage Inn, built on an old winery estate in the center of town, is a contemporary-styled luxury country inn. The brick-and-board exterior fronts a warm and handsome reception lounge, furnished with a brick fireplace, lavender couches, and shuttered windows. Guest rooms mimic this cozy style. Each contains a fireplace, cable color TV with HBO, oversize beds, a coffee maker, and a refrigerator. Did I mention the private Jacuzzi and plush bathrobes? You will be welcomed into your room with a complimentary bottle of wine to share on your secluded patio or veranda. The inn also provides nightly turndown service and sports a 60-foot, year-round heated swimming pool, an outdoor heated whirlpool, and tennis courts reserved for the exclusive use of the guests. A Californian-continental champagne breakfast (cereals, yogurt, pastries, egg salad, and fruit) is included with your stay and served daily in the Vintage Club, as is afternoon tea. Nice place.

WHERE TO DINE

Expensive

Domaine Chandon, California Drive. ☎ **707/944-2892.**

Cuisine: CALIFORNIAN/FRENCH. **Reservations:** Required. **Directions:** From Calif. 29 north, take the California Drive exit. The restaurant is on the west side of the highway.
Prices: Appetizers $7–$11; main courses $13–$19 at lunch, $22–$28 at dinner. AE, DC, MC, V.
Open: Summer, lunch daily 11:30am–2:30pm, dinner Wed–Sun 6–9pm; winter, lunch Wed–Sun 11:30am–2:30pm, dinner Wed–Sun 6–9pm. **Closed:** First 3 weeks of Jan.

Inside this French-owned champagne house is one of California's most exquisite restaurants, and one of the most celebrated. The winery building is a low, ultramodern stone-and-concrete structure that seems like part of the hillside. A creek shaded by large trees contributes to this idyllic setting. Domaine Chandon forsakes the usual old-fashioned Wine Country quaintness for understated modern elegance. Its multilevel interior contains several dining rooms with arched fir-paneled ceilings. It is one of the most dramatic and beautiful settings in the Wine Country. Large picture windows open onto vineyard views, while candles illuminate tabletops by night.

On nice days you can eat lunch outdoors, a meal that might begin with a salad of arugula with prosciutto, parmesan, truffle oil, and home-baked Calimyrna fig bread. Main courses change daily but might include lamb shank braised in Chardonnay and herbs, with garden vegetables. There are superb desserts, including such mouth-watering choices as the hot chocolate soufflé served with a white-chocolate sauce or the espresso and mascarpone ice cream terrine with a crunchy peanut-butter layer and bittersweet chocolate sauce. Ready for dinner? The roast California quail is served with chanterelles, soft polenta, and acorn squash. Sweetbreads come in shallot-prosciutto butter and truffle juice. The wine list is impeccable and includes some marvelous dessert wines and cognacs.

Moderate

California Cafe Bar and Grill, 6795 Washington St., Yountville. ☎ **707/944-2330.**

Cuisine: INTERNATIONAL. **Reservations:** Accepted. **Directions:** The restaurant is located directly on Highway 29 at Madison Street.
Prices: Appetizers $3–$8; main courses $10–$19; lunch $5–$11. AE, MC, V.
Open: Mon–Thurs 11:30am–9:30pm, Fri–Sat 11:30am–10pm, Sun 10am–9:30pm.

Both upscale and laid-back, California Cafe's big, bright, and airy dining room is as California as it gets. Smokey scents from the restaurant's wood-burning oven permeate the room; its products include smoked duck and hickory-roasted game hen. Spicy chili onion rings can be followed by pastas like black pepper fettuccini or rigatoni with mixed vegetables, or a respectable paella—mussels, shrimp, chicken, and spicy sausage mixed with saffron rice. A large selection of salads like warm cabbage with spicy beef, and sandwiches like fried-oyster on a baguette are available at lunch. Sunday brunches are popular. The dedicated menu features scrambled eggs with fried oysters, smoked bacon, spinach, and potatoes; and an omelet with artichokes, spinach, roasted peppers, and fontina cheese.

The Diner, 6476 Washington St. ☎ **707/944-2626.**

Cuisine: AMERICAN/MEXICAN. **Reservations:** Not accepted. **Directions:** From Calif. 29 north, take the Yountville exit and turn left on Washington Street.

Prices: Breakfast $4–$7; lunch $6–$10; dinner $8–$12. No credit cards.
Open: Tues–Sun 8am–3pm; dinner 5:30–9pm.

It's a diner, all right, decorated in shell pink, with track lighting, and boasting a friendly and unpretentious atmosphere. The restaurant features a functioning Irish Waterford wood stove, a collection of vintage diner water pitchers, and an art exhibit that changes monthly. Seating is at the counter or in wooden booths.

The menu is extensive, the portions are huge, and the food is good. Breakfast offerings include such California staples as huevos rancheros and Jalisco (eggs scrambled with fresh red and yellow peppers). French toast and eggs are also available.

Lunch and dinner dishes include a host of toothsome Mexican and American dishes, such as tamari-basted chicken breast salad on baby greens, grilled fresh fish, giant burritos, and thick sandwiches made with house-roasted meats and homemade bread. Homemade desserts usually include fresh-fruit cobblers and sundae sauces. The Diner has a cappuccino machine and stocks fresh-squeezed orange juice as well as natural-fruit sodas, along with beer and wine by the glass.

Mustards Grill, 7399 St. Helena Hwy. (Calif. 29). ☎ **707/944-2424.**

Cuisine: CALIFORNIAN. **Reservations:** Recommended.
Prices: Appetizers $3–$8; main courses $11–$18. CB, DC, MC, V.
Open: Apr–Oct daily 11:30am–10pm; Nov–Mar daily 11:30am–9pm.

Look for the humorous bronze sculpture of a bowler-topped gentleman on the west side of the road and you have found Mustards. As you enter this barnlike structure, you'll see beamed cathedral ceilings, a black-and-white tile floor, and a small bar. The main dining room is on two levels and includes an airy glass-enclosed outer dining area for a simulated al fresco experience.

The atmosphere is light, festive, and relaxed. Mustards is a favorite with local wine makers and growers. The blue-jeaned, white-shirted servers are friendly and knowledgeable. Specials are listed on a blackboard, along with featured local wines ranging from $5 to $6 a glass. If you bring your own bottle, the restaurant charges a $10 corkage fee. From the looks of things, I'd guess that more wine per table is consumed here than in any San Francisco restaurant.

Tables are immediately topped with sliced, warm, crusty baguettes, served with sweet butter. Among the starters are such gems as home-smoked salmon with cornmeal pancakes, warm goat cheese with roasted beets, and Chinese chicken salad. Sandwiches include chicken breast with guacamole and onion relish, and grilled Ahi tuna with basil mayonnaise and ginger. Main courses are reasonably priced and range from wood-burning-oven specialties—barbecued baby back ribs, pork chops with Thai marinade, or smoked Long Island duckling—to grilled items like Sonoma rabbit and "mallet" chicken with seasonal vegetables. The menu changes every three months to accommodate the season's offerings.

Oakville & Rutherford

Driving north again on the St. Helena Highway (Calif. 29) you soon come to the Oakville Cross Road. There you will find the **Oakville Grocery Co.,** 7856 St. Helena Hwy., Oakville, CA 94562 (☎ **707/944-8802**). Stop! Its name, its location, and its exterior disguise one of the finest gourmet food stores this side of New York's Dean and DeLucca. Here you can obtain provisions for a memorable picnic or for a very special custom gift basket. You'll find the best of breads, the choicest selection of cheeses in the Northern Bay Area, pâtés, fresh foie gras (domestic and French, seasonally), smoked Norwegian salmon, smoked sturgeon and smoked pheasant (by special order), fresh caviar (Beluga, Sevruga, Osetra), and an exceptional selection of California wines.

Hard-to-find wines and vintages are also available here. If you find the wine decision difficult, there are sampler sets to help you along. The Oakville Grocery Co. will prepare a picnic-basket lunch for you if you give them 24 hours' notice. Delivery service is available to some areas. It's open daily from 10am to 6pm.

WHERE TO STAY

Rancho Camus, 1140 Rutherford Rd. (P.O. Box 78), Rutherford, CA 94573.
☎ **707/963-1777.** Fax 707/963-5387. 26 suites. A/C TV TEL

Rates (including continental breakfast): $115–$135 single or double; from $225 Master Suite; $295 two-bedroom suite. AE, MC, V.

As restful as the quiet town of Rutherford itself, this Spanish Mediterranean–style inn is one of our top Wine Country picks. Every suite in the two-story, red-tile-roofed Rancho opens onto the hotel's plant-filled courtyard. It's a colorful place, outfitted with hand-carved black walnut furniture, stained glass windows, and bright bedspreads and wall hangings woven by Ecuadorian Otavalon Indians. Most suites have split-level sleeping areas and wood-burning adobe fireplaces. The extra-luxurious Master Suites also have kitchenettes and large Jacuzzi baths.

Breakfast, which includes fresh fruit and breads, coffee, and juice, is either delivered to your room, or served in the inn's Garden Grill restaurant.

WHERE TO DINE

Auberge du Soleil, 180 Rutherford Hill Rd., Rutherford. ☎ **707/963-1211.**

Cuisine: CALIFORNIAN. **Reservations:** Recommended. **Directions:** From Oakville, take the Oakville Crossroad east to the Silverado Trail, turn left, heading north to Rutherford Hill Road, then right, up to Auberge du Soleil.

Prices: Main courses $14–$18 at lunch, $25–$30 at dinner; desserts $7–$8; fixed-price dinner $52. AE, DISC, MC, V.

Open: Breakfast daily 7–11am; lunch daily 11:30am–2:30pm; dinner daily 6–9:30pm.

This romantic country hideaway, nestled in an olive grove, overlooking the lovely Napa Valley, is a stunning setting for Chef David Hale's classic Wine Country cuisine. Inside, a magnificent fireplace, huge wood pillars, pink tablecloths, and fresh flowers combine to create a warm rustic ambience. Light classical music plays in a room that opens out to a wisteria-decked, umbrella-topped terrace with a panoramic view of the valley below.

The food here is as good as the atmosphere is peaceful. Chef Hale employs the freshest local ingredients to create his delicacies.

Lunch appetizers may include a Dungeness crab quesadilla with local Sonoma Jack cheese or grilled venison-cranberry sausage served with pear-apricot chutney. Among the lunch entrées are gourmet pizzas, seafood pastas, and a particularly endorsable grilled pork chop served with onion rings and a spicy tomato sauce. A la carte dinner dishes run the gamut from grilled Hawaiian ahi with rosemary polenta to rack of lamb accompanied by goat cheese soufflé. As everything else on the menu, desserts are very tasty. A good selection of country concoctions—such as bread pudding, with brandy sauce and bittersweet chocolate, and hazelnut rum cake—are always on hand.

St. Helena

Reminiscent in some ways of the south of France, with its tall plane trees arching over the roads, St. Helena also suggests feudal England, with mansions overseeing the vineyards and valleys from high hillside perches. Many of the buildings in the main part of town date from the 1800s and are worth a look. The modern wares in a variety of shops are also worth browsing. This is a friendly place, with some excellent restaurants and inns.

WHAT TO SEE & DO

Literary buffs and other romantics won't want to miss the **Silverado Museum,** 1490 Library Lane (☎ **707/963-3757**), devoted to the life and works of Robert Louis Stevenson, author of *Treasure Island, Kidnapped,* and other classics. It was here that Stevenson honeymooned in 1880, at the abandoned Silverado Mine. More than 8,000 museum items include original manuscripts, letters, photographs, portraits of the writer, and the desk he used in Samoa. It's open Tuesday through Sunday from noon to 4pm. Admission is free.

WHERE TO STAY

Bartels Ranch and Country Inn, 1200 Conn Valley Rd., St. Helena, CA 94574. ☎ **707/963-4001.** 4 rms. A/C **Directions:** From downtown St. Helena, turn east on Pope St., cross Silverado Trail and continue onto Howell Mountain Road. After about 1 mile, bear right, onto Conn Valley Road. The inn is two miles ahead.

Rates: $135–$275 single or double. AE, DISC, MC, V.

Encompassing over one hundred acres of rolling meadows, Bartels is an alluring resort packed with beauty and charm. Innkeeper Jami Bartels, a hands-on proprietor, provides picnic baskets and blankets with each guest room, and can lend you bicycles, arrange massages or personal wine country tours, or just direct you to the lounge for the cookies, coffee, and tea that are served all day.

Although it's not particularly fancy, every room has private baths and terry robes, and two rooms have fireplaces. There's a communal sundeck as well as a game room filled with books, a billiard table, and a stereo. Complimentary wine, fruit, and cheese are served each afternoon.

Wine Country Inn, 1152 Lodi Lane, St. Helena, CA 94574. ☎ **707/963-7077.** Fax 707/963-9018. 21 rms, 3 suites (all with bath). A/C TEL **Directions:** From Calif. 29 north, turn right onto Lodi Lane, in the middle of St. Helena.

Rates (including continental breakfast): Jan 3–Apr 15 $91–$155 single or double, from $155 suite; the rest of the year $97–$160 single or double, from $205 suite. Extra person $20. AE, MC, V. **Parking:** Free.

The Wine Country Inn, set on a hillside overlooking the vineyards, is one of the most romantic hostelries I've ever seen. Its rooms are individually decorated in New England style. Many of them have fireplaces, balconies or patios, country antique furnishings, stitchery hangings on the walls, and patchwork quilts on the beds. And to add to the aura of quiet relaxation, the inn has an elegant pool and Jacuzzi. Don't stay here alone.

Zinfandel Inn, 800 Zinfandel Lane, St. Helena, CA 94574. ☎ **707/963-3512.** 3 rms. A/C TV TEL

Rates (including full breakfast): $150–$250 single or double. AE, MC, V.

Innkeepers Jerry and Diane have turned their own smoke-free home into a charming bed-and-breakfast that's thoroughly recommendable. There are only three rooms here. The Chardonnay Room, which features bay windows and a large stone fireplace, contains a king-size brass bed, a sofa, and its own private garden entrance. The huge Zinfandel Suite holds a king-size bed, a large sitting area, an old-fashioned blue-steel fireplace, a large private deck, and an enormous bathroom outfitted with a Jacuzzi tub positioned by an octagonal window with garden views; the adjacent shower has two heads. The Petite Sirah Room is the B&B's smallest, but it's charmingly decorated with antiques, a featherbed, and windows that overlook the Napa Valley.

The home's public areas are as well cared for as the rooms. The kitchen, with its well-stocked refrigerator, is open to all guests throughout their stay, and a casual family room is also available for guests' use. Outside, a wooden deck leads to the house's backyard, which contains a hot tub, lagoon pool, waterfall, and fish pond. A full breakfast is served in the formal dining room.

WHERE TO DINE

Tra Vigne Restaurant and Cantinetta, 1050 Charter Oak Ave., St. Helena. ☎ **707/963-4444.**

Cuisine: ITALIAN. **Reservations:** Recommended.
Prices: Appetizers $5–$8; main courses $9–$17; cantinetta $4–$8. CB, DC, DISC, MC, V.
Open: Daily noon–9:30pm; cantinetta daily 11:30am–6pm.

Looking like a small sandstone winery on the east side of Calif. 29, Tra Vigne has garnered raves throughout its half dozen years of existence. Dramatically large, green-marble columns on either side of the front door give way to a striking dining room, designed with immense curved windows that open onto a large veranda.

The food here is terrific, with many of the best items coming from a wood-burning oven. When guests are seated, a demi-loaf of freshly baked bread, which might be cracked wheat or rosemary raisin, is placed on the table. Entrées include house-smoked duck, braised oxtail, grilled Sonoma rabbit, and a small selection of fresh fish. Gourmet pizzas and a variety of pastas and salads are also available. Lunch is also available at the bar, where a large assortment of wines, beers, ports, grappas, cocktails, and coffees are served. Desserts, too, are usually on the mark, and include lasagna di ciccolatte (layers of whipped chocolate, sour cherries, and chocolate sponge cake with lemon sauce).

The restaurant's more casual side, called the Cantinetta, offers a small selection of sandwiches, pizzas, and lighter meals, such as chicken and vegetable stew. It also packs picnics and sells about 20 flavored olive oils infused with roasted garlic, basil, chilies, hazelnuts, lavender, rosemary, and mint; sprinkle a little on a crouton and see which ones you like best.

Calistoga

Sam Brannan became California's first millionaire by building a hotel and spa to take advantage of this area's natural geothermal springs. His entrepreneurial instincts combined "California" with "Saratoga," a popular East Coast resort, and in 1859 Calistoga was born. Located at the northern end of the lush Wine Country, the town remains popular. Today, Calistoga's main street is still only about six blocks long, and no building is higher than two stories. It's not fancy at all, but Calistoga is a delightfully simple place in which to relax and indulge in mineral waters, mud baths, sulfur steam baths, Jacuzzis, massages—and, of course, wines.

WHAT TO SEE & DO

A Mud Bath

The main thing to do here is what people have been doing for the last 150 years: take a bath. If you've never had a mud bath before, you might wonder how it feels. The bath is composed of local volcanic ash, imported peat, and naturally boiling mineral-hot-springs water, all mulled together to produce a thick mud at a temperature of about 104°F. Once you overcome the hurdle of deciding how best to place your naked body into the mushy stone tub, the rest is pure relaxation—you soak with surprising buoyancy for about 10 to 12 minutes. A warm mineral-water shower, a mineral-water whirlpool bath, and a mineral-water steam-room visit follow; these are then followed by a relaxing blanket-wrap to cool your delighted body down slowly. All of this takes about 1 1/2 hours and costs about $45; with a massage, add another half hour and $20. The outcome is a rejuvenated, revitalized, squeaky-clean you. Mud baths are not recommended for people with high blood pressure or for pregnant women.

All spas also offer a variety of other treatments, such as hand and foot massages, herbal wraps, acupressure face-lifts, skin rubs, and herbal facials. Prices range from $29 to $100, and appointments are necessary for all services; call at least a week in advance. Calistoga spas include **Dr. Wilkinson's Hot Springs,** 1507 Lincoln Ave. (**707/942-4102**); **Lincoln Avenue Spa,** 1339 Lincoln Ave. (**707/942-5296**); **Golden Haven Hot Springs Spa,** 1713 Lake St. (**707/942-6793**); and **Calistoga Spa Hot Springs,** 1006 Washington St. (**707/942-6269**).

Other Attractions

Calistoga Depot, 1458 Lincoln Ave. ☎ **707/942-5556.**

The tiny town's defunct railroad station now houses a variety of shops, a restaurant, and the Calistoga Chamber of Commerce. The Depot occupies the site of the original railroad station, which was built in 1868. Alongside it sit six restored passenger cars dating from 1916 to the 1920s; each of them also houses some enticing shops.

Old Faithful Geyser of California, 1299 Tubbs Lane. ☎ **707/942-6463.**

One of three Old Faithful geysers in the world, this one has been blowing off steam at regular intervals for as long as anyone can remember. The 350°F water spews out every 40 minutes or so, day and night (the frequency varies with natural influences, such as barometric pressure, the moon and tides, and earth tectonic stresses). The performance lasts about three minutes, and you'll learn a lot about the origins of geothermal steam. You can bring a picnic lunch with you and catch the show as many times as you wish. A gift and snack shop is open every day.

Admission: $5 adults, $4 seniors, $2 children 6–12, children under 6 admitted free.

Open: Summer, daily 9am–6pm; winter, daily 9am–5pm. **Directions:** Follow the signs from downtown Calistoga; it's situated between Calif. 29 and Calif. 128.

Petrified Forest, 4100 Petrified Forest Rd. ☎ **707/942-6667.**

Although you won't see thousands of trees turned into stone, you will find many interesting petrified specimens, including redwoods that have turned to rock through the slow infiltration of silicas and other minerals. Volcanic ash blanketed this area after the eruption of Mount St. Helena 3 million years ago. Earlier specimens of petrified seashells, clams, and marine life indicate that water covered this area even before the redwood forest.

Admission: $3 adults, $1 children ages 4–11, free for kids under 4.

Open: Summer, daily 10am–5:30pm; winter, daily 10am–4:30pm. **Directions:** From Calif. 128, turn right onto Petrified Forest Road, just past Lincoln Avenue.

WHERE TO STAY

Dr. Wilkinson's Hot Springs, 1507 Lincoln Ave., Calistoga, CA 94515. ☎ **707/942-4102.** 42 rms. A/C MINIBAR TV TEL

Rates: Winter, $44–$79 single, $49–$99 double; summer, $59–$84 single, $64–$94 double. Weekly discounts available. AE, MC, V. **Parking:** Free.

Another good Calistoga choice is Dr. Wilkinson's Hot Springs. On the main highway in the middle of Calistoga, near Fairway Street, it's a typical motel, distinguished mostly by the mud baths on the premises. All rooms have drip coffee makers, and some have kitchens. Facilities include three swimming pools (two outdoor and one indoor). Wilkinson's has any number of packages, from the Stress-Stopper to Magical Morning and Salon Sampler. Call for details.

Mount View Hotel, 1457 Lincoln Ave. (Calif. 29), Calistoga, CA 94515. ☎ **707/942-6877.** Fax 707/942-6904. 22 rms, 3 cottages, 8 suites. A/C TV TEL

Rates: $85–$120 single or double; $140–$165 suite. Packages available. AE, MC, V. **Parking:** Free.

Located on the main highway, near Fairway Street in the middle of Calistoga, the Mount View Hotel offers art-deco rooms, self-contained cottages, and eight glamorous suites named for movie idols of the past. The Carole Lombard suite has peach-colored walls and light-green carpeting, while the Tom Mix suite has a western theme. Facilities also include a heated swimming pool, European spa, and Jacuzzi.

Valeriano's, a northern Italian restaurant, serves dinner nightly. A fairly standard menu of pastas and meats is accompanied by an extensive and reasonably priced selection of local wines. A separate cafe serves breakfast and lunch daily; it has live entertainment on weekends.

WHERE TO DINE

All Seasons Café, 1400 Lincoln Ave. ☎ **707/942-9111.**

Cuisine: CALIFORNIAN. **Reservations:** Recommended on weekends.
Prices: Appetizers $4–$9; main courses $6–$17 at lunch, $9–$23 at dinner. MC, V.
Open: Continental breakfast Mon–Thurs 9–10:30am; brunch Fri–Sun 9–10:30am; lunch Thurs–Tues 11:30am–3pm; dinner Thurs–Mon 5–10pm; store Thurs–Mon 9am–4pm and 5–9pm, Tues 9am–4pm.

For a delightful meal served in a treasurehouse of wines, wend your way to the All Seasons Café, on the main highway at the corner of Washington Street, in the middle of Calistoga. You can choose to eat in or prearrange a box lunch or picnic platter. Don't overlook the luncheon and dinner specials and the fresh desserts. Recent luncheon dishes included a baked eggplant, tomato, and mozzarella sandwich served with tomato sauce, and penne pasta with mushrooms, smoked chicken, garlic, sun-dried tomatoes, and romano cheese. The cafe also serves homemade soup and a wide selection of appetizers.

2 Sonoma County

45 miles N of San Francisco; 20 miles W of Napa

GETTING THERE • By Car From San Francisco, cross the Golden Gate Bridge and stay on U.S. 101 north. Exit at Calif. 37 and after 10 miles turn north onto Calif. 121. After another 10 miles, turn north again onto Calif. 12 (Broadway), which will take you into town.

From the town of Napa, take Calif. 121 south to Calif. 12. The road is well marked with directional signs.

ESSENTIALS • Orientation The town of Sonoma's geographical and commercial center is called the Plaza and sits at the top of a T formed by Broadway (Calif. 12) and Napa Street. Most of the surrounding streets form a grid pattern around this axis, making Sonoma easy to negotiate.

• Information Before you begin your explorations of the area, visit the **Sonoma Valley Visitors Bureau,** 453 First St. East, Sonoma, CA 95476 (☎ **707/996-1090,** fax 707/996-9212). It's located right on the Plaza and offers free maps and brochures about local happenings. It's open daily from 9am to 5pm.

The **Sonoma County Convention and Visitors Bureau,** 5000 Roberts Lake Rd., Rohnert Park, CA 94928 (☎ **707/586-8100** or toll free **800/326-7666,** fax 707/586-8111), offers a free visitor's guide with information relating to the county as a whole. It also provides specialized information on historical attractions, wine tours, walking tours, carriage rides, hot-air ballooning, swimming, fishing, boating, bicycling, camping, golf, rock climbing . . . you name it. Write as far in advance as possible.

Sonoma is not far from Napa Valley, but it is special enough to warrant separate attention. The town of Sonoma is the seat of the county of the same name. Its pleasant mix of architectural styles looks like a cross between early California Mission and western Victorian. Sonoma is rich in history; much of the area is still preserved as it was in the mid-1800s, when a brilliant Mexican army officer, Gen. Mariano Guadalupe Vallejo, was in charge of the Sonoma mission. In fact, so many of the town's historical monuments and landmarks are intact that it almost seems as though time has stood still.

The center of town is the Plaza—the largest town square in California and the site of City Hall. The Plaza's Bear Flag Monument marks the spot where the crude Bear Flag was raised in 1846, signaling the end of Mexican rule. The symbol was later adopted by the state of California. The eight-acre park surrounding the Plaza contains two ponds full with ducks and geese, and is a lovely place for picnicking. Provisions are available directly across the street (see "Where to Dine" below).

On your way to or from Sonoma, visit the Old Sonoma Barn's World of Birds, 23570 Arnold Dr. (Hwy. 121), Sonoma (☎ **707/996-1477**). Rare parrots and $15,000 macaws are on display (and for sale) here, as are a small herd of llamas. Nearby, Angelo's Wine Country Deli, 23400 Arnold Dr., Sonoma (☎ **707/938-3688**), sells all types of smoked meats, special salsas, and homemade mustards. He's especially known for his half-dozen types of homemade beef jerky, meats that this closet enthusiast heartily endorses. It's open daily from 9am to 6pm.

What to See & Do

The best way to see the town of Sonoma is to pick up a free copy of *Sonoma Walking Tour*, available from the Sonoma Valley Visitors Bureau (see "Information" above). With the help of this pamphlet, you can learn about all the historic spots in and around Sonoma Plaza. Highlights include General Vallejo's 1852 Victorian-style home; Sonoma Barracks, erected in 1836 to house Mexican army troops; and the Blue Wing Inn, an 1840 hostelry built to accommodate tourists and new settlers while they built homes in Sonoma (John Frémont, Kit Carson, and Ulysses S. Grant were guests).

Mission San Francisco Solano de Sonoma.

Founded in 1823, Sonoma's mission is the northernmost and last mission built in California. It was the only one established on the northern coast by the Mexican rulers, who were afraid of expansionist Russian fur traders.

Admission: $2 adults, $1 children ages 6–12, free for children 5 and under.

Open: Daily 10am–5pm.

Arts Guild of Sonoma, 521 Broadway, Sonoma. ☎ **707/996-3115.**

Step in and treat yourself to some truly exceptional different works of art. Exhibits change frequently and include a wide variety of styles and media. Everything on display has been produced by local artists. The Arts Guild is a nonprofit organization run by its artist members. Since its organization in 1977, the guild has provided local professionals with an outstanding showcase. The guild also sponsors art shows by other county art groups, as well as international exhibitions.

Admission: Free.

Open: Spring–summer daily 10am–6pm; fall–winter daily 10am–5pm.

Jack London State Park, London Ranch Rd., Sonoma. ☎ **707/938-5216.**

About eight miles north of Sonoma (a mile west of Glen Ellen), this 800-acre park includes a museum built by Jack's wife, Charmian, in 1919 for the purpose of housing the considerable collection of objects and memorabilia from the author's life. The cottage of the Londons is also here, along with the ruins of their mansion, and their graves.

Admission: $5 per car, $4 per car for seniors over 62.

Open: Park, daily in winter 10am–5pm, summer 10am–7pm; museum, daily 10am–5pm.

Sonoma Cattle Company, Jack London State Park, Sonoma. ☎ **707/996-8566.**

The Sonoma Cattle Company offers guided tours on horseback. You'll ride on the same trails that author Jack London once followed, and pass through London's eucalyptus grove and wood-frame cottage on your way to the top of Mount Sonoma for magnificent views of the countryside. The stables are in Jack London State Park, located in the northern part of Sonoma Valley. Rides cost $35 for a two-hour ride.

Open: By appointment daily, weather permitting.

WINERIES

Sonoma is the site of California's first winery, founded in 1857. Chardonnay is the single white variety for which Sonoma is noted and represents almost one-quarter of the acreage in vines. Like Napa, the Sonoma Valley produces some of the finest wines in the United States. Nearly all the operations are small or medium-size, and many are family owned. But you won't see the polished, city-bred look of the Napa Valley here. As you head north out of Sonoma on Calif. 12, the scenery evolves from an untidy backyard finish to the rough-hewn look of ranch country. The terrain varies by the mile, and with each change small variations in climate—known as "microclimates"—create the differences in the wines.

Sebastiani Vineyards Winery, 389 Fourth St. E., Sonoma. ☎ **707/938-5532,** or toll free **800/888-5532.**

Sebastiani has the most interesting and informative guided tour, and its place in the development of the region is unique. It's the only winery in Sonoma Valley to offer both a guided tour and tastings from a full selection of wines that have won 95 awards. The tour, through stone aging cellars containing more than 300 carved casks, is fascinating and well worth the time. You can see the winery's original turn-of-the-century crusher and press, as well as the largest collection of oak-barrel carvings in the world. If you don't want to take the tour, go straight to the tasting room, where you can sample an extensive selection of wines. The tasting room also offers a large assortment of winery gifts. A picnic area is adjacent to the cellars. Tours are 25 minutes long.

Open: Daily 10am–5pm (last tour begins at 4pm).

Ravenswood Winery, 18701 Gehricke Rd., Sonoma. ☎ **707/938-1960.**

Built right into the hillside to keep it cool, this traditional, small stone winery crushed its first grapes in 1976 for its inaugural Zinfandel. Today, Ravenswood is best known for its red wines, including Zinfandel, Merlot, and Cabernet Sauvignon. Visitors are also offered younger wines, often blends, that are less expensive than older vintages. Tours include the oak-barrel aging rooms and follow the wine-making process from grape to glass. Reservations are required.

This winery is located in the Sonoma hills; follow the WINERY signs.

Buena Vista, 18000 Old Winery Rd., Sonoma. ☎ **707/938-1266.**

Buena Vista, the patriarch of California wineries, is located slightly northeast of the town of Sonoma. It was founded in 1857 by Count Agoston Haraszthy, the Hungarian émigré who is called the father of the California wine industry. A close friend of General Vallejo, Haraszthy returned from Europe in 1861 with 100,000 of the finest vine cuttings, which he made available to all wine growers. Although Buena Vista's wine making now takes place in an ultramodern facility outside Sonoma, the winery still maintains a tasting room here, inside the restored 1862 Press House.

Open: Daily 10am–5pm.

Château St. Jean, 8555 Sonoma Hwy. (Calif. 12), Kenwood, CA 95452. ☎ **707/833-4134.**

It's worth the 20-minute drive to visit Château St. Jean, founded in 1973 by a family of grape growers. The winery is situated at the foot of Sugarloaf Ridge, just north of Kenwood and east of Calif. 12 on a private drive, on what was once a private 250-acre country retreat built in 1920. Château St. Jean is notable for its exceptionally beautiful buildings, magnificent grounds, and elegant tasting room—all once part of an impressive country estate. A meticulously maintained lawn is now a picnic ground, complete with a fountain surrounded by grass and benches.

There is a self-guided tour with detailed and photographic descriptions of the wine-making process. At the end of the tour, be sure to walk up to the top of the tower for a magnificent view of the valley. Back in the tasting room, you are invited to sample a good range of St. Jean's wines at no charge. From each vintage, Château St. Jean offers several Chardonnays and Cabernet Sauvignon, as well as Fume blanc, merlot, Johannisberg Riesling, and Gewurztraminer. Since 1984 the winery has been part of the Suntory family of premium wineries.

The toll-free, interactive Château St. Jean "wine line" (☎ **800/332-WINE**) offers free recorded reports from the Sonoma Wine Country, including updated information on vineyard conditions, interviews with wine makers and growers, information on what's happening at the winery, and descriptions of currently available wines.

Open: Self-guided tour, daily 10:30am–4pm; tasting room, daily 10am–4:30pm. **Closed:** Major holidays.

SONOMA SHOPPING

Most of the town's multitude of shops, located around the Plaza, offer everything from clothing and food to wines, excellent sourdough, and books.

The Mercato, 452 First Street E.

Located around Sonoma's main plaza, The Mercato is a small shopping center with several good stores selling unusual wares. Interesting shops include **Papyrus** (☎ **707/935-6707**), which has a vast collection of lovely paper products and is open Monday through Saturday from 10am to 5:30pm and on Sunday from 11am to 4pm.

Wine Exchange, 452 First St. E., Sonoma, CA 95476. ☎ **707/938-1794.**

One of the most intriguing shops of its kind, this handsomely decorated establishment bears a slight resemblance to a proper old pub. Up front there's an old grape press and to the rear is a stack of casks behind a full tasting bar for trying wine by the glass. The Wine Exchange carries more than 600 California wines, plus some French wines and champagnes. The beer connoisseur will be happy to find more than 250 beers from around the world, including a number of exceptional domestic beers that I guarantee you've never seen before. Draught choices include Anchor Old, Fog Horn, Hübsh Brai, and Cellis white lager. The Wine Exchange has wine and beer tastings daily. It also has a number of useful books on wines, guides to the Wine Country, and copies of *The Wine Spectator* and *Wine Journal.* It's a great place to shop, and it ships everywhere in the United States via air freight. The shop is open daily from 10am to 6pm.

Where to Stay

EXPENSIVE

Sonoma Mission Inn & Spa, 18140 Calif. 12, Boyes Hot Springs, CA 94576. ☎ **707/938-9000,** or toll free **800/358-9022, 800/862-4945** in California. Fax 707/938-4250. 170 rms, 3 suites. A/C MINIBAR TV TEL **Directions:** From central Sonoma drive three miles north on Calif. 12.

Rates: Nov–Apr, $105–$225 Historic Inn room; $145–$310 Wine Country room. May–Oct, $145–$260 Historic Inn room; $175–$395 Wine Country room. Year round, from $325 suite. AE, DC, MC, V. **Parking:** Free.

This hostelry is off Calif. 12, set back on eight acres of lush landscaping and surrounded by a stucco wall. It's a sweeping, three-story pink structure with mission towers, beautifully groomed lawns, bougainvillea, pines, eucalyptus trees, and a pink fountain near the entry. The Sonoma Mission Inn & Spa's guest facilities and services are every bit as impressive as the entryway. The huge lobby sports an exposed-beam ceiling that hints of an old Spanish mission. Tall palms break up the length of the room, along with a large fireplace.

Guest rooms are spacious and designed with elegance and taste, from the attractively framed watercolors to the simple styling of the ceiling fans. There are few things I appreciate more than having a large bathroom replete with all the thoughtful touches that make for easy living. Each room has a scale, a hairdryer, oversize bath towels, and an ample supply of Mission Inn toiletries.

Wine Country rooms are in a newer building and are furnished with king-size beds, desks, and refrigerators. Some have fireplaces, and many have balconies. The older Historic Inn rooms are located in a historic building and are decorated in country style. They are slightly smaller and most are furnished with queen-size beds. All rooms have a VCR and come with a complimentary bottle of wine.

In 1993 the inn retapped underground hot springs. They now fill its pools and whirlpools.

Dining/Entertainment: Should you require superior sustenance, the Mission Inn offers excellent Wine Country cuisine in the Grille inside or on the outdoor Terrace Grille (weather permitting). Their casual bistro-style cafe serves Italian cuisine.

Services: Room service, concierge, laundry.

Facilities: There are body wraps, body scrubs, hair and scalp treatments, back treatments, and beauty-salon services beyond belief. After all that, if you're not too relaxed to care, strike out for the exercise class, an early-morning hike, a picnic hike, or the tennis courts. Private tennis lessons, fitness training, nutritional consultation, and slimming meals are all available. The tariff schedule of individual spa and salon services range from $14 to $155. The use of the spa's bathhouse, which includes a sauna, steam room, whirlpool, outdoor exercise pool, and gym with weight equipment costs $10 on weekdays and $20 on weekends.

MODERATE

El Dorado Hotel, 405 First St. W., Sonoma, CA 95476. ☎ **707/996-3030,** or toll free **800/289-3031.** Fax 707/996-3148. 27 rms. A/C TV TEL

Rates (including continental breakfast): $90–$145 single or double. AE, MC, V. **Parking:** Free.

The El Dorado Hotel is a true Californian beauty. The entrance to the hotel faces bucolic Sonoma Town Square and Park and has an inviting air that suggests comfort, warmth, and relaxed elegance.

Each guest room has expansive French windows and small terraces, some with lovely views of the town square, others overlooking the hotel's private courtyard and heated pool. The El Dorado's country-style rooms afford its guests continental luxury in a setting created for comfort. Light peach-tone walls surround terra-cotta floors, which are topped by wine-colored rugs and four-poster beds. Each guest room has a color TV with remote control and a private bath with plush towels. All rooms, with the exception of those for handicapped access, are on the second floor. The two lovely rooms on the ground floor are off the private courtyard, and each has its own partially enclosed patio.

Breakfast is served either inside or outside and includes coffee, fruits, and freshly baked breads and pastries. The regional Italian cuisine in the hotel's Ristorante Piatti

(☎ **707/996-2351**) is prepared in an open, wood-burning oven. The restaurant is open daily for lunch and dinner; reservations are recommended.

Sonoma Hotel, 110 W. Spain St., Sonoma, CA 94576. ☎ **707/996-2996.** 17 rms (5 with bath).

Rates (including continental breakfast): Winter, Mon–Fri $65 single or double without bath, $95 single or double with bath; Sat–Sun $75 single or double without bath, $115–$120 single or double with bath. Summer, $75–$85 single or double without bath, $115–$120 single or double with bath. AE, MC, V. **Parking:** Free.

Located on Sonoma Town Square, the Sonoma Hotel is a small, classic, historic beauty. Its accommodations evoke feelings of a different time—warm, romantic, and gracious. Each of its rooms is decorated in an early Californian style with magnificent antique furnishings, beautiful woods, and floral-print wallpapers—all with an emphasis on European elegance and comfort. Some of the rooms feature a handsome American brass bed. You may even choose to stay in no. 21—the third-floor room in which Maya Angelou wrote *Gather Together in My Name.* Five of the seven rooms on the second floor have private baths. Rooms on the third floor, in European tradition, share immaculate bathing quarters and toilet facilities off the hallway; all have private wash basins. Rooms with private baths have beautiful, deep, luxurious clawfoot tubs. The Sonoma Hotel has neither TVs nor phones in its rooms. However, for your convenience there is a hall phone on the second floor, or you can make a call at the downstairs desk.

When you arrive you're greeted as a friend with an offering of wine. Each evening there's turndown service; each morning there's a complimentary continental breakfast with fresh-baked pastries. And what more could you ask of staying in Sonoma than being situated right at the corner of the Plaza, within walking distance of picnic spots, art galleries, and historical landmarks? During the summer season, reserve at least a month in advance.

The superb dining room and saloon are both open daily. The food is something to write a long letter home about (see "Where to Dine" below for complete information).

BUDGET

El Pueblo Motel, 896 West Napa St., Sonoma, CA 95476. ☎ **707/996-3651,** or **707/996-3652.** 38 rms. A/C TV TEL

Rates: Sun–Thurs $66 single or double; Fri–Sat $77 single or double; during the Thanksgiving and Christmas holidays, $80 single or double. AE, MC, V. **Parking:** Free.

Low-cost lodgings in Sonoma are simply not that easy to come by. This place, on Sonoma's main east-west street, eight blocks from the center of town, offers just about the best-priced accommodations around. Rooms here are quite pleasant, having post-and-beam construction, exposed brick walls, and brown carpeting throughout. All have an early-American look with light wood headboards and furnishings, geometric print bedspreads, a desk and chairs. All rooms have two double beds or a king and individually controlled heat and air conditioning. A nice touch for early risers is a drip coffee machine supplied with packets of coffee. If possible, reservations should be made at least a month in advance during the spring and summer months.

Where to Dine

MODERATE

Depot 1870 Restaurant, 241 First Street W. ☎ **707/938-2980.**

Cuisine: NORTHERN ITALIAN. **Reservations:** Recommended.
Prices: Appetizers $5–$8; main courses $6–$12 at lunch, $7–$18 at dinner. AE, DC, DISC, MC, V.
Open: Lunch Wed–Fri 11:30am–2pm; dinner Wed–Sun 5–9pm.

This pleasant restaurant just one block north of Sonoma Plaza is in a handsome, historic stone building that has seen several lives. The original 1870 owners opened their living room as a bar. In 1900 eight hotel rooms were added to the second floor. During Prohibition all was closed and the building once again became a private residence. Restoration work was begun in 1962, and the Depot Hotel 1870 was reopened as a restaurant and wine bar. It now has a comfortable country finish polished to a fresh glow. To the rear you overlook a fenced-in terra-cotta patio with lots of greenery, plantings, and trees, and a small pool surrounded by dining tables. The main dining room is airy, with pink linen over burgundy cloths. A lovely antique chandelier with droplets of crystal hangs above the cozy room.

Chef Michael Ghilarducci, who has owned the restaurant since 1985, has received the honor of Grand Master Chef of America and is listed in the National Registry of Master Chefs, along with such well-known Californian names as Alice Waters, Wolfgang Puck, Jeremiah Towers, and Phillipe Jeanty (of Napa's Domaine Chandon).

A number of dishes, although not all, are northern Italian cuisine designed by chef Ghilarducci to feature the locally produced meats, poultry, seafood, bread, cheeses, and vegetables. At lunch there's a delicious sandwich of prosciutto and Sonoma Jack cheese served on French bread. You might also begin with an appetizer of paper-thin raw filet mignon slices and capers touched with parmesan cheese and olive oil. For those whose eyes gleam at the thought of a creamy pasta, the tortellini Ghilarducci is a path to sheer joy—stuffed with ricotta, veal, and chicken and touched with a delicate cream sauce and freshly grated parmesan cheese.

As for main courses, you may find such dishes as veal scaloppine, chicken and Italian sausage with polenta, and prawns sautéed with white wine, shallots, and lemon. For desserts, the tiramisu is a best seller. Here, it's a creation of sponge cake layered with freshly grated chocolate and Mascarpone (an imported Italian cream cheese) and sprinkled with espresso and rum. For those almost lacking a sweet tooth, there is always fresh fruit and cheese.

Old Swiss Hotel, 18 W. Spain St. ☎ **707/938-2884.**

Cuisine: CONTINENTAL. **Reservations:** Accepted.
Prices: Appetizers $5–$7; main courses $8–$16; lunch $3–$11. MC, V.
Open: Lunch Mon–Fri 11am–2:30pm; dinner nightly 5–9:30pm. Bar open daily 11am–2am.

The historic Old Swiss Hotel, located right in Sonoma's center, is one of the town's true landmarks. Now a restaurant (recently reopened after extensive restoration), the building retains its seasoned charm, complete with slanting floors and aged beamed ceilings. The turn-of-the-century long oak bar, located to the left of the entrance, is decorated with black-and-white photographs of pioneering Sonomians. Cold beers are kept in an antique wood-and-glass meat cooler.

The restaurant's bright white dining room and rear dining patio are both intimate and colorful. Lunch offerings include such entrées as penne pasta with chicken and mushrooms, as well as a variety of sandwiches and California-style pizzas fired in a wood-burning oven. Nights may start with a warm winter salad of pears, walnuts, radicchio, and blue cheese or with minestrone soup. Entrées run the gamut from linguine with a spicy tomato sauce to filet mignon wrapped in a cheese crust and duck in a red wine sauce.

Sonoma Hotel, 110 W. Spain St. ☎ **707/996-2996.**

Cuisine: CALIFORNIAN. **Reservations:** Strongly recommended.
Prices: Appetizers $6–$11; main courses $6–$9 at lunch, $15–$17.50 at dinner. AE, MC, V.
Open: Lunch daily 11:30am–3pm; dinner nightly 5:45–8:30pm (in summer to 9pm).

Dining at the Sonoma Hotel, on Sonoma Town Square, is truly a visual and gastronomic treat that you don't want to pass up. The Sonoma is a respectful restoration of the original hotel, which dates back to the 1880s. There's a magnificent old bar of oak and mahogany, plucked right out of the turn of the century. The Saloon is a guileless charmer—an inviting, relaxed, comfortable spot out of another time—great for wine tasting, cocktails, conversation, waiting for your dinner partner, or a pleasant after-dinner drink.

The dining room has antique oak tables, decorative panels of stained glass, fresh flowers, comfortable oak chairs, and simply superb food. The menu changes every two weeks and specials are offered each evening. There are always great choices, whether your taste that evening happens to be for an exceptional beef, seafood, veal, chicken, or pasta dish. And the chef always includes seasonal vegetables, herbs from the hotel's garden, and homemade or locally produced ingredients.

The wine list is first-rate and there's a good selection of wines for $3 to $4.50 per glass. Should you decide to bring a bottle you may have selected at one of the vineyards, the corkage charge is $7.

BUDGET

Feed Store Café and Bakery, 529 First St. W. ☎ **707/938-2122.**

Cuisine: CALIFORNIAN. **Reservations:** Accepted; recommended Sun.
Prices: Appetizers $4–$9; main courses $4–$8 at lunch, $8–$14 at dinner; breakfast $3–$9. MC, V.
Open: Daily 7am–9pm.

You'll first notice that the Feed Store, on Sonoma Plaza at the corner of West Napa Street, is attractive, airy, and fresh. The staff is particularly nice and is always full of suggestions on what to see and do in the Bay Area. The dining room is large, and features high ceilings typical of turn-of-the-century feed stores. An open kitchen adds to the spacious feel.

During warm weather you might enjoy al fresco dining on the lovely patio at the rear of the restaurant, beautifully done with lots of flowers and a genteel gurgling fountain. On warm summer nights the staff rolls back the multicolored awning so that you can dine under the stars.

Food here is first-rate, reasonably priced, and plentiful. For breakfast, the Feed Store Café has more varieties of eggs than you could eat in a month's stay. Choices also include such delectables as the Sonoma Mission Scrambler on tortilla strips, huevos rancheros, and a delicious special-recipe French toast. Lunch is designed to match any appetite from quesadillas to burgers or a grilled Mexican chicken breast. Dinner specials change daily, although the mainstays of the menu are seafood, chicken, and enormous salads. Burgers and sandwiches are also available.

Under the same roof is the Bakery at the Feed Store, offering a marvelous selection of baked goods from mini coffee cakes, and a variety of muffins, to New York cheesecake. Their homemade breads are perfect for picnics.

Home Grown Bagels, 122 W. Napa St. ☎ **707/996-0166.**

Cuisine: DELI.
Prices: Bagel sandwiches or salads $3–$6. No credit cards.
Open: Mon–Fri 6:30am–2:30pm, Sat–Sun 7am–2pm.

This small bakery/restaurant just half a block from Sonoma Plaza may not be visually impressive, but it offers a good selection of bagels and bialys filled with any number of tasty items. In addition to the traditional cream cheese and lox, you can have more substantial fillings like pastrami, turkey, salami, and cheese. If a somewhat more traditional breakfast is your style, there's ham and egg, bacon and egg, or Canadian bacon and egg on a bagel. Salads, veggies, and salad plates are always available.

As you might expect, the establishment serves the usual hot beverages, as well as cappuccino. Soft drinks are also to be had. The bagelry is on the breakfast circuit; it's a mob scene after 8:30am, so be prepared to wait or get there early.

La Casa, 121 E. Spain St. ☎ **707/996-3406.**

Cuisine: MEXICAN. **Reservations:** Recommended on weekends and summer evenings.
Prices: Appetizers $4–$6; main courses $4.95–$10; lunch or dinner specialties $5.95–$10.50. AE, CB, DC, MC, V.
Open: Daily 11:30am–9pm.

Located on Sonoma Town Square, across from the mission, this is a no-nonsense Mexican restaurant made to satisfy your urge for enchiladas, fajitas, and chimichangas. Did I mention margaritas? La Casa opens onto a lounge and bar, then to a two-tiered, softly lit dining area and onto a new patio overlooking the El Paseo courtyard.

When available, the ceviche is made of fresh snapper marinated in lime juice and served on two crispy tortillas. Tortilla soup is made from a base of homemade chicken soup. The real treats are to be found among the specialties de la casa. Tamales freshly made in La Casa's kitchen are prepared with corn husks spread with corn masa, stuffed with chicken filling, and topped with mild red chile sauce. Then there are the enchiladas Suiza—deep-dish enchiladas with corn tortillas filled with chicken or ground beef, served with rice and a green salad. But if the fresh snapper Veracruz is available, that tops the menu. The filet is grilled and topped with a mild tomato sauce, onions, bell peppers, olives, capers, and melted cheese, and served with refried beans, rice, and a green salad. Wine is available by the bottle or glass, as is both Mexican and American beer.

PICNIC FARE

Although Sonoma has plenty of restaurants, the Plaza park is a lovely place for a picnic, complete with tables.

Sonoma Cheese Factory, 2 Spain St. on the Plaza. ☎ **707/996-1000.**

Offering an extraordinary variety of imported meats and cheeses, the factory also sells caviar, gourmet salads, pâté, and homemade Sonoma Jack cheese. It makes sandwiches, too. While you're there, you can watch a narrated slide show about cheese making.

Open: Mon–Fri 8:30am–5:30pm, Sat–Sun 8:30am–6pm.

Sonoma Sausage Co., 453 First St. W. ☎ **707/936-8200.**

Follow your nose to Sonoma Sausage; the fragrance of handmade sausage wafts over Sonoma Plaza. In addition to making and selling smoked, cooked, and Louisiana-style sausages, the company purveys smoked meats, pâtés, and lunch meats. There are more than 85 delicious varieties of sausages and lunch meats in all. Smoked meats are fully cooked and ready for picnicking. While I admit that I haven't tried every sausage here, the ones that I have had are delicious. Sonoma sausages are made with 100% pure meat and contain no cereals, soy concentrates, or other fillers. They come with complete cooking instructions, along with excellent recipes. The company has won many awards over the past several years. Sonoma Sausage Company will ship orders to any state, although a few items are recommended to be hand carried.

Open: Daily 10am–5pm.

★ **Vella Cheese Company,** 315 Second St. E. ☎ **707/938-3232,** or toll free **800/848-0505.**

Located one block north of East Spain Street, this is where they make and sell the original Dry Jack cheese, a carefully aged perfect accompaniment to wine. Vella Cheese also makes a rich, buttery Monterey Jack, a naturally seasoned Jack, and a superb sharp white Cheddar. Among other cheeses for which Vella has become famous is Oregon Blue, made at Vella's factory in southern Oregon. It is a rich, buttery, spreadable blue cheese—one of the few great blues produced in this country. Any of these fine handmade, all-natural cheeses can be shipped directly from the store.

Open: Mon–Sat 9am–6pm, Sun 10am–5pm.

6 Northern California

HEADING NORTH FROM SAN FRANCISCO, TRAVELERS COME UPON A CALIFORNIA THAT is very different from the southern part of the state. It is different in landscape, in climate, in flora and fauna, and in human habitation. Still one of the least urbanized areas of the country, it comes closer than the rest of the state to looking pretty much as it did when the European conquerors arrived in the mid-1500s.

The region, you'll find as you drive along, consists of a series of scenic views fit for a postcard. It has rugged coasts and majestic mountain ranges, among them Mount Whitney, the highest summit in the United States outside Alaska; it is covered for miles on end by vineyards and farmlands and by large redwood forests, some of which boast the tallest trees in the world; it contains Yosemite National Park, one of the largest natural preserves in the world, and Lake Tahoe, an alpine wonder; it is dotted with picturesque small towns, many of them displaying a charming Victorian-style architecture.

Northern California is devoid of sprawling big cities and, therefore, of the problems associated with them: noise, smog, congestion, clogged freeways, and social unrest. It is a place where one can still appreciate, at the close of the 20th century, the quiet, pristine beauty of nature, unspoiled by modern development.

SEEING NORTHERN CALIFORNIA

The prettiest way to reach Mendocino, Little River, and Fort Bragg—all of which are situated right next to each other—is to drive north from San Francisco along the coast via Calif. 1. The larger freeway, U.S. 101, runs inland through Healdsburg and Cloverdale and is faster. If you decide to take this route, turn toward the coast on Calif. 20 at Willits.

The 33-mile-long Avenue of the Giants is located in southern Humboldt County, north of Fort Bragg. It's an easy drive from Mendocino: Proceed north along the coast on Calif. 1, which becomes U.S. 101 at Leggitt; continue on U.S. 101 north for about 10 more miles to the avenue.

It's a long way from the Avenue of the Giants to Lake Tahoe and Yosemite National Park, so long that you'd be better off returning to San Francisco before heading east to the lake or park.

1 Mendocino, Little River & Fort Bragg

125 miles N of San Francisco

GETTING THERE • **By Car** The fastest route from San Francisco is via U.S. 101 north to Cloverdale. From there, take Calif. 128 west to Calif. 1, then go north along the coast, about a four-hour drive. The prettiest route from the Bay Area is Calif. 1 north along the coast the entire way, about a five-hour drive.

ESSENTIALS • **Orientation** Located directly on Calif. 1, the pocket-size town of Mendocino sits directly on the ocean in the middle of a particularly scenic stretch of coastline. Little River, about two miles to the south, is situated at the western end of Van Damme State Park. Fort Bragg, 10 miles north of Mendocino, is the largest coastal city between San Francisco and Eureka. Still, it's tiny, and negotiating your way around is as easy as keeping one eye on the ocean.

• **Information** The **Fort Bragg/Mendocino Coast Chamber of Commerce,** 332 N. Main St., P.O. Box 1141, Fort Bragg, CA 95437 (☎ **707/961-6300** or toll free

What's Special About Northern California

Natural Wonders

- The Sierra Nevada, with its display of awe-inspiring beauty.
- Yosemite National Park, one of the prettiest protected areas in the world.
- Giant redwoods, the world's tallest trees.
- Lake Tahoe, in the heavily timbered Sierra Nevada, one of the most beautiful lakes in the world.
- The state's most rugged coastline, revealing new, picture-postcard cliffs at every turn.

Physical Adventure

- Skiing and boating on the same day in and around northern California.
- Ballooning over Nevada's Carson Valley, near South Lake Tahoe.
- Bungee jumping, from a 75-foot tower, in Squaw Valley.
- Hiking and climbing on Half Dome and other peaks in Yosemite.
- Camping in the national park and other wilderness locations.

Charming Towns

- Mendocino, one of the prettiest small towns in the state, unmarred by commercialism.
- Innumerable small villages with small stores, friendly residents, and gas stations where you don't have to pay first.

Historical Sights

- Old Sacramento, with its more than 100 restored buildings, many dating from the gold-rush era.
- The state capitol and former governor's mansion, in Sacramento, both fine examples of early California architecture.

800/726-2780), distributes information and literature on accommodations, shops, restaurants, current events, and more.

Despite (or because of) its relative isolation, Mendocino has emerged as one of northern California's major centers for the arts. It's easy to see why artists are attracted to this idyllic seaside community, with its backdrop of 19th-century charm and beauty, weathered barns, old mansions, deep-green forests, blue sea, and white surf.

Mendocino town was originally known as Meiggsville, named after settler Harry Meiggs, who visited the area in search of a wrecked off-shore cargo of Chinese silk. Meiggs never found the silk, but he did discover another treasure here: giant redwoods. Not a naturalist, Meiggs built the area's first sawmill, chopped down the centuries-old beauties, and began shipping cargoes of lumber back to fast-growing San Francisco. The lumber boom lasted over 50 years. (Interestingly, Meiggs later traveled to South America, where he built the first railroad across the Andes.) Meiggsville was settled by lumberjacks, most of whom came from the New England states. Today, eastern colonial architecture is still very much in evidence in Mendocino—many old houses have widow's walks and slanted roofs steeply pitched to shed snow, which, of course, never falls here.

Northern California

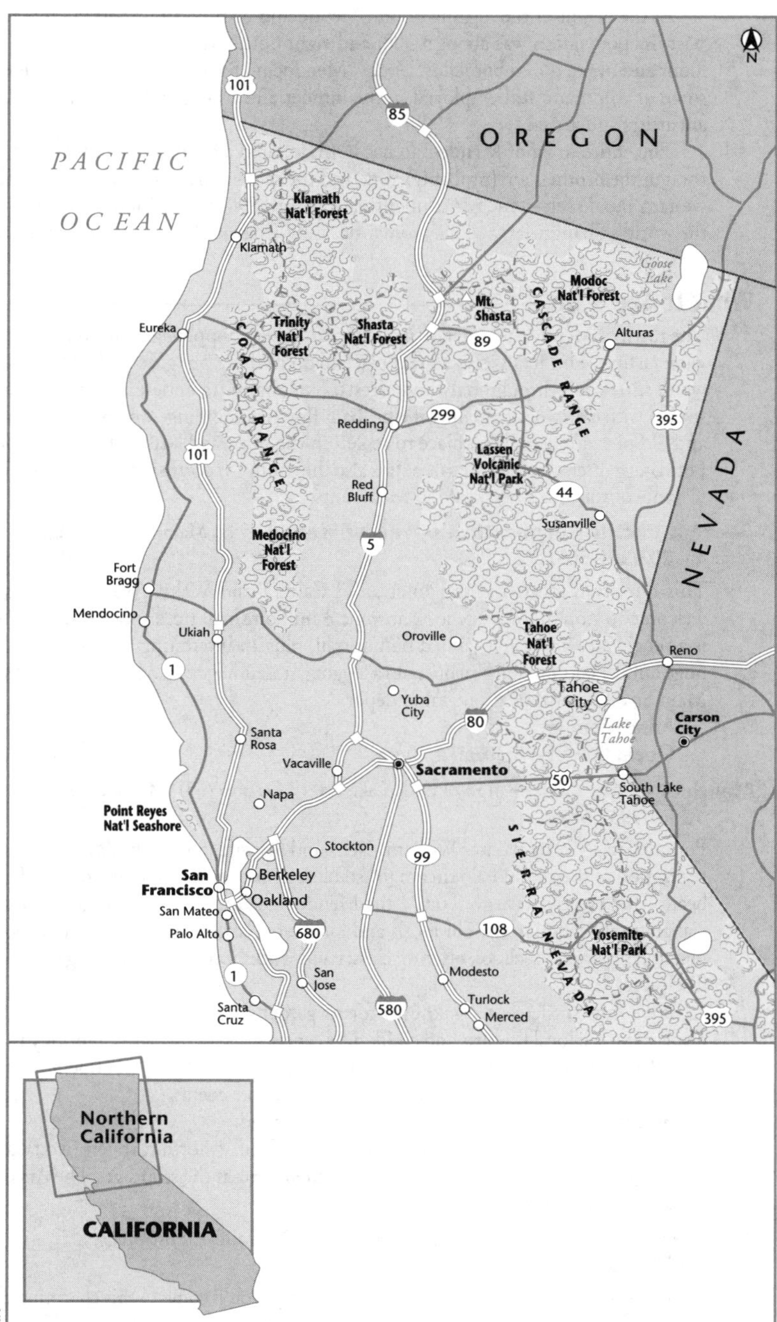

At the height of the logging boom, Mendocino became an important and active port. Its population was about 3,500, and eight hotels were built, along with 17 saloons and over a dozen bordellos. Today, Mendocino has only about 1,000 residents, some of whom are still employed in the lumber and fishing industries. Many more are artists and artisans.

The entire town of Mendocino has been declared a historic monument. And although the brothels are (probably) gone and the saloons are fewer, it still looks like a western movie set—much as it might have in an 1890 photo. Mendocino is one of the world's Shangri-las, a serene, romantic, away-from-it-all retreat, and a pleasure to visit.

What to See & Do

The town of Mendocino is tailor-made for art-gallery hopping and antiquing and for wine tasting. The area is also a great place to do nothing but gaze at the blue sea and white surf, stroll through redwood forests, or along miles of deserted sandy beaches strewn with driftwood, or enjoy the brilliant flowers blooming amid weathered barns and old picket fences. It's a place to replenish the spirit and bask in nature's bounty. Fort Bragg offers more of the same. It is also the county's sportfishing center and home to some of the area's best seafood restaurants.

Georgia-Pacific Corporation's Tree Nursery, 275 N. Main St. Fort Bragg. ☎ **707/964-5651.**

This nursery is located at the junction of Calif. 1 and Walnut Street. Visitors are welcome to stop in for a free look at some 3 million small trees and seedlings. There is a picnic area and a self-guided nature trail, plus an interesting visitor center. The huge lumber corporation also operates a logging museum located on Fort Bragg's North Main Street, near the Skunk Train depot.

Admission: Free

Open: Mon–Fri 8:30am–4:30pm.

Mendocino Art Center, 45200 Little Lake Rd. (P.O. Box 765), Mendocino. ☎ **707/937-5818.**

Founded in 1959 by painter William Zacha and his wife, Jenny, the Art Center is the realization of their long-held dream to establish a unique art school in an area of great beauty and creative energy. Today, the Mendocino Art Center is the town's unofficial cultural headquarters. For locals and long-term visitors, the center acts as both a meeting place and a school, offering classes and workshops in a broad range of artistic disciplines.

For tourists, the center is known for its gardens, three galleries, and shops that display and sell local fine arts and crafts. The center's free, informative monthly magazine *Arts and Entertainment* lists upcoming events throughout Mendocino. It also features interviews with local artists, short stories, and poems.

Admission: Free, though donations are requested.

Open: Daily 10am–5pm. **Directions:** From Calif. 1 north turn left (west) at the traffic signal (there's only one), and jog left, then right at the stop sign. The Art Center is two blocks ahead.

Mendocino Coast Botanical Gardens, 18220 N. Calif. 1, Fort Bragg. ☎ **707/964-4352.**

About six miles north of Mendocino, in Fort Bragg, you'll come to this charming clifftop public garden among the pines along the rugged coast. The gardens were fashioned by a retired nurseryman who spent years reclaiming wilderness and nurturing rhododendrons, fuchsias, azaleas, and a multitude of flowering shrubs. The area contains trails for easy walking, bridges, streams, canyons, dells, and picnic areas. Children under 12 must be accompanied by their parents.

Admission: $5 adults, $4 seniors age 60 and over, $3 children ages 13–17, free for children 12 and under.

Open: Mar–Oct daily 9am–5pm; Nov–Feb daily 9am–4pm.

Noyo's Fishing Center, 3245 North Harbor, Noyo. ☎ **707/964-7609.**

Located in the tiny village of Noyo, just south of Fort Bragg, this helpful, well-stocked shop is a good place to buy or rent tackle, and the best source of information on local fishing boats.

Russian Gulch State Park, Mendocino. ☎ **707/937-5804.**

Located directly on Hwy. 1, just north of Mendocino, Russian Gulch is one of the region's most spectacular parks. Fierce waves crash against craggy cliffs, which protect the park's magnificent California coastal redwoods. The most popular attraction at Russian Gulch is the Punch Bowl, a collapsed sea cave that forms a tunnel through which waves crash, creating throaty echoes. Visitors can also hike along miles of trails, including a gentle, well-marked three-mile Waterfall Loop that winds past tall redwoods and damp green foliage to a 36-foot-high waterfall.

Thirty wooded camping sites are available here from April through mid-October. Phone for reservations.

★ **Skunk Train,** Fort Bragg Depot, Laurel Ave., Fort Bragg. ☎ **707/964-6371.**

One of the best ways to see the redwoods is to "ride the Skunks"—California Western Railroad's self-powered diesel trains. They're nicknamed for their original gas engines, of which it was said "You can smell 'em before you can see 'em." The trains, which can be boarded at the foot of Laurel Avenue in Fort Bragg (two blocks from the Grey Whale Inn), travel 40 miles inland along the Redwood Highway (U.S. 101) to Willits. The journey through the very heart of California's most magnificent towering redwood forest is a truly spectacular route not accessible by car. Windows front and side make for some wonderful sightseeing. The ride takes you across 31 bridges and trestles and through two deep tunnels; its serpentine route encompasses scenery from forest to sunlit fields of wildflowers, grazing cattle, and apple orchards. The round trip takes six to seven hours, allowing plenty of time for lunch in Willits before you return on the afternoon train. Half-day trips are offered weekends throughout the year, and daily in summer from mid-June to early September. Call for reservations in the summer months. The trains run year round, and usually depart in the morning. Schedules vary; call for exact times.

Tickets: Adults $26 round-trip, $21 one-way; children ages 5–11 go for half price.

Sweetwater Gardens, 955 Ukiah St. (P.O. Box 337), Mendocino. ☎ **707/937-4140,** or toll free **800/300-4140.**

For a special non-touristy treat that seems particularly suited to Mendocino life, Sweetwater Gardens offers group and private saunas and hot tub soaks by the hour. Additional services include Swedish or deep-tissue massages. Reservations are recommended.

Private Tub Prices: $7.50 per person per half-hour, $10.50 per person per hour.
Group Tub Prices: $7.50 per person with no time limit. Special discounts on Wed.

Open: Mon–Thurs 2–10pm, Fri–Sun noon–11pm.

SHOPPING

The best shopping in the area is in Fort Bragg, where many small boutiques are clustered. Antiques shops line the 300 block of N. Franklin St., one block east of Main Street.

Fort Bragg Depot, 401 N. Main St., Fort Bragg. ☎ **707/964-6261.**

Fort Bragg's legendary historical train depot has been revived into a combination shopping center and historical museum exhibiting the town's railway history. The warehouse-size structure is filled with specialty shops and boutiques, and a small food court serving a variety of hot foods and espresso drinks. Organized tours of Fort Bragg, Mendocino, and the nearby redwood forests are also sold here. Historical artifacts include logging equipment and restored steam trains. Most shops are open daily from 10am to 6pm; the food court opens at 6:30am.

For the Shell of It, 344 N. Main St., Fort Bragg. ☎ **961-0461.**

Most of the handmade jewelry, baskets, and collectibles sold here are either made of shells, or have a nautical theme. It's open daily from 9am to 6pm.

Gallery Bookshop, at Main And Kasten Sts. (P.O. Box 270), Mendocino. ☎ **707/937-2665.**

This unusually large general-interest bookstore sells both new and used books, and includes an extensive childrens' section. It's open Sunday through Thursday from 10am to 6pm, Friday and Saturday from 10am to 9pm.

Glover Gallery, 226 East Redwood St., Fort Bragg. ☎ **964-6398.**

Jerry Glover's unique collection of sculpture, jewelry, collectibles, and fine art includes many pieces with marine mammal themes. Glover Gallery is open from 11:30am to 4:30pm by appointment only.

Highlight Gallery, 45052 Main St. (P.O. Box 1515), Mendocino. ☎ **707/937-3132.**

Only the luckiest local artists display their pieces in Clyde and Tigerlily Jones's clean, modern, bright gallery by the sea. Artful designs include wood pieces, lamps, cabinets, bronze sculptures, paintings, ceramics, and more. Located within sight of the magnificent Northern California coast, the store itself is almost as beautiful as the art it sells. It's open daily 10am to 5pm.

Hot Pepper Jelly Company, 330 N. Main St., Fort Bragg. ☎ **961-1422.**

Well known for their good supply of Mendocino-made foods, the company offers much more than dozens of varieties of pepper jelly. Local mustards, syrups, and biscotti are sold along with hand-painted porcelain bowls, unusual baskets, and more. It is open daily from 10am to 5:30pm.

Mendocino Chocolate Company, 542 Main St., Fort Bragg. ☎ **707/964-8800.**

Located adjacent to the train tracks, this small shop makes and sells wonderful homemade chocolates and truffles. They ship worldwide.

A second shop is located in Mendocino, at 10483 Lansing St. (☎ **707/937-1104**). Both are open daily 10am to 5pm.

Mendocino Gold, Lansing St. (P.O. Box 110), Mendocino. ☎ **707/937-2018.**

Only original handmade jewelry is sold here. Most, but not all, of the designs are created in gold—a few silver pieces are also available. It's open daily from 11am to 4:30pm.

Northcoast Artists, 362 North Main St., Fort Bragg. ☎ **964-8266.**

Painters, jewelers, sculptors, weavers, potters, and other local artists have joined together in this collective to display and sell their wares. An unusually large selection of good quality wares at relatively modest prices can be found here. Summer hours are Monday through Saturday from 10am to 6pm, Sunday from 10am to 3pm. The shop closes an hour earlier Monday through Saturday in winter.

Windsong, 324 N. Main St., Fort Bragg. ☎ **707/964-2050.**

A clutter of colorful kites, cards, candles, jazz music, and other gifts are sold here. The store is larger than it looks; browse towards the back, where additional rooms hold more gifts, plus used books and records. Open Monday through Saturday from 10am to 5:30pm, and Sunday 10am to 4pm.

Where to Stay

EXPENSIVE

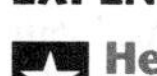

Heritage House, 5200 N. Calif. 1, Little River, CA 95456. ☎ **707/937-5885,** or toll free **800/235-5885.** 74 rms.

Rates (including breakfast and dinner): $175–$365 single or double. Additional person $65. Off-season discounted rates are available. MC, V. **Closed:** Dec–Jan. **Parking:** Free.

Most of the rooms in this idyllic retreat have wide-open views of the ocean and beautiful coastline. It's hard to say which is better—the ocean sunsets or falling asleep to the sound of the surf. Built in 1877 as a farmhouse, the main building's most infamous moment was as a hideout for bandit "Baby Face" Nelson. Only three guest rooms are located in the ivy-covered New England-style main building. The rest are in cottages tucked unobtrusively into the landscape. Accommodations are decorated with original antiques and locally hand-carpentered furnishings. The rooms are cozy and comfortable but are purposely devoid of phones and TV. There is no swimming pool either, just wooded walkways on one of the most dramatic coastlines in California. Accommodations include both breakfast and dinner.

Even if you're not staying here, though, it's worth showing up around mealtime. The Heritage House dining room is the country restaurant of everyone's dreams. Start with cocktails on the terrace while looking over potted geraniums onto the rocky shores below. Then move into the elegant interior dining room for an excellent $31 fixed-price dinner. A typical menu includes black mussel and saffron chowder, salad, crisp seared Cornish gamehen, two vegetables, homemade biscuits, cream puffs with hot fudge, fruit, cheese, and coffee. Other main courses often include grilled leg of lamb, filet mignon, and giant sea scallops. The accompanying wine list is outstanding. Men are requested to wear jackets and reservations are essential.

MODERATE

Grey Whale Inn, 615 N. Main St., Fort Bragg, CA 95437. ☎ **707/964-0640,** or toll free **800/382-7244**. 14 rms, 5 suites. TEL

Rates (including breakfast): $65–$145 single; $85–$165 double. Nov–Mar second consecutive weeknight, Sun–Wed, is half price. 20% discount on one-night stays Sun–Thurs, holidays excluded. AE, DISC, MC, V.

Looking to run a comfortable B&B in a slower moving town, former San Franciscans John and Colette Bailey came to Fort Bragg in 1978 and purchased this 1915 Mendocino Coast Landmark. Originally a hospital, the spacious and airy redwood building is now a perfectly run, relaxed inn, furnished partly with antiques and the requisite amount of local art. Each guest room is unique: several have ocean views, or a fireplace, or whirlpool tub; another has a private deck or a shower with wheelchair access. There is no smoking allowed in any of them. The inn itself is well-located, just six blocks from the beach and two blocks from the Skunk Train depot. The generous buffet breakfast includes homemade bread or coffeecake, juice or fresh fruit, and a selection of hot beverages, cereals, and brunch casseroles.

★ **MacCallum House,** Albion St. (P.O. Box 206), Mendocino, CA 95460. ☎ **707/937-0289.** 20 rms (8 with bath), 1 suite. **Directions:** From U.S. 101, turn right onto Albion Street in downtown Mendocino.

Rates (including continental breakfast): $75–$180 single or double; $180–$240 suite. Additional person $15. MC, V. **Parking:** Free.

A historic 1882 gingerbread Victorian mansion, MacCallum House is the town's top hostelry. Originally owned by local matriarch Daisy MacCallum, the house still has the imprint of this respected area resident. A teacher by trade, MacCallum helped start the town's fire department, studied horticulture, traveled extensively, and played a leading role in community affairs. The house remained in the family until 1974, when it was turned into a bed and breakfast. Now owned by resident proprietors Melanie and Joe Reding, the home has been preserved with all of its original furnishings and contents—right down to Daisy's Christmas cards and books of pressed flowers. Boasting an occasional Tiffany lamp or real Persian carpet, each uniquely decorated guest room is exquisitely furnished with many original pieces. Charming wallpaper surrounds a Franklin stove, handmade quilt, cushioned rocking chair, or child's cradle. Most rooms have sinks and share large baths. The luxurious barn suite, complete with a stone fireplace, can accommodate up to six adults.

The MacCallum House Restaurant (☎ **707/937-5763**) is open to the public and worth going out of your way for. Owner Rob Ferrero presides over made-to-order meals, which might start with broiled oysters bathed with garlic-basil butter and move on to a local salmon filet or pan-broiled tenderloin with shiitake mushrooms. Desserts are also homemade and may include a seasonal fruit tart, chocolate-nut torte, or puff pastry. Meals cost from $15 to $30 without wine. The restaurant is open for dinner Friday through Wednesday from 5:30 to 9pm.

Mendocino Hotel and Garden Suites, 45080 Main St., Mendocino, CA 95460. ☎ **707/937-0511,** or toll free **800/548-0513.** Fax 707/937-0513. 51 rms (37 with bath), 6 suites. TEL **Directions:** From Calif. 1, take the Jackson Street exit; this puts you on Lansing Street, which becomes Main Street.

Rates: $50–$80 single or double without bath, $65–$110 single or double with bath; $90–$180 deluxe single or double; $150–$225 suite. Additional person $20. Rates are slightly lower from Dec–Mar and on weekdays year-round. AE, MC, V. **Parking:** Free.

Beautiful beveled-glass doors open onto a lobby and public areas that evoke the Victorian opulence of Gold Rush days. The oak reception desk, from a demolished Kansas bank, is, like the other furnishings in this pretty 1878 wood hotel, part of a harmonious combination of antiques and reproductions that are liberally spread throughout. Guest rooms feature hand-painted French porcelain sinks with floral designs, quaint wallpapers, old-fashioned beds and armoires, and photographs and memorabilia of historic Mendocino. About half the rooms are located in four handsome small buildings across the road from the main house. Many of the deluxe rooms have fireplaces or wood-burning stoves, as well as more modern bathrooms and good views. Suites have an additional parlor, as well as a fireplace or balcony.

Moderately priced breakfasts and lunches are served in the lobby-level Garden Room, a cozy dining room featuring the standards of Californian-cuisine daily from

8am to 2:30pm. Dinner is served nightly in the Victorian main dining room until 9:30pm. Room service is available daily from 8am to 9pm.

Mendocino Village Inn, 44860 Main St., (P.O. Box 626), Mendocino, CA 95460. ☎ **707/937-0246,** or toll free **800/882-7029.** 13 rms. TEL

Rates (including breakfast): $65 double with shared bath; $85–$145 double with private bath; $190 suite. No credit cards.

Although there is a street running between the Mendocino Village Inn and the ocean, this bed-and-breakfast is just about as close to the water as an overnight visitor to Mendocino can get. A colorful garden of flowers, plants, ponds, and flags front the large blue-and-white guesthouse. Wooden stairs lead up to the B&B's front porch and main entrance. Built in 1882 by a local doctor who was also one of the region's lumber barons, and later occupied by famed local artist Emmy Lou Packard, the home's airy interior is just as welcoming.

Innkeepers Bill and Kathleen Erwin have decorated each room with a different, yet united, early California country decor. Skipper's Quarters is filled with internationally acquired treasures and trinkets. The vaguely Victorian-style Queen Anne Room features a four-poster canopy bed, and the sentimental Maggie's Room is named for a child who etched her name in the window glass almost a century ago—it's still there. Except for two attic rooms, every accommodation here has a private bath. Four rooms have private outside entrances, and all come with full breakfasts that include a main course, homemade baked goods, fresh fruit, juice, and coffee. Complimentary evening beverages are also served. The inn is completely non-smoking and prohibits pets and children under 10 years of age.

Pudding Creek Inn, 700 North Main Street, Fort Bragg, CA 95437. ☎ **707/964-9529,** or toll free **800/227-9529.** 10 rms.

Rates (including breakfast): $65–$125 single or double. AE, DISC, MC, V.

The pink Pudding Creek Inn is actually two separate small houses connected by an enclosed pebbled garden court filled with flowering plants, a stone fountain, and comfortable patio furnishings. Although many of the rooms here are quite small, each is uniquely decorated, comfortable and colorful, and comes with private baths.

Despite its name, the Main House contains fewer rooms than the adjacent two-story annex. The street-front Count's Room features a huge stone fireplace and a king-size brass bed. It's a beautiful room, but not far enough from the traffic noise of Highway 1. Rooms in back are quieter; the best is called Interlude, and contains a king bed and an oversized bathtub.

The B&B's only guest phone is located in the garden. A TV and recreation room is located on the ground floor of the Main House, near the breakfast parlor, which contains tall bay windows, antique tables, and a fireplace. Afternoon tea, wine, and cheese are served in a separate living room, or out in the garden on temperate days.

Where to Dine

EXPENSIVE

Café Beaujolais, 961 Ukiah St., Mendocino. ☎ **707/937-5614.**

Cuisine: AMERICAN/FRENCH. **Reservations:** Recommended. **Directions:** from Calif. 1 north, turn left at the traffic light onto Little Lake Road and continue left to Ukiah Street.

Prices: Appetizers $4.50–$9; main courses $7–$13 at lunch, $17–$22 at dinner; breakfast $5–$11. No credit cards.
Open: Lunch Thurs, Fri, and Mon 11am–2:30pm; brunch Sat–Sun 8:30am–2:30pm; dinner Thurs–Mon 5:45–9pm.

This charming French country–style inn is papered with the most beautiful Victorian reproduction wallpaper I've ever seen. Rose-colored carnival glass chandeliers hang over oak floors, a wood-burning stove, spindle-back chairs, and substantial oak pedestal tables adorned with flowers. There's more seating on an outdoor deck overlooking the garden.

You can begin the day with homemade coffee cake and excellent coffee, waffles with pure maple syrup, or eggs with chicken-apple sausage. Lunch menus change daily but usually offer everything from a terrific burger with country fries to local fish stew and an extraordinary black-bean chili. Dinners might include chicken stuffed with eggplant, mushrooms, cheese, garlic, and fresh herbs; or roast filet of beef. Among the specialties of the house are fresh salmon and roast leg of lamb. "Decadent" chocolate desserts are worth the splurge.

The newest addition to Café Beaujolais is The Brickery next door, noted for its wood-fired bread and pizza. This is where you can buy delicious crusty breads (baked daily) and pizzas to eat in or take out. And while you're there, grab a copy of the Café Beaujolais bakery catalog. Among the mouth-watering mail-order items are chicken-apple sausages, dried tomatoes, and pear barbecue sauce—a rich, naturally fruity, and mildly spicy marinade.

MODERATE

Bay View Cafe, 45040 Main St., Mendocino. ☎ **707/937-4197.**

Cuisine: AMERICAN. **Reservations:** Not accepted.
Prices: Breakfast $4–$7; lunch $5–$12; dinner $7–$15. No credit cards.
Open: Daily 8am–9pm.

True to the cafe's name, the magnificent bay view is the star at this otherwise mediocre eatery on Mendocino's Main Street. Bay View Cafe is one of the few places in town where you can dine overlooking the ruggedly awesome California coast. The restaurant's unspectacular soup-salad-and-sandwich coffee-shop fare is enlivened by good locally caught seafood entrées. Egg breakfasts are also recommendable, but the Bay View Cafe is at its best if you can luck into an outdoor table, then celebrate with a drink and a snack, and dinner elsewhere.

The Cafe, in The Old Coast Hotel, 101 N. Franklin St., Fort Bragg. ☎ **707/964-6446.**

Cuisine: INTERNATIONAL. **Reservations:** Accepted.
Prices: Appetizers $4–$8; main courses $10–$17. MC, V.
Open: Dinner only Wed–Sun 5:30–9:30pm.

Like many of Fort Bragg's finer restaurants, The Cafe is located within a hotel. Situated near the town's antique row, The Cafe serves good and serious meals in a decidedly casual setting. Flanked on one side by a long bar, the single dining room is simply furnished with light wood tables topped with red-and-white cloths.

Excellent appetizers include warm goat cheese smoked over vine cuttings and served on a bed of greens with mustard vinaigrette and oysters broiled in their shells with mushrooms, shrimp, garlic, white wine, and cheese. A selection of seafood, meat, and poultry entrées is always available; daily specials might include grilled cod with Créole spices, or a hotly peppered chicken. Vegetarians will be particularly pleased by items like grilled eggplant with creamy mushroom sauce and linguini with sun-dried and fresh tomatoes, basil, and mozzarella. Seasonally inspired desserts change nightly. There's a full bar, and a small selection of wines available by the glass.

Chocolate Mousse Cafe, 390 Kasten St., Mendocino. ☎ **707/937-4323.**

Cuisine: CONTINENTAL. **Reservations:** Accepted.
Prices: Lunch $5–$10; appetizers $4–$7; main courses $11–$16. No credit cards.
Open: Mon–Thurs 11:30am–9pm, Fri 11:30am–10:30pm, Sat 10am–10:30pm, Sun 10am–9pm.

The Chocolate Mousse Cafe, located a half-block off Mendocino's Main Street, is as whimsical as its name. The restaurant's light-hearted interior is a straightforward, crisp and clean renovation of an old house—white walls, large windows, and polished wood floors are light, wholesome, and bright. Menus, which appear to be planned with a mischievous wink, feature fresh twists on old favorites. A meatloaf sandwich is made with ground turkey and chicken sausage, flavored with Cajun spices, and served on a baguette. A roasted loin of pork is stuffed with dried fruit and wild rice, and lunch-time sandwiches are made with Armenian cracker-bread. Freshly caught seafood is always available, and homemade pâté is served gratis at both lunch and dinner.

The restaurant's considerable dessert list is heavy on chocolate, and includes the requisite house specialty—chocolate mousse.

North Coast Brewing Company, 444 N. Main St., Fort Bragg. ☎ **707/964-2739.**

Cuisine: AMERICAN. **Reservations:** Accepted for large parties only.
Prices: Appetizers $4–$7; main courses for lunch and dinner $6–$17. DISC, MC, V.
Open: Dinner only, Sun–Thurs 5–9:30pm, Fri–Sat 5–10pm.

This is the most "happening" place in an otherwise rather sleepy town—the large dark wood bar and adjacent tables are particularly busy during late afternoon happy hours. Beer is brewed on the premises, in large copper kettles that are displayed behind large plate-glass.

A pilsner, a stout, and a third seasonal brew are always available, served either in the lively bar, or a simpler wood-floored dining room. Standard brew-pub fare like burgers and barbecued chicken sandwiches, are augmented by more substantial dishes like linguini with smoked mushrooms, spiced cajun ham, and a North Coast mixed grill of Cajun-style prawns, chicken and sausage. Appetizers are also recommendable, especially the huge serving of nachos, layered with grated cheeses, fresh salsa, black beans, guacamole, and sour cream.

The Rendezvous Restaurant, 647 N. Main St., Fort Bragg. ☎ **707/964-8142.**

Cuisine: FRENCH. **Reservations:** Recommended.
Prices: Pasta $12–$17; meat and seafood $15–$19. DISC, MC, V.
Open: Tues–Sun 5:30–9pm. (Shorter hours during slower periods).

The Rendezvous Restaurant is romantic. Polished dark wood walls and lace curtains are warmly illuminated by a centerpiece brick fireplace. Elegant white tablecloths and oil lamps grace the tables, which are crowned with baskets of warm homemade wholegrain bread. Entrées are hearty, and each is served with either soup or salad, plus potatoes or pasta. A half-dozen chicken dishes include a baked breaded breast stuffed with crabmeat, or sautéed with mushrooms, scallions, and artichoke hearts. Charbroiled rib-eye steaks, scampi, veal, and pasta dishes are also served.

2 Avenue of the Giants

240 miles N of San Francisco

GETTING THERE • By Car Hop in the car again and head north to Sylvandale, six miles above Garberville on U.S. 101 (Calif. 1 and U.S. 101 converge at Leggett). Soon you'll come to a sign directing you to one of the most spectacular routes in the west, the Avenue of the Giants.

ESSENTIALS The Chimney Tree, Avenue of the Giants, P.O. Box 395, Garberville, CA 95549 (☎ **707/923-2265**), is the best place for information about the areas in and around the redwoods.

The giants are majestic coast redwoods (*Sequoia sempervirens*); over 50,000 acres of them make up the most outstanding display in the redwood belt. Their rough-bark columns climb 100 feet or more without a branch—some predate Christianity and are taller than a football field is long. The oldest dated coast redwood is over 2,200 years old. Thirty-three miles long, this scenic avenue, which roughly parallels U.S. 101, was left intact for sightseers when the freeway was built.

What to See & Do

Drive slowly, leaving your car occasionally for walks through the forest. En route you'll notice three public campgrounds: **Hidden Springs,** above Miranda; **Burlington,** two miles south of Weott; and **Albee Creek State Campground,** off to the left above Weott. You'll also come across picnic and swimming facilities, motels, resorts, restaurants, and numerous resting and parking areas.

The biggest attraction along the Avenue of the Giants is the **Chimney Tree,** where J.R.R. Tolkien's Hobbit is said to make his abode. This living, hollow redwood is over 1,500 years old. Nearby there is a gift shop, as well as a round building that offers sustenance in the form of gourmet beef burgers. At the south end of the avenue is another extraordinary sight—the **One-Log House,** a small apartment-like house built inside a log.

You can have lunch a few miles past the end of the road in Scotia (there are picnic areas and a grocery), where you can also take a tour of the **Pacific Lumber Company,** one of the world's largest mills. You can also drive your car through a living redwood at **Myers Flat Midway** along the Avenue of the Giants.

The village of **Ferndale,** 15 miles south of Eureka in the northernmost part of the Avenue of the Giants, is a historic landmark. Ferndale is a spectacle of Victoriana—gabled gingerbread houses, shops, a smithy, even a saddlery. It has a repertory company, artists, sculptors, dairy farms, hand-dipped chocolates for sale, and the annual World Champion Kinetic Sculpture Race in May. There are no parking meters, no traffic lights, and no mail deliveries.

Where to Stay

Gingerbread Mansion, 400 Berding St. (P.O. Box 40), Ferndale, CA 95536, ☎ **707/786-4000,** or toll free **800/952-4136.** 9 rms (all with bath). **Directions:** From U.S. 101 north, take the Fernbridge exit and continue 5 miles to Ferndale; the hotel is in the center of town.

Rates (including breakfast): $75–$195 single; $90–$205 double. $35 additional person. AE, MC, V.

Part of Ferndale's enchantment is this frequently photographed peach-and-yellow gabled inn with elaborate trimming. Run by Ken Torbert, the Victorian mansion is beautifully furnished with antiques; you may never sleep in more comfortable beds or feel more pampered. Some of the large guest rooms come with two old-fashioned clawfoot tubs for "his and her" bubble baths, and some rooms have fireplaces. Bathrobes and extra-large thick towels are provided. Two of the second-floor baths measure 200 square feet, and one has a mirrored ceiling and walls; hanging plants are all about and light filters through a lovely stained-glass window. (There is also a shower.) Beds are turned down for the night, and you will find hand-dipped chocolates on the nightstand.

When you rise, there's morning coffee or tea outside your door, enough to sustain you until a breakfast of fruit, cheese, muffins, breads, cakes, and a baked egg dish; afternoon tea with assorted baked items, candies, and fruit is also included in the rates.

The mansion has bicycles for the use of guests. Should it rain, there is also a supply of umbrellas. Smoking is permitted only on the verandas.

3 Sacramento

92 miles NE of San Francisco, 383 miles N of Los Angeles

GETTING THERE • **By Plane** Sacramento Metropolitan Airport (☎ **916/929-5411**), located 12 miles northwest of downtown Sacramento, is an international gateway for about a dozen airlines, including American (☎ toll free **800/433-7300**), Continental (☎ **916/369-2700**, or toll free **800/525-0280**), Delta (☎ **916/446-3464,** or toll free **800/221-1212**), Northwest (☎ toll free **800/225-2525**), and United (☎ toll free **800/241-6522**). Aero Shuttle (☎ **916/362-6232**) and Downtown Shuttle (☎ **916/448-8686**) are just two of the many share-ride services operating between the airport and downtown. Most charge about $10 to a hotel near the capital. Private taxis also ply this route, and charge $2.80 for the first mile and $2.20 for each additional mile—a total of about $30 from the airport to downtown.

• **By Train** Amtrak (☎ toll free **800/USA-RAIL**) services Sacramento daily, making California's capital one of the easiest cities in America to rail to. For a one-way trip from San Francisco, expect to pay about $15; from Los Angeles, about $75.

• **By Bus** Greyhound maintains a daily schedule into Sacramento from points around the compass. America's largest long-distance coach line no longer operates a nationwide toll-free telephone number, so consult your local directory for information.

• **By Car** From San Francisco, Sacramento is located about two hours east, a straight shot on I-80. From Los Angeles, take I-5 through the Central Valley directly into Sacramento. From North Lake Tahoe, take I-80 west, and from South Lake Tahoe take U.S. 50.

ESSENTIALS • **Orientation** Suburbia sprawls around Sacramento, but its touristy downtown area is relatively compact. Getting around the city is made easy by a gridlike pattern of streets that are designated by numbers or letters. The state capitol, on 10th Street between N Street and L Street, provides a terrific landmark. From the front of the capitol, M Street—which is at this point called Capitol Mall—runs 10 straight blocks to Old Sacramento, one of the city's oldest sections and a top sightseeing attraction.

• **Information** The **Sacramento Convention and Visitors Bureau,** 1421 K St., Sacramento, CA 95814 (☎ **916/264-7777**, fax 916/264-7788), produces and distributes an excellent visitor's guide and dispenses specialized information on sights, accommodations, and events. Once in the city, stop by the Sacramento Visitor Center, 1104 Front St. (☎ **916/264-7777, 442-7644** on weekends and holidays), in Old Sacramento for on-site information. It's usually open daily from 9am to 5pm.

As a city, Sacramento has one of the longest histories in California. Modern history began in 1839, when Johann Augustus Sutter received this property as part of a 48,000-acre land grant from Mexican Governor Juan Bautista Alvarado. In 1847, Sutter hired a carpenter, James Marshall, to build a sawmill on the nearby American River. It was here, on January 24, 1848, that Marshall discovered gold while inspecting the mill. Within six years, Sacramento's population grew from 150 into the tens of thousands, California was admitted to the Union, and Sacramento was named the state capital. Ironically, both Sutter and Marshall died penniless.

What to See & Do

Old Sacramento, Downtown At The Sacramento River, J Street exit off I-5.
☎ **916/443-7815.**

Four square blocks at the "foot" of downtown Sacramento contain the greatest concentration of historical buildings in California. More than 100 restored buildings, housing restaurants and shops, have collectively become the single most popular tourist attraction in the city. The area is visually fantastic, with cobblestone streets and gold-rush-era architecture; but its high concentration of T-shirt shops and other gimmicky stores has turned it into a sort of historical Disneyland.

Free guided tours are offered in the spring, summer, and fall; the tours depart from the California State Railroad Museum (see below) at 9:30am and 11am. Call **324-0040** for more information.

Admission: Free.

Open: Daily 24 hours; most shops open daily 9am–7pm.

California State Capitol, 10th St., between N St. And L St., Sacramento.
☎ **916/324-0333.**

Looking very much like a scale model of the U.S. Capitol in Washington, D.C., the dome-topped California state capitol, built in 1869, is Sacramento's most distinctive landmark. Massively renovated in 1976, the building has been restored to capture its palatial grandeur, designed along classical lines.

Daily guided tours, which are offered every hour on the hour, examine both the building's architecture and the workings of government. Visitors are led through seven historic, antique-filled offices into the Senate and Assembly chambers, where modern functions of government are carried out. Additional artifact-filled exhibit rooms and a film round out the tour.

Admission: Free.

Open: Daily 9am–5pm. **Tours:** Mon–Fri 9am–4pm, Sat–Sun 10am–4pm. **Closed:** Thanksgiving, Christmas, and New Year's Day.

California State Railroad Museum, 125 I St. at 2nd St.
☎ **916/552-5252** ext. 7245.

There are hundreds of railroad museums in the United States, and for good reason. The hulking engines and cars of beautifully restored trains are downright awesome.

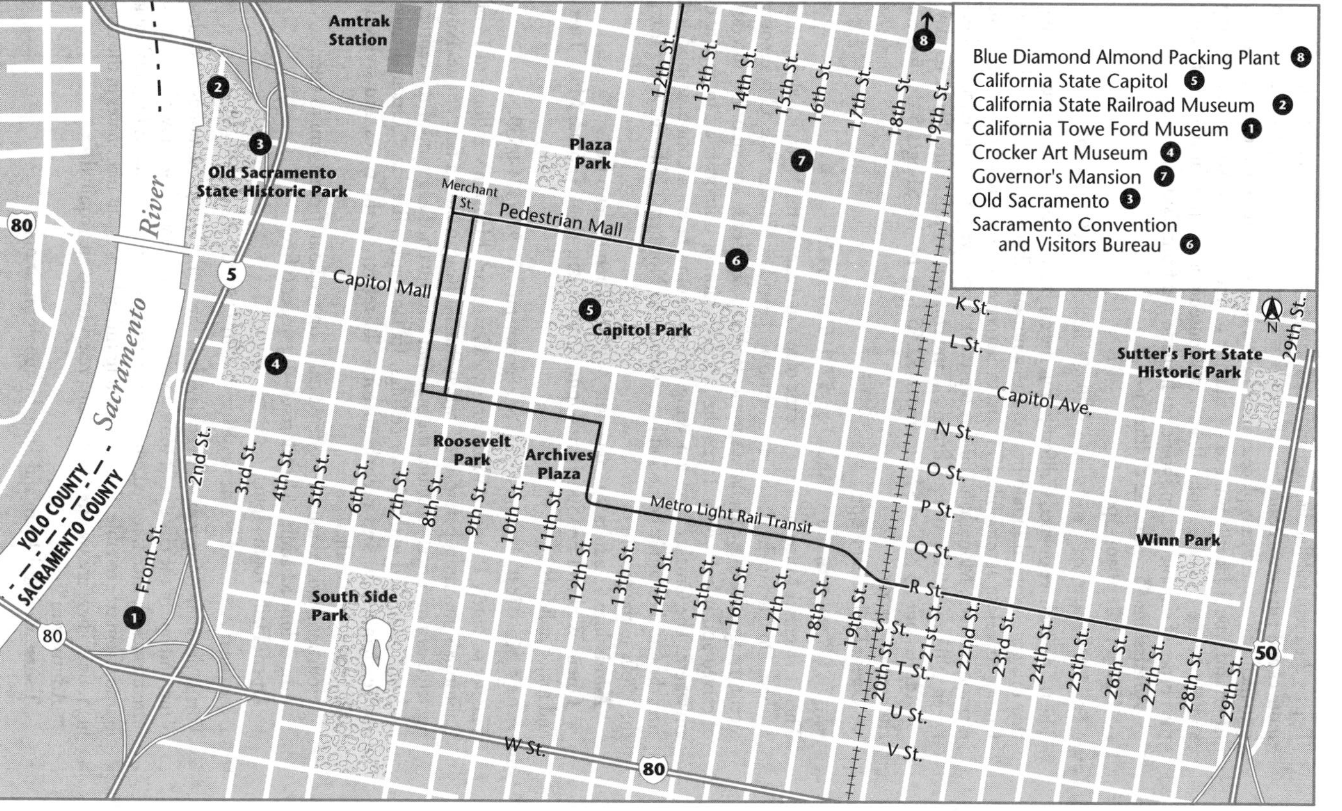

Downtown Sacramento

Bypass the memorabilia displays and head straight for the museum's 21 shiny locomotives and rail cars—beautiful antiques that are true works of art. You can't climb into them, but strategically placed mirrors allow bird's-eye views of the steam engines. Afterward, you'll actually want to see the film on the history of Western railroading and peruse the related exhibits. Really, this museum is not just for train buffs; even the hordes of schoolchildren shouldn't dissuade you from visiting.

Admission: $5 adults, $2 children 6–12.

Open: Daily 10am–5pm.

Towe Ford Museum of California, 2200 Front St. ☎ **916/442-6802.**

The train may have opened California, but the car built it. It is therefore quite fitting that this state's capital should be home to a museum that pays homage to the most famous American automobiles. This is, in fact, one of the world's largest collections of antique Fords. More than 180 cars represent nearly every Ford manufactured between 1903 and 1953. Antique fire, mail, and commercial trucks are also on display.

Admission: $5 adults, $4.50 seniors, $2.50 ages 14–18, $1 ages 5–13, free for children under 5.

Open: Daily 10am–6pm.

Crocker Art Museum, 3rd St. And O St. ☎ **916/264-5423.**

The Crocker Art Museum is not just the oldest museum in the West, it's also one of the best. Donated to the city of Sacramento by the widow of Judge E. B. Crocker over a century ago, the museum has a spectacular Victorian facade and an ornate interior of carved and inlaid woods. It has the best collection of California art to be found anywhere. The Crocker Mansion Wing, the museum's recent addition, is modeled after the Crocker family home and houses works by Northern California artists from the 1960s to the present day.

Admission: $3 adults, $1.50 youths 7–17, children under 6 free.

Open: Wed and Fri–Sun 10am–5pm, Thurs 10am–9pm. **Closed:** Mon, Tues, and major holidays.

Governor's Mansion, 16th St. And H St., Sacramento. ☎ **916/324-0539.**

The not so stately 15-room, Victorian-style Governor's Mansion was home to 13 of California's governors before 1967, when Ronald Reagan built a fancier one. Now operated as a historical museum, the mansion is maintained as a turn-of-the-century landmark, outfitted with 14-foot ceilings, Italian marble fireplaces, Oriental rugs, ornate chandeliers, and French mirrors—all reflecting the tastes and styles of California's first families.

Hour-long guided tours are offered daily, on the hour, from 10am to 4pm.

Admission: $2 adults, $1 children 6–12, under 6 free.

Open: Daily 10am–4pm.

Blue Diamond Almond Packing Plant, 1701 C St. ☎ **916/446-8439.**

This is not something you see everyday. It is the world's largest almond-packaging plant, and one of the city's most offbeat visitor sites. Here you'll see how almonds are sorted, cracked, sliced, halved, and roasted, and you'll learn all about the nuts' long journey from tree to table. Your guided tour through the plant terminates in the tasting room. There are two free tours daily; reservations are required.

Admission: Free.

Tours: Mon–Fri 10am and 1pm, by appointment only.

SPORTS & RECREATION

In a city bound by two rivers, the American and the Sacramento, water recreation tops the list of outdoor activities. Rafting is immensely popular, especially on weekends in the warmest months, and is a terrific activity that's very accessible to first-time visitors. Several Sacramento area outfitters rent rafts for 4 to 15 persons, along with life jackets and paddles. Their shuttles drop you and your entourage upstream and meet you three to four hours later at a predetermined point downstream. Recommended outfitters include **River Rat,** 4053 Pennsylvania Ave., Fair Oaks (☎ **916/966-6777**), and **American River Raft Rentals,** 11257 So. Bridge St., Rancho Cordova (☎ **916/635-6400**).

See "Alternative/Adventure Travel," in Chapter 2, for a list of outfitters offering guided river rafting trips.

WHERE TO SHOP

Old Sacramento, Downtown at the Sacramento River, J Street exit off I-5. ☎ **916/443-7815.**

There is no better place to shop at for tourist-oriented trinkets than in historical Old Sacramento (see "What to See and Do," above). Happily devoid of chain stores, this old-time mall features dozens of locally owned boutiques that sell all kinds of gifts and souvenirs.

Open: 24 hours; most shops open daily 9am–7pm.

Arden Fair Mall, 1689 Arden Way. ☎ **916/920-4809.**

Anchored by Nordstrom, Sears, and Weinstock's, Arden Fair houses over 150 specialty shops as well as restaurants, a theater, and a food court. By many locals reckoning, this is the best place to shop at in the entire city.

Open: Mon–Sat 10am–9pm, Sun 11am–6pm.

Where to Stay

EXPENSIVE

Amber House Bed and Breakfast, 1315 22nd St., Sacramento, CA 95816 ☎ **916/444-8085,** or toll free **800/755-6526.** Fax 916/447-1548. 9 rms. TV TEL

Rates (including breakfast): $85–$195 single or double. AE, CB, DC, DISC, MC, V.

Michael and Jane Richards' bucolic 1905 Amber House has just nine individually decorated rooms, named for famous artists and writers. Some of the rooms in the main house are a little cramped and offer no place for guests' baggage, but accommodations in the adjacent "Artists' Retreat" are thoroughly recommendable. The Renoir Room is the B&B's best, containing a canopied, king-size bed and a Jacuzzi big enough for three. The Van Gogh Room has a unique solarium bathroom with a huge, heart-shaped Jacuzzi tub, along with a TV and VCR.

A beautiful living room and intimate library are available for guests' use. A full breakfast is served each morning, in your room, in the large dining room, or outside on the front porch. Coffee is brought to your door early mornings.

Abigail's Bed and Breakfast, 2120 G St., Sacramento, CA 95816. ☎ **916/441-5007,** or toll free **800/858-1568.** 5 rms. A/C

Rates (including breakfast): $95–$135 single or double. AE, DISC, MC, V.

A boarding house for women during World War II, this 1912 Colonial Revival mansion has since been converted into a quaint B&B, overstuffed with furnishings and decor. A colorful clash of plush styles and patterns, Aunt Abigail's comes from the "more is better" school of design, crammed with furniture and items of virtu. There are several pretty sitting areas, an outdoor spa in the rear garden, and two house cats.

No smoking is allowed in any of the home's five rooms, which are outfitted with queen-size wood or brass beds and an assortment of antiques, including a chair or small settee. The Anne Room, the B&B's best, enjoys an enormous mahogany four-poster bed. Every room comes with terry robes and reproductions of antique radios. A telephone and TV are available upon request.

Hyatt Regency Sacramento, 1209 L St., Sacramento, CA 95814 ☎ **916/443-1234,** or toll free **800/233-1234.** Fax 916/321-6699. 500 rms, 30 suites. A/C TV TEL MINIBAR

Rates: $135–$175 single or double, $200 club level rooms, from $195 suite. AE, DC, DISC, MC, V. **Parking:** $6 self, $10 valet.

Sacramento's top hotel opened in 1988, right in the heart of downtown, directly across from the California state capitol. Lots of meeting space and the hotel's location within walking distance of Sacramento's convention center make this Spanish Mediterranean–style Hyatt popular with the name-tag crowd. Still, its facilities and services are unmatched in the city, leaving first-class independent travelers with little choice but to stay here. It's a pretty place, with intricately fashioned wrought iron railings wrapped around an airy lobby.

While the rooms themselves are not spectacular, they conform to a very high standard. The best are the ones with views facing the state capitol. All rooms are equipped with telephone, minibar, clock radio, full-length mirror, hairdryer, and cable TV with dozens of movies available on demand. The most expensive rooms are on the Regency Club floor; rent includes a private concierge and a private lounge where complimentary breakfast, beverage services, and hors d'oeuvres are provided.

Dining/Entertainment: Dawson's, the hotel's top restaurant, serves lunch and dinner and is worth a visit even if you're not staying at the Hyatt. Bugatti's serves breakfast, lunch, and casual dinners and is best known for its 18-foot-long antipasto bar. Amourath, the lobby bar, serves drinks all day.

Services: Room service, concierge, evening turndown, car rental desk, overnight laundry, lobby shoeshines.

Facilities: Swimming pool, Jacuzzi, exercise room, gift shop.

Radisson Sacramento, 500 Leisure Lane, Sacramento, CA 95815. ☎ **916/922-2020,** or toll free **800/333-3333.** Fax 916/649-9463. 309 rms, 27 suites. A/C TV TEL

Rates: $87–$107 single or double, from $184 suite. AE, CB, DC, DISC, MC, V.

Sprawling across 18 acres, Radisson Sacramento is a Mediterranean-style motel that combines the convenience of parking at your guest room door with the luxuries of a full-service resort. Built around an artificial lake about five miles from downtown, the hotel maintains hundreds of comfortable, if slightly dated, rooms that are popular with conventioneers, business trippers, and vacationers. Baths are stocked with the requisite soap package plus hairdryer. In spring and summer, locals show up for live music shows, held outdoors in the resort's amphitheater.

Dining/Entertainment: Palm Court Restaurant is a casual indoor-outdoor eatery overlooking the private lake. The Cabaña Room, the hotel's top eatery, also offers nightly entertainment. The Fanfare Bar is open nightly for drinks. The Petite Palm

Espresso Bar serves gourmet coffee, pastries, salads, and sandwiches.

Services: Round-the-clock room service, concierge, free airport shuttle, overnight laundry, shoeshine.

Facilities: Swimming pool, exercise room, Jacuzzi, paddle boat and bicycle rentals.

MODERATE

Best Western Ponderosa Inn, 1100 H St., Sacramento, CA 95814. ☎ **916/441-1314,** or toll free **800/528-1234**. 98 rms. A/C TV TEL

Rates (including continental breakfast): $72–$79 single or double. AE, CB, DC, DISC, MC, V.

You'd never know from the Ponderosa's plain motel-like exterior that this inn represents one of the best values in Sacramento. Rooms here are as up-to-date as any offered by the major national upscale players like Hilton and Sheraton, and include well-coordinated furnishings, in-room movies, voice-mail telephone, and valet and laundry service. There's a courtyard-enclosed swimming pool on the second floor, and complimentary coffee and Danish are served each morning in the lobby.

***Delta King* Riverboat,** 1000 Front St., Old Sacramento, CA 95814. ☎ **916/444-5464,** or toll free **800/825-5464.** 44 rms. A/C TV TEL

Rates (including continental breakfast): Sun–Thurs $85 single, $95 double, $200 captain's quarters; Fri–Sat $125 single, $135 double, $250 captain's quarters. AE, DC, DISC, MC, V.

With the exception of the *Queen Mary* in Long Beach, this big paddlewheeler is the only major floating hotel in California. The *Delta King* carried passengers between San Francisco and Sacramento in the 1930s. Permanently moored in Sacramento since 1984, it underwent a $9-million restoration that enlarged all the staterooms and refurbished a popular restaurant. Staying here is quite a novelty; the location, at the dock in Old Sacramento, can't be beaten. But the boat's cramped quarters can wear thin, especially if you're planning to spend a lot of time in your room. All rooms are nearly identical and have private baths and low ceilings. The captain's quarters, a particularly pricey suite, is a unique, mahogany-paneled stateroom, complete with a wet bar, observation platform, and private deck in the front of the boat.

The *Delta King's* Pilothouse Restaurant is popular with local office parties. When the weather is nice, there is dining on outside decks with views of Old Sacramento. The Paddlewheel Saloon, which overlooks the boat's 17-ton paddlewheel, features regular live entertainment.

INEXPENSIVE

The Sacramento Vagabond Inn, 909 Third St., Sacramento, Ca 95814. ☎ **916/446-1481,** or toll free **800/522-1555**. 107 rms. A/C TV TEL

Rates (including continental breakfast): $70 single or double. AE, CB, DC, DISC, MC, V.

Another recommendable choice within walking distance of the state capitol, the Vagabond Inn has a swimming pool, cable TV, and a host of free features, including local phone calls, weekday newspaper, and continental breakfast. There's an adjoining coffee shop as well as a cocktail lounge.

Where to Dine

EXPENSIVE

Capitol Grill, 2730 N St. ☎ **916/736-0744.**

Cuisine: AMERICAN/SEAFOOD. **Reservations:** Recommended.
Prices: Appetizers $5–$9; main courses $6–$22. AE, DC, DISC, MC, V.
Open: Mon–Fri 11:30am–10pm, Sat–Sun 5–10pm.

One of the liveliest restaurants in the city, Capitol Grill is popular with Sacramento's see-and-be-seen crowd—a good-looking throng of 20- and 30-somethings without any Los Angeles–style pretentiousness. The restaurant's warm redwood interior is backed by an extensive bar and wrapped with floor-to-ceiling windows that overlook a somewhat colorless corner.

An excellent selection of well-prepared dishes includes sea scallops with grilled scallions and ginger-soy butter, fresh crab tacos with diced vegetables and avocado cream, sesame-coated ahi tuna, and grilled pork chops with a spicy jicama-orange salad.

Paragary's Bar and Oven, 1401 28th St. ☎ **916/452-3335.**

Cuisine: ITALIAN. **Reservations:** Recommended.
Prices: Appetizers $4–$9; main courses $10–$17. AE, DC, DISC, MC, V.
Open: Mon–Thurs 11:30am–11pm, Fri 11:30am–midnight, Sat 5pm–midnight, Sun 5–10pm.

Occupying two distinctively different dining rooms just across the street from Capitol Grill (see above), Paragary's vies with its neighbor for best restaurant status in Sacramento's downtown district. The restaurant's fireplace room, which also contains a midquality fresco, is more formal than the brighter "cafe" room, which is outfitted with bentwood chairs and white Formica tables. During good weather, the best seats are on the sidewalk outside.

The same menu is served no matter where you sit, with the best dishes coming from the kitchen's wood-burning pizza oven. Some of the more unusual gourmet pizza toppings are prosciutto, new potatoes, goat cheese, roasted garlic, artichokes, smoked salmon, and grilled eggplant. Pizzas with pepperoni, cheese, tomato sauce, and mushrooms are also available. Typical appetizers include grilled asparagus wrapped with Parma prosciutto and roasted tomato-eggplant soup with basil. An assortment of California-style pastas are also served, along with grilled chicken, steak, and salmon.

MODERATE

Tower Café, 1516 Broadway. ☎ **916/441-0222.**

Cuisine: HEALTH FOOD. **Reservations:** Not accepted.
Prices: Appetizers $2–$6, main courses $7–$12. AE, MC, V.
Open: Sun–Thurs, breakfast 7:30am–10:30am; lunch 11:30am–4pm; dinner 5:30pm–10pm; dessert served until midnight. Fri–Sat, breakfast 7:30am–10:30am; lunch 11:30am–4pm; dinner 5:30–11pm; dessert until 1am.

Tower Café gets its name from the building in which it's located: a grand old movie house with a tall art-deco spire. The restaurant occupies the same space in which a small mom-and-pop music store once stood. This former resident, Tower Records, has since grown into America's second-largest record retailer.

While it's unlikely that Tower Café will share the phenomenal success of its predecessor, it's not because of the food or surroundings. Both are good, and even with perpetually sluggish service this restaurant remains my favorite place for lunch in Sacramento. On warm days it sometimes seems as though everyone in the city is lunching here, and crowd watching can be a real treat. Dishes are prepared somewhat health-consciously and include Chinese chicken salad, barbecued marinated shrimp served over soft rice noodles, jerk chicken, and lasagne layered with spinach, and other vegetables.

Wood'ys, 1379 Garden Hwy. ☎ **916/924-3434.**

Cuisine: AMERICAN. **Reservations:** Only for large parties.
Prices: Appetizers $3–$8, main courses $5–$12. AE, DC, DISC, MC, V.
Open: Mon–Thurs 11am–midnight, Fri–Sat 11am–2am, Sun 9:30am–midnight.

Wood'ys is the nicest of a handful of restaurants located at the Riverfront Complex, a small wooden mall on piers along the north bank of the American River. The ambience is a curious mélange of mediocrity: beautiful blond-wood floors, tropical-style bamboo chairs, industrial-style exposed ducts, and light rock music pumped through a low-fidelity sound system. If the weather is nice, sit outdoors, on a large deck that offers excellent, unobstructed river views.

The food, which is as festive as the surroundings, includes burgers, sandwiches, salads, pastas, Mexican specialties, and a cornucopia of other international dishes, such as Hawaiian chicken teriyaki, Cajun popcorn shrimp, and southern-style baby back ribs.

INEXPENSIVE

Fox and Goose Public House, 1001 R St. ☎ **916/443-8825.**

Cuisine: AMERICAN. **Reservations:** Not accepted.
Prices: Breakfast $2–$4, lunch $4–10. No credit cards.
Open: Mon–Fri 7am–2pm, Sat–Sun 9am–1pm.

Open only for breakfast and lunch, the Fox and Goose is basically a giant beerhall, with large wooden tables in a stark industrial interior. The restaurant gets mention here for its locally famous breakfasts; there's often a long wait on the weekends. Morning meal entrées include golden-brown waffles, raisin-walnut French toast, and a variety of omelets, including one that's stuffed with smoked salmon, cream cheese, and onions. Lunches are traditional British fare and include Cornish pasties, Welsh rarebit, burgers, bangers, and sandwiches. Wash it all down with one of over a dozen English beers on draught.

4 Lake Tahoe

191 miles NE of San Francisco, 99 miles NE of Sacramento

GETTING THERE • By Plane Reno Cannon International Airport, located 40 miles northeast of Lake Tahoe, offers regularly scheduled service from a number of airlines, including American (☎ toll free **800/433-7300**), Continental (☎ toll free **800/525-0280**), Delta (☎ toll free **800/221-1212**), and United/United Express (☎ toll free **800/241-6522**).

Tahoe Valley Airport, located in South Lake Tahoe, is a tiny airfield, offering commercial service from Los Angeles, San Diego, Portland, and Seattle via Trans World Express (☎ toll free **800/221-2000**). Prices range from $199 to $378 round-trip.

• **By Train** Amtrak (☎ toll free **800/USA-RAIL**) services both South Lake Tahoe, at the "bottom" of the lake, and Truckee, 10 miles north of the lake's "top" side. Trains connect with the rest of the state through Sacramento.

• **By Bus** Greyhound maintains a daily schedule into Truckee (☎ **916/587-3822**), about 10 miles north of Lake Tahoe. America's largest long-distance coach line no longer operates a nationwide toll-free telephone number, so consult your local directory for information.

• **By Car** From San Francisco—a four-hour drive—take either Interstate 50 through Sacramento to the lake's south shore or I-80 to Calif. 89 to reach the lake's north shore. From Los Angeles—a grueling nine-hour drive—take I-5 through California's Central Valley to I-80. If the weather is good and you can spare a few additional hours, it's really worth avoiding the interstate for the fantastically scenic drive on U.S. 395 and U.S. 50, which lie along the corridor between the towering peaks of the eastern Sierras and the humbling beauty of the Inyo Mountain Range.

ESSENTIALS • Orientation Of the several small towns that surround Lake Tahoe, the two most important are Tahoe City, located on the northwest side, and South Lake Tahoe, which abuts the Nevada border, at the southeast corner of the lake. Calif. 89 is Tahoe City's main commercial thoroughfare; most of the town's businesses are located near the Y in the road, where Calif. 89 meets Calif. 28. Similarly, most shops in South Lake Tahoe straddle I-50, which runs up the east side of the lake through Stateline, where most of the major casinos are located.

• **Information** Although the California-Nevada border divides Lake Tahoe into east and west sides, the region's primary population centers are split between the north and south sides of the lake. For this reason, the area's visitor information bureaus have divided their territories into north and south. Through the **Tahoe North Visitors & Convention Bureau,** P.O. Box 5578, Tahoe City, CA 96145 (☎ toll free **800/824-6348**), you can make reservations for car rental, lodging, and recreational

Winter Driving

Winter driving in the Sierra Nevada range can be dangerous. While the most hazardous roads are often closed, others are negotiable by four-wheel drive or with chained tires. Be prepared for sudden blizzards, and protect yourself by taking these important pretrip precautions:

- Check road conditions before setting out by calling toll free **800/427-7623**.
- If you're driving a rental car, let the rental company know you're planning to drive in snow, and ask whether the antifreeze is prepared for cooler climates.
- Make sure your heater and defroster work.
- Always carry chains.
- Recommended items include an ice scraper, a small shovel, sand or burlap for traction if your wheels should be ensnared in snow, warm blankets—and an extra car key (it's surprisingly common for motorists to lock their keys in the car while putting on tire chains).

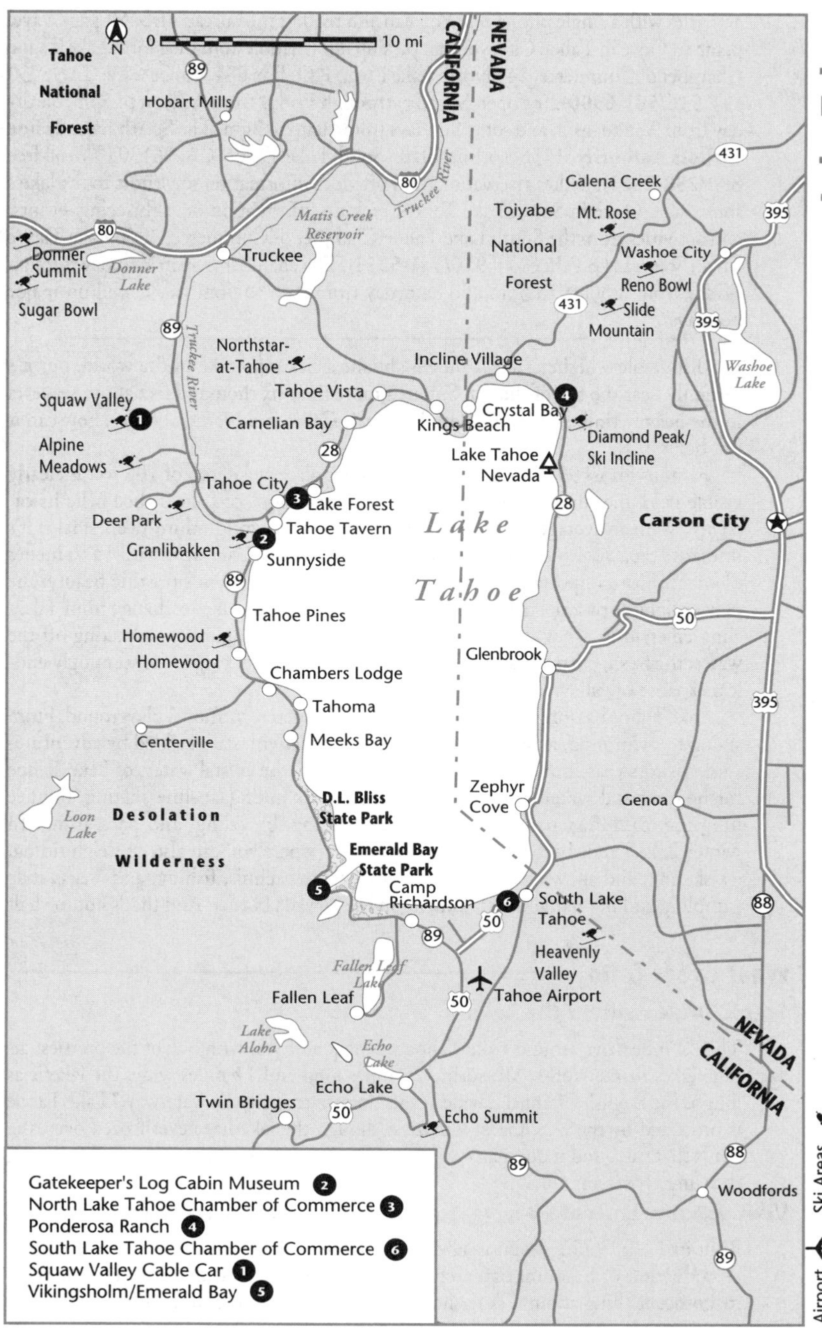

Lake Tahoe
0
10 mi
N
Tahoe National Forest
Hobart Mills
CALIFORNIA
NEVADA
Truckee River
Matis Creek Reservoir
Donner Summit
Donner Lake
Sugar Bowl
Truckee
Galena Creek
Toiyabe National Forest
Mt. Rose
Washoe City
Reno Bowl
Slide Mountain
Washoe Lake
Northstar-at-Tahoe
Incline Village
Tahoe Vista
Squaw Valley
Carnelian Bay
Kings Beach
Crystal Bay
Diamond Peak/ Ski Incline
Alpine Meadows
Lake Tahoe Nevada
Tahoe City
Lake Forest
Deer Park
Tahoe Tavern
Carson City
Granlibakken
Sunnyside
Lake Tahoe
Tahoe Pines
Homewood
Homewood
Glenbrook
Chambers Lodge
Tahoma
Centerville
Meeks Bay
D.L. Bliss State Park
Zephyr Cove
Genoa
Loon Lake
Desolation Wilderness
Emerald Bay State Park
Camp Richardson
South Lake Tahoe
Heavenly Valley
Fallen Leaf Lake
Fallen Leaf
Tahoe Airport
Lake Aloha
Echo Lake
Echo Lake
NEVADA
CALIFORNIA
Twin Bridges
Echo Summit
Woodfords
Gatekeeper's Log Cabin Museum 2
North Lake Tahoe Chamber of Commerce 3
Ponderosa Ranch 4
South Lake Tahoe Chamber of Commerce 6
Squaw Valley Cable Car 1
Vikingsholm/Emerald Bay 5
Ski Areas
Airport

activities with a single phone call. You can also request the bureau's free 50-page travel planner. Once in Tahoe City, you can pick up information from the North Lake Tahoe Chamber of Commerce, 245 North Lake Blvd., P.O. Box 884, Tahoe City, CA 95730 (☎ **916/581-6900**). It's open Monday through Friday from 8:30am to 5pm, Saturday from 9am to 4pm, and some Sundays from 10am to 2pm. The **South Lake Tahoe Visitors Authority,** 1156 Ski Run Blvd., South Lake Tahoe, CA, 96150 (☎ toll free **800/288-2463**), makes reservations and provides information to visitors to the lake's south side. Once in South Lake Tahoe, pick up information on sightseeing, events, and activities from the South Lake Tahoe Chamber of Commerce, 3066 Lake Tahoe Blvd., South Lake Tahoe (☎ **916/541-5255**). The chamber is open Monday through Friday from 8:30am to 5pm and Saturday from 9am to 4pm (it's closed on major holidays).

It's disputable whether Lake Tahoe is the most beautiful lake in the world, but it's certainly near the top of the list. Situated more than six thousand feet above sea level in the heavily timbered Sierra Nevada, on the California-Nevada border, how can it not be?

Famous for its 99.7% pure water—a dinner plate at a depth of 100 feet is clearly visible from the surface—the obvious visual dimensions of Lake Tahoe belie its capacity. With an average depth of 989 feet, Tahoe is the world's third-deepest lake; it's immense capacity is sufficient to cover the entire state of California with 14 $^1/_2$ inches of water. More important to the visitor, though, is the region's pristine beauty: the play of light during the day, which causes the color of the lake to change from a dazzling emerald to blues and rich purples; the snowy mountaintops reflecting off the water; the fresh, crisp air; and the green gleam of trees that carpet the seemingly endless expanse of valley.

Lake Tahoe has long been California's most popular recreational playground. From skiing to swimming, an almost endless catalog of activities are tackled by adventuresome visitors year-round. In summer you can enjoy the crystal waters of Lake Tahoe for boating and water sports; in addition, there's hiking, in-line skating, bungee jumping, camping, ballooning, horseback riding, bicycling, and parasailing. In winter Lake Tahoe becomes a popular ski resort, where you can also go sleigh riding, ice-skating, and snowmobiling. Year-round, there's tennis, fishing, and Vegas-style gambling and big-name entertainment on the Nevada border. And that's not the half of it.

What to See & Do

Scenic Drive Around the Lake

The 72-mile drive around Lake Tahoe will acquaint you with one of the prettiest alpine lakes in the world. Measuring 22 miles long and 12 miles wide, the lake is as long as the English Channel is wide. As an "interstate navigable waterway," Lake Tahoe is protected by the U.S. Coast Guard. Although the lake has never frozen over, the roads that surround it do; many are closed in winter, making this trip possible during the summer season only.

Vikingsholm/Emerald Bay, Hwy. 89. ☎ **916/525-7277** or **525-7232.**

Built in 1929, Vikingsholm is a 38-room mansion that's widely touted as the finest reproduction of Scandinavian architecture in America. And fine it is, but the most magnificent thing about Vikingsholm is its location, on the shores of Emerald Bay, truly one of the most picturesque spots anywhere. From the highway, which is hundreds of feet above lake level, visitors are treated to a striking panorama of the one-and-a-half-mile-long lake inlet, which is given perspective by tiny Fanette Island, itself punctuated by an old stone teahouse at its peak.

It's so pretty, they had to build a paved parking area on the highway for all the viewers. If you don't mind trekking back up, you can visit Vikingsholm by hiking down a steep 1½ mile trail. The mansion is open for tours, every hour on the half hour, during summer months only.

Admission: $2 adults, $1 children.

Open: July–Labor Day daily 10am–4pm.

Squaw Valley Cable Car, Squaw Valley. ☎ **916/583-6985.**

Not just for skiers, the Squaw Valley Cable Car takes sightseers and other recreational visitors up to a scenic High Camp 2,000 vertical feet above the valley floor. In addition to being treated to spectacular views of Lake Tahoe and the High Sierra, visitors to the top can take part in a variety of activities, including ice-skating, swimming, tennis, and bungee jumping at the High Camp Bath and Tennis Club. Squaw Valley is located about five miles north of Tahoe City; the cable car operates year-round.

Cable-Car Prices: $11 adults, $5 children 4–12, $9 seniors 65 and older, under 3 free.

Open: Daily 8am–4pm.

Ponderosa Ranch, Hwy. 28, Incline Village. ☎ **702/831-0691.**

If you've ever seen the 1960s' television show *Bonanza*, you'll probably recognize this movie-set ranch as the location for that hit series. Now operating as a sort of *Bonanza* tribute, Ponderosa is packed with show-oriented exhibits, including dozens of props and the original 1959 Cartwright Ranch House. You'll enjoy the various activities at the ranch, especially if you have kids in tow; activities include pony rides, staged gunfights, a petting farm, and a blacksmith's shop. The barbecue grill is almost always fired up, and breakfast hayrides, on tractor-pulled wagons, are offered for $2.

Admission: $8.50 adults, $5.50 children 5–11, under 5 free.

Open: Mid-Apr to Oct only, daily 9:30am–5pm.

The Gatekeeper's Log Cabin Museum, 130 W. Lake Blvd., Tahoe City. ☎ **916/583-1762.**

The gatekeeper regulates Lake Tahoe's water level by controlling the lake's flow into the Truckee River. Now that the flood gates are operated from an office tower in Reno, the rustic old gatekeeper's house endures as a museum operated by the North Lake Tahoe Historical Society. Restored to its original unremarkable state, the log cabin contains relics from its gate-guarding past, as well as Native American baskets and clothing, and mementos from Tahoe's logging days.

Admission: Free, donation requested.

Open: May–Oct, daily 11am–5pm.

Organized Tours

BY BOAT

M.S. *Dixie II*, Zephyr Cove Marina, NV. ☎ **702/588-3508.**

The recently launched M.S. *Dixie II* replaces the original M.S. *Dixie*, a 1927 Mississippi River cotton barge that had become something of a waterborne landmark. The new 550-passenger pleasure-craft is Lake Tahoe's largest, and features enclosed heated decks, an open promenade deck, bars, a dance floor, and a full dining room. Several different panoramic tours are offered daily from April through October, including breakfast, champagne brunch, and dinner tours. Zephyr Cove Marina is located on Hwy. 50, four miles north of Stateline in South Lake Tahoe.

Prices: Bay cruise, $12 adults, $4 children 11 and under; breakfast and brunch cruises, $16 adults, $7.50 children 11 and under; dinner cruises, $21–$31 adults, $9.50 children 11 and under.

Bay Cruises: Apr 17–Jun 18 and Oct 4–31 daily noon; Jun 19–Oct 3 daily 11am and 2:15pm. **Champagne Brunch Cruises:** Jun 19–Sept 5 Sun–Mon 9am; Apr 17–Jun 18 and Sept 5–Oct 31 Sun 9am. **Breakfast Cruises:** Jun 19–Sept 5 Tues–Thurs, and Sat 8:30am; Sept 6–Oct 3 Tues and Sat 8:30am. **Dinner Cruises:** Apr 17–Jun 18 daily 7pm; June 19–Sept 5 daily 7:30pm; Sept 6–Oct 31 daily 6:30pm.

Tahoe Queen, P.O. Box 14327, South Lake Tahoe, CA 95702. ☎ **916/541-3364,** or toll free **800/238-2463.**

There's enough room in Tahoe for two paddlewheelers. Both newer and larger than its competition (see above), the *Tahoe Queen* operates year-round, offering daily Emerald Bay cruises, sunset dinner dance cruises, and shuttle service between the lake's north and south shores during the ski season. There are large outdoor and indoor viewing decks and a glass bottom for peering deep into the lake.

The *Tahoe Queen* departs from Ski Run Marina, just south of Stateline. Call ahead to confirm rates and schedules.

Prices: Emerald Bay Cruise, $14 adults, $5 children 11 and under; Dinner Cruise, $18 adults, $9.50 children 11 and under (dinner optional, menu selections from $14.95); round-trip North/South Shore Ski Shuttle $18 adults, $9 children 11 and under.

Emerald Bay Cruises: Oct–May daily 12:30pm; the rest of the year 11am, 2:30pm, and 3:55pm. **Sunset Dinner Dance Cruises:** Oct–May daily 6:30pm; the rest of the year daily 7pm. North/South Shore Ski Shuttle Oct–May only Tues–Sat 8am and 5pm.

***Woodwind* Sailing Cruises,** in the Zephyr Cove Resort, on U.S. Hwy. 50, P.O. Box 1375 Zephyr Cove, NV 89448. ☎ **702/588-3000.**

Woodwind's 41-foot trihull craft takes up to 30 passengers on daily sailing tours of Lake Tahoe. The boat's glass bottom allows for views in every direction. Reservations are required.

Prices: $14 adults, $7 children under 12, under 2 free.

Departures: Apr 1–Oct 31, 11:30am, 1, 2:30, and 4pm.

BY PLANE

Seaplane Tours, P.O. Box 265, Homewood, Lake Tahoe, CA 96141. ☎ **916/525-7143.**

Small planes, which take off and land on the lake, offer a fun and exciting way to tour the Tahoe region. You can choose your own flight plan and buzz anyplace from South Lake Tahoe to Reno. There's usually a two-person minimum for each tour, but money is the ultimate arbiter. Call ahead for reservations. The seaplane base is in Homewood, six miles south of Tahoe City.

Prices: From $45–$81 per person.

Sports & Recreation

BICYCLING

It is said that, in Tahoe, for every mile of paved road there are five miles of mountain biking trails. Excellent paved trails—off-limits to motor vehicles—are also in abundance, both around the lake and along the Truckee River on Rte. 89. You can rent bikes in Tahoe City at **Porter's Ski and Sport,** 501 N. Lake Blvd. (☎ **916/583-2314**); and in Incline Village also at Porter's, 885 Tahoe Blvd. (☎ **702/831-3500**). Bike rentals usually cost $4 per hour, $11 for four hours, or $18 per day.

At both Northstar (☎ **916/587-0248**) and Squaw Valley (☎ **916/583-6985**), you can ride the cable car with your bike and cycle the trails all the way down. Call for complete information.

BUNGEE JUMPING

You've heard all about the "sport" that's sweeping the country, but could you tether yourself to a rubber band and dive head first toward the ground? At **Bungee Squaw Valley,** Squaw Valley (☎ **916/583-4000**), you can. Jumps here are as safe as they get; participants, who are strapped by waist and chest harnesses, leap from a 75-foot structure that towers over a giant safety airbag. The group is fully insured and allows jumpers from age 6 to 70 to fly. The price of the jump is $45. It's open year-around, Summer, daily noon to 5pm; winter, Thursday through Tuesday noon to 4pm.

FISHING

There are dozens of charter companies offering daily excursions on Lake Tahoe year-round. There's sportfishing here; most polers are deeplining for Mackinaw and toplining for Rainbows, Silvers, and Browns. **Mickey's Big Mack Charters,** P.O. Box 815, Tahoe City, CA 96145 (☎ **916/546-4444,** or toll free after 6pm, **800/877-1462**), is a well-respected outfit, led by experienced guide Mickey Daniels. All the fishing gear is provided, but you're responsible for your own fishing license. Write or call for requirements and reservations.

Mickey's boats depart from Sierra Boat Co., in Camelian Bay located about five miles north of Tahoe City. Trips cost $60 per person and depart daily year-round, in the early morning and late afternoon; exact times vary according to season.

HIKING

The mountains surrounding Lake Tahoe are criss-crossed with seemingly endless, marked hiking trails graded for all levels of experience. Before setting out, you may wish to contact the local visitors bureau (see "Information" above) for a map and more in-depth information on particular trails. Some of the most popular trails are:

Eagle Falls/Eagle Lake One of the best trails for novice hikers, the Eagle Falls walk offers a fabulous cascading reward for persistent walkers. The trail begins at Eagle Picnic Area, located directly on Hwy. 89 across from Emerald Bay.

Emerald Bay/Vikingsholm From the parking area, 1½ miles above Tahoe's prettiest inlet, you can hike down to Vikingsholm, a 38-room mansion that's widely touted as the finest reproduction of Scandinavian architecture in America (see "What to See and Do" above for complete information). The trail begins at the parking area on the north side of Emerald Bay, on Hwy. 89.

Loch Levin Lakes An easy, but beautiful walk, the Loch Levin trail is perfect for hikers who wish to stay on the beaten path. To reach the trailhead, take I-80 to the Big Bend exit and look for the sign PRIVATE ROAD PUBLIC TRAIL across from the Big Bend ranger station.

Shirley Lake Located in Squaw Valley, near the tram line, this excellent hike has the advantage of a one-way adventure; you can take the tram up and hike down or vice versa. The trail begins at the end of Squaw Peak Road, next to the tram building.

HORSEBACK RIDING

Northstar Stables, 2499 Northstar Dr. And Hwy. 267. ☎ **916/562-1230.**

Part of one of the most complete resorts in Tahoe, Northstar Stables offers a variety of trail rides, lessons, and pack trips. Special breakfast and dinner rides are also available. Children below the age of seven are not allowed on trail rides. Northstar is located on the north side of Lake Tahoe, between Kings Beach and Truckee.

Prices: $15 for 45 minutes, $28 for an hour and a half; breakfast and dinner rides $20–$25 per person. Call for pack trip information.

Open: Year-round, daily 9am–5pm; when winter prohibits trail rides, sleigh rides are available.

Squaw Valley Stables, 1525 Squaw Valley Rd. ☎ **916/583-7433.**

Trail rides and lessons are offered for all ages and riding levels. Squaw Valley is located about five miles north of Tahoe City.

Prices: $17–$64 per person.

Open: June–early Sept., daily 8:30am–4:30pm.

Sunset Ranch, Hwy. 50, South Lake Tahoe. ☎ **916/541-9001.**

Located a quarter of a mile west of the Lake Tahoe Airport, Sunset Ranch offers rides to both children and adults along the open meadows that abut the Truckee River. Guests can ride either with or without a guide, on horses that seem to know their own way around.

Prices: $20 per hour, or $30 per hour for two people on a single horse.

Open: Year-round, daily 8am–sunset.

ICE-SKATING

One of the world's most unusual ice rinks is located 8,200 feet above sea level at **Squaw Valley's High Camp,** Squaw Valley (☎ **916/583-6985**). The ice is accessible only by cable car—a scenic ride that's included with rink admission. Skating costs a hefty $17 for adults, $10 for children, including cable-car ride and skate rentals. After 4pm the prices drop to $9 for adults and $6 for children. The rink is open year-round, daily from 10am to 9pm. Call first, as the rink closes a few days in the spring and fall for repairs.

IN-LINE SKATING

Although there are trails all around Lake Tahoe, the best ones for blading are the well-paved PEDESTRIANS ONLY paths that hug the Truckee River and Calif. 89, between Tahoe City and Squaw Valley. Rollerblades and other in-line skates can be rented from the nearby **Squaw Valley Sport Shop,** Tahoe City (☎ **916/583-6278**). The shop charges $5 per hour (a $10 minimum) or $15 a day (the price covers wrist guards and other protective gear). Squaw Valley is open Sunday through Thursday from 9am to 6pm, Friday and Saturday from 9am to 7pm.

JETSKIING

Lighthouse Watersports Center, 950 N. Lake Blvd., Tahoe City (☎ **583-6000**), rents jet skis, paddle boats, and canoes during summer months only. Reservations are recommended for jet-ski rentals. Jet skis cost $35 per half hour and $60 per hour; paddle boats and canoes cost $15 per half hour and $20 for two hours. The watersports center is open June through September, daily from 9am to 6pm.

PARASAILING

Parasailing—flying from a parachute that's pulled by a motorboat—is a novel way to get a bird's-eye view of the lake. No experience is required, since the parasailors themselves don't really do anything but hang there. Because of this, anyone can parasail. You don't even get wet; sailors take off and land on the stern of the parasail boat. No one is an avid parasailor, but it's fun to do it once. **Tahoe Boat Co. Marina,** Tahoe City (☎ **916/583-7245**), charges $40 to $50 (depending on your time aloft) and $70 for tandem flight. Rides are offered from Memorial Day to Labor Day, daily from 8am to 3pm.

SKIING

Tahoe offers California's best skiing, on a dozen excellent mountains. The ski season lasts usually from November through May, but often lingers into the summer. In 1993 some Tahoe lifts were open until July 4th! Lift tickets usually cost about $40 per day, $27 per half day, and $5 for children under 13.

If you've come to ski, you'll be wise to contact both the Tahoe North Visitors & Convention Bureau, P.O. Box 5578, Tahoe City, CA 96145 (☎ toll free **800/824-6348**), and the South Lake Tahoe Visitors Authority, 1156 Ski Run Blvd., South Lake Tahoe, CA, 96150 (☎ toll free **800/288-2463**), for information on good-value ski packages offered by almost every hotel and resort on the lake. The following are some of Tahoe's most popular resorts.

Alpine Meadows, P.O. Box 5279, Tahoe City, CA 96145. ☎ **916/583-4232,** or toll free **800/441-4423**.

Alpine's high elevation (7,000 feet) gives it the most snow of any resort in Tahoe. Runs here are usually open later in the season than anywhere else. The resort features 11 chair lifts, and (thankfully) doesn't allow snowboarding.

Northstar-at-Tahoe, P.O. Box 129, Truckee, CA 96160. ☎ **916/562-1010,** or toll free **800/466-6784**.

Top-to-bottom snowmaking coverage and a full-time kids program make Northstar the top choice in Tahoe for families. Its location, close to the Nevada border, also puts it within close range to the casinos.

Squaw Valley USA, Squaw Valley, CA 96146. ☎ **916/583-6985,** or toll free **800/545-4350**.

Located at North Lake Tahoe, this was the site of the 1960 Olympic Winter Games. Some 70% of Squaw's terrain is geared for beginners and intermediates. There are 23 chairlifts and a 120-passenger cable car.

SNOWMOBILING

Snowmobiles are available for rent at several locations at the Lake Tahoe area. **Zephyr Cove Snowmobile Center,** Zephyr Cove (☎ **702/882-0788**), is located about five miles north of Stateline (Nevada), on the lake's east side. It offers two-hour guided snowmobile tours from November 26 through April 15 (weather permitting). Tours are scheduled usually thrice daily—at 10am, 12:15pm, and 2:45pm—and cost $69 for a single rider and $99 for two people on one snowmobile (limit 400 lb).

High Sierra Snowmobiling, Hwys. 267 and 28 (☎ **916/546-9909**), is open from November 15 through April 1 (again, weather permitting). It offers no trail tours, just a manicured track, for which it charges $30 per half hour. High Sierra is open daily from 10am to 4:30pm.

TENNIS

All the major resorts have tennis courts open to the public on a fee basis. Call the **Resort at Squaw Creek** (☎ **916/583-6300**) and **Northstar** (☎ **916/562-0321**) for information and reservations.

Budget-minded players looking for good local courts should visit **Tahoe Lake School,** Grove St., Tahoe City, where two lighted courts are available free, on a first-come, first-served basis.

South Tahoe Intermediate School, Lyons Avenue, off Hwy. 50, has eight lighted courts. It charges a manageable $3 per hour.

WATERSKIING

North Tahoe Marina, Hwy. 28, one mile west of Hwy. 267, Tahoe Vista. ☎ **916/546-8248.**

Skis and tow lines are rented along with 18- to 21-foot motor boats. Other powerboat toys, including tubes, kneeboards, and wetsuits, are also available.

Prices: $60–$85 per hour.

Open: June–Sept, daily 8am–6pm.

WINDSURFING

Although it may look easy, windsurfing is downright difficult. Easy winds and relatively calm conditions make Lake Tahoe a great place to learn. **Windsurfing at Carnelian Bay,** at Lakeside Chalets, 5240 N. Lake Blvd., Carnelian Bay (☎ **916/546-5857**), rents boards and offers lessons by appointment June through September. Windsurfers cost $20 per hour or $50 to $60 per day.

Where to Stay

The Lake Tahoe Visitors Authority (☎ toll free **800/288-2463**) can make hotel reservations for you at more than 80 properties in and around South Lake Tahoe. The Tahoe North Visitors Bureau (☎ toll free **800/824-6348**) can make accommodations reservations at dozens of hotels on the lake's north side.

EXPENSIVE

The Resort at Squaw Creek, 400 Squaw Creek Rd., P.O. Box 3333, Olympic Valley, CA 96146. ☎ **916/583-6300** or toll free **800/327-3353**. Fax 916/581-6632. 405 rms, 200 suites. A/C TV TEL MINIBAR

Rates: Apr 11–Jun 10 $165 single or double, from $235 suite; Jun 11–Sept 25 $190 single or double, from $275 suite; Sept 26–Dec 16 $175 single or double, from $235 suite; Dec 17–Apr 10 $250 single or double, from $350 suite. AE, CB, DC, DISC, MC, V. **Parking:** $10 valet, free self-parking.

Easily the nicest hotel resort in Tahoe, the $130-million Resort at Squaw Creek opened in January, 1990 amidst much environmentally based controversy. The results are mixed. The resort comprises two adjacent buildings. One, of a pleasing design inspired by Frank Lloyd Wright, houses public areas, restaurants, and meeting areas. The other building, a black-glass-and-steel, multistory cube, contains the guest rooms and offers a striking counterpoint that, however, is not quite so pleasing.

While accommodations here lack the plushness and elegance of a deluxe property, they are of a very high standard, and contain ample closet space, good lighting, remote-controlled TV, a minibar, and a speakerphone telephone. Suites come with spacious entertaining areas and additional TVs and telephones.

You can't beat the resort's ski-in/ski-out access to Squaw Valley mountains; a chair lift is located just outside the door. In addition, there are 30 kilometers of groomed cross-country skiing trails (marked for hiking and biking in the summer); an 18-hole golf course; three swimming pools; several outdoor, year-round hot tubs; an ice-skating rink (in the winter only); and an equestrian center with riding stables.

Dining/Entertainment: Glissandi, the resort's top restaurant, serves French-American cuisine in a window-wrapped dining room. Cascades, a more casual eatery, is open for all-day buffet-style dining. Ristorante Montagna is an Italian eatery, with tables both indoors and out. Sweet Potatoes Deli is open early for coffee and light accompaniments, before switching to picnic-style lunches and undemanding meals. Bullwhackers Pub, an English-style bar, has a pool table, regular live entertainment, and terrific happy-hour specials.

Services: Room service, concierge, overnight laundry, supervised children's activities.

Facilities: Golf course, ice skating rink, three heated swimming pools, three outdoor spas, eight tennis courts, fitness center, equestrian center, shopping arcade.

Fantasy Inn, 3696 Lake Tahoe Blvd., South Lake Tahoe, CA 96150. ☎ **916/541-6666,** or toll free **800/367-7736.** Fax 916/541-6798. 53 rms. A/C TV TEL

Rates: $98–$178 single or double weekdays; $138–$218 single or double weekends. AE, DISC, DC, MC, V. Special packages available.

One of Lake Tahoe's newest hotels is also the area's most talked about. Fantasy Inn, an unabashed "adult" hotel, features eight high-quality, provocatively named theme suites containing round or heart-shaped beds, mirrored ceilings, oversized spas, surround-sound stereo systems, and sensuous art. The Romeo and Juliet Suite features a nine-foot sunken tub, the Rain Forest Suite has a wild animal jungle theme, and Caesar's Indulgence Suite features a marble spa, zebra skin carpeting and silk furnishings.

Although the hotel's standard accommodations are themeless, they are outfitted with the same amenities as the themed rooms, including romantic lighting and twin shower heads. An on-site chapel can accommodate spontaneous weddings.

Harrah's, P.O. Box 8, U.S. 50 at Stateline, NV 89449. ☎ **702/588-6611,** or toll free **800/648-3773.** 535 rms. TV TEL MINIBAR

Rates: June–Sept 11 $139–$200 single or double; the rest of the year $119–$195 single or double. AE, CB, DC, DISC, MC, V.

One of four major casinos located just across the state line from South Lake Tahoe, Harrah's offers hundreds of nearly identical rooms to individuals and groups looking for consistently good standards. The accommodations are of good quality—comfortable bed, desk, bath amenities, remote-controlled TV, minibar—but they are not outstanding. The best things about this hotel are its proximity to the ski lifts and the service it provides: valet parking, 24-hour room service, concierge. Also worth noting is the entertainment, which includes, of course, gambling; the large, 65,000-square-foot casino offers blackjack, craps, slots, and all the other Vegas-style hits.

Dining/Entertainment: Harrah's has a total of seven restaurants. Big names headline at the casino's South Shore Room, where dinner is also available. The Summit Restaurant, open for dinner only, offers lovely panoramic views of the lake and mountains. Well-priced, all-you-can-eat breakfast, lunch, and dinner buffets are served in the Forest Restaurant. The Sierra Coffee Shop is open 24 hours.

Services: Round-the-clock room service, concierge, overnight laundry, shoe shine, ski shuttle, car-rental desk.

Facilities: Casino, glass-enclosed swimming pool, health-club, showroom.

Harvey's Resort Hotel & Casino, P.O. Box 128, Stateline, NV, 89449.
☎ **702/588-2411,** or toll free **800/648-3361**. 717 rms. TV TEL

Rates: July 2–Sept 5 $120–$185 single or double; the rest of the year $140–$210 single or double. AE, CB, DC, DISC, MC, V.

Harvey's is another megahotel, located on the same block as Harrah's. In addition to well-maintained guest rooms in a new, 18-story tower, the hotel features one of the lake's largest casinos, which contains more than 100 blackjack tables and 2,300 slot machines.

Dining/Entertainment: Llewellyn's is the casino's premiere eatery, serving conservative American dinners nightly. The Top of the Wheel, located 12 stories above Lake Tahoe, serves lunch, dinner, and cocktails nightly. The Sage Room Steak House is, as its name implies, a meat-and-potatoes kind of restaurant. There are also a Chinese restaurant, a Seafood place, and a Mexican-themed eatery called El Vaquero.

Services: Round-the-clock room service, concierge, overnight laundry, shoeshine, ski shuttle, car rental desk.

Facilities: Casino, swimming pool, three tennis courts, health-club, showroom.

MODERATE

Mayfield House, 236 Grove St., P.O. Box 5999, Tahoe City, CA 96145.
☎ **916/583-1001.** 6 rms. 1 suite.

Rates (including breakfast): $85–$95 single or double, $115 suite.

Built in 1932 by Norman Mayfield, one of the region's first contractors, this homey, wood-and-stone bed-and-breakfast is excellently located, being within walking distance of Tahoe City's restaurants and shops. There are only six rooms, and all are different from one another. Each is outfitted with down comforters and pillows, books, and fresh flowers. Most have a king- or queen-sized bed, and all come with morning breakfast and afternoon wine, cheese, and crackers. It's worth splurging on the Mayfield Room, the home's master suite, which contains a separate sitting area and dining area, a king-size bed, and a TV.

Meeks Bay Resort, P.O. Box 70248, Reno, NV 89570. ☎ **916/525-7242.** 21 units. TEL

Rates: $75 single or double, $650–$3,000 per week. No credit cards.

Located 10 miles south of Tahoe City, on Hwy. 89, Meeks Bay Resort is one of the oldest hostelries on the lake and somewhat of a historical landmark. This wide, sweeping lakefront curve fronts the best fine-sand beach in Tahoe. Known centuries ago to the

Washoe Indians, Meeks Bay was opened as a public campground in 1920. During the next 50 years the resort grew to include cabins and other improvements, and attracted many celebrities from southern California. Acquired by the U.S. Forest Service in 1974, the property is now operated, under a special-use permit, from June 15 to September 15 only. Most rentals are on a weekly basis and consist of cabins located both on the lake and on the adjacent hillside. Units vary in size, sleeping 2 to 12, and are modest without being austere. Each has a full kitchen, and some have fireplaces. The Kehlet Mansion is the resort's premiere accommodation. Owned at one time by William Hewlett, cofounder of the Hewlett-Packard Corporation, and later the summer residence of billionaire Gorden Getty, this pretty little house, on a rock that juts out into the lake, is one of the best places to stay at in all of Tahoe. The mansion has seven bedrooms, three bathrooms, a large kitchen and living room, and water on three sides. The entire house is rented by the week, sleeps a dozen, and costs just $3,000 from Wednesday to Wednesday.

Sunnyside Lodge, 1850 W. Lake Blvd., P.O. Box 5969, Tahoe City, CA 95730. ☎ **916/583-7200,** or California toll free **800/822-2754**. 23 rms.

Rates (including continental breakfast): Apr 4–May 27 and Oct 3–Dec 16 $100–$110 single or double; May 28–Oct 2 $125–$135 single or double; Dec 17–Apr 3 $115–$125 single or double. AE, MC, V.

Looking very much like a giant wooden cabin, the hotel offers almost two dozen individually decorated rooms, outfitted with homey bark-bearing tables and chairs and contemporary and antique-style prints. Since Sunnyside Lodge is located directly on Lake Tahoe, its best (and most expensive) rooms are practically hanging over the water. Some also have romantic stone fireplaces. Most of the lodge's ground floor is dominated by a popular restaurant that bustles throughout the day—especially in summer.

INEXPENSIVE

Lake of the Sky Motor Inn, P.O. Box 227, 955 N. Lake Blvd., Tahoe City, CA 95730. ☎ **916/583-3305.** 23 rms.

Rates: Apr 18–June 12 $50–$65 single or double; June 13–Sept 21 $70–$80 single or double; the rest of the year $95–$105 single or double. AE, CB, DC, DISC, MC, V.

Not much more than a 1950s-style A-frame motel in the heart of Tahoe City, Lake of the Sky Motor Inn offers decent accommodations in a terrific location, only steps away from shops and restaurants. There's a heated swimming pool as well as a barbecue area.

TraveLodge, Hwy. 28, P.O. Box 84, Tahoe City, CA 95730. ☎ **916/583-3766,** or toll free **800/255-3050**. 47 rms. TV TEL

Rates: $64–$135 single or double. AE, CB, DC, DISC, MC, V.

If it were anywhere else, this two-story, chalet-style motel would charge $25 per night. But this TraveLodge is not anywhere else—it's right in the heart of Tahoe City, a short stumble from several restaurants and bars. Inside, it's nothing special—the usual economy-motel look, complete with wall-mounted TVs, budget furnishings, and traditional motel art. But it's not at all shabby, and there's a heated swimming pool, as well as a small spa, for the guests' use.

Where to Dine

EXPENSIVE

Wolfdale's, 640 N. Lake Blvd., Tahoe City. ☎ **916/583-5700.**

Cuisine: CALIFORNIA. **Reservations:** Recommended.
Prices: Appetizers $7–$10; main courses $14–$20. MC, V.
Open: Wed–Mon 6–9pm, Fri–Sat 6–9:30pm. (July–Aug open Tues 6–9pm).

Although it's one of Tahoe's top restaurants, placed in an idyllic lakeside setting, Wolfdale's is visually modest. Behind a rather unassuming wood-shingle exterior is a simple, clean interior that combines country-style American furnishings with Japanese-style blond woods and screens.

Without a doubt, the skilled kitchen is more creative than the comfortably modest dining room. Meals here might begin with vegetable tempura, tea-smoked duck with peanut noodles and mango chutney, or sashimi with ginger and wasabi. Spinach salad tossed with smoked local trout, olives, and grated eggs is particularly memorable. Entrées are equally inventive and include grilled game hen with Thai dipping sauce, Alaskan halibut and sea scallops wrapped in Swiss chard with leek sauce, and roast filet mignon with herbed potatoes and morel mushroom sauce.

MODERATE

Fast Eddie's, 690 N. Lake Blvd., Tahoe City. ☎ **916/583-0950.**

Cuisine: TEXAS BARBECUE. **Reservations:** Not accepted.
Prices: Appetizers $2.50–$4.50; sandwiches $5–$7; main courses $9–$13. MC, V.
Open: Daily 11am–10pm.

Fast Eddie's good down-home feel is actually augmented by the colorful neon signs that hang in the windows. Behind bright orange awnings is a large dining room outfitted with about two dozen plastic-covered tables. The first whiff of Eddie's, from the parking lot outside, confirms that this is a family restaurant of the highest order. Slowly cooked chicken, ribs, sausage, and beef are smoked at low temperatures over black-oak firewood. The beef brisket must be cooked for not fewer than 10 hours, and like most everything else is served with french fries, beans, coleslaw, or corn-on-the-cob. A wide variety of beers and small selection of wines round out the offerings.

Sunnyside Restaurant, 1850 W. Lake Blvd., Tahoe City. ☎ **916/583-7200.**

Cuisine: SEAFOOD/AMERICAN. **Reservations:** Not accepted.
Prices: Appetizers $6–$9; main courses $13–$19.
Open: Oct–June dinner daily 5:30–10:30pm; July–Sept lunch daily 10am–2pm, dinner daily 5pm–10pm; Sunday brunch 9:30am–2pm.

Located about two miles south of Tahoe City, on Hwy. 89, Sunnyside Restaurant is the kind of place that's worth going out of your way for. In summer, when the sun is shining, there's no more highly coveted table in Tahoe than a table on Sunnyside's lakeside veranda. When it gets chilly, you can sit at one of the top dining room tables next to the large windows, which from a distance look like animated picture postcards.

Lunch offerings include fresh pastas, burgers, chicken, and fish sandwiches, together with a variety of soups and salads. Dinners are fancier with such entrées as

Australian lobster tail, oven-roasted shiitake pork tenderloin, steaks, chicken, and lamb chops (broiled and served with fresh mint). All dinners come with San Francisco–style sourdough bread, the chef's starch of the day, and a Caesar salad or cup of creamy fisherman's chowder.

Tahoe House, 625 W. Lake Blvd., Tahoe City. ☎ **916/583-1377.**

Cuisine: SWISS/CALIFORNIA. **Reservations:** Accepted.
Prices: Appetizers $3–$7; main courses $9–$18. AE, CB, DC, DISC, MC, V.
Open: Dinner from 5–10pm.

Fittingly, Tahoe, with its alpine scenery, boasts several Swiss restaurants. One of the oldest is Tahoe House, located at the "Y" in Tahoe City; it has served skiers and others for over 15 years. Chef-owner Peter Vogt's menu is not strictly Swiss: Pastas with sun-dried tomato, calamari strips with pesto aioli, and blackened chicken breasts intermingle with such traditional entrées as port-basted roast duckling, bratwurst, and rahmschnitzel (white veal with a creamy mushroom sauce). Meals are good and usually consistent, but the desserts, which include homebaked tortes, truffles, and chocolates, are always worth yodeling about.

Los Tres Hombres, 765 Emerald Bay Road, South Lake Tahoe. ☎ **916/544-1233.**

Cuisine: MEXICAN. **Reservations:** Not accepted.
Prices: Appetizers $3–$8; main courses $7–$13. MC, V.
Open: Daily 11:30am–10:30pm; bar usually stays open later.

While this restaurant's cavernous tiki-bar interior can easily be mistaken to represent the South Seas, the food is unmistakably south-of-the-border. Los Tres Hombres' bar and adjacent dining area are two of the busiest rooms in South Lake Tahoe. The menu is well priced and extensive, and diners *never* leave hungry. There's nothing too special, however, about the selection, which relies heavily on tried-and-true Californian Mexican specialties such as tacos, burritos, and enchiladas. The chili rellenos (cheese-stuffed peppers, battered and fried) get a thumbs-up, as does the crabmeat- and mushroom-stuffed enchilada.

INEXPENSIVE

Burger Spa, 126 W. Lake Blvd., Tahoe City. No phone.

Prices: Burger $4–$6. No credit cards.
Open: Mon–Fri 10am–7pm, Sat–Sun 10am–8pm.

It's just a simple, wooden A-frame building containing a small short-order grill, but Burger Spa flips an unusually hefty and tasty burger and an equally terrific grilled chicken breast sandwich. There are a few tables inside, but on a nice day the best seats are at the picnic tables set up out front.

The restaurant is located directly across from the Tahoe Yogurt Factory (see below).

The Galley Cafe, 700 N. Lake Blvd., Tahoe City. ☎ **916/581-3305.**

Cuisine: AMERICAN. **Reservations:** Recommended.
Prices: Breakfast entrées $3–$7, lunch entrées $5–$8, dinner entrées $7–$10. MC, V.
Open: Mon–Fri 11am–3pm, Sat–Sun 9am–3pm, times may vary according to season, call ahead.

The best place in town for breakfast has a beautiful country interior with floral prints and hardwood floors, and a slightly obstructed lake view. Good coffee is the first major test of an exceptional eggery, and the Galley passes with flying colors. All the customary morning meals are served, including French toast, eggs Benedict, pancakes, bagels, and a half dozen omelet selections (including one with grilled tomatoes, Jack cheese, dill, avocado, and sour cream). Large lunch sandwiches run the gamut from charbroiled chicken breast and hot pastrami to shrimp, veggie, and tuna. Philadelphia-style cheesesteaks (shaved sirloin tips and melted Jack cheese on a grilled French roll), a variety of salads, burgers, and other hot foods are served for both lunch and dinner.

Tahoe Yogurt Factory, 125 W. Lake Blvd., Tahoe City. ☎ **916/581-5253.**

Prices: Coffee $1; yogurt $1.75–$2.25; sandwiches $4–$5.75. No credit cards.
Open: Mon–Fri 6am–10pm, Sat–Sun 8am–11pm.

This small coffee shack, located at the "Y" in Tahoe City, gets mention as *the* best little cafe in Tahoe. There's not much more to it than basic croissants, muffins, and sandwiches—and excellent java. Small tables are placed outdoors in the summer.

Yellow Sub, Hwy. 50 and 983 Tallac Ave., South Lake Tahoe. ☎ **916/541-8808.**

Prices: Sandwiches $3–$6. No credit cards.
Open: Daily 10:30am–10pm.

When it comes to picnic supplies, there's stiff competition in South Lake Tahoe: three sandwich shops on this single block alone. But a recent independent taste test (mine) has named Yellow Sub the winner, with its 21 kinds of overstuffed subs, made in 6-inch and 12-inch varieties. The shop is hidden in a small shopping center, located across from the El Dorado Campground.

Evening Entertainment

Tahoe is not known particularly for its nightlife; perhaps visitors are too exhausted by the day's activities to be entertained all night. There's always something going on in the showrooms of the major casino hotels, located in Stateline, just north of South Lake Tahoe. Call Harrah's (☎ **588-6611**), Harvey's (☎ **588-2411**), Caesar's (☎ **588-3515**), and the Lake Tahoe Horizon (☎ **588-6211**) for current show schedules and prices.

There's usually live music nightly in **Bullwhackers Pub,** at the Resort at Squaw Creek (☎ **583-6300**), located five miles west of Tahoe City. The **Pierce Street Annex,** 850 N. Lake Blvd. (☎ **583-5800**), located behind the Safeway in Tahoe City, has pool tables, shuffleboard, and DJ dancing every night. It's one of the livelier places around.

5 Yosemite National Park

184 miles E of San Francisco, 307 miles N of Los Angeles

GETTING THERE • **By Plane** The nearest airport to Yosemite is in the town of Merced, about 40 miles east along winding Calif. 140. Several airlines, including United Express (☎ toll free **800/241-6522**) and USAir (☎ toll free **800/428-4322**) service the airport from both San Francisco and Los Angeles. The least expensive flights from the Bay Area cost about $120 each way.

• **By Train** Trains don't run into the Yosemite Valley itself, but they do come as close as Merced. California Greyline (☎ **209/383-1563**) buses connect with the

Yosemite National Park

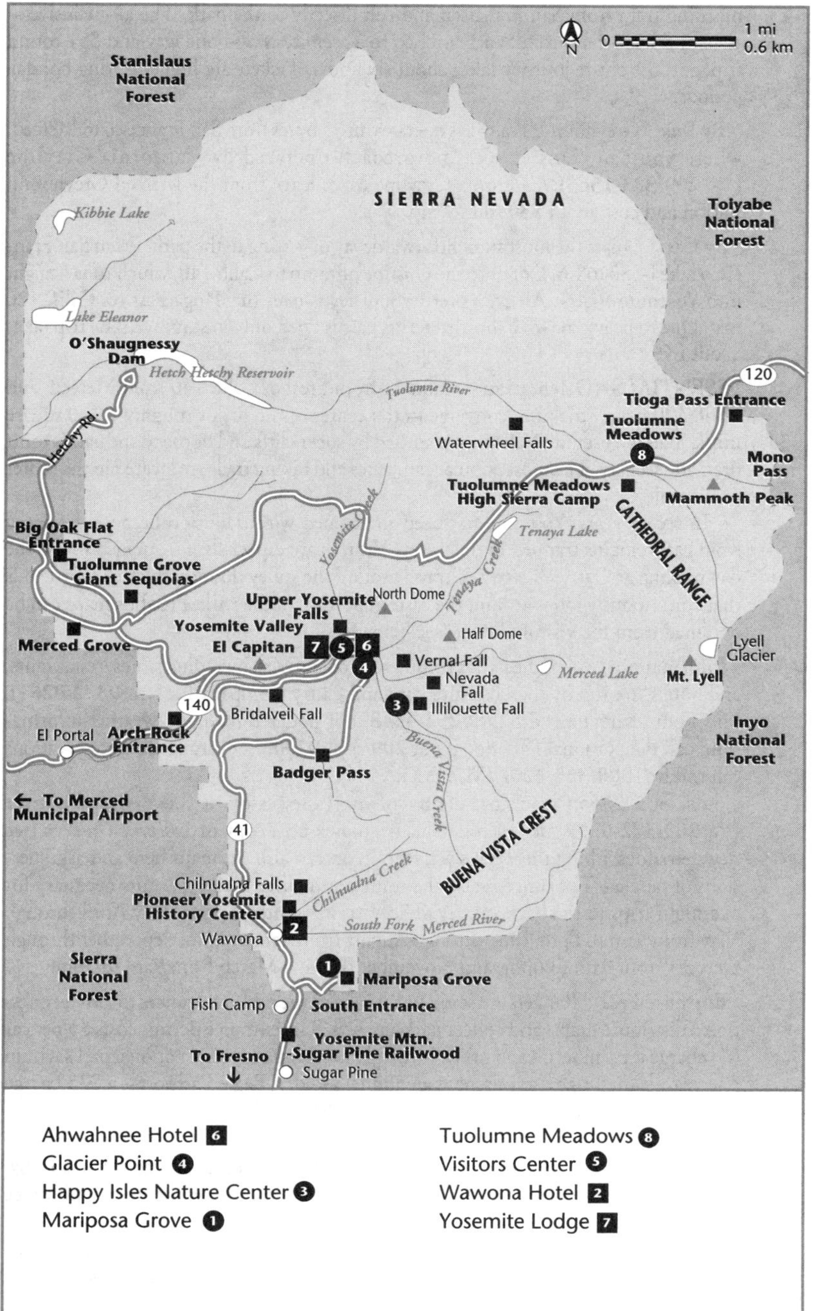

N
0
1 mi
0.6 km
Stanislaus National Forest
SIERRA NEVADA
Toiyabe National Forest
Kibbie Lake
Lake Eleanor
O'Shaugnessy Dam
Hetch Hetchy Reservoir
Hetchy Rd.
Tuolumne River
120
Tioga Pass Entrance
Tuolumne Meadows
Waterwheel Falls
Mono Pass
Tuolumne Meadows High Sierra Camp
Mammoth Peak
CATHEDRAL RANGE
Tenaya Lake
Big Oak Flat Entrance
Tuolumne Grove Giant Sequoias
Yosemite Creek
Tenaya Creek
Upper Yosemite Falls
North Dome
Yosemite Valley
Half Dome
Merced Grove
El Capitan
Vernal Fall
Lyell Glacier
Merced Lake
Mt. Lyell
Nevada Fall
140
Bridalveil Fall
Illilouette Fall
El Portal
Arch Rock Entrance
Inyo National Forest
Buena Vista Creek
Badger Pass
← To Merced Municipal Airport
41
BUENA VISTA CREST
Chilnualna Falls
Chilnualna Creek
Pioneer Yosemite History Center
South Fork Merced River
Wawona
Sierra National Forest
Mariposa Grove
Fish Camp
South Entrance
Yosemite Mtn. -Sugar Pine Railwood
To Fresno ↓
Sugar Pine
Ahwahnee Hotel 6
Glacier Point 4
Happy Isles Nature Center 3
Mariposa Grove 1
Tuolumne Meadows 8
Visitors Center 5
Wawona Hotel 2
Yosemite Lodge 7

morning train from San Francisco and run directly to the park. The all-inclusive—train and bus—fare from San Francisco to Yosemite is $44 one way and $51 round trip, and the entire journey takes about six hours. Tickets are higher during holiday periods.

• **By Bus** Greyhound/Trailways operates direct buses from San Francisco to Merced, where you can transfer to a motorcoach operated by California Greyline (☎ **209/383-1563**). California Greyline buses leave from the Merced Greyhound station and cost about $30 round-trip.

• **By Car** This is the most straightforward way of getting to the park. From San Francisco take I-580 to I-5. Exit onto the Gustine offramp to Calif. 140, which runs straight into Yosemite Valley. An even prettier journey is over the Tioga Pass on Calif. 120 east. Due to heavy snowfall, however, this pass is open only in summer. The trip takes about five hours.

ESSENTIALS • **Orientation** Calif. 41 from Fresno, Calif. 140 from Merced, and Calif. 120 from Stockton, converge in the center of the park's roughly 1,200 square miles. This is Yosemite Valley, surrounded by sheer cliffs and home to the park's most dramatic scenery. The most popular campsites and hiking trails are located in the center of the valley.

In recent years, Yosemite has been threatened with pollution because the smog from cars remains trapped in the valley. Visitors are especially encouraged to use the day parking at Curry Village and travel around the valley floor on the free shuttle bus that continuously loops around the eastern portion of the park. Free bus maps can be obtained from the visitors center (see below).

• **Information** All of the park's commercial operations, including stores, restaurants, and hotels, are run by the Yosemite Park and Curry Company (☎ **209/372-0264**). For room reservations call **209/252-4848**. For updated road and weather information, call the National Park Service at **209/372-0200**. For campground reservations call toll free **800/365-2267** (MISTIX).

As soon as you reach the center of the valley, stop at the **Visitors Center** (☎ **209/372-0299**) in Yosemite Village to pick up a copy of *Yosemite Guide,* a free newsletter describing the week's activities. You can also get maps here and ask questions of rangers. The office is also the source of the free hiking permits necessary for overnight trips to the backcountry. The Visitors Center is open daily April through May from 9am to 6pm, June through August from 8am to 8pm, September through October from 8am to 6pm, and November through March from 9am to 5pm.

• **Entrance Fees** Rangers are stationed at each of the park's entrances to answer questions, distribute maps, and collect park-use fees. The entrance permit costs $5 per car (no charge for seniors 62 and over). If you plan on visiting several national parks within one year, it might pay to purchase an annual Golden Eagle Passport—a $25 charge includes entrance to all the national parks that charge fees.

You might call Yosemite National Park breathtaking, spectacular, or awe-inspiring, but none of these words—however accurate—even begin to describe the magnificence of this country.

Yosemite Valley evolved when glaciers moved through the canyon, which had been created by the Merced River during repeated geological rises of the Sierras. When these glaciers began to melt, the moraine (accumulated earth and stones deposited by a glacier) dammed part of the Merced River to form Lake Yosemite in the new valley.

Eventually, sediment filled in the lake, thus accounting for the flat floor of Yosemite Valley. This same process, on a much smaller scale, is even now occurring with Mirror Lake at the base of Half Dome.

The Native American Ahwahneechees had been living in the valley for several thousand years before they first encountered Europeans in the middle of the 19th century. Members of the Joseph Reddeford Walker party were probably the first "foreigners" to see Yosemite Valley when they crossed from the east side of the Sierra in 1833. Later intrusions resulted in indiscriminate abuses of the environment. To forestall any commercial exploitation of the valley, President Abraham Lincoln granted Yosemite Valley and the Mariposa Grove of giant sequoias to California as a public trust. Federal legislation created Yosemite National Park in 1890.

Today, Yosemite Valley is, as it has been for thousands of years, a glacier-carved canyon with crashing waterfalls (in wet years) and sheer walls of granite extending thousands of feet upward from the valley's flat floor. It remains a sensual blend of open meadows, wildflowers, and woodlands with ponderosa pine, incense cedar, and Douglas fir. All kinds of wildlife, from monarch butterflies and a world of birds (223 species) to mule deer and black bear flourish in this protected environment.

What to See & Do

Although it occupies only 7 of the 1,200 square miles that make up the park, Yosemite Valley is the protected area's primary focal point, due to its incredible concentration of sheer beauty. Many of the park's campgrounds are here, making the valley a logical place to begin your visit. From here you can set out on your own to explore some of the park's most famous features, including Yosemite Falls, Mirror Lake, Half Dome, and El Capitan.

Visitors Center, Yosemite Village, ☎ **209/372-0299.**

The Visitors Center should be everyone's first stop. In addition to informative audio-visual programs and other exhibits relating to park history and activities, the center can recommend tours on Yosemite's 216 miles of paved road and point you toward the sequoia groves, granite summits, and waterfall bases.

Well over a dozen daily activities are offered here, beginning each morning around 8:30am and continuing until about 9pm. They might include lectures on photography, a ranger-led fireside discussion on bears, a guided luncheon hike to a waterfall, a geological history tour, or a puppet show with an environmental theme. There are fewer activities off-season.

Open: Apr–May daily 9am–6pm; Jun–Aug daily 8am–8pm; Sept–Oct daily 8am–6pm; Nov–Mar daily 9am–5pm.

TOURING THE PARK

The following park highlights are all accessible by automobile:

Tuolumne Meadows At an elevation of 8,600 feet, this is the largest alpine meadow in the High Sierras and a gateway to the High Country. Closed in winter, it's 55 miles from the valley by way of highly scenic Big Oak Flat and Tioga roads. A walk through this natural alpine garden makes a delightful day's excursion. In summer the park operates a large campground here, with a full-scale naturalist program.

Happy Isles Nature Center Another gateway to the high country, Happy Isles is also a trailhead for the John Muir Trail and for Vernal and Nevada falls (the Mist

Trail). Accessible by shuttle bus, the center is staffed by Yosemite Association employees who provide information about hiking to Nevada Falls and Mirror Lake.

Mariposa Grove One of the park's three groves of giant sequoias and the largest, this grove has hundreds of trees, over 200 of which measure 10 feet or more in diameter. Among them is the Grizzly Giant, the largest and oldest tree in the park (it takes 27 fifth-graders to reach around it, while 18 can reach around a school bus). Private vehicles can drive to the entrance of the grove; beyond that you can hike in or board a free shuttle bus. There are stops where you can get off to hear nature talks, stroll around, take photos, or just absorb the peaceful atmosphere of the forest. The Mariposa Grove (not to be confused with the community of Mariposa) is 35 miles south of the valley.

Glacier Point Offering a sweeping 180-degree panorama of the High Sierras and a breathtaking view from 3,200 feet above the valley, Glacier Point looks out over Nevada and Vernal falls, the Merced River, and the snow-covered Sierra peaks of Yosemite's backcountry. The approach road from the Badger Pass intersection (closed in winter) winds through verdant red-fir and pine forest and meadow. Many fine trails lead back down to the valley floor.

Sports & Recreation

A popular vacation destination in itself, Yosemite offers an exceptionally wide variety of visitor activities, from bicycling, backpacking, white-water trips, and mountaineering to more rugged snow-related pursuits.

The National Park Service and its rangers want you to have a marvelous time while you're in Yosemite. So here are a few common sources of trouble that can spoil the best vacation:

Streams in the Sierra Nevada can be dangerous, especially during the spring runoff when currents are fast, water is extremely cold, and rocks near the water are slippery. Children should be supervised closely.

Before you attempt to scramble or climb on Yosemite's walls, provide yourself with proper training and equipment and allow enough time.

Whenever possible, use only tap water for drinking. Water-borne parasites known as *Giardia lamblia* may contaminate lakes and streams. Symptoms associated with resulting infections include diarrhea, abdominal cramps, bloating, and fatigue.

Pay special attention when driving—park roads are narrow, steep, and winding. If you want to view the scenery and wildlife, pull off the roadway into a safe turnout. Park animals are wild—do not approach or feed them.

BICYCLING Why not see the sights on two wheels? Many trails are specially geared to cyclists, and you can rent a standard or multispeed bike from the Yosemite Lodge bike stand or the Curry Village bike stand. They cost about $15 per day.

FISHING Beautiful high-country lakes, miles of rivers (the Merced and Tuolumne are especially popular), streams, and tributaries provide anglers with excellent fishing and unsurpassed views. Various kinds of trout are the main catch here. Fishing licenses (required for anyone over 16) can be obtained at the Sports Shop in Yosemite Village.

HIKING Over 700 miles of trails offer opportunities for hiking—easy or very challenging and ranging from a leisurely stroll to a trip of a week or longer; and the terrain can range from plains to jagged mountains. If you wish to roam the less-traveled backcountry, a free wilderness permit is required. (Permits limit traffic to help keep the wilderness wild.) These can be obtained at any of the five permit stations in the park or by writing to Wilderness Office, P.O. Box 577, Yosemite, CA 95389.

HORSEBACK RIDING Yosemite has excellent stable facilities and over 30 miles of bridle paths in the valley. Located near Curry Village, the stables are open during the summer season only. Two-hour guided horseback rides leave several times daily. There are also half- and full-day guided mule trips to Clark's Point, Glacier Point, Half Dome, and other destinations.

Prices for horse and mule trips vary. For information on tours and rates, contact the Yosemite Concession Services (☎ **209/372-1248**).

MOUNTAIN CLIMBING With vertical granite walls surrounding two-thirds of the valley, Yosemite is considered by experts to be one of the finest climbing areas in the Western world. The **Yosemite Mountaineering School** at Curry Village has classes for beginning, intermediate, and advanced climbers. There are rock-climbing, ice-climbing, and natural-history trips, as well as beginning and advanced survival trips. Inquire at the visitor center.

SKIING **Badger Pass,** located 23 miles outside the valley, opened in 1935, making it the oldest ski resort in California. The terrain is mostly geared to intermediate-level skiers, with about 35% of the trails marked for beginners and 15% for experts. Ski instructors offer introductory and refresher courses, as well as children's ski lessons. Facilities include one triple-chair lift, three double-chair lifts, and a rope tow for beginners. The slopes are open from November or December through Easter (weather permitting).

Yosemite also encompasses over 90 miles of marked trails for cross-country skiing. Twenty-two miles of these trails are free, and machine-groomed track, set several times weekly from Badger Pass to Glacier Point. Skiers can stay overnight at the Glacier Point Ski Hut or at Ostrander Lake Ski Hut.

For information on Yosemite ski facilities, contact Badger Pass, Yosemite National Park, CA 95389 (☎ **209/372-1445** or **372-1332**). For a daily update on ski, road, and weather conditions, dial the Badger Pass snow phone: **209/372-1000.**

Where to Stay

From luxury hotel to simple tent, Yosemite offers a wide choice of accommodations. Unfortunately, space is very limited and demand is enormous. The park's hotels are regularly booked to capacity from May to September, and on weekends and holidays throughout the year. All Yosemite hotels take room reservations exactly 366 days in advance, and sell out within minutes for the most popular times of year. You might get lucky—rooms sometimes open up 30, 15, and 7 days in advance due to cancellations. To make reservations, contact **Yosemite Reservations,** 5410 E. Home Ave., Fresno, CA 93727 (☎ **209/252-4848**).

The Ahwahnee Hotel, Yosemite Village. ☎ **209/252-4848.** 123 rms, 5 suites. TV TEL

Rates: $201 single room or cottage; $208 double room or cottage; from $402 suite. Lower midweek winter rates are available. AE, DISC, MC, V.

A National Historic Landmark, the Ahwahnee Hotel is one of the finest hotels in the national park system. Built in 1927 with rock from just outside the park, this luxurious hotel is stocked with top-of-the-line in-room amenities that include TVs, refrigerators, bathrobes, and hairdryers. Each room has sturdy rustic wooden furniture, and is accented with original Native American designs. Suites have an additional sitting room. Ahwahnee Cottage Rooms are free-standing full-service cabins located in an adjacent wooded setting.

The hotel's celebrated dining and entertainment facilities include the Indian Bar room for drinks and the splendid Dining Room, where dinner reservations are recommended year round.

Wawona Hotel, 4 miles inside the south gateway. ☎ **209/252-4848.** 105 rms.

Rates: $63 single or double without bath, $86 single or double with bath. CB, DC, DISC, MC, V.

You won't be roughing it at the Wawona, near the southern end of Yosemite. This is the oldest hotel in continuous service in the national park system, dating from 1879. The pretty wooden gingerbread structures offer comfortable, if sparse, rooms; facilities include a swimming pool, a tennis court, and a nine-hole golf course, as well as nearby stables and hiking trails.

Yosemite Lodge, near the foot of Yosemite Falls. ☎ **209/252-4848.** 495 rms and cabins (405 with bath). TEL

Rates: $43 single or double without bath; $47 cabin without bath; $75 single or double with bath; $62 cabin with bath. MC, V.

Yosemite Lodge is within easy walking distance of most of the valley's attractions. It offers attractive but simple hotel rooms and small redwood cabins. Because it's priced so well, this place is popular, and reservations should be made as far in advance as possible. Facilities include a lounge, two restaurants, and a cafeteria, as well as several shops.

Camping

Yosemite's 300-plus year-round campsites expand to a whopping 2,000 sites in summer. Campground fees range from $7 to $14 per day. Sites are scattered over 17 different campgrounds, and split into two categories. The $10 to $14 Type A sites are the most elaborate, with well-defined roads, parking, drinking water, flush toilets, and, generally, a fireplace, table/bench combination, and tent space. The $7 Type B sites may be accessible by road or trail, and conveniences are limited to basic sanitary facilities and a smattering of fireplaces and tables.

From June 1 to September 15 camping permits are limited to 7 days in the valley and 14 days in the rest of the park. The rest of the year campers can stay for as long as 30 days.

For more details on campgrounds, contact the Campground Office, P.O. Box 426, Yosemite National Park, CA 95389 (☎ **209/372-4845**, or toll free **800/365-2267**).

7

The Monterey Peninsula & Big Sur Coast

LOCATED ABOUT 120 MILES DOWN THE COAST FROM SAN FRANCISCO, MONTEREY County's beautiful peninsula protrudes west into the Pacific like a puzzle piece. Part rustic New England, part aristocratic European, the cypress-covered peninsula, with its rugged shoreline and crescent-shaped bay, contains some of the prettiest coastal communities in the world.

The hamlets of Monterey and Pacific Grove spread across the northern half of the peninsula and front Monterey Bay. Pebble Beach, with its famous golf course, and the beautiful town of Carmel look out over Carmel Bay and hug the peninsula's south coast. Between the north and south coasts, which are only about five miles apart, are at least eight golf courses, some of the state's most stunning homes and hotels, and 17 Mile Drive, the most breathtaking coastal road in the world.

Big Sur is not the name of a town—it refers to an awe-inspiring 90-mile stretch of coast south of the Monterey Peninsula. Nestled between the Santa Lucia Mountains and the rocky Pacific shore, Big Sur is as grand as its name and as bold as its reputation.

SEEING MONTEREY & BIG SUR

There's no question that the best way to see this stretch of coast is by car. There is simply no acceptable alternative to exploring, at your own pace, the nooks and crannies of the shoreline and its accompanying towns.

The best sightseeing strategy? Drive from north to south, or vice versa, along Calif. 1. Leave the highway for secondary roads that lead into towns and unspoiled stretches of beach.

GETTING THERE The region's most convenient runway, at **Monterey Peninsula Airport (408/373-3731)**, is located three miles east of Monterey on Calif. 68. **American Eagle** (toll free **800/433-7300**), **Skywest** (toll free **800/453-9417**), **United Express** (toll free **800/444-9247**), and **USAir** (toll free **800/428-4322**) schedule daily flights in and out of Monterey. Many area hotels offer free airport shuttle service. Taxis also meet flights, and cost about $15 to $25 to a peninsula hotel. Several national car rental companies have airport locations, including **Dollar** (toll free **800/800-4000**) and **Hertz** (toll free **800/654-3131**).

Greyhound/Trailways offers daily bus service from both the north and south coasts. The Monterey bus station is at 351 Del Monte Ave. **(408/373-4735)**. Greyhound/Trailways no longer operates a nationwide toll free telephone number, so call your local office for fares and schedule information.

What's Special About Monterey & Big Sur

Scenery

- Dramatic coastlines around the peninsula and down the coast.
- The 17 Mile Drive, one of the most beautiful roads in the world.
- Tree-covered coasts, opening onto small, charming villages.

Golf Courses

- More than a half dozen greenways on the peninsula alone.
- Pebble Beach, one of the world's most famous links.

Towns

- Monterey, Pacific Grove, and Carmel are some of the prettiest, fanciest, and most expensive villages in the world.

Monterey-Salinas Transit (MST), Simoneau Plaza (**408/899-2558**), is a local bus line that connects the peninsula's neighboring cities to one another and to Big Sur on Calif. 1.

Driving your own car is the best way to go. Calif. 1, which hugs the California coast, runs right into the Monterey Peninsula. The beautiful but slow drive from San Francisco takes about three hours, depending on traffic. The peninsula is also connected to the rest of the state via U.S. 101, a two-hour journey from San Francisco.

1 Monterey

122 miles SE of San Francisco, 334 miles NW of Los Angeles

GETTING THERE See "Getting There" at the beginning of this chapter.

ESSENTIALS • **Orientation** The town of Monterey occupies the northeastern part of the peninsula to which it gives its name. The town's best sights are clustered along a mile of waterfront that runs from David Avenue to Figueroa Street. Cannery Row lies along the northern half of this stretch. Fisherman's Wharf, the Old Custom House, and many of the town's most important historical sites lie along the southern shore.

• **Information** The **Monterey Peninsula Visitors and Convention Bureau**, 380 Alvarado St. (P.O. Box 1770), Monterey, CA 93942 (☎ **408/649-1770**), has good maps and free pamphlets and publications, including an excellent visitors guide and two magazines with detailed listings, *Coast Weekly* and *Monterey Peninsula Review*. The office is located near the intersection of Pacific Street and Del Monte Avenue.

Originally settled in 1770, Monterey was one of the west coast's first European settlements. The town was the original capital of California under three flags—Spanish, Mexican, and American; its history, to a large extent, is the history of pre-Gold Rush California. Many architectural reminders of the past—including whitewashed adobe houses and pueblos—still stand. Combined with a stunning setting and a bustling wharf area, Monterey remains, both visually and economically, one of the state's most successful enclaves.

What to See & Do

★ **Cannery Row**, on Monterey Bay between David and Drake Aves. ☎ **408/649-6690**.

Author John Steinbeck singlehandedly brought fame to Cannery Row when he immortalized it in his 1945 book of the same name. At the time, the Row bustled with activity as workers packed sardines in 18 adjacent canneries. Steinbeck described the Row as "a poem, a stink, a grating noise, a quality of light, a tone, a habit, a nostalgia, a dream," and people came from all over to experience the same scenes.

Tragically, silver sardines suddenly disappeared from Monterey's waters in 1948: the combined result of overfishing, changing currents, and pollution. Fishermen left, canneries closed, and the Row fell into disrepair. Steinbeck's nostalgic dream was no more, but curious tourists, drawn by the author's *Cannery Row* and its sequel, *Sweet Thursday*, continued to visit the areas they had read about.

It didn't take long for entrepreneurs to take notice of—and cash in on—the Row's fantastic location and international fame. The seaside strip's canneries and warehouses were renovated and converted; they now hold harbor restaurants, local artists' galleries, touristy hotels, and visitor-oriented gift shops. Many of the larger buildings have become self-contained minimalls, containing myriad shops and eateries. It's a fun place to visit, and you can easily spend the day strolling along the row, visiting the surrounding museums and historical sites and even wandering barefoot along the rocky shoreline.

After visiting Cannery Row in the 1960s, Steinbeck wrote, "The beaches are clean where they once festered with fish guts and flies. The canneries which once put up a sickening stench are gone, their places filled with restaurants, antique shops, and the like. They fish for tourists now, not pilchards, and that species they are not likely to wipe out."

Fisherman's Wharf, 885 Abrego St. ☎ **408/373-0600.**

Lined with craft stores, gift shops, boating and fishing operations, and fish markets, the wharf remains perpetually busy year round. But it's the particularly large concentration of seafood restaurants that are the wharf's principal attraction. From before dawn to well past dusk, there's always a good selection of foods: from a simple cup of fresh shrimp to a full sit-down restaurant meal. During summer, many eateries tempt potential patrons with free samples of their homemade clam chowder. (See "Where to Dine" below for specific restaurant recommendations.)

★ **Monterey Bay Aquarium,** 886 Cannery Row. ☎ **408/648-4888.**

Monterey Bay Aquarium was not built in this particular region by accident. The aquatic research facility, and the California coast that surrounds it, sits on the border of one of the largest underwater canyons on earth—wider and deeper than even the Grand Canyon.

Opened in 1984, the Monterey Bay Aquarium quickly gained fame as one of the best exhibit aquariums in the world, and it's one of the largest, too. It was constructed at a cost of $55 million and is home to more than 6,500 marine animals. The living museum's main exhibit is a three-story, 335,000-gallon tank, the clear, acrylic walls of which give visitors an unmatched look at local sea life. A towering kelp forest, which rises from the floor of this oceanic zoo, gently waves with the water as hundreds of leopard sharks, sardines, anchovies, and other fish school back and forth in a seemingly endless game of hide-and-seek.

Additional wet exhibits re-create other undersea habitats found in Monterey Bay. There are coastal streams, tidal pools, a sand beach, and a petting pool, where you can touch living bat rays and handle sea stars. Visitors can also watch a live video link that continuously transmits from a deep-sea research submarine maneuvering thousands of feet below the surface of Monterey Bay.

A special exhibition, entitled "Mating Games: Reproduction and Survival in the Aquatic World," is scheduled to run to September 1995. The display, featuring a variety of ocean species, offers a fascinating look into the reproductive ways of marine animals.

Admission: $11.25 adults, $8.25 students and seniors over 65, $5 disabled and children ages 3–12, free for children under 3. You can avoid long lines at the gate by calling toll free **800/756-3737** and ordering tickets in advance. AE, MC, V.

Open: Daily 10am–6pm (summer and holidays open at 9:30am).

THE PATH OF HISTORY

About a dozen city buildings, clustered around Fisherman's Wharf and the adjacent waterfront, are preserved as historical monuments. Collectively, these structures comprise the Path of History and many are a part of the Monterey State Historic Park, 210 Olivier St. (☎ **408/649-7118**).

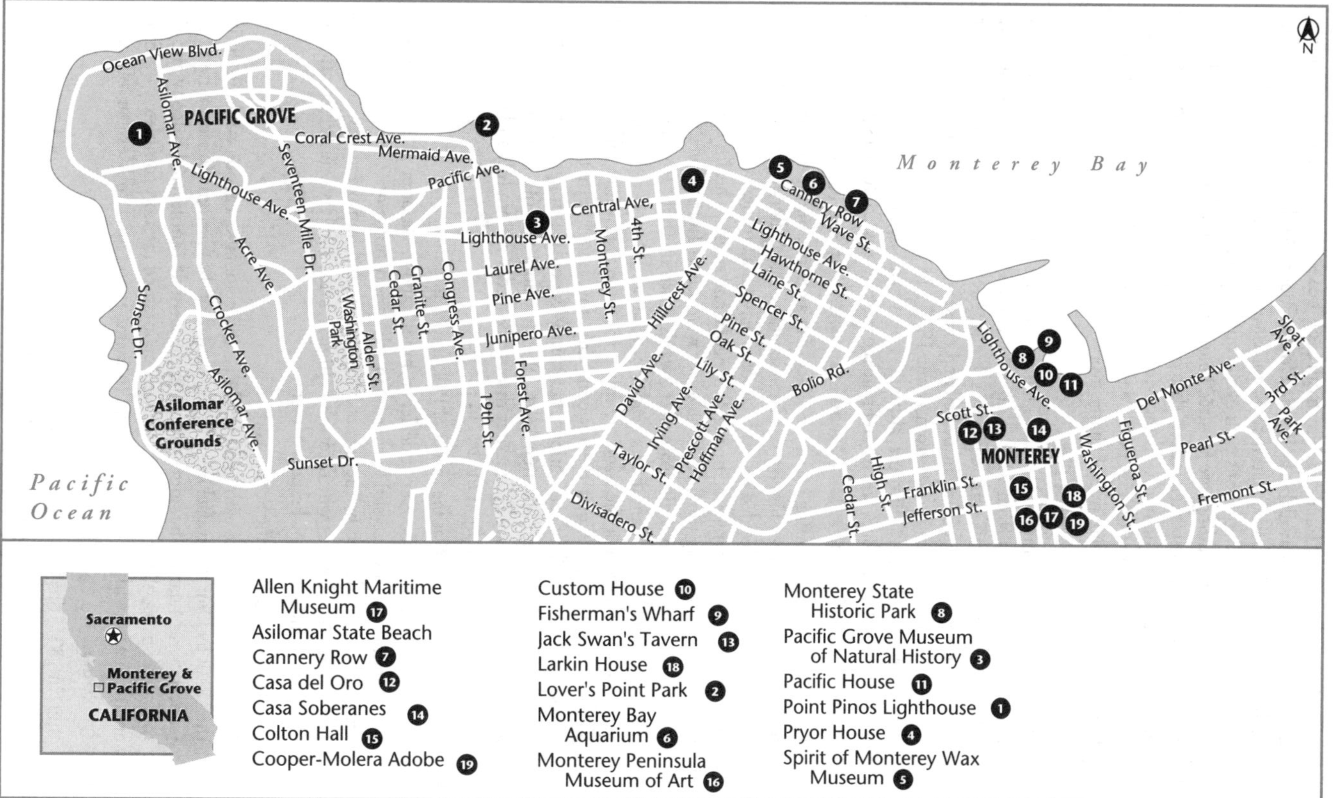

Monterey & Pacific Grove

Admission to all the buildings, which can easily be seen in a day, costs $4 for adults, $1 for children, and is available at Pacific House Cooper-Molera Adobe, and Colton Hall (see below). At these locations you might also wish to purchase a self-guided walking tour booklet that details each of the buildings on the tour.

The path's best buildings are featured below; many do not have formal addresses, so they're listed with street references. Path of History building hours vary from each other and change frequently. Call the Monterey State Historic Park for the latest information or visit the Orientation Center on Custom House Plaza. A Monterey history film is shown here free of charge every 20 minutes.

Custom House, 1 Custom House Plaza.

Until 1846, when Commodore John Drake Sloat raised the U.S. flag here, the Custom House, just across from what is now the entrance to Fisherman's Wharf, presided over Alta California's principal port. Under Mexican rule, customs duties were collected here; only after being inspected and taxed were the ships permitted to trade on the California coast. Dating from about 1827, the Custom House is the oldest government building in California, although it served as such for only about 40 years. It became obsolete in 1867, when San Francisco took over as California's primary port.

California's First Theater/Jack Swan's Tavern, Scott and Pacific Sts.

In 1847, Jack Swan, an English sailor of Scottish ancestry, built a lodging house and tavern on Pacific Street. Three years later several U.S. soldiers from the New York Volunteer Regiment decided to produce some plays as a business venture. They used blankets as curtains, barrels and boards as benches, and turned a healthy profit on their very first night. Among the first productions were scenes from *Romeo and Juliet.*

The building fell into disrepair after Swan's death in 1896. It was purchased by the California Historic Landmarks League in 1906 and then donated to the state for preservation, which kept the structure much the same as it was in earlier times. The Troupers of the Gold Coast theater company now stages authentic 19th-century melodramas here. Call for reservations after 1pm Wednesday through Saturday. Tickets cost $6 for adults, $5 for children 13 to 19 and seniors over 60, and $4 for kids 12 and under. Showtimes are Wednesday through Saturday at 8pm July and August, and Friday and Saturday at 8pm the rest of the year.

Cooper-Molera Adobe, at the corner of Polk and Munras Sts.

Captain John Rogers Cooper, a dealer in hides, tallow, sea otter pelts, and general merchandise, was a successful businessman. His pretty home on 2½ acres grew with his success, as evidenced by the successive additions and improvements. Built in the 1830s, the complex was willed to the National Trust for Historic Preservation by Cooper's granddaughter, Frances Molera.

Casa Soberanes, 336 Pacific St., at Scott St.

Often called the "House with the Blue Gate," this colonial-era adobe was built during the 1840s by Don José Rafael Estrada, the warden of the Custom House, for his bride, Concepcion Malarn. The home's Mediterranean-style cantilevered balcony and tile roof are of particular interest, as is the well-maintained interior, completely outfitted and decorated with early New England furnishings and modern Mexican folk art.

Larkin House, 510 Calle Principal, at Jefferson St.

Built in 1835, this balconied two-story adobe house was the home of Thomas Oliver Larkin, the U.S. consul to Mexico from 1843 to 1846. The house doubled as the consular office and is furnished with many fine antiques including some original pieces. Next door is the house used by William Tecumseh Sherman; it now contains a museum depicting the roles of the two men in California history.

Stevenson House, 530 Houston St.

The original portion of this two-story home dates to the late 1830s, when it sheltered Don Rafael Gonzales, the first administrator of customs of Alta California. In 1856 a French pioneer, Juan Giradin, and his wife became the home's owners. They made some additions and rented spare bedrooms to roomers, one of whom was Robert Louis Stevenson (he occupied a second-floor room during the autumn of 1879). Stevenson had come from Scotland to persuade Fanny Osbourne to marry him (she did). While here, he wrote *The Old Pacific Capital,* an account of Monterey in the 1870s. Poor, unknown, and in ill health, Stevenson was cared for by Jules Simoneau, in whose restaurant he had his one full meal of the day.

The building has been restored to its period look, and several rooms are devoted to Stevenson memorabilia.

Pacific House, 10 Custom House Plaza.

Built in 1847 by David Wight for Thomas O. Larkin, Pacific House was first used to house army offices and to store military supplies. Horses were corralled behind the building, which was also a popular spot for Sunday bull and bear fights. Pacific House later sheltered several small stores, and served successively as a public tavern, a courtroom, county clerk's office, newspaper office, law offices, a church—and a ballroom where a temperance society called the Dashaways held dances.

The Jacks family bought the property in 1880 and maintained the premises until 1954, when Miss Margaret Jacks made a gift of the historic building to the state. The first floor now houses a museum of California history; the second floor has an extensive collection of Native American artifacts plus a few Mexican-Indian and Inuit pieces.

Colton Hall, 522 Pacific St.

Named for the Rev. Walter Colton, a U.S. Navy chaplain who impaneled California's first jury, co-founded the state's first newspaper, and built the region's first public building, Colton Hall was originally built as the town hall and public school. California's constitutional congress convened here in 1849, and penned the state constitution and created California's great seal of the state. Old Monterey Jail adjoins the property, its grim cell walls still marked with prisoners' scribblings.

Casa del Oro, at the corner of Scott and Oliver Sts.

Originally built as a warehouse, barracks, and hospital for American seamen who were left at the port under consular care, this two-story adobe has enjoyed many lives. It's called Casa del Oro (house of gold) because miners supposedly stored their treasures in an iron safe here during Gold Rush days. In 1849 the building was leased to Joseph Boston and Company and operated as a general store.

Today, Casa del Oro is owned by the state and operated by the Monterey History and Art Association. It's still a general store, preserved as it was in the 19th century: stocked with and selling burlap sacks of coffee and beans, milk cans, ribbons, old tools, fabrics, dinnerware, and canisters of grains, noodles, and the like.

GUIDED TOURS

By Bus

Steinbeck Country Tours, Steinbeck Center Foundation, P.O. Box 2495, Salinas, CA 93902. ☎ **408/753-6411**.

Whole- and half-day tours of "Steinbeck Country" show visitors sites that were well-known to renowned American author and local legend John Steinbeck. Tours visit both Monterey and Salinas, and may include a guided walk along Cannery Row.

Prices: $15–$25 per person.

Times: Departures vary, phone for information.

By Semi-Submersible Submarine

Nautilus IV, 32 Cannery Row, Monterey, CA 93940. ☎ **408/647-1400**.

Nautilus IV, a semi-submersible submarine-like vessel allows visitors to view Monterey Bay from just below the waterline. A kind of real-life Disney-inspired ride, these undersea tours are augmented by experienced divers who swim along side the vessel and point out the particulars to the porthole viewers. On-board video screens broadcast images from cameras mounted on the sub's exterior. *Nautilus IV* is unusual "edutainment," as well as being an expensive thrill.

Prices: $24.95 adults, $14.95 children 5–12; under 5 free.

Times: Tours depart 5 times daily from 11am to 4pm; phone for times.

DEEP-SEA FISHING

The sardines may be gone, but Monterey is still a premiere jumping-off point for other catch of all kinds. Some of the best and most accessible charter boats depart from Fisherman's Wharf.

Chris' Fishing Trips, 48 Fisherman's Wharf. ☎ **408/375-5951**.

The largest party boats in Monterey, Chris' diesel-powered cruisers are equipped with fish finders, radar, ship-to-shore phone, and deck lounges. Cod and salmon are the main catches, with separate boats leaving daily. Call for a complete price list and sailing schedule.

Prices: Full-day excursions $25–$45 per person.

Sam's Fishing Fleet, 84 Fisherman's Wharf. ☎ **408/372-0577**.

Serving Monterey fisherfolk since 1914, Sam's four diesel-powered boats fish for cod, salmon, and whatever's running. Bring lunch and make reservations. Departures are at 7:30am Monday through Friday and at 6:30am on Saturday and Sunday. Check-in is 45 minutes prior to departure.

Prices: Mon–Fri $25 adults, $14 children under 12; Sat–Sun and holidays $28 adults, $17 children. Add $1 for credit cards, and $15 for equipment.

SHOPPING

Bayside Trading Co., 400 Cannery Row. ☎ **408/646-9944**.

It's an impressive backdrop for the variety of handsome objects displayed and sold here. Because Bayside selectively gathers handmade goods from around the world, there is nothing commonplace in its collection of colorful textiles, clothing, pottery, rugs, jewelry, glassware, carry-alls, and locally crafted furniture. Prices are reasonable, gift wrapping is complimentary, and shipping can be arranged.

Open: Daily 9am–9pm.

Where to Stay

EXPENSIVE

Monterey Bay Inn, 242 Cannery Row, Monterey, CA 93940. ☎ **408/373-6242,** or toll free **800/424-6242**. Fax 408/373-7603. 47 rms. MINIBAR TV TEL **Directions:** From Calif. 1. take the Pacific Grove Del Monte Avenue exit and follow signs to Cannery Row. The hotel is located near the aquarium.

Rates (including continental breakfast): $119–$329 single or double. AE, CB, DC, DISC, MC, V. **Parking:** Free.

Each guest room enjoys a water view and a private balcony; the best features of this conveniently located hotel. Inside, accommodations are decorated with light-toned woods and fabrics, augmented by photographs of local historical interest. Amenities include a minibar and refrigerator, full-length mirrors on the sliding closet doors, and plush terry-cloth robes. There is no dining room; complimentary breakfasts are delivered to your room. You might want to pass on the terrace hot tub in favor of the one on the fourth floor, which offers a spectacular view of the bay.

Facilities: Two hot tubs, sauna, scuba facilities, beach and dive access.

Monterey Plaza Hotel, 400 Cannery Row, Monterey, CA 93940. ☎ **408/646-1700,** or toll free **800/631-1339**, **800/334-3999** in California. Fax 408/646-0285. 290 rms, 15 suites. MINIBAR TV TEL **Directions:** From Calif. 1. take the Soledad Drive exit and follow signs to Cannery Row.

Rates: $150–$280 single or double; from $350 suite. Additional person $20. AE, CB, DC, MC, V. **Parking:** $10.

The Monterey Plaza is so close to the bay that it's on stilts to keep the water from lapping into the guests' quarters. This luxurious $69-million resort is just a short stroll from the Monterey Bay Aquarium. Public areas are elegantly decorated with a hodgepodge of 17th-century Ming vases, imported marble, McGuire Rattan furniture, hand-painted murals, and porcelain objets d'art. Guest rooms are contemporary in style, furnished with dark leathers and designer fabrics. Many have balconies overlooking the water.

Dining/Entertainment: Delfino's on the Bay, the hotel's flagship dining room, offers a diverse Italian menu. The old-world interior is augmented by sweeping views of the bay. The à la carte menu, prepared in an open Genovese exhibition kitchen, features homemade pastas, chicken, seafood, and veal dishes, and a number of traditional antipasti. Main courses cost from $15 to $25, and reservations are suggested.

Delfino's Lounge, decorated with Venetian amethyst glass wall appliques and marble tables, is an interesting setting for cocktails.

Services: Concierge, dry cleaning, fitness room.

★ **Old Monterey Inn,** 500 Martin St., Monterey, CA 93940. ☎ **408/375-8284,** or toll free **800/350-2344**. 10 rms, 2 suites. **Directions:** From Calif. 1, take the Soledad Drive exit and turn right onto Pacific Avenue, then left onto Martin Street.

Rates (including breakfast): $180–$240 single or double. MC, V. **Parking:** Free.

Ann and Gene Swett have done a masterful job of converting their comfortable family home into a lyrical country inn. Each guest room enjoys peaceful garden views and cozy beds with goose-down comforters and pillows, some even have feather beds, and others have wood-burning fireplaces. Accommodations are charmingly furnished, and unique in character. Special touches are evident throughout, including fresh flowers, sachets under the pillows, and books and magazines to read. Most of the rooms have wood-burning fireplaces, and one has a private patio. In addition to a toiletry package that includes deodorant, toothpaste, shampoo, and bath oil, bathrooms are equipped with electric hairdryers and curlers.

Breakfast is as impressive as the rooms: home-baked breads and perhaps a soufflé or Belgian waffles. It is served in your room, the dining room, or (weather permitting) in the garden. If you want to lunch on the beach, the Swetts provide guests with picnic baskets and towels. And when the clock hits 5pm, it's time for sherry, cheese, and crackers in the cozy living room in front of a blazing fireplace. Needless to say, reserve far in advance.

MODERATE

Fireside Lodge, 1131 10th St., Monterey, CA 93940. ☎ **408/655-5640.** Fax 408/655-5640. 24 rms. TV TEL

Rates (including continental breakfast): $59–$99 single or double. AE, MC, V.

A gas log fireplace in each room is the best thing about Fireplace Lodge, located close to Fisherman's Wharf and downtown. Except for the wicker chairs and lounges surrounding the brick mantles, room furnishings are relatively standard in terms of comfort and appearance. Cable TVs, and in-room coffee/tea makers round out the accoutrements. There's a hot tub on the premises, and continental breakfasts are served daily in the hotel's lobby.

Way Station, 1200 Olmsted Rd., Monterey, CA 93940. ☎ **408/372-2945.** 46 rms, 8 suites. TV TEL **Directions:** From Calif. 1, turn east on Calif. 68, continue straight to Olmsted Road, adjacent to the municipal airport.

Rates: $59 single, $69 double, $89 luxury room. Extra person $10. AE, CB, DC, MC, V. **Parking:** Free.

Set among manicured pines and well-groomed grounds, the Way Station is located in a noiseless grove close to Monterey Municipal Airport. Top accommodations at a reasonable rate are what you'll find at this attractive redwood motel. High-ceilinged guest rooms have a town-house appeal and are outfitted with shag carpeting and historical prints of local interest. A circular table, surrounded by leather chairs on rollers, sits below a simple chandelier in the corner of each bedroom. Several rooms have sliding glass doors that open onto comfortable balconies. Other accommodations have bay windows facing the pretty landscaping.

BUDGET

Motel 6, 2124 Fremont St., Monterey, CA 93940. ☎ **408/646-8585.** 51 rms. TV TEL

Rates: $50 single or double. AE, CB, DC, MC, V. **Parking:** Free.

What can one say about simple, good, clean accommodations in Monterey? A lot! It's a rare thing, and reservations for summer months should be made at least six months in advance. Not only are prices here rock-bottom, but there are plenty of extras, including laundry facilities, ice machines, and free local phone calls.

Where to Dine

Over 300 eateries cater to all palates—Italian, Japanese, Mexican, German, Scandinavian, French, Korean, Chinese, and more—and pocketbooks. Here's a short list of the best.

ON FISHERMAN'S WHARF

The following dining establishments are all located on Fisherman's Wharf. To get there from Calif. 1, exit at Soledad Avenue, turn right onto Pacific Avenue, and continue straight to the wharf.

Abalonetti Seafood Trattoria, 57 Fisherman's Wharf. ☎ **408/373-1851**.

Cuisine: ITALIAN. **Reservations:** Accepted.

Prices: Appetizers $3–$7; main courses $8–$17; lunch $6–$16. AE, CB, DISC, DC, MC, V.

Open: Daily 10am–10pm.

Open, airy, loud, and fun, family-owned Abalonetti is a great place for an informal meal. The restaurant has both indoor and outdoor seating; and its plain wood floor, simple decor and functional furnishings are mimicked by an equally straightforward menu.

Traditional Italian pastas include several fresh shellfish sauce selections, including prawns, clams, scallops, oysters, or crab. Landlubbers can always choose from the usual number of beef and chicken dishes or enjoy a product of the restaurant's wood-burning pizza oven. There's an antipasti bar, a full drinking bar, and a satisfactory selection of wines and beers by the bottle or glass.

Cove Restaurant, 46 Fisherman's Wharf. ☎ **408/373-6969**.

Cuisine: SEAFOOD. **Reservations:** Accepted.

Prices: Appetizers $3–$5; main courses $8–$16; breakfast $4–$7; lunch $5–$9. MC, V.

Open: Mon–Thurs 7am–4pm, Fri–Sun 7am–9pm.

The Cove Restaurant is easily identified by its small blue-gray awning and large bay window overlooking the wharf walk. Early risers will appreciate the hearty breakfasts served here. In addition to potatoes and toast, eggs the way you want them can be served with Italian sausage, squid, or fish. The best of their many omelets is an exceptional combination of shrimp and cheddar cheese.

Lunches here mean fish and chips made with Monterey Bay rock cod, a "Lucky Fisherman" platter of cod, squid, prawns, and scallops, and an oyster, and a selection of sandwiches.

Seafood is the specialty at dinner, too, but steaks and pastas are always available. Beer, wine, and cocktails are served daily starting at 11:30am.

Wharfside Restaurant and Lounge, 60 Fisherman's Wharf. ☎ **408/375-3956**.

Cuisine: SEAFOOD. **Reservations:** Accepted.

Prices: Appetizers $4–$9; main courses $9–$18; lunch $6–$11. AE, CB, DC, DISC, MC, V.

Open: Daily 11am–9:30pm. **Closed:** First two weeks of Dec.

The best thing about eating in the Wharfside's relaxed upstairs dining room is its terrific view from the end of Fisherman's Wharf and the adjacent busy marina. The decidedly nautical interior is enhanced by a polished sea-gray, post-and-beam construction, finished with maroon trim. The informal, downstairs dining room is somewhat more downscale. It's next to a small, efficient bar, which is divided from the main dining area by a discreet glass partition. There are also a few tables outside on the upper deck.

Seven different varieties of ravioli are made on the premises, as are homemade desserts. Daily specials usually include fresh seasonal fish, beef, and pasta; while clam chowder, sandwiches (including delicious hot crab), grilled squid, and pizzas are on the regular menu. A full bar, and a good selection of beers and Californian wines are available.

ON CANNERY ROW

Whaling Station Inn, 763 Wave St. ☎ **408/373-3778.**

Cuisine: CONTINENTAL. **Reservations:** Accepted, recommended on weekends. **Directions:** From Calif. 1, take the Soledad Drive exit and follow signs to Cannery Row, turn left on Wave Street one block before Cannery Row. The restaurant is located between Prescott and Irving Avenues.
Prices: Appetizers \$3–\$12; main courses \$17–\$30. AE, DC, MC, V.
Open: Dinner only, daily 5–9:30pm.

Diners enter the rustic-style Whaling Station through a wicker-furnished cocktail area, complete with barnwood walls and potted ferns. Similar in feel, the homey dining area is warmed by white linen tablecloths.

Every main course is preceded by an artichoke vinaigrette appetizer. A la carte main dishes range from prime rib, pastas, and shellfish, to a variety of fresh fish seared over a mesquite grill. Temptingly displayed desserts are prepared by a dedicated in-house pastry chef.

2 Pacific Grove

127 miles SE of San Francisco, 329 miles NW of Los Angeles

GETTING THERE See "Getting There" in the introduction to this chapter.

ESSENTIALS • Orientation In the northwest corner of the Monterey Peninsula, Pacific Grove (see map on p. 303) is compact and easy to negotiate. Most streets are laid out in a grid pattern, and are numbered from 1st to 19th, starting near the Monterey town line. Lighthouse Avenue is the Grove's principal thoroughfare, running from Monterey town to the lighthouse at the very point of the peninsula. Lighthouse Avenue is bisected by Forest Avenue, which runs from Calif. 1 (where it is called Holman Highway, or Calif. 68), to Lovers Point, a finger that sticks out into the bay in the middle of Pacific Grove.

• Information Although the town is small, Pacific Grove has its very own **Chamber of Commerce**, located at the corner of Forest and Central Avenues (P.O. Box 167), Pacific Grove, CA 93950 (☎ **408/373-3304**). The chamber is more than happy to point out local sights, help you negotiate your way around the town, show you specialized shops and services, and help you with any other questions you might have.

Little Pacific Grove is the best-kept secret on the Monterey Peninsula. The town first came into being in the 1870s as a seaside resort for the Methodist Retreat Association of San Francisco. Tents would spring up each summer, and church meetings would be held under the Pacific pines for which the town was named. It didn't take long for people to decide to settle in permanently; today, many area houses date from the late 19th century.

Pacific Grove is widely known as "Butterfly Town, U.S.A."—a reference to the thousands of monarch butterflies that migrate here each winter, traveling from as far away as Alaska. George Washington Park, at Pine Avenue and Alder Street, is particularly famous for its "butterfly trees." *Collectors beware:* The town imposes strict financial penalties for "molesting" butterflies.

What to See & Do

Pacific Grove's primary sight is itself. It's a charming town with an almost colonial character, and its streets deserve to be strolled. Walk around George Washington Park and along the waterfront around the point. **Point Pinos Lighthouse,** at the tip of the peninsula on Ocean View Boulevard, is the oldest working lighthouse on the west coast. It dates from 1855, when Pacific Grove was little more than a pine forest, and its grounds are open free to visitors daily.

Marine Gardens Park, a stretch of shoreline along Ocean View Boulevard on Monterey Bay and the Pacific, is renowned not only for its ocean views and colorful flowers, but also for its fascinating tidepool seaweed beds.

An excellent alternative, or complement, to 17 Mile Drive (see "Pebble Beach" below) is the fantastic drive around Pacific Grove's perimeter, along Ocean View Boulevard. This wonderful coastal stretch starts near Monterey's Cannery Row and follows the Pacific around the point where it turns into Asilomar Avenue. Take your time; the views along the way are nothing short of spectacular. During winter months, a furious sea rages and bounds against the rocks. The local cormorants, seals, and gulls, however, seem unfazed by this awesome sight of a less than passive Pacific.

SHOPPING On Monterey Bay, just one block west of the aquarium, the **American Tin Cannery Outlet Center,** 125 Ocean View Blvd. (☎ **408/372-1442**), is a warehouse of brand-name factory outlet shops. Top labels represented here include Anne Klein, Joan & David, Bass shoes, Carter's children's wear, Royal Doulton china, Maidenform, London Fog, Oneida stainless and silver-plated flatware, and Carole Little fashions, just to name a few. There are several good restaurants here, too. See "Where to Dine" below for complete information. American Tin Cannery shops are open Sunday through Thursday from 10am to 6pm, and Friday and Saturday from 10am to 8pm. Restaurant days and hours vary.

Where to Stay

Gosby House, 643 Lighthouse Ave. Pacific Grove, CA 93950. ☎ **406/375-1287**. Fax 408/655-9621. 22 rms (20 with bath). **Directions:** From Calif. 1, take the Pacific Grove exit, turn left on Lighthouse Avenue and drive 3 blocks to the hotel.

Rates (including breakfast): $85–$150 single or double. AE, MC, V.

Originally a boarding house for Methodist ministers, this pretty Victorian was built in the 1880s by cobbler J. F. Gosby. It's one of the oldest homes in the neighborhood; and although it is no longer a respite for Christian conferees, it's still one of the most charming Victorians on the Monterey Peninsula. Each room is uniquely decorated, with floral-print wallpapers, lacy pillows, and antique furnishings. Twelve guest rooms have private fireplaces, and all come with the inn's trademark teddy bears.

The house has a separate dining room and parlor, where guests congregate for breakfast in the morning and complimentary wine and snacks in the afternoon. Morning meals differ, but there's usually a good selection of fresh hot muffins and breads, egg dishes, cereals, yogurt, granola, fruit, juices, coffee and tea. As the sun sets, guests are invited to get to know one another with a glass of sherry and a homemade cookie. No smoking, please.

Green Gables Inn, 104 Fifth St., Pacific Grove, CA 93950. ☎ **408/375-2095**. 11 rms, 1 suite (7 with bath). **Directions:** From Calif. 1, take the Pacific Grove exit (Calif. 68) and continue to the Pacific Ocean, turn right on Ocean View Boulevard, and drive a half mile to Fifth Street.

Rates (including breakfast): $100–$160 single or double. AE, MC, V.

Until recently, the private home of Roger and Sally Post was open to visitors only during summer. Popularity prevailed, however, and the Green Gables is now a full-fledged, year-round inn. Managed by almost overly hospitable innkeepers, this little gem may not be fancy but it is comfortable. Rooms are divided between the main building and the carriage houses behind it. Most have an ocean view, and are individually decorated with dainty furnishings, including some antiques. Carriage rooms enjoy private baths, while most of those in the front house share two immaculate bathrooms.

There's an antique carousel horse in the pretty parlor, where complimentary wine, tea, and hors d'oeuvres are served each afternoon. No smoking is allowed.

★ **Pacific Grove Inn,** 581 Pine Ave., Pacific Grove, CA 93950, ☎ **408/375-2825,** or toll free **800/732-2825**. 16 rms, 3 suites. TV TEL **Directions:** From Calif. 1 take the Pacific Grove exit (Calif. 68) to the corner of Pine Avenue and Forest.

Rates (including continental breakfast): $70–$150 single, $85–$125 double, $95–$200 suite. AE, CB, DC, DISC, MC, V.

Located just five blocks from the beach, this stately renovated 1904 mansion is one of the town's architectural gems. Despite Victorian embellishments, this is no Dickensian inn. The elegant accommodations feel light, airy, and particularly roomy. Rooms come with queen- or king-size beds and no smoking is allowed.

Where to Dine

EXPENSIVE

Fandango, 223 17th St. ☎ **408/372-3456.**

Cuisine: MEDITERRANEAN. **Reservations:** Recommended. **Directions:** From Calif. 1, take the Pacific Grove exit (Calif. 68), turn left on Lighthouse Avenue and continue 2 blocks to 17th Street.

Prices: Appetizers $4–$7; main courses $14–$16; fixed-price dinner $20; lunch $5–$10. AE, CB, DC, DISC, MC, V.

Open: Lunch Mon–Sat 11am–2:30pm; brunch Sun 10am–2:30pm; dinner nightly 5–9:30pm.

For tapas-style appetizers, or grand main dishes, Fandango offers an exciting selection of provincial Mediterranean specialties. Recommendations include seafood paella, and North African couscous; the recipe for the latter has been in the owner's family for almost 200 years. Authentic spices are imported directly for these and other dishes including cassoulet maison, cannelloni niçoise, and a Greek-style lamb shank. If you decide on a main course, there is a good choice of pasta, mesquite-grilled rack of lamb, and fresh seafood dishes. There is a very respectable international wine list, and a dessert list that includes caramel custard, chocolate mousse, and a spectacular Grand Marnier soufflé served with fresh raspberry purée sauce and profiteroles.

The Sunday brunch menu includes omelets, blintzes, salads, and seafood dishes.

In winter, ask to be seated in the fireplace dining room. In summer, request the terrace room, made fragrant by a wood-burning grill.

The Tinnery, 631 Ocean View Blvd. ☎ **408/646-1040.**

Cuisine: CONTINENTAL. **Reservations:** Accepted for parties of six or more. **Directions:** From Calif. 1, take the Pacific Grove exit (Calif. 68) and turn left on Ocean View Boulevard.
Prices: Appetizers $3–$5; main courses $10–$17; lunch $5–$11. AE, DISC, MC, V.
Open: Breakfast daily 8–11am, lunch daily 11–4pm, dinner daily 4–11pm, bar daily 11am–2am.

The Tinnery has everything you could ask for in a seaside restaurant: fine food, efficient service, a handsome setting, a delightful view, and a bartender who knows how to pour a good drink. The contemporary, sea-gray interior is offset with wood paneling and large black-and-white photographs of old-time cannery operations. Track lights and ceiling fans hang over ficus plants, informal table settings, a large fireplace, and banks of flowers that separate the dining areas. Large windows reveal broad views of Lovers Point Park and Monterey Bay.

Breakfast, the fanciest meal of the day here, includes specialized items like scrambled eggs with calamari and toast with pineapple and bananas. Lunch includes a good selection of meaty sandwiches, fresh fish, thick chowders, and large salads. Dinner runs the gamut from Monterey Bay snapper to Chinese chicken salad with snow peas and ginger sauce, and a superior prime rib.

The restaurant's roomy lounge is set apart from the main dining room and is a comfortable place for predinner cocktails. A light, late-night menu is served from 11pm to 1am and is accompanied by live entertainment. As in the restaurant, a good selection of Californian wines by the bottle or glass is available.

After your meal, stroll along the waterfront. You may see dozens of harbor seals and black cormorants perched on the rocks below.

MODERATE

The Fishwife Restaurant, 1996 Sunset Dr. ☎ **408/375-7107.**

Cuisine: SEAFOOD. **Reservations:** Accepted. **Directions:** From Calif. 1, take the Pacific Grove exit (Calif 68) and stay left until it becomes Sunset Drive. The restaurant will be on your left about one mile ahead, as you approach Asilomar Beach.
Prices: Appetizers $4–$5; main courses $8–$12; lunch $5–$8. AE, DISC, MC, V.
Open: Mon, Wed–Sat 11am–10pm; Sun 10am–10pm.

Justifiably popular with locals, the Fishwife is arguably the best seafood restaurant in Pacific Grove. The foodery dates from the 1830s, when an enterprising sailor's wife began it as a small food market to provision ships. Famous for her Boston clam chowder and other seafood preparations, she became affectionately known as "the fishwife."

In addition to Boston clam chowder, the restaurant still serves a host of seafood main dishes, including Monterey rock cod, local salmon, Pacific swordfish steak, and Mississippi-grown catfish. Two bestsellers at dinner are calamari steak sautéed with shallots, garlic, and white wine; and prawns Belize, served sizzling with red onions, tomatoes, fresh serrano chilies, jicama, lime juice, and cashews. Beef and chicken preparations are always available and include fresh vegetables, French bread, and black beans and rice or air-fried potatoes. Over a half-dozen pastas are also available.

Lunch fare, which is usually lighter, includes unusual sandwiches, like duck sausage, crab salad, and hot Cajun sausage; and several kinds of pasta, including fettuccine Alfredo with crab, scallops, prawns, or clams.

The restaurant's light and airy look is markedly low key. The sedate dining room, with lots of wood, copper and brass, and colorful wall prints, is set apart from a similarly designed bar area.

The First Watch, in the American Tin Cannery, 125 Ocean View Blvd. ☎ **408/372-1125.**

Cuisine: AMERICAN. **Reservations:** Not accepted. **Directions:** From Calif. 1, take the Pacific Grove exit (Calif. 68) and turn right onto Lighthouse Avenue. After one mile turn left onto Eardley Avenue and take it to the corner of Ocean View Boulevard.
Prices: Breakfast $4–$7; lunch $5–$8. AE, MC, V.
Open: Daily 7am–2:30pm.

What was once a dank canning factory is now a fantastically bright, huge, open restaurant, flooded with light from an entire wall of windows. Ceilings don't get much taller than these, and they're topped with an enormous skylight and hung with plants and industrial overhead fans.

Breakfast, the most important meal of the day here, includes 11 varieties of omelets; granola with nuts, fruit, and yogurt; walnut and wheat pancakes; and raisin French toast. The excellent coffee is a real eye opener. At lunch there's a fine choice of salads, from mixed greens to taco salad with black beans and chorizo, and a foot-long list of sandwiches that encompasses everything from albacore to zucchini.

3 Pebble Beach

134 miles SE of San Francisco, 322 miles NW of Los Angeles

GETTING THERE See "Getting There" in the introduction to this chapter.

ESSENTIALS • Orientation Pebble Beach (see map on p. 317) doesn't really have a central downtown commercial district like its charming Peninsula neighbors. Rather, the area is a maze of stately homes, fancy resorts, immaculately manicured golf courses, and fantastically beautiful rugged coastline. Pebble Beach's most famous street is also the area's principal road. The 17 Mile Drive winds its way around the coast and is one of California's top attractions. See "What to See & Do" below for complete information.

• Information There is no dedicated Pebble Beach tourist office. Information, maps, pamphlets, and publications covering this area are available from the **Monterey Peninsula Visitors and Convention Bureau,** 380 Alvarado St. (P.O. Box 1770), Monterey, CA 93942 (☎ **408/649-1770**). See "Monterey," above, for complete information.

Unless you are staying at one of the area's expensive resorts, there's not much to do here . . . except marvel at the spectacular natural beauty.

What to See & Do

The whole Carmel–Pacific Grove–Monterey area, not to mention the breathtaking coast along Calif. 1, is so scenic that the ★ 17 Mile Drive may seem superfluous. But if you can't get enough of a good thing—and I can't—don't miss it. The drive, which winds its way through the Del Monte Forest, is a private road, and a $6 toll is charged to enter it. World famous for its magnificent land- and seascapes, it can be entered from any of three gates: Pacific Grove to the north, Carmel to the south, or Monterey to the east. The most convenient entrance from Calif. 1 is just off the main road at the Holman Highway exit. Admission to the drive includes an informative map that points out 26 points of interest along the way. Highlights include several picnic areas, six golf courses, the famous Lone Cypress, and Seal and Bird Rocks, where you can see countless gulls, cormorants, and other offshore birds. You may even spot offshore herds of harbor seals and California sea lions.

GOLF

Pacific Grove Municipal Golf Course, 77 Asilomar Ave., Pacific Grove. ☎ **408/648-3177.**

Actually located in Pacific Grove, this public green is an excellent and inexpensive alternative to the golf courses of Pebble Beach. The back nine holes of this 5,500-yard par 70 course overlook the sea and offer the added challenge of coping with the winds. Views are terrific, and the fairways and greens are better maintained than most semiprivate courses. There's a restaurant, pro shop, and driving range. Greens fees are $24 Monday through Thursday, and $28 Friday through Sunday; optional carts cost $20. No credit cards are accepted.

Pebble Beach Golf Links, at the Lodge at Pebble Beach, 17 Mile Drive. ☎ **408/624-3811,** or toll free **800/654-9300.**

Pebble Beach just might be the most famous golf course in the world. Built in 1919, this 18-hole course is 6,806 yards and par 72. It really is fantastically beautiful, precariously perched over a rugged ocean. It was also the site of the 1992 U.S. Open Championship. Greens fees cost $225, including mandatory cart rental—if you can get a slot.

Spyglass Hill Golf Course, Stevenson Dr. and Spyglass Hill Rd. ☎ **408/624-6611,** or toll free **800/654-9300.**

This 18-hole championship course is frequented by celebrities. It's a justifiably famous links: 6,810 yards and par 72. Greens fees are $175; $145 for guests of the Lodge (see "Where to Stay" below).

Where to Stay

★ **Inn at Spanish Bay,** 17 Mile Drive, Pebble Beach, CA 93953. ☎ **408/647-7500,** or toll free **800/654-9300.** Fax 408/624-6357. 270 rms, 17 suites. MINIBAR TV TEL **Directions:** From Calif. 1 south, turn west onto Calif. 68 and south onto 17 Mile Drive. The hotel is located on your right, just past the toll plaza.

Rates: $245–$350 single or double; from $550 suite. AE, CB, DC, MC, V. **Parking:** Free.

Surrounded by the Links at Spanish Bay, a golf course designed by Tom Watson and Robert Trent Jones, Jr., the Inn at Spanish Bay, built in 1987, is a plush three- and four-story low-rise. It is set on 236 magnificently manicured acres. Approximately half the rooms face the ocean, while the rest share lovely forest views. Each accommodation has a private fireplace, separate dressing area, and either an outdoor deck or a patio. Baths are finished in Italian marble and the furnishings, all of which are custom made, include four-poster beds with down comforters. Rooms with an ocean view are more expensive than those facing the forest.

Dining/Entertainment: The Dunes serves breakfast, lunch, and dinner on a seafront terrace or in a windowed salon. Californian cuisine main courses include grilled swordfish, New York steak, and exceptional pastas.

Traps and the adjacent lobby lounge serve light and casual meals of sandwiches, salads, pizzas, oysters on the half shell, and the like. They also have a fine selection of premium wines by the glass.

Bay Club, the hotel's premiere dining room, serves formal meals in a conservative setting. Only dinner is served, with a Mediterranean menu that includes pancetta-wrapped grilled prawns, salmon in parmesan crust with tomato-and-basil sauce, and veal with prosciutto, sage, tomato, and marsala.

Finally, you can also have breakfast or lunch at the nearby Clubhouse Bar and Grill, which overlooks the first fairway.

Services: 24-hour room service, concierge, evening turndown, overnight shoe shine, and laundry.

Facilities: Golf course, eight tennis courts (two lighted), pro shops, fitness center, and heated swimming pool.

★ **Lodge at Pebble Beach,** 17 Mile Drive, Pebble Beach, CA 93953.
☎ **408/624-3811,** or toll free **800/654-9300.** Fax 408/626-4468. 161 rms, 12 suites. MINIBAR TV TEL **Directions:** From Calif. 1 south, turn west on Calif. 68 and south onto 17 Mile Drive, follow the coastal road to the hotel.

Rates: $295–$450 single or double; from $800 suite. A 15% gratuity is added to your bill. AE, CB, DC, MC, V. **Parking:** Free.

Easily one of the most expensive hotels in the world, the overpriced, overly plush rooms at the Lodge are popular with monied Japanese, lucky expense account travelers, and the occasional honeymooning couple. A luxury resort, the hotel is located on the world-famous Pebble Beach Golf Links, features over a dozen tennis courts, and has access to nearby horseback riding.

The Lodge is really in a class of its own. Guest rooms here are fitted out with every possible amenity, including TVs, wet bars, refrigerators, and wood-burning fireplaces. Although a long stay here could wreak havoc on your budget, even a quick weekend should be booked far in advance.

Dining/Entertainment: The Cypress Room, which overlooks the 18th green and the bay beyond, is open from morning to night and serves traditional American favorites. The Tap Room is patterned after an English pub and decorated with golfing memorabilia. The menu changes daily, and includes everything from prime rib and wienerschnitzel to thick-crust pizza and grilled salmon. The Gallery restaurant and bar, which overlooks the first tee, is open only for breakfast and lunch. It serves a variety of eggs, burgers, hot dogs, fresh fruits, sandwiches, and German carrot cake that's to die for.

Club XIX, an extremely elegant classical French dining room, is opulently decorated with oak-paneled walls, burgundy and forest-green carpeting, and fresh flowers in silver vases at every table. While gazing at the golf course and bay you might begin with an appetizer of foie gras and truffles, followed by Bongo-Bongo—a creamy soup of oysters, spinach, herbs, and cognac. Main dishes are equally serious and include stuffed quail in a potato nest with brandy sauce, and poached Monterey salmon. Dinner for two will cost about $100, without wine. Reservations are recommended.

Services: 24-hour room service, concierge, priority golf tee times, evening turndown, complimentary airport transportation, massage, and laundry.

Facilities: Golf course, 14 tennis courts, jogging track, fitness room, horseback riding, beach, heated swimming pool, sauna, hiking trails, shopping arcade.

Carmel & Pebble Beach

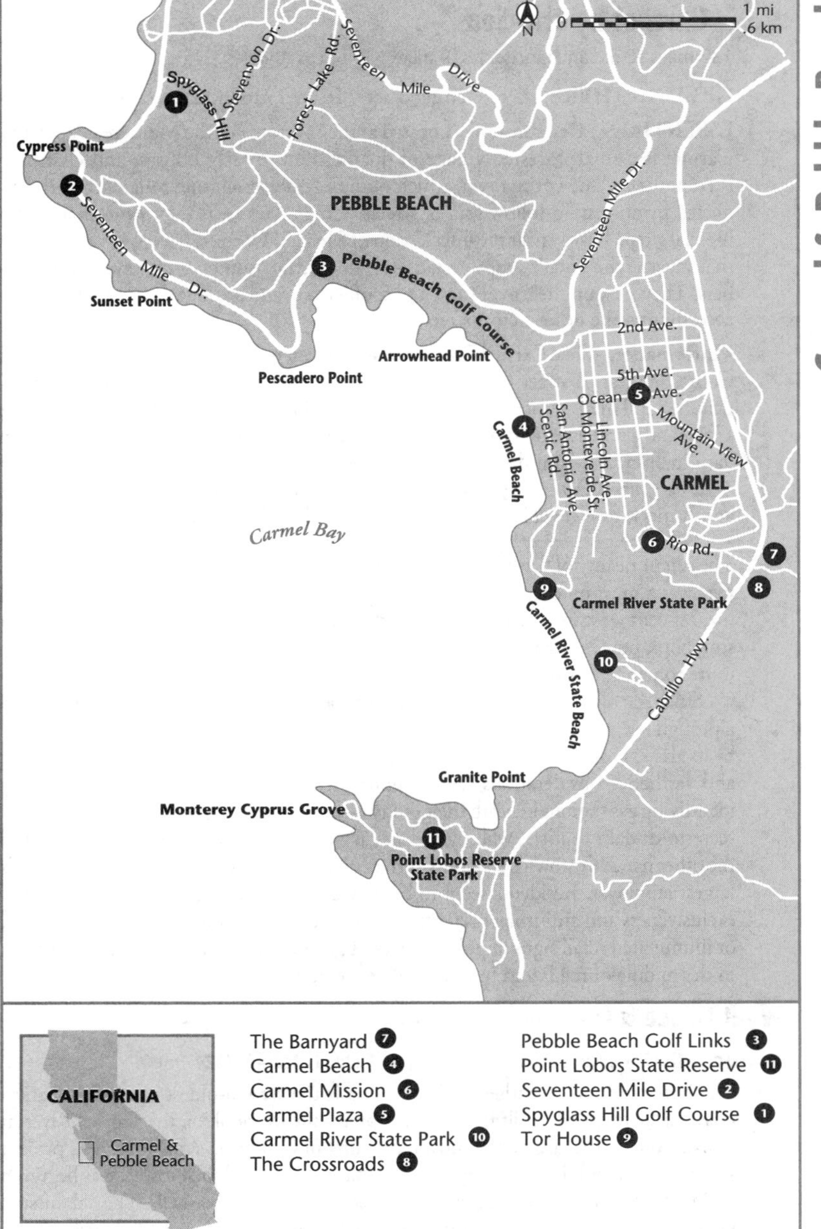

1 mi
.6 km
N
0
Spyglass Hill
Stevenson Dr.
Forest Lake Rd.
Seventeen Mile Drive
Cypress Point
PEBBLE BEACH
Seventeen Mile Dr.
Sunset Point
Pebble Beach Golf Course
Pescadero Point
Arrowhead Point
Seventeen Mile Dr.
2nd Ave.
5th Ave.
Ocean Ave.
Mountain View Ave.
Scenic Rd.
San Antonio Ave.
Monteverde St.
Lincoln Ave.
Carmel Beach
CARMEL
Carmel Bay
Rio Rd.
Carmel River State Park
Carmel River State Beach
Cabrillo Hwy.
Granite Point
Monterey Cyprus Grove
Point Lobos Reserve State Park
CALIFORNIA
Carmel & Pebble Beach
The Barnyard 7
Carmel Beach 4
Carmel Mission 6
Carmel Plaza 5
Carmel River State Park 10
The Crossroads 8
Pebble Beach Golf Links 3
Point Lobos State Reserve 11
Seventeen Mile Drive 2
Spyglass Hill Golf Course 1
Tor House 9

4 Carmel-by-the-Sea

137 miles SE of San Francisco, 319 miles NW of Los Angeles

GETTING THERE See "Getting There" in the introduction to this chapter.

ESSENTIALS • Orientation Located at the "bottom" of the Monterey Peninsula, Carmel is a small forested village of quaint shops, pretty houses, and charming surroundings. The entire town, which occupies only about one square mile, is connected by an easy-to-follow grid of streets. Ocean Avenue is the town's main commercial street, busiest near the intersection of San Carlos Street. It's important to know that most of the town's shops, restaurants, hotels, and houses don't have street numbers. They pick up their mail from a post office box and are identified geographically according to the nearest cross streets.

• Information The **Carmel Business Association,** on the second floor of Vandervort Court, San Carlos Street, between Ocean and 7th Avenues (☎ **408/624-2522**), distributes local maps, brochures, and publications. Pick up a copy of the *Carmel Gallery Guide* and a schedule of local events. The office is open Monday through Friday from 9am to 5pm, and Saturday from 10am to 3pm.

The *Carmel Pine Cone,* a thin local weekly, has faithfully informed locals of news and events for well over half a century. It's available from newsstands all around town.

The serene beauty of Carmel, a forest village encircled by mountains and rolling hills, makes it a must on every visitor's itinerary. White beaches, gnarly cypress trees, and magnificent seascapes are the background for a sleepy village of narrow streets, quaint storybook houses, charming hostelries, and cozy restaurants. It's hard to imagine a more romantic setting.

Since the turn of the century, Carmel has been a haven for artists and writers, and although few modern-day creatives can afford today's high prices, the town still lives by its artsy image. Modesty is preferred over flamboyance, serious art galleries abound, and aesthetic considerations are so important here that you might have difficulty identifying gas stations beneath their pretty wooden eaves. On the one hand Carmelites seem to disdain tourists, who by definition must live somewhere less desirable. On the other hand, the town's economy thrives on the business of tourism, easily the city's largest employer. Residents seem to bend over backward to protect Carmel's air of exclusiveness and antiurban pretentiousness. Local regulations prohibit large, gaudy, or illuminated retail signs in public places. A gladdening sight are the old trees smack in the middle of roads and in other unlikely places.

What to See & Do

Carmel Mission, Rio Rd., at Lasuen Dr., off Calif. 1. ☎ **408/624-3600.**

The burial ground of Father Junipero Serra is the second-oldest of the 21 Spanish missions he founded. Built in 1771 on a pretty site overlooking the Carmel River, it remains one of the largest and most interesting of California's missions. The present stone church, with its gracefully curving walls and Moorish bell tower, was begun in 1793. Its walls are covered with a lime plaster made of burnt seashells. The old mission kitchen, the first library in California, the high altar, and the beautiful flower gardens are all worth visiting. Over 3,000 Native Americans are buried in the adjacent cemetery; their graves are decorated with seashells.

Admission: $1 donation requested.

Open: Mon–Sat 9:30am–4:30pm, Sun 10:30am–4:30pm.

Tor House, Carmel Point, between Stewart Way and Ocean View Ave. ☎ **408/624-1813.**

One of Carmel's prettiest homes is this granite structure built by California poet Robinson Jeffers. Located on a picturesque bank of Carmel Bay, the house dates from 1918 and includes a spectacular 40-foot tower containing stones from the Pyramid of Cheops, Hadrian's Villa, and the Great Wall of China. Inside, an ancient porthole is reputed to have come from the ship on which Napoleon escaped from Elba in 1815. Admission is by guided tour only and reservations are required.

Admission: $5.

Open: Fri–Sat 10am–3pm, by reservation only.

SHOPPING

Carmel is a village of shops. Of the 600-plus stores in this tiny town, most seem to be little boutiques selling unique fashions, baskets, housewares, and imported goods. The rest are art galleries.

The town is made for strolling; its principal commercial attractions are clustered along Ocean Avenue and its attendant side streets between Junipero and San Antonio avenues. Pick up a copy of the *Carmel Gallery Guide* from the Carmel Business Association (see "Information" above), and poke into craft shops that grab your eye.

Carmel Plaza, a multilevel complex of boutiques, craft stores, restaurants, and gourmet food outlets on Ocean Avenue at Junipero Street, is a good place to begin your explorations.

The Barnyard, located on Calif. 1, at Carmel Valley Road, is a bit off the beaten track but unique and worth visiting. Authentic early-Californian barns house 60-plus unique shops and restaurants. There is no major department store "anchor" here; an historic windmill and water tank re-create an old-fashioned town rather than a contemporary shopping mall. **Thunderbird Bookshop** (☎ **408/624-1803**), in the middle of the complex, is a combination bookstore/cafe, selling over 50,000 titles and well-priced, hearty meals—but be careful with the gravy. It's open daily from 10am to 9pm.

Where to Stay

EXPENSIVE

Carriage House Inn, Junipero St., between Seventh and Eighth Aves. (P.O. Box 1900), Carmel, CA 93921. ☎ **408/625-2585,** or toll free **800/433-4732.** Fax 408/624-2967. 13 rms, 2 suites. MINIBAR TV TEL **Directions:** From Calif. 1, exit onto Ocean Avenue and turn left on Junipero Street.

Rates (including continental breakfast): $135–$240 single or double. Additional person $15. AE, CB, DC, DISC, MC, V.

The plush, quiet, country-style Carriage House offers beautifully decorated rooms furnished with wood-burning fireplaces, small refrigerators, cable TVs, and king-size beds with down comforters. Most of the second-floor rooms enjoy sunken tubs and pretty, vaulted beam ceilings. Guests are pampered with breakfast in bed that is delivered on blue willow china along with the morning newspaper. Complimentary wine and hors d'oeuvres are served in the library each evening.

★ **Quail Lodge Resort and Golf Club,** 8205 Valley Greens Dr., Carmel, CA 93923. ☎ **408/624-1581,** or toll free **800/538-9516.** Fax 408/624-3726. 100 rms, 4 suites. A/C TV TEL **Directions:** From Calif. 1 north, pass the Carmel exits after which the highway narrows to two lanes, turn left on Carmel Valley Road and continue for three miles to Valley Greens Drive.

Rates: Mar–Nov $195–$245 single or double; $285–$515 suite. Dec–Feb $155–$185 single or double; from $220 suite. Extra person $25. AE, CB, DC, MC, V.

Located not in downtown Carmel but in the nearby Carmel Valley, Quail Lodge is one of the most highly regarded resort hotels in the country. Its superb pastoral setting encompasses over 250 acres of sparkling lakes, secluded woodlands, and rolling meadows. Guests can make use of the lodge's private clubhouse on the Carmel Valley Golf and Country Club's 18-hole green.

Guest rooms are light and airy and have a southwestern feel. Higher-priced accommodations, located on the upper floors, have cathedral ceilings. Every room has a separate dressing area and an ample balcony. Some have fireplaces and wet bars. There's a coffee maker in every room, supplied with complimentary freshly ground beans. Afternoon tea is served in the lobby from 3 to 5pm.

Dining/Entertainment: The posh Covey Restaurant serves continental foods in warmly elegant surroundings. Tables are covered with Belgian linens, set with Sienna china, adorned with fresh flowers, and topped with romantic gas lamps. Main courses include Santa Barbara abalone and Muscovy duck with red currants and brandied cherries. Specialties of the house are rack of lamb and fresh seafood and, like most other dishes, cost $17 to $35. Jackets are required for men, and reservations are essential.

Services: Room service, concierge, evening turndown, complimentary morning newspaper.

Facilities: 18-hole golf course, clubhouse, four tennis courts, two swimming pools, sauna, redwood hot tub, gift shops, and beauty salon.

San Antonio House, San Antonio Ave., between Ocean and Seventh Aves. (P.O. Box 3683), Carmel, CA 93921. ☎ **408/624-4334.** 4 rms, 2 suites. TV TEL **Directions:** From Calif. 1 north, exit onto Carpenter Street and turn right on Ocean Avenue; after one mile, turn left onto San Antonio Avenue.

Rates (including breakfast): $120–$165 single or double. Extra person $20. MC, V.

Innkeepers Sarah Anne and Richard Lee's charming two- and three-room suites are comfortably furnished with art and antiques. Nestled in a private garden setting, all rooms have small refrigerators, private baths, fireplaces, and patios or gardens. All enjoy private entrances, which make them more private than the average B&B. There are fresh flowers in each room and complimentary morning newspapers are served with breakfast.

MODERATE

Normandy Inn, Ocean Ave., between Monte Verde and Casanova Aves. (P.O. Box 1706), Carmel, CA 93921. ☎ **408/624-3825,** or toll free **800/343-3825** in California. Fax 408/624-4614. 48 rms, cottages. TV TEL **Directions:** From Calif. 1, exit onto Ocean Avenue and continue straight for five blocks past Junipero Street.

Rates (including continental breakfast): $98–$155 single or double; $300 cottage with up to 4 guests. $10 per additional person. AE, MC, V.

This is a delightful provincial hostelry in a shingled Tudor building. The terrace patio beside the heated pool is lined with trees, shrubbery, and potted plants. Rooms are just lovely, too. About a quarter of them have fireplaces and/or kitchen areas, and most have tub/shower combinations and down comforters.

Cottages accommodate up to eight people and are an especially good buy. Each has three bedrooms, two bathrooms, a kitchen, a dining room, a living room with a fireplace, and a back porch. Be sure to reserve far in advance, especially in summer.

Pine Inn, Ocean Ave., between Lincoln St. and Monte Verde Ave. (P.O. Box 250),Carmel, CA 93921. ☎ **408/624-3851**, or toll free **800/228-3851**. Fax 408/624-3030. 49 rms, 6 suites. TV TEL **Directions:** From Calif. 1, exit onto Ocean Avenue and continue straight for four blocks past Junipero Street.

Rates: $95–$205 single or double. AE, CB, DC, MC, V.

I wouldn't choose the red-flocked wallpaper for my front room, but it fits in this midscale lobby/lounge, along with a blazing fireplace, plush furnishings, and a big grandfather clock. Rooms are individually designed, each with a turn-of-the-century motif that includes shuttered windows, lovely wallpapers, and antique furnishings. Some guest rooms have brass beds.

The Garden Room and the Gazebo Restaurant are open for breakfast, lunch, and an early dinner. Sunday brunch is also served: an inexpensive, fixed-price affair featuring a good selection of main dishes for under $15. Friday is Epicurean Feast night, when a seafood and roast beef buffet is served, along with an assortment of desserts, for under $20.

Sandpiper Inn at the Beach, 2408 Bay View Ave., Carmel, CA 93923. ☎ **408/624-6433**. Fax 408/624-5964. 16 rms.

Rates (including continental breakfast): $79–$180 single or double, MC, V.

A garden of flowers welcomes visitors to this quiet, mid-scale Carmel standby that's been welcoming visitors for over 60 years. The inn is within both sight and sound of the surf; the best rooms enjoy ocean views, and some also have fireplaces. The highest priced accommodations are the romantic free-standing cottages that, like other guest rooms, are decorated with handsome country antiques and fresh flowers that are changed daily.

Village Inn, Ocean Ave., at Junipero St. (P.O. Box 5275), Carmel, CA 93921. ☎ **408/624-3864,** or toll free **800/346-3864** in California. 34 rms, 2 suites. TV TEL **Directions:** From Calif. 1. exit onto Ocean Avenue and continue straight to Junipero Street.

Rates (including continental breakfast): $69–$135 single or double; $89–$189 triple or quad; from $89 suite. AE, MC, V.

Both well run and centrally located, Village Inn is a motor lodge all the same. Rooms are arranged around a courtyard/parking lot lined with potted geraniums and are outfitted with bland but functional decor. In addition to French country-style furniture, guest rooms come equipped with refrigerators and cable color TVs. Breakfast, along with the morning newspaper, is served in the downstairs lounge.

Where to Dine

EXPENSIVE

Casanova, Fifth Ave., between San Carlos and Mission Sts. ☎ **408/625-0501.**

Cuisine: NORTHERN ITALIAN. **Reservations:** Recommended. **Directions:** From Calif. 1, take the Ocean Avenue exit and turn right on San Carlos Street to 5th Avenue. **Prices:** Appetizers $4–$10; main courses $19–$33; lunch $8–$18; breakfast $4–$11. MC, V.

Open: Breakfast Mon–Sat 8–11am; lunch Mon–Sat 11:30am–3pm; dinner daily 5:30–10:30pm; Sun brunch 9am–3pm.

Casanova was designed by its Belgian owners to look like the European farmhouses of their childhood. Located in an old picturesque cottage that once belonged to Charlie Chaplin's cook, the restaurant is both cozy and provincial, with intimate dining under a low beamed ceiling. The dining room decor is completed with checkered curtains, French lampshades, bentwood chairs, and antique ceramic tiles embedded in the walls. Outdoor seating is also available, under heat lamps in a garden setting, with a fountain.

Breakfast, a veritable celebration of calories, includes French toast with Grand Marnier, Belgian waffles, and cheese blintzes. Lunch menus, which change seasonally, may include homemade linguine with prawns, scallops in a white-wine and Parmesan cream sauce, or braised veal with mushrooms, leeks, and polenta. Dinner might be rack of lamb rubbed with a mild garlic and Merlot-wine sauce, or any number of freshly prepared meats and fishes. All dinner main dishes include antipasto and a choice of appetizers like mushrooms in butter and herbs or gnocchi verde alla romana (pasta dumplings in a Parmesan cheese and cream sauce). Casanova's wine list is one of the most impressive on the peninsula; its more than 1,500 French, California, German, and Italian labels include some excellent buys.

L'Escargot, Mission St., between Fourth and Fifth Aves. ☎ **408/624-4914.**

Cuisine: FRENCH. **Reservations:** Recommended. **Directions:** From Calif. 1, take the Ocean Avenue exit and turn right onto Mission Street, one block past Junipero Street. **Prices:** Appetizers $4–$10; main courses $17–$25. AE, MC, V.

Open: Dinner Mon–Sat 5:30–9:30pm

Housed in one of the pretty shingle-roofed, stucco buildings that are so typical of Carmel, L'Escargot's exterior is as gentle as its neighbors. Under a beamed ceiling, the warm and cozy provincial-style interior includes hanging copperware, arrangements of dried and fresh flowers, leaded-glass windows, and shelves of decorative plates.

Dinner might begin with escargots; house-cured smoked salmon; herbed, braised fresh artichoke bottoms; or an excellent wild mushroom–stuffed puff pastry. Classical French main dishes include chicken with cream, foie gras, and truffles; braised breast of duck; and a number of choice seafood specialties such as sautéed scallops under orange-lemon butter. There's a full bar and an even fuller wine list that features both French and Californian vintages.

Desserts, which are as heavy as the other courses, are best when shared. Try the chilled Grand Marnier soufflé, which has the consistency of a light ice cream; the classic mousse au chocolat; or the utterly delicious crème caramel.

★ **Raffaello,** Mission St., between Ocean and Seventh Aves. ☎ **408/624-1541.**

Cuisine: ITALIAN. **Reservations:** Recommended. **Directions:** From Calif. 1, take the Ocean Avenue exit and turn left onto Mission Street, one block after Junipero Street.

Prices: Appetizers $6–$7; main courses $15–$22. AE, CB, DC, MC, V.
Open: Dinner Wed–Mon 6–10pm.

Men are required to wear jackets at this hushed and rather formal Florentine award-winner. The lights are low and the decor is subdued, with white linen cloths and fresh flowers on every table, and good Italian paintings and mirrors on the walls.

Main dishes include veal with fontina cheese and truffles, fettuccine romano, sweetbreads with cream-and-wine sauce, and shrimp-stuffed filet of sole poached in white wine and herbs. A glass of port and a small, assorted cheese plate makes the perfect dessert; sweet-tooths might have to opt for the light strawberry mousse or the rich and creamy zabaglione.

MODERATE

The Hog's Breath Inn, San Carlos St., between Fifth and Sixth Aves. ☎ **408/625-1044.**

Cuisine: AMERICAN. **Reservations:** Not accepted. **Directions:** From Calif. 1, take the Ocean Avenue exit and turn right onto San Carlos Street.
Prices: Appetizers $4–$7; main courses $9–$23; lunch $6–$13. AE, DC, MC, V.
Open: Lunch daily 11:30am–3pm; dinner daily 5–10pm; pub and patio daily 11am–2am.

The Hog's Breath's claim to fame is its celebrity owner, former Carmel mayor Clint Eastwood. The restaurant's name is meant to parody the almost excessive charm of most of the town's eateries. As it happens, the inn is a pretty relaxed place itself, despite perpetual mobs of tourists. Enter along a brick walkway and choose from a number of dining and drinking areas. During warm weather, the outdoor stone patio is best; there, you can pull a canvas director's chair up to a tree-trunk table near a warm, brick fireplace. Inside it's dark and rustic, decorated with farm implements, dried flowers, and a galaxy of celebrity photos.

When you finally get around to the food—a secondary concern here—choose the fresh catch of the day, a sirloin steak sandwich, or another one of the restaurant's straightforward meat-and-potatoes meals.

La Bohème, Dolores St., at 7th St. ☎ **408/624-7500.**

Cuisine: FRENCH COUNTRY. **Reservations:** Not accepted. **Directions:** From Calif. 1, exit onto Ocean Avenue and turn left on Dolores Street, three blocks past Junipero Street.
Prices: Fixed-price three-course dinner $18. MC, V.
Open: Dinner daily 5:30–10pm. **Closed:** Two weeks before Christmas.

Behind a bright blue awning, the interior of La Bohème is cleverly designed to look like a provincial French street, complete with a painted blue sky and shingled houses. Tables are set with floral-print cloths in bright colors, hand-painted dinnerware, and colorful floral bouquets.

Dinner is a three-course, fixed-price affair, consisting of a large salad, a tureen of soup, and a main dish—perhaps breast of chicken with ginger-shallot sauce or filet mignon with cognac-cream sauce. Vegetarian specials are available nightly. Homemade desserts and fresh coffee are sold separately, and usually worth the extra expense.

Patisserie Boissiere, Carmel Plaza, Mission St., between Ocean and Seventh Aves. ☎ **408/624-5008.**

Cuisine: FRENCH COUNTRY. **Reservations:** Recommended. **Directions:** From Calif. 1, take the Ocean Avenue exit and turn left on Mission Street, one block past Junipero Street.

Prices: Appetizers $5–$6; main courses, including soup and salad $14–$17; lunch, including soup and salad $8–$13. AE, MC, V.
Open: Mon–Tues 9am–4:30pm, Wed–Sun 9am–9pm.

For over 30 years, this charming little tearoom in a shingle-roofed stucco cottage has heralded passers-by with a real Parisian street sign reading "Rue Boissiere." A cozy, townish interior is enhanced by white stucco walls, a low-beamed ceiling, an antique maple sideboard, tiled fireplace, and Louis XV–style chairs. It's a relaxed venue for a light meal to be chosen from a wide variety of sandwiches, salads, and soups (including French onion). Hearty pasta and fresh fish main dishes are also available, like oven-baked salmon and braised rabbit. A long and reasonably priced wine list includes both Californian and French varieties.

Rio Grill, 101 Crossroads Blvd. ☎ **406/625-5436.**

Cuisine: AMERICAN. **Reservations:** Accepted. **Directions:** From Calif. 1, take the Rio Road exit west: after one block, turn right onto Crossroads Boulevard.
Prices: Appetizers $3–$8; main courses $5–$17 at lunch, $10–$25 at dinner. AE, MC, V.
Open: Sun–Thurs 10pm, Fri–Sat 11:30am–11pm.

You won't mind waiting to be seated here—the lively lounge is one of the best in Carmel. In addition to pouring a good drink, the bar attracts an interesting crowd and is lightly decorated with above-the-bar cartoons of famous locals like the late Bing Crosby and Clint Eastwood. Located in the Crossroads group of shops, the restaurant is fun and upbeat. The whimsical nature of the modern, southwestern-style dining room belies the kitchen's good and serious preparations, which include homemade soups; a rich quesadilla with almonds, cheeses, and smoked tomato salsa; barbecued baby back ribs from a wood-burning oven; and fresh fish from an open oak grill. A different pasta is offered each day, as are hamburgers and cheeseburgers, but consider the grilled eggplant sandwich with roasted red peppers, fontina cheese, and watercress. The most expensive item on the menu is a Rio Grill sweatshirt for $25—a cute design and a good buy. The restaurant's good selection of wines includes some rare Californian vintages and covers a broad price range.

BUDGET

Tuck Box English Room, Dolores St., at 7th St. ☎ **408/624-6365.**

Cuisine: ENGLISH. **Reservations:** Not accepted. **Directions:** From Calif. 1, exit onto Ocean Avenue and turn left on Dolores Street, which is three blocks past Junipero Street.
Prices: Breakfast $4–$7; lunch $5–$7. No credit cards.
Open: Wed–Sun 8am–4pm.

A longtime favorite spot for breakfast, Tuck Box is one of the most delightful restaurants in Carmel. Inside this small, shingle-roofed cottage is a clean and contemporary eatery with hardwood floors and light-gray walls livened with a whip of charcoal trim.

Meals are simple and elegant. A typical breakfast might include fresh-squeezed orange juice, fresh fruit, bacon and eggs, and homemade muffins or scones. Lunches are of similar quality and simplicity—for example, shepherd's pie, served with salad, a vegetable, and a muffin or scone. Homemade fruit pies are the restaurant's real specialty, usually topped with real whipped cream. You can dine on the patio during warm weather.

5 The Big Sur Coast

157 miles SE of San Francisco, 299 miles NW of Los Angeles

GETTING THERE • By Bus **Greyhound/Trailways** runs daily bus service up and down the coast from both north and south. The bus company no longer operates a nationwide toll free telephone number, so call your local office for fares and schedule information.

Monterey-Salinas Transit (MST), Simoneau Plaza, Monterey (☎ **408/899-2558**), is a local bus line that connects Big Sur with neighboring communities on the Monterey Peninsula. Call for prices and schedule information.

• By Car There can be no doubt that driving your own car is the best way to go. The magnificent but slow drive on Calif. 1 from San Francisco takes about 3½ hours, depending on traffic.

ESSENTIALS • Orientation Big Sur refers not to a town but to a region, one that encompasses about 90 miles of rugged Monterey County coast south of Carmel. Most of the stretch is state park, and Calif. 1 runs its entire length, hugging the ocean the whole way. Restaurants, hotels, and sights are easy to spot—most are situated directly on the highway—but without major towns as reference points, their addresses can be a little obscure. For the purposes of orientation, we will use the River Inn as our mileage guide. Located 29 miles south of Monterey on Calif. 1, the inn is generally considered to mark the northern end of Big Sur.

• Information The **Monterey Peninsula Visitors and Convention Bureau,** 380 Alvarado St. (P.O. Box 1770), Monterey, CA 93942 (☎ **408/649-1770**), also has specialized information on places and events in Big Sur. The office is located in Monterey, near the intersection of Pacific Street and Del Monte Avenue.

The most frequently asked question in these parts is "Where is Big Sur?" There is indeed a Big Sur Village, located approximately 25 miles south of Carmel. But when people refer to Big Sur, they mean the famously beautiful 90-mile stretch of coast between Carmel and San Simeon. Big Sur is a thin strip of land flanked on one side by the majestic Santa Lucia Range and on the other by the rocky Pacific coast. Drive through slowly on breathtakingly scenic Calif. 1, making frequent stops at viewing turnouts to "ooh" and "aah" at the feisty sea and jagged cliffs.

What to See & Do

Although the area attracts many tourists, Big Sur is in no way touristy. There are few artificial distractions—no big towns, few cute boutiques and art galleries, and no tennis or golf, shopping malls, or movie theaters. What Big Sur does have is unspoiled tranquility, and unparalleled natural beauty. Developers are kept at bay, while one of the coast's most expansive parcels of oceanfront property is left undeveloped to keep it safe for hiking, picnicking, camping, fishing, and beachcombing. Since its western beginnings, Big Sur has inspired a deep sense of spirituality among residents and visitors; even the tourist board describes the area as a place in which "to slow down . . . to meditate . . . to catch up with your soul." Take the board's advice and take your time—nothing better lies ahead.

Bixby Bridge, Calif. 1, 13 miles south of Carmel (16 miles north of the River Inn).

Perhaps the most photographed structure on the Big Sur coast, this vertigo-inducing bridge, towering nearly 260 feet above Bixby Creek Canyon, claimed to be the longest concrete arch span in the world when it was constructed in 1932. Several observation alcoves located at regular intervals along the bridge offer excellent views of the canyon below and the ocean beyond.

The Coast Gallery, Calif. 1, 37 miles south of Carmel (8 miles south of the River Inn). ☎ **408/667-2301.**

Big Sur's first, and only, art gallery can't hang anything prettier than its view. Rebuilt from redwood watertanks after a flood in 1973, this unique space displays the works of over 250 local and national artists and craftspeople. The art encompasses all media, including pottery, woodcarving, painting, sculpture, jewelry, and original water colors of Henry Miller. Candles made on the premises are sold here as well, adjacent to a cafe that features fine locally produced wines sold by the glass and by the bottle.

Open: Daily from 9am to 5pm.

The Henry Miller Memorial Library, Calif. 1, 30 miles south of Carmel (5 miles south of the River Inn). ☎ **408/667-2574.**

Henry Miller was one of Big Sur's most famous residents. The author came here in 1944 and watched the area grow from wilderness to a well-known artists' colony. Miller's writings, including his book *Big Sur and the Oranges of Hieronymus Bosch,* helped popularize the region. Emil White, an artist and Miller's longtime friend, transformed his own home into what is now the Henry Miller Memorial Library. This personal tribute to a truly great author is a small clutter of books that displays and sells all of Henry Miller's works—new, used, rare, and out of print.

The rear gallery room is a video-viewing space where films about Henry Miller can be seen. Emil White's original paintings are also on view. There is a sculpture garden plus tables on the adjacent lawn where visitors can rest and enjoy the surroundings.

Admission: Free.

Open: Usually Tues–Sun 11am–5pm; hours are informal, however, so call first.

Pfeiffer–Big Sur State Park, Sycamore Canyon Rd., off Calif. 1, 26 miles south of Carmel (3 miles north of the River Inn). ☎ **408/667-2315.**

Big Sur boasts a handful of wonderful beaches, but the one at Pfeiffer is the only beach accessible by car. Named for John Pfeiffer, an early settler, this 810-acre park is largely wooded and criss-crossed by well-tended nature trails.

Admission: $6.

Open: Daily, dawn to dusk.

Where to Stay

Few area accommodations offer the kind of pandering luxury you'd expect in a fine urban hotel; even direct-dial phones and TVs (often considered Philistine in these parts) are rare. Big Sur hotels are especially busy in summer, when advance reservations are required. To write to any of the places listed below, just address inquiries to the name of the establishment, Big Sur, CA 93920.

EXPENSIVE

Post Ranch Inn, Hwy. 1, P.O. Box 219, Big Sur, CA 93920. ☎ **408/667-2200,** or toll free **800/527-2200.** Fax 408/667-2824. 30 rms. TEL MINIBAR

Rates: $265–$525 single or double. AE, MC, V.

Some of the strictest development regulations in the United States mean that it's no easy task building anything on the Big Sur coast. Shepherding a major luxury hotel through the California Coastal Commission as well as local agencies is almost impossible. But that's exactly what Post Ranch has done; built the first resort permitted here in over 19 years. Constructed on a bluff overlooking Big Sur's spectacular coastline, the inn is a study in environmental consciousness. Designers took great care in preserving the pristine grounds, building guest cottages around existing trees, and elevating some on stilts, so as not to damage native redwood root structures.

Extensive use of wood and glass characterize the ultra-private guest rooms, some of which are recesses into the ridge and covered with wild flower sod roofs. Services and amenities are laid back, but top-of-the-line; rustic in feeling, yet impeccably attentive. The most popular (and most expensive) accommodations are the Ocean Houses, free-standing units that enjoy oceanfront views. Other cottages are also stratospheric in price, but face woodlands. Needless to say, Post Ranch Inn has become an immediate hit with Hollywood celebrities and wealthy San Franciscan business types. If you can get a reservation, count yourself among the lucky few.

Dining/Entertainment: The inn's dramatic Sierra Mar restaurant, with its floor-to-ceiling windows serves food that is almost as fantastic as the view. They also feature the area's most comprehensive wine list. Dinner reservations should be made in conjunction with your room request.

Ventana Inn, Calif. 1, Big Sur, CA 93920. ☎ **408/667-2331,** or toll free **800/628-6500.** Fax 408/667-2419. 56 rms, 4 suites. A/C MINIBAR TV TEL

Directions: from Carmel, take Calif. 1 28 miles south (4¼ miles south of the River Inn).

Rates (including breakfast): $175–$485 single or double; from $320 suite. AE, CB, DC, DISC, MC, V.

Ventana is the fanciest and most famous hotel in Big Sur. A luxurious wilderness resort on 243 mountainous, oceanfront acres, Ventana has an elegance that's atypical of the region. The hotel has continually attracted famous guests since its opening in 1975. Barbra Streisand, Goldie Hawn, and Francis Ford Coppola—among many others—have all stayed here.

Accommodations are worthy of the wild, blending in with the magical Big Sur countryside. Guest rooms are spread out among 12 contemporary natural-wood buildings with slanted roofs that work well with the landscape. The elegantly rustic and comfortable interiors have white-stucco and cedar walls, wicker furnishings, and firm beds covered with handmade quilted patchwork spreads. Each accommodation has a separate dressing room, VCR, and refrigerator, and private terrace or balcony overlooking the ocean or forest. Most rooms have private wood-burning fireplaces and some have hot tubs and high cathedral ceilings.

Breakfast—which includes fresh-baked croissants, Danish pastries, fresh-squeezed orange juice, homemade granola with yogurt and fresh fruit, and tea or coffee—is served in your room or in the main lobby. Make reservations well in advance.

Dining/Entertainment: Ventana Restaurant is a worthwhile splurge; its food is absolutely first rate. The airy raw-cedar interior has two large stone fireplaces, redwood tables, and cane and bentwood chairs, and is filled with ferns, potted plants, and colorful fruit baskets. The large outdoor patio offers good views over a dramatic expanse of ocean and 50 miles of Big Sur coast.

Lunch main courses range from $10 to $18 for such dishes as smoked Big Sur trout and salad niçoise. Dinners are about twice as expensive and include dishes such as roast glazed duckling and rack of lamb. Desserts, baked in the Ventana's own French bakery, are temptingly displayed and best chosen by sight. The restaurant is open daily from 11am to 3pm and 6 to 9:30pm. Reservations are recommended.

Services: Room service, concierge, and massage.

Facilities: Two 90-foot heated outdoor swimming pools, massage, bathhouse, Japanese hot bath, sauna, gift store, and art gallery.

MODERATE

Big Sur Lodge, Pfeiffer–Big Sur State Park, Calif. 1, Big Sur, CA 93920. ☎ **408/667-3100,** or toll free **800/424-4787.** Fax 408/667-3110. 61 cabins. **Directions:** From Carmel take Calif. 1 south 26 miles.

Rates: $69–$129 single or double; $89–$149 single or double with kitchen; $89–$149 single or double with fireplace. MC, V.

A terrific family hostelry, Big Sur Lodge, sheltered by towering redwoods, sycamores, and broad-leafed maples, is situated on 800-plus acres of pristine parkland. The accommodations are cabins, which are all quite large, with high peaked cedar- and redwood-beamed ceilings and walnut-paneled walls. They are clean and heated, and have private baths and reserved parking spaces. Most of the cabins have either fireplaces or kitchens, or both. All have porches or decks with views of the redwoods or the Santa Lucia Mountains.

A great advantage in staying here is that you are entitled to free use of all the facilities of the park, including hiking, barbecue pits, and picnic areas. In addition, the lodge has its own large, outdoor heated swimming pool, sauna, gift shop, grocery stores, and laundry facilities.

The lodge dining room is open for breakfast and dinner (and lunch in the summer). Evening menus feature fresh seafood, steaks, and pasta dishes. Reservations are recommended and should be made far in advance during summer months.

CAMPING

Big Sur Campground and Cabins, Calif. 1, 26 miles south of Carmel (a half mile south of the River Inn). ☎ **408/667-2322.**

Open year round, each campsite here has its own wood-burning fire pit, picnic table, and freshwater faucet within 25 feet of the pitching area. Facilities include bathhouses with hot showers, laundry facilities, a river for swimming, a playground area, a volleyball/basketball court, and a grocery store. Rates are $22 for two people in a car, $3 for each additional person. Electrical and water hookups are $3. Cabins range from $80–$130 double occupancy.

Fernwood, Calif. 1, 31 miles south of Carmel (2 miles south of the River Inn). ☎ **408/667-2422.**

This campground on 23 beautiful woodland acres has 60 sites, each of which has electricity, water, and a fire pit. About half the sites overlook the river. The restaurant on the premises is open daily from 11:30am to 10pm and serves burgers, ribs, and other camp fare. An adjacent, attractive bar/cocktail lounge features live music on the weekends. A grocery store sells wood, ice, beer, and other essentials. Rates are $21 a night with electricity, $19 without, for two people; $4 for each additional person.

Ventana Campground, Calif. 1, 28 miles south of Carmel (4¼ miles south of the River Inn). ☎ **408/667-2688.**

The 70 campsites on 40 acres of gorgeous redwood forest are spaced well apart for privacy. Each has a picnic table and fireplace, and 3 bathhouses with hot showers are conveniently located. The closest coastal access is at Pfeiffer Beach, three miles away. The entrance to Ventana Campground is located adjacent to the entrance to the resort of the same name (see above). Campsites cost $20 for two people and a car, $3 for each additional person, and $2 per dog.

Where to Dine

Glen Oaks Restaurant, Calif. 1, Big Sur. ☎ **408/667-2623.**

Cuisine: CONTINENTAL. **Reservations:** Recommended for dinner. **Directions:** From Carmel, take Calif. 1 south 26 miles.
Prices: Appetizers $5–$8; main courses $7–$19. MC, V.
Open: Dinner daily 6–9pm.

Marilee and Forrest Childs' well-known Glen Oaks Restaurant is a lovely eatery with beamed ceilings, flower-filled windows, a wood-burning copper-chimneyed fireplace, and fresh flowers on each table. Marilee's superb watercolors brighten every wall; Forrest's masterpieces are culinary. Dinner features such main dishes as gnocchi, cheese pillows in sage butter, and fettuccine with scallops and lobster. Bouillabaisse, New York steak, and sautéed Chinese vegetables with wild rice are other top picks. If you need more choices, there's fresh charcoal-broiled fish topped with a variety of sauces, according to the chef's mood. Desserts, which are fresh and homemade, are prepared daily on the premises, and a small selection of Californian wines is available.

★ **Nepenthe,** Calif. 1, Big Sur. ☎ **408/667-2345.**

Cuisine: AMERICAN. **Reservations:** Accepted for parties of 5 or more. **Directions:** From Carmel, take Calif. 1 south 30 miles (5 miles south of the River Inn).
Prices: Appetizers $6–$10; main courses $9–$25; lunch $9–$11. AE, MC, V.
Open: Daily 11:30am–10pm.

Traditionally, nepenthe was a mythical Egyptian drug that induced forgetfulness from grief (it is derived from the Greek word meaning "no sorrow"). The restaurant Nepenthe, one of the most famous restaurants in Big Sur, attempts to achieve emotional freedom through excellent food, an unmatched view, and a worry-free, laid-back philosophy.

According to its owners, the redwood-and-adobe building has become "one with the landscape and earth it stands on." Housed in a redwood-and-stucco structure, the dining room looks like a ski lodge, with a big wood-burning fireplace, wooden chairs at heavy wood tables, redwood-and-pine ceilings, and what seems like more windows than walls. Unless the weather is really bad, the best seats are outside on the ocean-view terrace; here, guests are afforded one of the most magnificent vistas anywhere. Nepenthe really is a magical place to laze away an afternoon; stay long enough to catch the sunset. Musicians often hang out here, trading fours with scores of gaily chirping birds.

A light lunch might consist of an assortment of cheeses, accompanied by fresh fruit, bread, and a liter of wine. Follow up with a pot of English tea and a dessert like homemade pumpkin spice cake or apple pie. During the day, you can also get hamburgers, salads, and sandwiches. Dinner main courses include steak dishes, broiled chicken, and fresh fish prepared any number of ways.

8

The Central Coast

CALIFORNIA'S CENTRAL COAST IS THE STATE'S MOST DIVERSE AREA. TOPOGRAPHically, the region encompasses beaches, lakes, and mountains, all within a few miles of each other. The narrow strip of coast that runs for more than 200 miles from Monterey to Ventura spans several climate zones and includes areas considered to be in northern as well as southern California. Economically, the central coast is one of the richest stretches of soil in the world. Last, but by no means least, the central coast is one of the state's most important tourist draws. Calif. 1, which follows the ocean cliffs, is perpetually packed with rental cars, recreational vehicles, bicyclists, and other visitors enjoying one of the most spectacular drives in the world.

SEEING THE CENTRAL COAST

Whether you're driving from Los Angeles or San Francisco, scenic Calif. 1 is the best way to travel along the coast. Most bicyclists peddle from north to south, the direction of the prevailing winds. Those in automobiles may prefer to drive south to north, so they can get a better look at the coastline as it unfolds toward the west.

1 San Simeon: Hearst Castle

214 miles SE of San Francisco, 242 miles NW of Los Angeles

GETTING THERE • By Car Hearst Castle is located directly on Calif. 1. From San Francisco or Monterey, take U.S. 101 south to Paso Robles, then Calif. 46 west to Calif. 1, and Calif. 1 north to the Castle. From Los Angeles, take U.S. 101 north to San Luis Obispo, then Calif. 1 north to the Castle.

ESSENTIALS • Orientation Located on Calif. 1, about 42 miles north of San Luis Obispo and 94 miles south of Monterey, there's not much else in this pretty coastal area besides Hearst Castle. Visitors park in the Visitor Center parking lot and take the tour bus five miles up the hill to the castle.

• Information Hearst Castle is administered by the **State of California Department of Parks & Recreation,** P.O. Box 942896, Sacramento, CA 94296. The direct line to the castle is ☎ **805/927-2020.**

A tour of San Simeon is a glimpse into a lifestyle that barely exists today. In the verdant Santa Lucia Mountains of San Simeon on a hill he called La Cuesta Encantada (The Enchanted Hill), William Randolph Hearst left an astounding monument to wealth, an ego trip par excellence. The mansion, which was donated to the state by the Hearst family in 1958, is now administered by the California Department of Parks & Recreation.

The history of Hearst Castle dates back to 1865, when 43-year-old George Hearst purchased a 40,000-acre Mexican land grant adjacent to San Simeon Bay. He built a comfortable ranch house, still standing today, on the property and ran large herds of cattle over its ranges and foothills. George Hearst often entertained at the ranch, and his only son, William Randolph, developed a great liking for the informal life at "Camp Hill." As a young man busy launching his newspaper career, he would often steal off to the San Simeon property for a quiet retreat. In 1919, William Randolph came into possession of the ranch, and the present castle was begun.

The focal point of today's estate is the incredible **Casa Grande,** a sprawling mansion with more than 100 rooms filled with priceless art and antiques: Flemish tapestries, 15th-century Gothic fireplaces, intricately carved 16th-century Spanish and

The Central Coast

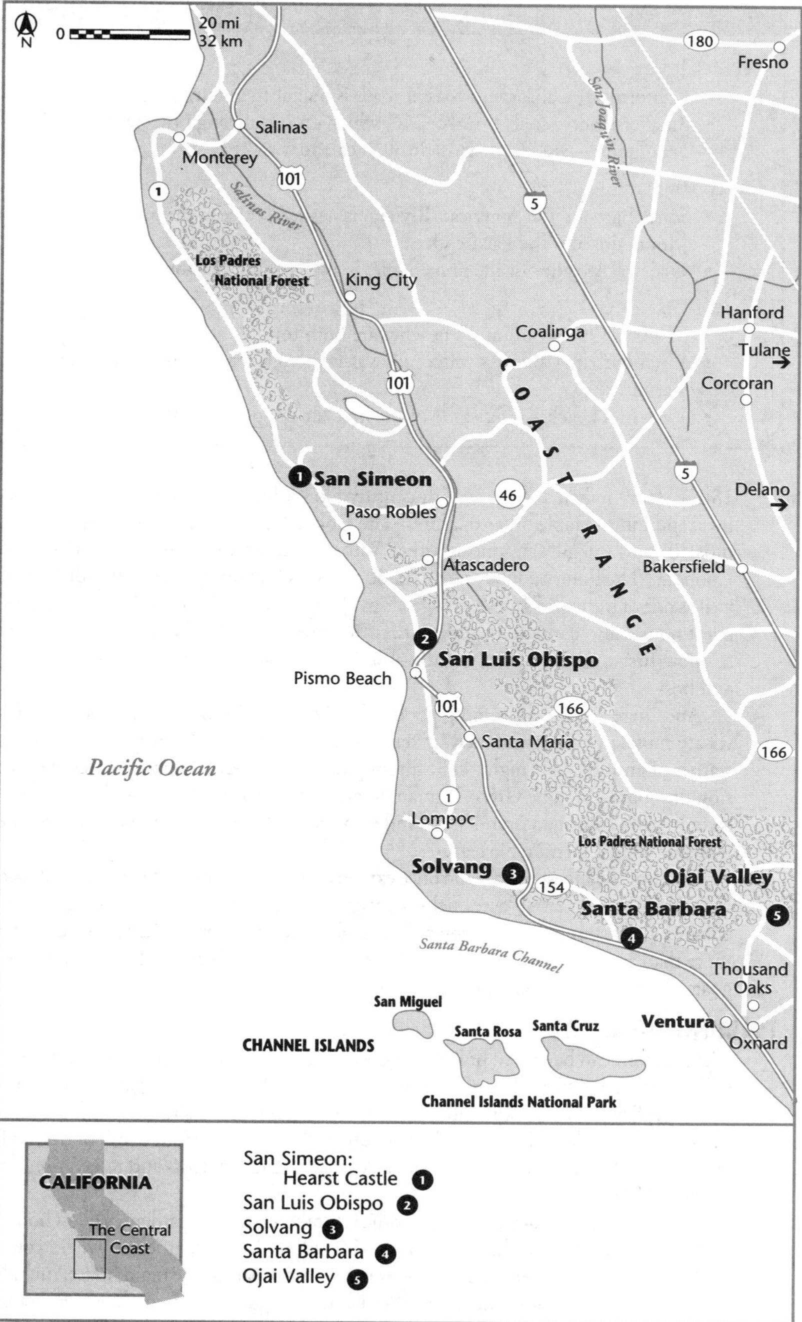
N
0
20 mi
32 km
180
Fresno
Salinas
Monterey
101
1
San Joaquin River
Salinas River
5
Los Padres
National Forest
King City
Hanford
Coalinga
Tulane
101
Corcoran
COAST RANGE
5
San Simeon
46
Delano
Paso Robles
1
Atascadero
Bakersfield
San Luis Obispo
Pismo Beach
101
166
Santa Maria
166
Pacific Ocean
1
Lompoc
Los Padres National Forest
Solvang
Ojai Valley
154
Santa Barbara
Santa Barbara Channel
Thousand
Oaks
San Miguel
Ventura
Santa Rosa
Santa Cruz
CHANNEL ISLANDS
Oxnard
Channel Islands National Park
CALIFORNIA
The Central
Coast
San Simeon:
Hearst Castle 1
San Luis Obispo 2
Solvang 3
Santa Barbara 4
Ojai Valley 5

What's Special About the Central Coast

Scenic Drives

- California 1, California's coastal road, is one of the prettiest in the world.
- Smaller roads—such as Calif. 246, which crosses through the Santa Ynez Mountains—are like driving through calendar art.

Pretty Towns

- Santa Barbara, the American Riviera, is nestled between the Santa Ynez Mountains and the Pacific Ocean.
- Ojai, in the valley of the same name, is as charming as a town gets.

Fantastic Beaches

- San Luis Obispo County's beaches are both touristy and fun.
- Santa Barbara County's waters are warm enough for swimming without a wetsuit.
- Ventura's beaches offer some of the best surfing on the coast.

18th-century Italian ceilings, a 16th-century Florentine bedstead, Renaissance paintings, and innumerable other treasures. The Doge's Suite was reserved for the house's most important guests, among them Winston Churchill and President Calvin Coolidge. The library contains over 5,000 volumes, including many rare editions, as well as one of the world's greatest collections of Greek vases. Three opulent "minicastle" guest houses also contain magnificent art treasures. A lavish private theater was used to show first-run films twice nightly—once for employees and again for the guests and host.

And there are two swimming pools. The Byzantine-inspired indoor pool has intricate mosaic work surrounded by replicas, in Carrara marble, of the most famous statues of antiquity. At night, light filtering through alabaster globes creates the illusion of moonlight. The Greco-Roman Neptune outdoor pool, flanked by Etruscan-style marble colonnades and surrounded by more Carrara statuary, is one of the mansion's most memorable features.

The world's largest private zoo once existed on the castle's magnificently landscaped grounds. Within a 2,000-acre enclosure were monkeys, cheetahs, giraffes, camels, elephants, bears, bison, llamas, zebras, deer, eagles, and other birds. Hearst had also kept more than 30 Arabian riding horses. Today only a few elk, Barbary sheep, Himalayan goats, deer, and zebra remain.

TOURING THE ESTATE

The mansion can be visited only by guided tour. Four separate tours are offered on a daily basis, each lasting almost two hours. They include some of the gardens as well as the magnificent outdoor and indoor pools. Wear comfortable shoes—you'll be walking about 1½ miles, which includes between 150 and 350 steps to climb or descend. (Visitors confined to wheelchairs may make special arrangements and reservations by calling **805/927-2020.**)

Tour I, recommended for the first-time visitor, includes the gardens, a guest house, and the ground floor of the main house—including the movie theater, where you'll see Hearst "home movies." Tour II takes in the upper part of the main house, including Hearst's private suite and office, libraries, duplex guest room, kitchen, and pools.

Tour III visits the guest wing, with its 36 bedrooms and sitting rooms, pools, and gardens, and deals with interior design changes over a 20-year period (300 stair steps). Tour IV, which is not offered in the winter, does not go inside the castle itself: it emphasizes the grounds and gardens and includes the wine cellar and the lower floor of the largest guest house.

Tours are conducted daily, beginning at 8:20am, except Thanksgiving Day, Christmas Day, and New Year's Day. Two to six tours leave every hour, depending on the season. Allow two hours between starting times if you plan on taking more than one tour. Reservations are recommended (arrive without them and you're guaranteed a long wait, if you get in at all) and can be made up to eight weeks in advance. Tickets can be purchased by telephone through **MISTIX** toll free at **800/444-4445.** They cost $14 for adults, $8 for children ages 6 to 12.

2 San Luis Obispo

230 miles S of San Francisco, 204 miles N of Los Angeles

GETTING THERE • By Plane Several major commuter airlines fly into **San Luis Obispo Municipal Airport,** including American Eagle (☎ toll free **800/433-7300**), and Skywest/Delta (☎ toll free **800/221-1212**). Ground transportation is provided by **Yellow Cab** (☎ **805/543-1234**) and costs about $15 to a downtown hotel.

• By Train **Amtrak** (☎ **800/USA-RAIL**) offers daily service from both San Francisco and Los Angeles. Trains depart from the San Luis Rail Station, 1011 Railroad Ave. (☎ **805/541-0505**), with fares as low as $60 to San Francisco and $30 to Los Angeles.

• By Bus **Greyhound/Trailways** maintains a daily schedule into San Luis Obispo from the north, south, and east. America's largest long-distance coach line no longer operates a nationwide toll-free telephone number, so consult your local directory for information.

• By Car U.S. 101, one of the state's primary north-south roadways, runs right through San Luis and represents the fastest land route to here from anywhere. If you're driving south down the coast, Calif. 1 is the way to go for its natural beauty and sheer oceanfront cliffs. If you're entering the city from the east, take Calif. 46 or 41.

ESSENTIALS • Orientation The city of San Luis Obispo, seat of the county of the same name, is located about 10 miles inland at the junction of Calif. 1 and U.S. 101. The downtown portion of the town is laid out in a grid roughly centered around the historic mission. Most of the main tourist sights are located around the mission, within the small triangle created by U.S. 101, Santa Rosa Street, and Marsh Street.

• Information The **San Luis Obispo Chamber of Commerce Visitors Center,** 1039 Chorro St. (☎ **805/781-2777,** or toll free **800/676-1772**), is located downtown between Monterey and Higuera Streets. Open seven days a week, this helpful office boasts one of the best-run visitors bureaus I have ever come across. Drop in to ask questions, pick up maps, get a calendar of events, or ask for specialized information on local sights. Ask for a "Path of History" map, this details many of the sights listed below. The office is open Tuesday through Friday 8am to 5pm, Monday 9am to 5pm, and Saturday and Sunday 10am to 5pm.

Located approximately halfway between San Francisco and Los Angeles, San Luis Obispo, often just called San Luis, is an easygoing, picturesque little college town that grew up around an 18th-century mission. In addition to its pretty setting—surrounded by the Los Padres Mountains—the city counts dozens of historical landmarks, quaint Victorian homes, shops, restaurants, and sporting facilities as its primary tourist attractions. Indeed, San Luis marks the northernmost outpost of southern California beach country—the first point south where you don't have to be a member of the Polar Bear Club to swim year round.

The town itself is easy enough to negotiate: you can reach most everything on foot. It also makes a good base for an extensive exploration of the country as a whole. To the west of town are some of the state's prettiest swimming beaches; turning east you enter the central coast's wine country, featuring dozens of respectable wineries.

What to See & Do

The Ah Louis Store, 800 Palm St. ☎ **805/543-4332.**

Practically unchanged since its opening in 1874, this century-old establishment is still in the hands of the original Cantonese family owners. Mr. Ah Louis was lured to California by gold fever in 1856. Returning from the mines empty-handed, he came to San Luis and took a job as a cook. Ah Louis soon began a lucrative career as a labor contractor, hiring and organizing Chinese crews to build the railroad. In addition to the store, he also started the first brickyard in the country, created county roads, had a vegetable and flower-seed business, bred racehorses, and was the overseer of eight farms.

Today, you can chat with his heir, Howard, who runs the store, while you browse through a clutter of Asian merchandise. Ask for a free brochure detailing the family's history. Hours are somewhat irregular since Howard often just closes up and goes fishing.

Admission: Free.

Open: Usually Mon–Sat 2–5:30pm, hours vary.

California Polytechnic State University. ☎ **805/756-1111,** or **805/756-1154.**

Cal-Poly, famous for its agriculture and architecture schools, occupies over 5,000 rolling acres, with the lion's share of campus space devoted to agricultural studies. The feed mill, meat-processing plant, dairy operation, ornamental horticulture greenhouse, barns, and chicken coops are all open to the public. School-produced milk, jams, salsa, and other products are sold at the campus store. From U.S. 101, take the Monterey exit and turn right onto Grand Avenue. Stop at the kiosk for a visitor permit and campus map, that outlines a self-guided tour. The bookstore and university student union are in the large building directly in front of you. To reach the campus store, continue onto Grand Avenue, turn right onto North Perimeter Drive, and right again onto Via Carta. The store is in the second building on your left.

★ **Farmer's Market,** Higuera St., between Osos and Nipomo Sts.

If you can, plan to be in San Luis on a Thursday, when the state's largest weekly street fair is held along four downtown city blocks. It's called Farmer's Market, but it's much more than fresh-picked produce. Every week, from 6:30 to 9pm, there's an ever-changing array of street entertainment, open-pit barbecues, food stands, and market stalls. Surrounding stores stay open until 9pm, and fresh flowers, cider, and other seasonal treats are sold.

★ **Mission San Luis Obispo de Tolosa,** 782 Monterey St. ☎ **805/543-6850.**

California's fifth mission, built with adobe bricks by Native American Chumash people, was completed in 1790. It remains one of the prettiest and most interesting structures in the Franciscan chain. Interior features of note include a 1793 statue of Saint Louis (San Luís) that tops the altar and a belfry that houses three large Peruvian-cast bells dating from 1818. Mass, held each morning at 7am and 8am, is open to the public. The Mission Museum, inside the main building, contains a plethora of historical artifacts including vestments, books, an 1831 Spanish wedding dress, and portraits and photos of mission workers. The best exhibits are of Native American origin and include flints, arrowheads, wampum beads, dolls, baskets, clothing, cooking pots, drums, and grinding stones for making flour.

Admission: $1 donation requested.

Open: Winter 9am–4pm; summer 9am–5pm (sometimes later).

Mission Plaza, adjacent to Mission San Luis Obispo de Tolosa.

The mission's parklike plaza is a pretty garden with brick paths and wooden benches fronting a meandering creek. Mission Plaza is the town square, the focal point for local festivities and activities ranging from live concerts to dance performances, poetry readings, and theater productions. Check at the Commerce Visitors Center to see what's on when you're in town.

San Luis Obispo Children's Museum, 1010 Nipomo St. ☎ **805/544-KIDS.**

Opened in late 1990, this terrific children's museum is one of the city's newest sights. There's a playhouse of interesting manipulatives for toddlers, an authentic reproduction of a Native American Chumash cave, an art center, computer corner, half-built house, and other activities.

Special events like mask making, sing-a-longs, and stage makeup classes are scheduled regularly. Call for current event information.

Admission: $3 for adults and children 2 and older, those under 2 are free.

Open: Sept–June Thurs–Fri 1–5pm, Sat–Sun 10am–5pm; July–Aug Thurs 2–7pm, Fri–Tues 10am–3pm.

San Luis Obispo County Historical Museum, 696 Monterey St. ☎ **805/543-0638.**

A wonderful place to browse, this little museum, run by the San Luis Obispo County Historical Society, is housed in the early-20th-century Carnegie Library building. The permanent exhibit includes artifacts from Native American Chumash and early European settlers. Special exhibitions on county history are often staged. The museum houses an extensive research library and owns thousands of historical photographs.

Admission: Free.

Open: Wed–Sun 10am–4pm.

St. Stephen's Episcopal Church, Pismo and Nipomo Sts.

Dating from 1867, this pretty, peaked, pine-and-redwood structure was one of the first Episcopal churches built in California. The church's original pipe organ was donated by Phoebe Apperson Hearst, Patty Hearst's great-grandmother.

NEARBY BEACH COMMUNITIES

There are three particularly fantastic beaches in San Luis Obispo County, each within minutes of downtown San Luis.

Avila Beach, about a 10-minute drive south, is a quaint seacoast village offering chartered deep-sea fishing and scenic pleasure cruises from its Port St. Luis Marina. The water here is some of the warmest in the county, which is still too cold for many. Barbecue and picnic facilities front directly on the beach.

Pismo Beach, about a 15-minute drive south, offers a spectacular 23-mile stretch of sandy beach. Explore isolated dunes, cliff-sheltered tidepools, caves, and old pirate coves by foot, horse, or all-terrain vehicle year-round. It is unclear whether the area's name comes from a Spanish word meaning "a place to fish," or from the Native Chumash *pismu,* which means "the place where blobs of tar wash up on the beach." Both are accurately descriptive. Fishing is permitted from Pismo Beach Pier, which is also packed with other amusements including arcade games, bowling, billiards, and the like. You'll also find a wide variety of restaurants and shops in the area, including several antiques stores and wineries.

The Pismo Beach Chamber of Commerce and Visitors Bureau, 581 Dolliver St., Pismo Beach, CA 93449 (☎ **805/773-4382,** or toll free **800/443-7778** in California), offers free brochures and information on local attractions. The office is open Monday through Friday from 9:30am to 5pm, Saturday from 10am to 4pm, and Sunday noon to 4pm.

Morro Bay, about 15 minutes north of downtown San Luis, is one of the most beautiful beaches, best known for its dramatic Morro Rock, part of a chain of long-extinct volcanoes. The huge domed rock is a winter and fall sanctuary for thousands of migrating birds, including cormorants, pelicans, sandpipers, and the rare peregrine falcon. It's wonderful to watch them from the beach or from a window table at one of the bay-view restaurants.

The beachside community of Morro Bay is centered around the Embarcadero, an oceanfront strip packed with tourist shops and seafood-with-a-view eateries. Commercial fishing boats often unload their catch here and sell to area markets. Other area attractions include boat and pier fishing facilities, shops, art galleries, and a nearby aquarium.

The Morro Bay Chamber of Commerce, 895 Napa St., Morro Bay, CA 93442 (☎ **805/772-4467,** or toll free 8**00/231-0592**), offers armfuls of area information. The chamber is open Monday through Friday from 8:30am to 5pm and Saturday from 10am to 3pm.

SHOPPING

San Luis has a couple of small malls, but, happily, the best shops are still the independent boutiques that are liberally scattered throughout the town. Stroll around downtown in the area surrounding the mission. The five blocks of Higuera Street from Nipomo to Osos streets and a short stretch of Monterey Street between Chorro and Osos streets are best.

The Creamery, 570 Higuera St. ☎ **805/541-0106.**

Originally the Golden State Creamery, this former factory at Nipomo Street was built in 1906 and functioned as one of the most important milk-producing centers in the state for over 40 years. Restored, remodeled, and opened in 1974 as a shopping and restaurant mall, the new complex is centered around the creamery's old cooling tower. Antique freezer doors, overhead workhouse lights, and milk-can lamps pointedly remind visitors of the structure's original function. An old nickelodeon (which costs a dime) shows scenes of devastation from the Great Earthquake of 1906.

The Network Mall, 778 Higuera St.

Two blocks from the Creamery, this small shopping center is a quaint collection of specialty shops and craft stores. It's worth a visit while strolling around downtown.

Where to Stay

MODERATE

Apple Farm Inn, 2015 Monterey St., San Luis Obispo, CA 93401. ☎ **805/544-2040,** or toll free **800/374-3705.** Fax 805/541-5497. 67 rms. A/C TV TEL **Directions:** from U.S. 101, take the Monterey Street exit; the hotel is located on your left.

Rates: $125–$200 single or double. Children under 18 stay free in parents' room. Extra person $15. AE, MC, V.

A delightful blend of country charm and traditional elegance can be found throughout this handsome turn-of-the-century Victorian inn. Rooms with pine furniture boast gas-log fireplaces, oversize tubs, and either a four-poster, canopied, or brass bed. Some bedrooms open onto cozy turreted sitting areas furnished with love seats, wing-back chairs, and romantic window seats. Others have bay windows and a view of San Luis Creek or the adjacent mill. The hotel's outdoor heated swimming pool incorporates a Jacuzzi and is open year round.

In San Luis Creek, an adjacent working mill spins its huge wheel. Set on the riverbank among giant sycamores, both the inn and mill were modeled after 19th-century structures. The mill's 14-foot wheel displaces about 600 gallons of water per minute and provides power to an apple cider press.

Hotel services include nightly turndown and a morning wake-up knock, delivered with complimentary coffee or tea. Cider is always available.

Madonna Inn, 100 Madonna Rd., San Luis Obispo, CA 93405. ☎ **805/543-3000.** Fax 805/543-1800. 109 rms, 25 suites. TV TEL **Directions:** From U.S. 101, take the Madonna exit and follow the signs to the hotel.

Rates: $72 single; $82–$140 double; from $170 suite. No credit cards.

Alex and Phyllis Madonna's unique motel is a festival of kitsch and one of the most famous (or infamous) hostelries on the California coast. Marring 1,500 hillside acres, the Madonna Inn, at the top of a road lined with bubble-gum-pink lampposts, is a perverted fairy-tale castle complete with outrageous turrets and exterior winding staircases. Each guest room is styled after a unique, eccentric thematic fantasy. One, for example, is canary yellow from floor to ceiling, with bright carpets and birdcage light fixtures. Several rooms are styled like caves, with dark interiors and choppy rock walls, working fireplaces and/or rock-walled waterfall showers. A particularly unusual bedroom features a bed that's five feet long on one side and six feet long on the other—customized sheets! If none of these rooms capture your fancy, you can choose Spanish, Italian, Irish, Alps, Currier and Ives, Native American, Swiss, or hunting decor. One of the most romantic is Love Nest, a honeymoon suite with a pink-carpeted winding stairway leading to a cupola hideaway. Morning Star is a two-room suite with a high, beamed cathedral ceiling, gold bed, gold tables, and gold-and-crystal chandelier.

Unfortunately, the motel has a reputation for sluggish service. Facilities include an enormous coffee shop, a pricey dining room, and two cocktail lounges, all as outlandishly ornate and plushly pink as the rest of the hotel.

BUDGET

Motel 6, 1625 Calle Joaquin, San Luis Obispo, CA 93401. ☎ **805/541-6992.** 117 rms (all with bath). A/C TV TEL **Directions:** From U.S. 101, take the Los Osos exit and turn right on Calle Joaquin.

Rates: $36 single, $40 double, AE, DISC, MC, V.

This money-saving beauty was finished in July 1988. Furnishings have a natural-wood finish, pastels predominate even to the pattern of the comforters, and the rooms are quite light. There is also a swimming pool.

Best Western Olive Tree, 1000 Olive St., San Luis Obispo, CA 93401. ☎ **805/544-2800,** or toll free **800/528-1234, 800/777-5847** in California. 36 rms, 2 suites. TV TEL **Directions:** From U.S. 101 south, exit at Santa Rosa Street and turn left onto Olive Street.

Rates: $42–$50 single; $49–$65 double; $68–$92 apt. suite. AE, CB, DC, MC, V.

These unremarkable, clean, competent rooms are both well located and well priced in an otherwise expensive community. The most unique feature of the Olive Tree is its eight apartment suites, housed in an attractive shingled building, all with large terraces or patios and big, fully equipped modern kitchens. The Olive Tree has a restaurant on the premises—the Stuffed Olive, a reasonably priced coffee shop. There's also a sauna along with the pool.

Lamp Lighter Inn, 1604 Monterey St., San Luis Obispo, CA 93401. ☎ **805/547-7777,** or toll free **800/547-7787.** Fax 805/547-7787. 40 rms, 11 suites. A/C TV TEL **Directions:** From U.S. 101, exit at Monterey Street; the hotel is 4 blocks ahead at Grove Street.

Rates (including continental breakfast): $45–$80 single or double; from $69 suite. AE, DISC, MC, V.

The neat and clean rooms at this motel all have cable color TVs with free HBO movies and coffee makers; clocks and irons are available on request. There's also a pool and heated whirlpool.

Motel 6, 1433 Calle Joaquin, San Luis Obispo, CA 93401. ☎ **805/549-9595.** 87 rms. A/C TV TEL **Directions:** From U.S. 101, take the Los Osos exit, turn right onto Calle Joaquin; the hotel is on your left, just past Denny's restaurant.

Rates: $36 single; $40 double. Extra adult $6. AE, DISC, MC, V.

Budget-minded travelers should consider this Motel 6—nothing fancy, just clean, comfortable rooms. Since the motel is slightly out-of-the-way, you'll need a car to reach it. There's a swimming pool on the premises.

Where to Dine

San Luis is not particularly known for its food; few restaurants in the area dish out unforgettable gourmet fare. But many eateries offer good honest meals served in very pleasant surroundings.

EXPENSIVE

McLintock's Saloon and Dining House, Shell Beach, 750 Mattie Rd. ☎ **805/773-1892.**

Cuisine: AMERICAN. **Reservations:** Accepted at all times, except dinner Fri–Sat. **Directions:** From U.S. 101, exit Shell Beach Road and continue to the restaurant.

Prices: Appetizers $3–$5; main courses $13–$27. DISC, MC, V.
Open: Brunch Sun 9am–1:30pm; dinner Mon–Fri 4–10pm, Sat 3pm–10:30pm, Sun 2pm–9:30pm.

Housed in what once was a real ranch house, McLintocks is still full of western spirit and style. A real stuffed buffalo greets diners in the lobby. Swinging saloon doors open into a room hung with hunting trophies and cowboy paraphernalia. Lantern-lit checker-board tablecloths, a blazing stone fireplace, and a craps table from speakeasy days round out the period decor. A separate covered, heated deck area is also available for dining. It's crammed with antique farm implements, blacksmith memorabilia, and a collection of old license plates and branding boards.

Meals are also meant to make you feel at home on the range. Main courses include hickory-smoked barbecued spareribs in pineapple-honey sauce, a 14-ounce top sirloin steak, and fresh abalone with drawn butter. Dinners include salad, Trail Camp beans, salsa, garlic bread, onion rings, ranch-fried potatoes, and an after-dinner liqueur or sherbet.

A second restaurant is located at 686 Higuera St. (☎ **805/541-0686**).

The Olde Port Inn, Avila Rd., Avila Beach. ☎ **805/595-2515.**

Cuisine: SEAFOOD. **Reservations:** Recommended. **Directions:** From downtown San Luis, take U.S. 101 south to Avila Beach exit. Turn right and continue to the end of the road; the restaurant is at the end of the third pier.
Prices: Appetizers $4–$7; main courses $12–$22. AE, MC, V.
Open: Dinner Mon–Fri 5:30–9pm, Sat–Sun 5:30–10pm.

In a superb location right out on the boat-filled bay, this two-story restaurant has windows everywhere and wonderful views of the water. The decor is rustic nautical—columns made of pier pilings, oil-can bar stools, weathered wood ceilings and beams, and walls lined with photos of local fisherfolk. Hanging lamps with red-glass shades and candle lamps made from cut-tin clam-juice cans warm to a cozy glow. The downstairs bar bounces, upstairs is quieter.

The restaurant has had the same owner for over 20 years, and the chef has always specialized in sautéeing and charbroiling. Fish dinners simply do not come fresher; evening meals are handpicked off local fishing boats. Steaks, pastas, and chicken are also available. Specialties of the house include bacon-wrapped prawns stuffed with jack cheese, seafood pasta, cioppino, and a steamed basket of crab claws, mussels, and clams. There's live entertainment nightly—rock, '40s swing, and sometimes jazz—in the downstairs cocktail area.

This Old House, Foothill Blvd. ☎ **805/543-2690.**

Cuisine: AMERICAN. **Reservations:** Recommended.
Prices: Appetizers $4–$9; main courses $12–$27. AE, DC, DISC, MC, V.
Open: Mon–Thurs 5–9pm, Fri 5–10pm, Sat 4–10pm, Sun 4–9pm.

Built in 1917, This Old House, named for the 1950s pop song, started life as a rowdy cowboy hangout complete with shooting contests and an occasional horse in the bar. Beer and whisky are still the drinks of choice here, but a model of Sputnik on the roof and a more refined clientele in the bar has altered the restaurant's image. Shootouts are now frowned upon here, but the bare oak floors, rodeo photos, and cowboy paraphernalia that adorn the walls still lend this place a western feel. There's a fireplace, a beamed barn-like ceiling, simulated gaslight chandeliers, and antique furnishings from country farms and ranches.

Barbecued beef, chicken, spareribs, and fish are served straight from an oak pit oven. All main courses are served with salad, ranch beans, Texas toast, salsa, potato, and sherbet. Children's portions are available.

MODERATE

Apple Farm, 2015 Monterey St. ☎ **805/544-6100.**

Cuisine: AMERICAN. **Reservations:** Accepted. **Directions:** From U.S. 101, take the Monterey Street exit; the restaurant is located on your left.
Prices: Appetizers $4–$7; main courses $9–$14; breakfast or lunch $5–$7. AE, MC, V.
Open: Daily 7am–9:30pm.

The touristy Apple Farm is a tribute to American country fare. Traditional breakfasts come with hash-brown potatoes or fresh fruit, plus freshly baked muffins and biscuits. Lunch, which includes homemade soups, chili, sandwiches, and salads, is accompanied by potato salad. Dinner means turkey pot pie, grilled fish, and prime rib. Desserts are the real specialty here; look for hot apple dumplings and apple pie.

Service and quality have reportedly been spotty here, so you might just want to visit the adjacent Apple Farm Bakery and choose from a wide selection of pies, cookies, brownies, and the like. A two-story gift shop sells wall hangings, books, toys, and canned foods like apple butter and boysenberry spread.

 **Linnaeas's Café,** 1110 Garden St. ☎ **805/541-5888.**

Cuisine: VEGETARIAN. **Reservations:** Not accepted. **Directions:** From U.S. 101, exit at Marsh Street and turn left on Garden Street.
Prices: Main courses $3–$5. No credit cards.
Open: Breakfast and lunch daily 7:30am–2pm; dessert only 2pm–midnight.

To many locals, Linnaeas Café is San Luis. The cafe, which has a wooden counter, simple stools, and small circular tables, doubles as an art gallery that features works for sale by local artists. In addition to the usual waffles or French toast, breakfast options include egg burritos (scrambled eggs, chopped tomatoes, scallions, black olives, and cheddar cheese in a flour tortilla, topped with salsa and sour cream), old-fashioned rice pudding with steamed milk, scones, muffins, and Linnaeas's own scrumptious coffee cake.

"SLO" rolls are lunch specialties made of Armenian crackerbread. They have various fillings, all with a cream cheese/mayonnaise base. The Mexican variety is filled with cheese, tomatoes, chiles, and onions; the Italian version features zucchini, mushrooms, green olives, and jack cheese, with touches of Parmesan and garlic. Rolls are sold by the inch—slices look like jelly rolls. Lunch choices also include freshly made soups and salads.

Linnaeas now features Illy Caffè, from Trieste, Italy, which they use for their espresso drinks, including cafe mochas. Linnaeas Café is not open for dinner, but an enormous selection of desserts are offered. Here are just a few examples of what you can choose from: fresh tortes, cheesecake topped with fresh fruit, and carrot cake. Live music begins nightly at about 8pm, and runs the gamut from classical to contemporary. More often than not there is no admission fee for the music.

3 Solvang

264 miles S of San Francisco, 170 miles N of Los Angeles

GETTING THERE • By Car From U.S. 101 north turn east (left) onto Calif. 246 at Buellton, a 20-minute drive from the freeway. From Santa Barbara in the south, take U.S. 101 to Calif. 154 over the San Marcos Pass, a 45-minute drive.

ESSENTIALS • Orientation Located in the Santa Ynez Mountains, the touristy part of the small town of Solvang is only about four square blocks big. Alisal Road, beginning at the traffic light at the corner of Calif. 246, is the main drag. Surrounding streets are laid out in a grid pattern and are best negotiated by foot.

• Information The **Solvang Chamber of Commerce Information Center,** 433 Alisal Rd., Solvang, CA 93463 (☎ **805/688-3317**), can supply you with maps, events schedules, and other information. It's open daily from 9am to 5pm. The visitor information booth on Copenhagen Drive, next to the Mid-State Bank, also offers literature and advice. The booth is open Monday through Friday from 10am to 4pm, Saturday and Sunday from 10am to 5pm.

The relatively compact and beautiful Santa Ynez Valley, surrounded by mountains of the same name, is home to five small towns: Buellton, Santa Ynez, Los Olivos, Ballard, and Solvang, the region's top tourist draw. Since it was founded by Danish-Americans in 1911, Solvang, or "sunny valley," has always had a Scandinavian bent. The original intention of town founders was to preserve the townspeople's heritage. As Solvang's popularity grew, however, cultural celebration became the town's primary economic engine. Today, the "quaint" village looks as if Disney did Denmark, with white and blue fringed buildings housing hokey import shops and innumerable pastry and pancake restaurants. Solvang's immense popularity has cost the town its charm. A trip here wouldn't ordinarily be worth going out of your way for, but since it is well located, right on an inland shortcut across the coast, it wouldn't hurt much to arrive in time for lunch.

What to See & Do

Strolling, eating, browsing, and buying are what this village is about, and not necessarily in that order. The town center, a cluster of wide streets offering ample parking, is lined with Scandinavian import shops, bars, restaurants, and even windmills. Wander, stop, shop, and wander some more.

Mission Santa Ines, 1760 Mission Dr.

Founded in 1804, this terrifically restored mission is easily the oldest structure in town. Number 19 in California's 21-mission series, Santa Ines still maintains an active congregation. After a series of restorations, the most recent of which was completed in 1988, Mission Santa Ines looks as it must have shortly after it was founded. The building houses a museum of early Native American and European mission artifacts. The church, chapel, museum, and surrounding grounds are open to the public.

Admission: $2 donation requested.

Open: Summer, Mon–Fri 9:30am–5pm, Sun noon–5pm; winter, Mon–Sat 9:30am–4:30pm, Sun noon–4:30pm. **Directions:** From downtown Solvang, take Calif. 246 one mile east to Mission Drive.

Where to Stay

MODERATE

Royal Scandanavian Inn, 400 Alisal Rd. (P.O. Box 30), Solvang, CA 93464. ☎ **805/688-8000,** or toll free **800/624-5572.** Fax 805/688-0761. 133 rms, 10 suites. A/C TV TEL **Directions:** From Calif. 246, turn onto Alisal Road and drive two blocks to the hotel.

Rates: $80–$125 single or double; from $135 suite. AE, CB, DC, DISC, MC, V.

While far from luxurious, this comfortable hotel is the fanciest in town. Pretty rooms with cable color TVs are augmented by a heated pool and spa, and a restaurant and cocktail lounge on the premises. It's easily the nicest hotel for miles around, well located, right in the center of things, and painted blue and white like neighboring buildings. The hotel is a popular rest stop for visitors on organized tours.

BUDGET

Motel 6, 333 McMurray Rd., Buellton, CA 93427. ☎ **805/688-7797.** 59 rms. A/C TV TEL **Directions:** From Solvang, take Calif. 246 west past U.S. 101 to the hotel.

Rates: $35 single; $42 double. Extra adult $6. Children under 18 stay free in parents' room. AE, CB, DC, MC, V.

The area's cheapest accommodations are in Buellton, about 20 minutes west of Solvang and just west of U.S. 101. This Motel 6 has the usual comforts and amenities associated with the chain; there's also a pool on the grounds and local calls from the rooms are free.

4 Santa Barbara

336 miles S of San Francisco; 96 miles N of Los Angeles

GETTING THERE • By Plane The **Santa Barbara Municipal Airport** (☎ **805/967-7111**) is located in Goleta, about 10 minutes north of downtown Santa Barbara. Major airlines servicing Santa Barbara include American Eagle (☎ toll free **800/433-7300**), Skywest/Delta (☎ toll free **800/453-9417**), United (☎ toll free **800/241-6522**), and USAir Express (☎ toll free **800/428-4322**). **Yellow Cab** (☎ **805/965-5111**) and other metered taxis line up outside the terminal and cost about $20 to a downtown hotel.

• **By Train** **Amtrak** (☎ **800/USA-RAIL**) offers daily service from both San Francisco and Los Angeles. Trains arrive and depart from the Santa Barbara Rail Station, 209 State St. (☎ **805/963-1015**); fares can be as low as $60 to San Francisco and $20 to Los Angeles.

• **By Bus** **Greyhound/Trailways** maintains a daily schedule into Santa Barbara from both the north and south. The central bus station is located in the middle of downtown at Cabrillo and Chapala Streets. America's largest long-distance coach line no longer operates a nationwide toll-free telephone number, so consult your local directory for information.

• **By Car** U.S. 101, one of the state's primary north-south roadways, runs right through Santa Barbara and represents the fastest land route to here from anywhere. From the north, you can take Calif. 154, which meets U.S. 101 at Los Olivos and cuts across the San Marcos Pass, a scenic route into Santa Barbara.

ESSENTIALS • Orientation State Street, the city's primary commercial thoroughfare, is in the geographical center of town; it ends at Stearns Wharf. Cabrillo Street runs along the ocean and separates the city's beaches from touristy hotels and restaurants.

• Information The **Santa Barbara Visitor Information Center,** 1 Santa Barbara St., Santa Barbara, CA 93101 (☎ **805/965-3021**), is on the ocean, at the corner of Cabrillo Street. This small but busy office distributes maps, literature, an events calendar, and excellent advice. Be sure to ask for their handy guide to places of interest and public parking. The office is open Monday through Saturday from 9am to 5pm, Sunday from 10am to 5pm; it closes one hour earlier in December and January and one hour later in July and August. A second Visitor Information Center, open 9am to 5pm Monday to Friday, is located in a storefront at 504 State St. in the heart of downtown.

Be sure to pick up a copy of *The Independent,* a free weekly available from sidewalk racks all around town.

Santa Barbara's geographical position has everything to do with its charm. Nature has smiled on this small notch of land between the Santa Ynez Mountains and the Pacific Ocean; the sun-blessed Southern Californian town is one of the world's most perfect places. Spoiled Santa Barbara is coddled by wooded mountains, caressed by baby breakers, and sheltered from tempestuous seas by rocky off-shore islands. Located 90 miles north of Los Angeles—just far enough to make the Big City seem at once remote and accessible—the town feels small, and growth is generally frowned upon. Because there are few employment opportunities, and real estate is expensive, demographics have favored college-age students and rich retirees; a situation locals refer to as "almost wed and almost dead."

Visually, downtown Santa Barbara is distinctive for its homogeneous Spanish-Mediterranean buildings, each of which sport matching red-tile roofs. But it wasn't always this way. Named in 1602 by a Carmelite friar sailing with Spanish explorer Sebástian Vizcaino, Santa Barbara had a thriving Native American Chumash population for hundreds, if not thousands, of years. The town's European era began in the late 18th century, around a presidio, or fort, that still stands reconstructed today, in its original town-center spot. The earliest architectural hodge-podge was destroyed in 1925, by a powerful earthquake that leveled Santa Barbara's business district. Out of the rubble rose Spanish-Mediterranean-style Santa Barbara, a stylish planned town that continues to rigidly enforce its strict building codes.

What to See & Do

County Courthouse, 1100 Anacapa St. ☎ **805/962-6464.**

Occupying a full city block and set in a lush tropical garden, this courthouse is a supreme example of Santa Barbara nouveau-Spanish architecture—a tribute to bygone days when style and elegance outweighed more practical considerations. Few would guess that it was built as late as 1929. The architect, William Mooser, was aided by his son who had spent 17 years in Spain and was well versed in Spanish-Moorish design. Towers and a turret, graceful arches, unexpected windows, brilliant Tunisian tilework, a winding staircase, intricately stenciled ceilings, palatial tile floors, lacy iron grillwork, heavy wood doors, and Spanish lanterns resembling hammered iron are among the impressive interior features. The magnificent historic murals by Dan Sayre Groesbeck that depict memorable episodes in Santa Barbara history are worth a visit in themselves. A compact elevator takes visitors up to the 85-foot-high observation deck roof of the clock tower. From here visitors are treated to good views of the ocean, mountains, and the red terra-cotta-tile roofs that cover the city.

A free guided tour is offered Wednesday and Friday at 10:30am, and Monday through Saturday at 2pm.

Admission: Free.

Open: Mon–Fri 8am–5pm, Sat–Sun and holidays 9am–5pm.

Moreton Bay Fig Tree, Chapala and Montecito Sts.

Famous for its massive size, Santa Barbara's best-known tree has a branch spread that would cover half a football field. It has been estimated that well over 10,000 people could stand in the tree's shade, while its roots run under more than an acre of ground. Planted in 1877, the *Figus macrophylla* is a native of Moreton Bay in eastern Australia. It is related to both the fig and rubber tree but produces neither figs nor rubber. The tree is hands-down the largest of its kind in the world. Once in danger of being leveled (for a proposed gas station) and later threatened by excavation for nearby U.S. 101, the revered tree is now the unofficial home of Santa Barbara's homeless community.

★ **Santa Barbara Mission,** Laguna and Los Olivos Sts. ☎ **805/682-4173** or **687-4149.**

Called the "Queen of the Missions," for its twin bell towers and graceful beauty, Santa Barbara's hilltop mission overlooks the town and the Channel Islands beyond. The structure is surrounded by green lawns with flowering trees and shrubs. The Santa Barbara Mission was established in 1786 and is still in use by a local parish. Displayed inside are a typical missionary bedroom, 18th- and 19th-century furnishings, paintings and statues from Mexico, and period kitchen utensils, including grinding stones, baskets, and copper kettles. The museum also displays Native American tools, crafts, and artifacts.

Admission: $2 adults, children under 16 free.

Open: Daily 9am–5pm. **Closed:** Christmas, Easter, and Thanksgiving.

Santa Barbara Museum of Natural History, 2559 Puesta del Sol Rd. ☎ **805/682-4711.**

Located roughly just beyond the mission, this museum is devoted to the display, study, and interpretation of Pacific Coast natural history: flora, fauna, and prehistoric life. The museum's architecture, in typical Santa Barbara style, reflects early Spanish and Mexican influence, with ivory-colored stucco walls, graceful arches, arcades, and a central patio. Exhibits range from diagrams to dioramas. Native American history is emphasized, including basketry, textiles, and a full-size replica of a Chumash canoe. Other displays encompass everything from fossil ferns to the complete skeleton of a blue whale. An adjacent planetarium projects sky shows every Saturday and Sunday. The museum store sells a good selection of books, jewelry, textiles, and a variety of handcrafted gifts.

Admission: $4 adults, $3 seniors and teens, $2 children.

Open: Mon–Sat 9am–5pm, Sun and holidays 10am–5pm.

Santa Barbara Museum of Art, 1130 State St. ☎ **805/963-4364.**

Considering the relatively small size of the community this museum serves, the Santa Barbara Museum of Art is extraordinary. From Egyptian reliefs to kinetic sculptures, there is something of interest for everyone. Top draws include Greek and Roman

Santa Barbara

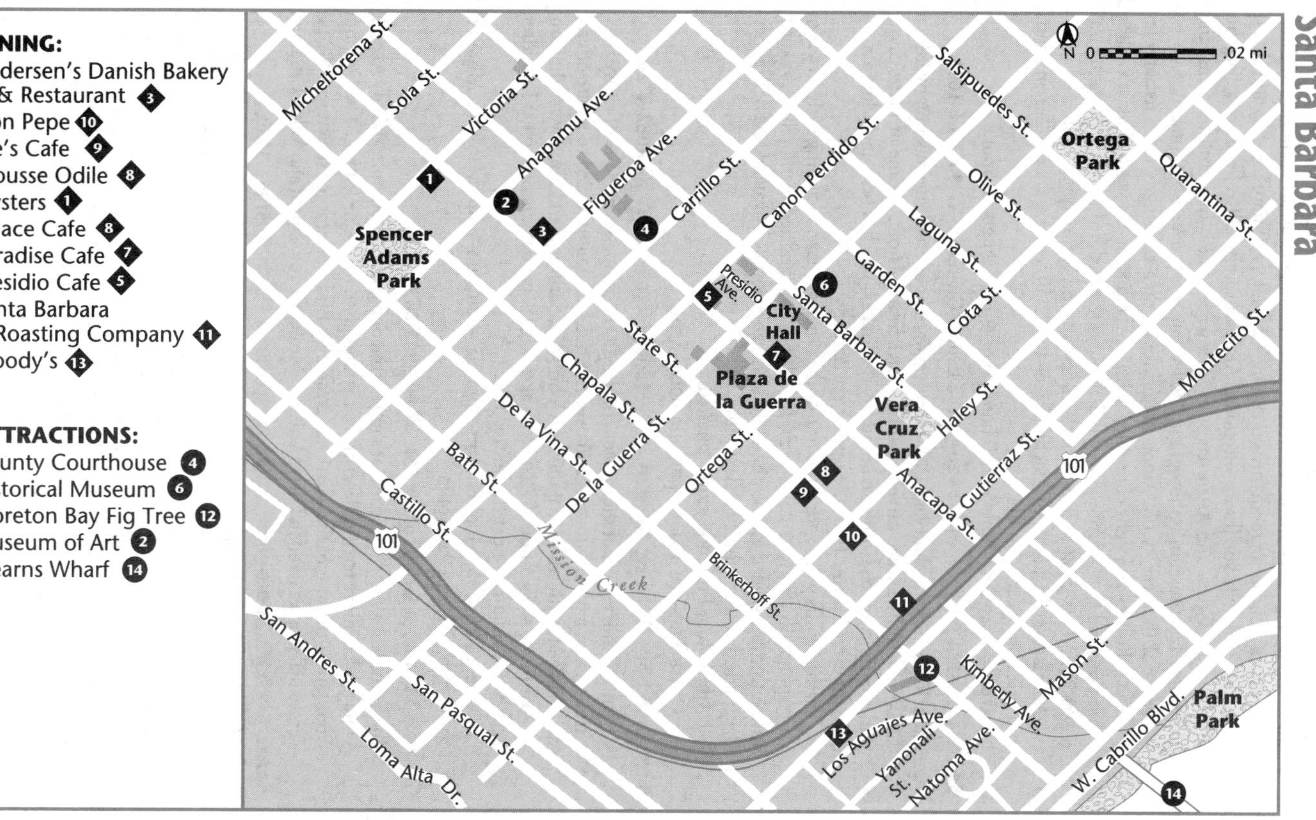

sculpture, representatives from the Italian Renaissance and Flemish schools; European impressionist paintings, including works by Monet and Degas, and paintings by early-20th-century European modernists including Chagall, Hoffmann, and Kandinsky. If all that isn't enough, you'll see a selection of American art by O'Keeffe, Eakins, Sargent, Hopper, and Grosz, and Asian sculpture, prints, ceramic ware, scrolls, screens, and paintings. The museum's photography collection boasts over 1,500 images.

Most of the over 15,000 works are exhibited on a rotating basis in recently remodeled climate- and light-controlled galleries. Temporary shows include travelling exhibitions and local features. Free guided tours are scheduled Tuesday through Sunday at 1pm. Focus tours are held on Wednesdays and Saturdays at noon.

Admission: $3 adults, $1.50 children 6–16, $2.50 seniors over 65, free on Thurs and first Sun of each month.

Open: Tues–Sat 11am–5pm, Thurs 11am–9pm, Sun noon–5pm.

Santa Barbara Historical Museum, 136 E. de la Guerra St. ☎ **805/966-1601.**

Local lore exhibits include late-19th-century paintings of California missions by Edwin Deakin; a 16th-century carved Spanish coffer from Majorca, home of Padre Serra; and objects from the Chinese community that once flourished here, including a magnificent carved shrine from the turn of the century.

History buffs will appreciate some of the other displays, including early letters of correspondence, antique dolls, period clothing, and assorted memorabilia. A most interesting free guided tour led by a knowledgeable docent is available every Wednesday, Saturday, and Sunday at 1:30pm.

Admission: Free, donation requested.

Open: Tues–Sat 10am–5pm, Sun noon–5pm.

Santa Barbara Botanic Garden, 1212 Mission Canyon Rd. ☎ **805/682-4726.**

About 1 1/2 miles north of the mission, the garden encompasses 65 acres of native trees, shrubs, cacti, and wildflowers, and over five miles of trails. Guided tours are offered daily at 2pm, with additional tours on Thursday, Saturday, and Sunday at 10:30am.

Admission: $3 adults, $2 children ages 13–19 and seniors over 64, $1 children ages 5–12, children under 5 admitted free.

Open: Nov–Feb, Mon–Fri 9am–4pm, Sat–Sun 9am–5pm; Mar–Oct, Mon–Fri 9am–5pm, Sat–Sun 9am–6pm.

Stearns Wharf, at the end of State St. ☎ **805/963-2633.**

In addition to a small collection of shops, attractions, and restaurants, the city's 1872-vintage pier enjoys terrific views of the city and good drop-line fishing. The Dolphin Fountain at the foot of the wharf was created by Bud Bottoms for the city's 1982 bicentennial (copies stand in Puerto Vallarta, Mexico; Toba, Japan; and Yalta, Ukraine).

Santa Barbara Zoological Gardens, 500 Ninos Dr. ☎ **805/962-5339,** or **962-6310** for a recording.

Sometimes, when you're driving around the bend on Cabrillo Beach Boulevard, the head of a giraffe can be spotted poking up through the palm trees. This is not your imagination, it's the intimate Santa Barbara Zoo, where all 700 animals can be seen in about 30 minutes. Most of the animals are displayed in open, naturalistic settings. The zoo encompasses a children's Discovery Area, a miniature train ride, a small carousel, and gift shop. Picnic areas, complete with barbecue pits are under-utilized, and especially recommendable. Beautiful botanic displays augment the animal exhibits.

Admission: \$5 adults, \$3 for seniors and children ages 2–12, children under 2 free.

Open: Jun–Aug 9am–6pm, Sept–May 10am–5pm; last admission is one hour prior to closing.

Sports & Recreation

One of the best things about Santa Barbara is the accessibility of almost every sport known to humankind, from mountain hiking to ocean kayaking. This is the southern California of the movies, where windsurfing and bunjee jumping are everyday activities. Pick up a free copy of "Things to See and Do" at the **Santa Barbara Visitor Information Center,** 1 Santa Barbara St., Santa Barbara, CA 93101 (☎ **805/965-3021**).

BICYCLING A relatively flat, four-mile palm-lined coastal pathway runs along the beach and is perfect for biking. More adventurous riders can pedal through town, up to the mission, or to Montecito, the next town over. **Beach Rentals,** 8 W. Cabrillo Blvd. (☎ **805/963-2524**), at State Street, rents well maintained one- and ten-speeds. They also have tandem bikes and surrey-cycles that can hold as many as four adults and two children. Rates vary depending on equipment. Bring an ID (driver's license or passport) to expedite your rental. Open daily from 8am to dusk.

GOLF The 18-hole **Santa Barbara Golf Club** course at 3500 McCaw Ave., at Las Positas Road (☎ **805/687-7087**), is 6,009 yards and encompasses a driving range. The golf shop and other nonplaying facilities were reconstructed and refurbished early in 1989. Unlike many municipal courses, the Santa Barbara Golf Course is well maintained and has been designed to present a good challenge for the average golfer. Greens fees are \$18 Monday through Friday, \$20 Saturday and Sunday; seniors pay \$13 weekdays, \$17 weekends. Optional carts cost \$20.

The 18-hole, 7,000-yard **Sandpiper,** 7925 Hollister Ave. (☎ **805/968-1541**), is a pretty oceanside course; it has a pro shop and driving range, plus a pleasant coffee shop. Greens costs are \$50 Monday through Friday, \$70 Saturday and Sunday. Carts cost \$22.

HIKING The hills and mountains surrounding Santa Barbara are riddled with excellent hiking trails. One of my favorites begins at the end of Mission Canyon Drive. Take Mission Canyon Road past the mission, turn right onto Foothill Road, and take the first left onto Mission Canyon Drive. Park at the end (where all the other cars are) and hike up. Purchase a trail map at the Santa Barbara Visitor Information Center or ask there for other trail information.

HORSEBACK RIDING Several area stables rent horses, including **San Ysidro Ranch Stables,** 900 San Ysidro Lane (☎ **805/969-5046, ext. 252**). They charge \$40 for a one-hour guided trail ride, and reservations are essential.

POWER BOATING & SAILING The **Sailing Center of Santa Barbara,** at the Santa Barbara Breakwater (☎ **805/962-2826**, or toll free **800/350-9090**), rents 40-horsepower boats and sailboats ranging from 13 to 50 feet. Both crewed and bare-boat charters are available by the day or hour. The center also offers sailing instruction for all levels of experience.

ROLLER SKATING At **Beach Rentals,** 8 W. Cabrillo Blvd. (☎ **805/963-2524**), you can rent conventional roller skates as well as Rollerblade in-line skates. The charge of $5 per hour includes wrist and knee pads.

SPORT FISHING, DIVING & WHALE WATCHING In the mood to do some fishing? **Sea Landing,** at the foot of Bath Street and Cabrillo Boulevard (☎ **805/963-3564**), makes regular sport fishing runs from specialized boats. They also offer a wide variety of other fishing and diving cruises. All boats are totally equipped with a stocked galley (food and drink served on board), and rental rods and tackle are available. Rates vary according to excursion, and reservations are recommended.

Whale-watching cruises are offered from February to the end of April, when the California gray whale makes its migratory journey from Baja, Mexico, to Alaska. Whale tours cost $22 for adults, $12 for children, and sightings of large marine mammals are guaranteed.

Shopping

State Street from the beach to Victoria Street is the city's chief commercial thoroughfare, and home to Santa Barbara's largest concentration of shops. Many of the stores here are tourist-oriented T-shirt and postcard shops, but there are still a few boutiques around. The best way to get to know the area is to walk; the entire stretch is less than a mile. If you get tired, hop on one of the city's free electric shuttle buses that run up and down State Street at regular intervals.

Brinkernoff Avenue, off Cota St., between Chapala and De La Vina Sts.

Santa Barbara's "antique alley" is packed with Victorian antique shops selling quilts, antique china, early American furnishings, jewelry, Orientalia, unusual memorabilia, bric-a-brac, and interesting junk. Most shops are open Tuesday through Sunday from 11am to 5pm.

El Paseo, 814 State St.

A picturesque shopping arcade, El Paseo is lined with stone walkways reminiscent of an old street in Spain. Built around the 1827 original adobe home of Spanish-born Presidio Commandante Jose de la Guerra, the mall is lined with charming shops and art galleries, each of which is worthy of a look.

Paseo Nuevo, State and Canon Perdido Sts.

Opened in mid-1990, this Spanish-style shopping mall in the heart of downtown is anchored by Nordstrom and The Broadway, two west coast–based department stores. Between these giant stores are smaller chain shops like The Sharper Image, Brentano's bookshop, and Express clothing store.

Where to Stay

VERY EXPENSIVE

★ **Four Seasons Biltmore,** 1260 Channel Dr., Santa Barbara, CA 93108. ☎ **805/969-2261,** or toll free **800/332-3442.** Fax 805/969-4682. 234 rms, 24 suites. A/C MINIBAR TV TEL **Directions:** From U.S. 101, exit onto Olive Mill Road, which turns into Channel Drive to the hotel.

Rates: $295–$360 single or double; from $595 suite. Special midweek and package rates are available. AE, DC, MC, V. **Parking:** $10.

The most elegant hotel in town is also one of the most prestigious hotels in California. The hotel's beautiful 21 acres of gardens front a private ocean beach. When the Biltmore opened in 1927, a concert orchestra played twice daily in the dining room, and separate quarters were available for personal servants accompanying guests. Although those days are long gone, the emphasis here is still on service.

Designed by Reginald Johnson, the hotel's award-winning Spanish architecture contains Portuguese, Basque, Iberian, and Moorish elements in a graceful combination of arcades, winding staircases, patios, and walkways, with lovely hand-painted Mexican tiles and grillwork throughout. The beauty of the estate is further enhanced by imposing views of the Pacific Ocean, the Santa Ynez Mountains, and the hotel's own palm-studded formal gardens. Updated with a $16-million renovation in 1988, this refined resort hotel features deluxe accommodations with plush, Iberian-style furnishings. Many of the rooms have romantic Spanish balconies and/or fireplaces, and some have private patios. All have ceiling fans and individual climate controls, as well as terry-cloth robes and hairdryers. Cottage suites are set back on the property and are as private as they are elegant.

Dining/Entertainment: La Marina restaurant offers elegant dining and a select list of California-inspired specialties such as their award-winning bouillabaisse with live Maine lobster, and lamb loin in puffed pastry, minted couscous, and natural jus. The patio, a glass-enclosed atrium, is more casual, serving breakfast, lunch, dinner, and Sunday brunch. Afternoon tea and evening cocktails are served in the La Salsa lounge. There's live piano music nightly.

Services: Concierge, 24-hour room service, evening turndown, overnight shoeshine, exercise classes, complimentary bicycle rental, video library, and special programs for children.

Facilities: Three lighted tennis courts, two swimming pools, 2 health clubs, putting green, shuffleboard and croquet courts, beachfront cabanas, sun deck, beauty salon, and gift shop.

★ **San Ysidro Ranch,** 900 San Ysidro Lane (off U.S. 101), Santa Barbara, CA 93108. ☎ **805/969-5046,** or toll free **800/368-6788.** Fax 805/565-1995. 45 cottages, 26 suites. MINIBAR TV TEL **Directions:** From U.S. 101, take the San Ysidro Lane exit and turn toward the mountains. Follow the road for about 2 miles to the ranch.

Rates: $225–$375 double; $475–$550 cottage room. AE, MC, V.

Since 1940, when Vivien Leigh and Sir Lawrence Olivier were married here, San Ysidro Ranch has won raves as one of southern California's most distinguished hotels. Its coveted location, at the top of a deceptively modest foothill road, is The Ranch's primary charm. Surrounded by tall oaks and gracious willows, the hotel feels as private as it is beautiful. Over the years, Winston Churchill, Sinclair Lewis, Rex Harrison, Groucho Marx, and Sidney Poitier have all signed the register at this quiet, beautifully landscaped 540-acre retreat. In 1953, John F. Kennedy and his bride Jacqueline chose to honeymoon here for a week.

The Ranch, as it is known locally, is Santa Barbara's top-rated hideaway hotel. Opened in 1893, The Ranch is comprised of about a dozen free-standing cottages nestled near the base of their own private mountain. Rooms are decorated with charming country inn–style antique furnishings. All have working fireplaces, most have private decks or patios, and some have outdoor hot tubs. Weddings are commonplace here, and are held most weekends amidst truly magnificent jasmine and honeysuckle-edged gardens that explode with year-round color.

Dining/Entertainment: The Stonehouse restaurant, in the old citrus-packing house, is a charming candlelit dining room with a beamed ceiling, shuttered windows, antique furnishings, and paintings of local landmarks adorning the white sandstone walls. A delightful and airy glass-enclosed cafe area adjoins, its view of the grounds enhanced by many hanging plants inside. The Plow and Angel bar is a good place for drinks. It draws a local crowd and features live music on the weekends.

Services: Room service, concierge.

Facilities: Two tennis courts, swimming pool, riding stables, badminton, croquet, and hiking and riding trails.

EXPENSIVE

★ **Upham,** 1404 De La Vina St., Santa Barbara, CA 93101. ☎ **805/962-0058,** or toll free **800/727-0876.** Fax 805/963-2825. 49 rms, 3 suites. TV TEL **Directions:** From U.S. 101, exit at Mission Street and turn right onto De La Vina Street. The hotel is 6 blocks ahead at Sola Street.

Rates (including continental breakfast): $100–$185 single or double, from $200 suite. Additional person $10. AE, CB, DC, DISC, MC, V.

Established in 1871, The Upham, located in the heart of town just two blocks from State Street, is one of the oldest hotels in Santa Barbara. It is also one of the most charming. Built by Amasa Lyman Lincoln, a Boston banker, the Upham's bed-and-breakfast design is reminiscent of an old-fashioned New England boarding house. A two-story clapboard structure, it has wide eaves and is topped by a glassed-in cupola and a widow's walk that faces the sea.

Fronted by a pair of immense ivy-entwined palms, the entrance is through a large colonnaded porch surrounded by a well-tended garden with neat flowerbeds. Refurbished in 1983, guest rooms are outfitted with antique armoires, brass or four-poster beds, and pretty pillow shams. Many rooms have private porches and fireplaces. The Master Suite features a fireplace, Jacuzzi, private yard, and king-size bed.

Complimentary wine, cheese, and crackers are served in the lobby and garden each afternoon. Louie's at the Upham, a cozy restaurant, is open for lunch and dinner.

MODERATE

Bath Street Bed and Breakfast Inn, 1720 Bath St., Santa Barbara, CA 93101. ☎ **805/882-9680,** or toll free **800/788-BATH, 800/549-BATH** in California. 10 rms. **Directions:** From U.S. 101, exit at Mission Street: turn right on De La Vina, then right on Valerio, and right again onto Bath Street.

Rates (including breakfast): $90–$150 single or double. AE, MC, V.

This handsome Queen Anne Victorian was built over a hundred years ago. The historic residence has two unusual features—a semicircular "eyelid" balcony and a hipped roof, unique even for Santa Barbara. The century-old trees, the flower-filled patio with white wicker furniture, and the brick courtyard add to the inn's charm, as does the graciousness of the innkeepers.

The living room is the heart of this home, comfortable and inviting, with a fireplace, Oriental rug, period prints, and fresh flowers. The dining area has a traditional blue-and-white floral-print paper that complements the finely crafted woodwork and furnishings.

Each individually decorated room has its own unique charm. One features a king-size canopied bed, from another under the eaves you can enjoy superb sunsets from a private balcony. Two new rooms, located in the Summer House, have fireplaces and one has a private Jacuzzi. Guests enjoy breakfasts of homemade granola with fruit and yogurt, egg frittatas with scones, or peach-topped cheese-stuffed French toast, as well as complimentary afternoon tea and evening refreshments, and access to the inn's bicycles. Pets are not accepted, and no smoking is allowed in the house.

Best Western Encina Lodge, 2220 Bath St., Santa Barbara, CA 93105. ☎ **805/682-7277,** or toll free **800/526-2262.** Fax 805/563-9319. 121 rms, 38 suites. A/C TV TEL **Directions:** From U.S. 101, exit at Mission Street and turn left onto Bath Street. The hotel is two blocks ahead at Los Olivos Street.

Rates: $102–$112 single; $106–$118 double; suite from $116. Additional person $6 AE, CB, DC, MC, V.

Set in a quiet residential area, this hotel is a short walk from the mission and a mere five-minute drive from the beach. All rooms are immaculate and tastefully decorated. Soft goods—furnishings, bedspreads, rugs—all look spanking new. Second-floor accommodations in the old building, outfitted with beamed raw-pine ceilings, are best. All rooms come with coffee makers, hairdryers, fresh fruit, candies, and cookies. Old-wing rooms have showers only; the rest have tub/shower combinations and dressing rooms.

Facilities include a swimming pool, whirlpool, sauna, lobby shop, beauty parlor, and barbershop. Additionally, there is complimentary airport and Amtrak pick-up. The ever-changing menu in the hotel restaurant might feature scallops sautéed in white wine and butter, a stuffed pork chop, or champagne chicken.

Miramar Hotel-Resort, 1535 S. Jameson Lane (P.O. Box 429), Montecito, CA 93102. ☎ **805/969-2203.** Fax 805/969-3163. 200 rms. A/C TV TEL **Directions:** From U.S. 101, take the San Ysidro exit and turn toward the ocean; Jameson Lane parallels the freeway right near the overpass.

Rates: $75–$145 single or double; from $130 cottage suite. AE, MC, V.

The Miramar's blue-roofed cottages, which can be seen from U.S. 101, have long been a famous Santa Barbara landmark. Actually located in Montecito, a ritzy area just south of Santa Barbara, the hotel dates from 1887, when the Doulton family began to augment their meager farm income by taking in paying guests. When a railroad was built, the property was split in two. The Miramar became an important rail station as affluent guests began arriving in their own private railroad cars. As the popularity of beach and ocean vacations grew, the hotel became a very chic place to stay.

The modern Miramar is set on 14 garden acres overlooking the Pacific Ocean. Guest room furnishings are indifferent at best, but accommodations are nevertheless comfortable. The best rooms are those on the second floor facing the ocean. Some of the attractive, homey cottages have fully equipped kitchens.

Facilities include two swimming pools, four tennis courts, a paddle-tennis court, 500 feet of private sandy beach, saunas, exercise rooms, bike rental, and table tennis. Golf and horseback riding are nearby. The dated Terrace Dining Room, filled with potted palms, is open for breakfast, lunch, and dinner. Sandwiches, salads, steaks, and seafood are featured. The Railroad coffee shop serves late breakfast and lunch. There's live music Tuesday through Saturday nights.

INEXPENSIVE

Franciscan Inn, 109 Bath St., Santa Barbara, CA 93101. ☎ **805/963-8845.** Fax 805/564-3295. 53 rms, 25 suites. TV TEL **Directions:** From U.S. 101, take the Castillo Street exit and turn toward the water, then turn left onto Mason Street and drive one block to the hotel.

Rates (including continental breakfast): $65–$155 single or double; from $100 suite. Extra person $8. AE, CB, DC, MC, V.

This excellent buy is just off Cabrillo Boulevard, one short block from the marina and beach. Each individually decorated room is airy, comfortable, and spacious; most have ceiling fans. Bathrooms come stocked with fat, fluffy towels. Several rooms have fully equipped kitchenettes. Suites are bi-level affairs, complete with a living room, a separate kitchen, and sleeping quarters that can accommodate up to four adults. One suite also has a fireplace.

Breakfast is served in the comfortable lobby. The inn is just steps from several area restaurants for other meals. There's also a heated swimming pool, Jacuzzi, and coin-operated laundry, and complimentary newspapers are distributed each morning. Reservations should be made well in advance, especially if you're traveling from May through September.

Tropicana Inn and Suites, 223 Castillo St., Santa Barbara, CA 93101. ☎ **805/966-2219,** or toll free **800/468-1988.** Fax 805/962-9428. 17 rms, 38 suites. TV TEL **Directions:** From U.S. 101, exit at Castillo Street and turn toward the water; the hotel is two blocks ahead between Montecito and Yanonali Streets.

Rates (including continental breakfast): $82–$122 single or double; $112–199 suite. Extra person $5. AE, CB, DC, DISC, MC, V.

This newly renovated pink stucco structure is just a short walk from the beach. Rooms are homey and attractive and equipped with AM/FM radios and refrigerators. Suites, which have a large bedroom and living room, sleep up to eight adults. They also have large eat-in kitchens that are fully equipped, right down to eggbeaters and potholders, not to mention ovens, full-size refrigerators, and toasters. Suites can be economical if you use them to do your own cooking. Facilities include a heated pool and Jacuzzi, both away from the street and very private, with lots of room for sunning. No smoking is allowed in any of the rooms.

BUDGET

Motel 6, 443 Corona del Mar, Santa Barbara, CA 93103. ☎ **805/564-1392.** 52 rms. TV TEL **Directions:** From U.S. 101, exit at Milpas Street and head toward the ocean, then turn left, drive one short block, then turn left again onto Corona del Mar.

Rates: $43 single; $47 double. Extra adult $7. AE, DISC, MC, V.

Inexpensive, clean accommodations near the beach are not easy to find, but this basic motel fits the bill. There's a small, heated swimming pool, cable color TVs, and no charge is made for local phone calls. Be sure to reserve far in advance, as this motel gets booked up quickly.

Motel 6, 3505 State St., Santa Barbara, CA 93105. ☎ **805/687-5400.** 60 rms. TV TEL **Directions:** From U.S. 101, exit at Mission Street and turn left onto State Street; the motel is about one mile ahead, between Las Positas and Hitchcock Way.

Rates: $44 single; $48 double. Extra adult $6. AE, CB, DC, DISC, MC, V.

On "upper" State Street, this property's location is not as desirable as those by the beach. But it is nice, featuring a large pool, and there is plentiful shopping nearby.

Mountain View Inn, 3055 De La Vina St., Santa Barbara, CA 93105. ☎ **805/687-6636.** 34 rms. TEL TV **Directions:** From U.S. 101, exit at Mission Street, turn toward the hills, and left onto State Street; the hotel is located about 10 blocks ahead, at the corner of State and De La Vina Streets.

Rates (including continental breakfast): Oct–May $60–$75 single or double; Jun–Aug $75–$87 single or double. Two-night stays are required on weekends. AE, DISC, MC, V.

Although it occupies a busy streetcorner, close to shops, sights, and restaurants, this well-priced inn maintains a hometown bed-and-breakfast atmosphere. Each room is individually decorated; some with lace tablecloths and ruffled pillow shams and matching comforters. Accommodations are bright and cheery, and are outfitted with both niceties and necessities like fresh flowers and small refrigerators. The inn surrounds a large, heated swimming pool, and is adjacent to a small park, complete with a children's playground.

Coffee, tea, fresh juice, and croissants are served each morning in the lobby.

Sandpiper Lodge, 3525 State St., Santa Barbara, CA 93105. ☎ **805/687-5326.** Fax 805/687-2271. 75 rms. TV TEL **Directions:** From U.S. 101, take the Las Positas exit and turn towards the mountains, then turn left onto State Street, and look for the motel on your left.

Rates: Oct–Jun $48–$58 single or double, $53–$63 triple; July–Aug $58–$68 single or double, $63–$73 triple. Weekly and monthly rates available. AE, CB, DC, MC, V.

Modest accommodations are counterbalanced by low rates, making this small hotel one of Santa Barbara's best buys. Nothing's fancy here, but the rooms are clean, and tastefully, if sparsely decorated. The lodge's "upper" State Street location means you'll have to drive to the beach and downtown shopping areas, but both are just 10 minutes away.

Coffee and tea are available all day, and some rooms include small refrigerators. There is also a swimming pool on the premises.

Where to Dine

MODERATE

Brophy Bros. Clam Bar & Restaurant, yacht basin and marina. ☎ **805/966-4418.**

Cuisine: SEAFOOD. **Reservations:** Not accepted. **Directions:** From Stearns Wharf, drive west on Cabrillo Boulevard past the Castillo Street traffic light, then turn left at the first light, which is Harbor Way; Brophy Bros. is a short walk along the yacht basin, on the second floor of the small light-gray building ahead on your right.
Prices: Appetizers $5.50–$9.50; main courses $7–$16. AE, MC, V.
Open: Sun–Thurs 11am–10pm, Fri–Sat 11am–11pm.

I am reluctant to tell even more people about one of my favorite restaurants in Santa Barbara. First-class seafood is served in beautiful surroundings that overlook the city's pretty marina from a second-floor location. The restaurant is a fun, friendly, noisy, convivial mix of locals and tourists almost every night of the week. Dress is very casual, service is excellent, and it's hard to beat the view of fishing boats, sailboats, and power launches. There are two dozen tables, and about 20 seats fronting an open oyster bar. Most of the chairs are always occupied, and the wait on a weekend night can be two hours long.

Portions are huge, and everything on the menu is good. Favorites include New England clam chowder, cioppino (California fish stew), and any one of an assortment of seafood salads. The scampi is consistently good, as are the tuna, shark, swordfish, salmon, and any fresh fish. A good assortment of beers and wines is available.

Joe's Cafe, 536 State St. ☎ **805/966-4638.**

Cuisine: AMERICAN. **Reservations:** Recommended, but not accepted Sat. **Directions:** From Stearns Wharf, drive up State Street; the restaurant is on your right at Cota Street.
Prices: Appetizers $2–$5; main courses $7–$19. AE, MC, V.
Open: Mon–Sat 11am–11pm, Sun 4–11pm.

Joe's food is not great, but there's something about this straightforward American eatery that's very appealing. Maybe it's the mixed drinks, some of the city's strongest. One of downtown's longest lived institutions, Joe's has been offering good home-cooking since 1928. Southern-style fried chicken, hefty 12-ounce charbroiled steaks, and pan-fried rainbow trout are menu staples. The ravioli is terrible, but addicting. And every Wednesday seems like Thanksgiving, as the kitchen turns out plate after plate of turkey, mashed potatoes, cranberry sauce, and stuffing.

The decor is as down home as the food; red-and-white-checked tablecloths, captain's chairs, mounted hunting trophies, and photos of old Santa Barbara on the walls. No desserts are served. "We give them enough starch without it," explains the owner.

Mousse Odile, 18 E. Cota St. ☎ **805/962-5393.**

Cuisine: FRENCH. **Reservations:** Accepted. **Directions:** From Stearns Wharf, drive up State Street and turn right onto Cota Street, 3 blocks past the U.S. 101 underpass.
Prices: Breakfast $4–$7; appetizers $4–$7; main courses $13.25–$17; lunch $4.25–$9.79. AE, MC, V.
Open: Breakfast Mon–Sat 8–11:30am; lunch Mon–Sat 11:30am–2:30pm; dinner Mon–Thurs 5:30–9pm, Fri–Sat 5–9:30pm.

The restaurant's brasserie side, nicely outfitted with oak flooring, red-and-blue checked tablecloths, and fresh flowers, is the setting for breakfasts and lunches. It's not fancy, though it does have a pleasant, simple French-provincial air. There's a bar along one wall, and a refrigerated case and counter to the rear.

Various quiches, waffles with crème anglaise (a delicious light custard sauce), and a variety of omelets are served with French bread, applesauce, and potatoes au gratin. Most *spécialtiés de la maison* are also served with fresh fruit—slices of banana, orange, and strawberries. Giant croissants can be ordered separately, along with one of the best cups of French roast coffee you've ever had. Lunch choices include cold pasta salad with smoked salmon and peas, and foot-long Parisian sandwiches of roast lamb or chicken and white veal sausage.

The simple, slightly formal adjoining dining room opens in the evening for dinner. An outdoor patio is open on balmy nights. The wood-and-window interior is illuminated by art deco lamps and brightened with green plants, fresh flowers, and candles on every table. Leg of lamb, roasted with garlic and herbs, is especially recommended. Other offerings might include Norwegian salmon poached in champagne and port wine, or filet mignon with pepper sauce and cognac. Appetizers include julienned celery root in mustard sauce, and marinated mussels or warm smoked salmon with pasta, caviar, and chives. There is a full bar, and a good selection of Californian and French wines is available. By the way, save room for dessert; mousse is the restaurant's specialty.

Oysters, Victoria Court, 9 W. Victoria St. ☎ **805/962-9888.**

Cuisine: CALIFORNIAN. **Reservations:** Recommended. **Directions:** From Stearns Wharf, drive up State Street and turn left onto Victoria Street, 10 blocks past the U.S. 101 underpass; the restaurant is immediately on your left.
Prices: Appetizers $4–$14; main courses $9–$17 at dinner, $6–$11 at lunch. AE, DC, DISC, MC, V.
Open: Lunch Mon–Sat 11:30am–2:30pm; dinner Tues–Sun 5–10pm; Sun brunch 10am–2:30pm.

Hidden behind lush bushes near the corner of State Street, Oysters' small, oddly shaped, window-wrapped dining room provides some of the best food in the city. Despite its name, the restaurant is not a shellfish bar; it's a select survey of Californian cuisine offered by Jerry and Laurie Wilson, a brother and sister team. Still, oyster appetizers are on the menu: grilled with cilantro butter, chopped into corn fritters, and stewed with spinach and shallots. Pasta, chicken, and veal main dishes are also available, but the best main meals are usually the daily fresh market specials like poached trout with salmon mousse, and saffron rice with Cajun sausage, lobster, and scallops. Desserts here are predictably decadent, but even the richest-looking chocolate torte should be passed up for the restaurant's home-churned ice cream.

Palace Cafe, 8 E. Cota St. ☎ **805/966-3133.**

Cuisine: CAJUN/CREOLE/CARIBBEAN. **Reservations:** Recommended. **Directions:** From Stearns Wharf, drive up State Street and turn right onto Cota Street, 3 blocks past the U.S. 101 underpass.
Prices: Appetizers $3.50–$8.50; main courses $12–$22. AE, MC, V.
Open: Dinner Sun–Thurs 5:30–10pm, Fri–Sat 5:30–11pm.

The Cajun-style Palace Cafe enhanced its reputation when it became a regular stop for the press corps that followed President Reagan to this nearby ranch. Both the food and atmosphere are far more casual than the prices. Terminally busy, the restaurant is divided into two similar rooms, both of which include high ceilings, overhead fans, simple wood tables, bentwood chairs, and various posters and paintings.

Tables are each topped with a huge bottle of Tabasco sauce, followed by a basket of hot muffins, including cheddar corn jalapeño. Favorite starters: Cajun popcorn (Louisiana crayfish tails dipped in cornmeal-buttermilk batter and flash fried), and Cuban black bean soup. Main courses emphasize seafood. Louisiana Bar-B-Que shrimp are sautéed with three-pepper butter and served with white rice. An assortment of blackened fish and filet mignon is served with a side of browned garlic butter. Although it's not on the menu, vegetarians should ask for the vegetable platter; it's terrific. For dessert, the tart, tasty Key lime pie is unusually good. Although the restaurant apparently has a liquor license, they offer only a single, nasty drink: the spicy-hot "Cajun" martini. Stick to beer and wine.

Pan e Vino, 1482 East Valley Road, Montecito. ☎ **969-9274.**

Cuisine: ITALIAN. **Reservations:** Recommended.
Prices: Appetizers $4–$9; pastas $8–$10; meat and fish $10–$18. No credit cards.
Open: Mon–Sat 11:30am–9:30pm, Sun 5–9:30pm.

Allow me to wax philosophical about my favorite restaurant in Santa Barbara, the perfect Italian trattoria. The food here is as good as what you'd serve in Rome, and the surroundings are far better. The simplest dish—spaghetti topped with basil-tomato sauce—is so delicious it's hard to understand why diners would want to distract their tastebuds with more complicated concoctions. Yet numerous tastings have proved that this kitchen is capable of most anything. A whole artichoke appetizer—steamed, chilled, and filled with breading and marinated tomatoes—is absolutely fantastic. Pasta puttanesca, with tomatoes, anchovies, black olives, and capers, is always tops, as are the nightly risotto, meat, and fish selections. Pan e Vino gets high marks for its terrific food, attentive service, and authentic and casual atmosphere. Although many diners prefer to eat outside, beneath heat lamps and a tarp on the restaurant's intimate patio, my favorite tables are inside, where waiters scurry between tables with obvious professional experience. The only drawback to this restaurant of superlatives is that they don't accept credit cards—but there's an ATM around the corner.

★ **Piatti's Ristorante,** 516 San Ysidro Rd. ☎ **805/969-7520.**

Cuisine: ITALIAN. **Reservations:** Recommended. **Directions:** From Stearns Wharf, take Cabrillo Boulevard east to U.S. 101, exit at San Ysidro Road, and follow toward the mountains about a half mile to the restaurant.
Prices: Appetizers $4–$8; main courses $8–$18. AE, MC, V.
Open: Sun–Thurs 11:30am–10pm, Fri–Sat 11:30am–11pm.

One of the area's best Italian restaurants is located 10 minutes south of downtown Santa Barbara, in the exclusive residential hideaway of Montecito. During warm weather, the best seats are at the faux marble–topped tables set under handsome cream-colored umbrellas on the outdoor patio.

The spacious interior is airy, comfortable, and relaxed. Everything is attractive here, from the small bar, to the exhibition kitchen, to the upscale good-looking clientele. The dining room has a polished country look, complete with pine sideboards, wall murals, and terra-cotta-tile floors.

Exceptional appetizers include fried calamari with spicy aioli sauce, fresh sweetbreads with porcini mushrooms, and parma prosciutto served with fresh fruit and parmesan cheese. Featured main dishes include homemade ravioli filled with spinach and ricotta cheese and served with a creamy lemon sauce, and lasagna al pesto—with layers of pasta, pesto, grilled zucchini, sun-dried tomatoes, pine nuts, and cheeses. Both are rich, but delicious. A specialty of the house is oak-wood-roasted chicken with roasted rosemary potatoes and vegetables.

There is an excellent selection of Californian and Italian wines. Many are available by the glass. There's also a full bar.

Paradise Cafe, 702 Anacapa St. ☎ **805/962-4416.**

Cuisine: AMERICAN. **Reservations:** Accepted for large parties. **Directions:** From Stearns Wharf, drive up State Street and turn right onto Ortega Street, five blocks past the U.S. 101 underpass: the restaurant is located one block from State Street on the corner of Ortega and Anacapa Streets.
Prices: Breakfast $4–$7; appetizers $4–$7; main courses $6–$18; lunch $5–$9. AE, MC, V.

White linen tablecloths and blondwood floors give this converted home a relaxed elegance that seems like quintessential Santa Barbara. The most coveted seats, however, are outside, on the open brick patio behind tall hedges and colorful wildflowers.

Excellent salmon, swordfish, half-pound burgers, and 22-oz. T-bone steaks are prepared on an open oak grill. Devoid of heavy sauces, meals here are consistently fresh and simple. Paradise Pie, an extremely decadent chocolate dessert, is an absolute must. The downstairs bar is well-known for strong drinks, and is especially popular with the local thirty-something crowd.

Your Place, 22A N. Milpas St. ☎ **805/956-5151.**

Cuisine: THAI. **Reservations:** Recommended. **Directions:** From Stearns Wharf, take Cabrillo Boulevard east and turn left onto Milpas Street; the restaurant is about one mile ahead on your right at Mason Street.
Prices: Appetizers $3–$7; main courses $5–$13. AE, DC, MC, V.
Open: Tues–Thurs and Sun 11am–10pm, Fri–Sat 11am–11pm.

There are an unusually large number of Thai restaurants in Santa Barbara; but when locals argue about which is best, Your Place invariably places high on the list. In addition to a tank of exotic fish, carved screens, and a serene Buddha, the restaurant's decor includes an impressive array of framed blowups of restaurant reviews.

Traditional dishes are prepared with distinctively fresh ingredients and represent a veritable survey of Thai cuisine. Over 100 menu listings include lemongrass soups, spicy salads, coconut curries, meat and seafood main dishes, and a variety of noodles. It's best to begin with soup, ladled out of a hotpot tableside, and enough for two or more. Tom kah kai, a hot-and-sour chicken soup with coconut milk and mushrooms is excellent. Siamese duckling, a top main dish, is prepared with sautéed vegetables, mushrooms, and ginger sauce. Like other dishes, it can be made mild, medium, hot, or very hot, according to your specifications. The restaurant serves wine, sake, beer, and a variety of non-alcoholic drinks, including hot ginger tea.

BUDGET

Andersen's Danish Bakery and Restaurant, 1106 State St. ☎ **805/962-5085.**

Cuisine: DANISH. **Reservations:** Accepted. **Directions:** From Stearns Wharf, drive up State Street; the restaurant is on your right, near Figueroa Street.
Prices: Breakfast $4–$9; lunches $5–$10. No credit cards.
Open: Wed–Mon 8am–6pm.

Only tourists eat here, but this small place is eminently suited to people-watching or reading the day's paper. You'll spot it by the red-and-white Amstel umbrellas protecting the outside diners seated on wrought-iron garden chairs. Even mid-November can be warm enough to eat outdoors at 9am.

The food is both good and well presented. Portions are substantial and the coffee is outstanding. A set breakfast includes eggs, bacon, cheese, fruit, homemade jam, and fresh-baked bread. Fresh fruit is also available.

For lunch, try soup and a sandwich, or liver pâté and quiche. Vegetarians can opt for an omelet with Danish Havarti cheese, a vegetable sandwich, or a cheese plate with fruit. Fresh fish and smoked Scottish salmon are also usually available. A daily changing selection of European dishes may include Hungarian goulash, frikadeller (Danish meatballs), schnitzel, duckling, chicken with caper sauce, Danish meat loaf, and roast turkey with caramel-sautéed potatoes. But if you yearn for smörgåsbord, Andersen's is a first-rate choice. Wine is available by the bottle or glass; beer is also served.

Cuca's, 315 Meigs Rd. ☎ **966-5951.**

Cuisine: MEXICAN.
Prices: Tacos $2–$3, burritos $3–$4. No credit cards.
Open: Daily 10am–10pm.

Around lunchtime, when Cuca's becomes the de facto "anchor" store of a particularly dull stripmall, it's hard to find a single seat at any of the restaurant's half-dozen outdoor tables. Though they're uncommon only in size, Cuca's extra-large, brick-weight burritos are packed solid with chicken or beef, rice, beans, and avocado. The truly excellent vegetarian variation, made with stir-fried vegetables, suggests a giant Chinese eggroll, and would be heralded as "genius" if it appeared on one of Spago-owner Wolfgang Puck's menus.

Cuca's is located atop an elevated area of the city known as "The Mesa." There's a second Cuca's at 626 W. Micheltorena (☎ **962-4028**).

Don Pepe, 617 State St. ☎ **962-4495.**

Cuisine: MEXICAN.
Prices: Appetizers $2–$5; main courses $5–$8; tacos and burritos $2–$4; breakfast $3–$5. MC, V.
Open: Sun–Thurs 8am–11pm, Fri–Sat 8am–2am.

Don Pepe is not just another burrito joint. In fact, it's not a burrito joint at all. With the exception of taking customers' orders at the front counter, Don Pepe is a full-service restaurant, serving traditional Mexican entrées to Mexican and American workers, and precious few adventurous tourists.

Appetizers include nachos, guacamole, and chicken or pork soup. Entrées include whole fish cooked in garlic butter, chicken with mole sauce, and grilled shrimp with wine and olives. Every meal starts with complimentary freshly-made tortilla chips, and most come with rice, beans, and salad. Of course Don Pepe's can also make meat or fish burritos. My favorite—chicken mole—isn't on the menu, but is always available.

La Super-Rica Taqueria, 622 N. Milpas St. ☎ **805/963-4940.**

Cuisine: MEXICAN. **Reservations:** Not accepted. **Directions:** From Stearns Wharf, take Cabrillo Boulevard east and turn left onto Milpas Street; the restaurant is about two miles ahead on your right between Cota and Ortega Streets.
Prices: Main courses $3–$6. No credit cards.
Open: Sun–Thurs 11am–9:30pm, Fri–Sat 11am–10pm.

Following celebrity chef Julia Child's lead, several south coast aficionados have deemed this place the best Mexican restaurant in California. The food is good, but slightly overrated. Excellent soft tacos are the restaurant's real forte; filled with any combination of chicken, beef, cheese, cilantro, and spices, they make a good meal. My primary complaint about this place is that the portions are really small; you have to order two or even three items to get a filling meal.

There's nothing grand about La Super-Rica except the food. The plates are paper, the cups Styrofoam, and the forks plastic. Unadorned wooden tables and plastic chairs are arranged under an unappealing tent; think about ordering your food "to go" and then finding a pretty beachside bench.

Santa Barbara Roasting Company, 321 Motor Way. ☎ **962-0320.**

Prices: Coffee $1.25, pastries $1–$2. No credit cards.
Open: Daily 7am–midnight.

The RoCo is a morning ritual for what seems like half of Santa Barbara. And for good reason. The beans are freshly roasted on the premises, and your choice of regular or unleaded is served bottomless. This is the coffee I dream of when I'm away; unfortunately, I can't say the same for their cakey baked goods, which used to be better.

Woody's Beach Club and Cantina, 229 W. Montecito St. ☎ **805/963-9326.**

Cuisine: AMERICAN BARBECUE. **Reservations:** Not accepted. **Directions:** From Stearns Wharf, go one block west on Cabrillo Boulevard, turn right onto Chapala Street, then left onto Montecito Street.
Prices: Appetizers $2–$5; main courses $4–$18. MC, V.
Open: Mon–Sat 11am–11pm, Sun 11am–10pm.

This place is woody all right—sort of "early cowpoke," with real wood paneling, post-and-beam construction, wood booths, and wood-plank floors. Order at the counter just inside the door, have a seat, and wait for your number to be called. Barbecued chicken and ribs head the large menu. A variety of burgers, tacos, pizzas, chili by the bowl, and french fries round out the offerings. Woody's home-smoked meats smothered in sauce might not be the best barbecue in the world, but it is easily the best in town. Children's portions are also available. Popular with fraternity types, Woody's sells beer by the glass, jug, bucket, or bottle.

A second Woody's is located in nearby Goleta, at 5112 Hollister Ave. (☎ **805/967-3775**).

Evening Entertainment

THEATERS

Arlington Theater, 1317 State St. ☎ **805/963-4408.**

Now primarily a movie theater, the Arlington regularly augments its film schedule with big-name theater and musical performances. The theater's interior is designed to look like an outdoor Spanish plaza, complete with trompe l'oeil artwork and a shimmering ceiling that winks like thousands of stars. The ornate theater, opened in 1931 at the birth of the talking-picture era, quickly became Hollywood's testing ground for unreleased movies; big stars flocked to Santa Barbara to monitor audience reaction at sneak previews. Ticket prices range from $7 to $40. The box office is open Monday through Saturday from 9am to 6pm, and Sunday from 9am to 4pm.

Center Stage Theater, Chapala St. and De La Guerra St., upstairs at Paseo Nuevo. ☎ **805/963-0408.**

The city's newest stage is a "black box" theater that can transform seating and sets into innumerable configurations. It's an intimate space that is often booked by local talent performing plays, music, and comedy. Call to see what's on when you're in town. Ticket prices run from $6 to $12. The box office is open Wednesday through Saturday from noon to 6pm and one hour before showtime.

Lobero Theater, 33 E. Canon Perdido St. ☎ **805/963-0761.**

Built by Italian immigrant Guiseppi Lobero in 1872, Santa Barbara's largest playhouse bankrupted its owner and quickly fell into disrepair. Rebuilt in 1924, the beautiful Lobero has struggled from season to season, boasting a spotty career at best. Many famous actors have performed here, including Lionel Barrymore, Edward G. Robinson, Clark Gable, Robert Young, Boris Karloff, and Betty Grable. More recent productions have included the Martha Graham dance company, concert luminaries like Andrés Segovia, Arthur Rubinstein, and Leopold Stokowski.

The box office is open Monday through Friday from noon to 5:30pm.

Earl Warren Showgrounds, Las Positas Rd. and U.S. 101. ☎ **805/687-0766.**

Whether it be a rodeo, circus, or factory-outlet sale, something's always happening at this indoor/outdoor convention center. Banquets, antique shows, barbecues, rummage sales, flower shows, music festivals, horse shows, dances, and cat shows are just some of the regular annual offerings. The Santa Barbara Fair and Expo, Santa Barbara's own county fair, is held in April, and features a carnival, livestock competitions, and entertainment. Call to find out what's on when you're in town. Admission ranges from free to $20. Opening times vary with the event. Call for event information.

BARS & CLUBS

Beach Shack, 500 Anacapa St. ☎ **966-1634.**

Live local bands most every night of the week attract a good-looking college crowd. Tikihut–themed bars are located both inside and out, away from the busy dance floor. Open Tuesday to Sunday from 7pm to 2am.

Admission: Free–$5.

Joe's, 536 State St. ☎ **966-4638.**

Packed on weekend nights with college-age locals, Joe's is known for its particularly powerful drinks and attractive beachy crowd. Food is served at tables and booths until 11pm, but mingling at the adjacent bar is best. Open Monday to Saturday from 11am to 11pm, Sunday from 4 to 11pm.

Mel's, in the Paseo Neuvo Mall, 6 W. De La Guerra. ☎ **963-2211.**

There seems to be no stigma against hard drinking at this dive located in the heart of downtown. The compact bar attracts a good cross-section of regulars. Open daily from 7am to 2am.

Revival, 18 E. Ortega. ☎ **730-7383.**

Santa Barbara's most alternative nightclub enjoys a Los Angeles–style warehouse setting, and a mixed gay/straight crowd. Scantily-clad dancers excite a dance-oriented crowd. Under high ceilings are two bars, a pool table, an indoor fountain, and the largest dance floor in town. Regular theme nights are interspersed with occasional live local bands. Open Sunday, Monday, and Wednesday to Friday from 9pm to 2am; on Saturday, from 7:30pm to 2am.

Admission: Free–$5.

The Wildcat Lounge, 15 W. Ortega. ☎ **962-7970.**

Duncan Wesley's Wildcat Lounge is easily the most happening place in town. The excellent CD jukebox and intentional-kitsch decor attract local twenty- and thirty-somethings to a nightspot that otherwise amounts to little more than a good bar with interesting lighting and a pool table. Open daily from 4pm to 2am.

5 Ojai Valley

371 miles S of San Francisco, 61 miles N of Los Angeles

GETTING THERE • By Car From Santa Barbara, take U.S. 101 south to Calif. 150, one of California's most gorgeous roadways. From Los Angeles, take U.S. 101 north to Calif. 33, which meets Calif. 150 and runs into Ojai.

ESSENTIALS • Orientation The town of Ojai is just 32 miles southeast of Santa Barbara, across the bucolic Casitas Pass and past sparkling Lake Casitas. Calif. 150 is called Ojai Avenue in the town center and is the village's primary thoroughfare. The post office is the main landmark. There's not much to the town—the surrounding countryside is this area's chief draw.

• Information The **Ojai Valley Chamber of Commerce,** 338 E. Ojai Ave. (P.O. Box 1134), Ojai, CA 93023 (☎ **805/646-8126**), distributes free area maps, brochures, and the informative *Visitor's Guide to the Ojai Valley,* which lists scenic drives, galleries, and current events. The office is open Monday through Friday from 9:30am to 4:30pm, Saturday and Sunday from 10am to 4pm.

It would be a shame to visit Santa Barbara and miss the nearby Ojai (pronounced "O-high") Valley, just 32 miles southeast of Santa Barbara along Calif. 150. The drive alone is scenic enough to justify the trip, but there are some fun things to do once you arrive.

What to See & Do

Lake Casitas, Santa Ana Rd. ☎ **805/649-2233.**

Created by Casitas Dam, the lake has almost 100 miles of shoreline. Located midway between Ojai town and the Pacific Ocean, Casitas is a breathtakingly beautiful opalescent body of fresh water, great for swimming, boating, or fishing. Rowboats and small powerboats can be rented year round at the **boathouse** (☎ **805/649-2043**) and cost $21 and $44 per day, respectively. From Ojai town, take Calif. 150, turn right onto Santa Ana Road, and follow the signs to the recreation area.

Los Padres National Forest. ☎ **805/646-4348.**

More than 140 square miles of mountains just north of town are accessible by hiking trails. The forest encompasses mountainous terrain, flat fields, rolling valleys, and over 140 miles of streams. Contact the **Forest Service Office** or the **Ojai Valley Chamber of Commerce** for trail maps and hiking and camping information.

Valley of "Shangri-la"

When Ronald Coleman saw Shangri-la in the movie *Lost Horizon,* he was really in the Ojai Valley. To visit the breathtakingly beautiful spot where Coleman stood, drive east up the hill on Ojai Avenue and stop at the bench near the top. It's a good place for a picnic.

Where to Stay

VERY EXPENSIVE

Ojai Valley Inn, Country Club Dr., Ojai, CA 93023. ☎ **805/646-5511,** or toll free **800/422-6524.** Fax 805/646-7969. 207 rms, 15 suites. A/C MINIBAR TV TEL **Directions:** Take U.S. 101 to Calif. 33 north and continue for about 12 miles. Turn right at Country Club Drive.

Rates: $195–$260 single or double; from $345 suite. Children stay free in parents' room. Packages available. AE, DC, MC, V.

Surrounded by the Topa Topa mountain range—200 acres of lush, green rolling hills that were the setting for *Lost Horizon*—the handsome adobe complex features refreshingly modern guest rooms and contemporary facilities that include a championship golf course.

Many of the unusually spacious rooms and suites enjoy private fireplaces, and most have secluded terraces or balconies that open onto expansive views of the valley and the magnificent Sierra Madre. Most accommodations are fitted with sofas and writing desks. Soft goods such as spreads and drapes are southwestern in style. Added comforts include coffee makers, plush terry-cloth robes, and hairdryers.

Golf on the 18-hole, 6,258-yard course costs $76 for guests, plus an additional $14 per player for a cart. Tennis charges are $12 per hour. Special children's programs include a supervised play area and activities during peak holiday periods, including movies and western-style, counselor-managed cookouts.

Dining/Entertainment: The first-rate Vista Room serves American-style dishes such as coho salmon and grilled beef tenderloin (see "Where to Dine," below). Additional facilities include the Oak Grill and Terrace, and the Club Bar.

Services: Concierge, 24-hour room service, and evening turndown.

Facilities: An 18-hole championship golf course (par 70), eight hard-surface tennis courts (four lighted), two pools (including a 60-foot lap pool), fitness center with exercise room, whirlpool, sauna, steam room, jogging trails, complimentary bicycles.

MODERATE

Best Western Casa Ojai, 1302 Ojai Ave., Ojai, CA 93023. ☎ **805/646-8175,** or toll free **800/528-1234.** Fax 805/640-8247. 45 rms. A/C TV TEL **Directions:** From U.S. 101 north, take Calif. 150 into Ojai town, where it becomes Ojai Avenue. The hotel is located across from Soule Golf Course by Shady Lane.

Rates (including continental breakfast): $60–$90 single or double. AE, CB, DC, DISC, MC, V.

Every room in this comfortable hotel is air conditioned, has cable TV, and a coffee maker. The hotel is a two-level ranch-style casa and has a heated swimming pool and adjacent spa. It's well located near the heart of town, and nonsmoking rooms are available.

Where to Dine

EXPENSIVE

Ranch House, 102 Besant Rd. ☎ **805/646-2360.**

Cuisine: AMERICAN. **Reservations:** Required. **Directions:** From the downtown post office (at the traffic light), take Ojai Avenue west about three miles and then turn right onto Tico Road.

Prices: Appetizers $4–$9; main courses $19–$24. AE, DISC, MC, V.

Open: Brunch Sun 11am–1:30pm; lunch Wed–Sat 11:30am–1:30pm; dinner Wed–Sun seatings 6 and 8:30pm.

One of Ojai's best and most-beloved restaurants was started by Alan and Helen Hooker, who, because of their interest in the philosopher Krishnamurti, came to Ojai in 1949. They rented an old ranch house, which they then turned into a boarding house and restaurant. Today's eatery is no longer in that first rented building—it's moved to a prettier location surrounded by an orchard, a bamboo thicket, and herb and flower gardens. Lunch is served in the serene and tranquil garden from May through September; dinner is served year-round.

You can begin a meal here with an appetizer like chicken liver pâté, dig into a soup of curried mushrooms or Vietnamese chicken and crab, and then enjoy prime rib, crab voisin, chicken champagne, or fresh fish. All main dishes come with two fresh vegetables and three kinds of fresh-baked breads. Be sure to leave room for one of the delicious desserts: rum trifle, applesauce cake, lime cheesecake, or ice cream with a choice of special Ranch House toppings—fudge, green ginger, pomegranate, or fresh coconut.

The restaurant has received *Wine Spectator* magazine's Grand Award for an impressive wine list that features more than 600 domestic and imported types.

If you can't get enough of the Ranch House while you're there, you can pick up a loaf of fresh-baked bread from the bakery along with a copy of one of Alan Hooker's cookbooks.

★ **Wheeler Hot Springs and Restaurant,** 16825 Maricopa Hwy., Ojai. ☎ **805/646-8131.**

Cuisine: CALIFORNIAN. **Reservations:** Recommended. **Directions:** From downtown Ojai, take Calif. 33 north about seven miles to the springs.
Prices: Appetizers $7–$9; main courses $13–$22; set brunch $15; Sat hot tub brunch for two $45; Thurs–Fri and Sun hot tub dinner for two $72. AE, MC, V.
Open: Brunch Sat–Sun 10am–2:30pm; dinner Thurs–Sun 5–9:30pm.

This soothing restaurant and bath is the Ojai Valley's most famous resident. A regular stop for the area's rich and famous, Wheeler Hot Springs offers mineral baths and massages, as well as a terrific restaurant; after a tub and a rub, you can dig into a fine meal. The setting is rustic, with comfortable wood-and-wicker furniture and large fireplaces for the nippy days.

The emphasis is on health; the menu changes weekly to take advantage of fresh local herbs, fruits, nuts, seafood, and vegetables. Brunch offerings include artichoke Benedict topped with sun-dried tomato–hollandaise sauce, and warm yellowtail salad with raspberry dressing. Live music accompanies weekend dinners where you might find fresh whole-wheat spaghetti with smoked duck, or lamb baked in a puff pastry. This place is popular; reserve several days in advance for baths and meals.

Hot tub prices are $10 per half hour; a massage costs $36 per half hour, $50 per hour. The spa is open Monday to Thursday from 9am to 9pm, and Friday to Sunday from 9am to 10pm.

MODERATE

L'Auberge, 314 El Paseo. ☎ **805/646-2288.**

Cuisine: BELGIAN. **Reservations:** Required at dinner. **Directions:** From the post office (at the traffic signal), walk 4 blocks west on Ojai Avenue and then turn right on Rincon Street. The restaurant is 1 block ahead.
Prices: Appetizers $6–$8; main courses $15–$19; lunch $7–$9. AE, MC, V.
Open: Lunch Sat–Sun 11am–2:30pm; dinner Wed–Mon 5:30–9pm.

L'Auberge's dining room, which occupies the ground floor of an old house, meanders through several small rooms and out onto a delightful terrace with a lovely view. Owner Paul Franssen offers an array of crêpes (asparagus and mushroom, curried chicken) and omelets (cheese, mushroom, vegetable), along with salads and soups for brunch. Dinner can begin with an appetizer of snails in garlic butter or smoked salmon. Main courses are varied—from filet of sole amandine, to frogs' legs, to sweetbreads, to a filet of beef with mushrooms, tomatoes, and madeira sauce. And for dessert there's white- or dark-chocolate mousse, cheesecake, or crème caramel.

Vista Room, Ojai Valley Inn & Country Club, Country Club Dr. ☎ **805/646-5511.**

Cuisine: CALIFORNIAN. **Reservations:** Recommended at lunch and dinner.
Prices: Appetizers $4–$9; main courses $11–$23; fixed-price dinner $34; lunch $9–$15; Sun brunch $28.50. AE, MC, V.
Open: Breakfast daily 6:30–10:30am; lunch or brunch daily 11:30am–2:30pm; dinner daily 6–9:30pm.

A pleasant culinary adventure, either in the relaxed candlelit dining room or on the pretty terrace, the Vista Room, part of the Ojai Valley Inn & Country Club, serves three meals daily. The lunch menu is varied enough to satisfy most any taste, and includes an interesting selection of soups, sandwiches, and salads such as smoked chicken with baby greens and nuts. Simple hamburgers and more complicated seafood dishes like seared Norwegian salmon fettuccine are served alongside vegetarian dishes, which are always available.

Dinner at the Vista might start with Cajun chicken–stuffed mushroom caps and lead to broiled Atlantic salmon with steamed spinach, garlic, bacon, and mushrooms. Sunday buffet brunches are especially popular. The list of goodies is extensive: omelets, pasta, barbecue, all sorts of salads and desserts, plus an ice cream–sundae bar.

9

Los Angeles

LOS ANGELES IS A SEEMINGLY UNRELATED STRING OF SUBURBS IN SEARCH OF A CITY; A megalopolis sprawl connected by 1,500-plus miles of sluggish freeway. This promised land of sea, sand, and year-round sunshine filtering through the smog is the stomping ground of the stars, and the most status-conscious city in America.

The variety of lifestyles, activities, and places to see is mind boggling. Don't waste time trying to understand this pleasure-oriented paradox. Forget your preconceptions and discover L.A. for what it is—a glitzy, grimy, glittery, and gritty study in contemporary Americana.

1 Orientation

ARRIVING

BY PLANE Some 36 international airlines, and all major American carriers, serve the **Los Angeles International Airport** (LAX)—one of the most heavily trafficked in the world. Domestic airlines flying in and out of LAX include **Alaska Airlines** (toll free **800/426-0333**), **American Airlines** (toll free **800/433-7300**), **Delta Air Lines** (toll free **800/221-1212**), **Northwest Airlines** (toll free **800/447-4747**), **Southwest Airlines** (toll free **800/435-9792**), **Trans World Airlines** (toll free **800/221-2000**), **United Airlines** (toll free **800/241-6522**), and **USAir Express** (toll free **800/428-4322**).

Los Angeles International Airport [LAX] Most visitors who arrive by plane fly into Los Angeles International Airport—better known as LAX—situated oceanside, southwest of downtown L.A., between Santa Monica and Manhattan Beach. One of the largest airports in the world, LAX (☎ **310/646-5252**) contains eight terminals, including the Tom Bradley International Terminal, named for a former mayor who was a frequent overseas traveler on official city business. Despite its size, the airport has a rather straightforward, easy-to-understand design. Free blue-and-green striped shuttle buses connect the terminals, and Travelers Aid of Los Angeles operates booths in each of them.

To reach Santa Monica and other northern beach communities, exit the airport, turn left onto Sepulveda Boulevard, then follow the signs to Calif. 1, Pacific Coast Highway north.

To reach Huntington, Newport, and other southern beach communities, turn right, onto Sepulveda Boulevard, then follow the signs to Calif. 1, Pacific Coast Highway south.

To reach Beverly Hills or Hollywood, exit the airport via Century Boulevard, then take I-405 north to Santa Monica Boulevard.

To reach Downtown, exit the airport via Century Boulevard, then take I-405 north to I-10 east.

To reach Pasadena, exit the airport, turn right onto Sepulveda Boulevard south, then take I-105 east to I-110 north.

Airport Transportation All of the major American car rental firms operate off-site offices that are reached via free van or bus from outside each terminal. See "Getting Around," later in this chapter for a list of major rental car companies.

Taxis line up outside each terminal and rides are metered. Expect to pay about $25 to Downtown and Hollywood, $22 to Beverly Hills, $20 to Santa Monica, and $45 to Pasadena. These prices include a $2.50 service charge for rides originating at LAX.

What's Special About Los Angeles

Film and TV Studios

- Universal Studios Hollywood—more an amusement park than a backstage tour, but fun!
- Warner Brothers Studios, an intimate look into the world of television production.
- Game-show tapings—fun to watch, even more fun to participate in as a contestant.

Museums

- The J. Paul Getty Museum, reputedly the richest in the world.
- The Rancho La Brea Tar Pits, a prehistoric find in the center of one of the world's most contemporary cities.
- The *Queen Mary* and the *Spruce Goose*—one of the largest ships in the world sits next to the largest airplane in the world.

Hollywood Sights

- The Walk of Fame, where you can see your favorite stars honored on the world's most famous sidewalk.
- Mann's Chinese Theatre, with unusual architecture but best known for the stars' hand- and footprints (and sometimes noses) pressed in cement in the theater's forecourt.
- The HOLLYWOOD sign, internationally known symbol of the city of film.

Shopping

- Rodeo Drive, the poshest street in Beverly Hills, contains the city's most chic shops.
- Santa Monica's Third Street Promenade, fun shopping by the sea.
- Melrose Avenue, the place to go for youth-oriented, cutting-edge street fashions.
- Malls, where Los Angeles really shops.

Beaches

- Zuma Beach, Malibu's famous sea-front stretch is one of the largest and most popular in Los Angeles.
- Santa Monica, easy to get to and jam-packed on hot summer weekends.
- Southern beaches, great for swimming and sunning.

Theme Parks

- Disneyland, the most famous of them all, is the state's largest single tourist attraction.
- Knott's Berry Farm, close to Disneyland, really was a farm that almost accidentally became a theme park.

The city's new Metro Green Line, scheduled for completion by 1995, will connect LAX with Downtown L.A. Fares had not been set by press time.

Many city hotels provide free shuttles for their guests; ask about transportation when you make reservations. **Super Shuttle** (☎ **310/782-6600**), a private ride-sharing service, offers regularly scheduled minivans from LAX to any location in the city. The set fare can range from about $10 to $50, depending on your destination. When traveling to the airport, reserve your shuttle at least one day in advance.

Unless you're staying at one of the nearby airport hotels, taxis are not recommended; the cost of a taxi often seems more like a down payment on one.

The city's **RTD** buses also go to and from LAX from many parts of the city. Phone RTD Airport Information (☎ **800/252-7433**) for the schedules and fares. Free **Blue, Green,** and **White Airline Connections** shuttle buses (☎ **310/646-2911**) connect the terminals at LAX and stop in front of each ticket building. Special handicapped-accessible minibuses are also available.

Other Airports LAX is the city's largest airport, but Los Angeles is full of smaller regional airports that are usually easier to get to, and may be closer to your destination. To the north is the **Burbank-Glendale-Pasadena Airport,** 2627 N. Hollywood Way, Burbank (☎ **818/840-8830**); to the south are the **Long Beach Municipal Airport,** 4100 Donald Douglas Dr., Long Beach (☎ **310/421-8293**), and the **John Wayne Airport,** 19051 Airport Way North, Anaheim (☎ **714/252-5200**); and to the east is the **Ontario International Airport,** Terminal Way, Ontario (☎ **909/988-2700**).

BY TRAIN Service is provided by **Amtrak** to and from San Diego in the south and Oakland and Seattle in the north, as well as to and from points in between. Amtrak operates out of the station at 800 N. Alameda (☎ **213/683-6987**), on the north side of downtown L.A.

BY BUS The **Greyhound** bus system serves most cities in California. In Los Angeles, the main terminal is downtown at 1716 E. 7th St., a half block east of Alameda (☎ **213/629-8430**), a rather seedy part of the city. There are other Greyhound stations around L.A., but not all of them are serviced by interstate buses. If you are planning on arriving by bus, tell the operator where you want to go, and see if there's a stop closer to your destination.

BY CAR Almost all of the interstate highways that crisscross L.A. run right through the downtown area. From the east, you'll arrive on I-10, the San Bernardino Freeway. From the north or south, the most direct route is via I-5. You may wish to avoid the clogged downtown area entirely, in which case you should turn off I-5 onto I-405, which runs by LAX. Non-interstate entries include U.S. 101, which comes into the downtown area from Santa Barbara and the north; and Calif. 1, which follows the coast through Santa Monica.

TOURIST INFORMATION

The **Los Angeles Convention & Visitors Bureau,** 633 W. Fifth St., Suite 600, Los Angeles, CA 90071 (☎ **213/624-7300**), is the city's main source for information. Write for a free visitors kit. The bureau staffs a visitors information center at 685 S. Figueroa St., between Wilshire Blvd. and Seventh St., which is open Monday through Friday from 8am to 5pm and Saturday 8:30am to 5pm.

Many Los Angeles–area communities also run their own tourist offices. They are:

The **Visitor Information Center Hollywood,** The Janes House, 6541 Hollywood Blvd., Hollywood, CA 90028 (☎ **213/689-8822**), open Monday through Saturday from 9am to 5pm.

Beverly Hills Visitors Bureau, 239 S. Beverly Dr., Beverly Hills, CA 90212 (☎ **310/271-8174,** or toll free **800/345-2210**).

The **Hollywood Arts Council,** P.O. Box 931056, Dept. 1991, Hollywood, CA 90093 (☎ **213/462-2355**), distributes the free magazine *Discover Hollywood.* It contains good listings of the area's many theaters, galleries, music venues, and comedy clubs.

Long Beach Convention & Visitors Council, 1 World Trade Center, Ste. 300, Long Beach, CA 90831 (☎ **310/436-3645,** or toll free **800/452-7829**).

Marina del Rey Chamber of Commerce, 14014 Tahiti Way, Marina del Rey, CA 90292 (☎ **310/821-0555**).

Pasadena Convention & Visitors Bureau, 171 S. Los Robles Ave., Pasadena, CA 91101 (☎ **818/795-9311,** fax 818/795-9656).

Santa Monica Convention and Visitors Bureau, 2219 Main St., Santa Monica, CA 90405 (☎ **310/393-7593**). The Santa Monica Visitors Center is located near the Santa Monica Pier, at 1400 Ocean Ave.

CITY LAYOUT

Downtown Los Angeles lies about 12 miles east of the Pacific Ocean on a direct line with the coastal town of Santa Monica. This is the city's primary business district, but by no means its only one. Greater Los Angeles is an untamed urban sprawl that radiates out from the downtown area in an ever-increasing number of suburbs. A vast network of freeways links the separate districts to each other and to the rest of the state.

MAIN ARTERIES & STREETS The city's main arteries are freeways that crisscross L.A. in a complicated maze. U.S. 101 runs across L.A. from the San Fernando Valley to the center of downtown. Interstate 5 bisects the city on its journey from San Francisco to San Diego. I-10 connects the downtown area with Santa Monica and nearby beach areas. And I-405 skirts the downtown area completely, connecting the San Fernando Valley with LAX and the city's southern beach areas.

Hollywood, located northwest of downtown, is best serviced by the Hollywood Freeway (U.S. 101). Beverly Hills, which adjoins Hollywood on the southwest, is best reached by taking the Hollywood Freeway from the Civic Center to Santa Monica Boulevard.

Wilshire Boulevard, L.A.'s main drag, connects the downtown area with Beverly Hills, then continues on through Westwood en route to Santa Monica. As Wilshire Boulevard enters Beverly Hills, it intersects La Cienega Boulevard. The portion of La Cienega that stretches north from Wilshire Boulevard to Santa Monica Boulevard is known as Restaurant Row.

Hollywood's Sunset Boulevard, between Laurel Canyon Boulevard and La Brea Avenue is the famed Sunset Strip. Just north of the strip lies the equally famous Hollywood Boulevard.

Farther north still, via the Hollywood Freeway, is the San Fernando Valley; here you'll find Universal City. A right turn on the Ventura Freeway takes you to downtown Burbank.

Venice, the yacht-filled harbors of Marina del Rey, and the Los Angeles International Airport (LAX) are located on Calif. 1, south along the shore from Santa Monica.

FINDING AN ADDRESS Use a map—there's no other way. It's important to know which area of the city the address you're looking for is located. When you know, for instance, that the hotel is in Santa Monica, finding it is much easier. For that reason, all Los Angeles addresses in this guide either include the city area or are listed under a helpful heading.

Neighborhoods In Brief

Hollywood The legendary city where actresses once posed with leashed leopards is certainly on everyone's must-see list. Unfortunately, the glamour—what's left of it—

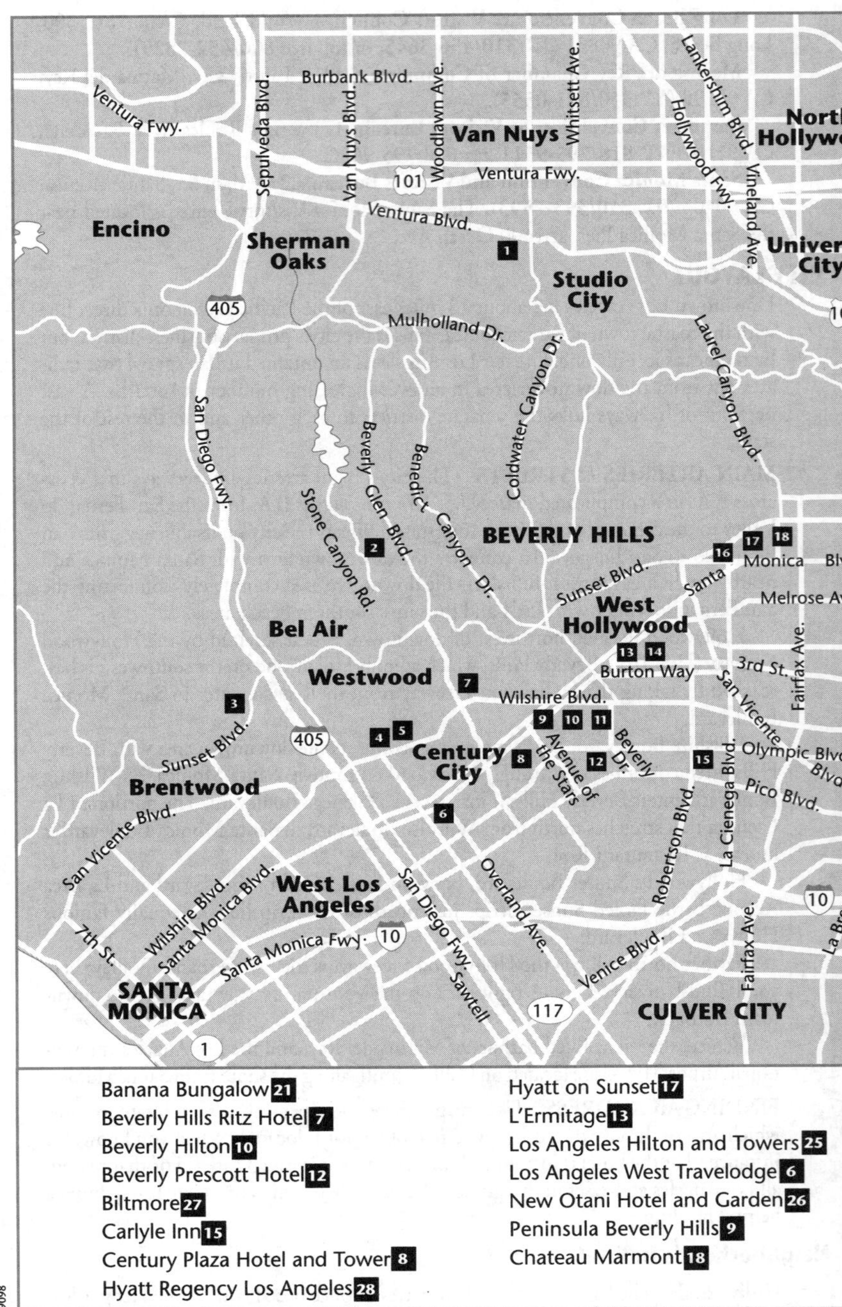

Burbank Blvd.
Ventura Fwy.
Sepulveda Blvd.
Van Nuys Blvd.
Woodlawn Ave.
Whitsett Ave.
Lankershim Blvd.
Hollywood Fwy.
Vineland Ave.
Van Nuys
101
Ventura Fwy.
Ventura Blvd.
Encino
Sherman Oaks
Studio City
405
Mulholland Dr.
Laurel Canyon Blvd.
Coldwater Canyon Dr.
San Diego Fwy.
Beverly Glen Blvd.
Benedict Canyon Dr.
Stone Canyon Rd.
BEVERLY HILLS
Sunset Blvd.
Santa Monica Blvd.
Melrose Ave.
West Hollywood
Bel Air
Westwood
Burton Way
3rd St.
Fairfax Ave.
San Vicente Blvd.
Wilshire Blvd.
405
Sunset Blvd.
Century City
Avenue of the Stars
Beverly Dr.
Olympic Blvd.
Pico Blvd.
Brentwood
San Vicente Blvd.
Robertson Blvd.
La Cienega Blvd.
Overland Ave.
West Los Angeles
San Diego Fwy.
Wilshire Blvd.
Santa Monica Blvd.
7th St.
10
Santa Monica Fwy.
Fairfax Ave.
Venice Blvd.
Sawtell
SANTA MONICA
117
CULVER CITY
1
Banana Bungalow 21
Beverly Hills Ritz Hotel 7
Beverly Hilton 10
Beverly Prescott Hotel 12
Biltmore 27
Carlyle Inn 15
Century Plaza Hotel and Tower 8
Hyatt Regency Los Angeles 28
Hyatt on Sunset 17
L'Ermitage 13
Los Angeles Hilton and Towers 25
Los Angeles West Travelodge 6
New Otani Hotel and Garden 26
Peninsula Beverly Hills 9
Chateau Marmont 18

9098

Accommodations in Beverly Hills, Hollywood & Downtown

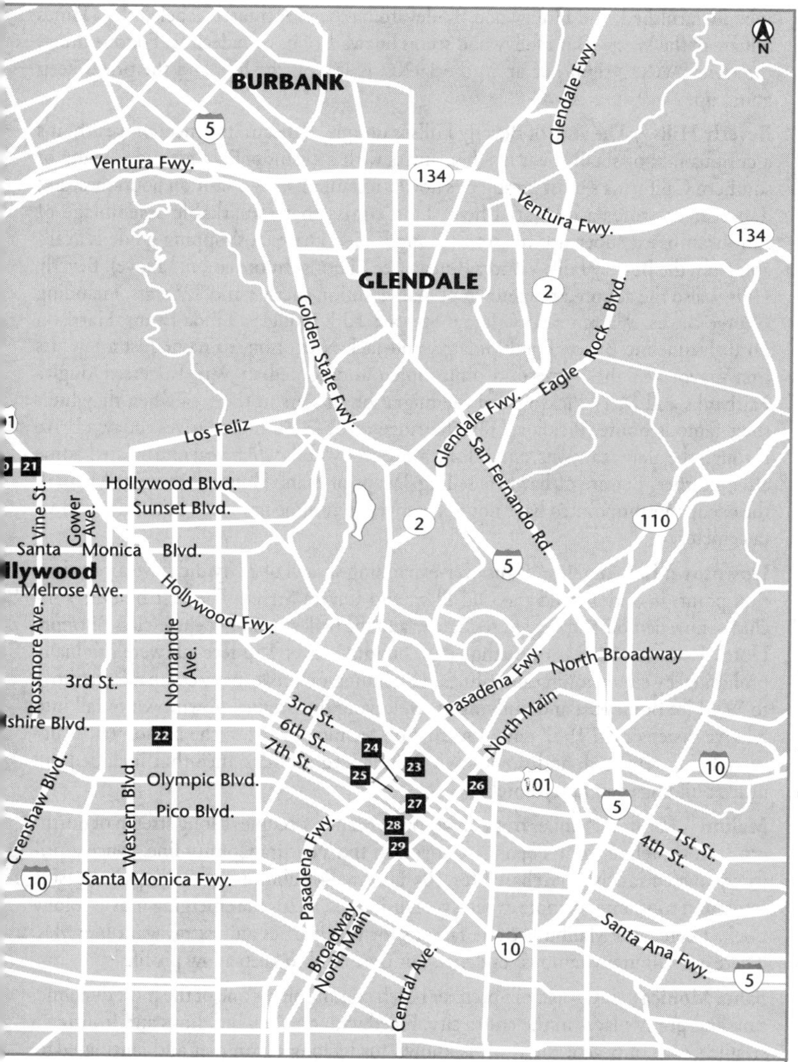

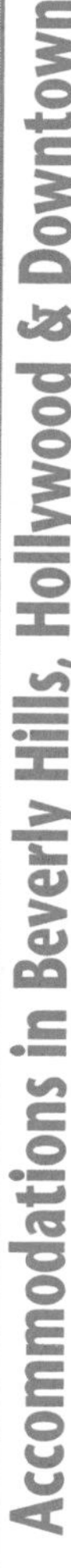

- Four Seasons Hotel Beverly Hills 14
- Holiday Inn Hollywood 20
- Holiday Inn Westwood Plaza 5
- Hollywood Celebrity Hotel 19
- Hotel Bel-Air 2
- Hotel Stillwell 29
- Radisson Bel Air Summit Hotel 3
- Regent Beverly Wilshire 11
- Royal Palace Westwood Hotel 4
- Sheraton Grande 23
- Sportsmen's Lodge 1
- Sunset Marquis Hotel and Villas 16
- Westin Bonaventure 24
- Wilshire Radisson Plaza 22

is badly tarnished, and Hollywood Boulevard has been accurately labeled the "Times Square of the West." But Hollywood seems unaware of its own decline. For one thing, the HOLLYWOOD sign, put up in the 1920s, is still on the hill, and the prices keep going up.

Beverly Hills The aura of Beverly Hills is unique. Beneath its veneer of wealth, it's a curious mix of small-town neighborliness with a cosmopolitan attitude. Many of southern California's most prestigious hotels, restaurants, high-fashion boutiques, and department stores are located here. Don't miss that remarkable assemblage of European-based super-upscale stores along Rodeo Drive. A shopping guide is available from the Beverly Hills Visitors Bureau (see "Tourist Information," above). Beverly Hills is also the adopted hometown of many motion-picture and TV stars, including George Burns, Warren Beatty, James Stewart, Kirk Douglas, Linda Evans, Harrison Ford, Jacqueline Bisset, Frank Sinatra, and Jack Nicholson, to name just a few. Its first mayor was the homespun philosopher and comedian Will Rogers. Douglas Fairbanks and Mary Pickford led the migration of stars to the area when they built their famous home, Pickfair, atop the ridge at 1143 Summit Drive; today a drive through the glens, canyons, and hillsides of Beverly Hills will reveal one palatial home after another. Beware of hawkers selling "Maps of Stars' Homes," though. Many of the occupants pinpointed have not only moved, but some have moved to Forest Lawn (a cemetery).

Downtown Los Angeles This ever-expanding sprawl of a city did have a germination point: in and around the Old Plaza and Olvera Street. The first buildings included now demolished elegant residences and the (still standing) deluxe-class Biltmore Hotel. Because of a fear of earthquakes, buildings over 150 feet tall were originally prohibited by city-planning authorities. This limitation drove many companies to move to Wilshire Boulevard and outlying areas, leaving the original downtown to fall into relative disrepair. In 1957 new construction technology led to the ban on tall structures being removed, and downtown experienced a renaissance that included tall office buildings and fancy hotels.

Malibu Located 25 miles from downtown, Malibu occupies a long stretch of northern L.A. shoreline from Topanga Canyon to the Ventura County line. Once a privately owned ranch—purchased for 10¢ an acre—Malibu is now a popular seaside resort and substantially more expensive. During the 1920s the emerging movie colony flocked here, and Malibu became famous for wild parties and extravagant lifestyles. There are still many famous residents, but they tend to keep a low profile.

Santa Monica Los Angeles's premier beach community is one of the most dynamic, fun, and pretty places in the entire city. Filled with art deco buildings and fronting a sizable swath of beach, the town is known for its long ocean pier and cutting-edge, artistic life-style. The new Third Street Promenade, lined with great shops and restaurants, is one of the most successful revitalization projects in the United States. Main Street, which runs south to Venice Beach, is also crammed with creative shops and eateries.

Redondo Beach and San Pedro In the 1880s Redondo Beach was the largest shipping port between San Diego and San Francisco. With the decline of commercial shipping, it became what it is now, a modest beach resort just a few minutes south of the Los Angeles International Airport.

Farther south along the beach, picturesque San Pedro, the bustling port of Los Angeles, handles an estimated 2-million tons of cargo annually.

Long Beach L.A.'s biggest beach town rates as the sixth-largest city in California. True to its name, it does, in fact, have a very long beach—5[1]/2 miles of sand. It's also well equipped with tennis, golf, sailing, fishing, and boating facilities.

Pasadena The grande dame of the Greater Los Angeles area, Pasadena is a residential city 11 miles northwest of the downtown district, hugging the foothills of the Sierra Madre mountain range in the San Gabriel Valley. It features street after street of large estates, surrounded by semitropical gardens—a haven for "old money." Old Pasadena is a 14-block, turn-of-the-century commercial district that has been transformed into one of the region's liveliest nightlife areas with specialty boutiques, movie theaters, pool halls, and more than 60 restaurants.

2 Getting Around

BY PUBLIC TRANSPORTATION

I've heard rumors about visitors to L.A. who have toured the city entirely by public transportation, and they might even be true. It's hard to believe that anyone can comprehensively tour Carland without an auto of their own, but if you're only in the city for a short time, are on a very tight budget, or don't expect to be moving around a lot, public transport might be for you. The city's trains and buses are operated by the Los Angeles County Metropolitan Transit Authority (MTA), 425 S. Main St., Los Angeles, CA 90013 (☎ **213/626-4455**). Stop in, write, or call MTA for maps, schedules, and detailed trip information. The office publishes a handy pamphlet outlining about two dozen self-guided MTA tours, including visits to Universal Studios, Beverly Hills, and Disneyland. A second, more convenient MTA office is located in ARCO Towers, 515 S. Flower St., adjacent to the Convention and Visitors Bureau.

BY BUS Spread-out sights, sluggish service, and frequent transfers make extensive touring of Los Angeles by bus impractical. For short hops, and occasional jaunts, however, buses could prove to be both economical and environmentally correct. Be sure to take a good book along to while away ride time (*War and Peace,* perhaps?).

The basic bus fare is $1.10 for all local lines, and transfers cost 25¢. Express buses, which travel along the freeways, and buses on intercounty routes charge higher fares. Phone for information.

The Downtown Area Short Hop (DASH) shuttle system operates buses throughout downtown and the west side of L.A. Service runs approximately every 5 to 20 minutes, depending on time of day, and costs just 25¢. Phone MTA for schedules and route information.

BY RAIL In June, 1990, the first line of a planned 300-mile network of commuter rail lines opened. The Metro Blue Line, an above-ground rail system, connects Downtown with Long Beach. Trains operate daily from 6am to 9pm and the fare is $1.10.

L.A.'s first subway, the Metro Red Line, which opened in 1993, currently runs just 4.4 miles, and makes just five stops in the downtown area. Fare is 25¢. The Red Line will be extended to Hollywood and the San Fernando Valley by 1999.

Construction of the Metro Green Line is scheduled for completion by 1995. The line will connect Norwalk in eastern Los Angeles County to LAX. The Green Line will connect with the Blue Line downtown.

BY TAXI

Distances are long in L.A. and cab fares are high. Even a short trip can cost $10 or more. Taxis charge $1.90 at the flagdrop, plus $1.60 per mile. A service charge is added to fares originating at LAX.

Except in the heart of downtown, passing cabs will usually not pull over when hailed. Cab stands are located at airports, Union Station, and at major hotels. To assure a ride, order a taxi in advance from Checker Cab (☎ **213/221-2355**), L.A. Taxi (☎ **213/627-7000**), or United Independent Taxi (☎ **213/483-7604**).

BY CAR

Need I tell you that Los Angeles is a car city? The elaborate network of freeways that connects this incredible urban sprawl is often jammed, especially during rush hours, when parking lots of traffic can seemingly slog along for hours. The golden rule of Los Angeles is always allow more time to get to your destination than you reasonably think it will take. See "Getting Around," in Chapter 2, for general information on rentals, driving rules, and other driving tips.

RENTALS Most of the large national car-rental firms have rental outlets in Los Angeles. See Section 8, "Getting Around," in Chapter 2, for information and toll-free telephone numbers. **Avis** (☎ toll free **800/331-1212**), **Budget** (☎ toll free **800/527-0700**), and **Hertz** (☎ toll free **800/654-3131**) all have offices at Los Angeles International Airport (LAX), as well as at Burbank and Long Beach airports and throughout the Greater Los Angeles area.

PARKING Parking throughout the city is usually ample. In most places you will be able to find metered street parking (carry plenty of quarters). Space gets scarce downtown and in West Hollywood, where you'll probably have to pay about $10 for a spot in an indoor garage. Most of the hotels listed in this book offer off-street parking, usually for an additional charge. This can get pricey—up to $20 per day. Check the listings and ask at the hotel before committing.

DRIVING RULES You may turn right at a red light (unless otherwise indicated) after yielding to traffic and pedestrians and making a complete stop. Pedestrians have the right-of-way at intersections and crosswalks. Pay attention to signs and arrows on the streets and roadways or you may find that you're in a lane that requires exiting or turning when you wanted to go straight. What's more, the city's profusion of one-way streets can create a few small difficulties; most road maps of the city, however, indicate which way traffic flows.

THE FREEWAYS Los Angeles has the most extensive freeway system in the world. In addition to a number, each freeway also has a name, or series of names, as it passes through various communities. Below is a list of major freeways, along with their locally-known names.

BY BICYCLE

If you care about your life, you won't try to bicycle in the city as a means of getting around. Traffic is heavy, and often you just can't get there from here with a bike. Cycles are terrific for recreation, however, especially along the car-free beach bike path in Santa Monica. See "Sports & Recreation," below, for complete information.

Freeway Number	Freeway Name(s)
2	Glendale
5	Golden State/Santa Ana
10	Santa Monica/San Bernardino
22	Garden Grove
57	Orange
60	Pomona
90	Marina
91	Artesia/Riverside
101	Ventura/Hollywood
105	Century
110	Pasadena/Harbor
118	Simi Valley–San Fernando Valley
134	Ventura
170	Hollywood
210	Foothill
405	San Diego
605	San Gabriel River
710	Long Beach

Fast Facts: Los Angeles

American Express There are several city American Express Travel Service offices, including 327 N. Beverly Dr. in Beverly Hills, and 901 W. 7th St. in downtown Los Angeles. To report lost or stolen cards call toll free **800/528-4800.** To report lost or stolen traveler's checks call toll free **800/221-7282.**

Area Code All phone numbers in this guide are prefaced with area codes. You'll need to use them when calling from one calling area to another.

There are three area codes in Los Angeles. Most numbers, including Hollywood and downtown are within the **213** code. Phone numbers in the city's beach communities, including the Los Angeles International Airport (LAX), Malibu, and Santa Monica begin with a **310** prefix. Many inland suburbs, including Pasadena, are within the **818** calling area.

Babysitters If you're staying at one of the larger hotels, the concierge can usually recommend a reliable babysitter. If they can't, call Baby Sitters Guild, P.O. Box 3418, South Pasadena, CA 91031 (☎ **818/441-4293**). This company, in business since 1948, provides mature, bonded sitters, on call 24 hours.

Business Hours Stores are usually open Monday through Saturday from 10am to 6pm; closed on Sunday.

Car Rentals See "Getting Around," earlier in this chapter.

Cleaners See "Laundry/Dry Cleaning," below.

Climate See "When to Go" in Chapter 2.

Currency Exchange Foreign-currency exchange services are provided by the Bank of America at 525 S. Flower St., B-level (☎ **213/228-4622**). Thomas Cook International, at 677 S. Figueroa, and Hilton Hotel Center, 900 Wilshire Blvd. (☎ **213/624-4221**), also offers foreign-currency exchange services.

Dentists Hotels usually have a list of dentists should you need one. For other referrals, you can call the Los Angeles Dental Society (☎ **800/422-8338**).

Doctors Here again, hotels usually have a list of doctors on call. For referrals, you can contact the Los Angeles Medical Association (☎ **213/483-6122**).

Drugstores Walgreens pharmacies are all over town. Ask at your hotel, or check the local phone directory for a location near you.

Embassies and Consulates See Chapter 3, "For Foreign Visitors."

Emergencies For police, fire, highway patrol, or in case of life-threatening medical emergencies, dial **911.**

Eyeglasses Lenscrafters makes glasses in about an hour. Offices include 301 Wilshire Blvd., Santa Monica (☎ **310/394-6692**); and 4518 Van Nuys Blvd., Sherman Oaks (☎ **818/501-6474**).

Film See "Photographic Needs," below.

Hairdressers/Barbers B.O.B.S, 230 S. Robertson Blvd., Beverly Hills (☎ **310/657-4232**), offers high-quality haircuts; an upscale, high-design atmosphere; and reasonable prices. Ronnie Romoff at Romoff, 1615½ Montana Ave., Santa Monica (**310/394-2709**), located in an alley, has just one chair and one mirror and offers no colors or perms, just professional cuts. Patrick Swayze, Michael Keaton, and Raquel Welch get clipped here. Cost: $250.

Holidays See "Fast Facts: For the Foreign Traveler," in Chapter 3.

Hospitals In an emergency, dial **911** from any phone. Santa Monica Hospital Medical Center, 1250 16th St., Santa Monica (☎ **310/319-4000**), is just one of many hospitals in the city. Ask at your hotel or check the front pages of a telephone directory for the hospital closest to you. For a free, confidential physician referral, call toll free **800/922-0000.**

Information See "Tourist Information," earlier in this chapter.

Laundry/Dry Cleaning Any one of the major hotels can take care of these services for you, but allow two days for the job.

Libraries Gutted by fire in 1986, the Los Angeles Central Library, 630 W. 5th St. (☎ **213/228-7000**), reopened in 1993 to become the third largest in America. There's a park atop the library's 1.5-acre parking garage.

Liquor Laws Liquor and grocery stores can sell packaged alcoholic beverages between 6am and 2am. Most restaurants, nightclubs, and bars are licensed to serve alcoholic beverages during the same hours. The legal age for purchase and consumption is 21, and proof of age is required. In California you can purchase packaged liquor with your credit card; however, most stores usually have a minimum dollar amount for charging.

Newspapers and Magazines The *Los Angeles Times* is distributed throughout the country. Its Sunday "Calendar" section is an excellent and interesting guide to the entire world of entertainment in and around Los Angeles, and includes listings of what's doing and where to do it. The free weekly listings magazine *L.A. Weekly* is packed with news of events and happenings around town. It's available from sidewalk newsracks and in many stores and restaurants around the city. Melrose News, at the corner of Melrose and Martel Avenues is one of the city's best outdoor newsstands.

Photographic Needs Photo finishing labs are located in every shopping mall and on major streets around the city. Fromex, 406 Broadway, Santa Monica (☎ **310/395-5177**), and other locations, is one of southern California's largest developers.

Police See "Emergencies," above.

Post Office Post offices are located all over the city. Call **213/586-1467** to find the one closest to you.

Radio Stations There are literally dozens of radio stations in L.A. FM classical music stations include KCSN (88.5), KCPB (91.1), KUSC (91.5), and KKGO (105.1). Country music stations include KFOX (93.5), KIKF (94.3), and KFRG (95.1). Rock music stations include KUCI (88.9), KLOS (95.5), KLSX (97.1), and KROQ (106.7). The top AM news and information station is KNX (1070).

Religious Services Los Angeles has hundreds of churches and synagogues, and at least a hundred denominations, formal and informal. Should you be seeking a house of worship, your hotel desk clerk or bell captain can usually direct you to the nearest church of most any denomination.

Restrooms Stores rarely let customers use the restrooms, and many restaurants offer their facilities for customers only. But most malls have bathrooms, as do the ubiquitous fast-food restaurants. Many public beaches and large parks provide toilets, though in some places you have to pay, or tip an attendant. If you have the time to find one, pull into a large hotel. Most have well-stocked, clean restrooms in their lobbies.

Safety Innocent tourists are rarely the victims of violent crime. Still, few locals would recommend walking alone late at night. East L.A., an inland area where tourists rarely venture, is the city's most infamous area. See the section on safety in Chapter 2 for additional safety tips.

Taxes Los Angeles County and California state sales taxes amount to 8.25%. Hotel tax is 14%–17%.

Taxis See "Getting Around," earlier in this chapter.

Television Stations All the major networks and several independent stations are represented. They are KCBS, Channel 2; KNBC, Channel 4; KTLA, Channel 5; KABC, Channel 7; KCAL, Channel 9; KTTV (Fox), Channel 11; and KCOP, Channel 13.

Transit Information See "Getting Around," earlier in this chapter.

Useful Telephone Numbers Call for the correct time at **213/853-1212.** For nonemergency police matters, phone **213/485-2121,** or, in Beverly Hills, **213/550-4951.**

Weather Call Los Angeles Weather Information at **213/554-1212** to find out that it will be 74°F and sunny today.

3 Accommodations

In Los Angeles, location is everything. When searching for a hotel here, think about in which areas you plan on spending the bulk of your time and locate nearby. In sprawling Los Angeles nothing is convenient to everything; wherever you stay, count on doing a lot of driving to somewhere else.

For the most part, the most elegant accommodations are in Beverly Hills and Bel Air. For hard-core tourists, Hollywood is probably the most central place to stay. Businesspeople would probably do best to locate downtown. Santa Monica and Marina del Rey are great areas right on the beach; they are coolest in summer and trendiest year round. Finally, families with kids might want to head straight to Anaheim or Buena Park, to bed down close to the theme parks.

You'll notice that more deluxe hostelries are listed here than in other chapters—there are simply more of them in star-studded L.A. than in other cities. Hotel listings are first broken down by area, then organized by price. Each entry has been measured by the strict yardstick of value and has earned a listing by providing travelers with the most for the money.

Downtown Los Angeles

VERY EXPENSIVE

Biltmore, 506 S. Grand Ave., Los Angeles, CA 90071. ☎ **213/624-1011,** or toll free **800/245-8673**. Fax 213/612-1545. 700 rms, 40 suites. A/C MINIBAR TV TEL **Directions:** From U.S. 101, take Grand Avenue exit; the hotel is located between Fifth and Sixth Streets.

Rates: $185–$275 single; $215–$275 double; from $450 suite. AE, CB, DC, MC, V. **Parking:** $18.

Built in 1923, this gracious and elegant hotel was the site of the Academy Award ceremonies during the 1930s and '40s, including the year *Gone with the Wind* swept them all (1940). The always-beautiful Biltmore now looks better than ever following a $40 million face-lift completed in 1987. Contemporary additions now complement traditional styles, including state-of-the-art door locks and other mechanical systems.

Lavishly appointed rooms are spacious and attractively decorated in pastel tones. Modern marble bathrooms, color TVs, and in-room minibars are offset by traditional French furniture.

Dining/Entertainment: The grand Rendezvous Court serves afternoon tea and evening cocktails. Its ornate cathedral-like vaulted ceiling was hand painted by Italian artist Giovanni Smeraldi. Bernard's, the hotel's top dining room, features fluted columns and hand-painted beamed ceilings. The cuisine combines classical French and regional American dishes. Smeraldi's Ristorante is open daily for breakfast, lunch, and dinner. The full-service dining room features homemade pastas and Californian cuisine with an Italian flair. The Grand Avenue Bar offers a cold lunch buffet, and showcases top-name entertainment in the evening.

Services: 24-hour room service, concierge, evening turndown, overnight shoeshine.

Facilities: Health club, including Roman spa pool, steam room, sauna, Jacuzzi, Nautilus equipment, and free weights; business center.

Sheraton Grande, 333 S. Figueroa St., Los Angeles, CA 90012. ☎ **213/617-1133,** or toll free **800/325-3535.** Fax 213/613-0291. 469 rms, 69 suites. A/C MINIBAR TV TEL **Directions:** From Calif. 110 (Harbor Freeway) exit onto Ninth Street, and turn left onto Figueroa Street; the hotel is located between Third and Fourth Streets.

Rates: $180–$210 single; $200–$235 double; from $275 suite. AE, CB, DC, DISC, MC, V. **Parking:** $17.

One of downtown's newest hotels, the Sheraton Grande is a splendid smoky-mirrored-glass structure located right in the heart of the hustle. The large open lobby and lounge is decorated with skylights and plants. A pianist entertains in the lounge daily from noon to 10:30pm.

Pastel-colored guest rooms are well lit and outfitted with the usual furnishings, including a writing desk, minibar, color TV, and firm mattresses. Bathrooms are equally functional, featuring good-quality fittings and hotel-quality Italian marble.

Dining/Entertainment: The Back Porch, an informal dining room overlooking the pool, serves three meals a day. The gourmet room, Scarlatti, features Italian cuisine Tuesday through Saturday nights.

Services: 24-hour room service, concierge, evening turndown, overnight shoeshine.

Facilities: Four movie theaters, heated outdoor swimming pool and sun deck, access to an off-premises health club.

EXPENSIVE

Hyatt Regency Los Angeles, 711 S. Hope St., Los Angeles, CA 90017. ☎ **213/683-1234,** or toll free **800/233-1234**. Fax 213/612-3179. 485 rms, 40 suites. A/C TV TEL **Directions:** From Calif. 110, exit at Ninth Street. Turn left at Hope Street; the hotel is on the corner of Seventh and Hope Streets.

Rates: $129–$209 single; $174–$234 double; from $225 suite. AE, CB, DC, DISC, MC, V. **Parking:** $13.50.

The 24-story Hyatt Regency is a dazzlingly ultramodern fixture in Broadway Plaza, a 21st century–style complex of shops, restaurants, offices, and galleries in the middle of downtown L.A. Topped by bright skylights, the two-story ground-floor lobby entrance has a garden plaza, lounges, and several boutiques. Wide escalators glide down to the lobby/reception area and lower gardens. Giant wall graphics and exposed brick surround potted plants, trees, old-fashioned gaslight streetlamps, and overstuffed furniture.

The hotel's guest rooms are of the same high comfort and unquestionable taste. Both innovative and attractive, accommodations boast enormous windows looking out onto surprisingly nice views for a downtown hotel. Deep pile carpeting, oversize beds, and small sofas, are all futuristic in design and utilize the same bold textures and russet-gold color scheme that's prevalent throughout the hotel.

Dining/Entertainment: Both the informal, lobby-level Brasserie and the more opulent Pavan restaurant are open for lunch and dinner Monday through Saturday. Additional eateries include the Lobby Bar, the Sun Porch, a sidewalk cafe–coffee shop.

Services: Room service, concierge, evening turndown service.

Facilities: Fitness center, business center, Jacuzzi, and sun deck.

Los Angeles Hilton and Towers, 930 Wilshire Blvd., Los Angeles, CA 90017. ☎ **213/629-4321**, or toll free **800/445-8667.** Fax 213/612-3987. 900 rms, 32 suites. A/C MINIBAR TV TEL **Directions:** From Calif. 110 north, exit onto Wilshire Boulevard; the hotel is located at the corner of Figueroa Street.

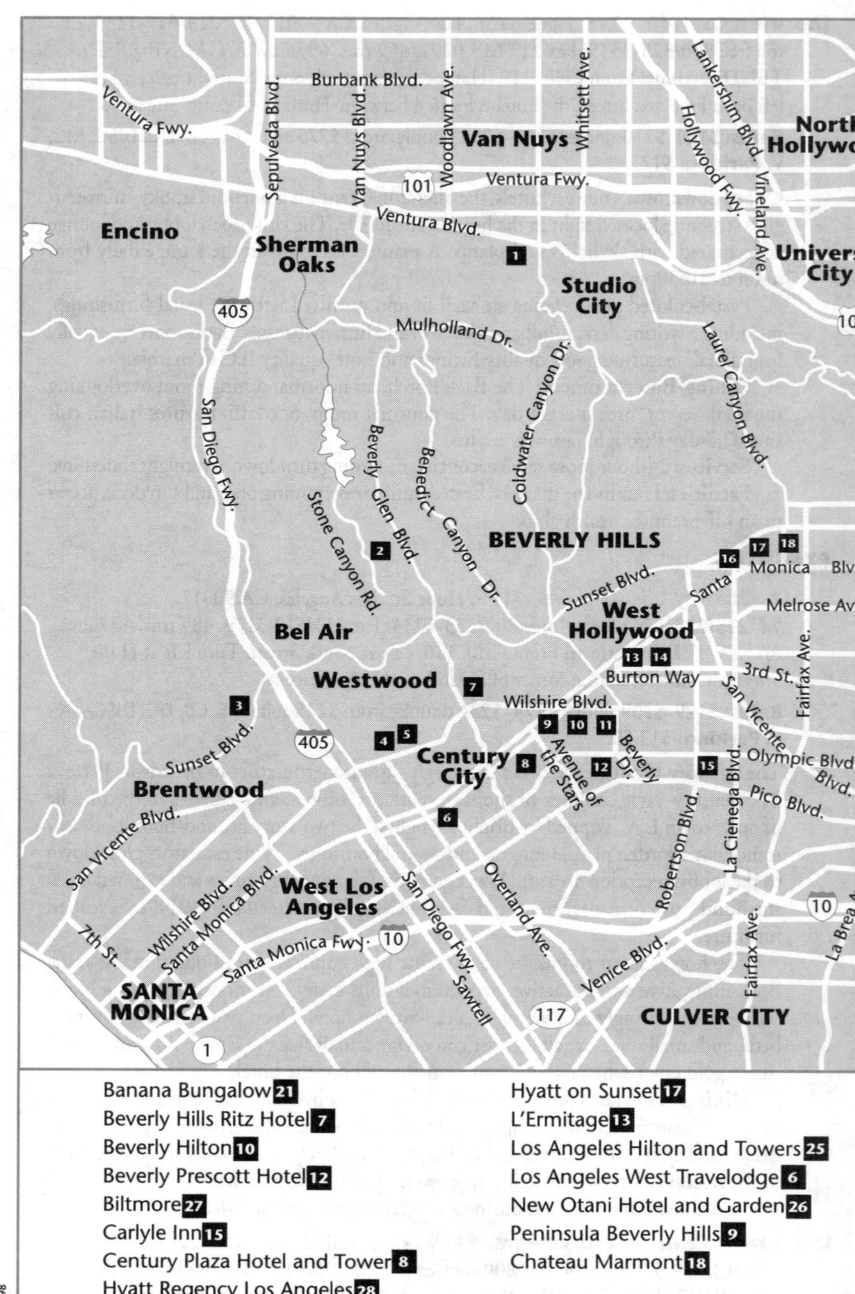

Burbank Blvd.
Ventura Fwy.
Sepulveda Blvd.
Van Nuys Blvd.
Woodlawn Ave.
Whitsett Ave.
Lankershim Blvd.
Hollywood Fwy.
Vineland Ave.
North Hollywo
Van Nuys
101
Ventura Fwy.
Ventura Blvd.
Encino
Sherman Oaks
1
Studio City
Univers City
405
101
Mulholland Dr.
Laurel Canyon Blvd.
Coldwater Canyon Dr.
San Diego Fwy.
Beverly Glen Blvd.
Benedict Canyon Dr.
Stone Canyon Rd.
2
BEVERLY HILLS
16
17
18
Santa Monica Blvd
Sunset Blvd.
Melrose Ave
West Hollywood
Bel Air
13
14
3rd St.
Burton Way
Westwood
7
Fairfax Ave.
3
Wilshire Blvd.
9
10
11
San Vicente Blvd.
405
4
5
Sunset Blvd.
Century City
8
Avenue of the Stars
12
Beverly Dr.
15
Olympic Blvd.
Brentwood
Pico Blvd.
San Vicente Blvd.
6
La Cienega Blvd.
Robertson Blvd.
Overland Ave.
West Los Angeles
San Diego Fwy.
Wilshire Blvd.
Santa Monica Blvd.
7th St.
10
10
La Brea Ave
Santa Monica Fwy.
Venice Blvd.
Fairfax Ave.
Sawtell
SANTA MONICA
117
CULVER CITY
1
Banana Bungalow 21
Beverly Hills Ritz Hotel 7
Beverly Hilton 10
Beverly Prescott Hotel 12
Biltmore 27
Carlyle Inn 15
Century Plaza Hotel and Tower 8
Hyatt Regency Los Angeles 28
Hyatt on Sunset 17
L'Ermitage 13
Los Angeles Hilton and Towers 25
Los Angeles West Travelodge 6
New Otani Hotel and Garden 26
Peninsula Beverly Hills 9
Chateau Marmont 18

Accommodations in Beverly Hills, Hollywood & Downtown

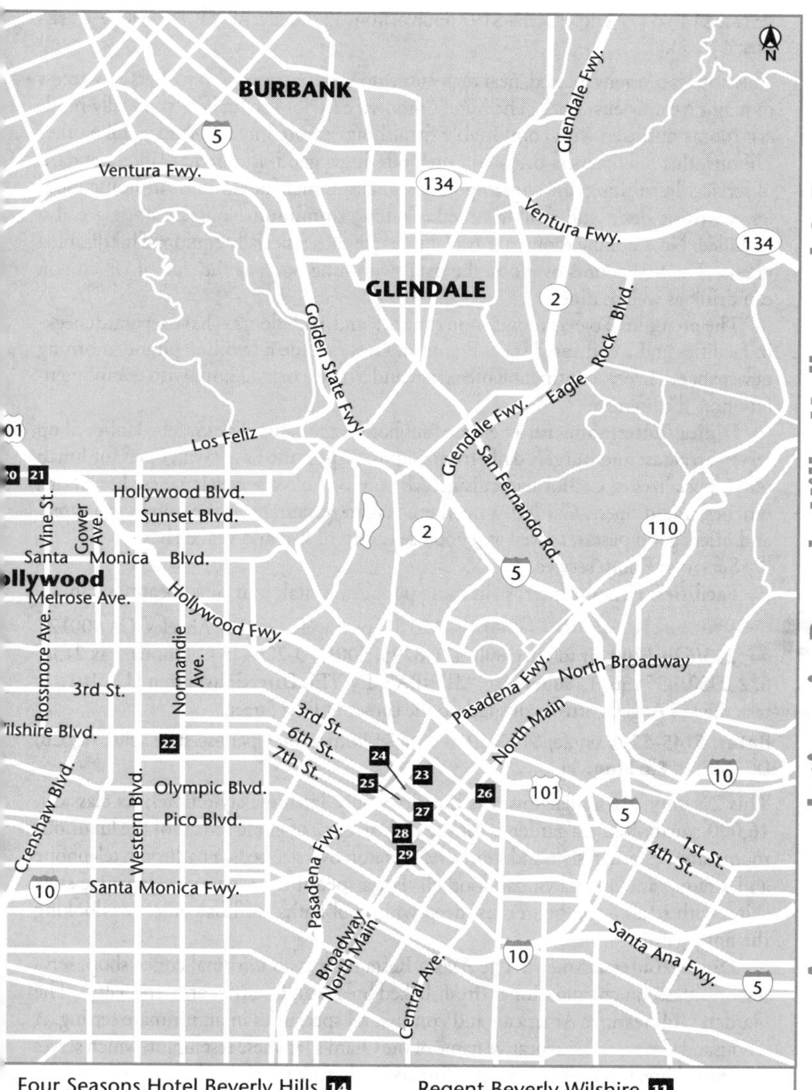

Four Seasons Hotel Beverly Hills 14
Holiday Inn Hollywood 20
Holiday Inn Westwood Plaza 5
Hollywood Celebrity Hotel 19
Hotel Bel-Air 2
Hotel Stillwell 29
Radisson Bel Air Summit Hotel 3
Regent Beverly Wilshire 11
Royal Palace Westwood Hotel 4
Sheraton Grande 23
Sportsmen's Lodge 1
Sunset Marquis Hotel and Villas 16
Westin Bonaventure 24
Wilshire Radisson Plaza 22

Rates: $147–$177 single; $167–$197 double; from $375 suite. AE, CB, DC, MC, V. **Parking:** $16.50.

This hotel is centrally located, near many downtown attractions, and it offers easy access to major freeway entrances. The hotel's modern exterior is matched by equally modern rooms outfitted with comfortable furnishings colored in soft shades. Like other Hiltons, this is a business-oriented hotel, offering a good, if unremarkable, standard of service. Furnishings are contemporary and clean; such amenities as in-house movies, a writing desk, and double-paned windows to minimize outside noise are also included. No-smoking rooms are available, as are those specially equipped for disabled guests. The best rooms overlook the oval swimming pool, at the side of which you can drink as well as dine.

The premium Towers rooms—on the 15th and 16th floors—have separate check-in facilities and a dedicated staff. Premium rates include a two-line phone, morning newspaper delivery, continental breakfast, and a daily cocktail hour with complimentary hors d'oeuvres.

Dining/Entertainment: There are four hotel restaurants. The Gazebo Coffee Shop serves breakfast and burgers daily from 6am to 11pm; the City Grill, open for lunch only, specializes in Californian cuisine; Minami of Tokyo serves Japanese breakfasts, lunches, and dinners. Cardini, a northern Italian restaurant, is the hotel's top eatery and offers good pastas, as well as a good selection of fish and veal dishes.

Services: Room service.

Facilities: Fitness center, swimming pool, car rental, tour desk, beauty salon.

★ **New Otani Hotel and Garden,** 120 S. Los Angeles St., Los Angeles, CA 90012. ☎ **213/629-1200,** or toll free **800/421-8795, 800/273-2294** in California. Fax 213/622-0980. 435 rms, 15 suites. A/C MINIBAR TV TEL **Directions:** From U.S. 101, take the Los Angeles Street exit south to the corner of First Street.

Rates: $145–$205 single; $170–$230 double; from $400 Japanese-style suite. AE, CB, DC, MC, V. **Parking:** $11.

This 21-story, triangular tower is the city's only Japanese-style hotel; its classical, 16,000-square-foot tea garden is for the exclusive use of guests. Most of the luxurious rooms are Western in style and sport a refrigerator, oversize beds, a bathroom telephone and a radio, and an individual doorbell. For a special treat, choose a Japanese-style suite, with tatami-mat bedrooms, deep whirlpool baths, and balconies overlooking the hotel garden.

Dining/Entertainment: The Azalea Restaurant is an informal coffee shop, serving breakfast, lunch, and dinner (fresh-baked breads and pastries are a specialty). The Garden Grill features American and continental specialties in an intimate setting. A Thousand Cranes is the evocative name of the Otani's Japanese restaurant, which serves traditional breakfasts, lunches, and dinners, including sushi.

Services: 24-hour room service, concierge, evening turndown, same-day valet cleaning.

Facilities: Japanese-style health club with saunas, baths, and shiatsu massages; shopping arcade with over 30 shops, car-rental desk, airport limousine service; golf and tennis are available in conjunction with a nearby country club.

Westin Bonaventure, 404 S. Figueroa St., Los Angeles, CA 90071. ☎ **213/624-1000,** or toll free **800/228-3000.** Fax 213/612-4800. 1,500 rms, 94 suites. A/C MINIBAR TV TEL **Directions:** From Calif. 110 (Harbor Freeway) exit onto Wilshire Boulevard, and turn left onto Figueroa Street; the hotel is located between Fourth and Fifth Streets.

Rates: $150–$195 single; $175–$215 double; from $335 suite. AE, DC, CB, MC, V. **Parking:** $18.

One of California's most innovative hotels, the space-age Westin Bonaventure is known for its five gleaming cylindrical towers that are one of downtown's most distinctive landmarks. Designed by architect John Portman (who is also known for San Francisco's Hyatt Regency), the Westin features a beautiful six-story skylight lobby that houses a large lake, trees, splashing fountains, and gardens. Twelve glass-enclosed elevators appear to rise from the reflecting pools.

The best city views are available from the highest guest rooms in this 35-story hotel. Like the lobby, accommodations are also elegantly modernistic, complete with floor-to-ceiling windows and every amenity you'd expect at a top big-city hotel. It's even nice to know that despite the hotel's great size, no bedroom is more than six doors from an elevator.

Dining/Entertainment: The Sidewalk Café, a Californian bistro, and the adjacent Lobby Court, with tables under large fringed umbrellas, are the focus of the hotel's nightly entertainment, which varies from jazz combos to cocktail-hour music to dancing. The Flower Street Bar, a mixture of marble, brass, and mahogany, is a popular spot for cocktails.

The rooftop Top of Five restaurant features panoramic views and gourmet continental cuisine. A revolving cocktail lounge, the Bona Vista, is located just below, on the 34th floor.

Services: 24-hour room service, concierge, shoeshine.

Facilities: The Shopping Gallery above the lobby contains five levels of shops and boutiques, an outdoor swimming pool and sun deck, tennis courts, health club.

BUDGET

$ **Hotel Stillwell,** 838 S. Grand Ave., Los Angeles, CA 90017. ☎ **213/627-1151,** or toll free **800/553-4774.** Fax 213/622-8940. 250 rms. A/C TV TEL **Directions:** From U.S. 101, exit Grand Avenue; the hotel is located between Eighth and Ninth Streets.

Rates: $35–$45 single; $45–$60 double. AE, DC, MC, V. **Parking:** $5.

Conveniently situated in the downtown area, the hotel is close to the Civic Center's Ahmanson Theater and Dorothy Chandler Pavilion. It's also close to the Museum of Contemporary Art, Little Tokyo, Olvera Street, Union Station, and a variety of exceptional restaurants.

Frommer's Smart Traveler: Hotels

1. A hotel room is a perishable commodity; if it's not sold, the revenue is lost forever. Always ask if a hotel has a lower rate, and make it clear that you're shopping around.
2. For the best rates, seek out business-oriented hotels on weekends and in the summer, and tourist-oriented bed and breakfasts during the off-season.
3. Ask about summer discounts, corporate rates, and special packages. Most hotel reservations offices don't tell you about promotional rates unless you ask.
4. Always inquire about telephone and parking charges. In Los Angeles, it could add $20 per night for your car and $1 per local call.

Decently decorated rooms include no-smoking accommodations, and larger rooms for guests traveling with children. The simple, yet comfortable, facilities are decorated in soft blue and gray tones. It's not a fancy place, but the Stillwell is relatively clean and a good pick for well-priced accommodations in an otherwise pricy neighborhood.

There are two restaurants on the premises: Gills Cuisine of India, serving competent northern Indian dishes; and Hank's American Grill, offering simple American meals. There's also a business center and tour desk.

Hollywood

VERY EXPENSIVE

Sunset Marquis Hotel and Villas, 1200 North Alta Loma Road, West Hollywood, CA 90069. ☎ **310/657-1333,** or toll free **800/858-9758.** Fax 310/652-5300. 118 suites. TV TEL **Directions:** From U.S. 101, exit onto Sunset Boulevard west, then turn left onto North Alta Loma Road, one block past La Cienega.

Rates: $215–$295 single or double; from $430 two-bedroom suites; from $450 villas. AE, DC, MC, V. **Parking:** Free.

Two things make the Sunset Marquis special: its villas and its clientele. This is the ultimate music industry hostelry, regularly hosting the biggest names in rock music in the hotel's homey villas and suites. Musicians and their hangers-on stay here while recording in the city. Sometimes they even record in the basement studios located in the hotel itself, then retire to the lobby bar, where their session can be piped-in directly.

The hotel's standard rooms are outfitted in traditional motel style—neither the bedrooms nor baths are particularly special. But each comes with an adjoining sitting area, outfitted with a VCR and a good sized refrigerator that pleases long-term guests. The villas represent a very different level of quality. These free-standing cottages overlooking the hotel's rolling three-acre grounds are top-of-the-line accommodations featuring wooden floors, sunken living rooms, opulent baths, canopied beds, and even grand pianos, fireplaces, and private saunas, steam rooms, or Jacuzzis.

Dining/Entertainment: Notes, a small Mediterranean restaurant with California influences serves either indoors or pool side. The Whiskey, the hotel's lobby bar, is one of the most exclusive rooms in Hollywood. Rock 'n' rollers like Mick Jagger, Axel Rose, and Robert Plant turn the bar into a celebrity-fest Wednesday through Saturday nights. Unless you're staying at the hotel, you'll probably never get in.

Services: 24-hour full-menu room service, concierge, business services, overnight laundry.

Facilities: Two swimming pools, health facilities, sauna, Jacuzzi.

EXPENSIVE

Hyatt on Sunset, 8401 Sunset Blvd., Hollywood, CA 90069. ☎ **213/656-1234,** or toll free **800/233-1234.** Fax 213/650-7024. 262 rms. A/C TV TEL **Directions:** From U.S. 101, exit onto Highland Avenue and turn right onto Sunset Boulevard; the hotel is located 2 blocks east of La Cienega Boulevard.

Rates: $119–$135 single; $144–$160 double; $350–$560 suite. Special weekend rates available. AE, CB, DC, DISC, MC, V. **Parking:** $7 self; $10 valet.

This lively place is well located: close to Restaurant Row on La Cienega Boulevard and to Sunset Strip nightlife. Spacious bedrooms on 13 floors have views of the Los

Angeles skyline and the Hollywood hills; many have private balconies. Rooms have modern furnishings and dressing areas, plus all the conveniences you'd expect from a Hyatt, including in-room movies on color TVs and large, modern bathrooms.

Dining/Entertainment: Enjoy the international selections of the Silver Screen Bistro, which is open for breakfast, lunch, and dinner and provides patio dining. Sip your favorite cocktail at the Sports Bar, while playing pool or viewing the big-screen TV (55 inches).

Services: Room service, concierge.

Facilities: Rooftop swimming pool/sun deck, business center, gift shop.

MODERATE

Chateau Marmont, 8221 Sunset Blvd., Hollywood, CA 90046.
☎ **213/656-1010,** or toll free **800/242-8328.** Fax 213/655-5311. 63 rms, 53 suites. A/C TV TEL **Directions:** From U.S. 101, exit onto Highland Avenue and turn right onto Sunset Boulevard; the hotel is located between La Cienega Boulevard and Crescent Heights Boulevard, at Marmont Lane.

Rates: $160 single or double; from $210 suite; from $495 bungalow. AE, CB, DC, MC, V.

There isn't enough space here to list all the famous people who have stayed at this château-style apartment hotel, situated on a cliff just above Sunset Strip. Humphrey Bogart, Jeanne Moreau, Boris Karloff, Al Pacino, James Taylor, Richard Gere, Bianca Jagger, John and Yoko, Sophia Loren, Sidney Poitier, and Whoopi Goldberg are just a few famous former guests. Carol Channing met her husband here; Greta Garbo used to check in under the name Harriet Brown; and even Howard Hughes once maintained a suite here.

Now a historical monument, the hotel was built in 1927. It mimics the architectural style of the French Normandy region and is surrounded by private gardens with views of the city and the Hollywood hills. Chateau Marmont is famous for its privacy and personal attention, not to mention its magnificently stocked wine cellar.

Guests often gather in the great baronial living room that is furnished with local antiques. On warm days, you might lounge around the oval swimming pool amid semitropical trees and shrubbery. Guest rooms are beautifully furnished in a tasteful English style. Suites have fully equipped kitchens, and most pets are welcome.

Services: Room service, concierge, twice-daily maid service.

Facilities: Swimming pool, fitness room.

Holiday Inn Hollywood, 1755 N. Highland Ave., Hollywood, CA 90028.
☎ **213/462-7181,** or toll free **800/465-4329.** Fax 213/466-9072. 470 rms, 22 suites. A/C TV TEL **Directions:** From U.S. 101, take the Franklin Avenue exit and head west to Highland Avenue, then turn left; the hotel is located between Franklin and Hollywood Boulevards.

Rates: $105–$145 single or double, from $135 suite. Extra person $12. Children 18 and under stay free in parents' room. AE, DC, DISC, MC, V. **Parking:** $5.50.

This 22-story hostelry in the heart of old Hollywood offers perfectly acceptable rooms that are both pleasant and comfortable. Each accommodation is equipped with a clock radio and a digital safe. There are also three laundry rooms and ice and soda machines on every floor. Suites here are a particularly good buy, since they include a small kitchenette that can save you on restaurant meals. There's a swimming pool and sun deck on the hotel's second floor.

A revolving circular rooftop restaurant, called Windows on Hollywood, features great Hollywood views while dancing and dining. The Show Biz Café, an unusually plush coffee shop, serves breakfast, lunch, and dinner. The Front Row Lounge, an intimate cocktail lounge, is open daily until 2am.

INEXPENSIVE

Hollywood Celebrity Hotel, 1775 Orchid Ave., Hollywood, CA 90028. ☎ **213/850-6464,** or toll free **800/222-7017, 800/222-7090** in California. Fax 213/850-7667. 39 rms. A/C TV TEL **Directions:** From U.S. 101, take the Highland Avenue exit and turn right onto Hollywood Boulevard, then take the first right onto Orchid Avenue.

Rates (including continental breakfast): $55 single; $60 double; $65 twin. Extra person $8. AE, CB, DC, DISC, MC, V. **Parking:** Free.

One of the best budget buys in Hollywood is this small but extremely centrally located hotel, just a half block behind Mann's Chinese Theatre. Spacious and comfortable units are decorated in an original art deco style. Breakfast is brought to your room along with the morning newspaper. Each room has cable TV and a radio. Small pets are allowed, but only if you present a $50 deposit.

BUDGET

Banana Bungalow, 2775 Cahuenga Blvd., West Hollywood, CA 90068. ☎ **213/851-1129,** or toll free **800/4-HOSTEL.** Fax 213/851-2022. 200 beds, 25 double rms. **Directions:** From U.S. 101, take the Cahuenga Boulevard exit and drive north to the well-signed hostel.

Rates: $15 per night in multi-bed room; $40 two people in private room. MC, V. **Parking:** Free.

Price notwithstanding, if you're under 35, Banana Bungalow is probably the most fun place to stay in all of Los Angeles. Nestled in a little Hollywood Hills valley, a short drive from the Walk of Fame and Universal Studios, the Bungalow has double and multi-share rooms, kitchen facilities, a restaurant, lounge, outdoor pool, movie theater, and arcade/game room. International guests always seem to be looking for a good time, and the atmosphere is always upbeat. The hostel offers free airport pick-up, and regular excursions to the beach, Disneyland, and other Los Angeles area destinations.

Beverly Hills & Century City

VERY EXPENSIVE

Beverly Hilton, 9876 Wilshire Blvd., Beverly Hills, CA 90210. ☎ **310/274-7777,** or toll free **800/445-8667.** Fax 310/285-1313. 581 rms, 90 suites. A/C MINIBAR TV TEL **Directions:** From Calif. 405 north, exit onto Santa Monica Boulevard and go east for three miles to the hotel at Wilshire Blvd.

Rates: $200–$240 single; $225–$265 double. Children and teens stay free in parents' room. Extra adult $25. AE, CB, DC, DISC, MC, V. **Parking:** $15.

Easily one of the poshest hotels in the Hilton chain, this luxuriously decorated hotel is like a minicity, complete with a small shopping mall and several restaurants that make leaving the property unnecessary.

Individually decorated rooms are full of amenities, including a refrigerator and in-room first-run movies. Most rooms have a balcony that overlooks an Olympic-size pool and the surrounding hillsides. The more expensive rooms are on higher floors.

Dining/Entertainment: L'Escoffier, the rooftop restaurant, combines gourmet French cuisine with a panoramic view of the city. It's open for dinner Tuesday to Saturday. The award-winning Trader Vic's sports a nautical theme, and serves South Seas and continental dishes along with exotic drinks. Mr. H, another elegant continental-style eatery is known for its Sunday champagne brunch and daily lunch and dinner buffets. Café Beverly and the lively lobby bar round out the offerings.

Services: 24-hour room service, concierge, evening turndown, overnight shoeshine.

Facilities: Two heated swimming pools, health club, business center, shops, including Princess Ermine Jewels, Cecily L. boutique, a gift and sundry shop.

Century Plaza Hotel and Tower, Avenue of the Stars, Los Angeles, CA 90067. ☎ **310/277-2000,** or toll free **800/228-3000.** Fax 310/551-3355. 1,072 rms and suites. A/C TV TEL **Directions:** From Santa Monica Boulevard, exit south onto the Avenue of the Stars; the hotel is two blocks ahead on your left.

Rates: Hotel $130–$165 single; $130–$190 double; from $250 suite. Tower $170–$200 single; $170–$220 double; from $900 suite. AE, CB, DC, MC, V. **Parking:** $10 self, $16 valet.

The imposing Century Plaza Hotel and Tower complex is composed of two separate and distinctive properties on 10 tropical plant–covered acres. Occupying a commanding position near Beverly Hills and right across the street from the ABC Entertainment Center and the 1,850-seat Shubert theater, the Westin managed hotel was built on what was once a Twentieth-Century-Fox back lot.

The 20-story, 750-room hotel is enormous—it appears to be roughly the size of New York's Grand Central Terminal, complete with vaulted cathedral ceilings, two-story windows, and sunken lounge areas. It has the feel of a bustling city of tomorrow. Rooms follow a garden motif with marble-topped oak furnishings and beautiful teal-blue or forest-green carpeting. Each has a balcony and is equipped with every amenity, including a color TV discreetly hidden in an oak armoire, three phones (bedside, tableside, and bath), refrigerator, AM/FM radio, clock, big closet, and tub/shower bath with marble sink, hairdryer, oversize towels, and scales. Special hotel extras range from a dedicated kitchen elevator in which food is kept warm on its way to your room, to the homey practice of leaving a mint and a good-night note from the management on each guest's pillow when the beds are turned down for the night.

The 30-story, $85-million Tower at Century Plaza (where former President Reagan once stayed) has 322 exceptionally spacious rooms—that's only 14 rooms per floor. All have a private balcony, a wet bar and refrigerator, three conveniently located phones, an all-marble bathroom with separate soak tub and shower, double vanity and washbasins, and a heat lamp. Writing desks have travertine marble tops, and there's a live tree or green plant in each room. All Tower guests receive a complimentary newspaper each morning, and deluxe bath amenities such as robes, slippers, and oversize bath towels. Tower suites are all fitted with marble Jacuzzis.

The tower and hotel are linked by a marble corridor hung with over $4 million worth of art. The property underwent a $16.5-million renovation in 1990.

Dining/Entertainment: The Lobby Court cocktail lounge is surrounded by two-story windows that overlook the hotel's pools and garden and features nightly entertainment. La Chaumière restaurant blends contemporary Californian ingredients and classic French techniques to produce an innovative cuisine in a setting reminiscent of a fine European club. The Terrace is an excellent choice for classic Mediterranean and Californian dining. Filled with greenery and located on the lobby level, it serves breakfast, lunch, and dinner daily, as well as a champagne brunch on Sunday. The Café Plaza, a provincial-style coffee shop with a simple bakery, deli, and charcuterie, is open from 6am to 1am.

Services: 24-hour room service, concierge, evening turndown, business center, multilingual staff, same-day laundry, complimentary car service to and from Beverly Hills.

Facilities: Two large outdoor heated swimming pools, three Jacuzzis, children's pool, 10 shops, airline desk, car-rental office, ticket agency, tour desk, free access to off-premises health club.

Four Seasons Hotel Beverly Hills, 300 S. Doheny Drive, Los Angeles, CA 90048. ☎ **310/273-2222.** Fax 310/859-3824. 179 rms, 106 suites. A/C TV TEL MINIBAR **Directions:** From Santa Monica Boulevard, exit onto Wilshire Boulevard east, then turn north onto Doheny Drive. The hotel is on your right, at the corner of Burton Way.

Rates: $280–$330 single; $310–$360 double; from $430 suite. AE, DC, MC, V. **Parking:** Valet $8, self free.

As the world's superintendent of traditionalist wealth, the ultra-conservative 16-story Four Seasons can always be counted on for impeccable service and standards. On the plus side, this means intense attention to details, butlers on 24-hour call, and high-quality furnishings and food. On the minus side it means muted beiges and browns, dull designs that are chosen for their inoffensiveness, and doting saccharine service.

The hotel is expensive and attractive to both the old and new kind of rich. Dated decor includes firm king-size beds, and three two-line telephones. French doors in each room lead to a private balcony. European art hangs throughout the hotel, and marble bathrooms are fitted with telephones, hairdryers, robes, and miniature TVs. They only contain a single sink, however, and rooms are devoid of stereos or VCRs—accoutrements that are increasingly common in more cutting-edge top-of-the-line hotels.

Dining/Entertainment: The Gardens Restaurant serves three California-inspired meals daily. In addition to light meals, Windows is open daily for cocktails and afternoon tea on Saturdays from 3 to 4pm. The less formal Cafe is open all day, and offers afternoon tea during the week from 3 to 4:30pm.

Services: 24-hour room service, concierge, overnight laundry, complimentary shoeshine, twice-daily maid service.

Facilities: Swimming pool, Jacuzzi, workout facilities, gift shop, florist, car rental desk.

L'Ermitage, 9291 Burton Way, Beverly Hills, CA 90210. ☎ **310/278-3344,** or toll free **800/800-2113**. Fax 310/278-8247. 112 suites. A/C MINIBAR TV TEL **Directions:** From Santa Monica Boulevard, exit onto Burton Way; the hotel is located 10 blocks ahead, at the corner of Maple Drive.

Rates: $285–$350 one-bedroom executive suite; $400–$475 one-bedroom townhouse suite; $600 two-bedroom townhouse suite; $1,500 three-bedroom townhouse suite. AE, CB, DC, MC, V. **Parking:** $15.

L'Ermitage is one of the finest hotels in the world. In addition to a kitchenette, each of the small suites includes a sunken living room, wet bar, dressing area, and powder room. Townhouse suites are slightly larger and have fully equipped kitchens.

Accommodations here are furnished residentially, like rooms in a fine home. The rooms and hallways are hung with oil paintings, and every unit has a fireplace.

Strawberries and brown sugar are delivered to each suite at 4pm, and complimentary caviar is served each afternoon in the elegant bar on the top floor.

Dining/Entertainment: The Club restaurant, which is hung with original paintings by Renoir, Braque, and De la Pena, caters exclusively to hotel guests.

Services: 24-hour room service, concierge, overnight shoeshine, limousine service, morning newspaper.

Facilities: Rooftop garden, spa, heated swimming pool, private solarium.

The Peninsula Beverly Hills, 9882 Santa Monica Blvd., Beverly Hills, CA 90212. ☎ **310/551-2888,** or toll free **800/462-7899**. Fax 310/788-2319. 162 rms, 48 suites. A/C TV TEL MINIBAR **Directions:** From I-405, exit onto Santa Monica Boulevard east. The hotel is located about 2 miles ahead, at the corner of Wilshire Boulevard.

Rates: $280–$425 single or double; from $500 suite. AE, CB, DC, DISC, MC, V. **Parking:** $17.

Los Angeles loves successful newcomers, and this monied recent arrival quickly found wide acceptance with Beverly Hills' fresh-face seekers. The Peninsula is a very good hotel that strives to be more personalized than most top-of-the-line business-oriented properties. The main building is only four stories tall. Fronted by a circular, flower hedged motorcourt, the squat French Renaissance–style structure houses a smallish but elegant lobby, and most of the hotel's rooms and suites.

Like the hotel itself, guest rooms are each decorated in a residential style, and feature French doors, marble baths, two-line voice-mail telephones, and ample closet space. Suites, many of which are located in five surrounding two-story villas, are particularly nice, and feature fireplaces, spas, and terraces.

Additional attractions include a heated rooftop lap pool, and a spa that includes body treatments, saunas, and steam rooms.

Dining/Entertainment: The Belvedere Restaurant serves heavy, continental-style meals all day. Afternoon tea and cocktails are served daily in the lobby-level Living Room. Light lunches are also served seasonally on The Roof Garden. The Club Bar serves cocktails in a, well, club-like setting.

Services: 24-hour room service, 24-hour concierge, business center, overnight dry cleaning, courtesy Rolls Royce service in the area.

Facilites: Lap pool, weight and exercise rooms, steam room, sauna, whirlpool, sundry shop.

★ **Regent Beverly Wilshire,** 9500 Wilshire Blvd., Beverly Hills, CA 90210. ☎ **310/275-5200,** or toll free **800/421-4354**. Fax 310/274-2851. 300 rms, 144 suites. A/C TV TEL **Directions:** From Santa Monica Boulevard, exit onto Wilshire Boulevard and continue east 8 blocks to the hotel.

Rates: $225–$315 single or double; $335–$405 deluxe single or double; from $425 suite. Additional person $30. Children under 15 stay free in parents' room. AE, DC, DISC, MC, V. **Parking:** $15.

This grand Beverly Hills hotel has long attracted international royalty, media celebrities, stage personalities, presidents, and the usual smattering of rich and famous. Parts of *Pretty Woman,* with Richard Gere and Julia Roberts, were filmed here. The spacious lobby contains French Empire (Directoire) furnishings, French and Italian marble flooring, restored bronze and crystal chandeliers, hand-wrought sconces, and two paintings by Verhoven.

Upon arrival, visitors are greeted by a guest-relations officer who personally escorts you to your room; luggage is recorded by computer and arrives by a separate lift. There is steward service on every floor (a concept that began with Regent's Hong Kong property), as well as 24-hour concierge service.

El Camino Real, a private cobblestone and gas lamp street, separates the Beverly and Wilshire wings of the hotel. On average, guest rooms here are larger than those in comparable hotels. Wilshire Wing rooms are largest, but many on the Beverly side are prettier, with balconies overlooking the pool area. Every room is beautifully appointed with a mix of period furniture, three phones, three cable color TVs, and special double-glazed windows that ensure absolute quiet.

Bathrooms are lined with marble and feature a large vanity, excellent lighting, a deep soaking tub, and a separate glass-enclosed shower that's large enough for three or more. Amenities include fresh flowers in each room, plush deep-pile white bathrobes, scales, hairdryer, and specially packaged toiletries.

Dining/Entertainment: The Café, an elegant, updated version of the old-fashioned soda fountain, serves lox and eggs, cheese blintzes, sandwiches, salads, and changing daily main courses. It's open from 7am to midnight. The Lobby Lounge is an elegant European-style salon for tea (served from 3 to 5pm), light menus, late-night dinner fare, and cocktails—a place "to be seen." There's live entertainment in the evening. The Dining Room, outfitted in lush woods and soft fabrics, offers a lengthy list of elegant American lunch and dinner fare. Reservations are recommended.

Services: 24-hour room service, concierge, evening turndown, overnight shoeshine.

Facilities: Health club, swimming pool, hot tubs, massage, business center, and shops, including Escada and Buccellati.

EXPENSIVE

Beverly Prescott Hotel, 1224 S. Beverwil Dr. (P.O. Box 3065), Beverly Hills, CA 90212. ☎ **310/277-2800,** or toll free **800/421-3212.** Fax 310/203-9537. 128 rms, 12 suites. A/C TV TEL **Directions:** From I-405, exit east onto Pico Boulevard, continue about 2 miles, then turn left onto Beverwil Drive.

Rates: $145–$195 single or double; from $250 suites. AE, DC, DISC, MC, V. **Parking:** $12.

After a multi-million renovation that rendered the former Beverly Hillcrest Hotel unrecognizable, the Beverly Prescott opened its doors in 1993, garnering raves from all quarters. Managed by the Kimpton Group, owners of about a dozen high quality "boutique" hotels in San Francisco, the Prescott is knowledgeably run and joyfully decorated, with comfortable, colorful, funky furnishings carefully chosen by a confident, competent designer. The Prescott's distinctiveness begins in the lobby, where an alluring sitting area is made particularly inviting with plush, mixed-print furnishings surrounding a working fireplace.

Rooms are decorated in salmon and cream stripes or black and tan checks, each accentuated with bright bedspreads and pillows. An emphasis on details means oversized TV screens, remote phones with up to three lines, and dimmer switches on most lights. Suites are fitted with down comforters, and most come with VCRs. Every room has a private balcony with good city views. All in all, the Beverly Prescott represents one of the best deals in town.

Dining/Entertainment: Röx, the lobby-level restaurant owned by celebrity chef Hans Röckenwagner serves top quality meals either indoors or out (see Section 4, "Dining," below, for complete information).

Services: 24-hour room service, concierge, chocolate turndown, free morning newspaper, complimentary shuttle service to nearby business centers and shopping, overnight laundry and shoeshine, massage and manicure service.

Facilities: Swimming pool, business services, health club.

MODERATE

Carlyle Inn, 1119 S. Robertson Blvd., Los Angeles, CA 90035. ☎ **310/275-4445,** or toll free **800/322-7595**. Fax 310/859-0496. 32 rms, 10 suites. A/C MINIBAR TV TEL

Rates: $95–$140 single or double; $160 suite. AE, DC, DISC, MC, V. **Parking:** Free.

Hidden away in a modest location just south of Beverly Hills, on an otherwise uneventful stretch of Robertson Boulevard, Carlyle Inn is one of the best-priced quality finds in Los Angeles. Cleverly designed, the hotel sports thoroughly contemporary rooms, complete with recessed lighting, deco wall sconces and lamps, clean pine furnishings, and well-framed Roman architectural monoprints. Facilities include a coffee- and teamaker (and a bottle of Evian to fill it with), a clock radio, and a TV with VCR. The hotel's only drawback is the view, or lack of it; and curtains must remain drawn to maintain privacy.

Suites are slightly larger and contain full-length mirrors and well-outfitted baths with telephone, lighted magnified mirror, hairdryer, and plenty of counter space for toiletries.

The small size of the hotel directly translates into great personal service.

Bel Air

Hotel Bel-Air, 701 Stone Canyon Rd., Bel-Air, CA 90077. ☎ **310/472-1211,** or toll free **800/648-4097**. Fax 310/476-5890. 52 rms, 39 suites. A/C MINIBAR TV TEL **Directions:** From I-405, exit onto Sunset Boulevard east; after two miles, turn left onto Stone Canyon Road.

Rates: $245–$395 single; $275–$435 double; from $495 suite. AE, CB, DC, MC, V. **Parking:** $12.50.

Yet another top hotel in one of the world's fanciest neighborhoods, the Spanish-style Hotel Bel-Air regularly wins praise from guests for its attentive service and ultra-deluxe guest rooms. Set on exquisite tropical grounds and surrounded by the Santa Monica hills, the Bel-Air is entered via a long awning-covered pathway, actually an arched stone bridge over a swan-filled pond. A large oval swimming pool is set amid the lush gardens and surrounded by a flagstone terrace. Inside, you'll find richly traditional public rooms furnished with fine antiques, and a fire that is kept burning in the entrance lounge.

The individually decorated rooms and garden suites, all of which have large picture windows, are equally stunning; many have a patio or terrace, and some have a wood-burning fireplace. Each room has two phones, and a VCR is delivered to your room on request.

Dining/Entertainment: Even if you're not staying here, it's worth showing up for a drink at the Bar or for dinner in the Restaurant. Main courses include beef filet with a Stilton cheese crust, and medallions of veal with Chanterelle-prawn risotto. Seating on the terrace, which is heated year-round, overlooks a small lake. The Bar, a cozy drinkery adjacent to The Restaurant, has a wood-burning fireplace and nightly entertainment.

Services: 24-hour room service, concierge, evening turndown.

Facilities: Swimming pool, access to off-premises health club.

Radisson Bel-Air Summit Hotel, 11461 Sunset Blvd., Los Angeles, CA 90049. ☎ **310/476-6571,** or toll free **800/333-3333**. Fax 310/471-6310. 161 rms, 6 suites. A/C MINIBAR TV TEL **Directions:** From I-405, exit onto Sunset Boulevard west; the hotel is immediately ahead on your right.

Rates: $109–$139 single; $119–$149 double; from $179 suite. Additional person $15. AE, CB, DC, DISC, MC, V. **Parking:** $5.

Set in an eight-acre garden estate, the Radisson Bel-Air Summit is just minutes away from Beverly Hills, Westwood Village and UCLA, and Century City, and eight miles north of LAX.

Spacious rooms and suites all feature large balconies and have subtle color schemes and understated decor. All rooms have hairdryer, refrigerator, coffeemaker, electronic security keys, radio, and two phones. With a heated swimming pool and a single unlit tennis court on the premises.

Dining/Entertainment: Echo, the hotel dining room, serves breakfast, lunch, dinner, and a fabulous Sunday brunch. The Oasis bar serves cocktails nightly, and complimentary hors d'oeuvres Monday through Saturday from 5 to 7pm.

Services: Room service, concierge, car rental, tour desk.

Facilities: Swimming pool, one tennis court, gift shop, fitness room, beauty salon with spa treatments.

Wilshire

Wilshire is a very long street that connects Beverly Hills with downtown L.A. The two listings below are on opposite ends of the street.

Beverly Hills Ritz Hotel, 10300 Wilshire Blvd., Los Angeles, CA 90024. ☎ **310/275-5575,** or toll free **800/800-1234**. Fax 310/278-3325. 116 rms, all suites. A/C MINIBAR TV TEL **Directions:** From I-405 south, exit onto Wilshire Boulevard east; the hotel is located just before Beverly Hills, at Comstock Street.

Rates: $175–$275 standard suite; $275–$350 1-bedroom kitchen suite; $395–$600 2-bedroom kitchen suite. Monthly rates available. AE, CB, DC, DISC, MC, V. **Parking:** $8.

Dedicated to the comfortable, homelike suite business, this quiet, peaceful hotel offers a standard of intimacy and privacy not usually available at larger hotels. Understandably, the Ritz, located just outside Beverly Hills, attracts a considerable celebrity clientele.

The large rooms are decorated in either a traditional hotel style or with a colorful Californian modern flair. The units, which surround a central courtyard pool and garden area, have private balconies or patios. There are phones and TVs in both bedrooms and bathrooms. Kitchen suites are particularly large, ranging in size from 1,000 to 2,000 square feet. These well-equipped accommodations have a living room, a dining area, and completely equipped kitchens with china service.

Dining/Entertainment: Le Petit Café, a continental restaurant, serves breakfast, lunch, and dinner, and has a full-service bar.

Services: Room service, concierge, overnight laundry.

Facilities: Swimming pool, Jacuzzi, access to off-premises health club.

Wilshire Radisson Plaza, 3515 Wilshire Blvd., Los Angeles, CA 90010. ☎ **213/381-7411,** or toll free **800/333-3333**. Fax 213/386-7379. 396 rms, 5 suites. A/C TV TEL **Directions:** From U.S. 101, take the Melrose/Normandy exit and turn south onto Normandy Avenue; the hotel is located about two miles ahead, at the corner of Wilshire Boulevard.

Rates: $110–$140 single, $120–$160 double; from $250 suite. AE, DC, DISC, MC, V. **Parking:** $8 self, $10 valet.

Located close to downtown, this 12-story luxury hotel is popular with businesspeople for its pushbutton comfort and convenient location. Rooms are attractively furnished in a modern style; each has a glass brick wall and functional furniture. One- and two-bedroom suites have two bathrooms and an additional living room.

Dining/Entertainment: Tulip's Restaurant is open for breakfast, lunch, and dinner, serving basic American fare like prime rib and grilled swordfish. Sake-E Restaurant serves authentic Japanese cuisine.

Services: Room service, concierge, car rental, tour desk, business center.

Facilities: Heated outdoor swimming pool, fitness center, barbershop.

Westwood & West Los Angeles

Wedged between Santa Monica and glamorous Beverly Hills, the UCLA student-dominated community of Westwood has over 400 shops, about 100 restaurants, and 15 first-run movie theaters. West Los Angeles, as a glance at your L.A. map will show you, is just slightly south of Westwood, and within easy access of Beverly Hills, Century City, and Santa Monica.

Holiday Inn Westwood Plaza, 10740 Wilshire Blvd., Los Angeles, CA 90024. ☎ **310/475-8711,** or toll free **800/472-8556**. Fax 310/475-5220. 295 rms, 8 suites. A/C MINIBAR TV TEL **Directions:** From I-405, take the Westwood exit and follow Wilshire Boulevard east 1 mile to the hotel, at the corner of Selby Avenue.

Rates: $100–$130 single or double; from $200 suite. Children 18 or under stay free in parents' room. AE, CB, DC, DISC, MC, V. **Parking:** Free.

Attractively furnished twin-bedded rooms are decorated according to an English Tudor theme, which includes hunting prints on most walls. Special touches include marble sinks in the bathrooms, and complimentary morning newspapers delivered to your door. Services include a tour desk, car rental, laundry, concierge, gift shop, and an exercise room. The hotel also provides complimentary shuttle service to anywhere within a 2½-mile radius.

Facilities include a swimming pool, sun deck, sauna, and Jacuzzi. The hotel restaurant, Café Le Dome, is best known for its cocktail lounge, which is popular with basketball and football players, many of whom stay at the hotel.

Los Angeles West Travelodge, 10740 Santa Monica Blvd., Los Angeles, CA 90025. ☎ **310/474-4576,** or toll free **800/578-7878**. Fax 310/470-3117. 36 rms. A/C TV TEL **Directions:** From I-405, exit onto Santa Monica Boulevard; the hotel is two miles ahead, at Overland Avenue.

Rates: $60–$90 single; $66–$96 double. Extra person $6. AE, CB, DC, MC, V. **Parking:** Free.

This clean and friendly establishment offers good value for the area. The pleasant, modern rooms are equipped with clock, in-room coffeemaker, and refrigerator. There are no restaurant or health facilities in the hotel, but there is an enclosed, private heated swimming pool with a sun deck, plus plenty of parking.

Royal Palace Westwood Hotel, 1052 Tiverton Ave., Los Angeles, CA 90024. ☎ **310/208-6677,** or toll free **800/631-0100**. Fax 310/824-3732. 36 rms, 6 suites. A/C TV TEL **Directions:** From I-405, take the Westwood exit and follow Wilshire Boulevard east a half mile, then turn left onto Glendon Avenue and bear right onto Tiverton Avenue to the hotel.

Rates: $60 single; $66–$76 double; from $96 suite. Extra person $8. AE, CB, DC, DISC, MC, V. **Parking:** Free.

Located between Beverly Hills, Century City, Santa Monica, West Los Angeles, and Bel Air, the Royal Palace is convenient to Hollywood, the beach, the airport, and most importantly, the San Diego Freeway. There are dozens of shops and restaurants within easy walking distance of the hotel.

This is not a fancy place by any stretch of the imagination, but each comfortable, redecorated room has a bed, desk, dresser, and color TV. Some accommodations have a stove, a refrigerator, and stainless steel countertops, while others have a microwave oven. There are marble vanities in the bathrooms. Facilities include a free exercise room, lounge, and a tour desk for area activity information and reservations.

Studio City

Sportsmen's Lodge, 12825 Ventura Blvd., Los Angeles, CA 91604. ☎ **818/769-4700,** or toll free **800/821-8511, 800/821-1625** in California. Fax 213/877-3898. 193 rms, 13 suites. A/C TV TEL **Directions:** From U.S. 101, take the Coldwater Canyon exit and continue to the corner of Ventura Boulevard.

Rates: $100–$110 single; $110–$140 double; poolside executive studio $165 single; $175 double. Extra person $10. AE, CB, DC, DISC, MC, V. **Parking:** Free.

When staying here, you'd hardly know you're in the middle of a big city. Located just west of Universal City, the Sportsmen's Lodge is surrounded by redwood trees, waterfalls, rock gardens, lush tropical greenery, and rustic wooden footbridges that cross freshwater ponds. In fact, the hotel's name derives from the fact that guests used to fish for trout right on the premises.

Rooms are large and comfortable, but not luxurious in any way. They have an AM/FM radio, many have balconies, and refrigerators are available. The poolside executive studios are the most attractive accommodations here.

The hotel's attractive restaurant features a glass-enclosed dining room overlooking a tropical lagoon-style pond and small waterfall. You might begin a meal here with an order of Oysters Rockefeller, then order a main dish of veal piccata or duckling à l'orange with wild rice, priced from $15 to $22. Cakes and rolls are baked fresh daily. An adjacent coffee shop serves simpler breakfasts, lunches, and dinners.

Facilities include an Olympic-size, heated swimming pool with a Jacuzzi and large sun deck. A well-equipped exercise room has life cycles, rowing machines, and weights. There are also a variety of shops and service desks in the hotel, and both bowling and golf are nearby. Complimentary afternoon tea is served in the lobby at 4pm.

Frommer's Cool for Kids: Hotels

Century Plaza Hotel and Tower (see p. 389) Although it is not inexpensive, older children will love exploring this labyrinthine hotel, which features two large outdoor heated swimming pools, three Jacuzzis, and a children's pool. Kids are given free amenity packs filled with games, crayons, coloring books, and an inflatable beach ball.

Hotel Stillwell (see p. 385) Ask for one of their larger guest rooms, and the kids will have plenty of room for romping. It's an inexpensive hotel in an otherwise pricey neighborhood.

Pasadena

EXPENSIVE

The Pasadena Hilton, 150 S. Los Robles Ave., Pasadena, CA 91101. ☎ **818/577-1000,** or toll free **800/445-8667**. Fax 818/584-3148. 291 rms, 15 suites. A/C MINIBAR TV TEL **Directions:** From I-210, take the Lake Avenue South exit and turn right on Cordova Street; the hotel is straight ahead, on the corner of Cordova Street and Los Robles Avenue.

Rates: $120–$150 single; $135–$165 double; from $250 suite. AE, CB, DC, MC, V. **Parking:** $8.

This 13-story hostelry is 15 minutes from downtown Los Angeles, and only a block and a half south of Colorado Boulevard, which is famed for the Rose Parade passing by on it. Rooms have been redecorated in soft earth tones. Some have beds with elaborate high headboards, and all have refrigerators and in-room movies. The higher rates are for accommodations with king-size beds and balconies.

The hotel does a lot of convention business. It also has an affiliation with the nearby exclusive La Cañada/Flintridge Country Club, allowing guests to use their facilities.

Dining/Entertainment: The Trevos restaurant, serving a Californian cuisine, offers breakfast, lunch, and dinner. There is an all-you-can-eat buffet, fresh daily. The lobby bar is a favorite rendezvous during happy hour.

Facilities: Outdoor swimming pool; exercise room with Universal equipment, StairMasters, life cycles, and free weights; business center.

Services: Room service, concierge, evening turndown, overnight laundry.

★ **The Ritz-Carlton Huntington Hotel,** 1401 S. Oak Knoll Ave., Pasadena, CA 91109. ☎ **818/568-3900,** or toll free **800/241-3333**. Fax 818/568-3700. 383 rms, 21 suites. A/C MINIBAR TV TEL **Directions:** From LAX, take I-105 east to 110 north (Pasadena Freeway). The freeway ends at the corner of Arroyo Parkway and Glenarm. Turn right onto Glenarm. Turn right onto El Molino, then left onto Elliott, and right onto Oak Knoll Avenue.

Rates: $160–$275 single or double; from $350 suite. AE, DC, MC, V. **Parking:** $12.

Originally built in 1906, the landmark Huntington Hotel quickly became the place to be seen, as celebrated writers and entertainers, members of society and royalty, and political and business leaders favored it for its elegance and matchless service. The hotel managed to survive the 1929 stock market crash, the Great Depression, and World War II, but it could not survive the major earthquake that struck in 1985. After a painstaking 2½-year restoration, the Huntington reopened in 1991 under the Ritz-Carlton banner. The fantastically beautiful hotel is set on 23 meticulously landscaped garden acres nestled in the shadows of the San Gabriel Mountains and overlooking the San Gabriel Valley.

Throughout the hotel, careful attention has been paid to re-create the genteel, timeless ambience of the original resort. Overstuffed sofas and club chairs upholstered in natural fabrics sit on Oriental carpets and are surrounded by fine 18th- and 19th-century oil paintings.

The hotel consists of a main building and six suite-filled cottages. Each room is oversized and elegantly appointed with a marble bathroom, a sitting area, a desk, large closets, and two phones. There are a remote-controlled color TV, thick terry bathrobes, and in-room minibars.

Dining/Entertainment: The Grill offers a comfortable clublike setting for grilled meats, chops, and fresh fish. The Café serves breakfast, lunch, and dinner, either inside or outdoors. The menu offers American standards, as well as light spa cuisine. Champagne brunch is served on Sundays. The lobby lounge offers continental breakfast, cocktails, and traditional afternoon tea with—a pleasant touch—classical music accompaniment.

Services: 24-hour room service, concierge, evening turndown, babysitting, car rental, mountain bike rental.

Facilities: Olympic-size swimming pool, outdoor whirlpool, fitness center, three tennis courts, pro shop, gift shop, Japanese gardens.

BUDGET

Saga Motor Hotel, 1633 E. Colorado Blvd., Pasadena, CA 91106. ☎ **818/795-0431.** 69 rms. A/C TV TEL **Directions:** From I-210, exit at Fair Oaks Avenue south, and turn left on Colorado Boulevard, the second major street; the hotel is about one mile ahead, between Allan Avenue and Sierra Bonita.

Rates (including continental breakfast): $55 single; $57 double; $59 single or double with king-size bed and refrigerator; $70 suite. AE, CB, DC, MC, V. **Parking:** Free.

The Saga Motor Hotel is about a mile from the Huntington Library, and reasonably close to Pasadena City College, Cal Tech, and the Jet Propulsion Lab. It's also within an easy distance of the Rose Bowl. But the bottom line is that the Saga has, by far, some of the most attractive rooms in its price range, as well as a very inviting, sunlit, and spotlessly clean reception area.

Comfortable accommodations, which include a cable TV, are nicely decorated with brass beds, blue-and-white-checked spreads, and blue-and-white tile baths with both showers and tubs. Guest rooms are split between two buildings; the first is a single-story structure wrapped around a swimming pool; the other is a small three-story building between the pool and a quiet street at the rear of the building.

Santa Monica

Not only does locating in Santa Monica mean living near the beach, it means getting away from the smog and staying in one of the most attractive, dynamic neighborhoods in L.A.

EXPENSIVE

Miramar Sheraton Hotel, 101 Wilshire Blvd., Santa Monica, CA 90401. ☎ **310/576-7777,** or toll free **800/325-3535**. Fax 310/458-7912. 301 rms, 61 suites. A/C MINIBAR TV TEL **Directions:** From the Santa Monica Freeway 10, exit west onto Fourth Street, and after five blocks, turn left onto Wilshire Boulevard; the hotel is four blocks ahead on your left, between Ocean Avenue and Second Street.

Rates: $195–$225 single or double; from $275 suite. Extra person $20. AE, CB, DC, MC, V. **Parking:** $11.

Miramar means "ocean view" and that's just what this hotel offers from its cliff-top perch overlooking Santa Monica beach. The hotel was originally built in the 1920s, and that era's elegance is clearly in evidence throughout the public areas. In the courtyard is a century-old fig tree that casts its shadow over the garden and adjacent swimming pool.

Guest rooms are split between older low buildings and the newer tower. Each is comfortable and luxurious for a beach hotel. Amenities include a king-size bed or two double beds, in-room safe, and digital clock radio. Bathrooms are plush, outfitted with extra phones, honor bars, special soaps and shampoos, and oversize towels.

Dining/Entertainment: The Miramar Grille, a California-style bistro, is open for lunch and dinner. Open all day from 6:30am to 11pm is The Cafe. The Stateroom Lounge offers live entertainment, cocktails, and dancing several nights a week.

Services: 24-hour room service, concierge, evening turndown, same-day laundry and valet service, complimentary newspaper, car rental, bike rental.

Facilities: Heated swimming pool, health center, gift shop, beauty salon, women's boutique.

Shutters on the Beach, 1 Pico Blvd., Santa Monica, CA 90405. ☎ **310/458-0030,** or toll free **800/334-9000**. Fax 310/458-4589. 186 rms, 12 suites. TV TEL MINIBAR **Directions:** From I-10, exit onto 4th Street and turn left. After one long block, turn right, onto Pico Boulevard, and continue all the way to the ocean, to the hotel.

Rates: $230–$350 single or double; from $550 suite. AE, DC, DISC, MC, V. **Parking:** $15.

The only luxury hotel in L.A. that's actually on the beach, light and bright Shutters enjoys one of the city's most enviable locations, a block from Santa Monica Pier. Opened in 1993, the hotel is ingeniously designed to optimize its space. Gray-shingled Shutters is divided into two connecting parts; squat beachfront cottage-like structures are separated from the taller building behind them by the hotel's swimming pool. And although the beach cottage rooms are plainly more desirable then those in the tower, when it comes to rates, the hotel doesn't distinguish between them.

The hotel is justifiably proud of their extensive contemporary art collection which is liberally and almost casually hung throughout the hotel. Ocean views and the sound of crashing waves are the most outstanding quality of the guest rooms. Some accommodations have fireplaces, most have Jacuzzi tubs, and all have sliding wooden shutters on floor-to-ceiling windows that open. Large TVs are connected to VCRs, and showers come with waterproof radios and biodegradable bath supplies.

Dining/Entertainment: One Pico, the hotel's premiere restaurant, enjoys panoramic views of Santa Monica beach. The more casual Pedals, located directly on the beach path serves three meals daily and has a wood-burning grill. The adjacent Handle Bar is an upbeat drinkery with good happy hour specials.

Services: 24-hour room service, concierge, overnight laundry, evening turndown, massage.

Facilities: Swimming pool, Jacuzzi, health facilities, sauna, beach equipment, and bicycle rentals.

MODERATE

Radisson-Huntley Hotel, 1111 Second St., Santa Monica, CA 90403. ☎ **310/394-5454,** or toll free **800/333-3333**. Fax 310/458-9776. 213 rms, 6 suites. A/C TV TEL **Directions:** From I-10 (Santa Monica Fwy.), exit west onto Fourth Street, then after 5 blocks, turn left onto Wilshire Boulevard, then right onto Second Street to the hotel.

Rates: $120–$145 single; $135–$160 double; from $160 suite. Ask about "Supersaver Rates" promotion. AE, CB, DC, DISC, MC, V. **Parking:** $5.50.

One of the tallest buildings in the neighborhood, the Radisson-Huntley offers nondescript rooms just two blocks from the beach. Accommodations are basic yet comfortable, attractive, with ocean or mountain views, and are equipped with an AM/FM radio, color TV, and other modern amenities. Toppers, the rooftop Mexican restaurant, has a great view, serves good margaritas, and offers free live entertainment nightly. The lobby-level Garden Café is a classy coffee shop serving American standards.

BUDGET

Santa Monica International AYH Hostel, 1436 Second St., P.O. Box 575, Santa Monica, CA 90401. ☎ **310/393-9913.** Fax 310/393-1769. 38 rms. **Directions:** From the Santa Monica Fwy., exit on Fourth Street and make a right turn, then turn left on Colorado and then right on Second Street.

Rates: $14 per person with an IYHF card, $17 per person without, $3 surcharge for twin rooms. MC, V. **Parking:** 50¢ per hour.

Opened in April 1990, the Santa Monica hostel is just two blocks from the beach and Santa Monica Pier, and about a mile from Venice beach. It's within walking distance of shops and restaurants and about two blocks from regional bus lines, including a direct bus to Los Angeles International Airport (about seven miles).

This is one of the largest purpose-built hostels in this country and can accommodate up to 200 guests, including groups and families on a space-available basis. Accommodations are dormitory style, with shared bedrooms and bathrooms. The hostel has guest kitchen facilities, a travel library, and a travel center. It's pretty nice too, designed in muted earth tones and centered around an open courtyard. Six twin rooms are reserved for couples, and four family rooms cater to families.

There is a TV lounge, laundry room, games room, information desk, vending machines, a dining room, library, and secure lockers. Sheets are required, you have to be quiet after 11pm, and no smoking or alcohol is permitted.

Reservations are highly recommended, especially from May to October. Write them at least two weeks in advance and include your dates of stay, number of males and females in your party, your name, address, and phone number, and the first night's deposit. To reserve by phone, call between 1pm and 5pm Monday through Saturday.

IYHF membership is required during peak times. Individual membership in the American Youth Hostel organization costs $25 per year and entitles you to discounted rates in any AYH-affiliated hostel. You can buy a membership at the hostel. Guests are limited to three-day stays; however, this can be extended to five nights with the approval of the manager.

Accommodations in Southern Los Angeles County

Hotel *Queen Mary* 10

Los Angeles Airport Marriott 9

Marina del Rey Hotel 7

Marina del Rey Marriott 6

Marina International 5

Miramar Sheraton Hotel 2

Radisson-Huntley Hotel 1

Santa Monica International AYH Hostel 3

Sheraton Los Angeles Airport Hotel 8

Shutters on the Beach 4

9098A

Marina del Rey

Sandwiched between Santa Monica and the Los Angeles International Airport, Marina del Rey is a very popular waterfront resort, just two minutes from major freeways that connect with most L.A. attractions. Over 6,000 pleasure boats dock here, making Marina del Rey's marina the world's largest small-craft harbor.

Marina del Rey Hotel, 13534 Bali Way, Marina del Rey, CA 90292.

☎ **310/301-1000,** or toll free **800/882-4000, 800/862-7462** in California. Fax 310/301-8167. 154 rms, 6 suites. A/C TV TEL **Directions:** From I-405, exit onto Calif. 90, which ends at Lincoln Boulevard, turn left onto Lincoln Boulevard, then right onto Bali Way to the hotel.

Rates: $125–$190 single; $140–$210 double; from $350 suite. AE, CB, DC, MC, V. **Parking:** Free.

Located at the tip of a pier jutting into the harbor, this hotel specializes in rooms that look out over one of the world's largest yacht-filled harbors. The only hotel located on a harbor pier, the Marina del Rey is almost completely surrounded by water. First-class guest rooms are decorated in a soothing blue-and-tan color scheme and are fitted with all the expected amenities. Most rooms have balconies or patios. If yours doesn't, go down to the heated waterside swimming pool where great views can be enjoyed from the beautifully landscaped sun deck area.

Dining/Entertainment: The Dockside Café, a coffee shop, is open daily for breakfast and lunch. The Crystal Seahorse serves continental dinners from 6 to 11pm daily. The restaurant overlooks the marina, and its mirrored tables, walls, and ceilings reflect the view.

Services: Room service, concierge, evening turndown, complimentary airport limousine, bicycle rental, car rental desk.

Facilities: Heated swimming pool, putting green, nearby tennis, golf, complimentary athletic club, and beach.

Marina del Rey Marriott, 13480 Maxella Ave., Marina del Rey, CA 90292.

☎ **310/822-8555,** or toll free **800/228-9290**. Fax 310/823-2996. 283 rms. 3 suites. A/C MINIBAR TV TEL **Directions:** From I-405, exit onto Calif. 90, which ends at Lincoln Boulevard, turn right onto Lincoln Boulevard, and right again onto Maxella Avenue.

Rates: $90–$135 single; $130–$160 twin or double; from $275 suite. AE, CB, DC, DISC, MC, V. **Parking:** Free.

This delightful, resort-like hotel offers excellently appointed rooms with AM/FM clock radio, first-run movies, and bright tropical-style rooms accented with splashy floral-design spreads and drapes. Tile bathrooms, in-room minibars, pretty furnishings, and good service make this an excellent place to locate. Many rooms have patios or balconies.

The hotel is conveniently located next to the Villa Marina Center, a small mall with about 30 shops.

Dining/Entertainment: Maxfield's Restaurant and Lounge serves American-continental dishes in cheery surroundings. The outdoor pool bar is in a landscaped courtyard complete with a rock waterfall, pond, and a bridge over a stream.

Services: Room service, concierge, evening turndown, airport transportation.

Facilities: Swimming pool, whirlpool, car and bicycle rental.

Marina International, 4200 Admiralty Way, Marina del Rey, CA 90292. ☎ **310/301-2000,** or toll free **800/882-4000, 800/862-7462** in California. Fax 310/301-6687. 135 rms, 24 suites, 25 bungalows. A/C TV TEL **Directions:** From I-405, exit onto Calif. 90, which ends at Lincoln Boulevard, turn left onto Bali Way, and then right onto Admiralty Way to the hotel.

Rates: $110–$160 single; $125–$298 double; from $180 suite; from $195 bungalow. AE, CB, DC, MC, V. **Parking:** Free.

Located at the top end of the harbor, the Marina International's lovely rooms are both bright and contemporary, many offering unobstructed water views. Suites have an additional sitting room, and an extra phone in the bathroom. The hotel's bungalows are located off a private courtyard. An especially good buy, the spacious bungalows offer very private accommodations. They're fitted with luxuriously appointed sitting areas, bedrooms, and bathrooms. Larger than suites, some bungalows have raised ceilings, while others are split-level duplexes. Most rooms are decorated in a warm, casual, very contemporary Californian style, with soft pastel colors and comfortable textured fabrics.

Dining/Entertainment: The Crystal Fountain features California cooking served indoors or out. It's open daily for breakfast and lunch.

Services: Room service, concierge, complimentary airport shuttle.

Facilities: Heated swimming pool, whirlpool, tour desk, business center, nearby golf and tennis.

Near L.A.X.

Los Angeles Airport Marriott, Century Blvd. and Airport Blvd., Los Angeles, CA 90045. ☎ **310/641-5700,** or toll free **800/228-9290**. Fax 310/337-5358. 1,020 rms, 19 suites. A/C TV TEL **Directions:** From I-405, take Century Boulevard west towards the airport; the hotel is on your right, at Airport Boulevard.

Rates: $99 single; $164 double; from $375 suite. AE, CB, DC, DISC, MC, V. **Parking:** $9.

Built in 1973 and last renovated in 1987, this business hotel is not on the cutting edge, but it is a good choice near the airport. The property offers cheerfully decorated bedrooms with AM/FM-stereo radio and alarm clock. It's made for travelers on the fly; you can even get an ironing board, iron, and hairdryer if you need them. There's also a guest laundry room on the premises.

Dining/Entertainment: The Lobby Bistro serves buffet breakfasts, lunches, and dinners. The Capriccio Room offers continental specialties in a Mediterranean ambience. The Fairfield Inn coffee shop serves American food and is open all day. Cocktails and entertainment are offered in Champions lounge.

Services: Room service, concierge, car rental, tour desk, complimentary airport limousine service.

Facilities: Giant swimming pool, swim-up bar, garden sun deck, whirlpool, business center.

Sheraton Los Angeles Airport Hotel, 6101 W. Century Blvd., Los Angeles, CA 90045. ☎ **310/642-1111,** or toll free **800/325-3535**. Fax 310/645-1414. 807 rms, 91 suites. A/C MINIBAR TV TEL **Directions:** From I-405, take Century Boulevard west towards the airport; the hotel is on your right, near Sepulveda Boulevard.

Rates: $115–$155 single; $135–$175 double; from $300 suite. AE, CB, DC, DISC, MC, V. **Parking:** $8.

The airport area has been developing in the last few years, and this Sheraton is one of the newer additions. Rooms have a quintessential California look, with rattan chairs and live plants; color-coordinated drapes and bedspreads are dark green and burgundy. All rooms are equipped with digital alarm clock, TV with free sports, news, and movie channels, and AM/FM radio. Bathrooms are carpeted and are fitted with shower heads over bathtubs.

Dining/Entertainment: The Plaza Brasserie, an airy, contemporary cafe, is open from 6am to 11pm. At Landry's, which is open for dinner, the focus is on steak, chops, and seafood, including a sushi bar. Landry's lounge serves cocktails nightly.

Services: 24-hour room service, concierge, evening turndown, tour desk, business center, same-day laundry, complimentary airport shuttle transportation, complimentary morning newspaper.

Facilities: Heated outdoor swimming pool, spa, shops, boutiques, unisex hair salon, car-rental counter, exercise room with Universal equipment.

Malibu

Casa Malibu, 22752 Pacific Coast Hwy., Malibu, CA 90265. ☎ **310/456-2219,** or toll free **800/831-0858**. Fax 310/456-5418. 21 rms. TV TEL **Directions:** From Santa Monica, take Calif. 1 north to Malibu; the hotel is located directly on Calif. 1 about 1/4 mile before the Malibu Pier.

Rates: $95–$110 single or double with garden view; $120–$130 single or double with ocean view, $145–$155 oceanfront single or double. $10 additional for rooms with kitchens. Extra person $10. AE, MC, V. **Parking:** Free.

Inexpensive accommodations in Malibu are hard to come by. Your best bet is the Casa Malibu, a little inn built around a palm-studded brick courtyard with well-tended flowerbeds and cuppa d'oro vines growing up the balcony. The squat hostelry sits directly on the ocean, in front of a large swath of private, sandy beach. The rooms are cheerful and newly redecorated—some have private balconies and others have fireplaces. Each is equipped with oversized beds, a coffeemaker, and a refrigerator. Oceanfront rooms are particularly lovely, as they have private decks hanging over the sandy beach.

Long Beach

Hotel *Queen Mary*, 1126 Queen's Highway, Long Beach, CA 90802-6390. ☎ **310/435-3511** or **310/432-6964,** or toll free **800/437-2934.** Fax 310/437-4531. TV TEL 348 rms, 17 suites. A/C TV TEL **Directions:** From I-405 west, take I-710 south to the end. Follow the signs to the ship.

Rates: $65-$160 single or double; from $350 suite. Additional person $15, AE, DC, MC, V. **Parking:** $5.

The *Queen Mary* is considered the most luxurious ocean liner ever to have sailed the Atlantic. The last survivor of the era of the great super liners, the ship is now permanently docked in Long Beach. In addition to being a popular tourist attraction, the ship functions as a working hotel.

While the rooms are the largest ever built aboard a ship, they are not exceptional compared to those on terra firma. And while the charm and elegance of the art deco era is recalled in each stateroom's decor, modern amenities like TVs and carpeting seem ready for replacement. Only outside rooms have portholes. While the accommodations themselves really can't compete with luxury land-based hotels, the *Queen Mary* is thoroughly recommendable for its upbeat originality and truly spectacular public areas. A historical treasure from a bygone era, the ship's beautifully carved interior is a festival for the eye and fun to explore. If you're planning to be in Long Beach during the week, the *Queen Mary*'s low room rates are hard to beat.

Dining/Entertainment: Sir Winston's offers a terrific view of the coastline through the large windows of its formal dining room. The Chelsea restaurant specializes in seafood dinners. The Promenade serves all day, Sunday Champagne brunch is served in the ship's Grand Salon. Cocktails are served each evening in the art deco Observation Bar.

Services: Room service, concierge, overnight laundry.

Facilities: Shops.

4 Dining

Although it is surprising to many, Los Angeles is one of the world's leading restaurant cities. Supported by a diverse range of ethnic eateries, year-round outdoor seating, and Californian-inspired imaginative interiors, the many eateries in the city are also blessed with creative and skilled chefs.

In the last decade or so, Angelenos have become more knowledgeable about their food. They eat well and love to discuss restaurants and their respective chefs. Dining out is an important part of the entertainment industry; it's where you see and are seen, meet important contacts, and, ultimately, strike important deals.

Keep in mind that many of the restaurants listed as "expensive" are moderately priced at lunch. Also, many of the hotel restaurants listed should be considered. Reservations are usually advised at most Los Angeles–area restaurants. (For the general location of restaurants, see the map on pp. 408–409.)

Downtown Los Angeles

EXPENSIVE

Horikawa, 111 S. San Pedro St. ☎ **213/680-9355.**

Cuisine: JAPANESE. **Reservations:** Recommended at dinner. **Directions:** From U.S. 101 exit onto Alameda Street south: after two blocks, turn right on First Street, then left on San Pedro Street.

Prices: Appetizers \$5–\$9; lunch \$8–\$15; main courses \$13–\$30; complete dinner \$25–\$75; Ryotei dinner, \$75–\$100. AE, CB, DC, MC, V.

Open: Lunch Mon–Fri 11:30am–2pm; dinner Mon–Fri 6–10pm, Sat 5–10pm. **Closed:** Sunday.

This tranquil restaurant is an excellent choice for good Japanese cooking. At the entrance there's a small fountain such as one usually finds in traditional Japanese gardens. Reproductions of works by the Japanese artist Shiko Munakata hang in the separate Teppan Grill Room. In the Dining Room are originals by Japanese-American artist Mike Kanemitsu. It's worth coming here just to see them.

You can begin your dinner at Horikawa with a sushi sampler or seafood teriyaki. A complete dinner might include shrimp tempura, sashimi appetizer, dobin-mushi (a seafood and vegetable soup served in a minipot), kani (crab) salad, filet mignon tobanyaki (served on a sizzling minicooker), rice, tea, and ice cream or sherbet. You can also order à la carte. In the Teppan Grill Room you might opt for filet mignon and lobster tail served with fresh vegetables.

Pacific Dining Car, 1310 W. Sixth St. ☎ **213/483-6000.**

Cuisine: AMERICAN. **Reservations:** Recommended. **Directions:** From U.S. 101, take Fwy. 110 south; exit at Wilshire, and turn right. Go four blocks to Witmer St., turn right; the restaurant is at the next corner.
Prices: Appetizers $7–$15; main courses $23–$45; lunch $15–$30; breakfast $11–$25. AE, MC, V.
Open: Daily 24 hours; breakfast served 11pm–11am, lunch served 11am–4pm, dinner served anytime.

Located just a few short blocks from the center of downtown Los Angeles, this restaurant has been authentically decorated to evoke the golden age of rail travel. Walls are paneled in warm mahogany with brass luggage racks (complete with luggage) overhead. Old menus and prints from early railroading days line the walls, and brass wall lamps with parchment shades light some tables.

Steaks are prime, aged on the premises, and cooked over a mesquite-charcoal fire. At dinner, top sirloin, a New York steak, fresh seafood, veal, and lamb are all available. For starters, try the excellent calamari, although weight watchers might prefer the beefsteak tomato and onion salad. Menu items are basically the same at lunch. On a recent visit I enjoyed a perfectly charbroiled boneless breast of chicken, with choice of potato or tomato. There's an outstanding wine list too. Desserts are simple fare, such as apple pie. There's also a breakfast menu featuring egg dishes, salads, and steaks.

A second restaurant is located in Santa Monica, at 2700 Wilshire Blvd., one block east of 26th Street (**310/453-4000**).

MODERATE

 **Cha Cha Cha,** 656 N. Virgil Ave., Silver Lake. ☎ **213/664-7723.**

Cuisine: CARIBBEAN. **Reservations:** Recommended, required on weekends. **Directions:** From U.S. 101, exit onto Vermont Avenue north, and turn right onto Melrose Avenue. The restaurant is at the corner of Melrose and Virgil Avenues.
Prices: Appetizers $3–$6; main courses $8–$15; breakfast and lunch $5–$9. AE, DC, DISC, MC, V.
Open: Sun–Thurs 7am–10pm, Fri–Sat 7am–11pm.

Cha Cha Cha serves the West Coast's best Caribbean food. Period. The very spicy black pepper jumbo shrimp gets top marks, as does the paella, a veritable festival of flavors. Other recommendations inspired by Jamaica, Haiti, Cuba, and Puerto Rico include garlic pizza, shrimp cakes, jerk pork, and corn tortillas wrapped abound black beans, chicken, and vegetables. Only beer and wine are served.

Hardcore Caribbean food eaters might visit for breakfast, when fare ranges from plantain, yucca, onion, and herb omelets to scrambled eggs and fresh tomatillos served on hot grilled tortillas.

Cha Cha Cha's location, on the fringes of seedy downtown, authenticate the restaurant's off-beat charm. Dining rooms, located inside a small Créole-like house and in a completely enclosed courtyard, are romantic island settings, made funky with Caribbean music, wild tiling, and a hodgepodge of colorful clutter.

Grand Star, 943 Sun Mun Way. ☎ **213/626-2285.**

Cuisine: CHINESE. **Reservations:** Recommended. **Directions:** From U.S. 101, exit to North Broadway and continue north about seven blocks to Sun Mun Way, between College and Bernard Streets.

Prices: Appetizers $3–$7; main courses $8–$16; fixed-price meals from $20. AE, CB, DC, MC, V.

Open: Fri 11:30am–10pm, Sun 2–10pm, Mon–Thurs and Sat 5–10pm.

Owned and operated by the Quon family since 1967, the Grand Star offers an unusual selection of top-notch Chinese cooking. There are four complete meals, including a gourmet selection of spicy shrimp in a lettuce shell, wonton soup, spicy chicken wings, Mongolian beef with mushrooms, lobster Cantonese, barbecued pork with snow peas, fried rice, tea, and dessert. If there are four or five people in your party, Mama Quon's chicken salad is added, along with larger portions of everything else. A la carte items are also available, ranging from rum-flamed dumplings to lobster sautéed in ginger and green onion. Steamed fish, priced according to size, is a house specialty, as are the cashew chicken, Mongolian beef, and Chinese string beans.

The building began life as a penny arcade. On the street level, the Grand Star looks more Italian than Chinese; it's dimly lit, with black-leather booths and big bunches of dried flowers here and there. I prefer to sit upstairs, where tables are covered with red cloth and the family's fine collection of Chinese embroideries adorns the walls. Entertainment—usually consisting of a female vocalist with piano accompaniment—is featured at cocktail time and on most evenings.

Little Joe's, 900 N. Broadway. ☎ **213/489-4900.**

Cuisine: ITALIAN. **Reservations:** Recommended. **Directions:** From U.S. 101, exit to North Broadway and continue north about five blocks to the restaurant, at the corner of College Street.

Prices: Appetizers $5–$8; main courses $10–$19; lunch $6–$14. AE, CB, DC, DISC, MC, V.

Open: Mon–Fri 11am–9pm, Sat 3–9pm.

Little Joe's, a vestige of this once-Italian neighborhood, now finds itself in touristy New Chinatown. Opened as a grocery in 1927, Joe's has grown steadily over the years; it now encompasses several bars and six dining rooms. It's a wonderfully cozy restaurant with sawdust on the floors, hand-painted oil murals of Rome and Venice, soft lighting, and seating in roomy leather booths.

A meal here ought to begin with a plate of the special hot hors d'oeuvres—fried cheese, zucchini, and homemade ravioli. A complete six-course meal will consist of soup, antipasto, salad, pasta, vegetable or potato, bread and butter, and dessert; main dishes include veal scaloppine, scallops, or halibut steak. You can also get a full pasta dinner, or order à la carte. Less expensive lunches include dishes like eggplant parmigiana, sausage and peppers, and rigatoni. Without a doubt, Little Joe's is the best Occidental restaurant in Chinatown.

Otto Rothschilds Bar and Grill, ground floor of the Dorothy Chandler Pavilion, 135 N. Grand Ave. ☎ **213/972-7322.**

Cuisine: CONTINENTAL. **Reservations:** Recommended. **Directions:** From U.S. 101, exit onto Grand Street and go one block to the music center.

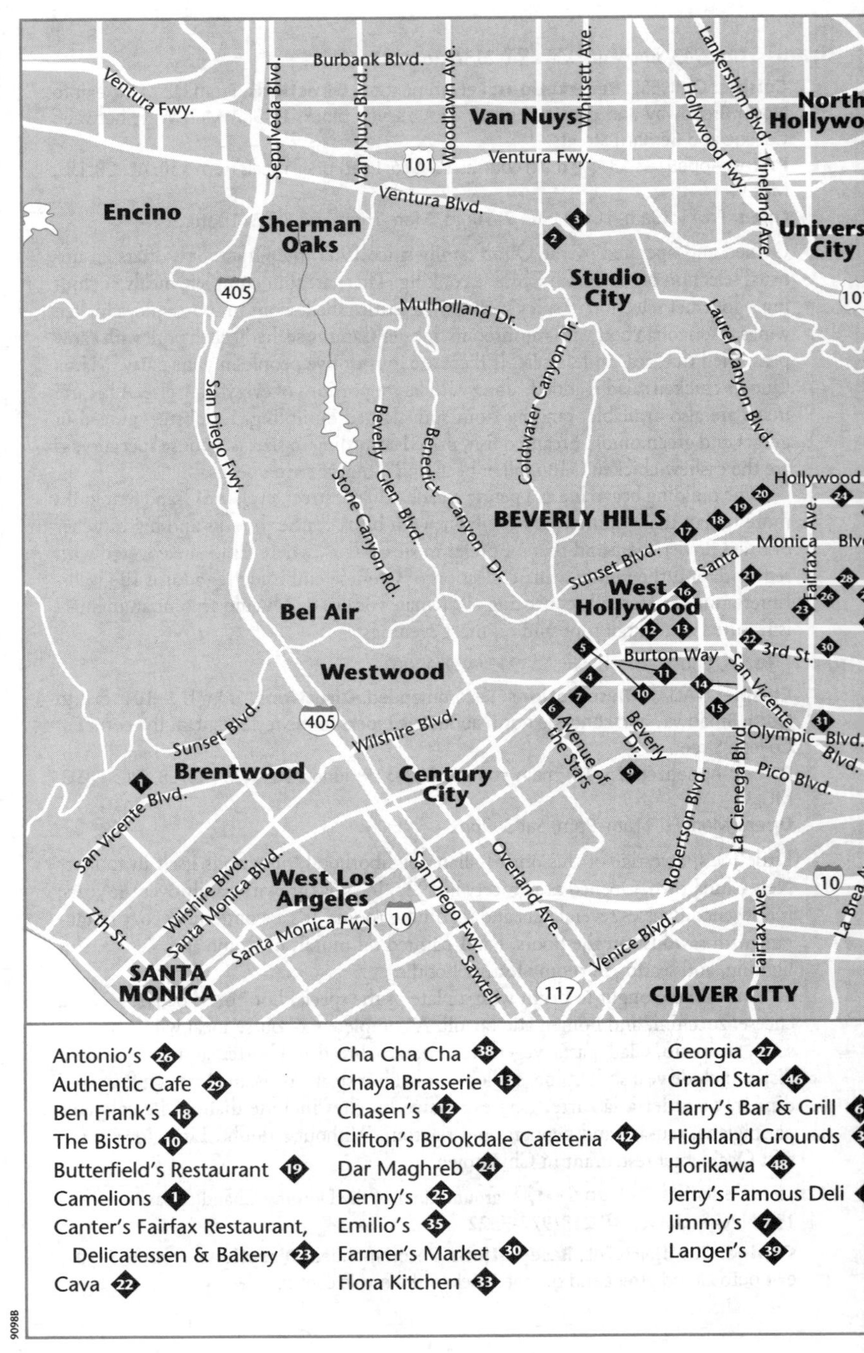

Burbank Blvd.
Ventura Fwy.
Sepulveda Blvd.
Van Nuys Blvd.
Woodlawn Ave.
Van Nuys
Whitsett Ave.
Lankershim Blvd.
Hollywood Fwy.
North Hollywo
101
Ventura Fwy.
Ventura Blvd.
Vineland Ave.
Encino
Sherman Oaks
Univers. City
Studio City
405
Mulholland Dr.
Coldwater Canyon Dr.
Laurel Canyon Blvd.
San Diego Fwy.
Beverly Glen Blvd.
Benedict Canyon Dr.
Stone Canyon Rd.
Hollywood
BEVERLY HILLS
Santa Monica Blvd.
Fairfax Ave.
Sunset Blvd.
West Hollywood
Bel Air
Burton Way
3rd St.
San Vicente Blvd.
Westwood
Beverly Dr.
Avenue of the Stars
Wilshire Blvd.
Sunset Blvd.
Olympic Blvd.
Brentwood
Century City
Pico Blvd.
San Vicente Blvd.
Robertson Blvd.
La Cienega Blvd.
Overland Ave.
Wilshire Blvd.
Santa Monica Blvd.
West Los Angeles
San Diego Fwy.
10
7th St.
Santa Monica Fwy.
Venice Blvd.
Fairfax Ave.
La Brea A.
SANTA MONICA
Sawtell
117
CULVER CITY
Antonio's 26
Authentic Cafe 29
Ben Frank's 18
The Bistro 10
Butterfield's Restaurant 19
Camelions 1
Canter's Fairfax Restaurant, Delicatessen & Bakery 23
Cava 22
Cha Cha Cha 38
Chaya Brasserie 13
Chasen's 12
Clifton's Brookdale Cafeteria 42
Dar Maghreb 24
Denny's 25
Emilio's 35
Farmer's Market 30
Flora Kitchen 33
Georgia 27
Grand Star 46
Harry's Bar & Grill
Highland Grounds
Horikawa 48
Jerry's Famous Deli
Jimmy's 7
Langer's 39

Dining in Beverly Hills, Hollywood & Downtown

BURBANK
GLENDALE
Hollywood
Ventura Fwy.
Glendale Fwy.
Golden State Fwy.
Eagle Rock Blvd.
Los Feliz
San Fernando Rd.
Hollywood Blvd.
Sunset Blvd.
Vine St.
Gower Ave.
Santa Monica Blvd.
Melrose Ave.
Hollywood Fwy.
Beverly Blvd.
Rossmore Ave.
Normandie Ave.
3rd St.
lshire Blvd.
North Broadway
Pasadena Fwy.
North Main
6th St.
7th St.
Crenshaw Blvd.
Western Blvd.
Olympic Blvd.
Pico Blvd.
Santa Monica Fwy.
1st St.
4th St.
Broadway
Central Ave.
Santa Ana Fwy.
5
134
2
110
101
10
cala & Boutique
estaurant 11
y Parker's 24-Hour Diner 19
ry's The Prime Rib 15
e Joe's 45
suhisa 14
ton's 16
so & Frank Grill 36
e & Al's 5
Noura Cafe 21
Original Pantry Cafe 41
Otto Rothschild's
Bar and Grill 43
Pacific Dining Car 40
Pinot Bistro 2
Ristorante Chianti
& Chianti Cucina 28
Roscoe's House of
Chicken 'n' Waffles 37
Röx 9
Shanghai Winter Garden 32
The Source 20
Spago 17
Tokyo Kaikan 47
Tom Bergin's Tavern 31
Trader Vic's 4

Prices: Appetizers $6–$9; main courses $14–$25; after-theater dinner $12–$19; lunch $8–$13. AE, CB, DC, MC, V.
Open: Mon 11am–6pm, Tues–Thurs 11am–9pm, Fri 7:30am–midnight, Sat–Sun 11:30am–midnight.

This restaurant celebrates the unparalleled visual history of the motion-picture industry and its stars. Photographs of stage and screen celebrities, taken by Otto Rothschild over a period of 40 years, adorn the walls of this handsome eatery.

There's nothing commonplace about lunch, either. I tend to focus on the appetizers and light dishes such as the jalapeño-tuna salad with jicama, green onion, and black bean salsa, or the prime rib chili served with corn chips. Heavier dishes include sautéed scallops with a rosemary-marinara over linguini, and Santa Fe chicken served with a black bean salsa and grilled scallions.

The list of dinner main courses includes excellent choices of prime meats and pastas. Herb-roasted prime rib is served with whipped horseradish sauce; the mixed grill contains a breast of chicken, sausage, and lamb chop.

An after-theater menu, served from 9pm to midnight, ranges from light main dishes (smoked ham and Cheddar omelet, a Rothschild burger, a salad) to the more substantive (pasta and a Black Angus steak).

Tokyo Kaikan, 225 S. San Pedro St. ☎ **213/489-1333.**

Cuisine: JAPANESE. **Reservations:** Recommended. **Directions:** From U.S. 101 exit onto Alameda Street south; after two blocks, turn right on First Street, then left onto San Pedro Street; the restaurant is located between Second and Third Streets.
Prices: Appetizers $4–$8; main courses $10–$17; complete dinner $16–$40; complete lunch $8–$30. AE, DISC, MC, V.
Open: Lunch Mon–Fri 11:30am–2pm; dinner Mon–Fri 6–10:30pm, Sat 5–10pm.

Tokyo Kaikan is among the most popular Japanese restaurants in Los Angeles. It's designed to look like a traditional Japanese country inn, with colored globe lights overhead, barnwood, and bamboo-and-rattan-covered walls adorned with straw baskets and other provincial artifacts.

A la carte dinner main dishes, served with soup and rice, include beef sukiyaki, shrimp and vegetable tempura, and chicken and beef teriyaki. Several combination plates let you try a number of native dishes without ordering everything on the menu. Green tea, sake, and beer is served at both lunch and dinner, as is ginger ice cream.

BUDGET

Clifton's Brookdale Cafeteria, 648 S. Broadway. ☎ **213/627-1673.**

Cuisine: AMERICAN. **Reservations:** Not accepted. **Directions:** From the Harbor Freeway 110, exit at Sixth Street and head east, turn right onto Spring Street, another right onto Seventh Street, and then right again onto Broadway.
Prices: Appetizers $1–$3; main courses $3–$7. No credit cards.
Open: Daily 7am–7pm.

This is one of a chain of economy cafeterias that has kept the less prosperous of Los Angeles nourished for over five decades. Clifford Clinton—not Clifton—founded the business on what, today, would seem to be a unique principle: "We pray our humble service be measured not by gold, but by the Golden Rule." During the Depression he kept thousands from starving by honoring an extraordinary policy: "No guest need go hungry. Pay what you wish, dine free unless delighted."

Frommer's Smart Traveler: Restaurants

1. Go ethnic. Los Angeles has some great, inexpensive ethnic dining.
2. Eat your main meal at lunch when prices are lower; you can sample gourmet hot spots for a fraction of the price charged at dinner.
3. Watch the liquor; it can add greatly to the cost of any meal.
4. Look for fixed-price menus, two-for-one specials, and coupons in local newspapers and magazines.

Those shopping or sightseeing downtown can enjoy a huge, economical meal that might consist of split-pea soup, hand-carved roast turkey with dressing, baked squash with brown sugar, and Bavarian cream pie—an excellent meal for under $10. There are over 100 à la carte items at modest prices. However, since there is a charge for everything, including bread and butter, you must limit your choices to make your meal economical. It's all fresh, delicious, and homemade, too; even the baking is done on the premises. Fresh bakery items are sold at the front counter.

A second Clifton's is located nearby, at 515 W. Seventh St. at Olive Street (☎ **213/485-1726**). It's open Monday through Saturday from 7am to 3:30pm.

Langer's, 704 S. Alvarado St. ☎ **213/483-8050.**

Cuisine: JEWISH. **Reservations:** Not accepted. **Directions:** From the Harbor Freeway 110, exit west onto Olympic Boulevard, and after 10 blocks turn right (north) on Alvarado Street: the restaurant is three blocks ahead, on the corner of Seventh Street.
Prices: Appetizers $4–$10; main courses $6–$14. MC, V.
Open: Daily 6:30am–9pm.

Dating from 1947, Langer's is a big, roomy place with counter seating and brown tufted-leather booths. The walls are lined with portraits of the Langer family and grandchildren, and the corner location (two windowed walls) is light and airy.

The food is kosher style rather than kosher, which means that you can mix milk and meat and order the likes of pastrami and Swiss cheese on rye. Stuffed kishka with soup or salad, vegetable, and potatoes, meat blintzes with gravy, and an interesting sandwich combination of cream cheese and cashews are among the main dishes.

The Original Pantry Cafe, 877 S. Figueroa St. ☎ **213/972-9279.**

Cuisine: AMERICAN. **Reservations:** Not accepted. **Directions:** From Calif. 110 (Harbor Freeway) exit onto Wilshire Boulevard and turn left onto Figueroa St; the restaurant is located at Ninth Street.
Prices: Appetizers $2–$4; main courses $6–$11. No credit cards.
Open: Daily 24 hours.

This place has been open 24 hours a day for over 60 years; they don't even have a key to the front door. Its well-worn decor consists of shiny cream-colored walls with old patinaed oil paintings and hanging globe lamps overhead; big stainless-steel water pitchers and bowls of celery, carrots, and radishes are placed on every Formica table. In addition to that bowl of raw veggies, you also get a whopping big portion of homemade creamy coleslaw and all the homemade sourdough bread and butter you want—a meal in itself—before you've even ordered. Owned by L.A. Mayor Richard Riordan, the Pantry is especially popular with politicos who come here for weekday lunches.

When you do order, you'll be amazed at the bountiful portions. A Pantry breakfast might consist of a huge stack of hotcakes, big slabs of sweet cured ham, home fries, and cup after cup of freshly made coffee. A huge T-bone steak, home-fried pork chops, baked chicken, and macaroni and cheese are served later in the day. The Pantry is an original—don't miss it.

Philippe the Original, 1001 N. Alameda St. ☎ **213/628-3781.**

Cuisine: AMERICAN. **Reservations:** Not accepted. **Directions:** From U.S. 101, exit onto Alameda; go north to the intersection of North Main, Alameda, and Ord Streets.
Prices: Appetizers $1–$3; main courses $3–$7. No credit cards.
Open: Breakfast daily 6–10:30am; lunch and dinner daily 10:30am–10pm.

Good old-fashioned value and quality is what this establishment is all about—people come here for the good beef, pork, ham, turkey, or lamb French-dip sandwiches served on the lightest, crunchiest French rolls. Philippe's has been around since 1908, and there's nothing stylish about the place. Stand in line while your French-dip sandwich is being assembled, then carry it to one of several long wooden tables. Other menu items include homemade beef stew, chili, two different soups daily, and pickled pigs' feet. A variety of desserts include New York–style cheesecake, cream and fruit pies, puddings, baked apples, and custards.

A hearty breakfast is served until 10:30am daily, including Philippe's special cinnamon-dipped French toast. All the egg dishes can be topped with their zesty homemade salsa. Beer and wine are available, and there's free parking in the rear and in a lot across the street.

Hollywood

EXPENSIVE

Dar Maghreb, 7651 Sunset Blvd. ☎ **213/876-7651.**

Cuisine: MOROCCAN. **Reservations:** Recommended. **Directions:** From U.S. 101, exit onto Sunset Boulevard and turn right; the restaurant is straight ahead between Fairfax and La Brea Avenues at the corner of Stanley Avenue.
Prices: Set dinners $18–$29. CB, DC, MC, V.
Open: Dinner daily 6–11pm.

When you pass through these immense carved brass doors, you enter an exotic Arab world. Step into a Koranic patio, at the center of which is an exquisite fountain under an open skylight. The floor is marble, and the carved wood-and-plaster walls are decorated with handmade tiles in geometric designs. A kaftaned hostess greets you and leads you to either the Rabat Room or the Berber Room. The former features rich Rabat carpets, marquetry tables, and silk cushions with spun-gold-thread designs. The Berber Room is more rustic, with warm earth tones, mountain rugs, and brass furniture from Marrakech. In both rooms diners sit on low sofas against the wall and on goatskin poufs (cushions). Berber and Andalusian music is played in the background, and there is belly dancing nightly.

The set meal is a multicourse feast, including a choice of chicken, lamb, turkey, beef, squab, quail, or shrimp, eaten with your hands and hunks of bread, and shared, from the same dish, with other members of your party. There are eight possible dinners, most of which come with Moroccan salads of cold raw and cooked vegetables, and b'stilla, an appetizer of shredded chicken, eggs, almonds, and spices wrapped in a flaky pastry shell and topped with powdered sugar and cinnamon. Other dishes include a tajine of chicken cooked with pickled lemons, onions, and fresh coriander; and couscous, with lamb and vegetables—squash, carrots, tomatoes, garbanzo beans, turnips, onions, and raisins.

MODERATE

Emilio's, 6602 Melrose Ave. ☎ **213/935-4922.**

Cuisine: ITALIAN. **Reservations:** Recommended. **Directions:** From U.S. 101, exit onto Highland Avenue and continue straight to the corner of Melrose Avenue, where you will find the restaurant.

Prices: Appetizers $5–$10; main courses $10–$24; Sun buffet $22. AE, CB, DC, MC, V.
Open: Lunch Thurs–Fri 11:30am–2:30pm; dinner daily 5–11:30pm.

This award-winning restaurant attracts a celebrity clientele with its authentic Italian cooking. The downstairs dining room centers around a colorfully lit "Fountain de Trevi," which is bathed in colored lights. The decor is ornate Italian, with marble columns from floor to lofty ceiling, brick archways, stained-glass windows, gilt-framed oil paintings, and fresh flowers on every table.

Order lavishly and savor every bite. You might begin with the antipasti of mussels with spicy tomato sauce and garlic, or the scallops with oil and garlic. For your second course, the brodetto adriadico (it's like cioppino) is heartily recommended, as are any of the several veal main dishes. Homemade pastas are also excellent, including linguine with shrimp and lobster, and rondelli stuffed with ricotta, mortadella, and spinach. Homemade noodles with sun-dried tomatoes, baby corn, carrots, and peas are less caloric, but good. Depending on the day, you may also find roast suckling pig or osso buco on the menu. An Italian countryside buffet is offered on Sundays from 5 to 9pm.

Georgia, 7250 Melrose Ave., ☎ **213/933-8420.**

Cuisine: SOUTHERN. **Reservations:** Recommended. **Directions:** From Santa Monica Boulevard, exit south onto Fairfax Avenue and turn left onto Melrose Avenue. The restaurant is about 10 blocks ahead at the corner of Alta Vista.

Prices: Appetizers $6–$9; main courses $13–$19; lunch $6–$15. AE, MC, V.
Open: Lunch Mon–Fri noon–3pm; dinner Mon–Sat 6:30–11pm, Sun 5:30–11pm.

Soul food and power ties commingle at this calorie-unconscious ode to southern cooking in the heart of Melrose's funky shopping district. Owned by a group of investors that includes actors Denzel Washington and Eddie Murphy, the restaurant is especially popular with Hollywood's African-American arts crowd—at least those who can afford to pay for L.A.'s highest-priced pork chops, fried chicken, and grits. Other offerings include turtle soup, fried oysters, blue-crab cakes, meat loaf, smoked babyback ribs, grilled Gulf shrimp, candied yams, and cornmeal mush. Some dishes, like catfish, are more delicately fried than is traditional. Others are smothered in onion gravy, and most are sided with corn pudding, string beans or cole slaw.

The dining room itself is built to resemble a fine southern house, complete with mahogany floors, Spanish moss, and wrought-iron gates. Palm tree artwork and a bourbon bar continue the theme.

Musso & Frank Grill, 6667 Hollywood Blvd. ☎ **213/467-7788.**

Cuisine: AMERICAN. **Reservations:** Recommended. **Directions:** From U.S. 101, exit onto Cahuenga Boulevard and continue to the restaurant near the corner of Hollywood Boulevard.

Prices: Appetizers $5–$9; main courses $10–$32. AE, CB, DC, MC, V.
Open: Tues–Sat 11am–11pm.

By the restaurant's estimation, this is Hollywood's oldest extant eatery, established in 1919. People keep coming back for the comfortable ambience, superb service, and consistently excellent food; Musso & Frank Grill is where Faulkner and Hemingway hung out during their screenwriting days. Today, it's a favorite dining spot of Jonathan Winters, Merv Griffin, and Ralph Edward, to name just a few.

The setting is richly traditional—oak beamed ceilings, red-leather booths and banquettes, mahogany room dividers (complete with coathooks), and soft lighting emanating from wall sconces and chandeliers with tiny shades.

The menu is extensive, and everything from soups to salads to seafood is served à la carte. Try the delicious seafood salads such as the chiffonade or shrimp Louie, perhaps with some Camembert that comes with crusty bread and butter. Diners desiring heartier fare might consider the veal scaloppine marsala, roast spring lamb with mint jelly or broiled lobster. Sandwiches and omelets are also available. The back of the menu lists an equally extensive liquor and wine selection.

Ristorante Chianti & Chianti Cucina, 7383 Melrose Ave. ☎ **213/653-8333.**

Cuisine: ITALIAN. **Reservations:** Recommended. **Directions:** From U.S. 101, exit onto Highland Avenue, turn right onto Melrose Avenue and continue straight for about 10 blocks to the restaurant, at the corner of Martel Avenue, between Fairfax and La Brea Avenues.
Prices: Appetizers $6–$8; main courses $13–$20. AE, CB, DC, MC, V.
Open: Ristorante Chianti, daily 5:30–11:30pm; Chianti Cucina Mon–Sat 11:30am–11:30pm, Sun 4pm–midnight.

Begun in 1938 by the famous New York restaurateur Romeo Salta, this charming northern Italian restaurant has a long history in Hollywood: the cast party for *Gone with the Wind* was held here. The restaurant has won several prestigious awards, including accolades for its excellent wine list. Although it operates as a single entity, Ristorante Chianti & Chianti Cucina offers two completely different dining experiences and menus.

Ristorante Chianti is traditional Italian in looks—quiet, intimate, complete with red-velvet seating and sepia-tone murals. Hot and cold appetizers range from fresh handmade mozzarella and prosciutto to lamb carpaccio with asparagus and marinated grilled eggplant filled with goat cheese, arugula, and sun-dried tomatoes. As for main dishes, the homemade pasta is both exceptional and deliciously untraditional. Try black tortelloni filled with fresh salmon, or giant ravioli filled with spinach, ricotta, and quail eggs topped with shaved black truffle. Other dishes include fresh fish and prawns, poultry, and a fine selection of meat dishes.

Chianti Cucina is bright, bustling, attractive, and loud; it feels like you are dining right in the kitchen. The menu changes frequently, but consistently features exceptional antipasti, pastas, and a pleasing main dish selection that is somewhat more limited than Ristorante Chianti's. Good first course selections include smoked duck with pearls of mozzarella and steamed spinach, and carpaccio with alfalfa sprouts and Parmesan cheese. Of the pasta dishes, you might try the lobster-and-shrimp-filled tortelli, or the simpler pasta dumplings with roasted pepper sauce, basil, and Parmesan.

Shanghai Winter Garden, 5651 Wilshire Blvd. ☎ **213/934-0505.**

Cuisine: CHINESE. **Reservations:** Accepted for parties of 4 or more. **Directions:** From U.S. 101, exit onto Highland Avenue, and turn right onto Sunset Boulevard; after about

one mile, turn left onto Fairfax Avenue, and after another mile turn right onto Wilshire Boulevard; the restaurant is about 10 blocks ahead at the corner of Hauser Boulevard.
Prices: Appetizers $4–$11; main courses $10–$25; lunch $6–$10. AE, DC, MC, V.
Open: Lunch Mon–Sat 11:30am–3pm; dinner daily 4–10:30pm.

This is one of my favorite Los Angeles Chinese restaurants. An archway depicting a phoenix and dragon, set in an intricately carved teak wall, separates the dining areas. Chinese paintings and wood carvings adorn the walls; large tasseled Chinese lamps hang overhead.

The menu features over 150 main dishes, including diced fried chicken sautéed with spinach, shrimp with bamboo shoots and green peas in a delicious sauce with crisp sizzling rice, crispy duckling made with five spicy ingredients, and crushed white meat chicken sautéed with diced ham, pine nuts, and green peas. As you can see, this is no ordinary take-out joint.

Tom Bergin's Tavern, 640 S. Fairfax Ave. ☎ **213/936-7151.**

Cuisine: IRISH. **Reservations:** Accepted. **Directions:** From U.S. 101, exit onto Highland Avenue, and turn right onto Sunset Boulevard; after about one mile, turn left onto Fairfax Avenue; the restaurant is located about one mile ahead, at Barrows Drive, between Wilshire and Olympic Boulevards.
Prices: Appetizers $5–$7; main courses $13–$20; bar lunch $4–$10. AE, DC, DISC, MC, V.
Open: Lunch Mon–Fri 11am–4pm; dinner daily 4–11pm; bar 11am–2am.

Tom Bergin's is L.A.'s Irish community's unofficial headquarters. Since 1936, this has also been a gathering place for sportswriters, athletes, and fans. Actors Bing Crosby and Pat O'Brien were early friends of the house. Bergin's was the first city restaurant to charter buses to pro football games—they still do, and they hold 230 seats to the games reserved five years in advance.

Mesquite-fired New York steak with onion rings, garlic cheese toast, salad, and potatoes is the specialty of the house. More traditional Irish fare like Dublin-style corned beef and cabbage with a steamed potato, or chicken Erin, simmered in cream and cider sauce, with bacon, leeks, mushrooms, and rice pilaf are also served, along with burgers and salads. For dessert you can choose from fresh fruit pies or Bailey's Irish Cream cheesecake, and wash it down with an Irish coffee.

INEXPENSIVE

Authentic Cafe, 7605 Beverly Blvd., Los Angeles. ☎ **213/939-4626.**

Cuisine: SOUTHWESTERN. **Reservations:** Not accepted. **Directions:** From Santa Monica Boulevard, turn south onto Fairfax, then right, onto Beverly Boulevard. The restaurant is about six blocks ahead at Curson Avenue.
Prices: Appetizers $2–$9; main courses $8–$13; lunch $5–$9. MC, V.
Open: Mon–Thurs 11:30am–10pm, Fri 11:30am–11pm, Sat 10am–11pm, Sun 10am–10pm.

True to its name, this excellent restaurant serves authentic Southwestern food in a casual cafe atmosphere, a winning combination. A trendy dining room that's terrific for people watching, very good food, and large portions translates into long waits almost every night of the week.

Chef Roger Hayot cooks up Southwestern American meals that sometimes have Asian influences—like brie, papaya, and chili quesadillas. Blue corn chile rellenos, pot stickers, and pizza bread round out the appetizers. A long list of entrées includes chicken casserole made with a cornbread crust; fettucini tossed with chicken, fresh corn, and red peppers in a chile cream sauce; and meat loaf made with caramelized onions. Lunches are lighter, and may include cheese-less pizza with tomato sauce, red onion, garlic, zucchini, eggplant, and basil; grilled sausage sandwiches, or Thai chicken salad.

Flora Kitchen, 460 S. La Brea Ave. ☎ **213/931-9900.**

Cuisine: AMERICAN. **Reservations:** Not accepted. **Directions:** From Santa Monica Blvd., exit east, onto Wilshire Boulevard, drive about four miles, then turn left, onto La Brea Avenue. The restaurant is one block ahead, at 6th Street.
Prices: Appetizers $2–$6; main courses $5–$10. AE, MC, V.
Open: Sun–Thurs 8am–10pm, Fri–Sat 8–11pm.

Imagine an upscale hip-happening bright funky cafeteria, and you've imagined Flora Kitchen. Known for its tuna and chicken salads served on most-exalted La Brea Bakery breads, the restaurant is equally comfortable dishing out more eclectic meals like Cayenne-spiced potato soup, poached salmon with dill sauce, and seared ahi with roasted vegetables.

Flora is popular with doyens of nearby art galleries by day, and with music lovers on warm summer nights who take the restaurant's dinners boxed, to the Hollywood Bowl.

Noura Cafe, 8479 Melrose Ave., Los Angeles. ☎ **213/651-4581.**

Cuisine: MIDDLE EASTERN. **Reservations:** Accepted for large parties only. **Directions:** From Santa Monica Boulevard, exit east onto Melrose Avenue. The restaurant is near the corner of La Cienega Boulevard.
Prices: Salads and pitas $4–$7; plates $5–$11. MC, V.
Open: Sun–Thurs 11am–11pm, Fri–Sat 11am–midnight.

The best find on Melrose, Noura Cafe is packed with thin, beautiful underweight people who love the restaurant's healthful, largely vegetarian, Middle Eastern cuisine. Seating is either inside, or out beside a warm firepit. Most meals are served with pita bread for stuffing with broiled lamb, beef, chicken, or one of a number of salads. Traditional Mediterranean salads include baba ghanoush (grilled eggplant with tahini and lemon), Turkish (tomatoes, green onions and spices), and tabbouli (cracked wheat, parsley, and tomatoes). The most disciplined customers just order a glass of fresh carrot juice and a home-baked muffin.

BUDGET

Roscoe's House of Chicken 'n' Waffles, 1514 N. Gower St. ☎ **213/466-7453.**

Cuisine: AMERICAN. **Reservations:** Not accepted. **Directions:** From U.S. 101, exit onto Highland Avenue, and turn left onto Sunset Boulevard; the restaurant is straight ahead, at Gower Street.
Prices: Main courses $4–$11. No credit cards.
Open: Sun–Thurs 8:30am–midnight; Fri–Sat 8:30am–3am.

Proximity to CBS Studios alone would probably guarantee a celebrity clientele. Roscoe's devotees have included Jane Fonda, Stevie Wonder, Flip Wilson, Eddie Murphy, Alex Haley, and the Eagles. The setting is very simple, with slanted cedar and white stucco walls, changing art exhibits, track lighting overhead, lots of plants, and good music in the background.

Only chicken and waffle dishes are served, though that includes eggs and chicken livers. A chicken-and-cheese omelet with french fries accompanied by an order of homemade biscuits makes for a unique and delicious breakfast. A specialty is a quarter chicken smothered in gravy and onions, served with waffles or grits and biscuits. You can also get chicken salad and chicken sandwiches. Homemade cornbread, sweet-potato pie, homemade potato salad, greens, and corn on the cob are all available as side orders, and wine and beer are sold.

A second Roscoe's is located at 4907 W. Washington Blvd., at La Brea Avenue (☎ **213/936-3730**).

West Hollywood

EXPENSIVE

Morton's, 8764 Melrose Ave., West Hollywood. ☎ **310/276-5205.**

Cuisine: CALIFORNIAN. **Reservations:** Suggested. **Directions:** From Santa Monica Boulevard, exit east onto Melrose Avenue. The restaurant is about one block ahead on your right.
Prices: Appetizers $7–$14; main courses $17–$29; lunch $7–$15. AE, MC, V.
Open: Mon–Fri noon–11:30pm, Sat 6–11:30pm.

In 1994, Hard Rock Cafe founder Peter Morton moved his successful self-named restaurant to a new, bigger location across the street. Surviving the odds, Morton's reopened to raves—especially from the entertainment community that has long been this restaurant's bread and butter. Morton's has long been an important part of the Hollywood "scene." In its new location, the restaurant has become the site of one of the most important post-Oscar celebrations. On Monday nights throughout the year, entertainment's high and mighty consider these the most highly-coveted tables in the city.

The restaurant's single, lofty, wood-ceiling dining room is spacious and open, yet dark enough to keep it feeling personal. Tables are spaced far enough apart to assure privacy, and servers are attentive without being obtrusive.

Meals at Morton's are straightforward and good. It's easy to understand every word on the menu, and meals arrive without a lot of visual fru fru. An emphasis on simplicity, quality, and freshness translates into appetizers like fresh Maryland soft-shell crabs, tuna sashimi, and lobster-stuffed sweet corn pancakes. Typical entrées on the seasonal menu include lime-grilled free range chicken, grilled swordfish, roasted pork tenderloin, and New York steak. Desserts, like hot fudge sundaes and warm fruit tarts, are equally forthright in taste and description.

Spago, 8795 Sunset Blvd. ☎ **310/652-4025.**

Cuisine: CALIFORNIAN. **Reservations:** Required. **Directions:** From U.S. 101, exit onto Highland Boulevard, and turn right onto Sunset Boulevard; the restaurant is about three miles ahead, at Horn Avenue.
Prices: Appetizers $10–$15; main courses $18–$28. DC, DISC, MC, V.
Open: Dinner daily 5:30–11:30pm.

Celebrity chef Wolfgang Puck has a flair for publicity and has made Spago one of the best-known restaurants in America. Famous across the land as the site of Swifty Lazar's annual Oscar-night party, this noisy L.A. restaurant is popular with celebrities, wannabes, and tourists throughout the year. Designed by Barbara Lazaroff, the restaurant is elegantly decorated in clean, light shades punctuated with armfuls of flowers. A huge picture window and an open kitchen gives diners an alternative view when they get tired of looking at each other.

Puck invented California-style gourmet pizza, baked in a wood-burning oven, and topped with exotic ingredients like duck sausage, shiitake mushrooms, leeks, artichokes, and even lox and sour cream. Pastas like black-pepper fettuccine with Louisiana shrimp, roasted garlic, and basil ratatouille, or angel-hair spaghetti with goat cheese and broccoli are also available, as are more substantial dishes like roast Sonoma lamb with braised shallots and herb butter, and grilled chicken with garlic and parsley. Despite all the hype, Spago is really terrific. Reservations should be made three to four weeks in advance.

MODERATE

Antonio's, 7472 Melrose Ave. ☎ **213/655-0480.**

Cuisine: MEXICAN. **Reservations:** Accepted. **Directions:** From U.S. 101, exit onto Highland Boulevard and turn right onto Melrose Avenue; the restaurant is located about one mile ahead, between Fairfax and La Brea Avenues.
Prices: Appetizers $5–$7; main courses $11–$15. AE, MC, V.
Open: Lunch Tues–Fri 11am–3pm; dinner Tues–Fri 5–11pm.

There's "gringo food"—fiery, with lots of cheese, sour cream, refried beans, tamales—and then there's the subtle, delicate, and delicious Mexican cooking of Antonio's. For almost 25 years, this gourmet Mexican restaurant has been serving top-notch food without the bright reds, yellows, and greens of the usual taco joint. The true cuisine of Mexico City is delicious, well seasoned, high in protein, low in cholesterol, and lean on calories. A variety of fresh seafood and meats with exotic vegetables are featured, and the majority of main dishes are steamed rather than fried.

The menu changes daily, but fresh fish is available at all times. Chicken is served in a variety of ways—Guadalajara style, in tamales stuffed with assorted fresh vegetables, or stewed in a delicate green sauce of tomatillos, green peppers, and exotic spices. Meat-stuffed cabbage, and spareribs with chile-and-herb sauce are both recommended.

Butterfield's Restaurant, 8426 Sunset Blvd., West Hollywood. ☎ **213/656-3055.**

Cuisine: CONTINENTAL. **Reservations:** Recommended. **Directions:** From Santa Monica Boulevard, turn north onto Fairfax Avenue, then turn left, onto Sunset Boulevard. The restaurant is about 10 blocks ahead on your left, at the corner of Olive Drive.
Prices: Appetizers $4–$8; main courses $9–$18; lunch $9–$12; weekend brunch $8–$10. AE, DC, MC, V.
Open: Lunch Mon–Fri 11:30am–3pm; brunch Sat–Sun 10:30am–3pm; dinner Sun–Thurs 6–10pm, Fri–Sat 6–11pm.

Tucked beneath the Sunset Strip, on the former estate of John Barrymore, Butterfield's is a woody oasis in the heart of the city. Dining al fresco here is like eating in the middle of a leafy forest. A small pond enlivened with mature Koi helps make this one of the most comfortable outdoor patios in L.A. The inside dining room, coveted only when the temperature drops, is located in a guest cottage that once housed Errol Flynn.

Dinners might begin with sea scallop ceviche, or tangy mushroom bisque. Of pastas, the best is topped with sun-dried tomatoes and red bell peppers, and an excellent meaty chicken breast is stuffed with cheddar cheese and apricots before it is baked with an apricot brandy glaze.

At lunch, cobb salads, fresh fruits, and sandwiches are the preferred meals. Patio brunches on warm weekend mornings include filling entrées like smoked salmon benedict; spicy scrambled eggs with prosciutto, bacon, venison sausage, and jalapeño; and Aztec eggs—poached, and served with cheese and black bean sauce on a blue corn burrito.

Frommer's Cool for Kids: Restaurants

Aunt Kizzy's Back Porch (see p. 428) This restaurant was practically invented for children. It serves fried chicken and has a down-home, fun atmosphere.

The Warehouse (see p. 428) Kids won't have any trouble finding something they like from this extensive international menu. The atmosphere is very leisurely, and the thousands of moored boats will keep the kids' interest.

BUDGET

The Source, 8301 W. Sunset Blvd. ☎ **213/656-6388.**

Cuisine: CALIFORNIAN HEALTH FOOD. **Reservations:** Not accepted. **Directions:** From U.S. 101, exit onto Highland Boulevard and turn right onto Sunset Boulevard; the restaurant is located about two miles ahead, at Sweetzer Avenue, between La Cienega and Fairfax Avenues.
Prices: Appetizers $3–$5; main courses $5–$11. AE, CB, DC, MC, V.
Open: Mon–Fri 8am–midnight, Sat–Sun 9am–midnight.

This is where Woody Allen met Diane Keaton for a typical L.A. lunch in *Annie Hall*—part of his New York–centric statement about southern California. Inside it's cozy, with curtained windows, tables set with fresh flowers, and a plant-filled stone fireplace in one corner. Those who want fresh air with their health food shouldn't be in L.A., but outdoor dining on the covered patio is available.

Cheese-walnut loaf, served with homemade soup or salad, and a basket of whole-wheat rolls and butter comprises a typical meal. Salads and sandwiches are also available. Most menu items are vegetarian, but chicken and fish are also served. Portions are huge. Drinks include yogurt shakes, beer, and wine. The homemade date-nut cheesecake is so good it's hard to believe it's healthy.

Beverly Hills & Century City

EXPENSIVE

The Bistro, 246 N. Canon Dr., Beverly Hills. ☎ **310/273-5633.**

Cuisine: CONTINENTAL. **Reservations:** Required. **Directions:** From Santa Monica Boulevard exit onto Canon Drive. The restaurant is two blocks ahead at Dayton Way.
Prices: Appetizers $8–$13; main courses $15–$27. AE, CB, DC, MC, V.
Open: Dinner only, Tues–Sat 6–10:30pm.

Conceived more than two decades ago by celebrated film director Billy Wilder and Romanoff's maitre d' Kurt Niklas, the Bistro is both elegant and charming. The restaurant is decorated in authentic Parisian belle epoque, with mirrored walls, hand-painted panels with classical motifs, tables set with gleaming silver, soft pink lighting, and fresh roses on every table.

Both the service and the cuisine are top notch. Mussel soup is outstanding, and the rich lobster bisque and cream of watercress soups are excellent. Two appetizers you won't want to overlook are the salmon and the pheasant pâté. You might choose a cold main dish of duck or quail salad, or one such as linguine with raddichio, asparagus, and scallops. The rack of lamb is also recommended. All the pasta is homemade and fresh. For dessert, I recommend the sumptuous chocolate soufflé. Jackets for men are required at dinner, when there is live piano music.

Chasen's, 9039 Beverly Blvd., West Hollywood. ☎ **310/271-2168.**

Cuisine: AMERICAN. **Reservations:** Recommended. **Directions:** From Santa Monica Boulevard, exit onto Beverly Boulevard and continue straight four blocks to the restaurant at Doheny Drive.
Prices: Lunch $11–$18; appetizers $9–$19; main courses $22–$37. AE, DISC, MC, V.
Open: Lunch Tues–Fri 11:30am–2pm; dinner Tues–Sun 6pm–1am.

The original Chasen's, a chili parlor, was financed by *New Yorker* editor Harold Ross, and early patrons at this "Algonquin West" included Jimmy Durante and James Cagney. James Thurber once spent hours drawing murals on the men's room wall—they were immediately removed by an overly industrious janitor. Chasens is a real restaurant, with professional waiters serving great American food. Even after all these years, it's thoroughly recommendable.

The main dining room of this enduring favorite is wood-paneled and softly lit, with beamed ceilings, brass reading lamps, and plush tufted red-leather booths. The menu has come a long way since chili dominated (Elizabeth Taylor's favorite—she's had it sent to her), but the continental fare still retains its American simplicity. Specialties include the exceptional hobo steak (not listed on the menu), veal bone chop, and rack of lamb. You can top off your meal with the house special: banana or strawberry shortcake.

Chaya Brasserie, 8741 Alden Dr., Los Angeles. ☎ **310/859-8833.**

Cuisine: CALIFORNIAN. **Reservations:** Recommended. **Directions:** From Santa Monica Boulevard, exit south onto Robertson, then turn right onto Alden Drive to the restaurant.
Prices: Appetizers $7–$15; main courses $11–$24; lunch $9–$16. AE, CB, DC, MC, V.
Open: Lunch Mon–Fri 11am–2:30pm; dinner Mon–Thurs 6–10:30pm, Fri–Sat 6–11pm, Sun 6–10pm.

Opened by a family of Japanese restaurateurs, Chaya has long been one of Los Angeles's best restaurants. Popular with film agents during lunch, the restaurant regularly packs in stars and stargazers who love great food served in a noisy, but homey atmosphere. On warm afternoons and evenings, the best tables are on the outside terrace, overlooking the busy street.

A continental bistro with Asian flair, the restaurant is best-known for its grilled items like seared soy-marinated Hawaiian tuna, and Long Island duckling. Hot and cold starters include seaweed salad with ginger soy rice vinaigrette, escargot with chopped mushrooms, and sautéed foie gras over hearts of daikon. Similarly styled entrées include lobster ravioli with pesto cream sauce, and a host of lunchtime salads and sandwiches.

Jimmy's, 201 Moreno Dr., Beverly Hills. ☎ **310/552-2394.**

Cuisine: FRENCH. **Reservations:** Recommended. **Directions:** From Santa Monica Boulevard, exit east onto Wilshire Boulevard and immediately turn right onto Lasky Drive; the restaurant is three blocks ahead at Moreno Drive.
Prices: Appetizers $8–$20; main courses $23–$30; lunch $13–$22. AE, CB, DC, MC, V.
Open: Lunch Mon–Fri 11:30am–3pm; dinner Mon–Sat 5pm–1am.

Jimmy Murphy—the long-time maitre d' at L.A.'s elite Bistro—struck out on his own several years ago, with backing from Johnny Carson and Bob Newhart. Jimmy's reputation has attracted a top staff, and he has created one of the prettiest and most comfortable restaurants in town. Baccarat crystal chandeliers hang from recessed ceilings, which have been painted to look like the sky. Tables are set with Limoges china, crystal glasses, and fresh flowers. One wall of windows overlooks the terrace with its small garden, fountain, shade trees, and tables under white canvas umbrellas. From the Chinoiserie statues at the entrance to the considered placement of mirrors, plants, and floral arrangements, Jimmy's is perfectly lovely in every detail, including the posh bar/lounge where a pianist entertains nightly.

You could begin lunch or dinner with an hors d'oeuvre of assorted shellfish or pheasant pâté with truffles. Dinner main dishes include filet mignon with Cognac and a green peppercorn sauce, and peppered salmon with Cabernet sauce. At lunch you might opt for seafood salad, cold salmon in aspic, whitefish with limes, or steak tartar with fresh asparagus.

Lawry's The Prime Rib, 100 N. La Cienega Blvd., Beverly Hills. ☎ **310/652-2827** or **310/655-8646.**

Cuisine: AMERICAN. **Reservations:** Recommended. **Directions:** From Santa Monica Boulevard, exit onto Wilshire Boulevard and continue straight for about two miles, then turn left onto N. La Cienega Boulevard; the restaurant is just a half block ahead.
Prices: Appetizers \$5–\$9; main courses \$19–\$26. AE, CB, DC, DISC, MC, V.
Open: Mon–Thurs 5–11pm, Fri–Sat 5pm–midnight, Sun 3–10pm.

A family enterprise begun in 1938, Lawry's enjoys an excellent Restaurant Row location, near Beverly Hills's eastern edge. The restaurant was created by Lawrence Frank and his brother-in-law, Walter Van de Kamp. Frank set out to offer the "greatest meal in America," serving just one main dish—the hearty prime rib he had enjoyed every Sunday for dinner as a boy (his father was in the meat business). Then the beef—showcased atop three gleaming silver carts, each costing as much as a Cadillac—was carved tableside by knowledgeable experts. Lawry's is also the home of the now famous seasoned salt invented as the perfect seasoning for prime rib.

Lawry's clubroom atmosphere begins in the homey cocktail lounge, where drinks are served from a pewter-topped wood-paneled bar. The dining room is equally opulent, decorated with original oil paintings, Persian-carpeted oak floors, and high-backed chairs at tables draped with orange-sherbet cloths.

In addition to the restaurant's main dish—a choice of four cuts of Lawry's award-winning prime ribs of beef, there is a seafood entrée. With both you get Yorkshire pudding, salad, mashed potatoes, and creamed horseradish. You can also get side dishes like creamed spinach, corn, or buttered peas, and a good wine list is available.

Matsuhisa, 129 N. La Cienega Blvd., Beverly Hills. ☎ **310/659-9639.**

Cuisine: JAPANESE/PERUVIAN. **Reservations:** Required. **Directions:** From Santa Monica Boulevard, exit onto Wilshire Boulevard east and turn left onto La Cienega Boulevard to the restaurant.
Prices: Appetizers \$6–\$14; main courses \$14–\$22; lunch \$7–\$13. AE, DC, MC, V.
Open: Lunch Mon–Fri 11:45am–2:45pm; dinner daily 5:45–10:15pm.

Japanese chef/owner Nobuyuki Matsuhisa arrived in Los Angeles via Peru and opened what may be the most creative restaurant in the entire city. A true master of fish cookery, Matsuhisa creates fantastic and unusual dishes by combining Japanese flavors with South American spices and salsas. Broiled sea bass with black truffles, sautéed squid with garlic and soy, and Dungeness crab tossed with chilies and cream are good examples of the masterfully-prepared delicacies you can expect here. Sushi dishes are equally eclectic, innovative, interesting.

Both tight and bright, the restaurant's cafeteria-like dining room suffers from bad lighting and precious lack of privacy. There's lots of action behind the sushi bar, and a frenetic waitstaff keeps the restaurant humming at a fiery pace. But Matsuhisa remains popular with hard-core foodies who continually return for the savory surprises that come with every bite.

Trader Vic's, in the Beverly Hilton Hotel, 9876 Wilshire Blvd., Beverly Hills. ☎ **310/274-7777,** or **310/276-6345.**

Cuisine: POLYNESIAN. **Reservations:** Accepted. **Directions:** From I-405 north, exit onto Santa Monica Boulevard and go east for three miles to the hotel at Wilshire Boulevard.
Prices: Appetizers $7–$12; main courses $16–$30. AE, DC, DISC, MC, V.
Open: Dinner Mon–Thurs 5pm–midnight, Fri–Sun 5pm–1am.

The interesting nautical interior of Trader Vic's features model ships and tropical shells. The restaurant has long been famous for its tropical rum drinks garnished with cute little umbrellas.

An eclectic South Pacific menu includes a host of delicious *pu pus* (hors d'oeuvres), among them singed ahi tuna and yakitori skewers of shrimp and chicken with a soya-ginger sauce. Two excellent main dishes are barbecued Mongolian New York steak and Indonesian lamb roast, completely trimmed and marinated and served with a peach chutney. The chateaubriand for two is an excellent cut of matured prime beef. Desserts include mud pie and passion-fruit sorbet.

MODERATE

Harry's Bar & Grill, 2020 Ave. of the Stars, Century City. ☎ **310/277-2333.**

Cuisine: ITALIAN. **Reservations:** Recommended. **Directions:** From Santa Monica Boulevard exit south onto the Avenue of the Stars.
Prices: Appetizers $5–$8; main courses $9–$20; lunch $10–$18. AE, CB, DC, MC, V.
Open: Lunch Mon–Sat 11:30am–5pm; dinner daily 5–11:30pm.

Located on the Plaza Level of the ABC Entertainment Center, Harry's is almost identical to its namesake in Florence, which is itself a spinoff of the Harry's in Venice, made famous by Ernest Hemingway in his novel *Across the River and Into the Trees.* The bar is very European, with high walnut counters and tall wooden stools. Former owners Larry Mindel and Jerry Magnin hand picked the paintings, tapestries, and furnishings on various trips to Italy. Artist Lazero Donati (who created an oil painting for the Florentine Harry's) was commissioned to do a similar painting for this establishment.

The northern Italian menu changes often but may include such entrées as salmon lasagna with fresh fennel, veal scaloppine sautéed with butter and lemon, and grilled beef tenderloin grilled with mustard, wine, and basil. All pastas are homemade, and taste like it.

La Scala & Boutique Restaurant, 410 N. Canon Dr., Beverly Hills. ☎ **310/275-0579.**

Cuisine: ITALIAN. **Reservations:** Accepted at lunch for groups of six or more; required at dinner. **Directions:** From Santa Monica Boulevard, exit onto Canon Drive; the restaurant is a half block ahead, before Brighton Way.
Prices: Appetizers $6–$12; main courses $13–$25; lunch $7–$15. AE, CB, DC, DISC, MC, V.
Open: Mon–Sat 11:30am–10:30pm.

Now an institution, Jean Leon's Scala is a busy restaurant catering primarily to customers in The Business. Easily identified by the name "La Scala" on the white bowed awnings, the restaurant's relatively small interior features faux orange trees, red-leather booths, amber mirrors, soft spot lighting, and fresh flowers. To the rear, directly above a small bar, are a number of those Gerald Price caricatures of famous Hollywood faces.

Lunch might begin with bean soup with olive oil (fagioli alla toscana con olio santo), followed by Leon's popular chopped salad. Excellent, more substantial main courses include cannelloni Gigi and grilled shrimp marinara. Sandwiches are on the menu, as well as a selection of cold plates.

At dinner try the marinated salmon with white truffles, and move on to a pasta dish like spaghetti alla checca, with chopped tomatoes, virgin olive oil, garlic, and basil. Beautifully prepared main courses include the grilled shrimp or langostines with white wine, duck sausage with Cannelli beans, and spring chicken with rosemary and white wine. Tiramisu and cappuccino are always available.

Nate & Al's, 414 N. Beverly Dr., Beverly Hills. ☎ **310/274-0101.**

Cuisine: JEWISH. **Reservations:** Not accepted. **Directions:** From Santa Monica Boulevard, exit onto Beverly Drive. The restaurant is half a block ahead at Brighton Way.
Prices: Appetizers $5–$11; main courses $8–$13. AE, DISC, MC, V.
Open: Daily 7:30am–9pm.

Nate & Al's has been slapping pastrami on fresh-baked rye since 1945, not to mention chopped liver and schmaltz (chicken fat), kosher franks, and hot corned beef. Seating is in comfortable booths and lighting is pleasantly low. A big counter up front handles take-out orders that include everything from halvah to Brie.

This place is kosher style rather than strictly kosher; the book-sized menu encompasses both meat and dairy items. Sandwiches only come in one size—huge—and are overstuffed with meats, cheeses, and traditional favorites. Other offerings include chicken soup with matzoh balls, potato pancakes, and cheese, cherry, or blueberry blintzes with sour cream and applesauce. Wine and beer are available.

Röx, in the Beverly Prescott Hotel, 1224 S. Beverwil Dr. ☎ **310/772-2999.**

Cuisine: CALIFORNIAN. **Reservations:** Recommended. **Directions:** From I-405, exit east onto Pico Boulevard, continue about two miles, then turn left onto Beverwil Drive.
Prices: Appetizers $5–$8; main courses $16–$20; lunch $10–$14. AE, DISC, MC, V.
Open: Mon–Thurs 7am–10pm, Fri 7am–11pm, Sat 8am–11pm, Sun 8am–9pm.

Until now, Hans Röckenwagner, one of America's greatest chefs, only had one uncomfortable Los Angeles dining room in which to show off his skills. The recent opening of Röx, a more personalized restaurant with a relaxed teak and denim interior, now means an all-around dining experience that's as comfortable as it is flavorful.

Ginger duck dumplings and tuna sashimi are two appetizing examples of Röckenwagner's Asian-influenced California cuisine. The latter is served with a spicy gazpacho vinaigrette. Beautifully presented entrées might include peppered pork chops with oregano pesto, grilled scallops with vegetable cous cous, or rice-crusted sea bass and sesame asparagus drizzled with soya-sake sauce.

Röx Loggia, an open-air piano bar adjacent to the restaurant is open nightly for light meals and drinks.

INEXPENSIVE

Cava, in the Beverly Plaza Hotel, 8384 W. 3rd. St. ☎ **213/658-8898.**

Cuisine: SPANISH. **Reservations:** Accepted. **Directions:** From Santa Monica Boulevard, exit south onto La Cienega, then turn left, onto 3rd Street. The restaurant is one block ahead.

Prices: Breakfast $3–$9; lunch $4–$14; appetizers $3–$7; main courses $8–$17. AE, CB, DC, DISC, MC, V.
Open: Daily 6:30am–midnight.

There are no Mexican meals at this all-Spanish winner in the Beverly Plaza Hotel at Orlando Avenue. Revelers in the mood for fun are attracted to Cava's great mambo atmosphere, made festive with flamboyant, colorful decorations, long shared tables, and loud, lively music, that's live on weekends. People get drunk here, then dance off dinner.

Although entrées like beef-stuffed green peppers, pork with sautéed apples, crispy red snapper with garlic, and sherry-glazed orange chicken are truly recommendable, the large assortment of tapas offers the most comprehensive party for the palate. Top picks include grilled shrimp in garlic sauce, mussels steamed in sweet sherry, lamb riblets in red wine, and eggplant rolled in cheese and chorizo. Paellas are available with or without meat. If you have room for dessert, try the ruby-colored pears poached in port, rice pudding, or flan.

San Fernando Valley

EXPENSIVE

Pinot Bistro, 12969 Ventura Blvd., Studio City. ☎ **818/990-0500.**

Cuisine: FRENCH. **Reservations:** Recommended. **Directions:** From U.S. 101, exit south onto Coldwater Canyon Avenue, then turn right onto Ventura Boulevard to the restaurant.
Prices: Appetizers $7–$12; main courses $16–$22; lunch $5–$14. AE, DC, DISC, MC, V.
Open: Lunch Mon–Fri 11:30am–2:30pm; dinner Mon–Thurs 6–10pm, Fri 6–10:30pm, Sat 5:30–10:30pm, Sun 5:30–9:30pm.

When Los Angeles' older, knowledgeable Valley crowd doesn't want to make the drive into town to Patina, they pack into Pinot Bistro, restaurateur Joachim Splichal's other hugely successful restaurant. The bistro's dark woods, etched glass, and cream-colored walls say "authentic French" almost as loudly as the rich, straightforward cooking.

Of the appetizers, the bistro's warm potato tart with smoked whitefish, baby lobster tails with creamy polenta, and duck liver mousse with grilled country bread are studies in culinary perfection. Generously portioned main dishes continue the theme with baby lobster risotto, braised oxtail with parsley gnocchi, and a puff pastry stuffed with bay scallops, manila clams, and roast duck. Daily specials, which are always as delicious as they are interesting, might include roasted suckling pig with braised cabbage, Pacific bouillabaisse, or beef strudel. Many regulars prefer Pinot Bistro at lunch, when a less expensive menu is served to a more easygoing crowd.

MODERATE

Jerry's Famous Deli, 12655 Ventura Blvd., Studio City. ☎ **818/980-4245.**

Cuisine: DELICATESSEN. **Directions:** From U.S. 101, exit onto Coldwater Canyon Boulevard south and continue to the restaurant at Ventura Boulevard.
Prices: Breakfast $2–$11; appetizers $5–$13; sandwiches and salads $4–$12; main courses $9–$14. AE, MC, V.
Open: Daily 24 hours.

Just east of Coldwater Canyon Avenue there's a simple yet sizable deli where all the young "happening" people go to relieve late-night munchies. The place probably has one of the largest menus in America—a tome that spans cultures and continents from Central America to China to New York. From salads to sandwiches to steak and seafood platters, everything, including breakfasts, are served all day. Jerry's is not the best deli in the world, but it's consistently good, and an integral part of Los Angeles's cultural landscape. They also have a full bar.

Pasadena

Miyako, in the Livingstone Hotel, 139 S. Los Robles Ave., Pasadena. ☎ **818/795-7005.**

Cuisine: JAPANESE. **Reservations:** Accepted. **Directions:** From 1-210, exit at Walnut Street east and turn right (south) on Los Robles Avenue; the restaurant is a half mile on your right, across from the Pasadena Hilton hotel, between Green and Cordova Streets. **Prices:** Appetizers $5–$8; main courses $10–$25; lunch $6–$13. AE, MC, V. **Open:** Lunch Mon–Fri 11:30am–2pm; dinner Mon–Sat 5:30–9:30pm, Sun 4–9pm.

The Miyako is on the same street as the Hilton, but it's been around much longer—since 1959. People come here for fine Japanese cuisine in an attractive setting. You can choose between the tatami room or table service; a view of a small Japanese garden is available from the latter.

If you're not used to eating raw fish, begin with a sashimi appetizer, a small portion of tuna slices. A full Imperial dinner offers a combination of shrimp tempura, chicken teriyaki, and sukiyaki.

Santa Monica & Venice

Camelions, 246 26th St., Santa Monica. ☎ **310/395-0746.**

Cuisine: CALIFORNIAN/FRENCH. **Reservations:** Accepted.
Directions: From Santa Monica, take Ocean Avenue west, turn right, onto San Vicente Boulevard, then left, onto 26th Street to the restaurant.
Prices: Appetizers $6–$14; main courses $14–$22; lunch $7–$13. AE, CB, DC, MC, V.
Open: Lunch Tues–Sun 11:30am–2:30pm; dinner Tues–Sun 6–9:30pm.

Located south of San Vicente Boulevard, Camelions is a little French cottage offering fireside dining in several small dining rooms, or outside on a hideaway patio. It's romantic throughout. Guests enter via iron gates garnished with creeping ivy.

Meals are on the expensive side, but for special occasions are well worth it. Winning appetizers, both hot and cold, include Norwegian salmon tartare prepared with lemon, soy sauce, capers, and dill; red lentil cakes with smoked salmon; and braised celery hearts tossed with capers, egg, and beet juice vinaigrette.

Creative entrées prepared by the capable kitchen include sautéed rabbit served in a clay pot, rice paper–wrapped salmon, and roasted veal chops. A large selection of salads are available at lunch, including spinach with warm new potatoes, bacon, and mustard vinaigrette. Sandwiches like grilled shrimp, avocado, and bacon are also served, along with creamed spinach omelets and grilled lamb chops.

★ **Chinois on Main,** 2709 Main St. ☎ **310/392-9025.**

Cuisine: CHINESE/CALIFORNIAN/FRENCH. **Reservations:** Required. **Directions:** From the Santa Monica Freeway, take the Fourth Street exit and turn left, then turn right onto Pico Boulevard and after two blocks, turn left onto Main Street; the restaurant is on your left.
Prices: Appetizers $9–$21; main courses $21–$29. AE, DC, MC, V.
Open: Lunch Wed–Fri 11:30am–2pm; dinner daily 6–10:30pm.

Wolfgang Puck's other place (see "Spago," above) is one of the trendiest spots in Santa Monica for moneyed diners. Decorated in a colorful Asian-tech, the stunning restaurant is as much an extravaganza to the eye as it is to the tongue. It's loud and lively and perpetually packed.

"Chinois," means Chinese in French, and that's sort of what you get; a delicious combination of Asian, French, and Californian cooking. The seasonal menu might offer stir-fried garlic chicken, whole sizzling catfish, or charcoal-grilled Szechuan beef, thinly sliced, with hot chile oil and cilantro sauce.

West Beach Cafe, 60 N. Venice Blvd. ☎ **310/823-5396.**

Cuisine: CALIFORNIAN. **Reservations:** Recommended. **Directions:** From the Santa Monica Freeway, take the Fourth Street exit and turn left, then turn right onto Pico Boulevard and after two blocks, turn left onto Neilson, which becomes Pacific Avenue; after about one mile, turn right onto Venice Boulevard and the restaurant is near the corner, one-half block from the beach.

Prices: Appetizers $6–$8; main courses $8–$22; lunch $8–$22; weekend brunch $8–$18; late night pizzas $13–$17. AE, CB, DC, MC, V.

Open: Dinner Sun–Thurs 6–10pm, Fri–Sat 6–10:45pm; brunch Sat–Sun 10am–2:45pm; late night snacks 11:30pm–1am.

This trendy, boxy eatery is minimally decorated with white cinder-block walls, track lighting, and simple wood chairs and white-clothed tables. The walls of the cafe serve as a gallery for an ever-changing variety of works by local artists, and the room features unobstructed views for easy table hopping.

Dinners are elaborate: favorites on the changing weekly menu are Chilean sea bass, lasagne and oxtails with mashed potatoes and roasted vegetables. A special brunch served on weekends includes eggs Benedict, Belgian waffles, and huevos rancheros. There's a fine wine list, and good late-night pizzas, made with whatever's left in the kitchen, are also available.

MODERATE

Caffe Delfini, 147 W. Channel Rd., Santa Monica. ☎ **310/459-8823.**

Cuisine: ITALIAN. **Reservations:** Required. **Directions:** From Santa Monica, take Highway 1 north, and turn right, onto Channel Road to the restaurant.

Prices: Appetizers $5–$16; main courses $9–$20. MC, V.

Open: Dinner 6–10pm.

When you enter Caffe Delfini, you just know you're with a hip crowd, though it's hard to see individual faces through the shadows of the darkened dining room. Exceedingly romantic, this candlelit, neighborhood Italian trattoria is the perfect date place, provided you can get a reservation. Cozy, intimate, and charming, the atmosphere is complemented by unobtrusive servers and solid, straightforward Italian cooking.

Mixed designer-green salads, fresh mozzarella and basil, and ripe tomatoes are typical of the restaurant's very traditional starters. Excellent pastas are full of Italian integrity, topped with tangy tomato-based sauces that can include garlic, anchovies, or clams. The all–à la carte menu includes veal and chicken standards, as well as a small selection of very recommendable seafood dishes that always includes fresh fish.

Dining in Southern Los Angeles County

- Anastasia's Asylum 1
- Aunt Kizzy's Back Porch 6
- The Beacon 8
- Chinois on Main 4
- Congo Square 2
- EATZ 3
- The Warehouse 7
- West Beach Cafe 5

9098C

Marina Del Rey

EXPENSIVE

The Warehouse, 4499 Admiralty Way. ☎ **310/823-5451.**

Cuisine: INTERNATIONAL. **Reservations:** Not accepted. **Directions:** From 1-405, exit onto Calif. 90, which ends at Lincoln Boulevard, then turn left onto Lincoln Boulevard, right on Bali Way, and then right onto Admiralty Way to the restaurant.
Prices: Appetizers $4–$10; main courses $14–$35. AE, DC, MC, V.
Open: Lunch Mon–Fri 11:30am–3pm; brunch Sat 11am–3pm, Sun 10am–3pm; dinner Mon–Thurs 4–10pm, Fri–Sat 4–11pm, Sun 5–10pm.

Admittedly, the leisurely ambience and terrific views are better than the food, but this is still a good place to eat. The owner, photographer Burt Hixson, traveled 23,000 tax-free miles, ostensibly in a quest to find the perfect decor for his dream restaurant. The result is a two-level dockside restaurant with cask-and-barrel seating, burlap-coffee-bag wall hangings, and a hodgepodge of nettings, ropes, peacock chairs, and the like. Hixson's photos line the walls, but the best views are in the other direction, towards the marina. During warm weather, the best tables are outside.

The cuisine is influenced by as many nations as the beer menu, and includes chicken Dijon, Malaysian shrimp, and steak teriyaki. There's also a raw bar serving oysters, and snacks like garlic bread, nachos, and quesadillas.

MODERATE

Aunt Kizzy's Back Porch, in the Villa Marina Shopping Center, 4325 Glencove Ave. ☎ **310/578-1005.**

Cuisine: AMERICAN. **Reservations:** Not accepted. **Directions:** From I-405, exit onto Calif. 90, which ends at Lincoln Boulevard, then turn right onto Lincoln Boulevard and right again onto Maxella Avenue; the Villa Marina Shopping Center is just ahead, on the corner of Glencove Avenue.
Prices: Appetizers $3–$6; main courses $8–$13; Sun brunch $12. No credit cards.
Open: Lunch Mon–Sat 11am–4pm; dinner Sun–Thurs 4–10pm, Fri–Sat 4–11pm; brunch Sun 11am–3pm.

Authentic southern-American, home-cooked meals are prepared from time-honed recipes by a chef from Cleveland, Mississippi. Menu options include fried chicken, chicken Créole, jambalaya, catfish with hush puppies, and some of the best smothered pork chops you've ever tasted. Most everything comes with two vegetables, cornbread, or rice and gravy. Whitebread desserts include peach cobbler and sweet-potato pie.

Sunday brunches are really special. Served buffet style, meals include meat and cheese omelets, grilled potatoes, smothered pork chops, barbecued beef ribs, and fried chicken (to name just a few options) and a choice of five vegetables.

Nothing is easy to find in the shopping center, though, Aunt Kizzy's is located to the right of Vons supermarket, across a small driveway.

Malibu & Topanga Canyon

MODERATE

Alice's, 23000 Pacific Coast Hwy., Malibu. ☎ **310/456-6646.**

Cuisine: CALIFORNIAN. **Reservations:** Recommended. **Directions:** From Santa Monica, take Calif. 1 north to Malibu; the restaurant is located directly on Calif. 1 about a quarter mile before the Malibu Pier.

Prices: Appetizers $6–$11; lunch main courses $6–$16; dinner main courses $8–$19. AE, MC, V.
Open: Mon–Sat 11:30am–10:30pm, Sun 11am–11pm.

Alice's has a 20-year history as one of the liveliest restaurants in Malibu. Facing the Malibu Pier, the dining area is glassed-in on three sides; rear tables are on a raised platform so that everyone can view the ocean. It's light and airy, and the menu is mostly seafood—as always, beautifully fresh.

Among the tempting luncheon main courses are yellowtail tuna with spinach, lemon, and tarragon butter; and grilled chicken breast marinated in garlic, soy, and spices, served with a tomato-cilantro relish. But don't overlook the pasta choices, especially the spaghetti with hot Créole sausage, zucchini, and a sweet red-pepper sauce. Alice's also has a good selection of salads, warm and cold. Consider also the Malibu sausage burger with sautéed onions and peppers, and mustard dressing.

For dinner, you might begin with the smoked Norwegian salmon served with caviar cream. Of the salads, my choice is the hot roasted goat-cheese salad with mixed greens, fresh herbs, walnuts, and a sherry vinaigrette. Great main dishes include grilled swordfish with herb butter and the stir-fried scallops with black-bean sauce and sweet peppers over pan-fried angel-hair pasta.

Inn of the Seventh Ray, 128 Old Topanga Canyon Rd., Topanga Canyon.
☎ **310/455-1311.**

Cuisine: AMERICAN NATURAL. **Reservations:** Required at dinner. **Directions:** From Santa Monica, take Calif. 1 north to Malibu, then turn right onto Calif. 27 (Topanga Canyon Boulevard), which, after about two miles, turns into Topanga Canyon Road.
Prices: Appetizers $6–$10; main courses $14–$28; lunch and brunch $7–$13. MC, V.
Open: Lunch Mon–Fri 11:30am–3pm; Sat 10:30am–3pm; brunch Sun 9:30am–3pm; dinner daily 6–10pm.

Located about four miles from Pacific Coast Calif. 1, this unusual and lovely creekside inn offers tranquil dining under the shade of an ancient canyon. About half of the seating is outdoors, at tables that overlook the creek and endless untamed foliage. Inside, tables are neatly arranged beneath a sloped shingle-and-stucco roof; a glass wall provides mountain views.

Although it is not vegetarian, the Inn of the Seventh Ray is the most orthodox, and the most beautiful, of L.A.'s natural-food restaurants. It was opened about 20 years ago by Ralph and Lucille Yaney as a place to practice and share their ideas about the relationship of food and energy. Main dishes are listed on the menu in order of their "esoteric vibrational value"; the lightest and least dense, hence more purifying, items get top billing. Everything is prepared from scratch on the premises. Soups are homemade, and chemical- and preservative-free foods are so important that even the fish is caught in deep water far offshore and served the same day. Lunch options include sandwiches such as avocado, cheese, and sprouts, as well as salads, omelets, quiche, and waffles. The dinner menu contains 10 main dishes, all served with soup or salad, complimentary hors d'oeuvres, steamed vegetables, baked potato or herbed brown rice, and stone-ground homemade bread. The lightest item is called Five Secret Rays: lightly steamed vegetables served with lemon-tahini and caraway-cheese sauces; the densest, vibrationally speaking, is a 10-ounce New York steak cut from naturally fed beef. A glass of fruit wine is suggested as an aperitif, and delicious desserts are also available. Even if you're not especially into natural foods, all the dishes are excellent and the setting is enjoyable.

Sand Castle, 28128 W. Pacific Coast Hwy. ☎ **310/457-2503.**

Cuisine: AMERICAN. **Reservations:** Accepted. **Directions:** From Santa Monica, take Calif. 1 north to Malibu; the restaurant is located directly on Calif. 1 at Paradise Cove.
Prices: Appetizers $5–$9; main courses $12–$35. AE, MC, V.
Open: Breakfast daily 6am–noon; lunch daily 11:30am–3:30pm; dinner Mon–Thurs 5–9pm, Fri–Sat 5–10pm, Sun 4–9pm.

Leisurely breakfasts and lunches are the best meals to eat in this gray New England–style shingled house, complete with weather vane and window's walk. The restaurant is located directly on the beach, and has a wall of widows overlooking the ocean. The rustic interior sports a nautical theme, with ship-light chandeliers, rigging decor, and the like. A giant fireplace separates the dining room from the lounge, which sees a lot of action on weekend nights.

Hearty egg breakfasts give way to lunches that can be anything from a Monte Cristo sandwich to scallops sautéed in white wine. Dinners are often meat-and-potatoes affairs, and include steak, fish, chicken, and the like.

BUDGET

Carlos and Pepe's, 22706 Pacific Coast Hwy. ☎ **310/456-3105.**

Cuisine: MEXICAN. **Reservations:** Not accepted. **Directions:** From Santa Monica, take Calif 1. north to Malibu. The restaurant is located directly on Calif. 1, about a quarter of a mile before the Malibu Pier.
Prices: Appetizers $3–$6; main courses $8–$16. AE, CB, DC, MC, V.
Open: Sun–Thurs 11:30am–10pm, Fri–Sat 11:30am–11pm.

Carlos and Pepe's is a delightful, weathered-wood seacoast structure. Inside you'll find a few touches from south of the border, including, at the bar, papier-mâché banana trees with tropical birds. The interior is designed so that each table has an ocean view. An immense aquarium filled with tropical fish separates the bar and dining areas. The best place to sit is on the plant-filled, glass-enclosed deck that directly overlooks the ocean.

The restaurant should be best known for their 16-ounce margaritas, made with freshly squeezed juices. But the sizable menu, which includes the usual enchiladas, chimichangas (a burrito fried crisp), and tacos, isn't too bad either. The fajitas are the restaurant's top ticket: grilled steak or chicken, served sizzling with peppers, onions, and tomatoes. Roll and fill your own tortillas with guacamole, salsa, lettuce, and beans. Hamburgers, omelets, and steaks are also available.

Specialty Dining

DINING COMPLEXES

EATZ, in Santa Monica Place, Colorado Ave. (at 2nd Street), Santa Monica. ☎ **310/394-5451.**

EATZ, the Santa Monica Place mall's ground-floor food pavilion, sells a world's array of fast foods from vendors like Charlie Kabob, Croissant de Paris, David Smith's Deli, Island Grille, Khyber Express, and Wok Inn. Röckenroll (☎ **310/587-1115**), owned by celebrity chef Hans Röckenwagner, specializes in upscale sandwiches like fresh mozzarella with basil, sun-dried tomatoes, and arugula on roasted onion bread.

Farmer's Market, Fairfax and 3rd Avenues. ☎ **213/933-9211.**

Open: Mon–Sat 9am–6:30pm, Sun 10am–5pm.

Located near West Hollywood, the fun Farmer's Market is one of America's best prepared food malls. In addition to endless isles of food stalls, the covered outdoor market is jam-packed with local produce, Norwegian cod roe, beef-blood pudding, and Japanese pin-head gunpowder—a type of green tea.

The market dates from 1934, when 18 *Grapes of Wrath*–era farmers began selling fresh produce here, right from the backs of their trucks. Who knows when the first Jane Darwell predecessor decided to fry a chicken, bake some raisin bread, and whip up an old-fashioned potato salad the way folks back home in Oklahoma liked it. Eventually, tables were set up under olive trees, where customers could consume the prepared food.

Today, dining is still al fresco, at one of the many outdoor tables. The variety of foods is staggering. Your selections might include fresh fruit juices; barbecued beef, chicken, ribs, or Texas chili; tacos; tamales; enchiladas; waffles; hundreds of cheeses; smoked fish; blintzes; hot roasted chestnuts; fruit salads; vegetable salads; seafood salads; roast meats; seafood entrées; pizza; fish and chips; burgers; stuffed cabbage; falafel; or Italian fare, from eggplant parmigiana to lasagna.

BRUNCH

Aunt Kizzy's Back Porch, in the Villa Marina Shopping Center, 4325 Glencove Ave., Marina del Rey. ☎ **213/578-1005.**

Cuisine: AMERICAN. **Reservations:** Not accepted. **Directions:** From I-405, exit onto Calif. 90, which ends at Lincoln Boulevard. Turn right onto Lincoln Boulevard and right again onto Maxella Avenue. The Villa Marina Shopping Center is just ahead, on the corner of Glencove Avenue.

Prices: Sun brunch $12. No credit cards.

Open: Brunch Sun 11am–3pm.

Authentic southern (American) home-cooked meals are prepared from time-honored recipes by a chef from Cleveland, Mississippi. Sunday brunches are really special. Served buffet style, dishes include meat and cheese omelets, grilled potatoes, smothered pork chops, barbecued beef ribs, fried chicken, and a choice of five vegetables.

The Beacon, in the Hyatt Regency, 200 S. Pine Ave., Long Beach. ☎ **310/491-1234.**

Cuisine: CALIFORNIAN. **Reservations:** Recommended. **Directions:** From the Long Beach Freeway (I-710) south, take the Shoreline Drive exit and turn left onto Pine Avenue.

Prices: Sun brunch $22.50 per person, children ages 4–12 half price.

Open: Brunch Sun 10am–2:30pm.

They serve other meals here, but Sunday brunch is what makes The Beacon special. Themed around a large glass lighthouse, the long and narrow dining room offers terrific views of the Long Beach Marina as well as the large ponds and walkways of the Hyatt Regency Hotel.

The buffet is an all-you-can-eat affair, and the offerings seem endless. There is an omelet bar, a ham and roast beef carving station, salads and seafood, including smoked salmon and peel-and-eat shrimp. Champagne and fresh juices are also bottomless. Did I mention the dessert section, which has at least seven different cakes and pies to choose from, as well as pastries and fresh fruit with hot chocolate fondue for dipping?

West Beach Cafe, 60 N. Venice Blvd., Venice. ☎ **213/823-5396.**

Cuisine: CALIFORNIAN. **Reservations:** Recommended. **Directions:** From the Santa Monica Freeway, take the 4th Street exit and turn left. Turn right onto Pico Boulevard and after two blocks, turn left onto Neilson, which becomes Pacific Avenue. After about one mile, turn right onto Venice Boulevard. The restaurant is near the corner, one-half block from the beach.
Prices: Weekend brunch $8–$18. AE, CB, DC, MC, V.
Open: Brunch Sat–Sun 10am–2:45pm.

This trendy, boxy eatery is an excellent choice for any meal, but brunches are really special. Served only on weekends, the brunch menu includes eggs Benedict, Belgian waffles, and huevos rancheros.

CAFES

Anastasia's Asylum, 1028 Wilshire Blvd., Santa Monica. ☎ **310/394-7113.**

Cuisine: CAFE. **Directions:** From the Santa Monica Freeway west, take the 4th Street exit and turn right. Turn right again onto Wilshire Boulevard. The cafe is near the corner of 11th Street.
Prices: Coffee and cakes $1–$4. No credit cards.
Open: Sun–Thurs 7am–2am, Fri–Sat 7am–3am.

Anastasia's upscale beatnik ambience is created by a hip, eclectic crowd that comes for good coffee and conversation. There's a terrific upstairs stage that's often accommodating musicians and poets.

Congo Square, 1238 3rd St., Santa Monica. ☎ **310/395-5606.**

Cuisine: CAFE. **Directions:** From the Santa Monica Freeway west, take the 4th Street exit and turn right. Turn left onto Broadway and park in the Santa Monica Place garage.
Prices: Coffee and cakes $1–$4. No credit cards.
Open: Sun–Thurs 8am–1am, Fri–Sat 8am–2am.

Located on Santa Monica's pedestrian-only Third Street Promenade, this contemporary, unfinished brick cafe gets high marks for its outside tables that are great for people watching. Good brewed coffee is served along with well made espresso drinks.

Espresso Bar, 34 S. Raymond St., Pasadena. ☎ **818/356-9095.**

Cuisine: CAFE. **Directions:** From I-210 east, take the Fair Oaks Avenue exit and turn right. Turn left onto Colorado Boulevard, then right, onto Raymond Street to the cafe.
Prices: Coffee and cakes $1–$4. No credit cards.
Open: Mon–Tues noon–1am, Wed–Thurs and Sun 9am–1am, Fri–Sat 9am–2am.

This simply named coffeehouse has been around so long, it almost seems as though Pasadena grew up around it. Hidden down a hard-to-find alleyway, the cafe is popular with punker poets who come here to read and emote in front of one of the area's most unusual audiences.

Highland Grounds, 742 N. Highland Ave., Hollywood. ☎ **213/466-1507.**

Cuisine: CAFE. **Reservations:** Not accepted. **Directions:** From U.S. 101, exit onto Highland Avenue. The cafe is located a half-block north of Melrose Avenue.
Prices: Coffee and cakes $1–$4. No credit cards.
Open: Mon–Sat 9am–midnight, Sun 10am–midnight.

In addition to excellent coffee drinks and occasional poetry readings, Highland Grounds is best known for their good line-up of local bands, playing to a young crowd almost every night of the week.

LATE-NIGHT EATING

Ben Frank's, 8585 Sunset Blvd., West Hollywood. ☎ **310/652-8808.**

Cuisine: AMERICAN. **Reservations:** Not accepted. **Directions:** From Santa Monica Boulevard, turn north onto La Cienega, then right, onto Sunset Boulevard. The restaurant is two blocks ahead.

Prices: Appetizers $4–$7; main courses $7–$13; lunch $5–$7; breakfast $4–$8. AE, MC, V.

Open: Daily 24 hours.

Although it's open all day, the most colorful time to go to this Sunset Strip joint is late at night, when it's jammed with long-haired rockers and their attendant pierced punk-babes.

The food is never as colorful as the crowd. Ben Frank's serves typical coffee shop fare: breakfasts of French toast and eggs benedict; lunches of hamburgers, salads, and sandwiches; and dinners of meat loaf, pot roast, pastas, and fish and chips. Shakes and malts are also sold, as well as beer and wine.

Canter's Farifax Restaurant, Delicatessen & Bakery, 419 N. Fairfax Ave., Los Angeles. ☎ **213/651-2030.**

Cuisine: JEWISH. **Reservations:** Not accepted.

Prices: Appetizers $3–$7; main courses $6–$12. MC, V.

Open: Daily 24 hours.

Popular with rock stars and other celebs, Canter's has also been a hit with late-nighters since it opened 65 years ago. In addition to a full range of sandwiches, diners can get matzoh ball soup, knishes, and other Jewish specialties. There's live music in the restaurant's Kibitz Room every Tuesday. (See "Evening Entertainment," below, for complete information).

Denny's, 7373 W. Sunset Blvd., West Hollywood. ☎ **213/876-6660.**

Cuisine: AMERICAN. **Reservations:** Not accepted.

Prices: Appetizers $2–$4; main courses $4–$7. AE, MC, V.

Open: Daily 24 hours.

When someone says "let's go to Rock-and-Roll Denny's," they don't mean just any restaurant in this nationwide chain; they're referring to the one at the corner of Sunset and Vista. On weekends between 2am and 4am a half-hour wait should be expected. You can get the same food at a dozen other Denny's citywide, but the crowd makes this one the best.

Larry Parker's 24-Hour Diner, 206 S. Beverly Dr., Beverly Hills. ☎ **310/274-5655.**

Cuisine: AMERICAN. **Reservations:** Not accepted.

Prices: Appetizers $3–$6; main courses $4–$8. AE, MC, V.

Open: Daily 24 hours.

On the weekend, don't be surprised to find a 45-minute wait at 4am. This is the most popular of the after-bar eateries. It blasts high-decibel hip-hop, sports a spinning disco ball, and attracts a flashy crowd. Patrons line up behind a doorman-watched velvet rope.

5 Attractions

There's plenty to do in L.A.; the only problem is that you have to drive everywhere to do it. Traffic makes it impossible to see everything in a day. Order your priorities and don't plan on seeing everything in a short time or you'll end up not seeing much of anything. Be sure and get a good map; any accordion-style foldout, sold in gas stations and drugstores all around town, will do. If you can, pick up a copy of the Sunday *Los Angeles Times* and refer to the "Calendar" for a good list of the week's events.

Suggested Itineraries

If You Have One Day

After spending the morning in Hollywood, visiting the Walk of Fame and Mann's Chinese Theatre, cruise along Sunset Boulevard or stop in at the Rancho La Brea Tar Pits. Spend the afternoon in Beverly Hills. Window-shop along Rodeo Drive, have a drink at the Polo Lounge, drive by famous homes, and cruise on the free Beverly Hills Trolley Tour.

If You Have Two Days

Spend the first day as above, then tour a television or film studio, or go shopping along Melrose Avenue and visit the world-famous Farmer's Market. In the evening, go to a baseball or football game, see a play, or visit the Griffith Observatory.

If You Have Three Days

Spend your third day exploring the city's beach communities, most notably Santa Monica, Venice, and Malibu. Don't miss the scene along the Venice Beach Walk.

If You Have Five Days Or More

Visit a theme park—Universal Studios, Disneyland, or Knott's Berry Farm—or try out as a contestant on a TV game show. Maybe just join a studio audience and watch your favorite show being taped. Museum-lovers should visit the J. Paul Getty Museum or dip into Forest Lawn Cemetery.

The Top Attractions

Griffith Observatory, 2600 E. Observatory Rd. ☎ **213/664-1191.**

More than 50 million people have visited Griffith Observatory since its doors opened in 1935. Located on the south slope of Mt. Hollywood, the observatory is still one of L.A.'s best evening attractions. Visitors are invited to look through the observatory's 12-inch telescope, one of the largest in California devoted to public viewing. On a clear night, you can see the moon, planets, and other celestial objects. Phone **213/663-8171** for the Sky Report—a recorded message on current planet positions and celestial events.

Admission: Free.

Viewing Times: Hall of Science, winter, Tues–Fri 2–10pm, Sat–Sun 12:30–10pm, summer, daily 12:30–10pm; telescope, winter, Tues–Sun 7pm–9:45pm, summer, daily dark–9:45pm. **Directions:** From U.S. 101, take the Vermont exit north to its end in Griffith Park.

"Hollywood" Sign, Hollywood.

The 50-foot-high white sheet-metal letters of the world-famous HOLLYWOOD sign have long been a symbol of the movie industry city. But it wasn't always that way.

Erected in 1923, it was originally built as an advertisement for an area real estate development, and the full text read "Hollywoodland" until 1949. Unfortunately, laws prohibit visitors from climbing up to the base, but that's O.K.—the best viewing is from down below, in Hollywood.

Walk of Fame, Hollywood Blvd. and Vine St., Hollywood.

Nearly 2,000 stars are honored in the world's most famous sidewalk. Bronze medallions set into the center of each star pay tribute to famous television, film, radio, live theater, and record personalities, from nickelodeon days to the contemporary celebrities. Some of the most popular include: Marilyn Monroe, 6744 Hollywood Blvd.; James Dean, 1719 Vine St.; John Lennon, 1750 Vine St.; and Elvis Presley, 6777 Hollywood Blvd. Each month another celebrity is awarded a star on the Walk of Fame, and the public is invited to attend. For dates and times, contact the Hollywood Chamber of Commerce, 7000 Hollywood Blvd., Suite 1, Hollywood, CA 90028 (☎ **213/469-8311**).

Directions: From U.S. 101, exit onto Highland Boulevard and turn left onto Hollywood Boulevard.

★ **J. Paul Getty Museum,** 17985 Pacific Coast Hwy., Malibu. ☎ **310/458-2003.**

The J. Paul Getty Museum is a spectacular reconstruction of the Roman Villa dei Papiri, which was buried in volcanic mud when Mount Vesuvius erupted in A.D. 79 destroying Pompeii and Herculaneum. Completed in 1974 with a hefty endowment, the 10-acre museum is the world's wealthiest.

The magnificent Italian-style museum is, fittingly, particularly strong on Greek and Roman antiquities. One of the most notable pieces in the collection is a 4th-century B.C. Greek sculpture, *The Victorious Athlete* (known as the Getty bronze), possibly done by Lysippus, court sculptor to Alexander the Great.

A second strength is pre-20th-century European paintings and decorative arts, major examples of which include 17th- and 18th-century French furniture, tapestries, silver, and porcelain. The galleries of paintings contain an extensive Italian Renaissance collection including Titan's *Venus and Adonis,* Pontormo's *Portrait of Cosimo I de'Medici,* and Andrea Mantegna's *Adoration of the Magi,* a Flemish baroque collection, and several important French paintings by such artists as Georges de la Tour, Nicolas Poussin, Jacques-Louis David, and Jean-François Millet.

Vincent van Gogh's masterpiece *Irises,* which is among the most important recent acquisitions, joins a growing number of impressionist and postimpressionist paintings that include works by Renoir, Monet, Pissaro, Cézanne, and Degas.

If that's not enough, the museum also displays medieval and Renaissance illuminated manuscripts, sculpture, and drawings; as well as 19th- and 20th-century European and American photographs.

Two incredible educational interactive videodiscs allow visitors to guide themselves through the rich and complex worlds of Greek vases and illuminated manuscripts with the touch of a finger. This new technology allows you to study these subjects in depth, depending on your level of interest, and have the otherwise forbidden luxury of leafing through a medieval manuscript or handling an ancient Greek vase. Game boxes for families, and a browsing room with books for young and old are some of the services available to visitors. Spanish-language materials and tours are also available.

Moderately priced snacks, salads, and sandwiches are sold in the Garden Tea Room, a cafeteria-style eatery. Picnics are not permitted on the premises.

Orientation lectures are given at the ocean end of the main garden every 15 minutes from 9:30am to 3:15pm. Details about educational tours are given at the Information Desk.

Important: Parking is free, but visitors are required to phone for a parking reservation 7 to 10 days in advance. Due to an agreement with local homeowners, walk-in visitors are not permitted. Carless visitors may enter the grounds by bicycle, motorcycle, taxi, or RTD bus 434 (phone the museum for information and request a museum pass from the driver).

In 1992, construction of a new, bigger Getty museum complex began on a seven-hundred-acre hilltop site in western Los Angeles. Scheduled to open in 1997, the $730 million museum will allow for 1.5 million visitors annually.

Admission: Free.

Open: Tues–Sun 10am–5pm (last entrance 4:30pm). **Directions:** From Santa Monica, take Calif. 1 (Pacific Coast Highway) north about five miles to the museum entrance.

★ **Mann's Chinese Theatre,** 6925 Hollywood Blvd., Hollywood. ☎ **213/461-3331.**

One of Hollywood's greatest landmarks, Grauman's Chinese Theatre was opened in 1927 by impresario Sid Grauman. Opulent both inside and out, the theater is a combination of authentic and simulated Chinese decor. Original Chinese heaven doves top the facade, and two of the theater's columns are actually from a Ming Dynasty temple. Despite its architectural flamboyance, the theater is most famous for its entry court, in which movie stars' signatures, and hand and foot prints are set in concrete. Sid Grauman, who was credited with originating the idea of the spectacular movie "premiere," was an excellent promoter. To this day countless visitors continue to match their hands and feet with those of Elizabeth Taylor, Paul Newman, Ginger Rogers, Humphrey Bogart, Frank Sinatra, and others. It's not always hands and feet, though; Betty Grable made an impression with her shapely leg; Gene Autry with the hoofprints of Champion, his horse; and Jimmy Durante and Bob Hope used (what else?) their noses. The theater's name was changed to Mann's in the 1970s. Movie tickets cost $7.50.

Open: Call for showtimes. **Directions:** From U.S. 101, exit onto Highland Boulevard and turn right onto Hollywood Boulevard; the theater is located three blocks ahead on your right.

★ ***Queen Mary,*** Pier J, Long Beach. ☎ **310/435-3511.**

The *Queen Mary,* permanently docked here since its 14,500-mile journey around South America in 1967, is quite an imposing sight. The black hull and white superstructure is a fifth of a mile long; its three vermilion stacks jut 150 feet into the air. Visitors can explore the ship's engine rooms, bridge, turbines, and machinery; as well as re-creations of all classes of accommodations. In addition to an extensive display on World War II, in which the ship took part as a troop carrier, there is a sound-and-light show that re-enacts a near-collision at sea; and there is a fine exhibit devoted to model-ship building. There are about 25 specialty shops on board and a chapel for "at sea" weddings.

Tickets: Admission is free; tours are $5 adults, $3 children.

Open: Daily 10am–6pm, last entry 5:30pm. **Parking:** $5. **Directions:** Take the Long Beach Fwy. (I-710) to its terminus at the marina.

Rancho La Brea Tar Pits/George C. Page Museum, Hancock Park, 5801 Wilshire Blvd. ☎ **213/857-6311.**

Even today a bubbling, odorous, murky swamp of congealed oil still oozes to the earth's surface in the middle of L.A. It's not pollution—it's the La Brea Tar Pits, an incredible, primal attraction right on the Miracle Mile in the Wilshire district. The pits date back some 40,000 years, when they formed a deceptively attractive drinking area for mammals, birds, amphibians, and insects, many of which are now extinct. Thousands of prehistoric animals crawled into the sticky sludge and stayed forever. Although the existence of the pits was known as early as the 18th century, it wasn't until 1906 that scientists began a systematic removal and classification of the fossils. Disengorged specimens have included ground sloths, huge vultures, mastodons (early elephants), camels, and prehistoric relatives of many of today's rodents, bears, lizards, and birds, as well as plants and freshwater shells.

There are currently six pits here, in which asphalt seeps to the surface to form sticky pools. Tar pit tours are offered on Saturdays and Sundays at 1pm, starting from the observation pit at the west end of Hancock Park.

More than two dozen specimens have been mounted and are exhibited in the George C. Page Museum of La Brea Discoveries, at the eastern end of Hancock Park. Skeletons of trapped birds and animals are also on display, as is a 15-minute documentary film documenting the tar pit discoveries. In the adjacent paleontology laboratory, you can watch scientists as they clean, identify, and catalog new fossils.

Admission: $5 adults, $2.50 seniors 62 and older and students with I.D., $2 children ages 5–12, kids 4 and under free. Admission is free the second Tues of every month.

Open: Museum, Tues–Sun 10am–5pm; paleontology laboratory, Wed–Sun 10am–5pm; observation pit, Sat–Sun 10am–5pm. **Directions:** From the Santa Monica Freeway 10, exit onto La Brea Avenue north, continue for three miles, and then turn left onto Wilshire Boulevard. The museum and tar pits are about 10 blocks ahead, between Fairfax and La Brea Avenues.

Universal Studios Hollywood, Hollywood Fwy., Lankershim Blvd. exit, Universal City. ☎ **818/508-9600.**

The largest and busiest movie studio in the world, Universal began offering tours to the public in 1964. Now a full-fledged amusement park, the "studio" attracts over five million visitors a year to ride the rides and get a behind-the-scenes look at the movies.

Visitors board a tram for the one-hour guided tour of the studio's 420 acres. You'll pass stars' dressing rooms and countless departments involved in film production.

Did You Know?

- Los Angeles encompasses 85 incorporated cities, of which Vernon (population 90) is the smallest and Los Angeles (population 3.4 million) is the largest.
- Los Angeles hosts more than 62 million visitors annually.
- Television and motion pictures constitute the *third*-largest industry in Los Angeles behind aerospace and tourism.

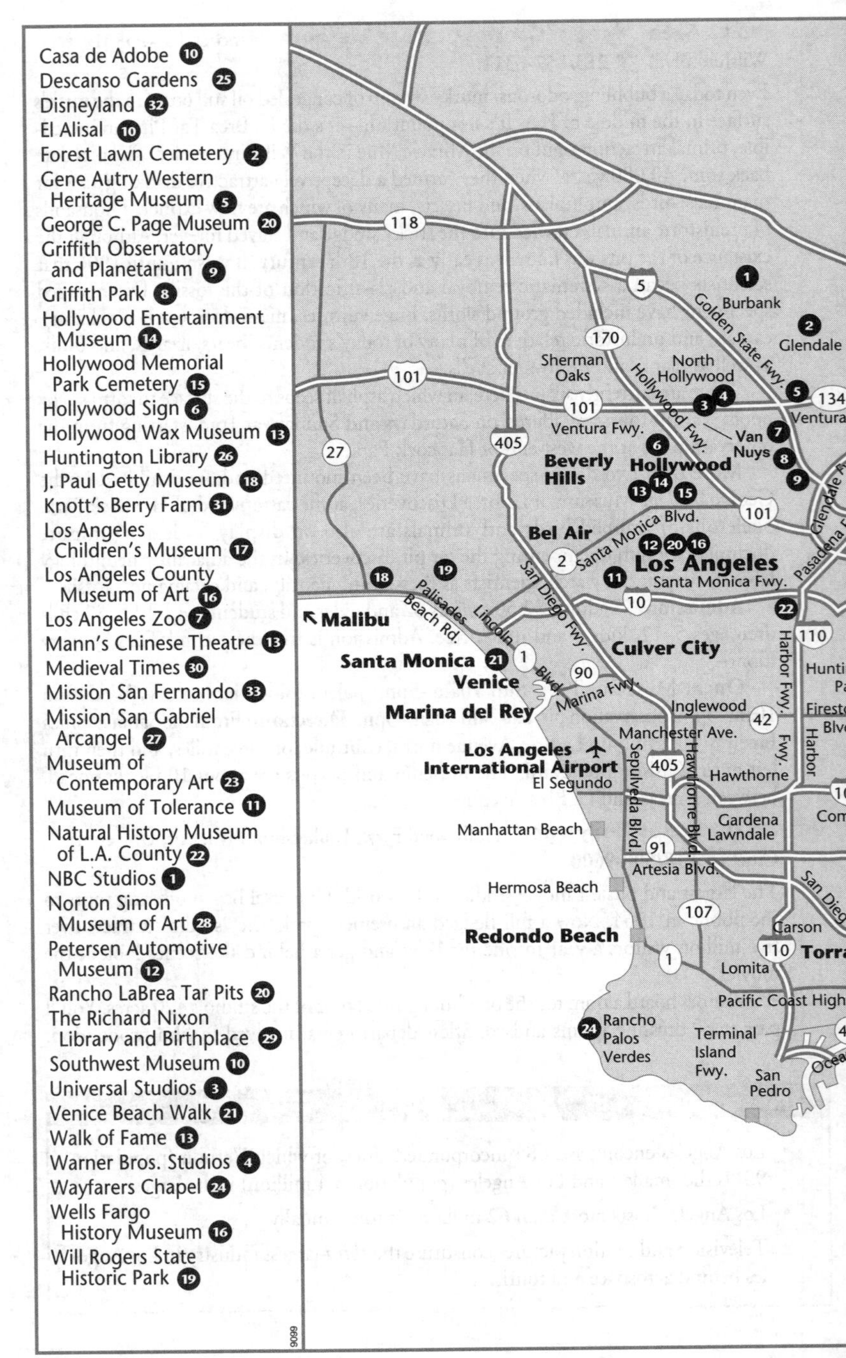

Casa de Adobe 10
Descanso Gardens 25
Disneyland 32
El Alisal 10
Forest Lawn Cemetery 2
Gene Autry Western Heritage Museum 5
George C. Page Museum 20
Griffith Observatory and Planetarium 9
Griffith Park 8
Hollywood Entertainment Museum 14
Hollywood Memorial Park Cemetery 15
Hollywood Sign 6
Hollywood Wax Museum 13
Huntington Library 26
J. Paul Getty Museum 18
Knott's Berry Farm 31
Los Angeles Children's Museum 17
Los Angeles County Museum of Art 16
Los Angeles Zoo 7
Mann's Chinese Theatre 13
Medieval Times 30
Mission San Fernando 33
Mission San Gabriel Arcangel 27
Museum of Contemporary Art 23
Museum of Tolerance 11
Natural History Museum of L.A. County 22
NBC Studios 1
Norton Simon Museum of Art 28
Petersen Automotive Museum 12
Rancho LaBrea Tar Pits 20
The Richard Nixon Library and Birthplace 29
Southwest Museum 10
Universal Studios 3
Venice Beach Walk 21
Walk of Fame 13
Warner Bros. Studios 4
Wayfarers Chapel 24
Wells Fargo History Museum 16
Will Rogers State Historic Park 19
118
5
Burbank
Golden State Fwy.
Glendale
170
Sherman Oaks
North Hollywood
Hollywood Fwy.
101
134
Ventura Fwy.
Ventura
Van Nuys
405
27
Beverly Hills
Hollywood
Glendale Fwy.
Pasadena Fwy.
Santa Monica Blvd.
Bel Air
Los Angeles
Santa Monica Fwy.
San Diego Fwy.
10
Malibu
Palisades Beach Rd.
Lincoln Blvd.
110
Culver City
Harbor Fwy.
Santa Monica
Venice
90
Marina Fwy.
Marina del Rey
Inglewood
42
Manchester Ave.
Los Angeles International Airport
El Segundo
Sepulveda Blvd.
Hawthorne Blvd.
Hawthorne
Harbor Fwy.
Manhattan Beach
Gardena Lawndale
91
Artesia Blvd.
Hermosa Beach
107
Carson
Redondo Beach
1
Lomita
Pacific Coast Highw
Rancho Palos Verdes
Terminal Island Fwy.
San Pedro
9099

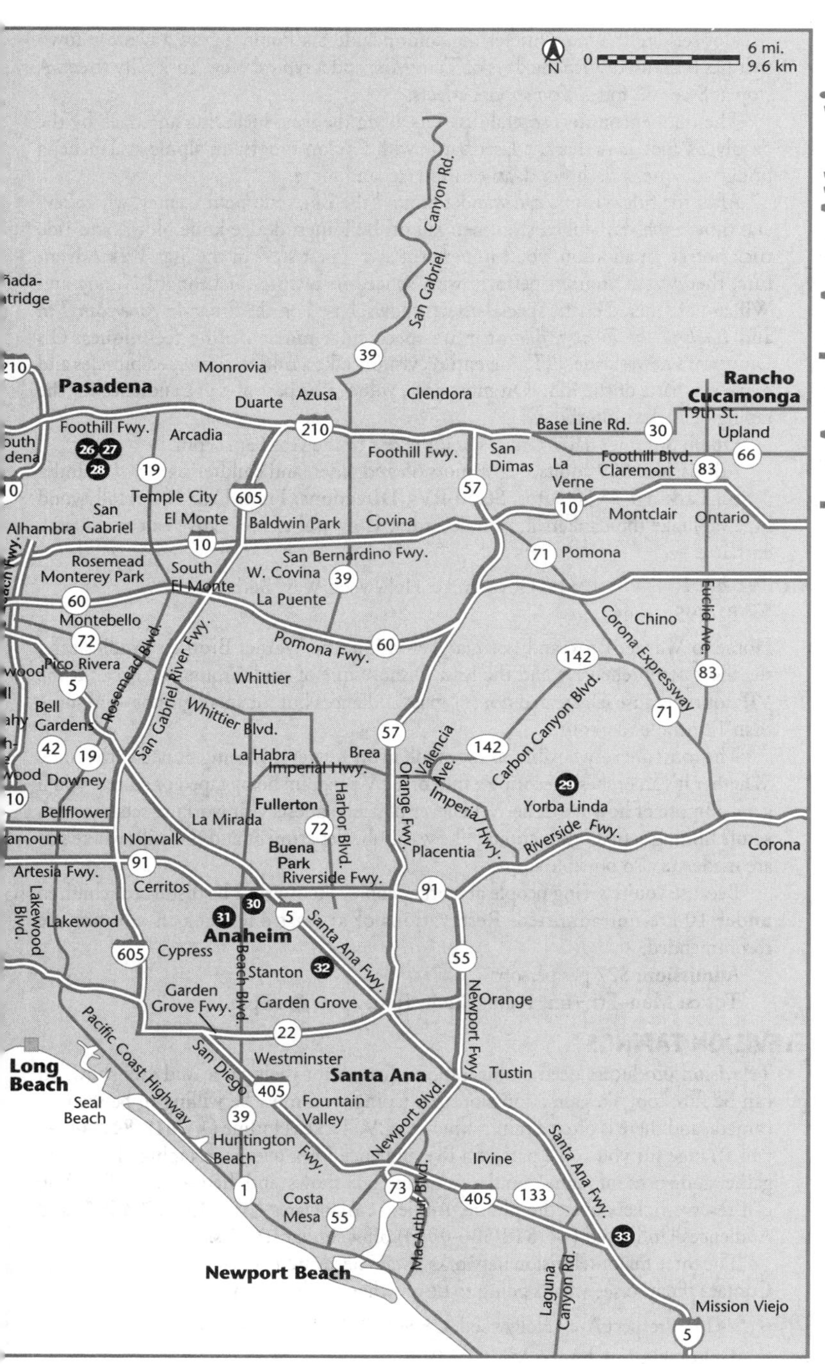

Los Angeles Area Attractions

Backlot sets are the most interesting, and include Six Point, Texas, a western town that has been used since the days of Tom Mix; and a typical New York City street. A stop at Stage 32 focuses on special effects.

The tram encounters several disasters along the way, including an attack by the deadly 24-foot *Jaws* shark, a laser battle with Cyclon robots, an alpine avalanche, a bridge collapse, a flash flood, an earthquake, and more.

After the ride, visitors can wander around the Entertainment Center, where several times each day skilled stuntmen fall off buildings, dodge knife blows, and ride trick horses. In addition, you can perform as a "guest star" in the Star Trek Adventure, then watch yourself perform with spliced-in pictures of Leonard Nimoy and William Shatner. Terrific special-effects shows, based on the films *An American Tail* and *Back to the Future,* demonstrate spectacular moviemaking techniques. On Universal's newest ride, E.T. Adventure, visitors take a ride on simulated bicycles and relive key parts of the film. On most days, you can be part of a live audience for the taping of a television show.

Open: Summer daily 7am–11pm, the rest of the year 9am–7pm.

Admission: $29 adults, $23 seniors 65 and older, and children ages 3–11, under 3 free. **Parking:** $5.50 autos, $6.50 RVs. **Directions:** From U.S. 101 (Hollywood Freeway) take the Lankershim Boulevard or Universal Center Drive exit to the park entrance.

Warner Brothers Studios, Olive Ave. at Hollywood Way, Burbank.
☎ **818/954-1744.**

Home to Warner Bros. and Lorimar Television, the Warner Brothers Studios offer the most comprehensive and the least Disneyesque of studio tours. They call it the VIP tour, because it's created not for mass audiences but for small groups—no more than 12 people to a tour.

The tours are very flexible, as they look in on whatever is being filmed at the time. Whether it's an orchestra scoring a film or a TV program being taped or edited, you'll get a glimpse of how it's done. Whenever possible, guests visit working sets to watch actors filming actual productions. The wardrobe department and the mills where sets are made are also possible stops.

Because you're seeing people at work, people who mustn't be disturbed, children under 10 are not admitted. Reservations of at least one week in advance are recommended.

Admission: $27 per person.

Tours: Mon–Fri 9am, 10am, 11am, 1pm, 2pm, and 3pm.

TELEVISION TAPINGS

Television producers need enthusiastic audiences for their game and talk shows. It can be fun, too. To gain admission to a taping, you must be willing to be seen on camera, and there is often a minimum age. T.V. Ticket Hotline (☎ **818/840-4444**) will arrange for you to be part of a live audience for a television taping. They help gather audiences for many popular game and talk shows, and their service is free. You can reserve tickets over the phone. Audience Associates (☎ **213/467-4697**) and Audiences Unlimited (☎ **818/506-0043**) offer similar services.

The three major television networks always need audiences for their show tapings. Contact them to see what's going to be on when you're in town.

ABC-TV, 4151 Prospect Ave., Hollywood, CA 90027 ☎ **213/520-1ABC.**

Ticket window hours: Mon–Fri 9am–5pm.

CBS-TV, 7800 Beverly Blvd., Los Angeles, CA 90036 ☎ **213/852-2458.**

Ticket window hours: Mon–Fri 9am–5pm, Sat–Sun 10am–5pm.

Universal Studios, 100 Universal City Plaza, Universal City, CA 91608. ☎ **818/777-3750.**

To see a television show being taped at Universal Studios without going to the theme park, write or call the ticket office. Be sure to give them your preferred dates; they will supply you with a taping schedule. Tickets are free.

Ticket office hours: Daily 8:30am–4pm.

NBC Studios, 3000 W. Alameda Ave., Burbank, CA 91523. ☎ **818/840-3537.**

For tickets to any of the shows taped at NBC Studios (including the "Tonight Show"), write to the address above. You'll receive a "guest letter," which can be exchanged for tickets on your arrival in Los Angeles. It does not guarantee entrance to a specific taping. Tickets are distributed on a first-come, first-served basis. Tickets for the "Tonight Show" are available on the day of the show only; tickets for other shows may be picked up in advance. Minimum age limits vary from 8 to 18; it's 16 for the "Tonight Show." Tickets are free.

Ticket office hours: Mon–Fri 8am–5pm.

TELEVISION GAME SHOWS

Have you ever dreamed of being a contestant on a television game show? Producers are picky, but if you have the look they are searching for, you may be picked to play. Since most contestants are from California, coordinators are especially pleased to see out-of-towners. If they like you, they will do everything they can to accommodate you. The average audition lasts about an hour, and usually consists of a written test. Callbacks are held anywhere from a few hours to a few days later.

With proper planning, you can audition for three or four shows in a single week, and still have plenty of time to tour the city. Shows looking for contestants advertise daily on the front page of the *Los Angeles Times* classified section. You can also contact production companies directly to see if they're currently auditioning. Below is a short list of major companies, followed by game shows they produce:

Merv Griffin Enterprises, 1541 North Vine St., Hollywood, CA 90028 (☎ **310/859-0188**). "Wheel of Fortune" and "Jeopardy!"

Mark Goodson Productions, 5757 Wilshire Blvd., Suite 206, Los Angeles, CA 90036 (☎ **213/965-6500**). "The Price is Right" and "Family Feud."

Dick Clark Productions, 3003 West Olive Ave., Burbank, CA 91510 (☎ **818/841-3033**).

More Attractions

CEMETERIES

Hollywood Memorial Park Cemetery, 6000 Santa Monica Blvd., Hollywood. ☎ **213/469-1181.**

This centrally located cemetery is a popular, if morbid, sightseeing excursion. Dedicated movie buffs can visit the graves of Valentino, Peter Lorre, Douglas Fairbanks, Sr., Norma Talmadge, Tyrone Power, Cecil B. DeMille, Marion Davies, and others.

Admission: Free.

Open: Daily 8am–5pm. **Directions:** From U.S. 101, exit onto Sunset Boulevard west; after five blocks, turn left onto Gower Street, then left at the cemetery to the entrance on Santa Monica Boulevard.

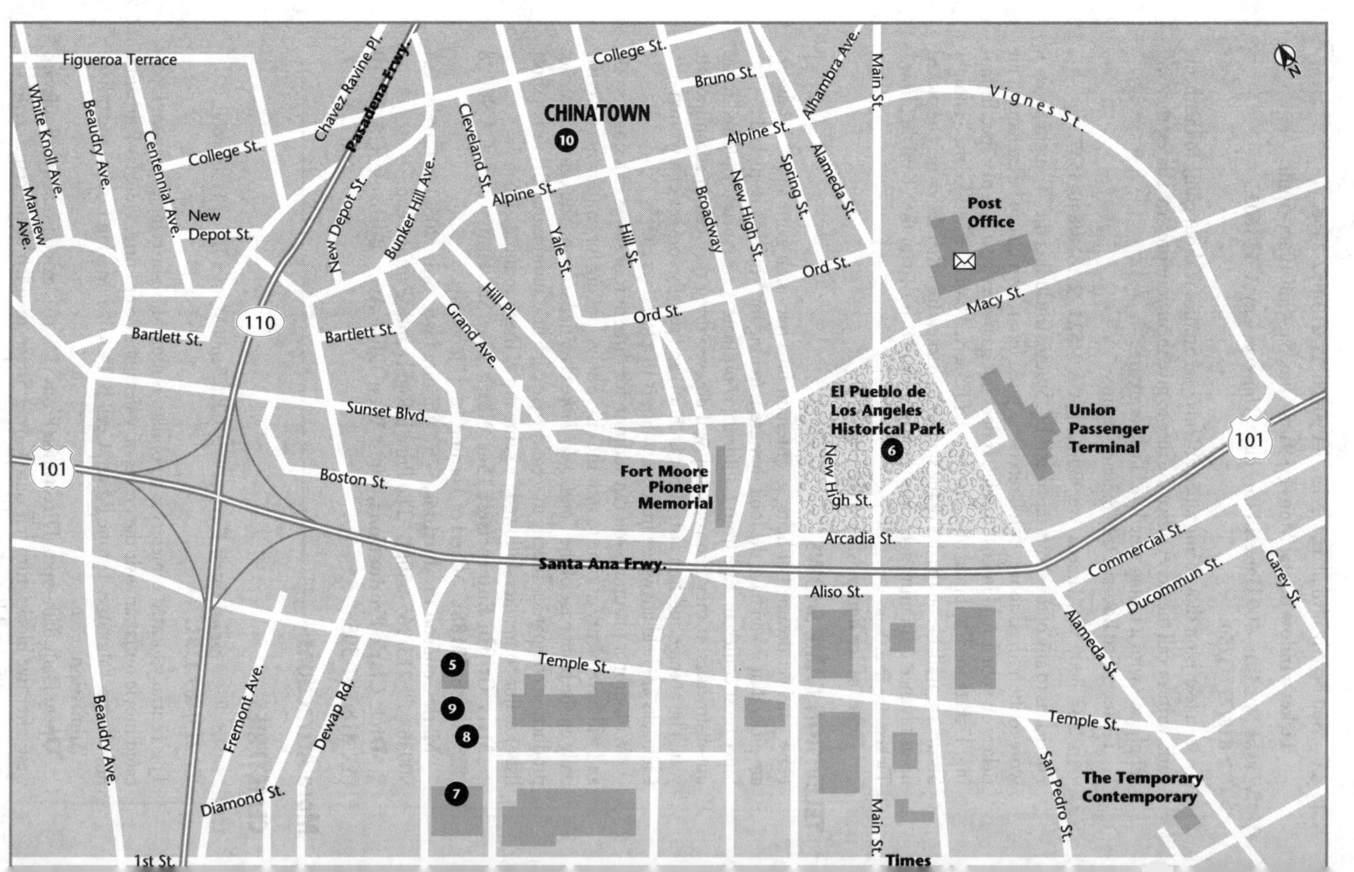

Figueroa Terrace
College St.
Bruno St.
Alhambra Ave.
Main St.
Vignes St.
CHINATOWN
10
Chavez Ravine Pl.
Pasadena Frwy.
White Knoll Ave.
Beaudry Ave.
Centennial Ave.
Marview Ave.
New Depot St.
Bunker Hill Ave.
Cleveland St.
Alpine St.
Yale St.
Hill St.
Broadway
New High St.
Spring St.
Alameda St.
Post Office
Ord St.
Macy St.
110
Bartlett St.
Grand Ave.
Hill Pl.
Sunset Blvd.
El Pueblo de Los Angeles Historical Park
6
Union Passenger Terminal
101
Boston St.
Fort Moore Pioneer Memorial
New High St.
Arcadia St.
Santa Ana Frwy.
Commercial St.
Ducommun St.
Garey St.
Aliso St.
Temple St.
5
9
8
7
Fremont Ave.
Dewap Rd.
Diamond St.
San Pedro St.
The Temporary Contemporary
1st St.
Times

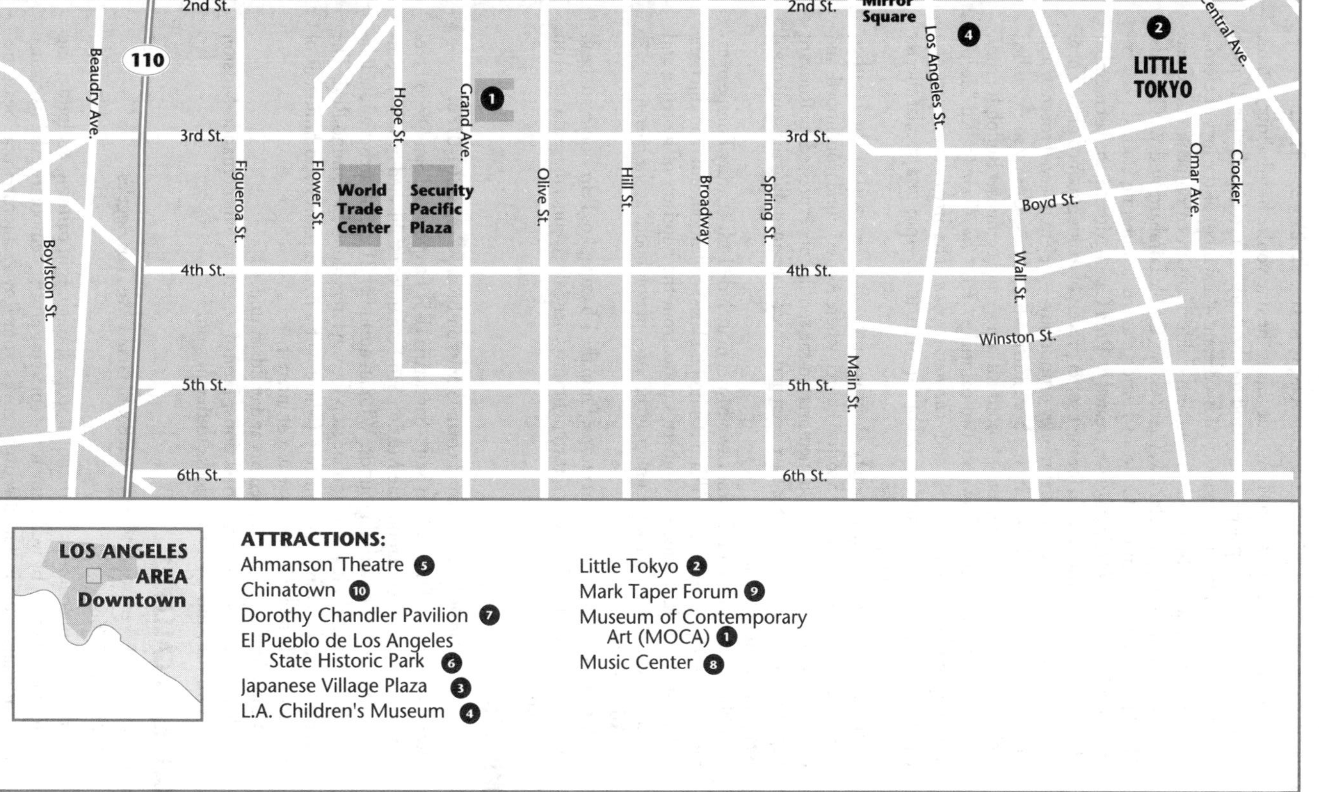
2nd St.
3rd St.
4th St.
5th St.
6th St.
Beaudry Ave.
Boylston St.
110
Figueroa St.
Flower St.
Hope St.
Grand Ave.
World
Trade
Center
Security
Pacific
Plaza
Olive St.
Hill St.
Broadway
Spring St.
Main St.
Mirror
Square
Los Angeles St.
Wall St.
Winston St.
Boyd St.
Omar Ave.
Crocker
Central Ave.
LITTLE
TOKYO
LOS ANGELES
AREA
Downtown
ATTRACTIONS:
Ahmanson Theatre 5
Chinatown 10
Dorothy Chandler Pavilion 7
El Pueblo de Los Angeles State Historic Park 6
Japanese Village Plaza 3
L.A. Children's Museum 4
Little Tokyo 2
Mark Taper Forum 9
Museum of Contemporary Art (MOCA) 1
Music Center 8
0016
Post Office

Downtown Los Angeles Attractions

Forest Lawn Cemetery, 1712 S. Glendale Ave., Glendale, ☎ **213/254-3131.**

There are five Forest Lawns in L.A., but this is the one you've heard about. Comic Lenny Bruce called this place "Disneyland for the dead," but to founder Dr. Hubert Eaton, Forest Lawn was the cemetery of his dreams—a symbol of the joys of eternal life. It's quite a place. Thousands of southern Californians are entombed in the Great Mausoleum, including Jean Harlow, Clark Gable, Carole Lombard, and W. C. Fields. The Mausoleum's Memorial Court of Honor features a stunning stained-glass re-creation of da Vinci's *The Last Supper,* created by Rosa Caselli Moretti, the last member of a Perugia, Italy, family known for their secret process of making stained glass. There are special crypts in the court that money cannot buy—they're reserved for men and women whose service to humanity has been outstanding. Those already so entombed include Gutzon Borglum, creator of Mount Rushmore and composer Rudolph Friml.

The cemetery's biggest draws are two paintings: *The Crucifixion* (called "deeply inspiring" by Pope John Paul II) and *The Resurrection.* The artworks are part of a narrated show, presented daily every hour from 10am to 4pm in a special theater specifically built for this purpose.

There are a number of cemetery churches, including Wee Kirk o' the Heather, modeled after the 14th-century Scottish church where Annie Laurie worshipped; and the Church of the Recessional, a memorial to the sentiments expressed by Rudyard Kipling. Over 30,000 marriages have been performed here, including that of Ronald Reagan and Jane Wyman.

Other attractions in the Forest Lawn Museum include 14th-century European cathedral stained glass from the William Randolph Hearst collection, and reproductions of famous artworks, including Ghiberti's doors from the Baptistry of Florence and Michelangelo's *David.* Pick up a map at the information booth at the entrance.

Admission: Free.

Open: Daily 8am–5pm. **Directions:** From the I-5 exit at Los Feliz Boulevard head east, then, at the end of the street, turn right into Glendale Avenue; the entrance is on your left.

A MISSION

Mission San Fernando, 15151 San Fernando Mission Blvd. ☎ **818/361-0186.**

Near the junction of the Golden State–Santa Ana (I-5) Freeway and San Diego Freeway (I-405) in San Fernando, the Mission San Fernando, established in 1797, occupies seven acres of beautiful grounds. With an arcade of 21 classic arches and adobe walls four feet thick, it was a familiar stop for wayfarers along El Camino Real. The museum and the adjoining cemetery (where half a dozen padres and hundreds of Shoshone Indians are buried) are also of interest.

Admission: $4 adults, $3 seniors and children under 15.

Open: Daily 9am–5pm. **Directions:** From I-5, exit at San Fernando Mission Boulevard east, and drive five blocks to the mission.

MUSEUMS & GALLERIES

Museum of Contemporary Art, 250 South Grand Ave., Los Angeles. ☎ **213/621-2766.**

A permanent collection of international scope specializes in painting, sculpture, and environmental works by well-known and emerging artists. Temporary exhibits change frequently and have included retrospectives from Roy Lichtenstein, a "Seascape" photograph series by Hiroshi Sugimoto, and an exploration of the relationship between film and art that included art objects, film excerpts, and installations.

Admission: $6 adults, $4 seniors and students, free for children under 12.

Open: Tues–Wed and Fri–Sun 11am–5pm, Thurs 11am–8pm.

Museum of Tolerance, 9786 West Pico Blvd., Los Angeles. ☎ **310/553-8403.**

Located in the Simon Wiesenthal Center, this extraordinary new museum features interactive exhibits that illustrate the history of racism and prejudice. One of the largest installations in this high-tech gallery focuses on the Holocaust. The contemporary layout of the building itself, its fast-paced contents, are designed to engage serious investigators as well as the MTV crowd.

Admission: $7.50 adults, $5.50 seniors, $3.50 students, $2.50 children 3–12. Advanced purchase is recommended.

Open: Mon–Wed 10am–5pm; Thurs 10am–8pm; Fri in Apr–Oct 10am–3pm, Fri in Nov–Mar 10am–1pm; Sun 11am–6:30pm.

The Southwest Museum, 234 Museum Dr., Highland Park. ☎ **213/221-2164,** or **213/221-2163** for a recording.

At the top of a steep hill overlooking Arroyo Seco, the Southwest Museum is Los Angeles's oldest museum. Founded in 1907 by historian and Native American expert Charles F. Lummis, the privately funded museum contains one of the finest collections of Native American art and artifacts in the United States.

Inside the two-story structure, the whole world of the original Americans opens onto a panoramic exhibition, complete with a Cheyenne summer tepee, rare paintings, weapons, moccasins, and other artifacts of Plains life. A separate two-level hall presents the culture of the native people of southeastern Alaska, Canada's west coast, and the northern United States. A major exhibition interprets 10,000 years of history of the people of the American southwest, featuring art and artifacts of the native peoples of Arizona, New Mexico, Colorado, and Utah. The California Hall offers insights into the life-styles of the first Californians. The Caroline Boeing Poole Memorial Wing exhibits a changing display of more than 400 examples of native North American basketry from the museum's 11,000-plus collection.

Frommer's Favorite Los Angeles Experiences

A Visit to a Film or TV Studio Nothing is more common to L.A. than a backstage tour of a film or television production facility. It's a lot of fun to see how your favorite TV show or a movie is actually made.

Dining at a Top Restaurant Splurge for an expensive dinner in a trendy restaurant. L.A. is one of America's great restaurant cities. Don't just go for the food—do as the locals do and make it an evening to see and be seen.

A Day at the Beaches Stroll along the Venice beach walk, cruise the Santa Monica Pier, and sunbathe in Malibu.

A Shopping Tour of the City You might only want to window-shop along Rodeo Drive but dig into the stores on Melrose Avenue and in trendy Santa Monica. Don't miss an excursion to the Beverly Center, the city's most famous shopping mall.

A Day at a Theme Park Whether it's Disneyland, Knott's Berry Farm, or Universal Studios Hollywood, these attractions mean fun for the entire family.

An exceptionally interesting calendar of events includes a Native American Film Festival; lectures on the sacred art of the Huichols; Mexican song, dance, and costumes; and Native American masks—to name just a few.

Admission: $5 adults, $3 seniors over 55 and students, $2 children ages 7–18, free for children under 7.

Open: Tues–Sun 11am–5pm. **Directions:** From the Pasadena Freeway, 110, exit onto Avenue 43. Turn right onto Figueroa and follow signs zigzagging up the hill to the museum at Museum Drive.

Natural History Museum of Los Angeles County, Exposition Park, 900 Exposition Blvd. ☎ **213/744-3466.**

The largest natural history museum in the west houses seemingly endless exhibits of fossils, minerals, birds, mammals, and the like. It's a warehouse of history, chronicling the Earth and its environment from 600 million years ago to the present day. Other permanent displays include the world's rarest shark, a walk-through vault containing priceless gems, a Childrens Discovery Center, insect zoo, and state-of-the-art bird hall. Dioramas depict animals in their natural habitats, and other exhibits detail human cultures, including one on American history from 1660 to 1914.

Free guided tours are offered daily at 1pm.

Admission: $8 adults; $5.50 children ages 12–17, seniors, and students with I.D.; $2 children ages 5–12; children under 5 free. Free admission first Tues of every month.

Open: Daily 10am–5pm. **Directions:** from the Pasadena Freeway, 110, exit onto Exposition Boulevard east; the museum is located three blocks ahead, one block west of Hoover Street.

Los Angeles County Museum of Art, 5905 Wilshire Blvd. ☎ **213/857-6111,** or **857-6000** for a recording.

A complex of five modern buildings around a spacious central plaza, the Los Angeles County Museum of Art in Hancock Park, is considered by some to be one of the finest art museums in the United States.

The **Ahmanson Building,** built around a central atrium, contains the permanent collection, which encompasses everything from prehistoric to 19th-century art. The museum's holdings include Chinese and Korean pieces; pre-Columbian Mexican art; American and European painting, sculpture, and decorative arts; ancient and Islamic art; a unique glass collection from Roman times to the 19th century; and the renowned Gilbert collection of mosaics and monumental silver. There's also one of the nation's largest holdings of costumes and textiles, and an important Indian and Southeast Asian art collection.

Major special loan exhibitions, as well as galleries for prints, drawings, and photographs, are in the adjacent Hammer Building.

The **Robert O. Anderson Building** features 20th-century painting and sculpture, as well as special exhibits. The **Leo S. Bing Center** has a 600-seat theater and a 116-seat auditorium where lectures, films, and concerts are held.

The **Pavilion for Japanese Art,** opened in September 1988, was designed by the late Bruce Goff specifically to accommodate Japanese art, though certain elements of the museum are somewhat reminiscent of New York's Frank Lloyd Wright–designed Guggenheim Museum—the curved rising ramp, the central treatment of light, the structure of the displays. An extraordinary touch by Goff was in the use of Kalwall (a translucent material) for the exterior walls; in addition to screening out ultraviolet light, these walls, like shoji screens, allow for a soft, delicate entry of natural light. The museum now houses the internationally renowned Shin'enkan collection of Edo Period (1615–1865) Japanese painting, rivaled only by the holdings of the former emperor of Japan. It also displays Japanese sculpture, ceramics, lacquerware, screens, scrolls, and prints.

Two sculpture gardens contain a dozen large-scale outdoor sculptures, as well as works by 19th-century French master Auguste Rodin and German artist George Kolbe.

Free guided tours covering the highlights of the permanent collections are given daily on a regular basis.

Admission: $6 adults, $4 students and seniors 62 and over, $1 children ages 6–17 years, free for children 5 and under. Free admission for regular exhibitions second Wed of every month.

Open: Wed–Thurs 10am–5pm, Fri 10am–9pm, Sat–Sun 11am–6pm. **Directions:** From the Hollywood Freeway, take the Santa Monica Boulevard exit west to Fairfax Avenue, then turn left onto Wilshire Boulevard to the museum.

The Gene Autry Western Heritage Museum, 4700 Western Heritage Way. ☎ **213/667-2000.**

A life-size bronze sculpture of Gene Autry (once called the "singing cowboy") and his horse, Champion, greet visitors to this museum of American nostalgia.

Opened in 1988, this remarkable repository is undoubtedly one of the most comprehensive historical museums in the world. More than 25,000 artifacts and art pieces, including 100 of Gene Autry's personal treasures, illustrate the everyday lives and occupations of the early pioneers who helped settle the west. There are antique firearms, common tools, saddles (some intricately tooled), clothing, stagecoaches, and many hands-on exhibits. As the tour progresses, visitors enter the west of romance and imagination, as seen by artists, authors, filmmakers, and in TV and radio productions. Show business is illustrated with items from Buffalo Bill's Wild West Show, movie clips from the silent days, contemporary films, and memorabilia from various TV western series.

There is also a hands-on children's gallery exploring the history of the ranch, city houses, and lives of a fictive Arizona Mexican-American family.

The museum shop is worth a visit in itself. Gifts include cowboy hats, western posters, books, shirts, bolo ties, and silver and turquoise jewelry.

The Golden Spur Cafe serves breakfast and lunch from 8am to 4:30pm every day the museum is open.

Admission: $7 adults, $5 seniors 60 and over and students ages 13–18, $3 children ages 2–12, children under 2 free.

Open: Tues–Sun 10am–5pm. **Directions:** From I-5, exit at Zoo Drive and follow signs to Griffith Park; the museum is located opposite the zoo.

Hollywood Entertainment Museum, 6433 Hollywood Blvd., Hollywood. ☎ **213/956-5469.**

Scheduled to open in late 1995, this museum is devoted to Hollywood's achievements in motion pictures, television, radio, and sound recording. The museum is located in the historic Hollywood Pacific Theater, a 1928 construction that was once the largest theater in Los Angeles. The museum has conserved much of the original theater, including about 90% of the original plaster ornamentation, and the planetarium-like ceiling.

The Entertainment Museum's displays include collections from the silent-film era, and exhibits relating to the advent of sound recording, television, special effects, animation, and computer graphics. Historical and interactive displays detail the development of the entertainment industry, while other hands-on exhibits detail other aspects of the arts, utilizing the latest technologies.

Admission and opening hours: Not set at press time; phone for information.

The Petersen Automotive Museum, 6060 Wilshire Blvd., Los Angeles. ☎ **213/744-3524.**

It's certainly fitting that there is a good car museum in Los Angeles; this recently opened ode to the automobile was long overdue.

The Peterson Automotive Museum, located at the corner of Fairfax Avenue, celebrates the history of motor vehicles and their influence upon American life. Named for its founder Robert Petersen, the publisher responsible for *Hot Rod* and *Motor Trend* magazines, the four-story museum displays over 200 automobiles. Cars on the first floor are depicted chronologically, in period settings. The three other floors are devoted to race cars, early motorcycles, and famous movie cars.

Admission: $7 adults; $5 seniors and students; $3 children ages 5–12; under age 5 free.

Open: Sat–Thurs 10am–6pm, Fri 10am–9pm.

PARKS & GARDENS

Descanso Gardens, 1418 Descanso Dr., La Cañada. ☎ **818/952-4402,** or **952-4400** for a recording.

E. Manchester Boddy began planting camellias in 1941 as a hobby. Today the Rancho del Descanso (Ranch of Rest) contains thousands of camellias, with over 600 varieties and over 100,000 plants—making it the world's largest camellia garden. The County of Los Angeles purchased the gardens in 1953, and today they are managed by the Descanso Gardens Guild.

In addition to the camellias, there is a five-acre International Rosarium that includes some 7,500 varieties. Paths and streams wind through a towering oak forest and a native plant collection. Each season features different plants: daffodils, azaleas, tulips, and lilacs in the spring; chrysanthemums in the fall; and so on. Monthly art exhibits are also held in the garden's hospitality house.

A Japanese-style teahouse is located in the camellia forest. Landscaped with money donated by the Japanese-American community, it features pools, waterfalls, azaleas, and camellias. The teahouse serves tea and cookies Saturday and Sunday from 11am to 4pm. Free docent-guided walking tours are offered every Sunday at 1pm; guided tram tours, which cost $1.50, run Tuesday through Friday at 1, 2, and 3pm, and on Saturday and Sunday at 11am, 1pm, 2pm, and 3pm. Picnicking is allowed in specified areas.

Open: Daily 9am–4:30pm.

Admission: $5 adults; $3 students and seniors (over 62); $1 children 5-12; children under 12, free.

Directions: Take Calif. 210 to the Angeles Crest exit, continue to the junction of the Glendale Freeway and Foothill Freeway.

★ **Griffith Park.** ☎ **213/665-5188.**

Encompassing over 4,000 acres of trees and hills, verdant Griffith Park claims to be the largest municipal park in the United States. Home of the Los Angeles Zoo and the Griffith Observatory, the park's facilities include golf courses, a bird sanctuary, tennis courts, a huge swimming pool, picnic areas, an old-fashioned merry-go-round, and large expanses of wilderness.

The park is located just northeast of Hollywood. Enter via Western Avenue for the beautiful Ferndell and children's playground. Vermont Avenue is the best entrance for the observatory, bird sanctuary, and Mount Hollywood.

Cool for Kids

Griffith Planetarium and Hall of Science, 2800 E. Observatory Rd. ☎ **213/664-1181,** or **213/664-1191** for a recording.

Griffith's "great Zeiss projector" flashes five different shows a year across a 75-foot dome. Excursions into interplanetary space might range from a search for extraterrestrial life to a quest into the origins of constellations. The 12-inch Zeiss refracting telescope is open to the public on clear evenings, free of charge. Shows last about an hour, but showtimes vary; call for information.

The Hall of Science, with many fascinating exhibits on galaxies, meteorites, and other cosmic subjects, includes a solar telescope that's trained on the sun, a Foucault Pendulum, which demonstrates the earth's rotation, 6-foot Earth and Moon globes, meteorites, a Cosmic Ray Cloud chamber, and more.

Admission: Hall of Science, free; planetarium, $4 adults, $3 seniors 65 and older, $2 children ages 5–12. Those under 5 are only admitted to the children's programs at 1:30pm on Sat and Sun.

Open: Summer, daily 12:30–10pm; all other times, Tues–Fri 2–10pm, Sat–Sun 12:30–10pm. **Closed:** Mon during winter, Thanksgiving, and Christmas. **Directions:** From U.S. 101, take the Vermont exit north to its end in Griffith Park.

The Los Angeles Zoo, 5333 Zoo Dr., in Griffith Park. ☎ **213/666-4090.**

Only in southern California would a zoo advertise its "cast of thousands." Here the stars include over 2,000 mammals, birds, and reptiles walking, flying, and slithering over 113 acres. Habitats are divided by continent: North America, South America, Africa, Eurasia, and Australia. Active in wildlife conservation, the zoo is also home to an intense research facility, and it houses about 50 endangered species. There's also an aviary with a walk-in flight cage, a reptile house, an aquatic section, and Adventure Island.

Adventure Island, the revamped children's zoo, is an unusual addition that looks nothing like a zoo. Four distinct habitats blend into one another in a space of about 2$^1/_2$ acres, where mountains, meadows, deserts, and shorelines are re-created. Especially popular with children, Adventure Island houses an aviary, tidepool, and animal nursery.

Admission: $8.25 adults, $5.25 seniors, $3.25 children ages 2–12, free for children under the age of 2.

Open: Daily 10am–5pm.

Directions: From I-5, exit at Zoo Drive and follow the signs to the zoo in Griffith Park.

Los Angeles Children's Museum, 310 N. Main St. ☎ **213/687-8800.**

This delightful museum is a place where children learn by doing. Everyday experiences are demystified in an interactive, playlike atmosphere; children are encouraged to imagine, invent, create, pretend, and work together. In the Art Studio they can make everything from Mylar rockets to finger puppets. There's a City Street where kids can sit on a police officer's motorcycle, play at driving a bus or at being a firefighter. Young visitors can become "stars" in the recording or TV studio; learn about health in an interactive "maze" of health-related activities; see their shadows frozen on walls in the Shadow Box; and play with giant foam-filled Velcro-edged building blocks in Sticky City.

In addition to the regular exhibits, there are all kinds of special activities and workshops, from cultural celebrations to T-shirt decorating and making musical instruments. There is a 99-seat theater for children where live performances or special productions are scheduled every weekend. Call the museum for upcoming events.

Admission: $5; free for children under 2.

Open: Summer, Mon–Fri 11:30am–5pm, Sat–Sun 10am–5pm; the rest of the year, Sat–Sun 10am–5pm. **Directions:** From U.S. 101 South, exit onto Los Angeles Street, turn right and the museum will be on the right-hand side; northbound 101 traffic should exit at Alameda, proceed straight past Alameda and turn left on Los Angeles Street.

Walking & Driving Tours

Unlike San Francisco, the city of Los Angeles—designed and built for the automobile—does not lend itself to walking tours. Many of the sights and attractions are so far apart that the only way you can get to see them is by traveling a good part of the day on the freeway—often frustratingly clogged—as you go from one point of interest to another. Yet, even in sprawling L.A., there are some areas where major sights are situated sufficiently near each other so as to enable you to visit them on foot. One area is Hollywood—not surprisingly, the most popular tourist attraction in L.A.

Visitors come to Hollywood hoping to catch a glimpse of some of their favorite stars. If you take the tour below, you may very well get to see them—in the Hollywood Wax Museum; for the city is no longer the home of the great studios and the playground of the stars.

You'll have a better chance of spotting a favorite actor or actress in Beverly Hills, the hometown of such motion-picture and TV stars as Warren Beatty, Jacqueline Bissett, George Burns, Kirk Douglas, Linda Evans, Harrison Ford, Jack Nicholson, Frank Sinatra, and Jimmy Stewart. Here, where you'll find many of southern California's most prestigious hotels, restaurants, and high-fashion boutiques (on fabled Rodeo Drive), you'll see not only where the stars live but also where they shop and dine and often entertain. For information on a **walking and driving tour** through the area, call or write to the Beverly Hills Chamber of Commerce and Visitors Bureau, 239 S. Beverly Dr., Beverly Hills, CA (☎ **213/271-8174,** or toll free **800/345-2210**). Consult also *Frommer's Los Angeles* (Macmillan).

Walking Tour
Hollywood

Start Mann's Chinese Theater, 6925 Hollywood Blvd.
Finish Capitol Records Building, 1756 N. Vine St.
Time About 1½ hours, not including shopping.
Best Times During the day, when shops are open and you can see the buildings.
Worst Times At night, when the area becomes even more seedy.

The legend of Hollywood as the movie capital of the world still persists, though many of its former studios have moved to less expensive and more spacious venues. The famous city where actresses once posed with leashed leopards is certainly on everyone's must-see list. And although the glamour is badly tarnished, and Hollywood

Boulevard has been accurately labeled the "Times Square of the West" (the city itself seems to be unaware of its decline), there is still plenty to see. Shopping is good here, too. Between the T-shirt shops and the frenzied pizza places, you'll find some excellent poster shops, film souvenir stores, and assorted Hollywood memorabilia outfits. See the section "Savvy Shopping" in this chapter for specifics.

If you're driving, exit from U.S. 101 onto Highland Boulevard and turn right onto Hollywood Boulevard. Park as soon as you can and go three blocks ahead on your right to:

1. **Mann's Chinese Theatre,** one of Hollywood's greatest landmarks. Opened in 1927 as Grauman's Chinese Theatre, the imposing structure was the brainchild of impresario Sid Grauman. Opulent both inside and out, the theater combines authentic and simulated Chinese decor. Original Chinese heaven doves top the facade, and two of the theater's columns actually come from a Ming Dynasty temple. Despite its architectural flamboyance, the theater is most famous for its entry court, in which movie stars' signatures, as well as hand- and footprints, are set in concrete. Sid Grauman, who was credited with originating the idea of the spectacular movie "premiere," was an excellent promoter. Countless visitors come to match their hands and feet with those of Elizabeth Taylor, Paul Newman, Ginger Rogers, Humphrey Bogart, Frank Sinatra, and others. It's not always hands and feet, though; Betty Grable made an impression with her shapely leg; Gene Autry with the hoofprints of Champion, his horse; and Jimmy Durante and Bob Hope with (what else?) their noses. The theater's name was changed to Mann's in the 1970s. Movie tickets cost $8.

   Walk east on Hollywood Boulevard. You're now trodding along the famous:

2. **Walk of Fame,** where nearly 2,000 stars are honored in the world's most famous sidewalk. Bronze medallions set into the center of each sidewalk star pay tribute to famous television, film, radio, and record personalities, from nickelodeon days to the present. Some of the most popular include: Marilyn Monroe, 6744 Hollywood Blvd.; James Dean, 1719 Vine St.; John Lennon, 1750 Vine St.; and Elvis Presley, 6777 Hollywood Blvd. Each month another celebrity is awarded a star on the Walk of Fame, and the public is invited to attend. For dates and times, contact the Hollywood Chamber of Commerce, 6255 Sunset Blvd., Suite 911, Hollywood, CA 90028 (☎ **213/469-8311**).

   As soon as you cross Highland Avenue you will encounter the:

3. **Hollywood Wax Museum,** 6767 Hollywood Blvd. (☎ **462-8860**). Cast in the Madame Tussaud mold, this museum features dozens of lifelike figures of famous movie stars and events. One of the most talked-about images pairs John F. Kennedy with Marilyn Monroe—dress blowing and all. A tableau of Leonardo da Vinci's *Last Supper,* as well as scenes depicting Queen Victoria and Martin Luther King, Jr., are on display. A "Chamber of Horrors" exhibit includes the coffin used in *The Raven* as well as a scene from Vincent Price's old hit, *The House of Wax.* It's open Sunday through Thursday from 10am to midnight, and Friday and Saturday from 10am to 2am.

   Farther along the block you will see the:

4. **Hollywood Egyptian Theater,** 6712 Hollywood Blvd., one of the area's top theaters and the site of Hollywood's first premiere: *Robin Hood,* starring Douglas Fairbanks.

Refueling Stop

Musso & Frank Grill, 6667 Hollywood Blvd. (☎ **213/467-7788**), may be Hollywood's oldest extant eatery. Established in 1919, the restaurant was a hangout for Faulkner and Hemingway during their screenwriting days. The setting is richly traditional, and the extensive continental menu features everything from salads to seafood.

Just down the block you'll reach the beautiful art-deco building that is the headquarters of:

5. **Frederick's of Hollywood,** 6608 Hollywood Blvd. (**213/466-8506**). Easily one of the most famous panty shops in the world, Frederick's is also one of Hollywood's top tourist attractions. Everything is sold here, from overtly tight spandex suits and skimpy bikini bras to sophisticated nighties. A small "museum" displays the undergarments of the stars. Even if you're not buying, stop in and pick up one of their informative catalogs.

Continue straight ahead, along several more tourist-oriented schlock shop blocks, and you'll be standing at the intersection of:

6. **Hollywood and Vine.** Once considered the heart of Hollywood, this corner is legendary not for its uneventful architecture but for the big-name stars who crossed the intersection. When Greta Garbo walked down the street in trousers and was widely photographed, the pictures shocked women all over America. After recovering from their horror and the headlines—GARBO WEARS PANTS—women rushed to their astonished dressmakers (or, in some cases, their husbands' tailors) to have the slacks duplicated.

Just east of Vine Street you'll see:

7. **Pantages Theatre,** 6233 Hollywood Blvd. (**213/468-1700**). Built in 1930, this luxurious theater was opened at the very height of Hollywood's heyday. For 10 years this art-deco beauty was the setting for the presentation of the Academy Awards, including the first televised Oscar ceremony. Since that time, the theater has been through several incarnations, and is now one of the city's leading legitimate theaters. Recent productions have included *Me and My Girl* and the *Will Rogers Follies,* as well as the televised Country/Western Music Awards.

Turn north on Vine Street and walk half a block to the:

8. **Capitol Records Building,** 1756 N. Vine St. The building's design, shaped like a stack of records and topped by a stylus, is said to have been conceived by songwriter Johnny Mercer and singer Nat "King" Cole. The round structure has been a Hollywood landmark since its opening in 1956.

Final Refueling Stop

Roscoe's House of Chicken 'N' Waffles, 1514 N. Gower St. (☎ **213/466-7453**), is really just a dive, but its devotees have included Jane Fonda, Stevie Wonder, the Eagles, and many other stars. It seems like a joke, but only chicken and waffle dishes are served. To reach the restaurant, continue east on Hollywood Boulevard for about five blocks and turn right onto Gower Street. Roscoe's will be about five blocks ahead.

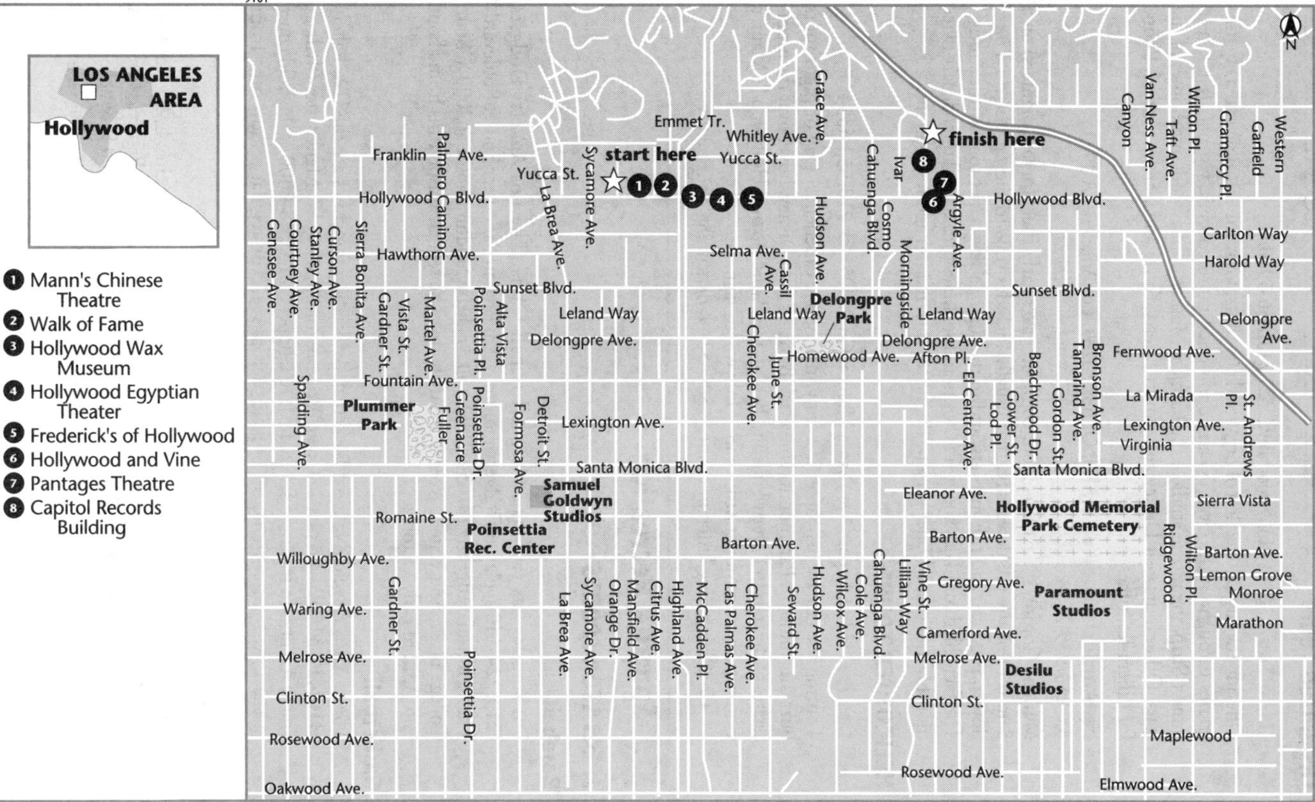

Walking Tour—Hollywood

Organized Tours

Gray Line Tours, 6541 Hollywood Blvd. ☎ **213/856-5900.**

Offering the largest selection of organized city tours, Gray Line runs several daily itineraries throughout the city. Via air-conditioned motorcoaches, visitors are taken to Sunset Strip, the movie studios, the Farmers Market, Hollywood, and homes of the stars. Other tours visit Disneyland, Knott's Berry Farm, and Catalina Island. Phone for itineraries, times, and prices.

The Insomniac's Tour of L.A., P.O. Box 35269, Los Angeles, CA 90035. ☎ **213/939-2688.**

Marlene Gordon's Next Stage tour company takes early risers (or late nighters) on a 3am tour of the pre-dawn city, that usually includes trips to the *Los Angeles Times,* flower, produce, and fish markets, and to the top of a skyscraper to view the sunrise. The fact-filled tour lasts about 6½ hours and includes breakfast. Tours depart twice monthly and cost $47 per person. Phone for information and reservations.

HELICOPTER TOURS

Heli La., Inc., 3200 Airport Ave., Santa Monica, CA 90405. ☎ **213/553-4354.**

Touring the city by helicopter is a truly memorable experience. Day or night tours buzz the studios of Paramount, Universal, Burbank, and Disney, hover over the mega-estates of the stars in Beverly Hills and Bel Air, then wind-up over Hollywood's Mann's Chinese Theater, Sunset Strip, and "Hollywood" sign.

Cost (including lunch or dinner): $99–$149, depending on itinerary.

6 Sports & Recreation

SPECTATOR SPORTS

Baseball

Los Angeles has two major-league baseball teams. The Los Angeles Dodgers (**213/224-1400**) play at Dodger Stadium, 1000 Elysian Park, near Sunset Boulevard. The California Angels (**714/634-2000**) call Anaheim Stadium home at 2000 S. State College Blvd., near Katella Avenue in Anaheim. The regular season runs from about mid-April to early October.

Basketball

The two Los Angeles National Basketball Association franchises are the L.A. Lakers (**310/419-3100**), who play in Great Western Forum, 3900 W. Manchester Blvd., at Prairie Avenue, in Inglewood; and the L.A. Clippers (**213/748-8000**), who hold court in the L.A. Sports Arena, 3939 S. Figueroa Ave. The regular season runs from November to April.

Football

The two Los Angeles–area NFL football teams are the L.A. Raiders (**310/322-5901**), playing at the L.A. Memorial Coliseum, 3911 S. Figueroa Ave., and the L.A. Rams (**310/277-4744**), playing in Anaheim Stadium, 2000 S. State College Blvd., near Katella Avenue in Anaheim. The regular season runs from August to December.

Horse Racing

Frequented by Hollywood personalities, the **Hollywood Park Racetrack,** 1050 S. Prairie Ave., Inglewood (**310/419-1500**), with its lakes and flowers, features Thoroughbred racing from early April through July and in November and December. The $1-million Hollywood Gold Cup is also run here. Well-placed monitors project views of the back stretch as well as stop-action replays of photo finishes. Races are usually held Wednesday through Sunday. Post times are 1pm in the summer (Fridays at 7:30pm), 12:30pm in the fall. Admission is $6 general, $9.50 clubhouse.

One of the most beautiful tracks in the country, the **Santa Anita Racetrack,** 285 W. Huntington Dr., Arcadia (**818/574-7223**), offers Thoroughbred racing from October through mid-November and December through late April. On weekdays during the racing season, the public is invited to watch morning workouts from 7:30 to 9:30am. Post time is 12:30 or 1pm. Admission is $3.

Ice Hockey

The NHL L.A. Kings (**310/673-6003**) play at the Great Western Forum at 3900 W. Manchester Blvd., at Prairie Avenue, in Inglewood. The regular season runs from September to March.

RECREATION

Beaches

Los Angeles County's 72-mile coastline sports over 40 miles of beaches, most of which are operated by the Department of Beaches & Harbors, 13837 Fiji Way, Marina del Rey (**310/305-9503**). County-run beaches usually charge for parking ($2–$4), and lifeguards are on duty year-round during daylight hours. Pets, alcohol, and bonfires are prohibited. Below is a selective list of some of the county's best beaches.

NORTH COUNTY LINE Fittingly located between Los Angeles and Ventura counties, this pristine beach, with no facilities or official parking, is a popular surf spot.

LEO CARILLO Located near the point at which Mullholland Drive meets Pacific Coast Highway, this beach is part of an adjacent, inland state park, where camping is permitted. It's good for tide pool watching at low tide, and for cookouts—fire pits are allowed.

EL PESCADOR, LA PIEDRA, and EL MATADOR These relatively rugged and isolated beaches front a four-mile stretch of Pacific Coast Highway between Broad Beach and Decker Canyon roads. It's very picturesque and perfect for picnicking.

ZUMA and POINT DUME Jam-packed on warm weekends, these two adjacent Malibu beaches offer wide stretches of sand, and plenty of parking and services. These are L.A.'s most popular beaches; Families go to Zuma while younger people head toward Point Dume.

PARADISE COVE This private beach in the 28000 block of Pacific Coast Highway charges $15 to park and $5 per person if you walk in. Changing rooms and showers are included in the price. The beach is often full by noon on weekends.

SURFRIDER One of the city's most popular surfing spots, this beach is located between Malibu Pier and the lagoon. Few "locals only" wave wars are ever fought here.

SANTA MONICA The beaches on either side of the Santa Monica Pier are popular for their sands and easy accessibility. There are big parking lots, eateries, and lots of well-maintained bathrooms. The paved beach path runs along here, allowing you to walk, bike, or blade to Venice and points south.

VENICE The paved boardwalk gets most of the attention here, but the broad beach would be alluring all on its own. Expensive parking lots abound on the small streets surrounding Windward Court.

MARINA DEL REY Located right in the middle of del Rey, this beach is popular with families, and offers shaded picnic tables and rather calm waters. Parking is just off Admiralty Way, at Via Marina.

MANHATTAN BEACH Locals sun south of the pier, and park in lots on 26th Street, or at the end of 45th Street. This is an excellent swimming beach.

HERMOSA BEACH One of my favorite beaches in L.A., Hermosa is popular with the younger volleyball crowd, and offers wide sands and a paved boardwalk called The Strand. There's plenty of street parking.

REDONDO BEACH Beach access here is south of King Harbor, at 200 Portofino Way. The Redondo Municipal Pier, located just north, is a family-oriented fun-filled "mall by the sea."

TORRANCE BEACH South of Redondo, beaches are bigger and less crowded, but offer excellent facilities including food and toilets. Local snorkelers swear by Malaga Cove, located just south of the beach.

LONG BEACH Running the entire length of the city along Ocean Boulevard, this calm, breakwater-protected beach is long indeed, and close to the good restaurants and shops that line 2nd Avenue. This is one of the city's best sunning beaches.

SEAL BEACH Both charming and quiet, smallish Seal Beach is a terrific place to steal away from the city. A "Tot-Lot" contains diversionary play-structures for the kiddies. Parking is available both at the pier and on 1st Street.

Bicycling

The best place to bike (or skate) is along the 22-mile auto-free beach path that runs along Santa Monica and Venice beaches. You can rent 10-speeds from Sea Mist Rental, 1619 Ocean Front, Santa Monica (**310/395-7076**).

Horseback Riding

The Griffith Park Livery Stables, 480 Riverside Dr., Burbank (**818/840-8401**), rents horses by the hour for western or English riding. There's a 200-pound weight limit, and children under 12 are not permitted to ride. Horses cost $13 per hour, and there's a two-hour rental limit maximum. The stables are open Monday through Friday from 8am to 7pm, Saturday and Sunday from 8am to 4pm.

Jetskiing

Nature Tours, 1759 9th St. #201, Santa Monica. ☎ **310/452-7508.**

Intensive two-hour lessons teach riders of all level how to get the most out of jetskis and wave runners. Beginners ski around Marina del Rey, while advanced jetters cruise up to Malibu. Midweek half-day trips to Pyramid Lake include jet ski rental, lessons, and a barbecued lunch.

Cost: About $150 per lesson or tour.

Sea Kayaking

Island Packers, 1867 Spinnaker Dr., Ventura. ☎ **805/642-1393.**

Island Packers arranges small groups who make the two-hour sail to Santa Cruz Island, then tour neighboring Anacapa Island by kayak. One-day excursions last about 10 hours, include continental breakfast and picnic lunch, and cost $135.

Longer adventures can also be arranged, include camping or lodging, and cost $215 to $445.

Southwind Sports Resource, 17855 Sky Park Circle, Ste. A., Irvine. ☎ **714/261-0200.**

Southwind combines sea kayaking with bird watching in their tours of Upper Newport Bay. Trips cost from $35 to $65. One-day Catalina Island kayaking trips are also arranged, and cost about $110.

Tennis

Public courts, administered by the City of Los Angeles Department of Recreation and Parks (☎ **213/485-5555**), are located all around the city. Call for the nearest location.

Windsurfing

Surfing meets sailing in this fun sport that is much more dificult than it looks. The Long Beach Windsurfing Center, 3850 E. Ocean Ave., Long Beach, rents boards by the hour. They're open daily from 10am to 6pm.

Malibu Ocean Sports, on the public beach in front of Marina del Rey's Cheesecake Factory. ☎ **310/821-8960.**

Windsurf rentals, including board, wet suit, and flotation devices, cost $15 per hour. Lessons are offered on weekends; the three-hour course costs $45, and is guaranteed to teach you the basics.

7 Savvy Shopping

One of the biggest cities in the United States, Los Angeles is well known for its plethora of top shops, trendy boutiques, and gaggle of shopping malls. Although the city is quite spread out, shopping areas are distinct; each is geared toward a particular market.

THE SHOPPING SCENE

GREAT HUNTING GROUNDS • Hollywood Boulevard One of Los Angeles' most famous streets is, for the most part, a sleazy strip. But between the T-shirt shops and frenzied pizza places you'll find some excellent poster shops, film souvenir stores, and assorted Hollywood memorabilia outfits.

• Melrose Avenue The area between Fairfax and La Brea Avenues is one of the best shopping streets in the country for young, trendy fashions. Hundreds of stores sell the latest in clothes, gifts, jewelry, and accessories.

• Venice Beach Walk Stalls and shops sell youth-oriented street fashions to beachgoers and tourists who come here to see and be seen. Even if you're not shopping, come here for the carnival of people showing off their unique talents and fashions.

• **Rodeo Drive** Beverly Hills' most famous street is known for its haute couture boutiques, expensive jewelry shops, top restaurants, and major department stores.

• **Third Street Promenade** Packed with chain stores and boutiques, as well as dozens of restaurants and a large movie theater, Santa Monica's Third Street, between Broadway and Wilshire Boulevard, has recently become one of the most popular shopping areas in the city. The Promenade is closed to vehicular traffic.

• **Downtown Garment District** The blocks surrounding Ninth Street are known as a host of shops selling clothes, luggage, and assorted goods at significantly discounted prices.

HOURS, TAXES & SHIPPING Store hours are generally Monday through Saturday from 10am to 6pm, and Sunday from noon to 5pm. Most department stores and malls stay open later: usually Monday through Friday from 10am to 9pm, Saturday from 10am to 6pm, and Sunday from 11am to 6pm.

Sales tax in Los Angeles is 7.75%, added on at the register for all goods and services purchased.

Most of the city's shops can wrap your purchase and **ship** it anywhere in the world via United Parcel Service (UPS). If they can't, you can send it yourself, either through UPS, 10690 Santa Monica Blvd. (☎ toll free **800/222-8333**), and other locations, or through the U.S. Mail (see "Fast Facts: Los Angeles," above).

SHOPPING A TO Z

Art Galleries

Brendan Walter Gallery, 1001 Colorado Ave., Santa Monica. ☎ **310/395-1155.**

A contemporary arts gallery specializing in furniture, vessels, paintings, and glass and metal sculpture.

Open: Tues–Sat 10:30am–5:30pm.

The Broadway Gallery Complex, 2022-2114 Broadway, Santa Monica. ☎ **310/829-3300.**

Ten galleries showing a wide range of work are housed in this single Santa Monica complex. Featured contemporary artists include Barbara Ackerman, Ruth Bloom, Mark Moore, and Sylvia White.

Open: Wed and Fri–Sat 11am–6pm, Thurs 11am–8pm, Sun noon–4pm.

Christopher Grimes Gallery, 916 Colorado Ave., Santa Monica. ☎ **310/587-3373.**

The emphasis here is contemporary American art in a wide range of media, including painting, sculpture, photography, and video.

Open: Tues–Sat 10am–5:30pm.

Gallery of Functional Art, 2429 Main St., Santa Monica. ☎ **213/450-2827.**

Tables, chairs, beds, sofas, lighting, screens, dressers, and bathroom fixtures are some of the functional art and art furniture pieces that are sold here. Smaller items such as jewelry, watches, flatware, candlesticks, ceramics, and glass are also shown.

Open: Tues–Fri 11am–7pm, Sat–Sun 11am–6pm.

Books

There are hundreds of bookshops in Los Angeles. Below is a select list of some of the more interesting.

Audubon Society Bookstore, 7377 Santa Monica Blvd., West Hollywood. ☎ **213/876-0202.**

A terrific selection of books on nature, adventure travel, and ecology is augmented by bird-watching paraphernalia and regular L.A. nature walks. Phone for information.

Open: Tues–Sat 10am–3pm.

Heritage Book Shop, Inc., 8340 Melrose Ave., Los Angeles. ☎ **310/659-3674.**

Specializing in rare books and manuscripts, Heritage is packed with first editions and special illustrations.

Open: Tues–Fri 9:30am–5:30pm, Sat 10am–4:30pm.

C. G. Jung Bookstore & Library, 10349 W. Pico Blvd., Los Angeles. ☎ **310/556-1196.**

Specializes in analytical psychology, folklore, fairy tales, alchemy, dream studies, myths, symbolism, and other related books. Tapes and videocassettes are also sold.

Mandala Bookstore, 616 Santa Monica Blvd., Santa Monica. ☎ **310/393-1953.**

In addition to crystals and Southeast Asian music, this store stocks many hard-to-find books on Buddhism and religion from Nepal, Tibet, and India.

Midnight Special Bookstore, 1318 Third St., Santa Monica. ☎ **310/393-2923.**

Located on Santa Monica's Third Street Promenade, this medium-sized general book shop is known for their good small press selection and regular poetry readings.

Open: Mon–Wed 10:30am–10pm, Thurs–Sat 10:30am–11:30pm, Sun 11am–10pm.

Mysterious Bookshop, 8763 Beverly Blvd., West Hollywood. ☎ **310/659-2959.**

Over 20,000 used, rare, and out-of-print titles make this the area's best mystery, espionage, detective, and thriller book shop. There are regular author appearances and other special events.

Open: Mon–Sat 10am–6pm, Sun noon–5pm.

Department Stores

Most department stores in the city have flagship stores or large branches in Beverly Hills or downtown. A large number of stores also serve as anchors in L.A.'s largest shopping malls. Here is a list of the largest.

The Broadway, Beverly Center, West Hollywood. ☎ **310/854-7200.**

Based in southern California, The Broadway sells moderately priced designer clothes, sportswear, and casual clothing, and has, as well, excellent cosmetics and cookware departments.

Bullock's, 10661 Weyburn Ave., near Westwood Blvd., Westwood. ☎ **310/208-4211.**

Upper-middle-class, fashion-conscious customers shop here for imported designer fashions and good-quality private label merchandise in all departments.

Neiman Marcus, 9700 Wilshire Blvd., Beverly Hills. ☎ **310/550-5900.**

Distinctive men's and women's fashions, world-famous furs, precious jewels, unique gifts, and legendary personal service have made this one of California's most successful department stores.

Open: Mon–Sat 10am–6pm.

Nordstrom, Westside Pavilion, West L.A. ☎ **310/470-6155.**

Emphasis on customer service has won this Seattle-based store a loyal following. Best known for shoes, the store also features some couture clothing and conservative men's and women's clothes.

Robinson's-May, 920 7th St., Downtown. ☎ **213/683-1144.**

Home accessories, furniture, and household supplies are featured here, along with sportswear for women and large selections of costume jewelry.

Eyewear

L.A. Eyeworks, 7407 Melrose Ave., Los Angeles. ☎ **213/653-8255.**

This home-town design shop has become world famous for their innovative Hollywood styles. This is their first storefront location.

Open: Mon–Fri 10am–7pm, Sat 10am–6pm, Sun noon–5pm.

Strictly Sunglasses, in the Westside Pavilion, 10800 Pico Blvd. ☎ **310/446-1668.**

More than 600 designer and house brands, including Revo, Serengeti, Ray-Ban, Vuarnet, Oakley, and Armani range in price from $20 to $400 a pair. They're often the first to get new models making this shop tops on trendsetters' hit lists.

Open: Mon–Fri 10am–9pm, Sat 10am–7pm, Sun 11am–6pm.

Fashion

Battle Dress, 7318 C Melrose Ave., Los Angeles. ☎ **213/935-7350.**

Selling some of the most unusual leather frocks, tops, pants, and boots, many of the handmade styles here are inspired by authentic Cherokee designs. Bring your checkbook.

Open: Tues–Sat noon–7:30pm, Sun noon–6pm.

Bijan, 420 N. Rodeo Dr., Beverly Hills. ☎ **310/273-6544.**

This top-quality menswear shop features exquisitely tailored clothing and accessories along with Bijan's fragrance collections.

Open: Mon–Sat 10am–6pm.

Giorgio Beverly Hills, 327 N. Rodeo Dr., Beverly Hills. ☎ **310/274-0200.**

Giorgio's signature yellow and white striped awnings mark the home of the designer's apparel, gift, and fragrance collections.

Open: Mon–Fri 10am–7pm, Sat 10am–6pm, Sun noon–5pm.

Hermes, 343 N. Rodeo Dr., Beverly Hills. ☎ **310/278-6440.**

This Beverly Hills branch of Paris' 155-year-old House of Hermes is known for its superlative handmade leather goods, hand-screened silk ties and scarves, perfumes, and other gift items.

Open: Mon–Sat 10am–6pm.

Hobie Sports, 1409 Third St., Santa Monica. ☎ **310/393-9995.**

In addition to swimwear, Hobie Sports specializes in colorful surfer dude–style shorts and T-shirts.

Open: Mon–Thurs 10am–10pm, Fri–Sat 10am–11pm, Sun 11am–8pm.

L.A. Equestrian Center's Dominion Saddlery, 480 Riverside Dr., Burbank. ☎ **818/842-4300.**

One of the largest assortments of riding wear includes stretch Equijeans, leather lace-up boots, lycra breeches, fox-hunting jackets, and riding crops. Nothing's cheap.

Open: Mon and Sat 9am–5pm, Tues 9am–8pm, Wed–Fri 9am–6pm, Sun 9am–4pm.

Louis Vuitton, 307 N. Rodeo Dr., Beverly Hills. ☎ **310/859-0457.**

Carrying the largest selection of Vuitton items in the United States, this tony shop stocks luggage, business cards, handbags, wallets, and a seemingly endless variety of accessories.

Open: Mon–Sat 10am–6pm, Sun noon–5pm.

Na Na, 1228 Third St., Santa Monica. ☎ **310/394-9690.**

This is what punk looks like in the 1990s: Clunky shoes, knit hats, narrow striped shirts, and baggy street wear.

Place and Company, 8820 S. Sepulveda Blvd., Westchester. ☎ **310/645-1539.**

Second-hand, mint-condition men's and women's designer duds include labels from Chanel, Armani, Blass, Ferré, Klein, Versace, and Valentino. $1,000-plus dresses and suits are sometimes priced as low as $350. Sport coats, shirts, and designer sweaters are also sold.

Open: Mon–Sat 10am–6pm.

Polo/Ralph Lauren, 444 N. Rodeo Dr., Beverly Hills. ☎ **310/281-7200.**

This Beverly Hills shop is the exclusive Los Angeles outlet for Polo/Ralph Lauren's apparel collections for men, women, and children. Selected home furnishings are also sold.

Open: Mon–Wed and Fri–Sat 10am–6pm, Sun noon–5pm, Thurs 10am–8pm.

Ragtime, 7952 Third St., Santa Monica. ☎ **213/655-1742.**

Vintage rags are given contemporary lives when they are dressed up by Ragtime owner Helen Levy. Old designer labels are sewn on T-shirts, and assorted fasteners decorate vintage vests.

Open: Mon–Sat 11am–6pm.

Red Balls on Fire, 7708 Melrose Ave., Los Angeles. ☎ **213/655-3409.**

Outrageous stagewear and head-turning streetwear include funky jackets and the wildest stretch pants. Try them on in the dressing rooms made of purple velvet-lined upright coffins.

Open: Mon–Sat 11am–8pm, Sun 11am–7pm.

Studio Wardrobe Services, 3953 Laurel Grove, Studio City. ☎ **818/508-7762.**

Although you may recognize some of the clothes from Dennis Quaid, Kathleen Turner, or Sylvester Stallone movies, most were worn by extras, before being turned over for public sale here. Prices range from $25 to $1,500, and new shipments arrive weekly.

Open: Mon–Sat 10am–6pm, Sun noon–5pm.

Texas Soul, 7515 Melrose Ave., Los Angeles. ☎ **213/658-5571.**

Men's and women's boots, jackets, jewelry, and belts are peddled at this Western leather shop. Plenty of working and walking boots are sold along with traditional cowboy styles.

Open: Món–Sat 11am–8pm, Sun noon–7pm.

Wasteland, 7428 Melrose Ave., Los Angeles. ☎ **213/653-3028.**

An enormous art-filled exterior fronts a large collection of vintage and contemporary clothes for men and women. Leathers, natural fibers, and dark colors predominate. Grandma's furniture is also for sale.

Open: Mon–Sat 11:30am–8:30pm, Sun noon–8pm.

Film Memorabilia

Book City Collectables, 6631 Hollywood Blvd., Hollywood. ☎ **213/466-0120.**

Over 70,000 color prints of stars past and present are sold, along with a good selection of autographs, movie and TV scripts, and cinema biographies.

Cinema Collectors, 1507 Wilcox Ave. (at Sunset Blvd.), Hollywood. ☎ **213/461-6516.**

Original movie posters, magazines, stills, head shots, and associated memorabilia are cross-referenced on computer. Helpful, uniformed employees can answer your questions and help you find your way around.

Hollywood Book and Poster Company, 6349 Hollywood Blvd., Hollywood. ☎ **213/465-8764.**

Owner Eric Caidin's excellent collection of movie posters is particularly strong in horror and exploitation flicks (about $20). Photocopies of about 5,000 movie and television scripts are also sold for $10 to $15 each.

The Last Moving Picture Show, 6307 Hollywood Blvd., Hollywood. ☎ **213/467-0838.**

Movie-related merchandise of all kinds is sold here, including stills from the 1950s and authentic production notes from a variety of films.

Star Wares on Main, 2817 Main St., Santa Monica. ☎ **310/399-0224.**

Owner Marcia Tysseling was governess to Joan Rivers' daughter. Now she is the proprietor of a unique resale boutique carrying celebrity clothes, props, movie wardrobes, and autographed items. Threads include Madonna's gown from her *Blond Ambition* tour, a tie clasp from Rudolph Valentino, Bette Davis's handbag and cigarette case, original artwork from *Star Trek,* a miniature batwing from *Batman Returns,* and various other items. Of every sale of celebrity-owned items, 10% goes to charity.

Gifts

Alamo Flags, 1349 A Third St., Santa Monica. ☎ **310/917-3344.**

In addition to country flags of all sizes, Alamo sells banners, ensigns, pennants, and standards emblazoned with all manner of signs and sayings. Nautical and special-occasion flags are some of their best sellers.

Open: Mon–Fri 9am–9pm, Sat–Sun 9am–10pm.

Beverly Hills Baseball Card Shop, 1137 S. Robertson Blvd., ☎ **310/278-4263.**

From Ty Cobbs and Lou Gehrigs to Tom Seavers and Mookie Wilsons, this warehouse of baseball history houses literally millions of cards, including rare rookie editions and other hard-to-find collectibles.

Open: Tues–Fri 11am–6pm, Sat 11am–5pm.

Brian Jeffrey's Design Greenhouse, 7556 Melrose Ave., Los Angeles. ☎ **213/651-2539.**

One of the most beautiful stores on Melrose, Brian Jeffrey's is a professional decorator's dream store for interior plants, baskets and containers, candle holders, and wind chimes. A festival for the senses, the shop is cluttered with terrific visuals, smells great, and resounds with ethereal music.

Open: Mon–Sun 11am–6pm.

Card de A, 1570 E. Rosecrans Ave., Manhattan Beach. ☎ **310/536-0040.**

No Hallmark greetings here, just highly stylized designer greetings and occasion cards from small presses and individual producers. Handmade art cards are their specialty.

Open: Mon–Fri 10am–7pm, Sat 10am–6pm, Sun 11am–5pm.

Details, 8625 Melrose Ave., Los Angeles. ☎ **310/659-1550.**

Appropriately located near West Hollywood's Pacific Design Center in a monstrous building known to locals as the "Blue Whale," Details offers huge selections of hard-to-find home decorating items including imaginative cabinet and door pulls, hooks, knobs, towel bars, and kitchen and bath accessories from Europe and Japan.

Open: Mon–Fri 10am–7pm, Sat 10am–6pm, Sun 11am–5pm.

Condomania, 7306 Melrose Ave., Los Angeles. ☎ **213/933-7865.**

A vast selection of condoms, lubricants, and kits creatively encourage safe sex. Glow-in-the-dark condoms anyone?

Open: Sun–Thurs 11am–8pm, Fri–Sat 11:30am–10:30pm.

Off the Wall, 7325 Melrose Ave., Los Angeles. ☎ **213/930-1185.**

Oversized antiques include kitschy statues, deco furnishings, carved wall reliefs, Wurlitzer juke boxes, giant restaurant and gas station signs, pinball machines, and lots and lots of neon.

Open: Mon–Sat 11am–6pm.

Mayhem, 1411 Third St., Santa Monica. ☎ **310/451-7600.**

Genuine autographed guitars and other entertainment-biz memorabilia from U2, Nirvana, Springsteen, Bon Jovi, Pearl Jam, and other rockers are sold to collectors that include the owners of the Hard Rock Cafes. It's as much a museum as a store.

Open: Sun–Thurs 11am–midnight, Fri–Sat 11am–2am.

Warner Brothers Studio Store, in Beverly Center, 8500 Beverly Blvd., Los Angeles. ☎ **310/289-7954.**

Warner Brothers has taken merchandising to the next level with its string of shops selling T-shirts, watches, baseball caps, and other items emblazoned with images from their film, television, and cartoon catalogues.

Open: Mon–Fri 10am–10pm, Sat 10am–8pm, Sun 11am–6pm.

Haircare

Melrose Beauty Center, 7419 Melrose Ave., Los Angeles. ☎ **213/651-4709.**

Aveda, Paul Mitchell, JoiCo, and other top haircare products that are labeled for "exclusive sale in salons" are sold here in economical larger sizes.

Open: Daily 11am–8pm.

Jewelry

King's Cross, 13045 Ventura Blvd., Studio City. ☎ **818/905-3382.**

King's Cross specializes in crosses, crucifixes, and rosaries made of gold, ivory, and pearl. Most are vintage models dating from the 1820s to 1930s, with an emphasis on Victoriana. Prices range from $200 to $2,000.

Open: Mon–Sat 10am–5pm, Sun noon–5pm.

Maya, 7452 Melrose Ave., Los Angeles. ☎ **213/655-2708.**

This rather plain looking store offers a huge variety of silver and turquoise rings and earrings from South America, Nepal, Bali, and central Asia. The shop's walls are cluttered with wooden Asian and South American ceremonial and ornamental masks.

Open: Mon–Sat 11am–9pm, Sun 11am–7pm.

Lingerie

Frederick's of Hollywood, 6608 Hollywood Blvd., Hollywood. ☎ **213/466-8506.**

The world's most famous lingerie shop includes a museum and celebrity lingerie Hall of Fame, where you can see vintage underwear dating from 1946, and gaze at photos of celebrities who glamorized them.

Malls/Shopping Centers

Beverly Center, 8500 Beverly Blvd., at La Cienega, Los Angeles. ☎ **310/854-0070.**

One of the city's best-known malls is also one of the best located. The 1991 film *Scenes from a Mall,* starring Woody Allen and Bette Midler, was shot here. About 170 shops occupy the huge, eight-story building, constructed with interesting exterior glass-covered escalators. Both The Broadway and Bullock's department stores anchor here, sandwiching dozens of shops, restaurants, and movie theaters. The Warner Brothers Studio Store and Aveda Esthetique are two of the mall's newest additions. Despite the mall's immense size, it's actually quite a pleasant place to shop.

The Broadway Plaza, Seventh and Flower Sts., Downtown. ☎ **213/624-2891.**

Anchored by the Hyatt Regency Los Angeles Hotel and The Broadway department store, the one-square-block-big Plaza encompasses over 25 shops and 17 restaurants. Most of the shops are middle-class-oriented clothing chain stores.

Farmer's Market, 6333 West Third St., near Fairfax, Wilshire. ☎ **213/549-2140.**

This city market, with its more than 120 restaurants, shops, and grocers, has been attracting locals and tourists since 1934. It's one of the area's top tourist draws, and is one of L.A.'s best places to spot celebrities, with retailers selling souvenirs, pet supplies, clothes, books, artworks, and anything else you can imagine. The best part of the market is the international food stands and restaurants—at least 23 in all. Admission and parking are free.

Glendale Galleria, Central Ave., at Hawthorne Ave., Glendale. ☎ **818/240-9481.**

Located in the eastern San Fernando Valley, the Glendale Galleria is one of the largest malls in the nation, occupying two levels on two wings, and housing about 250 retailers. Five department stores compete for business here, along with well-known name-brand shops like Benetton, Ann Taylor, and ACA Joe.

Ports O' Call Village, Berth 77, Samson Way, between 6th and 22nd Sts., San Pedro. ☎ **310/831-0287.**

This collection of shops sells crafts and clothing from around the world. Over 75 international specialty shops sell goods like hand-blown glass, Philippine jewelry, and Japanese gun-powder tea, while several restaurants offer myriad cuisines. You can watch a steady stream of yachts, luxury liners, tankers, freighters, schooners, and sailboats cruise by as you browse along the village's winding cobblestoned streets. Harbor/dinner cruises are available from here, as well as whale watching and boat charters.

Santa Monica Place, Colorado Ave. (at 2nd Street), Santa Monica. ☎ **310/394-5451.**

About 100 shops occupy three bright stories anchored by Robinson's-May and The Broadway department stores. Amid the usual mall shops are more unusual finds like Frederick's of Hollywood, which sells lingerie, and the KCET Public Television's Store of Knowledge, selling T-shirts, mugs, gifts, educational software, and documentary video tapes.

EATZ, the mall's ground-floor food pavilion, sells a world's array of fast foods, including several health-oriented eateries. See, "Dining," earlier in this chapter, for more information.

Sherman Oaks Galleria, 15301 Ventura Blvd., at Sepulveda Blvd., Sherman Oaks. ☎ **818/783-7100.**

This famous western San Fernando Valley mall is the hangout for dedicated Valley girls, popularized by the movie *Fast Times at Ridgemont High.* Trendy, mainstream clothes are in abundance, sold from about 60 storefronts.

Universal Citywalk, at Universal Studios, Universal City. ☎ **213/251-4638.**

Los Angeles's newest shopping/entertainment promenade is an ultra-stylized urban street that looks just slightly saner than Toontown. More than three dozen shops and specialty restaurants include the Museum of Neon Art, a Panasonic electronics pavilion and Wolfgang Puck Cafe. Both visually amazing, and one of the few places in L.A. where you can stroll without a car, CityWalk is definitely worth a look.

From U.S. 101, take the Universal City exit and follow the signs to CityWalk.

Music

Pyramid Music, 1340 Third St., Santa Monica. ☎ **310/393-5877.**

Seemingly endless bins of used tapes and compact discs line the walls of this long, narrow shop on Santa Monica's Third Street Promenade. LPs, posters, cards, buttons, and accessories are also sold.

Open: Mon–Thurs 11am–11pm, Fri–Sat 11am–1am, Sun noon–11pm.

Tower Records, 8811 W. Sunset Blvd., Hollywood. ☎ **310/657-7300.**

Tower insists it has L.A.'s largest selection of compact discs—over 125,000 titles. The shop's blues, jazz, and classical selections are definitely greater than the competition.

Open: Sun–Thurs 9am–midnight, Fri–Sat 9am–1am.

Virgin Megastore, 8000 Sunset Blvd., Hollywood. ☎ **213/650-8666.**

One-hundred CD "listening posts," and an in-store "radio station" make this megastore a music browser's paradise. They claim to stock 150,000 titles, including an extensive collection of hard-to-find artists.

Open: Sun–Thurs 9am–midnight, Fri–Sat 9am–1am.

Sports Equipment

Golf Exchange, 830 S. Olive St., Los Angeles. ☎ **213/622-0403.**

L.A.'s golf megastore sprawls across 10 rooms filled with clubs and accessories. An entire room is devoted to golf shoes, another to bags, and another to used clubs. There's also an indoor driving range so you can try before you buy.

Open: Mon–Fri 9am–5:30pm, Sat 9am–4:30pm.

Rip City Sports, 2709 Santa Monica Blvd., Santa Monica. ☎ **310/828-0388.**

Jim McDowell's top-rated designer skateboards are some of the world's most wanted. Many are hand-crafted with the highest quality wheels and bearings.

Open: Mon–Sat 10:30am–6pm, Sun noon–4pm.

Toys

F.A.O. Schwarz, in the Beverly Center, 8500 Beverly Blvd., Los Angeles. ☎ **310/659-4547.**

One of the world's greatest toy stores for both children and adults is filled with every imaginable plaything, from hand-carved, custom-painted carousel rocking horses, dolls, and stuffed animals, to gas-powered cars, train sets, and hobby supplies. The new Barbie collection includes hundreds of models—from a three-foot-tall fiber optically-lighted Barbie to a $200 doll dressed by designer Bob Mackie.

Open: Mon–Fri 10am–9pm, Sat–Sun 10am–7pm.

Travel Goods

California Map and Travel Center, 3211 Pico Blvd., Santa Monica. ☎ **310/829-6277.**

Like the name says, this center carries a good selection of domestic and international maps and travel accessories, including guides for hiking, biking, and touring. Globes and atlases are also sold.

Open: Mon–Fri 8:30am–6pm, Sat 9am–5pm, Sun noon–5pm.

8 Evening Entertainment

Once criticized as a cultural wasteland, Los Angeles has increasingly attracted serious arts houses worthy of its size. Without a doubt, the entertainment business—film, TV, records, theater—is still the best known industry in Los Angeles. Check the "Calendar" section of the Sunday *Los Angeles Times* for good, if not comprehensive, listings of the upcoming week's events. The *L.A. Weekly,* available free from sidewalk stands, shops, and restaurants, should also be consulted.

The Performing Arts

Theatre L.A. (☎ **213/688-ARTS**) sells discounted performing arts tickets for same-day seats for such venues as the Mark Taper, Doolittle, Pantages, Pasadena Playhouse, and other under-100-seat houses. Tickets are usually about half price. Callers are either referred to theater box offices, or can order by phone. Theatre L.A. is open Tuesday through Saturday noon to 5pm.

MAJOR PERFORMING ARTS COMPANIES

Los Angeles's five most prestigious performing arts companies all call The Music Center of Los Angeles County home (see "Major Concert Halls and All-Purpose Auditoriums," below).

The **Los Angeles Philharmonic** is the city's top symphony and the only really major name in Los Angeles. Many symphony watchers believe that the Philharmonic's music director Esa-Pekka Salonen will continue to concentrate on contemporary compositions in order to attract a younger concert audience. In addition to regular performances at the Music Center, the Philharmonic plays a popular summer season at the

Hollywood Bowl. Lesser-known resident companies of the Music Center are the **Center Theatre Group,** the **Los Angeles Music Center Opera,** the **Joffrey Ballet LA/NY,** and the **Los Angeles Master Chorale.**

MAJOR CONCERT HALLS & ALL-PURPOSE AUDITORIUMS

Dorothy Chandler Pavilion, the Music Center, 135 N. Grand Ave., downtown. ☎ **213/972-7211.**

Home of the Los Angeles Philharmonic, Master Chorale, Los Angeles Opera, Center Theatre Group, and the Joffrey Ballet, this 3,197-seat multipurpose theater hosts regular concerts, recitals, opera, and dance performances. The American premiere of the London hit musical *Me and My Girl* was presented here, as are regular televised ceremonies.

Prices: Ticket prices vary, depending on performance.

Greek Theatre, 2700 N. Vermont Ave., Griffith Park. ☎ **213/480-3232.**

The Greek Theatre is a place where the entertainment ranges from performances by Frank Sinatra to rock artists like The Red Hot Chili Peppers and the B-52s. The theater is patterned after the classical outdoor theaters of ancient Greece. Dance groups and national theater societies also perform here.

Prices: Tickets $25–$60, depending on performance.

Hollywood Bowl, 2301 N. Highland Ave. (at Odin St.). ☎ **213/850-2020.**

One of America's most famous outdoor amphitheaters, the Bowl is known for its outstanding natural acoustics. This is the summer home of the Los Angeles Philharmonic Orchestra, as well as the resident Hollywood Bowl Orchestra. Their seasons begin July 1 and end around mid-September.

Internationally known conductors and soloists often join the L.A. Philharmonic in classical programs on Tuesday and Thursday nights. Friday and Saturday concerts are often "pops" shows that feature orchestrated contemporary music.

Something is happening almost every night of the summer. The season also includes a jazz series, a Virtuoso series, and a Sunday Sunset series. Several weekend concerts throughout the season feature fireworks, including the traditional July 4th weekend Family Fireworks picnic concerts. For evening performances be sure to bring a sweater or jacket—it gets chilly in those hills.

Prices: Classical and virtuoso concerts $1 lawn, $23 bench, $42–$88 box. Other events vary. **Parking:** $7–$20, subject to availability and reserved in advance; free in off-site lots, then $2 per person for parking shuttle. **Box office hours:** May–June, Mon–Sat 10am–6pm; July–Sept, Mon–Sat 10am–9pm, Sun noon–6pm.

The Music Center of Los Angeles County, 135 N. Grand Ave. ☎ **213/972-7211.**

Los Angeles's largest and most prestigious performing arts facility encompasses three distinct theaters: the Dorothy Chandler Pavilion (see listing under this same heading), the Ahmanson Theatre, and the Mark Taper Forum (see "Theaters," below). Free tours are scheduled on a regular basis. Call **213/972-7483** for information and reservations. All theaters are handicapped accessible.

Prices: Ticket discounts available for students and senior citizens for most performances in each theater.

Universal Amphitheatre, 100 Universal City Plaza. ☎ **818/622-3931.**

This 6,251-seat enclosed theater is adjacent to the Visitors Entertainment Center at Universal Studios. It's well designed—no seat is more than 140 feet from the stage—and only top names perform here, usually for three to five days. Tickets are often sold out well before the concert dates, so haunt the box office in advance.

Prices: Tickets $25–$75.

Wilshire Theatre, 8440 Wilshire Blvd., Beverly Hills. ☎ **213/468-1716.**

The Wilshire opened in 1980 with *The Oldest Living Graduate,* starring Henry Fonda. More recent productions have included blockbuster musicals like *A Chorus Line.* Rock and jazz concerts are held here, too. Call to see what's on. Tickets run from $25 to $60.

THEATERS

Ahmanson Theatre, the Music Center, 135 N. Grand Ave. (at First Street), downtown. ☎ **213/972-7401.**

L.A.'s top legitimate playhouse has 2,071 seats and is the home base of the Center Theater Group, which stages a full season of plays each year, usually from mid-October to early May. Offerings have included Christopher Reeve in *Summer and Smoke,* Daniel J. Travanti in *I Never Sang for My Father,* and the west coast premiere of Neil Simon's *Broadway Bound.* Visiting productions are also offered here, including a special long run of *The Phantom of the Opera.* A variety of international dance companies and concert attractions rounds out the season.

Prices: Tickets $60; discounts available for students and seniors for specified performances.

James A. Doolittle Theatre, 1615 N. Vine St., Hollywood. ☎ **213/462-6666** or **972-0700.**

The Doolittle Theatre offers a wide spectrum of live theater productions, such as Amy Irving in the Pulitzer Prize– and Tony Award–winning *The Heidi Chronicles,* Neil Simon's Pulitzer Prize–winning *Lost in Yonkers,* and August Wilson's *Two Trains Running.*

Prices: Tickets $20–$44.

Mark Taper Forum, the Music Center, 135 N. Grand Ave. (at First St.), downtown. ☎ **213/972-0700.**

Adjacent to the Ahmanson Theater, this 747-seat circular theater is the Music Center's intimate playhouse. The emphasis here is on new and contemporary works, as the theater specializes in world and west coast premieres. Recent productions have included nationally acclaimed productions of *The Kentucky Cycle, Angels in America,* and *Twilight: Los Angeles, 1992.*

Prices: Tickets $22–$35, discounts available for students and seniors.

Pantages Theatre, 6233 Hollywood Blvd., Hollywood. ☎ **213/468-1770.**

This luxurious Hollywood landmark dates from 1930. For 10 years it was the setting for the presentation of the Academy Awards, including the first televised Oscar ceremony. It's been through several incarnations, including one as a fine movie house. In 1977 the Pantages returned as a leading legitimate theater with a production of *Bubbling Brown Sugar.* Recent productions have included *Les Misérables, Man of La Mancha,* and *Joseph and the Amazing Technicolor Dreamcoat,* as well as concerts by Bob Dylan and The Gypsy Kings.

Prices: Tickets $20–$60.

Major Concert & Performance Halls

Ahmanson Theatre, the Music Center, 135 N. Grand Ave. (at First St.), downtown. **213/972-7401.**

Dorothy Chandler Pavilion, the Music Center, 135 N. Grand Ave., downtown. **213/972-7211.**

Greek Theatre, 2700 N. Vermont Ave., Griffith Park. **213/665-1927.**

Hollywood Bowl, 2301 N. Highland Ave. (at Odin St.). **213/850-2020.**

James A. Doolittle Theatre, 1615 N. Vine St., Hollywood. **213/972-7372.**

L.A. Sports Arena, 3939 S. Figueroa St. **213/480-3232.**

Mark Taper Forum, the Music Center, 135 N. Grand Ave. (at First St.), downtown. **213/972-7373.**

Pantages Theatre, 6233 Hollywood Blvd., Hollywood. **213/480-3232.**

Shubert Theatre, in the ABC Entertainment Center, Century City. Toll free **800/233-3123.**

Universal Amphitheatre, 100 Universal City Plaza. **818/622-3931.**

Wilshire Theatre, 8440 Wilshire Blvd., Beverly Hills. **213/480-3232.**

Shubert Theatre, in the ABC Entertainment Center, Century City. ☎ toll free **800/447-7400.**

This opulent theater presents big-time musicals—like *Cats, Sunset Boulevard,* and *Les Misérables.* It's located directly across from the Century Plaza Hotel.

Prices: Tickets $25–$65.

Actors Circle Theatre, 7313 Santa Monica Blvd., West Hollywood. ☎ **213/882-8043.**

Winner of six "Dramalogue" awards in 1993, this 47-seat theater presents contemporary and original works throughout the year.

The Coast Playhouse, 8325 Santa Monica Blvd., West Hollywood. ☎ **213/650-8507.**

The 99-seat Coast presents contemporary and classical plays and musicals, staged Wednesday through Sunday.

The Lee Strasberg Theatre Institute, 7936 Santa Monica Blvd., West Hollywood. ☎ **213/650-7777.**

A well-known acting school, the Strasberg Institute sometimes presents productions for the public, including young people's programs. There are four theaters here, ranging from 25 to 99 seats.

Odyssey Theatre Ensemble, 2055 Sepulveda Blvd., Los Angeles. ☎ **310/477-2055.** Fax 310/444-0455.

For over 25 years, the Odyssey Theatre has been performing exploration-oriented pieces from contemporary, classical, and original sources, with a strong leaning toward international and multicultural works. They produce 10 to 20 productions per year.

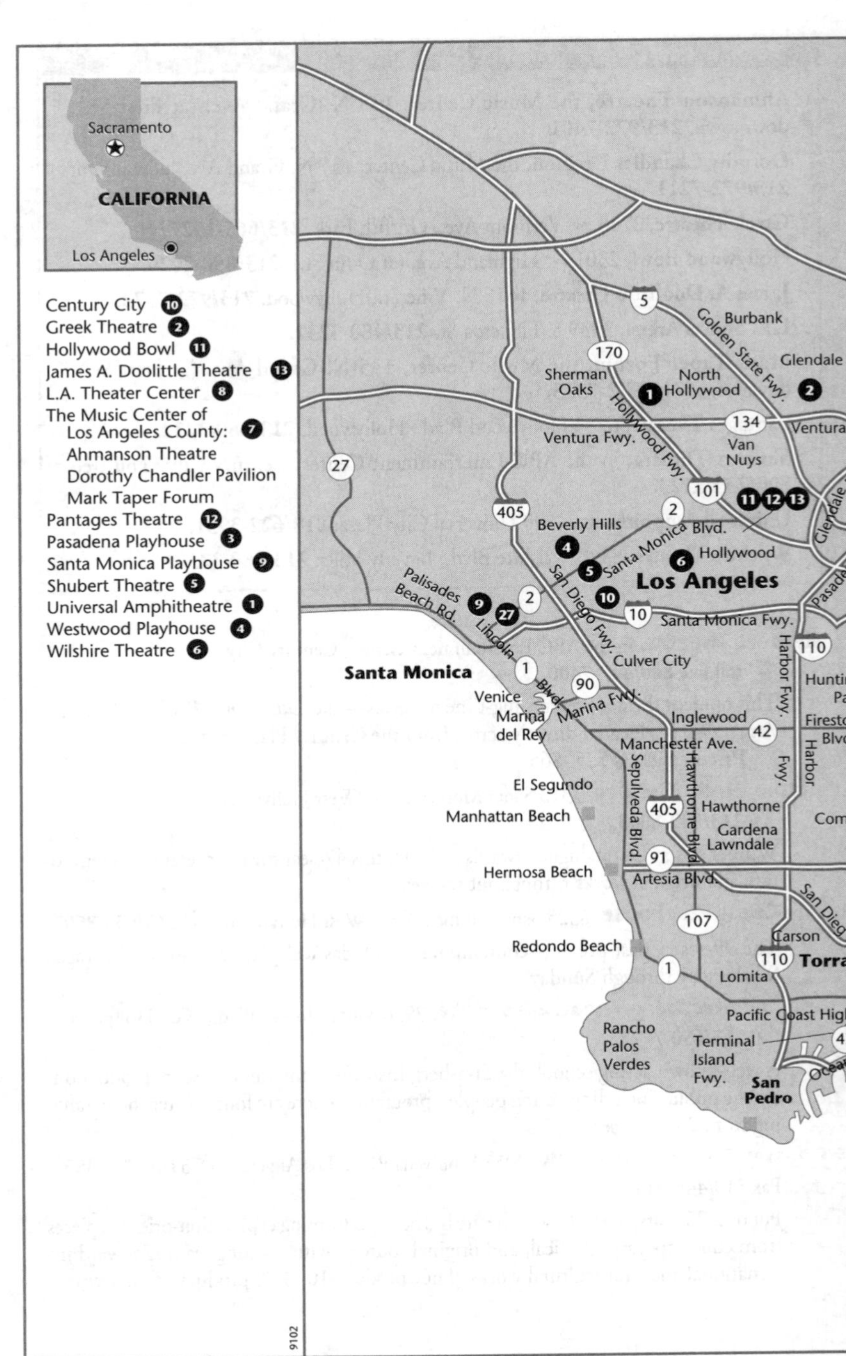
Sacramento
CALIFORNIA
Los Angeles
Century City 10
Greek Theatre 2
Hollywood Bowl 11
James A. Doolittle Theatre 13
L.A. Theater Center 8
The Music Center of Los Angeles County: 7
Ahmanson Theatre
Dorothy Chandler Pavilion
Mark Taper Forum
Pantages Theatre 12
Pasadena Playhouse 3
Santa Monica Playhouse 9
Shubert Theatre 5
Universal Amphitheatre 1
Westwood Playhouse 4
Wilshire Theatre 6
Burbank
Golden State Fwy.
Glendale
Sherman Oaks
North Hollywood
Hollywood Fwy.
Ventura Fwy.
Van Nuys
Beverly Hills
Santa Monica Blvd.
Hollywood
Los Angeles
San Diego Fwy.
Palisades Beach Rd.
Santa Monica Fwy.
Harbor Fwy.
Lincoln Blvd.
Culver City
Santa Monica
Venice
Marina del Rey
Marina Fwy.
Inglewood
Manchester Ave.
Sepulveda Blvd.
Hawthorne Blvd.
El Segundo
Manhattan Beach
Hawthorne
Gardena
Lawndale
Hermosa Beach
Artesia Blvd.
Carson
Redondo Beach
Lomita
Pacific Coast High
Rancho Palos Verdes
Terminal Island Fwy.
San Pedro
9102

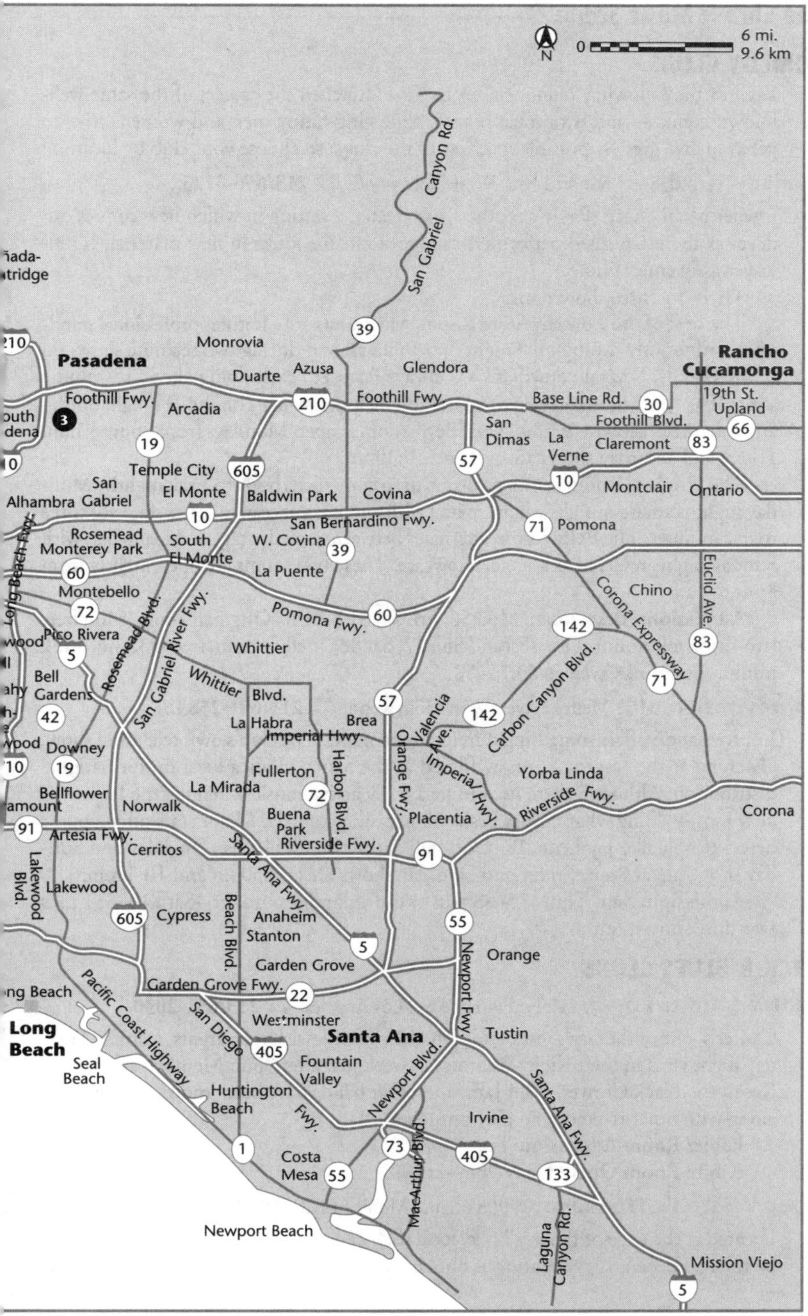

N
0
6 mi.
9.6 km
San Gabriel Canyon Rd.
Pasadena
Monrovia
Duarte
Azusa
Glendora
Rancho Cucamonga
Foothill Fwy.
Arcadia
Foothill Fwy
Base Line Rd.
19th St.
Upland
Foothill Blvd.
San Dimas
La Verne
Claremont
Temple City
San Gabriel
El Monte
Baldwin Park
Covina
Montclair
Ontario
Alhambra
San Bernardino Fwy.
Pomona
Rosemead
Monterey Park
South El Monte
W. Covina
La Puente
Euclid Ave.
Long Beach Fwy.
Montebello
Pomona Fwy.
Chino
Corona Expressway
Pico Rivera
Rosemead Blvd.
San Gabriel River Fwy.
Whittier
Carbon Canyon Blvd.
Bell Gardens
Whittier Blvd.
La Habra
Brea
Imperial Hwy.
Valencia Ave.
Orange Fwy.
Harbor Blvd.
Downey
Fullerton
Imperial Hwy.
Yorba Linda
Bellflower
La Mirada
Norwalk
Buena Park
Placentia
Riverside Fwy.
Corona
Artesia Fwy.
Cerritos
Riverside Fwy.
Santa Ana Fwy.
Lakewood Blvd.
Lakewood
Beach Blvd.
Cypress
Anaheim
Stanton
Newport Fwy.
Orange
Garden Grove
Garden Grove Fwy.
Pacific Coast Highway
San Diego Fwy.
Westminster
Long Beach
Santa Ana
Tustin
Seal Beach
Fountain Valley
Newport Blvd.
Santa Ana Fwy.
Huntington Beach
Irvine
MacArthur Blvd.
Costa Mesa
Laguna Canyon Rd.
Newport Beach
Mission Viejo
210
3
19
605
10
39
30
66
83
57
71
60
72
5
142
42
19
91
72
91
55
605
5
22
405
1
73
405
55
133
5

The Club & Music Scene

COMEDY CLUBS

Each of the following venues claims to have launched the careers of the same well-known comics—and it's probably true. Emerging funny men and women strive to get as many "gigs" as possible, playing all the clubs; so choose your club by location.

Comedy Store, 8433 Sunset Blvd., West Hollywood. ☎ **213/656-6225.**

Owner Mitzi Shore (Pauly's mother) has created a setting in which new comics can develop and established performers can work out the kinks in new material. It's always vastly entertaining.

There are three showrooms:

The **Best of the Comedy Store Room,** which seats 400, features professional stand-ups continuously through the night on Mondays, and during two separate shows on the weekends. Several comedians are always featured, each doing about 15-minute stints. The talent here is always first rate, and includes regulars on the "Tonight Show" and other television programs. The "Best" room is open Mondays from 8pm to 1am; Friday and Saturday shows are at 8 and 10:30pm.

The **Original Room** features a dozen or so comedians back-to-back nightly. Monday night is amateur night when anyone with enough guts can take the stage for three to five minutes. The **Belly Room** alternates between comedy stage and piano bar, with Sunday nights reserved as a singer showcase. These two rooms are open nightly from 8pm to 1am.

Admission: "Best" room, Mon $6, Fri–Sat $12–$14; "Original" room, Mon free, two-drink minimum, Tues–Fri and Sun $7, Sat $8; "Belly" room, free–$3, two-drink minimum. Drinks average $3.75–$7.

Improvisation, 8162 Melrose Ave., West Hollywood. ☎ **213/651-2583.**

Improvisation offers something different each night. The club's own television show, "Evening at the Improv," is now filmed at the Santa Monica location for national distribution. Although there used to be a fairly active music schedule, the Improv is now mostly doing what it does best—showcasing comedy. Major stars often appear here—people like Jay Leno, Billy Crystal, and Robin Williams. Thursday and Sunday shows are at 8pm; Friday and Saturday shows are at 8:30pm and 10:30pm.

Admission: Sun–Thurs $5–$8 plus two-drink minimum, Fri–Sat $10–$11 plus two-drink minimum.

ROCK & BLUES CLUBS

Canter's Kibitz Room, 419 N. Fairfax Ave., Los Angeles. ☎ **213/651-2030.**

Canter's, one of the city's most established 24-hour Jewish restaurants, features Tuesday night jams in their Kibitz Room each week just after 9pm. Members of Guns n' Roses, the Black Crowes, Pearl Jam, and other bands have been known to play here, along with other rockers who play until 2am.

Kibitz Room Admission: Free.

Kibitz Room Open: Daily 9pm–2am.

Doug Weston's Troubadour, 9081 Santa Monica Blvd. ☎ **310/276-6168.**

Located at the edge of Beverly Hills, local rock bands are usually served back-to-back by the half dozen. An adventurous booking policy ensures a good mix, and so many bands each night usually means there will be at least one you like. Hours are usually 8pm to 2am nightly.

Admission: $5–$15.

Gazzarri's on the Strip, 9039 Sunset Blvd. (near Doheny Dr.). ☎ **310/273-6606.**

Once self-described as "Hollywood's oldest disco," Gazzarri's has now changed to a live-music format, offering rock 'n' roll bands almost nightly. Sometimes it's hip hop and other nights it's rap. The age group is early 20s; dress is casual. No credit cards are accepted and you must be at least 18 to get in. Hours are usually 8pm to 2am Wednesday through Saturday.

Admission: $10–$14.

House of Blues, 8430 Sunset Blvd. ☎ **213/650-0247.**

Looking very much like a Disney-inspired shanty shack, this new blues joint owned in part by Harvard University, actors Dan Aykroyd and Jim Belushi, and members of the rock band Aerosmith, features daily live blues performances and southern-style cooking. The club is the third in a series of successful blues houses—founder Isaac Tigrett also helped originate the Hard Rock Cafe chain.

Tickets: Free–$30, depending on who's playing.

Open: Daily 11am–2am; bands usually start around 9pm.

McCabe's Guitar Shop, 3101 Pico Blvd., Santa Monica. ☎ **310/828-4497,** recorded information **310/828-4403.**

One of the most unusual music venues in the city, McCabe's is an actual guitar store that features regular live weekend performances in its small, 150-seat theater. Top-level performers include both new and established artists. No alcohol is sold, but coffee, tea, juices, and cookies are available. Phone to see what's on.

Admission: $12.50–$20, depending on who's playing.

The Roxy, 9009 Sunset Blvd., West Hollywood. ☎ **310/276-2229,** or **310/276-2222** for a recording.

Probably the top venue in L.A., the medium-sized Roxy specializes in showcasing the music industry's new signings, as well as smaller established bands, and occasionally, even superstars such as David Bowie and Bon Jovi. The roster is usually packed with Los Angeles bands you've never heard of, often three or four per night. There is no age limit for entry, but only those over 21 may legally purchase alcohol. It's usually open nightly from 8pm to 2am.

Admission: $5–$20.

DANCE CLUBS

Palladium Hollywood, 6215 Sunset Blvd., Hollywood. ☎ **213/962-7600.**

Lawrence Welk used to do his famous New Year's Eve show from here. Today the club is one of the best venues in town, featuring a $10,000 dance contest every Saturday, with live acts from the R&B chart every other week. The club can hold up to 4,000 patrons, most of whom dress up for the occasion.

Admission: $15–$25.

Roxbury, 8225 Sunset Blvd., Hollywood. ☎ **213/656-1750.**

A labyrinthine dance club, the Roxbury attracts a trendy crowd that dresses to impress. There are four full bars, and DJ dancing almost nightly. Hours are Tuesday through Saturday from 9:30pm to 2am.

Admission: $10.

BARS

Lava Lounge, 1533 La Brea Ave., Hollywood. ☎ **213/876-6612.**

Located at Sunset Boulevard, this retro dive bar with a very mixed crowd is slightly seedy, grungy, artsy, and fringy. Great jazz, often trios, play in a room with a sordid tiki-hut decor. Weekdays can be hit or miss, while weekends are always crowded.

Admission: Free.

Open: Nightly 9pm–2am.

Tatou, 233 N. Beverly Drive, Beverly Hills. ☎ **310/274-9955.**

Very L.A., Tatou is a trendy meeting place with three distinct atmospheres. A loud restaurant is fronted by a 1930s-style stage where great jazz and rock bands perform. The back bar enjoys a view of the table and stage action, but is both quieter and more interactive. An upstairs dance floor fills up on weekends when great-looking trendies bop to the latest beats.

Admission: $15–$20.

Open: Mon–Fri 6pm–2am, Sat 6:30pm–2am.

The Lobby Club Bar, at The Peninsula Beverly Hills, 9882 Santa Monica Blvd., Beverly Hills. ☎ **310/551-2888.**

Beverly Hills' best looking crowd comes here nightly to see, be seen, drink expensive drinks, and hear pianist George Bugatti tickle the ivories of his Kimball baby grand. Sinatra's even stopped in, and stayed after hours to croon.

Admission: Free.

Open: Daily 11:30am–2am.

Whiskey, at the Sunset Marquis Hotel and Villas, 1200 North Alta Loma Road, West Hollywood. ☎ **310/657-1333.**

The Whiskey is one of the most exclusive rooms in Hollywood. Rock 'n' rollers like Mick Jagger, Axel Rose, and Robert Plant cavort with model-actresses, Eurotrash, and guys who wear tank tops under sport jackets. Make sure you're either staying at the hotel, or you know somebody, or you probably won't get in.

Admission: Free.

Open: Nightly 9pm–2am.

POOL HALLS

Gotham Hall, 1431 Third St., Santa Monica. ☎ **310/394-8865.**

Grape- and mustard-colored walls, contemporary cut-steel railings and light coverings, and ultra-modern furniture make this futuristic pool hall one of the most interesting in L.A. Seventeen regulation size tables are overlooked by a balcony bar.

Pool Prices: $7–$14 per hour.

Open: Mon–Fri 4pm–2am, Sat–Sun noon–2am.

Yankee Doodles, 1410 Third St., Santa Monica. ☎ **310/394-4632.**

Grimier, if not noisier than Gotham Hall (see above), this sports bar–cum–pool hall features 32 pool tables on two levels, battling satellite televisions, and lousy food.

Pool Prices: $6–$12 per hour.

Open: Daily 11am–2am.

GAY BARS & CLUBS

Micky's, 8857 Santa Monica Blvd., West Hollywood. ☎ **310/657-1176.**

Both a dance club and restaurant, Micky's high energy atmosphere is popular with a youngish crowd. The good-looking club occupies two levels and serves full meals.

Admission: Free–$7.

Open: Daily noon–2am.

Spike, 7746 Santa Monica Blvd., West Hollywood. ☎ **213/656-9343.**

A pool- and pinball-playing Levi and leather crowd likes the bar's techno, house, and rock selections.

Admission: Free–$7.

Open: Sun–Thurs noon–2am, Fri–Sat noon–4am.

9 Easy Excursions from Los Angeles

Some people might say that Anaheim, Fullerton, Buena Park, and Irvine are among the most physically unprepossessing towns in California, but they nevertheless attract the most visitors. The natural surroundings may not be as inspiring as other parts of the state, but the specially created attractions are enchanting—transformed by the magic wand of Walt Disney into a wonderful world of make-believe. And Disneyland is just one of the spectacular sights in the area. There are also Knott's Berry Farm, the Movieland Wax Museum, and more. So take the kids—and if you don't have any kids, be a kid yourself for a while.

Santa Catalina Island

22 miles W of mainland Los Angeles

GETTING THERE • By Plane Valley Executive Charter (**310/982-1575**) flies from the Long Beach Municipal Airport, 4100 Donald Douglas Dr., Long Beach (**310/421-8293**) to Catalina's Airport in the Sky (**310/510-0143**), 1,600 feet above the sea-level town of Avalon. Tickets are $300 per person.

• By Boat The *Catalina Express* (**310/519-1212,** or toll free **800/995-4386**) operates almost 20 daily departures to Avalon and Two Harbors on Catalina Island. There is easy freeway access to the terminal in San Pedro and Long Beach, with secure parking. The trip takes about an hour. One-way fares from San Pedro are $17.75 for adults, $16 for seniors; $13.25 for children 2 to 11, $1 for infants. Long Beach fares are about 50¢ higher for all except infants, who are still charged $1. The *Catalina Express* departs from the Sea/Air Terminal at Berth 95, Port of L.A. in San Pedro: the *Catalina Express* port is at the *Queen Mary* in Long Beach. Call for information and reservations.

Note: There are very specific baggage restrictions on the *Catalina Express.* Luggage is limited to 50 pounds per person; reservations are necessary for bicycles, surfboards, and dive tanks; and there are restrictions on transporting domestic pets—call for information.

ESSENTIALS • Orientation The picturesque town of Avalon is the island's only city. Named for a passage in Tennyson's *Idylls of the King,* Avalon is also the port of entry for the island. From the ferry dock you can wander along Crescent Avenue, the main road along the beachfront, and easily dip into adjacent side streets. Visitors are not allowed to operate cars on the island; walk around Avalon and take tours to points inland (see "What to See and Do," below). About 86% of the island remains undeveloped. It's owned by the Santa Catalina Island Conservancy, which endeavors to preserve the island's natural resources.

• **Information** The **Catalina Island Chamber of Commerce & Visitor's Bureau,** Dept. FLA, P.O. Box 217, Avalon, CA 90704 (**213/510-1520**), located on Green Pleasure Pier, distributes brochures and information on island activities. It also offers information on local airlines, hotels, boat transport, and sightseeing tours, as well as brochures on camping, hiking, fishing, and boating. Write ahead for an extremely useful free 88-page visitor's guide.

Located 22 miles west of Long Beach, Catalina is a small, cove-fringed island famous for its laid-back resorts, largely unspoiled landscape, and crystal-clear waters. Because of its relative isolation, tourists don't crowd Catalina like they do the mainland. Visitors who do show up have plenty of elbow room to boat, fish, swim, scuba dive, and snorkel. There are miles of hiking and biking trails; and golf, tennis, and horseback-riding facilities abound.

Catalina is so different from mainland Los Angeles that it seems almost like a different country, remote and unspoiled. The island separated from the mainland over half a million years ago and evolved to meet environmental challenges. Even today there is unique plantlife here, and archeology has revealed traces of a Stone Age culture that existed here. From the time of its first sighting by Western explorers in the 1600s until the turn of the 20th century, Catalina was primarily a place for pirates and smugglers. The island was purchased by William Wrigley, Jr., the chewing gum manufacturer, in 1915 in order to develop a fashionable pleasure resort here. To publicize the new vacationland, Wrigley brought big-name bands to the Avalon Casino Ballroom, and he moved the Chicago Cubs baseball team, which he owned, to the island for spring training. His marketing efforts worked, and Catalina became a favorite resort vacation spot for wealthy mainlanders. It no longer takes spectacular marketing to entice visitors to Catalina; the island's hotels are often fully booked months in advance. But Catalina is still far from overtouristed, remaining a genuinely tranquil and charming retreat.

WHAT TO SEE & DO

Avalon Casino Building, at the end of Crescent Avenue. ☎ **800/428-2566.**

The most famous structure on the island is also one of the oldest. The casino was the first resort building erected to attract vacationers from the mainland. Built in 1929, the massive circular rotunda, topped by a red tile roof is its most famous feature, appearing on posters and postcards in shops all around town. Avalon Casino is best known for its beautiful art deco ballroom that once hosted top big bands like the Tommy Dorsey and the Glen Miller orchestras. You can see the inside of the building by attending a ballroom event or a film (the Casino is Avalon's primary movie theater). Otherwise, admission is by guided tour only, operated daily by Catalina Adventure Tours (see "Organized Tours," below).

Avalon Pleasure Pier, Crescent Ave. and Catalina St., Avalon.

Jutting out into Crescent Cove, the wood-plank pier offers excellent views of the town and surrounding mountains. Food stands and bait-and-tackle shops line the pier, selling fish to eat and cast.

Catalina Island Museum, at the end of Crescent Ave. ☎ **310/510-2414.**

Located on the ground floor of the Avalon Casino, the Catalina Island Museum features exhibits on island history, archeology, and natural history. The small museum also has an excellent relief map that details the island's interior.
Admission: $1 adults; children under 12 free.
Open: Daily 10:30am–4pm.

Lover's Cove, at the end of Crescent Ave., Avalon.

One of Catalina's top draws is its crystal-clear waters and abundant sea life. Lover's Cove is filled with colorful fish and rich kelp beds. Several Avalon companies rent scuba and snorkeling equipment. Santa Catalina Island Company, Avalon Harbor Pier (☎ toll free **800/626-7489**), offers glass-bottom boat tours of the area daily, leaving every hour from 11am to 4pm. The trip takes about 40 minutes and costs $7.50 for adults, and $3.75 for children. The company also offers tours of the underworld in their new semi-submersible submarine. This 60-foot, 50-ton vessel allows visitors to see panoramic underwater views. The trip costs $18 for adults and $12 for children, call for times.

Organized Tours

Visitors are not allowed to drive cars around the island, so it will be hard for you to tour Catalina on your own. Sign up for an organized tour. **Catalina Adventure Tours,** with ticket sales offices in Long Beach, San Pedro, and Avalon Boat Terminals and on the Green Pleasure Pier (☎ **310/510-2888**), operates several boat and bus tours.

The **Inside Adventure Tour** is a two-hour tour in luxury, air-conditioned buses, which explore the Catalina seldom seen by most island visitors. Enjoy the spectacular valleys, rolling hillsides, and scenic coastline—as well as the untamed wildlife, such as buffalo, bald eagles, and free-roaming deer, and plants native to Catalina—as you tour the interior of Catalina. This tour includes a 15-minute stop at the Nature Center at the Airport-in-the-Sky. Tours cost $13 for adults, $10.50 for seniors, and $7.50 for children ages 3–11, call for times.

The **Glass Bottom Boat Tour** is a 35-minute trip through which guests discover the wonders of undersea life. The boat glides over the California State Marine Preserve "Lover's Cove." Prices are $6 for adults, $4 for seniors, and $3.50 for children ages 3–11. Call for times.

The **City and Botanical Garden Tour** is a 1½-hour tour that details the history of Avalon. It includes a short stop at the Wrigley Memorial and Botanical Gardens. The Memorial and Gardens, developed in the early 1930s, are home to a stunning collection of desert plants found only in the California Channel Islands. The cost for adults is $9.50, $6.50 for seniors, and $4.25 for children ages 3–11; call for times.

WHERE TO STAY

Catalina's 30 or so hotels, all of which are beautifully situated, maintain an almost pretentious unpretentiousness. There are no large chain hotels here, and the hotels that are here somehow seem to go out of their way not to be quaint or charming. Don't worry about your hotel's decor (or lack of it), since there's nary an eyesore on the entire island. If you do plan on overnighting on Catalina, be sure to reserve a room in advance, as hotels fill up early.

Catalina Canyon Hotel, 888 Country Club Dr., Avalon, CA 90704. ☎ **310/510-0325,** or toll free **800/253-9361**. Fax 310/510-0900. 80 rms. No-smoking rooms available. A/C TV TEL **Directions:** From Avalon Pleasure Pier, go up Catalina Avenue, turn right onto Tremont Street and then left onto Country Club Drive to the hotel.

Rates: $83–$149 single or double. Extra person $20. AE, MC, V.

The Catalina Canyon Hotel is set on beautifully landscaped grounds in the foothills of Avalon. The guest rooms are tastefully decorated and comfortably furnished; all have an AM/FM radio and a balcony overlooking the outdoor pool and Jacuzzi. The Canyon Restaurant serves breakfast, lunch, and a continental dinner menu. Room service is available. Cocktails may be enjoyed in the lounge or on the outdoor terrace overlooking the pool. The hotel is adjacent to a golf course and tennis courts. A courtesy van meets guests at the air and sea terminals.

Catalina Island Inn, 125 Metropole, P.O. Box 467, Avalon, CA 90704. ☎ **310/510-1623.** Fax 310/510-7218. 35 rms and 1 suite. TV **Directions:** From the Avalon Pleasure Pier, go right on Crescent Ave., go two blocks to Metropole, and left to the hotel.

Rates (including continental breakfast): May–Sept and hols and weekends year round $75–$160 single or double, minisuite $155. AE, DISC, MC, V.

Innkeepers Martin and Bernadine Curtin have created some of the most attractive accommodations in town. Pale blue-gray rooms are accented in peach and set off by blue carpeting and teal green bedspreads. Shuttered windows and stained-glass lighting fixtures add further charm. All rooms have a color TV. There are no telephones in the rooms, but the front desk will take phone messages. There are ice and soda machines in the hall.

Hotel Macrae, 409 Crescent (P.O. Box 1517), Avalon, CA 90704. ☎ **310/510-0246,** or toll free **800/698-2266**. 23 rms. TEL

Rates (including continental breakfast): Summer $90–$170 single or double; winter $50–$110 single or double. MC, V.

This pleasant two-story hostelry is right across from the beach. It's decorated in bright, cheerful colors—parrot green, orange, yellow, red, and white. Rooms are individually equipped with heaters for chilly nights. In the center of the hotel is a large, open courtyard, perfect for lounging or sunning.

Zane Grey Pueblo Hotel, off Chimes Tower Rd. (P.O. Box 216), Avalon, CA 90704. ☎ **310/510-0966,** or toll free **800/378-3256**. 17 rms (all with bath). **Directions:** From the Avalon Pleasure Pier, go north on Crescent Avenue, turn left onto Hill Street and right onto Chimes Tower Road.

Rates (including continental breakfast): June–Sept $75–$125 single or double; Nov–Mar $55 single or double; rest of the year $65–$85 single or double. Weekends and hols may be slightly higher. Extra person $35. AE, MC, V.

The most superb views on the island are from the lofty Zane Grey Pueblo Hotel. This Shangri-la mountain retreat is the former home of novelist Zane Grey, who spent his last 20 years in Avalon, enjoying isolation with an ocean view. He wrote many books here, including *Tales of Swordfish and Tuna,* which tells of his fishing adventures off Catalina Island.

The hotel has teak beams that the novelist brought from Tahiti on one of his fishing trips. Most of the rooms also have large windows and ocean or mountain views. They have all been renovated with new furniture, carpeting, and ceiling fans. An outdoor patio has an excellent view, while the original living room has a grand piano, a fireplace and a TV. The hotel also offers a swimming pool and sun deck, with chairs overlooking Avalon and the ocean. Coffee is served all day, and there's a courtesy bus to town.

WHERE TO DINE

The Busy Bee, 306 Crescent. ☎ **310/510-1983.**

Cuisine: AMERICAN. **Reservations:** Not accepted. **Directions:** From the Avalon Pleasure Pier, walk 2 blocks north on Crescent to the end of Metropole.
Prices: Appetizers $3–$6; main courses $7–$15. AE, CB, DC, DISC, MC, V.
Open: Summer Mon–Fri 9am–10pm, Sat–Sun 9am–10pm; winter daily 9am–8pm.

The Busy Bee has been an Avalon institution since 1923. The restaurant is located on the beach directly over the water. You can eat in several locations, including a lovely wraparound outdoor patio.

The fare is light—deli style. Breakfast, lunch, and dinner are served at all times; the extensive menu includes omelets, various sandwiches and salads, and Buffalo burgers. The restaurant grinds its own beef and cuts its own potatoes for french fries. Salad dressings are also made on the premises. Even if you're not hungry, come here for a drink; it's Avalon's only bar on the water.

El Galleon, 411 Crescent. ☎ **310/510-1188.**

Cuisine: AMERICAN. **Reservations:** Accepted.
Prices: Appetizers $5–$12, lunch main courses $7–$18; dinner main courses $11–$37. AE, DISC, MC, V.
Open: Lunch daily 11am–2:30pm, dinner daily 5–10pm, bar daily 10am–1:30am.

El Galleon is large, warm, and woody, complete with portholes, rigging, anchors, big wrought-iron chandeliers, oversize tufted-leather booths, and tables with red-leather captain's chairs. There's additional balcony seating, plus outdoor café tables overlooking the ocean harbor. Lunches mean fresh seafood, burgers, steak, stews, salads, and sandwiches. The dinner menu features many seafood items, too, like fresh swordfish steak, and broiled Catalina lobster tails in drawn butter. "Turf" main dishes range from country-fried chicken and beef Stroganoff to broiled rack of lamb with mint jelly.

Sand Trap, Avalon Canyon Rd. ☎ **310/510-1349.**

Cuisine: CALIFORNIAN/MEXICAN. **Reservations:** Not accepted. **Directions:** From the Avalon Pleasure Pier, go up Catalina Avenue and turn right onto Tremont; take the next left onto Falls Canyon Road, which soon turns into Avalon Canyon Road.
Prices: Appetizers $2–$5; main courses $4–$12. No credit cards.
Open: Daily 7:30am–3:30pm.

Long a local favorite, the Sand Trap is a great place to escape from the bayfront crowds. Enjoy breakfast, lunch, or snacks while looking out over the golf course. The specialties of the house are delectable omelets served till noon and soft tacos served all day. Either can be made with any number of fillings, including cheese, mushrooms, turkey, homemade chorizo, spicy shredded beef, cheddar, sour cream, and salsa. Burgers, sandwiches, salads, and chili are also served. Beer and wine are available.

Disneyland, Knott's Berry Farm & Environs

27 miles SE of downtown Los Angeles

GETTING THERE • **By Plane** Most visitors who fly in to see Orange County theme parks arrive via **Los Angeles International Airport** (LAX), located about 30 miles west of Disneyland and Knott's Berry Farm.

John Wayne International Airport, located in Irvine, is Orange County's largest airport. Located about 15 miles from Disneyland, and 20 miles from Knott's Berry Farm, the airport is served by Alaska Airlines, American Airlines, Continental, Delta, Northwest, TWA, and United.

• **By Train** The nearest **Amtrak (800/USA-RAIL)** stations are located in San Clemente and San Juan Capistrano, near the coast in the southern part of the county. Trains travel both north and south between Los Angeles and San Diego. Call for fare and schedule information.

• **By Bus** **Greyhound** can get you here from anywhere. The company no longer operates a nationwide toll-free telephone number, so check your local directory for phone numbers.

• **By Car** From Los Angeles, take I-5 south. Exit south onto Beach Boulevard for Knott's Berry Farm. Continue for another five miles to the Harbor Boulevard exit for Disneyland. The theme parks are about an hour's drive from downtown Los Angeles.

ESSENTIALS • **Orientation** Located just blocks south of the Santa Ana Freeway (I-5), about five miles from each other, both Disneyland and Knott's Berry Farm are relatively compact theme parks completely surrounded by hotels and fast-food restaurants and other tourist-oriented facilities. The surrounding communities of Anaheim and Buena Park, respectively, are largely residential and not too exciting from a tourist's perspective.

• **Information** For information relating specifically to Disneyland, call the park at **714/999-4565.** The **Anaheim Area Visitor & Convention Bureau,** 800 W. Katella Ave. (P.O. Box 4270), Anaheim, CA 92803 (☎ **714/999-8999**), can fill you in on other area attractions, beaches, and activities.

For information relating specifically to Knott's Berry Farm, call the park at **714/220-5200.** The **Buena Park Convention & Visitors Office,** 6280 Manchester Blvd., Ste. 103 (☎ **714/562-3560**, or toll free **800/541-3953**), has other area information.

Despite tourist board protests to the contrary, Anaheim is Disneyland. What was once a sleepy little town in the Valencia orange-grove belt, Anaheim has developed into a playground of attractions, hotels, restaurants, and various other tourist-oriented facilities.

Knott's Berry Farm's Buena Park is just 5 miles west of Disneyland's Anaheim, but don't even think about conquering them both in the same day. Several hotel options are listed below so you can plan an extended visit and do all there is to do.

WHAT TO SEE & DO

 **Disneyland,** 1313 Harbor Blvd. ☎ **714/999-4565.**

Opened in 1955, this world-famous, ground-breaking 80-acre entertainment complex is divided into several themed "lands," each containing tailored rides and attractions. Many visitors tackle the park systematically, beginning at the entrance, and working their way clockwise around the park. But a better plan of attack is to arrive early and run to the most popular rides first—Space Mountain, Big Thunder Mountain Railroad, Splash Mountain, and Pirates of the Caribbean. Lines to get on the best rides can last an hour or more in the middle of the day.

Main Street U.S.A., the main drag of a small turn-of-the-century American town, is at the entrance to the park. This is a good area to save for the end of the day—particularly the "Great Moments with Mr. Lincoln" a patriotic look at America's 16th president, where you can rest your weary feet. You can start by touring the entire park by train—a 19th-century steamer departs from the Main Street Depot and completely encircles the park. After sunset during summer, there's a Main Street Electrical Parade spectacular—with fabulous whirling lights followed by Fantasy in the Sky fireworks.

Adventureland is inspired by exotic regions of Asia, Africa, and the South Pacific. Electronically animated tropical birds, flowers, and "tiki gods" present a musical comedy in the Enchanted Tiki Room. On the Jungle Cruise, which is within a spear's throw, passengers are threatened by wild animals and hostile natives. New Orleans square offers the ghost-packed Haunted Mansion; Pirates of the Caribbean, a hydroflume ride down a plunging waterfall and through pirate caves; and Splash Mountain, one of the largest towering log-flume attractions in the world.

Frontierland, which gets its inspiration from 19th-century America, is full of dense forests and broad rivers inhabited by hearty pioneers. You can ride a raft to Tom Sawyer's Island and take a ride on the Big Thunder Mountain Railroad, a roller coaster that races through a deserted 1870s mine.

Fantasyland's storybook theme is illustrated with several rides based on famous children's books, including Through the Looking Glass and Peter Pan. The seemingly unrelated Matterhorn Bobsleds, a roller-coaster ride through chilling caverns and drifting fog banks, is here, too; it's one of the park's most popular rides.

Tomorrowland explores the world of the future and offers some of the park's best attractions. Space Mountain, a pitch-black indoor roller coaster, is one of the best-known rides at Disneyland. Captain Eo, a 3-D motion picture musical, is a space adventure starring Michael Jackson. One of the newest attractions is Star Tours, a 40-passenger StarSpeeder that encounters a spaceload of misadventures on the way to the Moon of Endor.

The "lands" themselves are only half the adventure. Other attractions include Disney characters, penny arcades, restaurants and snack bars galore, fireworks (during summer only), mariachi bands, ragtime pianists, parades, shops, marching bands, and much more.

Admission (including unlimited rides and all entertainment): $31 adults and children over 12, $25 children ages 3–11, and seniors 60 and over. **Parking:** $5.

Open: Mid-Sept–May, Mon–Fri 10am–6pm, Sat–Sun 9am–midnight; Jun–mid-Sept plus Thanksgiving, Christmas, and Easter, daily 8–1am.

★ **Knott's Berry Farm,** 8039 Beach Blvd., Buena Park. ☎ **714/827-1776,** or **714/220-5200** for a recording.

In 1920, Walter and Cordelia Knott arrived in Buena Park in their old Model-T Ford and leased a small farm on 10 acres of land. Things got tough during the Great Depression, so Cordelia set up a roadside stand selling pies, preserves, and home-cooked chicken dinners. Within a year sales were up to about 90 meals a day. Lines became so long that Walter decided to create an old-west ghost town as a diversion for waiting customers, and that's how it all began. The Knott family now owns the farm that surrounds the world-famous Chicken Dinner Restaurant, an eatery that serves

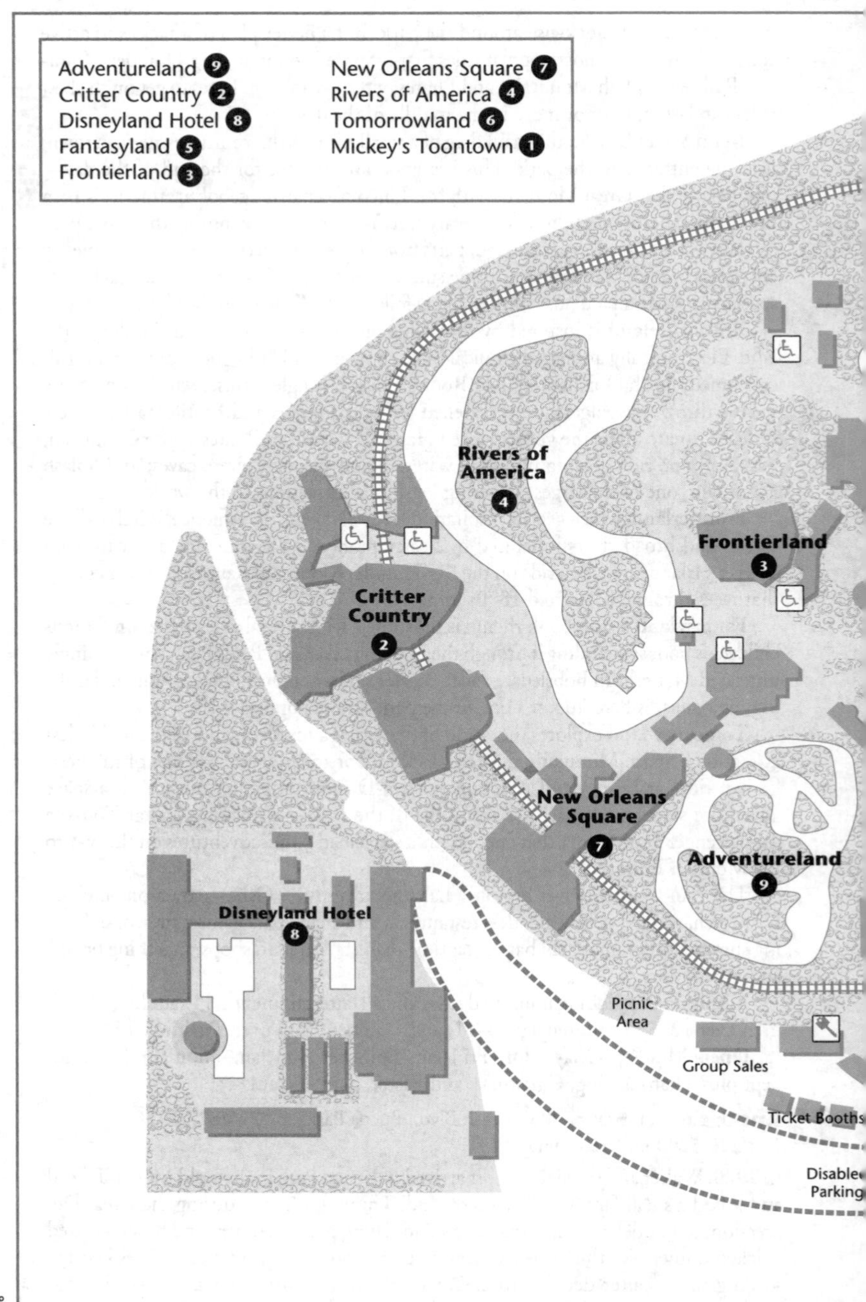

Adventureland 9
Critter Country 2
Disneyland Hotel 8
Fantasyland 5
Frontierland 3
New Orleans Square 7
Rivers of America 4
Tomorrowland 6
Mickey's Toontown 1
Rivers of America
4
Frontierland
3
Critter Country
2
New Orleans Square
7
Adventureland
9
Disneyland Hotel
8
Picnic Area
Group Sales
Ticket Booths
Disabled Parking

9106

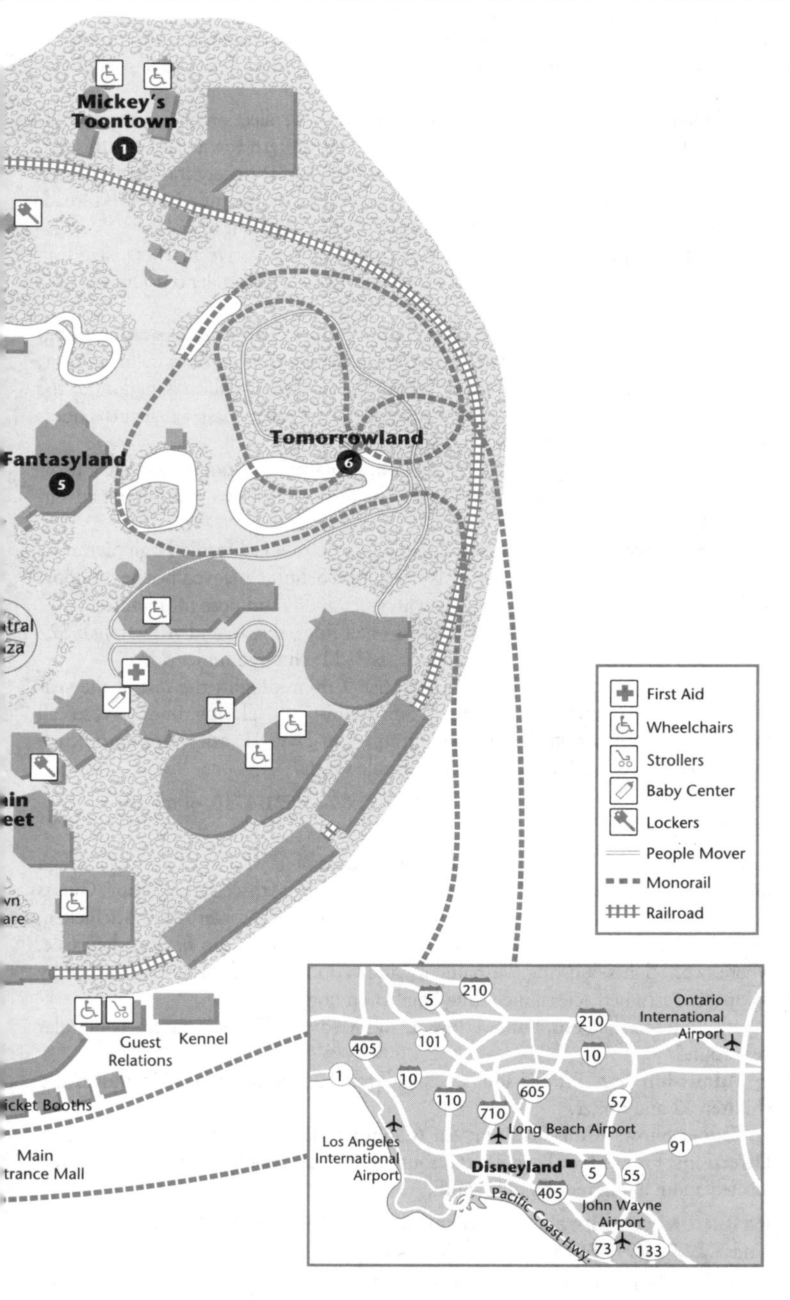
Mickey's Toontown
1
Fantasyland
5
Tomorrowland
6
tral
za
ain
eet
wn
are
Guest Relations
Kennel
icket Booths
Main
trance Mall
First Aid
Wheelchairs
Strollers
Baby Center
Lockers
People Mover
Monorail
Railroad
5
210
Ontario International Airport
210
405
101
10
1
10
605
110
710
57
Long Beach Airport
Los Angeles International Airport
91
Disneyland
5
55
405
Pacific Coast Hwy.
John Wayne Airport
73
133

over a million meals a year. And Knott's Berry Farm has emerged as the nation's third-best-attended family entertainment complex (after the two Disney facilities). The park still maintains its original old-west motif and is divided into five Old Time Adventures areas.

Old West Ghost Town, the original attraction, is a collection of authentic buildings that have been relocated from actual deserted western towns and refurbished. Visitors can pan for gold, climb aboard the stagecoach, ride rickety train cars through the Calico Mine, get held up aboard the Denver and Rio Grande Calico Railroad, and hiss at the villain during a melodrama in the Birdcage Theater.

Fiesta Village's south-of-the-border theme means festive markets, strolling mariachis, and wild rides like Montezooma's Revenge—a loop roller coaster that turns you upside down and goes backward.

Roaring '20s Amusement Area contains the thrilling Sky Tower, a parachute jump that drops riders into a 20-story free-fall. Other white-knuckle rides include XK-1, the ultimate flight simulator "piloted" by the riders; the $7 million Kingdom of the Dinosaurs ride; and the Boomerang, a state-of-the-art roller coaster that turns riders upside down six times in less than one minute.

Wild Water Wilderness is a $10 million, 3½-acre attraction styled like a turn-of-the-century California wilderness park. The top ride here is a white-water adventure called Bigfoot Rapids.

Camp Snoopy is meant to re-create the picturesque California High Sierra. Its six rustic acres are the playing grounds of Charles Schulz's beloved beagle, Snoopy, and his pals, Charlie Brown and Lucy, who greet guests and pose for pictures.

Admission (including unlimited access to all rides, shows, and attractions): $27 adults, $18 seniors over 60, $16 children ages 3–11, children under 3 free.

Open: Summer, Sun–Fri 9am–11pm, Sat 9am–midnight; the rest of the year Mon–Fri 10am–6pm, Sat 10am–10pm, Sun 10am–7pm. Closing times vary, so call for the latest information. **Directions:** From I-5 or Fwy. 91, exit south onto Beach Boulevard; the park is located about a half mile south.

Medieval Times, 7662 Beach Blvd., Buena Park. ☎ **714/521-4740,** or toll free **800/899-6600**.

Basically, Medieval Times is a dinner show for those of us who were unlucky enough not to have been born into a royal family somewhere in 11th-century Europe. Guests crowd into long wooden tables and enjoy a four-course "banquet" of roast chicken, spare ribs, herbed potatoes, and pastries. Over 1,100 people can fit into the castle, where sword fights, jousting tournaments, and various feats of skill are performed by colorfully costumed actors, including knights on horseback.

It's kind of ridiculous, but kids love it, and Medieval Times is extremely popular year-round.

Admission: Sun–Fri $32 adults, $20 children 12 and under; Sat $35 adults, $20 children 12 and under.

Open: Shows Mon–Fri 7pm; Sat 6:30pm and 8:45pm; Sun 2pm and 5pm. **Directions:** From I-5 or Fwy. 91, exit south onto Beach Boulevard. The attraction is located about a quarter of a mile south.

The Richard Nixon Library and Birthplace, 18001 Yorba Linda Blvd., Yorba Linda. ☎ **714/993-5075.** Fax 714/528-0544.

There has always been a warm place in the hearts of Orange County locals for Richard Nixon, the most vilified U.S. President in modern history. This presidential library, located in Nixon's boyhood town, celebrates the roots, life, and legacy of America's 37th President. The nine-acre site contains the actual modest farmhouse where Nixon was born, manicured flower gardens and a modern museum containing presidential archives. Nixon was buried here, next to his wife Pat on April 1, 1994.

Displays include videos of the famous Nixon-Kennedy TV debates, a statuary summit of world leaders, gifts-of-state, and exhibits on China, Russia, and Vietnam. There's also an exhibit of Pat's sparkling First Lady gowns. There's a 12-foot-high chunk of Berlin Wall symbolizing the defeat of Communism, but hardly a mention of Nixon's leading role in the anti-Communist McCarthy "witch hunts." There are exhibits on Vietnam, but no mention of Nixon's illegal expansion of that war into neighboring Cambodia. Only the Watergate Gallery is relatively forthright, where visitors can listen to actual White House tapes, and view a montage of the President's last day in the White House before he was forced to leave office in disgrace. Rotating exhibits include never-before-displayed photographs and Nixon memorabilia that illuminate this controversial president's private and public life.

Admission: $4.95 adults, $2.95 seniors, $1 children ages 8–11.

Open: Mon–Sat 10am–5pm, Sun 11am–5pm. **Directions:** To reach the Library & Birthplace from Los Angeles, take I-5 south to Highway 91 east. Exit north on Highway 57, then turn east onto Yorba Linda Boulevard to the museum.

WHERE TO STAY

Expensive

Disneyland Hotel, 1150 W. Cerritos Ave., Anaheim, CA 92802. ☎ **714/778-6600.** Fax 714/965-6582. 1,131 rms and 62 suites. No-smoking rooms available. A/C MINIBAR TV TEL **Directions:** From I-5, exit south onto Harbor Boulevard and turn right onto Katella Avenue, then pass the Disneyland parking lot and turn right onto West Street; the hotel is ahead on your left, at Cerritos Avenue.

Rates: $140–$245 single or double, suite from $425. AE, DC, MC, V. **Parking:** $10.

The "Official Hotel of the Magic Kingdom" offers its guests the most convenient transportation to the park via a monorail system that runs right through the hotel. Located on 60 attractively landscaped acres, the hotel offers six restaurants, five cocktail lounges, 20 shops and boutiques, every kind of service desk imaginable, a "wharfside" bazaar, a walk-under waterfall, three swimming pools, and 10 night-lit tennis courts. An artificial white sand beach is also adjacent to the hotel.

Rooms are not fancy, but they are very comfortable and attractively furnished with king-size beds, a table, and chairs. Many rooms feature framed reproductions of rare Disneyland conceptual art.

Moderate

Sheraton-Anaheim Hotel, 1015 W. Ball Rd., Anaheim, CA 92802. ☎ **714/778-1700,** or toll free **800/325-3535**. Fax 714/535-3889. 500 rms. 31 suites. No-smoking rooms available. A/C MINIBAR TV TEL **Directions:** From I-5 north, exit onto Ball Road west: the hotel is on your right as you reach the top of the ramp.

Rates: $95–$135 single, $120–$200 double, from $150 suite. Children 17 and under stay free in parents' room. AE, CB, DC, DISC, MC, V. **Parking:** Free.

Looking very much like an English Tudor castle, the Sheraton-Anaheim rises to the festive theme park occasion with an unusual architectural design and unique public facilities that include a restaurant open 24 hours, a lobby lounge and bar, a California-style delicatessen, and free shuttle service to and from Disneyland and the airport.

Rooms are completely modern and outfitted with separate dressing rooms, color TVs, and radios, some also have refrigerators. The hotel is adequate, but there's no question that guests are really paying for the location—just blocks from Disneyland.

Budget

Farm de Ville, 7800 and 7878 Crescent Ave., Buena Park, CA 90620.
☎ **714/527-2201.** Fax 714/826-3826. 130 rms. A/C TV TEL **Directions:** From I-5 exit, get onto Beach Boulevard south; after about two miles, turn right onto Crescent Avenue to the hotel.

Rates: $35 single, $40 double. Extra person $4. Units for 4–6 persons $80. AE, MC, V. **Parking:** Free.

Although it's just a motel, the Farm de Ville has a lot to offer. It's located close to Knott's Berry Farm's south entrance and is convenient to all the nearby attractions, including Disneyland (just 10 minutes away).

Although they are not immaculately clean, the rooms are spacious and well furnished; each has a radio, dressing area, and individually controlled heat and air conditioning. Facilities include two swimming pools, two wading pools for kids, two saunas, and a coin-op laundry.

WHERE TO DINE

Neither Anaheim nor Buena Park is famous for its restaurants. If you're visiting the area just for the day, you'll probably eat inside the theme parks; there are plenty of restaurants—in all price ranges—to choose from at both Disneyland and Knott's Berry Farm. For the most unusual dinner you've ever had with the kids, see Medieval Times, listed above under "What to See and Do."

Mr. Stox, 1105 E. Katella Ave. ☎ **714/634-2994.**

Cuisine: AMERICAN. **Reservations:** Accepted. **Directions:** From 1-5, exit onto Harbor Boulevard south and turn left onto Katella Avenue to the restaurant.
Prices: Appetizers $5am–$10; main courses $10–$30. AE, DC, MC, V.
Open: Lunch Mon–Fri 11:30am–2:30pm; dinner Mon–Sat 5:30–10pm, Sun 5:30–9pm.

Hearty steaks and fresh seafood are served in an early California setting. Main-dish specialties include Porterhouse steak, fresh seafood, osso buco, venison, and rack of lamb. Homemade desserts, ice cream, and fresh breads are made daily. Mr. Stox has an enormous wine cellar, and there is live entertainment every night.

Peppers Restaurant, 12361 Chapman Ave., Garden Grove. ☎ **714/740-1333.**

Cuisine: CALIFORNIAN/MEXICAN. **Reservations:** Accepted. **Directions:** From 1-5, exit south onto Harbor Boulevard and turn left onto Chapman Avenue to the restaurant.
Prices: Appetizers $3–$7; main courses $9–$14. AE, CB, DC, DISC, MC, V.
Open: Lunch Mon–Fri 11am–3pm; dinner daily 5:30–10pm; Sun brunch 10am–3pm.

Located just south of Disneyland, this colorful Californian/Mexican-themed restaurant features mesquite-broiled "Norteño" cuisine and fresh seafood daily. Mexican specialties include all types of tacos and burritos, but the grilled meats and fish are best.

There's dancing here nightly to Top 40 hits, starting at 8pm. A free shuttle to and from area hotels is available.

Newport Beach & Laguna Beach

30 miles SE of downtown Los Angeles

GETTING THERE • By Plane The **Los Angeles International Airport** (LAX) is located approximately 35 miles northwest of Newport, along the Pacific Coast Highway (Calif. 1). **John Wayne International Airport,** located in Irvine, is only about one mile from Newport Beach on the Costa Mesa Freeway 55.

• By Train The nearest **Amtrak (800/USA-RAIL)** station is located in San Juan Capistrano, at 26701 Verdugo St., about 15 miles from Newport Beach. Trains travel both north and south between Los Angeles and San Diego. Call for fare and schedule information.

• By Bus **Greyhound** can get you here from anywhere. The company no longer operates a nationwide toll-free telephone number, so check your local directory for information.

• By Car From Los Angeles, take I-5 or I-405 south. Exit south onto the Costa Mesa Freeway 55, and continue to the end in Newport Beach. It's about a one-hour drive from downtown Los Angeles.

ESSENTIALS • Orientation Newport Beach encompasses several islands and peninsulas, as well as a good-sized swath of mainland. Balboa Island and Lido Isle are the two largest, though each is only 10 to 20 blocks long and only three or four blocks wide. The islands are situated in a gentle harbor, protected by the giant Lido Peninsula that sticks out from the mainland like a gnarled finger.

• Information The **Newport Beach Conference and Visitors Bureau,** 366 San Miguel, Ste. 200 (☎ **714/644-1190**, or toll free **800/94-COAST**), distributes the requisite maps, brochures, and information. Write for a free visitors' package.

A jigsaw puzzle of islands and peninsulas, Newport Beach is a top southern California recreational resort. Once cattle-ranch land above an uncharted estuary, Newport is now a busy harbor town that embraces the delightful peninsula/island town. The phenomenal growth of hotel and restaurant facilities in the last few years indicates that Newport Beach is fast becoming one of southern California's most popular coastal towns. It's an excellent vacation base from which to explore other coastal beaches, as well as sights in Anaheim and Buena Park.

Laguna Beach, just south of Newport, is smaller, more charming, and somewhat quieter than its northerly neighbor. On weekends, especially, the town is packed with tourists who are attracted by beautiful beaches, terrific shops, top-of-the-line accommodations, and great restaurants. July and August are Laguna's brightest months, when a world-famous Festival of the Arts (**714/494-1145**) takes over the town. The Pageant of the Masters (**714/497-6582,** or toll free **800/487-3378**), in which live actors reenact famous artworks such as Steuben's *Orpheus* shouldn't be missed.

WHAT TO SEE & DO

Balboa Pavilion, 400 Main St., Balboa. ☎ **714/675-9444.**

Designated as a California Historical Landmark, Balboa Pavilion was built in 1905 and originally served as a bathhouse. Today, the cupola-topped structure is a major focus of activity. Restored to its original "waterfront Victorian" splendor, the pavilion serves as the Newport terminal for Catalina Island Passenger Service boats, harbor cruises, and whale-watching trips. It's also home to several restaurants and shops. For cruise and charter information, call **714/673-5245;** for sport-fishing information, call **714/673-1434.**

You can also ferry from here to Balboa Island, across the small bay. Rides cost 90¢ for cars and 40¢ for each adult passenger.

Directions: From Calif. 1, turn south onto Newport Boulevard, which becomes Balboa Boulevard on the peninsula; continue straight to the Pavilion.

Fashion Island, Newport Beach. ☎ **714/721-2000.**

One of the most successful malls in America, Fashion Island encompasses over 75 good-quality shops including Mondi, Victoria's Secret, Benetton, Boxer Bay, Nautica, and Cole Haan. The sprawling complex, which is anchored by Neiman Marcus, I. Magnin, The Broadway and Robinsons-May, includes a dozen restaurants and is surrounded by several luxury hotels.

Newport Bay Harbor Cruises, Balboa Pavilion, 400 Main St., Balboa. ☎ **714/673-5245.**

The best way to see Newport Beach is from the bay. Several 45-minute narrated harbor cruises are offered daily. The cruises pass the fancy homes that have made the area famous and give passengers a good historical background on the area. Cruise times vary, so call for information.

Ticket prices: $6–$8 adults, $4 seniors, $1 children under 12, children under 5 free.

Mission San Juan Capistrano, Ortega Hwy., San Juan Capistrano. ☎ **714/248-2049.**

The "miracle" of the Swallows of Capistrano takes place each year on March 19th, St. Joseph's Day. According to legend, the little birds wing their way back to this mission annually, arriving here at early dawn.

The seventh in California's chain of 21 missions, San Juan Capistrano is the state's most tourist-oriented. Full of small museums, and various stone rooms that are as quaint as they are interesting, the mission is a mix of old ruins and working buildings. Outdoor excavations reveal original 18th-century floorings, while the intimate mission chapel is still regularly used for religious services.

The swallows are said to take flight again on October 23, after bidding the mission "farewell." In reality, however, you can probably see the well-fed birds here any day of the week, winter or summer.

Admission: $4.

Open: Daily 8:30am–5pm. **Closed:** Thanksgiving, Christmas, Good Friday night.

Newport Harbor Art Museum, 850 San Clemente Rd. ☎ **714/759-1122.**

The museum presents rotating exhibitions of 20th-century artworks. The emphasis here is on Californian paintings, sculpture, installations, and photographs. Note that the galleries are closed between exhibitions; call for the current schedule before heading out.

Admission: $4 adults; $2 students, seniors age 65 and over; free for children under 12.

Open: Tues–Sun 10am–5pm. **Directions:** From Calif. 1, turn left onto Newport Center Drive and bear left around the oval to Santa Barbara Drive, then take the next right onto San Clemente Drive to the museum.

WHERE TO STAY

Expensive

Doryman's Inn Bed & Breakfast, 2102 W. Ocean Front, Newport Beach, CA 92663 ☎ **714/675-7300.** 8 rms, 2 suites.

Rates (including breakfast): $135–$230 single or double; from $185 suite. AE, MC, V.

Doryman's opulent rooms combine luxury with romance making it one of the nicest bed-and-breakfasts to be found anywhere. Rooms are outfitted with French and American antiques, floral draperies and spreads, beveled mirrors, and cozy furnishings. There are working fireplaces and sunken marble tubs in every room, some fitted with Jacuzzi jets. King or queen-size beds, lots of plants, and good ocean views round out the decor.

Doryman's location, directly on the Newport Beach Pier Promenade, is also enviable, though some may find it a bit too close to the action. Breakfast, which is served in a charming dining room, includes fresh pastries and fruit, brown eggs, yogurt, cheeses, and international coffees and teas.

Four Seasons Hotel Newport Beach, 690 Newport Center Drive, Newport Beach, CA 92660. ☎ **714/759-0808,** or toll free **800/332-3442** (☎ toll free **800/268-6282** from Canada). Fax 714/760-8073. 221 rms, 64 suites. A/C TV TEL MINIBAR

Rates: $195–$235 single; $225–$265 double; from $295 suite. Children under 18 stay free in parents' room. Additional person $30. AE, DC, MC, V.

Polished and professional, this member of the world-class Four Seasons group gets high marks for its comprehensive facilities. Rooms, conservatively designed in inoffensive beiges, have firm beds, terry bathrobes, oversized closets, and marble baths. Most rooms have small balconies, though the Newport skyline is nothing special to look at. Impeccable service means intense attention to details, butlers on 24-hour call, and high-quality furnishings and food.

The hotel is expensive and attractive to both the old and new kind of rich. Because of their larger size, rooms with two double beds are the hotel's best value. Guests are encouraged to bring their pets, and doggie biscuits and dog food are always available.

Dining/Entertainment: The Pavilion Restaurant serves French/California cuisine, and is popular with locals at lunch. Poolside Cabana Cafe enjoys a nice garden setting, and afternoon tea and evening cocktails are served in the lobby-level Conservatory Lounge.

Services: 24-hour room service, concierge, evening turn-down, complimentary transportation from the Orange County Airport, overnight laundry and shoeshine.

Facilities: Pool, whirlpool, fitness club, two lighted tennis courts, business center, gift shop.

★ **Hyatt Newporter,** 1107 Jamboree Rd., Newport Beach, CA 92660. ☎ **714/729-1234,** or toll free **800/233-1234**. Fax 714/644-1552. 410 rms, 20 suites. A/C TV TEL **Directions:** From Calif. 1, exit north onto Jamboree Road; the hotel is just ahead on your right, near Backbay Drive.

Rates: $139–$170 single; $164–$195 double; from $300 suite. AE, CB, DC, DISC, MC, V. **Parking:** Free.

Located on 26 landscaped acres, the Hyatt Newporter is a resort complex par excellence, and an important hub of activity in this beach town. The John Wayne Tennis

Club is on the premises, a top facility that includes 16 championship courts (all lit for night play), spa equipment, a steam/sauna, and a clubhouse. In addition, the hotel boasts a nine-hole, par-three golf course, three heated Olympic-size swimming pools, three whirlpools, and a children's pool, as well as a fitness room and volleyball court; also available are shuffleboard, Ping-Pong, jogging trails, and much more.

The rooms, decorated in pastel tones, have contemporary furnishings, marble baths, and deluxe amenities. All have balconies or terraces with a view of the back bay, gardens, or golf course.

In addition to offering a pretty view of the back bay, the three-bedroom villas have a separate living and dining area, fireplace, and access to a private swimming pool.

Dining/Entertainment: Three meals a day are offered in the Jamboree Café, a casual Californian-style eatery. Dinner is served both in Ristorante Cantori, a northern Italian dining room, and in the award-winning gourmet room, the Wine Cellar, the hotel's flagship restaurant.

Services: Room service, concierge, evening turndown.

Facilities: There are 16 lighted tennis courts, a nine-hole golf course, three heated swimming pools, three whirlpools, health spa, tour desk, car rental, gift shop, beauty salon.

Newport Beach Marriott Hotel and Tennis Club, 900 Newport Center Dr., Newport Beach, CA 92660. ☎ **71/640-4000,** or toll free **800/228-9290**. Fax 714/640-5055. 586 rms. A/C TV TEL **Directions:** From Calif. 1, turn left onto Newport Center Drive and continue straight to the hotel.

Rates: $139–$149 single; $139–$169 double. AE, CB, DC, DISC, MC, V. **Parking:** $6.

This 15-story hotel was built around a nine-story atrium—and a large 19th-century Italian Renaissance-style fountain; it's a clever design. A majority of the guest rooms, all strikingly decorated with cheerful drapes and spreads, offer ocean views. In addition to the usual features, each room is equipped with a radio, individual climate controls, and an iron and ironing board.

Two swimming and hydrotherapy pools are surrounded by a palm-lined sun deck. Eight tennis courts (all lit at night) are complemented by a well-stocked pro shop and snack bar. There's also a good health club, and golfing next door at the Newport Beach Country Club's 18-hole course.

Dining/Entertainment: J. W.'s California Grill is a pleasant and cheerful indoor/outdoor restaurant serving fresh seafood and American favorites.

Services: Room service, concierge, evening turndown.

Facilities: Two swimming pools, eight lighted tennis courts, health club, pro shop, off-premises golf course, tour desk, car rental.

Surf & Sand Hotel, 1555 South Coast Hwy., Laguna Beach, CA 92651. ☎ **714/497-4477,** or toll free **800/524-8621.** 157 rms. TV MINIBAR **Directions:** From Los Angeles, take I-5 to the Laguna Canyon offramp and head west to the ocean. Turn south on S. Coast Hwy., the hotel will be on your right.

Rates: Jan–Apr and Oct–Dec $160–$245 single or double; from $375 penthouses. May–Sept $200–$295 single or double; from $475 penthouses. Additional person $10.

What is today the best hotel in Laguna Beach started in 1937 as a modest little hotel with just 13 units. The Surf and Sand has come a long way. Still occupying the same fantastic touching-the-ocean location, the hotel now features dozens of top-of-the-line luxurious rooms that, despite their standard size, feel enormously decadent.

Decorated in whites—from walls, to linens, to furnishings, rooms are very bright and beachy. Purposeful architecture ensures that every room gets an oceanfront view. All have private balconies, marble baths, minibars, robes, in-room safes, and radio alarm clocks. Some have whirlpool tubs. Get a deluxe corner room, if you can.

Dining/Entertainment: Splashes Restaurant (see "Where to Dine," below) serves three meals daily in a beautiful oceanfront setting. The green and black Towers Restaurant, located on the hotel's ninth floor, offers contemporary Northern Italian cuisine. Because the windows don't open, a sound system was installed to pipe in the sounds of the surf below. It's open for dinner nightly from 5:30pm.

Services: Room service, concierge, overnight laundry and dry cleaning, complimentary morning newspaper, evening turndown service.

Facilities: Heated swimming pool, gift shop, hair salon, fashion boutique.

MODERATE

Laguna Riviera on the Beach, 825 S. Coast Hwy., Laguna Beach, CA 92651. ☎ **714/494-1196.** Fax 714/494-8421. 41 rms. TV TEL **Directions:** From Los Angeles, take I-5 to the Laguna Canyon offramp and head west to the ocean. Turn south on S. Coast Hwy, the hotel will be on your right, at the corner of St. Ann's Drive.

Rates (including continental breakfast): Sept–June 12 $63–$93 single or double; $90–$149 oceanfront single or double. June 13–Sept 11 $72–$123 single or double; $115–170 oceanfront single or double. MC, V.

What makes Laguna so special is the cliffs that drop straight down to the beach. This two-story pink and green motel takes full advantage of its cliff-top, oceanfront site, offering terrific views from each of its unobstructed oceanfront rooms. Large decks gulp in the views, and an offshore breeze always seems to blow. The Riviera is a truly magical place in which to fall asleep listening to ocean waves that are literally a skipping-stone's throw away.

Don't be misled, the hotel's guest rooms are rather plain; certainly they are no match for the views, as evidenced by the hotel's own motto: "You cannot be both grand and comfortable." But if you're looking for well-priced, down-to-earth accommodations that are walking distance from downtown Laguna Beach, oceanfront rooms at the Riviera are my highest recommendation. Rooms without a view are another matter entirely.

Facilities: Swimming pool, sauna.

Vacation Village, 647 South Coast Hwy., Laguna Beach, CA 92651 ☎ **714/494-8566,** or toll free **800/843-6895**. Fax 714/494-1386. 100 rms, 38 suites. TV

Rates: $80–$195 single or double; from $205 suite. AE, CB, DC, DISC, MC, V.

Vacation Village has something for everyone. A cluster of seven oceanfront and near-the-ocean three-to-five-story motels includes rooms, studios, suites, and apartments. Most of the accommodations are standard motel fare: bed, TV, table, basic bath. The best rooms are oceanfront, located in a four-story structure that overlooks the Village's private beach. Beach umbrellas and back rests for beachgoers are available in the summer months.

Dining/Entertainment: The Vacation Village Restaurant serves meals, cocktails, and refreshments all day.

Facilities: Private beach, two swimming pools, whirlpool.

WHERE TO DINE

The Cannery, 3010 Lafayette Ave. ☎ **714/675-5777.**

Cuisine: SEAFOOD. **Reservations:** Recommended. **Directions:** From Calif. 1, turn south onto Newport Boulevard, then, after you cross the bridge, turn left onto 31st St.; the restaurant is directly ahead, at Lafayette Avenue.
Prices: Appetizers $5–$7; main courses $12–$24; Sun brunch $9–$14. AE, CB, DC, DISC, MC, V.
Open: Lunch Mon–Sat 11:30am–3pm; dinner Mon–Sat 5–10pm, Sun 4:30–9pm. Sun brunch 10am–2:30pm.

The Cannery is housed in a remodeled 1934 fish cannery that used to turn out 5,000 cases of swordfish and mackerel a day. Now a historical landmark, the two-story restaurant is a favorite spot for locals and tourists alike—for good food, a colorful atmosphere, and friendly service. In the upper lounge, tables surround a corner platform where there's live entertainment every Thursday evening and Sunday afternoon.

Fresh fish and local abalone are specialties here. At dinner there's always a superfresh chef's catch of the day. Other good choices are prime rib, chicken teriyaki, and pasta dishes. At lunch you might ask for shrimp and fries, or sandwiches and salads.

The restaurant also serves a champagne buffet brunch while you cruise Newport Harbor aboard the Cannery's *Isla Mujeres;* the cost is $30. Call for information and reservations.

Chanteclair, 18912 MacArthur Blvd., Irvine. ☎ **714/752-8001.**

Cuisine: CONTINENTAL. **Reservations:** Recommended. **Directions:** From Newport Beach, take the Costa Mesa Freeway north one mile to San Diego Freeway 405 east, then go just one exit to MacArthur Boulevard south; the restaurant is straight ahead opposite the airport terminal, between Campus and Douglas drives.
Prices: Appetizers $5–$13; main courses $14–$25. AE, CB, DC, MC, V.
Open: Lunch Mon–Fri 11:30am–2:30pm; dinner Mon–Sat 5:30–11pm; Sun brunch 10:30am–2:30pm.

Chanteclair is expensive, and slightly hard to get to, but it is included here because it is really an excellent place. The restaurant is designed in the style of a provincial French inn. The rambling stucco structure, built around a central garden court, houses several dining and drinking areas: a grand and a petit salon, a boudoir, a bibliotheque, a garden area with a skylight roof, and a hunting lodge-style lounge. Furnished in antiques, it has five fireplaces.

At lunch you might order grilled lamb chops with an herb and garlic sauce, chicken and mushroom crêpes, or Cajun chard ahi. Dinner is a worthwhile splurge that might begin with a lobster bisque with brandy, or beluga caviar with blinis. For a main dish I recommend the rack of lamb with thyme sauce and roasted garlic. The captain will be happy to help you choose from the considerable selection of domestic and imported wines.

Five Feet Restaurant, 328 Glenneyre, Laguna Beach. ☎ **714/497-4955.**

Cuisine: CALIFORNIAN/ASIAN. **Reservations:** Recommended.
Prices: Appetizers $5–$10; main courses $14–$24.
Open: Lunch Fri only 11:30am–2:30pm; dinner Sun–Thurs 5–10pm, Fri–Sat 5–11pm. AE, MC.

If the atmosphere was as good as the food, Five Feet would be one of the best restaurants in California. Chef/proprietor Michael Kang has created one of the country's most innovative and interesting restaurants, combining the best in California cuisine, with Asian technique and ingredients. Outstanding appetizers include spicy Chinese shrimp ravioli, goat cheese wantons with raspberry couli, and foie gras and pear salad with truffle vinaigrette. Entrées run the gamut from tea-smoked filet mignon topped with roquefort cheese and candied walnuts, to a hot Thai-style mixed grill of veal, beef, lamb, and chicken stir-fried with sweet peppers, onions, and mushrooms in curry mint sauce.

Unfortunately, the dining-room's gray concrete walls are not much to look at, and the exposed vents on an airplane hangar–sized wooden ceiling just look unfinished, not trendy industrial. Aging metal chairs, and unspectacular faux marble tables complete the decor, which is only brightened by an exceedingly friendly staff, and truly unparalleled food.

Marrakesh, 1100 W. Coast Hwy. ☎ **714/645-8384.**

Cuisine: MOROCCAN. **Reservations:** Recommended. **Directions:** From Newport Boulevard turn east onto West Coast Calif. 1; the restaurant is directly ahead, near Dover Drive.
Prices: Appetizers $6–$8; main courses $19–$23. AE, CB, DC, MC, V.
Open: Dinner Sun–Thurs 5–10pm, Fri–Sat 5–11pm.

The decor is exotic, with dining areas divided into intimate tents furnished with Persian carpets, low cushioned sofas, and authentic Moroccan artworks.

Dinners here are something of a ritual feast that begins when a server comes around to wash your hands. Everyone in your party shares the same meal—an eight- or nine-course feast that is eaten with your hands. Meals start with Moroccan soup and a tangy salad that are scooped up with hunks of fresh bread. Next comes b'stila, a chicken-filled pastry topped with cinnamon; or kotban, a lamb shish kebab marinated in olive oil, coriander, cumin, and garlic. The choice of main dishes is squab with rice and almonds, chicken with lemon and olives, fish in a piquant sauce, and rabbit in garlic sauce. Leave room for the next course of lamb and vegetables with couscous, followed by fresh fruits, tea, and Moroccan pastries.

Splashes Restaurant and Bar, in the Surf & Sand Hotel, 1555 South Coast Hwy., Laguna Beach. ☎ **714/497-4477.**

Cuisine: MEDITERRANEAN. **Reservations:** Accepted for dinner.
Prices: Appetizers $5–$9; main courses $16–$22; lunch $8–$12. DC, DISC, MC, V.
Open: Daily 7am–10pm.

Sitting almost directly on the surf, this light and bright southwestern-styled restaurant basks in sunlight, and the calming crashing of the waves. Floor-to-ceiling windows maximize this view, and good food completes the stimulation of the senses. Splashes is truly stunning.

In addition to the usual egg and pastries, breakfasts include huevos rancheros and homemade duck hash. Lunchtime might offer crab cakes, eggplant cannelloni, pizzas topped with shrimp, spinach, roasted peppers, and fontina cheese. At dinner, a basket of warm, crusty, fresh-baked bread prefaces a long list of appetizers that might include wild mushroom ravioli with a lobster sauce, or sautéed Louisiana shrimp with red chilies and lemon. Gourmet pizzas also make great starters, and are topped with interesting combinations like grilled lamb, roasted fennel, artichokes, mushrooms, and feta cheese. Entrées also change daily, and might offer baked striped bass, roasted and braised duck with red wine, or risotto with vegetable and cheese ratatouille.

21 Oceanfront, at McFadden's Landing, 2100 West Oceanfront, Newport Beach. ☎ **714/675-2566.**

Cuisine: SEAFOOD. **Reservations:** Recommended.
Prices: Appetizers $5–$8; main courses $16–$24. MC, V.
Open: Daily 4–11pm.

If it weren't for the windows that overlook Newport Pier, you'd hardly know you're at the beach at this dark, clubby restaurant with turn-of-the-century decor. Occupying the second floor of a historic building, the dining room has an upscale New Orleans feel, with a mirrored black and purple decor that includes a cloth-covered ceiling, candlelit tables, and semicircular leatherette booths.

A truly terrific wine list complements thoroughly American dishes like Maryland softshell crab, rack of lamb, grilled abalone, porterhouse steaks, bouillabaisse, and swordfish. Meals are well-prepared and attractively presented. Get dessert elsewhere, then walk it all off on the promenade and pier.

Rockin' Baja Lobster, at the Newport Beach pier, 2104 West Oceanfront, Newport Beach. ☎ **714/723-0606.**

Cuisine: MEXICAN SEAFOOD. **Reservations:** Not accepted.
Prices: Appetizers $4–$10; main courses $9–$13; lunch $6–$11. MC, V.
Open: Sun–Thurs 10am–11pm, Fri–Sat 10am–1am.

A "margarita Mexican" joint, Baja Lobster is a fun, touristy restaurant that's especially popular during lunch and afternoon happy hours. Most of the dishes are deep-fried, including their signature Baja Bucket, a mountain of seasoned lobster tails, served with Caesar salad, beans, rice, and tortillas. Pastas and burgers are also offered as well as tacos, fajitas, and seafood-stuffed chili rellenos.

10

The Palm Springs Desert Resorts

ALMOST SYNONYMOUS WITH SUNNING STARS, PALM SPRINGS DESERT RESORTS IS THE general name of a half dozen adjacent resort towns located in the southern California desert. The largest and most famous of these villages are Palm Springs and Palm Desert, both of which are discussed in detail below. The smaller and lesser-known resort areas surrounding them are Cathedral City, Indian Wells, Indio, La Quinta, and Rancho Mirage.

Located just about 100 miles east of Los Angeles—an easy two-hour drive—the Desert Resorts prove to any doubter that the majority of California is indeed a desert; most of the land is made fertile by water diverted from as far away as Colorado. A true oasis albeit an artificial one, the resorts are crowded with holiday heat-seekers during the glorious winter before reverting into virtual ghost towns during the repressively hot summers.

Although Joshua Tree National Monument—one of our nation's unique parks—is not technically part of the Palm Springs Desert Resorts, its immense importance and close proximity to them warrant its entry here.

SEEING THE PALM SPRINGS DESERT RESORTS

The Palm Springs Desert Resorts are easily accessible from Los Angeles and San Diego. If you're driving from Los Angeles, take Interstate 10, a straight shot from L.A. directly into the heart of the resorts. If you're driving from San Diego, take I-15 north toward Las Vegas and change to I-10 about halfway into your drive.

Since the Desert Resorts are adjacent to one another, you can see them all in one fell swoop. Joshua Tree National Monument is a scenic, 45-minute drive northeast from Palm Springs. It makes for an excellent day out from the Desert Resorts.

1 Palm Springs

103 miles E of Los Angeles, 135 miles NE of San Diego

GETTING THERE • **By Plane** Several airlines service the **Palm Springs Municipal Airport,** 3400 E. Tahquitz-McCallum Way (☎ **619/323-8161**), including Alaska, America West, American, Delta, TWA, Skywest, USAir, United. Flights from Los Angeles International Airport take about 40 minutes.

• **By Bus** **Greyhound** can get you here from anywhere. The central terminal is located at 311 N. Indian Ave. (☎ **619/325-2053**). The company no longer operates a nationwide toll-free telephone number, so check your local directory for information.

• **By Car** From I-10, take the Calif. 111 turnoff to Palm Springs. You drive into town on East Palm Canyon Drive, the main thoroughfare. The trip from downtown Los Angeles takes about 2½ hours.

ESSENTIALS • **Orientation** Downtown Palm Springs stretches for about a half mile along Palm Canyon Drive, a wide storefront-lined boulevard of restaurants, clothing stores, and hotels. The mountains lie directly west, while the rest of Palm Springs is laid out in a grid to the east. Tahquitz—McCallum Way, a street as wide as Palm Canyon Drive, creates the town's primary intersection, and runs through the heart of downtown.

• **Information** The **Palm Springs Desert Resorts Convention and Visitors Bureau,** Atrium Design Centre, 69-930 Highway 111, Suite 201, Rancho Mirage, CA 92270 (☎ **619/770-9000** or toll free **800/417-3529**), offers maps, brochures, and advice. It's open Monday through Friday from 8:30am to 5pm.

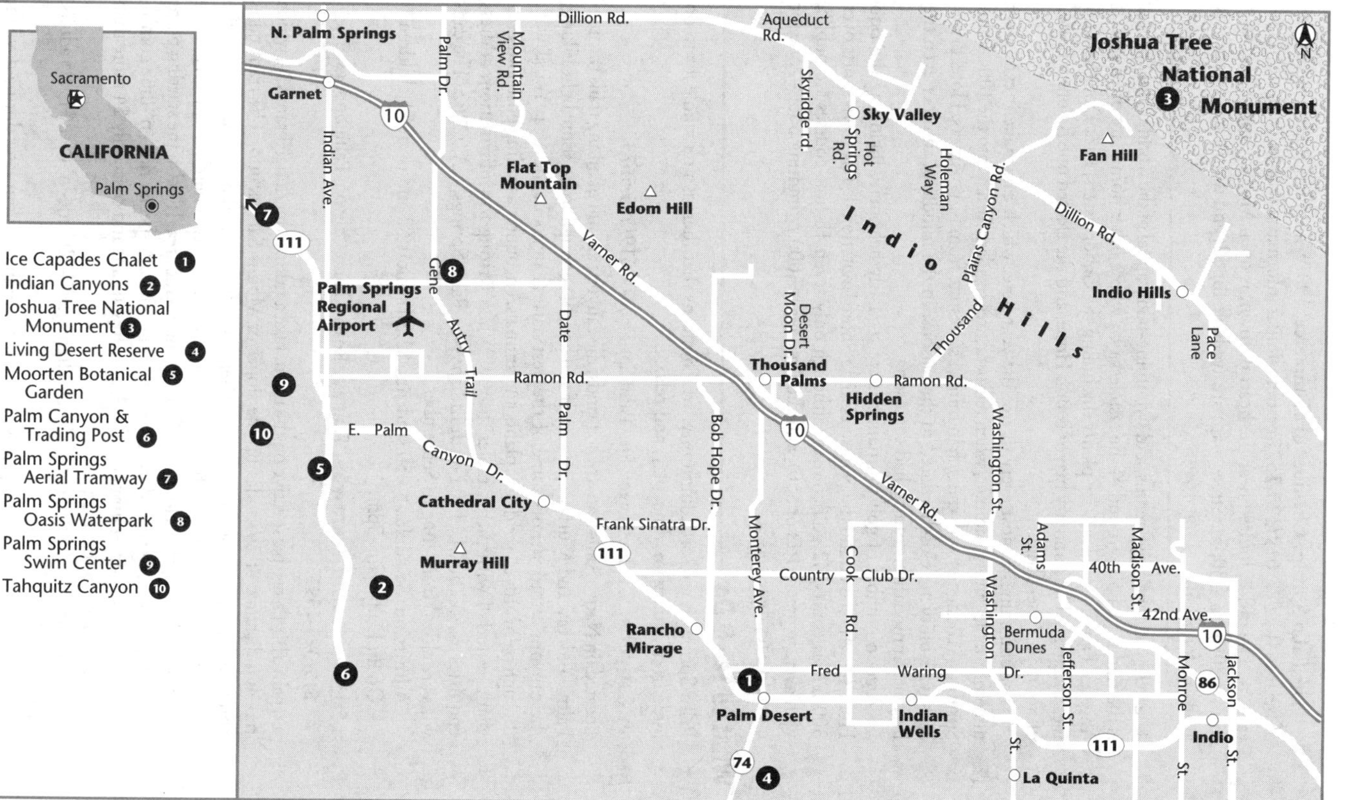

Palm Springs

The **Palm Springs Chamber of Commerce,** 190 W. Amado Rd., at the corner of Belardo Rd. (☎ **619/325-1577**), offers similar information, as well as hotel reservations. The office, located near the heart of town, is open Monday through Friday from 8:30am to 4:30pm. Street maps are available for $2, and tourist information is available for $3.50.

The self-proclaimed golf, tennis, and swimming-pool capital of the world, Palm Springs is the traditional playground of the tasteless rich whose other homes are often in Los Angeles. Famous residents are plenty, including the Gabor sisters, Kirk Douglas, and Dean Martin. The honorary mayor is Bob Hope, and the elected one is Sonny Bono, of Sonny & Cher fame.

The sun shines almost every day of the year here, which can make it extremely uncomfortable during summer, when temperatures regularly reach into the 100s. Palm Springs was designed with the rich in mind, as a respite from L.A. winters. Hotel prices and availability are closely related to the seasons; in the middle of summer even the best accommodations can be had for a song.

A good number of golf tournaments are regularly held here, including the Bob Hope Desert Classic and the Nabisco Dinah Shore Invitational. The town sports over 300 tennis courts, 42 golf courses (although only seven 18-hole courses are public, with average greens fees of $50), and there are over 7,000 swimming pools—one for every five residents!

What to See & Do

Palm Springs is a resort community, which means that there isn't a whole lot to do aside from sun, swim, dine, play, and relax.

Indian Canyons, S. Palm Canyon Dr., Palm Springs. ☎ **619/325-5673.**

Located on Native American–owned lands, the canyons are full of hiking trails through Palm, Andreas, and Murray canyons. If you are able enough to do some light hiking, the canyons afford visitors some of the best natural sights in the area. You'll walk through palm groves, see desert plants and animals, encounter a trading post, and even visit a waterfall with picnic tables nearby. When writing for information, address enquiries to A.C.B.C.I., 110 North Indian Ave., Palm Springs, CA 92262. The canyons are closed from June to September.

Admission: $5 adults, $3.50 students, $2.50 seniors 62 and over, $1 children.

Open: Daily 8am–5pm.

Palm Springs Aerial Tramway, Tramway Road–Chino Canyon, Palm Springs. ☎ **619/325-1391.**

To gain a bird's-eye perspective on the town, take a ride on the Aerial Tramway, which travels a distance of 2½ miles up the slopes of Mount San Jacinto. The tram takes you from the desert floor to cool alpine heights in less than 20 minutes; in winter the change is dramatic, from warm desert to deep snowdrifts. There's a cafeteria at the top, along with a cocktail lounge, gift shop, and picnic area. It's also the starting point of 54 miles of hiking trails dotted with campgrounds. A special ride-'n'-dine combination includes a sunset dinner at the Alpine Restaurant and costs only $4 more than the ride alone—a great bargain.

Admission: $15.95 adults, $10.95 children ages 5–12; Ride-'n'-dine $19.95 adults, $13.95 children.

Open: Mon–Fri 10am–8pm, Sat–Sun 8am–8pm; one hour later during daylight saving time.

ORGANIZED TOURS

Palm Springs Celebrity Tours, 333 N. Palm Canyon Dr., Suite 113A. ☎ **619/325-2682.**

Celebrity Tours has been around since 1963. Their professional guides know all the ins and outs of Palm Springs and specialize in personal tours and small groups; their air-conditioned deluxe coaches seat up to 31.

The one- and two-and-a-half-hour tours take comprehensive looks at Palm Springs and include homes of movie stars and celebrities. The longer tour includes everything you'd see during the one-hour version plus the estates of Frank Sinatra and businessman Walter Annenberg, who has his own golf course. You'll also see the Tamarisk, Canyon, and Thunderbird country clubs, where the international elite meet to play. Then it's on to the Eisenhower Medical Center and beautiful date groves, with a brief stop for refreshments.

The one-hour tour meets at the office at the above address. For the two-hour tour, Celebrity Tours will pick you up at any hotel in Palm Springs.

Reservations are required and should be made at least a day or two in advance. Tours go out daily; call for departure times.

Prices: One-hour tour $11 adults, $10 seniors, $6 children under 12. Two-and-a-half-hour tour $16 adults, $14 seniors, $8 children under 12.

Where to Stay

EXPENSIVE

Ingleside Inn, 200 W. Ramon Rd., Palm Springs, CA 92264. ☎ **619/325-0046,** or toll free **800/772-6655**. Fax 619/325-0710. 29 rms, 16 suites. A/C TV TEL

Rates (including continental breakfast): Oct–May $95–$265 single or double, from $295 suite; Jun–Sept $75–$235 single or double, from $225 suite. AE, DISC, MC, V.

Some of the most charming rooms in town are at this 65-year-old hideaway estate. Each room and suite is uniquely decorated with antiques—perhaps a canopied bed, or a 15th-century vestment chest. Many rooms have wood-burning fireplaces; all have in-room whirlpools, steambaths, and refrigerators stocked with complimentary light snacks and beverages. Once you pass the imposing wrought-iron gates, you leave the bustling world of the 20th century behind and enter an old-world era of luxurious relaxation and fine, unstuffy, remarkably friendly service.

If you decide to stay here, you'll join the ranks of Elizabeth Taylor, Howard Hughes, John Wayne, Bette Davis, Salvador Dalí, and Gary Cooper, all of whom have enjoyed the luxurious facilities at one time or another.

A major renovation was completed in 1990. Redecorated accommodations sport new drapes, spreads, and upholstery. Three rooms were gutted and rebuilt to include totally secluded patios blessed with a magnificent view of the mountains and with wood-burning fireplaces.

Dining/Entertainment: Melvyn's, one of Palm Springs's most prestigious "in" spots, is located downstairs, and definitely worth a visit even if you're not staying here. Frank and Barbara Sinatra hosted a dinner here on the eve of their wedding. The food is excellent, the celebrity-watching first-rate, and the decor is lovely.

Services: Room service, concierge, massage, complimentary limousine service.

Facilities: Swimming pool, Jacuzzi, croquet, shuffleboard, sundry boutiques, business center, tour desk, car rental.

★ **La Mancha,** 444 Avenida Caballeros, Palm Springs, CA 92262. ☎ **619/323-1773,** or toll free **800/647-7482.** Fax 619/323-5928. 47 villas. A/C MINIBAR TV TEL

Rates: $150–$800 single or double. AE, DC, MC, V.

It's hard to top La Mancha, one of the best places to stay in a town full of great hotels. Publicity seekers should stay away—La Mancha is built for privacy. The resort's highest-quality one- and two-bedroom villas are fitted with top-of-the-line amenities that include full kitchens, sunken living rooms, and walled swimming pools or spas that afford total privacy. Inside, large-screen TVs are connected to both VCRs and video disc players. Baths are fitted with double sinks, and bedrooms come equipped with expensive orthopedic mattresses.

On-site facilities include tennis courts, croquet, pitch 'n putt golf greens, saunas, a gym, and bicycles that are free for guests' use.

Palm Springs Hilton, 400 E. Tahquitz Canyon Way, Palm Springs, CA 92262. ☎ **619/320-6868,** or toll free **800/522-6900.** Fax 619/320-2126. 260 rms, 71 suites. A/C MINIBAR TV TEL

Rates: Dec–May $195–$225 single or double; from $265 suite. June–July 4 and Sept–Nov $145–$175 single or double; from $205 suite. July 5–Aug $90–$110 single or double; from $125 suite. Children under 17 stay free in parents' room. AE, CB, DC, DISC, MC, V. **Parking:** Self free, valet $4.

One of the town's most glittering resorts has the atmosphere of a busy country club. A large group-oriented hotel, the three-story Hilton blends into the natural environment and reflects the sand colors of the desert. The lobby, rooms, and restaurants are very contemporary, and are filled with original art, mostly contemporary serigraphs by David Weidman and sculptures by local artists.

Guest rooms—built around a central garden and swimming pool and decorated in soft earth tones—are large and residential in feel, with sitting areas and large window shutters. All rooms have patios or balconies, large baths with thermostatically regulated showers, brass fixtures, and individual temperature controls.

Dining/Entertainment: The Terrace Restaurant, overlooking the pool area, serves a continental cuisine for breakfast, lunch, and dinner daily. There's also a poolside dining facility for snacks, and Harvey's bar/lounge.

Services: Room service, concierge, complimentary airport transportation.

Facilities: Swimming pool, two Jacuzzis, six tennis courts, pro shop, exercise room, tour desk, car rental, beauty salon, video game room.

Spa Hotel & Mineral Springs, 100 N. Indian Canyon Dr., Palm Springs, CA 92263. ☎ **619/325-1461,** or toll free **800/854-1279.** Fax 619/325-3344. 230 rms, 20 suites. A/C MINIBAR TV TEL

Rates (including continental breakfast): Jan–May $135–$185 single or double, from $200 suite; June–Sept $55–$95 single or double, from $90 suite; Oct–Dec $95–$135 single or double, from $175 suite. Extra person $15–$25. Various spa packages available. AE, CB, DC, DISC, MC, V. **Parking:** Free.

Spa Hotel is the only full service "spa" resort in Palm Springs. The site was formerly a shrine for Native American Cahuilla Indians, who claimed that the springs which flow here had magical powers and cured illness. In 1993, the Cahuillas purchased Spa Hotel, and contracted with Nevada-based Caesar's World to build a $25 million casino on land adjacent to the hotel, just one block off Palm Canyon Drive. It's scheduled to open in 1995.

Even without the casino, Spa Hotel, having undergone a recent major renovation, is one of the more unusual accommodations choices in town. There are three pools on the premises. One is a conventional outdoor swimming pool; the other two are filled from underground natural springs brimming with revitalizing minerals. There are an additional 30 indoor, sunken Roman swirlpools, which are also fed from the springs.

The price of a guest room includes hot springs immersion, eucalyptus inhalation, sauna, cooling room, outdoor mineral pools, solarium, and gym. A variety of additional treatments are also available, including exercise classes, herbal wraps, herbal baths, loofah scrubs, salt glows, massages, computerized body stretches, and the like.

Dining/Entertainment: Caliente Dining Room serves both continental cuisine and a Californian-style spa menu.

Services: Evening turndown, massage, facials, manicures, pedicures, and other beauty treatments.

Facilities: Complete gym and spa, three night-lit tennis courts.

MODERATE

Casa Cody Country Inn, 175 S. Cahuilla Rd., Palm Springs, CA 92262. ☎ **619/320-9346,** or toll free **800/231-2639.** Fax 619/325-8610. 10 rms, 7 suites. A/C TV TEL **Directions:** From Palm Canyon Drive, turn west on Tahquitz Canyon Way and take the second left onto Cahuilla Road to the inn.

Rates: Mid-Dec–Apr $65–$175 single or double; May–June $60–$160; July–Sept $45–$105; Oct–mid-Dec $60–$160. Extra person $10. AE, MC, V. **Parking:** Free.

Originally built by Harriet Cody, a relative of Buffalo Bill Cody, Casa Cody is a newly restored, very attractive inn peacefully nestled in the heart of Palm Springs, at the base of the mountain. The hotel offers lovely, spacious ground-level accommodations, most with wood-burning fireplaces and private patios. Elegant touches include saltillo tile floors, dhurri rugs, and original artwork; furnishings are in a comfortable Santa Fe style.

There are two swimming pools and a tree-shaded whirlpool spa. Services include complimentary poolside breakfasts daily. Arrangements can be made for nearby tennis and golf, and access to a private health spa. Complimentary bicycles are available, and the Carl Lyken mountain trailhead is located within walking distance.

Estrella Park Inn, 415 S. Belardo Rd., Palm Springs, CA 92262. ☎ **619/320-4117.** Fax 619/323-3303. 74 rms and cottages. A/C TV TEL **Directions:** From Palm Canyon Drive, turn west on Tahquitz Way, then left onto Belardo Road to the hotel.

Rates (including continental breakfast): Jan to mid-Apr $110–$130 single or double; $160–$200 one-bedroom cottage; $185–$235 two-bedroom cottage. Mid-Apr to May and Oct–Dec $95–$105 single or double; $135–$160 one-bedroom cottage; $160–$185 two-bedroom cottage. Jun–Sept $79–$89 single or double; $119–$129 one-bedroom cottage; $129–$139 two-bedroom cottage. Monthly rates available. AE, DC, DISC, MC, V. **Parking:** Free.

One of the best moderately priced establishments, Estrella Inn is located on a quiet, secluded street that seems to be miles from everywhere, even though it's just a block from the center of town. The rooms vary widely in size—from very small quarters to suites with decks, wet bars, full kitchens, and fireplaces.

There are two swimming pools and a children's pool, two Jacuzzis, and a lawn and court games area. There's no restaurant, but the inn serves a complimentary continental breakfast every morning in the lobby lounge.

BUDGET

El Rancho Lodge, 1330 E. Palm Canyon Dr., Palm Springs, CA 92264. ☎ **619/327-1339.** 19 rms. A/C TV TEL

Rates (including continental breakfast): June–Sept $40–$60 single or double; Oct–May $61–$80 single or double. Monthly discounts available. AE, DISC, MC, V. **Parking:** Free.

Relatively small in size, El Rancho is most popular with guests over 50, which lends a congenial community feeling to the place. Accommodations are simple but pleasantly furnished, roomy, and nicely maintained. All rooms are situated around a large heated pool and spa.

Most of the rooms have one king-size bed or two twin beds. Some of the larger rooms also have full kitchens and some have two full baths—a luxury rarely found even in pricey hotels.

Ironside Hotel, 310 E. Palm Canyon Dr., Palm Springs, CA 92262. ☎ **619/325-1995.** 6 rms. A/C TV TEL

Rates: $40–$70 single or double. AE, MC, V. **Parking:** Free.

Excellent rates and a good Palm Springs location are the main draws of this otherwise basic hotel. Each of the six rooms here is very clean, with white furniture and contemporary floral prints. Rooms have either two double beds or one queen-size bed and a private, tiled bath. Look for the small, peach-colored hotel flying bright flags out front.

Westward Ho Hotel, 701 E. Palm Canyon Dr., Palm Springs, CA 92264. ☎ **619/320-2700,** or toll free **800/854-4345.** Fax 619/322-5354. 208 rms. A/C TV TEL

Rates: Nov–May $42 single, $52 double; Jun–Oct $34 single, $46 double. AE, MC, V. **Parking:** Free.

Rooms at this pleasant, comfortable, and well-priced motel have a modified western look. Most accommodations also have attractive Indian-print spreads, hanging cylinder lamps, upholstered chairs with casters, and dark-wood furnishings. A heated "therapy" pool for guests at the center of the complex is surrounded by comfortable lounges. There is also a small wading pool for children. During holiday periods and special events there is a two-night minimum stay, and rates are slightly higher.

One of the conveniences of the motel is that it adjoins Denny's, a coffee shop–style restaurant that's open 24 hours.

Where to Dine

There are many attractive restaurants in Palm Springs and more in the offing, but oftentimes the food is not as smart as the surroundings. Some of the best restaurants in town are in hotels—most notably Melvyn's at Ingleside Inn, and Caliente at the Spa Hotel. Other good choices are listed below.

EXPENSIVE

Alfredo's, 292 E. Palm Canyon Dr. ☎ **619/325-4060.**

Cuisine: ITALIAN. **Reservations:** Accepted.
Prices: Appetizers $4–$7; main courses $15–$20; lunch $7–$12. AE, DISC, MC, V.
Open: Daily 11:30am–11pm.

The exterior of Alfredo's has always attracted me. It's simple, uncluttered, and inviting, with a forthright "Alfredo's" sign in neon script. The restaurant is just as handsome inside—dusty-rose and cream walls, with complementary maroon-and-cream furnishings, scenic lithographs, smoked mirrors, and frosted-glass art deco lamps overhead.

Appetizers include Mama's fava beans, a Sicilian-style artichoke; and mozzarella marinara—deep-fried cheese cooked with the chef's special sauce. Interesting salads range from the house's dandelion salad (yes, dandelion) to a cold seafood-and-linguine combination.

Main courses range from veal marsala or filet mignon "Alfredo style" to pizza. And the spicy chicken wings have to be the best this side of Buffalo, N.Y. (Alfredo's hometown). They come in hot, medium, or mild, and are served authentically—with celery sticks and blue-cheese dip. If you thought that spaghetti and meatballs was hardly an inspired choice for dinner, try these. Not to be ignored either is veal Alfredo—veal cutlets and eggplant in light batter, sautéed, separated with prosciutto, topped with mozzarella, then baked and finished with Alfredo's special sauce.

MODERATE

Billy Reed's, 1800 N. Palm Canyon Dr. ☎ **619/325-1946.**

Cuisine: AMERICAN. **Reservations:** Accepted for large parties.
Prices: Appetizers $2–$4; main courses $8–$20. AE, CB, DC, DISC, MC, V.
Open: Daily 7am–11pm.

For hearty home cooking, a great selection, huge portions, and small-town ambience, you can't beat Billy Reed's. The entry has the characteristic Palm Springs hacienda look—small fountain, foliage, and cool patio—but the Spanish resemblance ends there. Wicker furniture graces the outer lobby, and the interior is American/Victorian, with lace curtains and Tiffany stained-glass lamp shades. Somehow it all works. And though the place is huge, the low ceilings and overhead pot-and-mug collections make it seem warm and friendly.

You can start your day here with a breakfast such as sausage and eggs served with hash browns, toast, and butter. At lunch you might order the shrimp Louis, served with garlic toast or cornbread, a delicious chicken pot pie, or a bowl of chili with cubed sirloin and beans. Among the main course options are jumbo prawns, top sirloin, fried chicken, prime rib, or broiled scallops and shrimp en brochette with bacon, mushroom caps, and onions.

Las Casuelas Terraza, 222 S. Palm Canyon Drive, Palm Springs. ☎ **619/325-2794.**

Cuisine: MEXICAN. **Reservations:** Accepted.
Prices: Appetizers $4–$7; main courses $7–$13; lunch $4–$9. AE, DC, DISC, MC, V.
Open: Daily 11am–10pm.

The upscale Mexican style that typifies much of Palm Springs is epitomized in this festive restaurant, outfitted with stone archways, terra-cotta floors, and white plaster walls. In addition to a busy bar—where live entertainment is featured on weekends—the piazzalike eatery encompasses several indoor dining rooms as well as a popular terrace, spiced with small tables, a stone fountain, and hanging ferns.

While Las Casuelas Terraza's food is not outstanding, it never takes a back seat to the bar—a situation that's typical of most California-Mexican "margarita" restaurants. All the "hits" are here: nachos, burritos, tacos, quesadillas, and the recommendable fajitas with chicken, steak, or shrimp. Huevos rancheros and a variety of Mexican-style omelets are also available for brunch.

Lyon's English Grill, 233 E. Palm Canyon Dr. ☎ **619/327-1551.**

Cuisine: ENGLISH/JEWISH. **Reservations:** Accepted.
Prices: Appetizers $3–$10; main courses $14–$20. AE, CB, DC, MC, V.
Open: Dinner daily 4–11pm. **Closed:** July.

Lyon's English Grill has an almost theatrical, woody, English-pub ambience composed of stained-glass windows, old pub signs and maps, Tudor-style beamed walls, and heraldic banners suspended from the ceilings. Even the menus were made in England, originally for a restaurant in Hampton Court.

One of the grill's most unusual menus combines English and Jewish specialties like steak-and-kidney pie, matzo ball soup, prime rib, and chicken in the pot. Starters include shrimp scampi, sautéed mushrooms, and potato skins. Main courses run the gamut from filet mignon and barbecued ribs, to roasted chicken and steak-and-kidney pie. But of course you are in California, so cobb salad and fresh fish are also available.

Sorrentino's, 1032 N. Palm Canyon Dr. ☎ **619/325-2944.**

Cuisine: SEAFOOD. **Reservations:** Recommended.
Prices: Appetizers $3–$12; main courses $11–$30. AE, CB, DC, MC, V.
Open: Dinner only, daily 5–10:30pm.

When you're in the mood for a truly fresh seafood dinner visit Sorrentino's, undoubtedly the best seafood restaurant in town. Its Italian-American origins are reflected by the decor: green banquettes against orange walls decked with oil paintings and wrought-iron-encased fixtures.

Virtually all the fish is fresh, and when it's "fresh frozen"—more often than not the case in Palm Springs—Sorrentino's tells you so. Some of the great choices on the extensive menu include a hearty cioppino with lobster, shrimp, clams, crab, squid, and fish, served with rice; king crab legs; abalone steak; and fresh fish broiled, poached, baked, and grilled. Several Italian-style meat choices are also available, as is a special children's dinner which offers a choice of four main courses. The wine list, both domestic and imported, is limited but good. Sorrentino's has a huge bar adjacent to the main dining room, so you won't mind the inevitable wait for a table.

BUDGET

El Mirasol, 140 E. Palm Canyon Dr. ☎ **619/323-0721.**

Cuisine: MEXICAN REGIONAL. **Reservations:** Accepted.
Prices: Appetizers $4–$7; main courses $6–$11; lunch $5–$9. MC, V.
Open: Lunch daily 11am–3pm, dinner daily 5–10pm.

A fine alternative to the better-known Mexican eateries in Palm Springs, El Mirasol is a well-priced family restaurant, simply decorated with dark-wood furniture, a beautiful desert mural on one wall, and potted plants. Classic Mexican combinations include tacos, enchiladas, chiles relleños, tostadas, and burritos, and for the benefit of brunchers, egg dishes, including huevos rancheros or chorizo and eggs, are also served. But the excellence of the menu is in the many "especialidades de la casa"—whether you choose the pork chile verde cooked with green chiles and tomatillos, or opt for the well-seasoned shrimp rancheros, a special treat prepared with bell peppers, onions, olives, and tomatoes.

The chefs cook with pure corn and olive oil and prepare their guacamole without salt or mayonnaise.

Louise's Pantry, 124 S. Palm Canyon Dr. ☎ **619/325-5124.**

Cuisine: AMERICAN. **Reservations:** Not accepted.
Prices: Appetizers $3–$6; main courses $8–$10; lunch $5–$7. DC, MC, V.
Open: Daily 7am–9pm. **Closed:** Mid-June to mid-Sept.

Louise's Pantry is a real fixture on the Palm Springs eating scene. It's a small place—just 47 seats—but it packs 'em in every day and night, and with good reason. It's hard to match Louise's quality and even harder to beat the price.

This is a real American diner kind of place: burgers, sandwiches, triple-deckers, and salads. The restaurant squeezes fresh orange juice daily, grinds its own beef, and bakes the sweet rolls, cornbread, pies, and cakes on the premises. There are three to six specials each evening, plus choices from a regular list of eight selections, like roast beef, homemade meatloaf, grilled pork chops, and fish and chips. Specials of the day may include lamb shanks, roast turkey, and pork tenderloin.

Louise's Pantry also serves breakfast, with all sorts of accompaniments. You can even create your own omelet from a lengthy mix-and-match list of goodies. Beer and wine are available.

Nate's Delicatessen and Restaurant, 100 S. Indian Ave. ☎ **619/325-3506.**

Cuisine: JEWISH. **Reservations:** Accepted.
Prices: Appetizers $3–$7; main courses $6–$9. AE, CB, DC, DISC, MC, V.
Open: Daily 8am–8pm.

One of the really enjoyable eating experiences in Palm Springs is Nate's Delicatessen and Restaurant, also known as Mister Corned Beef of Palm Springs. Unlike its New York, Los Angeles, or San Francisco deli counterparts, Nate's looks like a well-bred restaurant, but not to worry—it has all the great aromas of a super deli.

For breakfast, there are omelets in every conceivable combination—with salami, pastrami, corned beef, chopped liver, and the like—as well as eggs with onions, lox, whitefish, and even grilled knockwurst. French toast and pancakes are also available.

At lunch, sandwich fillings are piled high onto homemade warm rye bread (or whatever bread or roll you prefer). Everything comes with a relish tray of kosher pickles and old-world sauerkraut. They have eight varieties of salad, blintzes, gefilte fish, potato pancakes, and knishes, too.

The restaurant's $11, nine-course dinner includes juice or homemade chopped liver, soup or salad, and main dishes ranging from baked or fried chicken to corned beef, brisket, or seafood catch of the day. An extensive à la carte menu is also available.

2 Palm Desert

118 miles E of Los Angeles, 15 miles SE of Palm Springs

GETTING THERE • **By Plane** Palm Springs Municipal Airport, 3400 E. Tahquitz-McCallum Way (☎ **619/323-8161**), serves the entire Palm Springs Desert Resorts community. Flights from Los Angeles International Airport take about 40 minutes.

• **By Bus** **Greyhound** can get you here from anywhere. The closest stop is located at 311 N. Indian Ave., Palm Springs (☎ **619/325-2053**). The company no longer operates a nationwide toll-free telephone number, so check your local directory for information.

• **By Car** From Los Angeles, Palm Desert is an easy two-hour drive via the San Bernardino Freeway (Interstate 10). When approaching Palm Springs, exit onto Hwy. 111 (Palm Canyon Drive), which runs through all the resort towns before reconnecting with I-10 just past Indio.

ESSENTIALS • **Orientation** Palm Desert is small. El Paseo, the town's primary commercial thoroughfare, is shaped like a giant horseshoe that connects with East Palm Canyon Drive at both ends. In between are gridlike residential streets that are easy to negotiate.

• **Information** Visitor information is provided by the **Palm Springs Desert Resorts Convention and Visitors Bureau,** Atrium Design Centre, 69-930 Highway 111, Suite 201, Rancho Mirage, CA 92270 (☎ **619/770-9000**). The bureau can help you with maps, brochures, and advice. The office is open Monday through Friday from 8:30am to 5pm.

Located in the center of the Coachella Valley, Palm Desert is home to more golf courses than any other desert city. There's not that much to see and do here; shopping and sunning rank among the town's top activities.

What to See & Do

EL PASEO Palm Desert's main commercial thoroughfare is located one block from Hwy. 111. Dozens of specialty shops, selling everything from handcrafted jewelry and knickknacks to designer fashions, make this strip a fun place to walk and shop on. Many of the town's restaurants are also located on Hwy. 111; some are listed below. Hats are highly recommended for daytime strollers.

The Living Desert, 47-900 Portola Ave., Palm Desert. ☎ **619/346-5694.**

Located 15 miles southeast of Palm Springs, in Palm Desert, this largely outdoor museum is cleverly designed to acquaint visitors with the unique habitats that make up the southern California desert. Various components of this distinctive ecosystem are represented, including live tarantulas, scorpions, and snakes, as well as squirrels, bats, and lizards. Desert flora are also exhibited, along with informative displays about the effects of temperature, wind, and moisture on the desert community.

Although you'll rarely see them in the wild, native coyotes, foxes, bobcats, and other larger animals also make their home here. Fifty-minute guided tours are conducted daily, via motorized tram. Don't forget a hat and sunscreen. The museum is closed during most of the unbearably hot summer season.

Admission: $7 adults, $3.50 children 3–15, $6 for seniors 62 and over.

Open: Daily 9am–5pm, last admission at 4:30pm. **Closed:** June 16–Aug 31, Dec. 25.

Where to Stay

VERY EXPENSIVE

Marriott's Desert Springs Resort and Spa, 74885 Country Club Dr., Palm Desert, CA 92260. ☎ **619/341-2211,** or toll free **800/228-9290.** 844 rms, 51 suites. A/C MINIBAR TV TEL

Rates: Dec–May $195–$325 single or double, from $575 suite; June–July $110–$185 single or double, from $300 suite; Aug–Nov $95–$170 single or double, from $300 suite. AE, CB, DC, DISC, MC, V.

A tourist attraction in its own right, Marriott's Desert Springs Resort is worth a peek even if you're not lucky enough to stay here. Visitors enter this artificial desert oasis via a long palm tree–lined road that wends its way past a small pond "inhabited" by a gaggle of pink flamingos. Once inside, guests are greeted by a shaded marble lobby "rain forest" replete with running water and the squawk of tropical birds. Canopied water taxis congregate here, ready to float guests to their rooms.

While rooms here are not as fancy as the lobby would lead you to believe, they are exceedingly comfortable, decorated with muted pastels and contemporary furnishings. There is a large variety of accommodations, differing in size and location. Most have large bathrooms, outfitted with hairdryer, full-length mirror, and separate bathtubs. Suites have large sitting and dining areas furnished with Murphy beds.

Most of the resort's guests are attracted by excellent golf and tennis facilities. The spa is an added perk, offering massages, facials, aerobics classes, and supervised weight training. There are also the requisite Jacuzzis and swimming pools.

Dining/Entertainment: The Club Room is open for breakfast and lunch, serving eggs, sandwiches, and salads. Lunches are also served in the Lake View restaurant. Dining choices include Sea Grill and Oyster Bar, which features mesquite-grilled meat and fish; Tuscay's Ristorante, an Italian eatery; and Mikado, the resort's Japanese restaurant. Costa's lounge features dancing nightly.

Services: Room service, concierge, car-rental desk, babysitting, overnight laundry, and special children's programs.

Facilities: Two 18-hole golf courses, a putting course, a driving range, a full-service spa, 20 tennis courts (seven lighted), two outdoor swimming pools, one indoor lap pool, three outdoor Jacuzzis, a jogging trail, and games room.

MODERATE

Deep Canyon Inn, 74-470 Abronia Trail, Palm Desert, CA 92260. ☎ **619/346-8061,** or toll free **800/253-0004.** Fax 619/341-9120. 31 rms, 1 apt. A/C TV TEL

Rates (including continental breakfast): Jan–May $65–$150 single or double, $185 apt; the rest of the year $45–$110 single or double, $145 apt. AE, DC, DISC, MC, V.

The earth-toned Deep Canyon Inn, located a block from Hwy. 111, is a homey alternative to the many large chain hotels in the area. Behind a bevy of brightly colored flags are nicely remodeled rooms, each outfitted with dark rattan furnishings and natural-tone prints. Except for their exceptionally large size, guest rooms are in no way outstanding; still, accommodations are quite adequate and include clean, tiled baths. Higher-priced rooms include separate kitchens, stocked with cookware and dishes. French doors on second-story rooms open onto small balconies that overlook the hotel's central courtyard and swimming pool.

Shadow Mountain Resort and Racquet Club, 45-750 San Luis Rey, Palm Desert, CA 92260. ☎ **619/346-6123.** 60 rms, 100 suites. A/C TV TEL

Rates: May 31–Sept 24 $81–$100 single/double; from $150 suite. Sept 25–Nov 24, Nov 29–Dec 23, Jan 3–Feb 11, and Apr 18–May 27 $110–$135 single/double; from $167 suite. The rest of the year $134–$170 single/double; from $200 suite. Weekly and monthly rates available. AE, MC, V.

Shadow Mountain is a collection of individually owned condominiums that are rented out when their owners are away. There is a wide range of accommodations, from one-room studios with kitchenettes to large, two-bedroom units; all are uniquely decorated according to their owners' tastes. Don't worry, though. Each fully equipped apartment has to conform to the resort's good standards. Although the resort lacks many services that are usually identified with good hotels (for example, room service and concierge), it delivers the main ones, including a helpful staff and daily maid service. Particularly recommendable for families, homey Shadow Mountain happily dispenses with the pretensions and stuffiness that are sometimes associated with large resorts. In addition to 16 tennis courts, the resort encompasses four heated swimming pools and five whirlpools dotted across the property.

A small restaurant is open seasonally for light lunches and refreshments; a bar is open on weekend nights only.

BUDGET

Gala Villa Inn, 73-721 Shadow Mountain Dr., Palm Desert, CA 92260
☎ **619/346-6121.** 21 rms. A/C TV TEL

Rates: June–Oct $35–$42 single or double; Nov–Jan $55–$65 single or double; Feb–May $64–$72 single or double. AE, MC, V.

So what if the decor hasn't changed since the 1950s? Basic and totally serviceable Gala Villa Inn represents one of the best-priced picks in the area. Most of the inn's 21 rooms contain two double beds, and many also have kitchens. Most important, there's a swimming pool for quick desert relief.

Where to Dine

EXPENSIVE

La Quinta Cliffhouse, 78-250 Hwy. 111, La Quinta. ☎ **619/360-5991.**

Cuisine: CALIFORNIAN. **Reservations:** Recommended.
Prices: Appetizers $2–$7; main courses $14–$27; brunch $8–$13. AE, DISC, MC, V.
Open: Dinner Sun–Thurs 5–9:30pm, Fri–Sat 5–10pm; brunch Sunday, during the fall only, 10am–2pm.

King of its own little hill on the east side of Hwy. 111, La Quinta Cliffhouse successfully combines respectable food with a spirited site. The stairs that lead to the restaurant's entrance wind through a rocky waterfall. The best seats are at the thatched wood tables on the restaurant's outdoor terrace. The inside isn't shabby either, with oak tables atop a bright ethnic-print carpet. Residential-quality southwestern artwork, shaded chandeliers, and beamed ceilings round out the decor.

The entirely à la carte menu ensures that you'll pay handsomely for your dinner, but plenty of regulars affirm that it's worth it. A large, steamed artichoke, served with drawn butter, is my appetizer pick, followed by fresh mahi mahi prepared with soy and ginger and topped with razor-thin, stir-fried vegetables. Filet mignon, pork ribs, and several chicken selections keep the grill busy. Without exception, every dish is expertly handled and artfully presented.

Some of the more unusual Sunday brunch selections include crab cakes Benedict and a seafood quiche filled with bay shrimp, Dungeness crab meat, artichoke hearts, and Gruyère cheese.

MODERATE

Cedar Creek Inn, 73-445 El Paseo, Palm Desert. ☎ **619/340-1236.**

Cuisine: AMERICAN. **Reservations:** Recommended.
Prices: Appetizers $2–$5; main courses $7–$22; lunch $5–$9. AE, MC, V.

Open: Daily 11am–9pm.

The appropriately named Cedar Creek Inn sounds just like the quiet country hideaway it is. Choose to sit either inside, beside well-dressed windows and under wood-beamed ceilings, or on one of the two trellis-covered patios.

Straightforward soups and sandwiches are served throughout the day, along with a well-stocked salad bar. Reservations are encouraged at dinner, which is both more popular and more formal. Rack of lamb is the house specialty, but there is also a good selection of fresh fish and chicken.

Dakota Bar and Grill, 73-260 El Paseo, Palm Desert. ☎ **619/346-0744.**

Cuisine: AMERICAN. **Reservations:** Accepted.
Prices: Appetizers $5–$8; main courses $10–$24; lunch $6–$13. DC, MC, V.
Open: Daily 11:30am–10:30pm.

Smokey meats, burgers, chicken, and fish, served in a wild-west interior, combine to make the Dakota the desert's best barbecue. A country-and-western interior of buffalo horns, fake rocks, and fictitious wooden signs reminds diners of gold-rush days. Of the three different strengths of chili, "suicide" is hottest and requires plenty of ice water. Most items here are reasonably priced. Some items, however, such as the Cattle Baron's Special—two double cheeseburgers and a bottle of Dom Perignon champagne—are just a menu joke; there are few takers for the Cattle Baron's Special at $125 a pop.

Tsing Tao, 74-040 Hwy. 111, Suite E, Palm Desert. ☎ **619/779-9593.**

Cuisine: CHINESE. **Reservations:** Accepted.
Prices: Appetizers $5–$10; main courses $8–$18; fixed-price lunch $5–$7. MC, V.
Open: Lunch Mon–Fri 11:30am–2:30pm; dinner Sun–Thurs 5–9:30pm, Fri–Sat 5–10:30pm.

Located in a strip mall on Hwy. 111, this small Chinese restaurant offers a welcome alternative to the usual Cal-Mex fare that's so popular in this desert community. No red-and-white pagoda here. Contrasting black lacquer chairs and white-clothed tables are clean, elegant, and tastefully modern.

The restaurant's good-value fixed-price lunches include such entrées as almond chicken, shrimp mixed with Chinese greens, and curry chicken, all served with egg-flower soup, fried won tons, rice, fortune cookies, and tea. All the other Mandarin trademarks are also available for both lunch and dinner, including sweet-and-sour shrimp, moo shu pork, lobster Cantonese, and tangerine beef.

BUDGET

Mickey's Sandwich Shop, 73-655 El Paseo, Unit G, Palm Desert. ☎ **619/346-1072.**

Cuisine: SANDWICHES.
Prices: $3–$5 sandwiches, salads. No credit cards.
Open: Mon–Fri 10am–3pm.

For a good lunch at a reasonable price, it's hard to top Mickey's, where an arm-long list of sandwiches and salads offer plenty of choices for under $5. It's just a simple "to go" place, where all the usual meats and cheeses are augmented by seafood and vegetarian selections. Homemade salads include tuna, fruit, pasta, vegetable, and chicken. Brownies, cookies, and cheesecakes are available for dessert.

3 Joshua Tree National Monument

140 miles E of Los Angeles, 45 miles NE of Palm Springs

GETTING THERE • By Car There are two main entrances to Joshua Tree. The northwest entrance is located near Twentynine Palms. From Palm Springs, take Indian Avenue north and turn right onto Highway 62 north. Once in Twentynine Palms, turn right just past the traffic light onto National Monument Drive. To reach the park's southeast entrance, follow I-10 east 55 miles from Palm Springs.

ESSENTIALS • Orientation Half a million acres large, Joshua Tree National Monument connects the Mohave and the Colorado deserts. The Mohave, to the west, is high desert, with an average elevation over 3,000 feet. The eastern low desert is drier and more barren, receiving an average of six inches of rain per year.

• Information All queries regarding Joshua Tree National Monument should be addressed to 74485 National Monument Drive, Twentynine Palms, CA 92277 (☎ **619/367-7511**). Visitors' centers at both of the park's main entrances (see below) can supply you with information on hiking, camping, and exploring the monument.

The 558,000-acre Joshua Tree National Monument is located northeast of Palm Springs. Its main office is at 74485 National Monument Drive, Twentynine Palms, CA 92277 (☎ **619/367-7511**). The park takes its name from a large yucca belonging to the agave family that thrives in this region at elevations above 3,000 feet. These 20- to 30-foot tall cactus "trees," with spindly green knobs at the end of each branch, were named by early Mormon settlers, who thought their unusual forms looked like Joshua beckoning them farther west. The monument is comprised of two distinct halves, both deserts with average summer temperatures of 100 to 110 degrees. The eastern half is lower than the west's 3,000-plus-foot elevation and receives less than its neighbor's average annual eight inches of rain. Scattered about this arid region are five oases, where water can be found at or near the surface. Golden eagles, tarantulas, stinkbugs, sidewinders, and other desert animals are attracted to these watering holes, as are jackrabbits, coyotes, and rattlesnakes.

Over 3,500 established rock climbs make Joshua Tree one of the world's most popular climbing areas. Most visitors, however, come to hike and camp, and to experience Joshua's distinctive magnificence. Most of the western part of the park is relatively flat, so trails are not particularly strenuous. Still, be sure to carry an ample supply of water, as desert hiking leads quickly to dehydration. There are dozens of marked trails, and park rangers can suggest paths that are best suited for you. If your visit is short, however, and you want to get a good feel for the park's immense diversity, enter the park via the **Oasis Visitors Center** in Twentynine Palms and take the Barker Dam Trail, which wends its way through flatlands and large rock formations, past Native American petroglyphs, to a private little reservoir. It's incredibly picturesque. Alternatively, hike the short Hidden Valley Loop, an archetypical western walk, dotted with tall red rock formations, which will seem familiar to you if you are a fan of old cowboy movies.

Be aware that the desert is a very fragile ecosystem, and therefore vigilantly protected by the federal government. A half dozen plant species are threatened or endangered. The desert tortoise is one of the most imperiled; visitors are asked not to touch these or any other plants or animals in the park.

There are two main entrances to Joshua Tree. The most popular approach is via Twentynine Palms, 45 miles northeast of Palm Springs. At this north entrance, the Oasis Visitor's Center offers information and advice on visiting the park, along with trail maps and safety information. It's open daily from 8am to 4:30pm. Joshua Tree's less popular south entrance is served by the Cottonwood Visitor's Center and is located near Interstate 10, 55 miles east of Palm Springs. This Visitor Center is open daily from 8am to 4pm.

If you plan on camping in the park, call ahead, as reservations are required for some sites.

Admission is $5 per car and $3 per walk-in.

11 San Diego

MODERN CALIFORNIA BEGAN IN SAN DIEGO. PORTUGUESE EXPLORER JUAN CABRILLO dropped anchor at Point Loma in 1542, and Franciscan Father Junipero Serra established the first of California's chain of missions here in 1769. Yet, curiously, the historical relevance of this coastal city is not its most striking feature. San Diego's predominant impression is much more contemporary. The city is full of seemingly endless vistas of blue Pacific, boat-filled harbors, quiet coves, and sparkling warm water bays.

San Diego is the second-largest city in California, after Los Angeles, yet even if you stood at the city's busiest corner you'd never know it. San Diego's endless sunshine, perfect weather, soft winds, beautiful natural harbor, and fun, informal lifestyle combine to make it one of the best all-around vacation spots in the country.

1 Orientation

Although it is one of the largest cities in the United States, San Diego hardly feels like it. Downtown is fairly compact, but the tall buildings are not in a claustrophobic cluster, and the water is never too far away. Getting around is also relatively straightforward, with an easy-to-decipher street system, and many recognizable landmarks.

ARRIVING

BY PLANE The **San Diego International Airport,** 3707 N. Harbor Dr. (**619/231-7361**), locally known as Lindbergh Field, is just three miles from downtown. Most of the major domestic carriers fly here, including **Alaska Airlines** (toll free **800/426-0333**), **American** (toll free **800/433-7300**), **America West** (toll free **800/297-5692**), **Continental** (toll free **800/525-0280**), **Delta** (toll free **800/221-1212**), **Northwest** (toll free **800/447-4747**), **Southwest** (toll free **800/435-9792**), **Trans World Airlines** (☎ **619/295-7009**), **United** (toll free **800/241-6522**), and **USAir** (**619/574-6233,** or toll free **800/428-4322**)

There are two airport terminals, east and west, both of which are supported by a number of transportation options.

San Diego Transit's bus 2 stops at the center traffic aisle of the airport's East Terminal and at the far-west end of the West Terminal. The bus connects the airport with the downtown area, stopping at Broadway and Fourth Avenue. The no. 2 bus runs every 20 minutes from 5:30am to midnight (every 30 minutes on weekends) and costs $1.50.

Several airport shuttles run regularly from the airport to locations all over the county. They charge about $5 to any downtown location, and pick up from designated areas outside each terminal.

Taxis line up outside both terminals and cost about $7 to a downtown location.

Several major car rental companies operate at the airport, including Avis, Budget, Dollar, Hertz, and National. See Section 8, "Getting Around," in Chapter 2 for complete information and phone numbers.

If you are driving into the city from the airport, follow the signs to I-5/downtown; you will end up on Front Street, which links up with Broadway, the main east-west thoroughfare.

BY TRAIN **Amtrak** (**800/USA-RAIL**) trains connect San Diego to Los Angeles and the rest of the country. Trains pull into San Diego's pretty mission-style Santa Fe Station, 1850 Kettner Blvd. (at Broadway), within walking distance of many downtown hotels. See Section 7, "Getting There," in Chapter 2 for complete rail information.

What's Special About San Diego

Architecture

- Bazaar del Mundo, a former motel that has been remarkably transformed into a south-of-the-border corner of Old Town.
- The Gaslamp Quarter, a National Historic District that covers 16 downtown city blocks.
- Buildings in Balboa Park, enchanting vestiges of two world expositions.

Beaches

- Coronado, one of the cleanest and prettiest stretches of sand in California.
- La Jolla, stark, striking beauty, surrounded by pretty homes and great shops.
- Mission Beach, with its great boardwalk, and where the surf's usually up.
- Pacific Beach, for San Diego's top sunsets.
- Black's Beach, the area's best-known (unofficial) nude beach.

Zoo

- In Balboa Park, containing some of the world's most exotic wild animals.

BY BUS You can get to San Diego from anywhere, via **Greyhound.** Buses pull into the terminal at 120 W. Broadway, between Front Street and First Avenue (☎ toll free **800/231-2222**). The well-located station is within walking distance of several downtown hotels, Seaport Village, and Horton Plaza. America's largest interstate coach company no longer operates a nationwide toll-free telephone number, so check your local directory for the nearest office.

BY CAR You can't miss downtown's skyscrapers when driving into San Diego; they tell you you've made it to the heart of the city. From Los Angeles, you'll enter San Diego via I-5; from points northeast of the city, you'll come down on I-15; and from the east, you'll come in on I-8. The freeways are well marked, pointing the way to downtown streets. If you are heading to Coronado, take the Bay Bridge via Harbor Drive.

TOURIST INFORMATION

San Diego's excellent **International Visitors Information Center,** 11 Horton Plaza, at First Avenue and F Street (☎ **619/236-1212**), offers a free San Diego visitors guide, information on hotels, restaurants, entertainment, sightseeing, sporting activities, and excursions to Mexico. They employ a multilingual staff and sell San Diego street maps and the Annual Major Events Calender. The office is open Monday through Saturday 8:30am to 5pm, and June through August on Sunday 11am to 5pm. Travelers' aid booths are also located at both the East and West Terminal of the airport, and at the San Diego Cruise Terminal, B Street Pier.

Additional, specialized visitor information outlets include the Balboa Park Information Center, House of Hospitality, 1549 El Prado, San Diego, CA 92101 (☎ **619/239-0512**); the Coronado Visitor Information Center, 1111 Orange Ave., Suite A, Coronado, CA 92118 (☎ **619/437-8788**, or toll free **800/622-8300**); Old Town State Park Visitor & Information Center, 4002 Wallace St., San Diego, CA 92110 (☎ **619/220-5422**); and Mission Bay Visitors Information Center, 2688 E. Mission Bay Dr., San Diego, CA 92109 (☎ **619/276-8200**).

CITY LAYOUT

Downtown San Diego is pretty easy to negotiate. Avenues run north-south and are numbered from 1 to 12. Streets run east-west, and are lettered A to K. Outside the city center, street names get a little more complex, but most are laid out in a grid, making finding your way around very easy.

Harbor Drive is a good street to know; it runs along the Embarcadero, or waterfront, connecting downtown with the Coronado Bay Bridge. Interstate-5 doglegs around the city center and runs north to the airport and on to Mission Bay, Old Town, and La Jolla. Balboa Park and the Hillcrest area lie northeast of downtown, and are easily accessible via 12th Avenue, which becomes Park Boulevard.

MAIN ARTERIES & STREETS Interstate-5 is the most important road in San Diego, connecting each of the city's divergent parts with each other, and the entire region with the rest of the state.

Broadway and Fourth Avenue, which intersect in the heart of downtown, are the city's primary thoroughfares. Harbor Drive, which hugs the waterfront, connects downtown with the Coronado Bay Bridge. In other parts of the city, the primary streets run close to the water; if you're ever in doubt, just head toward the ocean.

FINDING AN ADDRESS It's easy to find an address when you're downtown. If the address is 411 Market St., for example, you'll find it between Fourth and Fifth avenues on Market Street. Make use of the maps provided in this guidebook to help you locate restaurants, hotels, and attractions. Listings in this guide are categorized by area to help you find them more efficiently.

STREET MAPS The International Visitors Information Center (see "Tourist Information" above) distributes an excellent map for free. Even more comprehensive maps are the foldout accordion types that are sold in gas stations and in pharmacies all around town.

Neighborhoods in Brief

Downtown San Diego's shopping, dining, and entertainment heart includes Horton Plaza, the Gaslamp Quarter, the Embarcadero (waterfront), and Seaport Village. There are several major hotels here, as well as a new convention center, the port, and some tourist attractions.

Old Town As its name implies, this area was the city's first commercial center and is now primarily a tourist attraction. It encompasses the Old Town State Historic Park, Presidio Park, Heritage Park, and numerous museums harking back to the turn of the century and the city's beginnings.

Hillcrest/Balboa Park A residential area with little cafes and shops adjacent to Balboa Park, the city's largest green space, famous for the San Diego Zoo and numerous museums.

Mission Bay The most colorful part of the city is this beautiful beach area located north of downtown. In addition to myriad outdoor activities, Mission Bay encompasses several attractions, including Sea World, and is known for its lively nightlife.

Coronado Tour leaders like to tell you that more retired admirals live here than anywhere else in the country. In this primarily residential neighborhood, real estate is expensive, but homes are not particularly impressive. Coronado is a peninsula, surrounded by water on three sides. It has one of the cleanest beaches in California,

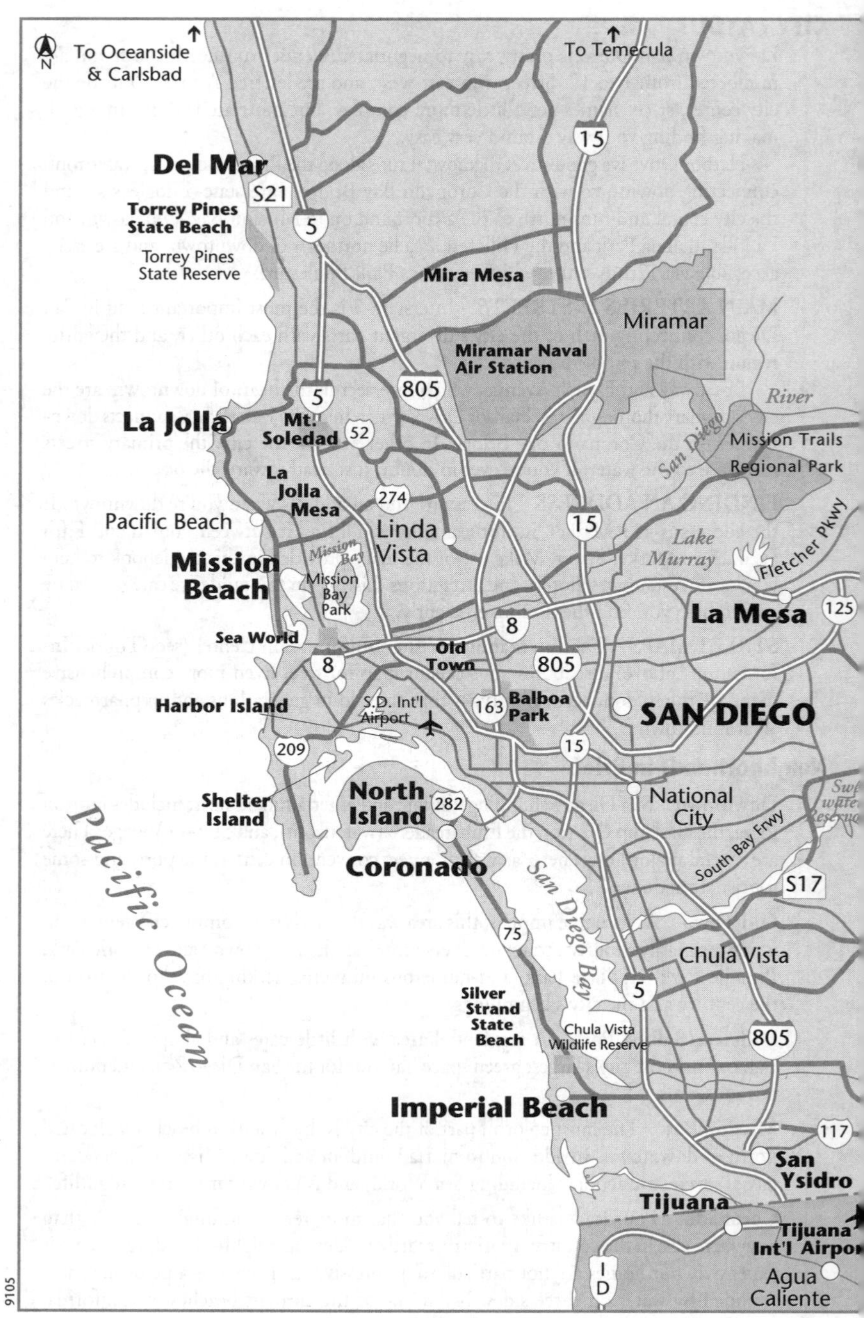

N
To Oceanside
& Carlsbad
To Temecula
15
Del Mar
S21
Torrey Pines
State Beach
Torrey Pines
State Reserve
5
Mira Mesa
Miramar
Miramar Naval
Air Station
5
805
River
La Jolla
Mt.
Soledad
52
San Diego
Mission Trails
Regional Park
La
Jolla
Mesa
274
Pacific Beach
Linda
Vista
15
Lake
Murray
Fletcher Pkwy
Mission
Beach
Mission
Bay
Mission
Bay
Park
La Mesa
125
8
Sea World
Old
Town
805
8
Harbor Island
S.D. Int'l
Airport
163
Balboa
Park
SAN DIEGO
209
15
National
City
Shelter
Island
North
Island
282
South Bay Frwy
Pacific Ocean
Coronado
San Diego Bay
S17
75
Chula Vista
5
Silver
Strand
State
Beach
Chula Vista
Wildlife Reserve
805
Imperial Beach
117
San
Ysidro
Tijuana
Tijuana
Int'l Airpor
I
D
Agua
Caliente

9105

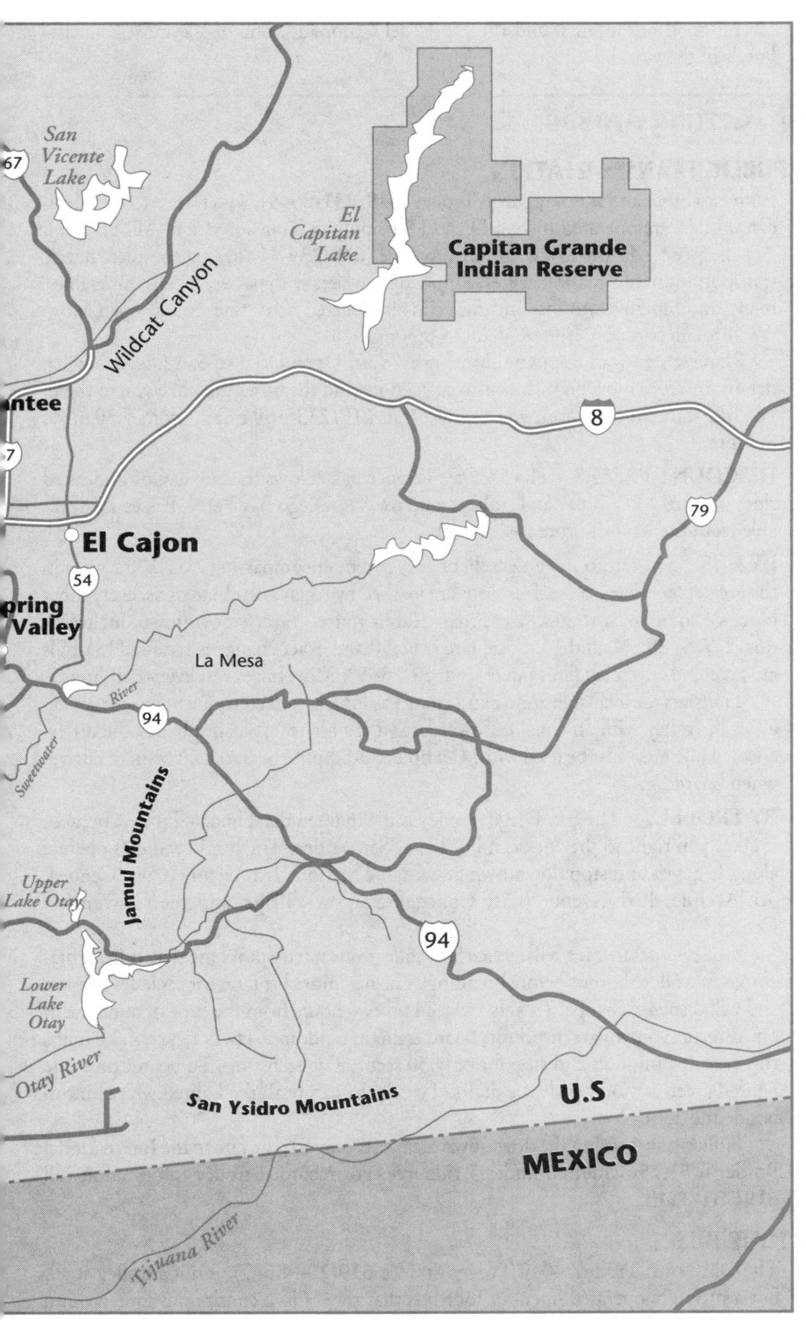

San Vicente Lake
67
El Capitan Lake
Capitan Grande Indian Reserve
Wildcat Canyon
antee
8
79
El Cajon
54
pring Valley
La Mesa
River
94
Sweetwater
Jamul Mountains
Upper Lake Otay
Lower Lake Otay
Otay River
San Ysidro Mountains
U.S
MEXICO
Tijuana River

several good restaurants, and the Hotel del Coronado, one of the most beautiful hotels in the world.

2 Getting Around

BY PUBLIC TRANSPORTATION

Both city buses and the San Diego Trolley (**619/231-8549**), which runs to the Mexican border, are operated by San Diego Metropolitan Transit System (MTS). Their Transit Store, 449 Broadway, at Fifth Avenue (**619/234-1060**), is a complete public transportation information center, supplying travelers with passes, tokens, timetables, maps, and brochures. A lost-and-found is also located here. The store is open Monday through Saturday from 8:30am to 5:30pm.

Request a copy of the useful brochure, "Your Open Door to San Diego," which details the city's most popular tourist attractions and the buses that take you to them. For bus route information, you can also call **619/233-3004** daily from 5:30am to 8:30pm.

DISCOUNT PASSES The $5 Day Tripper pass allows for one day of unlimited rides on local MTS buses and trolleys, and the San Diego Bay Ferry. Passes are available from the Transit Store (see above).

BY BUS San Diego has an excellent bus system encompassing over 100 routes in the greater San Diego Area. Bus stops are marked by rectangular blue signs, every other block or so on local routes. More than 20 bus routes traverse downtown, including nos. 2, 7, 9, 29, 34, and 35. Local fare is $1.50 and exact change is required ($1 bills are accepted). Express fares range from $1.75–$3. Most buses run every half hour.

Transfers are available at no extra charge as long as you continue your journey on a bus or trolley with an equal or lower fare (if it's higher, you simply pay the difference). Transfers must be used within an hour, and should be obtained from the driver when boarding.

BY TROLLEY The San Diego Trolley is nicknamed the Tijuana Trolley, because it takes you right to the Mexican border, at San Ysidro. The bright red cars operate along C Street and stop downtown at Santa Fe Station, 3rd Avenue (Civic Center), 5th Avenue, 12th Avenue (City College), Seaport Village, and the Convention Center.

Trolleys operate on a self-service fare-collection system; purchase tickets from machines in trolley stations before boarding. The machines list fares for each destination and will dispense change. Tickets are valid for two hours from the time of purchase in one direction only. Fare inspectors board trains at random to check tickets. The trains run every 15 minutes and stop for only 30 seconds at each stop. To board, push the lighted green button beside the doors. To exit the car, push the lighted white button beside the doors.

Trolley travel within the downtown area costs only $1; the fare to the International Border is $1.75. Children under 5 ride free. For recorded trolley information call **619/231-8549.**

BY TOUR BUS

The Old Town Trolley, 4040 Twiggs St. (☎ **619/298-8687**), is not a trolley at all, but a privately operated open-air tour bus that travels in a continuous loop around the city, stopping at tourist highlights. It's really designed for sightseeing, but the Old Town Trolley is actually a terrific and economical transportation vehicle.

The trolley stops at eight places around the city and you can hop on and off as many times as you please during one entire loop. A nonstop tour takes two hours. On the way, riders are treated to a live, fast-moving commentary on city history and sights. The trolley originates at the Old Town State Park, then goes to the Cruise Ship Terminal, Seaport Village, the Marriott Marinal Convention Center, Hotel del Coronado, the San Diego Zoo, and two stops at Balboa Park—at the Aero Space Museum and El Prado. Tours operate daily from 9am to dusk and cost $16 for adults, $7 for children ages 6 to 12 years; under 5 ride free.

BY TAXI

Five companies serve the San Diego area. They do not have standardized rates, except from the airport into town, which costs $1.50 per mile. Taxis may be hailed in the street, or phoned for a guaranteed pick-up. If you are at a hotel or restaurant, the front-desk attendant or maitre d' will call one for you. Taxi companies include **Orange Cab** (**619/291-3333**), **Coast Cab** (**619/226-TAXI**), and **Coronado Cab Company** (**619/435-6211**).

BY CAR

Although it is possible to tour the city without your own vehicle, San Diego is best navigated by car. Although streets tend to run one way, which may hamper you until you learn the lay of the land, in general, the city is pretty easy to negotiate.

RENTALS Most of the large, national car-rental firms have rental outlets at the airport and in the major hotels. Compare prices and services. The only car-rental company that will allow its cars into Mexico is **Courtesy Auto Rentals** (☎ **619/497-4800**, or toll free **800/285-2128**). Their cars may legally be driven as far as Ensenada, several hours south. See "Getting Around" in Chapter 2 for further information and toll-free telephone numbers.

PARKING For the most part you will find plenty of metered parking on streets throughout the city. Things tighten up somewhat downtown, where you will probably have to put your car in an enclosed garage. The garage at Horton Plaza, at G Street and Fourth Avenue, is free to shoppers for the first three hours, then costs $1 for each additional hour, it's free daily after 5pm. The parking lot at G Street and Sixth Avenue charges $3.25 for the day and $3 at night and on weekends and holidays.

DRIVING RULES You may turn right at a red light (unless otherwise indicated), after yielding to traffic and pedestrians, and making a complete stop. Pedestrians always have the right-of-way at intersections and crosswalks. Pay attention to signs and arrows on the streets and roadways or you may find that you're in a lane that requires exiting or turning when you wanted to go straight. What's more, San Diego's profusion of one-way streets can create a few small difficulties, but most road maps of the city indicate which way traffic flows.

Fast Facts: San Diego

American Express A convenient downtown office is located at 258 Broadway (**619/234-4455**). It's open Monday through Friday from 9am to 5pm.

Area Code The area code for all of San Diego County is **619.**

LEGEND

Express Routes

San Diego Trolley

San Diego Transit (Routes 20-150)

Rush Hours Service Only, Consult Timetable

County Transit Express Routes (800-820)

Local Routes

San Diego Transit (Routes 1-115), North County Transit (Routes 301-388), National City Transit (Routes 601-604), Chula Vista Transit (Routes 701-708), County Transit System (Routes 843-864) and contract service (Routes 901 and 932)

Infrequent Local Service

Other Map Symbols

3 Route Designation

7B Route Terminal

Trolley Station

Major Transit Point

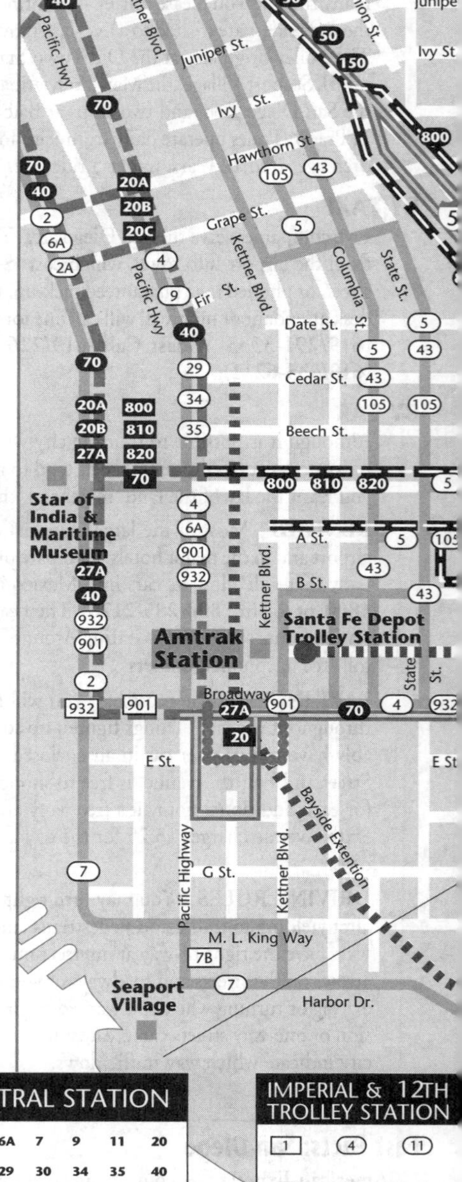

CENTRAL STATION

2	6A	7	9	11	20
27A	29	30	34	35	40
43	50	70	150	901	932

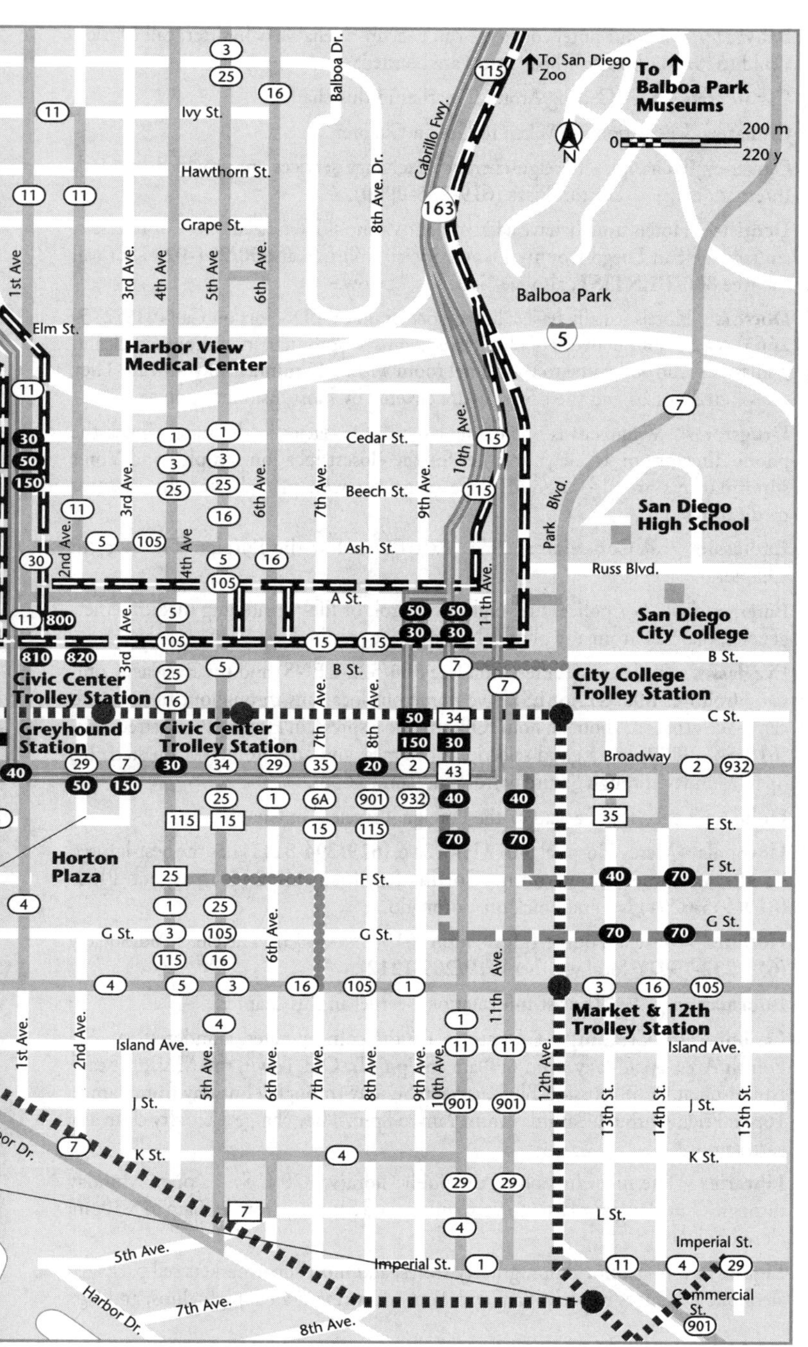

San Diego Bus Routes

Babysitters If your hotel concierge can't secure a reliable babysitter, call Marion Child (**619/582-5029**), whose sitters are bonded.

Car Rentals See "Getting Around," earlier in this chapter.

Climate See Section 2, "When to Go" in Chapter 2.

Currency Exchange Foreign-currency exchange services are provided by Deak International, 177 Horton Plaza (**619/235-0900**).

Dentists Hotels usually have a list of dentists should you need one. For referrals, contact the San Diego County Dental Society toll free at **800/201-0244,** or call toll free **800/DENTIST**; also see "Doctors," below.

Doctors Hotels usually have a list of doctors on call. Doctors on Call (**619/275-2663**) is a 24-hour network of physicians, dentists, optometrists, chiropractors, and podiatrists who will come to your hotel room within 45 minutes of your call. They accept credit cards and their services are covered by most insurance policies.

Drugstores Walgreens is one of the largest pharmacies in the state. Check the phone directory or ask at your hotel for the closest location. Ralph's and Von's supermarkets are also a good place to go for well-priced over-the-counter medications.

Embassies and Consulates See "Fast Facts: For the Foreign Traveler" in Chapter 3.

Emergencies For police, fire, highway patrol, or life-threatening medical emergencies, dial **911** from any phone. No coins are required.

Eyeglasses Both LensCrafters (toll free **800/522-LENS**) and the Eyeglass Company (toll free **800/GLASSES**) have numerous locations throughout the city and can make glasses in about an hour. Optometric Express, in Horton Plaza, street level (**619/544-9000**) has a good selection of frames, and an optometrist on staff. It's open Monday through Saturday from 9:30am to 6pm.

Holidays See "Fast Facts: For the Foreign Traveler" in Chapter 3.

Hospitals Mercy Hospital, 4077 Fifth Ave. (**619/294-8111**) has the best-located downtown emergency room. Coronado Hospital, 250 Prospect Place (**619/435-6251**) is a good pick on Coronado.

Hotlines Mexico Tourist Information (**619/298-4105**); Traveler's Aid Society (**619/232-7991**); local weather (**619/289-1212**).

Information See "Tourist Information," earlier in this chapter.

Laundry/Dry Cleaning Downtown try the coin-operated launderette at 724 Fourth Ave., open daily from 6:30am to 7pm. In Old Town, the Mission Beach Laundromat, 3758 Mission Blvd., is open Sunday through Thursday from 9am to 10pm, Friday through Saturday from 9am to 8pm. They charge $2 to dry clean any garment.

Libraries The main branch of the public library, 820 E St., is open Monday through Thursday from 10am to 9pm, Friday and Saturday from 9:30am to 5:30pm; closed holidays.

Liquor Laws Liquor shops, grocery stores, and most supermarkets sell packaged alcoholic beverages between 6am and 2am. Most restaurants, nightclubs, and bars are licensed to serve alcoholic beverages during the same hours. The legal age for purchase and consumption is 21, and proof of age is required.

Lost Property If you lost it on a bus or trolley, call San Diego Transit Lost and Found at **619/234-1060** or visit the Transit Store, 449 Broadway. If you lost it on an airplane, phone the airline directly.

Luggage Storage/Lockers Most area hotels will store baggage on a short-term basis at no charge. There are no luggage lockers at the airport, but you can find coin-operated facilities at the central bus station, on Broadway between First and Front Streets. They cost $1 for 24 hours.

Newspapers/Magazines *San Diego Union,* the city's largest daily is distributed each morning. Its Friday entertainment section is especially handy for the comprehensive listings. *San Diego Tribune* is published Monday through Saturday and is distributed county-wide in the afternoon. The best paper for events, listings, and advertisements, is the free weekly *Reader,* distributed each Thursday. It's available from cafes, clothing stores, and sidewalk racks all around town. *San Diego* magazine is an upscale glossy monthly filled with entertainment and dining listings. *San Diego This Week* is a tourist-oriented weekly filled with events listings and advertisements. It's available from hotels and tourist offices.

Photographic Needs You can buy film in most drugstores and supermarkets. Nelson Photo Supplies, 1909 India St. (**619/234-6621**), offers one-hour photo processing, repairs cameras, and sells supplies. It's open Monday through Friday from 8:30am to 5:30pm, Saturday 8:30am to 5pm.

Police In an emergency, dial 911 from any phone. No coins are needed. For other matters, contact the downtown precinct, 1401 Broadway (**619/531-2065**).

Post Office The main post office, 2535 Midway Dr., San Diego, CA 92110 (☎ toll free **800/333-8777**), is located near the Sports Arena and Sea World. Letters addressed to you and marked "General Delivery" can be picked up here. It is open to 1am Monday through Friday. Local branches are located all around town. A conveniently located downtown branch is at 815 E St., and open Monday through Friday from 8:30am to 5pm, on Saturday from 8:30am to noon.

Radio FM radio stations include 98.1 (KIFM) for jazz; 89.5 (KPBS) for NPR news and classical music; 94.1 (KFSD), classical; 97.3 (KSON), country; 105.3 (KCBQ), oldies; and 106.5 (KKLQ), Top 40. AM stations include 600 (KKLQ), Top 40; 690 (XTRA), ABC news and sports; 760 (KFMB) CBS news, music, and sports; and 1240 (KSON), country.

Religious Services Your hotel concierge or the Yellow Pages of the telephone book are the best sources for sorting out the plethora of churches and synagogues in San Diego. The San Diego Ecumenical Conference (**619/296-4557**) also keeps a list of county houses of worship. Catholic masses are held daily in the chapel of the historic Mission Basilica San Diego de Alcala, 10818 San Diego Mission Rd. Sunday masses are held on the hour from 7am to noon and again at 5:30pm; on weekdays they are at 7am and 5:30pm, on Saturday at 5:30pm.

Restrooms Stores rarely let customers use the restrooms, and many restaurants offer their facilities for customers only. But most malls, including Horton Plaza and Seaport Village, have bathrooms, as do the ubiquitous fast-food restaurants. Many public beaches and large parks provide toilets, though in some places you have to pay or tip an attendant. If you have the time to find one, pull into a large hotel. Most have well-stocked, clean restrooms in their lobbies.

Safety Innocent tourists are rarely the victims of violent crime. Still, you should use your common sense and avoid deserted streets and dark passageways. Use particular caution downtown late at night. In Balboa Park, stay on designated walkways and away from secluded areas.

Shoe Repairs Computerized Cobbler, in Horton Plaza, First and F Avenues (**619/231-3736**), will fix your shoes, boots, handbags, and other leather goods while you wait. American Shoe Repairing, 421 Broadway (**619/233-8776**), is another good pick downtown. It's open Monday through Friday from 8:30am to 5:30pm, Saturday from 9am to 5pm.

Taxes An 8¼% sales tax is added on at the register for all goods and services purchased in San Diego. The city hotel tax is 10%. No additional airport tax is charged to international travelers.

Taxis See "Getting Around," in this chapter.

Telegrams/Telex The Western Union office at 4351 University Ave. (**619/283-2020**), can send and receive telegrams and telexes worldwide. It is open daily 6am to midnight.

Transit Information Public transportation is operated by San Diego Regional Transit (**619/233-3004**). See "Getting Around" in this chapter for complete information.

Useful Telephone Numbers Time (**619/853-1212**); local highway conditions (toll free **800/427-7623**).

Weather For local weather information and beach weather and surf reports call **619/289-1212.**

3 Accommodations

San Diego's wide variety of accommodations appeals to every traveler's taste and pocketbook. There are always special rates for business travelers, and special packages are often available that represent significant savings.

Reservations are a good idea, especially on weekends or holidays. Price categories are arranged as follows, on a double-occupancy basis: expensive, over $140; moderate, $80 to $140; and budget, under $80.

Rates quoted below do not include the 10% hotel tax.

Downtown

EXPENSIVE

Hyatt Regency San Diego, 1 Market Place, San Diego, CA 92101.
☎ **619/232-1234,** or toll free **800/233-1234.** Fax 619/239-5678. 819 rms, 56 suites. A/C TV TEL MINIBAR

Rates: $149–$245 single or double; from $325 suite. Additional person $25. AE, CB, DC, MC, V.

Opened in December 1992, the brand-new Hyatt Regency enjoys a terrific location on San Diego Bay, within walking distance of the Gaslamp District, Seaport Village shops, and the convention center. The architecturally impressive, slender 40-story hotel features a three-story lobby of green marble and Italian limestone, enlivened by oversized floral arrangements and even larger oil paintings by San Diego artist Richard Garland Chase. Three floors of meeting space attract hordes of badge-wearing conventioneers (in my estimation, one of the hotel's few low points for independent guests).

While the rooms themselves are not spectacular, they conform to a very high standard. All are dressed with floral chintz bedspreads, a comfortable plaid armchair, 18th-century-style English furniture, and impressionist-style oil paintings. Each room is equipped with two telephones, dataports, a minibar, a full-length mirror, and cable TV with dozens of movies available on demand. Every room also enjoys a view of San Diego Bay. Spacious two-bedroom suites are located on the top floors and feature walk-in closets, whirlpool tubs, minikitchens, and wet bars. Fifty percent of all rooms are located on nonsmoking floors. The most expensive rooms are on the Regency Club floor, where rent includes the services of a private concierge and access to a private lounge that provides complimentary breakfast, beverage services, and hors d'oeuvres.

Dining/Entertainment: Sally's, an upscale seafood restaurant, is good enough to attract locals as well as guests. By special arrangement with the manager, you and nine of your closest friends can enjoy a really special meal at a table located inside the restaurant's kitchen. The less expensive and less formal Lael's is open for breakfast, lunch, and dinner and serves Mediterranean and American foods. Worthington's, a lobby lounge, serves drinks and light snacks. The clublike Top of the Hyatt serves drinks with a terrific 40th-floor view.

Services: 24-hour room service, concierge, laundry, shoeshine.

Facilities: Four tennis courts, outdoor swimming pool, whirlpool, health club, spa.

The Westgate Hotel, 1055 Second Ave., San Diego, CA 92101. ☎ **619/238-1818,** or toll free **800/221-3802.** Fax 619/557-3604. 223 rms, 11 suites. A/C MINIBAR TV TEL **Directions:** The hotel is located between Broadway and C Street; from I-5 south, take the Front Street/Civic Center exit, bear right and remain on Front Street, then make a wide left turn on C Street (crossing the trolley tracks); go 2 blocks to Second Avenue; the parking garage is straight ahead.

Rates: $144–$164 single; $154–$174 double; from $295 suite. Additional person $10. Children under 18 stay free in parents' room. AE, CB, DC, DISC, MC, V.

The Westgate is a luxury hostelry of the first order. The tone is obvious as soon as you set foot in the posh lobby, hung with Aubusson and Beauvais tapestries and furnished in priceless antiques. The pattern of the parquet floors is copied from that at Fontainebleau. Among the many fine works of art that hang in the lobby, *The Prodigal Son* by Velázquez is valued at half a million dollars.

Each of the spacious guest rooms is uniquely furnished, although the basic decor combines elements of the Louis XV, Louis XVI, Georgian, and English Regency periods. All rooms have a phone and scale in the bath. Many have speaker phones, private dressing areas, bathrobes, and hairdryers. The color TV is discreetly hidden in an elegant cabinet.

Dining/Entertainment: Le Fontainebleau, the Westgate's award-winning restaurant, is one of the most elegant dining rooms built in this century. The Westgate Dining Room is more casual and serves traditional American fare. The intimate Plaza Lounge is a local gathering spot for many of San Diego's most talented performers.

Services: 24-hour room service, concierge, evening turndown, complimentary airport, zoo, and Sea World transportation.

Facilities: Fitness center, barbershop, gift shop.

Mission Bay/Pacific Beach

EXPENSIVE

 **Catamaran,** 3999 Mission Blvd., San Diego, CA 92109. ☎ **619/488-1081,** or toll free **800/288-0770, 800/233-8172** in Canada. Fax 619/490-3328. 315 rms. No-smoking rooms available. A/C TV TEL **Directions:** From downtown San Diego, take I-5 north to the Grand and Garnet exit, turn left onto Grand Avenue at the first stoplight, then after three miles, turn left onto Mission Boulevard; the hotel is two blocks down on your left.

Rates: $120–$225 single or double. AE, DISC, MC, V. **Parking:** $4.

The Catamaran is beautifully situated on Mission Bay, just a scenic, few minutes' walk from the ocean. Looking like something out of Polynesia, the tropical-style hotel sports a 15-foot waterfall, full-size dugout canoe, colorful fish, and island artifacts in the large atrium lobby.

Each of the guest rooms, located in one 13-story building and six two-story bungalows, is decorated in soft tropical colors and has one king-size bed or two double beds. Each has a balcony or patio. Tower rooms have commanding views of the entire bay, the city skyline, La Jolla, and Point Loma. The hotel is popular at night with the bay crowd, and is within walking distance of many fine restaurants and nightspots.

Dining/Entertainment: The Atoll Restaurant serves light fare, along with a regular dinner menu that includes fresh fish, and grilled meats. The large, lively Cannibal Bar has bands and videos; there is a $4 cover for nonguests. Moray's, its counterpoint, is an intimate, crowded piano bar.

Services: Room service, concierge, evening turndown.

Facilities: Outdoor heated swimming pool, Jacuzzi, exercise room, water sports concessions.

San Diego Princess, 1404 West Vacation Rd., San Diego, CA 92109. ☎ **619/274-4630,** or toll free **800/344-2626.** Fax 619/581-5929. 462 rms, 103 suites. A/C TV TEL **Directions:** From downtown San Diego, take I-5 to Sea World Drive; pass the main entrance to Sea World, then turn right onto Ingraham Street; turn left at the second traffic light onto West Vacation Road, the resort entrance.

Rates: $130–$195 single or double; from $215 suite. AE, DC, DISC, MC, V. **Parking:** Free.

Owned by Princess Cruises, this exclusive resort spreads across 44 lushly landscaped tropical acres, including freshwater lagoons spanned by graceful bridges.

Every whim is catered to in modern rooms fitted with king-size beds, refrigerators, coffee makers, and patios. There are no stairs in the entire resort—everything is at ground level.

Dining/Entertainment: Continental dining with bay views is available at the Dockside Restaurant. The Barefoot Bar & Grill has a yacht club style atmosphere and features appetizers, salads, sandwiches, and pizza, and offers live evening and weekend entertainment. The Village Café offers casual breakfasts, lunches, and dinners.

Services: Room service, concierge, massage, bicycle and surrey cycle rentals, paddleboat.

Facilities: Five swimming pools, six tennis courts, fitness center, gift shop, sailboat marina, putting green, bicycle rental outlet.

MODERATE

The Beach Cottages, 4255 Ocean Blvd., San Diego, CA 92109. ☎ **619/483-7440.** Fax 619/273-9365. 28 rms, 3 suites, 12 studios, 18 apts, 17 cottages. TV TEL

Rates: May 14–June and Sept 7–Oct 3 $70–$85 single or double; $115–$155 apt and cottage; $85 studio; from $200 suite. July–Sept 6 $90–$110 single or double; $115–$163 apts and cottage; $75 studio; from $220 suite. Oct 4–May 13 $55–$75 single or double; $95–$135 apt and cottage; $85 studio, from $175 suite. Weekly rates available. AE, CB, DC, DISC, MC, V.

Lively, fun, and slightly noisy, the thoroughly enjoyable Beach Cottages are particularly suited for young couples and families who want to stay directly on the beach in Pacific Beach, San Diego's young, offbeat, beach haven. The hotel is within walking distance of shops and restaurants and has barbecue grills, shuffleboard courts, and Ping-Pong tables that actually get a lot of use.

In addition to regular motel rooms, the hotel offers cottages, apartments, studios, and suites. All accommodations except the motel rooms have a fully equipped kitchen. Cottages, which are literally sandside, contain either one or two bedrooms and sleep up to six; each cottage has a private patio. Apartments are nicer, outfitted with more contemporary interiors, but they are a bit farther from the waves. Studios, furnished with two queen-size beds, lack an additional sitting room. Suites, the newest additions to the property, are clean and contemporary, dressed condo-style with comfortable, durable furnishings.

To make a reservation, call between 9am and 9pm, when the office is open.

The Crystal Pier House, 4500 Ocean Blvd., San Diego, CA 92109. ☎ **619/483-6983,** or toll free **800/748-5894.** Fax 619/483-6811. 18 rms, 6 suites. TV TEL

Rates: June 15–Sept 15 $140 bungalow, $165–$180 suite; the rest of the year $85–$125 bungalow, $150–$180 suite.

One of the most unusual accommodations in San Diego, the Crystal Pier House occupies its own private pier, which juts into the Pacific Ocean in the center of Pacific Beach. The hotel is one of the area's oldest. Most of the rooms are quite similar to the way they were on opening day in 1936, outfitted with rattan furnishings, wooden shutters, vaulted ceilings, and large windows that gulp in vast stretches of ocean and beach. Suites are newer and crisper, but not necessarily better. Every accommodation comes with a fully equipped kitchenette, a separate bedroom and living room, and a private deck.

To make a reservation, call between 8am and 8pm, when the office is open.

Ocean Park Inn, 710 Grand Ave., San Diego, CA 92109. ☎ **619/483-5858,** or toll free **800/231-7735.** Fax 619/274-0823. 73 rms, 4 suites. TV TEL

Rates (including continental breakfast): May 30–Sept 6 $100–$145 single or double; from $130 suite. The rest of the year $80–$125 single or double; from $110 suite. Additional person $10. AE, DISC, MC, V.

Located directly on Pacific Beach's lively, circuslike beach path, this three-story sandfront standout is visually appealing both inside and out. Behind the hotel's modern Spanish-Mediterranean facade is a sharply designed marble lobby that gives way to 77 less splendid but completely comfortable guest rooms.

Accommodations are of the Hilton-meets-Motel-6 type—contemporary and with a thoroughly no-nonsense business quality. Every room has firm beds, good lighting, a table and chairs, a refrigerator, a clock radio, a direct-dial telephone, and lifeless motel art. The most expensive rooms have an oceanfront balcony. Suites are extra large and have a Roman tub; some also have a kitchenette. Hotel facilities include a sun deck, a heated swimming pool, an outdoor Jacuzzi, vending machines, and a coin laundry.

Surfer Motor Lodge, 711 Pacific Beach Dr., San Diego, CA 92109.
☎ **619/483-7070.** 52 rms. TV TEL **Directions:** From downtown San Diego, take I-5 to the Grand/Garnet exit, follow Grand Avenue, turn left onto Mission Boulevard, then right onto Pacific Beach Drive to the hotel.

Rates: Summer, $76–$90 single or double; winter, $65–$115 single or double. Weekly rates offered during winter. AE, DC, MC, V.

Practically situated close to shopping and dining, the lodge has a heated outdoor swimming pool. Almost all of the rooms have balconies and ocean views, and are cooled by ocean breezes. Fans are also available. The hotel can arrange fishing and golf outings.

BUDGET

Banana Bungalow, 707 Reed Ave., Mission Beach, San Diego, CA 92109.
☎ **619/273-3060,** or toll free **800/5-HOSTEL.** 71 beds.

Rates: $11–$15 per night in multi-bed room. MC, V. **Parking:** Free.

Banana Bungalow is the most fun place to stay in all of San Diego. The only hostel in California located directly on the beach, the Bungalow is always packed with international guests who always seem to be looking for a good time. The hostel offers free airport pick-up, and regular excursions to Tijuana. There are six or eight beds per room.

Mission Valley/Hotel Circle

Mission Valley is the most centrally located resort area in San Diego. Around its Hotel Circle are many restaurants, motels, hotels, and the largest shopping complex in the country, Fashion Valley Center.

From I-5, exit to I-8 east and take the Hotel Circle exit. Cross under the freeway to reach the hotels.

MODERATE

Hanalei Hotel, 2270 Hotel Circle, San Diego, CA 92108. ☎ **619/297-1101,** or toll free **800/882-0858.** Fax 619/297-6049. 450 rms. No-smoking rooms available. A/C TV TEL

Rates: $120–$150 single or double. AE, DC, DISC, MC, V. **Parking:** Free.

Under the same ownership as Town & Country, the Hanalei Hotel is best known for its eight-story open atrium complete with waterfalls and ponds. Glass elevators offer good views on the way up to the rooms, which are plushly furnished and excessively comfortable. Facilities include a large swimming pool and Jacuzzi, and a fun restaurant, Polynesian Islands Dining Room. A nearby health club is available to guests for a nominal fee.

Frommer's Smart Traveler: Hotels

Value-Conscious Travelers Should Take Advantage of the Following:

1. Off-season rates. While few downtown hotels lower their prices during the winter, beachside resorts often offer special deals to woo guests.
2. Complimentary shuttle service to the airport and area attractions; many hotels offer it.
3. Accommodations with kitchen facilities; they help keep costs down.

Questions to Ask If You're on a Budget:

1. Is the hotel tax included in the price?
2. Is there a surcharge for local telephone usage?
3. Is there a charge for parking? Rates can be as high as $15 per night in San Diego.

Town & Country, 500 Hotel Circle North, San Diego, CA 92108. ☎ **619/291-7131,** or toll free **800/854-2608, 800/542-6082** in California. Fax 619/291-3584. 960 rms. No-smoking rooms available. A/C MINIBAR TV TEL

Rates: $75–$110 single; $87–$125 double; from $195 suite. AE, MC, V. **Parking:** $5.

Town & Country, with over 1,000 rooms, is one of the largest hotels in San Diego. Every facility you could want or imagine exists within this "city within a city," including a gas station. There are shops, car-rental offices, airline and tour information desks, shuttle service to the airport and shopping, four swimming pools (one Olympic size), a sauna, four restaurants, two coffee shops, and two nightclubs.

Rooms are pleasantly decorated and outfitted with comfortable furnishings, large marble baths, in-room minibars, and other deluxe conveniences.

Dining/Entertainment: The Gourmet Room features giant portions of prime rib; Kelly's Steak House is also a meatery. Café Potpourri serves lighter fare for breakfast, lunch, and dinner. Crystal T's Live nightclub and Kelly's piano bar are nightspots at opposite ends of the spectrum. Abilene Country Saloon and Le Pavilion Lounge both present bands.

Services: Room service, concierge, evening turndown, morning newspaper delivery, tour desk, business center, car rental.

Facilities: Four swimming pools, two nightclubs, access to off-site health club.

BUDGET

Fabulous Inn, 2485 Hotel Circle Place, San Diego, CA 92108. ☎ **619/291-7700,** or toll free **800/647-1903.** Fax 619/297-6179. 175 rms. No-smoking rooms available. A/C TV TEL

Rates (including continental breakfast): $60–$65 single; $65–$75 double. AE, CB, DC, DISC, MC, V. **Parking:** Free.

This well-priced, modern four-story complex at the extreme western end of the Hotel Circle looks rather like a high-rise motel, complete with box-like balconies and a small free-form swimming pool. All rooms are large and attractively furnished. They have king- or queen-size beds, and baths with dressing areas; some have refrigerators. A heated outdoor swimming pool and Jacuzzi are on the premises, and a restaurant adjoins. There are good tennis facilities just across the street, as well as an 11-hole golf course (that's what I said, 11 holes).

Higher priced rooms have whirlpool bathtubs, individual refrigerators, and mini color TVs in the bath.

Motel 6, 2424 Hotel Circle North, San Diego, CA 92108. ☎ **619/296-1612.** 92 rms. No-smoking rooms available. A/C TV TEL

Rates: $38 single, $44 double. Extra person $6. AE, CB, DC, DISC, MC, V. **Parking:** Free.

As with all Motel 6 locations, rooms are efficient, clean, and comfortable, and there's a small pool on the premises. There is no charge for local calls.

Harbor Island & Shelter Island

These two artificial peninsulas—just minutes from the airport and downtown—are a hub of San Diego hotel, nightlife, and restaurant activity.

EXPENSIVE

Sheraton Harbor Island East, 1380 Harbor Island Dr., San Diego, CA 92113. ☎ **619/291-2900,** or toll free **800/325-3535.** Fax 619/296-5297. 1,005 rms, 45 suites. No-smoking rooms available. A/C MINIBAR TV TEL

Rates: $180–$225 single or double, suites from $250. AE, CB, DC, DISC, MC, V. **Parking:** $8 self, $11 valet.

The Sheraton Harbor Island East is actually one of two hotels that make up the Sheraton on Harbor Island. Together the properties boast a total of 1,050 handsomely furnished rooms with one king-size bed or two double beds. All rooms have balconies and most have marine views.

The combined facilities are extensive: health club, five pools (two for kids), saunas, whirlpools, four night-lit tennis courts, jogging course, boat and bike rental, shops, and launderette. At the Sheraton Harbor Island East, there are a variety of dining choices, too: Merlano's, an Italian restaurant; Café del Sol, the hotel's coffee shop; Spencer's, which serves specially prepared steaks and seafood; and, finally, Joe's Deli, which offers sandwiches and salads to go. There's also Telly's, a sports bar, and the poolside Island Bar.

MODERATE

Humphrey's Half Moon Inn, 2303 Shelter Island Dr., San Diego, CA 92106. ☎ **619/224-3411,** or toll free **800/542-7400.** Fax 619/224-3478. 182 rms, 54 suites. A/C TV TEL

Rates: $75–$140 single; $85–$150 double; from $110 suite. Children under 12 stay free in parents' room. AE, MC, V. **Parking:** Free.

Humphrey's Half Moon Inn is a favorite accommodation not just on Shelter Island but in all of San Diego. Its rooms, set amid lush tropical plantings, all have water views. Not only are the views lovely, but the interior of each room is very attractive, with beamed pine ceilings (especially nice on upper floors where ceilings are sloped), bamboo and rattan furnishings, and blue seashell-motif bedspreads. Amenities include double sinks and makeup lights in the bath. Also included are free in-room coffee, refrigerators, 24-hour switchboard, complimentary movie channel, and free transportation to the airport or the Amtrak station. As for facilities, there are heated pools for adults and children, a spa, table tennis, bicycles, and room for lawn games.

The adjacent restaurant, Humphrey's, has a very delightful garden decor and large windows providing views of the boat-filled marina. You can dine outdoors under white umbrellaed tables or inside where there's an abundance of plants and potted palms. Seafood is the specialty here. Humphrey's *Casablanca*-style lounge is also the setting for nightly entertainment, and a pianist plays during happy hour.

From June through October the hotel helps sponsor great jazz concerts with top-name performers in the park by the bay.

Coronado

EXPENSIVE

Hotel del Coronado, 1500 Orange Ave., San Diego, CA 92118. ☎ **619/522-8000,** or toll free **800/468-3533.** Fax 619/522-8262. 691 rms, 51 suites. No-smoking rooms available. A/C MINIBAR TV TEL

Rates: $154–$199 standard single or double; $220–$385 deluxe double; from $399 suite. AE, CB, DC, DISC, MC, V. **Parking:** $10.

The Hotel del Coronado opened its doors in 1888 and was designated a National Historic Landmark in 1977. The last of the extravagantly conceived seaside hotels, it is a monument to Victorian grandeur with its tall cupolas, turrets, and gingerbread trim. The register over the years has listed thousands of celebrity guests—12 U.S. presidents and such movie stars as Tony Curtis, Jack Lemmon, Robert Wagner, and Stefanie Powers.

I can't say enough good things about the Hotel Del. Accommodations are fittingly exquisite, with custom-made furnishings and all conveniences. The hotel also overlooks a beautiful white sand beach and a championship 18-hole golf course.

Dining/Entertainment: The hotel has four dining areas; the majestic Crown/Coronet Rooms, magnificently unchanged since the turn of the century; The Prince of Wales, for gourmet dining; the Del Deli; and the Ocean Terrace Restaurant and Lounge.

Facilities: Two swimming pools, six night-lit championship tennis courts, a health spa for men and women.

Frommer's Cool for Kids: Hotels

Beach Cottages (see p. 527) Kids enjoy the informality and the location near the beach.

Town & Country (see p. 529) Four swimming pools and 1,000 rooms make this a hide-and-seek paradise for older children. The hotel welcomes kids, has a games room, and offers plenty of activities.

Hotel del Coronado (see p. 531) In addition to a beautiful beach and a wonderful picture gallery that kids will enjoy, the hotel offers special supervised children's programs led by experienced counselors.

MODERATE

El Cordova Hotel, 1351 Orange Ave., Coronado, CA 92118. ☎ **619/435-4131,** or toll free **800/367-6467.** Fax 619/435-0632. 40 rms, 18 suites. TV TEL

Rates: Sept 12–June 10 $65–$90 single or double; from $115 suite. June 11–Sept 11 $75–$105 single or double; from $125 suite. AE, CB, DC, DISC, MC, V.

Built in 1902 and converted into a hotel in 1930, this pretty, salmon-colored, Spanish Mediterranean–style low-rise, represents one of the best buys in Coronado. Located across a busy street from the beachfront Hotel del Coronado, El Cordova is outfitted with Native American and Mexican furnishings that befit its historic interior.

Each room is slightly different from the next and, while not fancy, is nicely decorated with dusty earth tones and brightly tiled baths. Suites offer a separate living room and a small kitchenette.

Glorietta Bay Inn, 1630 Glorietta Blvd., Coronado, CA 92118. ☎ **619/435-3101,** or toll free **800/283-9383.** Fax 619/435-6182. 98 rms (17 suites). TV TEL **Directions:** From I-5 south, take the Coronado Bay Bridge to Orange Avenue, then turn left onto Glorietta Boulevard to the hotel.

Rates: $94–$130 single or double; from $129 suite. AE, DC, MC, V.

Once the summer mansion of John Spreckels, the 19th century multi-millionaire sugar baron and former owner of the Hotel del Coronado, the Glorietta Bay Inn is located across the street from the Hotel Del. The historic 1908 house, surrounded by lush gardens is beautifully restored with intricate moldings, and a fine brass and marble staircase that leads up to well-appointed rooms. The majority of the inn's accommodations are now located in a far less charming contemporary add-on that features bright furnishings and large windows that overlook Glorietta Bay. Except for a heated swimming pool, services and amenities are few. The hotel's dining room serves continental breakfast only.

BUDGET

El Cordova Hotel, 1351 Orange Ave., Coronado, CA 92118. ☎ **619/435-4131,** or toll free **800/367-6467.** Fax 619/435-0632. 50 rms, (25 suites). TV TEL

Rates: $60–$75 single or double; from $95 suite. AE, CB, DC, DISC, MC, V.

Except for the hotel's service, which is notoriously slow, El Cordova is one of the best budget hotels in San Diego. Both quality and location is far better than the hotel's low prices would lead you to believe, a situation that translates into few vacancies at any time of year.

Built in Spanish Mediterranean style in 1902, and made into a hotel in 1930, El Cordova's best accommodations are the suites built with oak floors and bay windows. Several come with kitchenettes, which like bathrooms and stairways are decorated with handcrafted Mexican designs.

A central courtyard holds a small swimming pool and barbecue. There is a Mexican restaurant and separate steakhouse on the premises. The hotel is located across the street from the Hotel del Coronado.

4 Dining

Expensive

Anthony's Star of the Sea Room, 1360 Harbor Dr. ☎ **619/232-7408.**

Cuisine: SEAFOOD. **Reservations:** Required.
Prices: Appetizers $7–$10; main courses $15–$28. AE, DC, MC, V.
Open: Dinner daily 5:30–10:30pm.

The Ghio and Weber families' Anthony's Star of the Sea Room is next to the three-masted *Star of India.* Dramatically set overlooking the San Diego harbor, the interior of Anthony's is handsomely decorated, elegant, and comfortable. Specialties include the cioppino à la Catherine (Catherine is Anthony Ghio's mother) and oven-baked sole stuffed with lobster, shrimp, and crab.

Tom Ham's Lighthouse, 2150 Harbor Island Dr., Harbor Island. ☎ **619/291-9110.**

Cuisine: AMERICAN. **Reservations:** Accepted.
Prices: Appetizers $5–$13; main courses $15–$34; lunch $7–$14. AE, DC, DISC, MC, V.
Open: Lunch Mon–Fri 11:15am–3:30pm; dinner Mon–Thurs 5–10pm, Fri–Sat 5–11pm, Sun 4–10pm; Sun brunch 10am–2pm.

Tom Ham's Lighthouse is built at the west end of Harbor Island beneath a lighthouse (the official Coast Guard no. 9 beacon). You can get good meals here and you enjoy the museum as well. A collection of marine artifacts has been gathered from around the world, forming a nostalgic reminder of San Diego in the early 1800s. Featured on the dinner menu are specialties such as seafood Newburg, scampi, and scallops tomatillo. A buffet lunch includes an elaborate salad bar and three hot main dishes, in addition to sandwiches, salads, and hot specialties. Be sure to save room for dessert; the apple pie is scrumptious.

Moderate

Café del Rey Moro, 1549 El Prado in Balboa Park. ☎ **619/234-8511.**

Cuisine: SOUTHWESTERN REGIONAL. **Reservations:** Recommended. **Directions:** Enter park at Sixth and Laurel, which becomes El Prado. Cross Cabrillo Bridge; the restaurant building fronts the first large parking plaza, Plaza de Panama.
Prices: Appetizers $4–$6; main courses $8–$15; lunch $5–$10. AE, MC, V.
Open: Lunch Mon–Fri 11am–4pm, Sat 11am–4:30pm; dinner Tues–Fri 4:30–8:30pm, Sat 5–8pm, Sun 4–8:30pm; Sun brunch 10am–3pm.

Located near the San Diego Museum of Art, in the historic House of Hospitality, a San Diego landmark since 1914, is Café Del Rey Moro. Set off from a central court-

Frommer's Smart Traveler: Restaurants

1. Go ethnic. San Diego has some great, inexpensive ethnic dining.
2. Eat your main meal at lunch when prices are lower; you can sample gourmet hot spots for a fraction of the price at dinner.
3. Watch for liquor; it can add greatly to the cost of any meal.
4. Look for fixed-price menus, two-for-one specials, and coupons in local newspapers and magazines.

yard somewhat like a Spanish hacienda—central fountain, small palms, wrought-iron benches—it's a perfect place to sit and relax on a warm summer day. The cafe rests serenely among gardens surrounded by high-flying eucalyptus and palm trees. You can dine outside on a brick terrace with white pillars and vine-covered trellises, overlooking a patio with a small fountain and lush gardens. Inside, the red-tile floors, the wall of glass doors, and greenery hanging from a latticework ceiling convey a sense of the outdoors.

The fare is generally light—fresh fish and seafood simply prepared with local vegetables, herbs, delicate sauces, and a touch of Mexico's spices. The brandy scallops are first-rate, served with oven-fresh sourdough bread for dipping. Among the meat dishes, one of my favorites is the loin of pork adobo—tender filets of pork loin marinated in a sauce of tomatoes, onion, garlic, and spices, then slowly braised. Specialties include brandy scallops and grilled fresh fish. The selection of luncheon main dishes is wide-ranging enough to satisfy any appetite; there are great sandwiches, salads, omelets, munchies, enchiladas, burritos, and soups mother never knew how to make.

Topping off the menu is a luscious list of desserts and exotic coffees. Try the irresistible raspberry-macaroon torte, or if you feel stuffed or righteous, polish off your meal with one of the restaurant's good coffees. Margaritas are always available, as is sangría; Café Del Rey Moro has a well-stocked bar.

Dakota Restaurant, 901 5th Ave. ☎ **619/234-5554.**

Cuisine: AMERICAN. **Reservations:** Recommended.
Prices: Appetizers \$4–\$7; main courses \$8–\$16.
Open: Lunch Mon–Fri 11am–3pm; dinner Sun 5–9pm, Mon–Thurs 5–10pm, Fri–Sat 5–11pm. Bar stays open late on the weekends.

This pretty, bilevel, glass-wrapped Gaslamp District eatery is San Diego's most upscale barbecue restaurant. Its succulent, mesquite-grilled chicken meats, and seafood are not the trendiest foods in the quarter, but they are consistently excellent and very fairly priced, and portions are large. Pizzas, pastas, and salads are also served. The atmosphere is casual but polished, and the service is unpolished but attentive. For good value, Dakota is definitely worth a letter home.

La Strada Restaurant, 705 5th Ave. ☎ **619/239-3400.**

Cuisine: ITALIAN. **Reservations:** Suggested.
Prices: Appetizers \$6–\$9; main courses \$12–\$21.
Open: Lunch Mon–Fri 11:30am–4pm; dinner Mon–Fri 5–midnight, Sat–Sun 5pm–2am.

All see-and-be-seen sizzle, La Strada is the Gaslamp's restaurant of the moment. Who cares if better meals can be had at several places up the street? The single, wide-open dining room offers excellent sightlines, and the food is good enough. Traditional antipasti are followed by competent pastas and simple meat dishes. You may pass on dessert but order a cappuccino—it's a small price to pay to linger.

Budget

Ichiban, 1441 Garnet Ave. ☎ **619/270-5755.**

Cuisine: JAPANESE. **Reservations:** Not accepted.
Prices: Appetizers \$1–\$3; main dishes \$3–\$8. No credit cards.
Open: Lunch Mon–Sat 11:15am–2:30pm; dinner Mon–Sun 5–9:30pm.

Trendy local twenty-somethings have claimed this budget sushi shop as their own, and for good reason. The fish is morning fresh, the service is excellent, and the crowd is always lively. While the decidedly downscale dining room may offend those who dislike black booths and pink tabletops, its uncalculated casualness is clearly one of the restaurant's main attractions.

Diners order at the counter and are then served at a table. In addition to raw fish, Ichiban cooks chicken teriyaki, ginger chicken, mixed fried seafood, vegetable sukiyaki, and fried salmon. Japanese beer and sake are also served.

Café 1134, 1134 Orange Ave., Coronado. No phone.

Cuisine: AMERICAN. **Reservations:** Not accepted.
Prices: $3–$5. No credit cards.
Open: Daily 8am–8pm.

Located at the curve in the road on the way to the Hotel del Coronado, Café 1134 serves the best coffee on the island, along with a small selection of sandwiches, snacks, and pastries. In the mornings, French toast, fruit granola, and stuffed croissants are served. The cafe's contemporary interior features bright wall art and comfortably cushioned wrought-iron bar stools and chairs. Even though there's no view—except of parked cars and a busy street—the outdoor sidewalk seats are highly coveted, especially on sunny Sundays.

La Piñata, 2836 Juan St., Old Town. ☎ **619/297-1631.**

Cuisine: MEXICAN. **Reservations:** Accepted; recommended on weekends.
Prices: Appetizers $3–$6; main courses $4–$11. MC, V.
Open: Sun–Thurs 11am–9pm, Fri–Sat 11am–9:30pm.

La Piñata is a cozy, friendly restaurant with a happy collection of the brightly colored Mexican toys that give it its name (donkeys, parrots, toros, rocket ships, elephants) hanging from the reed ceiling. It's just a bit out of the mainstream of people traffic, which makes it a pleasant alternative to the larger, somewhat noisy tourist emporiums. And it has a small outdoor patio where you can dine even on a coolish day and share your cheese quesadilla with the sparrows.

La Piñata is understandably popular among locals: it's attractive, the food is always good, prices are moderate, and service is pleasant and prompt. The restaurant prepares familiar dishes tastefully, be it fajitas, fajitadillas, tacos, tostados, or any combinations thereof. A compliments-of-the-house cheese quesadilla always precedes your order. The margaritas are delicious, offered in small, medium, or large (the large is about the size of a small bird bath). There's also a good selection of beer.

Frommer's Cool For Kids: Restaurants

La Piñata (see p. 535) A fun restaurant that will keep kids occupied both visually and gastronomically.

Café Del Rey Moro (see p. 533) The southwestern fare served here is unusual, but not too strange, spicy, or hot; good for an adventurous kid.

Tom Ham's Lighthouse (see p. 533) Straightforward American food means seafood and salads, as well as hamburgers and apple pie. Kids will also like the real lighthouse next door.

5 Attractions

San Diego is a city of the outdoors. Its best attraction is the city itself, sprawling across islands, peninsulas, and a vast swath of oceanfront. The streets are made for strolling, and even many of the top attractions are outdoors, including the San Diego Zoo and Sea World.

Suggested Itineraries

If You Have One Day

Start out at the San Diego Zoo, stroll around Balboa Park, and take in as many of the museums as you have time for. In the afternoon, tour Horton Plaza, then head toward the adjacent Gaslamp Quarter for dinner and evening entertainment.

If You Have Two Days

Spend Day One as outlined above. On your second day, visit Sea World or explore the beach areas by day and take in a play or concert by night.

If You Have Three Days

On your third day, visit Coronado, the Old Ferry Landing, and the Hotel del Coronado. Stroll along the beach, and if it's warm enough, you could even go swimming. If you have a car, think about driving out to Point Loma, or drive half an hour north to the Wild Animal Park.

If You Have Five Days

Definitely head north to the beautiful beachside towns of La Jolla and Del Mar. Alternatively, go south to Mexico, and experience life south of the border.

THE TOP ATTRACTIONS

In Balboa Park

Balboa Park. ☎ **619/235-1100.**

Balboa Park, covering approximately 1,200 acres, is one of the nation's largest municipal parks. Planned from its inception, the park encompasses walkways, gardens, historical buildings, a couple of restaurants, an ornate pavilion (housing one of the world's largest outdoor organs), and a world-famous zoo. The park's most distinctive feature is the architectural beauty of the Spanish-Moorish buildings lining El Prado, its main street, and the group of outstanding and diverse museums contained within it. Free organ concerts are given at the Organ Pavilion on Sundays at 2pm. The park is free, but most museums charge (see individual listings, below). A free park tram transports visitors around the park.

Open: Daily 10am–4:30pm. **Bus:** 7, 7B, 16, or 25.

Aerospace Museum & International Aerospace Hall of Fame, Balboa Park. ☎ **619/234-8291.**

Great achievers and achievements in the history of aviation and aerospace are celebrated by this superb collection of historical aircraft and related artifacts, including art, models, military accoutrements, dioramas, and filmstrip displays. The heroes honored range from the early experimenters to astronauts, and the planes cover the early gliders to spacecraft.

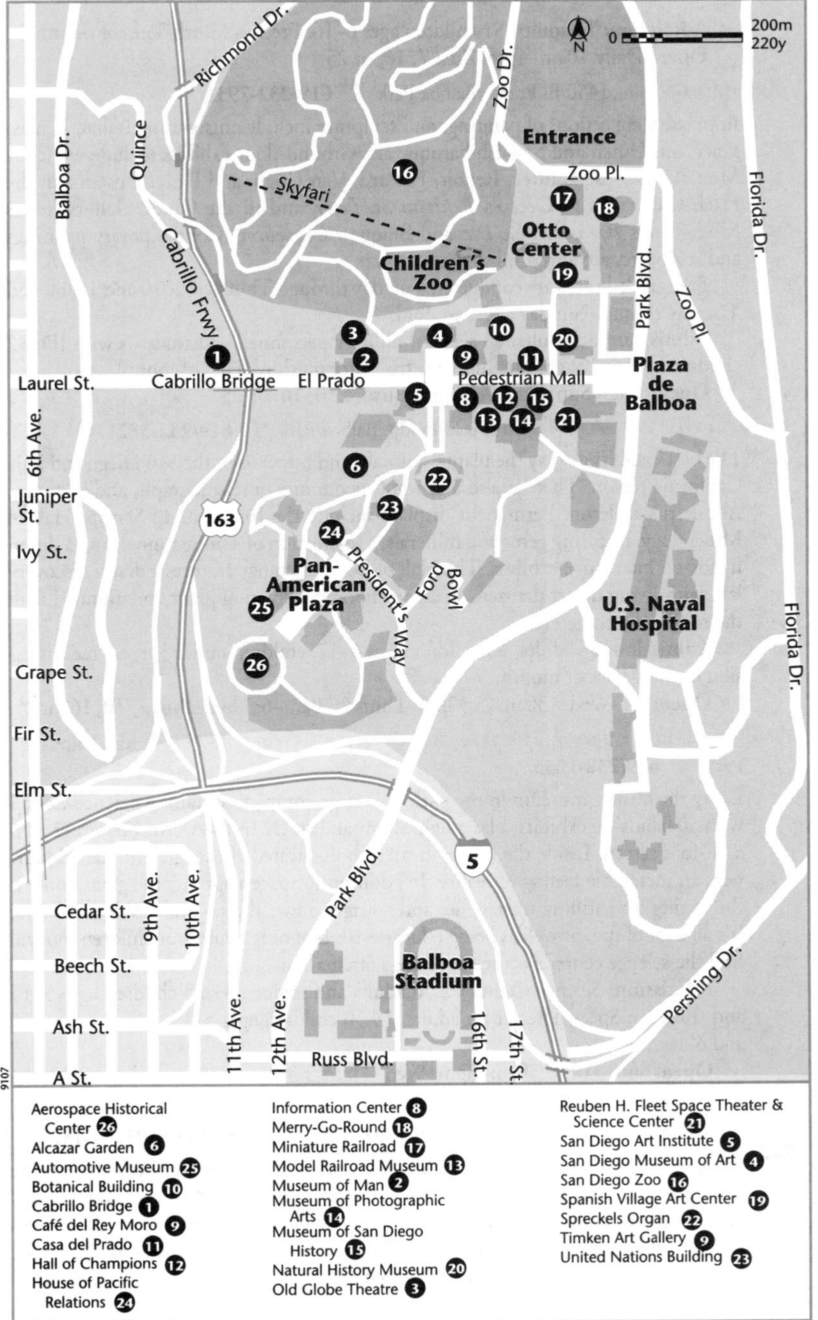
Richmond Dr.
Zoo Dr.
Entrance
Zoo Pl.
16
Skyfari
Quince
Balboa Dr.
Cabrillo Frwy.
17
18
Otto Center
Children's Zoo
19
Florida Dr.
Park Blvd.
Zoo Pl.
3
4
10
20
1
2
9
11
Plaza de Balboa
Laurel St.
Cabrillo Bridge
El Prado
Pedestrian Mall
5
8
12
15
13
14
21
6th Ave.
6
22
Juniper St.
23
163
Ivy St.
24
Pan-American Plaza
President's Way
Ford Bowl
25
U.S. Naval Hospital
Florida Dr.
26
Grape St.
Fir St.
Elm St.
5
Park Blvd.
Cedar St.
9th Ave.
10th Ave.
Beech St.
Balboa Stadium
Pershing Dr.
Ash St.
11th Ave.
12th Ave.
Russ Blvd.
16th St.
17th St.
A St.
200m
220y
0
N
Aerospace Historical Center 26
Alcazar Garden 6
Automotive Museum 25
Botanical Building 10
Cabrillo Bridge 1
Café del Rey Moro 9
Casa del Prado 11
Hall of Champions 12
House of Pacific Relations 24
Information Center 8
Merry-Go-Round 18
Miniature Railroad 17
Model Railroad Museum 13
Museum of Man 2
Museum of Photographic Arts 14
Museum of San Diego History 15
Natural History Museum 20
Old Globe Theatre 3
Reuben H. Fleet Space Theater & Science Center 21
San Diego Art Institute 5
San Diego Museum of Art 4
San Diego Zoo 16
Spanish Village Art Center 19
Spreckels Organ 22
Timken Art Gallery 9
United Nations Building 23
9107

Admission: $4 adults, $1 children ages 6–16. Free on fourth Tues of month.

Open: Daily 10am–4pm. **Bus:** 7, 16, or 25.

Museum of Art, 1450 El Prado, Balboa Park. ☎ **619/232-7931.**

Impressive collections of paintings and sculpture include outstanding Italian Renaissance and Dutch and Spanish baroque art. Ground-floor exhibits include works by Monet, Toulouse-Lautrec, Renoir, Pissarro, Van Gogh, and Dufy. Upstairs, in the Fitch Gallery, is El Greco's *Penitent St. Peter,* and in the Gluck Gallery hangs Modigliani's *Boy with Blue Eyes* and Braque's *Coquelicots.* Contemporary paintings and sculptures are also displayed.

Free guided tours are conducted Tuesday through Thursday at 10 and 11am, and Tuesday through Sunday at 1 and 2pm.

Admission: $5 adults, $4 seniors, military personnel, and students with ID; $2 children ages 6–17; children under 6 free. Free on third Tues of month.

Open: Tues–Sun 10am–4:30pm. **Bus:** 7, 7B, 16, or 25.

Natural History Museum, 1768 El Prado, Balboa Park. ☎ **619/232-3821.**

The best exhibits display the plants, animals, and minerals of the San Diego and Baja California region. There is also a foucault pendulum, a seismograph, and a life-size Allosaurus skeleton. Permanent displays include the Josephine L. Scripps Hall of Mineralogy, featuring gems and minerals, a re-creation of a mine tunnel, and a dozen hands-on interactive exhibits. The Hall of Desert Ecology features a desert discovery lab, with living desert denizens, a desert diorama depicting plant and animal life in the southwestern desert.

Admission: $6 adults, $2 children ages 6–17, children under 5 free. Free admission on first Tues of month.

Open: Fri–Wed 9:30am–5:30pm, Thurs 9:30am–6:30pm. **Bus:** 7, 7B, 16, or 25.

Reuben H. Fleet Space Theater and Science Center, 1875 El Prado, Balboa Park. ☎ **619/238-1233.**

Easily the busiest museum in the park, this large complex contains a Science Center with 50 hands-on exhibits, a laser light show, and an OMNIMAX movie theater with a 76-foot screen. Inside the movie theater, sophisticated effects give simulated journeys an incredible feeling of reality. In addition to space-tripping, the giant dome is the setting for thrilling travelogues and voyages under the sea and inside a volcano. It's all a lot of fun, as well as being educational. Not only adults but children too will find the science center a source of endless fascination.

Admission: Science Center $2.50 adults and seniors, $1.25 children ages 5–15 and students; Space Theater $6 adults, $3.50 children ages 5–15, $4.50 seniors 65 and older.

Open: Sun–Tues 9:30am–6pm, Wed–Thurs 9:30am–9:30pm, Fri–Sat 9:30am–10:30pm. **Bus:** 7, 7B, 16, or 25.

★ **San Diego Zoo,** 2920 Zoo Dr., Balboa Park. ☎ **619/234-3153** or **231-1515.**

Some of the most exotic wild animals in the world—over 3,500 of them—live at the San Diego Zoo. Set in a lavishly planted 100-acre tropical garden, the zoo is famous for its rare and exotic species: cuddly koalas, long-billed kiwis, wild Przewalski's horses from Mongolia, lowland gorillas, and Galapagos tortoises. The usual lions, elephants, giraffes, and tigers are present, too, not to mention a great number of tropical birds.

Most of the animals are housed in barless, moated enclosures that resemble their natural habitats. A simulated rain forest home has been added for the Sumatran tigers, a new aviary and gorilla jungle was completed in 1991.

A 40-minute guided bus tour—which costs $3 for adults and $2.50 for kids 3 to 15—provides a narrated overview of the park. Alternatively, you can get an aerial perspective via the Skyfari Tramway, which is included with zoo admission.

The Children's Zoo is scaled to a youngster's viewpoint. There is a nursery with baby animals, and a petting area where kids can cuddle up to sheep, goats, and the like.

Admission: $13 adults, $6 children ages 3–15.

Open: July–Labor Day daily 9am–5pm; after Labor Day–June daily 9am–4pm. **Bus:** 7 or 7B.

Timken Museum of Art, 1500 El Prado, Balboa Park. ☎ **619/239-5548.**

The Timken houses the Putnam Foundation's collection of American and European paintings, which includes works by Boucher, Rembrandt, and Brueghel. The private gallery also exhibits a rare collection of Russian icons and 19th-century American paintings.

Admission: Free.

Open: Tues–Sat 10am–4:30pm, Sun 1:30–4:30pm. **Closed:** Sept. **Bus:** 7, 7B, 16, or 25.

ELSEWHERE IN THE CITY

Sea World, 1720 S. Shores Rd., Mission Bay. ☎ **619/226-3901.**

The 150-acre, multimillion-dollar aquatic playground is a showplace for marine mammals, most notably Shamu, a four-ton black-and-white killer whale. The privately owned marine zoological park is a family entertainment center where the performers are dolphins, otters, sea lions, walruses, and seals.

Four shows are presented continuously throughout the day. There's also the Penguin Encounter, a Forbidden Reef, and Shark Encounter. A single admission price admits you to all shows and exhibits. During summer and on holidays there may be special entertainment, musical groups, or even fireworks.

Admission: $27.95 adults, $19.95 children ages 3–11, children under 3 free. **Parking:** $5.

Open: Mid-Jun–Aug daily 9am–11pm, the rest of the year daily 9am–dusk. **Bus:** 9 or 81. **Directions:** Exit I-5 west onto Sea World Drive.

Did You Know ?

- Tourism is San Diego's number three industry, right behind the military and manufacturing.
- San Diego County is one of the world's leading producers of honey, kelp, and avocados.
- The first U.S. passenger airline to operate year round, beginning in 1925, was Ryan Airlines of San Diego—the same firm that built the *Spirit of St. Louis.*
- The cavernous Hotel del Coronado, one of the world's largest wooden structures, was designed by architects whose only previous experience had been with railroad stations.

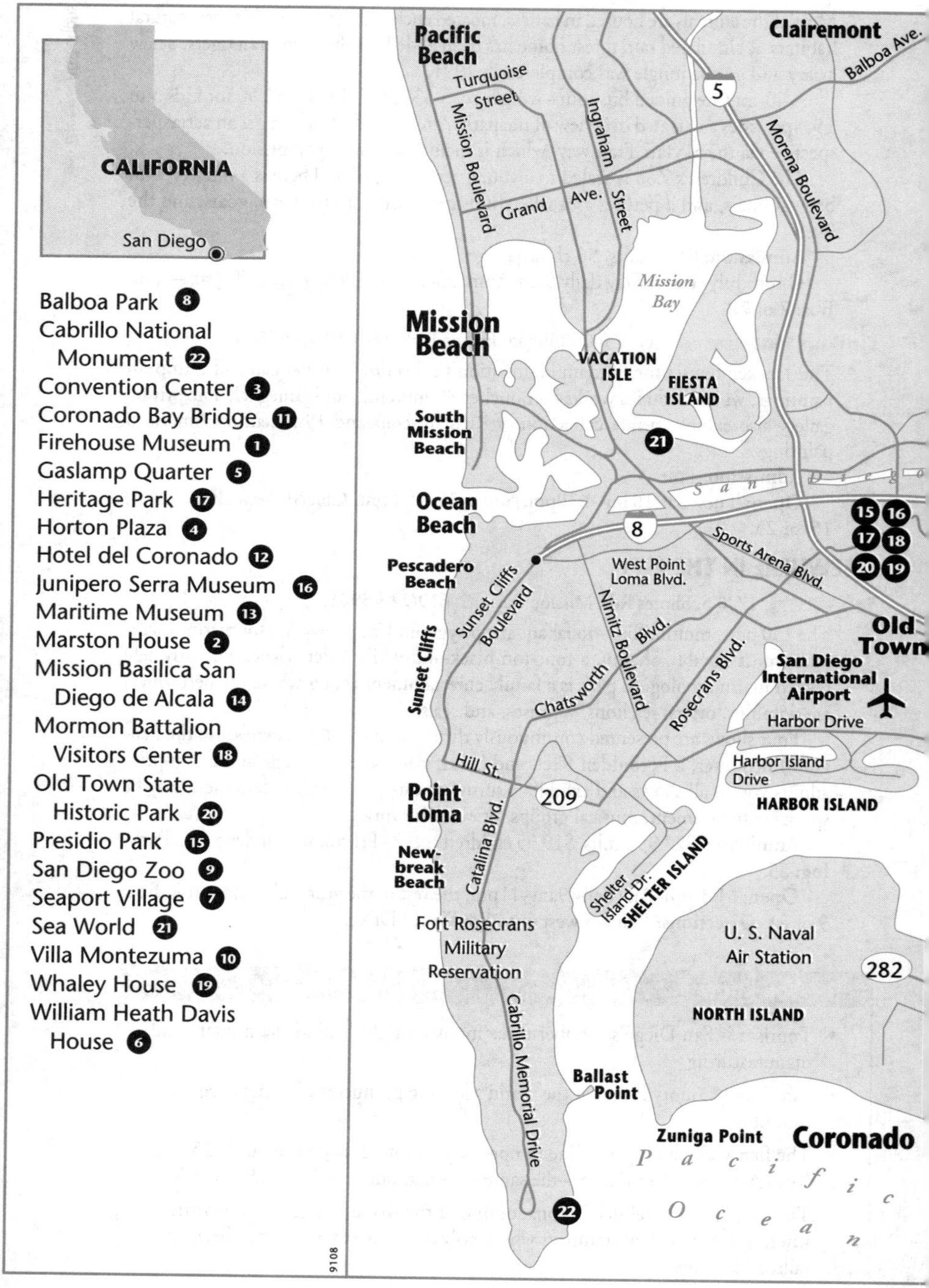

- Balboa Park 8
- Cabrillo National Monument 22
- Convention Center 3
- Coronado Bay Bridge 11
- Firehouse Museum 1
- Gaslamp Quarter 5
- Heritage Park 17
- Horton Plaza 4
- Hotel del Coronado 12
- Junipero Serra Museum 16
- Maritime Museum 13
- Marston House 2
- Mission Basilica San Diego de Alcala 14
- Mormon Battalion Visitors Center 18
- Old Town State Historic Park 20
- Presidio Park 15
- San Diego Zoo 9
- Seaport Village 7
- Sea World 21
- Villa Montezuma 10
- Whaley House 19
- William Heath Davis House 6

9108

Pacific Beach
Clairemont
Balboa Ave.
Turquoise Street
5
Mission Boulevard
Ingraham Street
Morena Boulevard
Grand Ave.
Mission Bay
Mission Beach
VACATION ISLE
FIESTA ISLAND
South Mission Beach
21
San Diego
Ocean Beach
8
15 16 17 18 20 19
Sports Arena Blvd.
West Point Loma Blvd.
Pescadero Beach
Sunset Cliffs Boulevard
Sunset Cliffs
Nimitz Boulevard
Chatsworth Blvd.
Rosecrans Blvd.
Old Town
San Diego International Airport
Harbor Drive
Hill St.
Harbor Island Drive
Point Loma
209
HARBOR ISLAND
Catalina Blvd.
New-break Beach
Shelter Island Dr.
SHELTER ISLAND
Fort Rosecrans Military Reservation
U. S. Naval Air Station
282
NORTH ISLAND
Cabrillo Memorial Drive
Ballast Point
Zuniga Point
Coronado
Pacific Ocean
22

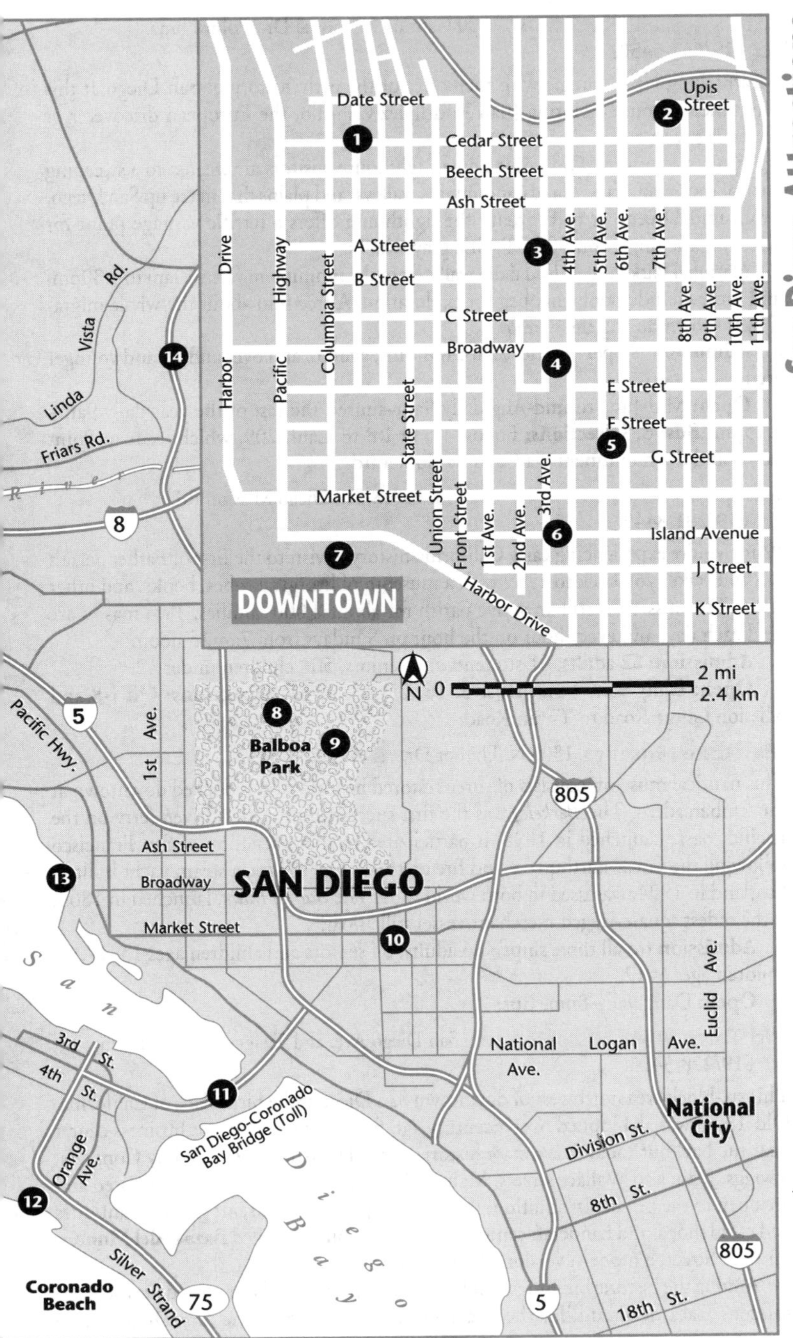

San Diego Attractions

Cabrillo National Monument, 1800 Cabrillo Memorial Dr., Point Loma. ☎ **619/557-5450.**

Breathtaking views mingle with memories of the early history of San Diego at this monument commemorating Juan Rodríguez Cabrillo, the European discoverer of America's west coast.

From the restored Old Point Loma Lighthouse, visitors are treated to a sweeping vista of the ocean, bays, islands, mountains, valleys, and plains that make up San Diego. From mid-December to February the lighthouse offers a terrific vantage point for watching the migration of the Pacific gray whales.

National Park rangers lead daily walks from the monument from 10am to 4:30pm, and there are tide pools that beg for exploration. A free film about the whale migration is shown during the winter.

Admission: $4 per vehicle, $2 for walk-ins; ages 62 and over and 16 and younger are free.

Open: Mid-June to mid-Aug daily 9am–sunset; the rest of the year daily 9am–5:15pm. **Bus:** 6. **Directions:** Follow I-5 or I-8 to Calif. 209, which leads to Point Loma and the monument via Catalina Boulevard.

Mission Basilica San Diego de Alcala, 10818 San Diego Mission Rd. ☎ **619/281-8449.**

While you're experiencing early California history, a visit to the first of Father Serra's missions takes you back to 1769 with a museum of liturgical robes, books, and other relics. The mission is still an active parish for about 2,000 families. Two masses are held each day, and every hour on the hour on Sundays from 7am to noon.

Admission: $2 adults, $1 students and seniors, 50¢ children under 12.

Open: Daily 9am–5pm. **Bus:** 6, 16, 25, 43, or 81. **Directions:** Off I-8 and Mission Gorge Road to Twain Road.

The Maritime Museum, 1306 N. Harbor Dr. ☎ **619/234-9153.**

This nautical museum consists of three restored historic vessels docked downtown at the Embarcadero. The *Berkeley* was the first successful propeller-driven ferry on the Pacific coast. Launched in 1898, it participated in the evacuation of San Francisco following the Great Earthquake and fire of 1906. The *Medea,* a steam yacht built in Scotland in 1904, was used in both world wars. The *Star of India,* launched in 1863, is the oldest square-rigged merchant vessel still afloat.

Admission (to all three ships): $6 adults, $4 seniors and children ages 13–17, $2 children ages 6–12.

Open: Daily 9am–8pm. **Bus:** 2.

★ **Old Town State Historic Park,** San Diego Ave. and Twiggs St., Old Town. ☎ **619/220-5423.**

This six-block area northwest of downtown San Diego is the birthplace of California. Old Town was abandoned over a century ago for a more convenient business center near the bay, but today it is a state historic park. The park is bounded by Congress, Twiggs, Juan, and Wallace streets. Many of its buildings have been fully restored and are open to the public. In addition, there are shops, restaurants, art galleries, antiques and curio shops, and handcraft centers, including a complex called **Bazaar del Mundo,** on Juan Street, a modern version of a Mexican street market.

Among the historic buildings that have been reconstructed or restored are the magnificent Casa de Estudillo, the Machado/Stewart Adobe, the *San Diego Union* newspaper office, the old one-room Mason Street schoolhouse, and the stables from which Alfred Seeley ran his San Diego–Los Angeles stagecoach line.

Just outside the boundary of the park is the "haunted" two-story Whaley House, once the focal point of high society.

There are two large parking areas at the entrance to the park. One is near the visitors information center, 4002 Wallace St. (☎ **220-5423**), which is open daily from 10am to 5pm. Here you can get maps and tour information. The Old Town State Historic Park offers free one-hour guided walking tours that leave from the center daily at 2pm.

Admission: $2 adults, $1 students, free ages 6 and under.

Open: Daily 10am–5pm. **Bus:** 4, 5, or 105.

ORGANIZED TOURS

See "By Tour Bus," under "Getting Around" above, for information on an excellent open-air bus tour of the city.

Cruise San Diego. ☎ **619/234-4111.**

The company offers daily harbor tours, plus a Sunday champagne jazz brunch. Dinner cruises with entertainment, as well as brunch cruises, are available on weekends. In summer there are cocktail cruises, and in winter, whale-watching excursions. Call for departure times and prices.

6 Sports & Recreation

SPECTATOR SPORTS

Baseball

San Diego Padres (NL), San Diego Jack Murphy Stadium, 9449 Friars Rd., Mission Valley. ☎ **619/283-4494.**

The team plays April through September. The Padres Express bus costs $4 round trip and, beginning two hours before the game, picks up fans at several locations throughout the city (**619/233-3004**). Admission is $5 to $11.

Football

San Diego Chargers (NFL), San Diego Jack Murphy Stadium, 9449 Friars Rd., Mission Valley. ☎ **619/280-2111.**

Frommer's Favorite San Diego Experiences

Strolling Through the Gaslamp Quarter Downtown's 16 blocks of Victorian commercial buildings are beautifully restored and house inviting shops, restaurants, and nightspots.

Riding the San Diego Trolley to Mexico For just $1.75 the bright red trolleys whisk passengers to the border in only half an hour.

Wandering Through Horton Plaza San Diego's centrally located shopping complex is one of the prettiest outdoor malls in the world. It's conducive to wandering—it was created purposely to keep you from getting directly from point A to point B.

The team plays August through December. The Chargers Express bus costs $5 round trip and, beginning two hours before game time, picks up fans at several locations throughout the city (**619/233-3004**). Tickets run from $15 to $23.

Horse Racing

Del Mar Racetrack, at the Del Mar Fairgrounds. ☎ **619/755-1141.**

Founded by Bing Crosby and Pat O'Brien in 1937, Del Mar is the most famous track in California. The racing season lasts just 43 days, from late July to mid-September. Tickets cost $3 to $5.

Soccer

San Diego Sockers (CISL), Sports Arena, 3500 Sports Arena Blvd. ☎ **619/224-4625.**

The season runs from June through September, and tickets run from $9 to $15.

RECREATION

Beaches

San Diego Country is blessed with 70 miles of sandy coastline and more than 30 public-access beaches that attract surfers, snorkelers, swimmers, and sunbathers. Listed below are some of the area's most popular beaches.

Bonita Cove, just south of Mission Beach, is perfect for families, with its calm waters, grassy areas for picnicking, and playground equipment.

Coronado Beach, lovely, wide, and sparkling white, is conducive to strolling and lingering, especially in the late afternoon. It fronts Ocean Boulevard and is especially lovely in front of the Hotel del Coronado.

Mission Bay, a 4,600-acre aquatic park, offers 27 miles of bayfront; 17 miles of oceanfront beaches; picnic areas; paths for biking, rollerskating, and jogging; and children's playgrounds.

Fishing

You can fish for no charge and with no license off the **Ocean Beach Pier,** at the foot of Niagara Street in Ocean Beach (**619/226-3474**). For information on lake fishing (where a daily recreation permit is required), contact the **Lakes Recreation Section** of the San Diego Water Utilities Department (**619/465-3474**).

San Diego's open-ocean fishing is among the finest on the Pacific coast. Many companies operate private charter boats.

H & M Landing, 2803 Emerson St., Point Loma. ☎ **619/222-1144.**

H & M offers the largest variety of fishing (they've been in the business since 1935) and whale-watching excursions. Their local fishing trips range from a half day at the Point Loma Kelp Beds to full-day fishing around the Coronado Islands. In summer and fall they go out for albacore tuna; in winter and spring it's for rock cod. The really exciting trips are on the 88-foot *Spirit of Adventure* (sleeps 30) for 2- to 10-day fishing trips. H & M has also been watching gray whales since 1955 (Pacific SeaFari Tours). This is also an opportunity to see sea lions, seabirds, and ocean life of all sorts.

7 Savvy Shopping

Department store names you'll recognize after only a brief stay in California include Nordstrom, Robinson's, and The Broadway, all of which are located in Horton Plaza.

Major shopping streets include Fifth Avenue and Broadway downtown, Orange Avenue in Coronado, and San Diego Avenue in Old Town.

Shops in San Diego tend to stay open late. Expect to find the welcome mat out until 9pm on weeknights, 8pm on Saturdays, and 6pm and sometimes 8pm on Sundays, particularly in shopping malls such as Horton Plaza and Seaport Village.

Purchases come with a $8^1/_4$% sales tax.

ANTIQUES

Olde Cracker Factory Antiques Shopping Center, 448 W. Market St. ☎ **619/233-1669.**

American and international antiques fill three floors of this warehouse at Columbia Street, one block north of Seaport Village, and three blocks from the San Diego Convention Center. Open Tuesday through Sunday from 11am to 5pm.

T&R Antiques Warehouse, 4630 Santa Fe St., Pacific Beach. ☎ **619/272-0437.**

Over 15,000 square feet of primarily European furniture and collectibles makes this one of the largest antiques warehouses in the state.

BOOKS

Doubleday Book Shop, 407 Horton Plaza. ☎ **619/696-9616.**

Heavy on paperback best-sellers, this well-known chain store is conveniently located in the busy Horton Plaza Center.

Rudolph Schiller's Books & Mercantile, Old Town State Historic Park. ☎ **619/298-0108.**

One of the city's most unusual bookshops celebrates people and places from the 1850s to the 1950s. Literature, coloring books, songbooks, and sewing books celebrate Shirley Temple, John Wayne, and turn-of-the-century America.

Upstart Crow, 835 Harbor Dr., Seaport Village. ☎ **619/232-4855.**

This bookstore/coffeehouse encourages patrons to browse and linger with a volume while sipping a cup of fresh-brewed coffee.

FASHIONS

For Men

Adventure 16, Horton Plaza. ☎ **619/234-1751.**

In addition to books and accessories, this is a terrific store for outdoor and adventure travel apparel.

Banana Republic, Horton Plaza. ☎ **619/238-0080.**

The casual clothes and footwear sold here are perfectly suited to San Diego's relaxed atmosphere.

Brady's, in the Fashion Valley Mall, 452 Fashion Valley. ☎ **619/296-8898.**

Contemporary clothes for middle-aged males that are both casual and elegant. Their excellent selection of ties is particularly notable.

For Women

Brady's, Hotel del Coronado, Coronado. ☎ **619/435-6766.**

Stylish evening wear and splashy poolside fashions are Brady's specialties.

GIFTS

The Nature Company, Horton Plaza. ☎ **619/231-1185.**

This popular shop sells all kinds of whimsical and serious items, from plastic insect keychains to high-powered telescopes. The emphasis is on the Earth, and several educational gifts are particularly suited for children.

United Nations International Gift Shop, Balboa Park. ☎ **619/233-5044.**

Under both the U.S. and U.N. flags you'll find a host of gifts from around the world, including Russian nesting dolls, Nepalese necklaces, Thai pottery, hand-carved boxes from Poland, and Japanese origami.

LUGGAGE

Luggage & Sunglasses, Etc., 419 Broadway. ☎ **619/231-1566.**

Located downtown, between Fourth and Fifth avenues, this well-stocked shop offers a good selection of hard- and soft-sided luggage, carry-on tote bags, backpacks, and leather goods for carrying extra gifts home. They also carry a large selection of sunglasses and prescription glasses.

MALLS

Bazaar del Mundo, 2754 Calhoun St., Old Town State Historic Park. ☎ **619/296-3161.**

Take a stroll down Mexico way through the arched passageways of this colorful part of Old Town. Always festive, its central courtyard vibrates with folkloric music, mariachis, and a splashing fountain. Shops feature one-of-a-kind folk art, home furnishings, clothing, and textiles from Mexico and Central America. Don't miss the Design Center and the Guatemala Store. Bazaar is open daily from 10am to 9pm.

Horton Plaza, 324 Horton Plaza. ☎ **619/238-1596.**

The city's largest shopping, dining, and entertainment cluster is the Disneyland of shopping malls. Located right smack in the heart of the city, Horton Plaza is more than a mall. It's the hearth of the city—the place where everyone gravitates to shop, eat, meet, and have fun. The more than 140 shops include both chain stores and specialty shops. In addition, there is a seven-screen cinema, live theatre, a Farmer's Market, and a variety of restaurants for all tastes and pocketbooks.

Seaport Village, 849 W. Harbor Dr., at Kettner Blvd. ☎ **619/235-4014.**

This 14-acre, waterfront mall is one of the city's major tourist shopping centers. Connected to the new San Diego Convention Center by a waterfront boardwalk, the complex is beautifully landscaped, adjacent to an eight-acre public park, and has more than 50 shops. Galleries and boutiques sell handcrafted gifts, collectibles, and many imported items. Two of my favorites are **Hug-A-Bear (619/230-1362)**, with a selection of plush bears and woodland animals, and **Kite Flite (619/234-5483)**, selling kites from around the world. I also enjoy the **Upstart Crow & Co. (619/232-4855)**, a delightful combination bookstore and coffeehouse.

Open: Sept–May daily 10am–9pm; Jun–Aug daily 10am–10pm.

8 Evening Entertainment

San Diego is hardly the nightlife capital of America, but pockets of entertainment—both cultural and otherwise—pulsate all around town. For a rundown of the week's events, consult the monthly listings magazine *San Diego Live!,* available from newsstands, and the Friday entertainment sections of the *San Diego Union* and the *San Diego Tribune.*

The Performing Arts

Half-price tickets to theater, music, and dance events are sold on the day of the show at **Times Arts Tix** (☎ **619/238-3810**), in Horton Plaza park, at Broadway and Broadway Circle. The kiosk is open Tuesday through Saturday from 10am to 7pm. Half-price tickets for Sunday performances are sold on Saturday. Only cash is accepted.

MAJOR PERFORMING ARTS COMPANIES

Opera and Classical Music

San Diego Civic Light Opera Association, Starlight Bowl. ☎ **619/544-STAR.**

Contemporary musicals like *Follies* and *Dreamgirls* are the mainstay of this fun company. The opera performs both indoors and outdoors at the Civic Theatre and the Starlight Bowl, respectively. Outdoor performances at the bowl are unique, due to its location in the flight path to Lindbergh Field; when airplanes pass overhead (and they often do), singers stop midnote at a cue from the conductor, wait for the noise to abate, then proceed with the performance. Outdoor shows are usually staged in the summer, and performances move inside in the spring and fall.

Prices: Tickets, $17–$32; $2 discount at box office. Seniors over 65 receive a 25% discount. **Box office hours:** Mon–Sat 10am–6pm, Sun noon–6pm.

San Diego Opera, Civic Theatre, 202 C St. ☎ **619/232-7636.**

Founded in 1964, the opera often showcases international stars. The season lasts from January through May, and includes several special recitals, in addition to major productions. The box office is located across the street from the theater.

Prices: Tickets $20–$90, $11 standing room tickets available a half hour prior to performance. Student and senior discounts are available one hour prior to performance. **Box office hours:** Mon–Fri 9am–5pm.

San Diego Symphony, Copley Symphony Hall, 750 B St. ☎ **619/699-4205.**

Israeli-born conductor Yoav Talmi leads the 83-member symphony during a season that lasts from October through May. Classical programs often feature internationally acclaimed guest soloists. The symphony is the only orchestra on the west coast that owns its performing hall (the former Fox Theatre, built in 1929). From June through September, the symphony puts on "pops" outdoor concerts at Embarcadero Marina Park South located behind the San Diego convention center in downtown San Diego.

Prices: Tickets $10–$50, half-price tickets for students and seniors 55 and over are available one hour prior to showtime. **Box office hours:** Mon–Fri 10am–6pm.

Dance

San Diego–based dance companies perform on erratic schedules and in several different venues around the city. Companies include the **California Ballet,** a traditional ballet troupe; **Malashock Dance & Co.** and **Three's Company,** both modern dance companies; **Jazz Unlimited,** a jazz group; and the **Al Germani Dance Co.,** which performs a mixture of modern and jazz dance. For specific performance information, call the **San Diego Area Dance Alliance Calendar** (☎ **619/239-9255**).

Theater

Gaslamp Quarter Theatre Company, 444 Fourth Ave. ☎ **619/232-9608,** box office **234-9583.**

Contemporary dramas have been this company's specialty since its beginning in 1980. Plays are regularly staged in the downtown 250-seat Hahn Cosmopolitan Theatre, 444 Fourth Ave.

Prices: Tickets $20–$22. **Box office hours:** Daily 10am–6pm.

San Diego Junior Theatre, Casa del Prado, Balboa Park. ☎ **619/239-8355.**

Founded in 1948, this is one of the country's oldest continuously operating children's theaters. Schoolchildren from grades 1 through 12 act in and serve as the technical crew for five productions each year.

Prices: Tickets $5–$7. **Box office hours:** Tues–Fri 12:30–4:30pm.

San Diego Repertory Theatre, Horton Plaza, 79 Horton Plaza. ☎ **619/235-8025.**

Now almost 17 years old, this well-known company stages a full season of contemporary plays in the bilevel Lyceum Theater in Horton Plaza. Call for current productions and showtimes.

Prices: Tickets $18–$24. **Box office hours:** Tues–Sun noon–6pm (until 8pm night of performance).

MAJOR CONCERT HALLS & AUDITORIUMS

Civic Theatre, 202 C St. ☎ **619/232-6510.**

Home to both the San Diego Playgoers and the San Diego Opera, the Civic also regularly hosts a variety of entertainment ranging from plays to dance performances to pop concerts.

Prices: Tickets $20–$37, depending on the show.

Copley Symphony Hall, 750 B St. ☎ **619/699-4205.**

Owned by the San Diego Symphony, this pretty theater was topped by the 34-story Symphony Hall Towers in 1989. The 80-foot mural in the lobby, by Denver artist James Jackson, depicts the intense concentration of a symphony orchestra. The San Diego Symphony Orchestra performs here October through May.

Prices: Vary depending on the show.

Major Concert & Performance Halls

Civic Theatre, 202 C St. (☎ **619/232-6510**).

Copley Symphony Hall, 750 B St. (☎ **619/699-4200**).

Simon Edison Complex for the Performing Arts, Balboa Park (☎ **619/239-2255**).

Spreckels Theater, 121 Broadway (☎ **619/235-9500**).

Old Globe Theatre/Simon Edison Centre for the Performing Arts, Balboa Park. ☎ **619/239-2255.**

This large complex incorporates the Tony Award–winning, 581-seat Old Globe Theatre, fashioned after Shakespeare's theater; the 612-seat, open-air Lowell Davies Festival Theatre; and the 225-seat Cassius Carter Centre Stage. The three theaters present stage plays, dance performances, music, and other events. Tours are offered most Saturdays and Sundays at 11am and cost $3.

Prices: Tickets $18–$32.

Spreckels Theatre, 121 Broadway. ☎ **619/235-9500.**

The city's oldest theater has been in almost continuous operation since it opened in 1912, when it was the largest theater of its kind west of New York. The 1,500-seat baroque building hosts theatrical and musical events.

Prices: Tickets $5–35.

THEATERS

La Jolla Playhouse, University of California at San Diego, La Jolla Village Dr. and Torrey Pines Rd. ☎ **619/550-1010.**

Co-founded in 1947 by Gregory Peck, this twin-stage playhouse encompasses both the 492-seat Mandell Weiss Theatre and the new 400-seat Weiss Forum. Dramas, musicals, and new plays are staged May through December.

Prices: Tickets $20–$37, special discounts available. **Box office hours:** Mon 10am–6pm, Tues–Sat 10am–8pm, Sun 10am–7pm.

Old Globe Theatre, in the Simon Edison Complex for the Performing Arts, Balboa Park. ☎ **619/239-2255.**

Reopened in 1982 after an arson fire, the theater often hosts well-known performers such as Sada Thompson, Hal Holbrook, and Marion Ross. Several shows have premiered here before moving on to Broadway, including *Into the Woods, Rumors, Jake's Women,* and *The Cocktail Hour.*

Prices: Tickets $18–$32. **Box office hours:** Mon 10am–5pm, Tues–Sat 10am–8:30pm, Sun noon–7:30pm.

The Club & Music Scene

COMEDY CLUBS

Comedy Store, 916 Pearl St., La Jolla. ☎ **619/454-9176.**

Top comics regularly visit from L.A. Monday and Tuesday are amateur nights; the acts improve as the week progresses. Showtime is 8pm Sunday through Thursday, 8 and 10:30pm Friday and Saturday.

Admission: Wed–Thurs and Sun $8, Fri–Sat $10 plus two-drink minimum.

The Improv, 832 Garnet Ave., Pacific Beach. ☎ **619/483-4520.**

A 1930s cabaret setting attracts performers and audiences from around the country. The club is part of a chain that includes stages in New York, Los Angeles, and Dallas, Dinner, which includes preferential seating, costs about $10–$13 extra. The show is at 8pm Sunday through Thursday, on Fridays and Saturdays shows are at 8 and 10:30pm.

Admission: Tues–Thurs $8, Fri–Sat $10, two-drink minimum additional.

ROCK/DANCE CLUBS

Sibyl's Down Under, 500 Fourth Ave. ☎ **619/239-9117.**

This Australian-themed club features the city's largest dance floor. Perpetually packed, it usually features Top 40 music, except on Thursdays, when DJs spin progressive rock discs. Open Thursday and Saturday 6pm to 2am, and Friday and Sunday from 5pm to 2am.

Admission: $5 after 9pm.

Cannibal Bar, in the Catamaran Hotel, 3999 Mission Blvd. ☎ **619/488-1081.**

Popular happy hours (with free hot and cold hors d'oeuvres) slip into busy nights, when dance videos and bands take center stage. Call for event information. Open Wednesday through Sunday from 5pm–1:30am.

Admission: Thurs–Sat $4–$7, depending on what's on.

Olé Madrid, 751 5th Ave. ☎ **619/557-0146.**

Most of the nightclubs in the Gaslamp District are relatively conservative adult-oriented places. This is not one of them. Its trilevel industrial/Gothic interior, hip-hop/house mix, and killer sangria are just the right blend to make Olé popular with a good-looking twenties crowd. The club also bills itself as a restaurant, but don't believe it. Open Sunday through Wednesday until 2am, Thursday through Saturday until 4am.

Admission: $3–$7.

JAZZ/BLUES

Croce's, 802 Fifth Ave. ☎ **619/233-4355.**

Half restaurant, half bar, this very popular jazzery is named after the late musician Jim Croce and is owned by his wife, Ingrid. Traditional jazz and rhythm and blues are offered nightly in two adjacent clubs. Croce's is open nightly.

Admission: $3–5.

The Bar Scene

Moose McGillicuddy's, 1165 Garnet Ave., Pacific Beach. ☎ **619/274-2323.**

One of Pacific Beach's largest clubs, Moose's packs 'em in on the weekends with high decibels and low-priced drink specials. It's really just a giant beer bar, with a largely wood interior. But lines can form down the block and the revelry can be positively raucous. Open Monday through Friday from 4pm to 1:45am and Saturday and Sunday from 11:30am to 1:45am.

Admission: Free–$5.

Society Billiard Cafe, 1051 Garnet Ave., Pacific Beach. ☎ **619/272-7665.**

Clean, bright, and relatively smoke-free, San Diego's poshest pool palace attracts young, upscale players more interested in fun than hustle—few of this hall's shooters come armed with their own sticks. There are 15 regulation tables, well-maintained rental cues, and an excellent beer selection, but only those suffering from famine should order from the meal menu. Open daily from 11am to 2am.

Prices: Billiard fees $5–$12 per hour; beer and wine $2–$7; sandwiches, salads, and pizza $5–$7.

Zanzibar Cafe, 976 Garnet Ave., Pacific Beach. ☎ **619/272-4762.**

Harleys, hippies, and assorted hangers-on make this the coolest cafe in town. The sidewalk in front of Zanzibar is always an interesting sociological study of American youth. Oh yeah, the coffee's pretty good, too. Open daily from 6am to midnight.

PIANO BARS

Marriott Suites Hotel, 701 A St. ☎ **619/696-9800.**

One of the prettiest bars in the city is located by the 12th-floor lobby of this elegant hotel. The pretty, plant-filled bar is an excellent place to meet for a drink. Drinks run $3 to $6.

Top O' the Cove, 1216 Prospect St., La Jolla. ☎ **619/454-7779.**

Gershwin is a favorite of resident pianist Kristi Rickert. Top O' the Cove provides an intimate setting, either inside or out on the idyllic patio, for the music that can be enjoyed Wednesday through Sunday from 7:30 to 11pm. Drinks are $4 to $7.

GAY BARS

The Flame, 3780 Park Blvd. ☎ **619/295-4163.**

Two bars and one large dance floor are dedicated entirely to women. Espresso is served, and regular theme nights are held. Call to see what's on. Hours are Monday to Thursday from 5pm to 2am, Friday and Sunday from 4pm to 2am, and Saturday from 5pm to 2am.

Admission: Sun–Thurs free, Fri–Sat $3.

Number One Fifth Avenue, 3845 Fifth Ave. ☎ **619/299-1911.**

One of the most popular men's bars, 1 Fifth, in the heart of Hillcrest, is decorated with brass and wood. Also enjoy their patio pool table, darts, pinball, and video games. Hours are daily from noon to 2am.

9 Easy Excursions from San Diego

La Jolla

12 miles N of downtown San Diego

GETTING THERE • By Bus Local buses 34 and 34A run from downtown San Diego to La Jolla. They stop in town at Silverado Street and Girard Avenue.

• By Car From San Diego to La Jolla is a leisurely 15-minute drive. Take I-5 to Ardath Road, turn left onto Torrey Pines Road, then right onto Prospect Place, which becomes Prospect Street, the main street in La Jolla.

ESSENTIALS • Orientation Prospect Street is the town's main commercial thoroughfare. It's pretty small, runs parallel to the coast, and contains about five blocks of boutiques, shops, restaurants, cafes, and art galleries. The ocean is only about a block away, and can be seen from Prospect Street.

• Information San Diego's excellent **International Visitors Information Center,** 11 Horton Plaza, at First Avenue and F Street (☎ **619/236-1212**), offers specialized information on La Jolla as well as the rest of the county. See "Tourist Information" at the beginning of this chapter for additional tourist information centers.

La Jolla (pronounced "La Hoya"), a residential coastal town just north of downtown San Diego, is one of the prettiest parcels in San Diego County. The aptly named seacoast village means "the jewel" in Spanish. For over half a century, wealthy seniors have chosen La Jolla for their beautiful retirement estates, having selected the site for its rugged coastline, lush plantings, pretty beaches, and proximity to the city. La Jolla is expensive real estate, and it retains its "old-money" image despite its openness to adventurous young people, Navy families, and retired citizens. If you can keep yourself from being jealous that you don't live here, the pretty town is definitely worth a look.

WHAT TO SEE & DO

La Jolla's primary attraction is itself—a beautiful piece of land hugging a pretty stretch of ocean. The town, known for its scenery, is meant to be strolled. The closest waterfront is known as La Jolla Cove; its clear, protected waters make it popular with families with small children, snorkelers, and scuba divers. The adjacent park is perfect for picnicking.

Scripps Aquarium Museum, 8602 La Jolla Shores Dr. ☎ **619/534-3474** for a recording.

Part of the Scripps Institution of Oceanography, a branch of the University of California at San Diego, the Aquarium Museum offers close-up views of local waters—the Pacific Ocean and the Gulf of California—in 22 marine-life tanks. World renowned for its oceanic research, Scripps offers visitors a chance to view its marine aquarium and artificial outdoor tidepools. The museum has 30 interpretive exhibits on the current and historical research done at the institution, which has been in existence since 1903. The bookshop is well stocked with textbooks, gifts, jewelry, and T-shirts. There are excellent beach and picnic areas nearby.

Admission: Free; suggested donation $6.50 adults, $2 children.

Open: Daily 9am–5pm. **Directions:** Take I-5 to La Jolla Village Drive West, which turns onto North Torrey Pines Road, then turn left at La Jolla Shores Drive; Scripps is at the bottom of the hill.

WHERE TO STAY

Expensive

La Valencia Hotel, 1132 Prospect St., La Jolla, CA 92037. ☎ **619/454-0771,** or toll free **800/451-0772.** Fax 619/456-3921. 100 rms, 11 suites. A/C MINIBAR TV TEL **Directions:** Take I-5 to Ardath Road, left onto Torrey Pines Road, then right onto Prospect Court, which becomes Prospect Street; the hotel is located at the corner of Herschel Avenue.

Rates: $180 partial ocean view single or double; $200–$285 full ocean view single or double; from $325 suite. Additional person $10. AE, DC, MC, V. **Parking:** $6.

La Valencia is a gracious old Mediterranean-style resort that delights the senses at every turn. Dramatically situated directly on an ocean beach, it was designed in archetypical early Californian-Spanish style by architect Reginald Johnson in 1926. From the colonnaded entrance with a vine-covered trellis to the lush gardens that surround the large swimming pool to the exquisite mosaic tilework within, it's a beauty. Old-world charm, outstanding personal service, and an impressive scenic location have made it a frequent haven for celebrities and entertainers. At the back of the hotel, garden

La Jolla

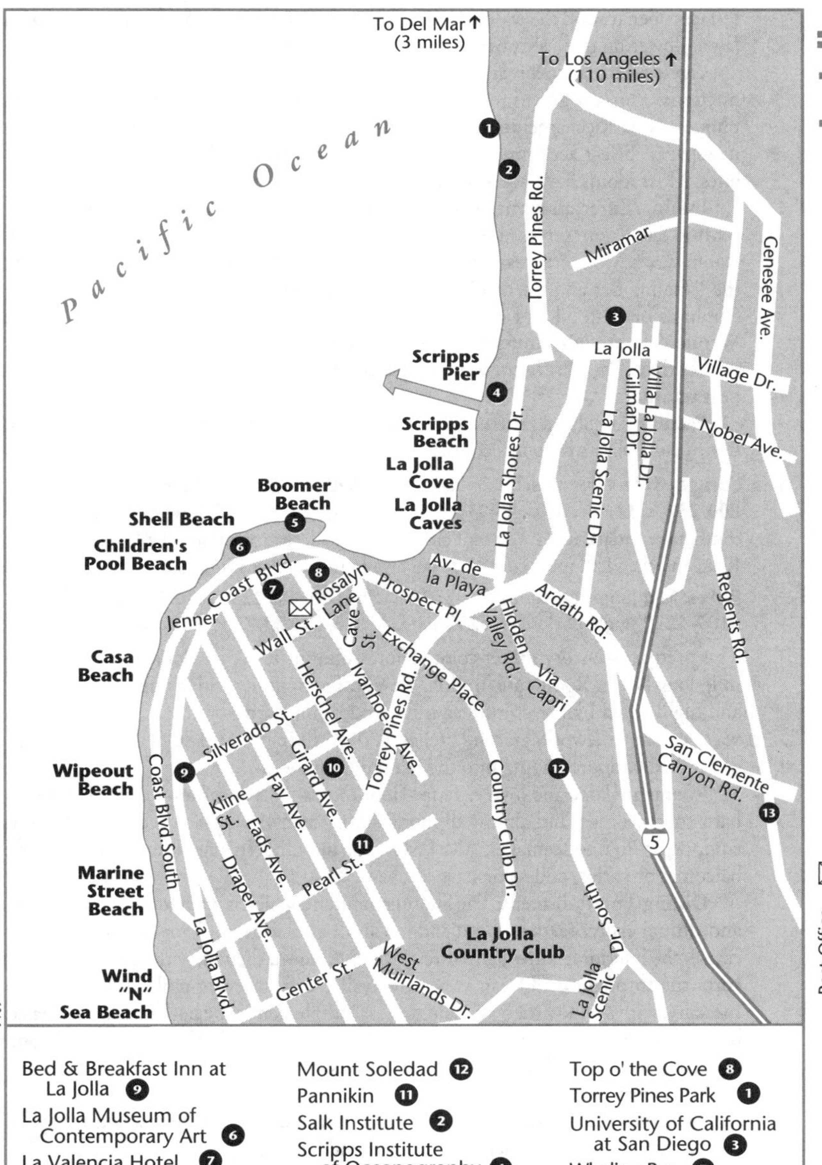

Bed & Breakfast Inn at La Jolla 9
La Jolla Museum of Contemporary Art 6
La Valencia Hotel 7
Mingei International Museum of World Folk Art 13
Mount Soledad 12
Pannikin 11
Salk Institute 2
Scripps Institute of Oceanography 4
Scripps Park 5
Star of the Sea Church 10
Top o' the Cove 8
Torrey Pines Park 1
University of California at San Diego 3
Whaling Bar 7

✉ Post Office

terraces open toward the ocean. Here, a free-form heated swimming pool is edged with lawn, flowering trees, shrubs, and a flagstone sunning deck.

Guest rooms are decorated in subdued tones and with European antique reproductions. Pleasant amenities include terry-cloth robes, oversize towels, bathroom phones, Nina Ricci amenities, nightly turndown service, and a daily complimentary newspaper. Select accommodations also have bathroom TVs, makeup mirrors, and safes. Most rooms have ocean views.

Dining/Entertainment: There are four delightful spots for dining. The elegant rooftop Sky Room serves lunch and a superb fixed-price dinner. The Mediterranean Room serves Mediterranean dishes either indoors or out on a pretty adjoining patio; the Whaling Bar and the adjoining Café La Rue serve international dishes, with an emphasis on seafood and grilled meats. There is piano music in the lobby lounge Wednesday through Saturday from 6 to 10pm.

Services: Room service, concierge, evening turndown, morning newspaper, airport transportation.

Facilities: Pool and Jacuzzi, sauna, exercise room, putting green, shuffleboard, mini health club, access to tennis courts.

Sea Lodge, 8110 Camino del Oro, La Jolla, CA 92037. ☎ **619/459-8271,** or toll free **800/237-5211.** Fax 619/456-9346. 128 rms, 8 suites. TV TEL **Directions:** From I-5 south, take Ardath Road west to Torrey Pines Road, turn right onto La Jolla Shores Road and then left onto Avenida de la Playa to the hotel at Camino del Oro.

Rates: Mid-June–mid-Sept $149–$309 single or double, $390 suite; the rest of the year, $109–$229 single or double, $290 suite. AE, CB, DISC, MC, V. **Parking:** Free.

This pretty three-story sunset-colored hotel, built in 1970, overlooks the Pacific on a mile-long beach. Rooms are in a long, low stucco building with a terra-cotta-tile roof and highlighted by fountains, beautiful landscaping and flowerbeds, open-air walkways, ceramic tilework, graceful arches, and Mexican antiques such as the 200-year-old cathedral doors leading into the main dining room.

Rooms are large and lovely. Third-floor rooms—my favorites—have high sloped barnwood ceilings, and almost all rooms have ocean views. Each accommodation is equipped with a coffeemaker, AM/FM radio, and modern amenities. All rooms have balconies or patios, and some have kitchens.

Dining/Entertainment: The Shores restaurant, which is open for breakfast, lunch, and dinner daily, features both indoor and patio seating. Both comfortable and casual, the interior features a mixture of Mediterranean themes, with handmade terra-cotta tile throughout. Ocean views are available from every table. Seafood is the specialty, with a wide variety of main dishes, complemented by both seafood and salad bars. In the Shores Lounge there's a good happy hour daily from 4:30 to 6:30pm, featuring drink specials and free hors d'oeuvres.

Services: Room service, concierge.

Facilities: Heated swimming pool, children's pool, sauna, tennis and volleyball courts, tour desk, complimentary underground parking.

Moderate

Bed & Breakfast Inn at La Jolla, 7753 Draper Ave., La Jolla, CA 92037. ☎ **619/456-2066.** Fax 619/453-4487. 16 rms (all with bath). **Directions:** Take I-5 to Ardath Road, left onto Torrey Pines Road, then right onto Prospect Street; turn left onto Draper Avenue to the inn.

Rates (including continental breakfast): $85–$225 single or double. MC, V.

In 1913, architect Irving Gill designed this house in his innovative "cubist" style. Located across from the Museum of Contemporary Art, the inn features unique cottage-style rooms located in two wings of a rambling house. Each beautifully kept accommodation contains a king- or queen-size bed or twin beds, and some have fireplaces. It's fun to ramble from the garden to the sun deck to the sitting room, where you can enjoy complimentary wine and cheese in the afternoon. In the guestbook, one traveler notes of the inn, "I have picked a bouquet and given it to myself."

WHERE TO DINE

Expensive

Top O' The Cove, 1216 Prospect St. ☎ **619/454-7779.**

Cuisine: CONTINENTAL. **Reservations:** Recommended.
Prices: Appetizers $7–$12; dinner main courses $25–$30; lunch $9–$20; Sun brunch $16. AE, CB, DC, MC, V.
Open: Lunch Mon–Sat 11:30am–2:30pm; dinner daily 5:30–10:30pm (jackets suggested); Sun brunch 10:30am–3pm.

The restaurant, located in a historic cottage with fig trees out front, has fireplaces glowing on chilly evenings, an intimate piano bar, and a gazebo and patio for dining on balmy days—perfect, in fact, for Sunday brunch with champagne, fruit, pastries, one of 10 main dishes, and coffee or tea. Lunch is on the light side—creative salads, fettuccine dishes, or a tenderloin burger on a sourdough bun—while dinner is more lavish, with fish, duck, veal, lamb, and venison prepared and served quite elegantly. A computerized wine list keeps track of the 10,000-plus bottles in the cellar. The upstairs bar and bistro is open until midnight. Proprietor and community dynamo Ron Zappardino heads a stellar staff.

Moderate

Sammy's, 702 Pearl St. ☎ **619/456-5222.**

Cuisine: CALIFORNIAN. **Directions:** From Prospect Street, take Girard Street to Pearl Street; the restaurant is a few blocks ahead on your right.
Prices: Pizzas $7–$10; pastas $8–$11; salads $5–$9. DC, MC, V.
Open: Sun–Thurs 11:30am–10pm, Fri–Sat 11:30am–11pm.

It's unusual to find an empty booth or table at this low-key, but lively eatery. Californian-style wood-fired pizzas take center stage here, and include favorites like five-cheese and sun-dried tomato pizzas. Among the pasta courses, fettuccine with chicken and angel hair with shrimp are both popular. The Thai chicken salad, which also gets raves, combines vegetables, tomatoes, roasted peanuts, sprouts, cilantro, and sesame chile dressing.

The Whaling Bar, in La Valencia Hotel, 1132 Prospect St. ☎ **619/454-0771.**

Cuisine: INTERNATIONAL. **Reservations:** Recommended.
Prices: Appetizers $4–$8; dinner main courses $11–$25; lunch $10–$13. AE, DC, MC, V.
Open: Daily 11:30am–10pm.

A La Jolla institution since 1947, 21 years after the founding of the hotel, The Whaling Bar was a popular haunt of movie stars Ginger Rogers and Charlton Heston, who came down from Los Angeles to perform at the La Jolla Playhouse. The restaurant features authentic New Bedford harpoons, pewter candle holders, wooden shutters, and scrimshaw. Meals are also sea oriented, and always include fresh fish and various seafood dishes. Chicken and choice cuts of steak are also available, accompanied by a good wine list.

Budget

Pannikin, 7467 Girard Ave. ☎ **619/454-5453.**

Cuisine: CONTINENTAL. **Reservations:** Not accepted.
Rates: Breakfast $3–$7; lunch $5–$8.
Open: Breakfast Mon–Fri 6–11am, Sat–Sun 7am–noon; lunch Mon–Sat 11am–5pm; coffee and pastries daily 3–10pm.

Opened in 1968, Pannikin remains unchanged. It is still in an old house with wood floors, a fireplace, and old movie-theater seats. Tiled tables stand on the porch and in the yard, which is trimmed with a hedge. It's extremely casual; you order and pay at the counter. The fare is simple and the coffee is terrific. Breakfast means Danish, eggs, or oatmeal. At lunch there are sandwiches, salads, pâtés, knishes, and bagels with lox. Cookies and desserts like cheesecake and chocolate mousse are always on hand.

Tijuana

20 miles S of San Diego

GETTING THERE • By Bus Daily round-trip bus service to downtown Tijuana is provided by Mexicoach (☎ **619/232-5049**). Buses depart from the San Diego Trolly stop at the International Border. The round-trip cost is $5; one-way is $2.50. Call for departure and return times.

• By Trolley The **San Diego Trolley** (☎ **619/231-8549**) departs from the corner of Kettner Boulevard and C Street, just across the street from the Amtrak station, every 15 minutes from 5am to 10pm, and every 30 minutes thereafter, with the last trolley returning from the border at 1am. The one-way trip to or from the border takes 45 minutes and costs $1.75 per person one-way from Kettner Boulevard; have exact change (machines do accept dollar bills). There are 18 stops on the line, since it doubles as commuter transportation, but it's a comfortable, interesting, and inexpensive way to reach the border. Once at the border you'll need a taxi to get into town, a $5 journey.

• By Car From San Diego, take 1-5 straight to the border. Most American auto insurance policies do not extend coverage to Mexico; you'll need to buy special insurance in San Ysidro, just north of the border. You might prefer to park in one of the many lots on the U.S. side (about $6), walk across the border, and take a taxi into town. You'll avoid long waits when return traffic jams up at the border.

ESSENTIALS • Entry Requirements U.S. citizens are not required to carry a passport when traveling within 72 miles of the border—which includes Tijuana—for visits of less than 72 hours. Citizens of other nations are required to carry passports. There is no need to exchange currency; U.S. dollars are accepted everywhere at a fair exchange rate.

• Orientation Tijuana is a large city—about 2 million inhabitants. But the part of the city that most tourists visit is rather small, almost confined to a single street, Avenida Revolución, located about one mile from the U.S. border.

• **Information** The **San Diego Convention & Visitors Bureau International Visitor Information Center,** 11 Horton Plaza, downtown at First Avenue and F Street (☎ **619/236-1212**), offers lots of information about traveling to Tijuana. Before strolling down Avenida Revolución, stop in at the city's new Tijuana Tourist Office, at Revolución 1 (☎ **88-05-55**), for information on sightseeing, restaurants, shopping, transportation, and the like. The exceedingly friendly staff is also under mandate from the Mexican government to defend tourists' rights, and are happy to intervene in disputes with shopkeepers, taxi drivers, and even the police. Keep their phone number handy, especially if you're traveling farther into Mexico. When calling Tijuana, dial **011-52-66** before the local number.

Because of its proximity to the United States, Tijuana is not like the rest of Mexico; you'll hear that time and again. The large and dirty city is packed with migrant workers, border-hoppers, and a vast number of citizens catering to the large tourist market. It is clear from the outset that the city is in an economically impoverished country—structures are rickety, cars are old, and many roads are unpaved. And Tijuana lacks the charm of most other points south; no charming town squares, few locals in colorful outfits, and a lack of flowers and foliage due to the dryness. Still, for someone who has never been in Mexico, or experienced the "Third World," Tijuana offers an interesting window into another lifestyle. There are also some good shops, offering inexpensive goods, and plenty of bars and restaurants catering to day trippers looking for cheap meals and a lower drinking age.

WHAT TO SEE & DO

Avenida Revolución, the city's primary tourist-oriented commercial thoroughfare, is lined with colorful shops and eateries of all description. It's easy to spend an entire day (and night) exploring this long and busy street, shopping, eating, drinking, and shopping some more. Many of the shops here accept major credit cards. At smaller stalls, bargaining is expected. Tolan, at Revolución and Calle 7, across from the Jai Alai Palace, is the best place to shop for craft items. Here you'll find clothing, wall hangings, glassware, and tinwork. Look also for glassware from Guadalajara, and Christmas ornaments from Oaxaca.

Jai alai, often called the fastest sport in the world, is played nightly (except Wednesday), starting at 8pm, at the **Fronton Palacio,** 1578 Avenida Revolución at Calle 7. Admission is $5. For information, call **619/231-1910.**

Thoroughbred racing is held at **Agua Caliente Racetrack,** on Boulevard Agua Caliente, every Saturday and Sunday at noon in winter, at 1:15pm the rest of the year; greyhound racing is scheduled Wednesday through Monday nights and there's never an admission charge.

Mexico's top matadors perform in two different **bullfight** rings every Sunday at 4pm from May through September. Ask a cab driver to take you there; the fare should never top $6, however.

You can also visit the **Tijuana Cultural Center,** located less than a mile from the border and across from the Plaza Ro Shopping Center, a cab ride away from Avenida Revolución. Designed to celebrate Mexico's heritage, it contains an anthropological museum, a bookstore, an arts and crafts center, and a performing arts center. Admission is only about $1. The center also houses an OMNIMAX Space Theater, with regular showings of *Pueblo del Sol* (village of the sun), an excellent film about the culture, beauty, and diversity of Mexico; admission is $3.35 for adults, $1.65 for children.

Tijuana's Wax Museum [Museo De Cera], 8281 1st St., on the corner of Madero Ave., Tijuana, Mexico. ☎ **88-24-78.**

Opened in 1993, Mexico's second wax museum (the first is in Mexico City) contains about a dozen unmarked tableaux with 60-plus lifelike models of famous and not so famous international figures. You'll recognize Michael Jackson and Madonna, but the identities of many others—important Mexicans of historical significance—will be appreciated more by Mexican-history buffs. The wax museum is not on a par with Madame Toussaud's in London, but it's worth at least a brief visit if you like viewing ceraceous effigies.

Open: Mon–Fri 10am–7pm, Sat–Sun 10am–8pm.
Admission: $3 adults, $2 children 6–12.

WHERE TO DINE

Expensive

★ **Pedrin's,** 1485 Avenida Revolución. ☎ **85-40-52.**

Cuisine: SEAFOOD. **Reservations:** Accepted. **Directions:** Located on the main commercial street between Calle 7 and Calle 8.
Prices: Appetizers $4–$11; main courses $7–$23. MC, V.
Open: Daily 10am–midnight.

Booths and tables overlook busy Avenida Revolución from the second-floor dining room. The restaurant is relatively fancy, with plenty of live plants and its white walls decorated with wood. On the bar there's an attractive seafood and wine display. Fish gets top billing here, starting with a hearty seafood soup. Other dishes include lobster, king crab, abalone, shrimp, oysters, and almost anything you can think of. It's a delightful place, a perfect spot to rest your feet after a long shopping spree.

Moderate

Guadalajara Grill, Diego Rivera 19. ☎ **34-30-65.**

Cuisine: MEXICAN. **Reservations:** Not accepted.
Prices: Appetizers $3–$8; main courses $6–$13. AE, MC, V.

It's zany, fun-loving, and welcoming—truly a plum spot to eat, drink, and be merry, especially at night, when the ceiling illusion makes you imagine you're seated under the stars. The decor is one big piece of whimsical artwork; don't miss the fountain made of tiles and pots, the cut-off ends of ties belonging to birthday celebrants, and the 50-foot-long bar. Amid a blasting mariachi band, diners are treated to good Mexican staples, such as burritos and tacos, along with several fish and chicken dishes. Portions are unusually large.

Tia Juana Tilly's, Avenida Revolución 1420. ☎ **85-60-24.**

Cuisine: MEXICAN. **Reservations:** Accepted. **Directions:** Right on the main commercial thoroughfare, at Calle 7.
Prices: Appetizers $3–$7; main courses $6–$12. MC, V.
Open: Fri–Wed 11am–11pm.

Centrally situated beside the Fronton Palacio (Jai Alai Palace), this place is huge, encompassing a large restaurant, bar, grill, and dance hall. Nicer than most of the other spots on the strip, Tilly's has cloth- and glass-topped tables and plenty of outdoor seating. A veritable survey of traditional Mexican cooking is offered, including chicken and beef dishes and any number of combination plates. Bring your appetite.

$ **Cafe la Especial,** Avenida Revolución 718. ☎ **85-66-54.**
Cuisine: MEXICAN. **Reservations:** Accepted.
Prices: Appetizers $2–$4, main courses $4–$10.
Open: Daily 9am–10:30pm.

Hidden down a staircase squeezed between two buildings, Especial is really worth finding, as it is one of the best moderately priced restaurants in Tijuana. The low ceilings, wood walls, and aging decor are far from fancy, but don't be misled—this is no hole in the wall. The professional—bow-tied and vested—waitstaff are proud of the restaurant's well-earned local reputation. The menu may offer a limited selection, but the food is impressive. Excellent tacos, enchiladas, and steaks are served with potatoes, rice, and beans. Whatever you order, start with the exceptional chicken soup. You'll also be impressed by the fine service.

Index

Please send me the books checked below:

FROMMER'S COMPREHENSIVE GUIDES

(Guides listing facilities from budget to deluxe,
with emphasis on the medium-priced)

	Retail Price	Code		Retail Price	Code
☐ Acapulco/Ixtapa/Taxco, 2nd Edition	$13.95	C157	☐ Jamaica/Barbados, 2nd Edition	$15.00	C149
☐ Alaska '94-'95	$17.00	C131	☐ Japan '94-'95	$19.00	C144
☐ Arizona '95 (Avail. 3/95)	$14.95	C166	☐ Maui, 1st Edition	$13.95	C153
☐ Australia '94-'95	$18.00	C147	☐ Nepal, 2nd Edition	$18.00	C126
☐ Austria, 6th Edition	$16.95	C162	☐ New England '95	$16.95	C165
☐ Bahamas '94-'95	$17.00	C121	☐ New Mexico, 3rd Edition (Avail. 3/95)	$14.95	C167
☐ Belgium/Holland/Luxembourg '93-'94	$18.00	C106	☐ New York State, 4th Edition	$19.00	C133
☐ Bermuda '94-'95	$15.00	C122	☐ Northwest, 5th Edition	$17.00	C140
☐ Brazil, 3rd Edition	$20.00	C111	☐ Portugal '94-'95	$17.00	C141
☐ California '95	$16.95	C164	☐ Puerto Rico '95-'96	$14.00	C151
☐ Canada '94-'95	$19.00	C145	☐ Puerto Vallarta/Manzanillo/ Guadalajara '94-'95	$14.00	C028
☐ Caribbean '95	$18.00	C148	☐ Scandinavia, 16th Edition (Avail. 3/95)	$19.95	C169
☐ Carolinas/Georgia, 2nd Edition	$17.00	C128	☐ Scotland '94-'95	$17.00	C146
☐ Colorado, 2nd Edition	$16.00	C143	☐ South Pacific '94-'95	$20.00	C138
☐ Costa Rica '95	$13.95	C161	☐ Spain, 16th Edition	$16.95	C163
☐ Cruises '95-'96	$19.00	C150	☐ Switzerland/Liechtenstein '94-'95	$19.00	C139
☐ Delaware/Maryland '94-'95	$15.00	C136	☐ Thailand, 2nd Edition	$17.95	C154
☐ England '95	$17.95	C159	☐ U.S.A., 4th Edition	$18.95	C156
☐ Florida '95	$18.00	C152	☐ Virgin Islands '94-'95	$13.00	C127
☐ France '94-'95	$20.00	C132	☐ Virginia '94-'95	$14.00	C142
☐ Germany '95	$18.95	C158	☐ Yucatan, 2nd Edition	$13.95	C155
☐ Ireland, 1st Edition (Avail. 3/95)	$16.95	C168			
☐ Italy '95	$18.95	C160			

FROMMER'S $-A-DAY GUIDES

(Guides to low-cost tourist accommodations and facilities)

	Retail Price	Code		Retail Price	Code
☐ Australia on $45 '95-'96	$18.00	D122	☐ Ireland on $45 '94-'95	$17.00	D118
☐ Costa Rica/Guatemala/Belize on $35, 3rd Edition	$15.95	D126	☐ Israel on $45, 15th Edition	$16.95	D130
☐ Eastern Europe on $30, 5th Edition	$16.95	D129	☐ Mexico on $45 '95	$16.95	D125
☐ England on $60 '95	$17.95	D128	☐ New York on $70 '94-'95	$16.00	D121
☐ Europe on $50 '95	$17.95	D127	☐ New Zealand on $45 '93-'94	$18.00	D103
☐ Greece on $45 '93-'94	$19.00	D100	☐ South America on $40, 16th Edition	$18.95	D123
☐ Hawaii on $75 '95	$16.95	D124	☐ Washington, D.C. on $50 '94-'95	$17.00	D120

FROMMER'S CITY $-A-DAY GUIDES

	Retail Price	Code		Retail Price	Code
☐ Berlin on $40 '94-'95	$12.00	D111	☐ Madrid on $50 '94-'95	$13.00	D119
☐ London on $45 '94-'95	$12.00	D114	☐ Paris on $45 '94-'95	$12.00	D117

FROMMER'S FAMILY GUIDES

	Retail Price	Code		Retail Price	Code
☐ California with Kids	$18.00	F100	☐ San Francisco with Kids	$17.00	F104
☐ Los Angeles with Kids	$17.00	F103	☐ Washington, D.C. with Kids	$17.00	F102
☐ New York City with Kids	$18.00	F101			

FROMMER'S CITY GUIDES

(Pocket-size guides to sightseeing and tourist accommodations and facilities in all price ranges)

	Retail Price	Code		Retail Price	Code
☐ Amsterdam '93-'94	$13.00	S110	☐ Minneapolis/St. Paul, 4th Edition	$12.95	S159
☐ Athens, 10th Edition (Avail. 3/95)	$12.95	S174	☐ Montreal/Quebec City '95	$11.95	S166
☐ Atlanta '95	$12.95	S161	☐ Nashville/Memphis, 1st Edition	$13.00	S141
☐ Atlantic City/Cape May, 5th Edition	$13.00	S130	☐ New Orleans '95	$12.95	S148
☐ Bangkok, 2nd Edition	$12.95	S147	☐ New York '95	$12.95	S152
☐ Barcelona '93-'94	$13.00	S115	☐ Orlando '95	$13.00	S145
☐ Berlin, 3rd Edition	$12.95	S162	☐ Paris '95	$12.95	S150
☐ Boston '95	$12.95	S160	☐ Philadelphia, 8th Edition	$12.95	S167
☐ Budapest, 1st Edition	$13.00	S139	☐ Prague '94-'95	$13.00	S143
☐ Chicago '95	$12.95	S169	☐ Rome, 10th Edition	$12.95	S168
☐ Denver/Boulder/Colorado Springs, 3rd Edition	$12.95	S154	☐ San Diego '95	$12.95	S158
☐ Dublin, 2nd Edition	$12.95	S157	☐ San Francisco '95	$12.95	S155
☐ Hong Kong '94-'95	$13.00	S140	☐ Santa Fe/Taos/Albuquerque '95	$12.95	S172
☐ Honolulu/Oahu '95	$12.95	S151	☐ Seattle/Portland '94-'95	$13.00	S137
☐ Las Vegas '95	$12.95	S163	☐ St. Louis/Kansas City, 2nd Edition	$13.00	S127
☐ London '95	$12.95	S156	☐ Sydney, 4th Edition	$12.95	S171
☐ Los Angeles '95	$12.95	S164	☐ Tampa/St. Petersburg, 3rd Edition	$13.00	S146
☐ Madrid/Costa del Sol, 2nd Edition	$12.95	S165	☐ Tokyo '94-'95	$13.00	S144
☐ Mexico City, 1st Edition	$12.95	S170	☐ Toronto '95 (Avail. 3/95)	$12.95	S173
☐ Miami '95-'96	$12.95	S149	☐ Vancouver/Victoria '94-'95	$13.00	S142
			☐ Washington, D.C. '95	$12.95	S153

FROMMER'S WALKING TOURS

(With routes and detailed maps, these companion guides point out the places and pleasures that make a city unique)

	Retail Price	Code		Retail Price	Code
☐ Berlin	$12.00	W100	☐ New York	$12.00	W102
☐ Chicago	$12.00	W107	☐ Paris	$12.00	W103
☐ England's Favorite Cities	$12.00	W108	☐ San Francisco	$12.00	W104
☐ London	$12.00	W101	☐ Washington, D.C.	$12.00	W105
☐ Montreal/Quebec City	$12.00	W106			

SPECIAL EDITIONS

	Retail Price	Code		Retail Price	Code
☐ Bed & Breakfast Southwest	$16.00	P100	☐ National Park Guide, 29th Edition	$17.00	P106
☐ Bed & Breakfast Great American Cities	$16.00	P104	☐ Where to Stay U.S.A., 11th Edition	$15.00	P102
☐ Caribbean Hideaways	$16.00	P103			

FROMMER'S TOURING GUIDES

(Color-illustrated guides that include walking tours, cultural and historic sites, and practical information)

	Retail Price	Code		Retail Price	Code
☐ Amsterdam	$11.00	T001	☐ Rome	$11.00	T010
☐ Barcelona	$14.00	T015	☐ Scotland	$10.00	T011
☐ Brazil	$11.00	T003	☐ Sicily	$15.00	T017
☐ Hong Kong/Singapore/Macau	$11.00	T006	☐ Tokyo	$15.00	T016
☐ Kenya	$14.00	T018	☐ Turkey	$11.00	T013
☐ London	$13.00	T007	☐ Venice	$ 9.00	T014
☐ New York	$11.00	T008			

Please note: If the availability of a book is several months away, we may have back issues of guides to that particular destination. Call customer service at (815) 734-1104.